Aboriginal Legal Issues
Cases, Materials & Commentary

Second Edition

Aboriginal Legal Issues
Cases, Materials & Commentary
Second Edition

John J. Borrows
B.A., M.A., LL.B., LL.M., D. Jur.
of the Ojibway/Anishinabe First Nation
Professor
Faculty of Law, University of Victoria

Leonard I. Rotman
B.A., LL.B., LL.M., S.J.D.
of the Ontario Bar
Professor
Faculty of Law, University of Windsor

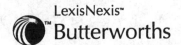
LexisNexis™
Butterworths

Aboriginal Legal Issues: Cases, Materials & Commentary, 2nd edition
© LexisNexis Canada Inc. 2003
September 2003

Members of the LexisNexis Group worldwide

Canada	LexisNexis Canada Inc, 75 Clegg Road, MARKHAM, Ontario
Argentina	Abeledo Perrot, Jurisprudencia Argentina and Depalma, BUENOS AIRES
Australia	Butterworths, a Division of Reed International Books Australia Pty Ltd, CHATSWOOD, New South Wales
Austria	ARD Betriebsdienst and Verlag Orac, VIENNA
Chile	Publitecsa and Conosur Ltda, SANTIAGO DE CHILE
Czech Republic	Orac sro, PRAGUE
France	Éditions du Juris-Classeur SA, PARIS
Hong Kong	Butterworths Asia (Hong Kong), HONG KONG
Hungary	Hvg Orac, BUDAPEST
India	Butterworths India, NEW DELHI
Ireland	Butterworths (Ireland) Ltd, DUBLIN
Italy	Giuffré, MILAN
Malaysia	Malayan Law Journal Sdn Bhd, KUALA LUMPUR
New Zealand	Butterworths of New Zealand, WELLINGTON
Poland	Wydawnictwa Prawnicze PWN, WARSAW
Singapore	Butterworths Asia, SINGAPORE
South Africa	Butterworth Publishers (Pty) Ltd, DURBAN
Switzerland	Stämpfli Verlag AG, BERNE
United Kingdom	Butterworths Tolley, a Division of Reed Elsevier (UK), LONDON, WC2A
USA	LexisNexis, DAYTON, Ohio

National Library of Canada Cataloguing in Publication

Borrows, John, 1963-
  Aboriginal legal issues : cases, materials & commentary / John J. Borrows, Leonard I. Rotman. — 2nd ed.

Includes bibliographical references and index.
ISBN 0-433-44010-4

  1. Native peoples—Legal status, laws, etc.—Canada—Cases.
I. Rotman, Leonard Ian   II. Title.

KE7709.B67 2003   342.71'0872   C2003-904927-2
KF8205.B67 2003

Printed and bound in Canada.

To our partners, Kim and Tammy,

thanks for your patience and support

About the Authors

John Borrows, B.A., M.A., LL.B., LL.M., D. Jur., is Professor of Law and Law Foundation Chair of Aboriginal Justice and Governance at the University of Victoria. Dr. Borrows is a recipient of the 2003 National Aboriginal Achievement Award for Law and Justice.

Leonard Rotman, B.A., LL.B., LL.M., S.J.D., is Professor of Law at the University of Windsor. Dr. Rotman is the author of numerous articles and casebook chapters in the areas of Aboriginal law, Fiduciary law, Trusts, and Corporate law and a former editor-in-chief of the *Windsor Yearbook of Access to Justice*.

PREFACE TO THE SECOND EDITION

MAUDJITAUWIN

In the five years since the first edition of Aboriginal Legal Issues was released, a number of prominent cases on important issues have been decided by the Supreme Court of Canada. There have also been some significant legislative and policy initiatives in this time. We have endeavoured, to the extent possible, to incorporate or otherwise account for these new developments in this new edition.

To keep the book at a manageable length, we set out to not simply add new material to the old, but to engage in a process of rethinking our earlier inclusions to determine their continued presence in the updated version of the book. Consequently, some of the materials from the first edition have been removed, while others have been re-edited. The result, we hope, is an improved and somewhat more streamlined product than its predecessor.

The purpose of the book remains the same. We continue to include materials on a variety of important topics to enable the book to serve as a useful resource while allowing instructors to customize their courses. Space constraints make it impossible to cover all of the pertinent issues concerning Aboriginal peoples and the law, resulting in the need for a certain amount of selectivity in coverage. Nonetheless, we hope that the materials contained herein provide something of value to the spectrum of individuals and institutions interested in this ever-expanding and complex area of law.

We extend thanks to Anand Ablack and Butterworths Canada for their encouragement of this second edition. Thanks also go to Tony Price for his help in putting this volume together, as well as to the Faculties of Law at the University of Victoria and the University of Windsor for their financial and other assistance.

As you read these materials, remember: Kegoh dae'b'awaetungaen kakinah gaego mishishuh nayaugook.

John Borrows
Victoria

Len Rotman
Windsor

July, 2003

ACKNOWLEDGEMENTS

A casebook on such a wide subject necessarily contains a great deal of references to the work of others. The authors and publishers of these articles and textbooks have been most generous in giving permission for the reproduction in this text of works already in print. References, of course, appear where necessary and possible in the text. It is convenient for us to list below, for the assistance of the reader, the publishers and authors for whose courtesy we are most grateful. The following is organized by author in alphabetical order.

Michael Asch and Patrick Macklem, "Aboriginal Rights and Canadian Sovereignty: An Essay on *R. v. Sparrow*" (1991) 29 Alta. L. Rev. 498 at 501-503, 505, 507-508, 510, 515-16. Reproduced with permission of Alberta Law Review.

Paul Barnsley, "Harvard Study Group Finds Fault with FNGA" (Windspeaker, Canada's National Aboriginal Newspaper, 1993). Reprinted with permission of The Aboriginal Multi-Media Society.

Richard H. Bartlett, *Indians and Taxation in Canada*, 3rd ed. (Saskatoon: Native Law Centre, 1992) 1-14, 47-56. Reproduced with permission of Native Law Centre, University of Saskatchewan.

Catherine Bell, "Métis Constitutional Rights in Section 35(1)" (1997) 36 Alta. L. Rev. 180 at 180-87, 189-92, 194-95. Reproduced with permission from the Alberta Law Review.

Catherine Bell, "Who are the Métis People in Section 35(2)?" (1991) 29 Alta. L. Rev. 351 at 353, 355-58, 370-71, 373-81. Reproduced with permission of Alberta Law Review.

John J. Borrows, "Wampum at Niagara: The Royal Proclamation, Canadian Legal History and Self-Government" in Michael Asch, ed., *Aboriginal and Treaty Rights in Canada: Essays on Law, Equality and Respect for Difference* (Vancouver: University of British Columbia Press, 1997) 161-65, 168-69. Reprinted with permission of the Publisher. All rights reserved by the Publisher.

John J. Borrows and Leonard I. Rotman, "The *Sui Generis* Nature of Aboriginal Rights: Does It Make a Difference?" (1997) 36 Alta. L. Rev. 9 at 43-44. Reproduced with permission from the Alberta Law Review.

Clem Chartier, "Aboriginal Rights and Land Issues: The Métis Perspective" in Menno Boldt and J. Anthony Long, eds., in association with Leroy Little Bear, *The Quest for Justice: Aboriginal Peoples and Aboriginal Rights* (Toronto: University of Toronto Press, 1988) 54 at 57-60. Reprinted by permission of University of Toronto Press Incorporated © 1988.

Governor Belcher's Proclamation, Nova Scotia, 1762, as reproduced in P.A. Cumming and N.H. Mickenburg, *Native Rights in Canada* (2nd ed.) (Toronto: Indian-Eskimo Association of Canada, 1972) Appendix I at 287-88.

Larry Chartrand, "Metis Identity and Citizenship" (2001) 12 Windsor Rev. Legal Soc. Issues. 5 at 6-10, 19-23, 25-26, 37-41, 47-52. Reproduced with permission of the Windsor Review of Legal and Social Issues.

Larry Chartrand, "Are We Metis or are We Indians? A Commentary on R. v. Grumbo" (1999-2000) 31 Ottawa L. Rev. 267 at 274-75, 281. Reproduced with permission of Ottawa Law Review.

A.C. Hamilton and C.M. Sinclair, *The Justice System and Aboriginal People: Report of the Aboriginal Justice Inquiry of Manitoba, Vol. 1* (Winnipeg: Queen's Printer, 1991), at 115-16, 127, 130-35, 137, 475-87, 509-520. Reproduced with permission of the Province of Manitoba.

Sonia Harris-Short, "The Road Back from Hell? Self-Government and the Decolonisation of Aboriginal Child Welfare in Canada" (2003, unpublished). Reprinted with permission of the author.

James [Sakej] Youngblood Henderson, "Empowering Treaty Federalism" (1994) 58 Sask. L. Rev. 241 at 250-69. Reproduced with permission of Saskatchewan Law Review.

Emma La Roque, "Re-examining Culturally Appropriate Models in Criminal Justice Applications" in Michael Asch, ed., *Aboriginal and Treaty Rights in Canada: Essays on Law, Equality and Respect for Difference* (Vancouver: University of British Columbia Press, 1997) at 75. Reprinted with permission of the Publisher. All rights reserved by the Publisher.

Andre Le Dressay, "A Brief Tax (on a me) of First Nations Taxation and Economic Development" in Sharing the Harvest: The Road to Self-Reliance, Report of the National Round Table on Aboriginal Economic Development and Resources at 218-23. Royal Commission on Aboriginal Peoples © 1993. Reproduced with the permission of the Minister of Public

Works and Government Services, 2003, and courtesy of the Privy Council Office.

Noel Lyon, "A Perspective on the Application of the Criminal Code to Aboriginal Peoples in Light of the Judgment of the Supreme Court in *R. v. Sparrow*" (1992) U. B.C. L. Rev. Special edition on Aboriginal Justice 306 at 306-11. Reproduced with permission of University of British Columbia Law Review.

Patrick Macklem, "First Nations Self-Government and the Borders of the Canadian Legal Imagination"(1991) 36 McGill L.J. 382 at 425. Reproduced with permission of McGill Law Journal.

Kent McNeil, "The Onus of Proof of Aboriginal Title" (1999) 37 Osgoode Hall L.J. 775 at 776-82, 800-803. Reprinted with permission of the Osgoode Hall Law School and the author.

Alan Pratt, "Aboriginal Self-Government and the Crown's Fiduciary Duty: Squaring the Circle or Completing the Circle?" (1992) 2 N.J.C.L. 163 at 166, 169, 180-83, 186-87. Reprinted by permission of Carswell, a division of Thomson Canada Limited, and the author.

Leonard I. Rotman, "Defining Parameters: Aboriginal Rights, Treaty Rights, and the *Sparrow* Justificatory Test" (1997) 36 Alta. L. Rev. 149 at 149-58, 161-71. Reproduced with permission from the Alberta Law Review.

Leonard I. Rotman, "Hunting for Answers in a Strange Kettle of Fish: Unilateralism, Paternalism and Fiduciary Rhetoric in *Badger* and *Van der Peet*" (1997) 8 Const. Forum Const. 40. Reproduced with permission from the Centre for Constitutional Studies.

Leonard I. Rotman, "Taking Aim at the Canons of Treaty Interpretation in Canadian Aboriginal Rights Jurisprudence" (1997) 46 U.N.B.L.J. 1 at 12-14, 26-27, 29-30, 32, 34-37, 40-41, 43-45, 47, 49-50.

Leonard I. Rotman, "Fiduciary Doctrine: A Concept in Need of Understanding" (1996) 34 Alta. L. Rev. 821 at 821-34, 838, 843-44, 846, 851. Reproduced with permission from the Alberta Law Review.

Leonard I. Rotman, *Parallel Paths: Fiduciary Doctrine and the Crown-Native Relationship in Canada* (Toronto: University of Toronto Press, 1996) at 3-4, 11-18, 192-93, 221, 238-39, 251-53, 279-80. Reprinted by permission of University of Toronto Press Incorporated.

Leonard I. Rotman, "Provincial Fiduciary Obligations to First Nations: The Nexus Between Governmental Power and Responsibility" (1994) 32 Osgoode Hall L.J. 735 at 743-45, 754-58, 760-63. Reproduced with permission of the Osgoode Hall Law Journal and the author.

Canada. Royal Commission on Aboriginal Peoples, Report of the Royal Commission on Aboriginal Peoples, Vol. I, Looking Forward, Looking Back at 128-30, 173-76; Vol. II, Restructuring the Relationship at 186-90, 535-39, 543, 544-49; Vol. III, Gathering Strength at 29-33, 52-53, 87, The Commission ©1996. Reproduced with the permission of the Minister of Public Works and Government Services, 2003, and Courtesy of the Privy Council Office; Vol. IV, Perspectives and Realities at 24-33, 33-36, 36-37, 39-42, 68-71, The Commission © 1996. Reproduced with the permission of the Minister of Public Works and Government Services, 2003, and Courtesy of the Privy Council Office; Bridging the Cultural Divide: A Report on Aboriginal People and Criminal Justice in Canada at xi, 7, 28-33, 159-67, Royal Commission on Aboriginal Peoples © 1996 (Ottawa: Privy Council Office, 1996). Reproduced with the permission of the Minister of Public Works and Government Services Canada, 2003, and Courtesy of the Privy Council Office.

Douglas Sanders, "We Intend to Live Here Forever: A Primer on the Nisga'a Treaty" (1999) U.B.C. L. Rev. 103-128. Reprinted with permission of University of British Columbia Law Review.

Bryan Schwartz, "A Separate Aboriginal Justice System?" (1990) 28 Man. L.J. 77-91.

Chief John Snow, *These Mountains are our Sacred Places: The Story of the Stoney Indians* (Toronto: Samuel Stevens, 1977) at 2-3, 12-13.

D. N. Sprague, "Canada's Treaties with Aboriginal Peoples" (1996) 23 Man. L.J. 341 at 341-44. Reproduced with permission of Manitoba Law Journal.

The Women's Press, "Retrospective", Enough is Enough: Aboriginal Women Speak Out (Toronto: The Women's Press, 1987). Reprinted with permission of Women's Press.

Janice Tibetts, "Adoptive Family Wins Custody of Native Boy Supreme Court will not Deliver Written Reasons for Ruling" *National Post* (18 February 1999). Reprinted with permission of Southam News.

Mary Ellen Turpel, "Home/land" (1991), 10 Can. J. Fam. L. 17 at 30. Reproduced with permission of Canadian Journal of Family Law.

Kerry Wilkins, "Still Crazy After All These Years: Section 88 of the Indian Act at Fifty" (2000) 38 Alta. L. Rev. 458. Reprinted with permission of Alberta Law Review.

William Wicken, "The Mi'kmaq and Wuastukwiuk Treaties" (1994), 44 U.N.B.L.J. 241 at 241-42, 249-53.

TABLE OF CONTENTS

Chapter 8: Aboriginal Women

Chapter 9: Governance

Chapter 12: Aboriginal Peoples and Criminal Justice

TABLE OF CASES

[A page number in boldface type indicates that a case has been excerpted in the text.]

CHAPTER 1

ABORIGINAL TITLE

A. INTRODUCTION

Land is a central element of Aboriginal societies. The sacredness of land to Aboriginal peoples is illustrated in the following statement made by the Shawnee leader Tecumseh:

> No tribe has the right to sell, even to each other, much less to strangers. ... Sell a country! Why not sell the great sea, as well as the earth? Did not the Great Spirit make them all for the use of his children?[1]

While not all Aboriginal issues revolve around land, Aboriginal rights, and some treaty rights, are strongly tied to Aboriginal relationships to land.

The link between Aboriginal rights and land exists because many of those rights stem from Aboriginal traditions, customs, or practices associated with land. Common examples are hunting, fishing, or trapping rights. These rights may exist either as Aboriginal rights or they may have been incorporated into a treaty as treaty rights. While these rights are derived from an association with land, their existence is not dependent upon a finding of Aboriginal title. As the Supreme Court of Canada decisions in *R. v. Adams*, [1996] 3 S.C.R. 101, 202 N.R. 89, 138 D.L.R. (4th) 657, 110 C.C.C. (3d) 97, 4 C.N.L.R. 1 and *R. v. Côté*, [1996] 3 S.C.R. 139, 202 N.R. 161, 138 D.L.R. (4th) 385, 110 C.C.C. (3d) 122, 4 C.N.L.R. 26 illustrate (see the excerpts of these cases in Chapter 4, *infra*), Aboriginal rights exist independently of title and may be exercised without the need to demonstrate title to a particular area. This same premise would also hold true of treaty rights that affirm pre-existing Aboriginal rights.

B. THE IMPORTANCE OF LAND TO ABORIGINAL CULTURES

Aboriginal peoples traditionally viewed land in a different manner than Europeans. They did not generally regard land as something to be owned, as Europeans did. Rather, they viewed land as something to be used and cared for. This notion of stewardship was a foreign concept to the Europeans of the 15th and 16th centuries. Because of the different conceptualizations of land possessed by Aboriginal and European peoples, each group viewed the others' actions regarding land according to their own conceptions of land use. Thus, when the Aboriginal peoples shared their lands with the Europeans, they did not imagine that what they regarded as sharing would be conceived of by the Europeans as a surrender of their interests.

THE JUSTICE SYSTEM AND ABORIGINAL PEOPLE: REPORT OF THE ABORIGINAL JUSTICE INQUIRY OF MANITOBA, VOL. 1

(Winnipeg: Queen's Printer, 1991)
(A.C. Hamilton and C.M. Sinclair, Commissioners) c. 5 at 115-16

When Europeans came to the Americas they were considered outsiders but, in accordance with the Aboriginal view, were permitted to share in the land and its resources. Elders have told us that, in the eyes of the Creator, the Europeans as outsiders could not enjoy the same rights as the original inhabitants. Whatever rights the Europeans wanted had to be sought from those who were placed upon the land first by the Creator. It is a belief common to many Aboriginal societies that the Creator placed Aboriginal people upon this land first for a reason, and that, as the first one on the land, they were placed in a special relationship to it. In the worldview of Aboriginal people, the Europeans were visitors and, as such, were bound to respect the obligations of that status.

For Aboriginal peoples, the land was part of their identity as a people. The earth was their Mother, the animals were their spiritual kin and all were part of the greater whole, which was life. Their culture was grounded in nature. Time was marked by the changing seasons and the rising and setting of the sun, rather than by numbers, and their existence was marked by an acceptance of and respect for their natural surroundings and their place in the scheme of things. The thinking of Aboriginal peoples was cyclical, rather than linear like that of the Europeans. Everything was thought of in terms of its relation to the whole, not as individual bits of information to be compared to one another. Aboriginal philosophy was holistic, and did not lend itself readily to dichotomies or categories as did European philosophy. So, for Aboriginal people, their rights were — and still are — seen in broad, conceptual terms.

The most fundamental of those rights is the right to their identity as Aboriginal people. Since that identity was derived largely from the land they used and occupied before the arrival of the Europeans, they believe they had — and still have — certain rights in regard to the land, including continuing habitation and use of the land, whether it be for hunting, fishing, trapping, gathering food and medicines, or for any other traditional pursuits.

This excerpt from the Manitoba Aboriginal Justice Inquiry report affirms the central role that land plays in the identity of Aboriginal peoples. Consequently, to be able to properly understand the basis of an Aboriginal claim to land, it is necessary to have an appreciation of the meaning of land to Aboriginal cultures. Of course, individual Aboriginal cultures will view land in their own way. In the following excerpt, Chief John Snow describes the centrality of land, in particular, the Rocky Mountains, to the Stoney Indians. Note that in describing the importance of land to his people, Chief Snow does not focus only on his people's relationship to the land, but on his people's way of life and their place within the natural order.

CHIEF JOHN SNOW, THESE MOUNTAINS ARE OUR SACRED PLACES: THE STORY OF THE STONEY INDIANS

(Toronto: Samuel Stevens, 1977) at 2-3, 12-13

Indian traditions and oral history say that my people were always present in this part of the Great Island (the native name for the North American continent), roaming along the foothills out onto the prairies to the east and deep into the Rocky Mountain country to the west. Our traditional hunting territory seems to have extended north to the Brazeau River-Jasper area, south a little past what is now the international border, east beyond the present-day city of Calgary, and west into the Rockies beyond what would become the British Columbia border.

In order to understand the vital importance the mountains had — and still have — to my people, it is necessary to know something of our way of life before the coming of the whiteman. It is not enough to say the mountains were the Stoneys' traditional place of prayer because our life was not a fragmented one with a compartment for religion. Rather, our life was one in which religion (and reverance for nature, which revealed religious truth) was woven throughout all parts of the social structure and observed in conjunction with every activity. Our forefathers were a proud people because they knew they had been selected by the Creator to receive a precious gift of special understanding and they have handed that gift down to us as a sacred trust.

In the days prior to the coming of the whiteman, we lived a nomadic way of life, hunting, fishing, and gathering from the abundance of this good land. There were literally millions of buffalo roaming on the western prairies, along the foothills, and even into the Rocky Mountains themselves. There were game animals of all kinds — moose, elk, deer, wild sheep, and goats — readily available for us to hunt and enjoy. The land was vast, beautiful, and rich in abundant resources. Our Mother Earth called us from the forests, the prairies, the valleys, the mountainous areas, the lakes, rivers, and springs: "Come, my children, anyone who is hungry, come and eat from the fruits and gather from the abundance of this land. Come, everyone who thirsts, come and drink pure spring waters that are especially provided for you." Everywhere the spirits of all living things were alive.

We talked to the rocks, the streams, the trees, the plants, the herbs, and all nature's creations. We called the animals our brothers. They understood our language; we, too, understood theirs. Sometimes they talked to us in dreams and visions. At times they revealed important events or visited us on our vision quests to the mountain tops. Truly, we were part of and related to the universe, and these animals were a very special part of the Great Spirit's creation.

· · · · ·

In our migrations, as in our vision quests, my people continued to observe the animals, plants, rocks, trees, streams, winds, sun, moon, stars, and all things. Our teaching has always been that everything was created for a purpose by the Great Spirit. We must, therefore, respect all things of creation and learn as much as we can. There are lessons hidden in creation that we must learn in order to live a good life and walk the straight path. Behind these lessons and teachings is the Creator. These things can only be understood through the Great Spirit.

Century after century, the rugged Rocky Mountains sat there in majesty, and nature seemed to say: "Your thoughts must be as firm as these mountains, if you are to walk the straight path. Your patience and kindness must be as solid as these mountains, if you are to acquire understanding and wisdom."

. . . . .

Upon these lofty heights, the Great Spirit revealed many things to us. Some of my people received powers to heal. They could heal the physical body with herbs, roots, leaves, plants, and mineral spring waters. They could also heal the broken and weary soul with unseen spiritual powers. Others received powers over the weather. These gifted religious men and women could call for a great storm or calm the weather; they could call on the winds, rain, hail, snow, or sleet, and they would come. From these mountain-top experiences my fellow tribesmen and women were given unique tasks to perform to help the tribe prepare for things to come.

Therefore the Rocky Mountains are precious and sacred to us. We knew every trail and mountain pass in the area. We had special ceremonial and religious areas in the mountains. In the olden days some of the neighbouring tribes called us the "People of the Shining Mountains." These mountains are our temples, our sanctuaries, and our resting places. They are a place of hope, a place of vision, a place of refuge, a very special and holy place where the Great Spirit speaks with us. *Therefore, these mountains are our sacred places.*

C. THE DOCTRINE OF ABORIGINAL TITLE

Aboriginal peoples used and occupied lands in what is now known as Canada long before the first arrival of Europeans to North America. During that time, they put the land to various uses in order to provide for the sustenance and continuation of their societies. When European traders and settlers arrived in North America, they required the assistance of the Aboriginal peoples in order to survive in a strange and distant land. The Aboriginals shared their land, resources, and knowledge with the Europeans. The groups also engaged in mutually-beneficial trade of fish, furs, and other resources.

As the number of Europeans grew significantly, disputes between the European and Aboriginal peoples arose over rights to land. The doctrine of

Aboriginal title in English common law originated from the historical circumstances arising from these competing European and Aboriginal land interests. The Europeans, who sought ownership and control of North American lands, laid claim to those lands through a variety of means. In actual fact, European claims to lands in the New World had been initiated prior to the Europeans' arrival on North American shores. In 1455, King Alfonso V of Portugal had been granted the exclusive "right" to conquer and enslave all "pagan" nations — and to seize their lands — by Pope Nicholas V in his bull *Romanus Pontifex*. When Spain ignored the exclusivity of this grant by sending Columbus to the New World in the latter stages of the 15th century, Pope Alexander VI divided the rights that had been granted to Portugal between it and Spain in his 1493 bull *Inter Caetera*. Being snubbed by the papacy once again, England and France sent explorers to claim lands in the New World on their own authorization. King Henry VII granted Letters Patent to John Cabot in 1496 which authorized him to "subdue, occupy and possess all such townes, cities, castles and isles of them found, which [he] can subdue, occupy and possess".[2] France, meanwhile, issued its own commission to Jean François de La Rocque, Sieur de Roberval, in 1541, which granted him "full power and authority over those *lands that he shall have been able to acquire for us in this voyage*".[3] Soon, Russia, the Netherlands, and Sweden also joined in the race to claim lands in the New World.

1. Aboriginal Title and the Law of Nations

Aside from papal bulls and royal charters, European nations attempted to reinforce their claims to lands in the New World through the doctrines of discovery, occupation/settlement, adverse possession, conquest, and cession. These concepts were creatures of the *jus gentium*, or Law of Nations, which governed controversies between its member states, including those surrounding their attempts to acquire new territories. The question remains, however, what the effects of these concepts were *vis-à-vis* the Aboriginal peoples of North America.

THE JUSTICE SYSTEM AND ABORIGINAL PEOPLE: REPORT OF THE ABORIGINAL JUSTICE INQUIRY OF MANITOBA, VOL. 1

(Winnipeg: Queen's Printer, 1991) (A.C. Hamilton and C.M. Sinclair, Commissioners) c. 5 at 127, 130-5, 137 (references omitted)

One of the primary issues with which Canadian society has to come to grips is the historical legacy of its acquisition of Aboriginal lands. ... The issue involves how Canadian and American legal systems have addressed the nature and form of the Aboriginal legal interest in the land now within Canada and the United States, and of the legal techniques used to assert dominion over lands which enjoyed some degree of legal protection in international law.

The Use of Doctrines of International Law

Since the beginning of the Age of Discovery, European states have engaged relentlessly in the process of divesting indigenous peoples of their lands, and have sought to justify and legitimate this practice through the use of the doctrines of discovery, occupation, adverse possession, conquest and cession. On the whole, domestic courts have either ignored or generally misapplied and misinterpreted these doctrines in their discussions of "Aboriginal title," thereby upholding the status quo of Aboriginal dispossession.

The starting point in determining what rights Aboriginal people had at international law when they first were in contact with Europeans requires an examination of the legal provisions applicable to those nations which asserted authority over North America after contact. We will examine in turn each of the rationales for European claims to sovereignty and underlying title to the discovered territories.

The Doctrine of Discovery

The doctrine of discovery has been — and still is — rigorously advanced by various authors, jurists, legal scholars, nation states and domestic courts as the foundation upon which English, Canadian or American sovereignty in North America is based. The basic premise is that the first state to "discover" an uninhabited region with no other claims to it automatically acquires territorial sovereignty. Originally, the doctrine was limited to *terra nullius* — literally, a barren and deserted area — as reflected by the noted English scholar of the common law, Blackstone, writing in his *Commentaries*. The concept of *terra nullius* was expanded later, without justification, to include any area devoid of "civilized" society. In order to reflect colonial desires, the New World was said by some courts to fall within this expanded definition.

The traditional doctrine of discovery has never been recognized as vesting a valid claim or title to a "discovered" territory. Since [16th-century Spanish scholar Francisco de] Vitoria's vehement rejection of the doctrine in the 16th century, such a claim has been seen only as establishing an initial and incomplete title to the territory in question. This traditional interpretation has been ratified and affirmed in decisions from international courts in this century. While there is some debate among academics about this claim's validity, the dominant view clearly is in favour of the traditional elaboration of this doctrine.

Although the doctrine of discovery has been advanced occasionally by European powers since the "discovery" of the New World, such a claim was based more upon expediency than international law. The validity of the claim is dependent upon the status of the territory as *terra nullius* — an uninhabited land. Because Indians already occupied the land at the arrival of the Europeans, Vitoria unequivocally rejected such a title when it was asserted in the New World. Although there were many attempts to found claims based on discovery, the doctrine, by itself, was not considered sufficient to establish a valid claim, and does not appear to have been accepted officially by the competing states themselves, unless the discoverer was able to demonstrate an actual and effective governmental presence.

In *Johnson v. M'Intosh*, 21 U.S. (8 Wheat.) 543 (1823), however, the United States Supreme Court applied the doctrine of discovery in order to justify American sovereignty over the land included in what is now the United States of America. The court held that:

- The principle of discovery was acknowledged by all Europeans because it was in their interests to do so.
- The nation making the "discovery" had "the sole right of acquiring the soil and establishing settlements on it."
- The rule regulated the relations among the competing interests of European powers.
- The original inhabitants had the right to retain possession of their land, but were without any powers of alienation other than to the "discoverers" who had obtained exclusive title by virtue of making the "discovery."

When one considers both the international legal reality of the time and state practice, this decision appears to be more an effort to justify the taking of Indian territory that had already occurred than a serious analysis and application of the principles demanded by international law. Quite simply, the concept that Aboriginal inhabitants could only alienate their interest in the land to the "discoverer" was a legal fiction, because that concept did not originally exist in international law. In the *Island of Palmas* case (1928), 2 R.I.A.A. 829, the doctrine of discovery, as a means to justify the taking of Aboriginal lands, was considered and rejected definitively in just such a situation by the Permanent Court of Arbitration.

The Doctrine of Occupation

It has been argued by some that if discovery was seen to vest only an imperfect title, then discovery plus occupation completed the claim. There was, however, a traditional requirement that the land so discovered and occupied had to be *terra nullius*. At one time, an area devoid of "civilized" society was alleged by some scholars to fall within the scope of such a requirement. The more accurate historical interpretation, which is reflected by the modern jurisprudence in international law, precludes the requirement's application to any region with an indigenous population that is organized socially and politically.

According to the *Island of Palmas* case, a claim based on discovery was incomplete until accompanied by "the effective occupation of the region claimed to be discovered." The term "effective occupation" incorporates the notion of "uninterrupted and permanent possession." Based on such a rule and interpretation, it would appear that the only ones capable of successfully advancing a claim based on discovery and occupation may be the Aboriginal peoples themselves, because they are the ones who could argue best that they first discovered and occupied the vacant territory many thousands of years ago.

There was much debate about the definition of *terra nullius* for some time. Although the term was commonly accepted as meaning "uninhabited," some decisions have held that certain tribal lands could be said to fall within the scope of "uninhabited" if the peoples of the area exhibited an unwillingness to exploit the land in a "civilized" fashion. Such decisions, like many of the European policies of dealing with indigenous peoples, were largely the result of expediency and ethnocentrism. The present state of international law, as expressed by the International Court of Justice in the *Western Sahara Case*, precludes a region from being termed "uninhabited" if nomadic or resident tribes with a degree of social and political organization are present in the area. The issue then becomes, in individual cases, whether a specific indigenous group meets the test by exhibiting a sufficient degree of internal organization to be recognized as a distinct society, so as to effectively occupy the land and administer it as its own.

It appears from the Canadian case law that probably every Aboriginal group would meet this test. The standard is not similarity to European civilization, and no particular level of "sophistication" is required. International law merely requires that the society was organized sufficiently to meet the needs of its members and was recognizable by others as a legal entity that inhabited the territory with a settled system of government.

. . . . .

It should be noted that the colonizing nations themselves applied this test in the 18th and 19th centuries, with the Indian treaties demonstrating its practical application. The *Western Sahara Case*'s adoption of it in 1975 indicates that it reflects current international law. This test, however, should not be confused with international law requirements established for recognition as a nation state, which include additional criteria.

The Doctrine of Adverse Possession

The doctrine of adverse possession has frequently been linked to the above two doctrines to consolidate a valid claim to territory. Adverse possession basically posits that you can acquire title to part of another state's land if you openly occupy it for an extended period of time and the original owner acquiesces to your presence. In order for such a claim to be valid, there must be a *de facto* exercise of sovereignty which is peaceful and unchallenged. This doctrine is similar to one that exists within the Canadian domestic law by virtue of provincial and territorial legislation (the relevant *Limitations Act*, which establishes a 10- or 20-year rule among private parties and 60 years versus the Crown) or through reception of English law (regarding federal Crown land).

It would take little effort to discover in Canadian or Manitoban history sufficient examples of Aboriginal resistance to European occupation of the land to refute the application of this doctrine. Significant European occupation of lands in Manitoba did not occur until the Selkirk Settlement of 1811. That settlement came about as a direct result of Aboriginal consent being negotiated with Indian Chief Peguis by Lord Selkirk prior to the arrival and occupation of the land by the European settlers. The Hudson's Bay Company, which constituted the only significant European presence prior to that era, acknowledged in its practices the Indian sovereignty in the territory, and deliberately did not interfere with Indian control over their territory. In fact, various instructions sent to the trading post managers in North America by the senior officials of the company always emphasized the importance of not interfering in the internal affairs of the Indians, and in ensuring that wherever trading posts were established, the "Indian title" was purchased. When the company transferred its interest in the territory to Canada, it specifically required that the new Dominion negotiate land surrenders with the Indians, and in 1872 the Canadian government began to do so. Those earlier negotiations between the company and the Indians, as well as the later treaties between the Dominion and the First Nations, enabled the land to be settled by Europeans with Indian consent, as the latter agreed to share their territory.

To the extent that they reflect only a surrender of exclusive Indian title to much of the land, the treaties also amount to a confirmation of the Indian right to retain all other aspects of their Aboriginal title (*i.e.*, their "other" Aboriginal rights), since only the land rights were surrendered.

What is clear, however, is that Canadian sovereignty in western Canada is dependent to a large degree upon the validity of the treaties in those areas covered by them.

The Doctrine of Conquest

With respect to its traditional interpretation, the doctrine of conquest allowed using force or waging war only if a nation's security or rights were threatened. Under traditional international law, a country was no more justified in exploiting another through force than was a private individual. Conquest gave the victorious nation the full right to colonize the vanquished nation and change its legal regime. These rights usually were described in the peace treaty that ended the war. The doctrine of conquest only operated, however, if the conquered territory actually was annexed and possessed by the conqueror. In terms of the indigenous lands in North America, these criteria normally were not met, as no state of war was declared, although hostilities were not infrequent.

The present interpretation of the doctrine of conquest was outlined by the Permanent Court of International Justice in the *Status of Eastern Greenland Case* (1933), 3 W.C.R. 148 at 171. According to this decision:

> [The doctrine of conquest] only operates as a cause of lack of sovereignty when there is a war between two states and by reason of the defeat of one of them sovereignty over territory passes from the loser to the victorious state.

The doctrine of conquest frequently has been confused with the doctrine of discovery. Both are also the cause of further confusion, as they have international and domestic law purposes. At international law, conquest can cause the vanquished to lose sovereignty when the conqueror chooses to annex part or all of the territory of the loser. As has been indicated already, discovery *per se* can justify only the acquisition of sovereignty over uninhabited territories, and even then mere discovery without actual occupation is insufficient.

These two doctrines are also used for an entirely different purpose: determining what law comes to be applied within the newly acquired territory, as opposed to the international law standards governing the legitimacy of the process of acquisition itself. The common law distinguishes among settled, ceded and conquered colonies for the purposes of defining precisely when and on what terms the common law becomes the basic foundational law of the colony. This function is embraced within the English doctrine of reception of laws. It is quite possible, therefore, for a territory to be treated as being acquired at international law by conquest or cession (treaty), and then for the common law to be applied on the basis that the land is treated as a settled colony.

Canada, in fact, is treated largely as a settled colony under the reception of laws doctrine, with the common law being "received" by each colony as it stood on the date the first local colonial statute was passed. The sole example of using the conquest theory for domestic purposes relates to the colony of New France, in which King George III imposed the common law through the *Royal Proclamation of 1763*. French civil law was restored in non-criminal matters through the *Quebec Act of 1774*.

It is clear from our history that conquest was rarely, if ever, relevant in the acquisition of sovereignty over Aboriginal peoples and title to their lands. While this was argued forcefully by the Province of Nova Scotia and a variety of other governments in the *Simon* case, the Supreme Court of Canada decisively rejected its application in relation to the Micmac treaties of 1725 and 1752. The court further stated in *R. v. Simon*, [1985] 2 S.C.R. 387 that the conquest doctrine could apply in Canada only if a declaration of war had been proclaimed previously by the Crown, and there was no evidence of this ever occurring in Aboriginal-Crown relations.

The Doctrine of Cession

From the discussion thus far, it would appear that the consent of indigenous peoples is a necessary precondition to the legitimate acquisition of their territory, except where war has been officially declared and the conquest doctrine applies. The signing of valid treaties would fulfil the requirement for consent but ... the exact legal nature and effect of the Indian treaties are plagued by uncertainty. In some instances, Aboriginal groups voluntarily surrendered their aboriginal title, but in other instances fraud, undue influence and misunderstanding would seem to invalidate the arrangement.

The history of Indian treaties is filled with injustice and dishonesty, if not in the negotiations themselves, then certainly in the implementation and interpretation of the treaties. ... Indian people generally believed that they were only signing an arrangement to share the land with the newcomers, not, as some government officials later asserted, that they were agreeing to an abject surrender of their land and sovereignty. If they had been told that that [the latter] was to be the case, there is much doubt that they ever would have agreed. In fact, there is considerable evidence that many of the assurances given during the treaty negotiations were deliberately ignored by governments.

The Application of International Law to Aboriginal Peoples in Canada

Proper respect for the principles of international law by Canadian governments would have protected Aboriginal people from the treatment they received during the treaty-making era and subsequently. The colonization of the "New World" essentially involved the assertion of territorial and jurisdictional sovereignty by the European governments. In order for each one to legitimate its claims in the eyes of its European competitors, it was necessary for the colonizer to demonstrate a valid legal claim or title to the territory in question. In order to do so, however, reliance had to be placed on international law, yet that law contained principles concerning Aboriginal people which made it clear that the Aboriginal interest in the land could not be ignored. The manner in which legal title was asserted as against the Aboriginal people in subsequent domestic court decisions is clouded by the obvious lack of attention to those principles.

Thus, the traditional international law doctrines of discovery, occupation, adverse possession, conquest and cession bore little resemblance to the way in which they came to be applied in American, English and Canadian case law.

---

2. *The Use of Symbolic Acts*

In addition to these international law doctrines, the European nations also used symbolic acts, such as the planting of crosses and/or the recitation of words of conquest, to legitimize their claims to sovereignty over such lands. One such act was Jacques Cartier's erection of a cross on the point of the entrance to Gaspé Bay in July of 1534:

> Upon the 25 of the moneth, wee caused a faire high Crosse to be made of the height of thirty foote, which was made in the presence of many of them, upon the point of the entrance of the sayd haven [Gaspé Bay], in the middest whereof we hanged up a Shield with three Floure de Luces in it, and in the top was carved in the wood with Anticke letters this posie, Vive le Roy de France. Then before them all we set it upon sayd point .... So soone as it was up, we altogether kneeled downe before them, with our hands towards Heaven, yeelding God thankes: and we made signes unto them, shewing them the Heavens, and that all our salvation dependeth onely on him which in them dwelleth ... And after wee were returned to our ships, their Captaine clad with an old Beares skin, with three of his sonnes, and a brother of his with him, came unto us in one of their boates ... there he made a long Oration unto us, shewing us the crosse we had set up, and making a crosse with two fingers, then did he shew us all the Countrey about us, as if he would say that all was his, and that wee should not set up any crosse without his leave .... Then did we shew them with signes, that the crosse was but onely set up to be as a light and leader which wayes to enter into the port, and that wee would shortly come againe.[4]

It should be noted that when the Aboriginals inquired about the reasons for Cartier's erection of the cross, the true purpose of the act — to claim the land for France — was denied.

Another surreptitious use of symbolic acts was the Spanish *requerimiento*, or "requirement". The *requerimiento* was to be read aloud to peoples over whom Spain sought to exercise control. The text of the document reads as follows:

On the part of the Kind, don Fernando, and of doña Juana, his daughter, Queen of Castille and Leon, subduers of the barbarous nations, we their servants notify and make known to you, as the best we can, that the Lord our God, Living and Eternal, created the heaven and the Earth, and one man and one woman, of whom you and I, and all the men of the world, were and are descendants, and all those who come after us. But, on account of the multitude which has sprung from this man and woman in the five thousand years since the world was created, it was necessary that some men should go one way and some another, and that they should be divided into many kingdoms and provinces, for in one alone they could not be sustained.

Of all the nations God our Lord gave charge to one man, called St. Peter, that he should be Lord and Superior of all the men in the world, that all should obey him, and that he should be head of the whole human race, wherever men should live, and under whatever law, sect, or belief they should be; and he gave him the world for his kingdom and jurisdiction.

And he commanded him to place his seat in Rome, as the spot most fitting to rule the world from; but also he permitted him to have his seat in any other part of the world, and to judge and govern all Christians, Moors, Jews, Gentiles, and all other sects. This man was called Pope, as if to say, Admirable Great Father and Governor of men. The men who lived in that time obeyed that St. Peter, and took him for Lord, King, and Superior of the universe; so also have they regarded the others who after him have been elected to the Pontificate, and so it has been continued even until now, and will continue until the end of the world.

One of these Pontiffs ... made donation of these isles and Terra-firme to the aforesaid King and Queen and to their successors, our lords, with all that there are in these territories, as is contained in certain writings which passed upon the subject as aforesaid, which you can see if you wish.

So their Highnesses are kings and lords of these islands and land of Terra-firme by virtue of this donation; and some islands, and indeed almost all those to whom this land has been notified, have received and served their Highnesses ... with good will, without any resistance, immediately, without delay, when they were informed of the aforesaid facts. And also they received and obeyed the priests whom their Highnesses sent to preach to them and to teach them our Holy Faith; and all these, of their own free will, without any reward or condition, have become Christians, and are so, and their Highnesses have joyfully and benignantly received them, and also have commanded them to be treated as their subjects and vassals; and you too are held and obliged to do the same. Wherefore as best we can, we ask and require you that you consider what we have said to you, and that you take the time that shall be necessary to understand and deliberate upon it, and that you acknowledge the Church as the Ruler and Superior of the whole world and the high priest called Pope, and in his name the King and Queen doña Juana our lords, in his place, as superiors and lords and kings of these islands and this Terra-firme by virtue of the said donation, and that you consent and give place that these religious fathers should declare and preach to you the aforesaid.

If you do so, you will do well, and that which you are obliged to do to their Highnesses, and we in their name shall receive you in all love and charity, and shall leave you your wives, and your children, and your lands, free without servitude, that you may do with them and yourselves freely that which you like and think best, and they shall not compel you to turn

Christians, unless you yourselves, when informed of the truth, should wish to be converted to our Holy Catholic Faith, as almost all the inhabitants of the rest of the islands have done. And besides this, their Highnesses award you many privileges and exceptions and will grant you many benefits.

But if you do not do this, and wickedly and intentionally delay to do so, I certify to you that, with the help of God, we shall forcibly enter into your country and shall make war against you in all ways and manners that we can, and shall subject you to the yoke and obedience of the Church and of their Highnesses; we shall take you and your wives and children, and shall make slaves of them, and as such shall sell and dispose of them as their Highnesses may command; and we shall take away your goods, and shall do all the harm and damage that we can, as to vassals who do not obey, and refuse to receive their lord, and resist and contradict him; and we protest that the deaths and losses which shall accrue from this are you fault, and not that of their Highnesses, or our, or of these cavaliers who come with us. And that we have said this to you and made this Requirement, we request the notary here present to give us his testimony in writing, and we ask the rest who are present that they should be witnesses of this Requirement.[5]

While the *requerimiento* was meant to be read aloud by the Spanish to the inhabitants of invaded territories, in practice this did not occur in the intended manner. As indicated by scholar Lewis Hanke:

... the Requirement was read to trees and empty huts when no Indians were to be found. Captains muttered its theological phrases into their beards on the edge of sleeping Indian settlements, or even a league away before starting the formal attack, and at times some leather-lunged Spanish notary hurled its sonorous phrases after the Indians as they fled into the mountains.[6]

Hanke's account of the practical implementation of the *requerimiento* demonstrates that, much like Cartier's erection of a cross illustrated above, there was a marked difference between the purported implications of the symbolic acts engaged in and the subsequent explanations of those actions provided to the Aboriginal peoples concerned.

It is legitimate to question how symbolic acts such as these could form a basis for legitimate claims to territory, superseding those of the Aboriginal peoples, if their very purposes were concealed from those same peoples.

3. The Doctrine of Discovery and Early Aboriginal Rights Jurisprudence

Of these various international law doctrines and symbolic acts, the primary vehicle used by the Europeans to justify their claims to land was discovery. In *Johnson v. M'Intosh*, 8 Wheat. 543 (U.S. 1823), a case involving a dispute over the ownership of former Indian lands, Chief Justice John Marshall explained the function of discovery as a basis for acquiring title to Aboriginal lands at 572-3:

On the discovery of this immense continent, the great nations of Europe were eager to appropriate to themselves so much of it as they could respectively acquire. ... But, as they were all in pursuit of nearly the same object, it was necessary, *in order to avoid conflicting settlements, and consequent war with each other*, to establish a principle, which all should acknowledge as the law by which the right of *acquisition*, which they all asserted, should be regulated *as between themselves*. This principle was, that discovery gave title to the government by whose subjects or by whose authority it was made, *against all other European governments*, which title might be consummated by possession. [Emphasis added]

The issues raised in *Johnson v. M'Intosh* were soon considered again in *Worcester v. State of Georgia*, 6 Pet. 515 (U.S. 1832), excerpted below. That case dealt with the authority of the state of Georgia to pass laws pertaining to territory that was occupied by the Cherokee Nation but situated within Georgia's state boundaries. Samuel Worchester had entered Cherokee territory, with authority of the United States government, to preach. He was arrested under Georgia law for being on Cherokee territory without state authority and sentenced to four years' hard labour. He appealed his sentence to the United States Supreme Court.

In declaring that Georgia had no authority for passing such laws in Cherokee territory, Chief Justice Marshall and Justice M'Lean rendered classic judgments on the nature of Aboriginal title and the interaction between European and Aboriginal peoples.

WORCESTER v. STATE OF GEORGIA

6 Pet. 515 (U.S. 1832) (references omitted)

Marshall C.J.: — America, separated from Europe by a wide ocean, was inhabited by a distinct people, divided into separate nations, independent of each other and of the rest of the world, having institutions of their own, and governing themselves by their own laws. It is difficult to comprehend the proposition, that the inhabitants of either quarter of the globe could have rightful original claims of dominion over the inhabitants of the other, or over the lands they occupied; or that the discovery of either by the other should give the discoverer rights in the country discovered, which annulled the pre-existing rights of its ancient possessors.

After lying concealed for a series of ages, the enterprise of Europe, guided by nautical science, conducted some of her adventurous sons into this western world. They found it in possession of a people who had made small progress in agriculture or manufactures, and whose general employment was war, hunting, and fishing.

Did these adventurers, by sailing along the coast and occasionally landing on it, acquire for the several governments to whom they belonged, or by whom they were commissioned, a rightful property in the soil, from the Atlantic to the Pacific; or rightful dominion over the numerous people who occupied it? Or has nature, or the great Creator of all things, conferred these rights over hunters and fishermen, on agriculturists and manufacturers?

But power, war, conquest, give rights, which, after possession, are conceded by the world; and which can never be controverted by those on whom they descend. We proceed, then, to the actual state of things, having glanced at their origin; because holding it in our recollection might shed some light on existing pretensions.

The great maritime powers of Europe discovered and visited different parts of this continent at nearly the same time. The object was too immense for any one of them to grasp the whole; and the claimants were too powerful to submit to the exclusive or unreasonable pretensions of any single potentate. To avoid bloody conflicts, which might terminate disastrously to all, it was necessary for the nations of Europe to establish some principle which all would acknowledge, and which should decide their respective rights as between themselves. This principle, suggested by the actual state of things, was, "that discovery gave title to the government by whose subjects or by whose authority it was made, against all other European governments, which title might be consummated by possession."

This principle, acknowledged by all Europeans, because it was the interest of all to acknowledge it, gave to the nation making the discovery, as its inevitable consequence, the sole right of acquiring the soil and making settlements on it. It was an exclusive principle which shut out the right of competition among those who had agreed to it. It regulated the right given by discovery among the European discoverers; but could not affect the rights of those already in possession, either as aboriginal occupants, or as occupants by virtue of a discovery made before the memory of man. It gave exclusive right to purchase, but did not found that right on a denial of the right of the possessor to sell.

. . . . .

Soon after Great Britain determined on planting colonies in America, the king granted charters to companies of his subjects who associated for the purpose of carrying the views of the crown into effect, and of enriching themselves. The first of these charters was made before possession was taken of any part of the country. They purport, generally, to convey the soil, from the Atlantic to the South Seas. This soil was occupied by numerous and warlike nations, equally willing and able to defend their possessions. The extravagant and absurd idea, that the feeble settlements made on the sea coast, or the companies under whom they were made, acquired legitimate power by them to govern the people, or occupy the lands from sea to sea, did not enter the mind of any man. They were well understood to convey the title, which, according to the common law of European sovereigns respecting America, they might rightfully convey, and no more. This was the exclusive right of purchasing such lands as the natives were willing to sell. The crown could not be understood to grant what the crown did not affect to claim; nor was it so understood.

. . . . .

[T]hese grants asserted title against Europeans only, and were considered as blank paper so far as the rights of the natives were concerned.

. . . . .

Fierce and warlike in their character, they [the Indians] might be formidable enemies, or effective friends. Instead of rousing their resentments, by asserting claims to their lands, or to dominion over their persons, their alliance was sought by flattering professions, and purchased by rich presents. The English, the French, and the Spaniards were equally competitors for their friendship and their aid. Not well acquainted with the exact meaning of words, nor supposing it to be material whether they were called the subjects, or the children of their father in Europe; lavish in professions of duty and affection, in return for the rich presents they received; so long as their actual independence was untouched, and their right to self government acknowledged, they were willing to profess dependence on the power which furnished supplies of which they were in absolute need, and restrained dangerous intruders from entering their country: and this was probably the sense in which the term was understood by them.

Certain it is, that our history furnishes no example, from the first settlement of our country, of any attempt on the part of the crown to interfere with the internal affairs of the Indians, farther than to keep out the agents of foreign powers, who, as traders or otherwise, might seduce them into foreign alliances. The king purchased their lands when they were willing to sell, at a price they were willing to take; but never coerced a surrender of them. He also purchased their alliance and dependence by subsidies; but never intruded into the interior of their affairs, or interfered with their self government, so far as respected themselves only.

. . . . .

Such was the policy of Great Britain towards the Indian nations inhabiting the territory from which she excluded all other Europeans; such her claims, and such her practical exposition of the charters she had granted: she considered them as nations capable of maintaining the relations of peace and war; of governing themselves, under her protection; and she made treaties with them, the obligation of which she acknowledged.

This was the settled state of things when the war of our revolution commenced. The influence of our enemy was established; her resources enabled her to keep up that influence; and the colonists had much cause for the apprehension that the Indian nations would, as the allies of Great Britain, add their arms to hers. This, as was to be expected, became an object of great solicitude to congress. Far from advancing a claim to their lands, or asserting any right of dominion over them, congress resolved "that the securing and preserving the friendship of the Indian nations appears to be a subject of the utmost moment to these colonies."

The early journals of congress exhibit the most anxious desire to conciliate the Indian nations. Three Indian departments were established; and commissioners appointed in each, "to treat with the Indians in their respective departments, in the name and on behalf of the United Colonies, in order to preserve peace and friendship with the said Indians, and to prevent their taking any part in the present commotions."

The most strenuous exertions were made to procure those supplies on which Indian friendships were supposed to depend; and every thing which might excite hostility was avoided.

. . . . .

The general law of European sovereigns, respecting their claims in America, limited the intercourse of Indians, in a great degree, to the particular potentate whose ultimate right of domain was acknowledged by the others. This was the general state of things in time of peace. It was sometimes changed in war. The consequence was, that their supplies were derived chiefly from that nation, and their trade confined to it. Goods, indispensable to their comfort, in the shape of presents, were received from the same hand. What was of still more importance, the strong hand of government was interposed to restrain the disorderly and licentious from intrusions into their country, from encroachments on their lands, and from those acts of violence which were often attended by reciprocal murder. The Indians perceived in this protection only what was beneficial to themselves — an engagement to punish aggressions on them. It involved, practically, no claim to their lands, no dominion over their persons. It merely bound the nation to the British crown, as a dependent ally, claiming the protection of a powerful friend and neighbour, and receiving the advantages of that protection, without involving a surrender of their national character.

· · · · ·

The Indian nations were, from their situation, necessarily dependent on some foreign potentate for the supply of their essential wants, and for their protection from lawless and injurious intrusions into their country. That power was naturally termed their protector. They had been arranged under the protection of Great Britain: but the extinguishment of the British power in their neighbourhood, and the establishment of that of the United States in its place, led naturally to the declaration, on the part of the Cherokees, that they were under the protection of the United States, and of no other power. They assumed the relation with the United States, which had before subsisted with Great Britain.

This relation was that of a nation claiming and receiving the protection of one more powerful: not that of individuals abandoning their national character, and submitting as subjects to the laws of a master.

· · · · ·

The Indian nations had always been considered as distinct, independent political communities, retaining their original natural rights, as the undisputed possessors of the soil, from time immemorial, with the single exception of that imposed by irresistible power, which excluded them from intercourse with any other European potentate than the first discoverer of the coast of the particular region claimed: and this was a restriction which those European potentates imposed on themselves, as well as on the Indians. The very term "nation," so generally applied to them, means "a people distinct from others." The constitution, by declaring treaties already made, as well as those to be made, to be the supreme law of the land, has adopted and sanctioned the ... treaties with the Indian nations, and consequently admits their rank among those powers who are capable of making treaties. The words "treaty" and "nation" are words of our own language, selected in our diplomatic and legislative proceedings, by ourselves, having each a definite and well understood meaning. We have applied them to Indians, as we have applied them to the other nations of the earth. They are applied to all in the same sense.

. . . . .

The actual state of things at the time, and all history since, explain these charters; and the king of Great Britain, at the treaty of peace, could cede only what belonged to his crown. These newly asserted titles can derive no aid from the articles so often repeated in Indian treaties; extending to them, first, the protection of Great Britain, and afterwards that of the United States. These articles are associated with others, recognizing their title to self government. The very fact of repeated treaties with them recognizes it; and the settled doctrine of the law of nations is, that a weaker power does not surrender its independence — its right to self government, by associating with a stronger, and taking its protection. A weak state, in order to provide for its safety, may place itself under the protection of one more powerful, without stripping itself of the right of government, and ceasing to be a state.

. . . . .

The Cherokee nation, then, is a distinct community occupying its own territory, with boundaries accurately described, in which the laws of Georgia can have no force, and which the citizens of Georgia have no right to enter, but with the assent of the Cherokees themselves, or in conformity with treaties, and with the acts of congress.

. . . . .

It is the opinion of this court that the judgment of the superior court for the country of Gwinnett, in the state of Georgia, condemning Samuel A. Worcester to hard labour, in the penitentiary of the state of Georgia, for four years, was pronounced by that court under colour of a law which is void, as being repugnant to the constitution, treaties, and laws of the United States, and ought, therefore, to be reversed and annulled.

M'lean J.: — With the decision, just given, I concur.

. . . . .

By the treaties and laws of the United States, rights are guarantied to the Cherokees, both as it respects their territory and internal polity. By the laws of Georgia these rights are abolished; and not only abolished, but an ignominious punishment is inflicted on the Indians and others; for the exercise of them. The important question then arises, which shall stand, the laws of the United States, or the laws of Georgia? No rule of construction, or subtlety of argument, can evade an answer to this question. The response must be, so far as the punishment of the plaintiff in error is concerned, in favour of the one or the other.

. . . . .

A reference has been made to the policy of the United States on the subject of Indian affairs, before the adoption of the constitution, with the view of ascertaining in what light the Indians have been considered by the first official acts, in relation to them, by the United States. For this object, it might not be improper to notice how they were considered by the European inhabitants, who first formed settlement in this part of the continent of America.

The abstract right of every section of the human race to a reasonable portion of the soil, by which to acquire the means of subsistence, cannot be controverted. And it is equally clear, that the range of nations or tribes, who exist in the hunter state, may be restricted within reasonable limits. They shall not be permitted to roam, in the pursuit of game, over an extensive and rich country, whilst in other parts, human beings are being crowded so closely together, as to render the means of subsistence precarious. The law of nature, which is paramount to all other laws, gives the right to every nation, to the enjoyment of a reasonable extent of country, so as to derive the means of subsistence from the soil.

In this view perhaps, our ancestors, when they first migrated to this country, might have taken possession of a limited extent of the domain, had they been sufficiently powerful, without negotiation or purchase from the native Indians. But this course is believed to have been nowhere taken. A more conciliatory mode was preferred, and one which was better calculated to impress the Indians, who were then powerful, with a sense of the justice of their white neighbours. The occupancy of their lands was never assumed, except upon the basis of contract, and on the payment of a valuable consideration.

This policy has obtained from the earliest white settlements in this country, down to the present time. Some cessions of territory may have been made by the Indians, in compliance with the terms on which peace was offered by the whites; but the soil, thus taken, was taken by the laws of conquest, and always as an indemnity for the expenses of the war, commenced by the Indians.

At no time has the sovereignty of the country been recognized as existing in the Indians, but they have been always admitted to possess many of the attributes of sovereignty. All the rights which belong to self government have been recognized as vested in them. Their right of occupancy has never been questioned, but the fee in the soil has been considered in the government. This may be called the right to the ultimate domain, but the Indians have a present right in possession.

From this discussion of early Crown-Aboriginal interaction and the use of international law doctrines to justify the dispossession of Aboriginal peoples, a number of questions arise. For one, how could the doctrine of discovery be used in relation to Aboriginal lands in North America if the doctrine required land to be *terra nullius*? Second, if discovery only granted to the "discovering" nation the right to *purchase* title from the Aboriginal inhabitants, does that entail that the latter "owned" the lands in their possession? If they did not "own" the lands, who did? Finally, if the Law of Nations was designed to govern controversies between its member states, was it binding on Aboriginal peoples who were not members?

D. THE BRITISH CROWN'S RESPONSE

The pre-emptive right to purchase land from the Aboriginal peoples was highly sought-after by Europeans seeking to establish colonies in North America. By acquiring this right, not only could a European nation obtain title, but it could exclude its European colonial competitors. The wars between Britain and France in North America resulted, in part, from those nations' attempts to acquire or maintain this pre-emptive right.

Following the conquest of New France in 1760-61, Britain endeavoured to consolidate its hold on its North American colonies and reinforce its right to purchase the Aboriginal peoples' interest in land that it laid claim to. The conquest had created concern for the Aboriginal allies of France, who were anxious about its effects on them politically and economically. Britain sought to smooth over these concerns by issuing a policy statement detailing the status of its relations with the Aboriginal peoples. This policy statement was the *Royal Proclamation of 1761*, Order of the King in Council on a Report of the Lords of Trade, 2 December 1761, issued by King George III at the request of the Lords of Trade. The report of the Lords of Trade, requesting that the king issue the proclamation, and the proclamation itself, are reproduced below.

1. The Report of the Lords of Trade, 23 November 1761

REPORT OF THE LORDS OF TRADE, 23 NOVEMBER 1761

in E.B. O'Callaghan, ed., *Documents Relative to the Colonial History of the State of New York*, 11 vols. (Albany: Weed, Parsons, 1853-61) VII at 472-6

Your Majesty, having been pleased to referr unto this Committee a Representation from the Lords Commissioners for Trade and Plantations dated the 11th of this Instant, Setting forth "That they have had under their consideration several letters and papers which they have received from Cadwallader Colden Esq' Lieutenant Governor and late Commander in Chief of Your Majesty's Province of New York in America.

. . . . .

"That the Said Lords Commissioners should not upon this occasion take upon them to controvert the general principles of Policy upon which either one or other of these general propositions is founded, but however expedient and constitutional they may appear in the abstract view and consideration of them. Yet they apprehend that when they come to be applied to the present State of Your Majesty's Colonies they will appear in a very different light and be found, the one to be dangerous to their Security and the other destructive to the Interest of the people, and subversive of the Policy by which alone Colonies can be kept in a just dependence upon the Government of the Mother Country.

That this is the General Light in which they see these measures, but as they are in their nature separate and distinct, so they will as the said Lords Commissioners apprehend require a separate and distinct consideration and therefore they humbly offer to Your Majesty what has occurred to them upon each in the order in which they have placed them That it is unnecessary as it would be tedious to enter into a Detail of all the Causes of Complaint which, our Indian Allies had against us at the commencement of the troubles in America, and which not only induced them thô reluctantly to take up the Hatchet against us and desolate the Settlement on the Frontiers but encouraged our enemies to pursue those Measures which have involved us in a dangerous and critical war, it will be sufficient for the present purpose to observe that the primary cause of that discontent which produced these fatal Effects was the Cruelty and Injustice with which they had been treated with respect to their hunting grounds, in open violation of those solemn compacts by which they had yielded to us the Dominion, but not the property of those Lands. It was happy for us that we were early awakened to a proper sense of the Injustice and bad Policy of such a Conduct towards the Indians, and no sooner were those measures pursued which indicated a Disposition to do them all possible justice upon this head of Complaint than those hostilities which had produced such horrid scenes of devastation ceased, and the Six Nations and their Dependants became at once from the most inveterate Enemies our fast and faithful Friends.

That their steady and intrepid Conduct upon the Expedition under General Amherst for the Reduction of Canada is a striking example of this truth, and they now, trusting to our good Faith, impatiently wait for the event which by putting an End to the War shall not only ascertain the British Empire in America but enable Your Majesty to renew those Compacts by which their property in their Lands shall be ascertained and such a system of Reformation introduced with respect to our Interests and Commerce with them as shall at the same time that it redresses their Complaints and establishes their Rights give equal Security and Stability to the rights and Interests of all Your Majesty's American Subjects.

That under these Circumstances and in this situation the granting Lands hitherto unsettled and establishing Colonies upon the Frontiers before the claims of the Indians are ascertained appears to be a measure of the most dangerous tendency, and is more particularly so in the present case, as these settlements now proposed to be made, especially those upon the Mohawk River are in that part of the Country of the Possession of which the Indians are the most jealous having at different times expressed in the strongest terms their Resolution to oppose all settlements thereon as a manifest violation of their Rights.

That the principles of Policy which the said Lord Commissioners have laid down are they apprehended in their nature so clear and uncontrovertible that it is almost unnecessary to add anything further to induce Your Majesty to give immediate Orders for putting a stop to all Settlements upon the Mohawk River and about Lake George until the Event of the War is determined and such Measures taken thereupon, with respect to our Indian Allies as shall be thought expedient, and yet it may be proper to observe that independent of what regards our Connection with the Indians the conduct of those who have in former times been intrusted with the Administration of the Government of New York has in reference to granting of Lands in general been very exceptionable and has held forth a very bad example to their Successors."

. . . . .

The Lords of the Committee this day took the said Representation into their consideration, and agreeing in opinion with the said Lord Commissioners for Trade and Plantations do humbly report to Your Majesty that they conceive it advisable that Your Majestys Pleasure should be made known upon the first point of Granting Lands, as well in the Colony of New York as in all other Your Majestys Colonies on the Continent of America, where such grants interfere with the Indians bordering on those Colonies. ... And therefore that Your Majesty may be graciously pleased to order the said Lord Commissioners to prepare Draughts of Instructions proper to be sent hereupon to the Governors or Commanders in Chief of all Your Majesty's Islands and Colonies in America accordingly, to the end that due obedience be given thereto and the matters complained of so detrimental to the public service, prevented for the future.

His Majesty taking the said Report into consideration was pleased by the advice of his Privy Council to approve of what is therein proposed and accordingly to order, as it is hereby ordered, that the Lord Commissioners for Trade and Plantations do prepare Draughts of Instructions proper to be sent with respect to the first point of granting Lands, as well to the Governor or Commander in Chief of the Colony of New York, as to the Governors or Commanders in Chief of all other His Majesty's Colonies on the Continent of America where such grants interfere with the Indians bordering on those Colonies. ... And that such Draughts of Instructions be laid before His Majesty at this Board for his Royal Approbation.

---

2. The Royal Proclamation of 1761

ORDER OF THE KING IN COUNCIL ON A REPORT OF THE LORDS OF TRADE, 2 DECEMBER 1761

in E.B. O'Callaghan, ed., *Documents Relative to the Colonial History of the State of New York*, 11 vols. (Albany: Weed, Parsons, 1853-61) VII at 478-9

Draft of an Instruction for the Governors of Nova Scotia, New Hampshire, New York, Virginia, North Carolina, South Carolina, and Georgia forbidding them to Grant Lands or make Settlements which may interfere with the Indians bordering on those Colonies.

WHEREAS the peace and security of Our Colonies and Plantations upon the Continent of North America does greatly depend upon the Amity and

Alliance of the several Nations or Tribes of Indians bordering upon the said Colonies and upon a just and faithful Observance of those Treaties and Compacts which have been heretofore solemnly entered into with the said Indians by Our Royall Predecessors Kings & Queens of this Realm, And whereas notwithstanding the repeated Instructions which have been from time to time given by Our Royal Grandfather to the Governors of Our several Colonies upon this head the said Indians have made and do still continue to make great complaints that Settlements have been made and possession taken of Lands, the property of which they have by Treaties reserved to themselves by persons claiming the said lands under pretence of deeds of Sale and Conveyance illegally fraudulently and surreptitiously obtained of the said Indians; And Whereas it has likewise been represented unto Us that some of Our Governors or other Chief Officers of Our said Colonies regardless of the Duty they owe to Us and of the Welfare and Security of our Colonies have countenanced such unjust claims and pretensions by passing Grants of the Lands so pretended to have been purchased of the Indians We therefor taking this matter into Our Royal Consideration, as also the fatal Effects which would attend a discontent amongst the Indians in the present situation of affairs, and being determined upon all occasions to support and protect the said Indians in their just Rights and Possessions and to keep inviolable the Treaties and Compacts which have been entered into with them, Do hereby strictly enjoyn & command that neither yourself nor any Lieutenant Governor, President of the Council or Commander in Chief of Our said [Colony/Province] of _____ do upon any presence whatever upon pain of Our highest Displeasure and of being forthwith removed from your or his office, pass any Grant or Grants to any persons whatever of any lands within or adjacent to the Territories possessed or occupied by the said Indians or the Property Possession of which has at any time been reserved to or claimed by them. And it is Our further will and Pleasure that you do publish a proclamation in Our Name strictly enjoining and requiring all persons whatever who may either wilfully or inadvertently have seated themselves on any Lands so reserved to or claimed by the said Indians without any lawfull Authority for so doing forthwith to remove therefrom And in case you shall find upon strict enquiry to be made for that purpose that any person or persons do claim to hold or possess any lands within Our said [Province/Colony] upon pretence of purchases made of the said Indians without a proper licence first had and obtained either from Us or any of Our Royal Predecessors or any person acting under Our or their Authority you are forthwith to cause a prosecution to be carried on against such person or persons who shall have made such fraudulent purchases to the end that the land may be recovered by due Course of Law And whereas the wholesome Laws that have at different times been passed in several of Our said Colonies and the instructions which have been given by Our Royal Predecessors for restraining persons from purchasing lands of the Indians without a Licence for that purpose and for regulating the proceedings upon such purchases have not been duly observed. It is therefore Our express Will and Pleasure that when any application shall be made to you for licence to purchase lands of the Indians you do forebear to grant such Licence untill you shall have first transmitted to Us, by Our Commissioners for Trade and Plantations the particulars of such applications as well as in respect to the situation as the extent of the lands so proposed to be purchased and shall have received Our further directions therein; And it is Our further Will and Pleasure that you do forthwith cause this Our Instruction to you to be made Publick not only within all parts of your said [Provinces/Colonies] inhabited by Our Subjects, but also amongst the Several Tribes of Indians living within the same to the end that Our Royal Will and Pleasure in the Premises may be known and that the Indians may be apprized of Our determin'd Resolution to support them in their just Rights, and inviolably to observe Our Engagements with them.

---

3. Governor Belcher's Proclamation

Under the authority of the *Royal Proclamation of 1761*, Governor Jonathan Belcher of Nova Scotia issued his own proclamation that set out the land rights of the Aboriginal peoples inhabiting Nova Scotia, as recognized by the British Crown.

GOVERNOR BELCHER'S PROCLAMATION, NOVA SCOTIA, 1762

in P.A. Cumming and N.H. Mickenberg, *Native Rights in Canada*, 2nd ed.
(Toronto: Indian-Eskimo Association of Canada, 1972)
Appendix I at 287-8

His Majesty by His Royal Instructions, Given at the Court of St. James, the 9th day of December, 1761, having been pleased to Signify,

THAT the Indians have made, and still do continue to make great Complaints, that Settlements have been made, and Possessions taken, of Lands, the Property of which they have by Treaties reserved to themselves, by Persons claiming the said Lands, under Pretence of Deeds of Sale & Conveyance, illegally, Fraudulently, and surreptitiously obtained of said Indians.

AND THAT His Majesty had taken this Matter into His Royal Consideration, as also the fatal Effects which would attend a Discontent among the Indians in the Present Situation of Affairs.

AND BEING determined upon all Occasions to support and protect the Indians in their just Rights and Possessions and to keep inviolable the treaties and Compacts which have been entered into with them, was pleased to declare His Majesty's further Royal Will and Pleasure, that His Governor or Commander in Chief in this Province should publish a Proclamation in His Majesty's Name, for this special purpose:

WHEREFORE in dutiful Obedience to His Majesty's Royal Orders I do accordingly publish this proclamation in His Majesty's Royal Name, strictly injoining and requiring all Persons what ever, who may either willfully or inadvertently have seated themselves upon any Lands so reserved to or claimed by the said Indians, without any lawful Authority for so doing, forthwith to remove therefrom.

AND, WHEREAS Claims have been laid before me in behalf of the Indians for Fronsac Passage and from thence to Nartigonneich, and from Nartigonneich to Piktouk, and from thence to Cape Jeanne, from thence to Emchih, from thence to Ragi Pontouch, from thence to Tedueck, from thence to Cape Rommentin, from thence to Miramichy, and from thence to Bay Des Chaleurs, and the environs of Canso. From thence to Mushkoodabwet, and so along the coast, as the Claims and Possessions of the said Indians, for the more special purpose of hunting, fowling and fishing, I do hereby strictly injoin and caution all persons to avoid all molestation of the said Indians in their said claims, till His Majesty's pleasure in this behalf shall be signified.

AND if any person or persons have possessed themselves of any part of the same to the prejudice of the said Indians in their Claims before specified or without lawful Authority, they are hereby required forthwith to remove, as they will otherwise be prosecuted with the utmost Rigour of the Law.

Given under my Hand and Seal at Halifax this fourth Day of May, 1762, and in the Second Year of His Majesty's Reign.

Shortly after Governor Belcher's proclamation was issued, he was replaced as governor and the copies of his proclamation were rounded up and destroyed. Nothing more was heard of either the *Royal Proclamation of 1761* or Governor Belcher's proclamation. Shortly afterwards, a second royal proclamation was issued. This later proclamation, dating from 1763, made no explicit mention of treaties or treaty relations, as its predecessor had. However, it did include the same sentiments regarding the British Crown's expression of its relationship with the Aboriginal peoples and the nature of its claim to title to North American lands.

4. *The Royal Proclamation of 1763*

The *Royal Proclamation of 1763* established British policy for its North American colonies. Following the defeat of New France, Britain had acquired new territories from France under the *Treaty of Paris, 1763*, February 10, 1763. Yet, Britain still faced a number of threats to its North American ambitions of empire. In addition to the potential threat stemming from the French population of the new colony of Quebec, other issues to contend with included deteriorating British-Indian relations that had led to Pontiac's Rebellion in 1763 and the American colonies' growing expansionist desires. The Proclamation was designed to curb American territorial expansion, establish control over Quebec, and prevent the outbreak of politically and economically costly Indian wars. This was to be accomplished by the creation of an immense Indian hunting ground in the Proclamation which was intended to placate Aboriginal concerns while functioning as a buffer between the French loyalists in Quebec and the agitated American colonists.

The relevant portions of the Proclamation dealing with Aboriginal land rights are reproduced below:

ROYAL PROCLAMATION OF 7 OCTOBER, 1763

R.S.C. 1985, App. II, No. 1

Whereas We have taken into Our Royal Consideration the extensive and valuable Acquisitions in America, secured to our Crown by the late Definitive Treaty of Peace, concluded at Paris, the 10th Day of February last; and being desirous that all Our loving Subjects, as well of our Kingdom as of our Colonies in America, may avail themselves with all convenient Speed, of the great Benefits and Advantages which must accrue therefrom to their Commerce, Manufactures, and Navigation, We have thought fit, with the Advice of our Privy Council, to issue this our Royal Proclamation, hereby to publish and declare to all our loving Subjects, that we have, with the Advice of our Said Privy Council, granted our Letters Patent, under our Great Seal of Great Britain, to erect, within the Countries and Islands ceded and confirmed to Us by the said Treaty, Four distinct and separate Governments, styled and called by the names of Quebec, East Florida, West Florida and Grenada. ...

And whereas it is just and reasonable, and essential to our Interest, and the Security of our Colonies, that the several Nations or Tribes of Indians with whom We are connected, and who live under our Protection, should not be molested or disturbed in the Possession of such Parts of Our Dominions and Territories as, not having been ceded to or purchased by Us, are reserved to them, or any of them, as their Hunting Grounds. — We do therefore, with the Advice of our Privy Council, declare it to be our Royal Will and Pleasure, that no Governor or Commander in Chief in any of our Colonies of Quebec, East Florida, or West Florida, do presume, upon any Pretence whatever, to grant Warrants of Survey, or pass any Patents for Lands beyond the Bounds of their respective Governments, as described in their Commissions; as also that no Governor or Commander in Chief in any of our other Colonies or Plantations in America do presume for the present, and until our further Pleasure be known, to grant Warrants of Survey, or pass Patents for any Lands beyond the Heads or Sources of any of the Rivers which fall into the Atlantic Ocean from the West and North West, or upon any Lands whatever, which, not having been ceded to or purchased by Us as aforesaid, are reserved to the said Indians, or any of them.

And We do further declare it to be Our Royal Will and Pleasure, for the present as aforesaid, to reserve under our Sovereignty, Protection, and Dominion, for the use of the said Indians, all the Lands and Territories not included within the Limits of Our said Three new Governments, or within the Limits of the Territory granted to the Hudson's Bay Company, as also all the Lands and Territories lying to the Westward of the Sources of the Rivers which fall into the Sea from the West and North West as aforesaid.

And We do strictly forbid, on Pain of our Displeasure, all our loving Subjects from making any Purchases or Settlements whatever, or taking Possession of any of the Lands above reserved, without our especial leave and Licence for that Purpose first obtained.

And, We do further strictly enjoin and require all Persons whatever who have either wilfully or inadvertently seated themselves upon any Lands within the Countries above described, or upon any other Lands which, not having been ceded to or purchased by Us, are still reserved to the said Indians as aforesaid, forthwith to remove themselves from such Settlements.

And whereas great Frauds and Abuses have been committed in purchasing Lands of the Indians, to the great Prejudice of our Interests, and to the great Dissatisfaction of the said Indians, In order, therefore, to prevent such Irregularities for the future, and to the end that the Indians may be convinced of our Justice and determined Resolution to remove all reasonable Cause of Discontent, We do, with the Advice of our Privy Council strictly enjoin and require, that no private Person do presume to make any purchase from the said Indians of any Lands reserved to the said Indians, within those parts of our Colonies where, We have thought proper to allow Settlement; but that, if at any Time any of the Said Indians should be inclined to dispose of the said Lands, the same shall be Purchased only for Us, in our Name, at some public Meeting or Assembly of the said Indians, to be held for that Purpose by the Governor or Commander in Chief of our Colony respectively within which they shall lie; and in case they shall lie within the limits of any Proprietary Government, they shall be purchased only for the Use and in the name of such Proprietaries, conformable to such Directions and Instructions as We or they shall think proper to give for that Purpose.

. . . . .

Given at our Court at St. James's the 7th Day of October 1763, in the Third Year of our Reign.

———————

In many respects, the *Royal Proclamation of 1763* may be viewed as similar in intention and effect to the version of discovery formulated by Chief Justice Marshall in *Johnson v. M'Intosh*, 21 U.S. (8 Wheat.) 543 (1823), and *Worcester v. State of Georgia*6 Pet. 515 (U.S. 1832). The Proclamation provided Britain with the exclusive right to treat with the Aboriginal peoples in those territories claimed by it; it did not provide a right of sovereignty over them and their lands. As the Royal Commission on Aboriginal Peoples has explained:

> [T]he Proclamation portrays Aboriginal nations as autonomous political units living under the Crown's protection and on lands that are already part of the Crown's dominions. Aboriginal nations hold inherent authority over their internal affairs and the power to deal with the Crown by way of treaty and agreement. In a word, it portrays the link between Aboriginal peoples and the Crown as broadly 'confederal'.[7]

The protection of Aboriginal interests in the Proclamation may be viewed as qualifications imposed by the Crown upon its own rights. These qualifications stem from the Crown's recognition and affirmation of the Aboriginal peoples' pre-existing right to land. Thus, the Proclamation did not grant new rights to the Aboriginal peoples, it simply affirmed existing rights. As explained in *R. v. Koonungnak* (1963), 42 C.R. 143, [1963-64] 45 W.W.R. 282 at 302 (N.W.T. Terr. Ct.):

This proclamation has been spoken of as the 'Charter of Indian Rights.' Like so many great charters in English history, it does not create rights but rather affirms old rights. The Indians and the Eskimos had their aboriginal rights and English law has always recognized these rights.

See also A.C. Hamilton, *A New Partnership* (Ottawa: Ministry of Public Works & Government Services Canada, 1995) at 7: "The Royal Proclamation of October 7, 1763 recited the legal principles of that day. It did not make new law."

Indeed, the Proclamation also carried on the British tradition of requiring Aboriginal peoples interested in alienating their lands to first surrender them to the Crown (see the discussion of surrenders, *infra*). This practice had existed previously in the 13 American colonies, as seen, for example, in legislation from Maryland in 1638 and 1649 and from Virginia in 1655.[8]

The Proclamation's recognition of Aboriginal land rights has been incorporated into section 25 of the *Constitution Act, 1982*, being Schedule B to the *Canada Act 1982* (U.K.), 1982, c. 11, which reads:

> The guarantee in this Charter of certain rights and freedoms shall not be construed so as to abrogate or derogate from any aboriginal, treaty, or other rights or freedoms that pertain to the aboriginal peoples of Canada including
>
> (a)   any rights or freedoms that have been recognized by the Royal Proclamation of October 7, 1763.

The effect of this recognition has yet to be judicially determined. However, there have been numerous disputes over the effect of the Proclamation's recognition of Aboriginal lands rights. The first of these came in the landmark case of *St. Catherine's Milling & Lumber Co. v. R.*, reproduced below.

E. CANADIAN ABORIGINAL TITLE JURISPRUDENCE

The *St. Catherine's* case was the first important consideration of Aboriginal title in Canada. It involved a dispute between the Province of Ontario and the Dominion of Canada over the ownership of former Indian lands and the rights to timber thereon.

ST. CATHERINE'S MILLING & LUMBER CO. v. R.

(1888), 14 App. Cas. 46 (P.C.)

The judgment of their Lordships was delivered by

Lord Watson: — On the 3rd of October, 1873, a formal treaty or contract was concluded between commissioners appointed by the Government of the Dominion of Canada, on behalf of Her Majesty the Queen, of the one part, and a number of chiefs and headmen duly chosen to represent the Salteaux tribe of Ojibbeway Indians, of the other part, by which the latter, for certain considerations, released and surrendered to the Government of the Dominion, for Her Majesty and her successors, the whole right and title of the Indian inhabitants whom they represented, to a tract of country upwards of 50,000 square miles in extent. By an article of the treaty it is stipulated that, subject to such regulations as may be made by the Dominion Government, the Indians are to have right to pursue their avocations of hunting and fishing throughout the surrendered territory, with the exception of those portions of it which may, from time to time, be required or taken up for settlement, mining, lumbering, or other purposes.

Of the territory thus ceded to the Crown, an area of not less than 32,000 square miles is situated within the boundaries of the Province of Ontario; and, with respect to that area, a controversy has arisen between the Dominion and Ontario, each of them maintaining that the legal effect of extinguishing the Indian title has been to transmit to itself the entire beneficial interest of the lands, as now vested in the Crown, freed from incumbrance of any kind, save the qualified privilege of hunting and fishing mentioned in the treaty.

Acting on the assumption that the beneficial interest in these lands had passed to the Dominion Government, their Crown Timber Agent, on the 1st of May, 1883, issued to the appellants, the St. Catherine's Milling and Lumber Company, a permit to cut and carry away one million feet of lumber from a specified portion of the disputed area. The appellants having availed themselves of that licence, a writ was filed against them in the Chancery Division of the High Court of Ontario, at the instance of the Queen on the information of the Attorney-General of the Province, praying — (1) a declaration that the appellants have no rights in respect of the timber cut by them upon the lands specified in their permit; (2) an injunction restraining them from trespassing on the premises and from cutting any timber thereon; (3) an injunction against the removal of timber already cut; and (4) decree for the damage occasioned by their wrongful acts. The Chancellor of Ontario, on the 10th of June, 1885, decerned with costs against the appellants, in terms of the first three of these conclusions, and referred the amount of damage to the Master in Ordinary. The judgment of the learned Chancellor was unanimously affirmed on the 20th of April, 1886, by the Court of Appeal for Ontario, and an appeal taken from their decision to the Supreme Court of Canada was dismissed on the 20th of June, 1887, by a majority of four of the six judges constituting the court.

Although the present case relates exclusively to the right of the Government of Canada to dispose of the timber in question to the appellant company, yet its decision necessarily involves the determination of the larger question between that government and the province of Ontario with respect to the legal consequences of the treaty of 1873.

. . . . .

The capture of Quebec in 1759, and the capitulation of Montreal in 1760, were followed in 1763 by the cession to Great Britain of Canada and all its dependencies, with the sovereignty, property, and possession, and all other rights which had at any previous time been held or acquired by the Crown of France. A royal proclamation was issued on the 7th of October, 1763, shortly after the date of the Treaty of Paris, by which His Majesty King George erected four distinct and separate Governments, styled respectively, Quebec, East Florida, West Florida, and Grenada, specific boundaries being assigned to each of them. Upon the narrative that it was just and reasonable that the several nations and tribes of Indians who lived under British protection should not be molested or disturbed in the "possession of such parts of Our dominions and territories as, not having been ceded to or purchased by us, are reserved to them or any of them as their hunting grounds," it is declared that no governor or commander-in-chief in any of the new colonies of Quebec, East Florida, or West Florida, do presume on any pretence to grant warrants of survey or pass any patents for lands beyond the bounds of their respective governments, or "until Our further pleasure be known," upon any lands whatever which, not having been ceded or purchased as aforesaid, are reserved to the said Indians or any of them. It was further declared "to be Our Royal will, for the present, as aforesaid, to reserve under Our sovereignty, protection, and dominion, for the use of the said Indians, all the land and territories not included within the limits of Our said three new Governments, or within the limits of the territory granted to the Hudson's Bay Company." The proclamation also enacts that no private person shall make any purchase from the Indians of lands reserved to them within those colonies where settlement was permitted, and that all purchases must be on behalf of the Crown, in a public assembly of the Indians, by the governor or commander-in-chief of the colony in which the lands lie.

The territory in dispute has been in Indian occupation from the date of the proclamation until 1873. During that interval of time Indian affairs have been administered successively by the Crown, by the Provincial Governments, and (since the passing of the British North America Act, 1867), by the Government of the Dominion. The policy of these administrations has been all along the same in this respect, that the Indian inhabitants have been precluded from entering into any transaction with a subject for the sale or transfer of their interest in the land, and have only been permitted to surrender their rights to the Crown by a formal contract, duly ratified in a meeting of their chiefs or head men convened for the purpose. Whilst there have been changes in the administrative authority, there has been no change since the year 1763 in the character of the interest which its Indian inhabitants had in the lands surrendered by the treaty. Their possession, such as it was, can only be ascribed to the general provisions made by the royal proclamation in favour of all Indian tribes then living under the sovereignty and protection of the British Crown. It was suggested in the course of the argument for the Dominion, that inasmuch as the proclamation recites that the territories thereby reserved for Indians had never "been ceded to or purchased by" the Crown, the entire property of the land remained with them. That inference is, however, at variance with the terms of the instrument, which shew that the tenure of the Indians was a personal and usufructuary right, dependent upon the good will of the Sovereign. The lands reserved are expressly stated to be "parts of Our dominions and territories;" and it is declared to be the will and pleasure of the sovereign that, "for the present," they shall be reserved for the use of the Indians, as their hunting grounds, under his protection and dominion. There was a great deal of learned discussion at the Bar with respect to the precise quality of the Indian right, but their Lordships do not consider it necessary to express any opinion upon the point. It appears to them to be sufficient for the purposes of this case that there has been all along vested in the Crown a substantial and paramount estate, underlying the Indian title, which became a plenum dominium whenever that title was surrendered or otherwise extinguished.

By an Imperial statute passed in the year 1840 (3 & 4 Vict. c. 35), the provinces of Ontario and Quebec, then known as Upper and Lower Canada, were united under the name of the Province of Canada, and it was, *inter alia*, enacted that, in consideration of certain annual payments which Her Majesty had agreed to accept by way of civil list, the produce of all territorial and other revenues at the disposal of the Crown arising in either of the united Provinces should be paid into the consolidated fund of the new Province. There was no transfer to the Province of any legal estate in the Crown lands, which continued to be vested in the Sovereign; but all moneys realized by sales or in any other manner became the property of the Province. In other words, all beneficial interest in such lands within the provincial boundaries belonging to the Queen, and either producing or capable of producing revenue, passed to the Province, the title still remaining in the Crown. That continued to be the right of the Province until the passing of the British North America Act, 1867. Had the Indian inhabitants of the area in question released their interest in it to the Crown at any time between 1840 and the date of that Act, it does not seem to admit of doubt, and it was not disputed by the learned counsel for the Dominion, that all revenues derived from its being taken up for settlement, mining, lumbering, and other purposes would have been the property of the Province of Canada. The case maintained for the appellants is that the Act of 1867 transferred to the Dominion all interest in Indian lands which previously belonged to the Province.

The Act of 1867, which created the Federal Government, repealed the Act of 1840, and restored the Upper and Lower Canadas to the condition of separate Provinces, under the titles of Ontario and Quebec, due provision being made (sect. 142) for the division between them of the property and assets of the United Province, with the exception of certain items specified in the fourth schedule, which are still held by them jointly. The Act also contains careful provisions for the distribution of legislative powers and of revenues and assets between the respective Provinces included in the Union, on the one hand, and the Dominion, on the other. The conflicting claims to the ceded territory maintained by the Dominion and the Province of Ontario are wholly dependent upon these statutory provisions. In construing these enactments, it must always be kept in view that, wherever public land with its incidents is described as "the property of" or as "belonging to" the Dominion or a Province, these expressions merely import that the right to its beneficial use, or to its proceeds, has been appropriated to the Dominion or the Province, as the case may be, and is subject to the control of its legislature, the land itself being vested in the Crown.

Sect. 108 enacts that the public works and undertakings enumerated in Schedule 3 shall be the property of Canada. As specified in the schedule, these consist of public undertakings which might be fairly considered to exist for the benefit of all the Provinces federally united, of lands and buildings necessary for carrying on the customs or postal service of the

Dominion, or required for the purpose of national defence, and of "lands set apart for general public purposes." It is obvious that the enumeration cannot be reasonably held to include Crown lands which are reserved for Indian use. The only other clause in the Act by which a share of what previously constituted provincial revenues and assets is directly assigned to the Dominion is sect. 102. It enacts that all "duties and revenues" over which the respective legislatures of the United Provinces had and have power of appropriation, "except such portions thereof as are by this Act reserved to the respective legislatures of the Provinces, or are raised by them in accordance with the special powers conferred upon them by this Act," shall form one consolidated fund, to be appropriated for the public service of Canada. The extent to which duties and revenues arising within the limits of Ontario, and over which the legislature of the old Province of Canada possessed the power of appropriation before the passing of the Act, have been transferred to the Dominion by this clause, can only be ascertained by reference to the two exceptions which it makes in favour of the new provincial legislatures.

The second of these exceptions has really no bearing on the present case, because it comprises nothing beyond the revenues which provincial legislatures are empowered to raise by means of direct taxation for Provincial purposes, in terms of sect. 92 (2). The first of them, which appears to comprehend the whole sources of revenue reserved to the provinces by sect. 109, is of material consequence. Sect. 109 provides that "all lands, mines, minerals, and royalties belonging to the several Provinces of Canada, Nova Scotia, and New Brunswick, at the union, and all sums then due or payable for such lands, mines, minerals, or royalties, shall belong to the several Provinces of Ontario, Quebec, Nova Scotia, and New Brunswick, in which the same are situate or arise, subject to any trusts existing in respect thereof, and to any interest other than that of the Province in the same." In connection with this clause it may be observed that, by sect. 117, it is declared that the Provinces shall retain their respective public property not otherwise disposed of in the Act, subject to the right of Canada to assume any lands or public property required for fortifications or for the defence of the country. A different form of expression is used to define the subject-matter of the first exception, and the property which is directly appropriated to the Provinces; but it hardly admits of doubt that the interests in land, mines, minerals, and royalties, which by sect. 109 are declared to belong to the Provinces, include, if they are not identical with, the "duties and revenues" first excepted in sect. 102.

The enactments of sect. 109 are, in the opinion of their Lordships, sufficient to give to each Province, subject to the administration and control of its own Legislature, the entire beneficial interest of the Crown in all lands within its boundaries, which at the time of the union were vested in the Crown, with the exception of such lands as the Dominion acquired right to under sect. 108, or might assume for the purposes specified in sect. 117. Its legal effect is to exclude from the "duties and revenues" appropriated to the Dominion, all the ordinary territorial revenues of the Crown arising within the Provinces. That construction of the statute was accepted by this Board in deciding *Attorney General of Ontario v. Mercer*, where the controversy related to land granted in fee simple to a subject before 1867, which became escheat to the Crown in the year 1871. The Lord Chancellor (Earl Selborne) in delivering judgment in that case, said: "It was not disputed, in the argument for the Dominion at the bar, that all territorial revenues arising within each Province from 'lands' (in which term must be compre-hended all estates in land), which at the time of the union belonged to the Crown, were reserved to the respective Provinces by sect. 109; and it was admitted that no distinction could, in that respect, be made between lands then ungranted, and lands which had previously reverted to the Crown by escheat. But it was insisted that a line was drawn at the date of the union, and that the words were not sufficient to reserve any lands afterwards es-cheated which at the time of the union were in private hands, and did not then belong to the Crown. Their Lordships indicated an opinion to the ef-fect that the escheat would not, in the special circumstances of that case, have passed to the Province as "lands;" but they held that it fell within the class of rights reserved to the Provinces as "royalties" by sect. 109.

Had its Indian inhabitants been the owners in fee simple of the territory which they surrendered by the treaty of 1873, *Attorney-General of Ontario v. Mercer* might have been an authority for holding that the Province of On-tario could derive no benefit from the cession, in respect that the land was not vested in the Crown at the time of the union. But that was not the character of the Indian interest. The Crown has all along had a present proprietary estate in the land, upon which the Indian title was a mere bur-den. The ceded territory was at the time of the union, land vested in the Crown, subject to "an interest other than that of the Province in the same," within the meaning of sect. 109; and must now belong to Ontario in terms of that clause, unless its rights have been taken away by some provision of the Act of 1867 other than those already noticed.

In the course of the argument the claim of the Dominion to the ceded territory was rested upon the provisions of sect. 91 (24), which in express terms confer upon the Parliament of Canada power to make laws for "In-dians, and lands reserved for the Indians." It was urged that the exclusive power of legislation and administration carried with it, by necessary im-plication, any patrimonial interest which the Crown might have had in the reserved lands. In reply to that reasoning, counsel for Ontario referred us to a series of provincial statutes prior in date to the Act of 1867, for the purpose of shewing that the expression "Indian reserves" was used in leg-islative language to designate certain lands in which the Indians had, after the royal proclamation of 1763, acquired a special interest, by treaty or otherwise, and did not apply to land occupied by them in virtue of the proclamation. The argument might have deserved consideration if the ex-pression had been adopted by the British Parliament in 1867, but it does not occur in sect. 91 (24), and the words actually used are, according to their natural meaning, sufficient to include all lands reserved, upon any terms or conditions, for Indian occupation. It appears to be the plain policy of the Act that, in order to ensure uniformity of administration, all such lands, and Indian affairs generally, shall be under the legislative control of one central authority.

Their Lordships are, however, unable to assent to the argument for the Dominion founded on sect. 92 (24) [sic]. There can be no a priori probabil-ity that the British Legislature, in a branch of the statute which professes to deal only with the distribution of legislative power, intended to deprive the Provinces of rights which are expressly given them in that branch of it which relates to the distribution of revenues and assets. The fact that the power of legislating for Indians, and for lands which are reserved to their use, has been entrusted to the Parliament of the Dominion is not in the least degree inconsistent with the right of the Provinces to a beneficial interest in these lands, available to them as a source of revenue whenever the estate of the Crown is disencumbered of the Indian title.

By the treaty of 1873 the Indian inhabitants ceded and released the territory in dispute, in order that it might be opened up for settlement, immigration, and such other purpose as to Her Majesty might seem fit, "to the Government of the Dominion of Canada," for the Queen and Her successors for ever. It was argued that a cession in these terms was in effect a conveyance to the Dominion Government of the whole rights of the Indians, with consent of the Crown. That is not the natural import of the language of the treaty, which purports to be from beginning to end a transaction between the Indians and the Crown; and the surrender is in substance made to the Crown. Even if its language had been more favourable to the argument of the Dominion upon this point, it is abundantly clear that the commissioners who represented Her Majesty, whilst they had full authority to accept a surrender to the Crown, had neither authority nor power to take away from Ontario the interest which had been assigned to that province by the Imperial Statute of 1867.

These considerations appear to their Lordships to be sufficient for the disposal of this appeal. The treaty leaves the Indians no right whatever to the timber growing upon the lands which they gave up, which is now fully vested in the Crown, all revenues derivable from the sale of such portions of it as are situate within the boundaries of Ontario being the property of that Province. The fact, that it still possesses exclusive power to regulate the Indians' privilege of hunting and fishing, cannot confer upon the Dominion power to dispose, by issuing permits or otherwise, of that beneficial interest in the timber which has now passed to Ontario. Seeing that the benefit of the surrender accrues to her, Ontario must, of course, relieve the Crown, and the Dominion, of all obligations involving the payment of money which were undertaken by Her Majesty, and which are said to have been in part fulfilled by the Dominion Government. There may be other questions behind, with respect to the right to determine to what extent, and at what periods, the disputed territory, over which the Indians still exercise their avocations of hunting and fishing, is to be taken up for settlement or other purposes, but none of these questions are raised for decision in the present suit.

Their Lordships will therefore humbly advise Her Majesty that the judgment of the Supreme Court of Canada ought to be affirmed, and the appeal dismissed.

The question of Aboriginal title was raised in *St. Catherine's Milling* simply because governmental and private interests hinged upon its resolution. The same principle held true for the majority of early Canadian Aboriginal rights jurisprudence. Consequently, while Aboriginal title was a primary element of early Aboriginal rights jurisprudence, the Aboriginal peoples whose title was the subject of litigation were rarely, if ever, represented in such litigation. They were neither afforded the direct opportunity to explain the significance of land to their cultures, nor the uses they made of the land. It was not until the decision in *Calder v. Attorney-General of British Columbia*, reproduced below, that Aboriginal conceptions of land and its use were given primary attention by the judiciary. Perhaps not coincidentally, this change in approach to the determination of Aboriginal title resulted in pronouncements that were more consistent with the nature of that title than previous judicial analyses had been.

CALDER v. ATTORNEY-GENERAL OF BRITISH COLUMBIA

(1973), 34 D.L.R. (3d) 145, [1973] S.C.R. 313 (*sub nom. Calder v. British Columbia (Attorney General)*), [1973] 4 W.W.R. 1

[**Martland** and **Ritchie JJ.** concur with **Judson J.**]

Judson J.: — The appellants sue, as representatives of the Nishga Indian Tribe, for a declaration "that the aboriginal title, otherwise known as the Indian title, of the Plaintiffs . . . has never been lawfully extinguished". The action was dismissed at trial. The Court of Appeal rejected the appeal. The appellants appeal from both decisions.

The appellants are member of the Nishga Nation, which is made up of four bands: Gitlakdami, Canyon City, Greenville and Kincolith. They are officers of the Nishga Tribal Council and councillors of each of the four Indian bands. They are descendants of the Indians who have inhabited since time immemorial the territory in question, where they have hunted, fished and roamed. It was agreed for purposes of this litigation that this territory consisted of 1,000 square miles in and around the Nass River Valley, Observatory Inlet, Portland Inlet and the Portland Canal, all located in north-western British Columbia. No other interest has intervened in this litigation to question the accuracy of this agreed statement of facts.

The Crown in right of the Province has made certain grants in this territory, some in fee simple; in other cases rights of pre-emption, mineral and mining rights, petroleum permits, forestry rights and titles, and tree farm licences. However, the vast bulk of the area remains still unalienated.

No treaty or contract with the Crown or the Hudson's Bay Company has ever been entered into with respect to the area by anyone on behalf of the Nishga Nation. Within the area there are a number of reserves but they comprise only a small part of the total land. The Nishga Nation did not agree to or accept the creation of these reserves. The Nishgas claim that their title arises out of aboriginal occupation; that recognition of such a title is a concept well embedded in English law; that it is not dependent on treaty, executive order or legislative enactment. In the alternative they say that if executive or legislative recognition ever was needed, it is to be found in the Royal Proclamation of 1763, in Imperial statutes acknowledging that what is now British Columbia was "Indian Territory", and in

Royal instructions to the Governor of British Columbia. Finally, they say that their title has never been extinguished.

. . . . .

In the agreed statement of facts, the mode of life of the Indians is set out in rather bald terms. This description is amplified in the material filed at the hearing. I refer to the *Indian History of British Columbia*, chapter 8, by Wilson Duff, published in 1964:

> It is not correct to say that the Indians did not 'own' the land but only roamed over the face of it and 'used' it. The patterns of ownership and utilization which they imposed upon the lands and waters were different from those recognized by our system of law, but were nonetheless clearly defined and mutually respected. Even if they didn't subdivide and cultivate the land, they did recognize ownership of plots used for village sites, fishing places, berry and root patches, and similar purposes. Even if they didn't subject the forests to wholesale logging, they did establish ownership of tracts used for hunting, trapping, and food-gathering. Even if they didn't sink mine shafts into the mountains, they did own peaks and valleys for mountain goat hunting and as sources of raw materials. Except for barren and inaccessible areas which are not utilized even today, every part of the Province was formerly within the owned and recognized territory of one or other of the Indian tribes.

The Nishga answer to Government assertions of absolute ownership of the land within their boundaries was made as early as 1888 before the first Royal Commission to visit the Nass Valley. Their spokesman said:

> David Mackay — What we don't like about the Government is their saying this: "We will give you this much land." How can they give it when it is our own? We cannot understand it. They have never bought it from us or our forefathers. They have never fought and conquered our people and taken the land in that way, and yet they say now that they will give us so much land — our own land. These chiefs do not talk foolishly, they know the land is their own; our forefathers for generations past had their land here all around us; chiefs have had their own hunting grounds, their salmon streams, and places where they got their berries; it has always been so. It is not only during the last four or five years that we have seen the land; we have always seen and owned it; it is no new thing, it has been ours for generations. If we had only seen it for twenty years and claimed it as our own, it would have been foolish, but it has been ours for thousands of years. If any strange person came here and saw the land for twenty years and claimed it, he would be foolish. We have always got our living from the land; we are not like white people who live in towns and have their stores and other business, getting their living in that way, but we have always depended on the land for our food and clothes; we get our salmon, berries, and furs from the land.

Any Canadian inquiry into the nature of the Indian title must begin with *R. v. St. Catherines Milling & Lumber Co. v. The Queen*.

. . . . .

There can be no doubt that [in *St. Catherine's Milling*] the Privy Council found that the Proclamation of 1763 was the origin of the Indian title —

"Their possession, such as it was, can only be ascribed to the . . . royal proclamation in favour of all Indian tribes then living under the sovereignty and protection of the British Crown."

I do not take these reasons to mean that the Proclamation was the exclusive source of Indian title. The territory under consideration in the *St. Catherines* appeal was clearly within the geographical limits set out in the Proclamation. It is part of the appellants' case that the Proclamation does apply to the Nishga territory and that they are entitled to its protection. They also say that if it does not apply to the Nishga territory, their Indian title is still entitled to recognition by the Courts. These are two distinct questions.

I say at once that I am in complete agreement with judgments of the British Columbia Courts in this case that the Proclamation has no bearing upon the problem of Indian title in British Columbia. I base my opinion upon the very terms of the Proclamation and its definition of its geographical limits and upon the history of the discovery, settlement and establishment of what is now British Columbia.

. . . . .

When the Colony of British Columbia was established in 1858, there can be no doubt that the Nishga territory became part of it. The fee was in the Crown in right of the Colony until July 20, 1871, when the Colony entered Confederation, and thereafter in the Crown in right of the Province of British Columbia, except only in respect of those lands transferred to the Dominion under the Terms of Union.

. . . . .

Although I think it is clear that Indian title in British Columbia cannot owe its origin to the Proclamation of 1763, the fact is that when the settlers came, the Indians were there, organized in societies and occupying the land as their forefathers had done for centuries. This is what Indian title means and it does not help one in the solution of this problem to call it a "personal or usufructuary right". What they are asserting in this action is that they had a right to continue to live on their lands as their forefathers had lived and that this right has never been lawfully extinguished. There can be no question that this right was "dependent on the goodwill of the Sovereign".

It was the opinion of the British Columbia Courts that this right, if it ever existed, had been lawfully extinguished, that with two societies in competition for land — the white settlers demanding orderly settlement and the Indians demanding to be let alone — the proper authorities deliberately chose to set apart reserves for Indians in various parts of the territory and open up the rest for settlements. They held that this had been done when British Columbia entered Confederation in 1871 and that the Terms of Union recognized this fact.

As to Vancouver Island, we have before us a collection of dispatches between the Colonial Office and Governor Douglas in connection with the Indian problem that was confronting him. The first, dated July 31, 1851,

contains an admonition that it should be an invariable condition in all bargains or treaties with the natives for the cession of lands possessed by
them that subsistence should be supplied in some other shape.

. . . . .

These dispatches are detailed and informative on both sides. They set
out the difficulties and problems as they arose and suggestions for their
solution. I quote from the last dispatch of the Governor, which conven-
iently summarizes his efforts:

Victoria, 25th March, 1861.
    My Lord Duke, — I have the honour of transmitting a petition from the
House of Assembly of Vancouver Island to your Grace, praying for the aid
of Her Majesty's Government in extinguishing the Indian title to the public
lands in this Colony; and setting forth, with much force and truth, the evils
that may arise from the neglect of that very necessary precaution.

    2. As the native Indian population of Vancouver Island have distinct
ideas of property in land, and mutually recognize their several exclusive
possessory rights in certain districts, they would not fail to regard the occupation of such portions of the Colony by white settlers, unless the full consent of the proprietary tribes, as national wrongs, and the sense of injury
might produce a feeling of irritation against the settlers, and perhaps disaf-
fection to the Government that would endanger the peace of the country.

    3. Knowing their feelings on that subject, I made it a practice up to the
year 1859, to purchase the native rights in the land, in every case prior to the
settlement of any district; but since that time in consequence of the termination of the Hudson's Bay Company's Charter, and the want of funds, it has
not been in my power to continue it. Your Grace must, indeed, be well
aware that I have, since then, had the utmost difficulty in raising money
enough to defray the most indispensable wants of Government.

. . . . . .

The reasons for judgment next deal with a series of Proclamations by
James Douglas as Governor of the Colony of British Columbia. The first is
dated December 2, 1858, and it is stated to be a Proclamation having the
force of law to enable the Governor of British Columbia to have Crown
lands sold within the said Colony. It authorized the Governor to grant any
land belonging to the Crown in the Colony.

The second Proclamation is dated February 14, 1859. It declared that all
lands in British Columbia and all mines and minerals thereunder belonged
to the Crown in fee. It provided for the sale of these lands after surveys
had been made and the lands were ready for sale, and that due notice
should be given of such sales.

The third Proclamation is dated January 4, 1860. It provided for British
subjects and aliens who take the oath of allegiance acquiring unoccupied
and unreserved and unsurveyed Crown land, and for the subsequent recognition of the claim after the completion of the survey.

The fourth Proclamation is dated January 20, 1860. It provided for the
sale of certain lands by private contract and authorized the Commissioner

of Land and all Magistrates and Gold Commissioners to make these sales at certain prices.

The fifth Proclamation of January 19, 1861, dealt with further details of land sales.

The sixth Proclamation, dated January 19, 1861, reduced the price of land.

The seventh Proclamation, dated May 28, 1861, dealt with conditions of pre-emption and limited the right to 160 acres per person.

The eighth Proclamation, dated August 27, 1861, was a consolidation of the laws affecting the settlement of unsurveyed Crown lands in British Columbia.

The ninth Proclamation, dated May 27, 1863, dealt with the establishment of mining districts.

Then follow four Ordinances enacted by the Governor by and with the consent of the Legislative Council of British Columbia. The first is dated April 11, 1865. It repeats what the Proclamation had previously said, namely, that all lands in British Columbia and all mines and minerals therein, not otherwise lawfully appropriated, belong [to] the Crown in fee. It goes on to provide for the public sale of lands and the price; that unless otherwise specially announced at the time of the sale, the conveyance of the lands shall include all trees and all mines and minerals within and under the same (except mines of gold and silver). It also deals with rights of pre-emption of unoccupied, unsurveyed and unreserved Crown lands "not being the site of an existent or proposed town, or auriferous land or an Indian reserve or settlement under certain conditions."

The next Ordinance, dated March 31, 1866, restricts those who may acquire lands by pre-emption under the Ordinance of April 11, 1865. British subjects or aliens who take the oath of allegiance have this right but it does not extend without special permission of the Governor to companies or "to any of the Aborigines of this Colony of the Territories neighbouring thereto".

The third Ordinance is dated March 10, 1869. It deals with the payment of purchase money for pre-emption claims.

The last Ordinance is dated June 1, 1870, and is one to amend and consolidate the laws affecting Crown lands in British Columbia.

The result of these Proclamations and Ordinances was stated by Gould, J., at the trial in the following terms [8 D.L.R. (3d) at pp. 81-2]. I accept his statement, as did the Court of Appeal:

> The various pieces of legislation referred to above are connected, and in many instances contain references *inter se*, especially XIII. They extend back well prior to November 19, 1866, the date by which, as a certainty, the delineated lands were all within the boundaries of the Colony of British Columbia, and thus embraced in the land legislation of the Colony, where the words were appropriate. All thirteen reveal a unit of intention to exercise, and the legislative exercising, of absolute sovereignty over all the lands of British Columbia, a sovereignty inconsistent with any conflicting interest, including one as to "aboriginal title, otherwise known as the Indian title", to quote the statement of claim. The legislation prior to November 19, 1866, is included to show the intention of the successor and connected legislation after that date, which latter legislation certainly included the delineated lands.

. . . . .

The Terms of Union under which British Columbia entered into Confederation with the Dominion of Canada are also of great significance in this problem. These terms were approved by Imperial Order in Council dated May 16, 1871 [see R.S.C. 1952, vol. VI, p. 6259; R.S.B.C. 1950, vol. V, p. 5223], which has, under s. 146 of the *B.N.A. Act*, the force of an Imperial statute. Term 13 reads:

> 13. The charge of the Indians, and the trusteeship and management of the lands reserved for their use and benefit, shall be assumed by the Dominion Government, and a policy as liberal as that hitherto pursued by the British Columbia Government shall be continued by the Dominion Government after the Union.
>
> To carry out such policy, tracts of land of such extent as it has hitherto been the practice of the British Columbia Government to appropriate for that purpose, shall from time to time be conveyed by the Local Government to the Dominion Government in trust for the use and benefit of the Indians on application of the Dominion Government; and in case of disagreement between the two Governments respecting the quantity of such tracts of land to be so granted, the matter shall be referred for the decision of the Secretary of State of the Colonies.

On the question of reserves, it is convenient to mention at this point, though it is out of chronological order, the McKenna-McBride Commission, its Report and the Dominion legislation which followed on its recommendations.

The Commission was established in 1913 to settle all differences between the Dominion and the Province of British Columbia respecting Indian lands and Indian affairs generally in the Province. Seven years later, the recommendations of this Commission were followed by Dominion legislation, 1920 (Can. 2nd Sess.), c. 51.

. . . . .

The recommendations of the Commission resulted in the establishment of new or confirmation of old Indian reserves in the Nass area. They are over thirty in number. Frank Calder, one of the appellants, says that this was done over Indian objections. Nevertheless, the federal authority did act under its powers under s. 91(24) of the *B.N.A. Act, 1867*. It agreed, on behalf of the Indians, with the policy of establishing these reserves.

In the Department of Indian Affairs and Northern Development there exists a Nass River Agency that administers the area in question. The reserves generally correspond with the fishing places that Indians had traditionally used. The Government of the original Crown colony and, since 1871, the Government of British Columbia have made alienations in the Nass Valley that are inconsistent with the existence of an aboriginal title. These have already been referred to and show alienations in fee simple and by way of petroleum and natural gas leases, mineral claims and tree farm licences.

Further, the establishment of the railway belt under the Terms of Union is inconsistent with the recognition and continued existence of Indian title.

. . . . .

There was no reservation of Indian rights in respect of the railway belt to be conveyed to the Dominion Government.

From what I have already said, it is apparent that before 1871 there were no treaties between the Indian tribes and the Colony relating to lands on the mainland. From the material filed, it appears that on Vancouver Island there were, in all, fourteen purchases of Indian lands in the area surrounding Fort Victoria. These are the ones referred to in the correspondence between James Douglas and the Colonial Office. In 1899, Treaty 8 was negotiated and certain tribes of north-eastern British Columbia were grouped with the Cree, Beaver, Chipewyan, Alberta and Northwest Territories' tribes, and included in the treaty. The area covered by this treaty is vast — both in the Northwest Territories and north-eastern British Columbia. There can be no doubt that by this treaty the Indians surrendered their rights in both areas.

. . . . .

In my opinion, in the present case, the sovereign authority elected to exercise complete dominion over the lands in question, adverse to any right of occupancy which the Nishga Tribe might have had, when, by legislation, it opened up such lands for settlement, subject to the reserves of land set aside for Indian occupation.

. . . . .

I would dismiss the appeal and would make no order as to costs.

[**Laskin** and **Spence JJ.** concur with **Hall J.**]

Hall J. (dissenting): — This appeal raises issues of vital importance to the Indians of northern British Columbia and, in particular, to those of the Nishga tribe. The Nishga tribe has persevered for almost a century in asserting an interest in the lands which their ancestors occupied since time immemorial. The Nishgas were never conquered nor did they at any time enter into a treaty or deed of surrender as many other Indian tribes did throughout Canada and in southern British Columbia. The Crown has never granted the lands in issue in this action other than a few small parcels later referred to prior to the commencement of the action. The claim as set out in the statement of claim reads as follows:

> WHEREFORE, the Plaintiffs claim a declaration that the aboriginal title, otherwise known as the Indian title, of the Plaintiffs to their ancient tribal territory hereinbefore described, has never been lawfully extinguished.

. . . . .

It was stated and agreed to by counsel at the hearing in this Court that Parliament had not taken any steps or procedures to extinguish the Indian right of title after British Columbia entered Confederation. The appeal was argued on this basis and on the representation of counsel that no constitutional question was involved.

Consideration of the issues involves the study of many historical documents and enactments received in evidence.... The Court may take judicial notice of the facts of history whether past or contemporaneous; *Monarch Steamship Co. Ltd. v. A/B Karlshamns Oljefabriker*, [1949] A.C. 196 at p. 234, and the Court is entitled to rely on its own historical knowledge and researches: *Read et al. v. Lincoln*, [1892] A.C. 644, *per* Lord Halsbury at pp. 652-4.

The assessment and interpretation of the historical documents and enactments tendered in evidence must be approached in the light of present-day research and knowledge disregarding ancient concepts formulated when understanding of the customs and culture of our original people was rudimentary and incomplete and when they were thought to be wholly without cohesion, laws or culture, in effect a subhuman species. This concept of the original inhabitants of America led Chief Justice Marshall in his otherwise enlightened judgment in *Johnson and Grahams' Lessee v. M'Intosh* (1823), 8 Wheaton 543, 21 U.S. 240, which is the outstanding judicial pronouncement on the subject of Indian rights to say [p. 590], "But the tribes of Indians inhabiting this country were fierce savages, whose occupation was war . . ." We now know that that assessment is ill-founded. The Indians did in fact at times engage in some tribal wars but war was not their vocation and it can be said that their preoccupation with war pales into insignificance when compared to the religious and dynastic wars of "civilized" Europe of the 16th and 17th centuries. Chief Justice Marshall was, of course, speaking with the knowledge available to him in 1823. Chief Justice Davey in the judgment under appeal [13 D.L.R. (3d) 64, 74 W.W.R. 481], with all the historical research and material available since 1823 and notwithstanding the evidence in the record which Gould, J. [8 D.L.R. (3d) 59, 71 W.W.R. 81], found was given "with total integrity", said of the Indians of the mainland of British Columbia [p. 66]:

> ... they were undoubtedly at the time of settlement a very primitive people with few of the institutions of civilized society, and none at all of our notions of private property.

In so saying this in 1970, he was assessing the Indian culture of 1858 by the same standards that the Europeans applied to the Indians of North America two or more centuries before.

. . . . .

The nature of the title of the interest being asserted on behalf of the Nishgas was stated in evidence by Calder in cross-examination as follows:

> From time immemorial the Naas River Nishga Indians possessed, occupied and used the Naas Valley, Observatory Inlet, and Portland Inlet and Canal, and within this territory the Nishgas hunted in its woods, fished in

its waters, streams and rivers. Roamed, hunted and pitched their tents in the valleys, shores and hillsides. Buried their dead in their homeland territory. Exercised all privileges of free men in the tribal territory. The Nishgas have never ceded or extinguished their aboriginal title within this territory.

. . . . .

When asked to state the nature of the right being asserted and for which a declaration was being sought, counsel for the appellants described it as "an interest which is a burden on the title of the Crown; an interest which is usufructuary in nature; a tribal interest inalienable except to the Crown and extinguishable only by legislative enactment of the Parliament of Canada". The exact nature and extent of the Indian right or title does not need to be precisely stated in this litigation. The issue here is whether any right or title the Indians possess as occupants of the land from time immemorial has been extinguished. ... Their position is that they possess a right of occupation against the world except the Crown and that the Crown has not to date lawfully extinguished that right. The essence of the action is that such rights as the Nishgas possessed in 1858 continue to this date. Accordingly, the declaratory judgment asked for implies that the *status quo* continues and this means that if the right is to be extinguished it must be done by specific legislation in accordance with the law.

The right to possession claimed is not prescriptive in origin because a prescriptive right presupposes a prior right in some other person or authority. Since it is admitted that the Nishgas have been in possession since time immemorial, that fact negatives that anyone ever had or claimed prior possession.

The Nishgas do not claim to be able to sell or alienate their right to possession except to the Crown. They claim the right to remain in possession themselves and to enjoy the fruits of that possession. They do not deny the right of the Crown to dispossess them but say the Crown has not done so. There is no claim for compensation in this action. The action is for declaration without a claim for consequential relief. ... However, it must be recognized that if the Nishgas succeed in establishing a right to possession, the question of compensation would remain for future determination as and when proceedings to dispossess them should be taken. British Columbia's position has been that there never was any right or title to extinguish, and alternatively, that if any such right or title did exist it was extinguished in the period between 1858 and Confederation in 1871. The respondent admits that nothing has been done since Confederation to extinguish the right or title.

The appellants do challenge the authority of British Columbia to make grants in derogation of their rights, but because the grants made so far in respect of Nishga lands are so relatively insignificant the appellants have elected to ignore them while maintaining that they were *ultra vires*.

Unlike the method used to make out title in other contexts, proof of the Indian title or interest is to be made out as a matter of fact. In *Amodu Tijani v. Secretary, Southern Nigeria*, [1921] 2 A.C. 399, Lord Haldane said at pp. 402-4:

Their Lordships make the preliminary observation that in interpreting the native title to land, not only in Southern Nigeria, but other parts of the British Empire, much caution is essential. *There is a tendency, operating at times unconsciously, to render that title conceptually in terms which are appropriate only to systems which have grown up under English law. But this tendency has to be held in check closely.* As a rule, in the various systems of native jurisprudence throughout the Empire, there is no such full division between property and possession as English lawyers are familiar with. *A very usual form of native title is that of a usufructuary right, which is a mere qualification of or burden on the radical or final title of the Sovereign where that exists. In such cases the title of the Sovereign is a pure legal estate, to which beneficial rights may or may not be attached.* But this estate is qualified by a right of beneficial users which may not assume definite forms analogous to estates. (Emphasis added.)

The appellant Calder who is a member of the Legislature of British Columbia testified as follows:

. . . . .

Q. Are you acquainted with the territory outlined in the map, exhibit 2?
A. Yes.
Q. Have the Nishga people every signed any document or treaty surrendering their aboriginal title to the territory outlined in the map, exhibit 2 ?
A. The Nishgas have not signed any treaty or any document that would indicate extinguishment of the title.

Gosnell, Chief Councillor of the Gitlakdamix band, said:

Q. Mr. Gosnell, have the Nishga people ever signed any treaty or document giving up their Indian title to the lands and the waters comprised in the area delineated on the map Exhibit 2 which I am showing you?
A. No.
MR. BROWN: I think I can save my friend some trouble, I think the Attorney-General is prepared to say while denying there is such a thing as an Indian title in the area, that the inhabitants never did give up or purport to give up that right.

The witnesses McKay, Nyce and Robinson confirmed the evidence of Calder and Gosnell.

. . . . .

At the second Royal Commission hearing in 1915 (the McKenna-McBride Commission), Gideon Minesque for the Nishgas said:

We haven't got any ill feelings in our hearts but we are just waiting for this thing to be settled and we have been waiting for the last five years — we have been living here from time immemorial — it has been handed down in legends from the old people and that is what hurts us very much because the white people have come along and taken this land away from us. I myself am an old man and as long as I have lived, my people have been telling me stories about the flood and they did not tell me that I was only to live here on this land for a short time. We have heard that some white men, it must have been in Ottawa; this white man said that they must be dreaming when they say they own the land upon which they live. It is not a dream — we are certain that this land belongs to us. Right up to this day the government never made any treaty, not even to our grandfathers or our great-grandfathers.

Wilson Duff, associate professor of anthropology at the University of British Columbia, testified as to the nature of the Nishga civilization and culture in great detail.

. . . . .

Dr. Duff is the author of vol. I of the *Indian History of British Columbia* published by the Government of British Columbia and admitted in evidence as ex. 25. Dr. Duff testified as follows, quoting from ex. 25 and related quotations applicable to the Nishgas:

Q. Now, are you able to tell the Court whether the Nishga Tribe made use of the land and the waters delineated on the map beyond the limits of the reserve that appear on this map in the MacKenna-McBride report?

A. Yes.

. . . . .

Q. Now, prior to the establishment of these reserves what use would the Indian people have made of the areas which flow into the mouths of the streams and rivers?

A. The general pattern in these cases would be that the ownership of the mouth of the stream and the seasonal villages, or habitations that were built there, signify the ownership and use of the entire valley. It would be used as a fishing site itself and a fishing site on the river, but in addition to that the people who made use of this area would have the right to go up the valley for berry picking up on the slopes, for hunting and trapping in the valley and up to forest slopes, usually for the hunting of mountain goats. In other words they made use, more or less intensive use of the entire valley rather than just the point at the mouth of the stream.

. . . . .

Q. To what extent would the use and exploitation of the resources of the Nishga territory have extended in terms of that territory? Would it have extended only through a limited part of the territory or through the whole territory?

A. To a greater or lesser degree of intensity it would extend through a whole territory except for the most barren and inaccessible parts, which were not used or wanted by anyone. But the ownership of an entire drainage basin marked out by the mountain peaks would be recognized as resting within one or other groups of Nishga Indians and these boundaries, this ownership would be respected by others.

. . . . .

On cross-examination he said:

. . . . .

Q. Well, now, I was asking you as to what documentary or other evidence there was that justifies you in using the word 'ownership'. I suggest that that was a concept that was foreign to the Indians of the Nass Agency?

A. I am an anthropologist, sir, and the kind of evidence with which I work is largely not documentary evidence. It is verbal evidence given by people who didn't produce documents and it is turned into documentary form in anthropological and historical reports and in the reports of various Commissions.

Q. All right. Well, that is what I want now.

A. Yes, okay.

Q. I want you to state, so I can go and look them up, the documents you rely upon to support your statement, your use of the word 'ownership', as 'belonging' in the Indian concept.

A. Anthropological reports which I understand Mr. Berger is going to enter into the record, one of them by Philip Drucker, is a general book on the Indians of the Northwest Coast and it would use the term. Another is a book by Viola Garfield as to the Tsimshian Indians in general and in this sense it includes the Nishga which would use a concept of ownership.

Q. Now, are you suggesting that this is anything other than a tribal concept?

A. It includes the tribal concept and it is more besides, yes.

. . . . .

Q. Well, in other words the Indians would speak of the fact that when they attended before a Commission, that they owned the land?

A. Yes.

Q. They would speak in those terms as "We" as a group.

A. Yes.

Q. "Own the land".

A. I think they would go beyond that and say, "And the chief owned that certain territory up Portland Inlet where we used to get this and that," and the whole list of things that I referred to before.

Q. Would one family defend its right like that against other families?

A. It could, yes.

Q. Well, is there evidence of that?

A. There are narratives to that effect, yes.

Q. In the Nishga Valley, in the territory you have marked off there?

A. Yes.

Q. Where? Can you point to that?

A. They are in the unpublished material that I have been referring to.

Possession is of itself at common law proof of ownership: Cheshire, *Modern Law of Real Property*, 10th ed. (1967), p. 659, and Megarry and Wade, *Law of Real Property*, 3rd ed. (1966), p. 999. Unchallenged possession is admitted here.

Dr. Duff also went into details of the Nishga system of succession to property based on a matrilineal line, showing that the Nishgas had a well-developed and sophisticated concept of property.

. . . . .

An interesting and apt line of questions by Gould, J., in which he endeavoured to relate Duff's evidence as to Nishga concepts of ownership of real property to the conventional common law elements of ownership must be quoted here as they disclose that the trial Judge's consideration of the real issue was inhibited by a preoccupation with the traditional *indicia* of ownership. In so doing, he failed to appreciate what Lord Haldane said in *Amodu Tijani*, [[1991] 2 A.C. at p. 402]:

> Their lordships make the preliminary observation that in interpreting the native title to land, not only in Southern Nigeria, but other parts of the British Empire, much caution is essential. There is a tendency, operating at times unconsciously, to render that title conceptually in terms which are appropriate only to systems which have grown up under English law. But this tendency has to be held in check closely.

The trial Judge's questions and Duff's answers were as follows:

THE COURT:

Q. I want to discuss with you the short descriptive concept of your modern ownership of land in British Columbia, and I am going to suggest to you three characteristics (1) specific delineation of the land, we understand is the lot.

A. Yes.

Q. Specifically delineated down to the lot, and the concept of the survey; (2) exclusive possession against the whole world, including your own family. Your own family, you know that, you want to keep them off or kick them off and one can do so; (3) to keep the fruits of the barter or to leave it or to have your heirs inherit it, which is the concept of wills. Now, those three characteristics — are you with me?

A. Yes.

Q. Specific delineation, exclusive possession, the right of alienation, have you found in your anthropological studies any evidence of that concept being in the consciousness of the Nishgas and having them executing such a concept?

A. My lord, there are three concepts.

Q. Yes, or a combination of them.

A. Could we deal with them one at a time?

Q. Yes, you can do it any way you like. You deal with it.

A. Specific delineation, I think, was phrased by Dr. —

Q. Touched upon by landmarks.

A. Physical landmarks, physical characteristics. The exclusive occupation did not reside in an individual. It rested in a group of people who were a sub-group of the tribe.

Q. The third one was alienation.

A. The owners in this sense had certain rights of alienation. They could give up the tract of land, lose it in warfare, but in practice it would not go to anybody outside of the tribe, that is, a tract of Nishga land might change hands but it wouldn't go to other than a Nishga family.

Q. So am I correct in assuming that there are similarities in the Nishga civilization in the first two characteristics, but not the third? All that alienation means, of course, is that you can sell it to anybody you like?

A. Yes.

Q. Generally speaking, I mean, that is what it does, Two of the three the Nishga Tribe — I don't want to put words in your mouth, now, I want you to tell me. I don't want to tell you anything.

A. Delineation but not by modern surveying methods.

Q. Of course, I understand, yes.

A. Exclusive ownership resting not in an individual.

Q. Possession or occupancy, not ownership?

A. Oh, I see. Possession or occupancy resting in a specific group rather than an individual. The right of alienation, which in practice would leave the land within the same tribe. It was limited.

Q. Could the group having exclusive occupancy select within the tribe, if they chose, another group to whom they wanted to either, to use the modern word, convey it, or would that go by general communal habit, customs or even law?

A. The group could do the thing you suggest. For example, in some cases the chief of a group might convey a property to his son, which would not be the normal way; it would be to his nephew in the normal way.

Q. Yes.

A. And that would , on rare occasions, be accepted.

Q. Always subject to the acceptance of what, the tribe?

A. The tribe, yes.

RE-EXAMINED BY MR. BERGER:

Q. His lordship put to you three characteristics of modern day real property concepts. Having regard to the territory of the Nishga Tribe outlined on the map, Exhibit 2, can you say whether or not there would have been specific delineation of that area in the sense in which it was put to you by his lordship?

A. Of the boundaries of that area?

Q. Yes.

A. Yes.

Q. What would the means of delineation have been?

A. As Dr. Drucker has described them here, landmarks.

Q. By landmarks. Do you mean the mountain tops?

A. Yes, geographical locations.

Q. Now, his lordship put to you the notion of exclusive possession. As regards the territory delineated on the map, Exhibit 2, the Nishga territory, what would have been the application of that concept if it had any in the time before the coming of the white man?

A. It would be recognized by all as Nishga territory. They would exercise exclusive possession of it.

MR. BERGER: I have no further questions.

THE COURT: I have some more now.

Q. I will give you two more characteristics of ownership, the right to destroy it at your own whim, if you like, and the other, that the exclusive possession should be of indeterminable time, that is, cannot be terminated by a person's life; that is, can be passed on to one's heirs. That makes five. Now, you have dealt with three. Now, the right to destroy at whim, set fire to your own house; these matters you have been dealing with, would a group within the Nishga have the right, if the buildings at the mouth of a certain river had been in their exclusive use some time and they will say, "Let's set fire to it," would the tribe prohibit that?

A. I would think that they would have that right.

Q. You would think they would have that right?

A. Yes.

Q. Now, what about the duration of the right, not to destroy, but the right of exclusive ownership, would it go to their heirs?

A. Yes.

Q. Or go back to the tribe for distribution?

A. In theory it belongs within that kinship group through time, with no duration in theory. It always remains with that same kinship group.

Q. There is a matrilineal line?

A. Yes.

THE COURT: Thank you.

In enumerating the *indicia* of ownership, the trial Judge overlooked that possession is of itself proof of ownership. *Prima facie*, therefore, the Nishgas are the owners of the lands that have been in their possession from time immemorial and, therefore the burden of establishing that their right has been extinguished rests squarely on the respondent.

What emerges from the evidence is the following: the Nishgas in fact are and were from time immemorial a distinctive cultural entity with concepts of ownership indigenous to their culture and capable of articulation under the common law.

· · · · ·

While the Nishga claim has not heretofore been litigated, there is a wealth of jurisprudence affirming common law recognition of aboriginal rights to possession and enjoyment of lands of aborigines precisely analogous to the Nishga situation here.

· · · · ·

The case most frequently quoted with approval dealing with the nature of aboriginal rights is *Johnson and Graham's Lessee v. M'Intosh* (1823), 8 Wheaton 543, 21 U.S. 240. It is the *locus classicus* of the principles governing aboriginal title.

· · · · ·

The dominant and recurring proposition stated by Chief Justice Marshall in *Johnson v. M'Intosh* is that on discovery or on conquest the aborigines of newly-found lands were conceded to be the rightful occupants of the soil with a legal as well as a just claim to retain possession of it and to use it according to their own discretion, but their rights to complete sovereignty as independent nations were necessarily diminished and their power to dispose of the soil on their own will to whomsoever they pleased was denied by the original fundamental principle that discovery or conquest gave exclusive title to those who made it.

· · · · ·

The view that the Indians had a legal as well as a just claim to the territory they occupied was confirmed as recently as 1946 by the Supreme Court of the United States in the case of *United States v. Alcea Band of Tillamooks et al.* (1946), 329 U.S. 40. In that case it was held that the Indian claims legislation of 1935 did not confer any substantive rights on the Indians, that is, it did not convert a moral claim for taking their land without their consent and without compensation into a legal claim, because they had already had a valid legal claim and there was no necessity to create one.... The judgment is based squarely on the recognition by the Court of "aboriginal Indian title" founded on their previous possession of the land.

· · · · ·

The aboriginal Indian title does not depend on treaty, executive order or legislative enactment. Sutherland, J., delivering the opinion of the Supreme Court of the Unites States in *Cramer et al. v. United States* (1923), 67 L. Ed. 622, 261 U.S. 219, dealt with the subject as follows [p. 626]:

> The fact that such right of occupancy finds no recognition in any statute or other formal governmental action is not conclusive. The right, under the circumstances here disclosed, flows from a settled governmental policy. *Broder v. Natoma Water & Min. Co.* 101 US 274, 276, 24 L. Ed. 790, 791, furnishes an analogy. There this Court, holding that the Act of July 26, 1866, 14 Stat. at L. 251, chap. 262 ss 9. Comp. Stat. ss 4647, 9 Fed. Stat. Anno. 2d ed p. 1349, acknowledging and confirming rights of way for the construction of ditches and canals, was in effect declaratory of a pre-existing right, said: "It is the established doctrine of this court that rights of . . . persons who had constructed canals and ditches . . . are rights which the government had, by its conduct, recognized and encouraged and was bound to protect, before the passage of the Act of 1866. We are of opinion that the section of the act which we have quoted was rather a voluntary *recognition of a pre-EXISTING RIGHT OF POSSESSION*, constituting a valid claim to its continued use, than the establishment of a new one. [Italic capitalization added.]

The Court of Appeal in its judgment cited and purported to rely on *United States v. Santa Fe Pacific R. Co.* (1941), 86 L. Ed. 260, 314 U.S. 339. This case must be considered to be the leading modern judgment on the question of aboriginal rights. In my view the Court of Appeal misapplied the *Santa Fe* decision. This becomes clear when the judgment of Douglas, J., in *Santa Fe* is read. He said [pp. 269-270]:

· · · · ·

> Nor it is true, as respondent urges, that a tribal claim to any particular lands must be based upon a treaty, statute, or other formal government action. As stated in the Cramer case, "The fact that such right of occupancy finds no recognition in any state or other formal governmental action is not conclusive", 261 U.S. at 229, 67 L. Ed. 626, 43 S. Ct. 342.

· · · · ·

Surely the Canadian treaties, made with much solemnity on behalf of the Crown, were intended to extinguish the Indian title. What other purpose did they serve? If they were not intended to extinguish the Indian right, they were a gross fraud and that is not to be assumed. Treaty 8 made in 1899 was entered into on behalf of Queen Victoria and the representatives of Indians in a section of British Columbia and the Northwest Territories. The treaty was ratified by the Queen's Privy Council in Canada. Certain statements in the treaty are entirely inconsistent with any argument or suggestion that such rights as the Indians may have had were extinguished prior to Confederation in 1871.

· · · · ·

If there was no Indian title extant in British Columbia in 1899, why was the treaty negotiated and ratified?

Parallelling and supporting the claim of the Nishgas that they have a certain right or title to the lands in question is the guarantee of Indian rights contained in the Proclamation of 1763. This Proclamation was an Executive Order having the force and effect of an Act of Parliament and was described by Gwynne, J., in *St. Catherines Milling* case at p. 652 as the "Indian Bill of Rights". ... Its force as a statute is analogous to the status of Magna Carta which has always been considered to be the law throughout the Empire. It was a law which followed the flag as England assumed jurisdiction over newly-discovered or acquired lands or territories. It follows, therefore, that the *Colonial Laws Validity Act*, 1865 (U.K.), c. 63, applied to make the Proclamation the law of British Columbia.

. . . . .

[It] cannot be challenged that while the west coast lands were mostly unexplored as of 1763 they were certainly known to exist and that fact is borne out by the wording of the ... Proclamation.

. . . . .

This important question remains: were the rights either at common law or under Proclamation extinguished? Tysoe, J.A., said in this regard at p. 95 [13 D.L.R. (3d)] of his reasons: "It is true, as the appellants have submitted, *that nowhere can one find express words extinguishing Indian title . . .*" (emphasis added).

The parties here agree that if extinguishment was accomplished, it must have occurred between 1858 and when British Columbia joined Confederation in 1871. The respondent relies on what was done by Governor Douglas and by his successor, Frederick Seymour, who became Governor in 1864.

Once aboriginal title is established, it is presumed to continue until the contrary is proven. This was stated to be the law by Viscount Haldane in *Amodu Tijani v. Secretary, Southern Nigeria*, [1921] 2 A.C. 399 at pp. 409-10.

. . . . .

The appellants rely on the presumption that the British Crown intended to respect native rights; therefore, when the Nishga people came under British sovereignty ... they were entitled to assert, as a legal right, their Indian title. It being a legal right, it could not thereafter be extinguished except by surrender to the Crown or by competent legislative authority, and then only by specific legislation. There was no surrender by the Nishgas and neither the Colony of British Columbia nor the Province, after Confederation, enacted legislation specifically purporting to extinguish the Indian title nor did Parliament at Ottawa.

. . . . .

[T]he onus of proving that the Sovereign intended to extinguish the Indian title lies on the respondent and that intention must be "clear and plain". There is no such proof in the case at bar; no legislation to that effect.

The Court of Appeal also erred in holding that there "is no Indian Title capable of judicial interpretation ... unless it has previously been recognized either by the Legislature or the Executive Branch of Government" [see p. 70]. Relying on *Cook et al. v. Sprigg*, [1899] A.C. 572 and other cases, the Court of Appeal erroneously applied what is called the Act of State Doctrine. This doctrine denies a remedy to the citizens of an acquired territory for invasion of their rights which may occur during the change of sovereignty. English Courts have held that a municipal Court has no jurisdiction to review the manner in which the Sovereign acquires new territory. The Act of State is the activity of the Sovereign by which he acquires the property. Professor D.P. O'Connell in his work *International Law*, 2nd ed. (1970), at p. 378 says:

> [T]he Act of State doctrine is no more than a procedural bar to municipal law action, and as such is irrelevant to the question whether in international law change of sovereignty affects acquired rights.

The Act of State doctrine has no application in the present appeal for the following reasons: (a) It has never been invoked in claims dependent on aboriginal title. An examination of its rationale indicates that it would be quite inappropriate for the Courts to extend the doctrine to such cases; (b) It is based on the premise that an Act of State is an exercise of the Sovereign power which a municipal Court has no power to review.

. . . . .

In the present case the appellants are not claiming that the origin of their title was a grant from any previous Sovereign, nor are they asking this Court to enforce a treaty of cession between any previous Sovereign and the British Crown. The appellants are *not* challenging an Act of State — they are asking this Court to recognize that settlement of the north Pacific coast did not extinguish the aboriginal title of the Nishga people.

. . . . .

Once it is apparent that the Act of State doctrine has no application, the whole argument of the respondent that there must be some form of "recognition"of aboriginal rights falls to the ground.

On the question of extinguishment, the respondent relies on what was done by Governors Douglas and Seymour and the Council of British Columbia. The appellants, as I have previously mentioned, say that if either Douglas or Seymour or the Council of the Colony of British Columbia did purport to extinguish the Nishga title that any such attempt was beyond the powers of either the Governors or of the Council and that what, if anything, was attempted in this respect was *ultra vires*.

. . . . .

[O]n October 19, 1861 [the Colonial Secretary wrote to Governor Douglas] as follows:

> Sir, — I have had under my consideration your despatch No. 24, of the 25th of March last, transmitting an Address from the House of Assembly of Vancouver Island, in which they pray for the assistance of Her Majesty's Government in extinguishing the Indian title to the public lands in the Colony, and set forth the evils that may result from a neglect of this precaution.
>
> I am fully sensible of the great importance of purchasing without loss of time the native title to the soil of Vancouver Island; but the acquisition of the title is a purely colonial interest, and the Legislature must not entertain any expectation that the British taxpayer will be burthened to supply the funds or British credit pledged for the purpose. I would earnestly recommend therefore to the House of Assembly, that they should enable you to procure the requisite means, but if they should not think proper to do so, Her Majesty's Government cannot undertake to supply the money requisite for an object which, whilst it is essential to the interests of the people of Vancouver Island, is at the same time purely Colonial in its character, and trifling in the charge that it would entail.

This reply, while refusing funds to acquire the native rights in land, did not authorize Douglas to take or extinguish those rights without compensation. If the lands were to be taken they had to be paid for by the Colony and not by the British taxpayer. If the Colony had intended extinguishing the Indian title to public lands as referred to in the foregoing letter, it could easily have said, "Indian title to public lands in the Colony is hereby extinguished". No such enactment or one with language to like effect was ever passed.

A number of other Acts, Ordinances and Proclamations were passed or issued between February 14, 1859, and June 1, 1870. All of these were repealed and consolidated by an Ordinance passed July 1, 1870. That Consolidation contained in part the following:

PRE-EMPTION

3. From and after the date of the proclamation in this Colony of Her Majesty's assent to this Ordinance, any male person being a British Subject, of the age of eighteen years or over, may acquire the right to pre-empt any tract of unoccupied, unsurveyed, and unreserved Crown Lands (not being an Indian settlement) not exceeding three hundred and twenty acres in extent in that portion of the Colony situate to the northward and eastward of the Cascade or Coast Range of Mountains, and one hundred and sixty acres in extent in the rest of the Colony. Provided that such right of pre-emption shall not be held to extend to any of the Aborigines of this Continent, except to such as shall have obtained the Governors' special permission in writing to that effect.

This is the provision chiefly relied on by Gould, J., and by the Court of Appeal in making the finding that the Indian title in British Columbia had been extinguished. It is obvious that this enactment did not apply to the Nishga lands on the Naas River. The north-west boundary of the Colony in that area was still in dispute. In any event, this provision is expansive and permissive in so far as it enables aborigines to get title in fee with the Governor's written permission.

If in any of the Proclamations or actions of Douglas, Seymour or of the Council of the Colony of British Columbia there are elements which the respondent says extinguish by implication the Indian title, then it is obvious from the Commission of the Governor and from the Instructions under which the Governor was required to observe and neither the Commission nor the Instructions contain any power or authorization to extinguish the Indian title, then it follows logically that if any attempt was made to extinguish the title it was beyond the power of the Governor or of the Council to do so and, therefore, *ultra vires*.

A further observation in respect of the Letter of Instructions of July 31, 1858, must be made of the phrase, "Let me not omit to observe, that it should be an invariable condition, in all bargains or treaties with the Natives for the *cession* of land possessed by them . . .". Having in mind the use of the word "cession" in this context, how can it logically be said that the Imperial Government was not at the time recognizing that the natives had something to cede? What they had to cede was their aboriginal right and title to possession of the lands, subject to the Crown's paramount title.

. . . . .

I would, therefore, allow the appeal with costs throughout and declare that the appellants' right to possession of the lands delineated in ex. 2 with the exceptions before mentioned and their right to enjoy the fruits of the soil of the forest, and of the rivers and streams within the boundaries of said lands have not been extinguished by the Province of British Columbia or by its predecessor, the Colony of British Columbia, or by the Governors of that Colony.

Pigeon J.: — ... I have to hold that the preliminary objection that the declaration prayed for, being a claim of title against the Crown in the right of the Province of British Columbia, the court has no jurisdiction to make it in the absence of a fiat of the Lieutenant-Governor of that Province. I am deeply conscious of the hardship involved in holding that the access to the Court for the determination of the plaintiff's claim is barred by sovereign immunity from suit without a fiat. However, I would point out that in the United States, claims in respect of the taking of lands outside of reserves and not covered by any treaty were not held justiciable until legislative provisions had removed the obstacle created by the doctrine of immunity. In Canada, immunity from suit has been removed by legislation at the federal level and in most provinces. However, this has not yet been done in British Columbia.

I would therefore dismiss the appeal and make no order as to costs.

Appeal dismissed.

After the *Calder* decision, a significant number of claims to Aboriginal title were placed before the Canadian judiciary. One of the most prominent of these post-*Calder* decisions on Aboriginal title came in *Baker Lake (Hamlet) v. Canada (Minister of Indian Affairs & Northern Development)*, reproduced below. The case concerned an action brought by a number of Inuit organizations and individuals who sought (1) a declaration that lands comprising the Baker Lake area in the Northwest Territories belonged to the Inuit residing in or near the area on the basis of Aboriginal title, as well as (2) a declaration of their Aboriginal rights to hunt and fish on those lands. In the end, a declaration was granted with respect to part of the lands included in the Baker Lake area. However, the primary legacy of the case remains its formulation of the requirements to prove the existence of Aboriginal title at common law.

The test devised by Justice Mahoney, and some commentary on it, are excerpted below. Although since superseded by the test established in *Delgamuukw v. British Columbia*, [1997] 3 S.C.R. 1010, the *Baker Lake* test remains noteworthy as the prime example of post-*Calder*, pre-*Delgamuukw* considerations of the necessary requirements for proving Aboriginal title.

BAKER LAKE (HAMLET) v. CANADA (MINISTER OF INDIAN AFFAIRS & NORTHERN DEVELOPMENT)

(1979), 107 D.L.R. (3d) 513 at 542, [1980] 1 F.C. 518, [1980] 5 W.W.R. 193, [1979] 3 C.N.L.R. 17 (T.D.); additional reasons at [1981] 1 F.C. 266 (T.D.)

Mahoney J.: —

. . . . .

The elements which the plaintiffs must prove to establish an aboriginal title cognizable at common law are:

1. That they and their ancestors were members of an organized society.
2. That the organized society occupied the specific territory over which they assert the aboriginal title.
3. That the occupation was to the exclusion of other organized societies.
4. That the occupation was an established fact at the time sovereignty was asserted by England.

. . . . .

Proof that the plaintiffs and their ancestors were members of an organized society is required by the authorities. In quoting Mr. Justice Judson's *Calder* judgment, I emphasized the phrase "organized in societies" and I repeated the emphasis Mr. Justice Hall had included in quoting the passage from *Worcester v. Georgia*: "having institutions of their own, and governing themselves by their own laws". The *rationale* of the requirement is to be found in the following *dicta* of the Privy Council in *Re Southern Rhodesia*, [1919] A.C. 211 at pp. 233-4:

> The estimation of the rights of aboriginal tribes is always inherently difficult. Some tribes are so low in the scale of social organization that their usages and conceptions of rights and duties are not to be reconciled with the institutions or the legal ideas of civilized society. Such a gulf cannot be bridged. It would be idle to impute to such people some shadow of the rights known to our law and then to transmute it into the substance of transferable rights of property as we know them. In the present case it would

make each and every person by a fictional inheritance a landed proprietor "richer than all his tribe". On the other hand, there are indigenous peoples whose legal conceptions, though differently developed, are hardly less precise than our own. When once they have been studied and understood they are no less enforcable [sic] than rights arising under English law. Between the two there is a wide tract of much ethnological interest, but the position of the natives of Southern Rhodesia within it is very uncertain; clearly they approximate rather to the lower than to the higher limit.

. . . . .

It is apparent that the relative sophistication of the organization of any society will be a function of the needs of its members, the demands they make of it. While the existence of an organized society is a prerequisite to the existence of an aboriginal title, there appears no valid reason to demand proof of the existence of a society more elaborately structured than is necessary to demonstrate that there existed among the aborigines a recognition of the claimed rights, sufficiently defined to permit their recognition by the common law upon its advent in the territory.

. . . . .

The nature, extent or degree of the aborigines' physical presence on the land they occupied, required by the law as an essential element of their aboriginal title is to be determined in each case by a subjective test.

. . . . .

The occupation of the territory must have been to the exclusion of other organized societies. In the *Santa Fe* case [*U.S. v. Santa Fe Pacific Rwy. Co.*, 314 U.S. 339 (1941)], at p. 345, Mr. Justice Douglas, giving the opinion of the court, held:

> Occupancy necessary to establish an aboriginal possession is a question of fact to be determined as any other question of fact. If it were established as a fact that the lands in question were, or were included in, the ancestral home of the Walapais in the sense that they constituted definable territory occupied exclusively by the Walapais (as distinguished from lands wandered over by many tribes), then the Walapais had "Indian title" which, unless extinguished, survived the railroad grant of 1866.

. . . . .

[I]n this context, "time immemorial" runs back from the date of assertion of English sovereignty over the territory which was probably no earlier than 1610 and certainly no later than May 2, 1670 [the date of the granting of the royal charter to the Hudson's Bay Company, giving it control over Rupert's Land].

. . . . .

In the result, I find, on the balance of probabilities on the evidence before me, that at the time England asserted sovereignty over the barren lands west of Hudson Bay, the Inuit were the exclusive occupants of the portion of the barren lands extending from the vicinity of Baker Lake north and east toward the Arctic and Hudson Bay to the boundaries of the Baker Lake R.C.M.P. detachment area as they were in 1954 .... An aboriginal title to that territory, carrying with it the right to freely move about and hunt and fish over it, vested at common law in the Inuit.

Shortly after the *Baker Lake* decision was rendered, and slightly more than a decade after *Calder*, the Supreme Court of Canada again took the opportunity to discuss the nature of Aboriginal title and the effects of the *Royal Proclamation of 1763* in *Guerin v. R.* That case, which dealt primarily with the fiduciary obligations of the federal Crown towards the Musqueam band upon the latter's surrender of reserve lands for leasing purposes, is discussed in greater detail in Chapter 3, but is excerpted here for its discussion of Aboriginal title.

GUERIN v. R.

(1984), 13 D.L.R. (4th) 321 at 335, [1984] 2 S.C.R. 325, [1984] 6 W.W.R. 481,
59 B.C.L.R. 301, [1985] 1 C.N.L.R. 120, 20 E.T.R. 6, 36 R.P.R. 1 (*sub nom.*
Guerin v. Canada), 55 N.R. 161

Dickson J.: —

. . . . .

In *Calder et al. v. A.-G. B.C.* (1973), 34 D.L.R. (3d) 145, [1973] S.C.R. 313, [1973] W.W.R. 1, this court recognized aboriginal title as a legal right derived from the Indians' historic occupation and possession of their tribal lands. With Judson and Hall JJ. writing the principal judgments, the court split three-three on the major issue of whether the Nishga Indians' aboriginal title to their ancient tribal territory had been extinguished by general land enactments in British Columbia. The Court also split on the issue of whether the Royal Proclamation of 1763 was applicable to Indian lands in that province. Judson and Hall JJ. were in agreement, however, that aboriginal title existed in Canada (at least where it has not been extinguished by appropriate legislative action) independently of the Royal Proclamation of 1763. Judson J. stated expressly that the Proclamation was not the "exclusive" source of Indian title (at pp. 152-3, 156 D.L.R., pp. 322-23, 328 S.C.R.). Hall J. said (at p. 200 D.L.R., p. 390 S.C.R.) that "aboriginal Indian title does not depend on treaty, executive order or legislative enactment".

. . . . .

In recognizing that the Proclamation is not the sole source of Indian title the *Calder* decision went beyond the judgment of the Privy Council in *St. Catherine's Milling & Lumber Co. v. The Queen* (1888), 14 App. Cas. 46. In that case Lord Watson acknowledged the existence of aboriginal title but said it had its origin in the Royal Proclamation. In this respect *Calder* is consistent with the position of Chief Justice Marshall in the leading American cases of *Johnson and Graham's Lessee v. M'Intosh* (1823), 8 Wheaton 543, 21 U.S. 240, and *Worcester v. State of Georgia* (1832), 6 Peters 515, 31 U.S. 530, cited by Judson and Hall JJ. in their respective judgments.

In *Johnson v. M'Intosh*, Marshall C.J., although he acknowledged the Royal Proclamation of 1763 as one basis for recognition of Indian title, was none the less of the opinion that the rights of Indians in the lands they traditionally occupied prior to European colonization both predated and survived the claims to sovereignty made by various European nations in the territories of the North American continent. The principle of discovery which justified these claims gave the ultimate title in the land in a particular area to the nation which had discovered and claimed it. In that respect at least the Indians' rights in the land were obviously diminished; but their rights of occupancy and possession remained unaffected.

·····

The principle that a change in sovereignty over a particular territory does not in general affect the presumptive title of the inhabitants was approved by the Privy Council in *Amodu Tijani v. Secretary, Southern Nigeria*, [1921] 2 A.C. 399. That principle supports the assumption implicit in *Calder* that Indian title is an independent legal right which, although recognized by the Royal Proclamation of 1763, none the less predates it. ... [The Indians'] interest in their lands is a pre-existing legal right not created by Royal Proclamation, by s. 18(1) of the *Indian Act*, or by any other executive order or legislative provision.

It does not matter, in my opinion, that the present case is concerned with the interest of an Indian band in a reserve rather than with unrecognized aboriginal title in traditional tribal lands. The Indian interest in the land is the same in both cases: see *A.-G. Que. v. A.-G. Can.* (1920), 56 D.L.R. 373 at pp. 378-9, [1921] 1 A.C. 401 at pp. 410-11 (the *Star Chrome* case).

·····

In the *St. Catherine's Milling* case, *supra*, the Privy Council held that the Indians had a "personal and usufructuary right" [p. 54] in the lands which they had traditionally occupied. Lord Watson said that "there has been all along vested in the Crown a substantial and paramount estate, underlying the Indian title, which became a *plenum dominium* whenever the title was surrendered or otherwise extinguished" (at p. 55). He reiterated this idea, stating that the Crown "has all along had a present proprietary estate in the land, upon which the Indian title was a mere burden" (at p. 58). This view of aboriginal title was affirmed by the Privy Council in the *Star Chrome* case. In *Amodu Tijani, supra*, Viscount Haldane, adverting to the *St. Catherine's Milling* and *Star Chrome* decisions, explained the concept of a usufructuary right as "a mere qualification of or burden on the radical or final title of the Sovereign" (p. 403). He described the title of the Sovereign as a pure legal estate, but one which could be qualified by a right of "beneficial user" that did not necessarily take the form of an estate in land. Indian title in Canada was said to be one illustration "of the necessity for getting rid of the assumption that the ownership of land naturally breaks itself up into estates, conceived as creatures of inherent legal principle" [p. 403]. Chief Justice Marshall took a similar view in *Johnson v. M'Intosh, supra,* saying, "All our institutions recognize the absolute title of the Crown, subject only to the Indian right of occupancy" (p. 588).

It should be noted that the Privy Council's emphasis on the personal nature of aboriginal title stemmed in part from constitutional arrangements peculiar to Canada. The Indian territory at issue in *St. Catherine's Milling* was land which in 1867 had been vested in the Crown subject to the interest of the Indians. The Indians' interest was "an interest other than that of the Province", within the meaning of s. 109 of the *Constitution Act, 1867.* Section 109 provides:

> 109. All Lands, Mines, Minerals, and Royalties belonging to the several Provinces of Canada, Nova Scotia, and New Brunswick at the Union, and all Sums then due or payable for such Lands, Mines, Minerals, or Royalties, shall belong to the several Provinces of Ontario, Quebec, Nova Scotia, and New Brunswick in which the same are situate or arise subject to any Trusts existing in respect thereof, and to any Interest other than that of the Province in the same.

When the land in question in *St. Catherine's Milling* was subsequently disencumbered of the native title upon its surrender to the federal government by the Indian occupants in 1873, the entire beneficial interest in the land was held to have passed, because of the personal and usufructuary nature of the Indians' right, to the Province of Ontario under s. 109 rather than to Canada. The same constitutional issue arose recently in this court in *Smith et al. v. The Queen* (1983), 147 D.L.R. (3d) 237, [1983] 1 S.C.R. 554, 47 N.R. 132 *sub nom. Government of Canada v. Smith,* in which the court held that the Indian right in a reserve, being personal, could not be transferred to a grantee, whether an individual or the Crown. Upon surrender the right disappeared "in the process of release".

No such constitutional problem arises in the present case, since in 1938 the title to all Indian reserves in British Columbia was transferred by the provincial government to the Crown in right of Canada.

It is true that in contexts other than the constitutional the characterization of Indian title as "a personal and usufructuary right" has sometimes been questioned. In *Calder, supra,* for example, Judson J. intimated at p. 156 D.L.R., p. 328 S.C.R., that this characterization was not helpful in determining the nature of Indian title. In *A.-G. Can. v. Giroux* (1916), 30 D.L.R. 123, 53 S.C.R. 172, Duff J., speaking for himself and Anglin J., distinguished *St. Catherine's Milling* on the ground that the statutory provisions in accordance with which the reserve in question in *Giroux* had been created conferred beneficial ownership on the Indian band which occupied the reserve. In *Cardinal v. A.-G. Alta.* (1973), 40 D.L.R. (3d) 553, [1974] S.C.R. 695, 13 C.C.C. (2d) 1, Laskin J., dissenting on another point, accepted the possibility that Indians may have a beneficial interest in a reserve. The Alberta Court of Appeal in *Western Industrial Contractors Ltd. v. Sarcee Developments Ltd.* (1979), 98 D.L.R. (3d) 424, [1979] 3 W.W.R. 631 *sub nom. Western Int'l Contractors Ltd. v. Sarcee Developments Ltd.,* 15 A.R. 309, accepted the proposition that an Indian band does indeed have a beneficial interest in its reserve. In the present case this was the view as well of Le Dain J. in the Federal Court of Appeal. See also the judgment of Kellock J. in *Miller v. The King*, [1950] 1 D.L.R. 513, [1950] S.C.R. 168, in which he seems implicitly to adopt a similar position. None of these judgments mentioned the *Star Chrome* case, however, in which the Indian interest in land specifically set aside as a reserve was held to be the same as the "personal and usufructuary right" which was discussed in *St. Catherine's Milling*.

It appears to me that there is no real conflict between the cases which characterize Indian title as a beneficial interest of some sort, and those which characterize it a personal, usufructuary right. Any apparent inconsistency derives from the fact that in describing what constitutes a unique interest in land the courts have almost inevitably found themselves applying a somewhat inappropriate terminology drawn from general property law. There is a core of truth in the way that each of the two lines of authority has described native title, but an appearance of conflict has none the less arisen because in neither case is the categorization quite accurate.

Indians have a legal right to occupy and possess certain lands, the ultimate title to which is in the Crown. While their interest does not, strictly speaking, amount to beneficial ownership, neither is its nature completely exhausted by the concept of a personal right. It is true that the *sui generis* interest which the Indians have in the land is personal in the sense that it cannot be transferred to a grantee, but it is also true, as will presently appear, that the interest gives rise upon surrender to a distinctive fiduciary obligation of the Crown to deal with the land for the benefit of the surrendering Indians. These two aspects of Indian title go together, since the Crown's original purpose in declaring the Indians' interest to be inalienable otherwise than to the Crown was to facilitate the Crown's ability to represent the Indians in dealings with third parties. The nature of the Indians' interest is therefore best characterized by its general inalienability, coupled with the fact that the Crown is under an obligation to deal with the land on the Indians' behalf when the interest is surrendered. Any description of Indian title which goes beyond these two features is both unnecessary and potentially misleading.

F. ISSUES RAISED BY ABORIGINAL TITLE JURISPRUDENCE

The *Guerin* decision was premised on the earlier Supreme Court of Canada decision in *Smith v. R.*, [1983] 1 S.C.R. 554, 47 N.R. 132, 147 D.L.R. (3d) 237, which it cited in its discussion of Aboriginal title. In *Smith*, the Aboriginal interest in land was characterized as a right that disappeared upon surrender (*i.e.* relinquishment of Aboriginal title) and could not be transferred to a grantee, whether the Crown or a private individual. There are problems with this characterization of Aboriginal title, however. If, as in *Guerin*, a band surrenders title for leasing purposes with the intention of having the land revert back to it at the conclusion of the lease, how is it possible for the band to regain the land if its interest vanished upon surrender? Furthermore, if the *Smith* characterization of Aboriginal title is accurate, does that not render the treaty-making process between the Crown and Aboriginal peoples redundant, at least with regard to the characterization of treaties as land surrender agreements?

The unique, or *sui generis*, nature of Aboriginal land rights indicated in *Guerin* was referenced in *St. Mary's Indian Band v. Cranbrook (City)*, [1997] 2 S.C.R. 657. In that case, Lamer C.J.C., for the Court, held, at para. 14, that the *sui generis* nature of Aboriginal land rights entailed that disputes concerning Aboriginal lands were not to be approached "by strict reference to intractable real property rules". As he further explained, *ibid.* at para. 16:

> The reason the Court has said that common law real property concepts do not apply to native lands is to prevent native intentions from being frustrated by an application of formalistic and arguably alien common law rules. Even in a case such as this where the Indian band received full legal representation ... we must ensure that form not trump substance. It would be fundamentally unjust to impose inflexible and technical land transfer requirements upon these "autonomous actors"...

The requirement that Aboriginal peoples surrender their interests in land before those interests may be alienated to third parties, a matter of fundamental importance in the *Guerin, Smith,* and *St. Mary's* cases and seen in the earlier discussion of the *Royal Proclamation of 1763*, is summarized in *Opetchesaht Indian Band v. Canada*, [1997] 2 S.C.R. 119.

OPETCHESAHT INDIAN BAND v. CANADA

[1997] 2 S.C.R. 119

Major J.: —

. . . . .

Any sale or lease of land to a third party can only be carried out after a surrender has taken place, with the Crown then acting on the band's behalf to effectuate the transfer to third parties. The Crown prior to the surrender holds the fee simple to the land subject to the Indians' *sui generis* interest. When a band surrenders land, or more correctly, its *sui generis* interest in land, to the Crown, the band's interest is said to merge in the fee held by the Crown. The Crown then holds the land free of the Indian interest. The Crown has a broad discretion in dealing with surrendered land but it is subject to an equitable obligation to deal with the land for the benefit of the Indians and subject to the terms of the surrender from the band: *Guerin, supra*, at pp. 353-54, *per* Wilson J., and at p. 385, *per* Dickson J.

Surrenders may be absolute or qualified, conditional or unconditional. *Smith, supra*, at p. 568, makes clear that upon unconditional and absolute surrender the Indians' rights in the land disappear. However, surrenders may also release only partially or temporarily the interest of the Indians. The point here is that surrenders are required as a general rule not only when the Indian band is releasing all its interest in the reserve forever, but whenever any interest is given up for any duration of time. Indeed, this has been recognized by the jurisprudence of this Court:

> That there can be a partial surrender of the "personal and usufructuary rights" which the Indians enjoy is confirmed by the *St. Catherine's Milling Company Limited v. The Queen* [(1888), 14 App. Cas. 46], in which there was retained the privilege of hunting and fishing; and I see no distinction in principle, certainly in view of the nature of the interest held by the Indians and the object of the legislation, between a surrender of a portion of rights for all time and a surrender of all rights for a limited time.

(*St. Ann's Island Shooting and Fishing Club Ltd. v. The King*, [1950] S.C.R. 211, at p. 219, *per* Rand J.)

That this is so is apparent from the face of s. 37. Section 37 is not restricted to sales or complete alienation of lands in a reserve from the Crown to third parties. Leases or other dispositions of "lands in a reserve" also require a surrender by the Indians of their interest to the Crown. Section 38 elaborates what exactly may be surrendered to the Crown:

> **38.** (1) A band may surrender to Her Majesty any right or interest of the band and its members in a reserve.
> (2) A surrender may be absolute or qualified, conditional or unconditional.

Section 38 provides that "any right or interest of the band and its members" in a reserve may be surrendered, obviously in reference to s. 37. The bundle of rights which may be surrendered is "any right or interest" in a reserve. Section 35, the expropriation power, specifies that the right to expropriate may similarly be exercised "in relation to lands in a reserve or any interest therein".

Also apparent on the face of s. 37 from the qualification at the beginning of s. 37 is the legislative intention that it operate in conjunction with and subject to other provisions of the *Indian Act*. There is in this qualification an express recognition that other provisions of the *Indian Act* also deal with sales, alienations, leases or other dispositions of lands in a reserve.

McLachlin J. (dissenting): —

. . . . .

Surrender is a formal process, accompanied by a formal vote by band members and other safeguards to ensure that the people understand and consent to the proposed alienation.

. . . . .

The starting point in an assessment of the relationship between aboriginals and the Crown on the question of land is the *Royal Proclamation, 1763*, R.S.C., 1985, App. II, No. 1. That document, affirmed by Hall J. in *Calder v. Attorney-General of British Columbia*, [1973] S.C.R. 313, at p. 395, as an "Indian Bill of Rights", established as governing principles in Canada (1) the

reservation of certain lands to Indians for their exclusive use and possession, and (2) the creation of a strict process for the purchase of Indian land:

> And whereas it is just and reasonable, and essential to our Interest, and
> the Security of our Colonies, that the several Nations or Tribes of Indians
> with whom We are connected, and who live under our Protection, should
> not be molested or disturbed in the Possession of such Parts of Our Domin-
> ions and Territories as, not having been ceded to or purchased by Us, are re-
> served to them, or any of them, as their Hunting Grounds. . . .

. . . . .

> And whereas great Frauds and Abuses have been committed in the pur-
> chasing Lands of the Indians, to the great Prejudice of our Interests, and to
> the great Dissatisfaction of the said Indians; In order, therefore, to prevent
> such Irregularities for the future, and to the end that the Indians may be
> convinced of our Justice and determined Resolution to remove all reason-
> able Cause of Discontent, We do, with the Advice of our Privy Council
> strictly enjoin and require, that no private Person do presume to make any
> purchase from the said Indians of any Lands reserved to the said Indians,
> within those parts of our Colonies where, We have thought proper to allow
> Settlement; but that, if at any Time any of the Said Indians should be in-
> clined to dispose of the said Lands, the same shall be Purchased only for Us,
> in our Name, at some public Meeting or Assembly of the said Indians, to be
> held for that Purpose. . . .

As a result of the *Royal Proclamation, 1763*, "lands could be surrendered
only on a nation-to-nation basis, from the Indian nation to the British
Crown, in a public process in which the assembled Indian population
would be required to consent to the transaction" (*Report of the Royal Commission on Aboriginal Peoples* (1996), vol. 1, at p. 261). The Report also notes
that the "present *Indian Act* continues to reflect the land surrender procedure first set out in the Royal Proclamation" (p. 261).

The 1952 *Indian Act*, as amended by S.C. 1956, c. 40, reflects the surrender requirements established by the Royal Proclamation. Section 37 of the
Act affirms the presence of the Crown as a go-between in transactions involving reserve land, stating that "lands in a reserve shall not be sold, alienated, leased or otherwise disposed of until they have been surrendered
to Her Majesty by the band for whose use and benefit in common the reserve was set apart". Section 39(1) mandates that surrenders of reserve
land must be made to the Crown, must be assented to by a majority of the
electors of the band, and must be accepted by the Governor in Council.
This requirement of <u>band</u> approval stands in contrast to the more limited
requirements of ss. 28(2) and 58(1) for consent of the <u>band council</u> and
Minister to the granting of a permit, or a lease for agricultural or grazing
purposes.

The *Indian Act* provisions governing the surrender of reserve lands were
created to strike "a balance between the two extremes of autonomy and
protection. The band's consent was required to surrender its reserve.
Without that consent the reserve could not be sold. But the Crown,
through the Governor in Council, was also required to consent to the surrender": *Blueberry River Indian Band v. Canada (Department of Indian Affairs
and Northern Development)*, [1995] 4 S.C.R. 344 at p. 370. The protection of

reserve lands for future generations may be seen as one of the fundamental purposes of the Act. Alienation was viewed as a grave matter, to be
effected only in accordance with a highly scrutinized and strictly regulated
procedure. The *Indian Act* confirms the general inalienability of Indian
lands (s. 37) and safeguards the sanctity of reserve lands, by prohibiting
their alienation except to the Crown, with the consent of the band membership as a whole.

While *Opetchesaht* raised the issue of the effect of land surrenders on
Aboriginal title, it simply affirmed the *Smith* decision without truly considering its effects on surrenders for lease versus surrenders for sale.
Opetchesaht's finding that surrenders may partially or temporarily release
the Indian interest in land, while consistent with sections 37-38 of the *Indian Act*, creates problems in light of *Smith's* statement that Indian land
interests may not be transferred, but simply vanish upon surrender and
cannot be resurrected. If *Smith's* characterization is correct, then a band
that has temporarily surrendered its land interests (as in a leasing situation) will still be understood to have had those interests eliminated, leaving in doubt the basis upon which the band may reclaim the land upon
the termination of the lease.

As a result of the incomplete analysis of this issue in *Opetchesaht*, the
Smith precedent and the problems it created remain. More generally,
Opetchesaht affirms the unique quality of Aboriginal title, but does not help
clarify its nature or what it amounts to. Other Supreme Court of Canada
judgments, such as *Delgamuukw v. British Columbia* and *Musqueam Indian
Band v. Glass* (both of which are excerpted below) have provided additional pieces of the puzzle, yet a number of questions remain.

G. RECENT JUDICIAL CONSIDERATIONS OF ABORIGINAL TITLE

Originally, the doctrine of Aboriginal title, as formulated by British colonial law, was a means of reconciling Aboriginal and European claims to
land designed to maintain peaceful relations between the parties. The
modern law of Aboriginal title is derived from the nature of the interaction
between Aboriginal and European people in North America, their competing claims to land, and the creation of a significant body of case law
dealing with Aboriginal rights to land.

In spite of important pronouncements such as *Calder* and *Guerin*, Canadian courts have not always provided a consistent basis upon which to appraise questions of Aboriginal title. For a variety of reasons, the courts
have evaded many of the primary issues surrounding Aboriginal title. These
issues, which include the legitimacy of the British Crown's claims to title
and/or sovereignty over Canada, are of primary importance to all Canadians, whether Aboriginal or non-Aboriginal. Questions of title and sover-

eignty were central to the issues at bar in the case of *Delgamuukw v. British Columbia*, below.

DELGAMUUKW v. BRITISH COLUMBIA

[1997] 3 S.C.R. 1010

Cory, McLachlin, and **Major JJ.** concur with

Lamer C.J.C.: —

I. *Introduction*

This appeal is the latest in a series of cases in which it has fallen to this Court to interpret and apply the guarantee of existing aboriginal rights found in s. 35(1) of the *Constitution Act, 1982.* Although that line of decisions, commencing with *R. v. Sparrow*, [1990] 1 S.C.R. 1075, proceeding through the *Van der Peet* trilogy (*R. v. Van der Peet*, [1996] 2 S.C.R. 507, *R. v. N. T. C. Smokehouse Ltd.*, [1996] 2 S.C.R. 672, and *R. v. Gladstone*, [1996] 2 S.C.R. 723), and ending in *R. v. Pamajewon*, [1996] 2 S.C.R. 821, *R. v. Adams*, [1996] 3 S.C.R. 101, and *R. v. Côté*, [1996] 3 S.C.R. 139, have laid down the jurisprudential framework for s. 35(1), this appeal raises a set of interrelated and novel questions which revolve around a single issue — the nature and scope of the constitutional protection afforded by s. 35(1) to common law aboriginal title.

... This appeal demands ... that the Court now explore and elucidate the implications of the constitutionalization of aboriginal title.

. . . . .

In addition to the relationship between aboriginal title and s. 35(1), this appeal also raises an important practical problem relevant to the proof of aboriginal title which is endemic to aboriginal rights litigation generally — the treatment of the oral histories of Canada's aboriginal peoples by the courts. In *Van der Peet*, I held that the common law rules of evidence should be adapted to take into account the *sui generis* nature of aboriginal rights. In this appeal, the Court must address what specific form those modifications must take.

Finally, given the existence of aboriginal title in British Columbia, this Court must address, on cross-appeal, the question of whether the province of British Columbia, from the time it joined Confederation in 1871, until the entrenchment of s. 35(1) in 1982, had jurisdiction to extinguish the rights of aboriginal peoples, including aboriginal title, in that province. Moreover, if the province was without this jurisdiction, a further question arises — whether provincial laws of general application that would otherwise be inapplicable to Indians and Indian lands could nevertheless extinguish aboriginal rights through the operation of s. 88 of the *Indian Act*, R.S.C. 1985, c. I-5. [This latter issue will be dealt with in Chapter 7, Federalism/Constitutional Issues.]

II. *Facts*

. . . . .

The Gitksan consist of approximately 4,000 to 5,000 persons, most of whom now live in the territory claimed, which is generally the watersheds of the north and central Skeena, Nass and Babine Rivers and their tributaries. The Wet'suwet'en consist of approximately 1500 to 2000 persons, who also predominantly live in the territory claimed. This territory is mainly in the watersheds of the Bulkley and parts of the Fraser - Nechako River systems and their tributaries. It lies immediately east and south of the Gitksan.

... [T]he Gitksan and Wet'suwet'en are not the only people living in the claimed territory. ... [T]here are other aboriginals who live in the claimed territory, notably the Carrier-Sekani and Nishga peoples. Some of these people have unsettled land claims overlapping with the territory at issue here. Moreover, there are also numerous non-aboriginals living there.

. . . . .

The fundamental premise of both the Gitksan and the Wet'suwet'en people is that they are divided into clans and Houses. Every person born of a Gitksan or Wet'suwet'en woman is automatically a member of his or her mother's House and clan. There are four Gitksan and four Wet'suwet'en clans, which are subdivided into houses. Each house has one or more Hereditary Chief as its titular head, selected by the elders of their house, as well as possibly the Head Chief of the other Houses of the clan.

. . . . .

V. *Analysis*

A. *Do the pleadings preclude the Court from entertaining claims for aboriginal title and self-government?*

[The appellants, 51 Chiefs representing most of the houses of the Gitksan and Wet'suwet'en nations, originally advanced 51 individual claims for "ownership" and "jurisdiction" over 133 distinct territories, comprising some 58,000 square kilometres of northwestern British Columbia. On appeal, the original claim was altered in two ways: (1) replacing the claims for ownership and jurisdiction with claims for Aboriginal title and self-government, and; (2) amalgamating the 51 individual claims into two communal claims, one for each nation. The first amendment was not formally made to the pleadings, but via a *de facto* amendment allowed by the trial judge which was not contested by the respondents. **Lamer C.J.C.** held that there was no prejudice to the respondents by virtue of the first alteration of the claims. No amendment whatsoever was made regarding the amalgamation of the 51 claims, though. Consequently, **Lamer C.J.C.** held that this lack of amendment unfairly prejudiced the respondents and that this defect in the pleadings prevented the Supreme Court from considering the merits of the appeal. The Chief Justice ordered a new trial as the correct remedy for this defect in the pleadings. The remainder of the judgment was dedicated to other reasons why a new trial ought to be ordered.]

B. *What is the ability of this Court to interfere with the factual findings made by the trial judge?*

(1) *General Principles*

... As a general rule, this Court has been extremely reluctant to interfere with the findings of fact made at trial, especially when those findings of fact are based on an assessment of the testimony and credibility of witnesses. Unless there is a "palpable and overriding error", appellate courts should not substitute their own findings of fact for those of the trial judge. ... The same deference must be accorded to the trial judge's assessment of the credibility of expert witnesses.

. . . . .

... [W]hile accepting the general principle of non-interference, this Court has also identified specific situations in which an appeal court can interfere with a finding of fact made at trial. For example, appellate intervention is warranted "where the courts below have misapprehended or overlooked material evidence" ... In cases involving the determination of aboriginal rights, appellate intervention is also warranted by the failure of a trial court to appreciate the evidentiary difficulties inherent in adjudicating aboriginal claims when, first, applying the rules of evidence and, second, interpreting the evidence before it. As I said in *Van der Peet*, at para. 68:

> In determining whether an aboriginal claimant has produced evidence sufficient to demonstrate that her activity is an aspect of a practice, custom or tradition integral to a distinctive aboriginal culture, *a court should approach the rules of evidence, and interpret the evidence that exists*, with a consciousness of the special nature of aboriginal claims, and of the evidentiary difficulties in proving a right which originates in times where there were no written records of the practices, customs and traditions engaged in. *The courts must not undervalue the evidence presented by aboriginal claimants simply because that evidence does not conform precisely with the evidentiary standards that would be applied in, for example, a private law torts case.* [Emphasis added.]

The justification for this special approach can be found in the nature of aboriginal rights themselves. I explained in *Van der Peet* that those rights are aimed at the reconciliation of the prior occupation of North America by distinctive aboriginal societies with the assertion of Crown sovereignty over Canadian territory. They attempt to achieve that reconciliation by "their bridging of aboriginal and non-aboriginal cultures" (at para. 42). Accordingly, "a court must take into account the perspective of the aboriginal people claiming the right. ... while at the same time taking into account the perspective of the common law" such that "[t]rue reconciliation will, equally, place weight on each" (at paras. 49 and 50).

In other words, although the doctrine of aboriginal rights is a common law doctrine, aboriginal rights are truly *sui generis*, and demand a unique approach to the treatment of evidence which accords due weight to the perspective of aboriginal peoples. However, that accommodation must be done in a manner which does not strain "the Canadian legal and constitutional structure" ... Both the principles laid down in *Van der Peet* — first, that trial courts must approach the rules of evidence in light of the evidentiary difficulties inherent in adjudicating aboriginal claims, and second, that trial courts must interpret that evidence in the same spirit — must be understood against this background.

A concrete application of the first principle can be found in *Van der Peet* itself, where I addressed the difficulties inherent in demonstrating a continuity between current aboriginal activities and the pre-contact practices, customs and traditions of aboriginal societies. ... [T]he requirement for continuity is one component of the definition of aboriginal rights. ... However, given that many aboriginal societies did not keep written records at the time of contact or sovereignty, it would be exceedingly difficult for them to produce (at para. 62) "conclusive evidence from pre-contact times about the practices, customs and traditions of their community". Accordingly, I held that (at para. 62):

> The evidence relied upon by the applicant and the courts may relate to aboriginal practices, customs and traditions *post-contact*; it simply needs to be directed at demonstrating which aspects of the aboriginal community and society have their origins *pre-contact*. [Emphasis added.]

The same considerations apply when the time from which title is determined is sovereignty.

This appeal requires us to apply not only the first principle in *Van der Peet* but the second principle as well, and adapt the laws of evidence so that the aboriginal perspective on their practices, customs and traditions and on their relationship with the land, are given due weight by the courts. In practical terms, this requires the courts to come to terms with the oral histories of aboriginal societies, which, for many aboriginal nations, are the only record of their past. Given that the aboriginal rights recognized and affirmed by s. 35(1) are defined by reference to pre-contact practices or, as I will develop below, in the case of title, pre-sovereignty occupation, those histories play a crucial role in the litigation of aboriginal rights.

· · · · ·

Many features of oral histories would count against both their admissibility and their weight as evidence of prior events in a court that took a traditional approach to the rules of evidence. The most fundamental of these is their broad social role not only "as a repository of historical knowledge for a culture" but also as an expression of "the values and mores of ... [that] culture": Clay McLeod, "The Oral Histories of Canada's Northern People, Anglo-Canadian Evidence Law, and Canada's Fiduciary

Duty to First Nations: Breaking Down the Barriers of the Past" (1992), 30
Alta. L. Rev. 1276, at p. 1279. Dickson J. (as he was then) recognized as
much when he stated in *Kruger v. The Queen*, [1978] 1 S.C.R. 104, at p. 109,
that "[c]laims to aboriginal title are woven with history, legend, politics
and moral obligations". The difficulty with these features of oral histories
is that they are tangential to the ultimate purpose of the fact-finding process at trial — the determination of the historical truth. Another feature of
oral histories which creates difficulty is that they largely consist of out-of-
court statements, passed on through an unbroken chain across the generations of a particular aboriginal nation to the present-day. These out-of-
court statements are admitted for their truth and therefore conflict with the
general rule against the admissibility of hearsay.

Notwithstanding the challenges created by the use of oral histories as
proof of historical facts, the laws of evidence must be adapted in order that
this type of evidence can be accommodated and placed on an equal footing
with the types of historical evidence that courts are familiar with, which
largely consists of historical documents. This is a long-standing practice in
the interpretation of treaties between the Crown and aboriginal peoples
[see the discussion of treaty interpretation in Chapter 2]. ... To quote Dickson C.J., given that most aboriginal societies "did not keep written records", the failure to do so would "impose an impossible burden of proof"
on aboriginal peoples, and "render nugatory" any rights that they have
(*Simon v. The Queen*, [1985] 1 2 S.C.R. 387, at p. 408). This process must be
undertaken on a case-by-case basis.

. . . . .

On a final note, it is important to understand that even when a trial
judge has erred in making a finding of fact, appellate intervention does not
proceed automatically. The error must be sufficiently serious that it was
"overriding and determinative in the assessment of the balance of probabilities with respect to that factual issue".

. . . . .

The trial judge's treatment of the various kinds of oral histories did not
satisfy the principles I laid down in *Van der Peet*. These errors are particularly worrisome because oral histories were of critical importance to the
appellants' case. They used those histories in an attempt to establish their
occupation and use of the disputed territory, an essential requirement for
aboriginal title. The trial judge, after refusing to admit, or giving no independent weight to these oral histories, reached the conclusion that the appellants had not demonstrated the requisite degree of occupation for
"ownership". Had the trial judge assessed the oral histories correctly, his
conclusions on these issues of fact might have been very different.

In the circumstances, the factual findings cannot stand. However, given
the enormous complexity of the factual issues at hand, it would be impossible for the Court to do justice to the parties by sifting through the record
itself and making new factual findings. A new trial is warranted, at which

the evidence may be considered in light of the principles laid down in *Van der Peet* and elaborated upon here.

.....

C. *What is the content of aboriginal title, how is it protected by s. 35(1), and what is required for its proof?*

(1) *Introduction*

The parties disagree over whether the appellants have established aboriginal title to the disputed area. However, since those factual issues require a new trial, we cannot resolve that dispute in this appeal. But factual issues aside, the parties also have a more fundamental disagreement over the content of aboriginal title itself, and its reception into the Constitution by s. 35(1). In order to give guidance to the judge at the new trial, it is to this issue that I will now turn.

... I believe that all of the parties have characterized the content of aboriginal title incorrectly. The appellants argue that aboriginal title is tantamount to an inalienable fee simple, which confers on aboriginal peoples the rights to use those lands as they choose and which has been constitutionalized by s. 35(1). The respondents offer two alternative formulations: first, that aboriginal title is no more than a bundle of rights to engage in activities which are themselves aboriginal rights recognized and affirmed by s. 35(1), and that the *Constitution Act, 1982*, merely constitutionalizes those individual rights, not the bundle itself, because the latter has no independent content; and second, that aboriginal title, at most, encompasses the right to exclusive use and occupation of land in order to engage in those activities which are aboriginal rights themselves, and that s. 35(1) constitutionalizes this notion of exclusivity.

The content of aboriginal title, in fact, lies somewhere in between these positions. Aboriginal title is a right in land and, as such, is more than the right to engage in specific activities which may be themselves aboriginal rights. Rather, it confers the right to use land for a variety of activities, not all of which need be aspects of practices, customs and traditions which are integral to the distinctive cultures of aboriginal societies. Those activities do not constitute the right *per se*; rather, they are parasitic on the underlying title. However, that range of uses is subject to the limitation that they must not be irreconcilable with the nature of the attachment to the land which forms the basis of the particular group's aboriginal title. This inherent limit, to be explained more fully below, flows from the definition of aboriginal title as a *sui generis* interest in land, and is one way in which aboriginal title is distinct from a fee simple.

(2) *Aboriginal title at common law*

(a) *General features*

The starting point of the Canadian jurisprudence on aboriginal title is the Privy Council's decision in *St. Catherine's Milling and Lumber Co. v. The Queen* (1888), 14 A.C. 46, which described aboriginal title as a "personal and usufructuary right". ... What the Privy Council sought to capture is that aboriginal title is a *sui generis* interest in land. Aboriginal title has been described as *sui generis* in order to distinguish it from "normal" proprietary interests, such as fee simple. However, as I will now develop, it is also *sui generis* in the sense that its characteristics cannot be completely explained by reference either to the common law rules of real property or to the rules of property found in aboriginal legal systems. As with other aboriginal rights, it must be understood by reference to both common law and aboriginal perspectives.

The idea that aboriginal title is *sui generis* is the unifying principle underlying the various dimensions of that title. One dimension is its *inalienability*. Lands held pursuant to aboriginal title cannot be transferred, sold or surrendered to anyone other than the Crown and, as a result, is inalienable to third parties. This Court has taken pains to clarify that aboriginal title is only "personal" in this sense, and does not mean that aboriginal title is a non-proprietary interest which amounts to no more than a licence to use and occupy the land and cannot compete on an equal footing with other proprietary interests: see *Canadian Pacific Ltd. v. Paul*, [1988] 2 S.C.R. 654, at p. 677.

Another dimension of aboriginal title is its *source*. ... [I]t arises from the prior occupation of Canada by aboriginal peoples. That prior occupation, however, is relevant in two different ways, both of which illustrate the *sui generis* nature of aboriginal title. The first is the physical fact of occupation, which derives from the common law principle that occupation is proof of possession in law .... What makes aboriginal title *sui generis* is that it arises from possession *before* the assertion of British sovereignty, whereas normal estates, like fee simple, arise afterward. ... This idea has been further developed in *Roberts v. Canada*, [1989] 1 S.C.R. 322, where this Court unanimously held at p. 340 that "aboriginal title pre-dated colonization by the British and survived British claims to sovereignty" (also see *Guerin, supra,* at p. 378). What this suggests is a second source for aboriginal title — the relationship between common law and pre-existing systems of aboriginal law.

A further dimension of aboriginal title is the fact that it is held *communally*. Aboriginal title cannot be held by individual aboriginal persons; it is a collective right to land held by all members of an aboriginal nation. Decisions with respect to that land are also made by that community. This is another feature of aboriginal title which is *sui generis* and distinguishes it from normal property interests.

(b) *The content of aboriginal title*

Although cases involving aboriginal title have come before this Court and Privy Council before, there has never been a definitive statement from either court on the *content* of aboriginal title.

. . . . .

Although the courts have been less than forthcoming, I have arrived at the conclusion that the content of aboriginal title can be summarized by two propositions: first, that aboriginal title encompasses the right to exclusive use and occupation of the land held pursuant to that title for a variety of purposes, which need not be aspects of those aboriginal practices, customs and traditions which are integral to distinctive aboriginal cultures; and second, that those protected uses must not be irreconcilable with the nature of the group's attachment to that land. For the sake of clarity, I will discuss each of these propositions separately.

> Aboriginal title encompasses the right to use the land held pursuant to that title for a variety of purposes, which need not be aspects of those aboriginal practices, cultures and traditions which are integral to *distinctive aboriginal cultures.*

The respondents argue that aboriginal title merely encompasses the right to engage in activities which are aspects of aboriginal practices, customs and traditions which are integral to distinctive aboriginal cultures of the aboriginal group claiming the right and, at most, adds the notion of exclusivity; *i.e.*, the exclusive right to use the land for those purposes. However, the uses to which lands held pursuant to aboriginal title can be put are not restricted in this way. This conclusion emerges from three sources: (i) the Canadian jurisprudence on aboriginal title, (ii) the relationship between reserve lands and lands held pursuant to aboriginal title, and (iii) the *Indian Oil and Gas Act*, R.S.C., 1985, c. I-7.

. . . . .

(i) *Canadian jurisprudence on aboriginal title*

Despite the fact that the jurisprudence on aboriginal title is somewhat underdeveloped, it is clear that the uses to which lands held pursuant to aboriginal title can be put is not restricted to the practices, customs and traditions of aboriginal peoples integral to distinctive aboriginal cultures. In *Guerin*, for example, Dickson J. described aboriginal title as "an interest in land" which encompassed "a legal right to occupy and possess certain lands" (at p. 382). The "right to occupy and possess" is framed in broad terms and, significantly, is not qualified by reference to traditional and customary uses of those lands. Any doubt that the right to occupancy and possession encompasses a broad variety of uses of land was put to rest in *Paul*, where the Court went even further and stated that aboriginal title was "more than the right to enjoyment and occupancy" (at p. 688). Once again, there is no reference to aboriginal practices, customs and traditions as a qualifier on that right. Moreover, I take the reference to "more" as emphasis of the broad notion of use and possession.

(ii) *Reserve Land*

Another source of support for the conclusion that the uses to which lands held under aboriginal title can be put are not restricted to those grounded in practices, customs and traditions integral to distinctive aboriginal cultures can be found in *Guerin*, where Dickson J. stated at p. 379 that the same legal principles governed the aboriginal interest in reserve lands and lands held pursuant to aboriginal title. ... [see the discussion of *Guerin, supra*]

The nature of the Indian interest in reserve land is very broad, and can found in s. 18 of the *Indian Act*. ... The principal provision is s. 18(1), which states that reserve lands are held "for the use and benefit" of the bands which occupy them; those uses and benefits, on the face of the *Indian Act*, do not appear to be restricted to practices, customs and traditions integral to distinctive aboriginal cultures. The breadth of those uses is reinforced by s. 18(2), which states that reserve lands may be used "for any other purpose for the general welfare of the band". The general welfare of the band has not been defined in terms of aboriginal practices, customs and traditions, nor in terms of those activities which have their origin pre-contact; it is a concept, by definition, which incorporates a reference to the present-day needs of aboriginal communities. On the basis of *Guerin*, lands held pursuant to aboriginal title, like reserve lands, are also capable of being used for a broad variety of purposes.

(iii) *Indian Oil and Gas Act*

. . . . .

The overall purpose of the statute is to provide for the exploration of oil and gas on reserve lands through their surrender to the Crown. The statute presumes that the aboriginal interest in reserve land includes mineral rights, a point which this Court unanimously accepted with respect to the *Indian Act* in *Blueberry River Indian Band v. Canada (Department of Indian Affairs and Northern Development)*, [1995] 4 S.C.R. 344. On the basis of *Guerin*, aboriginal title also encompass [*sic*] mineral rights, and lands held pursuant to aboriginal title should be capable of exploitation in the same way, which is certainly not a traditional use for those lands. This conclusion is reinforced by s. 6(2) of the Act, which provides:

6. (2) Nothing in this Act shall be deemed to abrogate the rights of Indian people or preclude them from negotiating for oil and gas benefits in those areas in which land claims have not been settled.

The areas referred to in s. 6(2), at the very least, must encompass lands held pursuant to aboriginal title, since those lands by definition have not been surrendered under land claims agreements. The presumption underlying s. 6(2) is that aboriginal title permits the development of oil and gas reserves.

. . . . .

In conclusion, the content of aboriginal title is not restricted to those uses which are elements of a practice, custom or tradition integral to the distinctive culture of the aboriginal group claiming the right. However, nor does aboriginal title amount to a form of inalienable fee simple, as I will now explain.

(c) *Inherent Limit: Lands held pursuant to aboriginal title cannot be used in a manner that is irreconcilable with the nature of the attachment to the land which forms the basis of the group's claim to aboriginal title.*

The content of aboriginal title contains an inherent limit that lands held pursuant to title cannot be used in a manner that is irreconcilable with the nature of the claimants' attachment to those lands. This limit on the content of aboriginal title is a manifestation of the principle that underlies the various dimensions of that special interest in land — it is a *sui generis* interest that is distinct from "normal" proprietary interests, most notably fee simple.

I arrive at this conclusion by reference to the other dimensions of aboriginal title which are *sui generis* as well. ... As I discussed earlier, aboriginal title arises from the prior occupation of Canada by aboriginal peoples. That prior occupation is relevant in two different ways: first, because of the physical fact of occupation, and second, because aboriginal title originates in part from pre-existing systems of aboriginal law. However, the law of aboriginal title does not only seek to determine the historic rights of aboriginal peoples to land; it also seeks to afford legal protection to prior occupation in the present-day. Implicit in the protection of historic patterns of occupation is a recognition of the importance of the continuity of the relationship of an aboriginal community to its land over time.

... The relevance of the continuity of the relationship of an aboriginal community with its land here is that it applies not only to the past, but to the future as well. That relationship should not be prevented from continuing into the future. As a result, uses of the lands that would threaten that future relationship are, by their very nature, excluded from the content of aboriginal title.

Accordingly, in my view, lands subject to aboriginal title cannot be put to such uses as may be irreconcilable with the nature of the occupation of that land and the relationship that the particular group has had with the land which together have given rise to aboriginal title in the first place. ... Occupancy is determined by reference to the activities that have taken place on the land and the uses to which the land has been put by the particular group. If lands are so occupied, there will exist a special bond between the group and the land in question such that the land will be part of the definition of the group's distinctive culture. It seems to me that these elements of aboriginal title create an inherent limitation on the uses to which the land, over which such title exists, may be put. For example, if occupation is established with reference to the use of the land as a hunting ground, then the group that successfully claims aboriginal title to that land may not use it in such a fashion as to destroy its value for such a use (*e.g.*, by strip mining it). Similarly, if a group claims a special bond with the land because of its ceremonial or cultural significance, it may not use the land in such a way as to destroy that relationship (*e.g.*, by developing it in such a way that the bond is destroyed, perhaps by turning it into a parking lot.)

It is for this reason also that lands held by virtue of aboriginal title may not be alienated. Alienation would bring to an end the entitlement of the aboriginal people to occupy the land and would terminate their relationship with it. I have suggested above that the inalienability of aboriginal lands is, at least in part, a function of the common law principle that settlers in colonies must derive their title from Crown grant and, therefore, cannot acquire title through purchase from aboriginal inhabitants. It is also, again only in part, a function of a general policy "to ensure that Indians are not dispossessed of their entitlements": see *Mitchell v. Peguis Indian Band*, [1990] 2 S.C.R. 85, at p. 133. What the inalienability of lands held pursuant to aboriginal title suggests is that those lands are more than just a fungible commodity. The relationship between an aboriginal community and the lands over which it has aboriginal title has an important non-economic component. The land has an inherent and unique value in itself, which is enjoyed by the community with aboriginal title to it. The community cannot put the land to uses which would destroy that value.

. . . . .

[T]he importance of the continuity of the relationship between an aboriginal community and its land, and the non-economic or inherent value of that land, should not be taken to detract from the possibility of surrender to the Crown in exchange for valuable consideration. On the contrary, the idea of surrender reinforces the conclusion that aboriginal title is limited in the way I have described. If aboriginal peoples wish to use their lands in a way that aboriginal title does not permit, then they must surrender those lands and convert them into non-title lands to do so.

The foregoing amounts to a general limitation on the use of lands held by virtue of aboriginal title. It arises from the particular physical and cultural relationship that a group may have with the land and is defined by the source of aboriginal title over it. This is not, I must emphasize, a limitation that restricts the use of the land to those activities that have traditionally been carried out on it. That would amount to a legal straitjacket on aboriginal peoples who have a legitimate legal claim to the land. The approach I have outlined above allows for a full range of uses of the land, subject only to an overarching limit, defined by the special nature of the aboriginal title in that land.

(d) *Aboriginal title under s. 35(1) of the Constitution Act, 1982*

Aboriginal title at common law is protected in its full form by s. 35(1). This conclusion flows from the express language of s. 35(1) itself, which states in full: "[t]he *existing* aboriginal and treaty rights of the aboriginal peoples of Canada are hereby recognized and affirmed" (emphasis added). On a plain reading of the provision, s. 35(1) did not create aboriginal rights; rather, it accorded constitutional status to those rights which were "existing" in 1982.

. . . . .

The acknowledgement that s. 35(1) has accorded constitutional status to common law aboriginal title raises a further question — the relationship of aboriginal title to the "aboriginal rights" protected by s. 35(1). ... [A]lthough aboriginal title is a species of aboriginal right recognized and affirmed by s. 35(1), it is distinct from other aboriginal rights because it arises where the connection of a group with a piece of land "was of a central significance to their distinctive culture" [*Adams*, [1996] 3 S.C.R. 101 at para. 26].

. . . . .

(e) *Proof of aboriginal title*

(i) *Introduction*

To date, the Court has defined aboriginal rights in terms of *activities*. As I said in *Van der Peet* (at para. 46):

> "in order to be an aboriginal right an *activity* must be an element of a practice, custom or tradition integral to the distinctive culture of the aboriginal group claiming the right." [Emphasis added.]

Aboriginal title, however, is a *right to the land* itself.

. . . . .

This difference between aboriginal rights to engage in particular activities and aboriginal title requires that the test I laid down in *Van der Peet* be adapted accordingly. ... Since the purpose of s. 35(1) is to reconcile the prior presence of aboriginal peoples in North America with the assertion of Crown sovereignty ... s. 35(1) must recognize and affirm both aspects of that prior presence — first, the occupation of land, and second, the prior social organization and distinctive cultures of aboriginal peoples on that land.

. . . . .

The adaptation of the test laid down in *Van der Peet* to suit claims to title must be understood as the recognition of the first aspect of that prior presence. ... [The distinction between the *Van der Peet* test for Aboriginal rights and the test for Aboriginal title, discussed immediately below, is also addressed in Chapter 4, Aboriginal Rights.]

(ii) *The test for the proof of aboriginal title*

In order to make out a claim for aboriginal title, the aboriginal group asserting title must satisfy the following criteria: (i) the land must have been occupied prior to sovereignty, (ii) if present occupation is relied on as proof of occupation pre-sovereignty, there must be a continuity between present and pre-sovereignty occupation, and (iii) at sovereignty, that occupation must have been exclusive.

The land must have been occupied prior to sovereignty

In order to establish a claim to aboriginal title, the aboriginal group asserting the claim must establish that it occupied the lands in question at the *time at which the Crown asserted sovereignty over the land subject to the title*.

... [I]n the context of aboriginal title, sovereignty is the appropriate time period to consider for several reasons. First, from a theoretical standpoint, aboriginal title arises out of prior occupation of the land by aboriginal peoples and out of the relationship between the common law and pre-existing systems of aboriginal law. Aboriginal title is a burden on the Crown's underlying title. However, the Crown did not gain this title until it asserted sovereignty over the land in question. Because it does not make sense to speak of a burden on the underlying title before that title existed, aboriginal title crystallized at the time sovereignty was asserted. Second, aboriginal title does not raise the problem of distinguishing between distinctive, integral aboriginal practices, customs and traditions and those influenced or introduced by European contact. Under common law, the act of occupation or possession is sufficient to ground aboriginal title and it is not necessary to prove that the land was a distinctive or integral part of the aboriginal society before the arrival of Europeans. Finally, from a practical standpoint, it appears that the date of sovereignty is more certain than the date of first contact. It is often very difficult to determine the precise moment that each aboriginal group had first contact with European culture. ... For these reasons, I conclude that aboriginals must establish occupation of the land from the date of the assertion of sovereignty in order to sustain a claim for aboriginal title. McEachern C.J. found, at pp. 233-34, and the parties did not dispute on appeal, that British sovereignty over British Columbia was conclusively established by the Oregon Boundary Treaty of 1846. This is not to say that circumstances subsequent to sovereignty may never be relevant to title or compensation; this might be the case, for example, where native bands have been dispossessed of traditional lands after sovereignty.

There was a consensus among the parties on appeal that proof of historic occupation was required to make out a claim to aboriginal title. However, the parties disagreed on how that occupancy could be proved. The respondents assert that in order to establish aboriginal title, the occupation must be the physical occupation of the land in question. The appellant

Gitksan nation argue, by contrast, that aboriginal title may be established, at least in part, by reference to aboriginal law.

. . . . .

This debate over the proof of occupancy reflects two divergent views of the source of aboriginal title. The respondents argue, in essence, that aboriginal title arises from the physical reality at the time of sovereignty, whereas the Gitksan effectively take the position that aboriginal title arises from and should reflect the pattern of land holdings under aboriginal law. However, as I have explained above, the source of aboriginal title appears to be grounded both in the common law and in the aboriginal perspective on land; the latter includes, but is not limited to, their systems of law. It follows that both should be taken into account in establishing the proof of occupancy. Indeed, there is precedent for doing so. In *Baker Lake, supra,* Mahoney J. held that to prove aboriginal title, the claimants needed both to demonstrate their "physical presence on the land they occupied" (at p. 561) and the existence "among [that group of] ... a recognition of the claimed rights. ... by the regime that prevailed before" (at p. 559).

. . . . .

As a result, if, at the time of sovereignty, an aboriginal society had laws in relation to land, those laws would be relevant to establishing the occupation of lands which are the subject of a claim for aboriginal title. Relevant laws might include, but are not limited to, a land tenure system or laws governing land use.

However, the aboriginal perspective must be taken into account alongside the perspective of the common law. Professor McNeil has convincingly argued that at common law the fact of physical occupation is proof of possession at law, which in turn will ground title to the land ... : *Common Law Aboriginal Title*, at p. 73. ... Physical occupation may be established in a variety of ways, ranging from the construction of dwellings through cultivation and enclosure of fields to regular use of definite tracts of land for hunting, fishing or otherwise exploiting its resources. ... In considering whether occupation sufficient to ground title is established, "one must take into account the group's size, manner of life, material resources, and technological abilities, and the character of the lands claimed": Brian Slattery, "Understanding Aboriginal Rights", at pp. 758.

In *Van der Peet*, I drew a distinction between those practices, customs and traditions of aboriginal peoples which were "an aspect of, or took place in" the society of the aboriginal group asserting the claim and those which were "a central and significant part of the society's culture" (at para. 55). The latter stood apart because they "made the culture of that society distinctive ... it was one of the things which truly made the society what it was" (at para. 55). The same requirement operates in the determination of the proof of aboriginal title. As I said in *Adams*, a claim to title is made out when a group can demonstrate "that their connection with the piece of land ... was of central significance to their distinctive culture" (at para. 26).

... [I]n the case of title, it would seem clear that any land that was occupied pre-sovereignty, and which the parties have maintained a substantial connection with since then, is sufficiently important to be of central significance to the culture of the claimants. As a result, I do not think it is necessary to include explicitly this element as part of the test for aboriginal title.

If present occupation is relied on as proof of occupation pre-sovereignty, there must be a continuity between present and pre-sovereignty occupation

... Conclusive evidence of pre-sovereignty occupation may be difficult to come by. Instead, an aboriginal community may provide evidence of present occupation as proof of pre-sovereignty occupation in support of a claim to aboriginal title. What is required, in addition, is a *continuity* between present and pre-sovereignty occupation, because the relevant time for the determination of aboriginal title is at the time before sovereignty.

Needless to say, there is no need to establish "an unbroken chain of continuity" (*Van der Peet*, at para. 65) between present and prior occupation. To impose the requirement of continuity too strictly would risk "undermining the very purposes of s. 35(1) by perpetuating the historical injustice suffered by aboriginal peoples at the hands of colonizers who failed to respect" aboriginal rights to land (*Côté, supra*, at para. 53). In *Mabo, supra*, the High Court of Australia set down the requirement that there must be "substantial maintenance of the connection" between the people and the land. In my view, this test should be equally applicable to proof of title in Canada.

... [T]here is a strong possibility that the precise nature of occupation will have changed between the time of sovereignty and the present. I would like to make it clear that the fact that the nature of occupation has changed would not ordinarily preclude a claim for aboriginal title, as long as a substantial connection between the people and the land is maintained. The only limitation on this principle might be the internal limits on uses which land that is subject to aboriginal title may be put, *i.e.*, uses which are inconsistent with continued use by future generations of aboriginals.

At sovereignty, occupation must have been exclusive

Finally, at sovereignty, occupation must have been exclusive. The requirement for exclusivity flows from the definition of aboriginal title itself, because I have defined aboriginal title in terms of the right to *exclusive* use and occupation of land. Exclusivity, as an aspect of aboriginal title, vests in the aboriginal community which holds the ability to exclude others from the lands held pursuant to that title. The proof of title must, in this respect, mirror the content of the right. Were it possible to prove title without demonstrating exclusive occupation, the result would be absurd, because it would be possible for more than one aboriginal nation to have aboriginal title over the same piece of land, and then for all of them to attempt to assert the right to exclusive use and occupation over it.

As with the proof of occupation, proof of exclusivity must rely on both the perspective of the common law and the aboriginal perspective, placing equal weight on each. ... Exclusivity is a common law principle derived from the notion of fee simple ownership and should be imported into the concept of aboriginal title with caution. As such, the test required to establish exclusive occupation must take into account the context of the aboriginal society at the time of sovereignty. For example, it is important to note that exclusive occupation can be demonstrated even if other aboriginal groups were present, or frequented the claimed lands. Under those circumstances, exclusivity would be demonstrated by "the intention and capacity to retain exclusive control" (McNeil, *Common Law Aboriginal Title, supra*, at p. 204). Thus, an act of trespass, if isolated, would not undermine a general finding of exclusivity, if aboriginal groups intended to and attempted to enforce their exclusive occupation. Moreover, as Professor McNeil suggests, the presence of other aboriginal groups might actually reinforce a finding of exclusivity. For example, "[w]here others were allowed access upon request, the very fact that permission was asked for and given would be further evidence of the group's exclusive control" (at p. 204).

. . . . .

In their submissions, the appellants pressed the point that requiring proof of exclusive occupation might preclude a finding of joint title, which is shared between two or more aboriginal nations. The possibility of joint title has been recognized by American courts: *United States v. Sante Fe Pacific Railroad Co.*, 314 U.S. 339 (1941). I would suggest that the requirement of exclusive occupancy and the possibility of joint title could be reconciled by recognizing that joint title could arise from shared exclusivity. ... However, since no claim to joint title has been asserted here, I leave it to another day.

> ... [I]f aboriginals can show that they occupied a particular piece of land, but did not do so exclusively, it will always be possible to establish aboriginal rights short of title. These rights will likely be intimately tied to the land and may permit a number of possible uses. However, unlike title, they are not a right to the land itself. Rather, as I have suggested, they are a right to do certain things in connection with that land.

[The Chief Justice then considered the test of justification for governmental infringements of Aboriginal title. He concluded that the general principles governing justification, as set out in the *Sparrow* and *Gladstone* decisions, applied to infringements of Aboriginal title with some modifications because of the unique nature of Aboriginal title. The matter of justification was not addressed, as the question of whether the appellants possessed title to the lands in question was sent back to trial for adjudication. The justificatory test for governmental infringement of Aboriginal rights, including title, may be found in Chapter 4, *Aboriginal Rights*.

The appellants' claim to self-government rights was also sent back to trial. The Chief Justice declined to lay down legal principles to guide future self-government litigation, other than to state that "rights to self-government, if they existed, cannot be framed in excessively general terms".

Finally, Lamer C.J.C. held that the province did not have the power to extinguish Aboriginal rights, including title, after its admission into Confederation in 1871, whether under its own jurisdiction or through the operation of section 88 of the federal *Indian Act*. See the discussion of these issues in Chapter 7, Federalism/Constitutional Issues.]

VI. *Conclusion and Disposition*

For the reasons I have given above, I would allow the appeal in part, and dismiss the cross-appeal. Reluctantly, I would also order a new trial.

. . . . .

[La Forest J., L'Heureux-Dubé J. concurring, agreed with Lamer C.J.C.'s conclusion, but disagreed with the methodology the Chief Justice used to demonstrate whether Aboriginal peoples possess Aboriginal title to land. In particular, La Forest J. disagreed with Lamer C.J.C.'s finding that statutory provisions governing reserve lands — such as section 18 of the *Indian Act* and the *Indian Oil and Gas Act* — should automatically apply to tribal lands. Sopinka J. took no part in the judgment.]

Appeal allowed in part; cross-appeal dismissed.

In *Delgamuukw*, the onus of proving Aboriginal title was placed squarely upon the Aboriginal claimants. This is nothing new, as evidenced both by *Calder* and the test established in *Baker Lake*. What was new, however, was the test set out by the Supreme Court for proof of Aboriginal title, as well as the Court's articulation of the key temporal frame of reference for such claims.

In the following excerpt, Kent McNeil questions why it is that Aboriginal peoples bear then onus of proving that they possess title to land, given the fact that Aboriginal peoples "were here first", and examines some reasons why this requirement remains in place.

KENT MCNEIL, "THE ONUS OF PROOF OF ABORIGINAL TITLE"

(1999) 37 Osgoode Hall L.J. 775 at 776-82, 800-3 (footnotes omitted)

In *Delgamuukw v. British Columbia*, the Supreme Court of Canada decided that, absent valid extinguishment or surrender, the Aboriginal peoples have Aboriginal title to the lands they exclusively occupied at the time of assertion of Crown sovereignty. The Court placed the onus of proving the requisite occupation on the Aboriginal peoples. Chief Justice Lamer, delivering the principal judgment, said that "[i]n order to establish a claim to aboriginal title, the aboriginal group asserting the claim must establish that it occupied the lands in question at the *time at which the Crown asserted sovereignty over the land subject to the title.*"

Chief Justice Lamer went on to say that present occupation can be relied on as proof of pre-sovereignty occupation; however, in that situation, continuity between present and pre-sovereignty occupation is required. ...

Chief Justice Lamer was careful, nonetheless, to avoid placing an impossible burden of proof on Aboriginal claimants in this respect. He said:

> Needless to say, there is no need to establish "an unbroken chain of continuity" (*Van der Peet*, at para. 65) between present and prior occupation. The occupation and use of lands may have been disrupted for a time, perhaps as a result of the unwillingness of European colonizers to recognize aboriginal title. To impose the requirement of continuity too strictly would risk "undermining the very purposes of s. 35(1) by perpetuating the historical injustice suffered by aboriginal peoples at the hands of colonizers who failed to respect" aboriginal rights to land (*Côté*, ... at para. 53). In *Mabo*, ... the High Court of Australia set down the requirement that there must be "substantial maintenance of the connection" between the people and the land. In my view, this test should be equally applicable to proof of title in Canada.

. . . . .

II. EXPLANATIONS FOR PLACING THE ONUS ON THE ABORIGINAL PEOPLES

Why, one might ask, is the onus of proving Aboriginal title on the Aboriginal peoples, and not on the Crown, when we all know that the Aboriginal peoples were here first? In *Calder v. British Columbia (A.G.)*, the very first Canadian case involving a direct assertion of Aboriginal title, Judson J. acknowledged that this prior presence is the basis for Aboriginal title. In an oft-quoted passage, he said that "the fact is that when the settlers came, the Indians were there, organized in societies and *occupying the land* as their forefathers had done for centuries. This is what Indian title means ... ." Given the undeniable fact of their pre-existing occupation of land, why do Aboriginal peoples have to prove their title? While to my knowledge Canadian courts have not answered this question directly, some possible explanations can be given, none of which are entirely satisfactory.

One explanation is that, in dominions of the Crown where the common law applies, the doctrine of tenures gives the Crown underlying or radical title to lands that are occupied or owned by others. ... As occupation and ownership are primarily questions of fact, whereas the Crown's title arises as a matter of law in this context, the onus is apparently on persons who allege occupation or ownership to rebut what amounts to a presumption of Crown title by proving their own occupation or ownership. Hence, Aboriginal peoples who claim title due to their occupation of lands prior to Crown assertion of sovereignty have to prove the occupation.

In *Delgamuukw*, Lamer C.J.C. held that the requisite occupation can be proven either by establishing physical occupation, or by showing that the Aboriginal laws of the claimants demonstrate their occupation of the claimed lands. Physical occupation, he said:

> may be established in a variety of ways, ranging from the construction of dwellings through cultivation and enclosure of fields to regular use of definite tracts of land for hunting, fishing or otherwise exploiting its resources: see McNeil, *Common Law Aboriginal Title*, at pp. 201-2. In considering whether occupation sufficient to ground title is established, "one must take into account the group's size, manner of life, material resources, and technological abilities, and the character of the lands claimed": Brian Slattery, "Understanding Aboriginal Rights," at p. 758.

Respecting Aboriginal law, Lamer C.J.C. said that

> if, at the time of sovereignty, an aboriginal society had laws in relation to land, those laws would be relevant to establishing the occupation of lands which are the subject of a claim for aboriginal title. Relevant laws might include, but are not limited to, a land tenure system or laws governing land use.

Given these criteria for occupation, the Aboriginal peoples probably occupied much, if not all, of what is now Canada at the time of Crown assertion of sovereignty. If so, is it appropriate to apply the presumption of Crown title in this context? Is not reliance on the feudal doctrine of tenures, which had already lost much of its importance in Britain by the time Canada was colonized, counter-intuitive and prejudicial where Aboriginal title is concerned? Why does the known fact of the Aboriginal presence not take precedence over a presumption based on this largely out-dated doctrine? And what of the Aboriginal perspective on this matter? In *Van der Peet*, Lamer C.J.C. said that, "[i]n assessing a claim for the existence of an aboriginal right, a court must take into account the perspective of the aboriginal people claiming the right . ... while at the same time taking into account the perspective of the common law." In placing the onus of proof of Aboriginal title on Aboriginal claimants in *Delgamuukw*, the chief justice does not appear to have taken account of the Aboriginal perspective at all.

One reason why the Supreme Court probably has not relied on the Aboriginal perspective and the historical record to presume that the Aboriginal peoples were in occupation of all of Canada, and so cast the burden on the Crown of rebutting that presumption by proving the opposite where particular lands are concerned, is that the Aboriginal peoples would then be presumed to have held all lands in Canada by Aboriginal title, and that might pose too great a threat to the economic, social, and political stability of the country. But there are legal rationalizations for the position the Court has taken on this matter as well. Aboriginal title is not a single title to all of Canada that is vested in the Aboriginal peoples as a whole. Rather, it relates to particular tracts of land, and is held by discrete Aboriginal nations or groups who occupied those tracts at the time of Crown sovereignty. This is evident not only from judicial decisions like *Delgamuukw*, but also from the fact that there are many instances where the land claims of Aboriginal nations overlap and conflict with one another. Consequently, even if the Aboriginal peoples occupied all of Canada, it would still be necessary to prove which nations occupied what parts in order to identify the actual Aboriginal titleholders. One could not presume that every nation occupied the lands they claim when so many claims overlap.

A second legal justification for placing the onus of proof on the Aboriginal peoples arises from the fact that they are typically the plaintiffs in actions for a declaration of Aboriginal title. As a general rule, in legal actions the plaintiffs bear the onus of proving the facts on which their claims depend. As the validity of an Aboriginal title claim depends on occupation of the claimed land at the time the Crown asserted sovereignty over the territory where the land is located, and occupation is a question of fact, it is not surprising that the courts have placed the onus of proving occupation of that specific land on the Aboriginal nation making the claim. But if the tables were turned and Aboriginal nations were the defendants rather than the plaintiffs, the onus should be the other way around. Moreover, if an Aboriginal nation brought an action, not for a declaration of Aboriginal title, but for trespass on their Aboriginal title lands, the evidentiary requirements would be different as well, because in that situation they would only have to prove their present possession, not their title. So the identity of the party initiating the legal proceedings, and the form of action, affect both the onus of proof and what has to be proven. ...

. . . . .

V. CONCLUSIONS

Despite the apparent unfairness of placing the onus of proving their title on the Aboriginal nations, it is unlikely that the Supreme Court will re-examine this issue and require the Crown to initially prove its own title when an Aboriginal title claim is brought to court. Nonetheless, Aboriginal nations should be able to rely on two fundamental common law rules to meet the onus the Court has placed on them: (1) title is presumed from possession; and (2) possession is title as against anyone who cannot prove that he or she has a better title. So in situations where they can establish either present or past possession of lands at any time *after* Crown assertion of sovereignty, Aboriginal nations should be presumed to have a valid Aboriginal title to those lands, and the burden of proving a better title should be cast on the Crown or its grantees.

Where past possession and the presumption of title arising from it are relied on, an action for recovery of land might be more appropriate and more likely to succeed than an action for declaration of Aboriginal title, as judgment in an action for recovery of land would not prejudice possible claims of persons not party to the action. For the same reason, where an Aboriginal nation seeks to protect *present* possession from interference, the preferable action would probably be an action for trespass rather than an action for declaration of title. If it resulted in a positive judgment, an action for recovery of land or for trespass would restore or secure the possession of the Aboriginal nation against the defendant who had wrongfully taken possession of or trespassed on the nation's lands. Such a judgment would presumably act as a deterrent to discourage others from wrongfully interfering with the nation's possession.

. . . . .

An Aboriginal nation that is in a position to rely on present possession of some or all of their lands could also support that possession with continuing uses and activities on and in relation to the land that would make their possession apparent to the world. Using the land in accordance with their traditional lifestyles, which might include fishing, hunting, gathering, horticulture, cutting trees for building houses, maintaining trails, visiting and conducting ceremonies at sacred sites, and so on, would all be means of supporting their possession. But any other uses of the land, whether "traditional" or not, would serve the same purpose. Examples might be constructing roads, controlling water flow, utilizing natural resources, erecting buildings and other structures, pasturing livestock, and putting up fences. Given that Lamer C.J.C. said in *Delgamuukw* that Aboriginal laws are also relevant to proving Aboriginal occupation, affirming or establishing laws in relation to the land would be another way for the nation to support their possession, while exercising their right of self-government. It would also be advisable to mark boundaries and put up signs or other indicators that the land belongs to the Aboriginal nation. Informing outsiders who intrude on the land that they are trespassing, and either asking them to leave or giving them limited permission to stay, would be another important way to make the nation's possession known to the world. In short, the Aboriginal nation could engage in as many uses and peaceful activities on and in relation to the land as practicable, and sustain those activities over time so that their possession would be maintained. This would require community organization and coordination, fostering a common enterprise that virtually every member of the nation could participate in. By means of this direct participation on the ground, they would be contributing to their community by helping to establish the factual basis for their nation's possession, on which the nation's right to the land may well depend.

The issues that were raised in *Delgamuukw* are not peculiar to the situation in Canada. Many of the same claims have been made in other countries. Australia, for instance, saw a rash of Aboriginal land claims following the Australian High Court's decision in *Mabo v. Queensland [No. 2]* (1992), 107 A.L.R. 1 (H.C. Aust.). The *Mabo* case repudiated principles that had all but eliminated Aboriginal land claims in Australia following the decision in *Milirrpum v. Nabalco Pty. Ltd.*, [1971] 17 F.L.R. 141 (Northern Terr. S.C.). However, as a result of subsequent events — including the judgments in *Wik Peoples v. Queensland* (1996), 187 C.L.R. 1 (H.C. Aust.) and *Fejo v. Northern Territory* (1998), 195 C.L.R. 96 (H.C. Aust.) and the promulgation of the *Native Title Act, 1993* (Cth.) and the *Native Title Amendment Act, 1998* (Cth.) which recognize the ability of the Australian government to extinguish Aboriginal title (including by unilateral action) — Aboriginal title claims in Australia have waned, leaving empty the initial promise set out in *Mabo*.

While not touching directly on the issues concerning Aboriginal title raised in *Delgamuukw*, the Supreme Court of Canada provided an interesting commentary on Canadian judicial understandings of the nature of Aboriginal land interests (particularly *vis-à-vis* non-Aboriginal title) in *Musqueam Indian Band v. Glass*, [2000] 2 S.C.R. 633.

MUSQUEAM INDIAN BAND v. GLASS

[2000] 2 S.C.R. 633

McLachlin C.J.C. (dissenting): — This case requires us to interpret a lease. The parties entered into the contract voluntarily and with counsel.

Thus our only task is to interpret their agreement. Two issues of interpretation arise — the meaning of "current land value" and the deductibility of servicing costs. I agree in principle with Justice Gonthier on the second issue but respectfully disagree on the first. In my view, "current land value" means the actual value of similar land held in fee simple, and should not be reduced by 50 percent because the Musqueam Indian Band ("Band") continues to hold the land as a reserve.

I. Background

In 1960, the Band surrendered approximately 40 acres of reserve land to the Crown for the purposes of leasing. On June 8, 1965, the Crown entered into an agreement ("Master Agreement") with the Musqueam Development Company Limited ("Company") under which the Company was to service and subdivide the land, and the Crown was then to provide the Company with an individual lease for each lot. Each lease was to have a term of 99 years, running from the date of the Master Agreement. The Company fulfilled its obligations under the Master Agreement, the Crown provided the leases, and in 1966 the Company assigned those leases to individuals, who built houses on the lots. Those individuals, or their assignees, are the appellants here.

Under the individual lease agreements, the lessees agreed to pay rent to the Crown in right of the Band, and in 1980 the Crown transferred management authority to the Band so that the Band now receives the rent directly. The rent for the first 30 years was specified in the leases, and increased from approximately $300 per year to approximately $400 per year over that period. The rent was subject to review after the first 30 years, and every 20 years thereafter. Thus the rent came up for review in 1995.

The rent review clause, identical in each of the individual leases, is the subject of this dispute. It provides:

> 2(2) The rent for each year of the three succeeding twenty (20) year periods and for the final nine (9) year period of the term hereof, shall be a fair rent for the land negotiated immediately before the commencement of each such period. In conducting such negotiations the parties shall assume that, at the time of such negotiations, the lands are
>
> (a) unimproved lands in the same state as they were on the date of this agreement;
>
> (b) lands to which there is public access;
>
> (c) lands in a subdivided area, and
>
> (d) land which is zoned for single-family residential use,
>
> . . . . .
>
> 2(4) An annual clear total rental which represents six percent (6%) of the current land value, calculated at the time of renegotiation, and on the basis set out in subparagraph (2) hereof, shall be regarded as a "fair rent" for the purposes thereof.

The lessees contend that "current land value", as used in clause 2(4), means the value of the land as it is currently held — that is, as reserve land. The Band, by contrast, argues that "current land value" refers to the value of fee simple title to similar land, absent factors associated with its reserve status.

.....

In construing a lease, our first consideration is the language of the lease itself. Here that language is clear. In a real estate document, "land" usually means "a right to receive a good title in fee simple". ... "Value" means the "fair market value" of the land or, equivalently, the "exchange value" of the land: what a willing buyer would pay for the land in the open market. ... Nothing in the leases at issue here suggests that either "land" or "value" should be assigned any definition other than the generally accepted one. Thus "current land value" means the price a willing buyer would pay for fee simple title to the land.

This construction of the disputed clause, which simply gives effect to the plain meaning of its words, is entirely consistent with the widely accepted rationale for a rent review provision like the one at issue here. Rents that are linked to the underlying value of the land ensure that the lessor gets a fair return on the asset. ...

.....

The advantages of linking rent to underlying land value are well illustrated by the circumstances of this case. In 1966, neither the Band nor the lessees could have known what course real estate prices would take over the next 30 years, let alone the next 99. If the parties had fixed the rent for each lot at a particular dollar amount per year (presumably escalating every year at some fixed rate), the lessees would have run the risk that their rent would escalate more quickly than land prices, and the Band would have run the risk that real estate prices would escalate more quickly than the rent. Having linked rent to the value of the land, however, the parties are now assured that their 30-year-old leases will reflect the contemporary market. The Band is assured that it will receive an income comparable to the income it would receive if it was unencumbered by the existing leases. And the lessees are assured they will pay no more than they would if they entered into a new lease with any other landowner today.

My colleague Gonthier J. agrees that the plain meaning of "current land value" is freehold value, and that the purpose of the rent review clause here was to ensure a fair return to the lessor and a fair rent to the lessee. However, he nonetheless affirms the trial court's valuation of the leased lands at 50 percent of freehold value. With respect, I cannot agree.

First, although my colleague agrees that "current land value" requires the assessment of the "exchange value" of the land, his result does not in fact assess the land on the basis of its potential sale. As he states, calculating fair market value requires determining the "highest and best use" for the land that is legally permissible, disregarding any restrictions imposed by the lease itself. One way the Band could legally use the land is to sell it for fair market value. ... The only impediment to the Band's selling its land is the leases themselves, whose restrictions my colleague Gonthier J. concedes should be disregarded. This removes the justification for discounting the value of the land. The fact that the Band has chosen not to sell its land cannot bear on the land's value. It follows that the "exchange value" of the land means what it could be sold for, not 50 percent of that amount.

The rationale for placing weight on the fact that the Band has chosen not to sell the land is said to be that fair market value "must reflect the legal restrictions on the land" (Gonthier J., at para. 46). However, the fact that land is part of a reserve is not a legal restriction within the ambit of this principle. This principle is properly applied to such restrictions as zoning laws, building codes, historical district or other non-zoning land-use controls, and environmental regulations. ... Adjusting fair market value to account for such restrictions makes sense, because usually a landowner has little or no control over them, and clearly a buyer is not going to pay the going rate for commercial land if the land is zoned only for residential use. By contrast, nothing stops the Band from surrendering the land to the Crown and selling the land just like any other freehold is sold, except the leases themselves, whose restrictions must be disregarded in determining "current land value". The reserve character of the land is therefore not a legal restriction. ...

Second, although my colleague Gonthier J. agrees that the rent review clause here was meant to assure the Band a market rate of return on its land, the reduction of land value for reserve related factors precludes this result. Rather, it assures that the Band will never get a market return on its land, by effectively reading "current land value" to mean 50 percent of current land value. As a result, the Band will get a 6 percent return on half the value of its asset, or, equivalently, a 3 percent return. ...

Third, the proposed 50 percent reduction for reserve related factors depends on the valuation of an interest that could simply never exist. As the trial court noted, reserve land can be converted to fee simple only by surrender to the Crown. Once reserve land is surrendered to the Crown, it loses all the characteristics of reserve land. Thus there can be no such thing as fee simple title to reserve land. Given that no such interest can ever exist, it is difficult to see how it could be valued in any principled way.

. . . . .

The combined fee simple/reserve factor approach, by contrast, is not susceptible of principled analysis. Because there is no such thing as a fee simple interest in reserve land, there is simply nothing to which the subject property can be compared. The comparison is not with real properties, but with something that cannot exist — a parcel of land that is both fee simple and reserve land. I cannot accept that this is what the parties intended when they referred to "current land value". If "current land value" means fee simple, and fee simple is inconsistent with reserve status — propositions with which my colleague Gonthier J. agrees — then it must be wrong to devalue fee simple for factors related to reserve status, such as speculation about unrest, limitations on non-natives' standing to be elected to the governing body, and uncertainty about property taxation. (This does not preclude consideration of the fact that the fee simple is <u>located</u> near reserve land, should this prove relevant to assessing the value of the fee simple.)

As my colleague notes, some leases for aboriginal land specifically provide that the subject property is to be valued by reference to comparable property located outside the reserve. ... It does not follow, however, that when the lease does not include an express indication that off-reserve property is the touchstone, the parties intended otherwise. "Current land value" generally means fee simple value, and common industry practice is to value land by assessing what the land would be worth on the open market. Except where the parties expressly provide for a different method of valuation, it is plain meaning and common practice that should provide the default.

In my view, the rent should be set at 6 percent of the current land value, and no discount should be applied merely because the subject land is on an Indian reserve. This construction accords with the leases' plain meaning, common industry practice, and the clear purpose of the rent review clause.

. . . . .

IV. Conclusion

I would dismiss the appeal and the cross-appeal and affirm the judgment of the Federal Court of Appeal.

The judgment of **Gonthier, Major, Binnie** and **LeBel JJ.** was delivered by

Gonthier J.: —

. . . . .

IV. Issues

1. What is the meaning of "current land value" in the Musqueam rent review clause 2(4)?

2. What is the meaning of "unimproved" and "this agreement" in clause 2(2)(a) of the leases?

V. Analysis

A. Construction of the Leases

I find that "current land value" in the rent review clause refers to fee simple or freehold as opposed to leasehold value, but that it refers to freehold on the reserve, not off the reserve. A freehold value for the Musqueam lands must be hypothetical because there is no such thing as freehold title on a reserve. But this does not mean that this hypothetical value cannot be assessed and then serve its function in the rent review calculation.

Unless the parties specify otherwise, the meanings of "land" and of "value" are well established in law. When land is sold, "land" refers to "a right to receive a good title in fee simple" unless the agreement states otherwise. ... "Land" is not given a special meaning in the Musqueam leases; in particular, it is <u>not</u> defined as a 99-year leasehold interest in the property under the lease.

"Value" in real estate law generally means the fair market value of the land, which is based on what a seller and buyer, "each knowledgeable and willing," would pay for it on the open market. ...

Market value generally is the <u>exchange</u> value of land, rather than its <u>use</u> value to the lessee. ... Land is valued without regard to the tenant's interest in it, for it does not reduce the land's exchange value if the tenant chooses not to use the land for its highest use. ...

... The leases do not refer to "current leasehold value" or to "the value of the land leased on the terms and conditions contained in this lease" as did the lease on reserve land in *Leighton, supra.* In the absence of any indication that the leasehold value is to be used to set the rent, "current land value" means freehold value.

. . . . .

Valuing the Musqueam land at its freehold value is consistent with an interpretation of the leases that sees the rent review clause as an attempt to generate an annual fair market return on a capital asset. The freehold value better approximates this return than does the leasehold value. But this reasoning does not lead to the Federal Court of Appeal's conclusion that it must be the freehold value of land outside the reserve that should be used to determine the rent. On the contrary, the capital asset here is reserve land surrendered for leasing, not land surrendered for sale. The nature of the capital asset at issue is reserve land.

Some leases on reserves specify that off-reserve land values go directly into the rent calculation. In *Rodgers v. Canada* (1993), 74 F.T.R. 164, and in *Devil's Gap Cottages (1982) Ltd. v. Canada*, [1991] F.C.J. No. 1142 (QL) (T.D.), for example, the leases require that comparison properties be "similar in area and character, but situate outside of the Reserve". Where the lease is clear, the Federal Court of Appeal is correct to insist that the courts adhere to the lease when determining rents. The Musqueam leases, however, do <u>not</u> specify that off-reserve land values should be used in the rent review formula.

. . . . .

Interpreting "current land value" as the value of reserve land is consistent with the economic rationale identified above. It is land which is part of the reserve that the Band owns as a capital asset. Although the Band could surrender the land for sale, thereby excluding it from the reserve (and presumably achieve market prices for non-reserve land), it has not chosen to do so. The asset it holds is reserve land, for which it must accept the realities of the market. Thus, in my view, the leases in stipulating "current land value" refer to the value of freehold land on the reserve.

B. *Appraising the Freehold Value*

It is difficult to appraise the value of a hypothetical fee simple interest on the Musqueam reserve. The trial judge found as a fact that the fee simple value of comparable lands off the reserve was $600,000 on average, and this finding was not disturbed by the Federal Court of Appeal. This figure was also accepted by expert appraisers for both parties; I accept it as well.

As I have explained above, the leases require the court to assess the value of a hypothetical fee simple ownership on the reserve. This value must reflect the legal restrictions on the land and market conditions. One cannot simply assume that either legal restrictions or market conditions are the same for reserve land as for off-reserve land. In fact, the legal restrictions on the reserve land differ from those on the comparable areas of Vancouver. So too the market may respond differently to Musqueam reserve land than it does to land off the reserve. To give effect to the leases, the land value in the rent review clause must pertain to the actual land in question.

Legal restrictions on land use, as opposed to restrictions found in the lease, may affect the market value of freehold property. ... To determine land value, whether as vacant or as improved, the appraiser (unless otherwise instructed by the lease) considers the highest and best use that is "legally permissible, physically possible, financially feasible, and maximally productive". Legal impediments include "[p]rivate restrictions, zoning, building codes, historic district or other non-zoning land use controls, and environmental regulations" ...

The legal restrictions on land use imposed by a band on its land are analogous to land laws imposed by a municipal government. ... The legal environment on a reserve should therefore be taken into account when appraising the land's value. Of course, like municipal zoning, band restrictions could either increase or decrease land value depending on how the market responds to them. In *Devil's Gap Cottages, supra*, Strayer J. (as he then was) noted that favourable zoning on that reserve increased its value dramatically over non-reserve land.

Like the trial judge, I am therefore of the opinion that the fee simple off-reserve value cannot simply be transposed to the Musqueam land. The chief difficulty in assessing the value of the Musqueam land is that there can be no actual market for the value expressed in the leases. As soon as reserve land is surrendered for sale, it loses its reserve features. There can therefore be no such thing as fee simple title on reserve land. To approximate it, one must use a hypothetical value. In this case, the value can be determined by adapting the off-reserve value to take into account the actual features of the land and of the market.

Because the direct comparison approach to land appraisal is not available here, the trial judge took the fee simple value for comparable non-reserve land of roughly $600,000 per lot. He then found at para. 86 that "[t]he actual value of such serviced land having regard to the long-term leasehold interest and Indian reserve features pertaining to it would be approximately 50% of the fee simple values".

The trial judge derived the 50 percent rate from a comparison of the sale of 99-year pre-paid leasehold interests in another subdivision on the

Musqueam reserve, Salish Park, to comparable off-reserve properties. The Salish Park properties were worth 50 percent less than the comparables. Because the leasehold and reserve features are similar for Salish Park and for Musqueam Park, the trial judge found that the 50 percent rate was transportable, and applied it to the Musqueam comparables.

The Salish properties are leasehold, not freehold, interests. Discounting the land because of its leasehold features is an error in law for, as I have explained above, "current land value" means freehold and not leasehold value. But this distinction does not significantly affect the market value of the land. ... It is worth noting that the amount of the reduction of 50 percent was not disputed before this Court. There were no submissions on the point. Although I would not disturb the trial judge's finding of a 50 percent reduction in this case, it does not follow that land on a reserve will necessarily bear that discount. It will be a question of fact what, if any, discount should be applied.

I find no error in the trial judge's findings on this question of fact, and agree that in 1995, the 50 percent reduction in value reflected the market value of the Musqueam reserve land. The trial judge accepted the evidence of the professional appraisers who testified at trial (both Mr. Johnston for the Band and Mr. Oikawa for the leaseholders, as well as the City of Vancouver Assessor Mr. Jones) who all agreed that uncertainty lowered the market price of the Musqueam lands. This fact cannot be dismissed or ignored. In the future, the market may respond differently. But when the market perceives uncertainty, it is cold comfort to the lessor to believe that the lessees' fears are unwarranted. The market value of the Musqueam lands in 1995 having been found to be 50 percent of that of comparable off-reserve lots, the rent should be based on this value as being their current land value under the terms of the leases.

. . . . .

VI. *Conclusion*

I would allow the appeal and dismiss the cross-appeal, both with costs.

. . . . .

Bastarache J.: — ... The Chief Justice disagrees with Gonthier J. because, in her opinion, he has chosen to ascribe to the land a value based on the existence of a hypothetical on-reserve fee simple — hypothetical because there can be no fee simple title in reserve land. The Chief Justice argues that since the Musqueam Indian Band ("Band") has the power to sell its land in fee simple, even if it has not chosen to do so, the value of the land should be viewed as if it were held under a fee simple title *simpliciter*. It is unlikely that the parties would ever have intended a hybrid freehold or fee simple land with its value calculated so as to include its reserve status. This hypothetical title requires attributing to the parties a far too unusual formulation when there is no indication that it was in fact intended by them. However, I cannot agree with the reasoning of the Chief Justice when she posits that the land must be valued as though it were not reserve land but had been converted to land held in fee simple. I believe that the fee simple value ascribed by the Chief Justice is also based on a hypothetical title.

It is my view that the "current land value" should be calculated as leasehold land, including its status as reserve land because (i) this is the best description of what the land in fact is, and (ii) this is consistent with the parties' intentions.

. . . . .

I would allow the appeal, dismiss the cross-appeal and affirm the judgment of the Trial Division of the Federal Court with costs.

Appeal allowed with costs.

The end result of the *Glass* decision was that Indian reserve lands were valued at one-half of what similarly situated, non-reserve lands would be valued at. This "discount" was intended to account for the land's reserve status and the restrictions created by that status. If the band wished to have the land valued without a discount, it would have to surrender the land to the Crown, which would deprive the band of the opportunity to develop the land while maintaining the land's traditional character.

In this sense, the *Glass* case affirms an idea previously articulated in cases from *St. Catherine's Milling* through to *Delgamuukw*, namely that Aboriginal land interests are inferior in Canadian law to non-Aboriginal land interests and are to be treated accordingly.

H. ALTERNATIVES TO ABORIGINAL TITLE LITIGATION

From the discussion in this chapter, it is evident that case law on Aboriginal title has not resulted in many favourable decisions for Aboriginal peoples. Nevertheless, Aboriginal title claims are still being pursued by Aboriginal groups in the courts. There are, however, alternatives to pursuing Aboriginal title claims through the litigation process. These alternatives were created by the federal government through its Comprehensive and Specific Claims processes. As the following excerpt from the Royal Commission on Aboriginal Peoples' Report illustrates, these processes suffer from their own deficiencies that reduce their usefulness as viable alternatives to Aboriginal title litigation.

REPORT OF THE ROYAL COMMISSION ON ABORIGINAL PEOPLES, RESTRUCTURING THE RELATIONSHIP, Vol. 2

(Ottawa: Ministry of Supply & Services Canada, 1996)
at 535-9, 543, 544-9 (references omitted)

The comprehensive claims process

As originally defined by government and set out in the 1982 publication, *In All Fairness*, a comprehensive claim is one based on unextinguished Aboriginal title and is, in effect, a request for the negotiation of a treaty. This is reinforced by subsection 35(3) of the *Constitution Act, 1982*, which recognizes and affirms existing Aboriginal and treaty rights: "'treaty rights' includes rights that now exist by way of land claims agreements or may be so acquired".

The comprehensive claims policy has three elements:

1. the criteria for acceptance under the policy;
2. the rights the Aboriginal group in question is asked to relinquish; and
3. the type and quantity of benefits the federal government will consider providing the Aboriginal group in exchange for the relinquishment of the group's rights.

Criteria for acceptance of claims

Under the comprehensive claims policy (as amended in 1986), the minister of Indian affairs will determine whether to accept a claim on advice from the minister of justice about its acceptability according to legal criteria. An Aboriginal group is therefore expected to submit a statement of claim that complies with the following requirements:

- the claimant has not previously adhered to treaty;
- the claimant group has traditionally used and occupied the territory in question, and this use and occupation continue;
- a description of the extent and location of such land use and occupancy together with a map outlining approximate boundaries; and
- identification of the claimant group, including the names of the bands, tribes or communities on whose behalf the claim is being made, as well as linguistic and cultural affiliation and approximate population figures.

This list might suggest relatively liberal criteria for accepting claims, but in practice the criteria used by the department of justice to assess validity are more rigorous, set out in the 1979 Federal Court decision in *Baker Lake*. Under this decision, as elaborated by the federal government, an Aboriginal group must demonstrate all of the following:

- It is, and was, an organized society.
- It has occupied the specific territory over which it asserts Aboriginal title from time immemorial. The traditional use and occupancy of the

territory must have been sufficient to be an established fact at the time of the assertion of sovereignty by European nations.

- The occupation of the territory is largely to the exclusion of other organized societies.
- There is continuing use and occupancy of the land for traditional purposes.
- Aboriginal title and rights to use of resources has not been dealt with by treaty.
- Aboriginal title has not been extinguished by other lawful means.

The last part of this test appears to have been somewhat altered by the 1990 *Sparrow* decision, which held that if the federal government's position is that Aboriginal title has been eliminated by "other lawful means", then its intention to extinguish Aboriginal title must have been "clear and plain". Federal policy continues to reflect other parts of the *Baker Lake* decision, however, despite Supreme Court decisions like *Simon* and *Bear Island* that implicitly reject evidentiary tests for Aboriginal claims that are impossible to meet in the absence of written evidence.

. . . . .

What Aboriginal people must relinquish

... [T]he Crown's interpretation of the treaty relationship was, historically, that Aboriginal nations had received specified benefits in exchange for a blanket extinguishment of their title or rights. In keeping with this practice, the original comprehensive claims policy specified that an Aboriginal group must surrender all Aboriginal rights in return for a grant of rights specified in a settlement agreement. The government has moved very little from this position.... [T]he amended federal policy allows for an "alternative" to the surrender of all Aboriginal rights — "the cession and surrender of Aboriginal title in non-reserved areas", while "allowing any Aboriginal title that exists to continue in specified reserve areas, granting to the beneficiaries defined rights applicable to the entire settlement area". This policy also notes that the only Aboriginal rights to be relinquished are those related to the use of and title to lands and resources. In practice, however, only one of the recent settlements, the Yukon Umbrella Final Agreement, comes under this "alternative". In that agreement the only Aboriginal rights that are not surrendered are surface interests in the lands that are retained as Indian lands. Thus, it would appear that the current policy allows for only minimal divergence from the basic position of requiring a total surrender of all Aboriginal rights.

Scope of the benefits Aboriginal groups can negotiate

Federal policy sets out a number of areas where benefits can be negotiated, including lands (including offshore lands), wildlife harvesting rights, subsurface rights, natural resources revenue sharing, environmental management, local self-government and financial compensation. Certain limitations on each of these areas are especially noteworthy.

First, until the recent federal announcement on self-government, these issues were based on delegated authority, not the inherent right, and were the
subject of separate negotiations governed by the federal policy on community self-government negotiations. Under the comprehensive claims policy,
issues of self-government will be contained in separate agreements and
separate enacting legislation. They will not receive constitutional protection
unless there is a general constitutional amendment to this effect.

Second, natural resources revenue-sharing provisions will be subject to
limitations, which might include an absolute dollar amount, the duration
of the revenue-sharing provisions or a reduction of the percentage of royalties generated. Thus, natural resources revenue-sharing arrangements
are seen more correctly as a way of spreading cash compensation over a
longer period of time, rather than securing a significant continuing source
of revenue for Aboriginal claimants.

Third, on the issue of Aboriginal participation in managing lands and
resources, the policy requires that any arrangements recognize the overriding powers of non-Aboriginal governments. While numerous management boards and committees have been set up under the various comprehensive land claims agreements, these bodies remain advisory, although
some have found innovative ways to prevent their recommendations from
being ignored. Nonetheless, non-Aboriginal governments retain full jurisdiction and final decision-making authority.

The lack of interim measures

One of the most significant weaknesses of comprehensive land claims
policy is the lack of any provision for interim measures before submission
of a comprehensive claim and during negotiations. Governments are free
to create new third-party interests on the traditional lands of Aboriginal
claimants right up until the moment a claims agreement is signed.

... It should not be necessary for Aboriginal people to mount blockades
to obtain interim measures while their assertions of title are being dealt
with.

. . . . .

The Commission cannot support the extinguishment of Aboriginal
rights, either blanket or partial. It seems to us completely incompatible
with the relationship between Aboriginal peoples and the land. This relationship is fundamental to the Aboriginal world view and sense of identity; to abdicate the responsibilities associated with it would have deep
spiritual and cultural implications. However, we recognize that there will
be circumstances where the Aboriginal party to a treaty may agree to a
partial extinguishment of rights in return for other advantages offered in
treaty negotiations. We would urge, however, that this course of action be
taken only after all other options have been considered carefully.

. . . . .

The specific claims process

As defined by government and set out in the 1982 publication, *Outstanding Business*, a specific claim is one based upon a "lawful obligation" of Canada to Indians. Claims based on unextinguished Aboriginal title are expressly excluded, as were pre-Confederation claims until 1991. A specific claim, from the government's point of view, is little more than a claim for compensation.

... [T]he concept of lawful obligation remains at the centre of specific claims policy, although there is no agreement upon what facts or relationships might constitute such an obligation. In a paper prepared for the department of Indian affairs before publication of the policy, G.V. La Forest suggested that "we are not so much concerned with a *legal obligation* in the sense of enforceable in the courts as with a *government obligation of fair treatment* if a lawful obligation is established to its satisfaction". ... The department of justice, however, assesses the validity of claims in terms of their chances of success in court and applies technical rules of evidence. Thus, legal validity informs the government's assessment of whether a claim properly falls within the scope of federal policy. This assessment is further informed, if not defined, by the examples of lawful obligations set out in the policy itself:

A lawful obligation may arise in any one of the following circumstances:

1. The non-fulfilment of a treaty or agreement between Indians and the Crown.
2. A breach of an obligation arising out of the *Indian Act* or other statutes pertaining to Indians and the regulations thereunder.
3. A breach of an obligation arising out of government administration of Indian funds or other assets.
4. An illegal disposition of Indian land.

The more restrictive view of lawful obligation is that a claim must fall within one of these examples in order to come within the policy. The most restrictive view is that a claim must fall within one of the examples and also within the compensation guidelines; that is, compensation in the form of money or land must be possible.

A narrow and restrictive reading of the policy leads to the exclusion of many claims based on non-fulfilment of treaty obligations. Assertions of the right to exercise hunting and fishing rights, for example, or of rights to education, health and other benefits, are not seen by government as coming within the policy even though they are justiciable rights. Even seemingly uncontroversial obligations, such as the provision of land under the terms of treaties, have been subject to the same narrow reading. ... It is the great irony of the policy, and the most common complaint against it, that it was intended to broaden the concept of negotiable claims beyond those that might be proven strictly in court. In fact, it does precisely the opposite. Nowhere is this more evident than in the failure to incorporate, as a basis of claim, breach of fiduciary obligation, which was established as actionable in 1984 by the Supreme Court of Canada.

In addition, the government's determination of validity involves a clear conflict of interest. The department of justice faces a conundrum, because the policy directs it to ignore technical rules of evidence and the issue of justiciability. Yet how can it advise government that a treaty includes one set of terms, with one meaning for purposes of claims policy, but another set of terms, with a different meaning, for purposes of litigation?

· · · · ·

As a result, the department of justice advises on treaties in the same way that it litigates them.

· · · · ·

The policy interpretations and practices noted here create the perception, if not the reality, of a policy that is arbitrary, self-serving and operating without due regard to established law. If negotiated settlements are meant to be achieved according to a broad range of rights and obligations than those otherwise enforceable in a court of law, then federal policy must set a clear standard by which their validity can be determined. ... At a minimum, Canada cannot continue to articulate standards that exclude justiciable claims from its policy for negotiated settlements.

The specific claims policy also contains restrictions on compensation, in the form of guidelines, which ensure much delay and confrontation in negotiations. The policy's first rule is that compensation will be based on "legal principles", but nine other guidelines qualify it. Of particular concern is guideline number 10:

> The criteria set out above are general in nature and the actual amount which the claimant is offered will depend on the extent to which the claimant has established a valid claim, the burden of which rests with the claimant. As an example, where there is doubt that the lands in question were ever reserve land, the degree of doubt will be reflected in the compensation offered.

In practice, guideline number 10 means that the federal government may, at any stage, reduce the amount of compensation being offered by 25 per cent, 50 per cent or 75 per cent. The perception is widespread that such determinations are made arbitrarily, or with a view to the budget rather than the facts.

· · · · ·

While it is possible to reach a negotiated claims settlement within the policies, it is far from clear that these settlements will deal ultimately with the underlying cause of grievance or implement any significant change over the long term. The Commission believes the number of settlements does not vindicate the specific claims policy or rebut the criticisms levelled against it. Our review of the specific claims policy and process shows that major change is needed.

Claims of a third kind

Claims of a third kind, acknowledged since 1993, are really a subset of specific claims. Such claims are intended to attract "administrative solutions or remedies to grievances that are not suitable for resolution, or cannot be resolved, through the Specific Claims process". The policy provides no definition of what kinds of claims might fall into this category.

... [N]o indication is given of the purpose of negotiation or the potential results. Quite simply, the problem with claims of a third kind is that there is no purpose, no definition, no process, no conclusion and no review.

An appropriate claims process would not require an unarticulated catch-all category like claims of a third kind. Such a policy would include these claims as part of an overall objective of achieving reconciliation and coexistence.

In the Royal Commission on Aboriginal Peoples' opinion — one that is shared by many Aboriginal groups — the federal government's claims processes are plagued by restrictive interpretations of claims, overly rigid applications of claims process criteria, and exclusive reliance on common law conceptions of land. In this sense, these processes replicate many of the problems that exist in Aboriginal title litigation. If the claims processes are to continue as meaningful alternatives to litigation, they need to be modified to account for both common law and Aboriginal understandings of land rights.

I. CONCLUSION

It may be seen that the law relating to Aboriginal title has undergone a number of changes since the decisions of the United States Supreme Court in the first half of the 19th century. Some of these changes may be observed by comparing the Privy Council's judgment in *St. Catherine's Milling* with that of Justice Hall in *Calder* or, to some extent, Chief Justice Lamer's judgment in *Delgamuukw*. In spite of these changes, can one truly say that there is much of a difference in judicial attitudes generally in dealing with Aboriginal title claims, especially after the decision in *Glass*?

In *Mabo*, Justice Brennan held that reliance on ancient doctrines of discovery and settlement as the basis for the Crown's claim to sovereignty may be challenged by contemporary courts. In many more decisions, however, the historic and legal basis of the Crown's claim to sovereignty is simply not questioned. The Supreme Court of Canada's decision in *R. v. Sparrow*, [1990] 1 S.C.R. 1075, [1990] 4 W.W.R. 410, 46 B.C.L.R. (2d) 1, 56 C.C.C. (3d) 263, 70 D.L.R. (4th) 385, 111 N.R. 241, [1990] 3 C.N.L.R. 160 is a prime example of this judicial practice. There, the unanimous judgment of the Court stated, at 404 D.L.R., that:

> It is worth recalling that while British policy toward the native population was based on respect for their right to occupy their traditional lands, a proposition to which the Royal Proclamation of 1763 bears witness, there

was from the outset never any doubt that sovereignty and legislative power, and indeed the underlying title, to such lands vested in the Crown.

None of the judgments rendered in the Supreme Court's consideration of *Delgamuukw*, altered this understanding; for that matter, neither did the decisions in *Opetchesaht*, *St. Mary's Indian Band v. Cranbrook*, or *Glass*. Consequently, while the law relating to Aboriginal title may have (at least rhetorically) discarded some of the obstacles that have impeded more contextual analyses of the legal nature of the Crown's claim to title and sovereignty over Canada, significant barriers remain.

ENDNOTES

1. In F.W. Turner III, ed., *The Portable North American Indian Reader* (Harmondsworth, England: Penguin, 1977) at 246.
2. Letters Patent to John Cabot, 4 March 1496, as reproduced in H.S. Commager, ed., *Documents of American History*, 8th ed. (New York: Appleton-Crofts, 1968) at 5.
3. See B. Slattery, "Did France Claim Canada Upon 'Discovery'?" in J.M. Bumsted, ed., *Interpreting Canada's Past*, Vol. I (Toronto: Oxford University Press, 1986) at 15.
4. From H.S. Burrage, ed., *Early English and French Voyages, Chiefly from Hakluyt, 1534-1608* (New York: Scribner's, 1906), as quoted in W.E. Washburn, *The Indian and the White Man* (Garden City, N.J.: Anchor Books, 1964) at 10-11.
5. As translated by L. Hanke, *History of Latin American Civilization: Sources and Interpretations*, Vol. I (Boston: Little, Brown, and Company, 1967) at 123-5.
6. L. Hanke, *The Spanish Struggle for Justice in the Conquest of America* (Philadelphia: University of Pennsylvania Press, 1949) at 34.
7. Royal Commission on Aboriginal Peoples, *Report of the Royal Commission on Aboriginal Peoples*, Volume I, Looking Forward, Looking Back (Ottawa: Ministry of Supply & Services, 1996) at 117.
8. L.I. Rotman, Parallel Paths: Fiduciary Doctrine and the Crown-Native Relationship in Canada (Toronto: University of Toronto Press, 1996) at 108-9.

CHAPTER 2

TREATIES

The language used in treaties with the Indians should never be construed to their prejudice. If words be made use of which are susceptible of a more extended meaning than their plain import, as connected with the tenor of the treaty, they should be considered as used only in the latter sense. To contend that the word "allotted," in reference to the land guarantied to the Indians in certain treaties, indicates a favour conferred, rather than a right acknowledged, would, it would seem to me, do injustice to the understanding of the parties. How the words of the treaty were understood by this unlettered people, rather than their critical meaning, should form the rule of construction.

Worcester v. State of Georgia, 6 Pet. 515 at 582 (U.S. 1832), *per* M' Lean J.

A. INTRODUCTION

Treaty relations between Britain and the Aboriginal peoples in North America have been a fundamental aspect of the interaction between the groups from earliest times. Treaties are foundational documents in the history of Crown-Native relations. Initially, they established parameters for peaceful intercourse. Later, they served as the basis for the parties' renewal of their historical commitments to each other.

Treaties were the primary means by which diplomatic relations were conducted between Britain and the Aboriginal peoples. Treaties signed between the groups took a variety of forms. Not all of them involved the cession of land, as conventional wisdom might suggest. Some were treaties of alliance, others of peace and friendship. What the treaties did share in common, at least in theory, was their creation or maintenance of mutually beneficial relationships between the Crown and the Aboriginal peoples.

REPORT OF THE ROYAL COMMISSION ON ABORIGINAL PEOPLES, LOOKING FORWARD, LOOKING BACK, VOL. 1

(Ottawa: Ministry of Supply & Services, 1996) at 173-6
(references omitted)

When Europeans landed on the shores of the Americas, they first sought shelter and sustenance, then pursued a lucrative trade with Aboriginal nations, and later made arrangements through treaties to live permanently in Aboriginal territories. These treaties varied in purpose and scope, depending on the circumstances and objectives of the parties making them. Early treaties were made for peace, trade, alliance, neutrality and military support. When settlement grew, treaties were made to establish relationships, as a way of living together in peaceful co-existence, and to acquire Aboriginal lands and resources.

. . . . .

Over time, treaties became more complex and difficult to negotiate. In the early period of contact, when Europeans were a minority and understanding one another was essential to survival, treaty relationships were cultivated and maintained carefully. As time went on and Europeans became a majority, negotiations became complex, difficult and vague in some areas, as the Crown pursued its goal of securing Aboriginal lands to build its new country. The different cultural views, values and assumptions of both parties conflicted in substantial ways. These contradictions were often not evident, or remained unspoken, in the negotiation and conclusion of solemn treaty agreements. In many cases, it is questionable whether the Indian parties understood the legal and political implications of the land conveyance documents they were asked to sign. Many of these transactions are the subject of land claims today.

It is also doubtful in many cases that the First Nations participating in the [post-Confederation] numbered treaties knew that the written texts they signed differed from the oral agreements they concluded. In fact, it was not evident to them until some years after treaties were made that the Crown was not honouring its treaty commitments or was acting in a way that violated treaty agreements. Their reaction to the imposition of government laws and restrictions upon them was seen as a violation of the Queen's promise to protect their way of life and not subject them to the Queen's laws (the *Indian Act*) or the Queen's servants (the Indian agent). The possibility that the party recording the oral agreements and preparing the written text took advantage of the other party's lack of understanding of the legal implications of written texts, or that those interpretations were not communicated to the party that did not read or write, is disturbing. If First Nations depended on the oral version of their treaties, it follows that the oral agreements reached must be compared to the written version to verify the nature and scope of these agreements today. The fact that in most cases the Indian parties were unable to verify the implications of the written text against the oral agreement, because of language and cultural barriers, must be given consideration when interpreting their meaning.

... [F]rom the perspective of the First Nations there were several basic elements or principles involved in the treaty-making process. In making treaties both parties recognized and affirmed one another's authority to enter into and make binding commitments in treaties. In addition, First Nations would not consider making a treaty unless their way of life was protected and preserved. This meant the continuing use of their lands and natural resources. In most, if not all the treaties, the Crown promised not to interfere with their way of life, including their hunting, fishing, trapping and gathering practices.

The Crown asked First Nations to share their lands with settlers, and First Nations did so on the condition that they would retain adequate land and resources to ensure the well-being of their nations. The Indian parties understood they would continue to maintain their traditional governments, their laws and their customs and to co-operate as necessary with the Crown. There was substantive agreement that the treaties established an economic partnership from which both parties would benefit. Compensation was offered in exchange for the agreement of First Nations to share. The principle of fair exchange and mutual benefit was an integral part of treaty making.

. . . . .

These principles, which were part and parcel of the treaty negotiations, were agreed upon throughout the oral negotiations for Treaties 1 through 11 [the post-Confederation numbered treaties]. They were not always discussed at length, and in many cases the written versions of the treaties are silent on them. In these circumstances, the parties based their negotiations and consent on their own understandings, assumptions and values, as well as on the oral discussions. First Nations were assured orally that their way of life would not change unless they wished it to. They understood that their governing structures and authorities would continue undisturbed by the treaty relationship. They also assumed, and were assured, that the Crown would respect and honour the treaty agreements in perpetuity and that they would not suffer — but only benefit — from making treaties with the Crown. They were not asked, and they did not agree, to adopt non-Aboriginal ways and laws for themselves. They believed and were assured that their freedom and independence would not be interfered with as a result of the treaty. They expected to meet periodically with their treaty partner to make the necessary adjustments and accommodations to maintain the treaty relationship.

Treaty negotiations were usually conducted over a three- to four-day period, with tremendous barriers created by two different cultures with very different world views and experiences attempting to understand and come to terms with one another. Negotiation and dialogue did not, and could not, venture into the meaning of specific terminology, legal or otherwise, and remained at a broad general level, owing to time and language barriers. Issues such as co-existence, non-interference with the Indian way of life, non-interference with hunting and fishing and retention of adequate lands would therefore have been understood at the broadest level. These were matters that would, presumably, be sorted out as time went on.

... [T]he parties had to rely on the trustworthiness, good intentions, and good faith of the other treaty partner and the ability to understand one another better through time. At the time of treaty making, First Nations would not have been sufficiently cognizant of British laws and perspectives, since their previous interaction and exchanges had been primarily through trading relationships. When treaty commissioners proposed a formula (usually called a land quantum formula) to determine how much land would be reserved for Indian nations, for example, it is doubtful that they would have understood the amount of land entailed in one square mile. Similarly, terms such as cede, surrender, extinguish, yield and forever give up all rights and titles appear in the written text of the treaties, but discussion of the meaning of these concepts is not found anywhere in the records of treaty negotiations.

Even as treaty commissioners were promising non-interference with the Indian way of life, treaty documents referred to the Indian nations as "subjects of the Crown". Since First Nations patterned their relationships along kinship lines, they would have understood the relationship they were entering as being more akin to "brothers" or "partners" of the Crown. The First Nations also assumed, since they were being asked for land, that they were the ones giving land to the Crown and that they were the owners of the land. Indeed, the notion that the Crown was in any position to "give" their land to them — for the establishment of reserves, for example — would have been ludicrous, since in many cases it had been their land since time immemorial.

Written texts also placed limits on the agreements and promises being made, unbeknownst to the Indian parties. For example, written texts limiting hunting and fishing to Crown lands stand in contradiction to the oral promise not to interfere, in any way, with their use of wildlife and fisheries resources. These inherent conflicts and contradictions do not appear to have been explained to the Indian parties.

However, it is also clear that both parties wanted to make treaties to secure their respective political and economic objectives. Both sides saw tangible rewards flowing from the treaties and each side worked to secure the terms and conditions they wanted in the treaty. Both parties pledged to honour and uphold their sacred and binding pacts. Each side brought something of value to bargain with — the First Nations brought capital in the form of their land and resources, and the Crown brought the promise of compensation and the promise not to interfere with their way of life and the use of their natural resources as they had in the past. Each believed they had secured their respective objectives — the Crown gained access to Indian lands and resources, and First Nations secured the guarantee of the survival and protection of their nationhood.

B. EARLY BRITISH-ABORIGINAL TREATY RELATIONS

The treaties solidified the relationship between the Crown and the Aboriginal peoples at strategic points in North American history. In addition to the mutual benefits received from trade, political, and military alliances, each side obtained valuable consideration from the other. This consideration came at a price, however. It was obtained only after giving up something equally desired by the other side. The forms of consideration exchanged included tangibles — such as land, goods, and money — and intangibles — guarantees of rights, or promises of peace, protection, or non-interference with another's affairs. For this reason, the treaties are properly viewed as negotiated compacts in which each side was promised certain benefits by the other.

The relationship between Britain and the Aboriginal peoples was not a static one, as the Royal Commission on Aboriginal Peoples has documented. Originally, Britain was heavily dependent upon the Aboriginal peoples. The Aboriginal peoples were more numerous than the British, possessed superior military strength, and had greater knowledge of the land. Over time, as the British presence in North America grew and the population and power of the Aboriginal peoples dwindled as a result of war and disease, the relations between the groups took on different forms.

1. The Treaty of Albany

The *Treaty of Albany, 1664* was the first formal alliance between Aboriginal peoples in North America and the British Crown. At the time of the treaty, the Iroquois were more numerous and powerful than the British in North America. Equally important, they had become catalysts in the struggle between Britain and France for economic and military pre-eminence in North America. The Iroquois had been allies of the Dutch prior to Britain's acquisition of New Netherland, renamed New York by Britain in 1664. Through the treaty, Britain sought to ally itself with a powerful ally. Meanwhile, the Iroquois sought to continue the relationship they had previously enjoyed with the Dutch.

ARTICLES BETWEEN COL. CARTWRIGHT AND THE NEW YORK INDIANS, 24 SEPTEMBER 1664

in E.B. O'Callaghan, ed., *Documents Relative to the Colonial History of the State of New York*, 11 vols. (Albany: Weed, Parsons, 1853-61), Vol. 3, at 67-8

ARTICLES made and agreed upon the 24th day of September 1664 in Fort Albany between Ohgehando, Shanarage, Soachoenighta, Sachamackas of yᵉ Maques; Anaweed Conkeeherat Tweasserany, Aschanoondah, Sachamakas of the Synicks, on the one part; and Colonell George Cartwright, in the behalf of Colonell Nicolls Governour under his Royall Highnesse the Duke of Yorke of all his territoryes in America, on the other part, as followeth, viz.ᵗ–

1. Imprimis. It is agreed that the Indian Princes above named and their subjects, shall have all such wares and commodities from the English for the future, as heretofore they had from the Dutch.
2. That if any English Dutch or Indian (under the proteccôn of the English) do any wrong injury or violence to any of yᵉ said Princes or their Subjects in any sort whatever, if they complaine to the Governor at New Yorke, or to the Officer in Chiefe at Albany, if the person so offending can be discovered, that person shall receive condigne punishmᵗ and all due satisfaccôn shall be given; and the like shall be done for all other English Plantations.
3. That if any Indian belonging to any of the Sachims aforesaid do any wrong injury or damage to the English, Dutch or Indians under the proteccôn of the English, if complaint be made to yᵉ Sachims and the person be discovered who did the injury, then the person so offending shall be punished and all just satisfaccôn shall be given to any of His Maᵗⁱᵉˢ subjects in any Colony or other English Plantacôn in America.

4.   The Indians at Wamping and Espachomy and all below the Manhatans, as also all those that have submitted themselves under the proteccôn of His Matie are included in these Articles of Agreement and Peace;

In confirmacôn whereof the partyes above mencôned have hereunto sett their hands the day and yeare above written.

GEORGE CARTWRIGHT

THESE ARTICLES following were likewise proposed by the same Indian Princes & consented to by Colonell Cartwright in behalfe of Colonell Nicolls the 25th day of September 1664.

1.   That the English do not assist the three Nations of the Ondiakes Pinnekooks and Pacamtekookes, who murdered one of the Princes of the Maques, when he brought ransomes & presents to them upon a treaty of peace.
2.   That the English do make peace for the Indian Princes, with the Nations down the River.
3.   That they may have free trade, as formerly.
4.   That they may be lodged in houses, as formerly.
5.   That if they be beaten by the three Nations above mencôned, they may receive accommodacôn from ye English.

The written version of the *Treaty of Albany* provided for separate British and Iroquois jurisdiction in criminal matters involving their own citizens. The written treaty provided Britain's understanding of the nature of the agreement between the parties. This understanding of the compact between the nations was affirmed by the Iroquois' own understanding of what transpired between them at Albany. In addition to the parchment treaty, a wampum belt was presented by the Iroquois to the British to mark the former's understanding of the compact between them. Wampum belts were created by making beads from shells, such as those from clams, that were then pierced and sewn into patterns on animal hides. The belt presented to the British at Albany became known as the Two-Row Wampum because of the pattern depicted on it.

The pattern of the Two-Row Wampum, and its significance, is described below:

> The belt showed two parallel rows of purple wampum on a background of white wampum. The white wampum symbolized the purity of the agreement. The two purple rows denoted the spirit of the nations' ancestors and the separate, but parallel paths which they would each take in their respective vessels. One vessel, a birch-bark canoe, was for the Iroquois people, their laws, customs, and way of life; the other, a ship, was for the British, their laws, customs, and way of life. Three beads of wampum — symbolizing peace, friendship, and respect — separated the two rows. The three beads were the link between the nations, but just as their paths never cross on the wampum belt, neither was to attempt to steer the other's vessel.[1]

As the first formal alliance between Britain and the Aboriginal peoples, the *Treaty of Albany* made use of forms existing within each culture that were duly representative of the solemnity with which the parties pledged their peace, friendship and respect. The use of formally written treaties on parchment was a practice that Britain had reserved for its relations with independent, sovereign powers. Meanwhile, the Iroquois' representation of the compact on a wampum belt, which was highly valuable and required great skill to fashion, demonstrated the sanctity with which they viewed their alliance with Britain. The use of formal agreements by Aboriginal peoples was also a practice that had been used prior to contact with European nations.

Future agreements between the Aboriginal peoples and Britain built upon the foundation provided by the *Treaty of Albany* and the Two-Row Wampum. Aboriginal peoples did not view treaties as disconnected agreements as the British tended to. Rather, they regarded individual treaties as continuations of earlier alliances. Thus, the *Treaty of Albany*, from the Aboriginal point of view, was not an isolated agreement. Rather, it provided the basis for the Covenant Chain alliance that was forged between them and that extended beyond the signing of the *Treaty of Niagara* in 1764.[2]

2. The Covenant Chain

The Covenant Chain alliance was a military, political, social, and economic alliance that existed initially between the Dutch and River Indians of the Hudson River region, but was later forged between the British and the Iroquois Confederacy and then extended to include other Aboriginal nations. The status of the *Treaty of Albany* as the foundation for the Covenant Chain alliance is supported by a statement made by the Onondaga Chief Canasatego in 1744:

> About two Years after the Arrival of the English, an English Governor came to Albany, and finding what great Friendship subsisted between us and the Dutch, he approved it mightily, and desired to make as strong a League, and to be upon as good Terms with us as the Dutch were, with whom he was united, and to become one People with us: and by his further Care in looking into what had passed between us, he found that the Rope which tied the Ship to the great Mountain was only fastened with Wampum, which was liable to break and rot, and to perish in a Course of Years; he thereafter told us, he would give us a Silver Chain which would be much stronger, and would last for ever. This we accepted, and fastened the Ship with it, and it has lasted ever since.[3]

As described by Chief Canasatego, the treaty relationship between Britain and the Iroquois was symbolized as a ship (Britain) that was tied to an immoveable object, such as a great tree (the Tree of Peace) or mountain (usually at Onondaga, the council fire of the Iroquois Confederacy). Each of the participants in the alliance was a link in the chain and their compact was symbolized by the notion of each party placing its arms through the chain's links.

The Covenant Chain was perhaps the primary example of the use of treaties building upon each other and serving as reminders of the alliance forged between the groups. While the Covenant Chain was designed as a permanent alliance, it was expected that the nations would regularly renew their respective undertakings. This process of renewal — which was often described as "polishing the chain" — was designed to remind the parties of the solemn compact that they had entered into. When the chain was neglected through a lack of renewed commitment, it was described as "tarnished" or "rusted."

Renewing the Covenant Chain was accomplished in different ways. It took the form of the exchange of presents or wampum belts, restating the nations' solidarity, by agreements of further undertakings of union, or the extension of the alliance to include other Aboriginal groups. The periodical renewal of historic alliances was a practice familiar to the Aboriginal peoples. In addition to giving the parties an opportunity to reaffirm the nature of their alliance, the renewal process enabled them to make any necessary alterations arising from changing circumstances or needs. As John Borrows explains in "Negotiating Treaties and Land Claims: The Impact of Diversity Within First Nations Property Interests"(1992) 12 Windsor Y.B. Access. Just. 179 at 191-2 (references omitted):

> Traditionally, First Nations did not allocate property in the exercise of their treaty decision-making powers by conducting their relations with other people in a static way. Relationships were continually renewed and reaffirmed through ceremonial customs. Renewal and re-interpretation were practised to bring past agreements into harmony with changing circumstances. First Nations preferred this articulation of treaty-making to exercise their powers of self-government because it was consistent with their oral tradition. The idea of the principles of a treaty being "frozen" through terms written on paper was an alien concept.
>
> · · · · ·
>
> Therefore, to convey the meaning of the treaties, First Nations sovereignty was exercised through the spoken word and Wampum belts, and not through written statements. The reception of presents was also a part of the traditional ceremonial and oral nature of treaties. The gathering for presents provided an opportunity to meet in council and exchange words and material goods to reaffirm or modify previous agreements according to changing conditions. This explains why First Nation leaders would travel such long distances to receive a few trinkets that were monetarily of trivial value.

C. THE PROCESS OF TREATY-MAKING

The process of initiating and renewing treaty relations that had commenced with the *Treaty of Albany* and was continued through the Covenant Chain alliance established the parameters of British-Aboriginal relations in North America. These treaties were compacts between independent nations, as the following excerpt indicates.

LEONARD I. ROTMAN, "TAKING AIM AT THE CANONS OF TREATY INTERPRETATION IN CANADIAN ABORIGINAL RIGHTS JURISPRUDENCE"

(1997) 46 U.N.B.L.J. 1 at 13-18 (references omitted)

... Although there is no firm definition of what constitutes a treaty in Canadian law, the parties' intentions, not their adherence to a certain protocol, is most relevant in ascertaining whether a valid treaty exists. Justice Lamer, as he then was, stated in the *Sioui* case that a treaty exists where there is an agreement between Aboriginal peoples and the Crown that demonstrates "the intention to create obligations, the presence of mutually binding obligations and a certain measure of solemnity."

. . . . .

Treaties were mutual compacts which recognized the independence of the European and Aboriginal nations that were parties to them. The very nature of the treaty-making process indicated the autonomy of the parties, since a nation did not need to treat with its own subjects. A letter from Sir William Johnson, British Superintendent-General of Indian Affairs, to the Lords of Trade in 1764 indicates that he regarded the Aboriginals as autonomous peoples who would not relinquish their independence by submitting to British sovereignty:

> I have just received from Genl Gage a copy of a Treaty lately made at Detroit by Coll. Bradstreet with the Hurons and some Ottawaes & Missisagaes; these people had subscribed to a Treaty with me at Niagara in August last, but by the present Treaty I find, they make expressions of subjection, which must either have arisen from the ignorance of the Interpreter, or from some other mistake; for I am well convinced, they never mean or intend, any thing like it, and that they can not be brought under our Laws, for some Centuries, neither have they any word which can convey the most distant idea of subjection, and should it be fully explained to them, and the nature of subordination punishment etc, defined, it might produce infinite harm, but could answer no purpose whatever ... I am impatient to hear the exact particulars of the whole transaction, and I dread its consequences, as I recollect that some attempts towards Sovereignty not long ago, was one of the principal causes of all our troubles, and as I can see no motive for proposing to them terms, which if they attended to them, they most assuredly never meant to observe, and 'tis out of our power to enforce, I am apt to think it may occasion a necessity for being sufficiently watchful over their motives.

During his tenure as Superintendent-General of Indian Affairs, Johnson continually represented that he dealt with the Aboriginal peoples as independent nations. This is illustrated by the "separate house" image conveyed in the following statement made by Johnson at the *Treaty of Niagara* in 1764:

> Brothers of the Western Nations, Sachems, Chiefs and Warriors: You have now been here for several days, during which time we have frequently met to renew and Strengthen our Engagements and you have made so many Promises of your Friendship and Attachment to the English that there now remains for us only to exchange the great Belt of the Covenant Chain that we may not forget our mutual Engagements.

I now therefore present you the great Belt by which I bind all your Western Nations together with the English, and I desire that you will take fast hold of the same, and never let it slip, to which end I desire that after you have shewn this Belt to all Nations you will fix one end of it with the Chipeweighs at St. Marys [Michilimackinac] whilst the other end remains at my house, and moreover I desire that you will never listen to any news which comes to any other Quarter. If you do it, it may shake the Belt.

As the Crown's duly-authorized emissary, Johnson's representations to the Aboriginals are binding on the Crown. The conclusion is that if he treated with the Aboriginal peoples as autonomous nations, then Britain can be regarded as treating with them as autonomous nations.

Britain's recognition of Aboriginal land interests and its protection of the rights flowing from those interests in the *Royal Proclamation of 1763* may also be seen to recognize and affirm the autonomy of the Aboriginal Peoples. As the Royal Commission on Aboriginal Peoples has noted:

[W]hile the Royal Proclamation asserted suzerainty over Aboriginal peoples living 'under Our Protection', it also recognized that these people were "Nations" connected with the Crown by way of treaty and alliance. ... [T]he Proclamation acknowledged the retained sovereignty of Aboriginal peoples under the Crown's protection, and adopted measures to secure and protect their Territorial rights. This arrangement is the historical basis of the enduring constitutional relationship between Aboriginal nations and the Crown and provides the source of the Crown's fiduciary duties to those nations.

The notion that the Aboriginal peoples dealt with Britain as independent nations is also illustrated in the representations made by the Aboriginal peoples themselves. The statement of the Onondaga and Cayuga Indians to the Governors of New York and Virginia on 2 August 1684 is indicative of this understanding:

Wee have putt our selves under the great Sachim Charles that lives over the great lake, and we do give you Two White Drest Dear Skins to be sent to the great Sachim Charles That he may write upon them, and putt a great Redd Seale to them ... And you great man of Virginia, meaning the Lord Effingham Governr of Virginia ... lett your freind that lives over the great lake know that we are a ffree people uniting our selves to what sachem we please, and do give you one beavor skinn.

That the Aboriginal peoples considered themselves independent actors, notwithstanding their alliances with particular European nations is also indicated in the statement of the Ojibway Chief Minavavana to English trader Alexander Henry at Michilimackinac in 1764, "Englishman, although you have conquered the French, you have not yet conquered us. We are not your slaves. These lakes, these woods and mountains, were left to us by our ancestors. They are our inheritance; and we will part with them to none."

In addition to recognizing the autonomy of the parties involved, the treaties also solidified the relationship between the Crown and the Aboriginal people. ... As the basis of the origins and continuation of Crown-Native relations, the treaties were the building blocks of the modern Canadian state.

As compacts between independent nations, the treaties provided the guidelines for the parties' interaction and governed disputes between them. In addition, they provided the basis for the reciprocal rights and obligations of the parties through the process that has been described as "treaty federalism."

JAMES [SAKEJ] YOUNGBLOOD HENDERSON, "EMPOWERING TREATY FEDERALISM"

(1994) 58 Sask. L. Rev. 241 at 250-69 (references omitted)

. . . . .

F. OUTLINE OF TREATY FEDERALISM

These written agreements between First Nations and the imperial Crown created nation to nation relationships. Each agreement comprises a central treaty and subsequent ratification treaties. Together these relationships are often called treaty federalism. Treaty federalism was the original Aboriginal-prerogative federation with Great Britain. It was an indispensable step that had to occur before the creation of colonial authority in British North America. Each treaty illustrated the spirit and intent of treaty federalism and its outline. The terms of treaty federalism were concerned with: (1) protection of inherent Aboriginal rights; (2) distribution of shared jurisdictions; (3) territorial management; (4) human liberties and rights; and (5) treaty delegations. A comparison between the Georgian and Victorian treaties shows the unity and distinctiveness of a right of self-determination and a limited delegation to the Crown.

1. Inherent Aboriginal Rights

Customary self-determination was the context of all treaties with the imperial Crown. The Treaty Commissioners repeatedly assured the Indians that the government had no intention of interfering with their way of life or their livelihood. Without manifested consent by the First Nations to the treaties, no alien conventions and laws applied to them. None of the Georgian and Victorian treaties clearly delegated the customary rights of Aboriginal self-determination to the imperial Crown. Instead, the treaties confirmed and reserved these rights to the Aboriginal peoples. The First Nations' autonomy existed by ancient family consent; it was not derived from a Crown grant.

Each First Nation began its relationship with the imperial Crown as an independent power in international law, exercising comprehensive authority over the territory and people. Most of these treaties explicitly recognized the supreme power of First Nations, affirming their inherent Aboriginal order. Their Aboriginal worldviews and their customary and implicate legal orders were protected by the imperial Crown under the treaty order. Thus, treaty federalism transformed inherent rights of an Aboriginal order into vested rights in the constitutional law of Great Britain, then the United Kingdom and then Canada.

Although the treaties could not affect the First Nations' international status, autonomy, identity or customary law, often the terms of the treaties consensually altered their relationship to other nations. The treaties united the First Nations as freely associated states of the United Kingdom, not as part of any colony, province or dominion. Consequently, treaty federalism united independent First Nations under one Crown, *but not under one law*.

. . . . .

Treaties created shared responsibilities rather than supreme powers. Indeed, a total transfer of Aboriginal authority over the members of First Nations is inconsistent with Aboriginal political thought. Such a concept requires a centralized ruler or king, a European tradition that is generally absent among Aboriginal peoples. Only positive law empires created around centralized rulers or aristocratic society can transfer total control to another ruler. This attribute was missing in First Nations. None of the First Nations had such an idea or structure. The First Nations' leaders were not superiors that directed the will of the inferiors; instead they were limited representatives of the people.

. . . . .

The terms of some of the treaties clearly affirm Aboriginal traditions. According to their ancient customs, the Aboriginal peoples selected the Chiefs and Headmen who would negotiate and sign the treaties, but they did not surrender any of their inherent right to self-determination. This tradition is confirmed in the Georgian treaties. In the ratification conferences for the Wabanaki Compact (1725), the spokesperson for the Wabanaki Confederacy objected to the terms of the written treaty. In particular, he challenged the addition of a statement that the Wabanaki acknowledged King George to be their King and "declar'd themselves to the Crown of England". The Wabanaki spokesperson wrote that during the treaty negotiations

> when you hae ask'd me if I acknowledg'd Him for king i answer'd yes butt att the same time have made you take notice that I did not understand to acknowledge Him for my king butt only that I own'd that he was king his kingdom as the king of France is king of His.

The Mikmaq Delegation at the Wabanaki Treaty Conference had asserted the same position. On December 1, 1725, Lieutenant Governor Mascarene read to the Mikmaq delegates a proposed ratification treaty (often labelled Number 239) to the Wabanaki Compact. The Mikmaq delegates stated their own understanding of the words: they said they would "pay all the respect & Duty to the King of Great Britain as we did to ye King of France, but we reckon our selves a free People and are not bound."

At the pre-treaty conference in 1750 to the Mikmaw Compact (1752), the Nova Scotia Council asked the Grand Chief about the process of making a treaty with the Mikmaw Nation. He replied that:

> he would return to his own people and inform them what he had done here, and then would go to the other Chiefs, and propose to them to renew the peace; and that he thought he should be able to perform it in a month, and would bring some of them with him if he could, and if not would bring their answer.

The Council accepted Cope's authority to carry the treaty proposal to the other Mikmaq chiefs.

. . . . .

Under the protection of the *Royal Proclamation of 1763*, the Aboriginal peoples in the Victorian treaties expressly affirmed their right to self-determination. The Victorian treaties recognized that the Aboriginal peoples properly selected Headmen and Chiefs to negotiate the treaties and that these Chiefs and Headmen would, through the internal structures of each First Nation, maintain the duty to ensure the treaty was fully performed:

> And whereas the Indians of the said tract, duly convened in Council as aforesaid, and being requested by Her Majesty's said Commissioners to name certain Chiefs and Headmen, who should be authorized on their behalf to conduct such negotiations and sign any treaty to be founded thereon ... And thereupon in open council the different bands, having presented the men of their choice to the said Commissioners as Chiefs and Headmen, for the purpose aforesaid, of the respective bands of Indians inhabiting the said district hereinafter described ... to become responsible to Her Majesty for their faithful performance by their respective bands of such obligations as shall be assumed by them.

These terms in the treaties illustrate the process of Aboriginal autonomy and choice in determining their political status. These indispensable acknowledgments are crucial to understanding the context of Aboriginal self-determination and the terms of the treaties. Since the First Nations only operated by consensual and limited delegations of authority from Aboriginal peoples, the Treaty Delegates did not have total authority. They only had limited and delegated authority, thus the necessity of a ratification or accession process to the central treaties. Treaty Delegates could not cede to the imperial Crown rights reserved to the people or families, such as the rights of self-determination or territorial livelihood. Operating by ancient customs or symbolic constitutions, the First Nations' source of authority was and remains the consent of the people through federated governments or councils of extended families.

As protected nations under their prerogative treaties, Aboriginal peoples were never subject to the authority of the imperial Parliament but remained as foreign jurisdictions under the prerogatives of the Crown. Under the terms of the treaties, certain imperial statutes transferred the implementation of treaty obligations to colonial representatives or agents of the Crown. These delegations of treaty obligations were not grants of legislative power over Aboriginal peoples.

2. *Distribution of Shared Jurisdictions*

In the shared territorial jurisdictions created by treaties, the dual system of law and government was continued. The shared jurisdictions created by the treaties did not alter the exercise of Aboriginal self-determination in a specific geographical area. The Georgian treaties of "peace, friendship and protection" authorized English laws applying to the existing settlements and civil law applying to all controversies between the two distinct peoples. A few treaties established English criminal jurisdiction within the settlements, but none established that English laws would apply within Aboriginal lands.

The Victorian treaties of "peace and goodwill" included jurisdictional promises by First Nations to maintain "peace and good order" in the ceded land among all peoples, to strictly observe the treaty, to respect, obey and abide by the law, and to aid in the prosecuting of certain violations by Indians in the ceded lands. The central and common article of the Victorian treaties concerning legal jurisdiction provided that:

> the undersigned Chiefs on their own behalf and on behalf of all other Indians inhabiting the tract within ceded, do hereby solemnly promise and engage to strictly observe this treaty, and also to conduct and behave themselves as good and loyal subjects of Her Majesty the Queen.
> *They promise and engage that they will in all respects obey and abide by the law, that they will maintain peace and good order between each other, and also between themselves and other tribes of Indians, and between themselves and others of Her Majesty's subjects, whether Indians or whites, now inhabiting or hereafter to inhabit any part of the said ceded tracts* and that they will not molest the person or property of any inhabitant of such ceded tracts, or the property of Her Majesty the Queen, or interfere with or trouble any person passing or travelling through the said tracts, or any part thereof, and that they will aid and assist the officers of Her Majesty in bringing to justice and punishment any Indian offending against the stipulations of this treaty, or infringing the laws in force in the country so ceded.

This treaty article affirms the inherent rights of Aboriginal self-determination and government through the Chiefs and Headmen. This article is of no less constitutional authority in North America than the original grants of the King's prerogative authority to the courts, the House of Lords and the House of Commons in England. Both the treaty article and the Crown grants are exercised in different contexts and territories but have the same constitutional significance. The treaty article is similar to the "Peace, Order, and good Government clause" in section 91 of the *Constitution Act, 1867*, which gives residual authority to the federal government. The authority that Chiefs and Headmen had initially exercised by Aboriginal right over the protected territory is now exercised by the treaties throughout the ceded land at the request of the Crown. Aboriginal authority to govern the ceded land is an inviolable and a vested prerogative right. However, its exercise in the ceded territory does not require any association with the imperial Crown.

The prerogative treaty order was a separate constitutional realm from imperial Parliament. It was also a separate realm from the colonial assemblies that were created by the Crown-in-Parliament, which ended prerogative authority over the British subjects. These derivative governmental bod-

ies had no constitutional capacity to extinguish or modify vested prerogative rights in treaty order since these rights continued as a distinct part of
the constitutional law of Great Britain. Dickson C.J. acknowledged the
separation of prerogative treaty federalism from provincial federalism. His
Lordship stated:

> [T]he Indians' relationship with the Crown or sovereign has never de-
> pended on the particular representatives of the Crown involved. From the
> Aboriginal perspective, any federal-provincial divisions that the Crown has
> imposed on itself are internal to itself and do not alter the basic structure of
> Sovereign-Indian relations. This is not to suggest that aboriginal peoples are
> outside the sovereignty of the Crown, nor does it call into question the divi-
> sions of jurisdiction in relation to aboriginal peoples in federal Canada.

3. Territorial Management

Aboriginal self-determination is also evidenced by the territorial management scheme in the treaties. ... Any comprehensive textual analysis of the
English version of the treaties shows that the First Nations were keepers of
the land. While ensuring the continued right of First Nations to their livelihood in all the reserved and ceded land, the treaties also permitted the
use of some of their land tenure as collateral for performance of treaty obligations.

The Georgian treaties reserved all land and governmental authority for
First Nations, but allowed the British coastal settlements to exist under
English law within the reserved tenure. These reserved tenures were sub-
sequently affirmed by prerogative legislation. Lamer J. clearly stated in
Sioui:

> The British Crown recognized that the Indians had certain ownership rights
> over their land ... [and] allowed them autonomy in their internal affairs, in-
> tervening in this area as little as possible.

Indian country in the West was under the general protection of the
Crown pursuant to the *Royal Proclamation* and the *Rupert's Land and North-
Western Territory Order*. Under these prerogative documents the First
Nations were protected against encroachments from the colonial govern-
ments and the settlers, but the First Nations had no consensual relation-
ship with the Crown. The Victorian treaties established that relationship.
The Chiefs and Headmen agreed to:

> open up [their reserved lands] for settlement, immigration, trade and such
> other purposes ... a tract of country ... so that there may be peace and good
> will between [the Chief and Headmen of the Indians] and Her Majesty and
> between them and Her Majesty's other subjects, and that Her Indian people
> may know and be assured of what allowance they are to count upon and re-
> ceive from Her Majesty's bounty and benevolence.

The English text of all eleven Victorian treaties provided that the First
Nations "cede, release, surrender, and yield up to the Government of the
Dominion of Canada, for Her Majesty the Queen, and Her successors for-
ever, all their rights, titles and privileges whatsoever, to the lands". The
First Nations' ratification treaties used the words "we transfer, surrender

and relinquish" to her Majesty the Queen for the use of the Government of the Dominion.

These treaties of cession are not purchases of Aboriginal land tenures by the imperial Crown. If a full sale and purchase of the Aboriginal tenures were intended in the Victorian treaties, it is hard to conceive of a more convoluted and sibylline way of stating it. The legal context around the selected words evidenced a transfer of Aboriginal tenure to the protection of the Crown consistent with the idea of shared territorial jurisdiction. The transfer is similar to placing the land in an imperial escrow account. The source and nature of the rights, titles and privileges to the land transferred to the Crown by these treaties were established by international law or a law common to both parties, not by English land law. In international law, treaties of cession create derivative entitlements in the grantee; these entitlements cannot create original tenures or titles for the imperial Crown.

... The First Nations' relationships with the land have always defined their identity, their spiritual ecology and their reality. The sale of the land, the sale of the rights of future generations, is beyond the linguistic comprehension of most Aboriginal languages. Under a treaty of cession, an imperial Crown may have had an international and ultimate pre-emptive interest in ceded territory against other European nations and peoples, but this future interest had no effect on Aboriginal dominion. What is clear is that, under a transfer of jurisdiction or territory to the Crown, the imperial Crown accepted a correlative *sui generis* fiduciary obligation to fully comply with the terms of the treaties.

Five other conditions in the treaties lend support to an argument for a continuing Aboriginal self-determination over the land and against its sale and purchase. First, there were no words of consideration or purchase price in the document. Second, these treaty cessions were not absolute since they were conditional. The validity of a cession depended on full compliance with the promises, obligations and with the rendering of services.

. . . . .

Third, as part of the continuing Aboriginal governmental authority in the ceded territory, the Chiefs agreed not to molest the person or property of any inhabitant of the ceded territory or any property of Her Majesty. This argues for the quiet enjoyment of settlers and against a purchase of the land by the Crown. It also demonstrates that any proprietary interest of the inhabitants and the Crown were under Aboriginal tenure and political jurisdiction. The quiet enjoyment of the settlers is related to the explicit purposes of settlement and trade as described in the treaties, not to absolute Crown authority.

Fourth, under their jurisdiction the Chiefs and Headmen agreed not to interfere with or trouble any person passing or travelling through the ceded territory. These provisions illustrate the Aboriginal peoples' right to control the ceded territory after the treaties and also protect minority interests within the ceded land.

Fifth, as explained previously, the Crown argued that the Chiefs and Headmen would continue to maintain "peace and good order" in the ceded land among all inhabitants. This allocation of authority created a distinction between title and government in the ceded land that defeats any purchase theory. The Crown may have had a protective title, but the Chiefs and Headmen had jurisdiction over the ceded land.

Together these terms manifest a distinction between title and jurisdiction in the ceded land that is incompatible with a purchase. ... The division of authority in the treaties between government and title reinforce the purpose and intent that the cession was of a protective, not proprietary, nature. The Chiefs and Headmen did not transfer all interests in the land. In fact, Lieutenant-Governor Alexander Morris, a Treaty Commissioner and agent for the Crown in Treaties 3 through 6, affirmed a continuing *sui generis* tenure in the Chiefs and Headmen when he described the resulting effects of the cession to the Treaty Delegates:

> Who made the earth, the grass, the stone, and the wood? The Great Spirit. He made them for all his children to use, and it is not stealing to use the gift of the Great Spirit. The lands are the Queen's under the Great Spirit.

For the purposes of this essay, it is sufficient to say that the essence of an Aboriginal *sui generis* tenure involves covenants with other life forms and their keepers. These spiritual and ecological worldviews created the context for customary management of the sacred place under Aboriginal peoples' care. To the Treaty Delegates, Morris' statement affirmed their vision of their original tenure and stressed the derivative interest of the Queen.

From an Aboriginal perspective, the treaties of cession between the First Nations and the Crown were not substantially different from the Crown's creation of derivative estates out of its original tenure in England. In English law, the King reserved some of the land for his estates while allowing others to use the land in exchange for certain services and taxes. In the Georgian and Victorian treaties, the First Nations reserved land for themselves and their guests, and they delegated other lands to the Crown to generate taxes and revenues to finance the treaty obligations of the Crown.

4. Human Liberties and Rights

All the treaties distinguish between Her Majesty's other subjects and Her Indian people. These categories affirm that the Aboriginal peoples are distinct from other British subjects. It affirms a basic constitutional distinction that recognizes their distinct character as peoples governing a distinct geographic territory. Also, these categories affirm the political separation of Aboriginal people from the colonizers and their political relationship to the Crown. In the treaties, Her Majesty's other subjects were not delegated any authority in the ceded territory.

... Provided Aboriginal peoples did not transgress the treaty or infringe on the treaty rights of others or violate their customary law, by virtue of the treaties they could do anything they pleased in their reserved or ceded territories. Conversely, the imperial Crown and its agents or other subjects could do nothing but what they were authorized to do by some positive delegation from the First Nations in the treaties. ...

The treaties transformed certain Aboriginal liberties into vested prerogative liberties.

· · · · ·

For example, in the Georgian treaties the imperial Crown granted the Eastern tribes the "free liberty" of hunting and fishing as usual (that is a royal franchise under prerogative law). Additionally, the Crown promised non-interference by the British settlements and governments in the exercise of that liberty. Beginning with Treaty 3, the Crown explicitly guaranteed Aboriginal liberties to hunt and fish on lands within the ceded area. These liberties enabled them to use resources of the land and waters as a means of maintaining ancient self-sufficiency. These liberties to livelihood were as necessary to their existence as was the atmosphere they breathed.

To assist the Aboriginal peoples in maintaining self-sufficiency, the Crown promised them performance of certain treaty delegations of authority, obligations and claims. By the terms of the treaties, the imperial Crown created the first equalization formulas in Canada to supplement and compensate Aboriginal peoples for the loss of their liberties on certain lands.

· · · · ·

5. Treaty Delegations

Express treaty delegations create specific obligations for the Crown. Lacking such express language, no implied authority exists in the Crown. The imperial Crown's authority over First Nations and the shared territory was clearly derivative, not inherent. Express treaty delegations coordinated the activities in the ceded lands. The treaty delegation principle is similar to the federal principle of Confederation. The federal principle asserts any power withheld from the federal Parliament by the imperial statutes is possessed by the provincial legislatures and vice versa. Under treaty federalism, any Aboriginal right not delegated to the Crown is retained by the First Nations. The retained Aboriginal authority within the shared territory is consistent with the classic theory of English common law, described in foreign jurisdictions as the doctrine of continuity. All legitimate British authority in North America is derived from the compacts and treaties with First Nations. Any Crown authority over First Nations is limited to the actual scope of their treaty delegations. If no authority or power is delegated to the Crown, this power must be interpreted as reserved to First Nations, respectively, and are protected by prerogative rights and the common law since neither can extinguish a foreign legal system. The ability of First Nations to delegate authority to the imperial Crown does not by itself affect First Nations' territorial authority.

· · · · ·

The First Nations submitted to different degrees of imperial control over Aboriginal rights. Some delegated to the Crown certain authority outside their reserved lands, while others retained all authority under customary law and refused to cede or delegate any authority to the Crown. No doubt some provisions may have been imposed, but most were generated out of concern for harmony with their environment.

6. Summary

These five categories in the treaties illustrate the process of Aboriginal autonomy and choice in pursuing their own economic, social and cultural development. Aboriginal self-determination is affirmed by the first principle of the rule of law in the United Kingdom — that all peoples, despite race or ethnicity, are to be secure in what the Crown has recognized as their liberties and entitlements. This principle of the sanctity of the Crown's promises, which is similar to Aboriginal concepts, established predictability and certainty in British law in North America. By any normal rule of law and by section 35(1) of the *Constitution Act, 1982*, each Aboriginal nation and the Crown is bound only by what it has agreed to in the treaties. They are not bound to unwritten customary law, to written constitutional norms or to imposed domestic law of each party. The treaty delegations to the Crown established the limits of Parliament and of the legislative assemblies. Additionally, the promises and terms of the treaties created a fiduciary duty in the Crown to protect the right of Aboriginal self-determination.

D. THE CHANGING FACE OF TREATIES

The nature of treaties — and, indeed, the entire treaty-making process — was fundamentally altered by the change in the political situation in North America following Britain's conquest of New France in 1760-61. The strategic importance of the Aboriginal peoples as allies or enemies during the battles between Britain and France for colonial supremacy in North America ended upon the conquest. As Leonard Rotman has explained:

> With Britain and France competing to achieve predominance in North America, the Indians were able to play the two European powers off against each other for their own benefit. They were shrewd negotiators who knew full well that they were the catalysts in the European struggle in North America. They also knew that their precarious interests were best served by maintaining the delicate balance of power between the two European nations.
>
> . . . . .
>
> The removal of France as a major power in North America forever changed the relationship between the Crown and Native peoples. The Indians could no longer occupy the enviable position of holding the balance of power between Britain and France.[4]

This change in the Aboriginals' position was described by General Thomas Gage, who stated that "All North America in the hands of a single power robs [the Aboriginals] of their Consequence, presents, & pay."[5]

Just as the relationship between Britain and the Aboriginal peoples did not remain static, the nature of their treaty relations also changed over time. As the following excerpt indicates, treaties have taken a variety of forms since their first use in North America.

D.N. SPRAGUE, "CANADA'S TREATIES WITH ABORIGINAL PEOPLES"

(1996) 23 Man. L.J. 341 at 341-4 (references omitted)

VII. The First Treaties, 1763-1850

... The first [treaties] in the eighteenth century were of "peace and friendship"negotiated by representatives of the crown and Native peoples, either for military alliance or neutrality towards competing colonial powers. The French entered such alliances earlier than the British, but more informally. Britain solemnised its simple arrangements with a written text: in return for Aboriginal peace and friendship, British negotiators promised not to disturb the other side in its essential hunting and fishing territories. At the end of the era of inter-imperial rivalry, from the time of Britain's occupation of the St. Lawrence valley in 1760, British generals made their peace with Native peoples formerly allied with the French.

Several "peace and friendship" treaties followed elsewhere in the Atlantic region after 1760. Supremacy of Great Britain in North America, formalised by the Peace of Paris in 1763, set the stage for a new kind of treaty-making announced by a royal proclamation on 7 October 1763. ... [T]he significance of the Royal Proclamation of 7 October 1763 for Canadian Aboriginal treaty matters was and continues to have primary importance.

. . . . .

What followed after 1763 was a new kind of negotiation with Native people: face to face meetings between specially commissioned agents and representatives of "the several Nations or Tribes" to negotiate lump-sum payments for lands needed by an expanding settler population. ... The first large-scale application of the treaty-making requirement enunciated in 1763 was ... to make land available for Loyalist refugees after the American Revolution. Over the next thirty years almost twenty other "land surrenders" negotiated purchases from Native people, prior to the crown opening such areas to settlers.

By the 1810s, imperial authorities complained that existing means of fulfilling the purpose of the Proclamation placed excessive demands on the colonial treasury. In 1818 a third kind of treaty replaced lump-sum payment for each surrender of Aboriginal land for settlement. J.R. Miller describes the new approach as one that shifted the cost of extinguishing Aboriginal title from the crown to the Natives themselves. What followed was a scheme of district by district promises of annual payments, "annuities," at first amply funded by revenue flowing to the crown from sales of Aboriginal lands to settlers. In Miller's characterisation, "the Indians indirectly funded most of the purchase price of their land through instalment payments made from revenues derived from the land." Almost twenty such arrangements, all in present-day southern Ontario, were made over the next several decades as the new norm for meeting the terms of the Proclamation of 1763.

II. The Robinson Treaties, 1850s

A final step in the evolution of Canadian treaty-making occurred in 1850. The newly autonomous Province of Canada, an experimental union of present-day Ontario and Quebec created in 1840, began to anticipate exploitation of mineral resources and pockets of agricultural land in the geographically enormous, thinly populated territory north of Lakes Huron and Superior (i.e., north of modern-day Sudbury and west beyond Thunder Bay). William Benjamin Robinson, the commissioner for the task, negotiated a surrender of Aboriginal title to the whole vast region in two brief meetings with representatives of Aboriginal occupants on 7 and 9 September 1850. Since the "Robinson treaties" affected twice as much territory as all previous treaties combined, in that aspect alone they signalled a bold departure from earlier practice. They represented an equally important step in the evolution of the Canadian form of treaty-making with Native people in another respect. In addition to the standard commitments to pay annuities, and ceremonial assurances that Native people could continue to hunt and fish on ancestral lands as before, the second innovation was a promise of a reserve of territory for each band signatory to the treaty. Robinson explained to his superiors that while the reserve-promise was a novelty, it was necessary as a cost-saving measure:

> In allowing the Indians to retain reservations of land for their own use I was governed by the fact that they in most cases asked for such tracts as they had heretofore been in the habit of using for purposes of residence and cultivation ... By securing these to them and the right of hunting and fishing over the ceded territory, they cannot say that the Government takes from their usual means of subsistence and therefore have no claims for support.

... The promise of reserves emerged, then, as the cost-effective means for securing extinguishment of Aboriginal title over much larger tracts than had been the case in any negotiations before 1850. The two Robinson treaties ... became normal legal form for the new Dominion of Canada ... In fact, every Canadian treaty after Confederation fit the basic Robinson recipe: negotiated by specially commissioned officers of the crown to extinguish title to relatively large expanses of territory, offering vague assurances for existing hunting and fishing rights, and promising reserves as well as annuities.

As Sprague highlights, treaties underwent a number of changes following the early days of Crown-Native relations. While the Aboriginal peoples continued to view treaties on the same basis as they had since the earliest treaties they had entered into with Britain, Canada's use of treaties after

Confederation was economically-focused. As Sprague notes, each of the post-Confederation numbered treaties from 1871 to 1921 paralleled some governmental economic interest:

> The one valid generalisation concerning the making of treaties was that extinguishment negotiations occurred sporadically, and only where Canada hoped for large returns from areas of expected boom: Treaties 1 to 7 (1871-1877) extinguished Aboriginal title to the Prairies and Northwestern Ontario to clear the way for the Canadian Pacific Railway and agricultural settlement; Treaty 8 (1899-1900) covered access to the Yukon Territory, established as an administrative district separate from the North West Territory in 1898 after the gold rush that began in 1897; Treaty 9 (1904) followed silver discoveries and expected hydroelectric, pulp and paper development along the routes of newly projected rail lines in northern Ontario; Treaty 10 (1909) served a similar purpose in northern Saskatchewan; and Treaty 11 (1921) followed Imperial Oil's first gusher at Norman Wells in 1920.[6]

E. CONCEPTUALIZING CROWN-NATIVE TREATIES

Once the Crown no longer relied upon the Aboriginal peoples as military or political allies, it tended to view the treaties it concluded with them much more like contractual agreements than compacts between nations.

Unlike this change in the Crown's attitude towards the treaties, the Aboriginal view remained consistent with the understanding emanating from the Covenant Chain, which was to regard treaties as a series of agreements and renewals that were relationship-based rather than individual agreements that were document-based. Thus, the Aboriginal understanding of treaties included oral promises or collateral representations made during treaty negotiations, not simply the final, written parchment copy. This more inclusive view is often referred to as the "spirit and intent" of the agreement.

REPORT OF THE ROYAL COMMISSION ON ABORIGINAL PEOPLES, LOOKING FORWARD, LOOKING BACK, VOL. 1

(Ottawa: Ministry of Supply & Services, 1996)
at 128-30 (references omitted)

To the Aboriginal nations, treaties are vital, living instruments of relationship. They forged dynamic and powerful relationships that remain in effect to this day. Indeed the spirit of the treaties has remained more or less consistent across this continent, even as the terms of the treaties have changed over time.

Canadians and their governments, however, are more likely to look on the treaties as ancient history. The treaties, to Canada, are often regarded as inconvenient and obsolete relics of the early days of this country. With respect to the early treaties in particular, which were made with the British or French Crown, Canadian governments dismiss them as having no relevance in the post-Confederation period. The fact remains, however, that Canada has inherited the treaties that were made and is the beneficiary of the lands and resources secured by those treaties and still enjoyed today by Canada's citizens.

A final source of misunderstanding about the treaties lies in the fact that the relationship created by treaty has meaning and precedent in the laws and way of life of the Indian nations for which there are no equivalents in British or Canadian traditions.

One aspect of treaty making that is little understood today is the spiritual aspect of treaties. Traditional Aboriginal governments do not distinguish between the political and spiritual role of the chiefs, any more than they draw a sharp demarcation line between the physical and spirit worlds. Unlike European-based governments, they do not see the need to achieve a separation between the spiritual and political aspects of governing:

> Everything is together — spiritual, and political — because when the Creator ... made this world, he touched the world all together, and it automatically became spiritual and everything come from the world is spiritual and so that is what leaders are, they are both the spiritual mentors and political mentors of the people.

This integration of spiritual and political matters extends to treaty making, where sacred wampum, sacred songs and ceremonies, and the sacred pipe are integral parts of making the commitment to uphold the treaty. In affirming these sacred pacts, the treaty partners assured one another that they would keep the treaty for as long as the sun shines, the grass grows and the waters flow.

What sacred pacts, symbols and things of concrete value did the Crown bring to treaty making? The Crown's representatives gave their word and pledged to uphold the honour of the Crown. The symbols of their honour and trustworthiness were the reigning king or queen in whose name the treaty was being negotiated and with whose authority the treaty was vested. Missionaries were a testament to the integrity of the vows that were made and witnesses to the promises that were to be kept. Outward symbols, like flags, the red coats, treaty medals, gifts and feasts were also part of the rituals.

While European treaties borrowed the form of business contracts, Aboriginal treaties were modelled on the forms of marriage, adoption and kinship. They were aimed at creating living relationships and, like a marriage, they required periodic celebration, renewal, and reconciliation. Also like a marriage, they evolved over time; the agreed interpretation of the relationship developed and changed with each renewal and generation of children, as people grew to know each other better, traded, and helped defend each other. This natural historical process did not render old treaties obsolete, since treaties were not a series of specific promises in contracts; rather they were intended to grow and flourish as broad, dynamic relationships, changing and growing with the parties in a context of mutual respect and shared responsibility.

Despite these differences, Europeans found no difficulty adapting to Aboriginal protocols in North America. They learned to make condolence before a conference with the Six Nations, to give and receive wampum, to smoke the pipe of peace on the prairies, to speak in terms of "brothers" (kinship relations), not "terms and conditions" (contract relations). Whatever may have come later, diplomacy in the first centuries of European contact in North America was conducted largely on a common ground of symbols and ceremony. The treaty parties shared a sense of solemnity and the intention to fulfil their promises.

The apparent common ground was real, but under the surface the old differences in world view still existed, largely unarticulated.

Early judicial interpretation of Crown-Native treaties tended to side with the Crown's more focused emphasis on the quid pro quo element of the treaties rather than their relationship basis emanating from the Covenant Chain. Consequently, to the courts, the written, parchment treaty handed to the aboriginal peoples by the Crown constituted the entirety of the agreement.

The fact that the judiciary did not account for Aboriginal understandings of the treaties was only part of the problem with early treaty jurisprudence. In the late 19th and early 20th centuries, treaties were regarded as simple promises existing at the sufferance of the Crown. As Lord Watson commented in *Attorney-General of Ontario v. Attorney-General of Canada: Re Indian Claims*, [1897] A.C. 199 at 213 (P.C.):

> Their Lordships have had no difficulty in coming to the conclusion that, under the treaties, the Indians obtained no right to their annuities ... beyond a promise and agreement, which was nothing more than a personal obligation by its governor.

Since the courts did not regard treaties as binding documents that vested legally enforceable rights in the Aboriginal peoples, the Crown could readily ignore the terms of treaties, either by failing to perform treaty obligations, or by passing legislation that was inconsistent with its treaty promises.

Some of these issues, and others typical of early treaty jurisprudence in Canada, are illustrated in *R. v. Syliboy*, which is a prime example of early judicial attitudes towards treaties.

R. v. SYLIBOY

[1929] 1 D.L.R. 307, 50 C.C.C. 389 (N.S. Co. Ct.) (references omitted)

Patterson (Acting) Co. Ct. J.: — The defendant, who is the grand chief of the Mick Macks of Nova Scotia was convicted under the Lands and Forests Act, 1926 (N.S.), c. 4, of having in his possession ... fifteen green pelts, fourteen muskrat and one fox. He made no attempt to deny having the pelts, indeed frankly admits having them, but claims that as an Indian he is not bound by the provisions of the Act, but has by Treaty the right to hunt and trap at all times. Every now and then for a number of years one has heard that our Indians were making these claims but, so far as I know, the matter has never been before a Court.

The Treaty relied upon is that of 1752, made between Governor Hopson of the Province of Nova Scotia and His Majesty's Council on behalf of His Majesty, and "Major Jean Baptiste Cope, chief Sachem of the Tribe of Mick

Mack Indians Inhabiting the Eastern Coast of the said Province, and Andrew Hadley Martin, Gabriel Martin & Francis Jeremiah, Members and Delegates of the said Tribe:" Article 4 in part says: — "It is agreed that the said Tribe of Indians shall not be hindered from but have free liberty to hunt and fish as usual."

Observe the date 1752. Cape Breton between 1748 and 1763 was not part of Nova Scotia. It was owned and governed by the French, while Nova Scotia was a colony of Great Britain. It will be remembered that defendant is a Cape Breton Indian and that the offence alleged against him was committed in Cape Breton. Assuming for the time that the Treaty is still in force in Nova Scotia proper, can defendant claim protection under it? Unless there is something more than I have stated, clearly not. But, say his counsel, the Mick Mack Tribe throughout Nova Scotia, including Cape Breton, is one and indivisible, and the Treaty was made with the tribe, and a very bright and intelligent young Indian testifies that two of the signatories to it were Cape Breton Indians. The language of the Treaty not only lends no support to this contention, but shows that it is untenable, and I am satisfied that the young Indian is mistaken.

"The following Treaty of Peace," reads the minute of Council, "was Signed, Ratifyed and Exchanged with the Mick Mack Tribe of Indians, Inhabiting the Eastern Parts of this Province:" computed to be ninety in number, — Cope himself claimed authority over only forty. Eight years before there had been three hundred Indians engaged in the attack on Canso, all from "the Eastern Parts of this Province" which shows that Cope and the others who joined with him in the Treaty, really represented only a small portion even of these very Indians they claimed to represent. Notice further, how Cope is described as "chief Sachem of the Tribe of Mick Mack Indians Inhabiting the Eastern Coast of the said Province," (*i.e.*, Nova Scotia proper) and his fellow signatories as "Members and Delegates of the said Tribe." Article 3 seems conclusive on the point. There it is provided: — "That the said Tribe" (*i.e.*, the tribe inhabiting the eastern coast of Nova Scotia) "shall use their utmost endeavours to bring in the other Indians to Renew and Ratify this Peace."

. . . . .

In the face of this evidence there can be no doubt, I think, that the Treaty relied upon was not made with the Mick Mack Tribe as a whole but with a small body of that tribe living in the eastern part of Nova Scotia proper, with headquarters in and about Shubenacadie, and that any benefits under it accrued only to that body and their heirs. The defendant being unable to show any connection, by descent or otherwise, with that body cannot claim any protection from it or any rights under it.

But there is much more than what I might not improperly call internal evidence to show that defendant's contention that the Treaty was a general and not a local one is untenable. Between 1752 and 1763 we find negotiations going on between the Governor and council and various tribes or local bodies of Indians for treaties: — for instance with the Fort Lawrence (Missiquash) Indians in 1753 and again in 1755; with the Cape Sable Indians in 1753; with Indians near Halifax in 1760; with Chibenaccadie Indians (the very Indians of our Treaty) in 1760. Between same dates we find treaties entered into with Lehéve (LaHave) Indians in 1753, 1760 and 1761; with the Chibenaccadie and Muscadoboit (Shubenacadie and Musquodoboit) Indians in 1760; with certain Indian chiefs in 1761; with the Missiquash Indians, and with the Pictouck and Malagonich (Pictou and Merigomishe) Indians in the same year. Why these negotiations — why these treaties if the Treaty of 1752 was general applying to all Nova Scotia?

In none of these treaties, or in the negotiations leading up to them is there any reference to the Treaty of 1752, while there are many to the Treaty of 1725. Indeed the only reference to the Treaty of 1752 that I have been able to find is in that infamous proclamation by Governor Lawrence dated May 14, 1756, wherein he offers a reward of £30 for the capture of any Indian, or £25 for any Indian woman. There it is mentioned as a treaty made with a tribe of Mick Macks.

. . . . .

That the Governor in Council of Nova Scotia knew that these treaties were of a local character is evident. On February 29, 1760, that body resolved "to make peace with each chief who came in, and afterwards to have a general treaty signed at Chignecto."

Counsel for the defendant suggest another way in which the benefits from the Treaty were or should be extended to their client and all other Cape Breton Indians. By Royal Proclamation after the Treaty of Paris [the *Royal Proclamation of 1763*], Cape Breton and St. John's (Prince Edward) Island were annexed to Nova Scotia and three years later the Parliament of Nova Scotia by statute declared that the laws of Nova Scotia extended to the Island of Cape Breton. But the expression, "the Laws of Nova Scotia" had reference only to the general laws of the Province and it would be misusing words to speak of the Treaty of 1752 as a law. At any rate the statute of 1766 (N.S.), c. 1, ceased to have any effect in 1784 when Cape Breton was disjoined from Nova Scotia and created a colony with authority to its Governor to convene the Assembly. Separate Cape Breton and Nova Scotia remained until 1820-21 (N.S.), c. 5. After their union in that year an Act was passed enacting that the administration of justice in the Island of Cape Breton should be conformable to the usage and practice of the Province of Nova Scotia. Nothing is said about general laws or treaties. Presumably no mention of general laws was necessary to make them effective, but surely that cannot be said of treaties.

I have referred to the proclamation after the Treaty of Paris. That is relied upon by the defendant for a reason other than that set out in the preceding paragraph. If that proclamation be examined it will be found that it deals only with those territories or countries, of which Nova Scotia was not one, that had been ceded to Great Britain by France. ... The references in it to the Indians are specifically limited to the Indians of the three first named governments [Quebec, East Florida, and West Florida]. One can understand an Indian in Quebec for example making a claim that he was guaranteed certain rights about hunting by the proclamation, but I confess I cannot understand a Cape Breton Indian making any such claim.

I might stop here. If the Treaty did not extend to Cape Breton and the Indians there could make no claim under it or derive any benefits from it, the prosecution must succeed and the conviction of the defendant be confirmed. I think, however, I should express my opinion on the other questions raised for I am in hopes that there will be an appeal from my decision and that upon so important a matter we may have the judgment of an Appeal Court.

Mr. McLennan for the prosecution, whose brief is a joy to read so complete and compact it is, contends that even if the Treaty relied upon by the defendant was made for the whole Mick Mack Tribe and did extend to Cape Breton and included the Indians there, it was almost at once put an end to by the breaking out of war. The ink was not much more than dry on the Treaty when Indians led by a son of Cope (let us hope not that son to whom the complacent Governor had sent a laced hat as a present) were carrying on in the characteristic Indian way a war against Britain. It was the very Indians who were parties to the Treaty that were responsible for the repeated raids upon Dartmouth, and it is a well-known and established fact that right down until the Treaty of Paris put an end to the war between England and France the Indians were on the side of France and were carrying on war in her behalf. Would that clause in the Treaty guaranteeing them the right to hunt be in consequence put an end to, or would it be merely suspended? ... I am inclined to hold it would only be suspended.

. . . . .

A treaty such as that with which we are dealing if made today is one that would require to be ratified by Parliament before becoming effective, and would be invalid until such ratification. Though there was authority in Cornwallis' commission to summon a parliament for Nova Scotia, we all know that none was summoned for some years after the treaty was signed. It is a fair inference I think that after parliament had been assembled and began to legislate this treaty should have been ratified, or otherwise it would lose its validity. At any rate it was not very long after Parliament assumed its functions that a statute was passed which ignored the Treaty and treated it as non-existent.

In 1794 the first of our many Game Acts was passed, 1794 (N.S.), c. 4. It provided that no person within a certain period each year should kill partridge or black duck but Indians and poor settlers. It might be argued that the exception goes to show that the Indians had a special right by treaty, but if they had such a right why mention it in the statute? It would seem to me that the proper interpretation would be that they having no such right by treaty were given it by statute. However that may be the next statute on the subject makes the point clear.

By s. 1 of R.S.N.S. 1851, c. 92, it was enacted that: —

> No person shall take or kill any partridge ... between the first of March and the first of September in any year; but Indians and poor settlers may kill them for their own use at any season.

Section 3 of that Act provides that: — "The sessions may make orders respecting the setting of snares or traps for catching moose," and by s. 5, "may make orders for regulating the periods ... within which moose may be killed." If the Indians were excepted as to the taking or killing of partridge because they had special right by treaty, why were they not so excepted as to setting snares or killing moose?

Then follows a series of statutes prohibiting everyone, Indians not excepted, from hunting during certain seasons until we come to that under which this prosecution was brought. Where a statute and treaty conflict a British Court must follow the statute ... The result therefore is that even assuming the so called Treaty of 1752 is a treaty; assuming that it was valid as such without ratification by parliament, and that any rights under it could be claimed by the Indians of all Nova Scotia as that Province is now constituted, the prosecution would still succeed, because the statute not the treaty prevails.

At the trial there was no discussion as to whether the so called treaty was really a treaty or not. Counsel for the defendant ... did not touch this point. Apparently they are content to accept the description in the document itself ... but the prosecution raised the question and I must deal with it. Two considerations are involved. First, did the Indians of Nova Scotia have status to enter into a treaty? And second, did Governor Hopson have authority to enter into one with them? Both questions must I think be answered in the negative.

(1) "Treaties are unconstrained Acts of independent powers." But the Indians were never regarded as an independent power. A civilized nation first discovering a country of uncivilized people or savages held such country as its own until such time as by treaty it was transferred to some other civilized nation. The savages' rights of sovereignty even of ownership were never recognized. Nova Scotia had passed to Great Britain not by gift or purchase from or even by conquest of the Indians but by treaty with France, which had acquired it by priority of discovery and ancient possession; and the Indians passed with it.

Indeed the very fact that certain Indians sought from the Governor the privilege or right to hunt in Nova Scotia as usual shows that they did not claim to be an independent nation owning or possessing their lands. If they were, why go to another nation asking this privilege or right and giving promise of good behaviour that they might obtain it? In my judgment the Treaty of 1752 is not a treaty at all and is not to be treated as such; it is at best a mere agreement made by the Governor and council with a handful of Indians giving them in return for good behaviour food, presents, and the right to hunt and fish as usual — an agreement that, as we have seen, was very shortly after broken.

(2) Did Governor Hopson have authority to make a treaty? I think not. "Treaties can be made only by the constituted authorities of nations or by persons specially deputed by them for that purpose." Clearly our treaty was not made with the constituted authorities of Great Britain. But was Governor Hopson specially deputed by them? Cornwallis' commission is the manual not only for himself but for his successors and you will search it in vain for any power to sign treaties.

Having called the agreement a treaty, and having perhaps lulled the Indians into believing it to be a treaty with all the sacredness of a treaty attached to it, it may be the Crown should not now be heard to say it is not a treaty. With that I have nothing to do. That is a matter for representations to the proper authorities — representations which if there is nothing else in the way of the Indians could hardly fail to be successful.

On behalf of the defendant one witness testified that all his life he had fished as he would without regard to the Fisheries Law, and defendant himself swears he has started hunting muskrat for the last thirty-four years on Hallowe'en, October 31. Neither of them had ever been interfered with. The suggestion was that they had not been interfered with because they were within their rights in doing what they did by virtue of the treaty. I say nothing about fishing, but as to the hunting it was not until 1927 that the close season was extended to November 15. Until that year whenever there had been a close season on muskrat it had ended on November 1. If defendant did not start his hunting until October 31, the reason he was not proceeded against before seems obvious.

There is abundant evidence also that the Indians have been for many years receiving food, blankets, etc., from the government through the Indian agent because, says the defendant, of this treaty. I cannot agree. Rather I think they received these goods, and other benefits as well, not because of the treaty but by virtue of the successive statutes in that behalf ... The good work so begun and carried on when Nova Scotia was a separate Province was taken over by the federal government at Confederation and one is glad to learn is being so generously continued.

On no ground that has been advanced, and I am sure everything has been said or done that with any chance of success could have been said or done, can defendant in my opinion succeed. Such sympathy as a Judge is permitted to have is with defendant. I would gladly allow the appeal if I could find any sound reason for doing so, but I cannot and must confirm the conviction. The very capable Magistrate who heard the case below has, I am pleased to see, fixed the penalty at the very lowest figure that the Act allows. Even so I venture to express the hope that the authorities will not enforce the conviction.

I have no doubt whatever that defendant honestly believed that the treaty was valid and that he was entitled under it to kill muskrat or have their pelts in his possession at any time, and as I pointed out, a year ago or rather in 1926 it was no offence on November 4 to have green muskrat pelts in one's possession. While everyone is presumed to know the law and to know the exact limits of the close season, it is more than likely — is it not a certainty — that the untutored mind of the defendant was not aware that in 1927 the close season had been lengthened to November 15? Of course, ignorance of the law excuses no one, but surely ignorance of the law under such circumstances can be urged as a plea for most lenient treatment — for in such a case as this waiving both penalty and costs.

Appeal dismissed.

Do you agree with Judge Patterson's characterization of the 1752 "treaty"? What of his statement that, "having perhaps lulled the Indians into believing it to be a treaty ... the Crown should not now be heard to say it is not a treaty"? Are there any merits to this argument? The 1752 treaty considered in *Syliboy* is reproduced, in its entirety, in *Simon v. R.*, [1985] 2 S.C.R. 387, 62 N.R. 366, 23 C.C.C. (3d) 238, 71 N.S.R. (2d) 15, 171 A.P.R. 15, [1986] 1 C.N.L.R. 153, 24 D.L.R. (4th) 390, excerpted, *infra*.

The English language and concepts implemented in the treaties were not always understood by the Aboriginal peoples. Where they were understood, they were not always understood by the Aboriginals in the same manner that they were by the Crown's representatives. Attempts at translation by the Crown's representatives were also affected by these problems. The Maritime peace and friendship treaties from the late 17th and 18th centuries, such as the 1752 agreement considered in *Syliboy*, are profound examples of the effects of such a lack of common understanding. Compare the approach to these treaties by historian William Wicken with that of either Lord Watson or Patterson J.

WILLIAM WICKEN, "THE MI' KMAQ AND WUASTUKWIUK TREATIES"

(1994) 44 U.N.B.L.J. 241 at 241-2, 249-53 (references omitted)

Between 1722 and 1786, Native people of the Atlantic region signed a series of treaties with the British Crown. In recent years, the Mi' kmaq and Wuastukwiuk have argued that the treaties supersede provincial statutes governing their hunting, fishing and trading rights. The resulting litigation has focused on two principal questions. Firstly, who signed the treaties, and therefore, who can claim their protection, and secondly, how are the treaties to be interpreted?

The courts are seeking answer to historical questions for which conclusive proof is lacking, but do not have the time and materials required to properly evaluate historical documents and testimony. The difficulties which this poses are suggested by errors in historical interpretation made in recent judgments in the Atlantic region. In *R. v. McCoy*, Justice Turnbull of New Brunswick stated that a treaty had been signed "with the Indians ... at Annapolis Royal in 1750." While treaties were signed in 1749 and 1752, both at Chebouctou (Halifax), none was concluded in 1750 at Annapolis Royal. Moreover, Justice Turnbull based his decision on a number of questionable historical interpretations.

. . . . .

While a court may not have time to grapple with the sometimes tortuous historical debates surrounding 18th century European-Indian relations, it does need to evaluate the historical documentation which is purported by both the treaty claimants and the Crown to validate their particular claims. This article outlines available 18th century documentation and points out some of the difficulties in using these materials to interpret the treaties.

Only by understanding the context in which documents are created is it possible to evaluate opposing interpretations critically. This requires knowing why the document was created, the context in which it was written and the identity of the author. From this it is possible to make some general comments regarding a document's biases, and therefore to evaluate the reliability of the information which it purports to describe. This assists historians in attempting to overcome their greatest difficulty: reconstructing an historical event using documents written by Europeans who are now dead and whose descendants have no memories of these events. What dialogue occurs must be created artificially by constantly questioning one's own assumptions. In doing so, historians must be sensitive to the particular historical context in which they live and question how this influences their perception of the past.

The Sources

Historians and anthropologists have long recognized the difficulties of reconstructing the histories of Native societies. As Native people did not generally produce written records or, in cases where they did, records have not survived, researchers rely almost exclusively on archaeological data to understand North American people prior to European contact, and on European produced documentation after this contact.

. . . . .

The Treaties

Collectively, these records provide the basis for our understanding of the Mi' kmaq and Wuastukwiuk society during the treaty-making period. As is evident, the records are fragmentary, with long silences between mentions of either people. Consequently, it is difficult to reconstruct the precise contours of either society during the 17th and 18th centuries. We do not know, for instance, such basic information as population sizes before and after contact. Indeed, one of the most important aspects of the records is that they show many, if not all, Mi' kmaq and Wuastukwiuk people lived far removed from the sight and pen of European officials. Because of the fragmentary character of this material, it is necessary to consult records produced after 1760. These sources, principally contained in British and Nova Scotian archival series, provide valuable insights into traditional fishing and hunting sites which, in some cases, had been abandoned temporarily in consequence of an expanding imperial rivalry between England and France in the Atlantic region between 1744 and 1760.

Interpretation is complicated further by the fact that the documentary evidence is not readily available. Because of the particular historical circumstances in which Mi' kmaq and Wuastukwiuk lands were invaded by European people, source materials tend to be scattered in archival series housed in Canada, England, France, Massachusetts, New Brunswick, Nova Scotia and Québec. Piecing together this information is a painstaking and time consuming process. Because of the vast quantity of historical documentation that must be read and analyzed, there may be a tendency, particularly in courtroom situations, to make general conclusions without first sifting through the available evidence. In the Atlantic region this point is particularly important since little new research on the Mi' kmaq and Wuastukwiuk has been published since the late 1970s, forcing an undue reliance on older academic interpretations.

The treaties signed between the British Crown and Mi' kmaq and Wuastukwiuk people illustrate these interpretative difficulties. There are, with one exception, no records of treaty negotiations. Generally, Europeans were not privy to discussions among sakamows and elders, and thus would not have known of community debates which preceded and followed a treaty signing. For example, the Governor of the Ile Royal, Saint-Ovide, wrote in November 1728 that during the previous year the Mi' kmaq had held great meetings at Antigoniche, but he had been unable to obtain much information regarding what had been said in council. Because of this lack of interaction between the Mi' kmaq and European colonial officials, we do not know what Mi' kmaq and Wuastukwiuk delegates were told by English officials about the treaty. This in turn forces reliance on European documentation and European interpretations to understand the treaty's meaning. Indeed, researchers have tended to accept that the English versions of treaties reflect how the Mi' kmaq and Wuastukwiuk understood them. As research on late 19th century treaties signed between Western Native people and the Canadian government has shown, however, there could be a significant difference between the written English document and how Native negotiators understood it. The 1725/26, 1749, 1752 and 1760/61 treaties are cases in point.

According to these treaties, the Mi' kmaq and Wuastukwiuk recognized the English Crown's "jurisdiction and Dominion Over the Territories of the said Province of Nova Scotia or Acadia." Subsequent articles implicitly made both people subjects of the English Crown. Given the lack of English military influence throughout the region before the Loyalist immigration of the early 1780s, such recognition appears unlikely. Indeed, from soon after the English conquest of Port-Royal (Annapolis Royal) through to the mid-1750s, a number of sakamows expressed that neither English nor other European powers held claim to Mi' kmaq land.

How are we to explain this apparent contradiction? One possible explanation is that during the negotiations, the precise content of the treaty was communicated incorrectly to Mi' kmaq and Wuastukwiuk delegates. This is suggested by representations made both by Loron, the speaker for the Penobscot people, and by French speaking delegates who attended the ratification of the 1725 Boston treaty by Abenaki people at Casco Bay in July 1726. In a letter addressed to the Lieutenant-Governor of Massachusetts, Loron stated that[:]

> Having hear'd the Acts read which you have given me I have found the Articles entirely differing from what we have said in presence of one another, 'tis therefore to disown them that I write this letter unto you.

Loron took exception to several of the treaty's articles. Though all of his objections were not included in the letter written to Dummer, Loron was particularly upset by those articles which purported that he and his people had acknowledged King George to be their King and had "declar'd themselves subjects to the Crown of England." According to Loron's memory of those negotiations,

> when you have ask'd me if I acknowedg'd Him for King I answer'd yes butt att the same time have made you take notice that I did not understand to acknowledge Him for my king butt only that I own'd that He was king his kingdom as the King of France is king in His.

Similarly, French-speakers present at the ratification at Casco Bay wrote that articles read to the Indians of Panaouamské had not included references to the fact that they came to submit themselves to the English King, that they accepted responsibility for beginning hostilities with the English, and that they would agree to live according to English law. Rather, the oral translation of these articles had emphasized that the Panaouamské had "come to salute the English Governor to make peace with him and to renew the ancient friendship which had been between them before."

Mistranslation of treaty articles might have occurred for several reasons. As Algonquian based languages, Micmac and Wuastukwiuk were fundamentally different from both English and French. Consequently, many of the words and ideas contained in the treaties could not be translated easily. In translating the treaties, interpreters, some of whom were likely ill-equipped to deal with the subtle nuances of the language, may have misinterpreted those articles of the 1725 treaty in which the Mi' kmaq and Wuastukwiuk recognized King George as their king and accepted his jurisdiction over their lands.

Translation difficulties were exacerbated by a general English distrust of Native people. To English officials, the Mi' kmaq were barbarous and culturally inferior. Native people were, as one New England minister wrote in 1724, a people "living in a state of Nature" who did not possess the two essential components of every civilized nation, agriculture and a system of government. They were unpredictable, unreliable, and therefore not to be trusted. Exemplifying this attitude are remarks made in August 1725 by Hibbert Newton, a member of Nova Scotia's Executive Council, and Captain John Bradstreet in conversation with the Governor of Ile Royal, Joseph de Saint-Ovide. In a frank exchange of views, Newton and Bradstreet said,

> we valued the Indians so very little and knew how little their word was to be depended on that we took no notice of them, nor never shall, till they come in with a method whereby we may be very well assured by hostages and other good pledges at their good behaviour.

Similarly, in October 1749, the governor of Nova Scotia, Edward Cornwallis wrote to the Board of Trade that treaties with Indians meant nothing, and nothing "but force will prevail."

To understand the treaties, we must first evaluate the sources available to interpret them. The usefulness of these sources is limited, as the documents were written by Europeans, and their depictions of Mi' kmaq and Wuastukwiuk society were sporadic and sometimes incorrect. This was particularly true of English documentation before 1760. We should be sceptical, for instance, of letters written by English colonial officials which purport to describe events occurring in Mi' kmaq society when little official contact occurred between the two societies. More useful are French records, as there were extensive cultural, social, economic and political interactions between Mi' kmaq and French-speaking communities in the 17th and 18th centuries. Indeed, it appears there were discrepancies between the English copy of a treaty and the oral understanding of the Mi' kmaq and Wuastukwiuk negotiators.

This complicates a court's task as it suggests that a literal interpretation of the treaties is not always valid. What we need to do, therefore, is move beyond the treaties' literal meaning and describe the context in which they were signed. In doing so, we may be able to visualize the world not only from the European view point, but also from the perspective of Mi' kmaq and Wuastukwiuk people. This can only be done, however, by first recognizing the limitations of the sources traditionally used to interpret the treaties.

What *Syliboy* and other early judicial pronouncements on treaties did not account for, largely because they did not look beyond the "four corners" of written treaties, was the significant discrepancies between the written treaties and the representations made to the Aboriginal peoples who signed them. Since the Aboriginal peoples could not read written documents, they were dependent upon the explanation of a treaty's terms provided to them by the Crown. As illustrated below, the nature of these explanations, as well as of the representations made by the Crown's representatives to the Aboriginal peoples, were not always consistent with the final, written version of the treaties.

The following account of the exchange between Alexander Morris, the Crown's chief negotiator for many of the early post-Confederation numbered treaties and Lieutenant-Governor of Manitoba and the North-West Territories, and representatives of the Ojibway Indians during the negotiations for Treaty No. 3 demonstrates the different understandings that the parties had regarding the purpose of the treaty. It also provides some insight into the process of Crown-Native treaty-making. It should be noted that this account is one that has been filtered through the eyes and ears of Governor Morris and his aides.

ALEXANDER MORRIS, THE TREATIES WITH THE INDIANS OF MANITOBA AND THE NORTH-WEST TERRITORIES, INCLUDING THE NEGOTIATIONS ON WHICH THEY WERE BASED, AND OTHER INFORMATION RELATING THERETO

(Toronto: Belfords, Clarke, 1880) at 55-65, 74-5

NORTH-WEST ANGLE,

October 1, 1873

The assembled Chiefs met the Governor this morning, as per agreement, and opened the proceedings of the day by expressing the pleasure they experienced at meeting the Commissioners on the present occasion. Promises had many times been made to them, and, said the speaker, unless they were now fulfilled they would not consider the broader question of the treaty.

Mr. S.J. Dawson, one of the Commissioners, reciprocated the expression of pleasure used by the Chiefs through their spokesman. ... He was, he continued, one of the Commission employed by the Government to treat with them and devise a scheme whereby both white men and Indians would be benefitted. ... He would explain to them the proposals he had to make. He had lived long amongst them and would advise them as a friend to take the opportunity of making arrangements with the Governor.

. . . . .

The Chief in reply said his head men and young men were of one mind, and determined not to enter upon the treaty until the promises made in the past were fulfilled; they were tired of waiting. What the Commissioners called "small matters" were great to them, and were what they wished to have settled.

. . . . .

His Excellency [Governor Morris] then addressed them at some length. ... Many of his listeners had come a long way, and he, too, had come a long way, and he wanted all the questions settled at once, by one treaty. He had a message from the Queen, but if his mouth was kept shut, the responsibility would rest on the Indians, and not with him if he were prevented from delivering it. He had authority to tell them what sum of money he could give them in hand now, and what he could give them every year; but it was for them to open his mouth. He concluded his remarks, which were forcibly delivered, with an emphatic, "I have said."

The Chief reiterated that he and his young men were determined not to go on with the treaty until the first question was disposed of. ... [I]t was the Indians' country, not the white man's. Following this the Governor told the Council that ... [h]e was bound by his Government, and was of the same mind to treat with them on all questions, and not on any one separately.

On seeing His Excellency so firm, and feeling that it would not do to allow any more time to pass without coming to business the Chief asked the Governor to open his mouth and tell what propositions he was prepared to make.

His Excellency then said — "I told you I was to make the treaty on the part of our Great Mother the Queen, and I feel it will be for your good and your children's. ... We are all children of the same Great Spirit, and are subject to the same Queen. I want to settle all matters both of the past and the present, so that the white and red man will always be friends. I will give you lands for farms, and also reserves for your own use. I have authority to make reserves such as I have described, not exceeding in all a square mile for every family of five or thereabouts. It may be a long time before the other lands are wanted, and in the meantime you will be permitted to fish and hunt over them. I will also establish schools whenever any band asks for them, so that your children may have the learning of the white man. I will also give you a sum of money for yourselves and every one of your wives and children for this year. I will give you ten dollars per head of the population, and for every other year five dollars-a-head. But to the chief men, not exceeding two to each band, we will give twenty dollars a-year for ever. I will give to each of you this year a present of goods and provisions to take you home, and I am sure you will be satisfied.

After consultation amongst themselves, the Councillors went to have a talk about the matter and will meet the Governor tomorrow morning, when it is expected the bargain will be concluded. Of course the Indians will make some other demands.

. . . . .

THIRD DAY

Proceedings were opened at eleven o'clock by the Governor announcing that he was ready to hear what the Chiefs had to say. The Fort Francis Chief acted as spokesman, assisted by another Chief, Powhassan.

MA-WE-DO-PE-NAIS — ... We think it a great thing to meet you here. What we have heard yesterday, and as you represented yourself, you said the Queen sent you here, the way we understood you as a representative of the Queen. All this is our property where you have come. We have understood you yesterday that Her Majesty has given you the same power and authority as *she* has, to act in this business; you said the Queen gave you her goodness, her charitableness in your hands. This is what we think, that the Great Spirit has planted us on this ground where we are, as you were where you came from. We think where we are is our property. I will tell you what he said to us when he ... planted us here; the rules that we should follow — us Indians — He has given us rules that we should follow to govern us rightly. ... I want to answer what we heard from you yesterday, in regard to the money that you have promised us yesterday to each individual. ... We ask fifteen dollars for all that you see, and for the children that are to be born in the future. This year only we ask for fifteen dollars; years after ten dollars; our Chiefs fifty dollars per year for every year, and other demands of large amounts in writing, say $125,000 yearly."

ANOTHER CHIEF — "I take my standing point from here. Our councillors have in council come to this conclusion, that they should have twenty dollars each; our warriors, fifteen dollars; our population, fifteen dollars. We have now laid down the conclusion of our councils by our decisions. We tell you our wishes are not divided. We are all of one mind." (Paper put in before the Governor for these demands.)

CHIEF — "I now let you know the opinions of us here. We would not wish that anyone should smile at our affairs, as we think our country is a large matter to us. If you grant us what is written on that paper, then we will talk about the reserves; we have decided in council for the benefit of those that will be born hereafter. If you do so the treaty will be finished, I believe."

GOVERNOR — "I quite agree that this is no matter to smile at. I think that the decision of to-day is one that affects yourselves and your children after, but you must recollect that this is the third time of negotiating. If we do not shake hands and make our Treaty to-day, I do not know when it will be done, as the Queen's Government will think you do not wish to treat with her. You told me that you understood that I represented the Queen's Government to you and that I opened my heart to you, but you must recollect that if *you* are a council there is another great council that governs a great Dominion, and they hold their councils the same as you hold yours. I wish to tell you that I am a servant of the Queen. I cannot do my own will; I must do hers. I can only give you what she tells me to give you. I am sorry to see that your hands were very wide open when you gave me this paper. I thought what I promised you was just, kind and fair between the Qeeen [*sic*] and you. It is now three years we have been trying to settle this matter. If we do not succeed to-day I shall go away feeling sorry for you and for your children that you could not see what was good for you and for them. I am ready to do what I promised you yesterday. My hand is open and you ought to take me by the hand and say, "yes, we accept of your offer." I have not the power to do what you ask of me. I ask you once more to think what you are doing, and of those you have left at home, and also of those that may be born yet, and I ask you not to turn your backs on what is offered to you, and you ought to see by what the Queen is offering you that she loves her red subjects as much as her white. I think you are forgetting one thing, that what I offer you is to be while the water flows and the sun rises. You know that in the United States they only pay the Indian for twenty years, and you come here to-day and ask for even more than they get for twenty years. Is that just? I think you ought to accept my offer, and make a treaty with me as I ask you to do. I only ask you to think for yourselves, and for your families, and for your children and children's children, and I know that if you do that you will shake hands with me to-day."

CHIEF — "I lay before you our opinions. Our hands are poor but our heads are rich, and it is riches that we ask so that we may be able to support our families as long as the sun rises and the water runs."

GOVERNOR — "I am very sorry; you know it takes two to make a bargain; you are agreed on the one side, and I for the Queen's Government on the other. I have to go away and report that I have to go without making terms with you. I doubt if the Commissioners will be sent again to assemble this nation."

. . . . .

CHIEF — "My terms I am going to lay down before you; the decision of our Chiefs; ever since we came to a decision you push it back. The sound of the rustling of the gold is under my feet where I stand; we have a rich country; it is the Great Spirit who gave us this; where we stand upon is the Indians' property and belongs to them. If you grant us our requests you will not go back without making the treaty."

ANOTHER CHIEF — "We understood yesterday that the Queen had given you the power to act upon, that you could do what you pleased, and that the riches of the Queen she had filled your head and body with, and you had only to throw them round about; but it seems it is not so, but that you have only half the power that she has, and that she has only half filled your head."

GOVERNOR — "I do not like to be misunderstood. I did not say yesterday that the Queen had given me all the power; what I told you was that I was sent here to represent the Queen's Government, and to tell you what the Queen was willing to do for you. You can understand very well; for instance, one of your great chiefs asks a brave to deliver a message, he represents you, and that is how I stand with the Queen's Government."

CHIEF — "It is your charitableness that you spoke of yesterday — Her Majesty's charitableness that was given you. It is our chiefs, our young men, our children and great grandchildren, and those that are to be born, that I represent here, and it is for them I ask for terms. The white man has robbed us of our riches, and we don't wish to give them up again without getting something in their place."

. . . . .

GOVERNOR — "I have told you already that I cannot grant your demands; I have not the power to do so. I have made you a liberal offer, and it is for you to accept or refuse it as you please."

CHIEF — "Our chiefs have the same opinion; they will not change their decision."

GOVERNOR — "Then the Council is at an end."

CHIEF (of Lac Seule) — "I understand the matter that he asks; if he puts a question to me as well as to the others, I say so as well as the rest. We are the first that were planted here; we would ask you to assist us with every kind of implement to use for our benefit, to enable us to perform our work; a little of everything and money. We would borrow your cattle; we ask you this for our support; I will find whereon to feed them. The waters out of which you sometimes take food for yourselves, we will lend you in return. If I should try to stop you — it is not in my power to do so; even the Hudson's Bay Company — that is a small power — I cannot gain my point with it. If you give what I ask, the time may come when I will ask you to lend me one of your daughters and one of your sons to live with us; and in return I will lend you one of my daughters and one of my sons for you to teach what is good, and after they have learned, to teach us. If you grant us what I ask, although I do not know you, I will shake hands with you. This is all I have to say."

GOVERNOR — "I have heard and I have learned something. I have learned that you are not all of one mind. I know that your interests are not the same — that some of you live in the north far away from the river; and some live on the river, and that you have got large sums of money for wood that you have cut and sold to the steamboats; but the men in the north have not this advantage. What the Chief has said is reasonable; and should you want goods I mean to ask you what amount you would have in goods, so that you would not have to pay the traders' price for them. I wish you were all of the same mind as the Chief who has just spoken. He wants his children to be taught. He is right. He wants to get cattle to help him to raise grain for his children. It would be a good thing for you all to be of his mind, and then you would not go away without making this treaty with me."

. . . . .

BLACKSTONE (Shebandowan) — "I am going to lay down before you the minds of those who are here. I do not wish to interfere with the decisions of those who are before you, or yet with your decisions. The people at the height of land where the waters came down from Shebandowan to Fort Frances, are those who have appointed me to lay before you our decision. We are going back to hold a Council."

. . . . .

GOVERNOR — "I think the nation will do well to do what the Chief has said. I think he has spoken sincerely, and it is right for them to withdraw and hold a Council among themselves."

. . . . .

The Governor decided that he would make a treaty with those bands that were willing to accept his terms, leaving out the few disaffected ones. A Council was held by the Indians in the evening ... After a very lengthy and exhaustive discussion, it was decided to accept the Governor's terms.

. . . . .

The treaty was finally closed on Friday afternoon, and signed on Saturday; after which a large quantity of provisions, ammunition and other goods were distributed.

. . . . .

The business of the treaty having now been completed, the Chief, Mawedopenais, who, with Powhassan, had with such wonderful tact carried on the negotiations, stepped up to the Governor and said: — "Now you see me stand before you all; what has been done here to-day has been done openly before the Great Spirit, and before the nation, and I hope that I may never hear any one say that this treaty has been done secretly; and now, in closing this Council, I take off my glove, and in giving you my hand, I deliver over my birth-right and lands; and in taking your hand, I hold fast all the promises you have made, and I hope they will last as long as the sun goes round and the water flows, as you have said."

The Governor then took his hand and said:

"I accept your hand and with it the lands, and will keep all my promises, in the firm belief that the treaty now to be signed will bind the red man and the white together as friends for ever."

A copy of the treaty was then prepared and duly signed, after which a large amount of presents, consisting of pork, flour, clothing, blankets, twine, powder and shot, etc., were distributed to the several bands represented on the ground.

Compare this exchange of words between Morris and the representative of the Aboriginal groups signing Treaty No. 3 with the written text of the treaty, reproduced below.

TREATY NO. 3

Between Her Majesty the Queen and the Saulteaux Tribe of the Ojibeway Indians at the northwest angle on the Lake of the Woods with adhesions

ARTICLES OF A TREATY made and concluded this third day of October, in the year of Our Lord one thousand eight hundred and seventy-three, between Her Most Gracious Majesty the Queen of Great Britain and Ireland, by Her Commissioners, the Honourable Alexander Morris, Lieutenant-Governor of the Province of Manitoba and the North-west Territories; Joseph Alfred Norbert Provencher and Simon James Dawson, of the one part, and the Saulteaux Tribe of the Ojibway Indians, inhabitants of the country within the limits hereinafter defined and described, by their Chiefs chosen and named as hereinafter mentioned, of the other part.

Whereas the Indians inhabiting the said country have, pursuant to an appointment made by the said Commissioners, been convened at a meeting at the north-west angle of the Lake of the Woods to deliberate upon certain matters of interest to Her Most Gracious Majesty, of the one part, and the said Indians of the other.

And whereas the said Indians have been notified and informed by Her Majesty's said Commissioners that it is the desire of Her Majesty to open up for settlement, immigration and such other purpose as to Her Majesty may seem meet, a tract of country bounded and described as hereinafter mentioned, and to obtain the consent thereto of Her Indian subjects inhabiting the said tract, and to make a treaty and arrange with them so that there may be peace and good will between them and Her Majesty and that they may know and be assured of what allowance they are to count upon and receive from Her Majesty's bounty and benevolence.

And whereas the Indians of the said tract, duly convened in council as aforesaid, and

being requested by Her Majesty's said Commissioners to name certain Chiefs and Headmen, who should be authorized on their behalf to conduct such negotiations and sign any treaty to be founded thereon, and to become responsible to Her Majesty for their faithful performance by their respective bands of such obligations as shall be assumed by them, the said Indians have thereupon named the following persons for that person, that is to say:—

KEK-TA-PAY-PI-NAIS (Rainy River.)
KITCHI-GAY-KAKE (Rainy River.)
NOTE-NA-QUA-HUNG (North-West Angle.)

NAWE-DO-PE-NESS (Rainy River.)
POW-WA-SANG (North-West Angle.)
CANDA-COM-IGO-WE-NINIE (North-West Angle.)
PAPA-SKO-GIN (Rainy River.)
MAY-NO-WAH-TAW-WAYS-KIONG (North-West Angle.)
KITCH-NE-KA-LE-HAN (Rainy River.)
SAH-KATCH-EWAY (Lake Seul.)
MUPA-DAY-WAH-SIN (Kettle Falls.)
ME-PIES (Rainy Lake, Fort Frances.)
OOS-CON-NA-GEITH (Rainy Lake.)
WAH-SHIS-ROUCE (Eagle Lake.)
KAH-KEE-Y-ASH (Flower Lake.)
GO-BAY (Rainy Lake.)
KA-MO-TI-ASH (White Fish Lake.)
NEE-SHO-TAL (Rainy River.)
KEE-JE-GO-KAY(Rainy River.)
SHA-SHA-GANCE (Shoal Lake.)
SHAH-WIN-NA-BI-NAIS (Shoal Lake.)
AY-ASH-A-WATH (Buffalo Point.)
PAY-AH-BEE-WASH (White Fish Bay.)
KAH-TAY-TAY-PA-E-CUTCH (Lake of the Woods.)

And thereupon, in open council the different bands having presented their Chiefs to the said Commissioners as the Chiefs and Headmen for the purposes aforesaid of the respective bands of Indians inhabiting the said district hereinafter described:

And whereas the said Commissioners then and there received and acknowledged the persons so presented as Chiefs and Headmen for the purpose aforesaid of the respective bands of Indians inhabiting the said district hereinafter described;

And whereas the said Commissioners have proceeded to negotiate a treaty with the said Indians, and the same has been finally agreed upon and concluded, as follows, that is to say:—

The Saulteaux Tribe of the Ojibbeway Indians and all other the Indians inhabiting the district hereinafter described and defined do hereby cede, release, surrender and yield up to the Government of the Dominion of Canada for Her Majesty the Queen and Her successors forever, all their rights, titles and privileges whatsoever, to the lands included within the following limits, that is to say:—

Commencing at a point on the Pigeon River route where the international boundary line between the Territories of Great Britain and the United States intersects the height of land separating the waters running to Lake Superior from those flowing to Lake Winnipeg; thence northerly, westerly and easterly along the height of land aforesaid, following its sinuosities, whatever their course may be, to the point at which the said height of land meets the summit of the watershed from which the streams flow to Lake Nepigon; thence northerly and westerly, or whatever may be its course, along the ridge separating the waters of the Nepigon and the Winnipeg to the height of land dividing the waters of the Albany and the Winnipeg; thence westerly and north-westerly along the height of land dividing the waters flowing to Hudson's Bay by the Albany or other rivers from those running to English River and the Winnipeg to a point on the said height of land bearing north forty-five degrees east from Fort Alexander, at the mouth of the Winnipeg; thence south forty-five degrees west to Fort Alexander, at the mouth of the Winnipeg; thence southerly along the eastern bank of the Winnipeg to the mouth of White Mouth River, thence southerly by the line described as in that part forming the eastern boundary of the tract surrendered by the Chippewa and Swampy Cree tribes of Indians to Her Majesty on the third of August, one thousand eight hundred and seventy-one, namely, by White Mouth River to White Mouth Lake, and thence on a line having the general bearing of White Mouth River to the forty-ninth parallel of north latitude, thence by the forty-ninth parallel of north latitude to the Lake of the Woods, and from thence by the international boundary line to the place beginning.

The tract comprised within the lines above described, embracing an area of fifty-five thousand square miles, be the same more or less. To have and to hold the same to Her Majesty the Queen, and Her successors forever.

And Her Majesty the Queen hereby agrees and undertakes to lay aside reserves for farming lands, due respect being had to lands at present cultivated by the said Indians, and also to lay aside and reserve for the benefit of the said Indians, to be administered and dealt with for them by Her Majesty's Government of the Dominion of Canada, in such a manner as shall seem best, other reserves of land in the said territory hereby ceded, which said reserves shall be selected and set aside where it shall be deemed most convenient and advantageous for each band or bands of Indians, by the officers of the said Government appointed for that purpose, and such selection shall be so made after conference with the Indians; provided, however, that such reserves, whether for farming or other purposes, shall in no wise exceed in all one square mile for each family of five, or in that proportion for larger or smaller families; and such selections shall be made if possible during the course of next summer, or as soon thereafter as may be found practicable, it being understood, however, that if at the time of any such selection of any reserve, as aforesaid, there are any settlers within the bounds of the lands reserved by any band, Her Majesty reserves the right to deal with such settlers as She shall deem just so as not to diminish the extent of land allotted to Indians; and provided also that the aforesaid reserves of lands, or any interest or right therein or appurtenant thereto, may be sold, leased or otherwise disposed of by the said Government for the use and benefit of the said Indians, with the consent of the Indians entitled thereto first had and obtained.

And with a view to show the satisfaction of Her Majesty with the behaviour and good conduct of Her Indians She hereby, through Her Commissioners, makes them a present of twelve dollars for each man, woman and child belonging to the bands here represented, in extinguishment of all claims heretofore preferred.

And further, Her Majesty agrees to maintain schools for instruction in such reserves hereby made as to Her Government of Her Dominion of Canada may seem advisable whenever the Indians of the reserve shall desire it.

Her Majesty further agrees with Her said Indians that within the boundary of Indian reserves, until otherwise determined by Her Government of the Dominion of Canada, no intoxicating liquor shall be allowed to be introduced or sold, and all laws now in force or hereafter to be enacted to preserve Her Indian subjects inhabiting the reserves or living elsewhere within Her North-west Territories, from the evil influences of the use of intoxicating liquors, shall be strictly enforced.

Her Majesty further agrees with Her said Indians that they, the said Indians, shall have right to pursue their avocations of hunting and fishing through-out the tract surrendered as hereinbefore described, subject to such regulations as may from time to time be made by Her Government of Her Dominion of Canada, and saving and excepting such tracts as may, from time to time, be required or taken up for settlement, mining, lumbering or other purposes by Her said Government of the Dominion of Canada, or by any of the subjects thereof duly authorized therefor by the said Government.

It is further agreed between Her Majesty and Her said Indians that such sections of the reserves above indicated as may at any time be required for Public Works or buildings of what nature soever may be appropriated for that purpose by Her Majesty's Government of the Dominion of Canada, due compensation being made for the value of any improvements thereon.

And further, that Her Majesty's Commissioners shall, as soon as possible after the execution of this treaty, cause to be taken an accurate census of all the Indians inhabiting the tract above described, distributing them in families, and shall in every year ensuring the date hereof at some period in each year to be duly notified to the Indians, and at a place or places to be appointed for that purpose within the territory ceded, pay to each Indian person the sum of five dollars per head yearly.

It is further agreed between Her Majesty and the said Indians that the sum of fifteen hundred dollars per annum shall be yearly and every year expended by Her Majesty in the purchase of ammunition and twine for nets for the use of the said Indians.

It is further agreed between Her Majesty and the said Indians that the following articles shall be supplied to any band of the said Indians who are now actually cultivating the soil or who shall hereafter commence to cultivate the land, that is to say: two hoes for every family actually cultivating, also one spade per family as aforesaid, one plough for every ten families as aforesaid, five harrows for every twenty families as aforesaid, one scythe for every family as aforesaid, and also one axe and one cross-cut saw, one hand-saw, one pit-saw, the necessary files, one grind-stone, one auger for each band, and also for each Chief for the use of his band one chest of ordinary carpenter's tools; also for each band enough of wheat, barley, potatoes and oats to plant the land actually broken up for cultivation by such band; also for each band one yoke of oxen, one full and four cows; all the aforesaid articles to be given once for all for the encouragement of the practice of agriculture among the Indians.

It is further agreed between Her Majesty and the said Indians that each Chief duly recognized as such shall receive an annual salary of twenty-five dollars per annum, and each, subordinate officer, not exceeding three for each band, shall receive fifteen dollars per annum; and each such Chief and subordinate officer as aforesaid shall also receive once in every three years a suitable suit of clothing; and each Chief shall receive, in recognition of the closing of the treaty, a suitable flag and medal.

And the undersigned Chiefs, on their own behalf and on behalf of all other Indians inhabiting the tract within ceded, do hereby solemnly promise and engage to strictly observe this treaty, and also to conduct and behave themselves as good and loyal subjects of Her Majesty the Queen. They promise and engage that they will in all respects obey and abide by the law, that they will maintain peace and good order between each other, and also between themselves and other tribes of Indians, and between themselves and others of Her Majesty's subjects, whether Indians or whites, now inhabiting or hereafter to inhabit any part of the said ceded tract, and that they will not molest the person or property of any inhabitants of such ceded tract, or the property of Her Majesty the Queen, or interfere with or trouble any person passing or travelling through the said tract, or any part thereof; and that they will aid and assist the officers of Her Majesty in bringing to justice and punishment any Indian offending against the stipulations of this treaty, or infringing the laws in force in the country so ceded.

IN WITNESS WHEREOF, Her Majesty's said Commissioners and the said Indian Chiefs have hereunto subscribed and set their hands at the North-West Angle of the Lake of the Woods this day and year herein first above named.

Signed by the Chiefs within named, in presence of the following witnesses, the same having been first read and explained by the Honorable James McKay.

The different understandings of the function of post-Confederation "land surrender" treaties held by the Crown and the Aboriginal peoples was not restricted to the scenario surrounding Treaty No. 3. Indeed, the disparate understanding of treaties by the Crown and the Aboriginal peoples is illustrated by the evidence led in *Paulette v. Registrar of Titles (No. 2)*(1973), 42 D.L.R. (3d) 8 (N.W.T.S.C.), rev'd on other grounds, [1976] 2 W.W.R. 193 (*sub nom. Paulette v. Register of Titles*), 63 D.L.R. (3d) 1 (N.W.T.C.A.), aff'd on other grounds (*sub nom. Paulette v. R.*), [1979] 2 S.C.R. 628, [1977] 1 W.W.R. 321, 12 N.R. 420, 72 D.L.R. (3d) 161, reproduced, *infra*, in which the effect of Treaties 8 and 11 as land surrender agreements was contemplated. Like Treaty No. 3, Treaties 8 and 11 have been implicated in a number of disputes between Aboriginal peoples and the Crown [note, for example, *R. v. Sikyea*, [1964] S.C.R. 642, 44 C.R. 266, 49 W.W.R. 306, [1965] 2 C.C.C. 129, 50 D.L.R. (2d) 80 and *R. v. Horseman*, [1990] 1 S.C.R. 901, [1990] 4 W.W.R. 97, 73 Alta. L.R. (2d) 193, 55 C.C.C. (3d) 353, 108 N.R. 1, 108 A.R. 1, [1990] 3 C.N.L.R. 95 cases, reproduced in Chapter 7]. The wording and structure of Treaties 8 and 11 take essentially the same form as Treaty No. 3, which was the blueprint for the numbered treaties that came after it.

Treaty No. 8 is notable, however, for the apparent disparity between its text and the representations made to the Aboriginal signatories documented in a report of the Treaty No. 8 Commissioners. Both Treaty No. 8 and the Commissioners' Report are excerpted below.

TREATY NO. 8

ARTICLES OF A TREATY made and concluded at the several dates mentioned therein, in the year of Our Lord one thousand eight hundred and ninety-nine, between Her most Gracious Majesty the Queen of Great Britain and Ireland, by Her Commissioners the Honourable David Laird, of Winnipeg, Manitoba, Indian Commissioner for the said Province and the Northwest Territories; James Andrew Joseph McKenna, of Ottawa, Ontario, Esquire, and the Honourable James Hamilton Ross, of Regina, in the Northwest Territories, of the one part; and the Cree, Beaver, Chipewyan and other Indians, inhabitants of the territory within the limits hereinafter defined and described, by their Chiefs and Headmen, hereunto subscribed, of the other part:—

WHEREAS, the Indians inhabiting the territory hereinafter defined have, pursuant to notice given by the Honourable Superintendent General of Indian Affairs in the year 1898, been convened to meet a Commission representing Her Majesty's Government of the Dominion of Canada at certain places in the said territory in this present year 1899, to deliberate upon certain matters of interest to Her Most Gracious Majesty, of the one part, and the said Indians of the other.

AND WHEREAS, the said Indians have been notified and informed by Her Majesty's said Commission that it is Her desire to open for settlement, immigration, trade, travel, mining, lumbering, and such other purposes as to Her Majesty may seem meet, a tract of country bounded and described as hereinafter mentioned, and to obtain the consent thereto of Her Indian subjects inhabiting the said tract, and to make a treaty, and arrange with them, so that there may be peace and good will between them and Her Majesty's other subjects, and that Her Indian people may know and be assured of what allowances they are to count upon and receive from Her Majesty's bounty and benevolence.

AND WHEREAS, the Indians of the said tract, duly convened in council at the respective points named hereunder, and being requested by Her Majesty's Commissioners to name certain Chiefs and Headmen who should be authorized on their behalf to conduct such negotiations and sign any treaty to be founded thereon, and to become responsible to Her Majesty for the faithful performance by their respective bands of such obligations as shall be assumed by them, the said Indians have therefore acknowledged for that purpose the several Chiefs and Headmen who have subscribed hereto.

AND WHEREAS, the said Commissioners have proceeded to negotiate a treaty with the Cree, Beaver, Chipewyan and other Indians, inhabiting the district hereinafter defined and described, and the same has been agreed upon and concluded by the respective bands at the dates mentioned hereunder, the said Indians DO HEREBY CEDE, RELEASE, SURRENDER AND YIELD UP to the Government of the Dominion of Canada, for Her Majesty the Queen and Her successors for every, all their rights, duties and privileges whatsoever, to the lands included within the following limits, that is to say:—

Commencing at the source of the main branch of the Red Deer River in Alberta, thence due west to the central range of the Rocky Mountains, thence northwesterly along the said range to the point where it intersects the 60th parallel of north latitude, thence east along said parallel to the point where it intersects Hay River, thence northeasterly down said river to the south shore of Great Slave Lake, thence along the said shore north-easterly (and including such rights to the islands in said lakes as the Indians mentioned in the treaty may possess), and thence easterly and north-easterly along the south shores of Christie's Bay and McLeod's Bay to old Fort Reliance near the mouth of Lockhart's River, thence southeasterly in a straight line to and including Black Lake, thence southwesterly up the stream from Cree Lake, thence including said Lake southwesterly along the height of land between the Athabasca and Churchill Rivers to where it intersects the northern boundary of Treaty Six, and along the said boundary easterly, northerly and southwesterly, to the place of commencement.

AND ALSO the said Indian rights, titles and privileges whatsoever to all other lands wherever situated in the Northwest Territories, British Columbia, or in any other portion of the Dominion of Canada.

To HAVE AND TO HOLD the same to Her Majesty the Queen and Her successors for ever.

And Her Majesty the Queen HEREBY AGREES with the said Indians that they shall have right to pursue their usual vocations of hunting, trapping and fishing throughout the tract surrendered as heretofore described, subject to such regulations as may from time to time be made by the Government of the country, acting under the authority of Her Majesty, and saving and excepting such tracts as may be required or taken up from time to time for settlement, mining, lumbering, trading or other purposes.

And Her Majesty the Queen hereby agrees and undertakes to lay aside reserves for such bands as desire reserves, the same not to exceed in all one square mile for each family of five for such number of families as may elect to reside on reserves, or in that proportion for larger or smaller families; and for such families or individual Indians as may prefer to live apart from band reserves, Her Majesty undertakes to provide land in severalty to the extent of 160 acres to each Indian, the land to be conveyed with a proviso as to non-alienation without the consent of the Governor General in Council of Canada, the selection of such reserves, and lands in severalty, to be made in the manner following, namely, the Superintendent General of Indian Affairs shall depute and send a suitable person to determine and set apart such reserves and lands, after consulting with the Indians concerned as to the locality which may be found suitable and open for selection.

Provided, however, that Her Majesty reserves the right to deal with any settlers within the bounds of any lands reserved for any band as She may see fit; and also that the aforesaid reserves of land, or any interest therein, may be sold or otherwise disposed of by Her Majesty's Government for the use and benefit of the said Indians entitled thereto, with their consent first had and obtained.

It is further agreed between Her Majesty and Her said Indian subjects that such portions of the reserves and lands above indicated as may at any time be required for public works, building, railways, or roads of whatsoever nature may be appropriated for that purpose by Her Majesty's Government of the Dominion of Canada, due compensation being made to the Indians for the value of any improvements thereon, and an equivalent in land, money or other consideration for the area of the reserve so appropriated.

And with a view to show the satisfaction of Her Majesty with the behaviour and good conduct of Her Indians, and in extinguishment of all their past claims, She hereby, through Her Commissioners, agrees to make each Chief a present of thirty-two dollars in cash, to each Headman twenty-two dollars, and to every other Indian of whatever age, of the families represented at the time and place of payment, twelve dollars.

Her Majesty also agrees that next year, and annually afterwards for ever, She will cause to be paid to the said Indians in cash, at suitable places and dates, of which the said Indians shall be duly notified, to each Chief twenty-five dollars, each Headman, not to exceed four to a large Band and two to a small Band, fifteen dollars, and to every other Indian, of whatever age, five dollars, the same, unless there be some exceptional reason, to be paid only to heads of families for those belonging thereto.

FURTHER, Her Majesty agrees that each Chief, after signing the treaty, shall receive a silver medal and a suitable flag, and next year, and every third year thereafter, each Chief and Headman shall receive a suitable suit of clothing.

Further, Her Majesty agrees to pay the salaries of such teachers to instruct the children of said Indians as to Her Majesty's Government of Canada may seem advisable.

FURTHER, Her Majesty agrees to supply each Chief of a Band that selects a reserve, for the use of that Band, ten axes, five hand-saws, five augers, one grindstone, and the necessary files and whetstones.

FURTHER, Her Majesty agrees that each Band that elects to take a reserve and cultivate the soil, shall as soon as convenient after such reserve is set aside and settled upon, and the Band has signified its choice and is prepared to break up the soil, receive two hoes, one spade, one scythe and two hay forks for every family so settled, and for every three families one plough and one harrow, and to the Chief, for the use of his Band, two horses or a yoke of oxen, and for each Band potatoes, barley, oats and wheat (if such seed be suited to the locality of the reserve), to plant the land actually broken up, and provisions for one month in the spring for several years while planting such seeds; and to every family one cow, and every Chief one bull, and one mowing-machine and one reaper for the use of his Band when it is ready for them; for such families as prefer to raise stock instead of cultivating the soil, every family of five persons, two cows, and every Chief two bulls and two mowing-machines when ready for their use, and a like proportion for smaller or larger families. The aforesaid articles, machines and cattle to be given one for all for the encouragement of agriculture and stock raising; and for such Bands as prefer to continue hunting and fishing, as much ammunition and twine for making nets annually as will amount in value to one dollar per head of the families so engaged in hunting and fishing.

And the undersigned Cree, Beaver, Chipewyan and other Indian Chiefs and Headmen, on their own behalf and on behalf of all the Indians whom they represent, DO HEREBY SOLEMNLY PROMISE and engage to strictly observe this Treaty, and also to conduct and behave themselves as good and loyal subjects of Her Majesty the Queen.

THEY PROMISE AND ENGAGE that they will, in all respects, obey and abide by the law; that they will maintain peace between each other, and between themselves and other tribes of Indians, and between themselves and others of Her Majesty's subjects, whether Indians, halfbreeds or whites, this year inhabiting and hereafter to inhabit any part of the said ceded territory; and that they will not molest the person or property of any inhabitant of such ceded tract, or of any other district or country, or inter-fere with or trouble any person passing or travelling through the said tract or any part thereof, and that they will assist the officers of Her Majesty in bringing to justice and punishment any Indian offending against the stipulations of this Treaty or infringing the law in force in the country so ceded.

IN WITNESS WHEREOF Her Majesty's said Commissioners and the Cree Chief and Headmen of Lesser Slave Lake and the adjacent territory, HAVE HEREUNTO SET THEIR HANDS at Lesser Slave Lake on the twenty-first day of June, in the year herein first above written.

Signed by the parties hereto, in the presence of the undersigned wit-nesses, the same having been first explained to the Indians by Albert Tate and Samuel Cunningham, Interpreters.

Compare the text of Treaty No. 8 with the representations made to the In-dian signatories by the treaty commissioners, as recorded in the following report.

REPORT OF COMMISSIONERS FOR TREATY NO. 8, 22ND SEPTEMBER, 1899

The Honourable CLIFFORD SIFTON, Superintendent General of Indian Affairs, Ottawa

SIR, —We have the honour to transmit herewith the treaty which, under the Commission issued to us on the 5th day of April last, we have made with the Indians of the provisional district of Athabasca and parts of the country adjacent thereto.

We met the Indians on the 20th, and on the 21st the treaty was signed.

As the discussions at the different points followed on much the same lines, we shall confine ourselves to a general statement of their import. ... There was expressed at every point the fear that the making of the treaty would be followed by the curtailment of the hunting and fishing privi-leges, and many were impressed with the notion that the treaty would lead to taxation and enforced military service. They seemed desirous of securing educational advantages for their children, but stipulated that in the matter of schools there should be no interference with their religious beliefs.

We pointed out that the Government could not undertake to maintain Indians in idleness; that the same means of earning a livelihood would continue after the treaty as existed before it, and that the Indians would be expected to make use of them. ... We promised that supplies of medicines would be put in the charge of persons selected by the Government at different points, and would be distributed free to those of the Indians who might require them. We explained that it would be practically impossible for the Government to arrange for regular medical attendance upon Indians so widely scattered over such an extensive territory. We assured them, however, that the Government would always be ready to avail itself of any opportunity of affording medical service just as it provided that the physician attached to the Commission should give free attendance to all Indians whom he might find in need of treatment as he passed through the country.

Our chief difficulty was the apprehension that the hunting and fishing privileges were to be curtailed. The provision in the treaty under which ammunition and twine is to be furnished went far in the direction of quieting the fears of the Indians, for they admitted that it would be unreasonable to furnish the means of hunting and fishing if laws were to be enacted which would make hunting and fishing so restricted as to render it impossible to make a livelihood by such pursuits. But over and above the provision, we had to solemnly assure them that only such laws as to hunting and fishing as were in the interest of the Indians and were found necessary in order to protect the fish and fur-bearing animals would be made, and that they would be as free to hunt and fish after the treaty as they would be if they never entered into it.

We assured them that the treaty would not lead to any forced interference with their mode of life, that it did not open the way to the imposition of any tax, and that there was no fear of forced military service. We showed them that whether treaty was made or not, they were subject to the law, bound to obey it, and liable to punishment for any infringements of it.

. . . . .

As to education, the Indians were assured that there was no need of any special stipulation, as it was the policy of the Government to provide in every part of the country, as far as circumstances would permit, for the education of Indian children, and that the law, which was as strong as a treaty, provided for non-interference with the religion of the Indians in schools maintained or assisted by the Government.

. . . . .

The Indians are given the option of taking reserves or land in severalty. As the extent of the country treated for made it impossible to define reserves or holdings, and as the Indians were not prepared to make selections, we confined ourselves to an undertaking to have reserves and holdings set apart in the future, and the Indians were satisfied with the promise that this would be done when required. There is no immediate necessity for the general laying out of reserves or the allotting of land. It will be quite time enough to do this as advancing settlement makes necessary the surveying of the land. Indeed, the Indians were generally averse to being placed on reserves. It would have been impossible to have made a treaty if we had not assured them that there was no intention of confining them to reserves. We had to very clearly explain to them that the provision for reserves and allotments of land were made for their protection, and to secure to them in perpetuity a fair portion of the land ceded, in the event of settlement advancing.

Treaty No. 11, which was concluded on 27 June 1921, with an adhesion on 17 July of that same year, between the Crown and the Slave, Dogrib, Loucheux, Hare and other Indians, was virtually identical to Treaty No. 8, save for the territory covered, the deletion of the option for the signatories to hold land in severalty and, in the place of the provision of agricultural implements, etc. the following inclusions:

> FURTHER, His Majesty agrees that, each band shall receive once and for all equipment for hunting, fishing and trapping to the value of fifty dollars for each family of such band, and that there shall be distributed annually among the Indians equipment, such as twine for nets, ammunition and trapping to the value of three dollars per head for each Indian who continues to follow the vocation of hunting, fishing and trapping.
>
> FURTHER, His Majesty agrees that, in the event of any of the Indians aforesaid being desirous of following agricultural pursuits, such Indians shall receive such assistance as is deemed necessary for that purpose.

The Treaty Commissioner's report for Treaty No. 11, as with the report accompanying Treaty No. 8, revealed additional information about the Aboriginals' concerns about signing the treaty and the effect that it would have upon them. Of these concerns, Commissioner H.A. Conroy wrote:

> I had several meetings with them, and explained the terms of the treaty. They were very apt in asking questions, and here, as in all the other posts where the treaty was signed, the questions asked and the difficulties encountered were much the same. The Indians seemed afraid, for one thing, that their liberty to hunt, trap and fish would be taken away or curtailed, but were assured by me that this would not be the case, and the Government will expect them to support themselves in their own way, and, in fact, that more twine for nets and more ammunition were given under the terms of this treaty than under any of the preceding ones; this went a long way to calm their fears. I also pointed out that any game laws made were to their advantage, and, whether they took treaty or not, they were subject to the laws of the Dominion. They also seemed afraid that they would be liable for military service if the treaty was signed, that they would be confined on the reserves, but, when told that they were exempt from military service, and that the reserves mentioned in the treaty would be of their own choosing, for their own use, and not for the white people, and that they would be free to come and go as they pleased, they were satisfied.

What is the relationship between a Treaty Commissioners' Report and the treaty that it corresponds to? Should the text of a Treaty Commissioners' Report be understood as part of a treaty? If not, what weight should it be given *vis-à-vis* the written treaty, if any?

These Treaty Commissioners' Reports reveal that the written text of Crown-Native treaties does not always accurately reflect the nature of the representations made by the Crown or the entirety of the agreement between the parties. This is illustrated as well by the judicial reception of Aboriginal oral history, an early example of which is seen in the *Paulette* case, excerpted below.

In *Paulette*, which was heard in 1973, Justice Morrow of the Northwest Territories Supreme Court received a significant amount of oral evidence from the Aboriginal peoples involved in the dispute. Morrow J.'s decision is interesting not only for its illustration of Aboriginal understandings of the purpose and effect of the treaties, but for its wholesale incorporation of these sentiments in his written reasons for judgment, something that had been infrequently done previously.

PAULETTE v. REGISTRAR OF TITLES (NO. 2)

(1973), 42 D.L.R. (3d) 8 at 14, [1973] 6 W.W.R. 97 (N.W.T. S.C.); rev'd on other grounds, [1976] 2 W.W.R. 193 (*sub nom. Paulette v. Register of Titles*), 63 D.L.R. (3d) 1 (N.W.T.C.A.); aff'd on other grounds (*sub nom. Paulette v. R.*) [1979] 2 S.C.R. 628, [1977] 1 W.W.R. 321, 12 N.R. 420, 72 D.L.R. (3d) 161

. . . . .

Morrow J.: — Chief Baptiste Cazon, chief of the Fort Simpson Band for some 20 years explained how the members of the present band at Fort Simpson were all descendants from his great-grandfather and that while his people had no written history, as far back as their memories down through each generation could go, his people had made their homes in the general area of Fort Simpson and that such lands had always been considered to be theirs. According to him, for thousands of years, his people had used the land for hunting and fishing, to obtain food and clothing. They roamed all over the country in pursuit of game. He explained that in his capacity as chief, he considered he had a responsibility to his people to take the place of their and his ancestors who had signed the treaty. There are still quite a few of his people even at this time who earn their living from the land in the time-honoured way.

. . . . .

Alexie Arrowmaker, chief at Fort Rae . . . stated that his people, the Dogribs, had never sold their land to anyone.

. . . . .

The chief of the Loucheux Band at Aklavik, Andrew Stewart, described pretty much the same state of affairs in respect of the Indians of his area as has been set forth above. About 12 years old at the time of the treaty he explained he had never heard any of the old people say they had given up their land to the Government.

Louis Norwegian, 64 years of age, was present at Fort Simpson in 1921 when "old" Norwegian as he describes his grandfather, was leader of the Fort Simpson Band and when the treaty was first "paid". He overheard some of the exchange of words between his grandfather and the Government representatives. According to this witness the Commissioner promised a letter on fishing and trapping. When his grandfather, the recognized leader, went home to eat, an Indian by the name of Antoine was left. He took the treaty and became the chief — the white men made him the chief. This man's evidence was to the effect that his grandfather "did not want to the take the money for no reason at all". The promises made that their hunting and fishing would be left to them as long as the sun shall rise and the rivers shall flow. He heard no mention of reserves but he did hear mention that once they took treaty the Government would receive the land. His memory was that the purpose of the treaty was to help the Indians live in peace with the whites and that the Indians would receive a grubstake each treaty payment. Once Antoine took the money, this witness testified the Commissioner said everybody had to take the treaty after that, Antoine was given a medal, the people took the money, and the people being "kind of scared" felt they had to keep Antoine on as chief after that.

Chief Vital Bonnetrouge, chief of the Fort Providence Band ... added a little more to the attitude of the people at the time the treaty was signed. As he states: "the land was not mentioned at the treaty. The old chief said "if this five dollars would be for my land, I am not taking it." This witness, by his testimony, left one with the same impression that came from the stories told by so many, namely, it was a deal to look after the people and nothing else.

. . . . .

Those Indians who had either taken part in the treaty negotiations or who had been present while the negotiations were under way and heard parts or all of the conversation, seemed to be in general agreement that their leaders were concerned about what they were giving up, if anything, in exchange for the treaty money, *i.e.*, they were suspicious of something for nothing; that up to the time of treaty the concept of chief was unknown to them, only that of leader, but the Government man was the one who introduced them to the concept of chief when he placed the medal over the Indian's head after he had signed for his people; that they understood that by signing the treaty they would get a grubstake, money, and the promised protection of the Government from the expected intrusion of white settlers. It is clear also that the Indians for the most part did not understand English and certainly there is no evidence of any of the signatories to the treaties understanding English. Some signatures purport to be what one would call a signature, some are in syllabic form, but most are by mark in the form of an "X". The similarity of the "X"s is suggestive that perhaps the Government party did not even take care to have each Indian make his own "X". Most witnesses were firm in their recollection that land was not to be surrendered, reserves were not mentioned, and the main concern and chief thrust of the discussions centred around the fear of losing their hunting and fishing rights, the Government officials always reassuring them with variations of the phrase that so long as the sun shall rise in the east and set in the west, and the rivers shall flow, their free right to hunt and fish would not be interfered with.

It seems also that very little if any reference to a map was made at any of the settlements. In several cases, also, it is apparent that fairly large segments of the Indian community were not present on the occasion of the first treaty and that the recognized leaders of the respective bands were not always there either.

. . . . .

An Order in Council of January 26, 1891 (never acted upon apparently according to Father Fumoleau's evidence), contained the following paragraph:

> On a Report dated 7th of January 1891, from the Superintendent General of Indian Affairs stating that the discovery in the District of Athabaska and in the Mackenzie River Country that immense quantities of petroleum exists within certain areas of those regions as well as the belief that other minerals and substances of economic value, such as sulphur on the South Coast of Great Slave Lake and Salt on the Mackenzie and Slave Rivers, are to be found therein, the development of which may add materially to the public weal, and the further consideration that several Railway projects in connection with this portion of the Dominion may be given effect to at no such remote date as might be supposed, appear to render it advisable that a treaty or treaties should be made with the Indians who claim those regions as their hunting grounds, with a view to the extinguishment of the Indian title in such portions of the same as it may be considered in the interest of the public to open up for settlement.

A second Order in Council enacted June 27, 1898, contains pretty much the same language in respect to "aboriginal title" and as to how the inhabitants "should be treated with for the relinquishment of their claim to territorial ownership".

The above language is repeated in the Order in Council of December 6, 1898, which deals with the extension of Treaty 8 into British Columbia. Finally on March 3, 1921, the Order in Council which authorized the negotiation of Treaty 11 contains the paragraph:

> The early development of this territory is anticipated and it is advisable to follow the usual policy and obtain from the Indians cession of their aboriginal title and thereby bring them into closer relation with the Government and establish securely their legal position.

Unless, therefore, the negotiation of Treaty 8 and Treaty 11 legally terminated or extinguished the Indian land rights or aboriginal rights, it would appear that there was a clear constitutional obligation to protect the legal rights of the indigenous people in the area covered by the proposed caveat, and a clear recognition of such rights.

5. *Treaty 8 and Treaty 11 could not legally terminate Indian land rights. The Indian people did not understand or agree to the terms appearing in the writ-*

*ten version of the treaties, only the mutually understood promises relating to
wild life, annuities, relief and friendship became legally effective committ-
ments.*

. . . . .

In the light of the evidence which was adduced during the present
hearing it is perhaps of interest to quote H. A. Conroy, the Treaty 11
Commissioner, where in his report to his Deputy Superintendent General,
Department of Indian Affairs, he states:

> They were very apt in asking questions, and here, as in all the other posts
> where the treaty was signed, the questions asked and the difficulties en-
> countered were much the same. The Indians seemed afraid, for one thing,
> that their liberty to hunt, trap and fish would be taken away or curtailed, but
> were assured by me that this would not be the case.

While the important phrase in respect to surrender of the land is in each
case camouflaged to some extent by being included in one of the pream-
bles, none the less the clear intention would seem to be to obtain from the
Indians "all their rights, titles and privileges whatsoever, to the lands . . .".
The actual words are: "the said Indians Do HEREBY CEDE, RELEASE,
SURRENDER AND YIELD UP". Read in conjunction with "all their rights,
titles and privileges" it is about as complete and all-embracing language as
can be imagined. If one was to stop there, of course, the Indians were left
nothing.

It seems to me that there are two possible qualifications:

(1) That really all the Government did was confirm its paramount title
and by assuring the Indians that "their liberty to hunt, trap and fish"
was not to be taken away or curtailed was in effect a form of declaration by the Government of continuing aboriginal rights in the Indians.

. . . . .

I am satisfied here that the Caveators have an arguable case under this
heading and have at least the possibility of persuading the Federal Court
or whichever other Court may be called upon to rule, that the two treaties
are not effective instruments to terminate their aboriginal rights for the
above reason. In other words the federal Government sought these treaties
to reassure their dominant title only.

(2) That, unlike perhaps the previous treaties, the manner of negotiation,
the "ultimatum" effect of the discussions between the parties in the
Northwest Territories was such as to make it possible for the Caveators to succeed in persuading a Court exercising the final say on these
matters that there was either a failure in the meeting of the minds or
that the treaties were mere "peace" treaties and did not effectively
terminate Indian title — certainly to the extent it covered what is normally referred to as surface rights — the use of the land for hunting,
trapping and fishing.

Under this subheading it is necessary to examine the evidence in somewhat closer detail than has been done heretofore in this judgment.

Throughout the hearings before me there was a common thread in the testimony — that the Indians were repeatedly assured they were not to be deprived of their hunting, fishing and trapping rights. To me, hearing the witnesses at first hand as I did, many of whom were there at the signing, some of them having been directly involved in the treaty making, it is almost unbelievable that the Government party could have ever returned from their efforts with any impression but that they had given an assurance in perpetuity to the Indians in the territories that their traditional use of the lands was not affected.

Ted Trindle, present at the signing of Treaty 11 at Fort Simpson, said:

> Well, they talked about land and the Indians were scared that by taking Treaty they would lose all of their rights but the Indians were told not, but if they were taking treaty they would get protection. They were told it was not to get the land but they would still be free to hunt and roam as usual, no interference.

At Fort Wrigley, Phillip Moses remembers that the Commissioner "said nothing would be changed, everything would be the same as way back, and everything would be the same in the future . . . ".

Pretty much the same assurance came at Fort Resolution. When Chief Snuff appeared to be holding out, according to Johnny Jean-Marie Beaulieu, who was there, he was told by the Treaty party: "we will pay out the Treaty to you here and it has no binding on your land or country at all. It has nothing to do with this land."

Almost each Indian witness affirmed how the Indian representatives only signed after being reassured that as one expressed it "If you don't change anything, we will take treaty."

As if the above was not enough, further examination of the evidence, including the material from the archives put in through Father Fumoleau, certainly leaves an impression of haste, almost an "ultimatum" as Bishop Breynat later reported. The uneasy feeling that the negotiations were not all as above-board as one would have hoped for is enhanced by statements like that of Pierre Michel who reported that at Fort Providence the Commissioner said: ". . . if didn't take money, there going to be some sort of trouble for the Indian people".

The comments of Mr. Harris in his report in 1925 for the Simpson Agency lends some credence to the anxiety. He reports:

> I believe it to be my duty to inform you that I know that certain promises were made these Indians at the first Treaty which in my opinion never should have been made. The Indians at Fort Simpson did not wish to accept the Treaty at first, and I think the wisest course would have been to let them alone till they asked for it themselves, though I do not in any way wish to criticise the action of my superiors in the Department.

Confirmation of haste and perhaps irregularities is easy to find from the suggestion put forth during the hearing that at Fort Simpson when the Indians led by Old Norwegian (their recognized spokesman) refused to sign and left, the Treaty party then appointed Antoine as chief and the treaty was signed. Again there is the testimony of Chief Yendo, who is shown as having signed for Fort Wrigley, but who has no memory of having signed and swears he cannot read or write.

The impracticability of expecting the indigenous peoples with whom the treaties were concerned here to be able to sustain themselves on the area of land each was to receive when reserves came to be allocated and set aside offers one more reason to suspect the *bona fides* of the negotiations. Perhaps the extreme south-western area might permit a bare subsistence living to be grubbed from the soil, but most of the area embraced by the treaties is as already described — rock, lake and tundra — with hunting, trapping and fishing offering the only viable method of maintaining life.

In examining agreements such as treaties where as in the present case one side, the Indians, were in such an inferior bargaining position, it is perhaps well to remember the cautionary words of Mr. Justice Matthews in *Choctaw Nation v. United States* (1886), 119 U.S. 1, where, at p. 28, he said:

> The recognized relation between the parties to this controversy, therefore, is that between a superior and an inferior, whereby the latter is placed under the care and control of the former, and which, while it authorizes the adoption on the part of the United States of such policy as their own public interests may dictate, recognizes, on the other hand, such an interpretation of their acts and promises as justice and reason demand in all cases where power is exerted by the strong over those to whom they owe care and protection. The parties are not on an equal footing, and that inequality is to be made good by the superior justice which looks only to the substance of the right, without regard to technical rules framed under a system of municipal jurisprudence, formulating the rights and obligations of private persons, equally subject to the same laws.

Justice Hall in *Calder et al. v. A.-G. B.C.* (1973), 34 D.L.R. (3d) 145 at p. 210, [1973] S.C.R. 313, [1973] 4 W.W.R. 1, in discussing onus, states:

> It would, accordingly, appear to be beyond question that the onus of proving that the Sovereign intended to extinguish the Indian title lies on the respondent and that intention must be "clear and plain". There is no such proof in the case at bar; no legislation to that effect.

With the above principle in mind I conclude under this heading that there is enough doubt as to whether the full aboriginal title had been extinguished, certainly in the minds of the Indians, to justify the Caveators attempting to protect the Indian position until a final adjudication can be obtained.

It has been shown that the Crown and the Aboriginal peoples did not always enter into treaty relations with common purposes or intentions. This reality was not necessarily recognized by the parties at the time. Combining this fact with the differences in the world views held by the parties — as evidenced, in part, by the disparate understandings of land discussed in Chapter 1 — resulted in the treaties being interpreted differently by the parties. This lack of uniformity in interpreting the purpose and effect of treaties has had significant effects on Canadian treaty jurisprudence. In the following excerpt, the duality of Crown-Native treaties is regarded in terms of the potential effects of those treaties.

PATRICK MACKLEM, "FIRST NATIONS SELF-GOVERNMENT AND THE BORDERS OF THE CANADIAN LEGAL IMAGINATION"

(1991) 36 McGill L.J. 382 at 425 (references omitted)

Though each is unique in its terms and scope of application, and apart from a few early peace and friendship treaties, virtually every treaty entered into by the Crown and native people involves the surrender of ancestral lands in return for certain benefits to be provided by state authorities. Treaties thus simultaneously frustrate and facilitate the aspiration of native peoples to have more control over their individual and collective destinies. On the one hand, the fact that the Crown has entered into agreements that have been held to deprive native people of their historic connection to their ancestral lands and involve the relocation of native people to reserves is a source of profound disempowerment. However much it may vary from context to context, the aspiration to self-government is inextricably tied to native peoples' relationship to ancestral lands. The severing of such a relationship through surrender and the relocation of native peoples to reserves has had a devastating effect on native peoples' ability to maintain native forms of life. On the other hand, treaties contain positive elements and entitlements for native people which, if read sympathetically, could facilitate the realization of self-government. The act of surrender, for example, need not be interpreted by reference to traditional Anglo-Canadian understandings of title transfers. A surrender need not be read as conveying an absolute right of exclusion and as automatically stripping native people of continued use and enjoyment of the land in question. Instead, a surrender could be viewed as the granting of consent to a system of priority of use, whereby native people, in return for benefits provided by the Crown, agree either that non-native use or native use will have priority in the event of a conflict between uses. When there is no conflict in use, namely, where one party can engage in activity that does not threaten the use put to the land by the other party enjoying priority, the act of surrender need not foreclose native use and enjoyment. The content of treaties also provides moments of possibility for the realization of aspects of self-government. The promise to maintain a school and a medicine chest on reserve lands in Treaty Six, for example, potentially binds the Crown to provide complete funding for educational and medical services to those covered by its terms. Judicial interpretation of treaties between the Crown and native peoples in Canada thus is critical to the success or failure of treaties to serve as instruments of self-government.

F.   MODERN CANADIAN TREATY JURISPRUDENCE – BEGINNING A NEW PROCESS OF INTERPRETATION

As indicated by the introductory quote to this chapter made by Justice M'Lean in *Worcester v. State of Georgia*, early American Aboriginal rights jurisprudence recognized the need to avoid interpreting treaties in a literal fashion. While this principle had become well-entrenched in American jurisprudence before the end of the 19th century, it did not achieve the same recognition in Canada for almost 150 years.

The traditional approach of interpreting treaties literally truly began to change in Canada in the second half of the 20th century. The case of *R. v. White and Bob*, was an early example of this change in judicial approach to treaty interpretation.

R. v. WHITE and BOB

(1964), 50 D.L.R. (2d) 613, 52 W.W.R. 193 (B.C.C.A.); aff'd. (1965), 52 D.L.R. (2d) 481*n* (S.C.C.)

Davey J.A.: — The Crown appeals from the respondents' acquittal by Swencisky, Co. Ct. J., on their appeal to him from their summary conviction by L. Beevor-Potts, Esq., P.M. of having game, namely, the carcasses of six deer, in their possession during the closed season without having a valid and subsisting permit under the *Game Act*, contrary to the provisions of that Act. The *Game Act* is an Act of the Provincial Legislature, R.S.B.C. 1960, c. 160.

The Crown concedes that if the respondents, who are native Indians, had a legal right to hunt for food for themselves and their families over the lands in question, they were lawfully in possession of the carcasses, no permit was required, and they were not guilty of the offence.

Section 18 of the *Game Act* forbids any person to kill deer except in open season, subject to certain specified exceptions within which the respondents do not fall. They contend that an agreement (ex. 8) between their ancestors, members of the Saalequun tribe, and Governor Douglas, dated December 23, 1854, for the sale of the land to the Hudson's Bay Company, gave them the right to hunt for food over the land in question and, alternatively, that as native Indians they possess the aboriginal right to hunt for food over unoccupied land lying within their ancient tribal hunting grounds.

For the purposes of this appeal it must be taken that the respondents are native Indians, members of the Saalequun tribe, and descendants of the members who signed ex. 8; that they killed the deer on unoccupied land comprised in the sale to the Hudson's Bay Co., and forming part of the ancient hunting grounds of the tribe, for the purpose of providing food for themselves and their families.

It is common ground that ex. 8 must be taken to include the following clause appearing in all other transfers of Vancouver Island Indian land, which, for reasons that need not be mentioned, does not appear in this instrument:

The condition of, or understanding of this sale, is this, that our village sites and enclosed fields, are to be kept for our own use, for the use of our children, and for those who may follow after us, and the lands shall be properly surveyed hereafter; it is understood however, that the land itself with these small exceptions, becomes the entire property of the white people forever, it is also understood that we are at liberty to hunt over the unoccupied lands, and to carry on our fisheries as formerly.

The Crown does not deny that the respondents are entitled to exercise and enjoy whatever rights or privileges there may be under ex. 8 until they have been effectively extinguished. It does contend that ex. 8 conferred no hunting rights, and if it did, that these rights have been extinguished by s. 87 of the *Indian Act*, R.S.C. 1952, c. 149, [now s. 88] first enacted in 1951, which the Crown says extends in effect the general provisions of the *Game Act* to Indians.

Section 87 reads as follows:

87. Subject to the terms of any treaty and any other Act of the Parliament of Canada, all laws of general application from time to time in force in any province are applicable to and in respect of Indians in the province, except to the extent that such laws are inconsistent with this Act or any order, rule, regulation or by-law made thereunder, and except to the extent that such laws make provision for any matter for which provision is made by or under this Act.

The Crown submits that ex. 8 does not fall within the prefatory saving clause of s. 87 because:

(1) Exhibit 8 did not create any hunting rights but merely recognized pre-existing privileges; that the alleged hunting rights were mere liberties which formed part of the aboriginal rights of the Indians over the soil, and that they existed when Vancouver Island became British territory, and continued until extinguished or abolished by valid legislation; that the saving clause refers only to rights created by Treaties.
(2) That even if ex. 8 did create or recognize rights that could be the subject of a Treaty within the meaning of the saving clause, the document is not such a Treaty.

The force of the first argument seems to depend upon the assumption that s. 87 should be read as if it were subject only to rights created by a Treaty; that would remove from the saving clause rights already in being and excepted from or confirmed by a Treaty. That argument fails to accord full meaning to the words, "subject to the *terms* of any treaty . . ." In my opinion an exception, reservation, or confirmation is as much a term of a Treaty as a grant, (I observe parenthetically that a reservation may be a grant), and the operative words of the section will not extend general laws in force in any Province to Indians in derogation of rights so excepted, reserved or confirmed.

Counsel for the Crown next submits that ex. 8 is not a Treaty. He contends that a Treaty within s. 87 is:

(1) A document that on its face is so described or one that uses that word in the text, and,

(2) deals with fundamental differences between the parties (quaere, political differences?) and not merely with private rights, such as in this case the sale of land, and,

(3) a formal document in which the terms are set out with some degree of formality, and,

(4) an agreement to which the Crown is a party, or which it has authorized one of the parties to make on its behalf.

Counsel submits that ex. 8 meets none of these requirements.

It is unnecessary to venture any extended definition of the word "Treaty" in this context, but it can be safely said that it does not mean an "executive act establishing relationships between what are recognized as two or more independent states acting in sovereign capacities . . .", per Rand, J., in *Francis v. The Queen* . ... It is also clear in my opinion that the word is not used in its widest sense as including agreements between individuals dealing with their private and personal affairs. Its meaning lies between those extremes.

. . . . .

In considering whether ex. 8 is a Treaty within the meaning of s. 87, regard ought to be paid to the history of our country: its original occupation and settlement; the fact that the Hudson's Bay Co. was the proprietor, and to use a feudal term contained in its charters, the Lord of the lands in the Northwest Territories and Vancouver Island; and, the part that company played in the settlement and development of this country. In the Charter granting Vancouver Island to the Hudson's Bay Co., it was charged with the settlement and colonization of that Island. That was clearly part of the Imperial policy to head off American settlement of and claims to the territory. In that sense the Hudson's Bay Co. was an instrument of Imperial policy. It was also the long standing policy of the Imperial government and of the Hudson's Bay Co. that the Crown or the company should buy from the Indians their land for settlement by white colonists. In pursuance of that policy many agreements, some very formal, others informal, were made with various bands and tribes of Indians for the purchase of their lands. These agreements frequently conferred upon the grantors hunting rights over the unoccupied lands so sold. Considering the relationship between the Crown and the Hudson's Bay Co. in the colonization of this country, and the Imperial and corporate policies reflected in those agreements, I cannot regard ex. 8 as a mere agreement for the sale of land made between a private vendor and a private purchaser. In view of the notoriety of these facts, I entertain no doubt that Parliament intended the word "Treaty" in s. 87 to include all such agreements, and to except their provisions from the operative part of the section. That being so, s. 87 does not extend the general provisions of the *Game Act* to the respondents in the exercise of their hunting rights under ex. 8 over the lands in question.

We have been referred to no other Act of Parliament or The Colonial Legislature that would have the effect of abrogating or curtailing the respondents' rights under ex. 8, and the only provincial legislation that might to do so is the *Game Act* itself.

Sections 8 [rep. & sub. 1961, c. 21, s. 3] and 15 [rep. & sub. 1961, c. 21, s. 6] of the *Game Act* specifically exempt Indians from the operation of certain provisions of the Act, and from that I think it clear that the other provisions are intended to be of general application and to include Indians. If these general sections are sufficiently clear to show an intention to abrogate or qualify the contractual rights of hunting notoriously reserved to Indians by agreements such as ex. 8 they would, in my opinion, fail in that purpose because that would be legislation in relation to Indians that falls within Parliament's exclusive legislative authority under s. 91(24) of the *B.N.A. Act*, and also because that would conflict with s. 87 of the *Indian Act* passed under that authority. Legislation that abrogates or abridges the hunting rights reserved to Indians under the treaties and agreements by which they sold their ancient territories to the Crown and to the Hudson's Bay Company for white settlement is, in my respectful opinion, legislation in relation to Indians because it deals with rights peculiar to them. Lord Watson's judgment in *St. Catherine's Milling & Lumber Co. v. The Queen* (1888), 58 L.J.P.C. 54, if any authority is needed, makes that clear. At p. 60 he observed that the plain policy of the *B.N.A. Act* is to vest legislative control over Indian affairs generally in one central authority. On the same page he spoke of Parliament's exclusive power to regulate the Indians' privilege of hunting and fishing. In my opinion, their peculiar rights of hunting and fishing over their ancient hunting grounds arising under agreements by which they collectively sold their ancient lands are Indian affairs over which Parliament has exclusive legislative authority, and only Parliament can derogate from those rights.

In the result, the right of the respondents to hunt over the lands in question reserved to them by ex. 8 are preserved by s. 87, and remain unimpaired by the *Game Act*, and it follows that the respondents were rightfully in possession of the carcasses. It becomes unnecessary to consider other aspects of a far-reaching argument addressed to us by the respondents' counsel.

I would dismiss the appeal.

Norris J.A. [at p. 648]: —

. . . . .

As to whether or not the document Exhibit 8 is a Treaty within Section 87 of the Indian Act:
On this branch of this appeal as has been stated, I agree with the conclusions of my brother Davey and substantially with his reasons. What I have to say following is by way of detail and in extension of those reasons. The question is, in my respectful opinion, to be resolved not by the application of rigid rules of construction without regard to the circumstances existing when the document was completed nor by the tests of modern day draftsmanship. In determining what the intention of Parliament was at the time of the enactment of s. 87 of the *Indian Act*, Parliament is to be taken to have had in mind the common understanding of the parties to the document at the time it was executed. In the section "Treaty" is not a word of art and in my respectful opinion, it embraces all such engagements made

by persons in authority as may be brought within the term "the word of the white man" the sanctity of which was, at the time of British exploration and settlement, the most important means of obtaining the good will and co-operation of the native tribes and ensuring that the colonists would be protected from death and destruction. On such assurance the Indians relied. In view of the argument before us, it is necessary to point out that on numerous occasions in modern days, rights under what were entered into with Indians as solemn engagements, although completed with what would now be considered informality, have been whittled away on the excuse that they do not comply with modern day formal requirements and with rules of interpretation applicable to transactions between people who must be taken in the light of advanced civilization to be of equal status. Reliance on instances where this has been done is merely to compound injustice without real justification at law. The transaction in question here was a transaction between, on the one hand, the strong representative of a proprietary company under the Crown and representing the Crown, who had gained the respect of the Indians by his integrity and the strength of his personality and was thus able to bring about the completion of the agreement, and on the other hand, uneducated savages. The nature of the transaction itself was consistent with the informality of frontier days in this Province and such as the necessities of the occasion and the customs and illiteracy of the Indians demanded. The transaction in itself was a primitive one — a surrender of land in exchange for blankets to be divided between the Indian signatories according to arrangements between them — with a reservation of aboriginal rights, the document being executed by the Indians by the affixing of their marks. The unusual (by the standards of legal draftsmen) nature and form of the document considered in the light of the circumstances on Vancouver Island in 1854 does not detract from it as being a "Treaty".

. . . . .

In determining the question as to whether ex. 8 is a "Treaty" within the meaning of s. 87 of the *Indian Act* of Canada the golden rule of construction is to be applied, *viz.*, that the grammatical and ordinary sense of the word is to be adhered to unless that would lead to some absurdity or some repugnance or inconsistency with the rest of the statute in which case the grammatical and ordinary sense of the word may be modified so as to avoid that absurdity, repugnance and inconsistency, but no further ... The Shorter Oxford dictionary, p. 2238, gives as a meaning of "treat", "To deal or carry on negotiations (*with* another) with a view to settling terms; to bargain, negotiate", and of "treaty", "A settlement arrived at by treating or negotiation; an agreement, covenant, compact, contract". In ex. 4, the instructions to Douglas under which ex. 8 was completed, words in the sense of the dictionary meaning quoted were used. The application of that meaning does not lead to any absurdity, repugnance or inconsistency, and indeed, in the light of the history and circumstances it is difficult to conceive of a term which would be more appropriate to describe the engagement entered into.

. . . . .

I have no doubt that in enacting s. 87 of the *Indian Act*, Parliament recognized the fact that Indian Treaties would have been completed in degrees of formality varying with the circumstances of each case — some with Government representatives, some with military commanders and others with frontier representatives of the great trading companies. It was necessary that those on the frontier be given wide powers and a wide discretion. So it was with Douglas.

. . . . .

In my opinion, therefore, the document (ex. 8) is a Treaty within the meaning of s. 87 of the Indian Act. As has already been indicated, the right could only be extinguished by Federal legislation.

———————

The Supreme Court of Canada dismissed an appeal from the British Columbia Court of Appeal, explaining that the majority's conclusion that the document in question was a treaty within the meaning of the term in s. 87 of the *Indian Act*, R.S.C. 1970, c. I-6 was correct.

Although the *White and Bob* decision initiated a different approach to treaty interpretation by providing for a more contextual analysis of the agreement made between the parties, it was not until the decision in *R. v. Taylor and Williams*, below, that the principles of treaty interpretation that had long existed in the United States truly took root in Canadian jurisprudence.

R. v. TAYLOR and WILLIAMS

(1981), 62 C.C.C. (2d) 228, 34 O.R. (2d) 360 (C.A.)

(references omitted)

MacKinnon A.C.J.O.: — The respondents, Indians by definition under the *Indian Act*, R.S.C, 1970, c. I-6, s. 2(1), were charged and convicted of taking bullfrogs during the closed season established under provincial legislation of general application. The respondents successfully argued on appeal to the Divisional Court that by virtue of s. 88 of the *Indian Act* and a treaty that the chiefs of their tribe had entered into with His Majesty the King in 1818, the provincial legislation did not apply to them. Section 88 reads:

> 88. Subject to the terms of any treaty and any other Act of the Parliament of Canada, all laws of general application from time to time in force in any province area applicable to and in respect of Indians in the province, except to the extent that such laws are inconsistent with this Act or any order, rule, regulation or by-law made thereunder, and except to the extent that such laws make provision for any matter for which provision is made by or under this Act.

The Divisional Court were also of the view that a 1923 treaty may have extinguished all fishing, hunting and trapping rights of the Indians in Ontario, and, accordingly, while agreeing with the respondents on the major issue before them, sent the matter back for a new trial to deal with the effect of the 1923 treaty [55 C.C.C. (2d) 172]. Counsel for the Crown advised us that if we agreed with the Divisional Court as to the effect of the 1818 treaty, he was not requesting a new trial to consider the effect of the 1923 treaty.

I

Ontario Regulation 576 of 1976 passed pursuant to s. 74 (rep. & sub. 1980, c. 47, s. 27) of the *Game and Fish Act*, R.S.O. 1970, c. 186 (now R.S.O. 1980, c. 182, s. 77), for the first time introduced throughout Ontario a closed season on the hunting of bullfrogs, commencing October 16, 1976, and ending June 30, 1977. The closed season thereafter ran from October 16th of one year until June 30th of the following year.

On June 11, 1977, the respondents took 65 bullfrogs from the waters of Crow Lake in the Township of Belmont in the County of Peterborough. It is agreed that the bullfrogs were taken from unoccupied Crown lands being the navigable waters of Crow Lake. It is also agreed that the respondents took bullfrogs for food for their families and not for any commercial purposes.

II

The respondents are descendants and members of the Indian tribes who were parties to "Articles of Provisional Agreement" (as it was described in its opening words) entered into at what is believed now to be Port Hope, Ontario on November 5, 1818, between the Honourable William Claus, Deputy Superintendent General of Indian Affairs, on behalf of His Majesty, and six chiefs of the Chippewa Nation, inhabiting the back parts of the Newcastle District. The document is known as Treaty No. 20. By this provisional agreement the Indians ceded a tract of land containing about 1,951,000 acres to the Crown. The bullfrogs taken by the respondents were within the area covered by this treaty. After setting out the names of the parties and describing the land to be surrendered, the treaty went on to say:

> And the said Buckquaquet, Pishikinse, Pahtosh, Cahgahkishinse, Cahgage-win and Pininse, as well for themselves as for the Chippewa Nation inhabiting and claiming the said tract of land as above described, do freely, fully and voluntarily surrender and convey the same to His Majesty without reservation or limitation in perpetuity.

The consideration for the conveyance was "yearly, and in every year, forever, the said sum of seven hundred and forty pounds currency in goods at the Montreal price, which sum the said Chiefs and Principal People, parties hereunto, acknowledge as a full consideration for the lands hereby sold and conveyed to His Majesty". In 1821 the consideration was restated as "being at the rate of ten dollars for each individual now living".

The payments have long since ceased. The question is whether there was other, and for the Indians, more material consideration given to them, namely, the reservation to them and their descendants of their aboriginal fishing and hunting rights.

A council meeting between the Deputy Superintendent of Indian Affairs and the chiefs of the six tribes who were parties to the provisional agreement was held the same day as the provisional agreement. The council meeting both preceded and followed the signing of the provisional agreement. Counsel for both parties to this appeal agreed that the minutes of this council meeting recorded the oral portion of the 1818 treaty and are as much a part of the treaty as the written articles of the provisional agreement. As these minutes are central to the issue in this appeal, they must be recited in whole:

> Minutes of a Council held as Smiths Creek, in the Township of Hope on Thursday the 5th of November 1818, with the Chippewa Nation of Indians, inhabiting & claiming a Tract of Land situate between the Western Boundary Line of the Midland District & the Eastern Boundary Line of the Home District, & extending Northerly to a Bay at the Northern Entrance of Lake Simcoe in the Home District.
>
> Present
> The Honbl. W. Claus Dep. Supt. General of Indian Affairs
> I. Givins Esq. Supt. of Indian Affairs for the Port of York
> W. Hands, Clerk Indn. Dept.
> W. Gruet, Interpreter
>
> After the ususal ceremonies the Dep. Supt. General addressed the Chiefs as follows:
>
> Children. I salute you in behalf of your Great Father & condole [sic] with you for the loss you have met with since I last met you — it is the will of the Great Spirit to remove our nearest & dearest connexions, we must submit to his will & not repine. I should have seen you before this, but I have had business with others of your Nation which has kept me until this day. My errand is, to put at rest the doubts with respect to the Lands in the back parts of this Country which you seem to think were never disposed of to the King & hope that hereafter none of your young men will be so idle as to remove the Posts or marks which will be put up by the Kings Surveyors. Your Great Father has directed me to lay before you a sketch of the Country in the back of this & you will point out to me the Land as far as the last purchase was, from the Waters edge from the Great Lake.
>
> Children. You must perceive the number of your Great Fathers children about here have no home, & out of pity for them, he wishes to acquire Land to give to them — He is charitable to all, does not like to see his children in distress. Your Land is not all that he has been purchasing, he has looked to the setting of Sun, as well as the rising, for places to put his Children, & when he asked your Country from you, he does not mean to do as formerly, to pay you at once, but as long as any of you remain on the Earth to give you Cloathing [sic] in payment every year, besides the presents he now gives you. You will go to your Camp & consult together & when you have made up your minds come & let me hear what it is.
>
> Buckquaquet, Principal Chief addressing the Dept. Supt. general, said

Father. We have heard your words, & will go to our Camp & consult & give you an answer to the request of our Great Father — But, Father, our Women & Children are very hungry, and desired me to ask you to let them taste a little of our Fathers Provisions & Milk —

After their return, Bucquaquet [*sic*] continued

Father. You see me here, I am to be pitied. I have no old men to instruct me. I am the Head Chief, but a young man. You must pity me, all the old people have gone to the other world. My hands are naked, I cannot speak as our Ancestors were used to.

Father. If I was to refuse what our Father has requested, our Women & Children would be more to be pitied. From our Lands we receive scarcely anything, & if your word are true we will get more by parting with them, than by keeping them — our hunting is destroyed, & we must throw ourselves on the compassion of our Great Father the King.

Father. Our young People & Chief have always thought of not refusing our Father any request he makes to us, & therefore do what he wishes.

Father. If it was not for our Brethren the Farmers about the Country we should near starve for our hunting is destroyed.

Father. *We hope that we shall not be prevented from the right of Fishing, the use of the Waters, & Hunting where we can find game. We hope that the Whites who are to come among us will not treat us ill*, some of young men are giddy, but we hope they will not hurt them.

Father. *The young men, I hope you will not think it hard at their requesting, that the Islands may be left for them that when we try to scratch the Earth, as our Brethren the Farmers do, & put anything in that it may come up to help our Women & Children.*

Father. *We do not say that we must have the Islands, but we hope our Father will think of us and allow us this small request* — that is all we have to say —

To which the Dept. Supt. general replied

Children — I have heard your answer, & in the name of your Great Father thank you for the readiness with which you have complied with his desire. Your words shall be communicated to him. *The request for the Islands, I shall inform him of, & have no doubt but that he will accede to your wish. The Rivers are open to all & you have an equal right to fish & hunt on them.* I am pleased to learn from you, that your Brothers the Whites have been so kind to you & hope those that will come among you will be as charitable. Keep from Liquor, & your young men will not be giddy. It is the ruin of your Nation. As soon as I get your Numbers you shall get something to eat, & some Liquor. Do not expect much, for I have so great a dread of it that I am at all times disinclined to give you any. We will now sign the Paper, it is merely to shew your Great Father our work, & when he agrees to our proceeding, you will then have to sign another Paper which Conveys the Country we now talk about to him, & the first payment will be made, an equal quantity of which you will receive every year —"

(Emphasis added.)

III

Cases on Indian or aboriginal rights can never be determined in a vacuum. It is of importance to consider the history and oral traditions of the tribes concerned, and the surrounding circumstances at the time of the treaty, relied on by both parties, in determining the treaty's effect. Although it is not possible to remedy all of what we now perceive as past wrongs in view of the passage of time, nevertheless it is essential and in keeping with established and accepted principles that the Courts not create, by a remote, isolated current view of events, new grievances.

In the instant appeal, both counsel were in agreement that we could, and indeed should, look at the history of the period and place, and at the Papers and Records of the Ontario Historical Society dealing with this particular treaty and the persons involved in it. The Crown was of the view that a historical analysis of the times and conditions supported its position that the Indians intended to surrender their hunting and fishing rights. Counsel for the respondents took the contrary view.

IV

In interpreting the treaty, accordingly, it is appropriate to have regard to the following matters. First, the tribe who were parties to the treaty had hunted and fished in the area covered by the treaty, and had taken bullfrogs for food there since earliest memory. It is part of the oral tradition of the tribes that this right was not only recognized at the time of the treaty, but that they continued to exercise the right without interruption up until the present. The respondents' evidence as to the oral traditions of the Indian tribes concerned was accepted by the trial Judge and was not disputed by the Crown.

Secondly, it appears that one of the reasons for the Crown entering into the treaty was to facilitate the Crown grants of land to settlers who were arriving in the country in 1818. From the histories of the period, it is clear that the early settlers in the area were in difficult material circumstances.

. . . . .

The minutes also make it clear that the Indians were equally suffering great privation at the time. ... The histories of the period indicate that the beaver hunting in the area had been destroyed and the Indians greatly relied on beaver skins for trading. As a result, ... they received scarcely anything from the lands and "we must throw ourselves on the compassion of our Great Father the King. ... Our young People & Chief have always thought of not refusing our Father any request he makes to us, & therefore do what he wishes".

Finally, it should be noted that William Claus, who represented the King, is described in vol. XXV of the Papers and Records of the Ontario Historical Society published by the Society in 1929 as "a valuable and highly esteemed public servant" who "made at least seven of the treaties of surrender with lands with the Indians from 1798 to 1818", and who "because of his familiarity with the Indians in all their ways and with their language, and his kindly attitude toward them, was trusted by them and exceptionally successful in dealing with them for the Crown".

V

The respondents argue that a proper interpretation of the treaty, when the relationship between the Crown and the Indians and their necessitous circumstances at the time is considered, is that the agreement and reassurance contained in the minutes was a clear reservation to the Indians of the time-honoured rights to hunt and fish over the lands now conveyed to the Crown — certainly so long as they we held by the Crown. If that is so then it follows, they submit, that the treaty comes within the opening words of s. 88 of the *Indian Act*.

The words that have caused the difficulty and which have to be interpreted in deciding whether the treaty reserved to the Indians the right to hunt and fish are the following (emphasized in the earlier quotation):

The Indian spokeman [*sic*] said:

> Father — We hope that we shall not be prevented from the right of Fishing, the use of the Waters, & Hunting where we can find game.

> . . . . .

> Father — The young men, I hope you will not think it hard at their requesting, that the Islands may be left for them that when we try to scratch the Earth, as our Brethren the Farmers do, & put any thing in that it may come up to help our Women & Children.

> Father — We do not say that we must have the Island, but we hope our Father will think of us & allow us this small request."

To these particular requests, Claus replied:

> The request for the Islands, I shall also inform him of, & have no doubt but that he will accede to your wish. The Rivers are open to all & you have an equal right to fish & hunt on them.

The request and the assurance were given before the treaty was signed. From the treaty it can be seen that there was no reservation established for the Indians. It is clear, on the other hand, that both parties expected the Indians to remain on the lands conveyed as the Indian spokesman said, "We hope that the Whites who are to come among us will not treat us ill, some of [the Indian] young men are giddy, but we hope they will not hurt them". No exception was taken to this statement by Claus but rather he said, "I am pleased to learn from you, that your Brothers the Whites have been so kind to you, and hope *those that will come among you* will be as charitable" (emphasis added).

If the Indians were to remain in the are one wonders how they were to survive if their ancient right to hunt and fish for food was not continued. Be that as it may, the question to be answered is whether this treaty can be interpreted so as to limit the applicability of the Ontario *Game and Fish Act* which, it is agreed, is a law of general application.

The principles to be applied to the interpretation of Indian treaties have been much canvassed over the years. In approaching the terms of a treaty quite apart from the other considerations already noted, the honour of the Crown is always involved and no appearance of "sharp dealing" should be sanctioned. Mr. Justice Cartwright emphasized this in his dissenting reasons in *R. v. George* ... where he said:

> We should, I think, endeavour to construe the treaty of 1827 and those Acts of Parliament which bear upon the question before us in such a manner that the honour of the Sovereign may be upheld and Parliament not made subject of the reproach of having taken away by unilateral action and without consideration the rights solemnly assured to the Indians and their posterity by treaty.

Further, if there is any ambiguity in the words or phrases used, not only should the words be interpreted as against the framers or drafters of such treaties, but such language should not be interpreted or construed to the prejudice of the Indians if another construction is reasonably possible: *R. v. White and Bob.*

. . . . .

Finally, if there is evidence by conduct or otherwise as to how the parties understood the terms of the treaty, then such understanding and practice is of assistance in giving content to the term or terms. As already stated, counsel for both parties to the appeal agreed that recourse could be had to the surrounding circumstances and judicial notice could be taken of the facts of history. In my opinion, that notice extends to how, historically, the parties acted under the treaty after its execution.

In my view, all the principles recited lead to the conclusion that the terms of the treaty, which include the oral terms recorded in the minutes, preserve the historic right of these Indians to hunt and fish on Crown lands in the lands conveyed and fall under the exception established by the opening words of s. 88 of the *Indian Act.*

The Crown's position was simply that "the terms of the treaty" did not preserve or grant the right to fish and hunt on Crown lands inconsistent with the application of provincial laws. The surrender of the Indian lands to the Crown, counsel submitted, included a surrender of their aboriginal hunting and fishing rights. Once it is accepted that the minutes of the council meeting between the representative of the Crown on the one hand and the Indian chiefs on the other is part of the treaty, it cannot be successfully argued that Treaty No. 20 is "silent" on the question of the right to hunt and fish.

With respect to the oral representation made in answer to the "hope" expressed by the Indians that they would not be prevented from hunting and fishing, it is argued that that representation was only to advise the Indians that they were to have an equal right with all others and was not a preservation of special rights. The transcript of the minutes cannot and should not be analyzed in minute detail. The use of certain words and their conciliatory tone only serve to emphasize the disparity in the positions of the two parties to the treaty, but do not lessen the force of the request nor the right to be attached to the assurance — quite the contrary.

The Indians' request for the continued right to hunt and fish was put on a higher plane than their request for the islands. In making their request for the islands their spokesmen said "We do not say that we *must* have the Islands" (emphasis added). No such qualification or limitation was put on their request that their traditional and historic right to hunt and fish for food continue. The representative of the Crown was clearly not intending to put any limitation on the rights of the Indians by saying that the rivers were open to "all" and that the Indians had an "equal" right to fish and hunt. These words immediately follow his dealing with the Indians' request for the islands to which he replied that no doubt "[your Great Father] will accede to your wish". It seems to me that rather than putting a limitation on the Indians' ancient right, William Claus, whose integrity was respected by the Indians, was emphasizing that that right would continue. The accepted evidence was that this understanding of the treaty has been accepted and acted on for some 160 years without interruption. In my view, it is too late now to deprive these Indians of their historical aboriginal rights: *R. v. White and Bob*.

VII

As noted, at the beginning of these reasons, there no longer is any request that consideration be given to the 1923 treaty and, accordingly, the appeal is dismissed without any reference back to the County Court as directed by the Divisional Court. I think it is appropriate in this type of case to ask the Crown to pay the costs of the respondents on a solicitor-and-client basis.

Appeal dismissed.

The articulation and adoption of these canons of treaty interpretation in *Taylor and Williams* marked an end to the traditionally restrictive interpretations of treaties that had been characteristic of the majority of previous Canadian judicial pronouncements. The subsequent Supreme Court of Canada decision in *R. v. Nowegijick* [1983] 1 S.C.R. 29, [1983] 2 C.N.L.R. 89, [1983] C.T.C. 20, 46 N.R. 41, 144 D.L.R. (3d) 193 at 198, in which Justice Dickson, as he then was, stated that "...treaties and statutes relating to Indians should be liberally construed and doubtful expressions resolved in favour of the Indian", affirmed the entrenchment of these canons of treaty interpretation as a fundamental element of Canadian treaty jurisprudence.

The following excerpt canvasses these canons of interpretation in greater detail.

LEONARD I. ROTMAN, "TAKING AIM AT THE CANONS OF TREATY INTERPRETATION IN CANADIAN ABORIGINAL RIGHTS JURISPRUDENCE"

(1997) 46 U.N.B.L.J. 1 at 12-14, 26-7, 29-30, 32, 34-7, 40-1, 43-5, 47, 49-50
(references omitted)

The recent decision of the Supreme Court of Canada in *R. v. Badger* affirmed that the existence of a number of canons of Aboriginal treaty interpretation is an integral aspect of treaty jurisprudence. The interpretive canons include the notion that treaties are to be given large, liberal and generous interpretations in favour of the Aboriginal peoples. Ambiguities in treaties are to be resolved in favour of the Aboriginals and the treaties ought to be construed as the Aboriginal signatories understood them. Also, treaties are to be interpreted in a flexible manner and extrinsic evidence should readily be used to determine the meaning and intent of treaties. Although these interpretive canons have existed as an explicit part of Canadian Aboriginal rights law for almost twenty years, they have not always been followed during that time. In a number of situations courts have explicitly affirmed the use of these principles, yet subsequently abandoned or ignored them altogether in their judgments. The result of this practice has been a general confusion regarding the status of these principles in Canadian law and how they ought to be implemented by the courts.

. . . . .

[T]hese interpretive principles ought to be recognized as permanent and vital fixtures in Canadian treaty jurisprudence. Understanding these principles as integral elements of treaty jurisprudence requires, however, that the judiciary give more than token attention to them. While it is important to articulate these principles, it is equally important to apply them to factual situations if they are to have any meaningful effect.

. . . . .

Part of the difficulty with the use of these principles is that while they are well-known, the reasons for their existence are not. ... Simply affirming that treaties are to be given large, liberal and generous interpretations does not explain why such an interpretation is necessary or what obstacles are to be overcome using this premise. These canons reveal much about treaty relationships and the respective attitudes of the Crown and Aboriginal peoples towards treaties and treaty-making processes.

. . . . .

(a) Large, Liberal and Generous Interpretation

The large, liberal, and generous interpretation of Aboriginal treaties is rooted in the recognition that literal readings of the written version of the treaties do not always provide accurate accounts of the agreements reached between the parties. Indeed, in some instances, after negotiations were concluded and treaty terms were agreed upon, the Aboriginal peoples affixed their signatures to blank pieces of paper, upon which the treaty's terms were filled in later. In other instances, treaties were written up prior to negotiations between the parties and agreed upon points that had not been included in the previously-prepared parchment versions were simply left out so that new documents would not have to be prepared. In these latter instances, the Aboriginal signatories were falsely assured that the written treaty presented for signing was representative of the agreement that had been reached.

· · · · ·

In addition to these problems with the actual text of written treaties, complications of interpretation abounded. ... The English language and concepts implemented in treaties were not always understood by the Aboriginal peoples in the same manner that they were by the Crown's representatives.

· · · · ·

The nuances of language and the different cultural understandings of land use and "ownership", as well as the concepts of "dominion" and "sovereignty" included in treaties, should raise yellow flags to those interpreting the meaning of these documents. Contemporary evidence suggests that treaties which make use of these and other like terms may not have been adequately understood by the Aboriginal peoples. ... [T]he Aboriginals' signing of treaties is to be viewed in light of the cultural and linguistic factors by which observers may legitimately question whether the treaties were truly understood and therefore agreed to at the time they were signed.

· · · · ·

(b) Ambiguities to be Resolved in Favour of Aboriginal Peoples

A key aspect of a large, liberal and generous interpretation of Aboriginal treaties is that where ambiguities exist, they are to be resolved in favour of the Aboriginal peoples. The basis for this canon of construction is similar to the rationale behind the use of the *contra proferentem* rule in contract law. ... Since the Crown drew up the treaties, in its own language in accordance with its legal system, implementing uniquely British concepts, this interpretive canon prevents the Crown from relying upon an ambiguity to its advantage. The reason for this approach is that the Crown had opportunities to provide sufficient clarity when it drafted the treaties. Additionally, the fact that the majority of evidence accepted by the courts is usually derived from the Crown and its representatives lends further support to the use of this interpretive canon.

· · · · ·

The notion of resolving treaty ambiguities in favour of the Aboriginal peoples led [the court] in *Taylor and Williams* to incorporate the "reserved rights doctrine". This doctrine is premised upon the notion that treaties did not grant rights to Aboriginal peoples, but merely recognized and affirmed pre-existing rights. Based upon this fundamental premise, the reserved rights doctrine holds that any Aboriginal rights which are not specifically extinguished by treaty remain in full force and vigour, including those rights which are not included in the treaty. The reserved rights doctrine has been described by the American scholar Felix Cohen as "perhaps the most basic principle of all Indian law." It can be seen as a cousin to both the interpretive canon that requires treaty ambiguities to be resolved in favour of the Indian parties and the *contra proferentem* rule.

Another close relative of these doctrines is the "clear and plain" test for demonstrating the extinguishment of Aboriginal rights. In some of its more prominent decisions, the Supreme Court of Canada has held that Aboriginal rights can only be extinguished when a clear and plain intention of the Crown to extinguish those rights exists. The onus of proof rests with the party claiming extinguishment. In the absence of such extinguishment, the rights remain in existence. Crown contentions of rights extinguishment must be put to a strict test due to the imbalance of power. Consequently there must be a clear and precise understanding of what is part of a treaty, what is not, and what rights are to be extinguished. If no such understanding exists, the benefit of doubt goes to the Aboriginal peoples. The relative positions of the Crown and the Aboriginal peoples also require that treaties be construed as the Aboriginals understood them.

(c) Treaties Construed as the Aboriginal Peoples Understood Them

... This canon of construction does not mean that only Aboriginal understandings of a treaty are relevant in ascertaining its meaning. Rather, this canon recognizes that Aboriginal understandings, which have long been neglected in treaty interpretation, play a vital role in obtaining a well-rounded, contextual understanding of treaties.

· · · · ·

Interpreting treaties in the manner that the Aboriginal peoples understood them also requires that the treaties not be interpreted in a technical or legalistic manner that would tend to benefit the Crown. As the *Report of the Select Committee on Aborigines, 1837* concluded, "a ready pretext for complaint will be found in the ambiguity of the language in which their agreements must be drawn up, and in the superior sagacity which the European will exercise in framing, in interpreting, and in evading them."

The idea that Aboriginal treaties ought to be construed as the Aboriginal peoples understood them was developed in accordance with the notion that treaties, as mutual compacts between the Crown and Aboriginal peoples, ought to be interpreted in a manner that is consistent with the understandings of the parties at the time the treaty was signed. As indicated in the *Sioui* decision, when interpreting the nature of an agreement between the Crown and Aboriginal peoples, it is necessary to strive towards the common intention of the parties and not merely rely upon the understanding possessed by one of the groups.

. . . . .

The construction of treaties in a technical manner based on European law cannot accurately be said to have been a part of this common understanding . ... Since the aboriginal peoples often could not read or write English, using the technical meaning of the terms of treaties favours the Crown's understanding over those of the Aboriginals. In order to achieve a more equitable understanding of what was being communicated by the Crown and what was understood by the Aboriginals, the courts have started to rely on the content of treaty negotiations. As well, historical records and oral evidence documenting the Aboriginal people's interpretation and understanding of the words or concepts used in the treaties are utilized.

. . . . .

[A]dhering to Aboriginal understandings of the meaning and intent of treaties does not corrupt the nature of the agreements nor result in an unacceptably biased version of those treaties. Rather, looking to Aboriginal understandings of the treaties in addition to those held by the Crown provides a reliable and accurate method by which the judiciary may conceptualize the nature of the agreement that was signed between the parties. ... [T]he Aboriginal understanding of the treaties must also include the reasonable expectations of the Aboriginal peoples in light of the various historical, political, social and economic factors in existence at the time that the treaties were signed. Such an analysis must not, however, allow treaty promises or the rights existing under the treaties to be frozen in time or restricted to the method in which those rights were exercised at the time the treaties were signed. Analysis of Aboriginal understandings and expectations must remain flexible enough to reflect the changing circumstances under which the treaties continue to operate. It must also provide for the evolution of Aboriginal treaty rights.

(d) Treaties Interpreted in a Flexible Manner

Treaties are living, evolving documents. Consequently, the Supreme Court of Canada has held that treaties should "be interpreted in a flexible way that is sensitive to the evolution of changes." ... Both the rights and obligations existing under treaties are ... of a continuing nature. While treaty rights continue, they are not restricted to the manner or method in which they were exercised at the time the treaty was signed. ... The notion that treaty rights may be exercised only in the manner in which they existed at the time of the treaty is called "frozen rights" theory. This theory has been expressly rejected on a number of occasions, most strikingly, by the Supreme Court of Canada in the *Sparrow* case.

. . . . .

The court's judgment in *Sparrow* demonstrates its recognition that judicial emphasis on temporal considerations as the sole determinants of the nature of Aboriginal and treaty rights is misguided. ... Aboriginal and treaty rights, as dynamic, evolving rights, ought not be restricted to their "primeval simplicity and vigour", but must be allowed to adapt to changing circumstances.

. . . . .

The notion that treaties must be interpreted in a flexible manner applies equally to the continued sustenance of rights. ... A contextually appropriate understanding of Aboriginal or treaty rights, such as fishing rights, must include the means necessary for the realization of those rights.

. . . . .

The notion that Aboriginal and treaty rights ought to be read to include those practices which are necessarily incidental to the exercise of the fundamental rights in question illustrates the proposition that those rights encompass more than the bare rights themselves. A strict interpretation of Aboriginal treaties would ostensibly preclude such incidental rights from receiving constitutional protection. Allowing for the flexible interpretation of Aboriginal treaties, as articulated by the Supreme Court, requires that these incidental rights be afforded the same protection where they are necessary to the exercise of the rights that are explicitly dealt with in the treaties. To ascertain whether there is a need to provide protection to these "incidental" rights requires discovering their existence and connection to the rights described in the treaties. Often, this necessitates the reception of evidence extrinsic to the written terms of the treaties themselves.

(e) The Use of Extrinsic Evidence

The use of extrinsic evidence in the interpretation of Aboriginal treaties is premised entirely upon the notion that the written versions of treaties are not generally sufficient to provide a contextual understanding of the agreement between the parties. ... The use of extrinsic evidence serves as a check upon the variety of difficulties of interpretation and helps to achieve accurate understandings of the nature of the bargains entered into at the time the treaties were signed. It allows for the admission of evidence as to the context of treaty negotiations, as well as Aboriginal understandings of what was agreed upon through the reception of oral history, written accounts by treaty negotiators and other seemingly secondary material.

. . . . .

To arrive at a more accurate picture of what actually transpired [during treaty negotiations] also requires that the extrinsic evidence used be critically appraised. What have traditionally been described as "secondary" sources by the courts, namely governmental records and the correspondence of governmental officials, are tainted by a variety of problems. Their function was to report on the success, or lack thereof, of governmental endeavours to conclude the treaties, not to try to understand Aboriginal perspectives on what transpired during treaty negotiations. Furthermore, their understandings and characterizations of Aboriginal societies and cultures were generally permeated with European value-laded biases.

To arrive at a more well-rounded, as well as contextually and culturally appropriate understanding of Aboriginal treaties, it is imperative to understand the limitations inherent in these sources as well as the court's traditional bias against evidence generated by the Aboriginal peoples. Government records and correspondence, and Aboriginal oral evidence ought to be afforded the same stature and importance as the written versions of the treaties.

. . . . .

IV CONCLUSION

... The unique nature of Crown-Aboriginal relations generally, as well as treaty relationships between the groups, demonstrate the need for a purposive, or pro-active, implementation of these treaty canons. ... It could be argued that the Crown's fiduciary obligations to Aboriginal peoples, which shape and inform the understanding of treaty rights in section 35(1) of the *Constitution Act, 1982*, provide a constitutional imperative to ensure that these canons are properly implemented.

. . . . .

The principles underlying the canons of Aboriginal treaty interpretation ... account for those elements of treaty rights which are not necessarily forthcoming from traditional, domestic contract or international law interpretations. They look to the background and circumstances of the treaties — including the events giving rise to them and the understandings that the respective parties had at the time they were signed — in order to achieve a well-rounded, culturally appropriate understanding of the nature of the agreements. They should, therefore, be entrenched as vital elements of Canadian Aboriginal rights jurisprudence in a manner that is consistent with the important place of Crown-Native treaties within Canadian law, as recognized by their inclusion in section 35(1) of the *Constitution Act, 1982*.

With the constitutional entrenchment of Aboriginal and treaty rights in section 35(1) of the *Constitution Act, 1982*, being Schedule B to the *Canada Act 1982* (U.K.), 1982, c. 11 both forms of rights that were in existence on 17 April, 1982 — the date that the Act took effect — enjoyed greater protection than ever before. The terms of section 35 read as follows:

35.(1)   The existing aboriginal and treaty rights of the aboriginal peoples of
Canada are hereby recognized and affirmed.

The effect of section 35(1) is dealt with in detail in Chapter 7.

With their constitutionalization in section 35(1), treaty rights were finally afforded the same solemn recognition at law that they had received
during the early stages of treaty relations between Britain and the Aboriginal peoples. Yet, the constitutionalization of treaty rights was not the only
change in the legal understanding of treaty rights following the adoption
of the canons of Aboriginal treaty interpretation. Other, equally significant
effects came about as a result of the Supreme Court of Canada's decision
in *Simon v. R.*, below.

In reading the *Simon* case, bear in mind that the treaty being discussed
therein is the very same treaty that was in issue in *Syliboy*. Note also Chief
Justice Dickson's comments on the *Syliboy* decision in the course of his
judgment in *Simon*.

SIMON v. R.

(1985), 24 D.L.R. (4th) 390 (S.C.C.)

Dickson C.J.C.: — This case raises the important question of the interplay
between the treaty rights of native peoples and provincial legislation. The
right to hunt, which remains important to the livelihood and way of life of
the Micmac people, has come into conflict with game preservation legislation in effect in the province of Nova Scotia. The main question before this
Court is whether, pursuant to a Treaty of 1752 between the British Crown
and the Micmac, and to s. 88 of the *Indian Act*, R.S.C. 1970, c. I-6, the appellant, James Matthew Simon, enjoys hunting rights which preclude his
prosecution for offences under the *Lands and Forests Acts*, R.S.N.S. 1967, c.
163.

I

Facts

The appellant is a member of the Shubenacadie Indian Brook Band (No. 2)
of the Micmac people and a registered Indian under the *Indian Act*. He was
charged under s. 150(1) of the *Lands and Forest Act* with possession of a
rifle and shot-gun cartridges. The two charges read:

On the 21st day of September, 1980 at West Indian Road, Hants County,
Nova Scotia, [he] did unlawfully commit the offence of illegal possession of
shotgun cartridge loaded with shot larger than AAA, contrary to s. 150(1) of
the *Lands and Forests Act*;

and that:

On the 21st day of September, 1980 at West Indian Road, Hants County,
Nova Scotia, [he] did unlawfully commit the offence of illegal possession of
a rifle during closed season contrary to s. 150(1) of the *Lands and Forests Act*.

Section 150(1) of the *Lands and Forests Act* provides:

150(1) Except as provided in this Section, no person shall take, carry or have in his possession any shot gun [shot-gun] cartridges loaded with ball or with shot larger than AAA or any rifle,

(a)   in or upon any forest, wood or other resort of moose or deer; or

(b)   upon any road passing through or by any such forest, wood or other resort; or

(c)   in any tent or camp or other shelter (except his usual and ordinary permanent place of abode) in any forest, wood or other resort.

. . . . .

Although all essential elements of the charges were admitted by Simon, it was argued on his behalf at trial that the right to hunt set out in the Treaty of 1752, in combination with s. 88 of the *Indian Act*, offered him immunity from prosecution under s. 150(1) of the *Lands and Forests Act*.

Section 88 of the *Indian Act* reads as follows:

88. *Subject to the terms of any treaty* and any other Act of the Parliament of Canada, all laws of general application from time to time in force in any province are applicable to and in respect of Indians in the province, except to the extent that such laws are inconsistent with this Act or any order, rule, regulation or by-law made thereunder, and except to the extent that such laws make provision for any matter for which provision is made by or under this Act.

(Emphasis added.)

The Treaty of 1752, the relevant part of which states at art. 4 that the Micmacs have "free liberty of hunting and Fishing as usual", provides:

Treaty or
Articles of Peace and Friendship Renewed
between

His Excellency Peregrine Thomas Hopson Esquire Captain General and Governor in Chief in and over His Majesty's Province of Nova Scotia or Acadie Vice Admiral of the same & Colonel of One of His Majesty's Regiments of Foot, and His Majesty's Council on behalf of His Majesty.

AND

Major Jean Baptiste Cope chief Sachem of the Tribe of Mick Mack Indians, Inhabiting the Eastern Coast of the said Province, and Andrew Hadley Martin, Gabriel Martin and Francis Jeremiah members & Delegates of the said Tribe, for themselves and their said Tribe their heirs and the heirs of their heirs forever. Begun made and Concluded in the manner form & Tenor following, viz.

1. It is agreed that the Articles of Submission & Agreements made at Boston in New England by the Delegates of the Penobscot Norridgwolk & St. John's Indians in the Year 1725 Ratifyed and Confirmed by all the Nova Scotia Tribes at Annapolis Royal in the Month of June 1726 and lately

Renewed with Governor Cornwallis at Halifax and Ratifyed at St. John's River, now read over Explained & Interpreted shall be and are hereby from this time forward renewed, reiterated and forever Confirmed by them and their Tribe, and the said Indians for themselves and their Tribe and their heirs aforesaid do make and renew the same Solemn Submissions and promises for the strict Observance of all the Articles therein Contained as at any time heretofore hath been done.

2. That all Transactions during the late War shall on both sides be buried in Oblivion with the Hatchet, And that the said Indians shall have all favour, Friendship & Protection shewn them from this His Majesty's Government.

3. That the said Tribe shall use their utmost Endeavours to bring in the other Indians to Renew and Ratify this Peace, and shall discover and make known any attempts or designs of any other Indians or any Enemy whatever against His Majesty's Subjects within this Province so soon as they shall know thereof and shall also hinder and Obstruct the same to the utmost of their power, and on the other hand if any of the Indians refusing to ratify this Peace shall make War upon the Tribe who have now Confirmed the same; they shall upon Application have such aid and Assistance from the Government for their defence as the Case may require.

4. It is agreed that the said Tribe of Indians shall not be hindered from, but have *free liberty of hunting and Fishing as usual* and that if they shall think a Truck house needful at the River Chibenaccadie, or any other place of their resort they shall have the same built and proper Merchandize, lodged therein, to be exchanged for what the Indians shall have to dispose of and that in the mean time the Indians shall have free liberty to bring to Sale to Halifax or any other Settlement within this Province, Skins, feathers, fowl, fish or any other thing they shall have to sell, where they shall have liberty to dispose thereof to the best Advantage.

5. That a Quantity of bread, flour, and such other Provisions, as can be procured, necessary for the Familys and proportionable to the Numbers of the said Indians, shall be given them half Yearly for the time to come; and the same regard shall be had to the other Tribes that shall hereafter Agree to Renew and Ratify the Peace upon the Terms and Conditions now Stipulated.

6. That to Cherish a good harmony and mutual Correspondence between the said Indians and this Government His Excellency Peregrine Thomas Hopson Esq. Capt. General & Governor in Chief in & over His Majesty's Province of Nova Scotia or Accadie Vice Admiral of the same & Colonel of One of His Majesty's Regiments of Foot hereby promises on the part of His Majesty that the said Indians shall upon the first day of October Yearly, so long as they shall Continue in Friendship, Receive Presents of Blankets, Tobacco, some Powder & Shott, and the said Indians promise once every year, upon the said first of October, to come by themselves or their Delegates and Receive the said Presents and Renew their Friendship and Submissions.

7. That the Indians shall use their best Endeavors to save the Lives & Goods of any People Shipwrecked on this Coast where they resort and shall Conduct the People saved to Halifax with their Goods, and a Reward adequate to the Salvadge shall be given them.

8. That all Disputes whatsoever that may happen to arise between the Indians now at Peace and others His Majesty's Subjects in this Province shall be tryed in His Majesty's Courts of Civil Judicature, where the Indians shall have the same benefits, Advantages & Priviledges as any others of His Majesty's Subjects.

In Faith & Testimony whereof the Great Seal of the Province is hereunto appended, and the Partys to these Presents have hereunto interchangeabley Set their Hands in the Council Chamber at Halifax this 22nd day of Nov. 1752 in the 26th Year of His Majesty's Reign.

[signatures deleted]

(Emphasis added.)

. . . . .

III

The issues

This appeal raises the following issues:
1.   Was the Treaty of 1752 validly created by competent parties?
2.   Does the treaty contain a right to hunt and what is the nature and scope of this right?
3.   Has the treaty been terminated or limited?
4.   Is the appellant covered by the treaty?
5.   Is the treaty a "treaty" within the meaning of s. 88 of the *Indian Act?*
6.   Do the hunting rights contained in the treaty exempt the appellant from prosecution under s. 150(1) of the *Lands and Forests Act?*

In addition, the following constitutional question was framed by Chief Justice Laskin:

Are the hunting rights referred to in the document entitled 'Treaty of Articles of Peace and Friendship Renewed' and executed November 22, 1752, existing treaty rights recognized and affirmed by s. 35(1) of the *Constitution Act, 1982?*

In his factum, the appellant asks this Court to dispose of the appeal on the sole basis of the effect of the Treaty of 1752 and s. 88 of the *Indian Act.* Therefore, if the treaty does not exempt the appellant from s. 150(1) of the *Lands and Forests Act,* he requests that the appeal be dismissed without prejudice to the Micmac position based on other treaties and aboriginal rights. The respondent agreed with this approach. I will, therefore, restrict my remarks to the Treaty of 1752 and s. 88 of the *Indian Act.* It will be unnecessary to deal with aboriginal rights, the Royal Proclamation of 1763, or other treaty rights.

IV

Was the Treaty of 1752 validly created by competent parties?

The respondent raised the issue of the capacity of the parties for two reasons which are stated at p. 8 of the factum:

> The issue of capacity is raised for the purpose of illustrating that the Treaty of 1752 was of a lesser status than an International Treaty and therefore is more easily terminated. The issue is also raised to give the document an historical legal context as this issue has been raised in previous cases.

The question of whether the Treaty of 1752 constitutes an international-type treaty is only relevant to the respondent's argument regarding the appropriate legal tests for the termination of the treaty. I will address this issue, therefore, in relation to the question of whether the Treaty of 1752 was terminated by hostilities between the British and the Micmac in 1753.

The historical legal context provided by the respondent consists primarily of the 1929 decision of Judge Patterson in *R. v. Syliboy* (1928), 50 C.C.C. 389, [1929] 1 D.L.R. 307 (Co. Ct.) and the academic commentary it generated immediately following its rendering. [Refer to the discussion of *Syliboy, supra.*]

. . . . .

It should be noted that the language used by Patterson J. ... reflects the biases and prejudices of another era in our history. Such language is no longer acceptable in Canadian law and, indeed, is inconsistent with a growing sensitivity to native rights in Canada. With regard to the substance of Judge Patterson's words, leaving aside for the moment the question of whether treaties are international-type documents, his conclusions on capacity are not convincing.

. . . . .

The treaty was entered into for the benefit of both the British Crown and the Micmac people, to maintain peace and order as well as to recognize and confirm the existing hunting and fishing rights of the Micmac. In my opinion, both the Governor and the Micmac entered into the treaty with the intention of creating mutually binding obligations which would be solemnly respected. It also provided a mechanism for dispute resolution. The Micmac Chief and the three other Micmac signatories, as delegates of the Micmac people, would have possessed full capacity to enter into a binding treaty on behalf of the Micmac. Governor Hopson was the delegate and legal representative of His Majesty the King. It is fair to assume that the Micmac would have believed that Governor Hopson, acting on behalf of His Majesty the King, had the necessary authority to enter into a valid treaty with them. I would hold that the Treaty of 1752 was validly created by competent parties.

V

Does the treaty contain a right to hunt and what is the nature and scope of this right?

Article 4 of the Treaty of 1752 states, "it is agreed that the said Tribe of Indians shall not be hindered from, but have free liberty of hunting and Fishing as usual . . .". What is the nature and scope of the "liberty of hunting and Fishing" contained in the treaty?

... In my opinion, the treaty, by providing that the Micmac should not be hindered from but should have free liberty of hunting and fishing as usual, constitutes a positive source of protection against infringements on hunting rights. The fact that the right to hunt already existed at the time the treaty was entered into by virtue of the Micmac's general aboriginal right to hunt does not negate or minimize the significance of the protection of hunting rights expressly included in the treaty.

Such an interpretation accords with the generally accepted view that Indian treaties should be given a fair, large and liberal construction in favour of the Indians.

. . . . .

Having determined that the treaty embodies a right to hunt, it is necessary to consider the respondent's contention that the right to hunt is limited to hunting for purposes and by methods usual in 1752 because of the inclusion of the modifier "as usual" after the right to hunt.

First of all, I do not read the phrase "as usual" as referring to the types of weapons to be used by the Micmac and limiting them to those used in 1752. Any such construction would place upon the ability of the Micmac to hunt an unnecessary and artificial constraint out of keeping with the principle that Indian treaties should be liberally construed. Indeed, the inclusion of the phrase "as usual" appears to reflect a concern that the right to hunt be interpreted in a flexible way that is sensitive to the evolution of changes in normal hunting practices. The phrase thereby ensures that the treaty will be an effective source of protection of hunting rights.

Secondly, the respondent maintained that "as usual" should be interpreted to limit the treaty protection to hunting for noncommercial purposes. It is difficult to see the basis for this argument in the absence of evidence regarding the purpose for which the appellant was hunting. In any event, art. 4 of the treaty appears to contemplate hunting for commercial purposes when it refers to the construction of a truck house as a place of exchange and mentions the liberty of the Micmac to bring game to sale.

. . . . .

It should be clarified at this point that the right to hunt to be effective must embody those activities reasonably incidental to the act of hunting itself, an example of which is travelling with the requisite hunting equipment to the hunting grounds. In this case, the appellant was not charged with hunting in a manner contrary to public safety in violation of the *Lands and Forests Act* but with illegal possession of a rifle and ammunition upon a road passing through or by a forest, wood or resort of moose or deer contrary to s. 150(1) of the same Act. The appellant was simply travelling in his truck along a road with a gun and some ammunition. He maintained that he was going to hunt in the vicinity. In my opinion, it is implicit in the right granted under art. 4 of the Treaty of 1752 that the appellant has the right to possess a gun and ammunition in a safe manner in order to be able to exercise the right to hunt. Accordingly, I conclude that the appellant was exercising his right to hunt under the treaty.

VI

Has the treaty been terminated or limited?

(a) *Termination by hostilities*

In accordance with the finding of the Nova Scotia Court of Appeal, the Crown argued that the Treaty of 1752 was terminated and rendered unenforceable when hostilities broke out between the Micmac and the British in 1753. The appellant maintained that the alleged hostilities were sporadic and minor in nature and did not, therefore, nullify or terminate the treaty. It was further argued by the appellant, relying on L. F. S. Upton, *Micmac and Colonists: Indian — White Relations in the Maritimes 1713-1867* (1979), that the English initiated the hostilities and that, therefore, the Crown should not be permitted to rely on them to support the termination of the treaty. Finally, the appellant submitted that, even if the Court finds that there were sufficient hostilities to affect the treaty, at most it was merely suspended and not terminated.

In considering the impact of subsequent hostilities on the peace Treaty of 1752, the parties looked to international law on treaty termination. While it may be helpful in some instances to analogize the principles of international treaty law to Indian treaties, these principles are not determinative. An Indian treaty is unique; it is an agreement *sui generis* which is neither created nor terminated according to the rules of international law.

. . . . .

It may be that under certain circumstances a treaty could be terminated by the breach of one of its fundamental provisions. It is not necessary to decide this issue in the case at bar since the evidentiary requirements for proving such a termination have not been met. Once it has been established that a valid treaty has been entered into, the party arguing for its termination bears the burden of proving the circumstances and events justifying termination. The inconclusive and conflicting evidence presented by the parties makes it impossible for this Court to say with any certainty what happened on the eastern coast of Nova Scotia 233 years ago. As a result, the Court is unable to resolve this historical question. The Crown has failed to prove that the Treaty of 1752 was terminated by subsequent hostilities.

. . . . .

I conclude from the foregoing that the Treaty of 1752 was not terminated by subsequent hostilities in 1753. The treaty is of as much force and effect today as it was at the time it was concluded.

(b) *Termination by extinguishment*

... The respondent submits that absolute title in the land covered by the treaty lies with the Crown and, therefore, the Crown has the right to extinguish any Indian rights in such lands. The respondent further submits ... that the Crown, through occupancy by the white man under Crown grant or lease, has, in effect, extinguished native rights in Nova Scotia in territory situated outside of reserve lands. As the appellant was stopped on a highway outside the Shubenacadie Reserve, the respondent argues that the Treaty of 1752 affords no defence to the appellant regardless of whether the treaty is itself valid.

In my opinion, it is not necessary to come to a final decision on the respondent's argument. Given the serious and far-reaching consequences of a finding that a treaty right has been extinguished, it seems appropriate to demand strict proof of the fact of extinguishment in each case where the issue arises. As Douglas J. said in *United States v. Sante Fe Pacific Ry. Co.*, *supra*, at p. 354, "extinguishment cannot be lightly implied".

In the present appeal the appellant was charged with the offence of possession of a rifle and ammunition on a road passing through or by a forest, wood or other resort. The agreed statement of facts does not disclose whether or where the appellant had hunted or was intending to hunt. In particular, there is no evidence to sustain the conclusion that the appellant had hunted, or intended to hunt, on the highway which might well raise different considerations.

. . . . .

It seems clear that, at a minimum, the treaty recognizes *some* hunting rights in Nova Scotia on the Shubenacadie Reserve and that any Micmac Indian who enjoys those rights has an incidental right to transport a gun and ammunition to places where he could legally exercise them. In this vein, it is worth noting that both parties agree that the highway on which the appellant was stopped "is adjacent to the Shubenacadie Indian Reserve" and "passes through or by a forest, wood, or other resource frequented by moose or deer".

The respondent tries to meet the apparent right of the appellant to transport a gun and ammunition by asserting that the treaty hunting rights have been extinguished. In order to succeed on this argument it is absolutely essential, it seems to me, that the respondent lead evidence as to where the appellant hunted or intended to hunt and what use has been and is currently made of those lands. It is impossible for this Court to consider the doctrine of extinguishment "in the air"; the respondent must anchor that argument in the bedrock of specific lands. That has not happened in this case. In the absence of evidence as to where the hunting occurred or was intended to occur, and the use of the lands in question, it would be impossible to determine whether the appellant's treaty hunting rights have been extinguished. Moreover, it is unnecessary for this Court to determine whether those rights have been extinguished because, at the very least, these rights extended to the adjacent Shubenacadie reserve. I do not wish to be taken as expressing any view on whether, as a matter of law, treaty rights may be extinguished.

VII

Is the appellant an Indian covered by the treaty?

The respondent argues that the appellant has not shown that he is a direct descendant of a member of the original Micmac Indian Band covered by the Treaty of 1752.

. . . . .

In my view, the appellant has established a sufficient connection with the Indian band, signatories to the Treaty of 1752. As noted earlier, this treaty was signed by Major Jean Baptiste Cope, Chief of the Shubenacadie Micmac tribe, and three other members and delegates of the tribe. The Micmac signatories were described as inhabiting the eastern coast of Nova Scotia. The appellant admitted at trial that he was a registered Indian under the *Indian Act*, and was an "adult member of the Shubenacadie — Indian Brook Band of Micmac Indians and was a member of the Shubenacadie Band Number 02". The appellant is, therefore, a Shubenacadie — Micmac Indian, living in the same area as the original Micmac Indian tribe, party to the Treaty of 1752.

This evidence alone, in my view, is sufficient to prove the appellant's connection to the tribe originally covered by the treaty. True, this evidence is not conclusive proof that the appellant is a *direct* descendant of the Micmac Indians covered by the Treaty of 1752. It must, however, be sufficient, for otherwise no Micmac Indian would be able to establish descendancy. The Micmacs did not keep written records. Micmac traditions are largely oral in nature. To impose an impossible burden of proof would, in effect, render nugatory any right to hunt that a present-day Shubenacadie Micmac Indian would otherwise be entitled to invoke based on this treaty.

The appellant, Simon, as a member of the Shubenacadie Indian Brook Band of Micmac Indians, residing in Eastern Nova Scotia, the area covered by the Treaty of 1752, can therefore raise the treaty in his defence.

VIII

Is the treaty a "treaty" within the meaning of s. 88 of the Indian Act?

Section 88 of the *Indian Act* stipulates that, "Subject to the terms of any treaty . . . all laws of general application from time to time in force in any province are applicable to and in respect of Indians in the province . . . ".

The majority of the Appellate Division held that it was extremely doubtful whether the Treaty of 1752 was a "treaty" within the meaning of s. 88, primarily because it was merely a general confirmation of aboriginal rights and did not grant or confer "new permanent rights". MacDonald J.A. also concluded that the 1752 document could not be considered a "treaty" under s. 88 because it was made by only a small portion of the Micmac Nation and it did not define any land or area where the rights were to be exercised. The respondent urges these views upon this Court. The respondent further submits that the word "treaty" in s. 88 of the *Indian Act* does not include the Treaty of 1752 even under the extended definition of "treaty" enunciated in *R. v. White and Bob* ... because the treaty did not deal with the ceding of land or delineation of boundaries.

... [T]he fact that the treaty did not *create* new hunting or fishing rights but merely *recognized* pre-existing rights does not render s. 88 inapplicable. On this point, Davey J.A. stated in *R. v. White and Bob, supra*, at p. 616:

> The force of the first argument seems to depend upon the assumption that s. 87 should be read as if it were subject only to rights created by a Treaty; that would remove from the saving clause rights already in being and excepted from or confirmed by a Treaty. That argument fails to accord full meaning to the words, "subject to the terms of any treaty . . ." *In my opinion an exception, reservation, or confirmation is as much a term of a Treaty as a grant*, (I observe parenthetically that a reservation may be a grant), and the operative words of the section will not extend general laws in force in any Province to Indians in derogation of rights so excepted, reserved or confirmed.

(Emphasis added.)

. . . . .

With respect to the respondent's submission that some form of land cession is necessary before an agreement can be described as a treaty under s. 88, I can see no principled basis for interpreting s. 88 in this manner. I would adopt the useful comment of Norris J.A. of the British Columbia Court of Appeal in *R. v. White and Bob, supra*, affirmed on appeal to this Court. In a concurring judgment, he stated at pp. 648-9:

> The question is, in my respectful opinion, to be resolved not by the application of rigid rules of construction without regard to the circumstances existing when the document was completed nor by the tests of modern day draftsmanship. In determining what the intention of Parliament was at the time of the enactment of s. 87 [now s. 88] of the *Indian Act*, Parliament is to be taken to have had in mind the common understanding of the parties to the document at the time it was executed. In the section "Treaty" is not a word of art and in my respectful opinion, it embraces all such engagements made by persons in authority as may be brought within the term 'the word of the white man' the sanctity of which was, at the time of British exploration and settlement, the most important means of obtaining the goodwill and co-operation of the native tribes and ensuring that the colonists would be protected from death and destruction. On such assurance the Indians relied.

In my view, Parliament intended to include within the operation of s. 88 all agreements concluded by the Crown with the Indians that would otherwise be enforceable treaties, whether land was ceded or not. None of the Maritime treaties of the eighteenth century cedes land. To find that s. 88 applies only to land cession treaties would be to limit severely its scope and run contrary to the principle that Indian treaties and statutes relating to Indians should be liberally construed and uncertainties resolved in favour of the Indians.

Finally, it should be noted that several cases have considered the Treaty of 1752 to be a valid "treaty" within the meaning of s. 88 of the *Indian Act* ... The treaty was an exchange of solemn promises between the Micmacs and the King's representative entered into to achieve and guarantee peace. It is an enforceable obligation between the Indians and the white man and, as such, falls within the meaning of the word "treaty" in s. 88 of the *Indian Act*.

IX

Do the hunting rights contained in the treaty exempt the appellant from prosecution under s. 150(1) of the Lands and Forests Act?

As a result of my conclusion that the appellant was validly exercising his right to hunt under the Treaty of 1752 and the fact he has admitted that his conduct otherwise constitutes an offence under the *Lands and Forests Act*, it must now be determined what the result is when a treaty right comes into conflict with provincial legislation. This question is governed by s. 88 of the *Indian Act*, which, it will be recalled, states that "Subject to the terms of any treaty, all laws of general application . . . in force in the province are applicable to . . . Indians".

. . . . .

Under s. 88 of the *Indian Act*, when the terms of a treaty come into conflict with federal legislation, the latter prevails, subject to whatever may be the effect of s. 35 of the *Constitution Act, 1982*. It has been held to be within the exclusive power of Parliament under s. 91(24) of the *Constitution Act, 1867*, to derogate from rights recognized in a treaty agreement made with the Indians.

. . . . .

Here, however, we are dealing with provincial legislation. The effect of s. 88 of the *Indian Act* is to exempt the Indians from provincial legislation which restricts or contravenes the terms of any treaty.

. . . . .

Therefore, the question here is whether s. 150(1) of the *Lands and Forests Act*, a provincial enactment of general application in Nova Scotia, restricts or contravenes the right to hunt in art. 4 of the Treaty of 1752. If so, the treaty right to hunt prevails and the appellant is exempt from the operation of the provincial game legislation at issue.

Section 150(1) states that no person shall take, carry or possess a rifle or shot-gun cartridges loaded with ball or with shot larger than AAA in certain areas of the province except as provided in the section.

. . . . .

In my opinion, s. 150 of the *Lands and Forests Act* of Nova Scotia restricts the appellant's right to hunt under the treaty. The section clearly places seasonal limitations and licensing requirements, for the purposes of wild-life conservation, on the right to possess a rifle and ammunition for the purposes of hunting. The restrictions imposed in this case conflict, there-fore, with the appellant's right to possess a firearm and ammunition in order to exercise his free liberty to hunt over the lands covered by the treaty. As noted, it is clear that under s. 88 of the *Indian Act* provincial leg-islation cannot restrict native treaty rights. If conflict arises, the terms of the treaty prevail. Therefore, by virtue of s. 88 of the *Indian Act*, the clear terms of art. 4 of the treaty must prevail over s. 150(1) of the provincial *Lands and Forests Act*.

. . . . .

I conclude that the appellant has a valid treaty right to hunt under the Treaty of 1752 which, by virtue of s. 88 of the *Indian Act*, cannot be re-stricted by provincial legislation. It follows, therefore, that the appellant's possession of a rifle and ammunition in a safe manner, referable to his treaty right to hunt, cannot be restricted by s. 150(1) of the *Lands and Forests Act*.

I would accordingly quash the convictions and enter verdicts of acquit-tal on both charges.

X

Constitutional question: s. 35 of the Constitution Act, 1982

... In my view, s. 88 of the *Indian Act* covers the present situation and provides the necessary protection to the appellant Simon. As a result, it is not necessary for the determination of this appeal to consider s. 35(1) of the *Constitution Act, 1982*.

. . . . .

Conclusions

To summarize:

1. The Treaty of 1752 was validly created by competent parties.
2. The treaty contains a right to hunt which covers the activities engaged in by the appellant.
3. The treaty was not terminated by subsequent hostilities in 1753. Nor has it been demonstrated that the right to hunt, protected by the treaty has been extinguished.
4. The appellant is a Micmac Indian covered by the treaty.
5. The Treaty of 1752 is a "treaty" within the meaning of s. 88 of the *Indian Act*.
6. By virtue of s. 88 of the *Indian Act*, the appellant is exempt from prose-cution under s. 150(1) of the *Lands and Forests Act*.

7. In light of these conclusions, it is not necessary to answer the constitutional question raised in this appeal.

I would, therefore, allow the appeal, quash the convictions of the appellant and enter verdicts of acquittal on both charges.

Appeal allowed; acquittals entered.

How did the Supreme Court's decision in *Simon* clarify the judicial understanding of treaties and treaty rights? What are the implications of its rejection of a "frozen rights" approach to treaty rights and its finding that activities "reasonably incidental" to the exercise of treaty rights must be embodied within the treaty right itself?

The rejection of frozen rights theory in *Simon* was subsequently affirmed by the Supreme Court of Canada in *R. v. Sparrow*, [1990] 1 S.C.R. 1075, [1990] 4 W.W.R. 410, 46 B.C.L.R. (2d) 1, 56 C.C.C. (3d) 263, 70 D.L.R. (4th) 385, 111 N.R. 241, [1990] 3 C.N.L.R. 160, which is reproduced in Chapter 4. However, compare the approach towards frozen rights theory in those cases with that endorsed by the Supreme Court's majority decision in *R. v. Van der Peet*, [1996] 9 W.W.R. 1, 23 B.C.L.R. (3d) 1, 50 C.R. (4th) 1, 137 D.L.R. (4th) 289, 109 C.C.C. (3d) 1, 200 N.R. 1, [1996] 4 C.N.L.R. 177 (S.C.C.), reproduced in Chapter 4. Note also how the majority's decision in *Van der Peet* treats activities that are "reasonably incidental" to the exercise of constitutionally protected rights versus the approach endorsed in *Simon*. Were the *Simon* and *Sparrow* precedents discussed here overturned by *Van der Peet*? If not, how are they affected by the *Van der Peet* decision?

G. MORE RECENT JUDICIAL CONSIDERATIONS OF TREATIES

Following the *Simon* decision, some confusion arose over the use of the canons of interpretation, initially as a result of the Supreme Court of Canada's decision in *R. v. Horse*, [1988] 1 S.C.R. 187, [1988] 2 W.W.R. 289, 39 C.C.C. (3d) 97, [1988] 2 C.N.L.R. 112, 82 N.R. 206, 65 Sask. R. 176, 47 D.L.R. (4th) 526 and, later, because of that Court's decision in *R. v. Howard*, [1994] 2 S.C.R. 299, 18 O.R. (3d) 384, [1994] 3 C.N.L.R. 146, 71 O.A.C. 278, 115 D.L.R. (4th) 312, 166 N.R. 282. The *Horse* decision, while outwardly affirming most of the canons of treaty interpretation, held that extrinsic evidence could be used only where there was an ambiguity in the terms of a treaty. In *Howard*, the Court stated that a 1923 treaty ought not be interpreted according to the canons of treaty interpretation because the treaty concerned lands close to urbanized Ontario and the Hiawatha signatories included businessmen and a civil servant and all were literate.

From these decisions, a number of questions arise. Are these decisions reconcilable with the canons of treaty interpretation? Ought different standards of treaty interpretation exist that would be applied based on the perceived or presumed knowledge of the Aboriginal treaty signatories? Should more recent treaties not receive the benefit of the canons of interpretation because of the Aboriginals' greater understanding of English and the concepts employed in treaties? In answering the latter question, it must first be asked what the bases of the canons of interpretation are: inequality in bargaining power? lack of Aboriginal understanding of English and legal concepts such as land surrenders? the parties' different understandings of language and concepts? the nature of the relationship between the parties? a combination of these?

The Supreme Court appeared to distance itself from the *Horse* judgment in its decision in *Sioui v. Quebec (Attorney General)* where it stated that "a more flexible approach is necessary as the question of the existence of a treaty within the meaning of s. 88 of the *Indian Act* is generally closely bound up with the circumstances existing when the document was prepared." Is it possible to interpret treaties in their historical context without looking beyond the four corners of the treaties? Consider what the Supreme Court had to say on this point in *Sioui*.

SIOUI v. QUEBEC (ATTORNEY GENERAL)

(1990), 70 D.L.R. (4th) 427, [1990] 1 S.C.R. 1025 (*sub nom. R. v. Sioui*), 109 N.R. 22, 56 C.C.C. (3d) 225, [1990] 3 C.N.L.R. 30, 30 Q.A.C. 280

The judgment of the court was delivered by

Lamer J.: —

I *Facts and relevant legislation*

The four respondents were convicted by the Court of Sessions of the Peace of cutting down trees, camping and making fires in places not designated in Jacques-Cartier park contrary to ss. 9 and 37 of the *Regulation respecting the Parc de la Jacques-Cartier* (Order in Council 3108-81 of November 11, 1981, (1981) 113 *O.G.* II 3518), adopted pursuant to the *Parks Act*, R.S.Q., c. P-9. The regulations state that:

> 9. In the Park, users may not:
>
> > **1.** destroy, mutilate, remove or introduce any kind of plant or part thereof.
>
> . . . . .
>
> However, the collection of edible vegetable products is authorized solely for the purpose of consumption as food on the site, except in the preservation zones where it is forbidden at all times;
>
> . . . . .
>
> **37.** Camping and fires are permitted only in the places designated and arranged for those purposes.

The *Parks Act*, under which the foregoing regulations were adopted, provides the following penalties for an offence:

11. Every person who infringes this act or the regulations is guilty of an offence and liable on summary proceedings, in addition to the costs, to a fine of not less than $50 nor more than $1,000 in the case of an individual and to a fine of not less than $200 nor more than $5,000 in the case of a corporation.

. . . . .

The respondents are Indians within the meaning of the *Indian Act*, R.S.C., 1985, c. I-5 (formerly R.S.C. 1970, c. I-6), and are members of the Huron band on the Lorette Indian Reserve. They admit that they committed the acts with which they were charged in Jacques-Cartier park, which is located outside the boundaries of the Lorette Reserve. However, they alleged that they were practising certain ancestral customs and religious rites which are the subject of a treaty between the Hurons and the British, a treaty which brings s. 88 of the *Indian Act* into play and exempts them from compliance with the regulations. Section 88 of the *Indian Act* states that:

> 88. Subject to the terms of any treaty and any other Act of Parliament, all laws of general application from time to time in force in any province are applicable to and in respect of Indians in the province, except to the extent that those laws are inconsistent with this Act or any order, rule, regulation or by-law made thereunder, and except to the extent that those laws make provision for any matter for which provision is made by or under this Act.

The document the respondents rely on in support of their contentions is dated September 5, 1760 and signed by Brigadier General James Murray. It reads as follows:

> THESE are to certify that the CHIEF of the HURON Tribe of Indians, having come to me in the name of His Nation, to submit to His BRITANNICK MAJESTY, and make Peace, has been received under my Protection, with his whole Tribe; and henceforth no English Officer or party is to molest, or interrupt them in returning to their Settlement at LORETTE; and they are received upon the same terms with the Canadians, being allowed the free Exercise of their Religion, their Customs, and Liberty of trading with the English: — recommending it to the Officers commanding the Posts, to treat them kindly.

> Given under my hand at Longueil, this 5th day of September, 1760.

> By the Genl's Command,   JA. MURRAY
> JOHN COSNAN,
> Adjut. Genl.

The Hurons had been in the Quebec area since about 1650, after having had to leave their ancestral lands located in territory which is now in Ontario. In 1760, they were settled at Lorette on land given to them by the Jesuits 18 years earlier and made regular use of the territory of Jacques-Cartier park at that time.

III *Points at issue*

The appellants are asking this court to dispose of the appeal solely on the basis of the document of September 5, 1760 and s. 88 of the *Indian Act*.

. . . . .

To decide the case at bar I will consider first the question of whether Great Britain, General Murray and the Hurons had capacity to sign a treaty, assuming that those parties intended to do so. If they had, I will then consider whether the parties actually did enter into a treaty. Finally, if the document of September 5, 1760 is a treaty, I will analyse its contents to determine the nature of the rights guaranteed therein and establish whether they have territorial application.

IV *Analysis*

A. *Introduction*

Our courts and those of our neighbours to the south have already considered what distinguishes a treaty with the Indians from other agreements affecting them. The task is not an easy one. In *Simon v. The Queen*, [1985] 2 S.C.R. 387, this court adopted the comment of Norris J.A. in *R. v. White and Bob* (1964), 50 D.L.R. (2d) 613 (B.C.C.A.) (affirmed in the Supreme Court (1965), 52 D.L.R. (2d) 481*n*, [1965] S.C.R. vi), that the courts should show flexibility in determining the legal nature of a document recording a transaction with the Indians. In particular, they must take into account the historical context and perception each party might have as to the nature of the undertaking contained in the document under consideration.

. . . . .

As the Chief Justice said in *Simon, supra*, treaties and statutes relating to Indians should be liberally construed and uncertainties resolved in favour of the Indians (at p. 410). In our quest for the legal nature of the document of September 5, 1760, therefore, we should adopt a broad and generous interpretation of what constitutes a treaty.

In my opinion, this liberal and generous attitude, heedful of historical fact, should also guide us in examining the preliminary question of the capacity to sign a treaty, as illustrated by *Simon* and *White and Bob*.

Finally, once a valid treaty is found to exist, that treaty must in turn be given a just, broad and liberal construction. This principle, for which there is ample precedent, was recently reaffirmed in *Simon*. The factors underlying this rule were eloquently stated in *Jones v. Meehan*, 175 U.S. 1 (1899), a judgment of the United States Supreme Court, and are I think just as relevant to questions involving the existence of a treaty and the capacity of the parties as they are to the interpretation of a treaty (at pp. 10-11):

> In construing any treaty between the United States and an Indian tribe, it must always . . . be borne in mind that the negotiations for the treaty are conducted, on the part of the United States, an enlightened and powerful nation, by representatives skilled in diplomacy, masters of a written language, understanding the modes and forms of creating the various technical estates known to their law, and assisted by an interpreter employed by themselves; that the treaty is drawn up by them and in their own language;

that the Indians, on the other hand, are a weak and dependent people, who have no written language and are wholly unfamiliar with all the forms of legal expression, and whose only knowledge of the terms in which the treaty is framed is that imparted to them by the interpreter employed by the United States; and that the treaty must therefore be construed, not according to the technical meaning of its words to learned lawyers, but in the sense in which they would naturally be understood by the Indians.

The Indian people are today much better versed in the art of negotiation with public authorities than they were when the United States Supreme Court handed down its decision in *Jones*. As the document in question was signed over a hundred years before that decision, these considerations argue all the more strongly for the courts to adopt a generous and liberal approach.

B. *Question of capacity of parties involved*

Before deciding whether the intention in the document of September 5, 1760 was to enter into a treaty within the meaning of s. 88 of the *Indian Act*, this court must decide preliminary matters regarding the capacity of Great Britain, General Murray and the Huron nation to enter into a treaty. If any one of these parties was without such capacity, the document at issue could not be a valid treaty and it would then be pointless to consider it further.

. . . . .

I will first examine the capacity of Great Britain to enter into a treaty and then consider that of Murray and the Hurons.

1. *Capacity of Great Britain*

At this preliminary stage of the analysis, and for purposes of discussion, it has to be assumed that the document of September 5, 1760 possesses the characteristics of a treaty and that the only issue that arises concerns the capacity of the parties to create obligations of the kind contained in a treaty.

The appellant argued that the British Crown could not validly enter into a treaty with the Hurons as it was not sovereign in Canada in 1760. The appellant based this argument on the rules of international law, as stated by certain 18th and 19th century writers, which required that a state should be sovereign in a territory before it could alienate that territory: see E. de Vattel, *The Law of Nations or Principles of the Law of Nature* (1760), vol. II, book III, para. 197; E. Ortolan, *Des moyens d' acquérir le domaine international ou propriété d' État entre les nations* (1851), para. 167.

Without deciding what the international law on this point was, I note that the writers to whom the appellant referred the court studied the rules governing international relations and did not comment on the rules which at that time governed the conclusion of treaties between European nations and native peoples. In any case, the rules of international law do not preclude the document being characterized as a treaty within the meaning of s. 88 of the *Indian Act*. At the time with which we are concerned relations with Indian tribes fell somewhere between the kind of relations conducted between sovereign states and the relations that such states had with their own citizens. The *Simon, supra,* decision, is clear in this regard: an Indian treaty is an agreement *sui generis* which is neither created nor terminated according to the rules of international law (p. 404).

Of course, if the document is a treaty, it could not have been binding on France if Canada had remained under its sovereignty at the end of the war. It would be fair to assume that the Hurons knew enough about warfare to understand that a treaty concluded with the enemy would be of little use to them if the French regained *de facto* control of New France.

Both *Simon* and *White and Bob* make it clear that the question of capacity must be seen from the point of view of the Indians at that time, and the Court must ask whether it was reasonable for them to have assumed that the other party they were dealing with had the authority to enter into a valid treaty with them. I conclude without any hesitation that the Hurons could reasonably have believed that the British Crown had the power to enter into a treaty with them that would be in effect as long as the British controlled Canada. France had not hesitated to enter into treaties of alliance with the Hurons and no one ever seemed to have questioned France's capacity to conclude such agreements. From the Hurons' point of view, there was no difference between these two European states. They were both foreigners to the Hurons and their presence in Canada had only one purpose, that of controlling the territory by force.

2. *General Murray's capacity*

The appellant disputes Murray's capacity to sign a treaty on behalf of Great Britain on the ground that he was at that time only Governor of the City and District of Quebec and a brigadier general in the British Army. As Governor, he was subject to the authority of His Majesty's Secretary of State for the Southern Department, and as a soldier he was the subordinate of General Amherst, the "Commander in Chief of His Britannic Majesty's Troops and Forces in North America". It is true that Murray's capacity to enter into this treaty is less obvious than that of Great Britain to "treat" with the Indians.

. . . . .

To arrive at the conclusion that a person had the capacity to enter into a treaty with the Indians, he or she must thus have represented the British Crown in very important, authoritative functions. It is then necessary to take the Indians' point of view and to ask whether it was reasonable for them to believe, in light of the circumstances and the position occupied by the party they were dealing with directly, that they had before them a person capable of binding the British Crown by treaty. To determine whether the Hurons' perception of Murray's capacity to sign a treaty on behalf of

Great Britain was reasonable, the importance of the part played by the latter in Canada in 1760 has to be established.

Although during the siege of Quebec James Murray was the fourth ranking officer in the British military hierarchy in Canada, after the death of Wolfe and the departure of Townshend and Monckton he became the highest ranking officer in the British Army stationed in Canada. General Amherst was the highest military authority in North America and his authority covered all British soldiers in Canada. Murray received the command of the troops at Quebec from him. A very important fact is that since 1759, Murray had also acted as Military Governor of the Quebec district, which included Lorette. He had used his powers to regulate, *inter alia*, the currency exchange rate and the prices of grain, bread and meat and to create civil courts and appoint judges (*Governor Murray's Journal of the Siege of Quebec* (1939), pp. 10-12, 14, and 16-17).

At the time the document under consideration was signed, General Amherst and his troops were occupied in crossing the rapids upstream of Montreal and it was not until some days later, probably on September 8, 1760, that they reached that city: see in this regard the work of F. X. Garneau, *Histoire du Canada français* (1969), vol. 3, at pp. 269-72. In my view, therefore, the respondents are correct in stating that on September 5, 1760, Murray was the highest ranking British officer with whom the Hurons could have conferred. The circumstances prevailing at the time, in my view, thus support the respondents' proposition that Murray in fact had the necessary capacity to enter into a treaty. Furthermore, if there is still any doubt, I think it is clear in any event that Murray had such authority in New France that it was reasonable for the Hurons to believe that he had the power to enter into a treaty with them.

. . . . .

In short, even apart from my conclusion with respect to Murray's actual authority to sign a treaty, I am of the view that the Hurons could reasonably have assumed that, as a general, Murray was giving them a safe conduct to return to Lorette, and that as Governor of the Quebec district, he was signing a treaty guaranteeing the Hurons the free exercise of their religion, customs and trade with the English. In either case no problems concerning Murray's capacity would invalidate the treaty, if there was one.

For all these reasons, therefore, I conclude that Murray had the necessary powers to enter into a treaty with the Hurons that would be binding on the British.

3. *Capacity of the Hurons*

The appellant argues that the Hurons could not enter into a treaty with the British Crown because this Indian nation had no historical occupation or possession of the territory extending from the St-Maurice to the Saguenay. Without going so far as to suggest that there cannot be treaties other than agreements under which the Indians cede land to the Crown, the appellant argues that a treaty could not confer rights on the Indians unless the latter could claim historical occupation or possession of the lands in question.

The appellant deduces this requirement from the fact that most of the cases involving treaties between the British and the Indians concern territories which had traditionally been occupied or held at the time in question by the Indian nation which signed the treaty. The academic commentary cited by the appellant also deals with the aspect of historical occupation or possession of land found in treaties with Indians.

There is no basis either in precedent or in the ordinary meaning of the word "treaty" for imposing such a restriction on what can constitute a treaty within the meaning of s. 88 of the *Indian Act*. In *Simon* [at p. 410], this court in fact rejected the argument that s. 88 applied only to land cession treaties. In the court's opinion that would limit severely the scope of the word "treaty" and run contrary to the principle that Indians treaties should be liberally construed and uncertainties resolved in favour of the Indians. The argument made here must be rejected in the same way. There is no reason why an agreement concerning something other than a territory, such as an agreement about political or social rights, cannot be a treaty within the meaning of s. 88 of the *Indian Act*. There is also no basis for excluding agreements in which the Crown may have chosen to create, for the benefit of a tribe, rights over territory other than its traditional territory. Accordingly, I consider that a territorial claim is not essential to the existence of a treaty.

I therefore conclude that all the parties involved were competent to enter into a treaty within the meaning of s. 88 of the *Indian Act*. This leads me to consider the next question: Did General Murray and the Hurons in fact enter into such a treaty?

C. *Legal nature of the document of September 5, 1760*

1. *Constituent elements of a treaty*

In *Simon* this court noted that a treaty with the Indians is unique, that it is an agreement *sui generis* which is neither created nor terminated according to the rules of international law. ... The following are two extracts illustrating the reasons relied on by the Chief Justice in concluding that a treaty had been concluded between the Micmacs and the British Crown (at pp. 401 and 410):

> In my opinion, both the Governor and the Micmac entered into the treaty with the intention of creating mutually binding obligations which would be solemnly respected. It also provided a mechanism for dispute resolution.

> . . . . .

> The treaty was an exchange of solemn promises between the Micmacs and the King's representative entered into to achieve and guarantee peace. It is an enforceable obligation between the Indians and the white man and, as such, falls within the meaning of the word "treaty" in s. 88 of the *Indian Act*.

From these extracts it is clear that what characterizes a treaty is the intention to create obligations, the presence of mutually binding obligations and a certain measure of solemnity.

. . . . .

In *White and Bob, supra,* Norris J.A. also discussed the nature of a treaty under the *Indian Act.* As he mentioned ... the word "treaty" is not a term of art. It merely identifies agreements in which the "word of the white man" is given and by which the latter made certain of the Indians' co-operation. Norris J.A. also wrote at p. 649:

> In view of the argument before us, it is necessary to point out that on numerous occasions in modern days, rights under what were entered into with Indians as solemn engagements, although completed with what would now be considered informality, have been whittled away on the excuse that they do not comply with present day formal requirements and with rules of interpretation applicable to transactions between people who must be taken in the light of advanced civilization to be of equal status. Reliance on instances where this has been done is merely to compound injustice without real justification at law. The transaction in question here was a transaction between, on the one hand, the strong representative of a proprietary company under the Crown and representing the Crown, who had gained the respect of the Indians by his integrity and the strength of his personality and was thus able to bring about the completion of the agreement, and, on the other hand, uneducated savages. The nature of the transaction itself was consistent with the informality of frontier days in this Province and such as the necessities of the occasion and the customs and illiteracy of the Indians demanded . . . The unusual (by the standards of legal draftsmen) nature and form of the document considered in the light of the circumstances on Vancouver Island in 1854 does not detract from it as being a "Treaty".

This lengthy passage brings out the importance of the historical context, including the interpersonal relations of those involved at the time, in trying to determine whether a document falls into the category of a treaty under s. 88 of the *Indian Act.* It also shows that formalities are of secondary importance in deciding on the nature of a document containing an agreement with the Indians.

The decision of the Ontario Court of Appeal in *R. v. Taylor and Williams* (1981), 62 C.C.C. (2d) 227, also provides valuable assistance by listing a series of factors which are relevant to analysis of the historical background. In that case the court had to interpret a treaty, and not determine the legal nature of a document, but the factors mentioned may be just as useful in determining the existence of a treaty as in interpreting it. In particular, they assist in determining the intent of the parties to enter into a treaty. Among these factors are:

1. continuous exercise of a right in the past and at present;
2. the reasons why the Crown made a commitment;
3. the situation prevailing at the time the document was signed;
4. evidence of relations of mutual respect and esteem between the negotiators, and
5. the subsequent conduct of the parties.

2. *Analysis of the document in light of these factors*

(a) *Wording*

. . . . .

Several aspects of the wording of the document are consistent with the appellant's position that it was an act of surrender and a safe conduct rather than a treaty. The following is a brief review of the appellant's five main arguments in this regard. First, the document opens with the words "These are to certify that ...", which would suggest that the document in question is a certificate or an acknowledgement of the Hurons' surrender, made official by Murray in order to inform the British troops. Bisson J.A. gave these introductory words an interpretation more favourable to the Hurons: the Hurons did not know how to write and the choice of words only makes it clear that the document of September 5, 1760 recorded an oral treaty.

Secondly, General Murray used expressions which appear to involve him only personally, which do not suggest that he was acting as a representative of the British Crown. Thus, the following expressions are used:

1. "having come to me",
2. "has been received under my Protection",
3. "By the General's Command".

Although the Hurons had surrendered to His Britannic Majesty, wording the document in this way could tend to show that Murray intended only to give his personal undertaking to protect the Hurons, without thereby binding the British Crown in the long term. Murray, it is argued, had only offered the Hurons military protection and had no intention of entering into a treaty.

Thirdly, the orders given to British soldiers stationed in Canada ("no English Officer or party is to molest, or interrupt them in returning to their Settlement at LORETTE ... recommending it to the Officers commanding the Posts, to treat them kindly ... By the Genl's Command") would more naturally form part of a document such as a safe conduct or pass than of a treaty.

These points bring out the unilateral aspect of the document of September 5th: it could be an administrative document issued by General Murray, recognizing that the Hurons had laid down their arms and giving orders to British soldiers accordingly. Finally, the document was signed only by the General's representative with no indication that it had been assented to by the Hurons' in one way or another. The main purpose of the document is thus, it is argued, to recognize the surrender, and what was more important to the Hurons, allow them to return to Lorette safely without fear of being mistaken for enemies by British soldiers they might meet along the way.

Fourthly, the reference to a specific event, namely the return journey to Lorette, as opposed to a document recognizing rights in perpetuity or without any apparent time-limit, could show that the purpose of this document was not to settle long-term relations between the Hurons and

the British. The temporary and specific nature of the document would indicate that the parties did not intend to enter into a treaty.

Fifthly, the document does not possess the formality which is usually to
be found in the wording of a treaty. First, it is not the General himself who
signed the document, but his adjutant on his behalf. Second, the language
used in the document does not have the formalism generally accompanying the signature of a treaty with Indians.

. . . . .

The appellant argues that the Hurons did not formalize the document
either by their signature (which would not be absolutely necessary to make
it a treaty) or by the use of necklaces or belts of shells which were the traditional method used by the Hurons to formalize agreements at the time.
Clearly, this argument has weight only if the document accurately indicates all the events surrounding the signature. Otherwise, extrinsic proof
of solemnities could help to show that the parties intended to enter into a
formal agreement and that they manifested this intent in one way or another.

While the analysis thus far seems to suggest that the document of September 5th is not a treaty, the presence of a clause guaranteeing the free
exercise of religion, customs and trade with the English cannot but raise
serious doubts about this proposition. It seems extremely strange to me
that a document which is supposedly only a temporary, unilateral and informal safe conduct should contain a clause guaranteeing rights of such
importance. As Bisson J.A. noted in the Court of Appeal judgment, there
would have been no necessity to mention the free exercise of religion and
customs in a document the effects of which were only to last for a few
days. Such a guarantee would definitely have been more natural in a
treaty where "the word of the white man" is given.

The appellant and the Attorney-General of Canada put forward certain
explanations for the presence of such guarantees in the document:

1. the free exercise of religion and customs was part of the protection under
   which General Murray received the Hurons;
2. the free exercise of religion and customs is mentioned because these
   benefits had been conferred on Canadians laying down their arms
   earlier.

As this Court recently noted in *R. v. Horse*, [1988] 1 S.C.R. 187 [at p. 201],
extrinsic evidence is not to be used as an aid to interpreting a treaty in the
absence of ambiguity or where the result would be to alter its terms by
adding words to or subtracting words from the written agreement. This
rule also applies in determining the legal nature of a document relating to
the Indians. However, a more flexible approach is necessary as the question of the existence of a treaty within the meaning of s. 88 of the *Indian Act*
is generally closely bound up with the circumstances existing when the
document was prepared ... In any case, the wording alone will not suffice
to determine the legal nature of the document before the court. On the one
hand, we have before us a document the form of which and some of whose
subject-matter suggest that it is not a treaty, and on the other, we find it to

contain protection of fundamental rights which supports the opposite conclusion. The ambiguity arising from this document thus means that the court must look at extrinsic evidence to determine its legal nature.

(b) *Extrinsic evidence*

It was suggested that the court examine three types of extrinsic evidence to assist it in determining whether the document of September 5th is a treaty. First, to indicate the parties' intent to enter into a treaty, the court was offered evidence to present a picture of the historical context of the period. Then, evidence was presented of certain facts closely associated with the signing of the document and relating to the existence of the various constituent elements of a treaty. Finally, still with a view to determining whether the parties intended to enter into a treaty, the court was told of the subsequent conduct of the parties in respect of the document of September 5, 1760.

I should first mention that the admissibility of certain documents submitted by the intervener the National Indian Brotherhood/Assembly of First Nations in support of its arguments was contested. The intervener was relying on documents that were not part of the record in the lower courts. The appellant agreed that certain of these documents, namely Murray's journal, letters and instructions, should be included in the record provided this court considered that their admissibility was justified by the concept of judicial notice. I am of the view that all the documents to which I will refer, whether my attention was drawn to them by the intervener or as a result of my personal research, are documents of a historical nature which I am entitled to rely on pursuant to the concept of judicial knowledge. As Norris J.A. said in *White and Bob* (at p. 629):

> The Court is entitled "to take judicial notice of the facts of history whether past or contemporaneous" as Lord du Parcq said in *Monarch Steamship Co., Ld. v. Karlshamns Oljefabriker (A/B)*, [1949] A.C. 196 at p. 234, [1949] 1 All E.R. 1 at p. 20, and it is entitled to rely on its own historical knowledge and researches, *Read v. Bishop of Lincoln*, [1892] A.C. 644, Lord Halsbury, L.C., at pp. 652-4.

The documents I cite all enable the court, in my view, to identify more accurately the historical context essential to the resolution of this case.

The appellant argues that the historical context at the time the document of September 5th was concluded shows that the parties had no intention to enter into a treaty. The respondents and the intervener, the National Indian Brotherhood/Assembly of First Nations, on the other hand, maintain that the historical background to this document supports the existence of a common intent to sign a treaty.

On September 5, 1760, France and England were engaged in a war begun four years earlier, which ended with the Treaty of Paris, 1763, signed on February 10, 1763. About a year earlier, the battle of the Plains of Abraham had allowed the British to take control of Québec City and the surrounding area. During the year following this victory, British troops had worked to consolidate their military position in Canada and to solve the supply and other practical problems engendered by the very harsh winter of 1759.

In his work *An Historical Journal of the Campaigns in North-America for the Years 1757, 1758, 1759 and 1760* (1769), at p. 382 (day of September 3, 1760), Captain Knox also relates the efforts of General Murray to win the loyalty of the Canadians. General Murray at that time invited French soldiers to surrender and Canadians to lay down their arms. He had made it widely known that he would pardon those who surrendered and allow them to keep their land. He had also promised them that he would make larger grants of land and protect them. He gave those who responded to his appeal and took the oath of allegiance to the British Crown safe conducts to return to their parishes. Steps were also taken to inform the Indians who were allies of the British of these changes of allegiance so as to ensure that they would not be attacked on the way back.

As the advantageous position and strength of the British troops became more and more apparent, several groups did surrender and it appears that this movement accelerated in the days preceding that on which the document at issue was signed.

. . . . .

In fact, the total defeat of France in Canada was very near: the "Act of Capitulation of Montreal", by which the French troops stationed in Canada laid down their arms, was signed on September 8, 1760, and signalled the end of France's *de facto* control in Canada.

. . . . .

From the historical situation I have just briefly outlined, the appellant deduced that the document at issue is only a capitulation and that the legal nature of such a document should not be construed differently depending on whether it relates to the Indians or to the French. The court has before it, he submitted, only a capitulation comparable to a capitulation of French soldiers or Canadians, which cannot be elevated to the category of a treaty within the meaning of s. 88 of the *Indian Act* simply because an Indian tribe was a party to it. In other words, as Murray signed the same kind of document with respect to the Indians, the French or the Canadians his intent could not have been any different. The appellant also maintains that, like the capitulations of the Canadians and the French soldiers, this document was only temporary in nature in that its consequences would cease when the fate of Canada was finally settled at the end of the war.

I consider that, instead, we can conclude from the historical documents that both Great Britain and France felt that the Indian nations had sufficient independence and played a large enough role in North America for it to be good policy to maintain relations with them very close to those maintained between sovereign nations.

The mother countries did everything in their power to secure the alliance of each Indian nation and to encourage nations allied with the enemy to change sides. When these efforts met with success, they were incorporated in treaties of alliance or neutrality. This clearly indicates that the Indian nations were regarded in their relations with the European nations which occupied North America as independent nations. The papers of Sir

William Johnson (*The Papers of Sir William Johnson*, 14 volumes), who was in charge of Indian affairs in British North America, demonstrate the recognition by Great Britain that nation-to-nation relations had to be conducted with the North American Indians. As an example, I cite an extract from a speech by Sir Johnson at the Onondaga Conference held in April, 1748, attended by the Five Nations (*The Papers of Sir William Johnson*, vol. I, (1921), p.157.):

> Brethren of the five Nations I will begin upon a thing of a long standing, our first *Brothership*. My Reason for it is, I think there are several among you who seem to forget it; It may seem strange to you how I a *Foreigner* should know this, But I tell you I found out some of the old Writings of our Forefathers which was thought to have been lost and in this old valuable Record I find, that our first *Friendship* Commenced at the Arrival of the first great Canoe or Vessel at Albany.

(Emphasis added.)

As the Chief Justice of the United States Supreme Court said in 1832 in *Worcester v. State of Georgia*, 31 U.S. 515 at pp. 548-9 (1832) (6 Pet.), about British policy towards the Indians in the mid-18th century:

> Such was the policy of Great Britain towards the Indian nations inhabiting the territory from which she excluded all other Europeans; such her claims, and such her practical exposition of the charters she had granted: *she considered them as nations capable of maintaining the relations of peace and war; of governing themselves, under her protection; and she made treaties with them, the obligation of which she acknowledged.*

(Emphasis added.)

Further, both the French and the English recognized the critical importance of alliances with the Indians, or at least their neutrality, in determining the outcome of the war between them and the security of the North American colonies.

Following the crushing defeats of the English by the French in 1755, the English realized that control of North America could not be acquired without the co-operation of the Indians. Accordingly, from then on they made efforts to ally themselves with as many Indian nations as possible. The French, who had long realized the strategic role of the Indians in the success of any war effort, also did everything they could to secure their alliance or maintain alliances already established: Jack Stagg, *Anglo-Indian Relations in North America to 1763* (1981); "Mr. Nelson's Memorial about the State of the Northern Colonies in America", September 24, 1696, reproduced in O' Callaghan (ed.) *Documents relative to the Colonial History of New York* (1856), vol. VII, at p. 206; "Letter from Sir William Johnson to William Pitt", October 24, 1760, in *The Papers of Sir William Johnson*, vol. III, (1921), at pp. 269 *et seq.*; "Mémoire de Bougainville sur l'artillerie du Canada", January 11, 1759, in *Rapport de l'archiviste de la Province de Québec pour 1923-1924* (1924), at p. 58; *Journal du Marquis de Montcalm durant ses campagnes en Canada de 1756 à 1759* (1895), at p. 428.

England also wished to secure the friendship of the Indian nations by treating them with generosity and respect for fear that the safety and development of the colonies and their inhabitants would be compromised by Indians with feelings of hostility. One of the extracts from Knox's work which I cited above reports that the Canadians and the French soldiers who surrendered asked to be protected from Indians on the way back to their parishes. Another passage from Knox, also cited above, relates that the Canadians were terrified at the idea of seeing Sir William Johnson's Indians coming among them. This proves that in the minds of the local population the Indians represented a real and disturbing threat. The fact that England was also aware of the danger the colonies and their inhabitants might run if the Indians withdrew their co-operation is echoed in the following documents: "Letter from Sir William Johnson to the Lords of Trade", November 13, 1763, reproduced in O' Callaghan, (ed.), *op. cit.*, at pp. 574, 579 and 580; "Letter from Sir William Johnson to William Pitt", October 24, 1760, in *The Papers of Sir William Johnson*, vol. III, at pp. 270 and 274; [M.] Ratelle, *Contexte historique de la localisation des Attikameks et des Montagnais de 1760 à nos jours* (1987); "Letter from Amherst to Sir William Johnson", August 30, 1760, in *The Papers of Sir William Johnson*, vol. X, (1951), at p. 177; "Instructions from George II to Amherst", September 18, 1758, National Archives of Canada (MG 18 L 4 file 0 20/8); C. Colden, *The History of the Five Indian Nations of Canada* (1747), at p. 180; Stagg, *op. cit.*, at pp. 166-7; and by analogy Murray, *Journal of the Siege of Quebec, ibid.*, entry of December 31, 1759, at pp. 15-6.

This "generous" policy which the British chose to adopt also found expression in other areas. The British Crown recognized that the Indians had certain ownership rights over their land, it sought to establish trade with them which would rise above the level of exploitation and give them a fair return. It also allowed them autonomy in their internal affairs, intervening in this area as little as possible.

Whatever the similarities between a document recording the laying down of arms by French soldiers or Canadians and the document at issue, the analogy does not go so far as to preclude the conclusion that the document was nonetheless a treaty.

Such a document could not be regarded as a treaty so far as the French and the Canadians were concerned because under international law they had no authority to sign such a document: they were governed by a European nation which alone was able to represent them in dealings with other European nations for the signature of treaties affecting them. The colonial powers recognized that the Indians had the capacity to sign treaties directly with the European nations occupying North American territory. The *sui generis* situation in which the Indians were placed had forced the European mother countries to acknowledge that they had sufficient autonomy for the valid creation of solemn agreements which were called "treaties", regardless of the strict meaning given to that word then and now by international law. The question of the competence of the Hurons and of the French or the Canadians is essential to the question of whether a treaty exists. The question of capacity has to be examined from a fundamentally different viewpoint and in accordance with different principles for each of these groups. Thus, I reject the argument that the legal nature of the document at issue must necessarily be interpreted in the same way as the capitulations of the French and the Canadians. The historical context which I have briefly reviewed even supports the proposition that both the British and the Hurons could have intended to enter into a treaty on September 5, 1760.

. . . . .

Let us now turn to the second type of extrinsic evidence proposed by the parties, namely evidence relating to facts which were contemporaneous with or which occurred shortly before or after the signing of the document of September 5, 1760.

The respondents first presented evidence that the document of September 5, 1760 was the outcome of negotiations between Murray and certain Indian nations, including the Hurons, who wished to make peace with the British Crown. Knox's journal, *ibid.*, reports the following events for September 6th (at p. 384):

> Eight Sachems, of different nations, lately in alliance with the enemy, have surrendered, for themselves and their tribes, to General Murray: these fellows, after conferring with his Excellency, *and that all matters had been adjusted to their satisfaction*, stepped out to the beach opposite to Montreal, flourished their knives and hatchets, and set up the war-shout; intimating to the French, that they are now become our allies and their enemies. While these Chieftains *were negotiating a peace*, two of our Mohawks entered the apartment where they were with the General and Colonel Burton.

(Emphasis added.)

. . . . .

The foregoing passage shows that the document of September 5th was not simply an expression of General Murray's wishes, but the result of negotiations between the parties.

. . . . .

Knox goes on to say that the Mohawks wanted to turn on the various Indian groups allied with the French who had just concluded peace with the British. Murray and Burton intervened and the Mohawks merely made threats against them. What is significant for purposes of this case is that these threats reflected the Mohawks' perception as to the nature of the agreement which had just been concluded between the eight Sachems and Murray. The Mohawks said the following (at p. 385):

> Do you remember, when you treacherously killed one of our brothers at such a time? Ye shall one day pay dearly for it, ye cowardly dogs, — *let the treaty be as it will*: — I tell you, we will destroy you and your settlement.

(Emphasis added.)

The view taken by these Indians was apparently shared by Murray himself. The note written by Murray in his journal, on September 5, 1760, indicates that he considered that a peace treaty had been concluded with the Indian nations in question:

Sepr. 5th. March'd with them myself and on the road, met the Inhabitants who were coming to deliver their arms, and take the oaths, there two nations of Indians, of Hurons and Iroquois, came in & *made their Pace.*

(Emphasis added.) (Knox, *Appendix to an Historical Journal or the Campaigns in North America for the Years 1757, 1758, 1759 and 1760* (1916), at p. 831.)

The accounts given by Knox and Murray himself of the events on the days that are critical for this case are quite consistent with British policy, which favoured alliance or at least neutrality for the greatest number of the Indian nations in the newly conquered territories. By holding negotiations to conclude a peace treaty between the Hurons and the British, Murray was only giving effect to this clear policy of Great Britain.

The intervener, the National Indian Brotherhood/Assembly of First Nations, provided the court with some very interesting evidence in this regard. It submitted the minutes of a conference between Sir William Johnson and the representatives of the Eight Nations, including the Lorette Hurons, held in Montreal on September 16, 1760: *The Papers of Sir William Johnson*, vol. XIII, 1962, at p. 163. Although the appellant objected to the court considering this document, I feel it is a reliable source which allows us to take cognizance of a historical fact. Its being submitted by the intervener does not in any way prevent the court from taking judicial notice of it. Indeed, I can only express my appreciation to the intervener for facilitating my research.

The minutes of this conference refer in several places to the peace recently concluded between the Eight Nations and the English and their allies (at pp. 163-4):

Br. Wy. [Brother Warrigheyagey, a term of endearment for Sir William Johnson, meaning "he who does much business"]

You desired of us to [see] deliver up your People who [may be] are still among us — [We] *As you have now settled all matters wth. us & we are become firm Friends. . . .*

a Belt

Br. W.

> *As we have now made a firm Peace wth. the English & ye. 6 Nats. we shall endeavour all in our Powr. to keep it inviolably.*

a large Belt."

(Emphasis added.)

These words were spoken by spokesmen for the Eight Nations and clearly show that the Indians and Sir William Johnson considered that relations between these Indian nations and the British would now take the form of an alliance ("firm friends"). This new situation was undoubtedly the outcome of the peace concluded between the parties, a peace desired by the Eight Nations as well as the British ("We have now made a firm Peace with the English").

Finally, it is worth noting that each of the contributions made by spokesmen at this conference was followed by the presentation of a belt to solemnize the content of the undertakings that had just been made or the words which had just been spoken. As we saw earlier, the appellant contends that the document of September 5, 1760 is not a treaty, *inter alia*, because the tokens of solemnity that ordinarily accompanied treaties between the Indians and the British are not present. I think it is reasonable to conclude that the circumstances existing on September 5th readily explain the absence of such solemnities. Murray was not given notice of the meeting, and *a fortiori* its purpose, and it was therefore largely improvised. Murray also had very little time to spend on ceremony: his troops were moving towards Montreal and were on a war footing. He himself was busy organizing the final preparations for a meeting between his army and that of Amherst and Haviland in Montreal, for the purpose of bringing down this last significant French bastion in Canada. Although solemnities are not crucial to the existence of a treaty, I think it is in any case reasonable to regard the presentation of belts at the conference on September 16th as a solemn ratification of the peace agreement concluded a few days earlier.

Lastly, the Court was asked to consider the subsequent conduct of the parties as extrinsic evidence of their intent to enter into a treaty. I do not think this is necessary, since the general historical context of the time and the events closely surrounding the document at issue have persuaded me that the document of September 5, 1760 is a treaty within the meaning of s. 88 of the *Indian Act*. The fact that the document has allegedly not been used in the courts or other institutions of our society does not establish that it is not a treaty. Non-use may very well be explained by observance of the rights contained in the document or mere oversight. Moreover, the subsequent conduct which is most indicative of the parties' intent is undoubtedly that which most closely followed the conclusion of the document. Eleven days after it was concluded, at the conference to which I have just referred, the parties gave a clear indication that they had intended to conclude a treaty.

I am therefore of the view that the document of September 5, 1760 is a treaty within the meaning of s. 88 of the *Indian Act*. At this point, the appellant raises two arguments against its application to the present case. First, he argues that the treaty has been extinguished. In the event that it has not been, he argues that the treaty is not such as to render ss. 9 and 37 of the *Regulation respecting the Parc de la Jacques-Cartier* inoperative. Let us first consider whether on May 29, 1982, the date on which the respondents engaged in the activities which are the subject of the charges, the treaty still had any legal effects.

V *Legal Effects of Treaty of September 5, 1760 on May 29, 1982*

The appellant argues that, assuming the document of September 5th is a treaty, it was extinguished by the following documents or events:

1. the Act of Capitulation of Montreal, signed on September 8, 1760;
2. the Treaty of Paris signed on February 10, 1763;
3. the Royal Proclamation of October 7, 1763;
4. the legislative and administrative history of the Hurons' land, and
5. the effect of time and non-use of the treaty.

Neither the documents nor the legislative and administrative history to which the appellant referred the court contain any express statement that the treaty of September 5, 1760 has been extinguished. Even assuming that a treaty can be extinguished implicitly, a point on which I express no opinion here, the appellant was not able in my view to meet the criterion stated in *Simon* regarding the quality of evidence that would be required in any case to support a conclusion that the treaty had been extinguished. That case clearly established that the onus is on the party arguing that the treaty has terminated to show the circumstances and events indicating it has been extinguished. This burden can only be discharged by strict proof, as the Chief Justice said at pp. 405-6:

> Given the serious and far-reaching consequences of a finding that a treaty right has been extinguished, it seems appropriate to demand strict proof of the fact of extinguishment in each case where the issue arises.

The appellant did not submit any persuasive evidence of extinguishment of the treaty. He argues, first, that the treaty had become obsolete because the "Act of Capitulation of Montreal" replaced all other acts of capitulation, thereby extinguishing them. This argument is based on art. 50 of the "Act of Capitulation", which reads as follows:

> The present capitulation shall be inviolably executed in all its articles, and bona fide, on both sides, notwithstanding any infraction, and any other pretence, with regard to the *preceding capitulations*, and without making use of reprisals.

(Emphasis added.)

As I have concluded that this is a peace treaty and not a capitulation, art. 50 has no application in this case, so far as extinguishment of the treaty of September 5th is concerned. That article was designed to ensure that the signatories would comply with the "Act of Capitulation", in spite of the existence of reasons for retaliation which the parties might have had as the result of breaches of an earlier act of capitulation. Article 50 can only apply to preceding acts signed on behalf of France, such as the "Act of Capitulation of Québec" in late 1759. I see nothing here to support the conclusion that this article was also intended to extinguish a treaty between an Indian nation and the British.

The appellant also cites art. 40 of the "Act of Capitulation of Montreal", which provides that:

> *The Savages or Indian allies* of his most Christian Majesty, shall be maintained in the Lands they inhabit; if they chuse to remain there; they shall not be molested on any pretence whatsoever, for having carried arms, and served his most Christian Majesty. They shall have, as well as the French, liberty of religion, and shall keep their missionaries.

(Emphasis added.)

France could not have claimed to represent the Hurons at the time the "Act of Capitulation" was made, since the latter had abandoned their alliance with the French some days before. As they were no longer allies of the French, this article does not apply to them.

· · · · ·

It would be contrary to the general principles of law for an agreement concluded between the English and the French to extinguish a treaty concluded between the English and the Hurons. It must be remembered that a treaty is a solemn agreement between the Crown and the Indians, an agreement the nature of which is sacred: *Simon, supra,* at p. 410, and *White and Bob, supra,* at p. 649. The very definition of a treaty thus makes it impossible to avoid the conclusion that a treaty cannot be extinguished without the consent of the Indians concerned. Since the Hurons had the capacity to enter into a treaty with the British, therefore, they must be the only ones who could give the necessary consent to its extinguishment.

The same reasoning applies to the appellant's argument that the Treaty of Paris of February 10, 1763 between France and England terminated the treaty of September 5, 1760 between the Hurons and the English. England and France could not validly agree to extinguish a treaty between the Hurons and the English, nor could France claim to represent the Hurons regarding the extinguishment of a treaty the Hurons had themselves concluded with the British Crown.

The appellant then argued that it follows that the Royal Proclamation of October 7, 1763 extinguished the rights arising out of the treaty of September 5, 1760, because it did not confirm them. I cannot accept such a proposition: the silence of the Royal Proclamation regarding the treaty at issue cannot be interpreted as extinguishing it.

· · · · ·

The proclamation confers rights on the Indians without necessarily thereby extinguishing any other right conferred on them by the British Crown under a treaty.

Legislative and administrative history also provides no basis for concluding that the treaty was extinguished.

· · · · ·

The appellant further argues that by adopting the Act to establish the Laurentides National Park, S.Q. 1895, and by making the territory in question a park, the Quebec legislator clearly expressed his intention to prohibit the carrying on of certain activities in this territory, whether or not such activities are protected by an Indian treaty.

Section 88 of the *Indian Act* is designed specifically to protect the Indians from provincial legislation that might attempt to deprive them of rights protected by a treaty. A legislated change in the use of the territory thus does not extinguish rights otherwise protected by treaty. If the treaty gives the Hurons the right to carry on their customs and religion in the territory of Jacques-Cartier Park, the existence of a provincial statute and subordinate legislation will not ordinarily affect that right.

Finally, the appellant argues that non-user of the treaty over a long period of time may extinguish its effect. He cites no authority for this. I do not think that this argument carries much weight: a solemn agreement cannot lose its validity merely because it has not been invoked to, which in any case is disputed by the respondents, who maintain that it was relied on in a seigneurial claim in 1824. Such a proposition would mean that a treaty could be extinguished merely because it had not been relied on in litigation, which is untenable.

In view of the liberal and generous approach that must be adopted towards Indians' rights and the evidence in the record, I cannot conclude that the treaty of September 5th no longer had any legal effect on May 29, 1982.

The question that arises at this point is as to whether the treaty is capable of rendering ss. 9 and 37 of the regulations inoperative. To answer this it will now be necessary to consider the territorial scope of the rights guaranteed by the treaty, since the appellant recognizes that the activities with which the respondents are charged are customary or religious in nature.

VI *Territorial scope of rights guaranteed by treaty of September 5, 1760*

Although the document of September 5th is a treaty within the meaning of s. 88 of the *Indian Act*, that does not necessarily mean that the respondents are exempt from the application of the *Regulation respecting the Parc de la Jacques-Cartier*. It is still necessary that the treaty protecting activities of the kind with which the respondents are charged cover the territory of Jacques-Cartier Park.

. . . . .

The respondents must therefore show that the treaty guaranteed their right to carry on their customs and religious rites in the territory of Jacques-Cartier Park.

The treaty gives the Hurons the freedom to carry on their customs and their religion. No mention is made in the treaty itself of the territory over which these rights may be exercised. There is also no indication that the territory of what is now Jacques-Cartier Park was contemplated. However, for a freedom to have real value and meaning, it must be possible to exercise it somewhere. That does not mean, despite the importance of the rights concerned, that the Indians can exercise it anywhere. Our analysis will be confined to setting the limits of the promise made in the treaty, since the respondents have at no time based their argument on the existence of aboriginal rights protecting the activities with which they are charged.

The respondents suggest that the treaty gives them the right to carry on their customs and religion in the territory of the park because it is part of the territory frequented by the Hurons in 1760, namely the area between the Saguenay and the St-Maurice. In their submission, customs as they existed at the time of the treaty and as they might reasonably be expected to develop subsequently are what the British Crown undertook to preserve and foster.

The appellant argued in the Court of Appeal that the free exercise of the customs mentioned in the document of September 5, 1760 has to be limited to the Lorette territory, a territory of 40 arpents by 40 arpents. ... In his intervention the Attorney-General of Canada argues that the respondents' claim is essentially a territorial one and that in order to establish their rights, the respondents must show a connection between the rights claimed and their exercise in a given territory.

. . . . .

In my view, the treaty essentially has to be interpreted by determining the intention of the parties on the territorial question at the time it was concluded. It is not sufficient to note that the treaty is silent on this point. We must also undertake the task of interpreting the treaty on the territorial question with the same generous approach toward the Indians that applied in considering earlier questions. Now as then, we must do our utmost to act in the spirit of *Simon*.

The historical context, which has been used to demonstrate the existence of the treaty, may equally assist us in interpreting the extent of the rights contained in it. As MacKinnon J.A. said in *Taylor and Williams, supra*, at p. 232:

> Cases on Indian or aboriginal rights can never be determined in a vacuum. It is of importance to consider the history and oral traditions of the tribes concerned, and the surrounding circumstances at the time of the treaty, relied on by both parties, in determining the treaty's effect.

. . . . .

The interpretation which I think is called for when we give the historical context its full meaning is that Murray and the Hurons contemplated that the rights guaranteed by the treaty could be exercised over the entire territory frequented by the Hurons at the time, so long as the carrying on of the customs and rites is not incompatible with the particular use made by the Crown of this territory.

. . . . .

I conclude that in view of the absence of any express mention of the territorial scope of the treaty, it has to be assumed that the parties to the treaty of September 5th intended to reconcile the Hurons' need to protect the exercise of their customs and the desire of the British conquerors to expand. Protecting the exercise of the customs in all parts of the territory frequented when it is not incompatible with its occupancy is in my opinion the most reasonable way of reconciling the competing interests. This, in my view, is the definition of the common intent of the parties which best reflects the actual intent of the Hurons and of Murray on September 5, 1760. Defining the common intent of the parties on the question of territory in this way makes it possible to give full effect to the spirit of conciliation, while respecting the practical requirements of the British. This gave the English the necessary flexibility to be able to respond in due course to the increasing need to use Canada's resources, in the event that Canada remained under British suzerainty. The Hurons, for their part, were protecting their customs wherever their exercise would not be prejudicial to the use to which the territory concerned would be put. The Hurons could not reasonably expect that the use would forever remain what it was in 1760. Before the treaty was signed, they had carried on their customs in accordance with restrictions already imposed by an occupancy incompatible with such exercise. The Hurons were only asking to be permitted to continue to carry on their customs on the lands frequented to the extent that those customs did not interfere with enjoyment of the lands by their occupier. I readily accept that the Hurons were probably not aware of the legal consequences, and in particular of the right to occupy to the exclusion of others, which the main European legal systems attached to the concept of private ownership. None the less I cannot believe that the Hurons ever believed that the treaty gave them the right to cut down trees in the garden of a house as part of their right to carry on their customs.

Jacques-Cartier Park falls into the category of land occupied by the Crown, since the province has set it aside for a specific use. What is important is not so much that the province has legislated with respect to this territory but that it is using it, is in fact occupying the space. As occupancy has been established, the question is whether the type of occupancy to which the park is subject is incompatible with the exercise of the activities with which the respondents were charged, as these undoubtedly constitute religious customs or rites. Since, in view of the situation in 1760, we must assume some limitation on the exercise of rights protected by the treaty, it is up to the Crown to prove that its occupancy of the territory cannot be accommodated to reasonable exercise of the Hurons' rights.

The Crown presented evidence on such compatibility but that evidence did not persuade me that exercise of the rites and customs at issue here is incompatible with the occupancy.

. . . . .

For the exercise of rites and customs to be incompatible with the occupancy of the park by the Crown, it must not only be contrary to the purpose underlying that occupancy, it must prevent the realization of that purpose. First, we are dealing with Crown lands, lands which are held for the benefit of the community. Exclusive use is not an essential aspect of public ownership. Secondly, I do not think that the activities described seriously compromise the Crown's objectives in occupying the park. Neither the representative nature of the natural region where the park is located nor the exceptional nature of this natural site are threatened by the collecting of a few plants, the setting up of a tent using a few branches picked up in the area or the making of a fire according to the rules dictated by caution to avoid fires. These activities also present no obstacle to cross-country recreation. I therefore conclude that it has not been established that occupancy of the territory of Jacques-Cartier Park is incompatible with the exercise of Huron rites and customs with which the respondents are charged.

VII *Conclusion*

For all these reasons, I would dismiss the appeal with costs.

Although it was decided in 1990, the *Sioui* decision, like *Simon* before it, did not contemplate the effects of the constitutionalization of treaty rights in section 35(1). The first treaty case decided by the Supreme Court of Canada that considered the effects of section 35(1) on treaties was *R. v. Badger* The *Badger* case focused on the rights of three Treaty No. 8 Indians to hunt on private lands. The treaty provided for the right to hunt over the territories surrendered, save for lands that had been taken up for settlement, mining, lumbering, trading, or other purposes. The key question to be determined was whether the appellants, Messrs. Badger, Kiyawasew, and Ominayak, had rights of access to the private lands they were hunting on when they were charged with different violations of the Alberta *Wildlife Act*, S.A. 1984, c. W-9.1.

Mr. Badger had been charged with shooting a moose outside of hunting season on brush land with willow regrowth and scrub. Although the land he was hunting on was private property, there were no fences or signs posted on the land which indicated that it was private property. There was, however, a farm house (that did not appear to be abandoned) located a quarter of a mile from where Badger had shot the moose. Mr. Kiyawasew was charged with hunting without a licence. He had shot a moose on an unfenced, snow-covered field. He testified that he had passed old, run-down barns and that signs were posted on the land, but he was unable to read them from the road. Evidence indicated that, in the fall, a crop had been harvested from the field. Mr. Ominayak was also charged with hunting without a licence. He had been hunting on uncleared muskeg, with no fences, signs, or buildings in the vicinity of where he shot a moose.

The brief extract from *Badger* reproduced below deals with the Court's explanation of the principles of treaty interpretation and their effects on the issues raised in *Badger*. The effect of the *Natural Resources Transfer Agreement, 1930*, S.C. 1930, c. 3 on the rights contained in Treaty No. 8, the other significant element of the *Badger* case, is examined in Chapter 7.

R. v. BADGER

(1996), 133 D.L.R. (4th) 324, [1996] 4 W.W.R. 457, 37 Alta. L.R. (3d) 153, 195 N.R. 1, 105 C.C.C. (3d) 289 (S.C.C.) (references omitted)

Sopinka J. (Lamer C.J.C. concurring): —

. . . . .

The key interpretive principles which apply to treaties are first, that any ambiguity in the treaty will be resolved in favour of the Indians and, second, that treaties should be interpreted in a manner that maintains the integrity of the Crown, particularly the Crown's fiduciary obligation towards aboriginal peoples.

. . . . .

Cory J. (La Forest, L'Heureux-Dubé, Gonthier and **Iacobucci JJ.** concurring): — Three questions must be answered on this appeal. First, do Indians who have status under Treaty No. 8 have the right to hunt for food on privately owned land which lies within the territory surrendered under that treaty? Secondly, have the hunting rights set out in Treaty No. 8 been extinguished or modified as a result of the provisions of para. 12 of the 1930 *Natural Resources Transfer Agreement, 1930 (Constitution Act, 1930*, Sch. 2)? Thirdly, to what extent, if any, do ss. 26(1) and 27(1) of the *Wildlife Act*, S.A. 1984, c. W-9.1, apply to the appellants?
[Only questions 1 and 2 will be dealt with in this extract. Question 3 is considered in the excerpt of the case in Chapter 6.]

. . . . .

The relevant part of Treaty No. 8, made June 21, 1899, provides:

> And Her Majesty the Queen HEREBY AGREES with the said Indians that they shall have right to pursue their usual vocations of hunting, trapping and fishing throughout the tract surrendered as heretofore described, subject to such regulations as may from time to time be made by the Government of the country, acting under the authority of Her Majesty, and saving and excepting such tracts as may be required or taken up from time to time for settlement, mining, lumbering, trading or other purposes.

The existing right to hunt for food

. . . . .

The hunting right provided by Treaty No. 8

...Treaty No. 8, made on June 21, 1899, involved the surrender of vast tracts of land in what is now northern Alberta, north-eastern British Columbia, north-western Saskatchewan and part of the Northwest Territories. In exchange for the land, the Crown made a number of commitments. ... However, it is clear that for the Indians the guarantee that hunting, fishing and trapping rights would continue was the essential element which led to their signing the treaties. The report of the commissioners who negotiated Treaty No. 8 on behalf of the government underscored the importance to the Indians of the right to hunt, fish and trap. The commissioners wrote:

> There was expressed at every point the fear that the making of the treaty would be followed by the curtailment of the hunting and fishing privileges.

. . . . .

> We pointed out ... that the *same means of earning a livelihood would continue after the Treaty as existed before it*, and that the Indians would be expected to make use of them.

. . . . .

Our chief difficulty was the apprehension that the hunting and fishing privileges were to be curtailed. The provision in the treaty under which ammunition and twine is to be furnished went far in the direction of quieting the fears of the Indians, for they admitted that it would be unreasonable to furnish the means of hunting and fishing if laws were to be enacted which would make hunting and fishing so restricted as to render it impossible to make a livelihood by such pursuits. But over and above the provision, *we had to solemnly assure them that only such laws as to hunting and fishing as were in the interest of the Indians and were found necessary in order to protect the fish and fur-bearing animals would be made, and that they would be as free to hunt and fish after the treaty as they would be if they never entered into it.*

(Emphasis added)

Treaty No. 8 then, guaranteed that the Indians "shall have the right to pursue their usual vocations of hunting, trapping and fishing". The treaty, however, imposed two limitations on the right to hunt. First, there was a geographic limitation. The right to hunt could be exercised "throughout the tract surrendered ... saving and excepting such tracts as may be required or taken up from time to time for settlement, mining, lumbering, trading or other purposes". Second, the right could be limited by government regulations passed for conservation purposes.

. . . . .

Principles of interpretation

At the outset, it may be helpful to once again set out some of the applicable principles of interpretation. First, it must be remembered that a treaty represents an exchange of solemn promises between the Crown and the various Indian nations. It is an agreement whose nature is sacred. ... Second, the honour of the Crown is always at stake in its dealing with Indian people. Interpretations of treaties and statutory provisions which have an impact upon treaty or aboriginal rights must be approached in a manner which maintains the integrity of the Crown. It is always assumed that the Crown intends to fulfil its promises. No appearance of "sharp dealing" will be sanctioned. ... Third, any ambiguities or doubtful expressions in the wording of the treaty or document must be resolved in favour of the Indians. A corollary to this principle is that any limitations which restrict the rights of Indians under treaties must be narrowly construed. ... Fourth, the onus of proving that a treaty or aboriginal right has been extinguished lies upon the Crown. There must be "strict proof of the fact of extinguishment" and evidence of a clear and plain intention on the part of the government to extinguish treaty rights. ...

These principles of interpretation must now be applied to this case.

. . . . .

Geographical limitations on the right to hunt for food

... In the present appeals, the hunting occurred on lands which had been included in the 1899 surrender but were now privately owned. Therefore, it must be determined whether these privately owned lands were "other lands" to which the Indians had a "right of access" under the treaty.

. . . . .

While some treaties contain express provisions with respect to hunting on private land, others, such as Treaty No. 8 do not. Under Treaty No. 8, the right to hunt for food could be exercised "throughout the tract surrendered" to the Crown "saving and excepting such tracts as may be required or taken up from time to time for settlement, mining, lumbering, trading or other purposes". Accordingly, if the privately owned land is not "required or taken up" in the manner described in Treaty No. 8, it will be land to which the Indians had a right of access to hunt for food.

[T]he applicable interpretive principles must be borne in mind. Treaties and statutes relating to Indians should be liberally construed and any uncertainties, ambiguities or doubtful expressions should be resolved in favour of the Indians. In addition, when considering a treaty, a court must take into account the context in which the treaties were negotiated, concluded and committed to writing. The treaties, as written documents, recorded an agreement that had already been reached orally and they did not always record the full extent of the oral agreement. ... The treaties were drafted in English by representatives of the Canadian government who, it should be assumed, were familiar with common law doctrines. Yet, the treaties were not translated in written form into the languages (here Cree and Dene) of the various Indian nations who were signatories. Even if they had been, it is unlikely that the Indians, who had a history of communicating only orally, would have understood them any differently. As a result, it is well settled that the words in the treaty must not be interpreted in their strict technical sense nor subjected to rigid modern rules of construction. Rather, they must be interpreted in the sense that they would naturally have been understood by the Indians at the time of the signing. This applies, as well, to those words in a treaty which impose a limitation on the right which has been granted.

. . . . .

The evidence led at trial indicated that in 1899 the Treaty No. 8 Indians would have understood that land had been "required or taken up" when it was being put to a use which was incompatible with the exercise of the right to hunt. Historian John Foster gave expert evidence in this case. His testimony indicated that, in 1899, Treaty No. 8 Indians would not have understood the concept of private and exclusive property ownership separate from actual land use. They understood land to be required or taken up for settlement when buildings or fences were erected, land was put into crops, or farm or domestic animals were present. Enduring church missions would also be understood to constitute settlement. These physical signs shaped the Indians' understanding of settlement because they were the manifestations of exclusionary land use which the Indians had witnessed as new settlers moved into the west. The Indians' experience with the Hudson's Bay Company was also relevant. Although that company had title to vast tracts of land, the Indians were not excluded from and, in fact, continued hunting on these lands. In the course of their trading, the Hudson's Bay Company and the Northwest Company had set up numerous posts that were subsequently abandoned. The presence of abandoned buildings, then, would not necessarily signify to the Indians that land was taken up in a way which precluded hunting on them. Yet, it is dangerous to pursue this line of thinking too far. The abandonment of land may be temporary. Owners may return to reoccupy the land, to undertake maintenance, to inspect it or simply to enjoy it. How "unoccupied" the land was at the relevant time will have to be explored on a case-by-case basis.

An interpretation of the treaty properly founded upon the Indians' understanding of its terms leads to the conclusion that the geographical limitation on the existing hunting right should be based upon a concept of visible, incompatible land use. This approach is consistent with the oral promises made to the Indians at the time the treaty was signed, with the oral history of the Treaty No. 8 Indians, with earlier case law and with the provisions of the Alberta *Wildlife Act* itself.

The Indian people made their agreements orally and recorded their history orally. Thus, the verbal promises made on behalf of the federal government at the times the treaties were concluded are of great significance in their interpretation.

. . . . .

Since the Treaty No. 8 lands were not well suited to agriculture, the government expected little settlement in the area. The commissioners ... indicated that "it is safe to say that so long as the fur-bearing animals remain, the great bulk of the Indians will continue to hunt and to trap". The promise that this livelihood would not be affected was repeated to all the bands who signed the treaty. Although it was expected that some white prospectors might stake claims in the north, this was not expected to have an impact on the Indians' hunting rights. For example, one commissioner ... stated:

> We are just making peace between Whites and Indians — for them to treat each other well. And we do not want to change your hunting. If Whites should prospect, stake claims, that will not harm anyone.

Commissioner Laird told the Indians that the promises made to them were to be similar to those made with other Indians who had agreed to a treaty. Accordingly, it is significant that the earlier promises also contemplated a limited interference with Indians' hunting and fishing practices. ... In negotiating Treaty No. 1, the Lieutenant-Governor of Manitoba, A.G. Archibald, made the following statement to the Indians ...:

> When you have made your treaty you will still be free to hunt over much of the land included in the treaty. Much of it is rocky and unfit for cultivation, much of it that is wooded is beyond the places where the white man will re-

quire to go, at all events for some time to come. *Till these lands are needed for use you will be free to hunt over them, and make all the use of them which you have made in the past. But when lands are needed to be tilled or occupied, you must not go on them any more. There will still be plenty of land that is neither tilled nor occupied where you can go and roam and hunt as you have always done,* and, if you wish to farm, you will go to your own reserve where you will find a place ready for you to live on and cultivate.

(Emphasis added.) With respect to Treaty 4, Lt. Gov. Morris made the following statement to the Indians ...:

We have come through the country for many days and we have seen hills and but little wood and in many places little water, and it may be a long time before there are many white men settled upon this land, and you will have the right of hunting and fishing just as you have now *until the land is actually taken up.*

(Emphasis added.) With respect to Treaty 6, Lt. Gov. Morris stated ...:

You want to be at liberty to hunt as before. I told you we did not want to take that means of living from you, you have it the same as before, on this, *if a man, whether Indian or Half-breed, has a good field of grain, you would not destroy it with your hunt.*

(Emphasis added.)

The oral history of the Treaty No. 8 Indians reveals a similar understanding of the treaty promises. Dan McLean, an elder from the Sturgeon Lake Indian Reserve, gave evidence in this trial. He indicated that the understanding of the treaty promise was that Indians were allowed to hunt anytime for food to feed their families. They could hunt on unoccupied Crown land and on abandoned land. If there was no fence on the land, they could hunt, but if there was a fence, they could not hunt there. This testimony is consistent with the oral histories presented by other Treaty No. 8 elders whose stories have been recorded by historians. The Indians understood that land would be taken up for homesteads, farming, prospecting and mining and that they would not be able to hunt in these areas or to shoot at the settlers' farm animals or buildings. No doubt the Indians believed that most of the Treaty No. 8 land would remain unoccupied and so would be available to them for hunting, fishing and trapping. ...

Accordingly, the oral promises made by the Crown's representatives and the Indians' own oral history indicate that it was understood that land would be taken up and occupied in a way which precluded hunting when it was put to a visible use that was incompatible with hunting. Turning to the case law, it is clear that the courts have also accepted this interpretation and have concluded that whether or not land has been taken up or occupied is a question of fact that must be resolved on a case-by-case basis.

Most of the cases which have considered the geographical limitations on the right to hunt have been concerned with situations where the hunting took place on *Crown* land. In those cases, it was held that Crown lands were only "occupied" or "taken up" when they were actually put to an active use which was incompatible with hunting. ...

A second but shorter line of cases has considered whether Indians have a treaty right of access to hunt on privately owned lands. While various factual situations have been considered, the courts have not settled the question as to whether the Treaty No. 8 right to hunt for food extends to privately owned land which is not put to visible use.

. . . . .

The "visible, incompatible use" approach, which focuses upon the use being made of the land is appropriate and correct. Although it requires that the particular land use be considered in each case, this standard is neither unduly vague nor unworkable.

In summary, then, the geographical limitation on the right to hunt for food is derived from the terms of the particular treaty if they have not been modified or altered by the provisions of para. 12 of the NRTA. In this case, the geographical limitation on the right to hunt for food provided by Treaty No. 8 has not been modified by para. 12 of the NRTA. Where lands are privately owned, it must be determined on a case-by-case basis whether they are "other lands" to which Indians had a "right of access" under the treaty. If the lands are occupied, that is, put to visible use which is incompatible with hunting, Indians will not have a right of access. Conversely, if privately owned land is unoccupied and not put to visible use, Indians, pursuant to Treaty No. 8, will have a right of access in order to hunt for food.

. . . . .

Permissible regulatory limitations on the right to hunt for food

Pursuant to the provisions of s. 88 of the *Indian Act*, R.S.C. 1985, c. I-5, provincial laws of general application will apply to Indians. This is so except where they conflict with aboriginal or treaty rights, in which case the latter must prevail. ... In any event, the regulation of Indian hunting rights would ordinarily come within the jurisdiction of the federal government and not the province. However, the issue does not arise in this case since we are dealing with the right to hunt provided by Treaty 8 as modified by the NRTA. [The NRTA's effect on treaty rights is discussed in Chapter 6.] Both the treaty and the NRTA specifically provided that the right would be subject to regulation pertaining to conservation.

Treaty No. 8 provided that the right to hunt would be "subject to such regulations as may from time to time be made by the Government of the country". In the west, a wide range of legislation aimed at conserving game had been enacted by the government beginning as early as the 1880s. Acts and regulations pertaining to conservation measures continued to be passed throughout the entire period during which the numbered treaties were concluded. In *Horseman, supra*, [reproduced in Chapter 6] the aim and intent of the regulations was recognized. ...:

> Before the turn of the century the federal game laws of the Unorganized Territories provided for a total ban on hunting certain species (bison and musk oxen) in order to preserve both the species and the supply of game for Indians in the future: see the *Unorganized Territories' Game Preservation Act, 1894*, S.C. 1894, c. 31, ss. 2, 4-8 and 26. ... Moreover, beginning in 1890, pro-

vision was made in the federal *Indian Act*, R.S.C. 1886, c. 43, for the Super-intendent-General to make the game laws of Manitoba and the Unorganized Territories applicable to Indians.

In light of the existence of these conservation laws prior to signing the treaty, the Indians would have understood that, by the terms of the treaty, the government would be permitted to pass regulations with respect to conservation.

. . . . .

[Cory J. went on to consider the licensing provisions in the Alberta *Wildlife Act, supra,* which it deemed to be only partially concerned with conservation matters. It found that these provisions infringed upon the hunting rights granted by Treaty No. 8, as modified by the NRTA. The Court then sought to apply the test for the legislative infringement of Abo-riginal rights developed in *R. v. Sparrow, supra* — which is discussed in Chapter 4 — to see whether the infringement of the Treaty No. 8 right to hunt by the *Wildlife Act* licensing requirements was justified. However, since the Crown had led no evidence at trial to justify the application of the regulations to Mr. Ominayak and the question of justification was not ad-dressed by the lower courts, a new trial was ordered. The charges against Mr. Ominayak were then stayed. The appeals of Messrs. Badger and Ki-yawasew were dismissed, as it was determined that the lands upon which they were hunting were put to a visible, incompatible use and were there-fore not lands to which they had a right of access for hunting under the treaty.]

The *Badger* decision raises a number of questions. Would the Treaty No. 8 signatories have understood (as Justice Cory suggests in *Badger*) that the government could regulate Aboriginal hunting (as long as that regulation was aimed at conservation) even though the signatories had been prom-ised by the treaty commissioners — as indicated in their own report (ex-cerpted earlier) — that "they would be as free to hunt and fish after the treaty as they would be if they never entered into it"? Is Justice Cory's con-clusion consistent with your interpretation of this treaty promise? Ought one answer this question only by reference to the Aboriginal understand-ing at the time the treaty was signed? Can extrinsic evidence properly be used in this situation?

In addition to demonstrating concern over Aboriginal understandings of treaties, the Supreme Court of Canada has also sanctioned expansive understandings of the rights associated with treaty promises. This is evi-denced particularly well in *R. v. Sundown*, [1999] 1 S.C.R. 393.

R. v. SUNDOWN

[1999] 1 S.C.R. 393 (references omitted)

Cory J. (for the court): — Like his ancestors John Sundown, a Cree Indian and a member of the Joseph Bighead First Nation, hunted and fished in Meadow Lake Provincial Park. In order to carry out these activities he constructed a log cabin in the Park. This act breached the Park Regulations. On this appeal it must be determined whether the cabin is reasonably incidental to the hunting and fishing rights of this First Nation. If it is, do the Park Regulations infringe upon the hunting rights of this First Nation set out in Treaty No. 6 and modified by the Natural Resources Transfer Agreement (NRTA)?

I. Factual Background

A. The Respondent

The respondent, John Sundown, is a Cree Indian and a member of the Joseph Bighead First Nation, which is a party to Treaty No. 6 by adhesion. In 1992, Mr. Sundown cut down some 25 mature white spruce trees in Meadow Lake Provincial Park and used them to build a one–storey log cabin, approximately 30 feet by 40 feet. The Parks Regulations, 1991, R.R.S. c. P-1.1, Reg. 6, prohibit both the construction of a temporary or permanent dwelling on park land without permission (s. 41(2)(j)) and the taking or damaging of trees without consent (s. 59(a)).

Pursuant to the provisions of Treaty No. 6, Mr. Sundown is entitled to hunt for food on land that is occupied by the provincial Crown, including Meadow Lake Provincial Park. He testified that he needed the cabin while hunting, both for shelter and as a place to smoke fish and meat and to skin pelts. At trial, evidence was presented of a long-standing Band practice to conduct "expedition hunts" in the area now included within the Park. In order to carry out these hunts shelters were built at the hunting sites. The shelters were originally lean-tos covered with moss. Later they were tents and log cabins.

· · · · ·

It is clear from the history of the negotiations between Alexander Morris and the First Nations who signed Treaty No. 6 that the government intended to preserve the traditional Indian way of life. Hunting and fishing were of fundamental importance to that way of life. This was recognized in the treaty negotiations and in the treaties themselves. At p. 193 of *The Treaties of Canada with the Indians, supra*, Morris writes:

> I then asked the Bear to tell the other two absent Chiefs, Short Tail and Sagamat, what had been done; that I had written him and them a letter, and sent it by Sweet Grass, and that next year they could join the treaty; with regard to the buffalo, the North–West Council were considering the question, *and I again explained that we would not interfere with the Indian's daily life except to assist them in farming.* [Emphasis added.]

The Joseph Bighead First Nation adhered to Treaty No. 6 in 1913.

.....

Meadow Lake Provincial Park is considered a "natural environment park". Recreational activities pursued within the park are intended to conform with the natural landscape of the park: *The Parks Act*, S.S. 1986, c. P-1.1, s. 4(4). The Park contains many lakes, including Mistohay Lake on which the respondent built the cabin, large tracts of forest and several roads including Provincial Highway 224. There is a cottage subdivision of 200 to 300 cottages. There are as well approximately 15 cottages located outside the subdivision. Some commercial activities are found within its boundaries. They include gas wells, pipeline clearings and a lodge offering accommodation. Finally, there are services to accommodate the park users, including lakeside fuel pumps, picnic and campground areas, landfill sites, boat launches and toilet facilities. This is a large park. Non-aboriginal persons can hunt in the park during the appropriate season. Aboriginal hunters can, as well, exercise their treaty hunting rights within the confines of the park. In short, Meadow Lake Provincial Park is not, as the respondent correctly points out, virgin forest.

.....

It is uncontested that the respondent, Mr. Sundown, had the right to hunt in Meadow Lake Provincial Park, as this Park is a "lan[d] to which the said India[n] may have a right of access". ...

.....

Mr. Sundown was charged with violating the Regulations that prohibit the cutting of trees or the building of cabins without permission from the Minister. He was convicted of both offences in Provincial Court. He appealed his convictions by way of summary conviction appeal to the Court of Queen's Bench. The conviction for building a permanent dwelling on park land (s. 41(2)(j)) was quashed and the conviction for cutting trees (s. 59(a)) was upheld. The Crown appealed the quashed conviction and the respondent appealed the conviction for cutting trees. The Court of Appeal dismissed the Crown appeal and allowed the respondent's appeal from conviction, entering an acquittal instead. Wakeling J.A., in dissent, would have restored the conviction for building a dwelling and quashed the conviction respecting the trees.

The charge of cutting down trees plays no part in this appeal. Mr. Sundown has admitted building a log cabin but claims that he was entitled to do so as it is an essential aspect of his right to hunt granted by Treaty No. 6 as modified by the NRTA.

.....

Treaties may appear to be no more than contracts. Yet they are far more. They are a solemn exchange of promises made by the Crown and various First Nations. They often formed the basis for peace and the expansion of

European settlement. In many if not most treaty negotiations, members of the First Nations could not read or write English and relied completely on the oral promises made by the Canadian negotiators. There is a sound historical basis for interpreting treaties in the manner summarized in *Badger*. Anything else would amount to be a denial of fair dealing and justice between the parties.

. . . . .

... [I]n addition to applying the guiding principles of treaty interpretation, it is necessary to take into account the circumstances surrounding the signing of the treaty and the First Nations who later adhered to it. For example, consideration should be given to the evidence as to where the hunting and fishing were done and how the members of the First Nation carried out these activities.

B. *The Nature of the Right to Hunt Under Treaty No. 6*

Meadow Lake Provincial Park is Crown land and members of the public can hunt in it during the specified season. The parties agree that Mr. Sundown has the right to hunt in the park. Like other adherents to Treaty No. 6 he is entitled to hunt for food. This he can do at any time so long as he does not endanger others and complies with the appropriate safety regulations and the conservation regulations, which are justifiable under *Sparrow*. ...

Both parties submitted that, in order to determine whether the right to shelter is reasonably incidental to the right to hunt, the test set out in *Simon, supra*, must be applied. ...

How should the term "reasonably incidental" be defined and applied? In my view it should be approached in this manner. Would a reasonable person, fully apprised of the relevant manner of hunting or fishing, consider the activity in question reasonably related to the act of hunting or fishing? It may seem old fashioned to apply a reasonable person test but I believe it is both useful and appropriate.

The reasonable person must be dispassionate and fully apprised of the circumstances of the treaty rights holder. That reasonable person must also be aware of the manner in which the First Nation hunted and fished at the time the treaty was signed. That knowledge must, of course, be placed to some extent in today's context. For example, in the past it was reasonably incidental to hunting rights to carry a quiver of arrows. Today it is reasonably incidental to hunting rights to carry the appropriate box of shotgun shells or rifle cartridges. A form of shelter was always necessary to carry out the expeditionary hunting of the Joseph Bighead First Nation. At the time of the treaty, the shelter may have been a carefully built lean-to. That shelter appropriately evolved to a tent and then a small cabin. Thus, the reasonable person, informed of the manner of hunting at the time of the treaty, can consider it in the light of modern hunting methods and can determine whether the activity in question — the shelter — is reasonably incidental to the right to hunt.

In order to determine what is reasonably incidental to a treaty right to hunt, the reasonable person must examine the historical and contemporary practice of that specific treaty right by the aboriginal group in question to see how the treaty right has been and continues to be exercised. That which is reasonably incidental is something which allows the claimant to exercise the right in the manner that his or her ancestors did, taking into account acceptable modern developments or unforeseen alterations in the right. The question is whether the activity asserted as being reasonably incidental is in fact incidental to an actually practised treaty right to hunt. The inquiry is largely a factual and historical one. Its focus is not upon the abstract question of whether a particular activity is "essential" in order for hunting to be possible but rather upon the concrete question of whether the activity was understood in the past and is understood today as significantly connected to hunting. Incidental activities are not only those which are essential, or integral, but include, more broadly, activities which are meaningfully related or linked.

It is uncontroverted that the Joseph Bighead First Nation has traditionally hunted in what was described as an expeditionary style. Like the spokes of a wheel the hunters radiate out from the base each day to search for game. The hunt may continue for two weeks. The base provides a place for dressing the game and smoking the fish. Further, it provides the hunters with shelter for the duration of the hunt. Without shelter, expeditionary hunting, the traditional method used by this First Nation, would be impossible. There is no doubt, in the context of this treaty and of this First Nation, that some form of shelter is in fact a necessary part of expeditionary hunting. Accordingly, shelter is also reasonably incidental to this method of hunting.

. . . . .

A hunting cabin is, in these circumstances, reasonably incidental to this First Nation's right to hunt in their traditional expeditionary style. This method of hunting is not only traditional but appropriate and shelter is an important component of it. Without a shelter, it would be impossible for this First Nation to exercise its traditional method of hunting and their members would be denied their treaty rights to hunt. A reasonable person apprised of the traditional expeditionary method of hunting would conclude that for this First Nation the treaty right to hunt encompasses the right to build shelters as a reasonable incident to that right. The shelter was originally a moss-covered lean-to and then a tent. It has evolved to the small log cabin, which is an appropriate shelter for expeditionary hunting in today's society.

C. The Issue of Permanency

The issue of the permanency of the cabin was raised by the Crown in this appeal ... It was argued that, by building a permanent structure such as a log cabin, the respondent was asserting a proprietary interest in park land. For a First Nation member to assert a proprietary right would, it is said, be contrary to the essential purpose of the Crown in negotiating the treaty and contrary to its terms.

I cannot accept this argument. Treaty rights, like aboriginal rights, must not be interpreted as if they were common law property rights. ... Aboriginal and treaty rights cannot be defined in a manner which would accord with common law concepts of title to land or the right to use another's land. Rather, they are the right of aboriginal people in common with other aboriginal people to participate in certain practices traditionally engaged in by particular aboriginal nations in particular territories.

Any interest in the hunting cabin is a collective right that is derived from the treaty and the traditional expeditionary method of hunting. It belongs to the Band as a whole and not to Mr. Sundown or any individual member of the Joseph Bighead First Nation. It would not be possible, for example, for Mr. Sundown to exclude other members of this First Nation who have the same treaty right to hunt in Meadow Lake Provincial Park.

Furthermore there are limitations on permanency implicit within the right itself. Three such limitations were properly conceded by the respondent.

First, provincial legislation that relates to conservation and that passes the justificatory standard set out in *Sparrow* ... could validly restrict the building of hunting cabins. ...

The second limitation on permanency is that imposed by the requirement that there be compatibility between the Crown's use of the land and the treaty right claimed. See *Sioui, supra*. ...

. . . . .

Thus, if the exercise of the respondent's hunting right were wholly incompatible with the Crown's use of the land, hunting would be disallowed and any rights in the hunting cabin would be extinguished. For example, if the park were turned into a game preserve and all hunting was prohibited, the treaty right to hunt might be entirely incompatible with the Crown's use of the land. ...

The third limitation on the treaty right to hunt is found in the term of the treaty that restricts the right to hunt to lands not "required or taken up for settlement". This is in essence a subset of the second limitation since by definition the use of lands taken up for settlement is a Crown use of land wholly incompatible with the right to hunt. Thus, if the park lands were to be converted into lands used for settlement, any rights in a hunting cabin would disappear if it was found that the right to hunt itself had been extinguished.

Neither the second nor the third of these three limitations applies in the case at bar to limit the rights of the respondent to hunt or to build a shelter to facilitate that hunt. Meadow Lake Provincial Park is not virgin forest. It currently contains many cabins, as well as numerous facilities to assist park users, including boat launches, picnic areas and gas stations. It is clear that the Crown's use of the land is not wholly incompatible with the respondent's right to hunt. In other words, the respondent's right to hunt does not prevent the realization of the Crown's purpose. Neither have the park lands been taken up for settlement. It remains to be seen whether the regulation in issue is related to conservation and was therefore contemplated by the treaty. If it was, the question then becomes whether it can be justified under the *Sparrow* test.

D. The Regulation at Issue

For ease of reference, I repeat the regulation under which the respondent was charged:

41(1) No person shall:

(a) occupy;

(b) undertake research on;

(c) alter;

(d) use or exploit any resource in, on or under; or

(e) develop;

park land without a disposition.

(2) Without limiting the generality of subsection (1), no person shall:

. . . . .

(j) construct or occupy a temporary or permanent dwelling on park land

. . . . .

without a disposition or the prior written consent of the minister.

These regulations prohibit the construction of either a temporary or permanent structure without the written permission of the minister.

The Crown has expressly disavowed the idea that these regulations are related to an overall scheme of conservation. ... It is possible that the Crown may be employing an unnecessarily restrictive definition of conservation. These regulations appear to have some environmental concerns. For example, a requirement that cabins be built at least 150 feet away from the shore may be concerned with possible pollution of the lake, the erosion of the shoreline and the effects of that erosion on water quality. It may well be that the conservation laws discussed in *Badger* should be construed generously to refer not only to the conservation of game and fish but also to the environment they inhabit. Legislation aimed at preserving habitat and biodiversity, the water quality of ground water and of lakes, rivers and streams, topsoil conservancy and the prevention of erosion may be laws in relation to conservation. However, in light of the Crown's concession, this issue should not be considered in this appeal.

This is not to foreclose the possibility that the Crown could, in properly drafted regulations, reasonably limit the hunting rights of Treaty No. 6 adherents. Regulations clearly aimed at conservation that carefully consider the treaty rights of the respondent and others in his position may very well pass the *Sparrow* justification test. However, both the purpose of the regulations and the accommodation of the treaty rights in issue would have to be clear from the wording of the legislation. It would not be sufficient for the Crown to simply assert that the regulations are "necessary" for conservation. Evidence on this issue would have to be adduced. The Crown would also have to demonstrate that the legislation does not unduly impair treaty rights. The solemn promises of the treaty must be fairly interpreted and the honour of the Crown upheld. Treaty rights must not be lightly infringed. Clear evidence of justification would be required before that infringement could be accepted.

. . . . .

A constitutional question was stated. It read:

Question:	Are ss. 41(2)(j) and 59(a) of *The Parks Regulations, 1991*, R.R.S. c. P-1.1, Reg. 6, constitutionally inapplicable to the respondent by virtue of his treaty right to hunt as recognized by s. 35 of the *Constitution Act, 1982*?

Answer:	As this appeal was resolved without reference to the *Constitution Act, 1982*, this question need not be answered.

Appeal dismissed.

The *Sundown* decision affirmed the principle found earlier in *Simon v. The Queen*, [1985] 2 S.C.R. 387, 24 D.L.R. (4th) 390 that practices incidental to the exercise of treaty rights are to be equally protected in order to give true meaning and effect to those rights. This reaffirms the principle that the rights protected in a treaty extend beyond the literal words on the parchment copy of the treaty.

H. TREATIES, TREATY INTERPRETATIONS, AND THE "HONOUR OF THE CROWN"

Modern treaty jurisprudence, as seen in cases such as *Badger* and *Sundown*, has made reference to the notion of the "honour of the Crown" in the process of interpreting Crown-Native treaties. This idea was reflected once again in *R. v. Marshall*, [1999] 3 S.C.R. 456, 177 D.L.R. (4th) 513, which is also the leading Canadian case on the principles of treaty interpretation and one of the most controversial Supreme Court of Canada decisions in recent years.

R. v. MARSHALL

[1999] 3 S.C.R. 456, 177 D.L.R. (4th) 513 (references omitted)

The judgment of **Lamer C.J.** and **L'Heureux-Dubé, Cory, Iacobucci** and **Binnie JJ.** was delivered by

Binnie J.: — On an August morning six years ago the appellant and a companion, both Mi'kmaq Indians, slipped their small outboard motor-boat into the coastal waters of Pomquet Harbour, Antigonish County, Nova Scotia to fish for eels. They landed 463 pounds, which they sold for $787.10, and for which the appellant was arrested and prosecuted.

On an earlier August morning, some 235 years previously, the Reverend John Seycombe of Chester, Nova Scotia, a missionary and sometime dining companion of the Governor, noted with satisfaction in his diary, "Two Indian squaws brought seal skins and eels to sell". That transaction was apparently completed without arrest or other incident. The thread of continuity between these events, it seems, is that the Mi'kmaq people have sustained themselves in part by harvesting and trading fish (including eels) since Europeans first visited the coasts of what is now Nova Scotia in the 16th century. The appellant says that they are entitled to continue to do so now by virtue of a treaty right agreed to by the British Crown in 1760. As noted by my colleague, Justice McLachlin, the appellant is guilty as charged unless his activities were protected by an existing aboriginal or treaty right. No reliance was placed on any aboriginal right; the appellant chooses to rest his case entirely on the Mi'kmaq treaties of 1760-61.

. . . . .

I would allow this appeal because nothing less would uphold the honour and integrity of the Crown in its dealings with the Mi'kmaq people to secure their peace and friendship, as best the content of those treaty promises can now be ascertained. In reaching this conclusion, I recognize that if the present dispute had arisen out of a modern commercial transaction between two parties of relatively equal bargaining power, or if, as held by the courts below, the short document prepared at Halifax under the direction of Governor Charles Lawrence on March 10, 1760 was to be taken as being the "entire agreement" between the parties, it would have to be concluded that the Mi'kmaq had inadequately protected their interests. However, the courts have not applied strict rules of interpretation to treaty relationships. …

The starting point for the analysis of the alleged treaty right must be an examination of the specific words used in any written memorandum of its terms. In this case, the task is complicated by the fact the British signed a series of agreements with individual Mi'kmaq communities in 1760 and 1761 intending to have them consolidated into a comprehensive Mi'kmaq treaty that was never in fact brought into existence. The trial judge, Embree Prov. Ct. J., found that by the end of 1761 all of the Mi'kmaq villages in Nova Scotia had entered into separate but similar treaties. Some of these documents are missing. Despite some variations among some of the documents, Embree Prov. Ct. J. was satisfied that the written terms applicable to this dispute were contained in a Treaty of Peace and Friendship entered into by Governor Charles Lawrence on March 10, 1760, which … provides as follows:

> … And I do further promise for myself and my tribe that we will not either directly nor indirectly assist any of the enemies of His most sacred Majesty King George the Second, his heirs or Successors, nor hold any manner

of Commerce traffick nor intercourse with them, but on the contrary will as much as may be in our power discover and make known to His Majesty's Governor, any ill designs which may be formed or contrived against His Majesty's subjects. <u>And I do further engage that we will not traffick, barter or Exchange any Commodities in any manner but with such persons or the managers of such Truck houses as shall be appointed or Established by His Majesty's Governor at Lunenbourg or Elsewhere in Nova Scotia or Accadia</u>.
...

The underlined portion of the document, the so-called "trade clause", is framed in negative terms as a restraint on the ability of the Mi'kmaq to trade with non-government individuals. A "truckhouse" was a type of trading post. The evidence showed that the promised government truck-houses disappeared from Nova Scotia within a few years and by 1780 a replacement regime of government licensed traders had also fallen into disuse while the British Crown was attending to the American Revolution.
...

The appellant's position is that the truckhouse provision not only incor-porated the alleged right to trade, but also the right to pursue traditional hunting, fishing and gathering activities in support of that trade. It seems clear that the words of the March 10, 1760 document, standing in isolation, do not support the appellant's argument. The question is whether the un-derlying negotiations produced a broader agreement between the British and the Mi'kmaq, memorialized only in part by the Treaty of Peace and Friendship, that would protect the appellant's activities that are the subject of the prosecution. ...

... [T]he Court was advised in the course of oral argument that the ap-pellant "was engaged in a small-scale commercial activity to help subsi-dize or support himself and his common-law spouse". ... [T]his characteri-zation ... is consistent with the scale of the operation, the amount of money involved, and the other surrounding facts. If at some point the appellant's trade and related fishing activities were to extend beyond what is reasona-bly required for necessaries, as hereinafter defined, he would be outside treaty protection, and can expect to be dealt with accordingly.

The Court of Appeal took a strict approach to the use of extrinsic evi-dence when interpreting the Treaties of 1760-61. Roscoe and Bateman JJ.A. stated at p. 194: "While treaties must be interpreted in their historical con-text, extrinsic evidence cannot be used as an aid to interpretation, in the absence of ambiguity". I think this approach should be rejected for at least three reasons.

Firstly, even in a modern commercial context, extrinsic evidence is available to show that a written document does not include all of the terms of an agreement. Rules of interpretation in contract law are in general more strict than those applicable to treaties, yet Professor Waddams states in *The Law of Contracts* (3rd ed. 1993), at para. 316:

> The parol evidence rule does not purport to exclude evidence designed to show whether or not the agreement has been "reduced to writing", or whether it was, or was not, the intention of the parties that it should be the exclusive record of their agreement. Proof of this question is a pre-condition to the operation of the rule, and all relevant evidence is admissible on it. This is the view taken by Corbin and other writers, and followed in the Sec-ond Restatement.

· · · · ·

Secondly, even in the context of a treaty document that purports to contain all of the terms, this Court has made clear in recent cases that extrinsic evidence of the historical and cultural context of a treaty may be received even absent any ambiguity on the face of the treaty.

Thirdly, where a treaty was concluded verbally and afterwards written up by representatives of the Crown, it would be unconscionable for the Crown to ignore the oral terms while relying on the written terms, *per* Dickson J. (as he then was) in *Guerin v. The Queen*, [1984] 2 S.C.R. 335. …

· · · · ·

"Generous" rules of interpretation should not be confused with a vague sense of after-the-fact largesse. The special rules are dictated by the special difficulties of ascertaining what in fact was agreed to. The Indian parties did not, for all practical purposes, have the opportunity to create their own written record of the negotiations. Certain assumptions are therefore made about the Crown's approach to treaty making (honourable) which the Court acts upon in its approach to treaty interpretation (flexible) as to the existence of a treaty (*Sioui, supra*, at p. 1049), the completeness of any written record (the use, e.g., of context and implied terms to make honourable sense of the treaty arrangement: *Simon v. The Queen*, [1985] 2 S.C.R. 387, and *R. v. Sundown*, [1999] 1 S.C.R. 393), and the interpretation of treaty terms once found to exist (*Badger*). The bottom line is the Court's obligation is to "choose from among the various possible interpretations of the <u>common</u> intention [at the time the treaty was made] the one which best reconciles" the Mi'kmaq interests and those of the British Crown (*Sioui, per* Lamer J., at p. 1069 (emphasis added)). …

[A discussion of the 1752 Mi'kmaq Treaty is omitted]

<u>Findings of Fact by the Trial Judge</u>

· · · · ·

… The treaty document of March 10, 1760 sets out a restrictive covenant and does not say anything about a positive Mi'kmaq right to trade. In fact, the written document does not set out any Mi'kmaq rights at all, merely Mi'kmaq "promises" and the Governor's acceptance. I cannot reconcile the trial judge's conclusion, at para. 116, that the treaties "gave the Mi'kmaq the right to bring the products of their hunting, fishing and gathering to a truckhouse to trade", with his conclusion at para. 112 that:

> The written treaties with the Mi'kmaq in 1760 and 1761 which are before me contain, and fairly represent, all the promises made and all the terms and conditions mutually agreed to.

It was, after all, the aboriginal leaders who asked for truckhouses "for the furnishing them with necessaries, in Exchange for their Peltry" in response to the Governor's inquiry "Whether they were directed by their Tribes, to propose any other particulars to be Treated upon at this Time".

It cannot be supposed that the Mi'kmaq raised the subject of trade concessions merely for the purpose of subjecting themselves to a trade restriction.
As the Crown acknowledges in its factum, "The restrictive nature of the
truckhouse clause was British in origin". The trial judge's view that the
treaty obligations are all found within the four corners of the March 10,
1760 document, albeit generously interpreted, erred in law by failing to
give adequate weight to the concerns and perspective of the Mi'kmaq people, despite the recorded history of the negotiations, and by giving excessive weight to the concerns and perspective of the British, who held the
pen. ...

... Such an overly deferential attitude to the March 10, 1760 document
was inconsistent with a proper recognition of the difficulties of proof confronted by aboriginal people, a principle emphasized in the treaty context
by *Simon*, at p. 408, and *Badger*, at para. 4, and in the aboriginal rights
context in *Van der Peet*, at para. 68, and *Delgamuukw*, at paras. 80-82. The
trial judge['s] ... narrow view of what constituted "the treaty" led to the
equally narrow legal conclusion that the Mi'kmaq trading entitlement,
such as it was, terminated in the 1780s. Had the trial judge not given undue weight to the March 10, 1760 document, his conclusions might have
been very different.

The Court of Appeal, with respect, compounded the errors of law. It not
only read the Mi'kmaq "right", such as it was, out of the trial judgment, it
also took the view, at p. 204, that the principles of interpretation of Indian
treaties developed in connection with land cessions are of "limited specific
assistance" to treaties of peace and friendship where "the significant
'commodity' exchanged was mutual promises of peace". While it is true
that there is no applicable land cession treaty in Nova Scotia, it is also true
that the Mi'kmaq were largely dispossessed of their lands in any event,
and (as elsewhere) assigned to reserves to accommodate the wave of
European settlement which the Treaty of 1760 was designed to facilitate. It
seems harsh to put aboriginal people in a worse legal position where land
has been taken without their formal cession than where they have agreed
to terms of cession. A deal is a deal. The same rules of interpretation
should apply. ...

The 1760 Negotiations

I propose to review briefly the documentary record to emphasize and amplify certain aspects of the trial judge's findings. He accepted in general
the evidence of the Crown's only expert witness, Dr. Stephen Patterson, a
Professor of History at the University of New Brunswick, who testified at
length about what the trial judge referred to (at para. 116) as British encouragement of the Mi'kmaq "hunting, fishing and gathering lifestyle".
That evidence puts the trade clause in context, and answers the question
whether there was something more to the treaty entitlement than merely
the right to bring fish and wildlife to truckhouses.

(i) *The Documentary Record*

I take the following points from the matters particularly emphasized by the trial judge at para. 90 following his thorough review of the historical background:

> 1. The 1760-61 treaties were the culmination of more than a decade of intermittent hostilities between the British and the Mi'kmaq. Hostilities with the French were also prevalent in Nova Scotia throughout the 1750's, and the Mi'kmaq were constantly allied with the French against the British.
>
> 2. The use of firearms for hunting had an important impact on Mi'kmaq society. The Mi'kmaq remained dependant on others for gun powder and the primary sources of that were the French, Acadians and the British.
>
> 3. The French frequently supplied the Mi'kmaq with food and European trade goods. By the mid-18th century, the Mi'kmaq were accustomed to, and in some cases relied on, receiving various European trade goods [including shot, gun powder, metal tools, clothing cloth, blankets and many other things].
>
> . . . . .
>
> 6. The British wanted peace and a safe environment for their current and future settlers. Despite their recent victories, they did not feel completely secure in Nova Scotia.

Shortly after the fall of Louisbourg in June 1758, the British commander sent emissaries to the Mi'kmaq, through the French missionary, Father Maillard (who served as translator at the subsequent negotiations), holding out an offer of the enjoyment of peace, liberty, property, possessions and religion ...

In the harsh winter of 1759-1760, so many Mi'kmaq turned up at Louisbourg seeking sustenance that the British Commander expressed concern that unless their demand for necessaries was met, they would become "very Troublesome" and "entirely putt a Stop to any Settling or fishing all along the Coast" or indeed "the Settlement of Nova Scotia" generally. ...

It is apparent that the British saw the Mi'kmaq trade issue in terms of peace, as the Crown expert Dr. Stephen Patterson testified, "people who trade together do not fight, that was the theory". Peace was bound up with the ability of the Mi'kmaq people to sustain themselves economically. Starvation breeds discontent. The British certainly did not want the Mi'kmaq to become an unnecessary drain on the public purse of the colony of Nova Scotia or of the Imperial purse in London, as the trial judge found. To avoid such a result, it became necessary to protect the traditional Mi'kmaq economy, including hunting, gathering and fishing. ...

The trial judge concluded that in 1760 the British Crown entered into a series of negotiations with communities of first nations spread across what is now Nova Scotia and New Brunswick. These treaties were essentially "adhesions" by different Mi'kmaq communities to identical terms because, as stated, it was contemplated that they would be consolidated in a more comprehensive and all-inclusive document at a later date, which never happened. The trial judge considered that the key negotiations took place not with the Mi'kmaq people directly, but with the St. John River Indians, part of the Maliseet First Nation, and the Passamaquody First Nation, who lived in present-day New Brunswick.

The trial judge found as a fact ... that the relevant Mi'kmaq treaty did "make peace upon the same conditions" (emphasis added) as the Maliseet and Passamaquody. Meetings took place between the Crown and the Maliseet and the Passamaquody on February 11, 1760, twelve days before these bands signed their treaty with the British and eighteen days prior to the meeting between the Governor and the Mi'kmaq representatives, Paul Laurent of LaHave and Michel Augustine of the Richibucto region, where the terms of the Maliseet and Passamaquody treaties were "communicated" and accepted.

The trial judge found ... that on February 29, 1760, at a meeting between the Governor in Council and the Mi'kmaq chiefs, the following exchange occurred:

> His Excellency then Ordered the Several Articles of the Treaty made with the Indians of St. John's River and Passamaquody to be Communicated to the said Paul Laurent and Michel Augustine who expressed their satisfaction therewith, and declar'd that all the Tribe of Mickmacks would be glad to make peace upon the same Conditions. [Emphasis added.]

Governor Lawrence afterwards confirmed, in his May 11, 1760 report to the Board of Trade, that he had treated with the Mi'kmaq Indians on "the same terms".

The genesis of the Mi'kmaq trade clause is therefore found in the Governor's earlier negotiations with the Maliseet and Passamaquody First Nations. In that regard, the appellant places great reliance on a meeting between the Governor and their chiefs on February 11, 1760 for the purpose of reviewing various aspects of the proposed treaty. The following exchange is recorded in contemporaneous minutes of the meeting prepared by the British Governor's Secretary:

> His Excellency then demanded of them, Whether they were directed by their Tribes, to propose any other particulars to be Treated upon at this time. To which they replied that their Tribes had not directed them to propose any thing further than that there might be a Truckhouse established, for the furnishing them with necessaries, in Exchange for their Peltry, and that it might, at present, be at Fort Frederick.
>
> Upon which His Excellency acquainted them that in case of their now executing a Treaty in the manner proposed, and its being ratified at the next General Meeting of their Tribes the next Spring, a Truckhouse should be established at Fort Frederick, agreable to their desire, and likewise at other Places if it should be found necessary, for furnishing them with such Commodities as shall be necessary for them, in Exchange for their Peltry & and that great care should be taken, that the Commerce at the said Truckhouses should be managed by Persons on whose Justice and good Treatment, they might always depend; and that it would be expected that the said Tribes should not Trafic or Barter and Exchange any Commodities at any other Place, nor with any other Persons. Of all which the Chiefs expressed their entire Approbation. [Emphasis added.]

It is true ... that the British made it clear from the outset that the Mi'kmaq were not to have any commerce with "any of His Majesty's Enemies". A Treaty of Peace and Friendship could not be otherwise. The subject of trading with the British government as distinguished from British settlers, however, did not arise until after the Indians had first requested truckhouses. The limitation to government trade came as a response to the request for truckhouses, not the other way around.

At a meeting of the Governor's Council on February 16, 1760 (less than a week later), the Council and the representatives of the Indians proceeded to settle the prices of various articles of merchandise ... Prices of "necessaries" for purchase at the truckhouse were also agreed ... At trial the Crown expert and the defence experts agreed that fish could be among the items that the Mi'kmaq would trade.

In furtherance of this trade arrangement, the British established six truckhouses following the signing of the treaties in 1760 and 1761... The existence of advantageous terms at the truckhouses was part of an imperial peace strategy. As Governor Lawrence wrote to the Board of Trade on May 11, 1760, "the greatest advantage from this [trade] Article . . . is the friendship of these Indians". The British were concerned that matters might again become "troublesome" if the Mi'kmaq were subjected to the "pernicious practices" of "unscrupulous traders". The cost to the public purse of Nova Scotia of supporting Mi'kmaq trade was an investment in peace and the promotion of ongoing colonial settlement. The strategy would be effective only if the Mi'kmaq had access *both* to trade *and* to the fish and wildlife resources necessary to provide them with something to trade.

. . . . .

By 1762 ... the number of truckhouses was reduced to three. By 1764, the system itself was replaced by the impartial licensing of private traders ... but that eventually died out as well...

In my view, all of this evidence, reflected in the trial judgment, demonstrates the inadequacy and incompleteness of the written memorial of the treaty terms by selectively isolating the restrictive trade covenant. Indeed, the truckhouse system offered such advantageous terms that it hardly seems likely that Mi'kmaq traders had to be compelled to buy at lower prices and sell at higher prices. At a later date, they objected when truckhouses were abandoned. The trade clause would not have advanced British objectives (peaceful relations with a self-sufficient Mi'kmaq people) or Mi'kmaq objectives (access to the European "necessaries" on which they had come to rely) unless the Mi'kmaq were assured at the same time of continuing access, implicitly or explicitly, to wildlife to trade. ...

. . . . .

In my view, the Nova Scotia judgments erred in concluding that the only enforceable treaty obligations were those set out in the written document of March 10, 1760, whether construed flexibly (as did the trial judge) or narrowly (as did the Nova Scotia Court of Appeal). The findings of fact made by the trial judge taken as a whole demonstrate that the concept of a disappearing treaty right does justice neither to the honour of the Crown nor to the reasonable expectations of the Mi'kmaq people. It is their common intention in 1760 — not just the terms of the March 10, 1760 document — to which effect must be given.

Ascertaining the Terms of the Treaty

Having concluded that the written text is incomplete, it is necessary to ascertain the treaty terms not only by reference to the fragmentary historical record, as interpreted by the expert historians, but also in light of the stated objectives of the British and Mi'kmaq in 1760 and the political and economic context in which those objectives were reconciled.

... The appellant asserts the right of Mi'kmaq people to catch fish and wildlife in support of trade as an <u>alternative</u> or supplementary method of obtaining necessaries. The right to fish is not mentioned in the March 10, 1760 document, nor is it expressly noted elsewhere in the records of the negotiation put in evidence. This is not surprising. As Dickson J. mentioned with reference to the west coast in *Jack, supra*, at p. 311, in colonial times the perception of the fishery resource was one of "limitless proportions".

The law has long recognized that parties make assumptions when they enter into agreements about certain things that give their arrangements efficacy. Courts will imply a contractual term on the basis of presumed intentions of the parties where it is necessary to assure the efficacy of the contract, e.g., where it meets the "officious bystander test" ... Here, if the ubiquitous officious bystander had said, "This talk about truckhouses is all very well, but if the Mi'kmaq are to make these promises, will they have the right to hunt and fish to catch something to trade at the truckhouses?", the answer would have to be, having regard to the honour of the Crown, "of course". If the law is prepared to supply the deficiencies of written contracts prepared by sophisticated parties and their legal advisors in order to produce a sensible result that accords with the intent of both parties, though unexpressed, the law cannot ask less of the honour and dignity of the Crown in its dealings with First Nations. The honour of the Crown was, in fact, specifically invoked by courts in the early 17th century to ensure that a Crown grant was effective to accomplish its intended purpose ...

An example of the Court's recognition of the necessity of supplying the deficiencies of aboriginal treaties is *Sioui, supra*, where Lamer J. considered a treaty document that stated simply (at p. 1031) that the Huron tribe "are received upon the same terms with the Canadians, being allowed the free Exercise of their Religion, their Customs, and Liberty of trading with the English". Lamer J. found that, in order to give real value and meaning to these words, it was necessary that a territorial component be supplied, as follows, at p. 1067:

> The treaty gives the Hurons the freedom to carry on their customs and their religion. No mention is made in the treaty itself of the territory over which these rights may be exercised. There is also no indication that the territory of what is now Jacques-Cartier park was contemplated. However, <u>for a freedom to have real value and meaning</u>, it must be possible to exercise it somewhere. [Emphasis added.]

Similarly, in *Sundown, supra*, the Court found that the express right to hunt included the implied right to build shelters required to carry out the hunt. See also *Simon, supra*, where the Court recognized an implied right to carry a gun and ammunition on the way to exercise the right to hunt. These cases employed the concept of implied rights to support the meaningful exercise of express rights granted to the first nations in circumstances where no such implication might necessarily have been made absent the *sui generis* nature of the Crown's relationship to aboriginal people. While I do not believe that in ordinary commercial situations a right to trade implies any right of access to things to trade, I think the honour of the Crown requires nothing less in attempting to make sense of the result of these 1760 negotiations.

Rights of the Other Inhabitants

... [I]t is ... true that a general right enjoyed by all citizens can nevertheless be made the subject of an enforceable treaty promise. ...

. . . . .

The Crown objects strongly to any suggestion that the treaty conferred *"preferential* trading rights". I do not think the appellant needs to show *preferential* trading rights. He only has to show *treaty* trading rights. The settlers and the military undoubtedly hunted and fished for sport or necessaries as well, and traded goods with each other. The issue here is not so much the content of the rights or liberties as the level of legal protection thrown around them. A treaty could, to take a fanciful example, provide for a right of the Mi'kmaq to promenade down Barrington Street, Halifax, on each anniversary of the treaty. Barrington Street is a common thoroughfare enjoyed by all. There would be nothing "special" about the Mi'kmaq use of a common right of way. The point is that the treaty rights-holder not only has the *right* or liberty "enjoyed by other British subjects" but may enjoy special treaty *protection* against interference with its exercise. So it is with the trading arrangement. On June 25, 1761, following the signing of the Treaties of 1760-61 by the last group of Mi'kmaq villages, a ceremony was held at the farm of Lieutenant Governor Jonathan Belcher, the first Chief Justice of Nova Scotia, who was acting in the place of Governor Charles Lawrence, who had recently been drowned on his way to Boston. In reference to the treaties, including the trade clause, Lieutenant Governor Belcher proclaimed:

> The Laws will be like a great Hedge about your Rights and properties, if any break this Hedge to hurt and injure you, the heavy weight of the Laws will fall upon them and punish their Disobedience.

Until enactment of the *Constitution Act, 1982*, the treaty rights of aboriginal peoples could be overridden by competent legislation as easily as could the rights and liberties of other inhabitants. The hedge offered no special protection, as the aboriginal people learned in earlier hunting cases such as *Sikyea v. The Queen*, [1964] S.C.R. 642, and *R. v. George*, [1966] S.C.R. 267. On April 17, 1982, however, this particular type of "hedge" was converted by s. 35(1) into sterner stuff that could only be broken down when justified according to the test laid down in *R. v. Sparrow*, [1990] 1 S.C.R. 1075, at pp. 1112 *et seq.*, as adapted to apply to treaties in Badger... The fact the *content* of Mi'kmaq rights under the treaty to hunt and fish and trade was no greater than those enjoyed by other inhabitants does not, unless those rights were extinguished prior to April 17, 1982, detract from the higher *protection* they presently offer to the Mi'kmaq people.

The Honour of the Crown

This appeal puts to the test the principle, emphasized by this Court on several occasions, that the honour of the Crown is always at stake in its dealings with aboriginal people. ...

This principle that the Crown's honour is at stake when the Crown enters into treaties with first nations dates back at least to this Court's decision in 1895, *Province of Ontario v. Dominion of Canada and Province of Quebec; In re Indian Claims* (1895), 25 S.C.R. 434. In that decision, Gwynne J. (dissenting) stated, at pp. 511-12:

> ... what is contended for and must not be lost sight of, is that the British sovereigns, ever since the acquisition of Canada, have been pleased to adopt the rule or practice of entering into agreements with the Indian nations or tribes in their province of Canada, for the cession or surrender by them of what such sovereigns have been pleased to designate the Indian title, by instruments similar to these now under consideration to which they have been pleased to give the designation of "treaties" with the Indians in possession of and claiming title to the lands expressed to be surrendered by the instruments, and further that the terms and conditions expressed in those instruments as to be performed by or on behalf of the Crown, have always been regarded as involving a trust graciously assumed by the Crown to the fulfilment of which with the Indians the faith and honour of the Crown is pledged, and which trust has always been most faithfully fulfilled as a treaty obligation of the Crown. [Emphasis added.]

. . . . .

In more recent times, as mentioned, the principle that the honour of the Crown is always at stake was asserted by the Ontario Court of Appeal in *Taylor and Williams, supra*. In that case, as here, the issue was to determine the actual terms of a treaty, whose terms were partly oral and partly written. ...

I do not think an interpretation of events that turns a positive Mi'kmaq trade demand into a negative Mi'kmaq covenant is consistent with the honour and integrity of the Crown. Nor is it consistent to conclude that the Lieutenant Governor, seeking in good faith to address the trade demands of the Mi'kmaq, accepted the Mi'kmaq suggestion of a trading facility while denying any treaty protection to Mi'kmaq access to the things that were to be traded, even though these things were identified and priced in the treaty negotiations. This was not a commercial contract. The trade arrangement must be interpreted in a manner which gives meaning and substance to the promises made by the Crown. In my view, with respect, the interpretation adopted by the courts below left the Mi'kmaq with an empty shell of a treaty promise.

. . . . .

... [T]he surviving substance of the treaty is not the literal promise of a truckhouse, but a treaty right to continue to obtain necessaries through hunting and fishing by trading the products of those traditional activities subject to restrictions that can be justified under the *Badger* test.

THE LIMITED SCOPE OF THE TREATY RIGHT

The Crown expresses the concern that recognition of the existence of a constitutionally entrenched right with, as here, a trading aspect, would open the floodgates to uncontrollable and excessive exploitation of the natural resources. Whereas hunting and fishing for food naturally restricts quantities to the needs and appetites of those entitled to share in the harvest, it is argued that there is no comparable, built-in restriction associated with a trading right, short of the paramount need to conserve the resource. … The ultimate fear is that the appellant, who in this case fished for eels from a small boat using a fyke net, could lever the treaty right into a factory trawler in Pomquet Harbour gathering the available harvest in preference to all non-aboriginal commercial or recreational fishermen. (This is indeed the position advanced by the intervener the Union of New Brunswick Indians.) This fear (or hope) is based on a misunderstanding of the narrow ambit and extent of the treaty right.

The recorded note of February 11, 1760 was that "there might be a Truckhouse established, for the furnishing them with <u>necessaries</u>" (emphasis added). What is contemplated therefore is not a right to trade generally for economic gain, but rather a right to trade for necessaries. The treaty right is a regulated right and can be contained by regulation within its proper limits.

The concept of "necessaries" is today equivalent to the concept of what Lambert J.A., in *R. v. Van der Peet* (1993), 80 B.C.L.R. (2d) 75, at p. 126, described as a "moderate livelihood". Bare subsistence has thankfully receded over the last couple of centuries as an appropriate standard of life for aboriginals and non-aboriginals alike. A moderate livelihood includes such basics as "food, clothing and housing, supplemented by a few amenities", but not the accumulation of wealth (*Gladstone, supra*, at para. 165). It addresses day-to-day needs. This was the common intention in 1760. It is fair that it be given this interpretation today.

… In this case, … it is not suggested that Mi'kmaq trade historically generated "wealth which would exceed a sustenance lifestyle". Nor would anything more have been contemplated by the parties in 1760.

Catch limits that could reasonably be expected to produce a moderate livelihood for individual Mi'kmaq families at present-day standards can be established by regulation and enforced without violating the treaty right. In that case, the regulations would accommodate the treaty right. Such regulations would *not* constitute an infringement that would have to be justified under the *Badger* standard.

. . . . .

Disposition

The constitutional question stated by the Chief Justice on February 9, 1998, as follows:

> Are the prohibitions on catching and retaining fish without a licence, on fishing during the close time, and on the unlicensed sale of fish, contained in ss. 4(1)(a) and 20 of the *Maritime Provinces Fishery Regulations* and s. 35(2) of the *Fishery (General) Regulations*, inconsistent with the treaty rights of the appellant contained in the Mi'kmaq Treaties of 1760-61 and therefore of no force or effect or application to him, by virtue of ss. 35(1) and 52 of the *Constitution Act, 1982*?

should be answered in the affirmative. I would therefore allow the appeal and order an acquittal on all charges.

The reasons of **Gonthier** and **McLachlin JJ.** were delivered by

McLachlin J. (dissenting): —

. . . . .

I conclude that the Treaties of 1760-61 created an exclusive trade and truckhouse regime which implicitly gave rise to a limited Mi'kmaq right to bring goods to British trade outlets so long as this regime was extant. The Treaties of 1760-61 granted neither a freestanding right to truckhouses nor a general underlying right to trade outside of the exclusive trade and truckhouse regime. The system of trade exclusivity and correlative British trading outlets died out in the 1780s and with it, the incidental right to bring goods to trade. There is therefore no existing right to trade in the Treaties of 1760-61 that exempts the appellant from the federal fisheries legislation. The charges against him stand.

Appeal allowed.

———

In *Marshall*, McLachlin C.J.C. codified the principles of treaty interpretation set out by the Supreme Court of Canada. This codification, while not a part of the majority's judgment in *Marshall*, has been positively cited in many subsequent treaty cases:

1. Aboriginal treaties constitute a unique type of agreement and attract special principles of interpretation: *R. v. Sundown*, [1999] 1 S.C.R 393, at para. 24; *R. v. Badger*, [1996] 1 S.C.R. 771, at para. 78; *R. v. Sioui*, [1990] 1 S.C.R. 1025, at p. 1043; *Simon v. R.*, [1985] 2 S.C.R. 387, at p. 404. See also: J. [Sákéj] Youngblood Henderson, "Interpreting *Sui Generis* Treaties" (1997), 36 Alta. L. Rev. 46; L.I. Rotman, "Defining Parameters: Aboriginal Rights, Treaty Rights, and the *Sparrow* Justificatory Test" (1997), 36 Alta. L. Rev. 149.

2. Treaties should be liberally construed and ambiguities or doubtful expressions should be resolved in favour of the Aboriginal signatories: *Simon, supra*, at p. 402; *Sioui, supra*, at p. 1035; *Badger, supra*, at para. 52.

3. The goal of treaty interpretation is to choose from among the various possible interpretations of common intention the one which best reconciles the interests of both parties at the time the treaty was signed: *Sioui, supra,* at pp. 1068-69.

4. In searching for the common intention of the parties, the integrity and honour of the Crown is presumed: *Badger, supra,* at para. 41.

5. In determining the signatories' respective understanding and intentions, the court must be sensitive to the unique cultural and linguistic differences between the parties: *Badger, supra,* at paras. 52-54; *R. v. Horseman,* [1990] 1 S.C.R. 901, at p. 907.

6. The words of the treaty must be given the sense which they would naturally have held for the parties at the time: *Badger, supra,* at paras. 53 *et seq.; Nowegijick v. The Queen,* [1983] 1 S.C.R. 29, at p. 36.

7. A technical or contractual interpretation of treaty wording should be avoided: *Badger, supra; Horseman, supra; Nowegijick, supra.*

8. While construing the language generously, courts cannot alter the terms of the treaty by exceeding what "is possible on the language" or realistic: *Badger, supra,* at para. 76; *Sioui, supra,* at p. 1069; *Horseman, supra,* at p. 908.

9. Treaty rights of Aboriginal peoples must not be interpreted in a static or rigid way. They are not frozen at the date of signature. The interpreting court must update treaty rights to provide for their modern exercise. This involves determining what modern practices are reasonably incidental to the core treaty right in its modern context: *Sundown, supra,* at para. 32; *Simon, supra,* at p. 402.

What, precisely, is meant by the "honour of the Crown?" Does *Marshall* define the term? Does the discussion in *Marshall* suggest a different interpretation than what was seen in *Badger* and/or *Sundown*? Perhaps more significantly, is this notion a new one, or is it a modern resurrection of a long-standing ideal? Consider this in light of the *Treaty of Albany* and the Covenant Chain alliance, *supra*.

In the aftermath of the *Marshall* decision, there were violent clashes between Aboriginal and non-Aboriginal fishers in the Maritimes and significant criticism of the Supreme Court's judgment as an example of the excesses of judicial activism. Perhaps not coincidentally, the Supreme Court of Canada revisited its judgment in *Marshall* two months later in the context of dismissing an intervener's motion for a rehearing and stay of the existing *Marshall* judgment pending that rehearing: see *R. v. Marshall,* [1999] 3 S.C.R. 533, 179 D.L.R. (4th) 193 ("*Marshall No. 2*").

Some commentators criticized the Court for its "reinterpretation" of the *Marshall* judgment in *Marshall No. 2* while others characterized the *Marshall No. 2* judgment as a method of responding to critics of the *Marshall* judgment. Consider the following excerpts from *Marshall No. 2* and decide for yourself:

> Those opposing the motion object in different ways that the Coalition's motion rests on a series of misconceptions about what the September 17, 1999 majority judgment decided and what it did not decide. These objections are well founded. The Court did not hold that the Mi'kmaq treaty right cannot be regulated or that the Mi'kmaq are guaranteed an open season in the fisheries. ...

> $\cdots\cdots$

> The September 17, 1999 majority judgment did not rule that the appellant had established a treaty right "to gather" anything and everything physically capable of being gathered. The issues were much narrower and the ruling was much narrower. ... It is of course open to native communities to assert broader treaty rights in that regard, but if so, the basis for such a claim will have to be established in proceedings where the issue is squarely raised on proper historical evidence, as was done in this case in relation to fish and wildlife. Other resources were simply not addressed by the parties, and therefore not addressed by the Court in its September 17, 1999 majority judgment. ...

> $\cdots\cdots$

> Other limitations apparent in the September 17, 1999 majority judgment include the local nature of the treaties, the communal nature of a treaty right, and the fact it was only hunting and fishing resources to which access was affirmed, together with traditionally gathered things like wild fruit and berries. ... [T]he Mi'kmaq treaty right to hunt and trade in game is not now, any more than it was in 1760, a *commercial* hunt that must be satisfied before non-natives have access to the same resources for recreational or commercial purposes. The emphasis in 1999, as it was in 1760, is on assuring the Mi'kmaq equitable access to identified resources for the purpose of earning a moderate living. ...

What is, perhaps, most curious about *Marshall No. 2* is that it unanimously affirmed the majority's judgment in *Marshall*, even though two of the judges participating in the *Marshall No. 2* judgment (McLachlin C.J.C. and Gonthier J.) had dissented in *Marshall*.

I. CONCLUSION

Treaty jurisprudence in Canada, like jurisprudence on Aboriginal title, has changed considerably in recent years, especially since the adoption and development of the canons of treaty interpretation in *R. v. Taylor and Williams, supra,* and *Simon, supra.* That change is still on-going, as witnessed by the criticism levied against the interpretive canons in cases such as *Horse* and *Howard* and their subsequent reaffirmation in *Marshall*. The constitutional entrenchment of treaty rights in section 35(1) of the *Constitution Act, 1982* has also had considerable effects on Canadian treaty jurisprudence. Nevertheless, governmental and judicial attitudes towards treaties continue to provide significant obstacles to achieving contextually and culturally appropriate understandings of treaties as solemn compacts between the Crown and Aboriginal peoples, as opposed to mere contractual agreements.

Consider the approach to treaties articulated in the following excerpt.

PATRICK MACKLEM, "FIRST NATIONS SELF-GOVERNMENT AND THE BORDERS OF THE CANADIAN LEGAL IMAGINATION"

(1991) 36 McGill L.J. 382 at 442-4 (references omitted)

Jurisprudence surrounding treaties negotiated between the Crown and native peoples is marked by a well-defined set of principles that speak to the legal status of treaties and the substantive rights established by the treaty-making process. With respect to the former, jurisprudence was originally based on the view that natives were different than, and inferior to, nonnative people. Native people were imagined as not possessing the authority to enter into binding reciprocal arrangements with the Crown. Treaties were imagined as not having the force of law, and amounted to little more than nonbinding, political arrangements entered into by the Crown with native people. Eventually, the law came to recognize the legal status of native people to enter into agreements which could be enforced in a court of law, by abandoning the view that native people are different than and inferior to nonnative people. Grounded in connotations of similarity, the enforceability of treaties is currently seen in contractual terms. Native people are imagined as similar to other subjects of the realm, entitled to enter into contractual arrangements with the Crown and sue for noncompliance. Yet, if treaties are imagined as little more than contractual arrangements, their contents will be subject to legislative regulation and extinguishment. At least prior to the passage of s. 35(1) of the *Constitution Act, 1982*, legislative initiatives were seen as paramount to the terms and conditions of treaties.

. . . . .

With respect to the way in which the judiciary has interpreted the content of treaty guarantees, the interpretive exercise was initially characterized by a refusal to treat native expectations differently than nonnative expectations. That is, vague treaty guarantees were infused with substantive meaning by unquestioned reference to a reliance on Anglo-Canadian categories of legal understanding. Notions of private property and freedom of contract guided the judiciary in interpretive movements from abstract treaty rights to concrete applications. The "plain meaning" of vague treaty guarantees was determined by a process which accepted without question the legitimacy of Anglo-Canadian legal categories of understanding. Recently, treaty jurisprudence has come to embrace native difference, with the acknowledgement that native expectations concerning the meaning of treaty entitlements may well have been markedly different than those entertained by the agents of the Crown. The interpretive process still places a high premium on the intent of the parties to the agreement, expanded to incorporate the original expectations of native negotiators. Yet Anglo-Canadian understandings concerning the meaning of land surrenders still permeate jurisprudence surrounding the interpretation of treaties with native people, legitimated by a vision of native people as the same as nonnative people.

Treaties that involve the surrender of land in return for certain specified benefits from the Crown are imagined as vesting in the Crown an absolute right to exclude native use and enjoyment of ceded land. Thus a set of assumptions steeped in Anglo-Canadian understandings concerning the ownership and the right of exclusion unquestionably informs treaty jurisprudence, to the detriment of alternative understandings of land surrenders which would acknowledge the possibility of joint use except in the case of actual conflict.

The above jurisprudential traits have the effect of maintaining and perpetuating a hierarchical relationship between native peoples and the Canadian state through the medium of treaty guarantees. Though the extremes of traditional acts of judicial interpretation have been eliminated by the new approach called for by Chief Justice Dickson in *Simon*, Anglo-Canadian conceptions are still imported into the process of interpreting treaty guarantees in the context of determining the meaning of land surrenders. Moreover, unless the Court holds to the contrary under s. 35(1) of the *Constitution Act, 1982*, Parliament remains free to regulate or extinguish rights guaranteed by treaties, and in the absence of specific federal legislation to the contrary, provincial legislatures are similarly empowered to regulate and even extinguish treaty rights. The end result is a set of principles that perpetuates a state of legal dependence by native peoples on the legislative good will of the Canadian state.

. . . . .

Justice Lamer's statement in *Sioui* that "[t]he very definition of a treaty ... makes it impossible to avoid the conclusion that a treaty cannot be extinguished without the consent of the Indians involved" ought to be taken seriously as precedential support for the proposition that federal and provincial legislation is not paramount over conflicting treaty guarantees: promises made to natives by the Crown ought to be imagined as setting the boundaries of permissible legislative activity in the future. Imagining treaties in this way forces reconsideration of traditional understandings of the nature of legislative authority; its end result would be to view treaties entered into by the Crown with native peoples as constitutional documents demarcating permissible and impermissible spheres of legislative authority as it intersects with native interests. Yet treaties ought to be imagined as constitutional documents; they represent historic agreements between Canada's First Nations and settling people as to the use and enjoyment of land and played a critical role in the constitution of Canada.

The Royal Commission on Aboriginal Peoples has recommended that the federal government take steps to demonstrate the Crown's commitment to the treaties. To that end, it proposed that the House of Commons and the Senate, by joint resolution, request that the Queen issue a royal proclamation that would establish "a new era of respect for the treaties". This proclamation would, among other things, reaffirm the principles espoused by the *Royal Proclamation of 1763*, R.S.C. 1985, App. II, No. 1, acknowledge the detrimental effects suffered by Aboriginal peoples from past governmental practices, and commit the Crown to redressing past breaches of treaty and other obligations.

Along with this royal proclamation, the Royal Commission has advocated the introduction of companion legislation to provide symbolic and legal force to the principles contained in the proclamation. It has recommended that this treaty legislation should achieve the following objectives:

1. It should provide for the implementation of existing treaty rights, including the rights to hunt, fish and trap.

2. It should affirm liberal rules of interpretation of treaties, having regard to the context of treaty negotiations, the spirit and intent of each treaty, and the special relationship between the treaty parties, and acknowledge the admissibility of oral and secondary evidence in the courts to make determinations with respect to treaty rights.

3. It should declare the commitment of Parliament and government of Canada to the implementation and renewal of each treaty on the basis of the spirit and intent of the treaty and the relationship embodied in it.

4. It should commit the government of Canada to treaty processes to clarify, implement and, where the parties agree, amend the terms of treaties so as to give effect to the spirit and intent of each treaty and the relationship embodied in it.

5. It should commit the government of Canada to a process of treaty-making with Aboriginal nations that do not yet have a treaty with the Crown and with treaty nations whose treaty does not purport to address land and resource issues.

6. It should clarify that defining the scope of governance for Aboriginal and treaty nations is a vital part of the treaties.

7. It should authorize establishment of the institutions necessary to fulfil the treaty process in consultation with treaty nations.[7]

The royal proclamation proposed would supplement and form a part of the Canadian Constitution, thus serving a similar function as the *Royal Proclamation of 1763* does through the incorporation of its principles in section 25 of the *Constitution Act, 1982* (as discussed in Chapter 1). Although the Commission's recommendations are geared towards federal legislation, it suggests that provincial and territorial governments also participate in this treaty affirmation and renewal process. It remains to be seen whether the federal government would be willing to consider adopting such proposals. In the meantime, it should be asked whether these proposals are feasible and what effect they would have, if any, on existing judicial interpretations of treaties.

In considering these questions, compare the Royal Commission's proposals with the treaty provisions contained in the failed Charlottetown Accord, reproduced in Chapter 7. Do they go further than those contained in the Accord or do they amount to essentially the same ideas?

Compare also these recommendations with Lord Woolf's statement about the contemporary approach to be taken towards treaties (specifically, the 1840 *Treaty of Waitangi*) in *New Zealand Maori Council v. A.-G. of New Zealand*, [1994] 1 A.C. 466 at 475 (P.C.):

> Both the Act of 1975 and the State-Owned Enterprises Act 1986 refer to the 'principles' of the Treaty. In their Lordships' opinion the 'principles' are the underlying mutual obligations and responsibilities which the Treaty places on the parties. They reflect the intent of the Treaty as a whole and include, but are not confined to, the express terms of the Treaty. ... With the passage of time, the 'principles' which underlie the Treaty have become much more important than its precise terms.

Does the answer to resolving problems of treaty interpretation lie in the "spirit and intent" of the treaties and the recognition of those agreements as creating and affirming lasting relationships between diverse groups with often equally diverse interests? Is this what the Royal Commission on Aboriginal Peoples was hinting at in the above proposals?

ENDNOTES

1. L.I. Rotman, *Parallel Paths: Fiduciary Doctrine and the Crown-Native Relationship in Canada* (Toronto: University of Toronto Press, 1996) at 32.
2. The formal elements of the *Treaty of Niagara* comprise a number of individual agreements made with various Aboriginal nations: see, for example, "Articles of Peace concluded with the Seneca Indians," 3 April, 1764, as reproduced in E.B. O'Callaghan, ed., *Documents Relative to the Colonial History of the State of New York*, 11 vols. (Albany: Weed, Parsons, 1853-61) VII at 621; "Articles of Peace between Sir William Johnson and the Huron Indians," 1 July, 1764, as reproduced, *ibid.* at 650; "Articles of Peace between Sir William Johnson and the Genesee Indians," 6 August, 1764, as reproduced, *ibid.*, at 652. For additional material on the *Treaty of Niagara*, see the documents contained in O'Callaghan, *ibid.*, as well as in *The Papers of Sir William Johnson*, 14 Vols. (Albany: University of the State of New York, 191-65) IV.
3. As quoted in F. Jennings, *The Founders of America* (New York: Norton, 1993) at 216.
4. Rotman, *supra*, note 1 at 38-9.
5. As quoted in R. White, *The Middle Ground: Indians, Empires, and Republics in the Great Lakes Region, 1650-1815* (Cambridge: Cambridge University Press, 1991) at 256.
6. D.N. Sprague, "Canada's Treaties with Aboriginal Peoples" (1996) 23 Man. L.J. 341 at 345-6.
7. Royal Commission on Aboriginal Peoples, *Report of the Royal Commission on Aboriginal Peoples, Volume II, Part I, Restructuring the Relationship* (Ottawa: Minister of Supply & Services Canada, 1996) at 67.

CHAPTER 3

FIDUCIARY LAW

A. INTRODUCTION

Fiduciary law is a relatively recent addition to Canadian Aboriginal rights jurisprudence. In the brief time that it has been a part of Aboriginal rights law, it has captured the imagination of scholars, judges, and Aboriginal peoples alike. The high profile that fiduciary law enjoys within Canadian Aboriginal rights jurisprudence cloaks the fact that the first Canadian judicial characterization of the relationship between the Crown and Aboriginal peoples as fiduciary occurred in 1984 in the Supreme Court of Canada's landmark decision in *Guerin v. R.*, [1984] 2 S.C.R. 335, [1984] 6 W.W.R. 481, 59 B.C.L.R. 301, [1985] 1 C.N.L.R. 120, 20 E.T.R. 6, 36 R.P.R. 1 (*sub nom. Guerin v. Canada*), 55 N.R. 161, 13 D.L.R. (4th) 321.

The casual manner in which fiduciary law is discussed in the context of Crown-Native relations implies a sophisticated understanding of the ramifications of applying fiduciary doctrine to that relationship. This picture painted by many existing judicial and academic commentaries on the subject is misleading. The application of fiduciary law to Crown-Native relations is neither a finished work nor even a nearly completed one. As illustrated in the following excerpt, fiduciary law's connection to Crown-Native relations remains a project in its infancy.

LEONARD I. ROTMAN, PARALLEL PATHS: FIDUCIARY DOCTRINE AND THE CROWN-NATIVE RELATIONSHIP IN CANADA

(Toronto: University of Toronto Press, 1996) at 3-4, 11-18
(references omitted)

In the 1984 landmark case of *Guerin v. R.*, the Supreme Court of Canada unanimously declared that the Crown is bound by fiduciary obligations to the aboriginal peoples of Canada. By determining that the nature of the Crown's obligation to aboriginal peoples is fiduciary, hence, legal rather than merely political or moral, the Supreme Court of Canada blazed a new path in Canadian aboriginal rights jurisprudence. Yet, more than ten years later, the Canadian judiciary remains poised at the perimeter of the Crown's duty, refusing to venture into its core.

The implementation of fiduciary doctrine to simultaneously describe and monitor the Crown-Native relationship has created difficulties both for the judiciary and legal scholars. Unlike many other areas of the law, such as contracts, the fiduciary relation — and it concomitant duties, obligations, rights, and benefits — is not very well understood. As one jurist has commented, "It is striking that a principle so long standing and so widely accepted should be the subject of the uncertainty that now prevails." Ironically, the confusion surrounding fiduciary doctrine has neither hampered the tremendous increase in the use of fiduciary arguments by litigants nor their acceptance by the judiciary in recent years.

. . . . .

The Crown's fiduciary duty to the aboriginal peoples applies to virtually every facet of the Crown-Native relationship. It has its basis in the historical relationship between the parties dating back to the time of contact, which describes the period ensuing immediately after the first meeting of Europeans and indigenous peoples in North America. It may also be noted in the terms of various treaties, compacts, and alliances between the groups. In addition to being judicially sanctioned in the *Guerin* case, the Crown's fiduciary duty to Native peoples has been constitutionally entrenched in Section 35(1) of the *Constitution Act, 1982*.

. . . . .

Unfortunately, in a number of judicial considerations since *Guerin*, Canadian courts have neither questioned the application of fiduciary doctrine to Native law nor have they attempted to explain the nature and extent of its application. Academic commentaries written in this area have been similarly plagued. As with existing judicial commentaries, these scholarly attempts to explain the application of fiduciary principles to the Crown-Native relationship have invariably been more descriptive than analytical. Even with all of these shortcomings, the application of fiduciary principles in Native law has become axiomatic. They are now presumed to exist as self-evident truths without ever having been put through any thorough examination of their applicability or appropriateness to the Crown-Native relationship. Indeed, the ramifications flowing from the existence of this relationship have yet to be fleshed out.

. . . . .

The continued application of fiduciary principles to the Crown-Native relationship based on the *Guerin* precedent may be seen to be inversely related to the perceived need to explain its application to that relationship. The more often *Guerin* is cited, without elaboration, for its proposition that the Crown owes fiduciary obligations to aboriginal peoples, the perceived need to explain the basis of the Crown's duty is reduced. Indeed, since *Guerin* has been used as the springboard for the imposition of fiduciary duties upon the Crown towards aboriginal peoples, judicial and academic analysis of the basis of the Crown's duty and its effects has decreased. However, it is of little benefit to state that a fiduciary relationship exists or that it has been breached without illustrating what the relationship encompasses or the ramifications of such a breach. Indeed, the portrayal of a relationship as fiduciary is only an initial step; the explanation of the resultant obligations arising by virtue of the relationship's existence is much more onerous.

. . . . .

The Crown-Native fiduciary relation has its origins in the interaction between the groups in the immediate, post-contact period. During the formative years, which roughly covers the period from contact until the removal of France as a major colonial power in North America in 1760-1, Crown-Native relations were based on mutual need, respect, and trust. Furthermore, when the fiduciary character of these relations was crystallized, the participants conducted themselves on a nation-to-nation basis. Consequently, the nature of the Crown's fiduciary obligations is founded on the mutually recognized and respected sovereign status of the Crown and the aboriginal peoples. This fact was recognized by the Royal Commission on Aboriginal Peoples, which stated: "When Europeans first came to the shores of North America, the continent was occupied by a large number of sovereign and independent Aboriginal peoples with their own territories, laws, and forms of government. These nations entered into relations with incoming European nations on the basis of equality and mutual respect, an attitude that persisted long into the period of colonization." Whereas there have been many changes in the nature of Crown-Native relations in the more than three hundred years that have passed since they were solemnified in the *Treaty of Albany, 1664*, their initial foundation forms the basis of the fiduciary aspect of their interaction.

Although the *Guerin* case may have been the first overt judicial recognition of the fiduciary nature of that relationship, it did not create a form of relationship that did not exist previously. *Guerin* merely gave a title and method of analysis for the subsequent treatment of the reciprocal rights, duties, and responsibilities existing between the groups. Therefore, in the nation-to-nation relationship between the Crown and aboriginal peoples, the interaction of the parties being governed by fiduciary law is not the product of an acceptance of the legitimacy of colonialism in Canada, but, rather, the rigorous, yet malleable principles of fiduciary law which are contextually appropriate to monitor the special needs of this *sui generis* situation.

The use of fiduciary doctrine is a valuable tool to ensure that the Crown performs the duties it owes to aboriginal peoples. It is rigorous in its demands of the Crown, protecting of the interests of the aboriginal peoples, and, as part of the common law, binding upon the Crown and enforceable in Canadian courts. Just as fiduciary doctrine is a part of the common law, though, it is also a part of the special, *sui generis* Crown-Native relationship.

The specific nature of a relationship and the situation under which it germinated is what renders it fiduciary, not the actors involved or whether it fits neatly into an already-established category of fiducial relations. Fiduciary doctrine, therefore, may be described as being *situation-specific*. Its situation-specificity insists that fiduciary principles be applied to a relationship only where the nature of the relationship warrants it. Even then, fiduciary doctrine is applicable only to the extent that its general characteristics and principles are relevant to the relationship under scrutiny.

The Crown-Native fiduciary relationship, in actuality, is comprised of two distinct types, or genres, of fiduciary relationships. The Crown owes a general, overarching fiduciary duty to aboriginal peoples as a result of the historical relationship between the parties dating back to the time of contact. In addition, the Crown also owes specific fiduciary duties or obligations to particular Native groups stemming from its relationships with those groups or from specific treaties, agreements, or alliances that it entered into. Depending on individual circumstances, it is possible for the Crown to owe both a general and one or more specific fiduciary duties to an aboriginal nation as a result of its intercourse with those people. As the Crown's fiduciary obligation may be recognized in the totality of its relationships with aboriginal peoples or in specific events or circumstances, such as treaties, initiatives, or legislation, an aboriginal nation's claim against the Crown for a breach of fiduciary obligation may be based either on the totality of events giving rise to the Crown's general fiduciary duty or on the obligations arising out of any one particular event or occurrence.

. . . . .

Because of the situation-specific basis on which fiduciary doctrine is premised, the unexplained application of fiduciary law to the Crown-Native relationship may clearly be seen to be detrimental to the understanding of that relationship. What is sorely needed before the Crown-Native fiduciary relationship may be truly understood is an explanation of why the relationship is a fiduciary one, who owes the obligations to the Native peoples, and what the ramifications of applying fiduciary doctrine to the Crown-Native relationship are. Thus far, no such commentary exists. It is not surprising, then, that the Crown-Native relationship is not more fully understood in the absence of any thorough examination of its fiduciary basis and effects.

The comfort exhibited by the juridical use of fiduciary rhetoric to characterize Crown-Native relations — and one of the inevitable questions raised as a result of its indiscriminate application — is illustrated in the Supreme Court of Canada's recent decision in *Ontario (Attorney- General) v. Bear Island Foundation*, [1991] 3 C.N.L.R. 79 (S.C.C.). It is insufficient to state, as the Supreme Court of Canada did in *Bear Island*, that "the Crown ... breached its fiduciary obligations to the Indians" without revealing which personifications of the Crown are bound by those obligations. In a juridical context, the phrase "the Crown" has a multitude of meanings which refer to a variety of personae. It may refer to the historical constitutional notion of the single and indivisible Crown, the British Crown in its various personalities, or, domestically, to the Crown in right of Canada or the Crown in right of a particular province.

. . . . .

Despite the manner in which it presents itself and is often regarded, the law is not acontextual. Laws come into being in response to external stimuli, not as a result of a priori assumptions. Consequently, any legal entrenchment of fiduciary obligations upon the Crown towards aboriginal peoples must also arise in response to particular events, circumstances, or requirements. In and of themselves, the *Royal Proclamation of 1763*, the

Indian Act, and the *Constitution Act, 1982* each provide one basis for ascertaining the nature of the Crown-Native relationship. However, a different light is shed on the legal entrenchment of the Crown's duty once these various components are placed within the context in which they originated.

Focusing exclusively on the legal effects of the *Royal Proclamation of 1763*, for example, provides only one element of the Crown's duty. Recognizing that the Proclamation affects the Crown's responsibilities to the aboriginal peoples renders another component of the Crown's duty. Examining the process by which the Proclamation was promulgated and the underlying rationale for its institution in law is a third component that provides additional information on which the fiduciary character of the Crown-Native relationship may be determined. The result of placing the concrete recognition of the Crown's fiduciary duty in context, then, is a multitiered view of the effect of any one component of the Crown-Native fiduciary relationship on that relationship.

By examining the entirety of events and documents that comprise various elements of the Crown's fiduciary duty, a much richer understanding of the nature of that duty may be obtained. Unless these events and documents are scrutinized for their effects on the legal entrenchment of the Crown's obligations, only a limited understanding of the Crown's duty may be achieved. To avoid this result, a proper accounting for these happenings must itself be well rounded. This includes a consideration of these events as understood by both the Crown and aboriginal peoples.

Traditionally, aboriginal understandings of the Crown-Native relationship are among the most neglected aspects of any examination of the applicability of fiduciary law to that relationship. One of the inherent flaws which has historically plagued the development of Canadian aboriginal rights jurisprudence has been its inability to account for or pay heed to Native perspectives. From an aboriginal standpoint, the nature of the Crown-Native relationship appears fundamentally different than it does from a strictly common law perspective, which is based on colonialist attitudes and the subjugation of aboriginal rights and claims to those more consistent with the common law's European origins and biases. Through the teachings of aboriginal elders and scholars, aboriginal understandings of the nature of their relationship with the Crown and the effects of various documents, events, alliances, and treaties on that relationship may begin to be more fully understood.

By examining the relationship between the Crown and aboriginal peoples in context, it is possible to address the untreated questions and issues arising from previous treatments of the Crown's fiduciary duty to aboriginal peoples. These range from the fundamental issues of the principles applicable to the Crown-Native fiduciary relationship and who is bound by the fiduciary duty to aboriginal peoples to the more specific issues of how the Crown is to discharge its duty and how it may avoid situations of conflict of interest. Only after these issues have been addressed may the full implications and ramifications of the imposition of fiduciary doctrine upon the relationship between the Crown and aboriginal peoples in Canada begin to be truly understood.

B. THE IMPLICATIONS OF FIDUCIARY LAW

A fiduciary relationship is comprised of at least two parties, one or more of whom possess equitable obligations to one or more others as a result of the nature of their interaction. The party owing those obligations is described as a fiduciary. The party that is owed fiduciary obligations is known as the beneficiary, or *cestui que trust*. The parties to fiduciary relationships need not be natural persons. They may be corporations, Indian bands, or the Crown itself.

In a fiduciary relationship, the beneficiary resposes trust and confidence in the honesty, integrity, and fidelity of the fiduciary and relies upon the latter's care of that trust. Fiduciary law exists to protect those who trust in the ability of others, whether voluntarily or out of necessity, from having that trust abused. Fiduciary law's primary purpose is to preserve the integrity of important, socially and/or economically valuable or necessary relationships that arise as a result of human interdependency. It also provides protection for beneficiaries who are involved in fiduciary relations from the potential for indecorous activities against their interests by unscrupulous fiduciaries.

The following excerpt provides an overview of the fiduciary concept generally as well as a blueprint for its contextual application.

LEONARD I. ROTMAN, "FIDUCIARY DOCTRINE: A CONCEPT IN NEED OF UNDERSTANDING"

(1996), 34 Alta. L. Rev. 821 at 821-34, 838, 843-4, 846, 851
(references omitted)

Fiduciary doctrine is an elusive concept. It has a lengthy existence, dating back over 250 years in English law to the celebrated case of *Keech v. Sandford*. Before that, it had been a well-established part of Roman law. The duration and frequency of fiduciary law's application to a wide variety of relationships fosters the impression that the fiduciary concept is one of the most well-understood of legal doctrines. Indeed, within the past thirty years or so, the Supreme Court of Canada has discussed the existence of fiduciary relationships between senior officers/directors and a corporation, custodial parent and non-custodial parent, solicitor and client, federal government and Indian band, doctor and patient, father and daughter, and financial advisor and client. Upon closer scrutiny, however, the frequent judicial application of fiduciary principles is only a thin veneer concealing the uncertainty which plagues fiduciary theory.

The law reports abound with descriptions of relationships as fiduciary when they actually bear little or no resemblance to such relationships. In fact, the judiciary has misapplied fiduciary law in a variety of instances: for remedial purposes in cases where there has been no demonstrated existence of a fiduciary relationship or where such a demonstration would prove impossible, and where heads of obligation exist independently of the fiducial relation.

Despite, or perhaps because of, the general confusion surrounding fiduciary doctrine, it has recently experienced a tremendous growth in use. Fiduciary arguments have become something of a "catch-all" — if all other claims are meritless or no other cause of action exists, a claim of breach of fiduciary duty is often resorted to. In *Burns v. Kelly Peters & Associates Ltd.*, Lambert J.A. highlighted the potential problem stemming from the indiscriminate use of fiduciary doctrine's malleable principles in this fashion:

> The danger, of course, with such a flexible remedy, is that it should be used as a catch-all for cases which offend against some of the more exacting standards of commercial morality. So the extra flexibility should promote a sense of caution in determining whether the fiduciary relationship exists. Or, as Viscount Haldane said in *Nocton v. Ashburton*, at 966: "... the special relationship must ... be clearly shown to exist...."

The increase in the use of fiduciary arguments has not escaped notice by the judiciary. In *Girardet v. Crease & Co.*, Southin J., as she then was, noted that "[t]he word 'fiduciary' is flung around now as if it applied to all breaches of duty by solicitors, directors of companies and so forth." In *LAC Minerals Ltd. v. International Corona Resources Ltd.*, La Forest J. stated that "[t]here are few legal concepts more frequently invoked but less conceptually certain than that of the fiduciary relationship." Judicial notice of the misapplication of the fiduciary concept illustrates the existence of a serious problem. What have often purported to be applications of fiduciary principles by the courts have too often been an amalgamation of unrelated rules, only some of which may be a part of fiduciary doctrine.

Part of the confusion surrounding fiduciary doctrine may be traced to judicial tendencies to incorrectly view the labeling of a person or relationship as fiduciary as the end of their investigatory process. The judiciary has often acted as though the mere description of a relationship as fiduciary was sufficient to enable it to apply a remedy. The American jurist Oliver Wendell Holmes once stated that "It is one of the misfortunes of the law that ideas become encysted in phrases and thereafter for a long time cease to provoke further analysis." Rather than denoting the end of judicial investigation, describing a person or a relationship as fiduciary creates the need for further inquiry. As Mr. Justice Felix Frankfurter explained in *Securities & Exchange Commission v. Chenery Corp.*:

> [T]o say that a man is a fiduciary only begins analysis; it gives direction to further inquiry. To whom is he a fiduciary? What obligation does he owe as a fiduciary? In what respect has he failed to discharge these obligations? And what are the consequences of his deviation from duty?

The judicial desire to describe relationships as fiduciary cannot ignore the ramifications of such a description en route to the imposition of one of fiduciary doctrine's desirable remedies. Without knowing what it is that renders a person or relationship fiduciary, that description is meaningless. The explanation of the obligations arising by virtue of the relationship's existence is what breathes life into the fiduciary characterization. This necessitates, however, an investigation into the nature of the interaction giving rise to the fiduciary relation.

It is pointless to describe a person — or for that matter a power — as being fiduciary unless at the same time it is said for the purposes of which particular rules and principles that description is being used. These rules are everything. The description "fiduciary," nothing.

This article rests upon twin premises: that fiduciary doctrine is both a valuable tool for the control and regulation of socially valuable or necessary relationships and that it has often been wrongfully characterized and misunderstood. Fiduciary law is not only "law's blunt tool" for the control of a fiduciary's discretion, but shapes the parameters of a beneficiary's ability to rely upon his or her fiduciary's good faith exercise of that discretion. Fiduciary relationships ought to be understood both for the duties and obligations possessed by fiduciaries as well as the benefits that flow to beneficiaries from the existence of such relationships. This necessitates a contextualization of fiduciary doctrine, something that has been omitted far too frequently from juridical examinations.

... What is needed ... is an explication of the underlying purpose of fiduciary doctrine, what it aims to promote, and how it attempts to do so through an examination of its theoretical underpinnings. Once these are understood, it is possible to apply the principles of fiduciary doctrine in a manner which is consistent with the doctrine's fundamental purpose.

II. A FUNCTIONAL APPROACH TO FIDUCIARY DOCTRINE

Traditionally, fiduciary relationships have been defined according to categories. Where questions of the fiduciary nature of particular relationships arose, juridical examinations would focus upon whether the relationship under scrutiny belonged to the list of relationships that were generally understood to be fiduciary in nature, such as trustee and beneficiary, parent and child, and guardian and ward. The nature of the particular relationship itself or the interaction of the parties involved in it was a secondary matter. Accordingly, there were no established guidelines for determining what constituted a fiduciary relationship.

. . . . .

The use of categories to determine the fiduciary nature of a relationship runs counter to the very basis of fiduciary doctrine. Fiduciary law has its origins in public policy, specifically the desire to protect certain types of relationships that are deemed to be socially valuable or necessary. The common elements to the relationships which come under its protection are the trust and confidence placed by one person in another within a given context. This reposing of trust by one person in the honesty, integrity, and fidelity of another, as well as the former's reliance upon the latter's care of that trust, is the basis for the creation of legal mechanisms such as fiduciary law and the law of trusts. These laws seek to protect those who trust in the ability of others from having that trust abused.

... Fiduciary law's preservation of relationships that come under its auspices requires that fiduciaries ascribe to a high standard of conduct. This is achieved through the imposition of certain restrictions upon fiduciaries' fulfillment of their special office, a requirement necessitated by virtue of the inherent inequality of the parties created by the nature of their interaction. Meanwhile, the ever-increasing degree of interdependency in societies governed by English common law or its derivatives has resulted in the commensurately-broadened mandate of fiduciary law within those spheres. Fiduciary doctrine has expanded its application to fill the increasing need to protect those who are dependent upon others for particular tasks and to ensure that relationships created by the push towards interdependency remain viable. Weinrib has suggested that:

> A sophisticated industrial and commercial society requires that its members be integrated rather than autonomously self-sufficient, and through the concepts of commercial and property law provides mechanisms of interaction and interdependence. The fiduciary obligation ... constitutes a means by which those mechanisms are protected.

Without individuals' need to rely upon others, there would be no need for fiduciary law. However, while fiduciary law exists because individuals rely upon each other, maintaining the viability of an interdependent society requires that that interdependency is closely monitored to avoid the potential for abuse existing within such relations. ... Therefore, the existence of fiduciary law protects the interests of individuals who rely upon others and allows for the continuation and proliferation of interdependent relationships which carry the possibility for *mala fide* activity by one party against the other.

. . . . .

[F]iduciary doctrine also ensures that the spirit, as well as the intent, of interdependent relations is maintained. In *McLeod and More v. Sweezey*, the defendant was to stake and record some asbestos mineral claims on behalf of the plaintiffs as part of a profit-sharing agreement. The defendant reported that there was no asbestos, whereupon the plaintiffs allowed the claims that had been staked under the agreement to lapse. When the defendant was no longer associated with the plaintiffs, he returned to the area — which had no asbestos, but which he knew was rich in chrome — and staked his own claims. The plaintiffs brought an action against the defendant for their share of the profit earned from the sale of his claims.

In finding in favour of the plaintiffs, the Supreme Court of Canada imposed a constructive trust upon the proceeds from the defendant's sale of the claims, with 75 percent allocated to the plaintiffs as per the agreement. In determining the nature of the defendant's undertaking pursuant to the agreement, the court held that the defendant's obligations were not limited to asbestos claims, but covered all minerals found in the area staked out:

> They had bargained for his mature judgment and for that not only on the possibility of asbestos. The expression in the memorandum agreement, 'asbestos mineral claims,' was description [sic] of what had been originally staked. The plaintiffs desired an expert opinion on those claims in the totality of their possibilities and not on one of them only. That, therefore, was the measure of the defendant's duty as the fiduciary of the plaintiffs in acting upon the disclosure of all the plaintiffs had of value; he undertook to apply his experience to everything found in the area of the claims.... He, therefore, owed to the plaintiffs the utmost good faith in his examination of the struc-

ture, formation, and other evidence of the land to which he was directed, and a duty to give them an unreserved account of what he had found and what, in his judgment, the mineral prospect was.

In the *McLeod* case, the existence of the defendant's fiduciary duties to the plaintiffs prohibited him from being able to take advantage of a technicality — no asbestos, but chrome — for personal gain at the expense of others. Had he not entered into the agreement with the plaintiffs, under which they reposed their trust and confidence in him and gave him key information, the defendant would not have known of the existence of the claims and, consequently, would not have discovered the chrome deposits. Essentially, the defendant's duty of utmost good faith to the plaintiffs entailed an obligation to live up to the spirit of the agreement — *i.e.* an obligation to report on the existence of all minerals, not just asbestos — and not merely its technical terms. Of course, the defendant's duty in this sense was not unlimited. Had he found the existence of an underground spring or a rare breed of truffle on the claimed lands and kept that information to himself for his own benefit, it is arguable that he would not have been found liable for a breach of fiduciary duty — the information would likely be deemed to be too far removed from his obligation to the plaintiffs for him to have to share it with them.

Two basic themes become evident from the theoretical basis of fiduciary doctrine. Initially, it is apparent that the fiduciary nature of any relationship arises from circumstances peculiar to that relationship and the interaction of its participants and not as a result of belonging to "traditional" categories of fiduciary relations. Secondly, since fiduciary relationships ought not be confined to already established categories and should be determined by a more functional approach, the categories of relationships that may be described as fiduciary should be viewed as open-ended.

A. THE SITUATION-SPECIFIC NATURE OF FIDUCIARY DOCTRINE

The most vital aspect of fiduciary doctrine, and what ought to receive the bulk of juridical attention, is its focus upon the specific characteristics of individual relationships. ... *A priori* assessments are therefore completely inappropriate within the realm of fiduciary law. Because of its implementation on a case-by-case basis, fiduciary doctrine is most appropriately described as *situation-specific*.

. . . . .

Since the determination of the fiduciary nature of any relationship is situation-specific, it follows that it is not possible to authoritatively determine the totality of relationships which may be deemed to be fiduciary. For these reasons, any attempt to create a taxonomic definition of fiduciary relations in the absence of context is impossible or, at the very least, unwise.

. . . . .

Subsequently, recognizing that fiduciary doctrine is situation-specific ought to be both a primary consideration and a precursor to its application to particular relationships.

B. THE CATEGORICAL OPEN-ENDEDNESS OF FIDUCIARY RELATIONSHIPS

The open-ended nature of fiduciary doctrine holds that no relationship may be precluded from being classified as fiduciary because it does not fit into established classes of fiduciary relationships or because the actors involved are not traditionally associated with fiduciary relations. It maintains that the only relevant consideration is whether the nature of the relationship is such that it ought to be considered fiduciary.

. . . . .

Even where particular types of relationships have been described by the courts as fiduciary, that does not necessarily entail that every instance of those relationships is fiduciary. Furthermore, not every aspect of a fiduciary relationship is fiduciary. Along this same line of reasoning, La Forest J. held in *LAC Minerals Ltd. v. International Corona Resources Ltd.* that it is far more important to look at the particulars of a relationship to ascertain whether it is fiduciary rather than simply observing who the parties to it are:

> The imposition of fiduciary obligations is not limited to those relationships in which a presumption of such an obligation arises. Rather, a fiduciary obligation can arise as a matter of fact out of the specific circumstances of a relationship. As such it can arise between parties in a relationship in which fiduciary obligations would not normally be expected.

What is truly meant by the open-endedness of the fiduciary relation, then, is that the categories of fiduciary relations are never closed and neither are their limits.

III. IMPLEMENTING THE FUNCTIONAL APPROACH

Whereas the integrity of fiduciary relations may be preserved by prescribing acceptable standards of fiduciaries' conduct, the success of such a regime is ultimately dependent upon a proper balance being struck between the desire to protect beneficiaries' interests and the sanctioning of fiduciaries' behaviour. The fiduciary office will remain vacant if the cost to prospective fiduciaries is so high that they are discouraged from accepting the position. Fiduciary doctrine attempts to provide an equitable balancing of the need to preserve the integrity of fiduciary relations by imposing strict standards of conduct upon fiduciaries which are sufficiently stringent to protect beneficiaries' interests, yet not so strict as to discourage others from accepting the fiduciary office.

. . . . .

Numerous relations between persons within any given society entail some form of dependence or potential for one person to positively or negatively affect the interests of another. These relationships take a variety of forms. Not all of them involve the reposing of trust, however. Moreover, not all of them ought to be treated as fiduciary in nature. The potential for one person's interests to be affected by the actions of another varies in degree according to a number of criteria. These include, among other things, the nature and scope of the relationship and the degree of trust and reliance involved. While the determination of the types of relationships that come under fiduciary law's protective sheath ought to be made according to the facts and requirements of the specific relationship under scrutiny and not be limited by general rules, this does not entail that all relationships involving degrees of dependency, reliance, or trust ought to be characterized as fiduciary.

. . . . .

The unprincipled application of fiduciary doctrine, whether under the categorical approach or otherwise, may result in the imposition of undeservedly-harsh sanctions upon persons who ought not to be made subject to them. Moreover, it also allows persons who would not otherwise be entitled to fiduciary remedies to be availed of them. Aside from acting as punishments or deterrents for fiduciaries and serving to maintain the integrity of fiduciary relations, fiduciary remedies exist to protect beneficiaries' interests by correcting fiduciaries' abuse of their positions in ways that go beyond ordinary remedies. Beneficiaries are only entitled to fiduciary remedies by virtue of their positions vis-à-vis their fiduciaries and due to fiduciary doctrine's perception that onerous penalties are required to ensure that fiduciaries live up to the high standards required of them. The reason why parties to a contract, for example, are neither imposed with the same high degrees of loyalty or availed of similarly far-ranging remedial aid is that the moral standards applied to contracting parties [are] far less exacting than those required of fiduciaries.

. . . . .

In general terms, fiduciary law exists to monitor the intercourse between those who give their trust and those who care for that trust. It ensures that fiduciaries live up to the high expectations required of them, provides beneficiaries with the means to enforce their fiduciaries' duties, and imposes remedies where fiduciaries fail to discharge their obligations. In all, fiduciary law seeks to ensure the equity of dealings between parties to relationships which, by their nature, are particularly susceptible to fraud, undue influence, and other activities which run afoul of public policy. Unfortunately, as a result of the tremendous scope of activity that fiduciary doctrine was designed to monitor, it has been particularly susceptible to incorrect usage.

V. FIDUCIARY THEORIES

... Traditional definitions of the term "fiduciary" have tended to focus upon the similarity of the fiduciary and the trustee and of the fiduciary relationship with the trust relationship. Indeed, "fiduciary" is derived from the Latin words "fiducia," which means trust, or reliance, and "fiduciarius," which translates to something that is entrusted or given in trust. Moreover, the latter two are derivatives of the verb "fido," which means "to trust." In the legal context, the notion of fiduciary relations was first conceived of by equity in relation to trustees, and was later expanded to include the actions of any person who occupies a position of trust or is entrusted by another for a particular purpose.

Both the fiduciary and trust relationship entail similar duties, benefits, and liabilities. The fiduciary relation involves the beneficiary's reposing of trust and confidence in the fiduciary to act in the former's best interests, with the utmost good faith, integrity, candour, and fidelity. The fiduciary is bound, meanwhile, to act selflessly for the benefit of the beneficiary and must not take unfair advantage of the beneficiary so as to prejudice the latter's interests.

. . . . .

An inherent aspect of fiduciary relationships is that fiduciaries possess the ability, by virtue of their positions, to positively or negatively affect the interests of their beneficiaries. Fiduciary law mandates that the fiduciary's actions adhere to the former; when they result in the latter, the beneficiary has legal recourse to seek appropriate sanctions against the fiduciary. The fiduciary's ability to affect the beneficiary's interests creates a situation of unequal power relations between the two within the confines of that relationship. However, the power of the parties vis-à-vis each other outside of the boundaries of their fiduciary relationship is irrelevant to the determination of whether any relationship is fiduciary:

> It cannot be the *sine qua non* of a fiduciary obligation that the parties have disparate bargaining strength.... [t]he fiduciary relation looks to the relative position of the parties that results from the agreement rather than the relative position that precedes the agreement.

In "The Vulnerable Position of Fiduciary Doctrine in the Supreme Court of Canada," I suggest that the best way to understand the relative positions of the parties in fiduciary relationships is to think of the fiduciary relationship as a transfer of powers from the beneficiary, B, to the fiduciary, F. The powers transferred by B to F originally belonged to the former and, in fact, still do. B has merely *loaned* the powers to F within the ambit of their fiduciary relationship; they do not become F's own possession. F is duty-bound to use these powers in the same manner as B would, subject to any constraints B imposes on their use. F may not exceed these imposed limits, otherwise he is liable for breach of duty; the purpose of F's duty is to act within the parameters established by B through the latter's transfer of powers, not to exceed them. When the fiduciary relationship is terminated, the powers return to B. A similar method of understanding the relative positions of fiduciaries and beneficiaries in fiduciary relationships was espoused by McLachlin J. in the Supreme Court of Canada's decision in *Norberg v. Wynrib*, where she explained that: "[i]t is as though the fiduciary has taken the power which rightfully belongs to the beneficiary on the condition that the fiduciary exercise the power entrusted exclusively for the good of the beneficiary."

The inequality in the relationship between fiduciary and beneficiary results from the transfer of powers from B to F. The inequality of this position is illustrated by the change in power relations between B and F within the boundaries of their fiduciary relationship. Originally both had complete and equal powers — Q. Upon the transfer of prescribed powers (P) from B to F, the fiduciary relationship came into being. However, within that fiduciary relationship, F's powers now amount to $Q+P$, whereas B only possesses $Q-P$, thereby resulting in a power inequality that did not exist prior to the creation of the fiduciary relation. Although the beneficiary's interests are protected by the law of fiduciaries, this protection serves only as a check on the fiduciary's ability to abuse the power transferred from the beneficiary.

· · · · ·

Fiduciary law ... has always been premised upon principles which are not limited or dictated by the actions of its participants. Moreover, it prescribes acceptable manners of conduct that are based upon a higher moral standard than that of the marketplace. The basis of the fiduciary standard is the mirror image of contract's reliance upon parties' self-interest. As Cardozo J. explained in *Meinhard v. Salmon*:

> Many forms of conduct permissible in a workaday world for those acting at arm's length, are forbidden to those bound by fiduciary ties. A trustee is held to something stricter than the morals of the marketplace. Not honesty alone, but the punctilio of an honor the most sensitive, is then the standard of behavior. As to this there has developed a tradition that is unbending and inveterate. Uncompromising rigidity had been the attitude of courts of equity when petitioned to undermine the rule of undivided loyalty by the "disintegrating erosion" of particular exceptions.... Only thus has the level of conduct for fiduciaries been kept at a level higher than that trodden by the crowd.

· · · · ·

VI. CONCLUSION

· · · · ·

Fiduciary doctrine is a vital element of law. It enjoys widespread application and has the potential to expand even further as the understanding of its theoretical basis and inherent purpose continues to evolve. However, rather than attempting to illustrate specific examples in which fiduciary doctrine has been held to apply, this paper has adopted a functional approach which is based upon an adherence to the purpose and intent of fiduciary doctrine.

... Fiduciary doctrine is not merely a set of loosely-fitting or entirely unrelated rules functioning in an *ad hoc* fashion. Rather, it is a blueprint for the protection and continued efficacy of interdependent societal relations.

C. FIDUCIARY LAW VS. TRUST LAW

It is almost impossible to discuss contemporary Aboriginal claims against the Crown without venturing into a discussion of fiduciary law. Responsibility for this rests upon the Supreme Court of Canada's decision in the *Guerin* case. Prior to *Guerin* there had been limited judicial consideration of Crown-Native relations rooted in trust law. There are, however, some fundamental problems associated with basing the Crown obligations in trust law, as demonstrated by the following excerpt.

PAWIS v. THE QUEEN

(1979), 102 D.L.R. (3d) 602 at 613-15, [1980] 2 F.C. 18 (T.D.)

Marceau J.: — The basic suggestion here is that the Lake-Huron Treaty of 1850 created a trust, the subject-matter of which was the "full and free privilege to hunt over the territory now ceded by them and to fish in the waters thereof as they have heretofore been in the habit of doing". It is, however, a suggestion that I am again unable to accept.

There is no doubt that the Crown can take upon itself trust obligations which are enforceable in a Court of Equity: *Tito v. Waddell (No. 2)*, [1977] 3 All E.R. 129. It is equally true that no specific form of words is necessary to create a trust, and that a treaty of that nature ought to be liberally construed. But I fail to see how one can find here the prerequisites for the existence of a proper trust that may be the subject-matter of an action before a Court. As was said by Cannon J., in *M.A. Hanna Co. v. Provincial Bank of Canada*, [1935] 1 D.L.R. 545 at p. 565, [1935] S.C.R. 144 at p. 167:

> To completely constitute a trust, four elements are required: —
> (a) A trustee;
> (b) A beneficiary;
> (c) Property the subject-matter of the trust;
> (d) An obligation enforceable in a Court of Equity on the trustee to administer or deal with the property for the benefit of the beneficiary. There must be an equitable interest based on a conscientious obligation which can be enforced against the legal owner of the property alleged to be the subject-matter of the trust. Otherwise there is no trust.

How can the privilege to hunt and to fish be the "property of a trust"? There is no subject-matter here capable of being "held" or "administered" by a trustee for the benefit of a beneficiary. Unless the lands said to be ceded, were to be considered as being the trust property? That suggestion, however, cannot hold since there never has been any doubt that the title to the lands was already vested in the Crown before 1850, and the Treaty cannot be construed as purporting to recognize in favour of the Indians a right different in nature than that of a licensee.

In *A.-G. Can. v. A.-G. Ont.; A.-G. Que. v. A.-G. Ont.*, [1897] A.C. 199, the Judicial Committee of the Privy Council, in deciding questions that turned upon the construction of the very treaty which forms the subject-matter of this trial, and its sister-treaty, the Lake-Superior Treaty, arrived at the following conclusion [at p. 213]:

> Their Lordships have had no difficulty in coming to the conclusion that, under the treaties, the Indians obtained no right to their annuities, whether original or augmented, beyond a promise and agreement, which was nothing more than a personal obligation by its governor, as representing the old province, that the latter should pay the annuities as and when they became due; that the Indians obtained no right which gave them any interest in the territory which they surrendered, other than that of the province; and that no duty was imposed upon the province, whether in the nature of a trust obligation or otherwise, to apply the revenue derived from the surrendered lands in payment of the annuities.

That case was concerned with the payment of the annuities promised in the treaties but it seems to me that the same reasoning must apply with respect to the other promise contained therein, that is the promise of a licence to fish and hunt.

In my view, it cannot be said that, by entering into the Lake-Huron Treaty, the Crown took upon itself a trust obligation. I mean, of course, a trust obligation in the technical sense. The expression "trust obligations" is sometimes used to refer to "governmental obligations" and in that sense it may perhaps be properly applied to the obligations created by the Treaty. But "trust obligations" of that type are not enforceable as such. The distinction between trust obligations enforceable in the Courts of Chancery and these governmental or trust obligations in the higher sense is referred to by Lord Selborne, LC., in *Kinloch v. Secretary of State for India* (1882), 7 App. Cas. 619 at pp. 625-6:

> Now the words 'in trust for' are quite consistent with, and indeed are the proper manner of expressing, every species of trust — a trust not only as regards those matters which are the proper subjects for an equitable jurisdiction to administer, but as respects higher matters, such as might take place between the Crown and public officers discharging, under the directions of the Crown, duties or functions belonging to the prerogative and to the authority of the Crown. In the lower sense they are matters within the jurisdiction of, and to be administered by, the ordinary Courts of Equity; in the higher sense they are not.

(See also *Tito v. Waddell (No. 2)* referred to above.)

In any event, assuming that true trust obligations were in fact created by the Treaty, the problem would remain as to the content thereof and the nature of the duties imposed on the Crown as trustee. ... The facts do not support the allegation of a breach of trust giving rise to an action for damages.

As seen above, Justice Marceau's chief difficulty in applying trust law to the treaty right to hunt and fish in *Pawis* was trust law's requirement that an express trust must have a legally recognizeable property interest that comprises the subject matter, or *res*, of the trust. The "privilege" to hunt and fish, as Marceau J. described it in *Pawis*, was not recognized as a common law property right, thus he found that no trust could exist. Could this situation have been avoided? See the following excerpt from *Guerin v. R.*, below.

D. THE TRIUMPH OF FIDUCIARY LAW OVER TRUST LAW

The *Guerin* case, like *Pawis* before it, began as an action against the Crown for breach of trust. At the Supreme Court of Canada, the *Guerin* decision initiated an entirely new way of conceptualizing Crown-Native relations by substituting the fiduciary concept as the basis for the Musqueam Band's claim against the federal Crown.

GUERIN v. R.

(1984), 13 D.L.R. (4th) 321 at 326, [1984] 2 S.C.R. 335, [1984] 6 W.W.R. 481,
59 B.C.L.R. 301, [1985] 1 C.N.L.R. 120, 20 E.T.R. 6, 36 R.P.R. 1
(*sub nom. Guerin v. Canada*), 55 N.R. 161

Dickson J.: — The question is whether the appellants, the chief and councillors of the Musqueam Indian Band, suing on their own behalf and on behalf of all other members of the band, are entitled to recover damages from the federal Crown in respect of the leasing to a golf club of land on the Musqueam Indian Reserve. Collier J., of the Trial Division of the Federal Court, declared that the Crown was in breach of trust .... He assessed damages at $10,000,000. The Federal Court of Appeal allowed a Crown appeal, set aside the judgment of the Trial Division and dismissed the action.

I. GENERAL

Before adverting to the facts, reference should be made to several of the relevant sections of the *Indian Act*, R.S.C. 1952, c. 149 as amended. Section 18(1) provides in part that reserves shall be held by Her Majesty for the use of the respective Indian bands for which they were set apart. Generally, lands in a reserve shall not be sold, alienated, leased or otherwise disposed of until they have been surrendered to Her Majesty by the band for whose use and benefit in common the reserve was set apart (s. 37). A surrender may be absolute or qualified, conditional or unconditional (s. 38(2)). To be valid, a surrender must be made to Her Majesty, assented to by a majority of the electors of the band, and accepted by the Governor in Council (s. 39(1)).

The gist of the present action is a claim that the federal Crown was in breach of its trust obligations in respect of the leasing of approximately 162 acres of reserve land to the Shaughnessy Heights Golf Club of Vancouver.

The band alleged that a number of the terms and conditions of the lease were different from those disclosed to them before the surrender vote and that some of the lease terms were not disclosed to them at all. The band also claimed failure on the part of the federal Crown to exercise the requisite degree of care and management as a trustee.

II. THE FACTS

... The following summary of the facts derives directly from the judgment at trial. Musqueam Indian Reserve (No. 2) in 1955 contained 416.53 acres, situated within the charter area of the City of Vancouver. The Indian Affairs Branch recognized that the reserve was a valuable one, "the most potentially valuable 400 acres in Vancouver today". In 1956 the Shaughnessy Heights Golf Club was interested in obtaining land on the Musqueam Reserve. There were others interested in developing the land, although the band was never told of the proposals for development.

On April 4, 1957, the president of the golf club wrote to Mr. Anfield, District Superintendent of the Indian Affairs Branch, setting forth a proposal for the lease of 160 acres of the Indian reserve, the relevant terms of which were as follows:

1. The club was to have the right to construct on the leased area a golf course and country club and such other buildings and facilities as it considered appropriate for its membership.
2. The initial term of the lease was to be for fifteen years commencing May 1, 1957, with the club to have options to extend the term for four successive periods of fifteen years each, giving a maximum term of seventy-five years.
3. The rental for the first fifteen year term was to be $25,000 per annum.
4. The rental agreement for each successive fifteen year period was to be detemined by mutual agreement, between the Department and the club and failing agreement, by arbitration, but the rental for any of the fifteen year renewal periods was in no event to be increased or decreased over that payable for the preceding fifteen year period by more than 15% of the initial rent.
5. At any time during the term of the lease, and for a period of up to six months after termination, the club was to have the right to remove any buildings and other structures it had constructed or placed upon the leased area, and any course improvements and facilities.

On April 7, 1957, a band council meeting was held. Mr. Anfield presided. The trial judge accepted evidence on behalf of the plaintiffs that not all of the terms of the Shaughnessy proposal were put before the band council at the meeting. William Guerin, a councillor, said copies of the proposal were not given to them; he did not recall any mention of the $25,000 per year for rental; he described it as a vague general presentation with reference to 15-year periods. Chief Edward Sparrow said he did not recall the golf club proposal being read out in full. At the meeting the band council passed a resolution which the trial judge presumed to have been drawn up by Mr. Anfield. The relevant part of the resolution reads:

That we do approve the leasing of unrequired lands on our Musqueam I.R. 2 and that in connection with the application of the Shaughnessy Golf Club, we do approve the submission to our Musqueam Band of surrender documents for leasing 160 acres approximately as generally outlined on the McGuigan survey in red pencil.

These events followed the band council meeting.

(a) Mr. Bethune, Superintendent of Reserves and Trusts of the Indian Affairs Branch, in Ottawa, questioned the adequacy of the $25,000 annual rental for the first 15 years.... Mr. Bethune suggested that the opinion of Mr. Alfred Howell be obtained. Mr. Howell, with the Veterans Land Act Administration, had earlier made an appraisal of the reserve lands at the request of the Indian Affairs Branch.

(b) On May 15, 1957, Mr. Anfield wrote Mr. Howell asking for the latter's opinion as to whether the $25,000 per year rental for the first 15 years was "just and equitable". Mr. Howell was not given all the details of the Shaughnessy proposal. He was not told that rent increases would be limited to 15%. Nor was he made aware that the golf club proposed to have the right to remove any buildings or improvements.

(c) In his reply to Mr. Anfield, Mr. Howell expressed the view that a 75-year lease, adjustable over 15 years and made with a financially sound tenant, eliminated any risk factor. On that basis he felt the then government bond rate of 3.75% was the most that could be expected.

At trial Mr. Howell said that if he had known the improvements would not revert to the band, he would have recommended a rate of return of 4-6%. He expressed shock at the 15% clause. He had assumed that at the end of the initial term the rental could be renegotiated on the basis of "highest and best use" without any limitation on rental increase.

(d) On September 27, 1957, a band council meeting was held at the reserve, attended by members of the band council, Mr. Anfield, two other officials of the Department of Indian Affairs and representatives of the golf club. Chief Sparrow stipulated for 5% income on the value of 162 acres, amounting to $44,000 per annum. The golf club people balked. They were asked to step outside while the band council and the Indian Affairs personnel had a private discussion. Mr. Anfield said the demand of $44,000 was unreasonable. Eventually, the band council reluctantly agreed to a figure of $29,000. William Guerin testified the councillors agreed to $29,000 because they understood the first lease period was to be 10 years; subsequent rental negotiations would be every five years; and the band council felt it could negotiate for 5% of the subsequent values.

Mr. Grant, officer in charge of the Vancouver agency of the Department of Indian Affairs, testified that there was "absolutely no question that the vote was for a specific lease to a specific tenant on specific terms" and that the band did not give Mr. Anfield "authority to change things around".

(e) On October 6, 1957, a meeting of members of the band was held at the reserve, the so-called "surrender meeting". The trial judge made these findings: (i) those present assumed or understood the golf club lease would be, aside from the first term, for 10-year periods, not 15 years; (ii) those present assumed or understood there would be no 15% limitation on rental increases; (iii) the meeting was not told that the golf club had proposed that it should have the right to remove any buildings, structures, course improvements and facilities.

The trial judge further found that two matters which subsequently found their way into the lease were not even put before the surrender meeting. They were not in the original golf club proposal. They first appeared in draft leases, after the meeting. The first of these terms was the method of determining future rents; failing mutual agreement, the matter was to be submitted to arbitration; the new rent would be the fair rent as if the land were still in an uncleared and unimproved condition and used as a golf club. The second term gave the golf club, but not the Crown, the right at the end of each 15-year period to terminate the lease on six months' prior notice. These two terms were not subsequently brought before the band council or the band for comment or approval.

The surrender, which was approved by a vote of 41 to 2, gave the land in question to Her Majesty the Queen on the following terms:

TO HAVE AND TO HOLD the same unto Her said Majesty the Queen, her Heirs and Successors forever in trust to lease the same to such person or persons, and upon such terms as the Government of Canada may deem most conducive to our Welfare and that of our people.

AND upon the further condition that all monies received from the leasing thereof, shall be credited to our revenue trust account at Ottawa.

AND WE, the said Chief and Councillors of the said Musqueam Band of Indians do on behalf of our people and for ourselves, hereby ratify and confirm, and promise to ratify and confirm, whatever the said Government may do, or cause to be lawfully done, in connection with the leasing thereof.

(f) On December 6, 1957, the surrender of the lands was accepted by the federal Crown by Order in Council P.C. 1957-1606, "in order that the lands covered thereby may be leased".

(g) On January 9, 1958, a band council meeting was held. A letter was read regarding the proposed golf club lease. The letter indicated the renewal periods were to be 15 years instead of 10 years. Chief Sparrow pointed out that the band had demanded 10-year periods. William Guerin said the council members were "flabbergasted" to learn about the 15-year terms. The band council then passed a resolution agreeing the first term should be 15 years, but insisting the renewal periods be 10-year terms.

(h) The lease was signed January 22, 1958. It provided, *inter alia*:

1. The term is for 75 years unless sooner terminated.

2. The rent for the first 15 years is $29,000 per annum.

3. For the succeeding 15-year periods, annual rent is to be determined by mutual agreement, or failing such agreement, by arbitration, such rent to be equal to the fair rent for the demised premises as if the same were still in an uncleared and unimproved condition and used as a golf course.

4. The maximum increase in rent for the second 15-year period (January 1, 1973 to January 1, 1988) is limited to 15% of $29,000, that is $4,350 per annum.

5. The golf club can terminate the lease at the end of any 15-year period by giving 6 months' prior notice.

6. The golf club can at any time during the lease and up to 6 months after termination, remove any buildings or other structures, and any course improvements and facilities.

The band was not given a copy of the lease, and did not receive one until 12 years later, in March, 1970.

(i) Mr. Grant testified that the terms of the lease ultimately entered into bore little resemblance to what was discussed at the surrender meeting. The judge agreed. He found that the majority of those who voted on Octo-ber 6, 1957, would not have assented to a surrender of the 162 acres if they had known all the terms of the lease of January 22, 1958.

. . . . . .

IV. FIDUCIARY RELATIONSHIP

The issue of the Crown's liability was dealt with in the courts below on the basis of the existence or non-existence of a trust. In dealing with the different consequences of a "true" trust, as opposed to a "political" trust, Le Dain J. noted that the Crown could be liable only if it were subject to an "equitable obligation enforceable in a court of law". I have some doubt as to the cogency of the terminology of "higher" and "lower" trusts, but I do agree that the existence of an equitable obligation is the *sine qua non* for liability. Such an obligation is not, however, limited to relationships which can be strictly defined as "trusts". As will presently appear, it is my view that the Crown's obligations *vis-à-vis* the Indians cannot be defined as a trust. That does not, however, mean that the Crown owes no enforceable duty to the Indians in the way in which it deals with Indian land.

In my view, the nature of Indian title and the framework of the statutory scheme established for disposing of Indian land places upon the Crown an equitable obligation, enforceable by the courts, to deal with the land for the benefit of the Indians. This obligation does not amount to a trust in the private law sense. It is rather a fiduciary duty. If, however, the Crown breaches this fiduciary duty it will be liable to the Indians in the same way and to the same extent as if such a trust were in effect.

The fiduciary relationship between the Crown and the Indians has its roots in the concept of aboriginal, native or Indian title. The fact that Indian bands have a certain interest in lands does not, however, in itself give rise to a fiduciary relationship between the Indians and the Crown. The conclusion that the Crown is a fiduciary depends upon the further proposition that the Indian interest in the land is inalienable except upon surrender to the Crown.

An Indian band is prohibited from directly transferring its interest to a third party. Any sale or lease of land can only be carried out after a surrender has taken place, with the Crown then acting on the band's behalf. The Crown first took this responsibility upon itself in the Royal Proclamation of 1763. ... It is still recognized in the surrender provisions of the *Indian Act*. The surrender requirement, and the responsibility it entails, are the source of a distinct fiduciary obligation owed by the Crown to the Indians. In order to explore the character of this obligation, however, it is first necessary to consider the basis of aboriginal title and the nature of the interest in land which it represents.

[This discussion of aboriginal title is reproduced in Chapter 1.]

. . . . .

(c) *The Crown's fiduciary obligation*

The concept of fiduciary obligation originated long ago in the notion of breach of confidence, one of the original heads of jurisdiction in chancery. In the present appeal its relevance is based on the requirement of a "surrender" before Indian land can be alienated.

The Royal Proclamation of 1763 provided that no private person could purchase from the Indians any lands that the Proclamation had reserved to them, and provided further that all purchases had to be by and in the name of the Crown, in a public assembly of the Indians held by the governor or commander-in-chief of the colony in which the lands in question lay. ... [T]his policy with respect to the sale or transfer of the Indians' interest in land has been continuously maintained by the British Crown, by the governments of the colonies when they became responsible for the administration of Indian affairs, and, after 1867, by the federal government of Canada. Successive federal statutes, predecessors to the present *Indian Act*, have all provided for the general inalienability of Indian reserve land except upon surrender to the Crown, the relevant provisions in the present Act being ss. 37-41.

The purpose of this surrender requirement is clearly to interpose the Crown between the Indians and prospective purchasers or lessees of their land, so as to prevent the Indians from being exploited. ... Through the confirmation in the *Indian Act* of the historic responsibility which the Crown has undertaken, to act on behalf of the Indians so as to protect their interests in transactions with third parties, Parliament has conferred upon the Crown a discretion to decide for itself where the Indians' best interests really lie. This is the effect of s. 18(1) of the Act.

This discretion on the part of the Crown, far from ousting, as the Crown contends, the jurisdiction of the courts to regulate the relationship between the Crown and the Indians, has the effect of transforming the Crown's obligation into a fiduciary one. Professor Ernest Weinrib maintains in his article "The Fiduciary Obligation", 25 U.T.L.J. 1 (1975), at p. 7, that "the hallmark of a fiduciary relation is that the relative legal positions are such that one party is at the mercy of the other's discretion". Earlier, at p. 4, he puts the point in the following way:

> [Where there is a fiduciary obligation] there is a relation in which the principal's interests can be affected by, and are therefore dependent on, the manner in which the fiduciary uses the discretion which has been delegated to him. The fiduciary obligation is the law's blunt tool for the control of this discretion.

I make no comment upon whether this description is broad enough to embrace all fiduciary obligations. I do agree, however, that where by statute, agreement, or perhaps by unilateral undertaking, one party has an obligation to act for the benefit of another, and that obligation carries with it a discretionary power, the party thus empowered becomes a fiduciary. Equity will then supervise the relationship by holding him to the fiduciary's strict standard of conduct.

It is sometimes said that the nature of fiduciary relationships is both established and exhausted by the standard categories of agent, trustee, partner, director, and the like. I do not agree. It is the nature of the relationship, not the specific category of actor involved that gives rise to the fiduciary duty. The categories of fiduciary, like those of negligence, should not be considered closed.

. . . . .

It should be noted that fiduciary duties generally arise only with regard to obligations originating in a private law context. Public law duties, the performance of which requires the exercise of discretion, do not typically give rise to a fiduciary relationship. ... [T]he Crown is not normally viewed as a fiduciary in the exercise of its legislative or administrative function. The mere fact, however, that it is the Crown which is obligated to act on the Indians' behalf does not of itself remove the Crown's obligation from the scope of the fiduciary principle. As was pointed out earlier, the Indians' interest in land is an independent legal interest. It is not a creation of either the legislative or executive branches of government. The Crown's obligation to the Indians with respect to that interest is therefore not a public law duty. While it is not a private law duty in the strict sense either, it is none the less in the nature of a private law duty. Therefore, in this *sui generis* relationship, it is not improper to regard the Crown as a fiduciary.

Section 18(1) of the *Indian Act* confers upon the Crown a broad discretion in dealing with surrendered land. ... When, as here, an Indian band surrenders its interests to the Crown, a fiduciary obligation takes hold to regulate the manner in which the Crown exercises its discretion in dealing with the land on the Indians' behalf.

I agree ... that before surrender the Crown does not hold the land in trust for the Indians. I also agree that the Crown's obligation does not somehow crystallize into a trust, express or implied, at the time of surrender. The law of trusts is a highly developed, specialized branch of the law. An express trust requires a settlor, a beneficiary, a trust corpus, words of settlement, certainty of object and certainty of obligation. Not all of these elements are present here. ... As the *Smith* decision [as discussed in Chapter 1] ... makes clear, upon unconditional surrender the Indians' right in the land disappears. No property interest is transferred which could constitute the trust *res*, so that even if the other *indicia* of an express or implied trust could be made out, the basic requirement of a settlement of property has not been met. Accordingly, although the nature of Indian title coupled with the discretion vested in the Crown are sufficient to give rise to a fiduciary obligation, neither an express nor an implied trust arises upon surrender.

Nor does the surrender give rise to a constructive trust. ... Any similarity between a constructive trust and the Crown's fiduciary obligation to the Indians is limited to the fact that both arise by operation of law.

. . . . .

The Crown's fiduciary obligation to the Indians is therefore not a trust. To say as much is not to deny that the obligation is trust-like in character. As would be the case with a trust, the Crown must hold surrendered land for the use and benefit of the surrendering band. The obligation is thus subject to principles very similar to those which govern the law of trusts concerning, for example, the measure of damages for breach. The fiduciary relationship between the Crown and the Indians also bears a certain resemblance to agency, since the obligations can be characterized as a duty to act on behalf of the Indian bands who have surrendered lands, by negotiating for the sale or lease of the land to third parties. But just as the Crown is not a trustee for the Indians, neither is it their agent; not only does the Crown's authority to act on the band's behalf lack a basis in contract, but the band is not a party to the ultimate sale or lease, as it would be if it were the Crown's principal. I repeat, the fiduciary obligation which is owed to the Indians by the Crown is *sui generis*. Given the unique character both of the Indians' interest in land and of their historical relationship with the Crown, the fact that this is so should occasion no surprise.

The discretion which is the hallmark of any fiduciary relationship is capable of being considerably narrowed in a particular case. This is as true of the Crown's discretion *vis-à-vis* the Indians as it is of the discretion of trustees, agents, and other traditional categories of fiduciary. The *Indian Act* makes specific provision for such narrowing in ss. 18(1) and 38(2). A fiduciary obligation will not, of course, be eliminated by the imposition of conditions that have the effect of restricting the fiduciary's discretion. A failure to adhere to the imposed conditions will simply itself be a *prima facie* breach of the obligation. In the present case both the surrender and the Order in Council accepting the surrender referred to the Crown leasing the land on the band's behalf. Prior to the surrender the band had also been given to understand that a lease was to be entered into with the Shaughnessy Heights Golf Club upon certain terms, but this understanding was not incorporated into the surrender document itself. The effect of these so-called oral terms will be considered in the next section.

(d) *Breach of the fiduciary obligation*

The trial judge found that the Crown's agents promised the band to lease the land in question on certain specified terms and then, after the surrender, obtained a lease on different terms. The lease obtained was much less valuable. As already mentioned, the surrender document did not make reference to the "oral" terms. I would not wish to say that those terms had none the less somehow been incorporated as conditions into the surrender. They were not formally assented to by a majority of the electors of the band, nor were they accepted by the Governor in Council, as required by s. 39(1)(*b*) and (*c*).

. . . . .

None the less, the Crown, in my view, was not empowered by the surrender document to ignore the oral terms which the band understood would be embodied in the lease. The oral representations form the backdrop against which the Crown's conduct in discharging its fiduciary obligation must be measured. They inform and confine the field of discretion within which the Crown was free to act. After the Crown's agents had induced the band to surrender its land on the understanding that the land would be leased on certain terms, it would be unconscionable to permit the Crown simply to ignore those terms. When the promised lease proved impossible to obtain, the Crown, instead of proceeding to lease the land on different, unfavourable terms, should have returned to the band to explain what had occurred and seek the band's counsel on how to proceed. The existence of such unconscionability is the key to a conclusion that the Crown breached its fiduciary duty. Equity will not countenance unconscionable behaviour in a fiduciary, whose duty is that of utmost loyalty to his principal.

While the existence of the fiduciary obligation which the Crown owes to the Indians is dependent on the nature of the surrender process, the standard of conduct which the obligation imports is both more general and more exacting than the terms of any particular surrender. In the present case the relevant aspect of the required standard of conduct is defined by a principle analogous to that which underlies the doctrine of promissory or equitable estoppel. The Crown cannot promise the band that it will obtain a lease of the latter's land on certain stated terms, thereby inducing the band to alter its legal position by surrendering the land, and then simply ignore that promise to the band's detriment.

. . . . .

In obtaining without consultation a much less valuable lease than that promised, the Crown breached the fiduciary obligation it owed the band. It must make good the loss suffered in consequence.

[Justice Dickson then considered the application of the relevant statutory limitation legislation and held that it did not bar the band's claim since there had been fraudulent concealment of the band's cause of action. He determined that Indian Affairs' conduct toward the band amounted to equitable fraud, thus suspending the operation of the limitation statute until March 1970, when the band first received a copy of the executed lease.]

VII. MEASURE OF DAMAGES

In my opinion, the quantum of damages is to be determined by analogy with the principles of trust law.... I am content to adopt the quantum of damages awarded by the [trial] judge, rejecting, as he did, any claim for exemplary or punitive damages.

I would therefore allow the appeal.

. . . . .

Wilson J. [at p. 356]: —

. . . . .

The appellants contend that the Federal Court of Appeal erred in failing to find that s. 18 of the *Indian Act* imposed on the Crown a fiduciary obligation enforceable in the courts. The section reads as follows:

> 18(1) Subject to the provisions of this Act, reserves shall be held by Her Majesty for the use and benefit of the respective bands for which they were set apart; and subject to this Act and to the terms of any treaty or surrender, the Governor in Council may determine whether any purpose for which lands in a reserve are used or are to be used is for the use and benefit of the band.

Mr. Justice Le Dain, after concluding on the authorities that there was nothing in principle to prevent the Crown from having the status of a trustee in equity, found that s. 18 nevertheless did not have that effect. It merely imposed on the Crown a governmental obligation of an administrative nature. It was a public law obligation rather than a private law obligation. Section 18 could not therefore afford a basis for an action for breach of trust.

While I am in agreement that s. 18 does not *per se* create a fiduciary obligation in the Crown with respect to Indian reserves, I believe that it recognizes the existence of such an obligation. The obligation has its roots in the aboriginal title of Canada's Indians as discussed in *Calder et al. v. A.-G. B.C.*

. . . . .

I think that when s. 18 mandates that reserves be held by the Crown for the use and benefit of the bands for which they are set apart, this is more than just an administrative direction to the Crown. I think it is the acknowledgment of a historic reality, namely, that Indians bands have a beneficial interest in their reserves and that the Crown has a responsibility to protect that interest and make sure that any purpose to which reserve land is put will not interfere with it. This is not to say that the Crown either historically or by s. 18 holds the land in trust for the bands. The bands do not have the fee in the lands; their interest is a limited one. But it is an interest which cannot be derogated from or interfered with by the Crown's utilization of the land for purposes incompatible with the Indian title unless, of course, the Indians agree. I believe that in this sense the Crown has a fiduciary obligation to the Indian bands with respect to the uses to which reserve land may be put and that s. 18 is a statutory acknowledgment of that obligation. It is my view, therefore, that while the Crown does not hold reserve land under s. 18 of the Act in trust for the bands because the bands' interests are limited by the nature of Indian title, it does hold the lands subject to a fiduciary obligation to protect and preserve the bands' interests from invasion or destruction.

The respondent submits, however, that any obligation imposed on the Crown by s. 18(1) of the *Indian Act* is political only and unenforceable in courts of equity. ... Mr. Justice Le Dain, delivering the judgment of the Federal Court of Appeal, adopted this approach.

. . . . .

With respect, while I agree with the learned justice that s. 18 does not go so far as to create a trust of reserve lands for the reasons I have given, it does not, in my opinion, exclude the equitable jurisdiction of the courts. The discretion conferred on the Governor in Council is not an unfettered one to decide the use to which reserve lands may be put. It is to decide whether any use to which they are proposed to be put is "for the use and benefit of the band". This discretionary power must be exercised on proper principles and not in an arbitrary fashion.

. . . . .

It seems to me that the "political trust" line of authorities are clearly distinguishable from the present case because Indian title has an existence apart altogether from s. 18(1) of the *Indian Act*. It would fly in the face of the clear wording of the section to treat that interest as terminable at will by the Crown without recourse by the band.

Continuing with the analysis of s. 18, it seems to me quite clear from the wording of the section that the Governor in Council's authority to determine in good faith whether any purpose to which reserve lands are proposed to be put is for the use and benefit of the band is "subject ... to the terms of any treaty or surrender". I take this to mean that if a band surrenders its beneficial interest in reserve lands for a specific purpose, then the Governor in Council's authority under the section to decide whether or not the purpose is for the use and benefit of the band is pre-empted. The band has itself agreed to the purpose and the Crown may rely upon that agreement. It will be necessary to consider this in greater detail in connection with the surrender which in fact took place in this case.

. . . . .

4. *The surrender*

Reference has already been made to the language of s. 18 and in particular to the fact that the Crown's fiduciary duty under it is "subject ... to the terms of any ... surrender". The implications of this have to be considered in the context of the learned trial judge's finding that the band surrendered the 162 acres to the Crown for lease to the golf club on specific terms which were not obtained.

. . . . .

It was submitted on behalf of the Crown that even if the surrender gave rise to a trust between the Crown and the band, the terms of the trust must be found in the surrender document and it was silent both as to the lessee and the terms of the lease. Indeed, it expressly gave the government complete discretion both as to the lessee and the terms of the lease and contained a ratification by the band of any lease the government might enter into.

I cannot accept the Crown's submission. The Crown was well aware that the terms of the lease were important to the band. Indeed, we have the trial judge's finding that the band would not have surrendered the land for the purpose of a lease on the terms obtained by the Crown. It ill becomes the Crown, therefore, to obtain a surrender of the band's interests for lease on terms voted on and approved by the band members at a meeting specially called for the purpose and then assert an overriding discretion to ignore those terms at will. ... It makes a mockery of the band's participation. The Crown well knew that the lease it made with the golf club was not the lease the band surrendered its interest to get. Equity will not permit the Crown in such circumstances to hide behind the language of its own document.

I return to s. 18. What effect does the surrender of the 162 acres to the Crown in trust for lease on specific terms have on the Crown's fiduciary duty under the section? It seems to me that s. 18 presents no barrier to a finding that the Crown became a full-blown trustee by virtue of the surrender. The surrender prevails over the s. 18 duty but in this case there is no incompatibility between them. Rather the fiduciary duty which existed at large under the section to hold the land in the reserve for the use and benefit of the band crystallized upon the surrender into an express trust of specific land for a specific purpose.

There is no magic to the creation of a trust. A trust arises, as I understand it, whenever a person is compelled in equity to hold property over which he has control for the benefit of others (the beneficiaries) in such a way that the benefit of the property accrues not to the trustee, but to the beneficiaries. I think that in the circumstances of this case as found by the learned trial judge the Crown was compelled in equity upon the surrender to hold the surrendered land in trust for the purpose of the lease which the band members had approved as being for their benefit. The Crown was no longer free to decide that a lease on some other terms would do. Its hands were tied.

What then should the Crown have done when the Golf Club refused to enter into a lease on the approved terms? It seems to me that it should have returned to the band and told them. It was certainly not open to it at that point of time to go ahead with the less favourable lease on the basis that the Governor in Council considered it for the benefit of the band. The Governor in Council's discretion in that regard was pre-empted by the surrender. I think the learned trial judge was right in finding that the Crown acted in breach of trust when it barrelled ahead with a lease on terms which, according to the learned trial judge, were wholly unacceptable to its *cestui que trust*.

· · · · ·

6. *The measure of damages*

· · · · ·

The position at common law concerning damages for breach of trust and, in particular, the difference between the principles in trust law from those applicable in tort and contract, are well summarized in the following passage from Mr. Justice Street's judgment in the Australian case of *Re Dawson; Union Fidelity Trustee Co. Ltd. v. Perpetual Trustee Co. Ltd.* (1966), 84 W.N. (Pt 1) (N.S.W.) 399 at pp. 404-6:

> The obligation of a defaulting trustee is essentially one of effecting a restitution to the estate. The obligation is of a personal character and its extent is not to be limited by common law principles governing remoteness of damage.
>
> · · · · ·
>
> *Caffrey v. Darby* (1801) 6 Ves. Jun. 488; 31 E.R. 1159 is consistent with the proposition that if a breach has been committed then the trustee is liable to place the trust estate in the same position as it would have been in if no breach had been committed. Considerations of causation, foreseeability and remoteness do not readily enter into the matter.
>
> · · · · ·
>
> The principles embodied in this approach do not appear to involve any inquiry as to whether the loss was caused by or flowed from the breach. Rather the inquiry in each instance would appear to be whether the loss would have happened if there had been no breach.
>
> · · · · ·
>
> The cases to which I have referred demonstrate that the obligation to make restitution, which courts of equity have from very early times imposed on defaulting trustees and other fiduciaries, is of a more absolute nature than the common-law obligation to pay damages for tort or breach of contract. ... [T]he distinction between common-law damages and relief against a defaulting trustee is strikingly demonstrated by reference to the actual form of relief granted in equity in respect of breaches of trust. The form of relief is couched in terms appropriate to require the defaulting trustee to restore to

the estate the assets of which he deprived it. *Increases in market values between the date of breach and the date of recoupment are for the trustee's account; the effect of such increase would, at common law, be excluded from the computation of damages but in equity a defaulting trustee must make good the loss by restoring to the estate the assets of which he deprived it notwithstanding that market values may have increased in the meantime. The obligation to restore to the estate the assets of which he deprived it necessarily connotes that, where a monetary compensation is to be paid in lieu of restoring assets, that compensation is to be assessed by reference to the value of the assets at the date of restoration and not at the date of deprivation.* In this sense the obligation is a continuing one and ordinarily, if the assets are for some reason not restored in specie, it will fall for quantification at the date when recoupment is to be effected, and not before.
(Emphasis added).

. . . . .

In this case the band surrendered the land to the Crown for lease on certain specified terms. The trial judge found as a fact that such a lease was impossible to obtain. The Crown's duty at that point was to go back to the band, consult with it, and obtain further instructions. Instead of doing that it went ahead and leased the land on unauthorized terms. In my view it thereby committed a breach of trust and damages are to be assessed on the basis of the principles enunciated by Mr. Justice Street. The lost opportunity to develop the land for a period of up to 75 years in duration is to be compensated as at the date of trial notwithstanding that market values may have increased since the date of breach. The beneficiary gets the benefit of any such increase. ... Since the lease that was authorized by the band was impossible to obtain, the Crown's breach of duty in this case was not in *failing* to lease the land, but in *leasing* it when it could not lease it on the terms approved by the band. The band was thereby deprived of its land and any use to which it might have wanted to put it. Just as it is to be presumed that a beneficiary would have wished to sell his securities at the highest price available during the period they were wrongfully withheld from him by the trustee ... so also it should be presumed that the band would have wished to develop its land in the most advantageous way possible during the period covered by the unauthorized lease. In this respect also the principles applicable to determine damages for breach of trust are to be contrasted with the principles applicable to determine damages for breach of contract. In contract it would have been necessary for the band to prove that it would have developed the land; in equity a presumption is made to that effect.

. . . . .

I cannot find that the learned trial judge committed any error in principle in approaching the damage issue on the basis of a lost opportunity for residential development.

... I do not think it is the function of this Court to interfere with the *quantum* of damages awarded by the trial judge if no error in principle in determining the measure of damages has been demonstrated. The trial judge was entitled to treat the termination of the lease by the club as a contingency tending towards diminution of the band's damages and it is not for this Court to substitute the value it would have put upon that contingency for his. I would not, therefore, interfere with the quantum.

Although *Guerin* single-handedly changed the characterization of Crown-Native relations from trust or quasi-trust to fiduciary, that does not necessarily entail that a specific Crown-Native relation cannot be described as a trust relationship: see *Cardinal v. R.* (1991), 44 E.T.R. 297 at 316 (*sub nom. Cardinal v. Canada*), 47 F.T.R. 203, [1992] 4 C.N.L.R. 1 (T.D.), rev'd. in part (1993), 72 F.T.R. 309, 164 N.R. 301 (*sub nom. Enoch Band of Stony Plain Indians v. Canada*), [1994] 3 C.N.L.R. 41 (Fed. C.A.), application for reconsideration refused (31 January 1994), Doc A-294-77, A-52-92 (Fed. C.A.) [unreported]. As seen in the *Pawis* excerpt, there are some difficulties with the use of trust law to describe Crown-Native relations that may be avoided by using fiduciary law instead.

Since fiduciary law does not require the existence of a legally recognizeable property interest, there is no doctrinal difficulty in having hunting, trapping, or fishing rights be the subject of a Crown fiduciary obligation to an Aboriginal group. Fiduciary law is thus capable of applying to a wider range of Aboriginal claims against the Crown than trust law. It may also avoid the difficulty of engaging judicial debate as to whether Aboriginal land rights are beneficial or non-beneficial in nature and therefore capable of constituting the *res* of a trust. Refer back to the discussion of *Smith v. R.*, [1983] 1 S.C.R. 554, 47 N.R. 132, 147 D.L.R. (3d) 237 in Chapter 1.

1. The Crown's Fiduciary Obligations and Conflict of Interest

As suggested in *Guerin, supra*, the application of fiduciary doctrine to Crown-Native relations entails that the Crown must act with the utmost good faith, or *uberrima fides*, in the best interests of the Aboriginal peoples. The Crown may not allow self-interest, or the interests of third parties, to interfere with its obligations to the Aboriginal peoples. This is known as the rule against conflict of interest.

The rule against conflict of interest imposes a number of restraints upon the Crown as a fiduciary towards Aboriginal peoples. In addition to foregoing personal benefit, the Crown must provide full disclosure of its actions while acting in its fiduciary capacity. A corollary of these two restraints is that the Crown must account for profits wrongfully made while in its fiduciary capacity. The Crown may also be found to be in conflict of interest in the absence of malevolent actions.

As a general rule, fiduciaries who depart from this standard of utmost good faith may be found in breach of duty and be subjected to harsh sanctions by the courts. In some circumstances, however, the Crown's fiduciary duty to Aboriginal peoples may conflict with its other responsibilities, such as the interest of the public at large. Where such potential conflict of interest situations exist, the Crown cannot ignore one interest in favour of the other. Rather, it must attempt to balance its competing responsibilities. In some situations, this may not be possible. Where such an irreconcilable conflict occurs, the judiciary may be required to balance those competing interests and the Crown's duties thereto. While, doctrinally, a fiduciary may not escape liability for a breach of duty by citing competing interests, this general rule may need to be modified, where appropriate, to account for the context of specific fact situations. However, any such modification must be consistent with the fiduciary concept's underlying principles.

The Crown's ability to avoid liability for breach of its fiduciary obligations by citing competing interests is a rather new issue in Canadian Aboriginal rights jurisprudence, but one that is likely to arise more frequently because of the unique position of the Crown as a fiduciary to Aboriginal peoples. This issue was a key element of the Federal Court of Appeal's decision in *Kruger v. R.* Although the *Kruger* case has not garnered significant attention in subsequent jurisprudence, it is a prime example of a Crown conflict of interest situation with regard to its fiduciary obligations to Aboriginal peoples.

KRUGER v. R.

(1985), 17 D.L.R. (4th) 591 at 595 [1986] 1 F.C. 3, 32 L.C.R. 65 (*sub nom. Kruger v. Canada*), 58 N.R. 241, [1985] 3 C.N.L.R. 15 (C.A.); leave to appeal to S.C.C. refused (1985), 33 L.C.R. 192*n*, 62 N.R. 102*n*

[In this case, the federal Crown had expropriated two parcels of land from the Penticton Indian Reserve No. 1 for use as an airport during World War II. One parcel, Parcel "A", was expropriated without surrender, with compensation paid three years after the expropriation. The second parcel, Parcel "B", was also initially expropriated without surrender, although a surrender was executed two years later and compensation paid to the band. The lands in question were fenced off, but never used as an airport. The band brought an action against the Crown, initially for breach of trust, alleging that the Crown failed to exercise the degree of care, stewardship, and prudent management required of a trustee.]

Heald J.: — ... One of the central issues in this appeal, as I see it, is the nature of the fiduciary duty owed by the respondent Crown to the appellants and whether the facts in this case demonstrate a breach of that fiduciary duty.
... [T]he learned trial judge held that the Crown stood as a fiduciary *vis-à-vis* the appellants ... Given the existence of such a duty, it is necessary to consider the nature and the parameters of that duty.

· · · · ·

I think it clear that the fiduciary obligation and duty being discussed in *Guerin* would also apply to a case such as this as well and that on the facts in this case, such a fiduciary obligation and duty was a continuing one — that is, it arose as a consequence of the proposal to take Indian lands and continued throughout the negotiations leading to the expropriations and thereafter including the dealings between the Crown and the Indians with respect to the payment of the compensation to the Indians in respect of Parcels "A" and "B".

. . . . .

... [E]quity will supervise the relationship by holding a fiduciary to the fiduciary's strict standard of conduct and "...will not countenance unconscionable behaviour in a fiduciary, whose duty is that of utmost loyalty to his principal" ...

. . . . .

... [T]he facts of this case clearly raise the issue of conflict of interest, in my view. It seems evident that two departments of the Government of Canada were in conflict concerning the manner in which the Indian occupants of Parcel "A" should be dealt with. The evidence seems to unquestionably establish that the officials of the Indian Affairs Branch were diligent in their efforts to represent the best interests of the Indian occupants. On the other hand, the Department of Transport was anxious to acquire the additional lands in the interests of air transport. This situation resulted in competing considerations. Accordingly, the federal Crown was in a conflict of interest in respect of its fiduciary relationship with the Indians. The law is clear that "one who undertakes a task on behalf of another must act exclusively for the benefit of the other, putting his own interests completely aside" and that "Equity fashioned the rule that no man may allow his duty to conflict with his interest." On this basis, the federal Crown cannot default on its fiduciary obligation to the Indians through a plea of competing considerations by different departments of government.

. . . . .

Based on the above-stated principles, and applying them to the facts in this case, I am unable to conclude that the federal Crown acted "exclusively for the benefit" of the Indians in the acquisition of Parcel "A". ...

In my view, the unmistakable inference to be drawn from this record is that, in the final decision-making process by the Governor in Council, the views of the Department of Transport prevailed over the views and representations of the Department of Indian Affairs. Undoubtedly, the Department of Transport had good and sufficient reason for requiring subject lands at an early date for its purposes but that circumstance did not relieve the federal Crown of its fiduciary duty to the Indians. Accordingly, I have no difficulty in concluding that the federal Crown has not discharged the onus cast upon it to show that no advantage was taken of the Indians in the transaction.

It follows, in my view, that there was a breach of fiduciary duty in respect of the acquisition of Parcel "A".

. . . . .

It is clear, in my view, that the conflict of interest between two departments of the Government of Canada which was so apparent in the dealings with respect to Parcel "A" is equally apparent when the dealings concerning the acquisition of Parcel "B" are scrutinized. Indian Affairs attempted valiantly to represent the Indians' best interests. On the other hand, National Defence and Transport were anxious to acquire Parcel "B" and enlarge the airport. An indication of their seeming indifference to the plight of the Indians is shown by the initial valuation — only $50 per acre; by the fact that they had possession for some 18 months without paying the Indians anything on account of compensation; by their rather leisurely approach to negotiations for compensation as compared to their great haste in taking possession and depriving the Indians of their means of livelihood. It seems clear from the evidence that Transport chose to ignore the considered opinions of officials of the Department of Indian Affairs as to value and made little effort to seriously negotiate a settlement. Their only answer was to expropriate first and then negotiate thereafter. Commissioner MacKay described their tactics most eloquently when he said that his suggestions for settlement were "born of sheer desperation" because of Transport's tactics of delay which frustrated a fair settlement. He also characterized Transport's attitude as "niggardly". Thus, after being out of possession of Parcel "B" for more than three and a half years, being deprived of their living therefrom, and having received only $6,500 on account of compensation, a minority of the Indians entitled to vote approved the surrender.

On these facts, can it be concluded that, in these negotiations culminating with the acquisition of Parcel "B", and settlement of compensation therefor, the federal Crown can be said to have been acting exclusively for the benefit of the Indians? I think not. Likewise, I am not satisfied that there was full disclosure to the Indians of all relevant facts. The evidence establishes that they were kept in the dark for very large periods of time. Their land was taken from them, no offers of compensation were forthcoming in a timely fashion. ... They were told that their land was expropriated, then they were told that, notwithstanding the expropriation, they would have to execute a surrender in respect of Parcel "B" but not in respect of Parcel "A". ... [T]he Governor in Council is not able to default in its fiduciary relationship to the Indians on the basis of other priorities and other considerations. If there was evidence in the record to indicate that careful consideration and due weight had been given to the pleas and representations by Indian Affairs on behalf of the Indians and, thereafter, an offer of settlement reflecting those representations had been made, I would have viewed the matter differently. Absent such evidence, I conclude that, as in the case of Parcel "A", there was also a breach of fiduciary duty in respect of the acquisition of Parcel "B".

[Heald J.A. then discussed the applicability of statutory limitations to the matter before him and concluded that the Penticton band's action was statute-barred. Because of this conclusion, he did not consider the defence of laches raised by the respondent. See the discussion of the effect of statutory limitations and laches on Aboriginal claims for breach of the Crown's fiduciary obligations, *infra*.]

Urie J. [at p. 627]: —

. . . . .

When the Crown expropriated reserve lands, being Parcels "A" and "B", there would appear to have been created the same kind of fiduciary obligation, *vis-à-vis* the Indians, as would have been created if their lands had been surrendered. The precise obligation in this case was to ensure that the Indians were properly compensated for the loss of their lands as part of the obligation to deal with the land for the benefit of the Indians ... How they ensured that lies within the Crown's discretion as a fiduciary and so long as the discretion is exercised honestly, prudently and for the benefit of the Indians there can be no breach of duty.

. . . . .

... Assuming, without deciding, that the rules applying to conflicts of interest between trustees and their *cestuis que trust* apply to fiduciaries, what was found by the learned trial judge is most pertinent. ... :

. . . . .

> The defendant's duty to the Band, as trustee, was by no means the only duty to be taken into account. The evidence is clear that those officials responsible for the administration of the *Indian Act* urged a lease while those responsible for the airport ultimately urged expropriation. The Governor in Council was entitled to decide on the latter. There was no breach of trust in doing so. ...

I agree with these findings. There was no breach of the fiduciary obligation of the Crown based on the alleged conflict existing between two of its departments — Mines and Resources, Indian Affairs Branch, and Transport. ... Ultimately a decision had to be taken which, unfortunately, may not have been wholly in accord with the view of the Indians as to the worth of their lands to them. ... That fact does not mean that there was a breach of fiduciary duty nor that there was a conflict of interest which had to be resolved in their favour, disregarding the obligations of the Department of Transport officials. ...

. . . . .

... [F]rom the perspective of the Crown in its Department of Transport incarnation, there were competing considerations. First, initially the requirement for an enlarged aerodrome as an emergency landing site for commercial aircraft, in a mountainous region where such sites were scarce, was important. Second, later on the more urgent requirement for an even larger aerodrome for western defence purposes in wartime was of at least equal importance.

From these considerations and facts, the question which must be posed is, did the fact that the competing considerations were resolved in respect of both Parcels "A" and "B", with the concurrence of the Indians, on terms which clearly were compromises, not entirely satisfactory to either of the branches of the Crown involved, result in a breach of the Crown's fiduciary duty to the Indians entitling them to the remedies sought in this action? I think not for the reasons which I have already given and for those which follow.

... If the submissions advanced by the appellants were to prevail, the only way that the Crown could successfully escape a charge of breach of fiduciary duty in such circumstances would have been, in each case, to have acceded in full to their demands or to withdraw from the transactions entirely. The competing obligations on the Crown could not permit such a result. The Crown was in the position that it was obliged to ensure that the best interests of all for whom its officials had responsibility were protected. The Governor in Council became the final arbiter. ...

IV

THE LIMITATION ACT AND LACHES

Since I have concluded that none of the attacks on the impugned judgment can succeed, it is, strictly speaking, unnecessary to deal with the Crown's contention that the band's claim is barred by s. 38 of the *Federal Court Act*, R.S.C. 1970, c. 10 (2nd Supp.), and the *Limitation Act*, R.S.B.C. 1979, c. 236, s. 3(4), because more than six years had elapsed between the date upon which the cause of action arose and ... the date upon which the action was commenced.

· · · · ·

Appeal dismissed.

Had the *Kruger* case been decided after the impact of the Supreme Court's decision in *Guerin* had been more fully digested and following the consideration of the Crown's fiduciary duty articulated in *R. v. Sparrow, infra,* which spoke of the need for the Crown to balance its actions taken with respect to Aboriginal peoples and their lands with its fiduciary duty to Aboriginal peoples, it is likely that a different result would have ensued. This issue was canvassed in the following excerpt.

LEONARD I. ROTMAN, PARALLEL PATHS: FIDUCIARY DOCTRINE AND THE CROWN-NATIVE RELATIONSHIP IN CANADA

(Toronto: University of Toronto Press, 1996) at 279-80
(references omitted)

The *Kruger* scenario could have been avoided entirely had the Crown taken reasonable steps to accommodate the band's wishes. Prior to expropriating the land, the Crown should have weighed the effects of its desire to expropriate the Penticton band's land with the anticipated effects that the taking of the land would have on the band. A careful consideration of the competing interests and costs involved — in a manner similar to the requirements outlined in the *Sparrow* test — would determine whether the band's land was absolutely needed. This would involve a consideration of the need to build the airport, to build it in that vicinity, and whether it had to be built on the band's land with no other sites being suitable or available in substitution. The Crown's fiduciary duty to the band required it to minimize any detrimental effects on the band. This required determining, before the act of expropriation in each instance, what the detrimental effects to the Penticton people would be and how to either avoid them entirely or minimize their impact. The greater the potential detriment to the Penticton band, the greater the onus would be on the Crown to demonstrate the need to take its lands.

If land in that vicinity was needed and no other land could have been substituted, the Crown was obliged to consult with the band to determine the method by which to adequately and swiftly compensate or otherwise accommodate it for its various losses suffered as a result of the taking of the land. If a voluntary settlement could not be reached, the Crown must have acted in accordance with the importance of its project to build the airport. The cost of compensating the Penticton band should have been directly tied to the importance of the project and the Crown's need to obtain the band's land. As the Crown's fiduciary duty required it to protect and promote the well-being of its beneficiaries, it was obliged to have provided fair and expeditious payment of compensation to the band.

Had the Crown heeded the advice given by the Department of Indian Affairs rather than concentrating exclusively on the Department of Transport's desire to obtain the band's land at the lowest possible price, the entire situation that arose could easily have been avoided. As Heald J.A. explained in his judgment: "If there was evidence in the record to indicate that careful consideration and due weight had been given to the pleas and representations by Indian Affairs on behalf of the Indians and, thereafter, an offer of settlement reflecting those representations had been made, I would have viewed the matter differently."

Until recently, the *Kruger* judgment was the only Crown-Native fiduciary case which considered, in any substantive way, the issue of competing Crown interests and the need for the Crown to balance them. Subsequent decisions have indicated that the Crown has a duty to balance the interests of its various constituents and beneficiaries and cannot avoid liability for breaching its obligations merely by citing competing interests, as was suggested by Urie J. in *Kruger, supra*.

For example, in *Wewaykum Indian Band v. Canada*, 2002 SCC 79 (excerpted *infra*), it was held that "as a fiduciary, it was the Crown's duty to be even-handed toward and among the various beneficiaries" (para. 97) and that "the role of honest referee does not exhaust the Crown's fiduciary obligation here. The Crown could not, merely by invoking competing interests, shirk its fiduciary duty." (para. 104)

2. The Scope of the Crown's Fiduciary Obligations

The release of the *Guerin* decision sparked a wave of litigation based on alleged breaches of the Crown's fiduciary obligations to Aboriginal peoples. The decision also sparked some controversy over the extent of fiduciary law's application to Crown-Native relations. It was questioned whether the Crown's fiduciary duty was restricted to the surrender of Aboriginal lands for leasing purposes, as in *Guerin*, or if it was of wider scope.

While the *Guerin* case did speak specifically to the existence of Crown fiduciary duties pertaining to the surrender of Aboriginal lands for lease, the limited scope of the decision was the result of the specific facts in issue, not because of the restricted nature of the Crown's fiduciary obligations. Justice Dickson, as he then was, expressly contextualized his examination of the Crown's duty in *Guerin* by stating that the relevance of the Crown's fiduciary duty "in the present appeal ... is based on the requirement of a surrender before Indian land can be alienated." Had he intended to limit the Crown's fiduciary obligations to land surrenders, his judgment would have been express on that point, which it clearly was not. This very point was affirmed in *Wewaykum, supra*, at para. 98:

> In *Guerin*, Dickson J. said the fiduciary "interest gives rise *upon surrender* to a distinctive fiduciary obligation on the part of the Crown" (p. 382). These dicta should not be read too narrowly. Dickson J. spoke of surrender because those were the facts of the *Guerin* case. As this Court recently held, expropriation of an existing reserve equally gives rise to a fiduciary duty: *Osoyoos Indian Band v. Oliver (Town)*, [2001] 3 S.C.R. 746, 2001 SCC 85. See also *Kruger v. The Queen*, [1986] 1 F.C. 3 (C.A.).

As indicated in the above quote from *Wewaykum*, this interpretation of the *Guerin* decision had been initially affirmed in *Kruger, supra*. Meanwhile, in the Supreme Court of Canada's decision in *R. v. Sparrow*, below, the scope of the Crown's fiduciary obligations to Aboriginal peoples was expanded considerably from what had been discussed in *Guerin*.

The *Sparrow* case was concerned more particularly with the scope of Aboriginal rights to fish and the extent to which those rights could be affected by governmental regulations. This aspect of the case will be discussed in Chapter 4. Within the scope of the Supreme Court's consideration of that issue, it made the following important pronouncement on the nature of the Crown's fiduciary obligations towards Aboriginal peoples.

R. v. SPARROW

(1990), 70 D.L.R. (4th) 385 at 389, [1990] 1 S.C.R. 1075, [1990] 4 W.W.R. 410, 46 B.C.L.R. (2d) 1, 56 C.C.C. (3d) 263, 111 N.R. 241, [1990] 3 C.N.L.R. 160

The judgment of the court was delivered by

Dickson C.J.C. and **La Forest J.:** — This appeal requires this court to explore for the first time the scope of s. 35(1) of the *Constitution Act, 1982*, and to indicate its strength as a promise to the aboriginal peoples of Canada.

. . . . .

The approach to be taken with respect to interpreting the meaning of s. 35(1) is derived from general principles of constitutional interpretation, principles relating to aboriginal rights, and the purposes behind the constitutional provision itself. Here, we will sketch the framework for an interpretation of "recognized and affirmed" that, in our opinion, gives appropriate weight to the constitutional nature of these words.

. . . . .

In our opinion, *Guerin*, together with *R. v. Taylor and Williams* (1981), 62 C.C.C. (2d) 227, 34 O.R. (2d) 360 (C.A.), ground a general guiding principle for s. 35(1). That is, the government has the responsibility to act in a fiduciary capacity with respect to aboriginal peoples. The relationship between the government and aboriginals is trust-like, rather than adversarial, and contemporary recognition and affirmation of aboriginal rights must be defined in light of this historic relationship.

. . . . .

There is no explicit language in the provision that authorizes this court or any court to assess the legitimacy of any government legislation that restricts aboriginal rights. Yet, we find that the words "recognition and affirmation" incorporate the fiduciary relationship referred to earlier and so import some restraint on the exercise of sovereign power. Rights that are recognized and affirmed are not absolute. Federal legislative powers continue, including, of course, the right to legislate with respect to Indians pursuant to s. 91(24) of the *Constitution Act, 1867*. These powers must, however, now be read together with s. 35(1). In other words, federal power must be reconciled with federal duty and the best way to achieve that reconciliation is to demand the justification of any government regulation that infringes upon or denies aboriginal rights. Such scrutiny is in keeping with ... the concept of holding the Crown to a high standard of honourable dealing with respect to the aboriginal peoples of Canada as suggested by *Guerin v. The Queen, supra*.

. . . . .

The way in which a legislative objective is to be attained must uphold the honour of the Crown and must be in keeping with the unique contemporary relationship, grounded in history and policy, between the Crown and Canada's aboriginal peoples.

. . . . .

[T]he honour of the Crown is at stake in dealings with aboriginal peoples. The special trust relationship and the responsibility of the government *vis-à-vis* aboriginals must be the first consideration in determining whether the legislation or action in question can be justified.

After the *Sparrow* decision, it was clear that the Crown's fiduciary obligations to Aboriginal peoples extended beyond the surrender of Aboriginal lands to Crown-Native relations more generally and that those obligations were constitutionally entrenched in section 35(1) of the *Constitution Act, 1982*, being Schedule B to the *Canada Act 1982* (U.K.), 1982, c. 11. It was not until 1995, however, that the Supreme Court of Canada released another judgment that contemplated the fiduciary nature of Crown-Native relations in the *Blueberry River* case, excerpted below.

BLUEBERRY RIVER INDIAN BAND v. CANADA

(1995), 130 D.L.R. (4th) 193, [1995] 4 S.C.R. 344, [1996] 2 C.N.L.R. 25, 190
N.R. 89, 102 F.T.R. 160n

[This case was concerned with the effects of certain surrenders of land by certain Aboriginal groups who were either Dunne-Za or Cree by linguistic grouping. The Dunne-Za Cree, as they had been described by the Federal Court of Appeal in *Apsassin v. Canada (Department of Indian Affairs and Northern Development)*, [1993] 3 F.C. 28, 2 C.N.L.R. 20, 15 N.R. 241, 100 D.L.R. (4th) 504, 61 F.T.R. 240n (C.A.), rev'd. on other grounds [1995] 4 S.C.R. 344, [1996] 2 C.N.L.R. 25, 190 N.R. 89, 102 F.T.R. 160n, had originally surrendered their traditional lands to the Crown in 1900 under the terms of Treaty No. 8. A reserve, designated as Indian Reserve No. 172 (IR 172), was set aside for them pursuant to the treaty.

In 1940, the federal Crown obtained a surrender of the Dunne-Za Cree's mineral rights to the reserve for the purposes of leasing them for the Dunne-Za Cree's benefit. The reserve itself was surrendered to the federal Crown in 1945 to be distributed to returning war veterans. Although it had been appraised at $93,000, the reserve was sold by the Department of Indian Affairs ("DIA") to the Director, *The Veterans' Land Act, 1942*, S.C. 1942-43, c. 33 (DVLA) for $70,000. Among the issues to be determined in the case was whether the sale of IR 172 below its appraised value constituted a breach of fiduciary obligation by the Crown. In addition, the Supreme Court was faced with determining whether the mineral rights to the reserve, which had been the subject of the 1940 surrender for lease, were included in the 1945 surrender of the reserve.

The Supreme Court of Canada was divided over whether the 1940 surrender of the mineral rights was subsumed under the 1945 surrender of IR 172. **Gonthier J.**, for the majority, held that it was, while **McLachlin J.**, with **Cory** and **Major JJ.** concurring, determined that the two surrenders were mutually exclusive. Despite this disagreement, the Court unanimously held that the Crown was under a fiduciary obligation to deal with both the surface and mineral rights in the best interests of the Dunne-Za Cree once they had been surrendered.

The Court determined that there was no breach of duty regarding the sale of the reserve for $70,000, since the price obtained was deemed to be reasonable in the circumstances. However, the Court held that the Crown breached its duty to the Dunne-Za Cree by transferring the mineral rights to IR 172 for no consideration. While this breach was held to be statute-barred, the Supreme Court did find that the transfer of the mineral rights by DIA to DVLA was an error or mistake. DIA had an opportunity to rectify its error via section 64 of the *Indian Act*, R.S.C. 1927, c. 98, which allowed the Crown to revoke any sale or lease issued in error or mistake, even against bona fide purchasers. However, DIA failed to make use of section 64, even after it discovered the error. The Court held that DIA had a fiduciary obligation to invoke section 64. Because of DIA's failure to correct its mistake, the Court held that DIA thereby breached its fiduciary duty to the Dunne-Za Cree. The portions of the decision concerning the Crown's fiduciary obligations are excerpted below.]

The judgment of **La Forest, L'Heureux-Dubé, Sopinka** and **Gonthier JJ.** was delivered by

Gonthier J.: —

I

INTRODUCTION

I have had the benefit of reading the reasons of my colleague, McLachlin J. While I agree with her analyses of the surrender of the surface rights in Indian Reserve 172 ("I.R. 172"), and the application of the British Columbia *Limitation Act*, R.S.B.C. 1979, c. 236, and with her ultimate disposition of the case, I find that I cannot agree with her conclusion that the 1945 surrender of I.R. 172 to the Crown did not include the mineral rights in the reserve. In my view, the 1945 agreement constituted a complete surrender to the Crown of the surface and mineral rights in the St. John Indian Reserve, in trust, "to sell or lease". The Beaver Band's intention at the time of the 1945 surrender, and the terms of the surrender instrument, bear this out. Moreover, while I agree with my colleague that in dealing with the mineral rights subsequent to the 1945 surrender, the Department of Indian Affairs ("DIA") committed a breach of fiduciary duty, my reasons are somewhat different. ...

II

THE EFFECT OF THE 1945 SURRENDER OF I.R. 172 ON THE 1940 SURRENDER OF THE MINERAL RIGHTS IN I.R. 172

McLachlin J.'s position, in brief, is that since there had already been a surrender of the mineral rights in I.R. 172 for "lease" in 1940, these mineral rights could not have been included in the 1945 surrender. The basis of her position lies in the *Indian Act*, R.S.C. 1927, c. 98, scheme governing the transfer of reserve lands to the Crown. ...

. . . . .

... My conclusion that the mineral rights in I.R. 172 were surrendered as part of the 1945 agreement rests on reasoning unrelated to the scope of the statutory surrender regime, and therefore holds even if the mineral rights had attained the status of "Indian lands" through the 1940 dealings. This is because the ultimate issue to be determined in this case is the impact of the 1945 surrender of I.R. 172 on the earlier 1940 surrender of the mineral rights in I.R. 172, regardless of the latter's effectiveness.

. . . . .

... [T]he legal character of the 1945 surrender, and its impact on the 1940 surrender, should be determined by reference to the intention of the Band. Unless some statutory bar exists (which, as noted above, is not the case here), then the Band members' intention should be given legal effect.

. . . . .

The Band's intention is evidenced by the terms of the 1945 surrender instrument, signed by Chief Succona, Joseph Apsassin and two councillors on behalf of the Band. This instrument states that the Band did "release, remise, surrender, quit claim and yield up unto our Sovereign Lord the King, his Heirs and Successors forever, ALL AND SINGULAR, that certain parcel or tract of land and premises ... composed of St. John Indian Reserve No. 172". Since this instrument effected the surrender of certain land forming a "reserve", it is reasonable to conclude that the term "Reserve", as used in the surrender instrument, was intended to have the same meaning as the term "reserve" in the *Indian Act*. ... [Section] 2(*j*) of the Act defines "reserve" as an unsurrendered tract of land including the "minerals ... thereon or therein". Therefore, the 1945 surrender included the tract of land forming I.R. 172, the minerals in that tract of land, and the right to exploit those minerals. ...

. . . . .

... I think that the true nature of the 1945 dealings can best be characterized as a *variation of a trust in Indian land*. In 1940, the Band transferred the mineral rights in I.R. 172 to the Crown in trust, requiring the Crown to lease those rights for the benefit of the Band. The 1945 agreement was also framed as a trust, in which the Band surrendered all of its rights over I.R. 172 to the Crown "to sell or lease". The 1945 agreement subsumed the 1940 agreement, and expanded upon it in two ways: first, while the 1940 surrender concerned mineral rights only, the 1945 surrender covered all rights in I.R. 172, including both mineral rights and surface rights; and second, while the 1940 surrender constituted a trust for "lease" , the 1945 surrender gave the Crown, as trustee, the discretion "to sell or lease". This two-pronged variation of the 1940 trust agreement afforded the Crown considerably greater power to act as a fiduciary on behalf of the Band. Of course, under the terms of the trust, and because of the Crown's fiduciary role in the dealings, the DIA was required to exercise its enlarged powers in the best interests of the Band.

. . . . .

I should also add that I would be reluctant to give effect to this surrender variation if I thought that the Band's understanding of its terms had been inadequate, or if the conduct of the Crown had somehow tainted the dealings in a manner which made it unsafe to rely on the Band's understanding and intention. However, neither of these situations arises here. ...

I therefore conclude that under the 1945 agreement, both the surface rights and the mineral rights in I.R. 172 were surrendered to the Crown in trust "to sell or lease".

III

BREACH OF FIDUCIARY DUTY BY THE DIA SUBSEQUENT TO THE 1945 SURRENDER

The terms of the 1945 surrender transferred I.R. 172 to the Crown "in trust to sell or lease the same to such person or persons, and upon such terms as the Government of the Dominion of Canada may deem most conducive to our Welfare and that of our people". By taking on the obligations of a trustee in relation to I.R. 172, the DIA was under a fiduciary duty to deal with the land in the best interests of the members of the Beaver Band. This duty extended to both the surface rights and the mineral rights.

In my view, it is critical to the outcome of this case that the 1945 agreement was a surrender in trust, *to sell or lease*. The terms of the trust agreement provided the DIA with the discretion to sell or lease, and since the DIA was under a fiduciary duty *vis-à-vis* the Band, it was required to exercise this discretion in the Band's best interests. Of equal importance is the fact that the 1945 surrender gave the DIA a virtual *carte blanche* to determine the terms upon which I.R. 172 would be sold or leased. The only limitation was that these terms had to be "conducive" to the "welfare" of the Band. Because of the scope of the discretion granted to the DIA, it would have been open to the DIA to sell the surface rights in I.R. 172 to the Director, *The Veterans' Land Act* ("DVLA"), while continuing to lease the mineral rights for the benefit of the Band, as per the 1940 surrender agreement.

. . . . .

The DIA's failure to continue the leasing arrangement could be excused if the Department had received a clear mandate from the Band to sell the mineral rights. ... There was ... no clear authorization from the Band which justified the DIA in departing from its long-standing policy of reserving mineral rights for the benefit of the aboriginals when surface rights were sold. This underscores the critical distinction between the Band's intention to include the mineral rights in the 1945 surrender, and an intention of the Band that the mineral rights must be sold and not leased by the Crown. Given these circumstances, the DIA was under a fiduciary duty to continue the leasing arrangement which had been established in the 1940 surrender. It was a violation of the fiduciary duty to sell the mineral rights to the DVLA in 1948.

IV

LIMITATION OF ACTIONS

. . . . .

As a fiduciary, the DIA was required to act with reasonable diligence. In my view, a reasonable person in the DIA's position would have realized by August 9, 1949 that an error had occurred, and would have exercised the s. 64 power to correct the error, reacquire the mineral rights, and effect a leasing arrangement for the benefit of the Band. That this was not done was a clear breach of the DIA's fiduciary duty to deal with I.R. 172 according to the best interests of the Band.

Thus, I conclude that the appellants may recover any losses stemming from transfers by the DVLA after August 9, 1949 as such losses fall within the 30-year limitation period imposed by the British Columbia *Limitation Act*, and are not barred by any other provision of that Act as explained in the reasons of McLachlin J.

. . . . .

McLachlin J. (**Cory** and **Major JJ**. concurring): —

I

INTRODUCTION

. . . . .

The appeal raises many issues relating to the duties on the Crown, the alleged breaches of those duties and whether the claims are statute-barred. I propose to consider them under the following headings: (1) Pre-surrender duties and breaches; (2) Post-surrender duties and breaches regarding surface rights; (3) Post-surrender duties and breaches regarding mineral rights; and (4) Limitations issues.

II

ANALYSIS

(1) *Pre-surrender duties and breaches*

. . . . .

(a)   *Whether the* Indian Act *imposed a duty on the Crown to prevent the surrender of the reserve*

... The answer to this question is found in *Guerin v. The Queen*, ... [1984] 2 S.C.R. 335, ... where the majority of this Court, *per* Dickson J. (as he then was), held that the duty on the Crown with respect to surrender of Indian lands was founded on preventing exploitative bargains.

. . . . .

Subject to the issue of the value of the reserve and the matter of mineral rights, which I deal with later, the evidence does not support the view that the surrender of the Fort St. John reserve was foolish, improvident or amounted to exploitation. In fact, viewed from the perspective of the Band at the time, it made good sense. The measure of control which the Act permitted the Band to exercise over the surrender of the reserve negates the contention that absent exploitation, the Act imposed a fiduciary obligation on the Crown with respect to the surrender of the reserve.

(b) *Whether the circumstances of the case gave rise to a fiduciary duty on the Crown with respect to the surrender*

If the *Indian Act* did not impose a duty on the Crown to block the surrender of the reserve, the further question arises of whether on the particular facts of this case a fiduciary relationship was superimposed on the regime for alienation of Indian lands contemplated by the *Indian Act*.

Generally speaking, a fiduciary obligation arises where one person possesses unilateral power or discretion on a matter affecting a second "peculiarly vulnerable" person ... The vulnerable party is in the power of the party possessing the power or discretion, who is in turn obligated to exercise that power or discretion solely for the benefit of the vulnerable party. A person cedes (or more often finds himself in the situation where someone else has ceded for him) his power over a matter to another person. The person who has ceded power *trusts* the person to whom power is ceded to exercise the power with loyalty and care. This is the notion at the heart of the fiduciary obligation.

The evidence supports the view that the Band trusted the Crown to provide it with information as to its options and their foreseeable consequences, in relation to the surrender of the Fort St. John reserve and the acquisition of new reserves which would better suit its life of trapping and hunting. It does not support the contention that the Band abnegated or entrusted its power of decision over the surrender of the reserve to the Crown.

. . . . .

I conclude that the evidence does not support the existence of a fiduciary duty on the Crown prior to the surrender of the reserve by the Band.

. . . . .

(2) *Post-surrender duties and breaches regarding surface rights*

The 1945 surrender conveyed the Band's lands to the Crown "in trust to sell or lease the same to such person or persons, and upon such terms as the Government of the Dominion of Canada may deem *most conducive to our Welfare and that of our people*" (emphasis added). The Crown concedes that this surrender imposed a fiduciary duty on the Crown with respect to the subsequent sale or lease of the lands: *Guerin, supra*. The only issue is whether the Crown breached that duty when in 1948 it sold the lands to the DVLA for $70,000.

· · · · ·

The trial judge was correct in finding that a fiduciary involved in self-dealing, i.e. in a conflict of interest, bears the onus of demonstrating that its personal interest did not benefit from its fiduciary powers ... The Crown, facing conflicting political pressures in favour of preserving the land for the Band on the one hand, and making it available for distribution to veterans on the other, may be argued to have been in a position of conflict of interest.

· · · · ·

... The Crown adduced evidence showing that the sale price lay within a range established by the appraisals. This raised a *prima facie* case that the sale price was reasonable. The onus then shifted to the Bands to show it was unreasonable. The Bands did not adduce such evidence. On this state of the record, a presumption of breach of the Crown's fiduciary duty to exact a fair price cannot be based on a failure to discharge the onus upon it. ...

I conclude that the trial judge erred in concluding that the Crown breached its fiduciary duty to the Band by selling the land for $70,000.

(c) *Failure to restore surface rights to the Band after the 1945 surrender*

The Bands argue that they should have been given their reserve back because of their apparent impoverishment between 1945 and 1961. The Crown, in the Bands' submission, should have realized that the surrender had been a mistake. Instead of confirming the mistake by selling the land to the DVLA, it should have cancelled the surrender and transferred the land back to the Band.

· · · · ·

Accepting that the Band was living in poverty, one cannot infer that the solution was to cancel the 1945 surrender or refuse to sell the Fort St. John reserve land. The Crown cannot be said to have breached the fiduciary duty it owed the Band after surrender of the Fort St. John reserve by failing to restore the land to the Indians.

(d) *Conclusions on post-surrender duty and breach with respect to surface rights*

I conclude that the Bands have not established breach of fiduciary duty with respect to the sale of the surface rights.

(3) *Post-surrender duties and breaches regarding mineral rights*

The Band surrendered "Petroleum and Natural Gas and the mining rights in connection therewith" in the Fort St. John reserve to the Crown in 1940, "in trust to lease the same to such person or persons, and upon such terms as the Government of Canada may deem most conducive to our welfare and that of our people". Section 54 of the 1927 *Indian Act* required the Crown to hold these lands for the purpose specified in the surrender — for lease for the benefit of the Band. The right to explore for minerals was leased in 1940 for $1,800. In 1948, by means which to this day remain the subject of debate, the mineral rights were transferred to the DVLA and hence to the veterans who took up the Fort St. John land. When oil and gas were discovered on the lands in 1976, it was not the Indians, but the veterans and their assigns, who obtained the revenues that flowed from the mineral rights.

To this résumé must be added two additional uncontested facts. First, at the time the mineral rights passed to the DVLA, and hence to the veterans, the Indians were unsophisticated and may not have fully understood the concept of different interests in land and how they might be lost. Second, they were never advised of the transfer of the mineral rights to the DVLA. They discovered it only in 1977, when an employee of the DIA brought to their attention that oil and gas had been discovered on their former lands and queried how the mineral rights had come to be transferred from the Band to the veterans.

. . . . .

(a) *The effect of the 1940 surrender of mineral rights*

The duties of the Crown with respect to the surrender of the mineral rights after the 1940 surrender are clear. The mineral rights were conveyed to the Crown in trust to *lease* for the welfare of the Band. The Crown owed the Band a fiduciary duty with respect to the minerals after the 1940 surrender as a matter of general law: *Guerin, supra*. Quite apart from this, the terms of the surrender and the Act, s. 54, make it clear that the Crown took the mineral rights as a fiduciary for the Band on terms which limited the Crown to leasing them for the Band's benefit.

(b) *The effect of the 1945 surrender on the mineral rights*

. . . . .

... Prior to 1940, the Band held a right in both the surface rights and the mineral rights of the reserve. The Band surrendered the mineral rights in the reserve to the Crown in 1940. The effect of this was to remove the mineral rights from the reserve. When the Band surrendered its interest in the Fort St. John reserve to the Crown in 1945, it could transfer only those rights in the reserve which it still possessed: *nemo dat quod non habet* — a person cannot give what he does not possess. The 1945 surrender could not therefore have included surrender of the Band's reserve rights over the minerals. Rather, it involved only the surrender of those rights which still belonged to the Band to surrender, namely the surface rights. The minerals remained in the Crown and the Crown remained bound by the terms of the 1940 surrender, even after the 1945 surrender of the Indian's remaining interest in the lands.

This result is dictated not only by the most basic principles of property transfer, but by the *Indian Act* itself. ...

. . . . .

The wording of the *Indian Act* and the regulations governing oil and gas which have been enacted under it, confirm that mineral rights in Indian reserves have consistently been viewed as capable of being transferred without transferring surface rights.

. . . . .

The basic purpose of the surrender provisions of the *Indian Act* is to ensure that the intention of Indian bands with respect to their interest in their reserves be honoured. One must wonder why, if the Band intended to alter the terms of the 1940 conditional surrender to make an absolute surrender, it did not avail itself of the provisions of the *Indian Act* for the proper legal expression of that intention? One may also ask why, if it was the intention of the Band to surrender the mineral rights for purposes of sale in 1945, mineral rights were never discussed in the negotiations leading to the 1945 surrender?

. . . . .

In my opinion, we should not overturn a deliberately executed and statutorily authorized surrender on the basis of no evidence. In determining something as nebulous as intention over 40 years later one must look to all available sources. Here the written source is silent where one would have expected clear wording to revoke the previous surrender and the oral testimony establishes that the issue was never even discussed. This cannot be evidence of intention and the Band should be entitled to the protection of the *Indian Act* and the common law which prevent the Crown from unilaterally changing the terms under which it held the property as fiduciary without obtaining the informed consent of the Band. In the words of Gonthier J., the DIA never received a clear mandate from the Band to sell the mineral rights. How then, one may ask, can one conclude that the Band intended that the mineral rights be surrendered for purposes of sale?

. . . . .

... [T]his is a case where the Crown, as fiduciary, has acted in a manner not authorized by the original surrender under which it became the fiduciary of the property. If the Crown wished to gain a broader discretion with respect to the property that it held in a "trust-like" manner there were certain steps it was required to follow. These steps included informing the Band specifically of the Crown's intention to alter the terms on which it held the mineral rights and following its own administrative procedures by revoking the 1940 surrender by order in council to allow for a new surrender in accordance with the *Indian Act*. Neither of these steps were taken here.

. . . . .

The Crown's own prior experience sufficed to establish that the mineral rights had actual and potential value. After taking the surrender in 1940, it issued a permit for prospecting for oil and gas on the property. The 1940 permit alone was worth $1,800, a not insignificant sum given that the annual interest of 5 percent on the $70,000 purchase price for the surface rights yielded about $3,500.

Moreover, the Crown had much earlier realized the potential value of mineral rights and routinely excluded them from its grants. ...

. . . . .

... [T]he trial judge's inference from low value of the absence of a duty to reserve the mineral from the 1948 transfer is suspect. If indeed the mineral rights had minimal sale value in 1948, it does not follow that a prudent person would give them away. It is more logical to argue that since nothing could be obtained for them at the time, and since it would cost nothing to keep them, they should be kept against the chance, however remote, that they might acquire some value in the future. The wisdom of the latter course is demonstrated by the Crown's policy with respect to its own mineral rights; it reserved them to itself, regardless of actual value. It lies ill in the mouth of the Crown to argue that it should have done less with the property entrusted to it as fiduciary to lease for the welfare of the Band.

The trial judge's emphasis on the apparent low value of the mineral rights suggests an underlying concern with the injustice of conferring an unexpected windfall on the Indians at the Crown's expense. This concern is misplaced. It amounts to bringing foreseeability into the fiduciary analysis through the back door. This constitutes an error of law. The beneficiary of a fiduciary duty is entitled to have his or her property restored or value in its place, even if the value of the property turns out to be much greater than could have been foreseen at the time of the breach ...

The matter comes down to this. The duty on the Crown as fiduciary was "that of a man of ordinary prudence in managing his own affairs": *Fales v. Canada Permanent Trust Co.*, [1977] 2 S.C.R. 302, at p. 315. A reasonable person does not inadvertently give away a potentially valuable asset which has already demonstrated earning potential. Nor does a reasonable person give away for no consideration what it will cost him nothing to keep and which may one day possess value, however remote the possibility. The Crown managing its own affairs reserved out its minerals. It should have done the same for the Band.

(d) *Conclusions on post-surrender duty and breach with respect to mineral rights*

I conclude that the 1940 surrender of the mineral rights imposed a fiduciary duty to the Band with respect to the mineral rights under the terms of the 1940 surrender, and that the DIA breached this duty by conveying the mineral rights to the DVLA.

(4) *Limitations issues*

The Crown argues that if it breached its fiduciary duty to the Band, by conveying the reserve to the DVLA, the action on the breach is statute-barred. The Bands dispute this contention.

[After considering the relevant statutory materials, **McLachlin J.** held that the Crown's breach of duty with respect to the sale of surface rights was, indeed, statute-barred. She then considered the Bands' mineral rights claims.]

. . . . .

An alternative argument, not considered below, is that the Crown had a statutory ability under s. 64 of the 1927 *Indian Act* to revoke any sale or lease issued in error or mistake, and that it was under a duty to exercise this power to correct the erroneous transfer of the mineral rights to the DVLA. Section 64 empowered the DIA to revoke erroneous sales or leases from the DIA to third parties:

> 64. If the Superintendent General is satisfied that any purchaser or lessee of any Indian lands, or any person claiming under or through him, has been guilty of any fraud or imposition, or has violated any of the conditions of the sale or lease, *or if any such sale or lease has been made or issued in error or mistake, he may cancel such sale or lease and resume the land therein mentioned*, or dispose of it as if no sale or lease thereof had ever been made. (Emphasis added.)

The Crown argues that s. 64 does not apply because the mineral rights were not transferred in error. The evidence does not support this contention. As discussed earlier, the transfer has never been described as intentional and has generally been attributed to inadvertence. This constitutes "error or mistake" within s. 64.

It follows that the DIA had the power to revoke the inadvertent, erroneous grant of the mineral rights to the DVLA up to the time they were transferred to veterans. ...

In my view, the DIA was under a duty to use this power to rectify errors prejudicing the interests of the Indians as part of its ongoing fiduciary duty to the Indians. The fiduciary duty associated with the administration of Indian lands may have terminated with the sale of the lands in 1948. However, an ongoing fiduciary duty to act to correct error in the best interests of the Indians may be inferred from the exceptional nature of s. 64. That section gave the DIA the power to revoke erroneous grants of land, even as against *bona fide* purchasers. It is not unreasonable to infer that the enactors of the legislation intended the DIA to use that power in the best interests of the Indians. If s. 64 above is not enough to establish a fiduciary obligation to correct the error, it would certainly appear to do so, when read in the context of jurisprudence on fiduciary obligations. Where a party is granted power over another's interests, and where the other party is correspondingly deprived of power over them, or is "vulnerable", then the party possessing the power is under a fiduciary obligation to exercise it in the best interests of the other ... Section 64 gave to DIA power to correct the error that had wrongly conveyed the Band's minerals to the DVLA. The Band itself had no such power; it was vulnerable. In these circumstances, a fiduciary duty to correct the error lies.

· · · · ·

I conclude that the Crown, having first breached its fiduciary duty to the Indians by transferring the minerals to the DVLA, committed a second breach by failing to correct the error on August 9, 1949 when it learned of the error's existence and the potential value of the mineral rights.

[**McLachlin J.** then found that this second breach of duty was not statute-barred.]

· · · · ·

Appeal and cross-appeal allowed.

Following *Blueberry River*, the Supreme Court of Canada issued two pronouncements which centred upon on the federal Crown's fiduciary duties to Aboriginal peoples: *Osoyoos Indian Band v. Oliver (Town)*, [2001] 3 S.C.R. 746 and *Wewaykum Indian Band v. Canada*, 2002 SCC 79, both of which are excerpted below.

OSOYOOS INDIAN BAND v. OLIVER (TOWN)

[2001] 3 S.C.R. 746 (references omitted)

[This case concerned the ability of an Indian band to tax lands taken from its reserve upon which an irrigation canal was built. The canal bisected the band's reserve, which was located near the town of Oliver in the Okanagan Valley of southern British Columbia. Authorization for the taking of the land was uncertain. No attempt to formalize the province's interest in the canal lands was undertaken until some 32 years after the canal was built, at which time a federal Order in Council enacted under section 35 of the 1952 *Indian Act* provided for the use of the land for "irrigation canal purposes" in exchange for the sum of $7,700 from the province. The land was never formally expropriated. In 1962, the canal lands were registered in the name of the Queen in right of the province. At the time of the litigation, the Town of Oliver operated and maintained the canal, although the basis of its authority to do so was uncertain.

Only those aspects of the judgment relevant to the issue of the Crown's fiduciary duty are reproduced below.]

The judgment of **McLachlin C.J.C.** and **Iacobucci, Binnie, Arbour** and **LeBel JJ.** was delivered by

Iacobucci J.: —

. . . . .

V. Issues and Submissions of the Parties

1. Can a taking pursuant to s. 35 of the *Indian Act* extinguish an Indian band's interest in reserve land such that the land is no longer "in the reserve" and falls outside the jurisdiction of the band?

2. Did Order in Council 1957-577 remove the land at issue in this case from the Osoyoos Indian Reserve Number 1?

... The appellant ... submits that because Indian interests are at stake, fiduciary principles constrain the discretion of the Governor in Council to transfer land under s. 35. Consequently, a minimal impairment rule should be applied in the interpretation of the Order in Council with the result that the Governor in Council could not have intended to, and did not in fact, remove the land at issue from the reserve. ...

... With respect to the interpretation of the Order in Council, the respondents submit that the Governor in Council is not under any fiduciary duty to the Band in the context of a taking of an interest in reserve land under s. 35. Therefore, a minimal impairment rule should not be applied in this case. ...

VI. Analysis

. . . . .

The determination of the rights and entitlements at issue in this case will significantly affect the interests of the parties. Yet, the factual basis upon which that determination must be made is somewhat unsatisfactory. I share the view of the Court of Appeal that the evidentiary record in this case is demonstrably incomplete. Important relevant evidence that could assist the Court in the interpretation and application of the Order in Council may be available but does not form part of the record of this case.

In particular, there is no evidence that explains under what authority, if any, the canal was initially constructed and operated prior to the enactment of the Order in Council. There is no evidence to indicate which interests in land were assessed or what methodology was used to calculate the value of the compensation received by the Band in 1955. The documentary evidence is thin: none of the correspondence, Band Council resolutions, minutes of meetings or other documents and reports that could offer external evidence of intention relating to the transfer effected by Order in Council 1957-577 was presented. Apart from the fact that the canal is "concrete lined", we do not know anything about how it was constructed. Similarly, apart from the fact that the canal lands cover an area of 56.09 acres, we do not know anything about its specific dimensions. There was no evidence that would explain what type of tenure is necessary to maintain and operate the canal or precisely what type of tenure is enjoyed by the Town of Oliver. There was no evidence of the activities carried on on the lands in question; whether it is fenced off or occupied exclusively by the Town of Oliver, or whether the Band members are permitted to cross the canal at certain points.

In my view, as a general matter the Court should be cautious in taking away interests in land in the absence of a complete evidentiary record. This is especially true when the interest at stake is the aboriginal interest in reserve land. ... In this case, we are faced with the difficult task of determining intention without supporting facts and evidence. Having said all this, as the appeal comes by way of a stated case, we must determine the rights of the parties as best we can using the evidence at hand.

. . . . .

Land may be removed from a reserve with the participation of the Crown, which owes a fiduciary duty to the band, as discussed below. Fiduciaries are held to a high standard of diligence. For this reason, as well as by reason of the foregoing principles, it follows that a clear and plain intention must be present in order to conclude that land has been removed from a reserve. ...

. . . . .

4. *The Content of the Crown's Fiduciary Duty in the Context of Section 35*

The intervener the Attorney General of Canada submits that when Canada's public law duty conflicts with its statutory obligation to hold reserve lands for the use and benefit of the band for which they were set apart, then a fiduciary duty does not arise. The Attorney General argues that the existence of a fiduciary duty to impair minimally the Indian interest in reserve lands is inconsistent with the legislative purpose of s. 35 which is to act in the greater public interest and that the opening phrase of s. 18(1) of the *Indian Act*, "Subject to the provisions of this Act . . .", effectively releases the Crown from its fiduciary duty in respect of s. 35 takings. In addition, the Attorney General contends that a fiduciary obligation to impair minimally the Indian interest in reserve lands is inconsistent with the principles of fiduciary law which impose a duty of utmost loyalty on the fiduciary to act only in the interests of the person to whom the duty is owed. Thus, the Attorney

General submits that the holding in *Guerin, supra,* that the surrender of an Indian interest of land gives rise to a fiduciary duty on the part of the Crown to act in the best interests of the Indians does not extend to the context of expropriation, and that the duty of the Crown to the band in the case of an expropriation of reserve land is similar to its duty to any other land holder — to compensate the band appropriately for the loss of the lands.

In my view, the fiduciary duty of the Crown is not restricted to instances of surrender. Section 35 clearly permits the Governor in Council to allow the use of reserve land for public purposes. However, once it has been determined that an expropriation of Indian lands is in the public interest, a fiduciary duty arises on the part of the Crown to expropriate or grant only the minimum interest required in order to fulfill that public purpose, thus ensuring a minimal impairment of the use and enjoyment of Indian lands by the band. This is consistent with the provisions of s. 35 which give the Governor in Council the absolute discretion to prescribe the terms to which the expropriation or transfer is to be subject. In this way, instead of having the public interest trump the Indian interests, the approach I advocate attempts to reconcile the two interests involved.

This two-step process minimizes any inconsistency between the Crown's public duty to expropriate lands and its fiduciary duty to Indians whose lands are affected by the expropriation. In the first stage, the Crown acts in the public interest in determining that an expropriation involving Indian lands is required in order to fulfill some public purpose. At this stage, no fiduciary duty exists. However, once the general decision to expropriate has been made, the fiduciary obligations of the Crown arise, requiring the Crown to expropriate an interest that will fulfill the public purpose while preserving the Indian interest in the land to the greatest extent practicable.

The duty to impair minimally Indian interests in reserve land not only serves to balance the public interest and the Indian interest, it is also consistent with the policy behind the rule of general inalienability in the *Indian Act* which is to prevent the erosion of the native land base: *Opetchesaht Indian Band v. Canada,* [1997] 2 S.C.R. 119, at para. 52. The contention of the Attorney General that the duty of the Crown to the Band is restricted to appropriate compensation cannot be maintained in light of the special features of reserve land discussed above, in particular, the facts that the aboriginal interest in land has a unique cultural component, and that reserve lands cannot be unilaterally added to or replaced.

As the Crown's fiduciary duty is to protect the use and enjoyment of the Indian interest in expropriated lands to the greatest extent practicable, the duty includes the general obligation, wherever appropriate, to protect a sufficient Indian interest in expropriated land in order to preserve the taxation jurisdiction of the band over the land, thus ensuring a continued ability to earn income from the land. Although in this case the taxation jurisdiction given to bands came after the Order in Council of 1957, the principle is the same, namely that the Crown should not take more than is needed for the public purpose and subject to protecting the use and enjoyment of Indians where appropriate.

[**Iacobucci J.** then turned his attention to the form of interest in the land necessary to operate the canal.]

... The evidence before the Court is insufficient to provide a clear answer. The respondents argue that since the canal is a permanent structure, they therefore must have the exclusive right to use and occupy the land. However, while the canal seems to be a permanent structure on the land, this fact should not be overstated. There was no evidence to indicate what kind of structure the canal is. Stripped to its essence, it is a ditch lined with concrete. Furthermore, it may be inferred that the fee simple to the land was not necessary to construct the canal since no transfer of title was made at the time of its construction. As well, since the canal was already built when the transfer was made, the interest in question is that which is reasonably required to operate and maintain the canal only. Moreover, it is obvious that the fee simple is not necessary to operate and maintain the canal since those activities are currently the responsibility of the Town of Oliver, which appears to have some kind of leasehold interest in the land. A canal is similar in nature to a railway in that both are permanent structures on the land involving operation and maintenance activities, and this Court has found that a grant of a statutory easement can be sufficient for the purposes of building and maintaining a railway (*Canadian Pacific Ltd. v. Paul*, [1988] 2 S.C.R. 654, at p. 671). As noted above, as a general matter the Court should be reluctant to take away interests in land in the absence of conclusive evidence.

. . . . .

I conclude that the Order in Council is ambiguous. There are no clear words of exclusion or limitation that make plain the extent of the interest being transferred. Some phrases in the recitals suggest that a transfer of a fee simple is contemplated ("a portion of Osoyoos Indian Reserve number one"), while others suggest a more restricted interest ("for irrigation canal purposes"). Indeed, the phrase "a portion of Osoyoos Indian Reserve number one" is not necessarily indicative of a fee simple transfer. Given that the law views property as a bundle of rights, that the Order in Council grants "a portion" of the reserve is not inconsistent with the granting of an easement or a right to use the land "for irrigation canal purposes". A right to use the land for a restricted purpose is part of the bundle of rights that make up the property interest in the reserve and so may be referred to as "a portion" of the reserve.

In its traditional sense, a "right of way" is a type of easement, and at common law the acquisition of a right of way does not give the holder a fee simple interest or the right to exclusive possession: E. C. E. Todd, *The Law of Expropriation and Compensation in Canada* (2nd ed. 1992). However, as noted by Newbury J.A. in the Court of Appeal, in modern usage the term right of way does not always correspond to the common law concept and in some circumstances may refer to a right to the exclusive use and occupation of a corridor of land. I acknowledge that the term "rights-of-way" can have two meanings and that the degree of occupation will be governed by the document conceding the grant. However, it is not clear from the context in which it appears in the Order in Council whether the term "rights-of-way" necessarily refers to an easement as it is traditionally known, or some greater interest in a corridor of land.

. . . . .

In finding that the Order in Council removed the land from the reserve, the majority of the Court of Appeal relied in part on the fact that there was no indication that the Province was acquiring anything less than exclusive rights to the land. However, this approach is contrary to the clear and plain intention test for extinguishment. While express language is not strictly necessary, courts should not take away an aboriginal interest in land by implication unless clearly and plainly supported by context.

. . . . .

To summarize, the Order in Council is ambiguous as to the nature of the interest conveyed. It is consistent with the granting of either a fee simple, or a statutory easement for irrigation canal purposes. In light of such ambiguity, resort must be had to the interpretive principles applicable to questions dealing with Indian interests, and the interpretation which impairs the Indian interests as little as possible is to be preferred. Thus, the Order in Council should be read as granting a statutory easement to the Province.

. . . . .

VII. CONCLUSION

I conclude that the Order in Council is ambiguous as to the nature of the interest transferred. It does not evince a clear and plain intent to extinguish the Band's interest in the reserve land. An interpretation of the instrument as granting only an easement over or right to use the canal lands is both plausible and consistent with the policies of the *Indian Act* relating to taxation (s. 83(1)(a)) and expropriation (s. 35). This interpretation is consistent with the minimal impairment of the Band's interest in reserve land. Accordingly, I find that the Order in Council effected a grant of an easement over the land occupied by the canal and did not take away the whole of the Band's interest in the reserve. Therefore, the canal land is still "in the reserve" for the purposes of s. 83(1)(a).

I would allow the appeal, set aside the judgment of the British Columbia Court of Appeal, and substitute therefor an order declaring that the canal land is in the reserve for the purposes of s. 83(1)(a). Since the appellant did not seek costs, I refrain from making an order for costs.

The reasons of **L'Heureux-Dubé**, **Gonthier**, **Major** and **Bastarache JJ.** were delivered by

Gonthier J. (dissenting): —

. . . . .

Without detailing the content of the Crown's fiduciary obligation, which will vary with the facts, it is fair to assume that the legislation that would guide a s. 35(1) expropriation might inform the extent of the interest and the tract of land that the government ought to transfer in keeping with its fiduciary obligation. In this respect, I agree with my colleague Iacobucci J.'s views expressed under the heading "The Content of the Crown's Fiduciary Duty in the Context of Section 35", though in this case, I cannot agree that the Crown's fiduciary obligation regarding its adoption of the Order in Council included a duty to protect an Indian interest in expropriated land sufficient to preserve the Band's taxation jurisdiction. The Band had no taxation jurisdiction to preserve in 1957, when the Order in Council was adopted. (The power to tax real property came into effect with the passage of what became s. 83 of the *Indian Act*, R.S.C. 1985, c. I-5, which allowed a band a limited power to tax contingent on a declaration by the Governor in Council that the "band has reached an advanced stage of development". It was not until the 1988 amendment to s. 83 (S.C. 1988, c. 23, s. 10) that all bands were given the broad jurisdiction to tax as exercized by the Band.)

. . . . .

V. CONCLUSION

I would answer the first stated question — Are lands, taken pursuant to s. 35 of the *Indian Act*, "land or interests in land" in a reserve of a Band within the meaning of s. 83(1)(*a*) of the *Indian Act* such that those lands are assessable and taxable pursuant to Band Assessment By-laws and taxable pursuant to Band Taxation By-laws — in the negative, where full ownership is expropriated.

I would answer the second stated question — If s. 35 of the *Indian Act* authorizes the removal of lands from reserve status, does federal Order in Council 1957-577, by which the Lands were transferred, remove the Lands from reserve status so that they are not assessable and taxable by the Osoyoos Indian Band — in the affirmative.

I would dismiss the appeal.

Appeal allowed.

The *Osoyoos* judgment is an illustration of the limitations imposed upon the Crown as a result of its fiduciary obligations to Aboriginal peoples. In *Wewaykum*, below, the issue of the Crown's fiduciary duty was connected to damages/loss of benefits alleged by two Indian bands to have occurred as a result of documentation errors by the Crown *vis-à-vis* two reserves.

WEWAYKUM INDIAN BAND v. CANADA

2002 SCC 79 (references omitted)

Binnie J.: — Two Indian bands on the east coast of Vancouver Island lay claim to each other's reserve land. The reserves, which have been in the possession of the incumbent band since about the end of the 19th century, are located two miles from each other. The inhabitants of both reserves are members of the Laich-kwil-tach First Nation which, in the mid-1800s, managed to displace the Comox First Nation from this area of British Columbia.

Each band claims that but for various breaches of fiduciary duty on the part of the federal Crown, its people would be in possession of *both* reserves. Members of the other band, on this view, should be in possession of neither.

. . . . .

Although the bands seek formal declarations of trespass and possession and injunctive relief against each other, each acknowledges the hardship that such a result would cause the other, and each band therefore says it would be satisfied with financial compensation from the federal Crown. The Cape Mudge appellants say *their* compensation should be in the range of $12.2 to $14.8 million for Reserve No. 11 and the Campbell River appellants say *their* claim is about $4 million for Reserve No. 12. In short, if the appellant bands' claims are allowed, each band will stay where it is but will receive substantial funds by way of "equitable compensation" plus costs on a solicitor-client scale.

We are therefore required to consider (i) the scope of the fiduciary duty of the Crown in the process of the *creation* of Indian reserve lands; (ii) whether the acts of government officials in this case breached any fiduciary duty; and (iii) what equitable remedies (including equitable compensation) are available to remedy such breaches, if any.

. . . . .

The legal requirements for the creation of a reserve within the meaning of the *Indian Act* were considered by this Court in *Ross River Dena Council Band v. Canada*, 2002 SCC 54 … At para. 68, LeBel J. noted "that the process of reserve creation, like other aspects of its relationship with First Nations, requires that the Crown remain mindful of its fiduciary duties and of their impact on this procedure, and taking into consideration the *sui generis* nature of native land rights". The role of the Crown's fiduciary duty in reserve creation was not argued in that case. It is squarely raised in the appeals now before us.

. . . . .

I think there is no doubt on the evidence that when the federal Crown received the B.C. Order-in-Council 1036 dated July 29, 1938, it intended to set apart each of the contested reserves for the beneficial use and occupation of the present incumbent. The claim of each appellant band to *both* reserves is misconceived.

. . . . .

Delay in the setting aside of reserves did in fact exacerbate the potential for conflict between Indians and the influx of settlers. In 1888, a dispute flared up at Campbell River between some homesteaders called Nunns and the resident Laich-kwil-tach Indians, each of whom claimed rights to some valuable timber in the vicinity of what is now Reserve No. 11. The most vocal figure in this dispute, at least on the Indian side, was Captain John Quacksister. ... Captain John's band affiliation was the subject of dispute between the parties. The trial judge concluded, at para. 289:

> Men and women passed from one group to another and clearly a person could be a member of more than one subgroup. The attempt to categorize Captain John's tribal affiliation epitomized this difficulty and he was appropriately known as "Smoke All Around".

... [T]he federal government authorized one of its surveyors, Mr. Ashdown Green, to sort out the boundary between Captain John and the homesteaders. It is his 1888 survey that forms the root of the Cape Mudge Band's claim in this litigation.

E. The Claim of the Cape Mudge Band (the "Wewaikai")

After visiting the Campbell River area, Ashdown Green recommended the creation of two additional reserves: Reserve No. 11 (Campbell River) and Reserve No. 12 (Quinsam). However, given the terms of his appointment, and the nature of his mandate (which was to resolve the point of contention between Indians and non-Indians), his report purported to settle only the "extent and boundaries" of Reserves Nos. 11 and 12. In the body of his Report, Reserves Nos. 11 and 12 were not identified as allocated to a particular band, but rather to the "Laich-kwil-tach (Euclataw) Indians". Moreover, in a copy of Green's Report filed with the McKenna McBride Commission, he explains his understanding of the reserve-creation process:

> The Laich-kwil-tach (Euclataw) reserves were re-allotted by Mr. O'Reilly in 1886. <u>No allotments were made to separate bands. The division into bands were made by the Agents</u>. [Emphasis in original.]

. . . . .

When a particular reserve was provisionally allocated at the band level, the practice was for a departmental official to write out a band's name in full for the first entry, and for every successive reference (in an unfortunate economy of effort) the official would simply put quotation or "ditto" marks. Thus by 1902, the Schedule (unlike the 1892 Schedule) showed an allocation to the Cape Mudge Band ("Wewayakay") of both Reserve No. 11 *and* Reserve No. 12 ... A note in the margin of the 1902 Schedule stated, "[a]llotted by Mr. Ashdown Green ... May 7, 1888. Surveyed, 1888. Final confirmation, May 18, 1889". As stated, the trial judge found this information to be erroneous. The only approval given by the Indian Superintendent was approval of the reserves for the Laich-kwil-tach First Nation and not for any of its subgroups. The approval was in any event provisional, as the Indian Superintendent must be taken to have been aware that British Columbia had still not agreed on what provincial Crown lands would be made available for that purpose.

The trial judge's findings of fact were clearly supported by the evidence and collectively are fatal to the Cape Mudge Band claim to both reserves. Appearance of the band name on an Indian Affairs document used for administrative purposes does not create in law a reserve in their favour, particularly where the document is based on erroneous information. ...

... No claim was made to Reserve No. 11 by the Cape Mudge Band either in 1914 when making submissions to the McKenna McBride Commission, or again in response to an Indian Affairs departmental inquiry in 1936. Having on those occasions acknowledged the beneficial interest in Reserve No. 11 to be in the Campbell River Band, equitable relief is not available to the Cape Mudge Band to achieve what would now be a most inequitable dispossession of its sister band. Nor, for the reasons to follow, is "equitable" compensation available against the Crown in substitution for the inequitable dispossession which, quite understandably, the Cape Mudge Band does not really desire.

F.   The Claim of the Campbell River Band ("Wewaykum")

The imputed allocation in the 1902 Schedule of both Reserves Nos. 11 and 12 to the Cape Mudge Band ("Wewayakay") created practical difficulties, as the Cape Mudge Band was not in occupation of Reserve No. 11, and never had been, whereas members of the Campbell River Band had been there for several years.

In 1905, a dispute between the two bands over fishing rights in the Campbell River led to a dispute over possession of Reserve No. 11. At about the same time, the International Timber Company expressed an interest in using the area in conjunction with their logging operations. It thus became necessary to sort out who was (provisionally) entitled to what. The Indian Agent William Halliday reported to Ottawa that "I deemed it necessary to get an expression of opinion from the Indians regarding ownership of this reserve (i.e., Reserve No. 11)".

It is important to note that Halliday did not consider it his mandate to impose a solution. It was "to get an expression of opinion from the Indians". The result was the *1907 Resolution* in March of that year wherein the Cape Mudge Band "ceded" to the Campbell River Band any claim to Reserve No. 11, subject to retaining fishing rights in the area. ...

. . . . .

For my purposes, the key points made in the Resolution adopted by the Cape Mudge Band can be summarized as follows:

1.   The Cape Mudge Band acknowledges that Reserve No. 11 is recorded in the departmental Schedule as allocated to it. (There was other corroborating evidence of disclosure by the Crown of the facts known to it as at 1907.)

2. There was however a "difference of opinion" between the bands which needed to be resolved (i.e., the issue here was not one of surrender or alienation but to resolve the "difference of opinion").

3. The members of the Cape Mudge Band recognize that Reserve No. 11 is occupied by the Campbell River Band, who were the first to reside there. (This is consistent with Indian Agent Pidcock's 1896 letter and arguably confirms that in Cape Mudge's then view, Captain John Quacksister was a member of the Campbell River Band.)

4. Members of the Cape Mudge Band acknowledge that it would "entail hardship on the members" of the Campbell River Band "to be obliged to move". (This too is important because it acknowledges that the Campbell River Band had "started to make use of the lands" as contemplated in *Ross River* as an element of reserve creation (para. 67).)

5. The interest of the Cape Mudge Band in Reserve No. 11 "was to have the use of the river for fishing purposes" (i.e., not the reserve for residential purposes).

6. The Cape Mudge Band "in council here assembled, do cede all right to the Campbell River Reserve [No. 11] to the Wewaiaikum [Campbell River] Band forever". (This seems to be in the nature of a quit claim deed rather than a "surrender" or purported conveyance of any interest.)

7. Reserving to the Cape Mudge Band "the undisputed right to catch any and all fish in the waters of Campbell River, this right to be in common with" the Campbell River Band.

8. The Indian Agent Halliday was "hereby authorized to take what steps are necessary to have this resolution made official and properly carried out".

The trial judge concluded that Halliday must have assumed that no reciprocal Resolution was required from the Campbell River Band disclaiming any interest in Reserve No. 12 because the Schedule at Indian Affairs already listed that reserve as allocated to the Cape Mudge Band and there was at that time no dispute about it.

. . . . .

The effect of the *1907 Resolution* was ineptly recorded by Indian Affairs in Ottawa in a handwritten addition to the 1902 Schedule ...

As is apparent, through a further unfortunate economy of effort, the handwritten note of "We-way-akum band" opposite Reserve No. 11 was not accompanied by any amendment to the Schedule to clarify the status of Reserve No. 12, whose ditto marks remained unchanged. ... On a correct interpretation, therefore, the ditto marks opposite Reserve No. 12 *continued* to refer to the "Wewayakay" (Cape Mudge) Band, despite the confusion introduced by the subsequent handwritten notation against Reserve No. 11.

. . . . .

In my view, the Campbell River Band's claim to a "legislated entitlement" is misconceived, but in any event it is seeking *equitable* relief against the Crown, and equity has always looked to substance not form ...

. . . . .

G. The McKenna McBride Commission, 1912

The continuing disagreements between the federal and provincial governments about the size and number of reserves in British Columbia led to the establishment in 1912 of the McKenna McBride Commission. ...

The McKenna McBride Commission visited the proposed reserves in the Campbell River area. In their analysis of the evidence gathered there, the Commissioners acknowledged that Reserve No. 11 was properly allocated in the federal Schedule to the Campbell River Band, but noted the error with respect to Reserve No. 12 ...

In their respective appearances before the McKenna McBride Commission in 1914, the Campbell River Band made no claim to Reserve No. 12 and the Cape Mudge Band made no claim to Reserve No. 11.

... The McKenna McBride Commission neither added acreage nor subtracted acreage from Reserve No. 11 or Reserve No. 12. ...

H. The Ditchburn Clark Commission

Unfortunately, the McKenna McBride Report also failed to obtain provincial approval. The federal and provincial governments then enacted mirror legislation establishing the Ditchburn Clark Commission to attempt to bring closure for a federal-provincial wrangle that at that stage had dragged on for almost 50 years ... With respect to Reserves Nos. 11 and 12, it basically restated the position already proposed in the McKenna McBride Report.

In 1924, the British Columbia government as well as the federal government finally adopted the McKenna McBride recommendations, as modified by the Ditchburn Clark Report. ... This eventually led to the issuing of provincial Order-in-Council No. 1036 on July 29, 1938 which transferred administration and control of the subject lands to the Crown in right of Canada. ... More importantly, given the critical role of "intention" in the creation of reserves (*Ross River, supra*, at para. 67), it was clear that at the highest levels of both governments the *intention* was to proceed by way of mutual agreement. An intention to create a reserve in 1907 on land that might be withdrawn from the federal-provincial package at any time prior to such agreement being concluded cannot reasonably be attributed to the federal Crown.

The position of the Campbell River Band is that the series of orders-in-council appending the faulty Schedules placed a legislative seal of approval ("legislative entitlement") on the "ditto mark error", and that the courts are now bound to give it full effect by dispossessing the Cape Mudge Band from Reserve No. 12 (not its preferred solution) or obtaining "equitable compensation" from the Crown in lieu thereof.

Orders-in-council are certainly presumptive proof of the Crown's intention to create a reserve as therein stated but they are not conclusive: *Ross River*, at para. 50. The trial judge found that the federal Crown, in whose jurisdiction the final act of reserve creation resided, *intended* that Reserve No. 12 be allocated to the Cape Mudge Band. As stated, substance not form prevails.

Counsel for the Campbell River Band is correct, of course, that a conventional reading of the ditto marks would give both reserves to his client. If this were the usual real estate battle between multinational corporations, which had negotiated extensively each word and punctuation mark in the documentation, the ditto mark argument might be considered a solid point, except that here his client is seeking *equitable* relief, and even as between multinational corporations such an outcome might be regarded as wholly inequitable in light of the factual findings of the trial judge.

I. Correction of the "Ditto Mark Error"

The apparent conflict between the official records and the *status quo* occupation by the appellant bands was bound to lead to a measure of agitation.

In 1928, Indian Commissioner Ditchburn wrote to the Secretary of the Department of Indian Affairs that

> As Quinsam Reserve No. 12 has always been claimed by the We-way-akay (Cape Mudge) Band and the claim has not been disputed by the We-wayakum (Campbell River) Band, I would recommend that it be officially decided as belonging to the We-way-akay Indians and notations made in the Schedule accordingly.

Both bands retained legal counsel in 1932 to investigate. In 1934, Indian Agent Todd, Halliday's replacement, was asked to contact the bands to ascertain accuracy of the sub-tribal allocations in the federal Schedule. The trial judge found as a fact that during the ensuing discussions, both appellant bands "were informed of the Department's position with respect to Reserves Nos. 11 and 12, including the circumstances and full text of the 1907 ceding resolution" (para. 131).

After the relevant facts had been ascertained and discussed, both bands confirmed the correctness of the *status quo*.

On November 23, 1936, a declaration was signed by the chief and principal men of the Wewaikai Band stating: "We the Chiefs and Principal Men of the Cape Mudge Band, do hereby state under oath that the Reserves shown below are the only reserves belonging to this band <u>and this list is complete</u>" (emphasis added). Among these reserves were Reserve No. 10 (Cape Mudge) and Reserve No. 12 (Quinsam). The Campbell River Reserve No. 11 was not mentioned in their list.

A parallel declaration was sworn by members of the Campbell River Band in 1937 indicating that "We the Chiefs and Principal Men of the Campbell River Band, do hereby state under oath that the reserves shown below are the only reserves belonging to this band <u>and that this list is complete</u>" (emphasis added). The list referred to in their declaration, while it mentions "Reserve No. 11", makes no claim to Reserve No. 12.

That is, both bands made declarations that corresponded to their actual incumbency. The various attacks now made on these declarations and the Indian agents by the respective sets of appellants were rejected by the trial judge. No reason has been shown to interfere with the trial judge's finding in that regard. ...

. . . . .

J. Recent Developments

The dispute resurfaced in the 1970s. ...

In 1985, the Campbell River Band initiated action against the Crown and the Cape Mudge Band. It did so, as stated in para. 30 of its factum, because of the perceived impact of the decision of this Court in *Guerin v. The Queen*, [1984] 2 S.C.R. 335, where a precedent was set of financial compensation to an Indian band for breach of fiduciary duty in the disposition of part of its reserve. The Cape Mudge Band counterclaimed for exclusive entitlement to both reserves and, in 1989, added a claim against the Crown. In October 1989, the actions were consolidated.

. . . . .

The solution to these appeals, in my opinion, does not lie in the law of rectification but in the law governing the fiduciary duty alleged and the equitable remedies sought by the appellant bands, as will now be discussed.

M. The Sui Generis Fiduciary Duty

If, as we affirm, neither band emerged from the reserve-creation process with both reserves, the issue arises whether this outcome establishes in the case of either appellant band a breach of fiduciary duty on the part of the federal Crown.

Prior to its watershed decision in *Guerin, supra*, this Court had generally characterized the relationship between the Crown and Indian peoples as a "political trust" or "trust in the higher sense". ...

The enduring contribution of *Guerin* was to recognize that the concept of political trust did not exhaust the potential legal character of the multitude of relationships between the Crown and aboriginal people. A quasi-proprietary interest (e.g., reserve land) could not be put on the same footing as a government benefits program. The latter will generally give rise to public law remedies only. The former raises considerations "in the nature of a private law duty" (*Guerin*, at p. 385). Put another way, the existence of a public law duty does not exclude the possibility that the Crown undertook, in the discharge of that public law duty, obligations "in the nature of a private law duty" towards aboriginal peoples.

. . . . .

[In *Guerin*], Dickson J. … pointed out that fiduciary duty was imposed on the Crown *despite* rather than *because* of its government functions … Wilson J., in a concurring opinion, made similar comments …

. . . . .

The *Guerin* concept of a *sui generis* fiduciary duty was expanded in *R. v. Sparrow*, [1990] 1 S.C.R 1075, to include protection of the aboriginal people's pre-existing and still existing aboriginal and treaty rights within s. 35 of the *Constitution Act, 1982*. In that regard, it was said at p. 1108:

> The *sui generis* nature of Indian title, and the <u>historic powers and responsibility assumed by the Crown</u> constituted the source of such a fiduciary obligation. In our opinion, *Guerin*, together with *R. v. Taylor and Williams* (1981), 34 O.R. (2d) 360, ground a general guiding principle for s. 35(1). That is, the Government has the responsibility to act in a fiduciary capacity with respect to aboriginal peoples. The relationship between the Government and aboriginals is trust-like, rather than adversarial, and contemporary recognition and affirmation of aboriginal rights must be defined in light of this historic relationship. [Emphasis added.]

The "historic powers and responsibility assumed by the Crown" in relation to Indian rights, although spoken of in *Sparrow*, at p. 1108, as a "general guiding principle in s. 35(1)", is of broader importance. All members of the Court accepted in *Ross River* that potential relief by way of fiduciary remedies is not limited to the s. 35 rights (*Sparrow*) or existing reserves (*Guerin*). The fiduciary duty, where it exists, is called into existence to facilitate supervision of the high degree of discretionary control gradually assumed by the Crown over the lives of aboriginal peoples. As Professor Slattery commented:

> The sources of the general fiduciary duty do not lie, then, in a paternalistic concern to protect a "weaker" or "primitive" people, as has sometimes been suggested, but rather in the necessity of persuading native peoples, at a time when they still had considerable military capacities, that their rights would be better protected by reliance on the Crown than by self-help.

This *sui generis* relationship had its positive aspects in protecting the interests of aboriginal peoples historically (recall, e.g., the reference in *Royal Proclamation, 1763*, R.S.C. 1985, App. II, No. 1, to the "great Frauds and Abuses [that] have been committed in purchasing Lands of the Indians"), but the degree of economic, social and proprietary control and discretion asserted by the Crown also left aboriginal populations vulnerable to the risks of government misconduct or ineptitude. The importance of such discretionary control as a basic ingredient in a fiduciary relationship was underscored in Professor E. Weinrib's statement, quoted in *Guerin, supra*, at p. 384, that: "… the hallmark of a fiduciary relation is that the relative legal positions are such that one party is at the mercy of the other's discretion." … Somewhat associated with the ethical standards required of a fiduciary in the context of the Crown and Aboriginal peoples is the need to uphold the "honour of the Crown" …

But there are limits. The appellants seemed at times to invoke the "fiduciary duty" as a source of plenary Crown liability covering all aspects of the Crown-Indian band relationship. This overshoots the mark. The fiduciary duty imposed on the Crown does not exist at large but in relation to specific Indian interests. In this case we are dealing with land, which has generally played a central role in aboriginal economies and cultures. Land was also the subject matter of *Ross River* ("the lands occupied by the Band"), *Blueberry River* and *Guerin* (disposition of existing reserves). Fiduciary protection accorded to Crown dealings with aboriginal interests in land (including reserve creation) has not to date been recognized by this Court in relation to Indian interests other than land outside the framework of s. 35(1) of the *Constitution Act, 1982*.

Since *Guerin*, Canadian courts have experienced a flood of "fiduciary duty" claims by Indian bands across a whole spectrum of possible complaints, for example:

(i)   to structure elections (*Batchewana Indian Band (Non-resident members) v. Batchewana Indian Band*, [1997] 1 F.C. 689 (C.A.), at para. 60; subsequently dealt with in this Court on other grounds);

(ii)   to require the provision of social services (*Southeast Child & Family Services v. Canada (Attorney General)*, [1997] 9 W.W.R. 236 (Man. Q.B.));

(iii)   to rewrite negotiated provisions (*B.C. Native Women's Society v. Canada*, [2000] 1 F.C. 304 (T.D.));

(iv)   to cover moving expenses (*Paul v. Kingsclear Indian Band* (1997), 137 F.T.R. 275); *Mentuck v. Canada*, [1986] 3 F.C. 249 (T.D.); *Deer v. Mohawk Council of Kahnawake*, [1991] 2 F.C. 18 (T.D.));

(v)   to suppress public access to information about band affairs (*Chippewas of the Nawash First Nation v. Canada (Minister of Indian and Northern Affairs)* (1996), 116 F.T.R. 37, aff'd (1999), 251 N.R. 220 (F.C.A.); *Montana Band of Indians v. Canada (Minister of Indian and Northern Affairs)*, [1989] 1 F.C. 143 (T.D.); *Timiskaming Indian Band v. Canada (Minister of Indian and Northern Affairs)* (1997), 132 F.T.R. 106);

(vi)   to require legal aid funding (*Ominayak v. Canada (Minister of Indian Affairs and Northern Development)*, [1987] 3 F.C. 174 (T.D.));

(vii)   to compel registration of individuals under the *Indian Act* (rejected in *Tuplin v. Canada (Indian and Northern Affairs)* (2001), 207 Nfld. & P.E.I.R. 292 (P.E.I.T.D.));

(viii) to invalidate a consent signed by an Indian mother to the adoption of her child (rejected in *G. (A.P.) v. A. (K.H.)* (1994), 120 D.L.R. (4th) 511 (Alta. Q.B.)).

I offer no comment about the correctness of the disposition of these particular cases on the facts, none of which are before us for decision, but I think it desirable for the Court to affirm the principle, already mentioned, that not all obligations existing between the parties to a fiduciary relationship are themselves fiduciary in nature (*Lac Minerals, supra*, at p. 597), and that this principle applies to the relationship between the Crown and aboriginal peoples. It is necessary, then, to focus on the particular obligation or interest that is the subject matter of the particular dispute and whether or not the Crown had assumed discretionary control in relation thereto sufficient to ground a fiduciary obligation.

· · · · ·

I do not suggest that the existence of a public law duty necessarily excludes the creation of a fiduciary relationship. The latter, however, depends on identification of a cognizable Indian interest, and the Crown's undertaking of discretionary control in relation thereto in a way that invokes responsibility "in the nature of a private law duty", as discussed below.

N. Application of Fiduciary Principles to Indian Lands

For the reasons which follow, it is my view that the appellant bands' submissions in these appeals with respect to the existence and breach of a fiduciary duty cannot succeed:

1. The content of the Crown's fiduciary duty towards aboriginal peoples varies with the nature and importance of the interest sought to be protected. It does not provide a general indemnity.

2. Prior to reserve creation, the Crown exercises a public law function under the *Indian Act* — which is subject to supervision by the courts exercising public law remedies. At that stage a fiduciary relationship may also arise but, in that respect, the Crown's duty is limited to the basic obligations of loyalty, good faith in the discharge of its mandate, providing full disclosure appropriate to the subject matter, and acting with ordinary prudence with a view to the best interest of the aboriginal beneficiaries.

3. Once a reserve is created the content of the Crown's fiduciary duty expands to include the protection and preservation of the band's quasi-proprietary interest in the reserve from exploitation.

4. In this case, as the appellant bands have rightly been held to lack any beneficial interest in the other band's reserve, equitable remedies are not available either to dispossess an incumbent band that is entitled to the beneficial interest, or to require the Crown to pay "equitable"compensation for its refusal to bring about such a dispossession.

5. Enforcement of equitable duties by equitable remedies is subject to the usual equitable defences, including laches and acquiescence.

I propose to discuss each of these propositions in turn.

1. The content of the Crown's fiduciary duty towards aboriginal peoples varies with the nature and importance of the interest sought to be protected. It does not provide a general indemnity.

In *Ross River, supra*, the Court affirmed that "[a]lthough this is not at stake in the present appeal, it should not be forgotten that the exercise of this particular power [of reserve creation] remains subject to the fiduciary obligations of the Crown as well as to the constitutional rights and obligations which arise under s. 35 of the *Constitution Act, 1982*" (LeBel J., at para. 62). Further, "it must not be forgotten that the actions of the Crown with respect to the lands occupied by the Band will be governed by the fiduciary relationship which exists between the Crown and the Band. It would certainly be in the interests of fairness for the Crown to take into consideration in any future negotiations the fact that the Ross River Band has occupied these lands for almost half a century" (para. 77).

In the present case the reserve-creation process dragged on from about 1878 to 1928, a period of 50 years. From at least 1907 onwards, the Department treated the reserves as having come into existence, which, in terms of actual occupation, they had. It cannot reasonably be considered that the Crown owed no fiduciary duty during this period to bands which had not only gone into occupation of provisional reserves, but were also entirely dependent on the Crown to see the reserve-creation process through to completion.

The issue, for present purposes, is to define the content of the fiduciary duty "with respect to the lands occupied by the Band" (*Ross River, supra*, at para. 77) at the reserve-creation stage insofar as is necessary for the disposition of these appeals.

. . . . .

As stated, even in the traditional trust context not all obligations existing between the parties to a well-recognized fiduciary relationship are themselves fiduciary in nature: *Lac Minerals, supra, per* Sopinka J., at pp. 597 *et seq.* Moreover, as pointed out by La Forest J. in *McInerney v. MacDonald*, [1992] 2 S.C.R. 138, not all fiduciary relationships and not all fiduciary obligations are the same: "These are shaped by the demands of the situation" (p. 149). ... These observations are of particular importance in a case where the fiduciary is also the government, as the Court in *Guerin* fully recognized (p. 385). (In the case of rival bands asserting overlapping claims to s. 35 aboriginal title over the same land, for example, the Crown is caught truly and unavoidably in the middle, but that is not the case here.)

The starting point in this analysis, therefore, is the Indian bands' interest in specific lands that were subject to the reserve-creation process for their benefit, and in relation to which the Crown constituted itself the exclusive intermediary with the province. The task is to ascertain the content of the fiduciary duty in relation to those specific circumstances.

2. Prior to reserve creation, the Crown exercises a public law function under the *Indian Act* — which is subject to supervision by the courts exercising public law remedies. At that stage its fiduciary duty is limited to the basic obligations of loyalty, good faith in the discharge of its mandate, providing full disclosure appropriate to the subject matter, and acting with a view to the best interest of the beneficiaries.

... In a substantive sense the imposition of a fiduciary duty attaches to the Crown's intervention the additional obligations of loyalty, good faith, full disclosure appropriate to the matter at hand and acting in what it reasonably and with diligence regards as the best interest of the beneficiary. In *Blueberry River* McLachlin J. (as she then was), at para. 104, said that "[t]he duty on the Crown as fiduciary was 'that of a man of ordinary prudence in managing his own affairs'". See also D. W. M. Waters, *Law of Trusts in Canada* (2nd ed. 1984), at pp. 32-33; *Fales v. Canada Permanent Trust Co.*, [1977] 2 S.C.R. 302, at p. 315. Secondly, and perhaps more importantly, the imposition of a fiduciary duty opens access to an array of equitable remedies, about which more will be said below.

In this case the intervention of the Crown was positive, in that the federal government sought to create reserves for the appellant bands out of provincial Crown lands to which these particular bands had no aboriginal or treaty right. ... [T]he people of the Laich-kwil-tach First Nation arrived in the Campbell River area at about the same time as the early Europeans (1840-1853). Government intervention from 1871 onwards was designed to protect members of the appellant bands from displacement by the other newcomers.

When exercising ordinary government powers in matters involving disputes between Indians and non-Indians, the Crown was (and is) obliged to have regard to the interest of all affected parties, not just the Indian interest. The Crown can be no ordinary fiduciary; it wears many hats and represents many interests, some of which cannot help but be conflicting: *Samson Indian Nation and Band v. Canada*, [1995] 2 F.C. 762 (C.A.). As the Campbell River Band acknowledged in its factum, "[t]he Crown's position as fiduciary is necessarily unique" (para. 96). In resolving the dispute between Campbell River Band members and the non-Indian settlers named Nunns, for example, the Crown was not solely concerned with the band interest, nor should it have been. The Indians were "vulnerable" to the adverse exercise of the government's discretion, but so too were the settlers, and each looked to the Crown for a fair resolution of their dispute. At that stage, prior to reserve creation, the Court cannot ignore the reality of the conflicting demands confronting the government, asserted both by the competing bands themselves and by non-Indians. ...

Here, as in *Ross River*, the nature and importance of the appellant bands' interest in these lands prior to 1938, and the Crown's intervention as the exclusive intermediary to deal with others (including the province) on their behalf, imposed on the Crown a fiduciary duty to act with respect to the interest of the aboriginal peoples with loyalty, good faith, full disclosure appropriate to the subject matter and with "ordinary" diligence in what it reasonably regarded as the best interest of the beneficiaries. As the dispute evolved into conflicting demands between the appellant bands themselves, the Crown continued to exercise public law duties in its attempt to ascertain "the place they wish to have" (as stated at para. 24), and, as a fiduciary, it was the Crown's duty to be even-handed towards and among the various beneficiaries. An assessment of the Crown's discharge of its fiduciary obligations at the reserve-creation stage must have regard to the context of the times. The trial judge concluded that each of these obligations was fulfilled, and we have been given no persuasive reason to hold otherwise.

3.   Once a reserve is created, the content of the fiduciary duty expands to include the protection and preservation of the band's interest from exploitation.

The content of the fiduciary duty changes somewhat after reserve creation, at which the time the band has acquired a "legal interest" in its reserve, even if the reserve is created on non-s. 35(1) lands. In *Guerin*, Dickson J. said the fiduciary "interest gives rise upon surrender to a distinctive fiduciary obligation on the part of the Crown" (p. 382). These dicta should not be read too narrowly. Dickson J. spoke of surrender because those were the facts of the *Guerin* case. As this Court recently held, expropriation of an existing reserve equally gives rise to a fiduciary duty: *Osoyoos Indian Band v. Oliver (Town)*, [2001] 3 S.C.R. 746, 2001 SCC 85. See also *Kruger v. The Queen*, [1986] 1 F.C. 3 (C.A.).

At the time of reserve *disposition* the content of the fiduciary duty may change (e.g. to include the implementation of the wishes of the band members). In *Blueberry River*, McLachlin J. observed at para. 35:

> It follows that under the *Indian Act*, the Band had the right to decide whether to surrender the reserve, and its decision was to be respected. At the same time, if the Band's decision was foolish or improvident – a decision that constituted exploitation – the Crown could refuse to consent. In short, the Crown's obligation was limited to preventing exploitative bargains.

It is in the sense of "exploitative bargain", I think, that the approach of Wilson J. in *Guerin* should be understood. Speaking for herself, Ritchie and McIntyre JJ., Wilson J. stated that prior to any disposition the Crown has "a fiduciary obligation to protect and preserve the Bands' interests from invasion or destruction" (p. 350). The "interests" to be protected from invasion or destruction, it should be emphasized, are legal interests, and the threat to their existence, as in *Guerin* itself, is the exploitative bargain (e.g. the lease with the Shaughnessy Heights Golf Club that in *Guerin* was found to be "unconscionable"). This is consistent with *Blueberry River* and *Lewis*. Wilson J.'s comments should be taken to mean that ordinary diligence must be used by the Crown to avoid invasion or destruction of the band's quasi-property interest by an exploitative bargain with third parties or, indeed, exploitation by the Crown itself. (Of course, there will also be cases dealing with the ordinary accountability by the Crown, as fiduciary, for its administrative control over the reserve and band assets.)

The Cape Mudge appellants contend that the Crown breached its fiduciary duty with respect to its two reserves (while attacking the trial judge's rejection of this factual premise) by permitting (or even encouraging) the *1907 Resolution*. They have been deprived of their legal interest in Reserve No. 11, they say, by an "exploitative bargain". They gave away 350 acres for nothing.

While the reserves were not constituted, as a matter of law, until 1938, I would be prepared to assume that, for purposes of this argument, the fiduciary duty was in effect in 1907. The Cape Mudge Band argument is nevertheless unconvincing. I do not accept what, with respect, is its shaky factual premise, i.e., that the band "gave away" Reserve No. 11 as opposed to entering a quit claim in favour of a sister band with a superior interest. More importantly, this argument rests on a misconception of the Crown's fiduciary duty. The Cape Mudge forbears, whose conduct is now complained of, were autonomous actors, apparently fully informed, who intended in good faith to resolve a "difference of opinion" with a sister band. They were not dealing with non-Indian third parties (*Guerin*, at p. 382). It is patronizing to suggest, on the basis of the evidentiary record, that they did not know what they were doing, or to reject their evaluation of a fair outcome. Taken in context, and looking at the substance rather than the form of what was intended, the *1907 Resolution* was not in the least exploitative.

While courts applying principles of equity rightly insist on flexibility to deal with the unforeseeable and infinite variety of circumstances and interests that may arise, and which will fall to be decided under equitable rules, it must be said that the bold attempt of the appellant bands to extend their claim to fiduciary relief on the present facts is overly ambitious.

On the other hand, the trial judge and the Federal Court of Appeal adopted, with respect, too restricted a view of the content of the fiduciary duty owed by the Crown to the Indian bands with respect to their existing quasi-proprietary interest in their respective reserves. In their view, the Crown discharged its fiduciary duty with respect to existing reserves by balancing "the interests of both the Cape Mudge Indians and the Campbell River Indians and to resolve their conflict regarding the use and occupation of the [Laich-kwil-tach] reserves ... [without favouring] the interests of one Band over the interest of the other" (para. 493 F.T.R. and para. 121 N.R.). With respect, the role of honest referee does not exhaust the Crown's fiduciary obligation here. The Crown could not, merely by invoking competing interests, shirk its fiduciary duty. The Crown was obliged to preserve and protect each band's legal interest in the reserve which, on a true interpretation of events, had been allocated to it. In my view it did so.

4. As the appellant bands have been held to lack any beneficial interest in the other band's reserve, equitable remedies are not available either to dispossess an incumbent band that is entitled to the beneficial interest, or to require the Crown to pay compensation for its refusal to bring about such a dispossession.

The various technical arguments arrayed by the bands are, in any event, singularly inappropriate in a case where they seek equitable remedies. As noted, each band has, over the past 65 or more years, reasonably relied on the repeated declarations and disclaimers of its sister band, and on the continuance of the *status quo*, to reside on and improve its reserve.

Reserves Nos. 11 and 12 were formally created when the federal Crown obtained administration and control of the subject lands in 1938. At that time, as outlined above, the appellant bands had manifested on several occasions their acknowledgement that the beneficial interest in Reserve No. 11 resided in the Campbell River Band and the beneficial interest in Reserve No. 12 resided in the Cape Mudge Band. The equitable remedies sought by the appellant bands necessarily address the disposition of the *beneficial* or equitable interest. The trial judge found as a fact (although not using these precise terms) that the equitable interests are reflected in the *status quo*. A mandatory injunction is not available to dispossess the rightful incumbent. Nor is there any requirement on the Crown to pay *equitable* compensation to a claimant band to substitute for an equitable or beneficial interest that does not belong to it.

[**Binnie J.** proceeded to discuss the application of equitable and statutory limitations to the bands' claims, which is excerpted, *infra*.]

. . . . .

Disposition

I would therefore dismiss the appeals with costs.

What did Justice Binnie mean when he said "Somewhat associated with the ethical standards required of a fiduciary in the context of the Crown and Aboriginal peoples is the need to uphold the honour of the Crown ...?" Is this akin to saying that a corpse is "somewhat dead?"

E.   TO WHOM DO THE CROWN'S FIDUCIARY OBLIGATIONS BELONG?

A great deal of uncertainty about the nature and scope of the Crown's fiduciary obligations to Aboriginal peoples remains in spite of the continued application of the fiduciary concept to Crown-Native relations since the *Guerin* decision. None of *Guerin*, *Sparrow*, *Blueberry River*, *Osoyoos* or *Wewaykum* have addressed the fundamental question of which emanation(s) of the Crown owe fiduciary obligations to Aboriginal peoples in Canada.

1. The Provincial Crowns' Fiduciary Obligations

To this point in Canadian Aboriginal rights jurisprudence, the Supreme Court of Canada has yet to definitively state that provincial Crowns owe fiduciary obligations to Aboriginal peoples (although a number of pronouncements at the provincial court of appeal level have done so). There are also valid constitutional arguments that justify the imposition of fiduciary obligations on provincial Crowns, as indicated in the following excerpt.

LEONARD I. ROTMAN, "PARALLEL PATHS: FIDUCIARY DOCTRINE AND THE CROWN-NATIVE RELATIONSHIP IN CANADA"

(Toronto: University of Toronto Press, 1996) at 221, 238-9, 251-3
(references omitted)

In the aftermath of the *Guerin* decision, the existence of the Crown's fiduciary duty to the aboriginal peoples is no longer in question. In the majority of post-*Guerin* decisions, judicial attention to the fulfilment of the fiduciary duties owed to aboriginal people has been directed to the Crown. However, these decisions have not addressed the issues of which emanations of the Canadian Crown — the Crown in right of Canada, the Crown in right of a province, or both — possess fiduciary obligations to the aboriginal peoples.

. . . . .

When the *British North America Act, 1867* [now the *Constitution Act, 1867* (U.K.), 30 & 31 Vict., c. 3] created federal and provincial Crowns in Canada, it did not affect the existing constitutional understanding of the Crown or the nature and extent of its pre-Confederation obligations and responsibilities. It merely divided the powers, responsibilities, and benefits of a single and indivisible Canadian Crown among the newly created federal and provincial Crowns. This division included the Crown's pre-existing fiduciary obligations to Native peoples. Therefore, the allocation of powers in the *British North America Act, 1867* did not remove or reduce the Crown's fiduciary obligations to the Native peoples, but simply redistributed them.

The fact that the Canadian Crown remained single and indivisible prevented it from escaping its obligations to Native peoples by donning a provincial — or federal — Crown "hat" at its convenience. The Crown could not escape, moreover, liability for adequately discharging its fiduciary duties by virtue of jurisdictional problems, such as those surrounding the establishment of Indian reserves from Indian lands surrendered by treaty: "Each level of government has an independent constitutional role and responsibility.... Both are, however, subject to the demands of the honour of the Crown, and this must mean, at a minimum, that the aboriginal people to whom the Crown in all its emanations owes an obligation of protection and development, must not lose the benefit of that obligation because of federal-provincial jurisdictional uncertainty."

Mutual power entails mutual responsibility and it is this mutual responsibility, founded in part on the sharing of legislative and executive powers by the federal and provincial Crowns, that underlies the Crown's fiduciary obligations to aboriginal peoples. If a provincial Crown obtains exclusive proprietary and administrative rights over Indian lands surrendered by treaty, then it must, by necessity or logical implication, also obtain a portion of the fiduciary duties owed to the aboriginal signatories to the treaty. Section 109 of the *British North America Act, 1867* is the conduit by which this transfer is effected. Once this transfer takes place, the province is legally bound to cooperate with the federal Crown in fulfilling the terms of the treaty. Brian Slattery has expressed similar sentiments in "First Nations and the Constitution: A Question of Trust": "Where the benefiting Province has the exclusive constitutional authority to fulfill the Crown's promises, it cannot take the benefit of the surrender without incurring corresponding fiduciary obligations. Thus, if the Federal Crown has undertaken to set aside reserves out of the lands surrendered, this promise binds the Province to which the lands pass, because it alone has the power to carry out the promise."

. . . . .

Because of the absence of provincial participation in the majority of the events giving rise to the Crown's fiduciary duties towards Native peoples, provincial obligations stem primarily from the federal-provincial distribution of legislative and authoritative responsibilities in Canada. Areas of provincial jurisdiction in the *British North America Act, 1867* which have direct effects on aboriginal and treaty rights include section 92(5) (management and sale of public lands and timber), section 92(13) (property and civil rights), section 92A (natural resources), and section 109 (ownership of lands, mines, minerals, and royalties). The distribution of legislative and authoritative responsibility between the federal and provincial Crowns entails provincial acceptance of both benefits and obligations from the actions of the federal Crown after 1867 and from its predecessors, including the British Crown, prior to 1867. Provincial obligations also arise from direct provincial actions towards and interaction with aboriginal peoples.

The sharing of legislative responsibility over aboriginal affairs may be seen, for example, in the ability of provinces to pass legislation affecting aboriginal peoples through section 88 of the *Indian Act*. Even though legislative jurisdiction over "Indians, and Lands reserved for the Indians" is an exclusive federal power under section 91(24) of the *British North America Act, 1867*, section 88 of the *Indian Act* allows for provincial laws of general application to be applied to status Indians by referential incorporation, subject to the terms of Indian treaties, the *Indian Act* itself, or other federal legislation.

. . . . .

Where provinces intrude on the federal Crown's section 91(24) legislative sphere, they cannot do so without affecting the nature and scope of their own obligations to Native peoples. As Brian Slattery explains: "[S]o long as the Provinces have powers and rights enabling them to affect adversely Aboriginal interests protected by the relationship, they hold attendant fiduciary obligations." Provinces thereby acquire some measure of the federal Crown's fiduciary responsibility where they pass legislation referentially under section 88 of the *Indian Act*, play an active role in the formulation of land agreements concerning the establishment of Indian reserves, or actively participate in the negotiation of Indian treaties and agreements.

. . . . .

The line between federal and provincial jurisdictional boundaries is becoming increasingly blurred because of the effects of the *Constitution Act, 1982*. For this reason, it is likely that provinces will continue to encroach even further upon the federal Crown's section 91(24) jurisdiction over "Indians, and Lands reserved for the Indians" without reproach. As Dickson C.J.C. noted in *Mitchell* [*Mitchell v. Sandy Bay Indian Band*, [1990] 2 S.C.R. 85, [1990] 3 C.N.L.R. 46, 3 T.C.T. 5219, 110 N.R. 241, 67 Man. R. (2d) 1 (*sub nom. Mitchell v. Peguis Indian Band*), [1990] 5 W.W.R. 97, 71 D.L.R. (4th) 193] the "fluidity of responsibility across lines of jurisdiction accords well with the fact that the newly entrenched s. 35 of the *Constitution Act, 1982* applies to all levels of government in Canada." However, if there is to be a point beyond which provincial action that is consistent with or in fulfilment of its obligation to aboriginal peoples is deemed to be *ultra vires*, some judicial definition of that line and of provincial fiduciary responsibilities to the aboriginal peoples is necessary. Otherwise, instances that approach or even cross that line will be difficult, if not impossible to regulate.

———————

From the above excerpt, federal and provincial Crown fiduciary responsibilities to the Aboriginal peoples are shown to have derived from the Crown's historical relationship with the Aboriginal peoples and the treaties and other alliances that it entered into with them. Consequently, it is apparent that these obligations predate the existence of Canadian federal and provincial Crowns. The question, then, is to whom did they belong previously?

The obvious answer to this question is that those duties had belonged to the British Crown. It was the entity in whose name relationships were forged with the Aboriginal peoples and treaties concluded. The British Crown's historical relationship with the Aboriginal peoples and the many treaties and other alliances that it entered into with them — such as the Covenant Chain alliance discussed in Chapter 2 — carried with them continuing obligations of a fiduciary nature. What remains to be answered is whether those historic obligations survived the devolution of British powers over Canadian affairs culminating in the repatriation of the Canadian Constitution in 1982.

2. The British Crown's Obligations

While the British Crown's divestment of its responsibilities for Canadian affairs entails that Britain no longer holds constitutional power over Canada, the devolution of powers from Britain to Canada would not have absolved Britain of the entirety of her fiduciary obligations to the Aboriginal peoples of Canada. Under the principle *delegatus non potest delegare* (a delegate must not re-delegate), the British Crown would retain ultimate responsibility for any delegations of fiduciary responsibilities it made, whether by formalized constitutional processes or otherwise. While the British Crown may delegate the entirety of its fiduciary *powers*, it may not divest itself of the totality of its fiduciary *responsibilities*. Although these conclusions are consistent with the dictates of the fiduciary concept, they have not been recognized in existing case law.

In two cases launched by Aboriginal groups in the English courts prior to the repatriation of the Canadian Constitution — *R. v. Secretary of State for Foreign & Commonwealth Affairs*, [1982] 2 All E.R. 118, [1982] Q.B. 892, [1982] 2 W.L.R. 641 (C.A.) and *Manuel v. Attorney General*, [1982] 3 All E.R. 786 (Ch. Div.), aff'd. [1982] 3 All E.R. 822, [1983] 1 Ch. 77, [1982] 3 W.L.R. 821 (C.A.) — the English courts held that while Britain once possessed certain obligations towards the Aboriginal peoples of Canada, it no longer held any such responsibility; those duties, such as they were, were deemed to have been transferred to Canada. It should be emphasized, however, that neither of these cases dealt with the issue of the British Crown's fiduciary obligations towards the Aboriginal peoples, nor did they address the principle of *delegatus non potest delegare*.

While the passage of time does not forgive a breach of fiduciary duty, allegations of breaches of fiduciary duty may be defeated by applicable statutory limitation periods or equitable bars, such as laches (these are discussed, *infra*). Practically speaking, any attempt to obtain a remedy from the British Crown for a breach of fiduciary duty at this late date would be seriously impeded by its devolution of responsibility over Canadian affairs to the Canadian federal and provincial Crowns. For more detailed consideration of the British Crown's duty and its ramifications, see Rotman, *Parallel Paths, supra*.

F.   EQUITABLE AND STATUTORY BARS TO BREACH OF FIDUCIARY DUTY CLAIMS

As seen in many of the cases discussed herein, often a band's claim against the Crown for breach of its fiduciary obligations arises long after the alleged breach of duty occurred. This creates problems for contemporary breach of fiduciary duty claims, insofar as many bands were unaware of their rights for considerable periods of time and, at one time, were statutorily prevented from commencing legal actions against the federal Crown under the *Indian Act*.[1] The problems associated with the use of breach of fiduciary duty actions by Aboriginal peoples against the Crown have been addressed in a limited way by the Alberta *Limitations Act*, R.S.A. 2000, c. L-12, s. 13, which exempts certain claims for breach of fiduciary duty brought by Aboriginal peoples against the Crown from the application of the current Act and its ultimate limitation period (although they are still subject to the limits established by its predecessor). Section 13 states:

> 13. An action brought on or after March 1, 1999 by an aboriginal people against the Crown based on a breach of a fiduciary duty alleged to be owed by the Crown to those people is governed by the law on limitation of actions as if the *Limitation of Actions Act*, R.S.A. 1980 c. L-15, had not been repealed and this Act were not in force.

Note that the reference in the Act to "the Crown" does not distinguish between federal and provincial Crowns.

In addition, the Ontario *Limitations Act*, R.S.O. 1990, c. L.15 does not presently contain a limitation period applicable to actions based upon alleged breaches of fiduciary duty. While Ontario has passed new limitations legislation (which was not proclaimed in force at the time this book went to press) that will cover equitable causes of action including breach of fiduciary duty, section 2(3) expressly excludes from its operation "proceedings based on equitable claims by Aboriginal peoples against the Crown," thereby maintaing the status quo in respect of such claims.

In the *Wewaykum* case, below, the Supreme Court of Canada addressed some of the concerns associated with the use of equitable and statutory bars to allegations of breach of fiduciary duty brought by Aboriginal peoples against the Crown.

WEWAYKUM INDIAN BAND v. CANADA

2002 SCC 79 (references omitted)

[The facts and issues in *Wewaykum* are detailed in the excerpt of the case found earlier in this chapter. The following discussion concerns only the effect of equitable and statutory bars to breach of fiduciary duty claims brought by Aboriginal peoples against the Crown.]

5. Enforcement of equitable duties by equitable remedies is subject to
the usual equitable defences, including laches and acquiescence.

One of the features of equitable remedies is that they not only operate "on the conscience" of the wrongdoer, but require equitable conduct on the part of the claimant. They are not available as of right. Equitable remedies are always subject to the discretion of the court ...

Equity has developed a number of defences that are available to a defendant facing an equitable claim such as a claim for breach of fiduciary duty. One of them, the doctrine of laches and acquiescence, is particularly applicable here. This equitable doctrine applies even if a claim is not barred by statute. ...

. . . . .

The doctrine of laches is applicable to bar the claims of an Indian band in appropriate circumstances ...

It seems to me both branches of the doctrine of laches and acquiescence apply here, namely: (i) where "the party has, by his conduct done that which might fairly be regarded as equivalent to a waiver", and (ii) such conduct "results in circumstances that make the prosecution of the action unreasonable" (*M. (K.) v. M. (H.), supra,* at pp. 76 and 78). Conduct equivalent to a waiver is found in the declaration, representations and failure to assert "rights" in circumstances that required assertion, as previously set out. Unreasonable prosecution arises because, relying on the *status quo*, each band improved the reserve to which it understood its sister band made no further claim. All of this was done with sufficient knowledge "of the underlying facts relevant to a possible legal claim" (*M. (K.) v. M. (H.), supra*, at p. 79).

I conclude therefore that the claims of the appellant bands were rightly rejected on their merits by the trial judge.

O. In Any Event, the Claims of the Appellant Bands are Statute Barred

Having rejected the appellants' claims to each other's lands on their merits I need not, strictly speaking, address the limitations issue. However, as this ground was extensively canvassed in the courts below and in argument before this Court, it should be dealt with.

This case originated in the Federal Court. It is therefore subject to the limitation provisions contained in the *Federal Court Act* and, in particular, s. 39(1):

> **39.** (1) Except as expressly provided by any other Act, the laws relating to prescription and the limitation of actions in force in any province between subject and subject apply to any proceedings in the Court in respect of any cause of action arising in that province.

Section 39(1) effectively incorporates by reference the applicable British Columbia limitation legislation, but the relevant provisions apply as federal law not as provincial law ...

1. Constitutionality of the Prescription Period

The appellant bands raise the threshold objection that provincial law cannot "extinguish" the Indian interest, which is a matter of exclusive federal legislative competence, *Canadian Pacific Ltd. v. Paul*, [1988] 2 S.C.R. 654, at p. 673. Section 9 of the B.C. Act provides for extinguishment of the cause of action, but, as stated, it applies as federal law.

Parliament is entitled to adopt, in the exercise of its exclusive legislative power, the legislation of another jurisdictional body, as it may from time to time exist: *Coughlin v. Ontario Highway Transport Board*, [1968] S.C.R. 569; *Ontario (Attorney General) v. Scott*, [1956] S.C.R. 137. This is precisely what Parliament did when it enacted what is now s. 39(1) of the *Federal Court Act*.

. . . . .

4. Alleged Harshness of the Prescription Ban

The Cape Mudge Band argues that the limitation periods otherwise applicable in this case should not be allowed to operate as "instruments of injustice" (factum, at para. 104). However, the policies behind a statute of limitations (or "statute of repose") are well known ... Witnesses are no longer available, historical documents are lost and difficult to contextualize, and expectations of fair practices change. Evolving standards of conduct and new standards of liability eventually make it unfair to judge actions of the past by the standards of today. ...

The need for repose is evident in this case. Each band had settled and legitimate expectations with respect to the reserve it now inhabits. Each band still recognizes the need for repose of its sister band (thus seeking compensation from the Crown rather than dispossession of its sister band). Each band claims repose for itself, thus pleading the limitation period in its own defence against the other band.

This is not to say that historical grievances should be ignored, or that injustice necessarily loses its sting with the passage of the years. Here, however, the bands had independent legal advice at least by the 1930s, and were aware at that time of the material facts, if not all the details, on which the present claims are based. While the feeling may not have been unanimous, each band membership elected not to disturb its neighbours. The conduct of each band between 1907 and 1936 suggests that not only was the other band's open and notorious occupation of its reserve acknowledged, but such occupation was considered, as between the bands, to be fair and equitable.

The Campbell River Band at para. 30 and again at para. 133 of its factum links initiation of these proceedings to a new awareness precipitated by the release of the *Guerin* decision in 1984 of the possibility of financial compensation against the Crown. Awareness of the availability of a claim in equity for financial compensation against the Crown does not, however, turn what the band regarded as an equitable situation into an inequitable situation.

5. Applicable Limitation Period

The causes of action at issue in the present appeal arose prior to July 1, 1975, the date on which the new B.C. *Limitations Act* came into force. If the appellants' causes of action were already extinguished by July 1, 1975 (*Limitation Act* (1979), s. 14(1)), it is *prima facie* the 1897 version of the B.C. *Statute of Limitations*, R.S.B.C. 1897, c. 123, which was in force in British Columbia between 1897 and 1975, that applies. If not so extinguished, the provisions of the new version of this *Limitations Act* apply.

. . . . .

With respect to the claims against the Crown based on breach of fiduciary duty, the 1897 Act imposed no limitation, and the case therefore falls to be decided under the transitional provisions of the 1975 Act. While the new Act is also silent with respect to an action for breach of fiduciary duty, or an action for declaration as to the title to property by a person that is not in possession of it, s. 3(4) of the B.C. *Limitations Act* provides a general six-year limitation period:

> 3(4) Any other action not specifically provided for in this Act or any other Act shall not be brought after the expiration of 6 years after the date on which the right to do so arose.

Section 14(3) of the 1975 *Limitations Act* therefore applied to bar actions for breach of fiduciary duty at the expiry of the grace period on July 1, 1977: *Bera v. Marr* (1986), 1 B.C.L.R. (2d) 1 (C.A.); *Squamish Indian Band v.*

Canada (2001), 207 F.T.R.1 , at paras. 724-30; *Kruger, supra.* The appellants' causes of action in these respects were therefore statute barred when they filed their respective statements of claim.

In any event, the claims asserted in these proceedings are all caught by the "ultimate limitation period" in s. 8 of the 1975 *Limitations Act* which says that "no action to which this Act applies shall be brought after the expiration of 30 years from the date on which the right to do so arose". The applicability of this limitation was affirmed in *Blueberry River*, at para. 107. The 30-year "ultimate" limit is subject to very limited exceptions, none of which apply here.

Finally, it is appropriate to note in support of the limitations policy an observation made by the trial judge, at para. 520:

> ... for much of the century, members of both bands had first hand knowledge of the important events which are the subject of these actions. Unfortunately, within the last 30 years, those band members as well as the Indian Agents, have died and many of their documents have been lost or destroyed.

6. The Assertion of Continuing Breach

The appellants contend that every day they are kept out of possession of the other band's reserve is a fresh breach, and a fresh cause of action. As a result, their respective claims are not yet statute barred (and could never be). ...

Acceptance of such a position would, of course, defeat the legislative purpose of limitation periods. For a fiduciary, in particular, there would be no repose. In my view such a conclusion is not compatible with the intent of the legislation. ... It was open to both bands to commence action no later than 1943 when the Department of Indian Affairs finally amended the relevant Schedule of Reserves. There was no repetition of an allegedly injurious act after that date. The damage (if any) had been done. There is nothing in the circumstances of this case to relieve the appellants of the general obligation imposed on all litigants either to sue in a timely way or to forever hold their peace.

Similarly, the "ultimate limitation" in s. 8(1) runs "from the date on which the right to [initiate proceedings] arose". All of the necessary ingredients of the causes of action pleaded in these proceedings could have been asserted more than 30 years prior to the date on which the actions were eventually commenced. The trial judge found that no new or fresh cause of action had arisen at any time within the 30-year period. None of the legislated exceptions being applicable, the 30-year "ultimate limit" applies by reason of its incorporation by reference into federal law.

This conclusion accords with the result on this point reached in *Semiahmoo Indian Band v. Canada*, [1998] 1 F.C. 3 (C.A.), *per* Isaac C.J., at para. 63; *Costigan v. Ruzicka* (1984), 13 D.L.R. (4th) 368 (Alta. C.A.), at pp. 373-74; *Lower Kootenay Indian Band, supra; Fairford First Nation v. Canada (Attorney General)*, [1999] 2 F.C. 48 (T.D.), at paras. 295-99.

The following excerpt amplifies the concepts of laches and acquiescence addressed in *Wewaykum*.

LEONARD I. ROTMAN, "PARALLEL PATHS: FIDUCIARY DOCTRINE AND THE CROWN-NATIVE RELATIONSHIP IN CANADA"

(Toronto: University of Toronto Press, 1996) at 192-3
(references omitted)

Laches and Acquiescence

The applicability of the doctrine of laches to a breach of fiduciary duty is quite rare. Laches is an equitable doctrine which estops, or prevents, a plaintiff from asserting a right or claim by virtue of the combination of having taken too long to assert that right or claim and the prejudice that would result to the adverse party if the allegation was allowed to proceed after such a delay. It should be noted that mere delay alone is insufficient to ground a defence of laches. The delay must have the effect of demonstrating the plaintiff's acquiescence to the defendant's conduct, thereby implying the waiver of any rights or claims belonging to the plaintiff arising from the defendant's conduct. Acquiescence, in this context, entails the plaintiff's objective knowledge of the existence of and right to bring forth any equitable rights or claims based on certain facts — as opposed to merely having knowledge of the facts, but not knowing that they give rise to any right or claim. The plaintiff, therefore, must know of the existence of the defendant's conduct, the wrongfulness of that conduct, and that the wrongful conduct creates the basis of an equitable action. It should also be noted that acquiescence, on its own, may constitute a defence to a claim of breach of fiduciary duty by virtue of the prospective plaintiff's knowledge of and deemed acquiescence to the wrongful activity.

· · · · ·

... [L]aches may only be successfully pleaded by a defendant to an equitable proceeding where there is a demonstration of prejudice to the defendant occasioned by the delay in bringing the proceedings caused by the plaintiff's action or inaction. The time from which the reasonableness of any delay is determined is the time at which the plaintiff first acquires sufficient knowledge of the facts which give rise to a cause of action. The determination of whether there has been unreasonable delay sufficient to constitute the basis of a claim of laches is, like all other equitable doctrines, situation-specific. It must, therefore, be made in light of the facts which give rise to the situation leading up to the allegation of delay.

The equitable doctrine of laches prevents a remedy from being granted where it would be unjust to do so in the circumstances. ... Consequently, where a beneficiary asserts a claim against a fiduciary, the doctrine of laches will generally not apply.

G. THE TENTATIVE APPLICATION OF FIDUCIARY PRINCIPLES

In spite of the widespread acknowledgment of the Crown-Native fiduciary relationship and its constitutionalization in section 35(1) of the *Constitution Act, 1982*, the judiciary has remained tentative in its application of fiduciary principles to Crown-Native relations. This tentativeness has prolonged the uncertainty that has surrounded the application of fiduciary law to Crown-Native relations since the *Guerin* decision.

Because of this uncertainty, a great deal of speculation about the future application of fiduciary law to Crown-Native relations exists. In "Aboriginal Peoples in Canada and the United States and the Scope of the Special Fiduciary Relationship" (1996), 24 Man L.J. 137, David Elliott suggests that post-*Guerin* and *Sparrow* case law has created two distinct strands of fiduciary law's application to Crown-Native relations. One strand, flowing from *Guerin*, is based on some relationship with Aboriginal land and related interests. The other, based on *Sparrow*, has been applied primarily to governmental regulation of Aboriginal hunting and fishing. Unlike the *Guerin* obligation, it is a governmental obligation to apply constitutionally protected rights in favour of Aboriginal peoples. Does your reading of the *Sparrow* case suggest that the fiduciary duty it contemplates is different than that articulated in *Guerin*? Alternatively, does *Sparrow* adopt and extend the understanding of the fiduciary concept and its application to Crown-Native relations set out in *Guerin*?

In *Guerin*, the Supreme Court of Canada rooted its finding of a Crown-Native fiduciary relationship in the historical interaction between the parties. The *Sparrow* decision also determined that the Crown's fiduciary obligations emanated from historical Crown-Native relations. As the Supreme Court explained, "The relationship between the government and aboriginals is trust-like, rather than adversarial, and contemporary recognition and affirmation of aboriginal rights must be defined in light of this historic relationship." Thus, it would appear that the findings of Crown-Native fiduciary relations in both *Guerin* and *Sparrow* are premised upon the historical interaction between the parties. The fiduciary relationship is simply one aspect of a broader Crown-Native relationship that includes fiduciary relations, treaty relations, and nation-to-nation relations (under which Aboriginal self-government falls).

There is considerable overlap between these different forms of Crown-Native relations. For instance, some Crown-Native fiduciary relations stem from treaties signed between the parties, while treaties may be perceived as concrete manifestations of Crown fiduciary obligations. Therefore, while the Crown's fiduciary obligations encroach into these other relations, not every aspect of Crown-Native relations is tinged by fiduciary obligations. Rather, the specific facts of individual interactions must be scrutinized in order to determine whether any component(s) of those interactions are fiduciary.

This relationship-based conception of the Crown's fiduciary obligations is shared by Alan Pratt, who suggests that Crown-Native fiduciary relations and aboriginal self-government are complementary.

ALAN PRATT, "ABORIGINAL SELF-GOVERNMENT AND THE CROWN'S FIDUCIARY DUTY: SQUARING THE CIRCLE OR COMPLETING THE CIRCLE?"

(1992), 2 N.J.C.L. 163 at 166, 169, 180-3, 186-7 (references omitted)

Self-government has so far been a product of political processes, although there has been a great deal of speculation as to extent of the right in law. The fiduciary relationship, and the Crown's fiduciary duties that derive from that relationship, have, by contrast, been the product of the judicial process. In considering the legal and political aspects of the special relationship between the Crown and aboriginal peoples, this is in my view entirely appropriate.

Both are perspectives on a relationship between the Crown and aboriginal peoples that is usually described as special, or in legalese "sui generis." Fiduciary law is the mechanism whereby the *legal* component of the special relationship has been given expression. By contrast, self-government is by its very nature the political aspect of the special relationship.

. . . . .

[B]oth the right of self-government and the fiduciary relationship are *sui generis*. ... My contention is that they are two ways of looking at the same unique relationship, one perspective being primarily legal and the other primarily political.

The two concepts together form a braid. They are part of each other, and they make sense only when they are considered together; when they are analyzed in isolation from each other, each of them can be made into a great lie. The most dangerous lie is that self-government means the end of all government responsibility toward aboriginal communities. This is the view that the fiduciary duty is like an umbilical cord, and upon the achievement of self-government the cord must necessarily be cut.

. . . . .

Undoubtedly, to make any sense of the fiduciary concept and to understand why these legal issues are *sui generis*, let alone to render any legal advice to the application of these principles, it is necessary to understand the theory which underpins aboriginal and treaty rights. It is now clear that the centrepiece of this is the relationship which gives rise to them.

. . . . .

It cannot be forgotten that this law is the product of the European legal and political tradition of Canada. It is not the product of the aboriginal world-view. Therefore, while it can and does respect the existence and vitality of aboriginal legal and political orders within Canada, it is alien to those traditions and cannot directly define the rights and obligations within those aboriginal orders. The fiduciary duty is the "blunt tool" which can police and discipline the Crown, and provide remedies when the Crown has acted dishonourably. It is a body of law which concentrates upon the obligations of the Crown to protect aboriginal peoples from intrusion.

The Canadian law of aboriginal and treaty rights now gives rise to an uncomfortable conundrum. On one hand, the courts of law have been instrumental in giving recognition and affirmation to the right of aboriginal peoples. ... Through the imposition of fiduciary duties, the courts have stimulated the conscience of the Crown and contributed to aboriginal peoples' pride and their arousal as a political force. There is now a rapidly maturing body of law which may be adequate for resolving past grievances such as land claims. Similarly, ongoing rights under treaties to occupy reserve lands and to harvest wildlife may now be given satisfactory scope as the direct result of *Sparrow*.

On the other hand, we must confront the possibility that we are close to the limits of the legitimate role of the law in defining the incidents of the political relationship within which the system of aboriginal and treaty rights, and corresponding obligations, exists. That special relationship as now described by Canadian law is one which is sympathetic to aboriginal peoples and their rights, but it is undoubtedly Eurocentric. It is based on the *de jure* and *de facto* dominance by the Euro-Canadian order, with its central component the fiduciary principle. In turn this principle dictates that the Crown adhere to the principles of *protection* and *respect* in dealings with aboriginal peoples.

. . . . .

The fiduciary duty owed by the Crown is, we know from *Guerin*, "trust-like." This leads some to assume that the aboriginal beneficiaries of this duty are analogous to the beneficiaries of a trust. Namely, that they are somehow incompetent to handle their own affairs; and less than fully mature.

... I do not believe that the "trust-like" analogy means that First Nations are incompetent at all. It means simply that the aboriginal peoples have been colonized. Because their sovereignty has been dominated — one need not say superseded or extinguished — by colonizing powers, they have lost the effective use of their own institutions, at least in the eyes of the dominant legal and political order. The fiduciary duty is only *indirectly* about the rights of aboriginal nations themselves. It is in reality about the responsibility assumed by the Crown in its acts of domination, or imposed upon the Crown as a consequence of those acts.

. . . . .

The fiduciary theory is the guiding force behind the liability of the Crown for various wrongs committed in the course of its extraordinary powers over Indians, and as a result has perhaps overwhelmed the evolution of a political theory based on inherent aboriginal sovereignty. Similarly, judicial decisions often arise from the paternalistic acts of the government in dealings with Indians in the past. A great danger therefore is that the *political* component of aboriginal and treaty rights and the relationship in which they exist may be obscured by legalism. By this I mean that the success of the fiduciary theory, with its analogies to trust law, can distort the real relationship between the fiduciary and self-government strands of the braid, unless it is counterbalanced by an equally strong political accommodation.

Thus what is needed is the reconciliation of these two great ideas. Perhaps the courts can do the reconciling, but probably not. If it is left to the courts to do this then the politicians have failed. When political or even partly political questions are answered by the courts, there are inevitable losers, and the losers equally inevitably reject and resent the decision. The law itself becomes an instrument not of reconciliation and justice but of oppression.

. . . . .

There is no question that the fiduciary duties applicable to the Crown in its dealings with aboriginal peoples arise from a special relationship and that the content of those duties derives from the content and the nature of that relationship. Since that relationship is one between polities or nations, the fiduciary duties must also have relevance to that relationship. At the core of the relationship, as we understand from *Guerin* and *Sparrow*, are the pre-existing rights of aboriginal peoples, the Crown's undertakings to protect aboriginal peoples in the enjoyment of those rights, and the law's concern that the Crown's honour must be upheld in the course of the relationship.

———

While the courts have used fiduciary rhetoric to characterize Crown-Native relations in a number of cases since *Guerin*, they have not truly discussed the implications of describing Crown-Native relations as fiduciary in a particular context. This has reinforced the stasis that characterizes the application of fiduciary law to Crown-Native relations. Judicial use of fiduciary rhetoric without considering the implications of applying the fiduciary concept to Crown-Native relations is not only unsatisfying to litigants, but may appear disingenuous. This idea is raised in the following excerpt.

LEONARD I. ROTMAN, "HUNTING FOR ANSWERS IN A STRANGE KETTLE OF FISH: UNILATERALISM, PATERNALISM AND FIDUCIARY RHETORIC IN BADGER AND VAN DER PEET"

(1997), 8 Constitutional Forum 40 (references omitted)

The Crown's fiduciary duty to the Aboriginal peoples of Canada is a fundamental part of the special, *sui generis* Crown-Native relationship. It requires that the Crown act selflessly, with honesty, integrity and the utmost good faith towards its Aboriginal beneficiaries' interests. This duty, which is binding upon both federal and provincial levels of government, also entails that the Crown must avoid placing itself or being placed in situations that would compromise the Aboriginal peoples' interests. While the extent of the

Crown's fiduciary duty has not yet been judicially considered, it arguably permeates virtually every aspect of Crown-Native relations.

The Crown's fiduciary duty to Aboriginal peoples ... has become a firmly entrenched, vital aspect of Canadian Aboriginal rights jurisprudence. Indeed, since the fiduciary nature of Crown-Native relations was first articulated by the Supreme Court of Canada in *Guerin v. R.*, fiduciary doctrine has been present in a substantial number of that court's Aboriginal rights decisions — the most notable being *R. v. Sparrow* in 1990. The *Sparrow* decision made clear that the Crown's fiduciary duty to Aboriginal peoples applies to Crown-Native relations generally; that it exists as a guiding principle in the consideration of the Aboriginal and treaty rights in section 35(1) of the *Constitution Act, 1982*; and that the duty is, itself, an entrenched element of section 35(1).

As a result of its decision in *Sparrow*, the Supreme Court effectively dictated that all future judicial considerations of the Aboriginal and treaty rights encompassed within section 35(1) had to take into account the existence of the Crown's fiduciary obligations. The majority of post-*Sparrow* Aboriginal rights cases have incorporated fiduciary rhetoric into their discussions of Aboriginal and treaty rights. The limited discussion of fiduciary doctrine and its application to the points in dispute in those cases suggest, however, that post-*Sparrow* judicial references to the Crown's fiduciary duty demonstrate a profound reluctance to apply and enforce the Crown's obligations. While Canadian courts may feel obliged to make use of fiduciary rhetoric, their sense of obligation appears to begin and end at recognising the Crown's duty and its incorporation in section 35(1). The recent Supreme Court of Canada decisions in *R. v. Badger* and *R. v. Van der Peet* are clear examples of this phenomenon.

The Supreme Court's discussion of the Crown's fiduciary duty in *Badger* and *Van der Peet* was limited to its recognition as an interpretive principle to guide the Court's analysis of the facts and issues arising in each case. In neither of these cases did the Supreme Court canvass the existence of the Crown's fiduciary obligations as they pertain directly to the respective points in issue. In *Badger*, for example, the Court failed to consider the effect of the Crown's actions on its existing fiduciary obligations under Treaty No. 8. Meanwhile, in *Van der Peet*, the Court did not consider the impact of its conclusions on the Crown's fiduciary obligations to Aboriginal peoples generally. ... [T]he manner in which fiduciary doctrine was used in these decisions strongly indicates that the Supreme Court's invocation of fiduciary rhetoric was more symbolic than real.

R. v. BADGER

In *Badger*, three Treaty No. 8 Indians were charged under the Alberta *Wildlife Act* while hunting on privately-owned land within the boundaries of tracts surrendered under the treaty.

. . . . .

In the course of its judgment, the Supreme Court held that the federal government possessed the ability to override or alter treaty rights guaranteed to Aboriginal peoples by way of unilateral enactments. Specifically, the Court held that the Alberta *Natural Resource Transfer Agreement, 1930* (hereinafter "NRTA"), an amendment to the Canadian Constitution, could override existing treaty rights guaranteed to the Aboriginal signatories to Treaty No. 8 where the treaty's terms were inconsistent or incompatible with the NRTA.

. . . . .

The *Badger* case clearly indicates that treaty rights are considered by the Supreme Court of Canada to be inferior to unilateral constitutional enactments, such as the NRTA. Justice Cory ... held that the NRTA modified treaty rights where they came into conflict with the NRTA, but did not supplant those rights. In a separate concurring judgment ... Sopinka J. determined that the NRTA entirely replaced Treaty No. 8 rights.

. . . . .

Whether adopting the conclusions of Cory or Sopinka JJ., the Supreme Court's analysis in *Badger* explicitly approves the notion that the Crown may enact legislation that infringes upon or eliminates treaty rights without the need to consult or negotiate with Aboriginal peoples or, more importantly, to obtain their consent. What is troubling about this conclusion is that the Court came to it without first considering the effects of the Crown's fiduciary obligations to the Treaty No. 8 signatories. While Canadian courts have held that it was within the Crown's legislative ability to extinguish, modify, or alter treaty rights prior to 17 April, 1982, those courts have never answered whether taking such action offends the Crown's pre-existing fiduciary obligations to the Aboriginal peoples.

In its decision in *Guerin*, the Supreme Court found that the Crown's fiduciary obligations to Aboriginal peoples were rooted in the *Royal Proclamation of 1763*. Consequently, it cannot presently be questioned whether the Crown possessed fiduciary obligations to the Aboriginal peoples when it promulgated the NRTA. Even if the Crown was unaware of the fiduciary nature of its obligations in 1930 — given the fact that those duties were only described as fiduciary in 1984 — it should have recognised that the solemn nature of Aboriginal treaties carried with them legally binding obligations. These treaty obligations ought to have prevented the Crown from unilaterally altering its historical treaty commitments. It should be noted, though, that the Canadian judiciary generally did not recognise treaty obligations as binding in law at that time.

By virtue of the *Guerin* and *Sparrow* decisions, contemporary courts are obliged to render the application of the NRTA subject to the Crown's fiduciary obligations even though the Crown may not have been aware of the fiduciary nature of its duties at that time. While this may appear to be a historical anachronism created by the common law, what is important to consider in this context is not the precise name given to the Crown-Native relationship, but the ramifications of the parties' interaction and whether that gave rise to legally enforceable obligations. This notion is consistent with the theoretical underpinnings of fiduciary doctrine. A relationship's dynamics are what truly causes it to be described as fiduciary, not whether it fits into already-established categories of fiduciary relations. On this basis, it is legitimate to hold the Crown to fiduciary obligations relating to the NRTA's effect on treaties in the present day since the Crown ought to have been aware in 1930 that it could not depart from its treaty promises without being legally bound to account for such a breach.

By upholding the Crown's ability to unilaterally eliminate or override existing treaty rights, the Supreme Court in *Badger* effectively sanctioned the Crown's breach of its general fiduciary duty to act in the best interests of Aboriginal peoples as well as its specific obligations under Treaty No. 8. It is simply not possible for the Crown to have maintained fidelity to its fiduciary duty to act in the best interests of the Aboriginal peoples while it was unilaterally eliminating rights guaranteed to them in treaties. Maintaining the honour of the Crown and avoiding sharp practice in all dealings with the Aboriginal peoples, principles explicitly endorsed in *Badger*, are clearly offended by finding that the NRTA may, without consultation or consent, override or alter the nature of solemn, pre-existing arrangements. The Crown's actions in this regard contradict the solemn and binding nature of Crown-Native treaties, as well as the representations of the Crown therein and in the negotiations leading up to their conclusion. Equally important, the constitutional affirmation and protection of Aboriginal and treaty rights in section 35(1), which incorporates the Crown's fiduciary duty to Native peoples, is itself offended by the Crown's powers as described in *Badger*.

R. v. VAN DER PEET

More recently, the Supreme Court made reference to the Crown's fiduciary obligations in *Van der Peet*, an Aboriginal fishing rights case, where a member of the Sto:lo nation had been charged with selling ten salmon for $50 while fishing under the authority of an Indian food fishing licence. In the course of determining whether the appellant possessed an Aboriginal right to sell fish, Lamer C.J.'s majority judgment held that an activity could only be considered an Aboriginal right if it was an element of a practice, tradition or custom integral to the distinctive culture of the Aboriginal group claiming the right; moreover, that right had to be traceable to pre-contact practices. Under this formulation of Aboriginal rights, any activity arising after contact with Europeans was incapable of being classified as a constitutionally-protected Aboriginal right under section 35(1).

In establishing the framework for his analysis of the right claimed by the appellant, Lamer C.J. emphasised the importance of adopting a purposive approach to section 35(1), as suggested by the Supreme Court in *Sparrow*. He found that this purposive approach, which entailed giving section 35(1) a generous and liberal interpretation in favour of the Aboriginal peoples, stemmed from the fiduciary nature of the relationship between the Crown and Aboriginal peoples. Additionally, he stated that this approach was intended to inform the court's analysis of the purposes underlying section 35(1), as well as that section's definition and scope. Chief Justice Lamer held that the Crown's fiduciary relationship with the Aboriginal peoples required that any doubt or ambiguity as to what ought to properly fall within the scope and definition of section 35(1) was to be resolved in favour of the Aboriginal peoples. Above all, he determined that the fiduciary nature of Crown-Native relations meant that the honour of the Crown was at stake in its dealings with Aboriginal peoples.

Chief Justice Lamer's finding that the appellant did not possess an Aboriginal right to sell fish because that practice was initiated entirely in response to non-Aboriginal settlement contradicts his own statements regarding the fiduciary nature of Crown-Native relations. Arbitrarily limiting the definition of Aboriginal rights to pre-contact practices prohibits the creation of new Aboriginal rights arising from the necessity to maintain the viability of distinctive Aboriginal cultures in the face of European interference with traditional Aboriginal ways of life. This is inconsistent with maintaining the honour of the Crown.

It is circular reasoning to suggest that Aboriginal rights must encompass only those practices that are integral to the distinctive cultures of Aboriginal societies and then, when the presence of European settlement interferes with or renders those practices ineffective, prevent the recognition as Aboriginal rights [of] those new practices arising in response to that European settlement. Insofar as Aboriginal rights are dynamic and evolving, they ought not be restricted to their "primeval simplicity and vigour." Rather, they must be allowed to adapt to changing circumstances. If, as in *Van der Peet*, the fact of European settlement created the cultural and physical need for the Sto:lo people to engage in the sale or barter of fish, then that activity ought to be regarded as a protected Aboriginal right regardless of whether it was induced and driven by European influences. To hold otherwise would be to deny the purposive application of the interpretive principles derived from the Crown's fiduciary obligations to Aboriginal peoples.

Chief Justice Lamer's determination in *Van der Peet* that "incidental" Aboriginal practices that "piggyback" on Aboriginal rights are not deserving of constitutional protection also has the potential of allowing the Crown to escape its fiduciary obligations to protect fundamental Aboriginal rights. It presents the possibility that Aboriginal rights that are dependent on conditions precedent may be indirectly denied simply by refusing to protect those prior conditions. Where an Aboriginal group has a recognised right to fish, protecting that right necessitates protecting the means necessary for the realisation of that right. Such a requirement would prevent, for example, allowing a marina to be built upstream from where those fishing rights are exercised that destroys the fishing stock. To hold otherwise would render any protection of the right meaningless.

. . . . .

The dissenting judgments of L'Heureux-Dubé and McLachlin JJ. in *Van der Peet* are more faithful to the recognition and enforcement of the Crown's fiduciary obligations than the majority judgment of Lamer C.J. Justice L'Heureux-Dubé recognised that the definition of Aboriginal rights must take place within "the broader context of the historical aboriginal reality in Canada," one aspect of which entails that Aboriginal rights must be construed in light of the special fiduciary relationship that exists between the Crown and Aboriginal peoples in Canada. Justice McLachlin emphasised that the determination of whether a practice constituted an Aboriginal right had to "remain true to the position of the Crown throughout Canadian history as trustee or fiduciary for the first peoples of this country." In paying heed to the fiduciary nature of Crown-Native relations, both dissenting judgments found that the existence of Aboriginal rights could not be arbitrarily limited to practices arising prior to contact.

CONCLUSION

The *Badger* and *Van der Peet* cases illustrate that simple judicial recognition of or professed adherence to the Crown's fiduciary obligations to Aboriginal peoples is not identical to the courts' enforcement of those obligations. Effecting the latter necessitates scrutinising the Crown's actions in light of its fiduciary responsibilities. The use of fiduciary rhetoric by the judiciary is rendered meaningless without a commitment to enforce its application in practice. Sanctioning the NRTA's effects on existing treaty rights, as in *Badger*, or the ability of the Crown to circumvent the recognition of legitimate Aboriginal rights, as in *Van der Peet*, is inconsistent with the Crown's historical undertakings towards Aboriginal peoples and their rights. It also trivialises the Crown's fiduciary duty to the point where it appears as nothing more than empty rhetoric.

. . . . .

The existence of the Crown's fiduciary duty in section 35(1) of the *Constitution Act, 1982* is a constitutional imperative to ensure that the Crown lives up to the historical obligations it owes to the Aboriginal peoples. It prescribes onerous obligations on the part of the Crown in its dealings with the Aboriginal peoples. It also provides the Aboriginal peoples with legally enforceable means to ensure either that the Crown lives up to its obligations or furnishes them with remedies where the Crown is found to have breached those obligations. Since the Crown's duty is entrenched within section 35(1), the Canadian judiciary is bound to enforce the Crown's obligations. This constitutional imperative requires more of the courts, rather, than the proliferation of empty rhetoric offered by the Supreme Court of Canada in *Badger* and *Van der Peet*.

Do you agree with Rotman's suggestion that the courts are simply using fiduciary rhetoric to maintain a surface adherence to the dictates of decisions such as *Guerin* and *Sparrow*? Ought fiduciary principles be extended to situations other than *Guerin*- and *Sparrow*-type scenarios? Finally, to what extent did fiduciary law actually form a part of the *Badger* and *Van der Peet* decisions? See the discussion of *Badger* in Chapters 2 and 7 and *Van der Peet* in Chapter 4.

H. CONCLUSION

The application of the fiduciary concept to Crown-Native relations is still in its developmental stages. To this point, fundamental questions surrounding the application of fiduciary principles to Crown-Native relations have yet to be adequately addressed. Instead, the courts have been content to rely on *Guerin* as the basis for their discussion of fiduciary doctrine without engaging in substantive discussions of what the imposition of fiduciary principles upon Crown-Native relations entails. *Wewaykum* looks to be somewhat of a departure from this practice, but it is rather restricted in its articulation of the fiduciary concept's application to Crown-Native relations.

The legacy of post-*Guerin* fiduciary case law remains remarkably short on substance and abundant in confusion. Perhaps not surprisingly, this situation is not entirely different than what the Supreme Court of Canada initially left after its decision in *Guerin*. What is, however, surprising is the continuation of this status quo for such a significant period of time, particularly in light of the importance of the fiduciary concept to the understanding of Crown-Native interaction.

ENDNOTE

1. R.S.C. 1906, c. 81, as amended by *An Act to Amend the Indian Act*, S.C. 1926-27, c. 32, s. 6. The section in question, numbered as s. 149A in the 1906 Act, became s. 141 of the *Indian Act*, R.S.C. 1927, c. 98 and was later repealed by the 1951 consolidation of the *Indian Act*, R.S.C. 1951, c. 29.

CHAPTER 4

ABORIGINAL RIGHTS

A. INTRODUCTION

Aboriginal rights are unlike other forms of rights that exist in Canadian society. Aboriginal rights are a part of Canadian common law, as well as Canadian constitutional law (being enshrined in sections 25 and 35(1) of the *Constitution Act, 1982,* being Schedule B to the *Canada Act 1982* (U.K.), 1982, c. 11). The text of section 35(1) reads as follows:

> 35.(1) The existing aboriginal and treaty rights of the aboriginal peoples of Canada are hereby recognized and affirmed.

Aboriginal rights have sometimes been described as "rights plus", insofar as they exist in addition to Aboriginal people's other common law rights, including those enumerated in the *Canadian Charter of Rights and Freedoms* [Part I of the *Constitution Act, 1982,* being Schedule B to the *Canada Act 1982* (U.K.), 1982, c. 11].

Aboriginal rights differ from other common law rights in another significant respect. Generally, rights in a democratic society are dependent upon their recognition or affirmation by governmental authority or law. Aboriginal rights exist because they are derived from Aboriginal practices, customs, and traditions. They exist in Canadian law not because of governmental recognition, but because they were not extinguished upon British or French assertions of sovereignty or their establishment of governmental authority in what is now Canada. By a process known as the Doctrine of Continuity, the rights of the Aboriginal peoples remained in place and were, in fact, received into British law where they were not explicitly altered or abrogated or where they were not incompatible with British law.[1]

In most instances, pre-existing Aboriginal rights were not altered or abrogated; rather, they were affirmed through treaties and historical practices (as evidenced, for example, by the *Royal Proclamation of 1761,* and documents such as the *Royal Proclamation of 1763,* R.S.C. 1985, App. II, No. 1). Whether received into the common law through treaties or under the Doctrine of Continuity, these Aboriginal rights became enforceable under the common law. The extent to which the common law recognized and enforced these rights, however, was rather limited in practice until after 1982.

Since Aboriginal rights are derived from Aboriginal practices, customs, and traditions, it would appear logical that they ought to be examined in accordance with the circumstances under which they originated and evolved and the manner in which they were exercised by the Aboriginal peoples. However, Canadian courts have not always looked to Aboriginal cultures or societies in their attempts to understand the content of Aboriginal rights.

The Supreme Court of Canada's decision in *Jack and Charlie v. R.*, below, provides a good illustration both of the difficulties faced by Canadian courts in addressing Aboriginal rights claims as well as those courts' methods of examining such rights.

JACK and CHARLIE v. R.

(1985), 21 D.L.R. (4th) 641, [1985] 2 S.C.R. 332, [1986] 1 W.W.R. 21, 69 B.C.L.R. 201, [1985] 4 C.N.L.R. 88, 21 C.C.C. (3d) 481, 62 N.R. 14, [1986] D.L.Q. 81 (references omitted)

Beetz J.: —

. . . . .

II — *The facts*

For the most part, the facts are not in dispute. They can be read in the judgments of the courts below, all of which have now been reported.

... [In the British Columbia Court of Appeal's decision in the case] Taggart J.A. thus began the recital of the facts:

> The appellants are both members of the Tsartlip Band of Indians and live on the Tsartlip Indian Reserve in Saanich, British Columbia. The Tsartlip Band is one of the bands making up the Coast Salish people. Elizabeth Jack is the wife of the appellant Anderson Jack and the sister of the appellant George Louie Charlie. She was present when her brother shot a deer on Pender Island at a place which is not within an Indian reserve. Anderson Jack helped George Louie Charlie load the dead deer into the trunk of their car. The three then drove to the place where they had been staying on Pender Island and there cleaned and dressed the deer. Later as they were driving to the ferry which would take them to Saanich they were stopped by police officers who found the deer carcass in the trunk of the car.

... [T]he trial judge said: "The two accused testified they had committed the act in order to help Elizabeth Jack obtain raw deer meat for a burning ceremony for her great-grandfather."

. . . . .

[T]he county court judge wrote:

> They freely admitted to the killing and possession; their plea before the provincial court, and here, is one of confession and avoidance. The deer, they contend (and the evidence on this point is accepted in its entirety by the Crown) was killed in preparation for a religious ceremony, in which the meat thereof would be burned to satisfy the requirements of an ancestor by means of a sort of reverse transubstantiation.

The religious ceremony and its meaning were described by several defence witnesses. Here is what Taggart J.A. wrote about this:

The religious ceremony was described by witnesses who were members of the Tsartlip Band and by Dr. Barbara Lane. Dr. Lane is an anthropologist who since 1948 has studied the Coast Salish people and especially their religious beliefs and practices. She said that the Coast Salish people were believed to have lived in British Columbia for about 20,000 years. The Coast Salish believe that members of their people who die do not go to another world but that their spirits remain close to where they lived. The belief is that the spirits have the same kinds of needs and desires as living people. Dr. Lane explained the belief in this way:

> They become lonely and want to visit their relatives, they become hungry and want to have the kind of foods that they had before, and they have desires for things that they've left behind here, and they transmit these desires to their close relatives through dreams and other kinds of experiences, and these needs are satisfied and the desires of the deceased relatives are met by the living providing to them the things that they request.

. . . . .

As I was attempting to suggest earlier, the entire world view of the Coast Salish Indian people is quite different from that which those of us who are raised in the Judaeo-Christian tradition have. Coast Salish Indian people perceive of the world as an intimately inter-related phenomenon in which the living and the dead animals and humans, all things are intimately connected and belong together in this place and do not leave it. And the function of burning food for the dead is to carry on the mutual responsibilities and respect that Indian people here try to accord to all of the other parts of the world as they see it. One of the things that always seems to be incomprehensible to Indian people is how the rest of us can pick ourselves up from one part of the world and move to another and abandon and cut ourselves off from our dead relatives because they perceive of themselves as being in continuous association with and having ongoing responsibilities to the dead.

Dr. Lane described the practice of serving the spirits of the dead by burning food.

> A   Well, this is a very ancient traditional practice among all Coast Salish people and the essence of the ceremony is to provide food for deceased relatives by burning it and the essence of the food, as I understand it, is transmitted through the smoke to the essence of the deceased person.

Dr. Lane said that the practice of burning food for the dead had been described in articles by other anthropologists who had studied the practices of the Coast Salish people.

The religious practices described by Dr. Lane were also spoken of by elders of the Tsartlip Band and by the appellants and Elizabeth Jack. The latter said she had been visited by the spirit of her great-grandfather who had asked that she burn raw meat for him. She sought the assistance of her husband and her brother to obtain raw deer meat for the burning ceremony.

There can be no doubt about the sincerity of the appellants' religious beliefs. Here is what the trial judge held on this subject:

> That evidence was interesting, revealing the religious beliefs and practices of the Coast Salish Indians and of the Saanich people, part of the Coast

Salish tribe or culture, to which people the two accused and Mrs. Elizabeth Jack belong, as well as the witnesses for the defence Louie Charlie, David Elliott, Tom Sampson, Samuel Sam, Louie Charlie and Philip Paul. I should also say at the outset that I believe the defence is put forward sincerely by these people and that they are, so far as appears, quite law abiding persons who committed the act rather fearfully, but apparently in the *bona fide* effort to obtain deer meat for a religious ceremony. The impression I obtained from the evidence was that they were fearful of breaking the law, because they are law abiding persons usually.

. . . . .

I must say, also, that I found the elders of the Saanich people impressive. Some of those who spoke in English are very articulate, although they are naturally inclined to use few words, but ingenuously poetic in a manner which obviously springs from deep sincerity.

III — *The defences offered by the appellants*

The submissions made by counsel for the appellants to this Court appear to have been substantially the same as those made to the courts below. They can be summarized in three propositions:

1. The *Wildlife Act* interferes with the appellants' freedom of religion and ought to be read down so as not to apply to them in the circumstances of this case.
2. In interfering with aboriginal religion, the *Wildlife Act* goes to the root of Indianness, and purports to regulate the appellants *qua* Indians; it accordingly should be held inapplicable to them.
3. Apart from religion, hunting is at the root of the culture and way of life of the Coast Salish people so that its prohibition attains the appellants *qua* Indians and ought to be held inapplicable to them.

I must observe however that the reading of the reasons given by the courts below does not clearly disclose whether the third proposition was advanced there as distinct from the second one.

More should be also said about the legal basis relied upon for the freedom of religion invoked in the first proposition.

This basis is not a statutory one ... there was no ... statutory provision relating to the freedom of worship or religion in force in British Columbia at the time the offence was committed.

This basis is not either a paramount constitutional or *quasi*-constitutional instrument. The *Canadian Charter of Rights and Freedoms* had not been enacted at the time the offence was committed. As for the *Canadian Bill of Rights*, counsel for the appellants expressly declined to rely upon it on the ground that it applied only to federal legislation whereas the *Wildlife Act* was a provincial statute. ... Neither before the trial judge, nor before the other courts below, nor before this Court was it considered whether the *Canadian Bill of Rights* might govern the *Wildlife Act* if the latter Act applied to Indians not *ex proprio vigore* but by referential adoption under s. 88 of the *Indian Act*, R.S.C. 1970, c. I-6.

The legal basis relied upon for the freedom of religion invoked by the appellants, as I understand it, is a fundamental principle of law ... of the same nature as the freedom of the press ... This fundamental freedom, while not absolute and subject to some legal restrictions, possesses, it is claimed, a degree of paramountcy over or exempting force from provincial law of general application, provided certain conditions are satisfied in what is called a balancing test. Here is how counsel for the appellants express themselves on this point in their factum:

> That in construing the application of a valid Provincial law of general application against a fundamental freedom, the Courts should apply a balancing test. The balancing test may be stated as follows: where the religious belief is held to be in good faith, and where the conduct is held to be justified to the practice of the religion, and where no compelling state interest is found to justify the curtailment of the religious practice, the general legislation must be applied so as to preserve the fundamental freedom.

It will readily be seen that this balancing test resembles closely the one which would be required if s. 1 of the *Canadian Charter of Rights and Freedoms* were applicable. In their factum, counsel for the appellants concede that there is no direct authority for their submission but argue that, even prior to the coming into force of the *Canadian Charter of Rights and Freedoms*, the balancing test has been used implicitly as the framework for analysis in some cases which need not be reviewed in these reasons, given the view I take of the case at bar.

IV — *The judgments of the courts below*

The trial judge ... relied upon the decision of this Court in *Kruger and Manuel v. The Queen* ... and thereafter made what in my opinion are crucial findings:

> In *Kruger and Manuel v. The Queen* (1977), 34 C.C.C. (2d) 377, 75 D.L.R. (3d) 434, [1978] 1 S.C.R. 104, the Supreme Court of Canada considered the very statute which is said to have been breached here, and decided unanimously that it was a statute of general application and a valid enactment, having as its object the conservation and management of provincial wildlife resources and that the accused, who were Indians, were subject to its provisions so long as the Act, in its policy, did not seek to impair the status and capacities of the accused *as Indians*. It is here contended that the effect of the provision which is sought by the Crown to be enforced is to impair the status of the accused *as Indians* by preventing them from exercising their *bona fide* religious practices. I am unable to accept that contention. To do so may well prevent the effective management and conservation of provincial wildlife resources. If Indians wish to exercise their historic religious practices there are ways within the bounds of the provincial statute in which to exercise those religious practices. They can, for example, retain a supply of deer meat in storage for such purposes. Section 9 [rep. & sub. 1971, c. 69, s. 9] of the *Wildlife Act* makes provision for that. The purposes of the Act is what matters. This Act has been held to be and is, clearly, I think, of general application and was certainly not aimed at preventing the Coast Salish from exercising any religious practice, and the act of burning food as an offering to the spirit of an ancestor is not prohibited. If it is exercised within the limits of the general law it may be freely carried out by the Saanich people.

. . . . .

V — *The submissions of the Crown*

· · · · ·

The fundamental issue in this case, says the Crown, is "whether hunting by Indians for the propitiation of the dead enjoys higher constitutional protection than hunting for sustenance of the living". If it does not, then the judgment of this Court in the *Kruger and Manuel* case is indistinguishable and conclusive. It was decided in that case that Indians hunting for food had no constitutional defence to a charge under s. 4(1)(c) of the *Wildlife Act*, — hunting in close season — the very section at issue in the case at bar.

The Crown submits that, for two reasons, the *Kruger and Manuel* case cannot be distinguished on the basis that s. 4(1)(c) of the *Wildlife Act* interferes with the appellants' freedom of religion. The two reasons are that

(a) the hunting itself was not a religious practice;
(b) the intended use of the deer meat in a religious ceremony amounts to "motive" and is therefore irrelevant to legal culpability.

In my opinion, which I express with the greatest of respect, the learned dissenting judge erred in stating that the "the hunting and killing was a part of a religious ritual". And the appellants' counsel are also in error in writing in their factum that there was an undisputed and unchallenged finding of fact to that effect at trial. There is no such finding in the reasons of the trial judge. In fact he expressly found that the *Wildlife Act* did not interfere with or prohibit appellants' religious practices which could be carried out with deer meat retained in storage and he referred to a section of the *Wildlife Act* which makes provision for that. The trial judge wrote ... that "the fact that the deer was killed to obtain deer meat for use in a religious ceremony, as here, is no defence".

This was confirmed in appeal by the country court judge who ... accepted appellants' contentions, unchallenged by the Crown, that the deer had been killed "in preparation for a religious ceremony". There is no suggestion that the deer was killed as part of the ceremony.

These conclusions are entirely consistent with the evidence which is detailed and precise in the description of the ceremony itself but bare and perfunctory in the description of the killing.

There was some evidence that the type of food to be burned was of significance and that raw deer meat was required in this case but no evidence as to the circumstances or methods of obtaining it, except by theft, which would render the meat unsuitable. There was no evidence that the use of defrosted raw deer meat was sacrilegious as is alleged in the appellants' factum. There was evidence that the food had to be disposed in several plates to provide for the guests of the honoured spirit, that the shaman presiding over the ceremony pronounced a name over each plate, that attendants had to remain at a certain distance from the fire, that cedar wood was preferred for the burning.

By contrast, there was no evidence that the killing of the deer was part of the religious ceremony. Mrs. Jack has previously hired two men to get her a deer. Since they failed to do so, she asked her husband and her brother for assistance. When the three of them saw the deer, her brother came out of the car and shot the deer five or six times with an automatic rifle. If he had shot two deers on the same spot, in the same manner, at the same time, one deer for a burning and one for food, there is no indication that any one of them was more suitable for one purpose than for the other.

As to the analogy drawn by the dissenting justice of appeal with the drinking of wine for sacramental purposes, here is what the Crown has to say in its factum:

> The offence in question relates to the circumstances of obtaining meat for the ceremony, not the conduct of the ceremony itself, hence the analogy of the clergyman committing an offence under the *Liquor Act* by conducting the sacrament of Holy Communion, drawn by Hutcheon, J.A. in the Court of Appeal (in dissenting reasons relied upon by the Appellants) is inapt.

> The *Wildlife Act* does not in any way prohibit or regulate the burning ceremony, it regulates the killing of deer, meat from which may be used for such a ceremony.

> To draw the parallel analogy, the obtaining of wine for sacramental purposes is not part of the sacrament of Holy Communion, and regulation of the sale of wine does not, therefore, prohibit the exercise of that religious ceremony. Such regulation cannot, therefore, be said to affect religious freedom.

> No clergyman could raise a defence based on religious freedom, to a charge of obtaining wine illegally while liquor stores were closed, simply because it was intended to use the wine for the sacrament of Holy Communion. Similarly a defence based on 'freedom of religion' must fail the Appellants in this case, where the charge is killing a deer in the closed season. Since killing a deer is not, in itself, ceremonial, the *actus reus* of the offence cannot be regarded as a religious observance. If it is not such an observance, then logically, its prohibition by the *Wildlife Act* raises no question of religious freedom.

I agree with the statement and with its conclusion that the prohibition of deer killing by the *Wildlife Act* raises no question of religious freedom.

It follows that appellants' main defence, relating to freedom of religion, as well as their second defence, relating to aboriginal religion, are without substance and must be dismissed.

In addition, I find no error in the Crown's second submission which is presented as follows in its factum:

> The intention of the Appellants that the deer meat be used for the burning ceremony was their 'ulterior intention' or 'motive'. As such, it is irrelevant to legal responsibility for the commission of the offence: *Lewis v. The Queen*, [1979] 2 S.C.R. 821 at 833.

> This can be illustrated as follows: if the two men hired by Mrs. Jack to 'get [her] a deer' had killed a deer without knowledge of Mrs. Jack's intended use of it, the defence raised by the Appellants would be unavailable to them, even if the deer had actually been ceremonially burned. The ultimate, actual or intended 'end' of killing the deer is ulterior to the *mens rea* of the offence, and is therefore irrelevant.

> Since the 'ulterior intention' of the Appellants is irrelevant as an element of the offence, the fact it is based on a religious belief, however *bona fide*,

must logically be irrelevant as well, and can therefore provide no basis for the defence advanced by the Appellants.

VI — *The third defence offered by the appellants*

That defence to the effect that, apart from religion, hunting is at the root of the culture and way of life of the Coast Salish people so that its prohibition attains the appellants *qua* Indians is indistinguishable from the defence dismissed in *Arthur Andrew Dick and Her Majesty the Queen*, in which judgment is being delivered today. It should accordingly be dismissed for the same reasons in the case at bar.

VII — *Conclusions*

I would dismiss the appeal and make no order as to costs.

Appeal dismissed.

The *Jack and Charlie* case, above, raises a number of issues relating to the Court's treatment of the Aboriginal rights in question. Some of these issues are discussed in the following excerpt.

JOHN BORROWS & LEONARD I. ROTMAN, "THE SUI GENERIS NATURE OF ABORIGINAL RIGHTS: DOES IT MAKE A DIFFERENCE?"

(1997), 36 Alta. L. Rev. 9 at 43–44 (references omitted)

What the court in *Jack and Charlie* failed to appreciate is that the *sui generis* content of Aboriginal rights encompasses more than the specific practice itself. The killing of the deer has consequences beyond its "fact" as an isolated Aboriginal practice; it has significance as a Salish legal exigency, and as an event related to the cultural survival of the group. The Supreme Court's description of the specific practice of burning the raw deer meat fails to recognize these elements. For example, the burning of the deer meat entails more than the actual tracking and killing of an animal and offering its flesh. The activity includes the entire process leading up to and including that specific practice, and is enmeshed in the web of legal obligations required within the Salish nation. It is an experience that sustains the cultural and physical survival of the group.

Considering the practice by sole reference to the deer meat (and thus suggesting that frozen deer could be a substitute), misses the cultural and legal context within which the ceremony is performed. There is no appreciation of the matrix of family responsibilities and relationships that are triggered by the requirement of obtaining fresh deer meat for this ceremony. There is no understanding of how the people plan for the trip, discuss its purpose, remember the great-grandfather, share their food and supplies, and experience nature together. There is no acknowledgment of the internal contractual and constitutional legal principles which govern the parties' conduct within Salish society. The event's narrow construction overlooks community participation that would accompany the preparation and dressing of a newly killed deer. The Court did not account for the people lifting the deer from the truck, taking it in the house or shed, skinning it, sitting around the table working at it, and discussing their routines and relationships in very specific ways.

Finally, the Court did not mention how the use of fresh deer meat for the ceremony would draw the community together in a way that retrieving frozen deer meat from a freezer never would. The immediacy of life and death would not be as culturally poignant if frozen deer meat were used. These understandings provide the "Aboriginal perspective on the meaning of the right at stake" and illustrate the reasons the Court must look beyond specific fact and site determinations in defining Aboriginal rights. The practices for which protection is sought can not be understood in the same way as one would individual rights. The practices have a collective purpose which underpins their recognition and affirmation – cultural and physical survival. The courts must gain a greater appreciation of this difference. Therefore, in making *sui generis* determinations of Aboriginal rights, courts must look to notions of collective physical and cultural survival, as well as specific Aboriginal laws, customs and practices. Reading both these elements into the jurisprudence would serve as a more appropriate interpretive prism through which the courts may find resolutions to Aboriginal rights disputes.

B. THE CHARACTERIZATION OF ABORIGINAL RIGHTS BY THE COURTS

Since Aboriginal rights exist because of circumstances that arose independently of Europeans' arrival in North America, it would appear logical that the existence of Aboriginal rights would not be dependent upon their recognition by European governments or laws. Yet, Canadian courts have only recently recognized that the existence of those rights is not dependent upon such positive, external recognition.

One of the first cases to recognize that Aboriginal rights had an independent existence and did not have to be recognized by the common law or governmental authority was *Calder v. British Columbia (Attorney General)*, [1973] S.C.R. 313, [1973] 4 W.W.R. 1, 34 D.L.R. (3d) 145, which is reproduced in Chapter 1. The same assertion was made more recently in Lamer C.J.C.'s majority judgment in the Supreme Court of Canada's decision in *R. v. Adams*, [1996] 3 S.C.R. 101, 4 C.N.L.R. 1 at para. 33:

> ... [T]he fact that a particular practice, custom or tradition continued following the arrival of Europeans, but in the absence of the formal gloss of legal recognition from the European colonizers, should not undermine the protection accorded to aboriginal peoples. Section 35(1) would fail to achieve its noble purpose of preserving the integral and defining features of distinctive aboriginal societies if it only protected those defining features

which were fortunate enough to have received the legal approval of British and French colonizers.[2]

The *Adams* decision and its companion case *R. v. Côté*, [1996] 3 S.C.R. 139, 202 N.R. 161, 138 D.L.R. (4th) 385, 110 C.C.C. (3d) 122, [1996] 4 C.N.L.R. 26 are excerpted later in this chapter.

One of the leading cases on the understanding of Aboriginal rights in Canadian law is *R. v. Sparrow*, below (which is also discussed in Chapter 3). The *Sparrow* case focused on the ability of fishing regulations enacted pursuant to the federal *Fisheries Act*, R.S.C. 1970, c. F-14 [now R.S.C. 1985, c. F-14] to restrict the ability of an Aboriginal person to exercise Aboriginal fishing rights.

R. v. SPARROW

(1990), 70 D.L.R. (4th) 385, [1990] 1 S.C.R. 1075, [1990] 4 W.W.R. 410, 46 B.C.L.R. (2d) 1, 56 C.C.C. (3d) 263, 11 N.R. 241, [1990] 3 C.N.L.R. 160

The judgment of the court was delivered by

Dickson C.J.C. and **La Forest J.**: —

. . . . .

The context of this appeal is the alleged violation of the terms of the Musqueam food fishing licence which are dictated by the *Fisheries Act*, R.S.C. 1970, c. F-14, and the regulations under that Act. The issue is whether Parliament's power to regulate fishing is now limited by s. 35(1) of the *Constitution Act, 1982*, and, more specifically, whether the net length restriction in the licence is inconsistent with that provision.

Facts

The appellant, a member of the Musqueam Indian Band, was charged under s. 61(1) of the *Fisheries Act* of the offence of fishing with a drift-net longer than that permitted by the terms of the band's Indian food fishing licence. The fishing which gave rise to the charge took place on May 25, 1984 in Canoe Passage which is part of the area subject to the band's licence. The licence, which had been issued for a one-year period beginning March 31, 1984, set out a number of restrictions including one that drift-nets were to be limited to 25 fathoms in length. The appellant was caught with a net which was 45 fathoms in length. He has throughout admitted the facts alleged to constitute the offence, but has defended the charge on the basis that he was exercising an existing aboriginal right to fish and that the net length restriction contained in the band's licence is inconsistent with s. 35(1) of the *Constitution Act, 1982* and therefore invalid.

. . . . .

The Appeal

... On November 24, 1987, the following constitutional question was stated:

> Is the net length restriction contained in the Musqueam Indian Band Indian Food Fishing Licence dated March 30, 1984, issued pursuant to the *British Columbia Fishery (General) Regulations* and the *Fisheries Act*, R.S.C. 1970, c. F-14, inconsistent with s. 35(1) of the *Constitution Act, 1982*?

. . . . .

Analysis

We will address first the meaning of "existing" aboriginal rights and the content and scope of the Musqueam right to fish. We will then turn to the meaning of "recognized and affirmed", and the impact of s. 35(1) on the regulatory power of Parliament.

"Existing"

The word "existing" makes it clear that the rights to which s. 35(1) applies are those that were in existence when the *Constitution Act, 1982* came into effect. This means that extinguished rights are not revived by the *Constitution Act, 1982*. A number of courts have taken the position that "existing"' means being in actuality in 1982.

. . . . .

Further, an existing aboriginal right cannot be read so as to incorporate the specific manner in which it was regulated before 1982. The notion of freezing existing rights would incorporate into the Constitution a crazy patchwork of regulations. Blair J.A. in *Agawa, supra* [(1988), 53 D.L.R. (4th) 101 (S.C.C.)] had this to say about the matter:

> Some academic commentators have raised a further problem which cannot be ignored. The *Ontario Fishery Regulations* contain detailed rules which vary for different regions in the province. Among other things, the *Regulations* specify seasons and methods of fishing, species of fish which can be caught and catch limits. Similar detailed provisions apply under the comparable fisheries *Regulations* in force in other provinces. These detailed provisions might be constitutionalized if it were decided that the existing treaty rights referred to in s. 35(1) were those remaining after regulation at the time of the proclamation of the *Constitution Act, 1982*.

As noted by Blair J.A., academic commentary lends support to the conclusion that "existing" means "unextinguished" rather than exercisable at a certain time in history. Professor Slattery, "Understanding Aboriginal Rights" (1987), 66 Can. Bar Rev. 727, at pp. 781-82, has observed the following about reading regulations into the rights:

> This approach reads into the Constitution the myriad of regulations affecting the exercise of aboriginal rights, regulations that differed considerably from place to place across the country. It does not permit differentiation between regulations of long-term significance and those enacted to deal

with temporary conditions, or between reasonable and unreasonable restrictions. Moreover, it might require that a constitutional amendment be
enacted to implement regulations more stringent than those in existence on
17 April 1982. This solution seems unsatisfactory.

. . . . .

The unsuitability of the approach can also be seen from another perspective. Ninety-one other tribes of Indians, comprising over 20,000 people
(compared with 540 Musqueam on the reserve and 100 others off the reserve) obtain their food fish from the Fraser River. Some or all of these
bands may have an aboriginal right to fish there. A constitutional patchwork quilt would be created if the constitutional right of these bands were
to be determined by the specific regime available to each of those bands in
1982.

Far from being defined according to the regulatory scheme in place in
1982, the phrase "existing aboriginal rights" must be interpreted flexibly so
as to permit their evolution over time. To use Professor Slattery's expression, in "Understanding Aboriginal Rights," *ibid.*, at p. 782, the word "existing" suggests that those rights are "affirmed in a contemporary form
rather than in their primeval simplicity and vigour". Clearly, then, an approach to the constitutional guarantee embodied in s. 35(1) which would
incorporate "frozen rights" must be rejected.

The Aboriginal Right

We turn now to the aboriginal right at stake in this appeal. The Musqueam
Indian Reserve is located on the north shore of the Fraser River close to the
mouth of that river and within the limits of the City of Vancouver. There
has been a Musqueam village there for hundreds of years. This appeal
does not directly concern the reserve or the adjacent waters, but arises out
of the band's right to fish in another area of the Fraser River estuary
known as Canoe Passage in the South Arm of the river, some 16 kilometres
(about 10 miles) from the reserve. The reserve and those waters are separated by the Vancouver International Airport and the Municipality of
Richmond.

The evidence reveals that the Musqueam have lived in the area as an
organized society long before the coming of European settlers, and that the
taking of salmon was an integral part of their lives and remains so to this
day. Much of the evidence of an aboriginal right to fish was given by Dr.
Suttles, an anthropologist, supported by that of Mr. Grant, the Band ad-
ministrator. The Court of Appeal thus summarized Dr. Suttles' evidence:

> Dr. Suttles was qualified as having particular qualifications in respect of
> the ethnography of the Coast Salish Indian people of which the Musqueams
> were one of several tribes. He thought that the Musqueam had lived in their
> historic territory, which includes the Fraser River estuary, for at least 1,500
> years. That historic territory extended from the north shore of Burrard Inlet
> to the south shore of the main channel of the Fraser River including the wa-
> ters of the three channels by which that river reaches the ocean. As part of
> the Salish people, the Musqueam were part of a regional social network cov-
> ering a much larger area but, as a tribe, were themselves an organized social
> group with their own name, territory and resources. Between the tribes

there was a flow of people, wealth and food. No tribe was wholly self-sufficient or occupied its territory to the complete exclusion of others.

Dr. Suttles described the special position occupied by the salmon fishery in that society. The salmon was not only an important source of food but played an important part in the system of beliefs of the Salish people, and in their ceremonies. The salmon were held to be a race of beings that had, in "myth times", established a bond with human beings requiring the salmon to come each year to give their bodies to the humans who, in turn, treated them with respect shown by performance of the proper ritual. Toward the salmon, as toward other creatures, there was an attitude of caution and respect which resulted in effective conservation of the various species.

While the trial for a violation of a penal prohibition may not be the most appropriate setting in which to determine the existence of an aboriginal right, and the evidence was not extensive, the correctness of the finding of fact of the trial judge "that Mr. Sparrow was fishing in ancient tribal territory where his ancestors had fished from time immemorial in that part of the mouth of the Fraser River for salmon" is supported by the evidence and was not contested. The existence of the right, the Court of Appeal tells us, was "not the subject of serious dispute". It is not surprising, then, that, taken with other circumstances, that court should find that "the judgment appealed from was wrong in . . . failing to hold that Sparrow at the relevant time was exercising an existing aboriginal right".

In this Court, however, the respondent contested the Court of Appeal's finding, contending that the evidence was insufficient to discharge the appellant's burden of proof upon the issue. It is true that for the period from 1867 to 1961 the evidence is scanty. But the evidence was not disputed or contradicted in the courts below and there is evidence of sufficient continuity of the right to support the Court of Appeal's finding, and we would not disturb it.

What the Crown really insisted on, both in this Court and the courts below, was that the Musqueam Band's aboriginal right to fish had been extinguished by regulations under the *Fisheries Act*.

[The Court then summarized the progressive restriction and regulation of the fisheries.]

It is this progressive restriction and detailed regulation of the fisheries which, respondent's counsel maintained, have had the effect of extinguishing any aboriginal right to fish. The extinguishment need not be express, he argued, but may take place where the sovereign authority is exercised in a manner "necessarily inconsistent" with the continued enjoyment of aboriginal rights. ... The consent to its extinguishment before the *Constitution Act, 1982* was not required; the intent of the sovereign could be effected not only by statute but by valid regulations. Here, in his view, the regulations had entirely displaced any aboriginal right. There is, he submitted, a fundamental inconsistency between the communal right to fish embodied in the aboriginal right, and fishing under a special licence or permit issued to individual Indians (as was the case until 1977) in the discretion of the Minister and subject to terms and conditions which, if breached, may result in cancellation of the licence. The *Fisheries Act* and its regulations were, he argued, intended to constitute a complete code inconsistent with the continued existence of an aboriginal right.

At bottom, the respondent's argument confuses regulation with extinguishment. That the right is controlled in great detail by the regulations does not mean that the right is thereby extinguished.

. . . . .

The test of extinguishment to be adopted, in our opinion, is that the sovereign's intention must be clear and plain if it is to extinguish an aboriginal right.

There is nothing in the *Fisheries Act* or its detailed regulations that demonstrates a clear and plain intention to extinguish the Indian aboriginal right to fish. The fact that express provision permitting the Indians to fish for food may have applied to all Indians and that for an extended period permits were discretionary and issued on an individual rather than a communal basis in no way shows a clear intention to extinguish. These permits were simply a manner of controlling the fisheries, not defining underlying rights.

We would conclude then that the Crown has failed to discharge its burden of proving extinguishment. In our opinion, the Court of Appeal made no mistake in holding that the Indians have an existing aboriginal right to fish in the area where Mr. Sparrow was fishing at the time of the charge. This approach is consistent with ensuring that an aboriginal right should not be defined by incorporating the ways in which it has been regulated in the past.

The scope of the existing Musqueam right to fish must now be delineated. The anthropological evidence relied on to establish the existence of the right suggests that, for the Musqueam, the salmon fishery has always constituted an integral part of their distinctive culture. Its significant role involved not only consumption for subsistence purposes, but also consumption of salmon on ceremonial and social occasions. The Musqueam have always fished for reasons connected to their cultural and physical survival. As we stated earlier, the right to do so may be exercised in a contemporary manner.

The British Columbia Court of Appeal in this case held that the aboriginal right was to fish for food purposes, but that purpose was not to be confined to mere subsistence. Rather, the right was found to extend to fish consumed for social and ceremonial activities. The Court of Appeal thereby defined the right as protecting the same interest as is reflected in the government's food fish policy.

. . . . .

[I]t was contended before this Court that the aboriginal right extends to commercial fishing. While no commercial fishery existed prior to the arrival of European settlers, it is contended that the Musqueam practice of bartering in early society may be revived as a modern right to fish for commercial purposes. The presence of numerous interveners representing commercial fishing interests, and the suggestion on the facts that the net length restriction is at least in part related to the probable commercial use of fish caught under the Musqueam food fishing licence, indicate the possibility of conflict between aboriginal fishing and the competitive commercial fishery with respect to economically valuable fish such as salmon. We recognize the existence of this conflict and the probability of its intensification as fish availability drops, demand rises and tensions increase.

Government regulations governing the exercise of the Musqueam right to fish, as described above, have only recognized the right to fish *for food* for over a hundred years. This may have reflected the existing position. However, historical policy on the part of the Crown is not only incapable of extinguishing the existing aboriginal right without clear intention, but is also incapable of, in itself, delineating that right. The nature of government regulations cannot be determinative of the content and scope of an existing aboriginal right. Government policy *can* however regulate the exercise of that right, but such regulation must be in keeping with s. 35(1).

In the courts below, the case at bar was not presented on the footing of an aboriginal right to fish for commercial or livelihood purposes. Rather, the focus was and continues to be on the validity of a net length restriction affecting the appellant's *food fishing licence*. We therefore adopt the Court of Appeal's characterization of the right for the purpose of this appeal, and confine our reasons to the meaning of the constitutional recognition and affirmation of the existing aboriginal right to fish for food and social and ceremonial purposes.

"Recognized and Affirmed"

We now turn to the impact of s. 35(1) of the *Constitution Act, 1982* on the regulatory power of Parliament and on the outcome of this appeal specifically.

. . . . .

[I]n finding the appropriate interpretive framework for s. 35(1), we start by looking at the background of s. 35(1).

It is worth recalling that while British policy towards the native population was based on respect for their right to occupy their traditional lands, a proposition to which the Royal Proclamation of 1763 bears witness, there was from the outset never any doubt that sovereignty and legislative power, and indeed the underlying title, to such lands vested in the Crown.... And there can be no doubt that over the years the rights of the Indians were often honoured in the breach.

. . . . .

For many years, the rights of the Indians to their aboriginal lands — certainly as *legal* rights — were virtually ignored. The leading cases defining Indian rights in the early part of the century were directed at claims supported by the Royal Proclamation or other legal instruments, and even these cases were essentially concerned with settling legislative jurisdiction or the rights of commercial enterprises. For fifty years after the publication of Clement's *The Law of the Canadian Constitution*, 3rd ed. (1916), there was a virtual absence of discussion of any kind of Indian rights to land even in academic literature. By the late 1960s, aboriginal claims were not even recognized by the federal government as having any legal status. Thus the *Statement of the Government of Canada on Indian Policy* (1969), although well meaning, contained the assertion (at p. 11) that "aboriginal claims to land . . . are so general and undefined that it is not realistic to think of them as specific claims capable of remedy except through a policy and program that will end injustice to the Indians as members of the Canadian community". In the same general period, the James Bay development by Quebec Hydro was originally initiated without regard to the rights of the Indians who lived there, even though these were expressly protected by a constitutional instrument: see *The Quebec Boundary Extension Act, 1912*, S.C. 1912, c. 45. It took a number of judicial decisions and notably the *Calder* case in this court (1973) to prompt a reassessment of the position being taken by government.

In the light of its reassessment of Indian claims following *Calder*, the federal Government on August 8, 1973 issued "a statement of policy" regarding Indian lands. By it, it sought to "signify the Government's *recognition and acceptance* of its continuing responsibility under the British North America Act for Indians and lands reserved for Indians", which it regarded "as an historic evolution dating back to the Royal Proclamation of 1763, which, whatever differences there may be about its judicial interpretation, stands as a basic declaration of the Indian people's interests in land in this country". (Emphasis added.) See *Statement made by the Honourable Jean Chrétien, Minister of Indian Affairs and Northern Development on Claims of Indian and Inuit People*, August 8, 1973. The remarks about these lands were intended "as an expression of acknowledged responsibility". But the statement went on to express, for the first time, the government's willingness to negotiate regarding claims of aboriginal title, specifically in British Columbia, Northern Quebec, and the Territories, and this without regard to formal supporting documents. "The Government", it stated, "is now ready to negotiate with authorized representatives of these native peoples on the basis that where their traditional interest in the lands concerned can be established, an agreed form of compensation or benefit will be provided to native peoples in return for their interest."

It is obvious from its terms that the approach taken towards aboriginal claims in the 1973 statement constituted an expression of a policy, rather than a legal position.

. . . . .

It is clear, then, that s. 35(1) of the *Constitution Act, 1982*, represents the culmination of a long and difficult struggle in both the political forum and the courts for the constitutional recognition of aboriginal rights. The strong representations of native associations and other groups concerned with the welfare of Canada's aboriginal peoples made the adoption of s. 35(1) possible and it is important to note that the provision applies to the Indians, the Inuit and the Métis. Section 35(1), at the least, provides a solid constitutional base upon which subsequent negotiations can take place. It also affords aboriginal peoples constitutional protection against provincial legislative power. We are, of course, aware that this would, in any event, flow from the *Guerin* case ... but for a proper understanding of the situation, it is essential to remember that the *Guerin* case was decided after the commencement of the *Constitution Act, 1982*. In addition to its effect on aboriginal rights, s. 35(1) clarified other issues regarding the enforcement of treaty rights.

. . . . .

In our opinion, the significance of s. 35(1) extends beyond these fundamental effects. Professor Lyon in "An Essay on Constitutional Interpretation" (1988), 26 Osgoode Hall L.J. 95, says the following about s. 35(1), at p. 100:

> . . . the context of 1982 is surely enough to tell us that this is not just a codification of the case law on aboriginal rights that had accumulated by 1982. Section 35 calls for a just settlement for aboriginal peoples. It renounces the old rules of the game under which the Crown established courts of law and denied those courts the authority to question sovereign claims made by the Crown.

The approach to be taken with respect to interpreting the meaning of s. 35(1) is derived from general principles of constitutional interpretation, principles relating to aboriginal rights, and the purposes behind the constitutional provision itself. Here, we will sketch the framework for an interpretation of "recognized and affirmed" that, in our opinion, gives appropriate weight to the constitutional nature of these words.

. . . . .

. . . The nature of s. 35(1) itself suggests that it be construed in a purposive way. When the purposes of the affirmation of aboriginal rights are considered, it is clear that a generous, liberal interpretation of the words in the constitutional provision is demanded. . . .

In *Nowegijick v. The Queen*, [1983] 1 S.C.R. 29 [at p. 36], the following principle that should govern the interpretation of Indian treaties and statutes was set out:

> . . . treaties and statutes relating to Indians should be liberally construed and doubtful expressions resolved in favour of the Indians.

In *R. v. Agawa, supra*, Blair J.A. stated that the above principle should apply to the interpretation of s. 35(1). He added the following principle to be equally applied:

> The second principle was enunciated by the late Associate Chief Justice MacKinnon in *R. v. Taylor and Williams* (1981), 34 O.R. (2d) 360. He emphasized the importance of Indian history and traditions as well as the perceived effect of a treaty at the time of its execution. He also cautioned against determining Indian rights 'in a vacuum'. The honour of the Crown is involved in the interpretation of Indian treaties and, as a consequence, fairness to the Indians is a governing consideration.

. . . In our opinion, *Guerin*, together with *R. v. Taylor and Williams* (1981), 34 O.R. (2d) 360, ground a general guiding principle for s. 35(1). That is, the Government has the responsibility to act in a fiduciary capacity with respect to aboriginal peoples. The relationship between the Government and aboriginals is trust-like, rather than adversarial, and contemporary recognition and affirmation of aboriginal rights must be defined in light of this historic relationship.

We agree with both the British Columbia Court of Appeal below and the Ontario Court of Appeal that the principles outlined above, derived from *Nowegijick, Taylor and Williams* and *Guerin*, should guide the interpretation of s. 35(1). As commentators have noted, s. 35(1) is a solemn commitment that must be given meaningful content.

. . . . .

In response to the appellant's submission that s. 35(1) rights are more securely protected than the rights guaranteed by the *Charter*, it is true that s. 35(1) is not subject to s. 1 of the *Charter*. In our opinion, this does not mean that any law or regulation affecting aboriginal rights will automatically be of no force or effect by the operation of s. 52 of the *Constitution Act, 1982*. Legislation that affects the exercise of aboriginal rights will none-the-less be valid, if it meets the test for justifying an interference with a right recognized and affirmed under s. 35(1).

There is no explicit language in the provision that authorizes this court or any court to assess the legitimacy of any government legislation that restricts aboriginal rights. Yet, we find that the words "recognition and affirmation" incorporate the fiduciary relationship referred to earlier and so import some restraint on the exercise of sovereign power. Rights that are recognized and affirmed are not absolute. Federal legislative powers continue, including, of course, the right to legislate with respect to Indians pursuant to s. 91(24) of the *Constitution Act, 1867*. These powers must, however, now be read together with s. 35(1). In other words, federal power must be reconciled with federal duty and the best way to achieve that reconciliation is to demand the justification of any government regulation that infringes upon or denies aboriginal rights. Such scrutiny is in keeping with the liberal interpretive principle enunciated in *Nowegijick, supra*, and the concept of holding the Crown to a high standard of honourable dealing with respect to the aboriginal peoples of Canada as suggested by *Guerin v. The Queen, supra*.

We refer to Professor Slattery's "Understanding Aboriginal Rights", *ibid.*, with respect to the task of envisioning a s. 35(1) justificatory process. Professor Slattery, at p. 782, points out that a justificatory process is required as a compromise between a "patchwork" characterization of aboriginal rights whereby past regulations would be read into a definition of the rights, and a characterization that would guarantee aboriginal rights in their original form unrestricted by subsequent regulation. We agree with him that these two extreme positions must be rejected in favour of a justificatory scheme.

Section 35(1) suggests that while regulation affecting aboriginal rights is not precluded, such regulation must be enacted according to a valid objective. Our history has shown, unfortunately all too well, that Canada's aboriginal peoples are justified in worrying about government objectives that may be superficially neutral but which constitute *de facto* threats to the existence of aboriginal rights and interests. By giving aboriginal rights constitutional status and priority, Parliament and the provinces have sanctioned challenges to social and economic policy objectives embodied in legislation to the extent that aboriginal rights are affected. Implicit in this constitutional scheme is the obligation of the legislature to satisfy the test of justification. The way in which a legislative objective is to be attained must uphold the honour of the Crown and must be in keeping with the unique contemporary relationship, grounded in history and policy, between the Crown and Canada's aboriginal peoples. The extent of legislative or regulatory impact on an existing aboriginal right may be scrutinized so as to ensure recognition and affirmation.

The constitutional recognition afforded by the provision, therefore, gives a measure of control over government conduct and a strong check on legislative power. While it does not promise immunity from government regulation in a society that, in the twentieth century, is increasingly more complex, interdependent and sophisticated, and where exhaustible resources need protection and management, it does hold the Crown to a substantive promise. The government is required to bear the burden of justifying any legislation that has some negative effect on any aboriginal right protected under s. 35(1).

In these reasons, we will outline the appropriate analysis under s. 35(1) in the context of a regulation made pursuant to the *Fisheries Act*. We wish to emphasize the importance of context and a case-by-case approach to s. 35(1). Given the generality of the text of the constitutional provision, and especially in light of the complexities of aboriginal history, society and rights, the contours of a justificatory standard must be defined in the specific factual context of each case.

Section 35(1) and the Regulation of the Fisheries

Taking the above framework as guidance, we propose to set out the test for *prima facie* interference with an existing aboriginal right and for the justification of such an interference.

. . . . .

The first question to be asked is whether the legislation in question has the effect of interfering with an existing aboriginal right. If it does have such an effect, it represents a *prima facie* infringement of s. 35(1). Parliament is not expected to act in a manner contrary to the rights and interests of aboriginals, and, indeed, may be barred from doing so by the second stage of s. 35(1) analysis. The inquiry with respect to interference begins with a reference to the characteristics or incidents of the right at stake. Our earlier observations regarding the scope of the aboriginal right to fish are relevant here. Fishing rights are not traditional property rights. They are rights held by a collective and are in keeping with the culture and existence of that group. Courts must be careful, then, to avoid the application of traditional common law concepts of property as they develop their understanding of what the reasons for judgment in *Guerin* ... referred to as the "*sui generis*" nature of aboriginal rights: See also Little Bear, "A Concept of Native Title," [1982] 5 Can. Legal Aid Bul. 99.

While it is impossible to give an easy definition of fishing rights, it is possible, and, indeed, crucial, to be sensitive to the aboriginal perspective itself on the meaning of the rights at stake. For example, it would be artificial to try to create a hard distinction between the right to fish and the particular manner in which that right is exercised.

To determine whether the fishing rights have been interfered with such as to constitute a *prima facie* infringement of s. 35(1), certain questions must be asked. First, is the limitation unreasonable? Secondly, does the regulation impose undue hardship? Thirdly, does the regulation deny to the holders of the right their preferred means of exercising that right? The onus of proving a *prima facie* infringement lies on the individual or group challenging the legislation. In relation to the facts of this appeal, the regulation would be found to be a *prima facie* interference if it were found to be an adverse restriction on the Musqueam exercise of their right to fish for food. We wish to note here that the issue does not merely require looking at whether the fish catch has been reduced below that needed for the reasonable food and ceremonial needs of the Musqueam Indians. Rather the test involves asking whether either the purpose or the effect of the restriction on net length unnecessarily infringes the interests protected by the fishing right. If, for example, the Musqueam were forced to spend undue time and money per fish caught or if the net length reduction resulted in a hardship to the Musqueam in catching fish, then the first branch of the s. 35(1) analysis would be met.

If a *prima facie* interference is found, the analysis moves to the issue of justification. This is the test that addresses the question of what constitutes legitimate regulation of a constitutional aboriginal right. The justification analysis would proceed as follows. First, is there a valid legislative objective? Here the court would inquire into whether the objective of Parliament in authorizing the department to enact regulations regarding fisheries is valid. The objective of the department in setting out the particular regulations would also be scrutinized. An objective aimed at preserving s. 35(1) rights by conserving and managing a natural resource, for example, would be valid. Also valid would be objectives purporting to prevent the exercise of s. 35(1) rights that would cause harm to the general populace or to aboriginal peoples themselves, or other objectives found to be compelling and substantial.

The Court of Appeal below held ... that regulations could be valid if reasonably justified as "necessary for the proper management and conservation of the resource *or in the public interest*". (Emphasis added.) We find the "public interest" justification to be so vague as to provide no meaningful guidance and so broad as to be unworkable as a test for the justification of a limitation on constitutional rights.

The justification of conservation and resource management, on the other hand, is surely uncontroversial.

. . . . .

[T]he value of conservation purposes for government legislation and action has long been recognized. Further, the conservation and management of our resources is consistent with aboriginal beliefs and practices, and, indeed, with the enhancement of aboriginal rights.

If a valid legislative objective is found, the analysis proceeds to the second part of the justification issue. Here, we refer back to the guiding interpretive principle derived from *Taylor and Williams* and *Guerin, supra*. That is, the honour of the Crown is at stake in dealings with aboriginal peoples. The special trust relationship and the responsibility of the government *vis-à-vis* aboriginals must be the first consideration in determining whether the legislation or action in question can be justified.

The problem that arises in assessing the legislation in light of its objective and the responsibility of the Crown is that the pursuit of conservation in a heavily used modern fishery inevitably blurs with the efficient allocation and management of this scarce and valued resource. The nature of the constitutional protection afforded by s. 35(1) in this context demands that there be a link between the question of justification and the allocation of priorities in the fishery. The constitutional recognition and affirmation of aboriginal rights may give rise to conflict with the interests of others given the limited nature of the resource. There is a clear need for guidelines that will resolve the allocational problems that arise regarding the fisheries. We refer to the reasons of Dickson J., [as he then was], in *Jack v. The Queen*, [1980] [1 S.C.R. 294] for such guidelines.

In *Jack*, the appellants' defence to a charge of fishing for salmon in certain rivers during a prohibited period was based on the alleged constitutional incapacity of Parliament to legislate such as to deny the Indians their right to fish for food. They argued that art. 13 of the *British Columbia Terms of Union* imposed a constitutional limitation on the federal power to regulate. While we recognize that the finding that such a limitation had been imposed was not adopted by the majority of this Court, we point out that this case concerns a different constitutional promise that asks this Court to give a meaningful interpretation to recognition and affirmation. That task requires equally meaningful guidelines responsive to the constitutional priority accorded aboriginal rights. We therefore repeat the following passage from *Jack*, at p. 313:

> Conservation is a valid legislative concern. The appellants concede as much. Their concern is in the allocation of the resource after reasonable and necessary conservation measures have been recognized and given effect to. They do not claim the right to pursue the last living salmon until it is caught. Their position, as I understand it, is one which would give effect to an order of priorities of this nature: (i) conservation; (ii) Indian fishing; (iii) non-Indian commercial fishing; or (iv) non-Indian sports fishing; the burden of conservation measures should not fall primarily upon the Indian fishery.
>
> I agree with the general tenor of this argument.... With respect to whatever salmon are to be caught, then priority ought to be given to the Indian fishermen, subject to the practical difficulties occasioned by international waters and the movement of the fish themselves. But any limitation upon Indian fishing that is established for a valid conservation purpose overrides the protection afforded the Indian fishery by art. 13, just as such conservation measures override other taking of fish.

The constitutional nature of the Musqueam food fishing rights means that any allocation of priorities after valid conservation measures have been implemented must give top priority to Indian food fishing. If the objective pertained to conservation, the conservation plan would be scrutinized to assess priorities. While the detailed allocation of maritime resources is a task that must be left to those having expertise in the area, the Indians' food requirements must be met first when that allocation is established. The significance of giving the aboriginal right to fish for food top priority can be described as follows. If, in a given year, conservation needs required a reduction in the number of fish to be caught such that the number equalled the number required for food by the Indians, then all the fish available after conservation would go to the Indians according to the constitutional nature of their fishing right. If, more realistically, there were still fish after the Indian food requirements were met, then the brunt of conservation measures would be borne by the practices of sport fishing and commercial fishing.

. . . . .

We acknowledge the fact that the justificatory standard to be met may place a heavy burden on the Crown. However, government policy with respect to the British Columbia fishery, regardless of s. 35(1), already dictates that, in allocating the right to take fish, Indian food fishing is to be given priority over the interests of other user groups. The constitutional entitlement embodied in s. 35(1) requires the Crown to ensure that its regulations are in keeping with that allocation of priority. The objective of this requirement is not to undermine Parliament's ability and responsibility with respect to creating and administering over-all conservation and management plans regarding the salmon fishery. The objective is rather to guarantee that those plans treat aboriginal peoples in a way ensuring that their rights are taken seriously.

Within the analysis of justification, there are further questions to be addressed, depending on the circumstances of the inquiry. These include the questions of whether there has been as little infringement as possible in order to effect the desired result; whether, in a situation of expropriation, fair compensation is available; and, whether the aboriginal group in question has been consulted with respect to the conservation measures being implemented. The aboriginal peoples, with their history of conservation-consciousness and interdependence with natural resources, would surely be expected, at the least, to be informed regarding the determination of an appropriate scheme for the regulation of the fisheries.

We would not wish to set out an exhaustive list of the factors to be considered in the assessment of justification. Suffice it to say that recognition and affirmation requires sensitivity to and respect for the rights of aboriginal peoples on behalf of the government, courts and indeed all Canadians.

Application to this Case — Is the Net Length Restriction Valid?

The Court of Appeal below found that there was not sufficient evidence in this case to proceed with an analysis of s. 35(1) with respect to the right to fish for food. In reviewing the competing expert evidence, and recognizing that fish stock management is an uncertain science, it decided that the issues at stake in this appeal were not well adapted to being resolved at the appellate court level.

· · · · ·

According to the Court of Appeal, the findings of fact were insufficient to lead to an acquittal. There was no more evidence before this Court. We also would order a re-trial which would allow findings of fact according to the tests set out in these reasons.

The appellant would bear the burden of showing that the net length restriction constituted a *prima facie* infringement of the collective aboriginal right to fish for food. If an infringement were found, the onus would shift to the Crown which would have to demonstrate that the regulation is justifiable. To that end, the Crown would have to show that there is no underlying unconstitutional objective such as shifting more of the resource to a user group that ranks below the Musqueam. Further, it would have to show that the regulation sought to be imposed is required to accomplish the needed limitation. In trying to show that the restriction is necessary in the circumstances of the Fraser River fishery, the Crown could use facts pertaining to fishing by other Fraser River Indians.

In conclusion, we would dismiss the appeal and the cross-appeal and affirm the Court of Appeal's setting aside of the conviction. We would accordingly affirm the order for a new trial on the questions of infringement and whether any infringement is nonetheless consistent with s. 35(1), in accordance with the interpretation set out here.

· · · · ·

Appeal and cross-appeal dismissed. The constitutional question should be sent back to trial to be answered according to the analysis set out in these reasons.

In *Sparrow*, the Supreme Court affirmed that section 35(1) of the *Constitution Act, 1982* prevented the extinguishment of Aboriginal rights found to exist on or after 17 April 1982. It also affirmed that section 35(1) was not subject to the limitation on rights provided by section 1 of the *Canadian Charter of Rights and Freedoms*. Nevertheless, it did allow for the limitation of Aboriginal rights on or after 17 April 1982 through the justificatory test it created.

From the *Sparrow* decision, the Court held that Aboriginal rights were those practices that were "integral to the distinctive cultures" of Aboriginal peoples. The Court also explained that Aboriginal rights could not be frozen at a particular point in time (as discussed in relation to treaty rights in Chapter 2). On these points, the *Sparrow* decision marked a significant departure from previous judicial decisions on Aboriginal rights and their status in law.

C. ABORIGINAL RIGHTS: INHERENT RIGHTS OR CONTINGENT RIGHTS?

While the *Sparrow* decision illustrated a variety of judicial interpretations of Aboriginal rights, a key element of the decision was predicated upon pre-*Calder*
characterizations about the nature of Aboriginal rights. In fact, the underlying basis of the *Sparrow* decision raises questions about the Court's understanding of Aboriginal rights and whether they exist independently of the common law or governmental recognition. In the following excerpt from their article "Aboriginal Rights and Canadian Sovereignty: An Essay on *R. v. Sparrow*," Michael Asch and Patrick Macklem address this through the characterizations of Aboriginal rights as "inherent" or "contingent".

MICHAEL ASCH & PATRICK MACKLEM, "ABORIGINAL RIGHTS AND CANADIAN SOVEREIGNTY: AN ESSAY ON R. v. SPARROW"

(1991), 29 Alta. L. Rev. 498 at 501-3, 505, 507-8, 510, 515-16
(references omitted)

. . . . .

II. TWO THEORIES OF ABORIGINAL RIGHT

. . . . .

A contingent rights approach views the existence or non-existence of aboriginal rights to be contingent upon the exercise of state authority. It therefore assumes the legitimacy of executive and legislative authority over First Nations and imagines rights as emanating from state recognition of a valid aboriginal claim to freedom from state interference. An aboriginal right to fish, for example, is dependent upon the state conferring such a right on the relevant aboriginal population by legislative or executive action.

. . . . .

A contingent theory of aboriginal right gives rise to a particular conception of the meaning of First Nations sovereignty and self-government. Under a contingent rights approach, First Nations sovereignty would not exist as a constitutional right until expressed by way of constitutional amendment. Until such a time, aboriginal self-government exists only to the extent it is given force by legislation or executive action. ... Thus, under a contingent theory of aboriginal rights, self-government is a label for a bundle of rights that attach to Native people as a result of legislative or executive action or constitutional amendment, and is not dependent upon a prior acceptance of First Nations sovereignty. In fact, a contingent theory of aboriginal right implicitly denies any assertion of First Nations sovereignty by viewing the existence or non-existence of aboriginal rights, including rights of self-government, as dependent upon the exercise of Canadian sovereign authority.

. . . . .

An inherent theory of aboriginal right generates an approach to First Nations sovereignty and self-government that stands in stark contrast to that envisioned by a contingent rights perspective. According to an inherent rights approach, First Nations sovereignty is a term used to describe the totality of powers and responsibilities necessary or integral to the maintenance and reproduction of aboriginal identity and social organization. Under an inherent rights theory, First Nations sovereignty and aboriginal forms of government, as the means by which aboriginal identity and social organization are reproduced, pre-existed the settlement of Canada and continue to exist notwithstanding the interposition of the Canadian state. The Canadian state may choose to recognize aspects of First Nations sovereignty and aboriginal forms of self-government through executive, legislative or judicial action. Unlike a contingent theory of aboriginal right, however, such action is not necessary for the existence of First Nations sovereignty and native forms of self-government, only their recognition in Canadian law.

The debate ... as to the legal nature of aboriginal rights was initially put to rest in 1984 by Dickson J. (as he then was) in *Guerin v. The Queen*. Describing the nature of the Musqueam Indian Band's interest in their land as "a pre-existing legal right not created by Royal Proclamation, by s. 128(1) of the *Indian Act*, or by any other executive order or legislative provision," Dickson J. in *Guerin* firmly opted for an inherent theory of aboriginal right. Yet, prior to the passage of the *Constitution Act, 1982*, the legal embrace of an inherent theory of aboriginal right was restricted to the common law. Although aboriginal rights in *Guerin* were conceived as not contingent upon the exercise of legislative or executive authority, they nonetheless existed only at common law. Common law aboriginal rights were therefore always subject to regulation or extinguishment by the appropriate legislative authority. The judicial recognition of the inherent nature of aboriginal rights thus occurred in the context of a tacit acceptance of the sovereign authority of the Canadian state over its indigenous population. As a result, the vision of First Nations sovereignty and native forms of self-government generated by an inherent theory of aboriginal right remained outside the purview of Canadian law.

III. THE *SPARROW* DECISION

. . . . .

In *R. v. Sparrow* ... the Supreme Court of Canada was provided with the occasion to give meaning to s. 35(1). As stated previously, the Court accepted that Canada enjoys sovereignty and is therefore entitled to exercise legislative authority over First Nations. The court held, however, that aboriginal rights that exist at common law are now "recognized and affirmed" by s. 35(1), and that, as a result, laws that interfere with the exercise of such rights must conform to constitutional standards of justification.

. . . . .

In so holding, the Court re-affirmed Dickson J.'s holding in *Guerin* that aboriginal rights are not contingent upon the exercise of legislative or executive authority, and to this extent the Court in *Sparrow* embraced an inherent theory of aboriginal right. In the Court's view, the reason for concluding that the Musqueam Nation enjoys a right to fish lies not in the presence of state action conferring such a right, but instead arises from the fact that fishing is integral to Musqueam self-identify and self-preservation. ...

. . . . .

The Court avoided some of the above implications of adopting an inherent theory of aboriginal right by making two critical moves, First, the Court unquestioningly accepted that the British Crown, and thereafter Canada, obtained territorial sovereignty over the land mass that is now Canada by the mere fact of European settlement. The Court's acceptance of the settlement thesis appears to exclude any possibility of the recognition and affirmation of a constitutional right to aboriginal sovereignty. Second, the embrace of the settlement thesis permitted the Court to rein in the scope of s. 35(1) by relying on a contingent rights approach to s. 35(1)'s requirement that aboriginal rights be "existing".

. . . . .

With respect to the assertion of Canadian sovereignty, the Court made the following crucial statement:

> It is worth recalling that while British policy toward the native population was based on respect for their right to occupy their traditional lands, a proposition to which the Royal Proclamation of 1763 bears witness, there was from the outset never any doubt that sovereignty and legislative power, and indeed the underlying title, to such lands vested in the Crown.

With this statement, the Court has indicated that it is of the view that, whatever the meaning given to s. 35(1), Canadian sovereignty over the indigenous population that finds itself within Canada is unquestioned. If Canadian sovereignty was "never in doubt," its assertion likely had the effect of subsuming pre-existing aboriginal sovereignty to the overarching authority of the Canadian state. Thus, unlike other aboriginal rights, the Court appears to accept the proposition that the right to sovereignty, however acceptable under an inherent theory of aboriginal right, is to be excluded *a priori* from the scope of s. 35(1). It is important to note that underlying this interpretation of s. 35(1) is a contingent theory of aboriginal right, which views the existence of an aboriginal right, in this case a right to aboriginal sovereignty, as dependent upon legislative or executive action. Since the Canadian state decided not to respect aboriginal sovereignty, such sovereignty cannot achieve the status of right.

The Court also implicitly relies on a contingent theory of aboriginal right in the definition it gives s. 35(1)'s requirement that aboriginal rights be "existing" before they receive constitutional recognition and affirmation. An inherent theory of aboriginal right would suggest that the existence of aboriginal rights is not to be determined by reference to actions of the Canadian state. The Court, however, held that prior to 1982 aboriginal rights could be extinguished by the Canadian state. If extinguished prior to 1982, aboriginal rights no longer "exist" within the meaning of s. 35(1) and their exercise is not protected against state action. If such rights were only regulated, they continue to exist within the meaning of s. 35(1) despite their regulation and can serve to check subsequent legislative or executive curtailment. State action, in other words, defines the parameters of s. 35(1) rights, which is a central tenet of a contingent theory of aboriginal right.

. . . . .

In sum, although the Court in *Sparrow* pays attention to an inherent theory of aboriginal right, its reasons ultimately betray a reliance on a contingent rights perspective, which serves to rein in the scope of s. 35(1) rights. The assertion of Canadian sovereignty is sufficient to nullify and render non-existent any pre-existing claims of aboriginal sovereignty, which would otherwise constitute an "existing aboriginal right" within the meaning of s. 35(1). ...

. . . . .

In our view, the assertion of Canadian sovereignty over aboriginal peoples, as well as the contingent theory of aboriginal right that it generates, ultimately rest on unacceptable notions about the inherent superiority of European nations. If this is true, unquestioned acceptance of Canadian sovereignty and a contingent theory of aboriginal right does violence to fundamental principles of justice and human rights in the modern world, such as the assumed equality of peoples, especially of their ability to govern themselves, and the basic right of a people to self-determination. We believe it abhorrent that Canada was constituted in part by reliance on a belief of inequality of peoples and that such a belief continues to inform political and legal practice in 1991.

. . . . .

... [W]e are drawn to the following statement by Justice Hall in the *Calder* case written more than twenty years ago:

> [t]he assessment and interpretation of the historical documents and enactments tendered in evidence must be approached in the light of present-day research and knowledge disregarding ancient concepts formulated when understanding of the customs and culture of our original people was rudimentary and incomplete and when they were thought to be wholly without cohesion, laws or culture, in effect a subhuman species.

... In our view, it is equally applicable to the invocation of a contingent theory of aboriginal right in the context of s. 35(1) of the *Constitution Act, 1982*. The stability of a contingent rights approach to s. 35(1) ultimately depends on a belief in the superiority of European nations. In our view, Canada ought not to be constituted by a reliance on such a belief, and constitutional interpretation surrounding Canada's relation with First Nations should heed Justice Hall's sage advice. An inherent theory of aboriginal right remains true to the belief of equality of peoples and as such should form an integral part of Canada's constitutional identity.

How do Asch and Macklem's views sit with those expressed by Binnie J. in *Mitchell v. M.N.R.*, [2001] 1 S.C.R. 911, where he said:

> The common law concept of aboriginal rights is built around the doctrine of sovereign succession in British colonial law. The framers of the *Constitution Act, 1982* undoubtedly expected the courts to have regard in their interpretation of s. 35(1) to the common law concept. This point was made by McLachlin J. (as she then was) (dissenting in the result) in *Van der Peet*, *supra*, at paras. 227 and 262:
>
> > The issue of what constitutes an aboriginal right must, in my view, be answered by looking at what the law has historically accepted as fundamental aboriginal rights. ...
> >
> > ... The *Constitution Act, 1982* ushered in a new chapter but it did not start a new book. Within the framework of s. 35(1) regard is to be had to the common law ("what the law has historically accepted") to enable a court to determine what constitutes an aboriginal right.

How do Justice Binnie's comments mesh with those of Noel Lyon, which were expressly adopted by the Supreme Court of Canada in *Sparrow*? Did section 35(1) usher in a new chapter in the approach to Aboriginal rights or did it begin a new book? What do you think? Does your answer differ if you consider only the approach to be taken with respect to those rights as opposed to the content of those rights?

D. POST-*SPARROW* CONSIDERATIONS OF ABORIGINAL RIGHTS

Until the Supreme Court of Canada's decisions in the *Van der Peet* trilogy — *R. v. Van der Peet*, below; *R. v. Gladstone*, *infra*, p. 380 and *R. v. N.T.C. Smokehouse Ltd.*, [1996] 2 S.C.R. 672, [1996] 4 C.N.L.R. 130, [1996] 9 W.W.R. 114, 23 B.C.L.R. (3d) 114, 137 D.L.R. (4th) 528, 50 C.R. (4th) 181, 109 C.C.C. (3d) 129, 200 N.R. 321 — the Supreme Court of Canada had not undertaken a substantive discussion of the effects of section 35(1) of the *Constitution Act, 1982* since its decision in *Sparrow* some six years previously. Through these decisions, in particular *Van der Peet* and *Gladstone*, the Supreme Court may be seen to have made some fundamental changes to its characterization of Aboriginal rights in *Sparrow*.

R. v. VAN DER PEET

[1996] 4 C.N.L.R. 177, [1996] 9 W.W.R. 1, 23 B.C.L.R. (3d) 1, 50 C.R. (4th) 1, 137 D.L.R. (4th) 289, 109 C.C.C. (3d) 1, 200 N.R. 1 (S.C.C.)

La Forest, Sopinka, Gonthier, Cory, Iacobucci and **Major JJ.** concur with

Lamer C.J.C.: —

I. *Introduction*

This appeal, along with the companion appeals in *R. v. N.T.C. Smokehouse Ltd.*, [1996] 2 S.C.R. 672, and *R. v. Gladstone*, [1996] 2 S.C.R. 723, raises the issue left unresolved by this Court in its judgment in *R. v. Sparrow*, [1990] 1 S.C.R. 1075: How are the Aboriginal rights recognized and affirmed by s. 35(1) of the *Constitution Act, 1982* to be defined?

In *Sparrow*, Dickson C.J. and La Forest J., writing for a unanimous Court, outlined the framework for analyzing s. 35(1) claims. First, a court must determine whether an applicant has demonstrated that he or she was acting pursuant to an Aboriginal right. Second, a court must determine whether that right has been extinguished. Third, a court must determine whether that right has been infringed. Finally, a court must determine whether the infringement is justified. In *Sparrow*, however, it was not seriously disputed that the Musqueam had an Aboriginal right to fish for food, with the result that it was unnecessary for the Court to answer the question of how the rights recognized and affirmed by s. 35(1) are to be defined. It is this question and, in particular, the question of whether s. 35(1) recognizes and affirms the right of the Sto:lo to sell fish, which must now be answered by this Court.

In order to define the scope of Aboriginal rights, it will be necessary first to articulate the purposes which underpin s. 35(1), specifically the reasons underlying its recognition and affirmation of the unique constitutional status of Aboriginal peoples in Canada. Until it is understood why Aboriginal rights exist, and are constitutionally protected, no definition of those rights is possible.

. . . . .

This judgment will thus, after outlining the context and background of the appeal, articulate a test for identifying Aboriginal rights which reflects the purposes underlying s. 35(1), and the interests which that constitutional provision is intended to protect.

II. *Statement of Facts*

The appellant Dorothy Van der Peet was charged under s. 61(1) of the *Fisheries Act*, R.S.C. 1970, c. F-14, with the offence of selling fish caught under the authority of an Indian food fish licence, contrary to s. 27(5) of the *British Columbia Fishery (General) Regulations*, SOR/84-248. At the time at which the appellant was charged s. 27(5) read:

> 27. . . .

> (5) No person shall sell, barter or offer to sell or barter any fish caught under the authority of an Indian food fish licence.

The charges arose out of the sale by the appellant of ten salmon on September 11, 1987. The salmon had been caught by Steven and Charles

Jimmy under the authority of an Indian food fish licence. Charles Jimmy is the common law spouse of the appellant. The appellant, a member of the Sto:lo, has not contested these facts at any time, instead defending the charges against her on the basis that in selling the fish she was exercising an existing Aboriginal right to sell fish. The appellant has based her defence on the position that the restrictions imposed by s. 27(5) of the Regulations infringe her existing Aboriginal right to sell fish and are therefore invalid on the basis that they violate s. 35(1) of the *Constitution Act, 1982*.

. . . . .

V. *Analysis*

Introduction

I now turn to the question which, as I have already suggested, lies at the heart of this appeal: How should the Aboriginal rights recognized and affirmed by s. 35(1) of the *Constitution Act, 1982* be defined?

In her factum the appellant argued that the majority of the Court of Appeal erred because it defined the rights in s. 35(1) in a fashion which "converted a Right into a Relic"; such an approach, the appellant argued, is inconsistent with the fact that the Aboriginal rights recognized and affirmed by s. 35(1) are *rights* and not simply Aboriginal practices. The appellant acknowledged that Aboriginal rights are based in Aboriginal societies and cultures, but argued that the majority of the Court of Appeal erred because it defined Aboriginal rights through the identification of pre-contact activities instead of as pre-existing legal rights.

While the appellant is correct to suggest that the mere existence of an activity in a particular Aboriginal community prior to contact with Europeans is not, in itself, sufficient foundation for the definition of Aboriginal rights, the position she would have this Court adopt takes s. 35(1) too far from that which the provision is intended to protect. Section 35(1), it is true, recognizes and affirms existing aboriginal *rights*, but it must not be forgotten that the rights it recognizes and affirms are *Aboriginal*.

In the liberal enlightenment view, reflected in the American *Bill of Rights* and, more indirectly, in the *Charter*, rights are held by all people in society because each person is entitled to dignity and respect. Rights are general and universal; they are the way in which the "inherent dignity" of each individual in society is respected.

. . . . .

Aboriginal rights cannot, however, be defined on the basis of the philosophical precepts of the liberal enlightenment. Although equal in importance and significance to the rights enshrined in the *Charter*, Aboriginal rights must be viewed differently from *Charter* rights because they are rights held only by Aboriginal members of Canadian society. They arise from the fact that Aboriginal people are *Aboriginal*. As academic commentators have noted, Aboriginal rights "inhere in the very meaning of Aboriginality", Michael Asch and Patrick Macklem, "Aboriginal Rights and

Canadian Sovereignty: An Essay on *R. v. Sparrow*" (1991), 29 *Alta. Law Rev.* 498, at p. 502; they are the rights held by "Indians *qua* Indians", Brian Slattery, "Understanding Aboriginal Rights" (1987), 66 *Can. Bar Rev.* 727, at p. 776.

The task of this Court is to define Aboriginal rights in a manner which recognizes that Aboriginal rights are *rights* but which does so without losing sight of the fact that they are rights held by Aboriginal people because they are *Aboriginal*. The Court must neither lose sight of the generalized constitutional status of what s. 35(1) protects, nor can it ignore the necessary specificity which comes from granting special constitutional protection to one part of Canadian society. The Court must define the scope of s. 35(1) in a way which captures *both* the Aboriginal and the rights in Aboriginal rights.

The way to accomplish this task is, as was noted at the outset, through a purposive approach to s. 35(1). It is through identifying the interests that s. 35(1) was intended to protect that the dual nature of Aboriginal rights will be comprehended. ... A purposive approach to s. 35(1), because ensuring that the provision is not viewed as static and only relevant to current circumstances, will ensure that the recognition and affirmation it offers are consistent with the fact that what it is recognizing and affirming are "rights". Further, because it requires the court to analyze a given constitutional provision "in the light of the interests it was meant to protect"(*Big M Drug Mart Ltd.*, [1985] 1 S.C.R. 295 at p. 344), a purposive approach to s. 35(1) will ensure that that which is found to fall within the provision is related to the provision's intended focus: Aboriginal people and their rights in relation to Canadian society as a whole.

. . . . .

General Principles Applicable to Legal Disputes Between Aboriginal Peoples and the Crown

Before turning to a purposive analysis of s. 35(1), however, it should be noted that such analysis must take place in light of the general principles which apply to the legal relationship between the Crown and Aboriginal peoples. In *Sparrow, supra*, this Court held ... that s. 35(1) should be given a generous and liberal interpretation in favour of Aboriginal peoples:

> When the purposes of the affirmation of Aboriginal rights are considered, it is clear that a generous, liberal interpretation of the words in the constitutional provision is demanded. [Emphasis added.]

This interpretive principle, articulated first in the context of treaty rights ... arises from the nature of the relationship between the Crown and Aboriginal peoples. The Crown has a fiduciary obligation to Aboriginal peoples with the result that in dealings between the government and Aboriginals the honour of the Crown is at stake. Because of this fiduciary relationship, and its implication of the honour of the Crown, treaties, s. 35(1), and other statutory and constitutional provisions protecting the interests of Aboriginal peoples, must be given a generous and liberal interpretation. ... This general principle must inform the Court's analysis of the purposes underlying s. 35(1), and of that provision's definition and scope.

The fiduciary relationship of the Crown and Aboriginal peoples also means that where there is any doubt or ambiguity with regards to what falls within the scope and definition of s. 35(1), such doubt or ambiguity must be resolved in favour of Aboriginal peoples.

. . . . .

Purposive Analysis of Section 35(1)

I now turn to a purposive analysis of s. 35(1).

When the court identifies a constitutional provision's purposes, or the interests the provision is intended to protect, what it is doing in essence is explaining the rationale of the provision; it is articulating the reasons underlying the protection that the provision gives. With regards to s. 35(1), then, what the court must do is explain the rationale and foundation of the recognition and affirmation of the special rights of Aboriginal peoples; it must identify the basis for the special status that Aboriginal peoples have within Canadian society as a whole.

In identifying the basis for the recognition and affirmation of Aboriginal rights it must be remembered that s. 35(1) did not create the legal doctrine of Aboriginal rights; Aboriginal rights existed and were recognized under the common law: *Calder v. Attorney-General of British Columbia*, [1973] S.C.R. 313. At common law Aboriginal rights did not, of course, have constitutional status, with the result that Parliament could, at any time, extinguish or regulate those rights: *Kruger v. The Queen*, [1978] 1 S.C.R. 104, at p. 112; *R. v. Derriksan* (1976), 71 D.L.R. (3d) 159 (S.C.C.); it is this which distinguishes the Aboriginal rights recognized and affirmed in s. 35(1) from the Aboriginal rights protected by the common law. Subsequent to s. 35(1) Aboriginal rights cannot be extinguished and can only be regulated or infringed consistent with the justificatory test laid out by this Court in *Sparrow, supra*.

. . . . .

... The pre-existence of Aboriginal rights is relevant to the analysis of s. 35(1) because it indicates that Aboriginal rights have a stature and existence prior to the constitutionalization of those rights and sheds light on the reasons for protecting those rights; however, the interests protected by s. 35(1) must be identified through an explanation of the basis for the legal doctrine of Aboriginal rights, not through an explanation of why that legal doctrine now has constitutional status.

In my view, the doctrine of Aboriginal rights exists, and is recognized and affirmed by s. 35(1), because of one simple fact: when Europeans arrived in North America, Aboriginal peoples *were already here*, living in communities on the land, and participating in distinctive cultures, as they had done for centuries. It is this fact, and this fact above all others, which separates Aboriginal peoples from all other minority groups in Canadian society and which mandates their special legal, and now constitutional, status.

More specifically, what s. 35(1) does is provide the constitutional framework through which the fact that Aboriginals lived on the land in distinctive societies, with their own practices, traditions and cultures, is acknowledged and reconciled with the sovereignty of the Crown. The substantive rights which fall within the provision must be defined in light of this purpose; the Aboriginal rights recognized and affirmed by s. 35(1) must be directed towards the reconciliation of the pre-existence of Aboriginal societies with the sovereignty of the Crown.

[The Court's review of authorities is omitted.]

. . . . .

The Test for Identifying Aboriginal Rights in Section 35(1)

In order to fulfil the purpose underlying s. 35(1) — i.e., the protection and reconciliation of the interests which arise from the fact that prior to the arrival of Europeans in North America Aboriginal peoples lived on the land in distinctive societies, with their own practices, customs and traditions — the test for identifying the Aboriginal rights recognized and affirmed by s. 35(1) must be directed at identifying the crucial elements of those pre-existing distinctive societies. It must, in other words, aim at identifying the practices, traditions and customs central to the Aboriginal societies that existed in North America prior to contact with the Europeans.

In *Sparrow, supra*, this Court did not have to address the scope of the Aboriginal rights protected by s. 35(1); however, in their judgment at p. 1099 Dickson C.J. and La Forest J. identified the Musqueam right to fish for food in the fact that:

> The anthropological evidence relied on to establish the existence of the right suggests that, for the Musqueam, the salmon fishery has always constituted an *integral part of their distinctive culture*. Its significant role involved not only consumption for subsistence purposes, but also consumption of salmon on ceremonial and social occasions. The Musqueam have always fished for reasons connected to their cultural and physical survival. [Emphasis added.]

The suggestion of this passage is that participation in the salmon fishery is an Aboriginal right because it is an "integral part" of the "distinctive culture" of the Musqueam. This suggestion is consistent with the position just adopted; identifying those traditions, customs and practices that are integral to distinctive Aboriginal cultures will serve to identify the crucial elements of the distinctive Aboriginal societies that occupied North America prior to the arrival of Europeans.

In light of the suggestion of *Sparrow, supra*, and the purposes underlying s. 35(1), the following test should be used to identify whether an applicant has established an Aboriginal right protected by s. 35(1): in order to be an Aboriginal right an activity must be an element of a practice, custom or tradition integral to the distinctive culture of the Aboriginal group claiming the right.

. . . . .

Factors to be Considered in Application of the Integral to a Distinctive Culture Test

The test just laid out — that Aboriginal rights lie in the practices, traditions and customs integral to the distinctive cultures of Aboriginal peoples — requires further elaboration with regards to the nature of the inquiry a court faced with an Aboriginal rights claim must undertake. I will now undertake such an elaboration, concentrating on such questions as the time period relevant to the court's inquiry, the correct approach to the evidence presented, the specificity necessary to the court's inquiry, the relationship between Aboriginal rights and the rights of Aboriginal people as Canadian citizens, and the standard that must be met in order for a practice, custom or tradition to be said to be "integral".

Courts must take into account the perspective of Aboriginal peoples themselves

In assessing a claim for the existence of an Aboriginal right, a court must take into account the perspective of the Aboriginal people claiming the right. In *Sparrow, supra,* Dickson C.J. and La Forest J. held, at p. 1112, that it is "crucial to be sensitive to the Aboriginal perspective itself on the meaning of the rights at stake". It must also be recognized, however, that that perspective must be framed in terms cognizable to the Canadian legal and constitutional structure. As has already been noted, one of the fundamental purposes of s. 35(1) is the reconciliation of the pre-existence of distinctive Aboriginal societies with the assertion of Crown sovereignty. Courts adjudicating Aboriginal rights claims must, therefore, be sensitive to the Aboriginal perspective, but they must also be aware that Aboriginal rights exist within the general legal system of Canada.

. . . . .

> *Courts must identify precisely the nature of the claim being made in determining whether an Aboriginal claimant has demonstrated the existence of an Aboriginal right*

Related to this is the fact that in assessing a claim to an Aboriginal right a court must first identify the nature of the right being claimed; in order to determine whether a claim meets the test of being integral to the distinctive culture of the Aboriginal group claiming the right, the court must first correctly determine what it is that is being claimed.

. . . . .

The nature of an applicant's claim must be delineated in terms of the particular practice, tradition or custom under which it is claimed; the significance of the practice, tradition or custom to the Aboriginal community is a factor to be considered in determining whether the practice, tradition or custom is integral to the distinctive culture, but the significance of a practice, tradition or custom cannot, itself, constitute an Aboriginal right.

To characterize an applicant's claim correctly, a court should consider such factors as the nature of the action which the applicant is claiming was done pursuant to an Aboriginal right, the nature of the governmental regulation, statute or action being impugned, and the tradition, custom or practice being relied upon to establish the right. In this case, therefore, the Court will consider the actions which led to the appellant's [*sic*] being charged, the fishery regulation under which she was charged and the traditions, customs and practices she invokes in support of her claim.

It should be acknowledged that a characterization of the nature of the appellant's claim from the actions which led to her being charged must be undertaken with some caution. In order to inform the court's analysis the activities must be considered at a general rather than at a specific level. Moreover, the court must bear in mind that the activities may be the exercise in a modern form of a tradition, custom or practice that existed prior to contact, and should vary its characterization of the claim accordingly.

In order to be integral a practice, custom or tradition must be of central significance to the Aboriginal society in question

To satisfy the integral to a distinctive culture test the Aboriginal claimant must do more than demonstrate that a practice, tradition or custom was an aspect of, or took place in, the Aboriginal society of which he or she is a part. The claimant must demonstrate that the practice, tradition or custom was a central and significant part of the society's distinctive culture. He or she must demonstrate, in other words, that the practice, tradition or custom was one of the things which made the culture of the society distinctive — that it was one of the things that truly *made the society what it was*.

This aspect of the integral to a distinctive culture test arises from the fact that Aboriginal rights have their basis in the prior occupation of Canada by distinctive Aboriginal societies. To recognize and affirm the prior occupation of Canada by distinctive Aboriginal societies it is *to what makes those societies distinctive* that the court must look in identifying Aboriginal rights. The court cannot look at those aspects of the Aboriginal society that are true of every human society (e.g., eating to survive), nor can it look at those aspects of the Aboriginal society that are only incidental or occasional to that society; the court must look instead to the defining and central attributes of the Aboriginal society in question. It is only by focusing on the aspects of the Aboriginal society that make that society distinctive that the definition of Aboriginal rights will accomplish the purpose underlying s. 35(1).

. . . . .

A practical way of thinking about this problem is to ask whether, without this practice, tradition or custom, the culture in question would be fundamentally altered or other than what it is. One must ask, to put the question affirmatively, whether or not a practice, tradition or custom is a defining feature of the culture in question.

The practices, customs and traditions which constitute Aboriginal rights are those which have continuity with the traditions, customs and practices that existed prior to contact

The time period that a court should consider in identifying whether the right claimed meets the standard of being integral to the Aboriginal community claiming the right is the period prior to contact between Aboriginal and European societies. Because it is the fact that distinctive Aboriginal societies lived on the land prior to the arrival of Europeans that underlies the Aboriginal rights protected by s. 35(1), it is to that pre-contact period that the courts must look in identifying Aboriginal rights.

The fact that the doctrine of Aboriginal rights functions to reconcile the existence of pre-existing Aboriginal societies with the sovereignty of the Crown does not alter this position. Although it is the sovereignty of the Crown that the pre-existing Aboriginal societies are being reconciled with, it is to those pre-existing societies that the court must look in defining Aboriginal rights. It is not the fact that Aboriginal societies existed prior to Crown sovereignty that is relevant; it is the fact that they existed *prior to the arrival of Europeans in North America*. As such, the relevant time period is the period prior to the arrival of Europeans, not the period prior to the assertion of sovereignty by the Crown.

That this is the relevant time should not suggest, however, that the Aboriginal group claiming the right must accomplish the next to impossible task of producing conclusive evidence from pre-contact times about the practices, customs and traditions of their community. It would be entirely contrary to the spirit and intent of s. 35(1) to define Aboriginal rights in such a fashion so as to preclude in practice any successful claim for the existence of such a right. The evidence relied upon by the applicant and the courts may relate to Aboriginal practices, customs and traditions post-contact; it simply needs to be directed at demonstrating which aspects of the Aboriginal community and society have their origins pre-contact. It is those practices, customs and traditions that can be rooted in the pre-contact societies of the Aboriginal community in question that will constitute Aboriginal rights.

. . . . .

Where an Aboriginal community can demonstrate that a particular practice, custom or tradition is integral to its distinctive culture today, and that this practice, custom or tradition has continuity with the practices, customs and traditions of pre-contact times, that community will have demonstrated that the practice, custom or tradition is an Aboriginal right for the purposes of s. 35(1).

The concept of continuity is also the primary means through which the definition and identification of Aboriginal rights will be consistent with the admonition in *Sparrow, supra*, at p. 1093, that "the phrase 'existing Aboriginal rights' must be interpreted flexibly so as to permit their evolution over time". The concept of continuity is, in other words, the means by which a "frozen rights" approach to s. 35(1) will be avoided. Because the practices, traditions and customs protected by s. 35(1) are ones that exist today, subject only to the requirement that they be demonstrated to have continuity with the practices, customs and traditions which existed pre-contact, the definition of Aboriginal rights will be one that, on its own terms, prevents those rights from being frozen in pre-contact times. The evolution of practices, traditions and customs into modern forms will not, provided that continuity with pre-contact practices, customs and traditions is demonstrated, prevent their protection as Aboriginal rights.

I would note that the concept of continuity does not require Aboriginal groups to provide evidence of an unbroken chain of continuity between their current practices, traditions and customs, and those which existed prior to contact. It may be that for a period of time an Aboriginal group, for some reason, ceased to engage in a practice, tradition or custom which existed prior to contact, but then resumed the practice, tradition or custom at a later date. Such an interruption will not preclude the establishment of an Aboriginal right. Trial judges should adopt the same flexibility regarding the establishment of continuity that, as is discussed, *infra,* they are to adopt with regards to the evidence presented to establish the prior-to-contact practices, customs and traditions of the Aboriginal group making the claim to an Aboriginal right.

Further, I would note that basing the identification of Aboriginal rights in the period prior to contact is not inconsistent with the fact that s. 35(2) of the *Constitution Act, 1982* includes within the definition of "Aboriginal peoples of Canada" the Métis people of Canada.

. . . . .

Courts must approach the rules of evidence in light of the evidentiary difficulties inherent in adjudicating Aboriginal claims

In determining whether an Aboriginal claimant has produced evidence sufficient to demonstrate that her activity is an aspect of a practice, custom or tradition integral to a distinctive Aboriginal culture, a court should approach the rules of evidence, and interpret the evidence that exists, with a consciousness of the special nature of Aboriginal claims, and of the evidentiary difficulties in proving a right which originates in times where there were no written records of the practices, customs and traditions engaged in. The courts must not undervalue the evidence presented by Aboriginal claimants simply because that evidence does not conform precisely with the evidentiary standards that would be applied in, for example, a private law torts case.

Claims to Aboriginal rights must be adjudicated on a specific rather than general basis

Courts considering a claim to the existence of an Aboriginal right must focus specifically on the traditions, customs and practices of the particular Aboriginal group claiming the right. In the case of *Kruger, supra,* this Court rejected the notion that claims to Aboriginal rights could be determined on a general basis. This position is correct; the existence of an Aboriginal right will depend entirely on the traditions, customs and practices of the *particular Aboriginal community claiming the right.* As has already been suggested, Aboriginal rights are constitutional rights, but that does not negate the central fact that the interests Aboriginal rights are intended to protect relate to the specific history of the group claiming the right. Aboriginal

rights are not general and universal; their scope and content must be determined on a case-by-case basis. The fact that one group of Aboriginal
people has an Aboriginal right to do a particular thing will not be, without
something more, sufficient to demonstrate that another Aboriginal community has the same Aboriginal right. The existence of the right will be
specific to each Aboriginal community.

*For a practice, custom or tradition to constitute an Aboriginal right it must be
of independent significance to the Aboriginal culture in which it exists*

In identifying those practices, customs and traditions that constitute the
Aboriginal rights recognized and affirmed by s. 35(1), a court must ensure
that the practice, custom or tradition relied upon in a particular case is independently significant to the Aboriginal community claiming the right.
The practice, custom or tradition cannot exist simply as an incident to another practice, custom or tradition but must rather be itself of integral significance to the Aboriginal society. Where two customs exist, but one is
merely incidental to the other, the custom which is integral to the Aboriginal community in question will qualify as an Aboriginal right, but the
custom that is merely incidental will not. Incidental practices, customs and
traditions cannot qualify as Aboriginal rights through a process of piggy-
backing on integral practices, customs and traditions.

*The integral to a distinctive culture test requires that a practice, custom or tra-
dition be distinctive; it does not require that that practice, custom or tradition
be distinct*

The standard which a practice, custom or tradition must meet in order to
be recognized as an Aboriginal right is *not* that it be *distinct* to the Aboriginal culture in question; the Aboriginal claimants must simply demonstrate
that the practice, custom or tradition is *distinctive*. A tradition or custom
that is *distinct* is one that is unique — "different in kind or quality, unlike"
(*Concise Oxford Dictionary, supra*). A culture with a distinct tradition must
claim that in having such a tradition it is different from other cultures; a
claim of distinctness is, by its very nature, a claim relative to other cultures
or traditions. By contrast, a culture that claims that a practice, custom or
tradition is *distinctive* — "distinguishing, characteristic" — makes a claim
that is not relative; the claim is rather one about the culture's own practices, customs or traditions considered apart from the practices, customs or
traditions of any other culture. It is a claim that this tradition or custom
makes the culture *what it is*, not that the practice, custom or tradition is
different from the practices, customs or traditions of another culture. The
person or community claiming the existence of an Aboriginal right protected by s. 35(1) need only show that the particular practice, custom or
tradition which it is claiming to be an Aboriginal right is distinctive, not
that it is distinct.

That the standard an Aboriginal community must meet is distinctiveness, not distinctness, arises from the recognition in *Sparrow, supra*, of an
Aboriginal right to fish for food. Certainly no Aboriginal group in Canada
could claim that its culture is "distinct" or unique in fishing for food; fish-

ing for food is something done by many different cultures and societies around the world. What the Musqueam claimed in *Sparrow, supra,* was rather that it was fishing for food which, in part, made Musqueam culture what it is; fishing for food was characteristic of Musqueam culture and, therefore, a *distinctive part* of that culture. Since it was so it constituted an Aboriginal right under s. 35(1).

The influence of European culture will only be relevant to the inquiry if it is demonstrated that the practice, custom or tradition is only integral because of that influence

The fact that Europeans in North America engaged in the same practices, customs or traditions as those under which an Aboriginal right is claimed will only be relevant to the Aboriginal claim if the practice, custom or tradition in question can only be said to exist because of the influence of European culture. If the practice, custom or tradition was an integral part of the Aboriginal community's culture prior to contact with Europeans, the fact that that practice, custom or tradition continued after the arrival of Europeans, and adapted in response to their arrival, is not relevant to determination of the claim; European arrival and influence cannot be used to deprive an Aboriginal group of an otherwise valid claim to an Aboriginal right. On the other hand, where the practice, custom or tradition arose solely as a response to European influences then that practice, custom or tradition will not meet the standard for recognition of an Aboriginal right.

Courts must take into account both the relationship of Aboriginal peoples to the land and the distinctive societies and cultures of Aboriginal peoples

As was noted in the discussion of the purposes of s. 35(1), Aboriginal rights and Aboriginal title are related concepts; Aboriginal title is a subcategory of Aboriginal rights which deals solely with claims of rights to land. The relationship between Aboriginal title and Aboriginal rights must not, however, confuse the analysis of what constitutes an Aboriginal right. Aboriginal rights arise from the prior occupation of land, but they also arise from the prior social organization and distinctive cultures of Aboriginal peoples on that land. In considering whether a claim to an Aboriginal right has been made out, courts must look at both the relationship of an Aboriginal claimant to the land *and* at the practices, customs and traditions arising from the claimant's distinctive culture and society. Courts must not focus so entirely on the relationship of Aboriginal peoples with the land that they lose sight of the other factors relevant to the identification and definition of Aboriginal rights.

. . . . .

Application of the Integral to a Distinctive Culture Test to the Appellant's Claim

The first step in the application of the integral to a distinctive culture test requires the court to identify the precise nature of the appellant's claim to have been exercising an Aboriginal right. In this case the most accurate characterization of the appellant's position is that she is claiming *an Aboriginal right to exchange fish for money or for other goods*. She is claiming, in other words, that the practices, customs and traditions of the Sto:lo include as an integral part the exchange of fish for money or other goods.

That this is the nature of the appellant's claim can be seen through both the specific acts which led to her being charged and through the regulation under which she was charged. Mrs. Van der Peet sold ten salmon for $50. Such a sale, especially given the absence of evidence that the appellant had sold salmon on other occasions or on a regular basis, cannot be said to constitute a sale on a "commercial" or market basis. These actions are instead best characterized in the simple terms of an exchange of fish for money. It follows from this that the Aboriginal right pursuant to which the appellant is arguing that her actions were taken is, like the actions themselves, best characterized as an Aboriginal right to exchange fish for money or other goods.

. . . . .

The appellant herself characterizes her claim as based on a right "to sufficient fish to provide for a moderate livelihood". ... The *significance* of the practice, custom or tradition is relevant to the determination of whether that practice, custom or tradition is integral, but cannot itself constitute the claim to an Aboriginal right. As such, the appellant's claim cannot be characterized as based on an assertion that the Sto:lo's use of the fishery, and the practices, customs and traditions surrounding that use, had the significance of providing the Sto:lo with a moderate livelihood. It must instead be based on the actual practices, customs and traditions related to the fishery, here the custom of exchanging fish for money or other goods.

Having thus identified the nature of the appellant's claim, I turn to the fundamental question of the integral to a distinctive culture test: Was the practice of exchanging fish for money or other goods an integral part of the specific distinctive culture of the Sto:lo prior to contact with Europeans? In answering this question it is necessary to consider the evidence presented at trial, and the findings of fact made by the trial judge.

. . . . .

The facts as found by Scarlett Prov. Ct. J. do not support the appellant's claim that the exchange of salmon for money or other goods was an integral part of the distinctive culture of the Sto:lo. ... The findings of fact made by Scarlett Prov. Ct. J. suggest that the exchange of salmon for money or other goods, while certainly taking place in Sto:lo society prior to contact, was not a significant, integral or defining feature of that society.

First, Scarlett Prov. Ct. J. found that, prior to contact, exchanges of fish were only "incidental" to fishing for food purposes. ... Thus, while the evidence clearly demonstrated that fishing for food and ceremonial purposes was a significant and defining feature of the Sto:lo culture, this is not sufficient, absent a demonstration that the exchange of salmon was *itself* a significant and defining feature of Sto:lo society, to demonstrate that the exchange of salmon is an integral part of Sto:lo culture.

. . . . .

Second, Scarlett Prov. Ct. J. found that there was no "regularized trading system" amongst the Sto:lo prior to contact. ... Given that the exchange of salmon was not widespread it cannot be said that, prior to contact, Sto:lo culture was defined by trade in salmon; trade or exchange of salmon took place, but the absence of a market demonstrates that this exchange did not take place on a basis widespread enough to suggest that the exchange was a defining feature of Sto:lo society.

Third, the trade engaged in between the Sto:lo and the Hudson's Bay Company, while certainly of significance to the Sto:lo society of the time, was found by the trial judge to be qualitatively different from that which was typical of the Sto:lo culture prior to contact. ... The trade of salmon between the Sto:lo and the Hudson's Bay Company does not have the necessary continuity with Sto:lo culture pre-contact to support a claim to an Aboriginal right to trade salmon. Further, the exchange of salmon between the Sto:lo and the Hudson's Bay Company can be seen as central or significant to the Sto:lo primarily as a result of European influences; activities which become central or significant because of the influence of European culture cannot be said to be Aboriginal rights.

Finally, Scarlett Prov. Ct. J. found that the Sto:lo were at a band level of social organization rather than at a tribal level. As noted by the various experts, one of the central distinctions between a band society and a tribal society relates to specialization and division of labour. In a tribal society there tends to be specialization of labour — for example, specialization in the gathering and trade of fish — whereas in a band society division of labour tends to occur only on the basis of gender or age. The absence of specialization in the exploitation of the fishery is suggestive, in the same way that the absence of regularized trade or a market is suggestive, that the exchange of fish was not a central part of Sto:lo culture.

. . . . .

For these reasons, then, I would conclude that the appellant has failed to demonstrate that the exchange of fish for money or other goods was an integral part of the distinctive Sto:lo society which existed prior to contact. The exchange of fish took place, but was not a central, significant or defining feature of Sto:lo society. The appellant has thus failed to demonstrate that the exchange of salmon for money or other goods by the Sto:lo is an Aboriginal right recognized and affirmed under s. 35(1) of the *Constitution Act, 1982*.

The Sparrow Test

Since the appellant has failed to demonstrate that the exchange of fish was an Aboriginal right of the Sto:lo, it is unnecessary to consider the tests for extinguishment, infringement and justification laid out by this Court in *Sparrow, supra*.

VI. *Disposition*

Having concluded that the Aboriginal rights of the Sto:lo do not include the right to exchange fish for money or other goods, I would dismiss the appeal.

. . . . .

L'Heureux-Dubé J. (dissenting): —

. . . . .

In my view, the definition of Aboriginal rights as to their nature and extent must be addressed in the broader context of the historical Aboriginal reality in Canada.

. . . . .

I. *Historical and General Background*

[P]rior to the first contact with the Europeans, the native people of North America were independent nations, occupying and controlling their own territories, with a distinctive culture and their own practices, traditions and customs.

. . . . .

[I]t has become accepted in Canadian law that Aboriginal title, and Aboriginal rights in general, derive from *historic occupation and use of ancestral lands by the natives* and do not depend on any treaty, executive order or legislative enactment.

. . . . .

Aboriginal people's occupation and use of North American territory was not static, nor, as a general principle, should be the Aboriginal rights flowing from it. ... Accordingly, the notion of Aboriginal rights must be open to fluctuation, change and evolution, not only from one native group to another, but also over time.

. . . . .

Aboriginal rights can be incidental to Aboriginal title but need not be; these rights are severable from and can exist independently of Aboriginal title. ...

... A treaty ... does not exhaust Aboriginal rights; such rights continue to exist apart from the treaty, provided that they are not substantially connected to the rights crystallized in the treaty or extinguished by its terms.

. . . . .

III. *Interpretation of Aboriginal Rights*

. . . . .

Aboriginal rights must be construed in light of the special trust relationship and the responsibility of the Crown *vis-à-vis* Aboriginal people: see *Taylor, supra,* and *Guerin, supra.* This fiduciary obligation attaches because of the historic power and responsibility assumed by the Crown over Aboriginal people.

. . . . .

[M]ost importantly, Aboriginal rights protected under s. 35(1) have to be interpreted in the context of the history and culture of the specific Aboriginal society and in a manner that gives the rights meaning to the natives. ... Unlike the Chief Justice, I do not think it appropriate to qualify this proposition by saying that the perspective of the common law matters as much as the perspective of the natives when defining Aboriginal rights.

. . . . .

Characteristics of Aboriginal rights

The issue of the nature and extent of Aboriginal rights protected under s. 35(1) is fundamentally about characterization. Which Aboriginal practices, traditions and customs warrant constitutional protection? It appears from the jurisprudence developed in the courts below (see the reasons of the British Columbia Court of Appeal and the decision in *Delgamuukw v. British Columbia* (1993), 104 D.L.R. (4th) 470) that two approaches to this difficult question have emerged. The first one, which the Chief Justice endorses, focuses on the particular Aboriginal practice, tradition or custom. The second approach, more generic, describes aboriginal rights in a fairly high level of abstraction. For the reasons that follow, I favour the latter approach.

The approach based on Aboriginal practices, traditions and customs considers only discrete parts of aboriginal culture, separating them from the general culture in which they are rooted. The analysis turns on the *manifestations* of the "integral part of [aboriginals'] distinctive culture" introduced in *Sparrow, supra,* at p. 1099. Further, on this view, what makes Aboriginal culture distinctive is that which differentiates it from non-Aboriginal culture.

. . . . .

Accordingly, if an activity is integral to a culture other than that of Aboriginal people, it cannot be part of Aboriginal people's distinctive culture. This approach should *not* be adopted.

. . . . .

[A]ll that "distinctive culture" requires is the characterization of Aboriginal culture, not its differentiation from non-Aboriginal cultures.

. . . . .

[A]n approach based on a dichotomy between Aboriginal and non-Aboriginal practices, traditions and customs literally amounts to defining Aboriginal culture and Aboriginal rights as that which is left over after features of non-Aboriginal cultures have been taken away. Such a strict construction of constitutionally protected aboriginal rights flies in the face of the generous, large and liberal interpretation of s. 35(1) of the *Constitution Act, 1982* advocated in *Sparrow*.

. . . . .

[T]he notion of "integral part of [aboriginals'] distinctive culture" ... constitutes a general statement regarding the purpose of s. 35(1). Instead of focusing on a particular practice, tradition or custom, this conception refers to a more abstract and profound concept.

. . . . .

Accordingly, s. 35(1) should be viewed as protecting, not a catalogue of individualized practices, traditions or customs, as the Chief Justice does, but the "distinctive culture" of which Aboriginal activities are manifestations. Simply put, the emphasis would be on the *significance* of these activities to natives rather than on the activities themselves.

. . . . .

The practices, traditions and customs protected under s. 35(1) should be those that are sufficiently significant and fundamental to the culture and social organization of a particular group of Aboriginal people.

. . . . .

Put another way, the Aboriginal practices, traditions and customs which form the core of the lives of native people and which provide them with a way and means of living as an organized society will fall within the scope of the constitutional protection under s. 35(1).

. . . . .

Period of time relevant to Aboriginal rights

. . . . .

[C]rystallizing Aboriginal practices, traditions and customs at the time of British sovereignty creates an arbitrary date for assessing existing Aboriginal rights.

. . . . .

[A]boriginal rights must be permitted to maintain contemporary relevance in relation to the needs of the natives as their practices, traditions and customs change and evolve with the overall society in which they live.

. . . . .

Consequently, in order for an Aboriginal right to be recognized and affirmed under s. 35(1), ... the determining factor should only be that the Aboriginal activity has formed an integral part of a distinctive Aboriginal culture ... *for a substantial continuous period of time.*

. . . . .

The substantial continuous period of time for which the Aboriginal practice, tradition or custom must have been engaged in will depend on the circumstances and on the nature of the Aboriginal right claimed.

. . . . .

In short, the substantial continuous period of time necessary to the recognition of Aboriginal rights should be assessed based on (1) the type of aboriginal practices, traditions and customs, (2) the particular Aboriginal culture and society, and (3) the reference period of 20 to 50 years. Such a time frame does not minimize the fact that in order to benefit from s. 35(1) protection, Aboriginal activities must still form the core of the lives of native people.

. . . . .

The most appreciable advantage of the "dynamic right" approach to defining the nature and extent of Aboriginal rights is the proper consideration given to the perspective of Aboriginal people on the meaning of their existing rights. It recognizes that distinctive Aboriginal culture is not a reality of the past, preserved and exhibited in a museum, but a characteristic that has evolved with the natives as they have changed, modernized and flourished over time, along with the rest of Canadian society. This, in the Aboriginal people's perspective, is no doubt the true sense of the constitutional protection provided to Aboriginal rights through s. 35(1) of the *Constitution Act, 1982.*

. . . . .

An Aboriginal activity does not need to be undertaken for livelihood, support and sustenance purposes to benefit from s. 35(1) protection.

. . . . .

In the instant case, this Court is only required to decide whether the Sto:lo's right to fish includes the right to sell, trade and barter fish for livelihood, support and sustenance purposes, and *not* whether it includes the right to make commercial use of the fish.

. . . . .

V. THE CASE

. . . . .

At the British Columbia Supreme Court, Selbie J. was of the view that the trial Judge committed such an error and, as a consequence, substituted his own findings of fact:

> In my view, the evidence in this case, oral, historical and opinion, looked at in the light of the principles of interpreting aboriginal rights referred to earlier, is more consistent with the aboriginal right to fish including the right to sell, barter or exchange than otherwise and must be found so. ... We are speaking of an aboriginal "right" existing in antiquity which should not be restrictively interpreted by today's standards. ... *The Indian right to trade his fish is not frozen in time to doing so only by the medium of the potlatch and the like; he is entitled, subject to extinguishment or justifiable restrictions, to evolve with the times and dispose of them by modern means, if he so chooses, such as the sale of them for money. It is thus my view that the aboriginal right of the Sto:lo peoples to fish includes the right to sell, trade or barter them after they have been caught. It is my view that the learned judge imposed a verdict inconsistent with the evidence and the weight to be given it.* [Emphasis added.]

. . . . .

The ... historical evidence on the record reveals that there was trade of salmon for livelihood, support and sustenance purposes among the Sto:lo and with other native people and, more importantly, that such activities formed part of, and were undoubtedly rooted in, the distinctive Aboriginal culture of the Sto:lo. In short, the fishery has always provided a focus for life and livelihood for the Sto:lo and they have always traded salmon for the sustenance and support of themselves and their families. Accordingly, to use the terminology of the test propounded above, the sale, trade and barter of fish for livelihood, support and sustenance purposes was sufficiently significant and fundamental to the culture and social organization of the Sto:lo.

. . . . .

Furthermore, there is no doubt that these activities did form part of the Sto:lo's distinctive Aboriginal culture for a substantial continuous period of time. In that respect, we must consider the type of Aboriginal practices, traditions and customs, the particular Aboriginal culture and society, and the reference period of 20 to 50 years. Here, the historical evidence shows that the Sto:lo's practices, traditions and customs relating to the trade of salmon for livelihood, support and sustenance purposes have existed for centuries before the arrival of Europeans. As well, it appears that such activities have continued, though in modernized forms, until the present day. Accordingly, the time requirement for the recognition of an Aboriginal right is also met in this case.

As a consequence, I conclude that the Sto:lo Band, of which the appellant is a member, possess an Aboriginal right to sell, trade and barter fish for livelihood, support and sustenance purposes. Under s. 35(1) of the *Constitution Act, 1982* this right is protected.

. . . . .

McLachlin J. (dissenting): —

. . . . .

1. DO THE STO:LO POSSESS AN ABORIGINAL RIGHT TO SELL FISH PROTECTED UNDER SECTION 35(1) OF THE CONSTITUTION ACT, 1982?

A. *Is a Prima Facie Right Established?*

I turn first to the principles which govern the inquiry into the existence of an Aboriginal right.

(i)   *General Principles of Interpretation*

. . . . .

[A] court approaching the question of whether a particular practice is the exercise of a constitutional Aboriginal right under s. 35(1) must adopt an approach which: (1) recognizes the dual purposes of s. 35(1) (to preclude extinguishment and to provide a firm foundation for settlement of Aboriginal claims); (2) is liberal and generous toward Aboriginal interests; (3) considers the Aboriginal claim in the context of the historic way of life of the people asserting it; and (4) above all, is true to the position of the Crown throughout Canadian history as trustee or fiduciary for the first peoples of this country.

(ii)   *The Right Asserted — the Right to Fish for Commercial Purposes*

. . . . .

On the view I take of the case, the critical question is not whether the sale of the fish is commerce or non-commerce, but whether the sale can be defended as the exercise of a more basic Aboriginal right to continue the aboriginal people's historic use of the resource.

. . . . .

(iii)   *Aboriginal Rights versus the Exercise of Aboriginal Rights*

It is necessary to distinguish at the outset between an Aboriginal right and the exercise of an Aboriginal right. Rights are generally cast in broad, general terms. They remain constant over the centuries. The exercise of rights, on the other hand, may take many forms and vary from place to place and from time to time.

If a specific modern practice is treated as the right at issue, the analysis may be foreclosed before it begins. This is because the modern practice by which the more fundamental right is exercised may not find a counterpart in the Aboriginal culture of two or three centuries ago. So if we ask whether there is an Aboriginal *right* to a particular kind of trade in fish, i.e., large-scale commercial trade, the answer in most cases will be negative. On the other hand, if we ask whether there is an Aboriginal right to use the fishery resource for the purpose of providing food, clothing or other needs, the answer may be quite different. Having defined the basic underlying right in general terms, the question then becomes whether the modern *practice* at issue may be characterized as an *exercise* of the right.

This is how we reconcile the principle that Aboriginal rights must be ancestral rights with the uncompromising insistence of this Court that Aboriginal rights not be frozen. The rights are ancestral; they are the old rights that have been passed down from previous generations. The *exercise* of those rights, however, takes modern forms. To fail to recognize the distinction between rights and the contemporary form in which the rights are exercised is to freeze Aboriginal societies in their ancient modes and deny to them the right to adapt, as all peoples must, to the changes in the society in which they live.

. . . . .

(iv)   *The Time Frame*

. . . . .

I agree with the Chief Justice that history is important. A recently adopted practice would generally not qualify as being Aboriginal.

. . . . .

I cannot agree with the Chief Justice, however, that it is essential that a practice be traceable to pre-contact times for it to qualify as a constitutional right. Aboriginal rights find their source not in a magic moment of European contact, but in the traditional laws and customs of the Aboriginal people in question. ... One finds no mention in the text of s. 35(1) or in the jurisprudence of the moment of European contact as the definitive all-or-nothing time for establishing an Aboriginal right. The governing concept is simply the traditional customs and laws of people prior to imposition of European law and customs. What must be established is continuity between the modern practice at issue and a traditional law or custom of the native people.

. . . . .

The modern exercise of a right may be quite different from its traditional exercise. To deny it the status of a right because of such differences would be to deny the reality that Aboriginal cultures, like all cultures, change and adapt with time. ...

. . . . .

(vi)   *The "Integral-Incidental" Test*

I agree with the Chief Justice ... that to qualify as an Aboriginal right "an activity must be an element of practice, custom or tradition integral to the distinctive culture of the Aboriginal group claiming the right". I also agree with L'Heureux-Dubé J. that an Aboriginal right must be "integral" to a "distinctive Aboriginal group's culture and social organization". To say this is simply to affirm the foundation of Aboriginal rights in the laws and customs of the people. It *describes* an essential quality of an Aboriginal right. But, with respect, a workable legal test for determining the extent to which, if any, commercial fishing may constitute an Aboriginal right, requires more. The governing concept of integrality comes from a description in the *Sparrow* case where the extent of the Aboriginal right (to fish for food) was not seriously in issue. It was never intended to serve as a test for determining the extent of disputed exercises of Aboriginal rights.

... The Chief Justice attempts to narrow the concept of "integral" by emphasizing that the proposed right must be part of what makes the group "distinctive", the "specific" people which they are, stopping short, however, of asserting that the practice must be unique to the group and adhere to none other. But the addition of concepts of distinctness and specificity do not, with respect, remedy the overbreadth of the test. Minor practices, falling far short of the importance which we normally attach to constitutional rights, may qualify as distinct or specific to a group. Even the addition of the notion that the characteristic must be central or important rather than merely "incidental", fails to remedy the problem; it merely poses another problem, that of determining what is central and what is incidental to a people's culture and social organization.

. . . . .

The historically based test for Aboriginal rights which I propose, by contrast, possesses its own internal limits and adheres more closely to the principles that animated *Sparrow*, as I perceive them.

(vii)   *The Empirical Historic Approach*

. . . . .

... Rather than attempting to describe *a priori* what an Aboriginal right is, we should look to history to see what sort of practices have been identified as Aboriginal rights in the past. From this we may draw inferences as to the sort of things which may qualify as Aboriginal rights under s. 35(1). Confronted by a particular claim, we should ask, "Is this *like* the sort of thing which the law has recognized in the past?". This is the time-honoured methodology of the common law. Faced with a new legal problem, the court looks to the past to see how the law has dealt with similar situations in the past. The court evaluates the new situation by reference to what has been held in the past and decides how it should be characterized. In this way, legal principles evolve on an incremental, pragmatic basis.

. . . . .

(ix)   *The Nature of the Interests and Customs Recognized by the Common Law*

. . . . .

Generally speaking, Aboriginal rights in Canada were group rights. A particular Aboriginal group lived on or controlled a particular territory for the benefit of the group as a whole. The Aboriginal rights of such a group inure to the descendants of the group, so long as they maintain their connection with the territory or resource in question.

. . . . .

[T]he common law and those who regulated the British settlement of this country predicated dealings with Aboriginals on two fundamental principles. The first was the general principle that the Crown took subject to existing Aboriginal interests in the lands they traditionally occupied and their adjacent waters, even though those interests might not be of a type recognized by British law. The second, which may be viewed as an application of the first, is that the interests which Aboriginal peoples had in using the land and adjacent waters for their sustenance were to be removed only by solemn treaty with due compensation to the people and its descendants. This right to use the land and adjacent waters as the people had traditionally done for its sustenance may be seen as a fundamental Aboriginal right. It is supported by the common law and by the history of this country. It may safely be said to be enshrined in s. 35(1) of the *Constitution Act, 1982*.

(x)   *The Right to Fish for Sale*

Against this background, I come to the issue at the heart of this case. Do Aboriginal people enjoy a constitutional right to fish for commercial purposes under s. 35(1) of the *Constitution Act, 1982*? The answer is yes, to the extent that the people in question can show that it traditionally used the fishery to provide needs which are being met through the trade.

If an Aboriginal people can establish that it traditionally fished in a certain area, it continues to have a similar right to do so, barring extinguishment or treaty. The same justice that compelled those who drafted treaties with the Aboriginals in the nineteenth century to make provision for the continuing sustenance of the people from the land, compels those dealing with Aboriginals with whom treaties were never made, like the Sto:lo, to make similar provision.

The Aboriginal right to fish may be defined as the right to continue to obtain from the river or the sea in question that which the particular Aboriginal people have traditionally obtained from the portion of the river or sea. If the Aboriginal people show that they traditionally sustained themselves from the river or sea, then they have a *prima facie* right to continue to do so, absent a treaty exchanging that right for other consideration. At its base, the right is not the right to trade, but the right to continue to use the resource in the traditional way to provide for the traditional needs, albeit in their modern form. However, if the people demonstrate that trade is the only way of using the resource to provide the modern equivalent of what they traditionally took, it follows that the people should be permitted to trade in the resource to the extent necessary to provide the replacement goods and amenities. In this context, trade is but the mode or practice by which the more fundamental right of drawing sustenance from the resource is exercised.

The right to trade the products of the land and adjacent waters for other goods is not unlimited. The right stands as a continuation of the Aboriginal people's historical reliance on the resource. There is therefore no justification for extending it beyond what is required to provide the people with reasonable substitutes for what it traditionally obtained from the resource. In most cases, one would expect the Aboriginal right to trade to be confined to what is necessary to provide basic housing, transportation, clothing and amenities — the modern equivalent of what the Aboriginal people in question formerly took from the land or the fishery, over and above what was required for food and ceremonial purposes. Beyond this, Aboriginal fishers have no priority over non-Aboriginal commercial or sport fishers.

. . . . .

(xi)   *Is an Aboriginal Right to Sell Fish for Commerce Established in this Case?*

. . . . .

[T]he evidence conclusively establishes that over many centuries, the Sto:lo have used the fishery not only for food and ceremonial purposes, but also to satisfy a variety of other needs. Unless that right has been extinguished, and subject always to conservation requirements, they are entitled to continue to use the river for these purposes. To the extent that trade is required to achieve this end, it falls within that right.

. . . . .

For these reasons I conclude that Mrs. Van der Peet's sale of the fish can be defended as an exercise of her Aboriginal right, unless that right has been extinguished.

B. *Is the Aboriginal Right Extinguished?*

The Crown has never concluded a treaty with the Sto:lo extinguishing its Aboriginal right to fish. However, it argues that any right the Sto:lo people possess to fish commercially was extinguished prior to 1982 through regulations limiting commercial fishing by licence. ...

For legislation or regulation to extinguish an Aboriginal right, the intention to extinguish must be "clear and plain": *Sparrow, supra*, at p. 1099.

. . . . .

[T]he regulatory scheme in place since 1908, far from extinguishing the Aboriginal right to fish for sale, confirms that right and even suggests recognition of a limited priority in its exercise. I conclude that the Aboriginal right of the Sto:lo to fish for sustenance has not been extinguished.

. . . . .

2. IS THE ABORIGINAL RIGHT INFRINGED?

. . . . .

[T]he Crown, by denying the Sto:lo the right to sell *any* quantity of fish, denies their limited Aboriginal right to sell fish for sustenance. The conclusion of *prima facie* infringement of the collective Aboriginal right necessarily follows.

. . . . .

3. IS THE GOVERNMENT'S LIMITATION OF MRS. VAN DER PEET'S RIGHT TO FISH FOR SUSTENANCE JUSTIFIED?

. . . . .

[T]he framers of s. 35(1) deliberately chose not to subordinate the exercise of Aboriginal rights to the good of society as a whole. In the absence of an express limitation on the rights guaranteed by s. 35(1), limitations on them under the doctrine of justification must logically and as a matter of constitutional construction be confined, as *Sparrow* suggests, to truly compelling circumstances, like conservation, which is the *sine qua non* of the right, and restrictions like preventing the abuse of the right to the detriment of the native community or the harm of others — in short, to limitations which are essential to its continued use and exploitation. To follow the path suggested by the Chief Justice is, with respect, to read judicially the equivalent of s. 1 into s. 35(1), contrary to the intention of the framers of the Constitution.

. . . . .

I have argued that the broad approach to justification proposed by the Chief Justice does not conform to the authorities, is indeterminate, and is, in the final analysis unnecessary. Instead, I have proposed that justifiable limitation of Aboriginal rights should be confined to regulation to ensure their exercise conserves the resource and ensures responsible use.

. . . . .

I therefore conclude that a government limitation on an Aboriginal right may be justified, provided the limitation is directed to ensuring the conservation and responsible exercise of the right. Limits beyond this cannot be saved on the ground that they are required for societal peace or reconciliation. Specifically, limits that have the effect of transferring the resource from Aboriginal people without treaty or consent cannot be justified. Short of repeal of s. 35(1), such transfers can be made only with the consent of the Aboriginal people.

. . . . .

4. CONCLUSION

I would allow the appeal to the extent of confirming the existence in principle of an Aboriginal right to sell fish for sustenance purposes, and set aside the appellant's conviction.

. . . . .

Appeal dismissed.

The Supreme Court's characterization of Aboriginal rights in *Van der Peet* as arising only where an activity was an element of a practice, tradition, or custom integral to the distinctive culture of the Aboriginal group claiming the right and traceable to pre-contact practices may be seen to have marked a significant departure from the previous standard, as set out in *Sparrow*. It also gives rise to a variety of questions:

1. Is Lamer C.J.C.'s restriction of Aboriginal rights to pre-contact practices evidence of an adherence to frozen rights theory?
2. Are temporal considerations key determinants in establishing Aboriginal rights?
3. When is "contact" for the purposes of establishing the existence of Aboriginal rights? What ought this be based upon?
4. Can post-contact practices created to replace pre-contact practices rendered ineffective by European settlement be protected under Lamer C.J.C.'s analysis in *Van der Peet*?

While the *Van der Peet* decision made significant changes to *Sparrow*'s characterization of Aboriginal rights, the Supreme Court of Canada's decision in *R. v. Gladstone, supra,* also altered the precedent that had been established in *Sparrow*. The key elements of *Gladstone*, as reproduced below, are those aspects of the decision relating to the justificatory standard that had been established in *Sparrow*.

R. v. GLADSTONE

[1996] 4 C.N.L.R. 65, [1996] 2 S.C.R. 723, [1996] 9 W.W.R. 149, 23 B.C.L.R. (3d) 155, 50 C.R. (4th) 111, 200 N.R. 189, 137 D.L.R. (4th) 648, 109 C.C.C. (3d) 193, 79 B.C.A.C. 161, 129 W.A.C. 161 (references omitted)

Sopinka, Gonthier, Cory, Iacobucci and **Major JJ.** concur with

Lamer C.J.C.: —

I. *Facts*

Donald and William Gladstone, the appellants, are members of the Heiltsuk Band. The appellants were charged under s. 61(1) of the *Fisheries Act*, R.S.C. 1970, c. F-14, with the offences of offering to sell herring spawn on kelp caught under the authority of an Indian food fish licence, contrary to s. 27(5) of the *British Columbia Fishery (General) Regulations*, SOR/84-248 and of attempting to sell herring spawn on kelp not caught under the authority of a Category J herring spawn on kelp licence, contrary to s. 20(3) of the *Pacific Herring Fishery Regulations*, SOR/84-324. Only the charges arising under s. 20(3) of the *Pacific Herring Fishery Regulations* are still at issue in this appeal.

The charges arose out of events taking place in April of 1988. On approximately April 27, 1988 the appellants shipped 4,200 pounds of herring spawn on kelp from Bella Bella to Richmond, a suburb of Vancouver. On

April 28, 1988 the appellants took a pail containing approximately 35 pounds of herring spawn on kelp to Seaborn Enterprises Limited, a fish store in Vancouver. At Seaborn Enterprises the appellants had a conversation with Mr. Katsu Hirose, the owner of the store, in which they asked Mr. Hirose if he was "interested" in herring spawn on kelp. Mr. Hirose informed the appellants that he did not purchase herring spawn on kelp from Native Indians. Upon leaving Seaborn Enterprises the appellants, who had been under surveillance by fisheries officers throughout these events, were arrested and the entire 4,200 pounds of herring spawn on kelp was seized. Upon arrest the appellant William Gladstone produced an Indian food fish licence permitting him to harvest 500 pounds of herring spawn on kelp.

. . . . .

Justification

In *Sparrow*, Dickson C.J. and La Forest J. articulated a two-part test for determining whether government actions infringing Aboriginal rights can be justified. First, the government must demonstrate that it was acting pursuant to a valid legislative objective.

. . . . .

Second, the government must demonstrate that its actions are consistent with the fiduciary duty of the government towards Aboriginal peoples. This means, Dickson C.J. and La Forest J. held, that the government must demonstrate that it has given the Aboriginal fishery priority in a manner consistent with this Court's decision in *Jack v. The Queen*, [1980] 1 S.C.R. 294, at p. 313, where Dickson J. (as he then was) held that the correct order of priority in the fisheries is "(i) conservation; (ii) Indian fishing; (iii) non-Indian commercial fishing; or (iv) non-Indian sports fishing".

. . . . .

Dickson C.J. and La Forest J. also held at p. 1119 that the Crown's fiduciary duty to Aboriginal peoples would require the Court to ask, at the justification stage, such further questions as:

> ... whether there has been as little infringement as possible in order to effect the desired result; whether, in a situation of expropriation, fair compensation is available; and, whether the aboriginal group in question has been consulted with respect to the conservation measures being implemented.

. . . . .

In this case, where, particularly at the stage of justification, the context varies significantly from that in *Sparrow*, it will be necessary to revisit the *Sparrow* test and to adapt the justification test it lays out in order to apply that test to the circumstances of this appeal.

Two points of variation are of particular significance. First, the right recognized and affirmed in this case — to sell herring spawn on kelp commercially — differs significantly from the right recognized and affirmed in *Sparrow* — the right to fish for food, social and ceremonial purposes. That difference lies in the fact that the right at issue in *Sparrow* has an inherent limitation which the right recognized and affirmed in this appeal lacks. The food, social and ceremonial needs for fish of any given band of Aboriginal people are internally limited — at a certain point the band will have sufficient fish to meet these needs. The commercial sale of the herring spawn on kelp, on the other hand, has no such internal limitation; the only limits on the Heiltsuk's need for herring spawn on kelp for commercial sale are the external constraints of the demand of the market and the availability of the resource. This is particularly so in this case where the evidence supports a right to exchange fish on a genuinely commercial basis; the evidence in this case does not justify limiting the right to harvest herring spawn on kelp on a commercial basis to, for example, the sale of herring spawn on kelp for the purposes of obtaining a "moderate livelihood".

·····

The significance of this difference for the *Sparrow* test relates to the position taken in that case that, subject to the limits of conservation, Aboriginal rights holders must be given priority in the fishery. In a situation where the Aboriginal right is internally limited, so that it is clear when that right has been satisfied and other users can be allowed to participate in the fishery, the notion of priority, as articulated in *Sparrow*, makes sense. In that situation it is understandable that in an *exceptional* year, when conservation concerns are severe, it will be possible for Aboriginal rights holders to be alone allowed to participate in the fishery, while in more ordinary years other users will be allowed to participate in the fishery after the Aboriginal rights to fish for food, social and ceremonial purposes have been met.

Where the Aboriginal right has no internal limitation, however, what is described in *Sparrow* as an exceptional situation becomes the ordinary: in the circumstance where the Aboriginal right has no internal limitation, the notion of priority, as articulated in *Sparrow*, would mean that where an Aboriginal right is recognized and affirmed that right would become an exclusive one. Because the right to sell herring spawn on kelp to the commercial market can never be said to be satisfied while the resource is still available and the market is not sated, to give priority to that right in the manner suggested in *Sparrow* would be to give the right-holder exclusivity over any person not having an Aboriginal right to participate in the herring spawn on kelp fishery.

In my view, such a result was not the intention of *Sparrow*. The only circumstance contemplated by *Sparrow* was where the Aboriginal right was internally limited; the judgment simply does not consider how the priority standard should be applied in circumstances where the right has no such internal limitation.

. . . . .

Where the Aboriginal right is one that has no internal limitation then the doctrine of priority does not require that, after conservation goals have been met, the government allocate the fishery so that those holding an Aboriginal right to exploit that fishery on a commercial basis are given an exclusive right to do so. Instead, the doctrine of priority requires that the government demonstrate that, in allocating the resource, it has taken account of the existence of Aboriginal rights and allocated the resource in a manner respectful of the fact that those rights have priority over the exploitation of the fishery by other users. This right is at once both procedural and substantive; at the stage of justification the government must demonstrate both that the process by which it allocated the resource and the actual allocation of the resource which results from that process reflect the prior interest of Aboriginal rights holders in the fishery.

The content of this priority — something less than exclusivity but which nonetheless gives priority to the Aboriginal right — must remain somewhat vague pending consideration of the government's actions in specific cases. ... [P]riority under *Sparrow*'s justification test cannot be assessed against a precise standard but must rather be assessed in each case to determine whether the government has acted in a fashion which reflects that it has truly taken into account the existence of Aboriginal rights. ... [U]nder *Sparrow*'s priority doctrine, where the Aboriginal right to be given priority is one without internal limitation, courts should assess the government's actions not to see whether the government has given exclusivity to that right (the least drastic means) but rather to determine whether the government has taken into account the existence and importance of such rights.

That no blanket requirement is imposed under the priority doctrine should not suggest, however, that no guidance is possible in this area, or that the government's actions will not be subject to scrutiny. Questions relevant to the determination of whether the government has granted priority to Aboriginal rights holders are those enumerated in *Sparrow* relating to consultation and compensation, as well as questions such as whether the government has accommodated the exercise of the Aboriginal right to participate in the fishery (through reduced licence fees, for example), whether the government's objectives in enacting a particular regulatory scheme reflect the need to take into account the priority of Aboriginal rights holders, the extent of the participation in the fishery of Aboriginal rights holders relative to their percentage of the population, how the government has accommodated different Aboriginal rights in a particular fishery (food *versus* commercial rights, for example), how important the fishery is to the economic and material well-being of the band in question, and the criteria taken into account by the government in, for example, allocating commercial licences amongst different users. These questions, like those in *Sparrow*, do not represent an exhaustive list of the factors that may be taken into account in determining whether the government can be said to have given priority to Aboriginal rights holders; they give some indication, however, of what such an inquiry should look like.

. . . . .

[W]here a right has no adequate internal limitations, the notion of exclusivity of priority must be rejected. Certainly the holders of such Aboriginal rights must be given priority, along with all others holding Aboriginal rights to the use of a particular resource; however, the potential existence of other Aboriginal rights holders with an equal claim to priority in the exploitation of the resource, suggests that there must be some external limitation placed on the exercise of those Aboriginal rights which lack internal limitation. Unless the possibility of such a limitation is recognized, it is difficult to see how the government will be able to make decisions of resource allocation amongst the various parties holding prioritized rights to participate in the fishery.

. . . . .

[I]t was not contemplated by *Sparrow* that the recognition and affirmation of Aboriginal rights should result in the common law right of public access in the fishery ceasing to exist with respect to all those fisheries in respect of which exist an Aboriginal right to sell fish commercially. As a common law, not constitutional, right, the right of public access to the fishery must clearly be second in priority to Aboriginal rights; however, the recognition of Aboriginal rights should not be interpreted as extinguishing the right of public access to the fishery.

. . . . .

I now turn to the second significant difference between this case and *Sparrow*. In *Sparrow*, while the Court recognized at p. 1113 that, beyond conservation, there could be other "compelling and substantial" objectives pursuant to which the government could act in accordance with the first branch of the justification test, the Court was not required to delineate what those objectives might be. Further, in delineating the priority requirement, and the relationship between Aboriginal rights-holders and other users of the fishery, the only objective considered by the Court was conservation. This limited focus made sense in *Sparrow* because the net-length restriction at issue in that case was argued by the Crown to have been necessary as a conservation measure (whether it was necessary as such was not actually decided in that case); in this case, however, while some aspects of the government's regulatory scheme arguably relate to conservation — setting the total allowable catch at 20 per cent of the estimated herring stock, requiring the herring roe fishery to bear the brunt of variations in the herring stock because it is more environmentally destructive — other aspects of the government's regulatory scheme bear little or no relation to issues of conservation. Once the overall level of the herring catch has been established, and allocated to the different herring fisheries, *it makes no difference in terms of conservation* who is allowed to catch the fish. Conservation of the fishery is simply not affected once, after the herring spawn on kelp fishery is set at 2,275 tons, 224 tons or 2,275 tons is allocated to the commercial fishery or to some other use. This is not to suggest that these decisions are unimportant or made pursuant to unimportant objectives, but simply that, whatever objectives the government is pursuing in making such decisions, conservation is not (or is only marginally) one of them. As such, it is necessary in this case to consider what, if any, objectives the government may pursue, other than conservation, which will be sufficient to satisfy the first branch of the *Sparrow* justification standard.

Considering this question is made more difficult in this case because, as will be discussed below, almost no evidence has been provided to this Court about the objectives the government was pursuing in allocating the herring resource as it did. Absent some concrete objectives to assess, it is difficult to identify the objectives other than conservation that will meet the "compelling and substantial" standard laid out in *Sparrow*. That being said, however, it is possible to make some general observations about the nature of the objectives that the government can pursue under the first branch of the *Sparrow* justification test.

· · · · ·

Aboriginal rights are recognized and affirmed by s. 35(1) in order to reconcile the existence of distinctive Aboriginal societies prior to the arrival of Europeans in North America with the assertion of Crown sovereignty over that territory; they are the means by which the critical and integral aspects of those societies are maintained. Because, however, distinctive Aboriginal societies exist within, and are a part of, a broader social, political and economic community, over which the Crown is sovereign, there are circumstances in which, in order to pursue objectives of compelling and substantial importance to that community as a whole (taking into account the fact that Aboriginal societies are a part of that community), some limitation of those rights will be justifiable. Aboriginal rights are a necessary part of the reconciliation of Aboriginal societies with the broader political community of which they are part; limits placed on those rights are, where the objectives furthered by those limits are of sufficient importance to the broader community as a whole, *equally* a necessary part of that reconciliation.

The recognition of conservation as a compelling and substantial goal demonstrates this point. Given the integral role the fishery has played in the distinctive cultures of many Aboriginal peoples, conservation can be said to be something the pursuit of which can be linked to the recognition of the existence of such distinctive cultures. Moreover, because conservation is of such overwhelming importance to Canadian society as a whole, including Aboriginal members of that society, it is a goal the pursuit of which is consistent with the reconciliation of Aboriginal societies with the larger Canadian society of which they are a part. In this way, conservation can be said to be a compelling and substantial objective which, provided the rest of the *Sparrow* justification standard is met, will justify governmental infringement of Aboriginal rights.

Although by no means making a definitive statement on this issue, I would suggest that with regards to the distribution of the fisheries resource after conservation goals have been met, objectives such as the pursuit of economic and regional fairness, and the recognition of the historical reliance upon, and participation in, the fishery by non-Aboriginal groups, are the type of objectives which can (at least in the right circumstances) satisfy this standard. *In the right circumstances, such objectives are in the interest of all Canadians and, more importantly, the reconciliation of Aboriginal societies with the rest of Canadian society may well depend on their successful attainment.*

I now turn to the application of the *Sparrow* justification test to the government regulatory scheme challenged in this case. As has already been noted, the government's regulatory scheme has four constituent parts, which, for ease of reference, I will reiterate here: (1) the government determines the amount of the herring stock that will be harvested in a given year; (2) the government allots the herring stock to the different herring fisheries (herring roe, herring spawn on kelp and other herring fisheries); (3) the government allots the herring spawn on kelp fishery to various user groups (commercial users and the Indian food fishery); and, (4) the government allots the commercial herring spawn on kelp licences.

Other than with regards to the first aspect of the government's regulatory scheme, the evidence and testimony presented in this case is insufficient for this Court to make a determination as to whether the government's regulatory scheme is justified. The trial in this case concluded on May 7, 1990, several weeks prior to the release of this Court's judgment in *Sparrow*. Perhaps as a result of this fact, the testimony, evidence and argument presented at the trial simply do not contain the information that is necessary for this Court to assess whether, in allocating the 40,000 tons of herring allotted to the herring fishery, the government has either acted pursuant to a compelling and substantial objective or has acted in a manner consistent with the fiduciary obligation it owes to Aboriginal peoples. It is not that the Crown has failed to discharge its burden of demonstrating that the scheme for allocating the 20 per cent of the herring stock was justified; it is simply that the question of whether or not that scheme of allocation was justified was not addressed at trial, at least in the sense necessary for this Court to decide the question of whether, under the *Sparrow* test, it was justified.

The lack of evidence is problematic with regards to both aspects of the *Sparrow* analysis. First, in so far as an evaluation of the government's objective is concerned, no witnesses testified, and no documents were submitted as evidence, with regards to the objectives pursued by the government in allocating the herring, and the herring spawn on kelp, amongst different user groups.

. . . . .

Second, with regards to priority, there is no evidence as to how much (if any) Aboriginal participation there is in the herring roe fishery or as to whether there are any existing Aboriginal rights to participate in the herring roe fishery, whether for food or commercial purposes. ...

Obviously a new trial will not necessarily provide complete and definitive answers to all of these questions; however, given that the parties simply did not address the justifiability of the government scheme, other than the setting of the herring catch at 20 per cent of the total herring stock, a new trial will almost certainly provide the court with better information than currently exists. Prior to *Sparrow* it was not clear what the government, or parties challenging government action, had to demonstrate in order to succeed in s. 35(1) cases; this lack of clarity undoubtedly contributed to the deficiency of the evidentiary record in this case. A new trial on the question of justification will remedy this deficiency.

A new trial is not, however, necessary with regards to the first aspect of the government's scheme; the evidentiary record clearly demonstrates that this aspect of the government's scheme was justified. Witnesses testified as to the conservation objectives of setting the stock at 20 per cent and as to the difficulties encountered by the herring fishery when the catch was set at much higher levels, as was the case in the 1960s. Moreover, the defence witness Dr. Gary Vigers testified that "fisheries management is full of uncertainty"; in the context of such uncertainty this Court must grant a certain level of deference to the government's approach to fisheries management.

Although the evidence regarding consultation is somewhat scanty, and more will hopefully be presented at a new trial on the justification issue, there is some evidence to suggest that the government was cognizant of the views of Aboriginal groups with regards to the herring fishery. The correspondence between the Native Brotherhood and the Department is indicative of the existence of such consultation. Finally, the setting of the herring catch at 20 per cent of the fishable herring stock, because aimed at conservation, and not affecting the priority of Aboriginal versus non-Aboriginal users of the fishery, is consistent with the priority scheme as laid out in *Sparrow* and as elaborated in this judgment.

V. *Disposition*

In the result, the appeal is allowed and a new trial directed on the issue of guilt or innocence and, with regards to the constitutionality of s. 20(3), on the issue of the justifiability of the government's allocation of herring.

. . . . .

[La Forest J., dissenting, dismissed the appeal, holding that the right of the Heiltsuk band to sell herring spawn on kelp, assuming that it was an Aboriginal right, had been extinguished by the Crown.]
[L'Heureux-Dubé J., delivering separate reasons, concurred with the result reached by the Chief Justice.]

McLachlin J.: —

. . . . .

My conclusions in this appeal may be summarized as follows. Following the reasons I set out in *Van der Peet*, *supra*, the appellants, as members of the Heiltsuk Band, have established that they have an Aboriginal right to harvest and sell herring spawn on kelp for sustenance purposes. That right was not extinguished by any regulatory legislation prior to 1982, and is therefore confirmed by the *Constitution Act, 1982*. The right is limited by the Heiltsuk's traditional reliance on the resource, which was to secure sustenance. It is also limited by the power of the Crown to limit or prohibit exploitation of the resource that is incompatible with its continued use. There is insufficient evidence to determine whether the current regulatory framework satisfies the sustenance needs of the Heiltsuk people. Therefore, the questions of whether the Heiltsuk's right to sell herring spawn on kelp for sustenance was infringed and, if so, whether any such infringement is justified by the Crown, must be decided at a new trial.

The extension of the *Sparrow* justificatory standard in *Gladstone* has garnered significant criticism. In particular, Lamer C.J.C.'s majority judgment has been criticized for allowing infringements of Aboriginal rights based on public interest standards, something that the unanimous decision in *Sparrow* had rejected as being "so vague as to provide no meaningful guidance and so broad as to be unworkable as a test for the justification of a limitation on constitutional rights".[3] As McLachlin J. explained in her judgment in *Van der Peet*:

> The extension of the concept of compelling objective to matters like economic and regional fairness and the interests of non-Aboriginal fishers, by contrast, would negate the very Aboriginal right to fish itself, on the ground that this is required for the reconciliation of Aboriginal rights and other interests and the consequent good of the community as a whole. This is not limitation required for the responsible exercise of the right, but rather limitation on the basis of the economic demands of non-Aboriginals. It is limitation of a different order than the conservation, harm prevention type of limitation sanctioned in *Sparrow*.

Kent McNeil has also commented that the former Chief Justice's approach to justification allows Aboriginal rights to be overridden "on broad policy grounds relating to economic and regional fairness, and even to support the economic interests of particular groups such as commercial fishers whose historic use of the fishery may well have been a violation of aboriginal rights all along".[4]

While *Gladstone* altered *Sparrow's* justificatory standard for legislative infringements of Aboriginal rights, the Supreme Court in *Delgamuukw v. British Columbia, infra,* further altered that test to render it applicable to infringements of Aboriginal title. Lamer C.J.C. held that proof of Aboriginal title did not require that the land be integral to the distinctive culture of the group claiming the title, but that the group was in exclusive occupation of the land.[5] Further, while Aboriginal rights had to be identifiable prior to European contact under the *Van der Peet* standard, Aboriginal title — specifically, the group's exclusive occupancy of the land in question — only had to be demonstrated to exist at the time the Crown asserted sovereignty over the land. Alternatively, Lamer C.J.C. held that proof of title could also be satisfied by demonstrating evidence of continuity between present occupation and pre-sovereignty occupation.[6] The discussion of the justificatory standard for Aboriginal title in *Delgamuukw* is also important for its summary of the standard for infringements of Aboriginal rights from *Sparrow* through *Gladstone*.

DELGAMUUKW v. BRITISH COLUMBIA

[1997] 3 S.C.R. 1010

Cory, McLachlin, and **Major JJ.** concur with

Lamer C.J.C.: —

(f) *Infringements of Aboriginal Title: the Test of Justification*

(i) Introduction

The aboriginal rights recognized and affirmed by s. 35(1), including aboriginal title, are not absolute. Those rights may be infringed, both by the federal (e.g., *Sparrow*) and provincial (e.g., *Côté*) governments. However, s. 35(1) requires that those infringements satisfy the test of justification. In this section, I will review the Court's nascent jurisprudence on justification and explain how that test will apply in the context of infringements of aboriginal title.

(ii) General Principles

The test of justification has two parts, which I shall consider in turn. First, the infringement of the aboriginal right must be in furtherance of a legislative objective that is compelling and substantial. I explained in *Gladstone* that compelling and substantial objectives were those which were directed at either one of the purposes underlying the recognition and affirmation of aboriginal rights by s. 35(1), which are (at para. 72):

> ... the recognition of the prior occupation of North America by aboriginal peoples or ... the reconciliation of aboriginal prior occupation with the assertion of the sovereignty of the Crown.

I noted that the latter purpose will often "be most relevant" (at para. 72) at the stage of justification. I think it important to repeat why (at para. 73) that is so:

> Because ... distinctive aboriginal societies exist within, and are part of, a broader social, political and economic community, over which the Crown is sovereign, there are circumstances in which, in order to pursue objectives of compelling and substantial importance to that community as a whole (taking into account the fact that aboriginal societies are part of that community), some limitation of those rights will be justifiable. *Aboriginal rights are a necessary part of the reconciliation of aboriginal societies with the broader political community of which they are part; limits placed on those rights are, where the objectives furthered by those limits are of sufficient importance to the broader community as a whole, equally a necessary part of that reconciliation.* [Emphasis added; "equally" emphasized in original.]

The conservation of fisheries, which was accepted as a compelling and substantial objective in *Sparrow*, furthers both of these purposes, because it simultaneously recognizes that fishing is integral to many aboriginal cultures, and also seeks to reconcile aboriginal societies with the broader community by ensuring that there are fish enough for all. But legitimate government objectives also include "the pursuit of economic and regional fairness" and "the recognition of the historical reliance upon, and participation in, the fishery by non-aboriginal groups" (para. 75). By contrast, measures enacted for relatively unimportant reasons, such as sports fishing without a significant economic component (*Adams, supra*) would fail this aspect of the test of justification.

The second part of the test of justification requires an assessment of whether the infringement is consistent with the special fiduciary relationship between the Crown and aboriginal peoples. What has become clear is that the requirements of the fiduciary duty are a function of the "legal and factual context" of each appeal (*Gladstone, supra,* at para. 56). *Sparrow* and *Gladstone,* for example, interpreted and applied the fiduciary duty in terms of the idea of *priority*. The theory underlying that principle is that the fiduciary relationship between the Crown and aboriginal peoples demands that aboriginal interests be placed first. However, the fiduciary duty does not demand that aboriginal rights always be given priority. As was said in *Sparrow, supra,* at pp. 1114-15:

> The nature of the constitutional protection afforded by s. 35(1) *in this context* demands that there be a link between the question of justification and the allocation of priorities in the fishery. [Emphasis added.]

Other contexts permit, and may even require, that the fiduciary duty be articulated in other ways (at p. 1119):

> Within the analysis of justification, there are further questions to be addressed, depending on the circumstances of the inquiry. These include the questions of whether there has been as little infringement as possible in order to effect the desired result; whether, in a situation of expropriation, fair compensation is available; and, whether the aboriginal group in question has been consulted with respect to the conservation measures being implemented.

Sparrow did not explain when the different articulations of the fiduciary duty should be used. Below, I suggest that the choice between them will in large part be a function of the nature of the aboriginal right at issue.

In addition to variation in the *form* which the fiduciary duty takes, there will also be variation in degree of scrutiny required by the fiduciary duty of the infringing measure or action. The degree of scrutiny is a function of the nature of the aboriginal right at issue. The distinction between *Sparrow* and *Gladstone,* for example, turned on whether the right amounted to the exclusive use of a resource, which in turn was a function of whether the right had an internal limit. In *Sparrow,* the right was internally limited, because it was a right to fish for food, ceremonial and social purposes, and as a result would only amount to an exclusive right to use the fishery in exceptional circumstances. Accordingly, the requirement of priority was applied strictly to mean that (at p. 1116) "any allocation of priorities after valid conservation measures have been implemented must give top priority to Indian food fishing".

In *Gladstone,* by contrast, the right to sell fish commercially was only limited by supply and demand. Had the test for justification been applied in a strict form in *Gladstone,* the aboriginal right would have amounted to an exclusive right to exploit the fishery on a commercial basis. This was not the intention of *Sparrow*, and I accordingly modified the test for justification, by altering the idea of priority. ... After *Gladstone*, in the context of commercial activity, the priority of aboriginal rights is constitutionally satisfied if the government had taken those rights into account and has allocated a resource "in a manner respectful" (at para. 62) of that priority. A court must be satisfied that "the government has taken into account the existence and importance of [aboriginal] rights" (at para. 63) which it determines by asking the following questions (at para. 64):

> Questions relevant to the determination of whether the government has granted priority to aboriginal rights holders are ... questions such as whether the government has accommodated the exercise of the aboriginal right to participate in the fishery (through reduced licence fees, for example), whether the government's objectives in enacting a particular regulatory scheme reflect the need to take into account the priority of aboriginal rights holders, the extent of the participation in the fishery of aboriginal rights holders relative to their percentage of the population, how the government has accommodated different aboriginal rights in a particular fishery (food *versus* commercial rights, for example), how important the fishery is to the economic and material well-being of the band in question, and the criteria taken into account by the government in, for example, allocating commercial licences amongst different users.

(iii)   Justification and Aboriginal Title

... In the wake of *Gladstone*, the range of legislative objectives that can justify the infringement of aboriginal title is fairly broad. Most of these objectives can be traced to the *reconciliation* of the prior occupation of North America by aboriginal peoples with the assertion of Crown sovereignty, which entails the recognition that "distinctive aboriginal societies exist within, and are a part of, a broader social, political and economic community" (at para. 73). In my opinion, the development of agriculture, forestry, mining, and hydroelectric power, the general economic development of the interior of British Columbia, protection of the environment or endangered species, the building of infrastructure and the settlement of foreign populations to support those aims, are the kinds of objectives that are consistent with this purpose and, in principle, can justify the infringement of aboriginal title. Whether a particular measure or government act can be explained by reference to one of those objectives, however, is ultimately a question of fact that will have to be examined on a case-by-case basis.

The manner in which the fiduciary duty operates with respect to the second stage of the justification test — both with respect to the standard of scrutiny and the particular form that the fiduciary duty will take — will be a function of the nature of aboriginal title. Three aspects of aboriginal title are relevant here. First, aboriginal title encompasses the right to *exclusive* use and occupation of land; second, aboriginal title encompasses *the right to choose* to what uses land can be put, subject to the ultimate limit that those uses cannot destroy the ability of the land to sustain future generations of aboriginal peoples; and third, that lands held pursuant to aboriginal title have an inescapable *economic component*.

The exclusive nature of aboriginal title is relevant to the degree of scrutiny of the infringing measure or action. For example, if the Crown's fiduciary duty requires that aboriginal title be given priority, then it is the altered approach to priority that I laid down in *Gladstone* which should apply. What is required is that the government demonstrate ... "both that the process by which it allocated the resource and the actual allocation of the resource which results from that process reflect the prior interest" of the holders of aboriginal title in the land. By analogy with *Gladstone*, this might entail, for example, that governments accommodate the participation of aboriginal peoples in the development of the resources of British Columbia, that the conferral of fee simples for agriculture, and of leases and licences for forestry and mining reflect the prior occupation of aboriginal title lands, that economic barriers to aboriginal uses of their lands (e.g., licensing fees) be somewhat reduced. This list is illustrative and not exhaustive. This is an issue that may involve an assessment of the various interests at stake in the resources in question. No doubt, there will be dificulties in determining the precise value of the aboriginal interest in the land and any grants, leases or licences given for its exploitation. These difficult economic considerations obviously cannot be solved here.

Moreover, the other aspects of aboriginal title suggest that the fiduciary duty may be articulated in a manner different than the idea of priority. This point becomes clear from a comparison between aboriginal title and the aboriginal right to fish for food in *Sparrow*. First, aboriginal title encompasses within it a right to choose to what ends a piece of land can be put. The aboriginal right to fish for food, by contrast, does not contain within it the same discretionary component. This aspect of aboriginal title suggests that the fiduciary relationship between the Crown and aboriginal peoples may be satisfied by the involvement of aboriginal peoples in decisions taken with respect to their lands. There is always a duty of consultation. Whether the aboriginal group has been consulted is relevant to determining whether the infringement of aboriginal title is justified, in the same way that the Crown's failure to consult an aboriginal group with respect to the terms by which reserve land is leased may breach its fiduciary duty at common law: *Guerin*. The nature and scope of the duty of consultation will vary with the circumstances. In occasional cases, when the breach is less serious or relatively minor, it will be no more than a duty to discuss important decisions that will be taken with respect to lands held pursuant to aboriginal title. Of course, even in these rare cases when the minimum acceptable standard is consultation, this consultation must be in good faith, and with the intention of substantially addressing the concerns of the aboriginal peoples whose lands are at issue. In most cases, it will be significantly deeper than mere consultation. Some cases may even require the full consent of an aboriginal nation, particularly when provinces enact hunting and fishing regulations in relation to aboriginal lands.

Second, aboriginal title, unlike the aboriginal right to fish for food, has an inescapably economic aspect, particularly when one takes into account the modern uses to which lands held pursuant to aboriginal title can be put. The economic aspect of aboriginal title suggests that compensation is relevant to the question of justification as well, a possibility suggested in *Sparrow* and which I repeated in *Gladstone*. Indeed, compensation for breaches of fiduciary duty are a well-established part of the landscape of aboriginal rights: *Guerin*. In keeping with the duty of honour and good faith on the Crown, fair compensation will ordinarily be required when aboriginal title is infringed. The amount of compensation payable will vary with the nature of the particular aboriginal title affected and with the nature and severity of the infringement and the extent to which aboriginal interests were accommodated. Since the issue of damages was severed from the principal action, we received no submissions on the appropriate legal principles that would be relevant to determining the appropriate level of compensation of infringements of aboriginal title. In the circumstances, it is best that we leave those difficult questions to another day.

A number of questions arise from the modification of the justificatory standard in *Delgamuukw*. Is there a substantial difference between the justificatory test for governmental legislative infringements of title established in *Delgamuukw* versus that for Aboriginal rights created in *Sparrow* and modified in *Gladstone*? What role does the Crown's fiduciary duty play in the *Delgamuukw* test? Is this different than the role of the Crown's duty under the modified *Sparrow* test? Finally, does Lamer C.J.C.'s discussion of the importance of governmental consultation with Aboriginal peoples in *Delgamuukw* differ from the Court's earlier statements of the role of consultation in the justification process?

In addition to these questions, one may also query whether the distinction between the requirement for proof of Aboriginal rights — that they must be integral to the distinctive culture of the group claiming the right and identifiable prior to European contact under the *Van der Peet* standard — versus that for proof of Aboriginal title — that the group claiming title must have been in exclusive occupancy of the land in question at the time the Crown asserted sovereignty over the land — under section 35(1) is an appropriate one. Are there valid reasons for looking to contact to determine Aboriginal rights, but looking to the time of the Crown's assertion of sovereignty to determine Aboriginal title? In *Delgamuukw*, [1997] 3 S.C.R. 1010, Lamer C.J.C. provided the following explanation at 1098:

> [I]n the context of Aboriginal title, sovereignty is the appropriate time period to consider for several reasons.... Aboriginal title is a burden on the Crown's underlying title. However, the Crown did not gain this title until it asserted sovereignty over the land in question. Because it does not make sense to speak of a burden on the underlying title before that title existed, aboriginal title crystallized at the time sovereignty was asserted. Secondly, aboriginal title does not raise the problem of distinguishing between distinctive, integral aboriginal practices, customs and traditions and those influenced or introduced by European contact. Under common law, the act of occupation or possession is sufficient to ground aboriginal title and it is not necessary to prove that the land was a distinctive or integral part of the aboriginal society before the arrival of Europeans. Finally, from a practical standpoint, it appears that the date of sovereignty is more certain than the date of first contact. It is often very difficult to determine the precise moment that each Aboriginal group had first contact with European culture. ... For these reasons, I conclude that Aboriginals must establish occupation of the

land from the date of the assertion of sovereignty in order to sustain a claim for Aboriginal title.

In Lamer C.J.C.'s explanation of why the time period for establishing Aboriginal title differs from that in which to establish Aboriginal rights, his final point is one of expediency — that the date of sovereignty is more certain than the date of first contact and the former is easier to demonstrate. If expediency is a legitimate rationale for establishing a particular temporal period as a basis for the existence of a right, is there any reason why it ought to apply only to Aboriginal title and not to Aboriginal rights?

Although the *Delgamuukw* decision is significant for its differentiation of the test for demonstrating Aboriginal title versus that for Aboriginal rights, the Supreme Court of Canada also considered the relationship between Aboriginal rights and Aboriginal title in its decisions in *R. v. Adams* and *R. v. Côté* (both of which are excerpted below). As these decisions indicate, many of the principles discussed in Chapter 1 in relation to Aboriginal title are equally applicable to Aboriginal rights.

R. v. ADAMS

[1996] 4 C.N.L.R. 1, [1996] 3 S.C.R. 101, 202 N.R. 89, 138 D.L.R. (4th) 657, 110 C.C.C. (3d) 97 (references omitted)

The judgment of **Lamer C.J.C.** and **La Forest, Sopinka, Gonthier, Cory, McLachlin, Iacobucci** and **Major JJ.** was delivered by

The Chief Justice: —

I. *Introduction*

This appeal and the appeal of *R. v. Côté*, [1996] [3 S.C.R. 139] have been released simultaneously and should be read together in light of the closely related issues raised by both cases.

The appellant, a Mohawk, was charged with the regulatory offence of fishing without a licence in Lake St. Francis in the St. Régis region of Quebec. He challenges his conviction on the basis that he was exercising an Aboriginal right to fish as recognized and affirmed by s. 35(1) of the *Constitution Act, 1982*.

In resolving this appeal and the appeal in *Côté*, this Court must answer the question of whether Aboriginal rights are necessarily based in Aboriginal title to land, so that the fundamental claim that must be made in any Aboriginal rights case is to Aboriginal title, or whether Aboriginal title is instead one sub-set of the larger category of Aboriginal rights, so that fishing and other Aboriginal rights can exist independently of a claim to Aboriginal title.

In the trilogy of *R. v. Van der Peet*, [1996] 2 S.C.R. 507, *R. v. N.T.C. Smokehouse Ltd.*, [1996] 2 S.C.R. 672, and *R. v. Gladstone*, [1996] 2 S.C.R. 723, this Court had opportunity to consider the question of the scope of the Aboriginal rights recognized and affirmed by s. 35(1). This case and *Côté* will require the application of the principles articulated in those cases to the question of the relationship between Aboriginal title and the other Aboriginal rights, particularly fishing rights, recognized and affirmed by s. 35(1). Furthermore, these two related appeals involve the claim of an Aboriginal right to fish within the historical boundaries of New France. As such, this Court must answer the question of whether, under the principles of the *Van der Peet* trilogy, the constitutional protection of s. 35(1) extends to Aboriginal customs, practices, and traditions which may not have achieved legal recognition under the colonial regime of New France prior to the transition to British sovereignty in 1763.

. . . . .

V. *Analysis*

Aboriginal Title and Aboriginal Rights

. . . . .

In *Van der Peet* ... Aboriginal rights were said to be best understood as,

> ... first, the means by which the Constitution recognizes the fact that prior to the arrival of Europeans in North America the land was already occupied by distinctive Aboriginal societies, and as, second, the means by which that prior occupation is reconciled with the assertion of Crown sovereignty over Canadian territory.

From this basis the Court went on to hold ... that Aboriginal rights are identified through the following test:

> ... in order to be an Aboriginal right an activity must be an element of a practice, custom or tradition integral to the distinctive culture of the Aboriginal group claiming the right.

What this test, along with the conceptual basis which underlies it, indicates, is that while claims to Aboriginal title fall within the conceptual framework of Aboriginal rights, Aboriginal rights do not exist solely where a claim to Aboriginal title has been made out. Where an Aboriginal group has shown that a particular activity, custom or tradition taking place on the land was integral to the distinctive culture of that group then, *even if they have not shown that their occupation and use of the land was sufficient to support a claim of title to the land*, they will have demonstrated that they have an Aboriginal right to engage in that practice, custom or tradition. ... *Van der Peet* establishes that s. 35 recognizes and affirms the rights of those peoples who occupied North America prior to the arrival of the Europeans; that recognition and affirmation is not limited to those circumstances where an Aboriginal group's relationship with the land is of a kind sufficient to establish title to the land.

To understand why Aboriginal rights cannot be inexorably linked to Aboriginal title it is only necessary to recall that some Aboriginal peoples were nomadic, varying the location of their settlements with the season and changing circumstances. ...

Moreover, some Aboriginal peoples varied the location of their settlements both before and after contact. The Mohawks are one such people ...

That this is the case may (although I take no position on this point) preclude the establishment of Aboriginal title to the lands on which they settled; however, it in no way subtracts from the fact that, wherever they
were settled before or after contact, *prior to contact the Mohawks engaged in
practices, traditions or customs on the land which were integral to their distinctive culture.*

. . . . .

The recognition that Aboriginal title is simply one manifestation of the
doctrine of Aboriginal rights should not, however, create the impression
that the fact that some Aboriginal rights are linked to land use or occupation is unimportant. Even where an Aboriginal right exists on a tract of
land to which the Aboriginal people in question do not have title, that
right may well be site specific, with the result that it can be exercised only
upon that specific tract of land. For example, if an Aboriginal people demonstrates that hunting on a specific tract of land was an integral part of
their distinctive culture then, even if the right exists apart from title to that
tract of land, the Aboriginal right to hunt is nonetheless defined as, and
limited to, the right to hunt on the specific tract of land. A site-specific
hunting or fishing right does not, simply because it is independent of Aboriginal title to the land on which it took place, become an abstract fishing
or hunting right exercisable anywhere; it continues to be a right to hunt or
fish *on the tract of land in question.*

Aboriginal Rights and The Colony of New France

The respondent raises another important question concerning the doctrine
of Aboriginal rights under s. 35(1). The Aboriginal right to fish claimed in
this instance relates to a tract of territory, specifically Lake St. Francis,
which falls within the boundaries of New France prior to 1763. The respondent argues that this claimed right should be rejected as the French
colonial regime never legally recognized the existence of Aboriginal title or
any incident Aboriginal right to fish prior to the commencement of British
sovereignty.

Under the British law governing colonization, the Crown assumed
ownership of newly discovered territories subject to an underlying interest
of indigenous peoples in the occupation and use of such territories. By
contrast, it is argued that under the French regime of colonization, the
French monarch assumed full and complete ownership of all newly discovered territories upon discovery and symbolic possession. In the absence
of a specific concession, colonists and Aboriginal peoples were only entitled to enjoy the use of the land through the grace and charity of the
French monarch, but not by any recognized legal right. ... In brief, the respondent submits that regardless of the actual fishing practices of the Mohawks both prior to and during the French regime, the French Crown
never formally recognized any legal right of the Mohawks to fish in Lake
St. Francis, and thus no such right was received into the common law with
the transition to British sovereignty in 1763.

For the reasons developed in *Côté, supra,* this argument must be rejected. The respondent's characterization of the status of Aboriginal rights under French colonial law is open to question, although, as in *Côté,* I need not decide the point here. What is important is that, as explained in *Van der Peet, supra,* the purpose of the entrenchment of s. 35(1) was to extend constitutional protection to the practices, customs and traditions central to the distinctive culture of Aboriginal societies prior to contact with Europeans. If the exercise of such practices, customs and traditions effectively continued following contact in the absence of specific extinguishment, such practices, customs and traditions are entitled to constitutional recognition subject to the infringement and justification test outlined in *Sparrow, supra,* and more recently, in *Gladstone, supra.* The fact that a particular practice, custom or tradition continued following the arrival of Europeans, but in the absence of the formal gloss of legal recognition from the European colonizers, should not undermine the protection accorded to Aboriginal peoples. Section 35(1) would fail to achieve its noble purpose of preserving the integral and defining features of distinctive Aboriginal societies if it only protected those defining features which were fortunate enough to have received the legal approval of British and French colonizers.

. . . . .

VI. *Disposition*

In the result the appeal is allowed and the appellant's conviction is set aside.

For the reasons given above, the constitutional question must be answered as follows:

Question :   Is s. 4(1) of the *Quebec Fishery Regulations,* as they read on May 7, 1982, of no force or effect with respect to appellant in the circumstances of these proceedings in virtue of s. 52 of the *Constitution Act, 1982* by reason of the Aboriginal rights within the meaning of s. 35 of the *Constitution Act, 1982* invoked by appellant.

Answer :   Yes.

L'Heureux-Dubé J.: —

... I have had the benefit of the Chief Justice's opinion and I agree with the result he reaches. I also agree generally with his reasons, subject to the following comments about the relationship between Aboriginal rights and Aboriginal title, and about the proper approach to the definition of the nature and extent of Aboriginal rights.

. . . . .

Although the point is implicit in the Chief Justice's reasons, I believe it is important in this case to state clearly that Aboriginal rights can be incidental to Aboriginal title but need not be: they are severable from and can exist independently of Aboriginal title. ... Put another way, the strict conditions for recognition of Aboriginal title at common law are not applicable when, as in this case, the appellant seeks, not the broadest right to occupy and use a tract of land, but only the limited right to fish upon it. In such cases, the only requirements are those set out in *Van der Peet*, regarding the recognition of an Aboriginal right under s. 35(1) of the *Constitution Act, 1982*.

With respect to the approach to the interpretation of the nature and extent of Aboriginal rights, the test utilized by the Chief Justice centres on the individualized practices of the particular Aboriginal group prior to contact with the Europeans. I must distance myself from this approach. ...

. . . . .

In the result, I would dispose of the appeal in the manner stated by the Chief Justice and answer the constitutional question as he suggests.

Appeal allowed.

As the *Adams* decision indicates, it was considered jointly with the appeal of the decision in *Côté*, below. Thus, it is necessary to consider both decisions together in order to acquire a true appreciation of the entirety of the issues considered by the Supreme Court of Canada therein.

R. v. CÔTÉ

[1996] 4 C.N.L.R. 26, [1996] 3 S.C.R. 139, 202 N.R. 161, 138 D.L.R. (4th) 185, 110 C.C.C. (3d) 122 (references omitted)

The judgment of **Lamer C.J.C.** and **Sopinka, Gonthier, Cory, McLachlin, Iacobucci** and **Major JJ.** was delivered by

The Chief Justice: —

I. Introduction

This appeal and the appeal of *R. v. Adams*, [1996] 3 S.C.R. 101, have been released simultaneously and should be read together in light of the closely related issues raised by both cases.

The appellants, members of the Algonquin people, were convicted of the offence of entering a controlled harvest zone in the Outaouais region of Quebec without paying the required fee for motor vehicle access. The appellant Côté was additionally convicted of the offence of fishing within the zone in the absence of a valid licence. The appellants jointly challenge their convictions on the basis that they were exercising an aboriginal right and a concurrent treaty right to fish on their ancestral lands as recognized and protected by s. 35(1) of the Constitution Act, 1982.

The appellant Côté was convicted under the same federal fishing regulation as the accused in Adams. In resolving both this appeal and Adams, this Court must answer the question of whether an aboriginal fishing or other right must be necessarily incident to a claim of aboriginal title in land, or whether an aboriginal right may exist independently of a claim of aboriginal title. ...

Additionally, these two related appeals involve the claim of an aboriginal right within the historic boundaries of New France. As such, this Court must answer the question of whether, under the principles of the Van der Peet trilogy, the constitutional protection of s. 35(1) extends to aboriginal practices, customs and traditions which did not achieve legal recognition under the colonial regime of New France prior to the transition to British sovereignty in 1763.

. . . . .

A. *Aboriginal Rights*

Aboriginal Rights and Aboriginal Title

Throughout the proceedings below, the appellants framed their ancestral right to fish on the Z.E.C. territory as an aboriginal right incidental to a claim of aboriginal title.

. . . . .

For the reasons I have given in the related appeal in *Adams, supra*, I find that aboriginal rights may indeed exist independently of aboriginal title. As I explained in *Adams* ... aboriginal title is simply one manifestation of the doctrine of aboriginal rights.

. . . . .

However, as I stressed in *Adams* ... a protected aboriginal right falling short of aboriginal title may nonetheless have an important link to the land. An aboriginal practice, custom or tradition entitled to protection as an aboriginal right will frequently be limited to a specific territory or location, depending on the actual pattern of exercise of such an activity prior to contact. As such, an aboriginal right will often be defined in site-specific terms, with the result that it can only be exercised upon a specific tract of land.

. . . . .

Aboriginal Rights within New France

In the proceedings below, the respondent adopted the position that the Algonquins could not assert the existence of aboriginal title within the former boundaries of New France in light of the process of French colonization and the legal transition to British sovereignty following capitulation.

. . . . .

The argument of the respondent is fairly straightforward. Under the British law of discovery, the British Crown assumed ownership of newly discovered territories subject to an underlying interest of indigenous peoples in the occupation and use of such territories. Accordingly, the Crown was only able to acquire full ownership of the lands in the New World through the slow process of negotiations with aboriginal groups leading to purchase or surrender.

Unlike the British process of colonization, however, it is suggested that the French Crown did not legally recognize any subsisting aboriginal interest in land upon discovery. Rather, the French Crown assumed full ownership of all discovered lands upon symbolic possession and conquest. Accordingly, French colonizers never engaged in the consistent practice of negotiating formal territorial surrenders with the aboriginal peoples. G. F. G. Stanley, summarized this process in "The First Indian 'Reserves' in Canada", *Revue d'histoire de l'Amérique française*, 4, 2 (1950): 178-210:

> One point of interest emerges with respect to the Indian reserves of the Ancien Régime. At no time was there any recognition on the part of the French crown of any aboriginal proprietary rights in the soil. The French settler occupied his lands in Canada without any thought of compensating the native. There were no formal surrenders from the Indians, no negotiations, and no treaties such as marked the Indian policy of the British period. The lands which were set aside for the Indians were granted not of right but of grace, not to the Indians themselves but to the religious orders who cared for them. The nearest approach to any grant to the Indians themselves was the Sillery grant of 1651. Whatever rights the Indians acquired flowed not from a theoretical aboriginal title but from the clemency of the crown or the charity of individuals.

... The French monarch did cede important specific lands to missions for the purpose of organizing and evangelizing the indigenous residents of New France. As well, colonial authorities did indeed tolerate the fact that aboriginal peoples occupied and engaged in traditional practices and activities (such as fishing and hunting) on Crown lands. However, it is contended that the toleration of such activities represented a general liberty accorded to all of the King's subjects, rather than the recognition of a special right enjoyed by aboriginal peoples.

The respondent further argues that following capitulation, pre-existing French colonial law was fully received under the terms of *The Quebec Act, 1774* and under the general principles of the British law of conquest.... In the absence of a formal renunciation of the French colonial system, it is submitted that the common law thus incorporated the non-existence of aboriginal rights within New France in its doctrine of aboriginal title.

... I am not persuaded that the status of French colonial law was as clear as the respondent suggests. As H. Brun admitted in "Les droits des Indiens" ... while French law never explicitly recognized the existence of a *sui generis* aboriginal interest in land, [TRANSLATION] "nor did it [explicitly] state that such an interest did not exist". Indeed, some legal historians have suggested that the French Crown never assumed full title and ownership to the lands occupied by aboriginal peoples in light of the nature and pattern of French settlement in New France.

According to this historical interpretation, from the time of Champlain to 1763, French settlements within New France fell almost exclusively within the St. Lawrence Valley. At the date of Champlain's arrival in the Montreal area in 1603, the surrounding region was largely devoid of indigenous inhabitants. In one of the mysteries of the history of New France, the Iroquois people who occupied the region at the date of Jacques Cartier's visit in 1534 had simply disappeared by 1603. The French colonists thus claimed and occupied this particular area as *terra nullius*. But these historians argue that the French chose not to further encroach on the traditional lands of the aboriginal peoples surrounding the valley. In the west of New France, for instance, French seigneuries did not extend further than the Long-Sault, stopping well before the vague eastern boundary of the ancestral lands of the Algonquins. The French, of course, had good reason for not encroaching upon these lands, as they were both outnumbered and surrounded by potentially hostile forces in the Valley. Content with occupation of the *terra nullius* of the Valley, the French thus never engaged in a pattern of surrender and purchase similar to British colonial policy. In this interpretation, it is argued that the French Crown only assumed ownership of the lands lining the St. Lawrence River which it actually occupied and organized under the Seigneurial system. ... This argument is supported by the fact that, in its diplomatic relations, the French Crown maintained that aboriginal peoples were sovereign nations rather than mere subjects of the monarch. As Cumming and Mickenberg chronicle in *Native Rights in Canada* ... in the diplomatic period following the Treaty of Utrecht, 1713, the French officially maintained that they could not cede title to lands occupied by aboriginal peoples in the Maritimes and Upper New York State as such peoples were independent nations allied with the French Crown, rather than mere royal subjects. The French similarly disavowed responsibility for Indian attacks on the British, on the grounds that aboriginal nations were independent allies of the French monarch rather than his royal subjects. ... While such assertions were raised in the context of subtle diplomatic manoeuvring between the two European powers, they do not appear to have been received as entirely hollow.

Furthermore, even under the assumption that the respondent's characterization of French colonial system is accurate, it is not at all clear that French colonial law governing relations with aboriginal peoples was mechanically received by the common law upon the commencement of British sovereignty. It is true that under *The Quebec Act, 1774*, and under the legal principles of British conquest, the pre-existing laws governing the acquired territory of New France were received and continued in the absence of subsequent legislative modification. It is by these legal means that the distinct civilian system of private law continues to operate and thrive within the modern boundaries of the province of Quebec. But while the new British regime received and continued the former system of colonial law governing the proprietary relations between private individuals, it is less clear that the advent of British sovereignty continued the French system of law governing the relations between the British Crown and indigenous societies. In short, the common law recognizing aboriginal title was arguably a necessary incident of British sovereignty which displaced the pre-existing colonial law governing New France. As Professor Slattery argues in "Understanding Aboriginal Rights":

> The doctrine of aboriginal rights, like other doctrines of colonial law, applied automatically to a new colony when the colony was acquired. In the same way that colonial law determined whether a colony was deemed to be 'settled' or 'conquered', and whether English law was automatically introduced or local laws retained, it also supplied the presumptive legal structure governing the position of native peoples. The doctrine of aboriginal rights applied, then, to every British colony that now forms part of Canada, from Newfoundland to British Columbia. Although the doctrine was a species of unwritten British law, it was not part of English common law in the narrow sense, and its application to a colony did not depend on whether or not English common law was introduced there. Rather the doctrine was part of a body of fundamental constitutional law that was logically prior to the introduction of English common law and governed its application in the colony.

Indeed, this Court has held that the law of aboriginal title represents a distinct species of federal common law rather than a simple subset of the common or civil law or property law operating within the province.

. . . . .

However, I do not rely on such reasoning to reject the position of the respondent on the reception of French colonial law. Rather, I believe that the respondent's submission is best addressed under the terms and purpose of the constitutional enactment of s. 35(1) of the *Constitution Act, 1982*.

I do not believe that the intervention of French sovereignty negated the potential existence of aboriginal rights within the former boundaries of New France under s. 35(1). The entrenchment of aboriginal ancestral and treaty rights in s. 35(1) has changed the landscape of aboriginal rights in Canada. As explained in the *Van der Peet* trilogy, the purpose of s. 35(1) was to extend constitutional protection to the practices, customs and traditions central to the distinctive culture of aboriginal societies prior to contact with Europeans. If such practices, customs and traditions continued following contact in the absence of specific extinguishment, such practices, customs and traditions are entitled to constitutional recognition subject to the infringement and justification tests outlined in *Sparrow, supra*, and *Gladstone, supra*.

As such, the fact that a particular practice, custom or tradition continued, in an unextinguished manner, following the arrival of Europeans *but* in the absence of the formal gloss of legal recognition from French colonial law should not undermine the constitutional protection accorded to aboriginal peoples. Section 35(1) would fail to achieve its noble purpose of preserving the integral and defining features of distinctive aboriginal societies if it only protected those defining features which were fortunate enough to have received the legal recognition and approval of European colonizers. I should stress that the French Regime's failure to recognize legally a specific aboriginal practice, custom or tradition (and indeed the French Regime's tacit toleration of a specific practice, custom or tradition) clearly cannot be equated with a "clear and plain" intention to extinguish such practices under the extinguishment test of s. 35(1).

. . . . .

The respondent's view, if adopted, would create an awkward patchwork of constitutional protection for aboriginal rights across the nation, depending upon the historical idiosyncrasies of colonization over particular regions of the country. In my respectful view, such a static and retrospective interpretation of s. 35(1) cannot be reconciled with the noble and prospective purpose of the constitutional entrenchment of aboriginal and treaty rights in the *Constitution Act, 1982.* Indeed, the respondent's proposed interpretation risks undermining the very purpose of s. 35(1) by perpetuating the historical injustice suffered by aboriginal peoples at the hands of colonizers who failed to respect the distinctive cultures of pre-existing aboriginal societies.

. . . . .

Therefore, even on the assumption that the French Crown did not legally recognize the right of the Algonquins to fish within the Z.E.C. prior to the commencement of British sovereignty, it remains open to the appellants to establish that they enjoyed an aboriginal right to fish within the Z.E.C. under the principles of *Van der Peet*, *Gladstone*, and *N.T.C. Smokehouse Ltd.*

. . . . .

La Forest J.: — I have had the advantage of reading the reasons of the Chief Justice, and while I agree with his conclusion and much of what he says, I am concerned about the possible reach of some parts of his reasons and I, therefore, find it advisable to succinctly set forth my own views.

As in the companion case of *R. v. Adams* ..., the issue in the present case is whether the traditional use, by a tribe of Indians, that has continued from pre-contact times of a particular area for a particular purpose can be recognized as an aboriginal right even though the Indians have no general right of occupation (often referred to as the "Indian title") of the affected land. As in *Adams*, I agree that this type of servitude (to use a generic term) should be recognized where the Indians exercise the right as an aspect of their particular way of life in pre-contact times. I think that was sufficiently established here. The fact that Quebec once fell under the French regime does not affect the matter in the present case. It was not established — and certainly not in clear and plain terms — that this aboriginal right was extinguished either during the French regime or later. The right claimed is, therefore, an "existing right" under s. 35(1) of the *Constitution Act, 1982.* I agree with the Chief Justice for the reasons he gives that this right was infringed by the *Quebec Fishery Regulations* but not by the *Regulation respecting controlled zones.* I also agree with what he has to say under the headings "Treaty Rights" and "Amendment of Informations and Constitutional Questions". It follows, therefore, that I would dispose of the case in the manner proposed by him.

L'Heureux-Dubé J.: — Subject to my remarks in *R. v. Adams* ... I agree with the Chief Justice's analysis and would dispose of the appeal as he suggests.

Appeal allowed in part.

As *Adams, supra*, and *Côté, supra*, indicate, Aboriginal title is a species of Aboriginal right. Thus, the "clear and plain" test for extinguishing Aboriginal title, for example, pertains equally to Aboriginal rights. Therefore, as the Supreme Court explained in *Côté*, "... the French Regime's failure to recognize legally a specific Aboriginal practice, custom or tradition (and indeed the French Regime's tacit toleration of a specific practice, custom or tradition) clearly cannot be equated with a clear and plain intention to extinguish such practices. ..."[7]

The *Adams* and *Côté* decisions also indicate, however, that Aboriginal rights exist independently of Aboriginal title. Thus, an Aboriginal group claiming the existence of Aboriginal rights such as hunting or fishing rights does not need to first demonstrate the existence of Aboriginal title to the land upon which those rights are exercised. Yet, because Aboriginal rights do not need to be tied to Aboriginal title does not necessarily mean that those rights are entirely unconnected to land, as the Court explained in *Adams*.

Interestingly, neither *Adams* nor *Côté* definitively address the question of whether Aboriginal rights may be portable rights, as opposed to rights exercisable only on particular lands, thus leaving the question to be dealt with at another time.

Another issue raised by the *Côté* decision was the extent of the application of the *Sparrow* justificatory test. In *Côté*, Chief Justice Lamer held that the *Sparrow* test applied equally to Aboriginal and treaty rights. He relied upon the Supreme Court of Canada's earlier decision in *R. v. Badger*, [1996] 4 W.W.R. 457, 37 Alta. L.R. (3d) 153, 195 N.R. 1, 105 C.C.C. (3d) 289, 133 D.L.R. (4th) 324 (S.C.C.) to support this proposition. This was subsequently affirmed in the *Marshall* cases — *R. v. Marshall*, [1999] 3 S.C.R. 456, 177 D.L.R. (4th) 513 and *R. v. Marshall*, [1999] 3 S.C.R. 533, 179 D.L.R. (4th) 193 ("*Marshall No. 2*") – where the applicable test was referred to as the "*Badger* test".

The following excerpt explains that there are substantive reasons to question the application of the *Sparrow* test to treaty rights. The primary point of emphasis is that since Aboriginal and treaty rights are distinct, any attempt to limit them must properly account for this distinctiveness.

LEONARD I. ROTMAN, "DEFINING PARAMETERS: ABORIGINAL RIGHTS, TREATY RIGHTS, AND THE SPARROW JUSTIFICATORY TEST"

(1997), 36 Alta. L. Rev. 149 at 149-58, 161-71 (references omitted)

In the landmark case of *R. v. Sparrow*, the Supreme Court of Canada instituted a justificatory scheme for legislation that infringed upon Aboriginal rights. In the recent Supreme Court decision in *R. v. Côté*, Chief Justice Antonio Lamer declared that the *Sparrow* justificatory test applied equally to treaty rights. The Chief Justice premised his findings on the Supreme Court's earlier decision in *R. v. Badger*, where both the majority and minority judgments discussed the application of the *Sparrow* test to treaty rights. Notwithstanding the definitiveness of Chief Justice Lamer's findings in *Côté*, this article suggests that applying the *Sparrow* test to treaty rights — although not prohibited by the *Sparrow* decision — is inappropriate because of the significant distinctions between Aboriginal and treaty rights.

While this article will assert that the *Sparrow* test ought not be applied to treaty rights, it does not propose to comment on the appropriateness of the *Sparrow* justificatory standard to Aboriginal rights. Whether the *Sparrow* test is or is not an appropriate response to the balancing of Aboriginal rights versus governmental legislative initiatives — especially in light of the Supreme Court of Canada's recent commentary on that test in *R. v. Gladstone* — is a matter for another day. Instead, the article will focus on the reasons provided in the case law for the application of the *Sparrow* justificatory standard to treaty rights. It will also examine the differences between Aboriginal and treaty rights. It will then propose a different justificatory standard for legislative infringements of treaty rights that accounts for the *sui generis* nature of the treaty making process between the Crown and the Aboriginal peoples in Canada.

II. THE *SPARROW* DECISION AND THE *SPARROW* JUSTIFICATORY TEST

The *Sparrow* case was concerned with the traditional rights of Aboriginal peoples to fish and whether those rights fell under the regulatory scheme established by federal fishing legislation. Framed more broadly, the primary question before the Court in *Sparrow* was whether constitutionally-protected Aboriginal rights could be limited by legislation. The unanimous judgment of the Supreme Court of Canada held that Aboriginal rights could be limited by governmental legislative initiatives, but only under certain circumstances. The circumstances set out by the Court comprise what is now known as the *Sparrow* justificatory test.

. . . . .

The test established in *Sparrow* was discussed in relation to Aboriginal rights as a result of the matter in issue before the Court. Soon after the *Sparrow* decision, the justificatory test that the Supreme Court had established began to be applied to situations involving both Aboriginal and treaty rights. Insofar as the Court in *Sparrow* had not limited the application of its justificatory test to Aboriginal rights, this process appeared to be a logical extension of the *Sparrow* judgment. Indeed, the Supreme Court had stated in *Sparrow* that the application of its justificatory standard was to be implemented on a case-by-case basis because of the generality of s. 35(1) of the *Constitution Act, 1982* and the "complexities of Aboriginal history, society and rights." However, as the limited reasoning provided in subsequent cases indicates, the application of the *Sparrow* test to treaty rights was presumed as a matter of fact rather than having been reasoned from the nature of treaty versus Aboriginal rights or the *dictum* of the Supreme Court in *Sparrow*.

III. CASES ON THE APPLICATION OF THE *SPARROW* TEST TO TREATY RIGHTS

. . . . .

A closer examination of some of the cases in which the *Sparrow* justificatory test has been used for Aboriginal and treaty rights provides little guidance as to why that test ought to be applied equally to both forms of rights. It appears as though the significant distinction between Aboriginal and treaty rights was not given its proper due in those judgments. For example, in *R. v. Bombay*, Austin J.A. dealt with the issue in the following, cursory manner:

> The *Sparrow* case dealt with the Aboriginal rights. The language of the decision of the Supreme Court of Canada in that case, however, is equally applicable to treaty rights. In *R. v. Joseph*, [1990] 4 C.N.L.R. 59 (B.C.S.C.) Murphy J. held that the framework provided by the Supreme Court in *Sparrow* 'applies also to treaty rights.' I agree.

Later, in *R. v. Fox*, the Ontario Court of Appeal again affirmed the application of the *Sparrow* justificatory test to treaty rights. It simply held that: "In *R. v. Sparrow, supra*, the Supreme Court of Canada set out the framework analysis for assessing the constitutionality of legislation affecting treaty and Aboriginal rights recognized and affirmed under s. 35(1)."

It may be seen that there was no consideration given in the *Bombay* and *Fox* judgments to the significant distinction between Aboriginal and treaty rights. Instead, it appears as though the placing together of those rights in s. 35(1) was solely responsible for the *Sparrow* test's application to treaty rights, not because of any reasoned analysis of why treaty rights should be treated like Aboriginal rights with respect to their limitation by governmental legislative initiatives.

. . . . .

It was not until the Supreme Court of Canada's recent decision in *Badger* that that court had an opportunity to comment on the application of the *Sparrow* test to treaty rights. In *Badger*, Cory J.'s majority decision concluded that although the *Sparrow* decision dealt with Aboriginal rights, the test formulated therein applied equally to treaty rights "in most cases." Why the application of the *Sparrow* test to treaty rights was qualified to render it applicable only to "most cases," as opposed to all cases, was not discussed in the judgment.

In finding the *Sparrow* test to be applicable to treaty rights in *Badger*, Cory J. expressly noted the distinction between Aboriginal and treaty rights. As he explained:

> There is no doubt that Aboriginal and treaty rights differ in both origin and structure. Aboriginal rights flow from the customs and traditions of the Native peoples. To paraphrase the words of Judson J. in *Calder* ... they embody

the right of Native people to continue living as their forefathers lived. Treaty rights, on the other hand, are those contained in official agreements between the Crown and the Native peoples. Treaties are analogous to contracts, albeit of a very solemn and special, public nature. They create enforceable obligations based on the mutual consent of the parties. It follows that the scope of treaty rights will be determined by their wording, which must be interpreted in accordance with the principles enunciated by this Court.

Cory J. also found that there were "significant aspects of similarity" between Aboriginal rights and treaty rights. Specifically, he held that:

> Although treaty rights are the result of mutual agreement, they, like Aboriginal rights, may be unilaterally abridged. See *Horseman, supra*, at p. 936; *R. v. Sikyea*, [1964] 2 C.C.C. 325 (N.W.T.C.A.), at p. 330, 642; and *Moosehunter, supra*, at p. 293. It follows that limitations on treaty rights, like breaches of Aboriginal rights, should be justified.
>
> In addition, both Aboriginal and treaty rights possess in common a unique, *sui generis* nature. ... In each case, the honour of the Crown is engaged through its relationship with the Native peoples.

On the basis of these similarities, as well as the wording of s. 35(1) — which he found "supports a common approach to infringements of Aboriginal and treaty rights" — Cory J. held that the *Sparrow* test was applicable to the treaty situation in *Badger*.

Cory J.'s consideration of Aboriginal and treaty rights in *Badger* makes it appear that his conclusion rests upon the same premise as that seen in *Bombay* and *Fox* — namely the placing together of Aboriginal and treaty rights in s. 35(1). Despite offering a cursory discussion of the nature of Aboriginal and treaty rights, Cory J. provides no additional reasoning beyond that offered in *Bombay* and *Fox* on which to found his conclusion. In any event, it would appear that Cory J. did not want his judgment to be understood as an authoritative proposition that the *Sparrow* test automatically applies to potential legislative infringement of both Aboriginal and treaty rights. Just as he had stated earlier in his judgment that the *Sparrow* test applies equally to treaty rights "in most cases," he prefaced his conclusions by stating that, in justifying legislative infringements of treaty rights, "the recognized principles to be considered and applied in justification should *generally* be those set out in *Sparrow*." While Cory J. found that the principles established in *Sparrow* were not exhaustive, he explained that they "may serve as a rough guide when considering the infringement of treaty rights." From the tone of his judgment, as well as its self-imposed qualifications, Cory J.'s decision in *Badger* can hardly be understood as a hearty endorsement of the *Sparrow* test's application to treaty rights.

In the Supreme Court's most recent consideration of the *Sparrow* test's use *vis-à-vis* treaty rights in *Côté*, Lamer C.J.C. also found that the *Sparrow* test was applicable. As he explained:

> As a general rule, where a claimant challenges the application of a federal regulation under s. 35(1), the characterization of the right alternatively as an Aboriginal right or as a treaty right will not be of any consequence once the existence of the right is established, as the *Sparrow* test for infringement and justification applies with the same force and the same considerations to both species of constitutional rights: *R. v. Badger*, [1996] 1 S.C.R. 771, at paras. 37, 77 and 78 and 79.

The Chief Justice later reaffirmed this position in making the following statement:

> In *Sparrow*, the Court set out the applicable framework for identifying the infringment of an Aboriginal right or treaty right under s. 35(1) of the *Constitution Act, 1982*. It should be noted that the test in *Sparrow* was originally elucidated in the context of a federal regulation which allegedly infringed an Aboriginal right. The majority of recent cases which have subsequently invoked the *Sparrow* framework have similarly done so against the backdrop of a federal statute or regulation. ... But it is quite clear that the *Sparrow* test applies where a provincial law has infringed an Aboriginal or treaty right in a manner which cannot be justified. ... The text and purpose of s. 35(1) do not distinguish between federal and provincial laws which restrict Aboriginal or treaty rights, and they should both be subject to the same standard of constitutional scrutiny.

Although the Chief Justice's focus in this latter statement is on the distinction between federal and provincial legislation, he once again affirmed, without reasons, the application of the *Sparrow* test to Aboriginal and treaty rights. His statement that s. 35(1) does not distinguish between federal and provincial legislation can be contrasted with the fact that s. 35(1) does distinguish between Aboriginal and treaty rights.

An interesting aspect of the Chief Justice's decision in *Côté* is that it appears to be far more conclusive on the question of the *Sparrow* test's application to treaty rights than the *Badger* judgment upon which it rests. Although he prefaces his application of the *Sparrow* test to treaty rights by stating that his finding is a "general rule," the language he uses is unequivocal — "the characterization of the right alternatively as an Aboriginal right or as a treaty right will not be of any consequence once the existence of the right is established." Once again, as in the cases discussed previously, the Chief Justice failed to provide any rationale for why the *Sparrow* test ought to apply to treaty rights.

The failure of case law to explain why the *Sparrow* test ought to apply to treaty rights posits either of two scenarios: that the application of the *Sparrow* test to treaty rights is so obvious as to negate the need for explanation, or that there is no informed basis upon which to apply the *Sparrow* test to treaty rights. It is suggested that the latter is the more accurate statement. There are significant distinctions between Aboriginal and treaty rights which militate against using the same justificatory standard for the limitation of those rights. The following section will examine some of these distinctions.

IV. ABORIGINAL RIGHTS AND TREATY RIGHTS

The distinction between Aboriginal and treaty rights is an important one. That the protection of Aboriginal peoples' rights in s. 35(1) specifically distinguishes between Aboriginal and treaty rights illustrates the distinctiveness of those forms of rights. This distinctiveness ought to be reflected in the standard that applies to legislative initiatives that may limit existing treaty rights from that applied to legislation affecting Aboriginal rights. The standard for limiting treaty rights should reflect an awareness of the special nature of treaty rights and what distinguishes them from Aboriginal rights. ...

· · · · ·

The most significant distinction between Aboriginal rights and treaty rights is their origins. Aboriginal rights are derived from Aboriginal customary laws and traditions. Accordingly, they are not dependent upon recognition or affirmation by the common law for their existence. As Hall J. explained in *Calder v. Attorney General of British Columbia* in relation to Aboriginal title, Aboriginal rights are not dependent upon treaty, executive order, or legislative enactment. This conclusion was premised on two American decisions which held that governmental recognition of Aboriginal land rights was not necessary for those rights to exist. This element of the *Calder* decision was subsequently affirmed by the Supreme Court of Canada in *Guerin*, and, most recently, in *Coté*. The independent existence of Aboriginal rights has also been explained by the Manitoba Aboriginal Justice Inquiry in the following manner:

> To the extent that Aboriginal rights of Aboriginal people have been confirmed in other Canadian or British laws, it has another form of recognition, but the state of the law in Canada, as we understand it, is that Aboriginal people and their rights did not depend upon non-Aboriginal recognition in order to exist.

Treaty rights, meanwhile, are rights that are enshrined within the terms of various treaties entered into between the Crown and Aboriginal nations. Treaties were a fundamental part of early European-Aboriginal diplomacy in North America. When the first formal treaty between Britain and the Aboriginal peoples of North America — the *Treaty of Albany* — was signed in 1664, British-Aboriginal alliances had already existed on a less formal basis for quite some time. ...

As negotiated rights, treaty rights may be comprised of any rights agreed to by the parties involved. This may include pre-existing Aboriginal rights which have been incorporated into a treaty, rights obtained from the Crown as a part of the treaty making process which did not exist previously, or both. For instance, an existing Aboriginal right to hunt may have been explicitly incorporated into the term of a treaty to ensure that the Crown both knew of and respected the continued existence of that right. Examples of rights included in a treaty that did not exist previously include the establishment of a reserve, the payment of money or an annuity, specified quantities of grain, blankets, horses, or other implements, and the right to a medicine chest or schooling.

· · · · ·

Insofar as treaty rights do not have an independent existence like Aboriginal rights, but arise by way of negotiated compacts between the Crown and Aboriginal peoples, they are to be understood differently than Aboriginal rights. The canons of treaty interpretation prevent treaty rights from being restricted to their literal description in the treaties by incorporating Aboriginal understandings of those rights. However, the use of Aboriginal understandings of treaty rights does not result in the same method of analysis used in the interpretation of Aboriginal rights. Instead of forming the primary basis of analysis under examinations of Aboriginal rights, Aboriginal understandings in the context of treaty rights must be weighed against the Crown's understandings. As the Supreme Court of Canada explained in *R. v. Sioui*, the common intention of the parties is what is sought in defining the terms of a treaty.

This common intention must be arrived at through a contextual examination of the parties' goals and ambitions, their conduct previous to, during, and after the negotiation of the treaties, as well as what would be reasonable to conclude from the aforementioned in light of the relative positions and strengths of the parties during the periods in question. In striving towards this common intention, however, one must not look only for any overlap between Crown and Aboriginal perspectives. If, for example, one party adopts a broad understanding of a treaty and the other adopts a narrow understanding, the only point of overlap would be the narrow understanding.

As a result of the significant distinctions between Aboriginal and treaty rights described above, the two forms of rights ought not be treated as interchangeable. If they were generally interchangeable, there would have been no need to consider them separately within s. 35(1). Consequently, where a judgment about the interpretation or regulation of Aboriginal rights is made, that judgment should not be automatically used as a precedent for treaty rights and vice versa. ...

V. THE IMPLICATIONS OF THE *SPARROW* DECISION

The *Sparrow* decision itself was unclear as to whether the justificatory test it created applies to both Aboriginal and treaty rights contained in s. 35(1). While the *Sparrow* case dealt only with Aboriginal rights, specifically the Aboriginal right to fish, it neither restricted the application of its justificatory test to those rights nor expanded the test's application to treaty rights. ...

It could be argued that limiting the *Sparrow* test's application to Aboriginal rights would improperly abridge the test's application. Similar arguments were made regarding the scope of the Crown's fiduciary duty following its entrenchment in the *Guerin* decision. However, there is a significant difference between the *Guerin* and *Sparrow* scenarios that demonstrates the necessity to read *Guerin* broadly and *Sparrow* narrowly.

In *Guerin*, the Supreme Court of Canada was faced with questions regarding the nature and extent of the federal Crown's obligations to the Musqueam band in leasing part of that band's reserve lands to a third party. The Court determined that a fiduciary relationship existed between the Crown and the band because of: the history of Crown-Native relations leading up to the *Royal Proclamation of 1763*; the nature of Aboriginal title; the relationship between the band and the Crown; and the surrender requirements contained within the *Indian Act*. The Court then found that the Crown had breached its duty to the band by failing to lease the land in accordance with terms specified by the band.

The *Guerin* case spoke specifically to the surrender of Aboriginal reserve lands to the federal Crown for lease purposes. ... However, the limited scope of the *Guerin* decision was the result of the context in which it arose, not because of the narrowness of the Crown's obligations to Native peoples. There was no other compelling reason to restrict the Crown's fiduciary duty to the surrender of land for leasing purposes. Indeed, Dickson J., as he then was, expressly contextualized the limited scope of his examination of the Crown's fiduciary duty in the *Guerin* case by stating that the relevance of the Crown's fiduciary duty "in the present appeal ... is based on the requirement of a 'surrender' before Indian land can be alienated." Had he wanted to indicate that the Crown only possessed fiduciary obligations to Native peoples within the context of the surrender of reserve lands, he would have specifically limited the Crown's obligations to that context. The Federal Court of Appeal's decision in *Kruger v. R.*, which was released shortly after the Supreme Court of Canada's pronouncement in *Guerin*, affirmed this interpretation of the *Guerin* decision.

· · · · ·

While it may be seen that limiting the *Guerin* precedent to situations involving the surrender of reserve lands by Aboriginal bands to the Crown is improper, limiting the application of the *Sparrow* justificatory test to Aboriginal rights issues does not create a similar injustice. As discussed earlier, Aboriginal rights are inherent rights, whereas treaty rights may be obtained only through negotiation with the Crown. Therefore, it could be argued that, as solemn engagements resulting from mutual agreements between the Crown and Aboriginal peoples, treaties cannot be limited in the manner contemplated by the *Sparrow* test. As negotiated rights, treaty rights should not be susceptible to being arbitrarily or unilaterally derogated from by the Crown. Indeed, as negotiated rights, they may take any form which is agreed to by the parties (in a manner similar to arguments in favour of freedom of contract).

If one accepts the fact that rights existing in a democratic society cannot be absolute, treaty rights, like Aboriginal rights, should also be caught by some form of restriction. Yet, once again, the distinction between Aboriginal rights as inherent rights and treaty rights as negotiated rights comes into play. Even in situations where treaty rights are identical to existing Aboriginal rights, the solemn nature of the treaties and the mutuality with which they were negotiated and signed militates against enabling the Crown to limit treaty rights without the consent of the Aboriginal peoples affected.

· · · · ·

Since treaties are negotiated instruments which the Crown has pledged its honour to uphold, it would be unseemly to allow those negotiated rights to be unilaterally altered by Crown legislation. As Gwynne J. explained in *St. Catherine's Milling and Lumber Co. v. The Queen*:

> Now it is to be observed, that the faith of Her Majesty is solemnly pledged to the faithful observance of this treaty, and the government of the Dominion of Canada is made the instrument by which the obligations contained in it, which are incurred by and on behalf of Her Majesty, are to be fulfilled.

. . . . .

If treaty rights are subject to alteration at the whim of the Crown, the solemn nature of the treaties in which they are contained is necessarily ignored ... and its honour tarnished. Judicial recognition of the solemn nature of treaties between the Crown and Aboriginal peoples has resulted in the promulgation of special canons of treaty interpretation that apply to the compacts between the Crown and Native peoples. The Supreme Court of Canada has demonstrated its recognition of the solemn nature of treaties when it held that treaty rights could only be deemed to have been extinguished by strict proof thereof and then only with the consent of the Aboriginal signatories.

. . . . .

... Allowing the application of the *Sparrow* test to treaty rights blurs the distinction between Aboriginal and treaty rights and provides the latter with no greater protection than the former. This is particularly true where pre-existing Aboriginal rights, such as hunting, fishing, or trapping rights, were expressly included in the terms of treaties.

The purpose of including Aboriginal rights within the treaties, from the Aboriginals' perspective, was to have a greater measure of protection of those rights. That does not suggest that the Aboriginal peoples viewed those rights as subject to being trumped at will by the Crown without their inclusion in a treaty. The Aboriginals were aware, though, that their rights were being ignored and sought to include them in treaties so that there would be more concrete recognition of those rights. The Aboriginal peoples' desire to have their rights included in treaties demonstrates their expectation that the Crown would honour the terms of the treaties. ...

Section 35(1)'s preservation of the distinction between Aboriginal and treaty rights serves the purpose of protecting all rights of the Aboriginal peoples that remained in existence on 17 April 1982. Therefore, s. 35(1) protects both the existing rights of Aboriginal peoples who were not parties to treaties or groups who had rights that were not included in the terms of treaties they were party to. With the equal protection of Aboriginal and treaty rights under s. 35(1), are those rights now to be considered interchangeable? If one is to remain faithful to the significant distinctions between Aboriginal and treaty rights, the answer clearly is no.

. . . . .

Questioning the *Sparrow* test's application to treaty rights is not intended to suggest that treaty rights are absolute whereas Aboriginal rights are not. As with Aboriginal rights, treaty rights also vie for space with competing rights. Consequently, they must be balanced, in some reasoned way, with those other rights. In providing an appropriate framework for this balancing act, it must be recognized that the breadth and extent of Aboriginal rights is dependent upon the practices of the Aboriginal peoples themselves, whereas treaty rights are dependent upon the extent of their recognition in the treaties, broadly construed. However, where certain rights exist as Aboriginal and treaty rights, as with Aboriginal rights replicated in the terms of a treaty, they benefit from both forms of protection. The reasonable balancing of competing rights neither entails the subjugation of treaty rights to those other rights, nor does it mean that treaty rights are to be viewed as any less solemn than the nature of the treaties indicates.

. . . . .

The solemn nature of treaties as representative of the agreements made between the Crown and Aboriginal peoples and their existence as negotiated compacts suggest that any attempt to abrogate the rights contained within them ought to be subject to a more onerous test than that applied to Aboriginal rights. As Wildsmith has stated:

> The *Sparrow* principle emphasizing that the Crown must act honourably and in a manner consistent with its fiduciary/trust responsibilities is particularly onerous when regard is had to treaty rights. Breaking an express 'solemn engagement' arrived at as a *quid pro quo* for promises on the part of the Aboriginal nations is *prima facie* dishonourable.

For this reason, it is suggested that the rationale for understanding treaties established in *Sioui*, which focuses upon the common intention of the parties at the time a treaty was signed, ought to be used as the basis for justifying legislative abrogations of treaty rights rather than the test developed in *Sparrow*. The *Sioui* standard is far more consistent with the notion of treaties as negotiated compacts than the *Sparrow* test, which places its emphasis upon justifying unilateral legislative initiatives.

VI. R. v. SIOUI

. . . . .

The *Sioui* decision is important for its statements regarding the Crown's obligation to consult or involve Aboriginal peoples and to obtain their consent prior to being able to alter their rights under treaties. The Supreme Court explicitly recognized that treaties are not unilateral documents and, as such, the Crown may not alter or extinguish rights that it had agreed to protect within them without involving the Aboriginal signatories. As the court explained, "[t]he very definition of a treaty thus makes it impossible to avoid the conclusion that a treaty cannot be extinguished without the consent of the Indians concerned." From this statement, two things may be ascertained. Initially, it may be seen that treaties and the rights contained within them are, indeed, capable of being altered or extinguished. However, if treaties or treaty rights are to be altered or extinguished, that may only take place with the consent of the Aboriginal peoples concerned. In light of this statement, it would appear that where strict proof of the extinguishment of a treaty is provided, that would necessarily have to entail proof of the Aboriginal peoples' consent to that extinguishment. Simply demonstrating that contrary legislation had effectively nullified existing treaty rights or that the promulgation of legislation provided a "clear and plain" intent to extinguish those rights is, in light of the *Sioui* decision, insufficient, in the absence of a demonstrated indication of Aboriginal consent.

What occurred in *Sioui* was the balancing of the Lorette band's treaty rights with competing interests — namely the Crown's interests in the park and its regulation. While the treaty stated that the Huron tribe would be able to maintain the free exercise of their religion and customs, it did not provide a territorial limitation for the exercise of those rights. Consequently, the Supreme Court held that the intention of the parties at the time the treaty was signed would provide the parameters for defining the rights' territorial restrictions. The Court found that the treaty itself was an attempt to balance the Crown's rights with those of the Huron people. By failing to indicate the territorial scope of the treaty, the Court surmised that the treaty was intended to reconcile the Crown's desire to expand its territorial acquisitions with the Hurons' endeavour to protect their customs and religion. Placing this compromise within the modern setting that led up to the charges being laid against the respondents resulted in a finding which allowed the Hurons to exercise their customs within all parts of their traditional territory where such exercise was not incompatible with the Crown's right of occupancy.

The balancing of competing interests in *Sioui* is different than that imposed by the Supreme Court in *Sparrow*. Whereas the *Sparrow* test imposes procedural requirements that the Crown's legislative initiatives must pass to be valid restrictions upon the exercise of Aboriginal rights, the *Sioui* model represents an attempt at conciliation that is based upon the intentions of the parties at the time a treaty is signed. These intentions may be discovered through a contextual examination of the parties' goals and ambitions, their conduct previous to, during, and after the negotiation of the treaties, as well as what would be reasonable to conclude from the aforementioned, paying heed to the relative positions and strengths of the parties during the period in question. On this basis, the *Sioui* model is more consistent with the good faith observance of Aboriginal treaties in their negotiated form — as well as the negotiated form of treaty rights — than is the *Sparrow* test. Rather than looking at whether legislative infringements of rights are justifiable under the *Sparrow* test, the *Sioui* model adopts as its starting point the desire to find appropriate methods of maintaining the exercise of rights protected under the treaties in a manner that attempts to reconcile treaty intentions with contemporary realities.

Do you agree with Rotman's contention that the *Sparrow* test ought not be applied to treaty rights? Is the consensual nature of treaties sufficient to distinguish treaty rights from Aboriginal rights? Aside from the consent-based nature of treaty rights, are there other reasons for the separation of Aboriginal and treaty rights in section 35(1) of the *Constitution Act, 1982*?

Despite holding in cases such as *Badger*, *Côté*, and *Marshall* that the test originating in *Sparrow* — renamed the "*Badger* test" with regard to its application to treaty rights in *Marshall* — applies with equal force to treaty rights, the Supreme Court of Canada has not entertained the issue in the manner it is presented in the above excerpt, notwithstanding Cory J.'s explicit acknowledgement of the distinction between Aboriginal and treaty rights in *Badger*. What is particularly curious about this *"Badger* test" is that there is no mention of any "test" in *Badger*, or, for that matter, in *Côté*. As suggested in the above excerpt, the *Sparrow* test was simply applied to treaty rights in those cases; it was never put through any substantive analysis of its appropriateness *vis-à-vis* treaty rights.

Returning more generally to the issue of Aboriginal rights and their definition rather than their limitation, a useful synopsis of the Supreme Court of Canada's understanding of the status of Aboriginal rights may be seen in the majority's judgment in *Mitchell v. M.N.R., supra*, at paras. 9-13, as excerpted below:

MITCHELL v. M.N.R.

[2001] 1 S.C.R. 911 (references omitted)

McLachlin C.J.C.: —

. . . . .

Long before Europeans explored and settled North America, aboriginal peoples were occupying and using most of this vast expanse of land in organized, distinctive societies with their own social and political structures. The part of North America we now call Canada was first settled by the French and the British who, from the first days of exploration, claimed sovereignty over the land on behalf of their nations. English law, which ultimately came to govern aboriginal rights, accepted that the aboriginal peoples possessed pre-existing laws and interests, and recognized their continuance in the absence of extinguishment by cession, conquest, or legislation ... At the same time, however, the Crown asserted that sovereignty over the land, and ownership of its underlying title, vested in the Crown: Sparrow, supra. With this assertion arose an obligation to treat aboriginal peoples fairly and honourably, and to protect them from exploitation, a duty characterized as "fiduciary" in Guerin ...

Accordingly, European settlement did not terminate the interests of aboriginal peoples arising from their historical occupation and use of the land. To the contrary, aboriginal interests and customary laws were presumed to survive the assertion of sovereignty, and were absorbed into the common law as rights, unless (1) they were incompatible with the Crown's assertion of sovereignty, (2) they were surrendered voluntarily via the treaty process, or (3) the government extinguished them ... Barring one of these exceptions, the practices, customs and traditions that defined the various aboriginal societies as distinctive cultures continued as part of the law of Canada ...

The common law status of aboriginal rights rendered them vulnerable to unilateral extinguishment, and thus they were "dependent upon the good will of the Sovereign": see *St. Catherine's Milling and Lumber Co. v. The Queen* ... This situation changed in 1982 when Canada's Constitution was amended to entrench existing aboriginal and treaty rights ... The enactment of s. 35(1) elevated existing common law aboriginal rights to constitutional status (although, it is important to note, the protection offered by s. 35(1) also extends beyond the aboriginal rights recognized at common law: *Delgamuukw v. British Columbia* ...). Henceforward, aboriginal rights falling within the constitutional protection of s. 35(1) could not be unilaterally abrogated by the government. However, the government retained the jurisdiction to limit aboriginal rights for justifiable reasons, in the pursuit of substantial and compelling public objectives: see *R. v. Gladstone* ...

In the seminal cases of *R. v. Van der Peet* ... and *Delgamuukw* ... this Court affirmed the foregoing principles and set out the test for establishing an aboriginal right. Since s. 35(1) is aimed at reconciling the prior occupation of North America by aboriginal societies with the Crown's assertion of sovereignty, the test for establishing an aboriginal right focuses on identifying the integral, defining features of those societies. Stripped to essentials, an aboriginal claimant must prove a modern practice, tradition or custom that has a reasonable degree of continuity with the practices, traditions or customs that existed prior to contact. The practice, custom or tradition must have been "integral to the distinctive culture" of the aboriginal peoples, in the sense that it distinguished or characterized their traditional culture and lay at the core of the peoples' identity. It must be a "defining feature" of the aboriginal society, such that the culture would be "fundamentally altered" without it. It must be a feature of "central significance" to the peoples' culture, on [*sic*] that "truly *made the society what it was*" ... This excludes practices, traditions and customs that are only marginal or incidental to the aboriginal society's cultural identity, and emphasizes practices, traditions and customs that are vital to the life, culture and identity of the aboriginal society in question.

Once an aboriginal right is established, the issue is whether [an] act ... is an expression of that right. Aboriginal rights are not frozen in their pre-contact form: ancestral rights may find modern expression. The question is whether the impugned act represents the modern exercise of an ancestral practice, custom or tradition. ...

Does this synopsis in *Mitchell* add or detract from anything that had been said in cases such as *Sparrow* and *Van der Peet*?

E. CONCLUSION

The judiciary's focus on Aboriginal rights in cases such as *Sparrow* and *Van der Peet* has often appeared to be more on the limitation of those rights than on facilitating their understanding or protection. Moreover, the restrictive understandings of Aboriginal rights in the majority judgments in the *Van der Peet* trilogy, as well as in *Adams* and *Côté*, appear to have eliminated the sensitivity to Aboriginal perspectives that had been recognized in *Sparrow*.[8] This approach is inconsistent with the purposive approach to interpreting section 35(1) of the *Constitution Act, 1982* indicated in both *Sparrow* and *Van der Peet*. If Aboriginal rights are to have substantive protection from section 35(1), Canadian courts must infuse their understandings of Aboriginal rights with more meaningful content that pays heed to

Aboriginal perspectives and understandings. As a constitutional protection of Aboriginal rights, section 35(1) clearly provides a constitutional imperative for the judiciary to engage in such activity.

ENDNOTES

1. See *Campbell v. Hall* (1774), 1 Cowp. 204, 98 E.R. 1045, [1558-1774] All E.R. Rep. 252 (K.B.); *Re Southern Rhodesia*, [1919] A.C. 211 at 233 (P.C.); *Amodu Tijani v. Southern Nigeria (Secretary)*, [1921] 2 A.C. 399 at 407 (P.C.); *Oyekan v. Adele*, [1957] 2 All E.R. 785 at 788, [1957] 1 W.L.R. 876 (P.C.); B. Slattery, ed., "The Doctrine of Continuity," in *Ancestral Lands, Alien Laws: Judicial Perspectives on Aboriginal Title* (Saskatoon: University of Saskatchewan Native Law Centre, 1983) at 10-11.
2. *R. v. Adams*, [1996] 3 S.C.R. 101, 4 C.N.L.R. 1 at 14. See also *R. v. Côté*, [1996] 3 S.C.R. 139, 4 C.N.L.R. 26 at 48, in which this quotation is repeated almost verbatim; also *Delgamuukw v. British Columbia*, [1997] 3 S.C.R. 1010, at 1093: "the existence of a particular aboriginal right at common law is not a *sine qua non* for the proof of an aboriginal right that is recognized and affirmed by s. 35(1)." The *Adams* and *Côté* decisions are notable for their findings that Aboriginal rights still exist in the former French colony of New France, notwithstanding longstanding arguments to the contrary by historians and jurists.
3. *R. v. Sparrow*, [1990] 1 S.C.R. 1075, [1990] 4 W.W.R. 410, 46 B.C.L.R. (2d) 1, 56 C.C.C. (3d) 263, 82 N.R. 206, 65 Sask. R. 176, 70 D.L.R. (4th) 385 at 412.
4. K. McNeil, "How Can Infringements of the Constitutional Rights of Aboriginal Peoples be Justified?" (1997), 8 Constitutional Forum 33 at 39.
5. As Lamer C.J.C. explained in *Delgamuukw, supra*, note 2 at p. 1098: "... [T]he act of occupation or possession is sufficient to ground aboriginal title and it is not necessary to prove that the land was a distinctive or integral part of the aboriginal society before the arrival of the Europeans." Refer back to the excerpt of the case in Chapter 1, Aboriginal Title.
6. *Ibid.* at p. 1103. As Lamer C.J.C. further explained at p. 1102, this continuity does not need to be in the form of an unbroken chain, for to require such a standard "would risk 'undermining the very purposes of s. 35(1) by perpetuating the historical injustice suffered by aboriginal peoples at the hands of colonizers who failed to respect' aboriginal rights to land."
7. *Côté, supra*, note 2 at 48.
8. Interestingly, the Supreme Court's judgment in *Delgamuukw, supra*, note 2 was arguably more sensitive to Aboriginal perspectives, even in the establishment of a justificatory standard for legislative infringements on Aboriginal title, than those in either the *Van der Peet* trilogy, *Adams*, or *Côté*.

CHAPTER 5

INUIT RIGHTS

A. INTRODUCTION

Section 35(2) of the *Constitution Act, 1982,* being Schedule B to the *Canada Act 1982* (U.K.), 1982, c. 11 identifies "Aboriginal Peoples of Canada" as including the "Indian, Inuit, and Métis Peoples of Canada". This definition is indicative of at least two things. Initially, it informs us that the contemplation of Aboriginal and treaty rights in section 35(1) is not restricted to those rights pertaining to "Indians", but to any Aboriginal or treaty rights belonging to the Aboriginal Peoples of Canada. Second, section 35(2) tells us that Inuit (and Métis) peoples, while considered "Aboriginal Peoples of Canada," are recognized by the Canadian Constitution as distinct peoples.

This chapter will examine the distinctiveness of the Inuit through an investigation of who Inuit peoples are and some of the issues that are most pertinent to them. Some of these issues have been illustrated elsewhere — for example, the Inuit claim to title in *Baker Lake (Hamlet) v. Canada (Minister of Indian Affairs and Northern Development),* [1980] 1 F.C. 518, [1980] 5 W.W.R. 193, 107 D.L.R. (3d) 513, [1979] 3 C.N.L.R. 17 (T.D.), additional reasons at [1981] 1 F.C. 266 (T.D.), discussed in Chapter 1. While there has been some litigation and negotiation over Inuit issues, these have yet to provide much in the way of significant or authoritative pronouncements on issues unique to Inuit peoples.

B. INUIT BACKGROUND

The Inuit have lived in harsh, northern climes for thousands of years. They live in parts of Alaska, Greenland, Siberia, and Canada. In Canada, they occupy western and central portions of the Arctic, the Keewatin region of the barren lands, Baffin Island and the high Arctic, the coastal areas of Hudson Bay and parts of northern Quebec and Labrador. There are between 115,000 and 128,000 Inuit living in the circumpolar north. According to the 1991 Aboriginal Peoples Survey, some 38,000 Inuit live in Canada. The distinct origins of the Inuit are briefly described below by the Royal Commission on Aboriginal Peoples.

REPORT OF THE ROYAL COMMISSION ON ABORIGINAL PEOPLES, LOOKING FORWARD, LOOKING BACK, VOL. 1

(Ottawa: Ministry of Supply & Services, 1996) at 78-9, 82
(references omitted)

Inuit of the Canadian Arctic are a distinct people, different from other Aboriginal peoples in Canada by virtue of their origins and physical make-up, their language and their technology.

. . . . .

The archaeological record of the Arctic and oral accounts of Inuit support each other in affirming that Inuit inhabiting what is now Alaska, Canada and Greenland — who speak variations of the common language, Inuktitut — descend from a people who migrated from what is now Alaska to Canada and Greenland. These were the Thule people, whose arrival in Canada archaeologists date at approximately 1000 AD. However, the Thule did not arrive in an empty land, for there were already people living in these northern regions. These earlier people, called Dorset by archaeologists and Tunit by Inuit, were the descendants of an earlier migration, around 2500 BC, that also originated in Alaska or Siberia.

... The distinguishing characteristic of historical Inuit culture is their way of life, which has enabled them to live year-round on the tundra, north of the tree line, in conditions demanding great resourcefulness, inner strength and quiet patience. Inuit oral tradition links these qualities with the requirements of survival in a harsh environment. Thus, Inuit used snow, animal skins, bone and stone, the elements indigenous to their environment, to fashion "a technology more complex than that of any other pre-industrial culture, which allowed not only an economically efficient but also a comfortable way of life throughout arctic North America."

. . . . .

Inuit of different regions clearly share many characteristics rooted in their common ancestry. Variations in culture apparently derive from adaptations to local conditions, whether created by changing climate or intercultural contact. Inuit oral history has received little attention in reconstructing the story of the Inuit past, with the result that written reports are erratic in coverage and rely heavily on archaeological finds and on European or southern Canadian perspectives more generally.

A publication of the Canadian Museum of Civilization suggests that distinct Inuit culture groups can be identified with nine regions: Labrador, Arctic Quebec, Southern Baffin Island, Northern Baffin Island and Foxe Basin, Southampton Island, Western Hudson Bay and the Barren Grounds, Central Arctic Coast, Mackenzie Delta, and the High Arctic. ... The culture of each of these groups has been shaped by the land and its particular historical experience.

C. INUIT AS "INDIANS" UNDER SECTION 91(24) OF THE *CONSTITUTION ACT, 1867*

One key question of concern to government and to Inuit people was whether they were considered to be "Indians" for the purpose of section 91(24) of the *Constitution Act, 1867* (U.K.), 30 & 31 Vict., c. 3 and thereby fell under federal jurisdictional powers. This issue was judicially resolved in the case of *Reference re Term "Indians"*.

REFERENCE RE TERM "INDIANS"

[1939] 2 D.L.R. 417 (*sub nom. Eskimos, Re*), [1939] S.C.R. 104
(references omitted)

REFERENCE to Supreme Court of Canada on the question: "Does the term 'Indians' as used in head 24 of the *B.N.A. Act, 1867*, include Eskimo inhabitants of the Province of Quebec?"

The judgment of **Duff C.J.C., Davis** and **Hudson JJ. (Crocket J.** concurring) was delivered by

Duff C.J.C.: — The reference with which we are concerned arises out of a controversy between the Dominion and the Province of Quebec touching the question whether the Eskimo inhabitants of that Province are "Indians" within the contemplation of head no. 24 of s. 91 of the *B.N.A. Act* which is in these words, "Indians and Lands Reserved for Indians;" and under the reference we are to pronounce upon that question.

Among the inhabitants of the three provinces, Nova Scotia, New Brunswick and Canada that, by the immediate operation of the *B.N.A. Act*, became subject to the constitutional enactments of that statute there were few, if any, Eskimo. But the *B.N.A. Act* contemplated the eventual admission into the Union of other parts of British North America as is explicitly declared in the preamble and for which provision is made by s. 146 thereof.

The Eskimo population of Quebec, with which we are now concerned, inhabits (in the northern part of the Province) a territory that in 1867 formed part of Rupert's Land; and the question we have to determine is whether these Eskimo, whose ancestors were aborigines of Rupert's Land in 1867 and at the time of its annexation to Canada, are Indians in the sense mentioned.

In 1867 the Eskimo population of what is now Canada, then between four and five thousand in number, occupied, as at the present time, the northern littoral of the continent from Alaska to, and including part of, the Labrador coast, within the territories under the control of the Hudson's Bay Co., that is to say, in Rupert's Land and the North-Western Territory which, under the authority given by s. 146 of the *B.N.A. Act* were acquired by Canada in 1871. In addition to these Eskimo in Rupert's Land and the North-Western Territory, there were some hundreds of them on that part of the coast of Labrador (east of Hudson Strait) which formed part of, and was subject to the Government of Newfoundland.

The *B.N.A. Act* is a statute dealing with British North America and, in determining the meaning of the words "Indians" in the statute, we have to consider the meaning of that term as applied to the inhabitants of British North America. In 1867 more than half of the Indian population of British North America were within the boundaries of Rupert's Land and the North-Western Territory; and of the Eskimo population nearly 90% were within those boundaries. It is, therefore, important to consult the reliable sources of information as to the use of the term "Indian" in relation to the Eskimo in those territories. Fortunately, there is evidence of the most authoritative character furnished by the Hudson's Bay Co. itself.

It will be recalled that the Hudson's Bay Co., besides being a trading company, possessed considerable powers of government and administration. Some years before the passing of the *B.N.A. Act*, complaints having been made as to the manner in which these responsibilities had been discharged, a committee of the House of Commons in 1856 and 1857 investigated the affairs of the company. Among the matters which naturally engaged the attention of the Committee was the Company's relations with and conduct towards the aborigines; and for the information of the Committee a census was prepared and produced before it by the officers of the company showing the Indian populations under its rule throughout the whole of the North American continent. This census was accompanied by a map showing the "locations" of the various tribes and was included in the Report of the Committee; and was made an appendix to the Committee's Report which was printed and published by the order of the House of Commons. It is indisputable that in the census and in the map the "Esquimaux" fall under the general designation "Indians" and that, indeed, in these documents, "Indians" is used as synonymous with "aborigines."

. . . . .

Seven years later, the scheme of Confederation, propounded in the Quebec Resolutions of October 10th, 1864, included a declaration that provision should be made "for the admission into the Union on equitable terms of Newfoundland, the North-West Territory, British Columbia, and Vancouver." This declaration was renewed in the Resolutions of the London Conference in December, 1866, and in the *B.N.A. Act* specific provision was made, as we have seen, in s. 146 for the acquisition of Rupert's Land as well as the North-west Territory and, in 1868, a statute of the Imperial Parliament conferred upon the Queen the necessary powers as respects Rupert's Land.

The *B.N.A. Act* came into force on July 1, 1867, and, in December of that year, a joint address to Her Majesty was voted by the Senate and House of Commons of Canada praying that authority might be granted to the Parliament of Canada to legislate for the future welfare and good government of these regions and expressing the willingness of Parliament to assume the duties and obligations of government and legislation as regards those territories. In the Resolution of the Senate expressing the willingness of that body to concur in the joint address is this paragraph:

Resolved that upon the transference of the Territories in question to the Canadian Government, it will be the duty of the Government to make adequate provisions for the protection of the Indian Tribes, whose interest and well being are involved in the transfer.

By Order in Council of June 23, 1870, it was ordered that from and after July 15, 1870, the North-West Territory and Rupert's Land should be admitted into, and become part of, the Dominion of Canada and that, from that date, the Parliament of Canada should have full power and authority to legislate for the future welfare and good government of the territory. As regards Rupert's Land, such authority had already been conferred upon the Parliament of Canada by s. 5 of the *Rupert's Land Act* of 1868.

The vast territories which by these transactions became part of the Dominion of Canada and were brought under the jurisdiction of the Parliament of Canada were inhabited largely, indeed almost entirely, by aborigines. It appears to me to be a consideration of great weight in determining the meaning of the word "Indians" in the *B.N.A. Act* that, as we have seen, the Eskimo were recognized as an Indian tribe by the officials of the Hudson's Bay Co. which, in 1867, as already observed, exercised powers of government and administration over this great tract; and that, moreover, this employment of the term "Indians" is evidenced in a most unequivocal way by documents prepared by those officials and produced before the Select Committee of the House of Commons which were included in the Report of that Committee. ... It is quite clear from the material before us that this Report was the principal source of information as regards the aborigines in those territories until some years after Confederation.

I turn now to the Eskimo inhabiting the coast of Labrador beyond the confines of the Hudson's Bay territories and within the boundaries and under the Government of Newfoundland. As regards these, the evidence appears to be conclusive that, for a period beginning about 1760 and extending down to a time subsequent to the passing of the *B.N.A. Act*, they were by governors, commanders-in-chief of the navy and other naval officers, ecclesiastics, missionaries and traders who came into contact with them, known and classified as Indians.

First, of the official documents. In 1762, General Murray, then Governor of Quebec, who afterwards became first Governor of Canada, in an official report of the state of the Government of Quebec, deals under the sixth heading with "Indian nations residing within the government." He introduces the discussion with this sentence:

In order to discuss this point more clearly I shall first take notice of the Savages on the North shore of the River St. Lawrence from the Ocean upwards, and then of such as inhabit the South side of the same River, as far as the present limits of the Government extend on either side of it.

In the first and second paragraphs he deals with the "Savages" on the North Shore and he says: "The first to be met with on this side are the Esquimaux." In the second paragraph he deals with the Montagnais who inhabited a "vast tract" of country from Labrador to the Saguenay.

It is clear that here the Eskimo are classified under the generic term Indian. They are called "Savages," it is true, but so are the Montagnais and so also the Hurons settled at Jeune Lorette. It is useful to note that he speaks in the first paragraph of the Esquimaux as "the wildest and most untamable of any" and mentions that they are "emphatically styled by the other Nations, Savages."

Then there are two reports to His Majesty by the Lords of Trade. The first, dated June 8, 1763, discusses the trade carried on by the French on the coast of Labrador. It is said that they carried on "an extensive trade with the Esquimaux Indians in Oyl, Furs, & ca. [*sic*] (in which they allowed Your Majesty's Subjects no Share)."

In the second, dated April 16, 1765, in dealing with complaints on the part of the Court of France respecting the French fishery on the coast of Newfoundland and in the Gulf of St. Lawrence, their observations on these complaints are based upon information furnished by Commodore Palliser who had been entrusted with the superintendency of the Newfoundland fishery and the Government of the island. In this report, this sentence occurs:

> The sixth and last head of complaint contained in the French Ambassador's letter is, that a captain of a certain French vessel was forbid by your Majesty's Governor from having commerce with the Eskimaux Indians;

and upon that it is observed that the Governor "is to be commended for having forbid the subjects of France to trade or treat with these Indians." "These Indians" are spoken of as "inhabitants ... who are under the protection of and dependent upon your Majesty."

Then there is a series of proclamations by successive Governors and Commanders-in-Chief in Newfoundland, the first of which was that of Sir Hugh Palliser of July 1, 1764. The Proclamation recites, "... Advantages would arise to His Majesty's Trading Subjects if a Friendly Intercourse could be Established with the Esquimeaux Indians, Inhabiting the Coast of Labradore ..." and that the Government "has taken measures for bringing about a friendly communication between the said Indians and His Majesty's subjects." All His Majesty's subjects are strictly enjoined "to treat them in the most civil and friendly manner."

The next is a Proclamation by the same Governor dated April 8, 1765, which recites the desirability of "friendly intercourse with the Indians on the Coast of Labrador" and that "attempts hitherto made for that purpose have proved ineffectual, especially with the Esquimaux in the Northern Ports without the Straits of Belle Isle" and strictly enjoins and requires "all His Majesty's subjects who meet with any of the said Indians to treat them in a most civil and friendly manner."

On April 10, 1772, Governor Shuldham in a Proclamation of that date requires "all His Majesty's subjects coming upon the coast of Labrador to act towards the Esquimaux Indians in a manner agreeable to the Proclamation issued at St. John's the 8th day of July 1769 respecting the savages inhabiting the coast of Labrador." In this Proclamation it should be noted that "Esquimaux savages" and "Esquimaux Indians" are used as convertible expressions.

In 1774, the boundaries of Quebec were extended, and the north eastern coast of Labrador and the Eskimo population therein came under the jurisdiction of the Governor of Quebec and remained so until 1809. Nevertheless, the Governor and Commander-in-Chief of Newfoundland, who at the date was Admiral Edwards, acting under the authority of that Order in Council of March 9, 1774, took measures to protect the missionaries of the Unitas Fratrum and their settlements on the coast of Labrador from molestation or disturbance and, on May 14, 1779, Admiral Edwards issued a Proclamation requiring "all His Majesty's subjects coming upon the Coast of Labrador to act towards the Esquimaux Indians justly, humanely and agreeably to these laws, by which His Majesty's subjects are bound." Here again it is to be observed that the words "savages" and "Indians" are used as equivalents.

A further Proclamation by Admiral Edwards on January 30, 1781, employs the same phrases, the Eskimo being described as "Esquimaux savages" and as "Esquimaux Indians."

On May 15, 1774, Governor Campbell, as Governor and Commander-in-Chief, issued a Proclamation in terms identical with that of 1781.

On December 3, 1821, a Proclamation was issued by Governor Hamilton as Governor and Commander-in-Chief of Newfoundland (now again including the Labrador coast) relating to a "fourth settlement" by the Moravian missionaries requiring all His Majesty's subjects "to act towards the missionaries and the Esquimaux Indians justly and humanely."

. . . . .

Evidence as to subsequent official usage is adduced in a letter of 1824 from the Advocate General of Canada to the Assistant Civil Secretary on some matter of a criminal prosecution in which "Esquimaux Indians" are concerned; and in a report of 1869 by Judge Pinsent of the Court of Labrador to the Governor of Newfoundland in which this sentence occurs: "In this number about 300 Indians and half-breeds of the Esquimaux and Mountaineer races are included."

Reports from missionaries and clergymen are significant. I refer particularly to two. There is a communication in 1821 by the Unitas Fratrum sent to Admiral Hamilton, Governor and Commander-in-Chief of Newfoundland and Labrador, on a visit by H.M.S. "Clinker" to their settlements. In this the Eskimo are mentioned as "Esquimaux Indians" and "Esquimaux Tribes".

. . . . .

In 1849, a report from the Bishop of Newfoundland was printed and published in London for the Society for the Propagation of the Gospel by the Bishop of London ... Extracts from this report, which describes a visit to Labrador ... exemplify in a remarkable way the use of the term Indian, as designating the Eskimo inhabitants of Labrador as well as other classes of Indians there ...

Having regard to the well established usage of designating the Esquimaux of Labrador as Indians or Esquimaux Indians, evidenced by the Proclamations of the Governors of Newfoundland, and other official and unofficial documents, one finds little difficulty in appreciating the significance of the phraseology of the correspondence, in 1879, between Sir John

A. Macdonald and Sir Hector Langevin on the subject of the Eskimo on the north shore of the St. Lawrence. The phrase "Esquimaux Indians" is employed in this correspondence as it had been employed for a hundred years in official and other documents to designate the Labrador Esquimaux.

. . . . .

Newfoundland, including the territory inhabited by these Labrador Eskimo was, as already pointed out, one of the British North American colonies the union of which with Canada was contemplated by the *B.N.A. Act*. Thus it appears that, through all the territories of British North America in which there were Eskimo, the term "Indian" was employed by well established usage as including these as well as the other aborigines; and I repeat the *B.N.A. Act*, in so far as it deals with the subject of Indians, must, in my opinion, be taken to contemplate the Indians of British North America as a whole.

. . . . .

Nor do I think that the fact that British policy in relation to the Indians, as evidenced in the Instructions to Sir Guy Carleton and the Royal Proclamation of 1763, did not contemplate the Eskimo (along with many other tribes and nations of British North American aborigines) as within the scope of that policy is either conclusive or very useful in determining the question before us.

. . . . .

Nor can I agree that the context (in head no. 24) has the effect of restricting the term "Indians". If "Indians" standing alone in its application to British North America denotes the aborigines, then the fact that there were aborigines for whom lands had not been reserved seems to afford no good reason for limiting the scope of the term "Indians" itself.

For these reasons I think the question referred to us should be answered in the affirmative.

———————

Although the *Reference re Term "Indians"* case determined that Inuit people were "Indians" for the purposes of section 91(24) of the *Constitution Act, 1867*, the Inuit had far different experiences with Canadian governmental bodies than did Aboriginal peoples residing to the south.

Because of their geographic locations, Inuit did not have significant interaction with Canadian governmental authorities until the 1950s. Also, they were specifically excluded from the scope of the federal *Indian Act*. Section 4(1) of the current *Indian Act*, R.S.C. 1985, c. I-5 is illustrative of this fact: "4(1) A reference in this Act to an Indian does not include any person of the race of aborigines commonly referred to as Inuit."

As a result of their exclusion from the *Indian Act*, the Inuit did not experience many of the benefits and burdens imposed or supported by the *Indian Act*, including the reserve system. The absence of the reserve system or the recognition of Inuit land rights created uncertainty in the legal status of Inuit peoples' relationship to their lands. This uncertainty began to be addressed with the negotiation of modern land claims agreements.

D. INUIT LAND CLAIMS AND SELF-GOVERNMENT AGREEMENTS

The negotiation of land claims and self-government agreements with the federal government has been a part of Inuit reality for more than two decades, beginning with the *James Bay and Northern Quebec Agreement* (JBNQA) in 1975. The JBNQA was followed in 1984 by the *Inuvialuit Final Agreement*, 1984, approved and given effect by the *Western Arctic (Inuvialuit) Claims Settlement Act*, S.C. 1984, c. 24 [as am. S.C. 1988, c. 16], and, most recently, the *Nunavut Land Claims Agreement* (1993), approved and given effect by the *Nunavut Land Claims Agreement Act*, S.C. 1993, c. 29; and *Nunavut Act*, S.C. 1993, c. 28. These agreements are discussed in greater detail in the following excerpt.

REPORT OF THE ROYAL COMMISSION ON ABORIGINAL PEOPLES, PERSPECTIVES AND REALITIES, VOL. 4

(Ottawa: Ministry of Supply & Services, 1996) at 430-6, 440-1
(references omitted)

For two decades Inuit have been negotiating land claims agreements and self-government with Canadian governments. In most of the Inuit territories, Inuit are the large majority of the population. ... Nevertheless, like other Aboriginal peoples in Canada, they have sought constitutional protection and legal guarantees of self-governing institutions.

. . . . .

Within Canada, Inuit have exercised their right of self-determination by choosing various public forms of self-government. ... [I]n the public government model, eligibility to participate as a citizen in governing institutions is based on long-term residency rather than membership or Aboriginal ancestry.

. . . . .

Public government has certain definite advantages. It permits Inuit (in concert with other residents of the jurisdiction) to control land use and wildlife management over large land areas. ...

But public government forms also carry certain risks. By choosing a form of public government now, Inuit have not ceded the right to choose a different form of self-government (on the nation-based model) at some time in the future.

. . . . .

In all the Inuit territories with land claims settlements — Nunavik, the lands of Inuvialuit and Nunavut — comprehensive claims agreements complement plans for self-government. We turn now to a brief look at how the land claims process unfolded in these three Inuit homelands and to the situation of the Labrador Inuit.

Inuit of Nunavik and the James Bay and Northern Quebec Agreement

The Inuit experience with land claims and self-government began with plans to build the James Bay hydroelectric complex. Announced in 1971, the project ... called for the creation of a series of dams and reservoirs and the flooding of large tracts of land.

The Northern Quebec Inuit Association (later to become Makivik Corporation) promptly began negotiations with the Quebec government, the federal government, and the three companies involved in the project. ... In 1975, the parties signed the James Bay and Northern Quebec Agreement (JBNQA), which recognized Inuit title to 8,400 square kilometres of land and gave them $90 million in compensation for loss of the use of certain traditional lands. It also included some provisions for regional government, a school board, and regimes for environmental protection and wildlife management. The agreement created a hunter income support program, which supports country food production by purchasing harvested wildlife and distributing it in Inuit communities and in the south.

JBNQA was ratified by Quebec Inuit in a referendum in February 1976, after considerable internal debate. Following ratification, the Northern Quebec Inuit Association was reorganized and renamed Makivik Corporation. Makivik was given responsibility for managing the compensation fund and fostering economic, social, political and cultural development of Inuit in Nunavik.

. . . . .

JBNQA provides for a regional administration under the auspices of the Kativik regional government (KRG) and also for a Kativik school board, both of which have been established. KRG has an elected council made up of members from the 14 Inuit communities and has powers over various matters of local administration. Inuit have continued to work toward a greater degree of self-government in negotiations with the province of Quebec.

. . . . .

JBNQA was the first comprehensive claims agreement. Not only was it negotiated rather speedily, compared to other agreements, but it was negotiated by individuals who had no experience with agreements of this type. Thus, it is not surprising that various matters of interpretation and implementation have emerged in the 20 years since the parties reached initial agreement.

. . . . .

Inuvialuit and self-government in the western Arctic

In 1984, Inuvialuit became the first Aboriginal people in the territorial North to sign a comprehensive land claims agreement. The Inuvialuit Final Agreement recognized Inuvialuit title to 91,000 square kilometres of land in the western Arctic and provided compensation of $152 million for the surrender of other land and $17.5 million for economic development and social programs. There was also provision for a joint wildlife management regime. Although the 1984 agreement included a clause extinguishing the Aboriginal land rights of Inuvialuit in the territory, Inuvialuit were successful in negotiating one provision related to self-government. This provision of the Inuvialuit Final Agreement (IFA) guarantees that Inuvialuit will not be treated less favourably than any other Aboriginal group with respect to governmental powers and authority. Section 4(3) of IFA states that

> Canada agrees that where restructuring of the public institutions of government is considered for the Western Arctic Region, the Inuvialuit shall not be treated less favourably than any other native group or native people with respect to the governmental powers and authority conferred on them.

. . . . .

Inuit of Nunavut

The creation of Nunavut will change the face of the North. Given the publicity it has received nationally and internationally, it will be watched closely as an example of Aboriginal self-government through public government.

. . . . .

A number of features will mark the development of Nunavut:

- The government of Nunavut will have province-type powers that are important to the social, cultural and economic well-being of Inuit.
- The government will be able to manage wildlife and resources effectively because it will have jurisdiction over a large territory. Inuit will have strong and usually dominant representation on the relevant boards.
- Representatives will be elected by and accountable to a predominantly Aboriginal electorate.
- It is likely that Aboriginal people will continue to form a majority of the population for the foreseeable future and so will continue to have a major influence in economic, political and cultural life, whatever institutional changes are made.
- Fiscal relations with the federal government will take into account the cost of providing existing levels of government services.

... Nunavut was first proposed in 1976. Since then, in response to federal unwillingness to negotiate self-government arrangements as part of the comprehensive claims process, Inuit have pursued a two-track strategy. They have negotiated comprehensive claims agreements with an eye to realizing all possible progress toward self-government, including securing an adequate resource base. At the same time, they have participated in available political forums, including the process to patriate and amend the Canadian constitution and the legislative assembly of the Northwest Territories.

· · · · ·

In 1990, the Government of the Northwest Territories signed an agreement in principle with Tungavik Federation of Nunavut (now Nunavut Tungavik Inc.), entrenching their joint commitment to division of the Northwest Territories. Agreement on a boundary was achieved after a special commission proposal was accepted by the Minister of Indian Affairs in 1991, and the proposed division line was supported in a second plebiscite, held on 4 May 1992.

Through the 1980s, while these political events unfolded, comprehensive claims negotiations continued, ultimately producing an agreement that made direct reference to the creation of Nunavut. In November 1992, Inuit of Nunavut ratified the land claims agreement.

· · · · ·

The Nunavut Agreement was signed by both parties in Iqaluit on 25 May 1993.

In June 1993, Parliament passed the *Nunavut Land Claims Agreement Act* and the *Nunavut Act*. These two laws provide the framework for establishing Nunavut by dividing the Northwest Territories in 1999 and for the development of governing institutions, beginning immediately.

The land claims agreement recognizes Inuit title to 350,000 square kilometres of land and provides compensation of $580 million and a $13 million training trust fund; it also includes provisions for joint management and resource revenue sharing. New agencies include the Nunavut Wildlife Management Board, the Nunavut Planning Commission, the Nunavut Impact Review Board and the Nunavut Water Board. These agencies will be composed of an equal number of federal, territorial and Inuit representatives. Since these bodies were created through the comprehensive claims agreement, they will have constitutional protection.

· · · · ·

Pursuant to the *Nunavut Act*, the Nunavut Implementation Commission (NIC) was established in December 1993. NIC includes representatives of the federal and territorial governments and of Nunavut Tungavik Inc., the body that represents Inuit of Nunavut and is responsible for implementing the land claims agreement. The mandate of NIC is to advise the three parties (federal, territorial and Inuit) on implementation questions, and it is likely the forum in which the stickier issue of implementation will be decided.

. . . . .

The Labrador Inuit

The Labrador Inuit Association (LIA), founded in 1971, represents Inuit and Kablunangajuit in the northern Labrador communities of Nain, Hopedale, Makkovik, Postville and Rigolet.

. . . . .

Labrador is the only Inuit region without a completed land claims settlement. In part, this is because Labrador Inuit were the last Inuit region to submit a comprehensive claim proposal (in 1977), and in part it is because a willingness to negotiate on the part of both the federal and the Newfoundland government was required. Federal acceptance of the claims proposal came in 1978, but the province did not join the process until 1980.

For various reasons, formal negotiations were not opened until January 1988. A framework agreement was reached in March 1990, with the condition that an intergovernmental memorandum of understanding be signed by the end of May 1992. The Minister of Indian Affairs was supposed to have reached an agreement with the province on cost-sharing arrangements. When a memorandum of understanding was not reached before the deadline, negotiations were suspended.

This excerpt from the Royal Commission on Aboriginal Peoples (RCAP report) describes briefly some of the agreements that Inuit people have signed with the federal government. In addition to transfers of land, administrative bodies have been established under these agreements to oversee important matters such as wildlife conservation and sustainable development. Although these agreements delineate the powers of the Inuit administrative bodies established, the interplay between these bodies and federal governmental departments and policy have yet to be fully experienced.

Since the RCAP report was released, Nunavut has become a reality. Meanwhile, the Labrador Inuit Association (LIA) reached a tentative verbal agreement for an Agreement-in-Principle (AIP) with Canada and Newfoundland on December 18, 1998. The final text of the AIP was initialized by the chief negotiators for the parties on May 10, 1999. The LIA ratified the AIP on July 26, 1999. Once it is signed, the AIP would become the basis for negotiating a final agreement, although the AIP itself is not legally binding.

The AIP provides that the Newfoundland government will contribute 72,520 square kilometres in northern Labrador — including 15,800 square kilometres of Inuit fee simple owned lands (known as Labrador Inuit Lands (LIL)) — for a Labrador Inuit Settlement Area (LISA). Canada is to provide a capital transfer of $140 million and $115 million in implementation costs once the comprehensive claim process has been finalized and a final agreement brought into effect. Other costs associated with self-government provisions, such as health, education, and social assistance, are to be explored during the final agreement negotiations.

The Voisey's Bay area, which the LIA call *Tasiujatsoak*, is located within traditional Labrador Inuit territory, but has not been included in LIL or LISA. However, the AIP provides that the parties will negotiate rights in relation to the Voisey's Bay area, the location of significant mining activity, before a final agreement is reached. The AIP does provide, though, that the Labrador Inuit will receive 3 per cent of provincial revenues from the Voisey's Bay project.

E. CREATING AN INUIT-FOCUSED JURISPRUDENCE

In addition to these land claims and self-government agreements, there is an emerging body of Inuit jurisprudence that sheds some light on the unique nature of Inuit rights. The *Kadlak* case, excerpted below, is one such example. *Kadlak* is also illustrative of the clashes between new Inuit administrative regimes and the exercise of traditional rights by Inuit people.

KADLAK v. NUNAVUT
(MINISTER OF SUSTAINABLE DEVELOPMENT)

[2001] 1 C.N.L.R. 147, 6 W.W.R. 276 (Nunavut Ct. Just.)
(references omitted)

Kilpatrick J.: — Noah Kadlak lives on Southampton Island in the vastness of Canada's eastern arctic. He is an experienced Inuk hunter, and a beneficiary under the Nunavut Land Claims Agreement. He lives his life close to the land. In this unforgiving landscape, Noah carries on the proud hunting traditions of his people; traditions that have ensured the survival of the Inuit from time immemorial.

Mr. Kadlak wishes to hunt a polar bear using the traditional methods and technology of his ancestors. The taking of a bear with spear or harpoon is a risky business. There is little room for mistake. The strength, agility and cunning of the bear make it an extremely dangerous and formidable adversary. This form of hunt requires exceptional skill and courage. It is perhaps the ultimate test of the Inuit hunter.

Noah Kadlak has been denied the opportunity to participate in this traditional hunt. The Minister of Sustainable Development for the Government of Nunavut has determined that this form of hunting presents an unwarranted risk to public safety and has refused to grant Mr. Kadlak any exemption from the provisions of section 42(1) of the *Wildlife Act* R.S.N.W.T. 1988, c. W-4. Mr. Kadlak now brings this application to review the Minister's decision. He asks the Court to find that the Minister's exercise of discretion in this case was unreasonable and contrary to law.

Procedural History:

In November 1997, Noah Kadlak applied to the Nunavut Wildlife Management Board (NWMB) for permission to hunt a bear using a spear or harpoon. This application was necessary because section 42(1) of the *Wildlife Act*, RSNWT 1988, c. W-4, permits hunting of bears only with certain prescribed weapons. A spear or harpoon is not an approved weapon for this purpose. Article 5.6.48 of the Nunavut Land Claim Agreement gives the NWMB the power to modify or remove this type of restriction in the Nunavut Settlement Area (defined as a non-quota limitation by Article 5.1.1).

In response to Noah Kadlak's application, the NWMB granted Mr. Kadlak permission to carry out the traditional hunt, but made this subject to a number of conditions. These conditions included the following:

a. That the person be at least 19 years of age and be an experienced polar bear hunter;
b. That the person sign a comprehensive Release and Indemnity Agreement;
c. That the person be accompanied by at least one other experienced hunter with a firearm that complies with section 42 of the *Wildlife Act*;
d. That the person first obtain the written endorsement of their HTO and the NWMB.

In accordance with the procedure provided for in the Nunavut Land Claims Agreement, the NWMB forwarded its decision granting permission for the traditional hunt to the Minister of Resources, Wildlife and Economic Development of the NWT by letter dated June 3rd 1998.

On July 17th 1998, The NWT Minister advised the NWMB that he was exercising his jurisdiction under Article 5.3.11 of the Nunavut Land Claims Agreement to disallow the Board's decision. This decision was made on the basis that the proposed hunt presented an unwarranted risk to public safety within the meaning of Article 5.3.3 of the Nunavut Land Claims Agreement.

The NWMB then reconsidered its original decision as required by Article 5.3.12. The Board reaffirmed the original decision granting the applicant permission to conduct a traditional hunt. This was communicated to the Minister by letter dated September 16th 1998.

The Minister of Sustainable Development for the new Nunavut Territory responded on October 25th, 1999. He confirmed that he was disallowing the Board's decision to grant permission for a traditional bear hunt on the grounds of public safety. It is this decision by the Minister of Sustainable Development that is now under review in this Court.

The Social and Legal Context of The Nunavut Land Claims Agreement:

Before the coming of organized government, the Inuit lived in scattered camps in the remote regions of what is now the new Territory of Nunavut. They survived in this harsh environment through nomadic hunting activities. The Inuit have developed a close symbiotic relationship to the land, and all the creatures of the air, sea and land upon which they have traditionally depended as a people for their survival. The traditions of the hunt are an important focus of Inuit culture. Even today, Inuit language, art, diet and clothing celebrate the hunt and the animals of the hunt. The preservation of Inuit culture remains closely linked to this traditional way of life. The Inuit right to hunt is understandably the central focus of the Nunavut Land Claims Agreement. This is key to their social and cultural identity as a people.

The Inuit right to harvest wildlife is set out in Article 5.6.1 of the Nunavut Land Claims Agreement. This Article provides that:

> ... an Inuk shall have the right to harvest up to the full level of his or her economic, social and cultural needs, subject to this Article.

Article 5.1.42 further provides that:

> An Inuk may employ any type, method, or technology to harvest pursuant to the terms of this Article that does not ... conflict with the laws of general application regarding humane killing of wildlife, public safety and firearms control.

The provisions of this Agreement were intended by the signatories to be understood and applied in a larger social/legal context that recognized Inuit traditional harvesting practices. As an aid to interpretation, Article 5.1.3 thus proclaims that the Agreement seeks to achieve as one of its objectives:

> ... the creation of a system of harvesting rights that reflects the traditional and current levels, patterns and character of Inuit harvesting.

Under the heading "Principles", Article 5.1.2 acknowledges that:

> a. Inuit are traditional and current users of wildlife;
> b. The rights of Inuit to harvest wildlife flow from their traditional and current use.

The Inuit right of harvest proclaimed in the Nunavut Land Claims Agreement is constitutionally protected by virtue of the incorporation of this Agreement into section 35 of Canada's *Constitution Act* 1982. In keeping with common law principles of constitutional law and statutory interpretation, the provisions of the Nunavut Land Claims Agreement are to be afforded a large, liberal and purposive interpretation so as to best attain the objectives of this legislation.

The Appropriate Standard of Judicial Review:

The "pragmatic and functional approach" to judicial review of administrative decisions is well entrenched in Canadian jurisprudence. This approach recognizes a continuum of judicial review with certain types of administrative decisions being entitled to more deference from the reviewing Court than others. At the highest end of this continuum, is the standard of correctness. A decision reviewed on this standard will be overturned if it does not fully and strictly comply with the law. At the lowest end, is a standard of patent unreasonableness, where the decision under review can only be overturned if it cannot be rationally supported from the standpoint of a reasonable person. A review conducted on this standard will thus accord significant deference to the administrative body that made the original decision.

It is argued on behalf of the Nunavut Government that the Court should review the Minister's decision in this case on the basis of the lowest possible standard of judicial review; that of patent unreasonableness. It is argued that the fact that the Minister's decision was made in the context of an aboriginal land claims agreement is not helpful in determining the appropriate standard of review.

I disagree with both these submissions. The decision made by the Minister in this case restricts or limits a constitutionally protected right of harvest that I have found to be the central focus of the Nunavut Land Claims Agreement. The decision under review does not involve a delicate balancing of polycentric rights as in the Turbot case recently before the Federal Court (see *NTI v. Minister of Fisheries and Oceans* (1997), 149 D.L.R. (4th) 519). It involves an individual's right of harvest. I find that the individual's right to determine the method of harvest has been directly impacted by the impugned decision. There is a "prima facie infringement of an aboriginal right" within the meaning of the *Sparrow* judgment of the Supreme Court of Canada, [1990] 3 C.N.L.R. 160, 70 D.L.R. (4th) 385.

I find that the highest level of judicial review, the standard of correctness, is demanded by the facts of this case. Any lesser standard of review would not be adequate to effectively protect the right proclaimed under the Nunavut Land Claims Agreement; a right that is both recognized and affirmed by section 35 of the *Constitution Act*. Any lesser standard of review would potentially undermine and erode the very objective that the Nunavut Land Claims Agreement seeks to protect.

In this case, there is no privative clause to limit Court reviews of Ministerial decisions made under Part 6 that limit or restrict the Inuit right of harvesting. The decision under review does not involve difficult technical issues, or issues involving special expertise or competence. It does involve the application of broad public policy considerations to the proposed exercise by the applicant of his right of harvest. It does involve consideration of the legal meaning to attach to the phrase "public safety" as this is found in Article 5.3.3 of the Nunavut Land Claims Agreement. I find that there is nothing about the issues behind this decision that cannot be closely examined by a reviewing Court on a standard of correctness.

The Supreme Court of Canada in the *Pushpanathan* case (160 D.L.R. (4th) 193) identified a number of factors that should be considered in determining the standard of review. The list of factors identified by Justice Bastarache was not intended to be complete or comprehensive. This case did not involve the review of a decision that impacted directly upon a constitutionally protected right. Nor was the Supreme Court called upon to consider the application of section 35 of the *Constitution Act* to the decision then under review. Yet the majority found that the decision of the Immigration and Refugee Board was subject to review on a standard of correctness. In, *Pushpanathan*, the Supreme Court of Canada asked the reviewing Court to look to the overall purpose of the legislation in question, and to examine the nature of the issue behind the decision under review.

I infer that a primary objective of the Nunavut Land Claim Agreement is to protect Inuit harvesting rights from unwarranted state interference through the incorporation of these rights into section 35 of the *Constitution Act*. It is entirely appropriate to ask the Court to intervene when government decisions adversely impact, or infringe upon those rights protected by the Constitution of this country. By conferring constitutional status and priority upon the Inuit right to harvest wildlife, Parliament and this Territory have sanctioned challenges to social and economic policy objectives embodied in legislation to the extent that this right is, has been, or will be affected. This Court finds that it is well equipped to monitor and maintain the delicate balance between the public interest represented by government and the private interests defined and protected by the Constitution, on the other. Curial deference has very little place in a review involving constitutional issues of this kind.

Counsel for the Government points to the absence of a right of appeal from the Minister's decision as being a significant indicator of legislative intention to minimize curial review. I disagree. An individual right that is both "recognized and affirmed" by its incorporation into the *Constitution Act* would be meaningless without a means of enforcement or redress. I find that no right of appeal is necessary to justify a standard of correctness on this review for the reasons that I have identified.

The Standard of Correctness:

Section 35(1) of the *Constitution Act* does not promise that the rights under the Nunavut Land Claim Agreement will be immune from all forms of government regulation. It does require the Territorial and Federal Crown to justify any decision that impacts adversely upon the promises made and rights conferred in the Land Claims Settlement. A decision by government that affects the exercise of a substantive aboriginal right will only be upheld if it meets the test for justifying an interference with a right recognized and affirmed under section 35(1). This test, and the analysis that precedes it, has been outlined by the Supreme Court of Canada in the case of *R. v. Sparrow*, [1990] 3 C.N.L.R. 160; (1990) 70 D.L.R. (4th) 385. The Territorial Crown thus has the burden in this case of justifying a decision that clearly restricts the right of harvest, and the right to determine the means of harvest, conferred upon Inuit by the Nunavut Land Claim Agreement.

It is common ground that the only lawful justification for the Minister's decision to deny the traditional hunt in this case must be found in the provision related to "public safety". Unfortunately, the Nunavut Land Claim Agreement does not define this phrase as it appears in Article 5.3.3.

Counsel for the Government argues that the phrase "public safety" should be given a broad and expansive definition. This would allow the regulation of risks assumed by individual hunters as members of the public. Such an interpretation would permit the Minister to effectively regulate a dangerous and risky harvesting activity. It is argued that in the case now before the Court, compelling public policy justified Ministerial intervention. It is argued that a prohibition of this activity is necessary to ensure that public health care and public welfare systems are not burdened by having to support individuals and their dependants who are injured or killed in the course of pursuing these risky hunting activities. It is suggested that the same public policy considerations that ultimately resulted in seat belt legislation being upheld as constitutionally valid are analogous to the case at bar.

The applicant, on the other hand, argues that a very restricted or narrow meaning should attach to the phrase "public safety". It is argued that the Ministerial power to restrict Inuit harvesting should only be allowed to the extent that the hunting activity presents an identifiable risk to the community or public at large. Such a power would thus allow for the imposition of "proximity restrictions" to a harvesting activity in the vicinity of known human population. It would not extend to the risks incurred by individual hunters while pursuing their harvesting activities.

It is argued that to allow the Minister to restrict hunting activities on the basis of risks assumed by individual hunters would "open the door" to significant regulation of the harvesting activities of Inuit. Many Inuit hunting activities contain an element of personal risk. Whaling with a harpoon, walrus hunting on the flow edge, polar bear hunting with a bow and arrow, or crossbow, for example, all pose significant risks, even to the experienced hunter. It is thus argued that the adoption of the "expansive" definition advocated by government could have a significant adverse affect upon the Inuit harvesting rights recognized under section 35(1) of the *Constitution Act*.

The second stage of the "Sparrow" analysis outlined by the Supreme Court of Canada requires that this Court examine the legislative objective behind the impugned decision. I am satisfied that the decision to restrict the Inuit harvesting right in this case was made pursuant to a "valid" legislative objective within the meaning of the *Sparrow* case. I further find that the decision to prohibit Noah Kadlak from pursuing the bear with a spear falls lawfully within this valid legislative objective of "public safety."

In making this finding, the Court accepts that the broader definition of public safety advanced by the government is correct in law. If this Court adopted the narrow definition advanced by the applicant, then many of the restrictions initially imposed by the NWMB upon Noah Kadlak would also be rendered "invalid". These restrictions appear to have been imposed in an effort to address the risk to the individual hunter pursuing the traditional bear hunt. The provisions of Article 5.3.3 of the Nunavut Land Claim Agreement equally bind the Minister and the NWMB. If the Minister cannot validly restrict hunting activities on the basis of risks assumed by individual hunters, then the NWMB had no basis in law to do so.

While the Court is thus prepared to accord the phrase "public safety" with a broad and expansive definition that would include the assumption of risks by individual hunters, the 2nd stage of the Sparrow type analysis requires that the Minister strictly comply with a "principle" of minimal interference when making his or her decision. Was the Minister's decision to effectively prohibit the traditional hunt the minimum infringement or restriction of the harvesting right possible in order to achieve the desired objective of public safety as I have defined it? Are there reasonable conditions, short of outright prohibition, that could substantially address the Minister's concerns? The principle of minimal interference is to be applied liberally, in accordance with constitutional principles of interpretation, to ensure that the rights recognized and affirmed by section 35 of the *Constitution Act* are not unduly restricted or denied through overzealous government regulation. This Court finds that the concerns raised by the applicant in argument are best addressed in this second stage of analysis.

The "principle" of minimal interference is well entrenched in constitutional litigation in this country. It is a principle adverted to by the majority of the Supreme Court of Canada at p. 187 of the *Sparrow* judgment. I find that it is also a "principle" that has been expressly built into the criteria circumscribing the Minister's decision under Article 5.3.3 of the Nunavut Land Claim Agreement. This Article provides as follows:

> Decisions of the NWMB or the Minister made in relation to part 6 shall restrict or limit Inuit harvesting only to the extent necessary:
>
> a. To effect a valid conservation purpose;
>
> b. To give effect to the allocation system outlined in this Article, to other provisions of this Article and to Article 40; or
>
> c. To provide for public health or public safety.

Before any decision is made to prohibit a particular form of harvesting activity, traditional or otherwise, the NWMB or the Minister must first consider whether other reasonable conditions could effectively address the legitimate public safety or public health concerns arising from the activity. It is clear that the NWMB did this when first authorizing the traditional hunt subject to conditions. There is no evidence before me that the Minister has done so.

The outright prohibition of a traditional Inuit harvesting activity is a drastic step. It is a step of last resort. This is so particularly given the principles and objectives of the Nunavut Land Claim Agreement that appear to recognize and accept the validity of traditional harvesting activities, and their continued importance to contemporary Inuit society. For the reasons given earlier, Government must be prepared to have the justification for such a decision closely scrutinized by the Courts. I am not satisfied on the evidence before me that the Minister's decision to disallow the NWMB decision in this case satisfied this principle of minimal interference. I am not satisfied in the circumstances of this case, and on the evidence now before me, that reasonable conditions could not have been crafted to address the Minister's concerns. In the result, the decision of the minister disallowing the NWMB authorization for a traditional hunt is quashed. It has not met the necessary standard of correctness. The Crown has failed to discharge the burden of justifying the decision under review. This matter is accordingly remitted back to the Minister for his further consideration.

The *Kadlak* case demonstrates that it is not only non-Aboriginal governmental bodies that Aboriginal peoples exercising traditional rights may come into conflict with. Here, the Nunavut government was faced with the difficult task of balancing traditional practices with the rights of others (both Aboriginal and non-Aboriginal) and the exercise of its governmental responsibilities. As with other cases involving the exercise of Aboriginal rights, *Kadlak* demonstrates that such rights are not absolute, regardless of where they may be practised or whether they are used within the jurisdiction of Aboriginal or non-Aboriginal governmental regimes.

The unique circumstances and geographic locations of Inuit peoples play an important role in judicial decision-making where Inuit rights or Inuit persons are brought before the courts. Consider, for example, the following case in which the sentencing judge heeded the unique circumstances of Inuit people in determining how to sentence an Inuit woman convicted of aggravated assault. (Note that further discussion of the relevant considerations associated with the sentencing of aboriginal offenders may be seen in Chapter 12, "Aboriginal Peoples and Criminal Justice", *infra*.)

R. v. EVALOARDJUK

[1999] Nu.J. No. 11 (Nunavut Ct. Just.) (references omitted)

Kilpatrick J. (orally): — Suzanne Evaloardjuk stands charged with a single count of aggravated assault arising out of an incident that occurred in Iqaluit on December 18, 1998. She is now before the court for sentencing, having entered an early guilty plea to the offence on April 19, 1999.

The facts before me are these: Suzanne had been drinking. She attends the apartment of the complainant and victim, one Blanchard Burns Wolfe. I am advised that this is a man with whom she maintained a relationship. Suzanne is invited inside. There is an argument. Suzanne confronts the complainant with allegations that he had been unfaithful to her. During this argument, Suzanne grabs a steak knife and stabs the complainant once in the abdomen. She does so while uttering the words, "Let's see if God is going to protect you now." Following the stabbing, the complainant asks Suzanne to leave, and she does so without further incident. Suzanne then cleans the knife and returns it to a kitchen drawer prior to departing.

The complainant is taken to the hospital where it is learned that the knife had perforated his bowel. Emergency medical intervention is required to stabilize his condition. Blanchard Burns Wolfe remains in hospital until December 24, recovering from his wound.

There is no suggestion on the evidence that the injury sustained in the assault will have any lasting or permanent medical implications for this complainant. No victim impact statement was available to the court to better understand how this offence has impacted on the life of the complainant.

The Crown has urged the court to impose a sentence of jail for this offence in the range of 8 to 12 months. The Crown points to a number of aggravating features, namely:

1. the breach of trust by the accused;

2.   the accused's resort to a weapon in the course of a domestic dispute;

3.   the infliction of serious injury to the complainant; and

4.   the high degree of moral culpability because the accused was clearly
     conscious of the great risk to the complaint associated with her use of
     the knife, as evidenced by her comment.

It is conceded by the Crown that the offence is out of character for the
accused. Suzanne has no record of criminal convictions.

It is conceded as well that the early guilty plea is mitigating and that
there is genuine remorse on Suzanne's part for having committed the offence.

It is argued by the Crown, however, that the aggravating features of the
offence itself demand that the court place greater emphasis on the sentencing principles of denunciation and general deterrence than on the rehabilitation of the accused as a first offender. It is said that the application
of these principles to the facts of this case must result in the imposition of a
deterrent jail term. It is further argued that a conditional sentence order
will not adequately address the need to denounce the conduct in question
or to deter others. The Crown has referred this Court to the decision of the
Alberta Court of Appeal in *R. v. Brady* (1998), 121 C.C.C. (3d) at p. 504. The
Crown asks this court to adopt the reasoning of the Alberta Court of Appeal as expressed in *Brady* to find that a conditional sentence order lacks
sufficient deterrent value for a crime of this magnitude.

On Suzanne's behalf it is argued that a community-based sentence in
the form of a suspended sentence or conditional sentence order will adequately address the purpose and principles of sentencing set out in s. 718
through 718.2 of the *Criminal Code*. The defence asks this court to consider
and apply the recent Supreme Court of Canada judgment in *Jamie Tanis
Gladue* (1999), 133 C.C.C. (3d) p. 385. In support of this position, the defence points to, first, the disadvantaged background of Suzanne as an Inuit
person; second, the early guilty plea and remorse; and, third, the absence
of any prior criminal record.

The court has given anxious consideration to the purpose and principles
of sentencing as set out in the *Criminal Code* and to the submissions of
counsel. The court finds itself in agreement with the Crown that the facts
of this case demand emphasis upon denunciation and general deterrence,
in addition to the obvious need to assist with Suzanne's rehabilitation.

Domestic violence is, unfortunately, very common in the Inuit communities of Nunavut territory and particularly in this community, the community of Iqaluit. Courts of appeal throughout the country have repeatedly stressed the need to emphatically repudiate this type of conduct
through deterrent sentences. When weapons are introduced into a volatile
domestic dispute, the potential for serious bodily harm and even death is
very high. This is so particularly where the weapon is wielded by an assailant who is under the influence of alcohol. Serious bodily harm was in
fact the result of the assault in this case, and it can be said that it was simply good luck and not good planning that death did not result. This court

accepts that the resort to weapons in a domestic dispute must be denounced and deterred through the sentencing process, particularly where the use of the weapon results in serious bodily harm to the victim of the domestic assault.

This court is satisfied on the facts of this case that some form of custodial sanction in the range suggested by the Crown is not only appropriate but necessary in order to effectively achieve the goals of sentencing.

Having arrived at this conclusion, however, the court does not find that an immediate sentence of imprisonment is necessary in this case to protect the public. Suzanne does not presently pose a danger to the community at large or to the complainant. It is agreed that the act in question is out of character for her. It appears that she is both willing and able to comply with court orders. There is apparently a history of approximately six months' compliance with the condition that she abstain from the use of alcohol. I am satisfied, therefore, that the threshold test for a conditional sentence order is made out on the facts of this case.

Before the court can impose a conditional sentence order, however, it must also be satisfied that the imposition of a conditional sentence, on the facts of this case, would also be consistent with the purpose and principles of sentencing as set out in s. 718.1 of the *Criminal Code*. It is on this point the Crown argues that the deterrence and denunciation objectives that I have found to be applicable in this case cannot be met by allowing Suzanne to remain in her community on a conditional sentence order.

Sentencing is very much an individualized process. It is a process that must reflect not only the infinite variety and great complexity of the human condition, it is a process that must also be sensitive to differences in the relative severity of crimes. It must respond with equal sensitivity, however, to the varying needs of offenders, their victims and the communities that are affected by criminal misconduct. In the 1996 decision of the Supreme Court of Canada in *M. (C.A.)*, [1996] 1 S.C.R. p. 500 Mr. Justice Lamer observed that the appropriateness of a sentence will depend on the particular circumstances of the offence, the offender, and the community in which the offence took place. The Supreme Court of Canada recognized that a disparity of sentence for similar crimes was a natural consequence of this individualized focus. Chief Justice Lamer at p. 567 of the judgment says this:

> It has been repeatedly stressed that there is no such thing as a uniform sentence for a particular crime....Sentencing is an inherently individualized process, and the search for a single appropriate sentence for a similar offender and a similar crime will frequently be a fruitless exercise of academic abstraction. As well, sentences for a particular offence should be expected to vary to some degree across various communities and regions of this country, as the "just and appropriate" mix of accepted sentencing goals will depend on the needs and current conditions of and in the particular community where the crime occurred.

This passage from Mr. Justice Lamer's judgment in *M.(C.A.)* was quoted with approval by the majority of the Supreme Court of Canada in the recent *Gladue* decision. There, Justices Cory and Iacobucci reaffirmed the individualized approach to sentencing and go on to state, at p. 417:

The comments of Lamer C.J. are particularly apt in the context of aboriginal offenders. As explained herein, the circumstances of aboriginal offenders are markedly different from those of other offenders, being characterized by unique systemic and background factors. Further, an aboriginal offender's community will frequently understand the nature of a just sanction in a manner significantly different from that of many non-aboriginal communities. In appropriate cases, some of the traditional sentencing objectives will be correspondingly less relevant in determining a sentence that is reasonable in the circumstances, and the goals of restorative justice will quite properly be given greater weight. Through its reform of the purpose of sentencing in s. 718, and through its specific directive to judges who sentence aboriginal offenders, Parliament has, more than ever before, empowered sentencing judges to craft sentences in a manner which is meaningful to aboriginal peoples.

Suzanne is Inuit. The offence for which she is to be sentenced occurred in a predominantly Inuit community. Her victim is also Inuit.

The views expressed by the Alberta Court of Appeal in *Brady* with respect to the appropriateness of the conditional sentence order then under appeal are clearly applicable to a non-aboriginal offender on a drug-related offence occurring in a large urban community in the Province of Alberta. In the view of the Nunavut Court of Justice, however, the sentencing of an Inuit person in an Inuit community demands particular attention, not only to the life circumstances and hardships associated with life in remote northern communities, but also the unique cultural perspectives of the Inuit community of which both Suzanne and her victim are a part.

When applying this cultural context to the facts of this case, the court is satisfied that the sentencing goals of denunciation and general deterrence that I have determined to be applicable can be achieved by allowing Suzanne to remain in the community, subject to a conditional sentence order.

The conditions of this sentence will be tough. They will impose real restrictions on Suzanne's liberty. The sentence will include conditions that not only include a period of close confinement to her home, but will also restrict her ability to take part in traditional on-the-land activities enjoyed by most Inuit. I am satisfied that the deterrent effect of this type of structured community-based sentence in a small Inuit community will probably be many times greater than a similar sentence imposed in the larger communities in the south. The anonymity associated with urban living in the south is simply not a feature common in the smaller and close-knit communities of Nunavut territory. Social conditions in these smaller communities make a community-based sentence, in many cases, a more effective way of achieving general deterrence because the sanction remains a consequence readily visible to others in the community on an on-going basis. Removal of an offender from a community through imprisonment, on the other hand, may not only impair the offender's ability to reintegrate back into his or her community and so further marginalize the offender, but will also likely result in the offender and the lessons implicit in the sentencing process being quickly forgotten by the community itself.

In the aftermath of the court process, most offenders in the Nunavut territory return to their communities where they will again live in close proximity to their victims and their extended families. To the extent that the removal of an offender from the community impairs the restorative processes leading to reconciliation with victims, the sentence of imprisonment may, in the long run, place the victim in even greater danger. Given the prevailing social conditions in Nunavut's communities, the sentence of the court must be sensitive to the obvious need to restore harmony and balance, to these communities in the aftermath of crime.

Many of the Inuit inhabitants of Nunavut have grown up on the land. This was true in Suzanne's case, at least in her formative years. I am told that Suzanne was born in a traditional hunting area in northern Baffin Island. Most Inuit retain a close association with traditional on-the-land activities. Many remain dependent upon these activities as their primary source of recreation. Hunting and fishing, and the foods generated by these activities provide not only a major staple of Inuit diet, but the activity itself constitutes a way of life. I am confident that many, if not most Inuit would perceive close confinement in a house as a significant hardship, particularly where this restricts access to the land. I am confident that such an order, in an appropriate case, will serve as a meaningful deterrent to others. This is so particularly where the sentence falls in the summer months when most Inuit, and northerners generally, take advantage of the long daylight hours and warmer weather to escape the confines of their houses.

The Alberta Court of Appeal in the *Brady* judgment at p. 522 had this to say about a sentence of house arrest:

> In theory, maybe a conditional sentence could be very restrictive. One example sometimes offered is called "house arrest". Neither Mr. Brady's sentence nor any of the cases argued with it contained any such terms. And even if they did, we question the degree of house arrest's severity and hence its deterrent or denunciatory value. For hundreds of years, Anglo-Canadian law has decreed that a man's home is his castle. It is not his prison. What is staying in the comfort of one's own home, sleeping in one's own bed, remaining with one's family, phoning, watching T.V., listening to the radio or stereo, and reading whenever one wants? In essence it is carrying on with one's life, except possibly for working. We cannot equate that with actual imprisonment. Saying that such a conditional sentence is tantamount to imprisonment does not make it so. The citizens of this country would never equate house arrest with prison. And with good reason. Staying at home means more comfort, more options, more flexibility; in short, considerably more freedom than jail.

This court notes that many Inuit do not enjoy the same level of comfort that is associated with urban living as is apparent in the south. Many of Nunavut's citizens do not have adequate housing and, though this situation is slowly improving, overcrowding is not uncommon. Illiteracy is high and reading as a source of recreation is not available to many. A significant percentage of Nunavut's citizens are unilingual. They speak only Inuktitut. To the extent that most of the visual and printed media continue to be published in English or French, the recreational value of these mediums is limited. The sad reality is that poverty, chronic unemployment, and inadequate housing combines with a lack of recreational outlets and substance abuse to draw many of Nunavut's citizens into a life of crime. To many of these citizens, prison offers material comforts that may not be available in the offenders' own homes, if indeed they have homes.

The Court of Appeal in *Brady* was not called upon to address the social conditions and cultural context prevailing in Nunavut in its judgment. The *Brady* decision is therefore distinguishable, and this court declines to follow it for the reasons advanced above.

I am satisfied that a consequence that is meaningful to an Inuit person living in a remote northern community may well be perceived differently by residents of larger urban communities in the south.

It is clear that Suzanne has had a disadvantaged background. The court will not review this in detail, as it was outlined at some length by her counsel in speaking to sentence. Yet, despite all of the hardships, all of the setbacks, the disappointments and frustrations, Suzanne had continued her efforts to better herself. She has been a social worker, a teacher, a broadcaster, and a mother. She is a person of tremendous ability. She has the potential to help others and to help her community.

There will be a conditional sentence order of nine months' duration. It will have the following conditions:

You shall keep the peace and be of good behaviour. You shall appear before the court when required to do so and you shall report back to court on the next available docket date, which is September 7, at 9:30 a.m., for a review of this conditional sentence order.

You shall report in person to your supervisor today and be under his or her supervision.

You shall report thereafter to your supervisor as and when directed to do so and in a manner directed by your supervisor.

You shall remain within the Nunavut territory unless permission to go outside of the jurisdiction is first obtained from the court.

You shall notify your supervisor in advance of any change in address, and promptly notify him or her of any change in your employment or occupation.

You shall abstain absolutely from the possession and consumption of any alcohol.

You shall submit such samples of your breath as are suitable for analysis to any peace officer or your supervisor if they have reasonable grounds to believe that you have been drinking in violation of this order.

You will not enter any premises licensed to sell alcohol under the *Liquor Act* except a restaurant, and then only for the purpose of consuming food.

You will reside at house 1690A in Iqaluit until further order.

You will attend school or such other educational or recreational programs as may be directed by your supervisor and not be absent from those programs without the written permission of your supervisor.

From now until midnight on August 31, 1999 you will remain inside your residence or within 10 meters of your residence, seven days a week with the following exceptions: firstly, for two hours a day between the hours of 1:00 p.m. and 3:00 p.m. you are permitted to be outside your residence; and, secondly, at any other time where you have first obtained permission in writing from your supervisor. If you have been given written permission by your supervisor to be outside your residence at any other time, you will carry on your person the written letter of permission when you are away from your house and provide this letter to any peace officer or your supervisor immediately upon their request.

During periods of confinement, you will present yourself to the front door of your residence at any time on request of a peace officer or your supervisor.

You will perform 200 hours of community work service when and as directed by your supervisor and to his or her satisfaction.

For the first six months of this order you will not leave the municipal boundaries of the community of Iqaluit, Nunavut without the prior written permission of your supervisor.

You will have no contact, directly or indirectly, with the complainant named in this Information unless this contact is initiated by him or by the Justice Committee in consultation with your supervisor.

You will not attend within 50 meters of the complainant's residence or any place at which he is employed.

As directed by your supervisor, you will attend any meetings of the Justice Committee arranged for the purpose of providing, in person, an apology to the complainant; or to receive guidance or counselling from the committee itself.

A firearms prohibition order appears to be mandatory under the circumstances. Defence, you are not asking for any exemption, I take it?

Ms. Cooper: No, I am not, sir. I discussed that matter with my client.

The Court: There will be a firearms prohibition order, commencing today, for a period of 10 years. You are required to surrender, within 24 hours, any firearms, ammunition or explosive substances now in your possession, together with any firearms acquisitions certificate that you may possess.

Suzanne, as I am sure your lawyer will explain to you, if you are found to be in violation of any of these conditions, you can be arrested and brought before the court, and the court then has the option of sending you to jail.

The court has found that you present no danger to your community at this time, but you should be aware that this court takes breaches of conditional sentence orders very seriously. The court has every reason to believe that you will do well on a conditional sentence order, and the court intends to follow your progress through regular reviews of this conditional sentence order, at least for the immediate future.

That is the sentence of the court.

The considerations accounted for by the sentencing judge in *Evaloardjuk* illustrate the contextual and culturally appropriate sentencing of Inuit offenders in the far north. While allowing the offender to remain in her community — albeit restricting her liberty and ability to engage in traditional, on-the-land activities — may appear lenient to some, as the sentencing judge indicated, small, close-knit Inuit communities in Nunavut do not allow offenders to remain anonymous as is more often the case in large urban centres. Thus, deterrence may, in fact, be facilitated by having the offender remain in her community rather than being sent away; restoring community harmony may also be achieved by the same process, depending, of course, on the nature of the offence. Additionally, requiring the offender, who was raised in a traditional hunting area, to maintain close proximity to her home, thereby restricting her ability to engage in traditional hunting activities, imposed a significant hardship upon her — far more than would usually be the case in a sentence involving house arrest where the offender did not possess such a strong cultural attachment to the land.

F. CONCLUSION

The geographic location of Inuit communities has meant that the Inuit have only recently been exposed to issues that have confronted other Aboriginal peoples in Canada for quite some time. The relative isolation of the Inuit has allowed Inuit communities to maintain greater connections to their traditional lifestyles and activities than many Aboriginal communities farther south and not be confronted with the same degree of interference from non-Aboriginal authorities as the latter. Not surprisingly, then, the Inuit's recent forays into modern land claims and self-government agreements are, for the most part, their first experiences in formal dealings with the federal government on matters concerning their rights.

As seen in the discussion of Inuit land claims and self-government agreements, the Inuit people have been able to negotiate the protection of some of their rights *vis-à-vis* the federal government. That progress has been hampered, though, by government refusals to negotiate agreements that would recognize non-delegated, inherent, or nation-based forms of self-government, as discussed in Chapter 1.

While the Inuit do share certain commonalities with other Aboriginal peoples in Canada and may draw upon the situations and precedents involving those other peoples, one must be mindful of the unique situation, rights, and practices of the Inuit. Indeed, as illustrated by the *Kadlak* and *Evaloardjuk* cases, the uniqueness of Inuit rights and practices, as well as the *sui generis* requirements of their geographic locations, have already been factored into Inuit rights jurisprudence and in the area of criminal sentencing.

CHAPTER 6

MÉTIS RIGHTS

A. INTRODUCTION

Métis peoples, like the Inuit whose rights are discussed in Chapter 5, fall under the definition of "aboriginal peoples of Canada" in section 35(2) of the *Constitution Act, 1982*, being Schedule B to the *Canada Act 1982* (U.K.), 1982, c. 11. Although for the purposes of section 35(2) Métis peoples are grouped with the Inuit and status Indians (see Chapter 8 for a discussion of the distinction between status and non-status Indians), this chapter will illustrate that the Métis possess distinct practices and cultures that are derived from their unique backgrounds. Indeed, as will be discussed further in the process of determining who Métis persons are, the unique histories of various Métis groups provide for a rich and diverse collectivity within the definition of "Métis".

This chapter will begin by examining the issue of Métis identity, a long-standing matter of debate within and without Métis communities. It will then consider the issue of Métis land rights, including the process and implications of bringing the Red River Métis into Confederation through the *Manitoba Act, 1870*. Finally, the chapter will focus on Métis Aboriginal rights as separate and distinct rights from the Aboriginal rights belonging to non-Métis groups. In the process of this latter examination, the dilemma faced by some Métis groups as they strive for recognition of their rights and traditions — do they wish to be treated as "Indians" under section 91(24) of the *Constitution Act, 1867* or do they seek to carve out their own status and rights as Métis under section 35(1) of the *Constitution Act, 1982* — will be considered.

B. MÉTIS IDENTITY

Because of the Métis' unique origins, a great deal of controversy has surrounded the definition of "Métis" and the nature and extent of their rights. This part of the chapter will examine Métis identification issues as well as disputes over the origins and scope of Métis rights.

REPORT OF THE ROYAL COMMISSION ON ABORIGINAL PEOPLES, PERSPECTIVES AND REALITIES, VOL. 4

(Ottawa: Ministry of Supply & Services, 1996)
"Métis Perspectives," at 199-203 (references omitted)

In 1982, the Constitution of Canada was amended to state that Canada's Aboriginal peoples include the Métis. Métis people did not need to be told that: they have always known who they are. They have always known, too, that Canada would be a different place today if they had not played a

major role in its development. Modern Canada is the product of a historical partnership between Aboriginal and non-Aboriginal people, and Métis
people were integral to that partnership.

Intermarriage between First Nations and Inuit women and European
fur traders and fishermen produced children, but the birth of new Aboriginal cultures took longer. At first, the children of mixed unions were
brought up in the traditions of their mothers or (less often) their fathers.
Gradually, however, distinct Métis cultures emerged, combining European
and First Nations or Inuit heritages in unique ways. Economics played a
major role in this process. The special qualities and skills of the Métis
population made them indispensable members of Aboriginal/non-
Aboriginal economic partnerships, and that association contributed to the
shaping of their cultures. Using their knowledge of European and Aboriginal languages, their family connections and their wilderness skills, they
helped to extend non-Aboriginal contacts deep into the North American
interior. As interpreters, diplomats, guides, couriers, freighters, traders
and suppliers, the early Métis people contributed massively to European
penetration of North America.

The French referred to the fur trade Métis as *coureurs de bois* (forest run-
ners) and *bois brulés* (burnt-wood people) in recognition of their wilderness
occupations and their dark complexions. The Labrador Métis (whose culture had early roots) were originally called "livyers" or "settlers", those
who remained in the fishing settlements year-round rather than returning
periodically to Europe or Newfoundland. The Cree people expressed the
Métis character in the term *Otepayemsuak*, meaning the "independent
ones".

. . . . .

1.2 Métis Identity

... Being Métis ... can mean different things in different contexts: one
context may speak to an individual's inner sense of personal identity; another may refer to membership in a particular Métis community; a third
may signal entitlement to Métis rights as recognized by section 35 of the
Constitution Act, 1982. Throughout the following discussion of Métis identity, the meaning of the term is governed largely by the context in which it
is used.

. . . . .

It is primarily culture that sets the Métis apart from other Aboriginal
peoples. Many Canadians have mixed Aboriginal/non-Aboriginal ancestry, but that does not make them Métis or even Aboriginal. ... What distinguishes Métis people from everyone else is that they associate themselves
with a culture that is distinctly Métis.

Historically, Métis cultures grew out of ways of life dictated by the resource industry roles of the early Métis. For those who served the fur
trade, the birth of the unique Métis language, Michif, was a consequence of
using both French and Indian languages. The need to travel inspired mo-

bile art forms: song, dance, fiddle music, decorative clothing. The periodic return to fixed trading bases, the seasonal nature of the buffalo hunt and discriminatory attitudes all shaped settlement patterns. For Métis people of the east, seasonal hunting and gathering expeditions combined with influences that stemmed from a fishing economy. In all cases, the cultures developed organically, their characteristics determined by the social and economic circumstances that germinated and nourished them.

. . . . .

Individual identity is a matter of personal choice. ... For acceptance of that identification, however, it is necessary to win the approval of the people or nation with which one identifies. It would be inappropriate for anyone outside that nation to intervene. Therefore, when a government wishes to know a nation's membership for the purpose of engaging in nation-to-nation negotiations, it can legitimately consider only two criteria: self-identification and acceptance by the nation.

This does not mean that other governments can never legitimately concern themselves with who is or is not Métis. Suppose that the government of Canada agreed through negotiation to provide a benefit to Métis residents of a particular area. In the absence of an agreed definition of Métis, it would be necessary for the government to decide who did and did not qualify for the benefit. Or if, pending the negotiated settlement of a Métis issue, it were agreed that a government should administer a program related to the issue, the program's beneficiaries would necessarily have to be identified. It might also be appropriate for a government to identify the membership of an Aboriginal nation in order to assess the ramifications of a decision recognizing its status as a nation. Beyond such purposes, the composition of an Aboriginal nation should be the business of no one other than that nation and its members.

In her article "Who Are the Métis People in Section 35(2)?", Catherine Bell attempts to clarify who fits within the definition of "Métis" in section 35(2) of the *Constitution Act, 1982*. Like the excerpt from the Royal Commission on Aboriginal Peoples Report above, Bell concludes that Métis peoples must be defined according to logical and political considerations in addition to self-identification based on racial, cultural, and historical criteria.

CATHERINE BELL, "WHO ARE THE METIS PEOPLE IN SECTION 35(2)?"

(1991), 29 Alta. L. Rev. 351 at 353, 355-8, 370-1, 373-81
(references omitted)

[In footnote 1 of this article, Bell explains that "For the purposes of this paper, a distinction is drawn between small "m" and capital "M" Métis. Written with a small "m" the term is a racial term referring to self-identifying Métis of mixed Indian-European ancestry including the Métis

Nation discussed in this paper. The term "Metis" in quotation marks refers to the term as it appears in s. 35(2) of the *Constitution Act, 1982.*"]

... A survey of the alternative definitions suggest that the term "Metis" as a contemporary legal concept cannot be given a single definition. However, this does not mean it is impossible to derive identification criteria. Rather specification of criteria is possible if the term "Metis" is limited in its application to one of two possible groups:

(a) the descendants of the historic Metis nation, or
(b) people associated with, and accepted by, self-identifying contemporary metis collectivities.

· · · · ·

Among the metis, there is disagreement whether the "Metis" in s. 35(2) are a single people or several peoples. However, it is clear that a variety of mixed-blood aboriginal collectivities identify as "Metis."

· · · · ·

The word "peoples" is not defined in the Constitution nor has it been defined in Canadian law. One possible interpretation is the word "peoples" refers to indigenous nations. This interpretation arises from claims of Canada's aboriginal peoples to recognition as nation states. As the notion of indigenous nationhood was part of the national and international climate within which s. 35 was negotiated, it is properly considered in a purposive interpretation of s. 35.

· · · · ·

Prior to the definition of aboriginal peoples in s. 35(2), four main categories of aboriginal peoples were commonly used in legal and political spheres. These categories were status Indians, non-status Indians, Inuit and Metis. ... The central issue debated among groups purporting to represent the Metis is whether non-status persons of mixed origins that have not been reinstated to Indian status, who identify as metis but are not descendants of the Metis nation, can properly be brought within the constitutional definition of "Metis." Essential to the resolution of this debate is the scope of the term "Indian" in s. 35(2). If "Indian" refers to the same class of persons referred to in s. 91(24) of the *Constitution Act, 1867*, a narrow definition of Metis peoples focusing on a common political, national, and historic background may not affect the constitutional recognition of non-status Indians. Although the term "Indian" has been interpreted to refer only to *Indian Act* Indians, this position has been subject to strong criticism and cannot be applied to s. 91(24) in the face of the *Eskimo* decision.

· · · · ·

If one accepts that the interpretation of s. 35(2) need not be analyzed by employing an "either-or" logic (that is, *either* it encompasses Indians re-

ferred to in s. 91(24) *or* it does not), then those persons who are not affiliated with the Metis Nation but identify as metis can logically be included
in the reference to "Indians".

Who are "the Metis people" in this context? ... The "Metis" referred to
in s. 35(2) may have been included as a matter of political expediency. The
definition section was inserted primarily to satisfy the claims of the N.C.C.
[Native Council of Canada] for recognition of their metis constituents as a
distinct aboriginal people. They were included, without a prior determination of whether they had aboriginal and treaty rights. Further, the decision was made without determining who the Metis are. ...

There are several broad choices from which to choose a definition for
the term "Metis." Among them are:

1. anyone of mixed Indian/non-Indian blood who is not a status Indian;
2. a person who identifies as Metis and is accepted by a successor community of the Metis Nation;
3. a person who identifies as Metis and is accepted by a self-identifying
   Metis community;
4. persons who took, or were entitled to take, half-breed grants under the
   Manitoba Act or *Dominion Lands Act*, and their descendants; and
5. descendants of persons excluded from the *Indian Act* regime by virtue
   of a way of life criterion.

. . . . .

B. HISTORICAL, POLITICAL AND LEGAL USAGE OF THE TERM "MÉTIS"

Basic to an understanding of the difficulties associated with defining the
term "Metis" is an appreciation of the history and use of the term. The
word "metis" is a French word meaning "mixed" and was first used to
refer to the French-speaking "half-breeds" of the Red River settlement and
surrounding areas. The term was used to refer to the French- and Cree-
speaking descendants of the French-Catholic Red River Metis as distinct
from the descendants of English-speaking "half-breeds" or "country
born," who lived a more agrarian lifestyle and identified themselves as
Protestant and British. Later, both native and non-native scholars writing
histories of the Red River area used the term collectively to refer to French-
and English-speaking "half-breeds" who emerged as a distinct cultural
group in the West and spoke of themselves as the "New Nation".

By the 1970s the term had extended beyond its religious, geographic,
and linguistic boundaries to encompass "any person of mixed Indian-
white blood who identified him or herself and was identified by others as
neither Indian or white, even though he or she might have no provable
link to the historic Red River Metis." The identification was a negative
identification used interchangeably with the word "half-breed". They were
Metis or half-breeds because they were not somebody else. More recent
historical works, focusing on the ethnic origins and changing dimensions
of Metis identity, use the term to refer to

those individuals, frequently of mixed Indian, Western European and other ancestry, who are in the St. Lawrence-Great Lakes trading system, including its extension to the Pacific and Arctic coasts and chose to see themselves in various collectivities as distinct from members of the 'white' community.

Some suggest that the contemporary usage should be extended to persons of mixed metis/Indian ancestry.

. . . . .

... [T]he N.C.C. ... argue that Metis people include "both blood relatives of the Red River Metis and completely distinct Metis populations which pre- and- post-date both the history and the people of the Red River." They contend the term "Metis" in s. 35(2) refers to their constituents who identify themselves as metis and were never included in treaty, or were excluded from treaty as half-breed, or were refused scrip on a residency basis or are descendants of the above. The M.N.C. [Metis National Council] has rejected both the contemporary and traditional usage of the term metis and has adopted a definition consistent with the legislative and political purposes of the federal government with respect to half-breeds living in Rupert's Land and the Northwest Territories. The M.N.C. define "Metis" as follows:

1. The Metis are:
   — an aboriginal people distinct from Indian and Inuit;
   — descendants of the historic Metis who evolved in what is now Western Canada as a people with a common political will
   — descendants of those aboriginal[s] who have been absorbed by the historic Metis.
2. The Metis community comprises members of the above who share a common cultural identity and political will.

The provincial organizations comprising the M.N.C. adopt similar definitions but also accept non-status Indians who have been accepted as members of the provincial organization. For example, when the Alberta Metis Association was founded in 1932 it offered membership to anyone of native ancestry. As recent as 1987, any person of native ancestry could be a member so long as a member of the Association was willing to take a sworn statement that the applicant was a metis. In Manitoba, the Manitoba Metis Federation was created because of a split between status and non-status Indians. The Federation constitution provided that a non-registered person of Indian descent could become a member of the Federation. A non-native person could also become a member provided he or she was married to a metis. It is likely the flexible nature of the membership criteria for prairie political organizations ... gave rise to the self-identification element in the M.N.C. definition of the Metis Nation.

The result is that today "Metis" can be defined in many different ways. A metis person is described as a person of mixed-blood, one who considers herself a metis, a non-status Indian, one who received land scrip or money scrip, one who is identified with a group that identifies as metis, or a non-native married to a metis. None of the definitions standing alone is satisfactory to all persons who identify themselves as metis. These potential usages and definitions have created the identity debate and have resulted in major divisions in native political organizations.

IV. RESOLUTION OF THE DEFINITION DEBATE

Given the complexity of the definition debate, is it possible to define the term "Metis" in s. 35(2)?

. . . . .

Taking into consideration the minimal criteria set out in s. 35 and the difficulty of identifying a single metis people, the most logical solution to the definition debate is to define the "metis" in s. 35(2) as belonging to one of two possible groups.

1. The descendants of the historic Metis Nation.
2. People associated with ongoing metis collectivities.

A refusal to select identifying criteria by freezing cultural idioms at a given point in history allows the interpreter of s. 35(2) to define "Metis" for constitutional purposes as small "m" metis. ... The result is that the constitutional term "Metis" does not refer to a homogeneous cultural or political group but a large and varied population characterized by mixed aboriginal ancestry and self-identification as "Metis." This conclusion should not be surprising as the term "Indian" clearly encompasses a variety of Indian nations with different political, cultural and historical backgrounds. The common factor shared by all of these groups is their aboriginal ancestry.

So when does the distinction between small "m" metis and the Metis Nation become significant for constitutional purposes? It is significant in the context of establishing entitlement to specific aboriginal rights recognized and affirmed under s. 35(1).

. . . . .

If inclusion in s. 35(2) does not automatically give rise to rights under s. 35(1), what is the benefit of inclusion? ... First, recognition as an aboriginal people provides a solid constitutional base upon which negotiations for the recognition and compensation of rights can begin. Second, it incorporates a fiduciary relationship between the federal government and aboriginal peoples and so imports some restraint on the exercise of federal power. This latter point is of particular importance to metis groups who have been excluded from programs designed to benefit Indian peoples and over whom the federal government refuses to accept responsibility. Should a narrow interpretation of "Metis peoples" be adopted as advocated by the M.N.C., these benefits and the potential for constitutional protection of existing rights under s. 35(1) may be denied to other metis groups that do not constitute part of the Metis nation and do not identify as Indian.

Given the continuation of federal policy to refuse responsibility for metis claims south of the 60th parallel, recognition may be of little practical significance to many metis without the strong arm of the court. It is un-likely inclusion will be taken as lightly by the courts. In *Sparrow*, the court stated that it was important that s. 35(1) applied to Inuit, Indian, and Metis. The court stated s. 35 was a solemn commitment to aboriginal peoples and should be given meaningful content. In *Dumont*, [which is excerpted, *infra*] the Supreme Court of Canada recognized that claims relating to the extinguishment of metis title were justiciable and not merely claims of a moral and political nature. Although Canadian courts have yet to decide on the existence, nature and continuance of Metis rights, it is clear their inclusion in s. 35(2) will be accorded some legal significance and will not be treated simply as a cruel deception or historical mistake.

A Métis view on the Métis identity debate which also looks at its social, political, and legal contexts is offered in the following excerpt.

LARRY CHARTRAND, "METIS IDENTITY AND CITIZENSHIP"

(2001), 12 W.R.L.S.I. 5 at 6-10, 19-23, 25-6, 37-41, 47-52 (references omitted)

. . . . .

... [O]ne of the objectives of this article is to examine the various current initiatives to identity and citizenship in the Metis context through the lens of international human rights law relevant to citizenship. The international law regarding citizenship will be contrasted with political definitions and judicial pronouncements on Metis identity. In light of this analysis, a model citizenship code that is consistent with international law and the unique circumstances of the Metis will be offered. Relevant policy implications will be highlighted in light of the issues surrounding Metis identity and citizenship.

. . . . .

II. BACKGROUND

Before entering into a discussion of Metis identity and citizenship, it is useful to place such a discussion within the contemporary Metis political and social context. This section of the article presents a brief sketch of Metis political organization and current social circumstances. This overview is useful to provide a context for appreciating the current debate surrounding Metis identity.

There are a number of organizations that presently claim to represent Metis people in Canada. Indeed, there are serious divisions among self-identifying Metis people about which political organizations are justified in identifying themselves as true Metis organizations. The issue of "Metis identity" is controversial and has generated considerable debate and conflict between various "Metis" organizations.

However, at the outset, it is important to keep in mind an important distinction between those entities that are capable of exercising rights of self-determination, including the right to determine citizenship, and those entities that are incorporated under various federal and provincial statutes as non-profit organizations representing Metis people according to the by-laws of the corporation.

. . . . .

A. Metis Political Representation in Canada

Metis peoples are purported to be represented by two national organizations: the Metis National Council and the Congress of Aboriginal Peoples. Each national organization has a number of provincial affiliates that comprise the membership of the national body. There also exists a Metis Settlements General Council that represents the Metis who are situated on the eight land settlements in northern Alberta. This Metis settlement regime is unique to Alberta. In addition, there are some independent regional organizations that purport to represent a particular Metis constituency. ...

. . . . .

B. Social, Cultural and Economic Circumstances

According to the 1996 Census report, 210,190 people identified themselves as Metis. This represents 25.9 per cent of the Aboriginal population and 0.715 per cent of the overall Canadian population. In general, the Metis are similar to First Nations people with respect to their social conditions, unemployment and lack of educational attainment. In other words, the Metis have not weathered the storm of social disruption and oppression caused by colonialism any better than Indians or the Inuit. Indeed, in terms of cultural survival, there is every indication that the Metis were particularly hard hit by the pressures of Canadian policies of assimilation.

For example, data from the 1991 Aboriginal Peoples Survey indicated that over 73 per cent of the Metis population never spoke an Aboriginal language at home. In addition, the percentage of Metis that participate in some form of traditional activity is considerably less than the average for all Aboriginal groups. Only 40 per cent of Metis participate in traditional activities compared to 50 per cent for all Aboriginal peoples. One can only speculate as to why there is a low participation rate. Reasons could be due to personal choice. For example, those who live in urban environments have fewer opportunities to pursue traditional activities. More importantly, the impact of public attitude towards the Metis after the war of 1885 may be the major reason for these statistics.

. . . . .

Although Metis continued to practice their culture, the social circumstances of the time no doubt dramatically affected their ability to do so at a level that would ensure maximum freedom and opportunity to pass on their culture to subsequent generations. Another factor relevant to the western Metis that may, in part, have caused such a disparity of culture and language maintenance is the "scrip" program for the Metis living in western Canada. Unlike Indian communities that acquired collective ownership of various tracts of land under the Indian reserve system, the Metis were forced to acquire individual plots of land, often at some distance from their home communities. Although there are problems with the paternalistic nature of the reserve system, at a minimum they at least allow Indian communities to continue practising their culture and maintain a sense of community identity and belonging. Unfortunately, the individualized and alienating scrip system denied the Metis this important condition of cultural continuity.

. . . . .

Except for the Metis Settlements in Alberta, the Metis, as communities, are a landless people. Without land, Metis communities have little to no control over their destiny. The important local decision-making is left in the hands of non-aboriginal authorities. Furthermore, without land the Metis have no financial security or control over resources to protect their traditional avocations for the present or for their children's future. Currently, Metis must often gather as a group to promote collective activities and events either in the basements of churches or community halls when they can afford to rent them.

Furthermore, Metis social and political institutions are often poorly funded. As a result, efforts to provide Metis specific services, such as child care, education and economic development are difficult to establish. Of particular concern is the lack of being able to plan for the long term because of the short-term nature of most funding programs. Agencies, such as Metis Child and Family Services in Edmonton are often put in difficult positions financially, because government funding programs are either temporary, pilot project oriented and administratively complicated due to varying funding criteria and requirements from different funding programs. These problems, in addition to delays and cutbacks, makes it extremely difficult to plan for future expansion and to meet new challenges and needs of the Metis community as they arise.

Much of the problem in developing Metis specific programs is due to the jurisdictional vacuum in which the Metis find themselves. Because of historical circumstances, the federal government denies that they are responsible for the Metis. Likewise, the provinces are not generally prepared to provide Metis-specific funding or services because they run the risk that, if they do so, they might be perceived as accepting jurisdictional responsibility over the Metis which they argue is a federal government responsibility.

Another social concern of the Metis has to do with the public's understanding of the Metis and their history, culture and legal status in Canadian society. This failure to understand who the Metis are often exacerbates problems associated with program service and delivery. Furthermore, government's lack of understanding often causes inequitable responses to Aboriginal issues. For example, an agreement between the

Province of Saskatchewan and the Federation of Saskatchewan Indians [FSIN] over the control of Casino revenues in the province excluded the Metis. The FSIN has representation on the Board of the Casino Corporation and are guaranteed 25 per cent of the profits through the First Nations Fund set up under the legislation. Yet the Metis Nation of Saskatchewan was left out of the picture almost entirely, but for a minor reference to the fact that like other charities, they may be eligible for some funding upon application. There is no representation on the Board, no special Metis Nation fund and no guarantee of funds. This is a form of discrimination against the Metis people.

This inequity is well illustrated in the child welfare area. There are several provinces that have legislation requiring child welfare authorities to contact the Indian Band office to which a child belongs if the child is going to become a ward of the state. Similar protections for the Metis do not exist.

Hunting and fishing rights have also been difficult for the Metis to establish and receive equity with First Nations' rights to hunt. …

. . . . .

Thus, even though the Metis have faced and continue to face racism and discrimination because they are Aboriginal, they also face discrimination because they are not Indians. They are doubly discriminated. They do not get the same level of recognition, as do Indians, in the acquisition of resources and culturally sensitive programs.

. . . . .

… The social circumstances facing Metis communities are often exacerbated by Metis exclusion from relevant federal government policies, programs and services that have benefited Indian and Inuit. Provinces, with the exception of Alberta, have denied any jurisdictional responsibility regarding the Metis and have consistently maintained that the Metis are the responsibility of the federal government. Thus, over much of the last 100 years, the Metis have been unable to communicate with the Crown on a nation to nation level — their existence as an Aboriginal people denied. And with that denial, a refusal by both levels of government to recognise the inherent rights of the Metis that exist independent of state or government action. In many cases, the Metis have, out of necessity, only been able to access financial support for their organisations like any other charitable organisation in the province.

. . . . .

IV. MEMBERSHIP AND CITIZENSHIP

Before examining the relevance of the concept of citizenship to the Metis nation in particular, it is appropriate at this point to discuss the distinction between the concepts of membership and citizenship. There are very real and important distinctions between the two concepts. Membership is a broad ideal and theoretically includes an unrestricted notion of belonging, which can legitimately apply many groups, whether religious, social, or personal interest in nature. ... [C]itizenship has "come to signify rights and privileges, duties and responsibilities in a political community ." As Professor Elkins notes, "citizenship goes beyond membership because it involves a sense of commitment, of being engaged by the actions related to that community. It is a concept that takes us beyond individualism, self-interest, and self-centredness, and thus it is inherently related to concepts of community." Consequently "political communities" can only exercise the determination of citizenship, as opposed to membership.

However, the concept of citizenship is a fluid one. It is not, as many people expect, one restricted to notions of community as defined by territory. A political community can be territorially defined, but it need not be. It is possible to belong to a political community that is non-territorial based and be a citizen of such a political community. History is replete with examples of political societies that for one reason or another existed without a recognized territorial base. As Professor Elkins aptly puts it, the concepts of citizenship will, it appears, "broaden in a global sense while becoming more focused in our identities. The implicit equation of citizenship with status as members of a territorial nation-state will increasingly give way to growing obligations implicit in our belief in human rights" which are transnational in nature.

. . . . .

The question that arises is which level of Metis political organization is authorized or appropriate to determine citizenship? At first, it would seem logical that Metis citizenship must be the responsibility of the Nation as a whole. To rest such a determination on Metis locals or provincial affiliates would be akin to saying that municipalities or provinces will determine Canadian citizenship. Arguably, the idea makes little sense.

In so far as citizenship is the common bond of a people, is it contrary to the concept of citizenship to allow units within a larger unit to independently determine the criteria of citizenship in the larger unit. Allowing such decision-making at the local level could literally break-up the larger Metis nation. The larger nation could not effectively govern if an individual Metis for the purposes of one local community was not Metis for the purposes of another local community. Movement back and forth within the Nation and the receipt of consistent treatment and services is one of the expectations of citizenship within a Nation. The larger Metis nation could not guarantee such a fundamental right of citizenship; thus, citizenship would only prove an illusion within the larger Metis nation.

However, there is an alternative view of citizenship that may not only respect the integrity of the larger Metis nation but also locate primary decision-making authority regarding citizenship at the local community level. There is nothing about the concept of citizenship that requires decision making responsibilities to be located in only one governing entity. Authority can be shared. The concept of citizenship is capable of being multi-dimensional as local Metis communities could determine citizenship, but also carry the presumption that individuals possessing Metis citizenship in one community, save extenuating circumstances, will acquire citizenship as of right in other local Metis communities. Thus, Metis citizenship, by means of a refutable presumption, is assumed to be universal throughout the Metis nation as a whole — yet primary decision-making authority rests with local communities and respects local history and patterns of identity formation.

. . . . .

Unfortunately, the current judicial approach to Metis identity makes it necessary to recognize that the definition of Metis, for the purposes of determining s. 35 rights, may be different from the definition of Metis for citizenship purposes.

Under s. 35(2) of the Constitution, the Metis are listed as one of the Aboriginal peoples of Canada; however, the provision does not specifically define who the Metis are. The Constitution could have read that a "Metis for the purposes of s. 35(2) is anyone who belongs to a Metis Nation according to the laws of a Metis Nation." This would have allowed the definition of Metis in s. 35(2) to be synonymous with Metis citizenship. But, as the above discussion indicates, a distinction between Metis identity for the purposes of s. 35(2), and Metis citizenship itself, is likely to materialize. To allow such incongruence to prevail will no doubt lead to significant confusion and unneeded administrative complexity.

There is also the danger that two classes of Metis will emerge wherein some Metis will have greater rights than others, not unlike the distinction that currently exists in s. 6 of the *Indian Act*, where s. 6(1) Indians have greater rights (to pass on status) than s. 6(2) Indians. This inequality in status has been the subject of considerable criticism and is the subject of ongoing court action. The same mistakes should not be made in the context of Metis identity and rights.

In addition, distinctions among Metis over rights may also lead to further uncertainty over the question of what constitutes Metis status. The courts can avoid such an outcome if they are cognizant of which level of Metis political organization is appropriate for determining Metis identity, and respect the decisions of the Metis political communities in exercising such authority.

From the perspective of both the federal government and the Metis, certainty is a desirable outcome; this can be best achieved if Metis citizenship and Metis identity for the purposes of s. 35(2) of the Constitution are synonymous.

The preferred option may be to avoid the uncertainty of the judicial route altogether by having the federal government, and if possible the provincial governments, agree to a Metis citizenship codes and accompanying processes for registration. In order to be respectful of a Metis Nation's right to self-determination, the Metis nation must be given complete latitude as to the criteria it would adopt for determining citizenship. It is important to realize that the determination of Metis citizenship is correctly regarded as an inherently political decision and one that only the nation itself can determine. It is political in the sense that the courts should not determine the criteria of citizenship. Courts can and do determine if individuals in any given case meet the criteria of citizenship, however, they should have no role in the determination of the criteria itself. Of course, the Metis nation would need to be cognizant of the concerns of the federal or provincial governments in formulating their definitions, as benefits may flow to Metis citizens by virtue of this identity. Once bilateral, or trilateral, political agreements have been reached with a Metis nation, the federal and provincial governments would then agree that they would respect the decisions of the Metis Nation regarding citizenship.

In summary, the concept of citizenship is very much appropriate for a Metis nation to identify those who are said to belong. Metis communities are no less political communities than other nations. Their lack of territories (with the exception of the Alberta Metis Settlements) does not disqualify them from describing their people as the citizens of a Metis nation possessing all the assumptions and entitlements that such a concept entails.

· · · · ·

VIII. THE SCOPE OF THE CORE OF METIS CITIZENSHIP

This paper assumes that there is more than one mixed-blood group that self-identifies as Metis. The position of the Metis National Council is that there is only one Metis Nation and that they are the only group that can legitimately call themselves Metis. Whether there is one Metis Nation or more than one does not detract from the need for each Metis group to determine who are its core group. In the prairies, there is a long history of distinct Metis national consciousness as an autonomous political society. In determining the core of the Metis nation of the prairies, there can be no doubt that they include individuals who are descendants of this historical nation that occupied Red River and the Northwest Territories during the late 1770s to 1900s. No one can reasonably deny that such ancestors are Metis citizens. A Metis citizen Acceptance Process could be undertaken to identify and register such individuals. This would be a one-time process.

The difficulty lies, however, in the fact that since the early 1900s, Metis political organizations have included within their past and existing membership individuals who are not ancestors of the historic Metis Nation of the prairies. Many non-status Indians, who are ethnically and culturally Indian, have for one reason or another, joined the Metis associations of various provinces. Indeed, as described earlier, the common concerns of Metis and non-status Indians over recognition of their Aboriginal rights facilitated the creation of the all-inclusive Native Council of Canada in the first place. For many years, the interests of the Metis and non-status Indian populations could be accommodated in a single organization. However, a sizable portion of the Metis membership of the NCC eventually thought that their interests would best be promoted by having a separate national organization that represented only Metis and, in particular, those who are descendants of the historic Metis Nation. Despite this regrouping and focus, the affiliates of the Metis National Council, still have members who are not descendants of the historic Metis Nation. Although these members have the option of joining the NCC affiliates from the various Prairie

Provinces, such individuals, may nonetheless, still maintain their identity as Metis. They may participate in Metis activities and gatherings and be accepted as members. Do such members belong to the core group?

This, of course, is a matter for the Metis to decide. However, under such circumstances, it may be politically expedient to allow all current members of the affiliate Metis associations of the MNC to become core Metis citizens. The other option is to include only those who are descendants of the historic Metis Nation, and to then allow those who are not, to apply for Metis citizenship under the naturalization process. This may be a divisive issue. But, since non-historic Metis, who identify as being Metis and participate in Metis activities, are likely to succeed in a fair naturalization process regardless, they should arguably be accepted as core Metis citizens under this one time acceptance process.

What becomes even more controversial is the question of whether Metis citizens can belong to another Aboriginal registry such as the *Indian Act*. Such individuals may be Metis culturally and socially, but have Indian status. Indeed, they may primarily associate with Metis and self-identify as Metis. Indeed, such an individual may even be a descendant of the historic Metis Nation. Should such individuals be excluded from possessing Metis citizenship by reason of having Indian status?

. . . . .

… [O]nce a person has Indian Status in Canada, the "current law in the *Indian Act* is that the person can never lose or forgo that status as an 'Indian'." … Regardless, the Metis Nation need not exclude such individuals. It is perfectly in accordance with international law for an individual to have more than one nationality. Alternatively, the Metis Nation might want to consider that such individuals are not automatically excluded from citizenship but that they could lose citizenship if they do not maintain a genuine connection to the Metis Nation.

. . . . .

X. CONCLUSION AND POLICY IMPLICATIONS

Recent uncertainty regarding Metis status has not caused significant concern for the federal government, as historically no programs or services specifically existed for them as a nation. Nonetheless, things are changing as the Metis gain recognition through successful claims based on s. 35 of the Constitution. Consequently, provincial and federal governments are now required to deal with the Metis as Metis.

It is in the interests of all the parties involved that certainty over status, and citizenship, be achieved; clearly, both the federal and provincial governments will benefit by ensuring that obligations owed to the Metis are not unduly compromised. By ensuring that governmental officials only recognize as Metis those that have been granted citizenship according to rules of a Metis nation, integrity of service delivery can be achieved.

As indicated in the above excerpts, historically, Métis people were often seen to fit neither entirely within Aboriginal societies nor within non-Aboriginal society, notwithstanding the fact that Métis people trace their ancestry to both groups. The unique position of the Métis people sometimes worked in their favour, but, at other times, was a hindrance to their relations with other groups. One of the ways in which this notion of "otherness" affected Métis people was in the understanding of Métis rights to land.

C. MÉTIS LAND RIGHTS

The problem of defining Métis is not only a modern phenomenon. Providing a means of definition was equally important when Manitoba was admitted into Confederation in 1870 by way of the *Manitoba Act, 1870* (U.K.), 32 & 33 Vict., c. 3. The *Manitoba Act* provided for the creation of the Province of Manitoba upon the admission of Rupert's Land and the North-West Territories into the Dominion of Canada. These lands were included in the Dominion via the *Rupert's Land and North-Western Territory Order, 1870.*

In addition to creating the Province of Manitoba, the *Manitoba Act* included certain provisions for Métis land rights, specifically in sections 30 to 32 of the Act. These provisions read as follows:

30. All ungranted or waste lands in the Province shall be, from and after the date of the said transfer, vested in the Crown, and administered by the Government of Canada for the purposes of the Dominion, subject to, and except and so far as the same may be affected by, the conditions and stipulations contained in the agreement for the surrender of Rupert's Land by the Hudson's Bay Company to Her Majesty.

31. And whereas, it is expedient, towards the extinguishment of the Indian Title to the lands in the Province, to appropriate a portion of such ungranted lands, to the extent of one million four hundred thousand acres thereof, for the benefit of the families of the half-breed residents, it is hereby enacted, that, under regulations to be from time to time made by the Governor General in Council, the Lieutenant-Governor shall select such lots or tracts in such parts of the Province as he may deem expedient, to the extent aforesaid, and divide the same among the children of the half-breed heads of families residing in the Province at the time of the said transfer to Canada, and the same shall be granted to the said children respectively, in such mode and on such conditions as to settlement and otherwise, as the Governor General in Council may from time to time determine.

32. For the quieting of titles, and assuring to the settlers in the Province the peaceable possession of the lands now held by them, it is enacted as follows:—

    (1) All grants of land in freehold made by the Hudson's Bay Company up to the eighth day of March, in the year 1869, shall, if required by the owner, be confirmed by grant from the Crown.

(2)   All grants of estates less than freehold in land made by the Hudson's Bay Company up to the eighth day of March aforesaid, shall, if required by the owner, be converted into an estate in freehold by grant from the Crown.

(3)   All titles by occupancy with the sanction and under the license and authority of the Hudson's Bay Company up to the eighth day of March aforesaid, of land in that part of the Province in which the Indian Title has been extinguished, shall, if required by the owner, be converted into an estate in freehold by grant from the Crown.

(4)   All persons in peaceable possession of tracts of land at the time of the transfer to Canada, in those parts of the Province in which the Indian Title has not been extinguished, shall have the right of pre-emption of the same, on such terms and conditions as may be determined by the Governor in Council.

(5)   The Lieutenant-Governor is hereby authorized, under regulations to be made from time to time by the Governor General in Council, to make all such provisions for ascertaining and adjusting, on fair and equitable terms, the rights of Common, and rights of cutting Hay held and enjoyed by the settlers in the Province, and for the commutation of the same by grants of land from the Crown.

The *Manitoba Act* was confirmed by the *Constitution Act, 1871*, section 6 of which prohibited the Dominion government from altering the provisions of the *Manitoba Act*:

6.   Except as provided by the third section of this Act, it shall not be competent for the Parliament of Canada to alter the provisions of the last-mentioned Act of the said Parliament in so far as it relates to the Province of Manitoba, or of any other Act hereafter establishing new Provinces in the said Dominion, subject always to the right of the Legislature of the Province of Manitoba to alter from time to time the provisions of any law respecting the qualification of electors and members of the Legislative Assembly and to make laws respecting elections in the said Province.

The above-cited provisions were prominent in *Dumont v. Canada (Attorney General)*, which is excerpted below.

DUMONT v. CANADA (ATTORNEY-GENERAL)

(1988), 52 D.L.R. (4th) 25, 52 Man. R. (2d) 291, [1998] 5 W.W.R. 193, [1988] 3 C.N.L.R. 39 (C.A.); revd [1990] 1 S.C.R. 279, [1990] 4 W.W.R. 127, 67 D.L.R. (4th) 159, 65 Man. R. (2d) 291, [1990] 2 C.N.L.R. 19, 105 N.R. 228 (references omitted)

Huband, Philp, and **Lyon JJ.A.** concur with

Twaddle J.A.: — The plaintiffs challenge the constitutional validity of several pieces of federal legislation enacted between 1871 and 1886. They say the legislation was unconstitutional because it altered provisions of the *Manitoba Act, 1870*, S.C. 1870, c. 3, contrary to the prohibition against such alteration contained in the *Constitution Act, 1871*, 1871 (U.K.), c. 28. The Attorney-General of Canada seeks to abort the challenge on the ground, amongst others, that the validity of the impugned legislation is a matter of academic interest only.

The learned judge in motions court, who dismissed the Attorney-General's application to strike out the claim, understood the plaintiffs' claim to be that the allegedly invalid legislation had deprived the plaintiffs' forebears of a community of interest in land which, but for the legislation, would have been inherited by the plaintiffs as the descendants of those to whom the community of interest was given. Based on this understanding of the plaintiffs' case, the learned judge dismissed the application to strike out the claim. It is from the order dismissing his application that the Attorney-General of Canada now appeals.

Historical background is helpful to an understanding of the issues which are raised on this appeal.

Rupert's Land was granted to the Hudson's Bay Company by Charles II in 1670. By 1867, the effective authority of the company in Rupert's Land was on the decline. The United Kingdom Parliament was thus able to foresee, and provide for, the eventual union of Rupert's Land with Canada. Provisions for this union are to be found in the *Constitution Act, 1867* and the *Rupert's Land Act, 1868*, 1868 (U.K.), c. 105.

. . . . .

In anticipation of the union of Rupert's Land with Canada, the Parliament of Canada enacted the *Rupert's Land Act, 1869*, S.C. 1869, c. 3, by which it made provision for the future government of the territory. Also in anticipation of the union, the Government of Canada sent survey teams into the territory.

In August, 1869, a number of half-breeds, fearful of the effect the proposed union would have on their use of land, opposed the making of surveys. What followed was, from Canada's viewpoint, rebellion. A number of local inhabitants openly disputed Canada's right to annex the territory, although others were anxious for union. A state of unrest prevailed. The authority of the Company had been weakened by its own inaction. In the absence of an effective ruling power, a provisional government was formed by some of the people.

The Provisional Government (as it styled itself) sent delegates to Ottawa to negotiate the terms on which the territory might be united with Canada. A draft bill resulted from the negotiations. Before its enactment as the *Manitoba Act, 1870* it was approved by what was known as the Assembly of the Provisional Government. This Act, assented to in May, 1870, preceded the effective date on which legislative authority for the government of the territory was vested in the Parliament of Canada by the Order of Her Majesty in Her Imperial Council dated June 23, 1870.

Land rights within the province were provided for in sections 30, 31 and 32 of the *Manitoba Act, 1870* ...

Doubts having been expressed as to the authority of the Parliament of Canada to establish the Province of Manitoba, the United Kingdom Parliament enacted the *Constitution Act, 1871*, which retroactively validated the *Manitoba Act, 1870*. ...

Subsequent legislation enacted by the Parliament of Canada and by the Governor General in Council regulated the allocation of land to half-breed children and the making of claims to land under s. 32 of the *Manitoba Act, 1870*. The plaintiffs allege that the subsequent legislation went beyond mere regulation. They say that it altered or embellished the original statutory provisions. They also say that this alteration or embellishment was contrary to the provisions of s. 6 of the *Constitution Act, 1871*.

I must say that, when I read the impugned legislation, I do not find provisions which can readily be regarded as alterations to the original enactment. Indeed, one of the impugned statutes actually conferred additional rights on individual half-breeds ("Act respecting the appropriation of certain Dominion Lands in Manitoba", S.C. 1874, c. 20). I do not find it necessary, however, to decide this appeal on the basis that the plaintiffs do not have a reasonable cause of action. It is my view that this appeal can be decided on the question of whether the issue which the plaintiffs wish to raise is justiciable.

Before turning to that question, let me make it clear that, for the purpose of this appeal, I assume the truth of all allegations of fact contained in the statement of claim. Those allegations include the allegation that all half-breeds of 1870 were "Métis"; that the Métis of 1870 were a distinct people; and that all their descendants are included within the undefined group of persons constitutionally recognized today as "the Métis people." These allegations which I assume as true also include the allegation that some half-breeds of 1870 did not receive, or were deprived of, constitutionally entrenched rights and the allegation that their loss of those rights was a result of the impugned legislation.

The plaintiffs do not assert any rights of their own. They acknowledge, at least in argument, that the land of which their forebears were deprived cannot be restored to them and that they, the plaintiffs, have no legal right to compensation for the loss. What they seek is a declaration that the impugned legislation was invalid. They seek this declaration not to establish rights arising from that loss, but for a collateral purpose. That purpose is stated in the statement of claim in these terms:

> [I]t would be greatly to the advantage of the Métis, in seeking to achieve a land claims agreement pursuant to s. 35(3) of the *Constitution Act, 1982*, as amended, to obtain a declaration that the federal ... statutes and orders-in-council ... were unconstitutional measures that had the purpose and effect of stripping the Métis of the land base promised to them under Sections 31 and 32 of the *Manitoba Act, 1870*.

The land claims agreement which the Métis seek is being sought extrajudicially. The land claim is rooted in the aboriginal status of the Métis people, a status recognized by s. 35 of the *Constitution Act, 1982*. ...

The fact that the Métis might acquire a community of interest in land under a land claims agreement does not mean that the plaintiffs are claiming that such an interest in the land was given to half-breeds by the *Manitoba Act, 1870*. I can find no allegation in the statement of claim which suggests that the plaintiffs are asserting in this action a community of interest in any land.

Any doubt as to what the plaintiffs are alleging is removed when one reads para. 13 of the statement of claim. It reads in part:

> Approximately 85% of Métis persons entitled to rights under sections 31 and 32 of the Manitoba Act failed to receive or were deprived of such rights by reason of the unconstitutional ... legislation ...

It must follow that some 15% of Métis retained their rights. Such a result is totally inconsistent with a collective grant to a community of persons. Such a grant must stand or fall as an entirety.

It is, in any event, impossible to construe s. 31 of the *Manitoba Act, 1870* as conferring on half-breed children generally a community of interest in the 1,400,000 acres appropriated for the benefit of the families of half-breed residents. The section makes it quite clear that the land was to be divided "among the children of the half-breed heads of families residing in the Province" and "granted to the said children respectively."

The plaintiffs argue that, by reason of the loss of individual land rights, their forebears were unable to assemble the land which should have been theirs into townships. The argument proceeds on the notion that, but for the impugned legislation, individual titles to land within the townships would have been handed down from one generation to the next so that the present generation of Métis people would not only have enjoyed land rights inherited by them as individuals, but would also have enjoyed the social and economic benefits to be derived from belonging to an integrated community. That argument is purely speculative of what might have been. It offers no justification for a finding that the plaintiffs have a community of interest in some unspecified land or that their own rights are at issue.

. . . . .

The plaintiffs are not entitled to a declaration merely for the purpose of demonstrating that their forebears were deprived of their rights unconstitutionally. It is a well-established principle that a declaration is not available as a cure for past ills. ...

The rationale for the grant of a declaration in this case can only be its potential utility to the parties in the resolution of the Métis land claim. The granting of a declaration in aid of an extra-judicial claim is illustrated by a number of cases ...

. . . . .

... [T]he declaration sought in this case will not decide an issue essential to the resolution of the extra-judicial claim. The settlement of the Métis claim will not be promoted in any real sense by the making of the declaration sought by the plaintiffs.

For these reasons, I am of the opinion that the appeal should be allowed, the order made in motions court set aside and an order made striking out the plaintiffs' claim against the Attorney-General of Canada.

. . . . .

O'Sullivan J.A. (dissenting): —

. . . . .

... [W]hat we have before us in court at this time is not the assertion of bundles of individual rights but the assertion of the rights and status of the half-breed people of the western plains.

The problem confronting us is how can the rights of the Métis people as a people be asserted. ...

Whatever may have been the case prior to 1982, I think it is indisputable that the Canadian Constitution recognizes the existence of aboriginal peoples of Canada and that the Métis are an aboriginal people. ...

I know there is a school of thought that says that the framers of the Constitution were of the view that the Métis people as such had no rights and that a cruel deception was practised on them and on the Queen whose duty it is to respect the treaties and understandings that she has entered into with her Métis people. But I do not subscribe to this school of thought.

In my opinion, it is impossible in our jurisprudence to have rights without a remedy and the rights of the Métis people must be capable of being asserted by somebody. If not by the present plaintiffs, then by whom?

. . . . .

One of the difficulties in enforcing the rights of native peoples is that they, are difficult to define in common-law terms. Even the question of membership in a people may provide perplexing issues. But that a half-breed people existed as a people in the western plains of British North America in 1869 can hardly be doubted by those familiar with the history of this country. The half-breeds formed the overwhelming majority of the population of the Red River colony and had achieved such a degree of self-awareness as a people that ... were able to form a provisional government which maintained law and order for many months in 1870. This provisional government may not have been recognized by some of the Canadian settlers in Rupert's Land, but it was recognized by the British government which entered into negotiations with delegates appointed by the convention that sanctioned and elected the provisional government.

The *Manitoba Act, 1870* sanctioned by Imperial legislation, is not only a statute; it embodies a treaty which was entered into between the delegates of the Red River settlement and the Imperial authority. Although some historians have suggested that concessions made to the Métis were "granted" by Macdonald, the truth is that the negotiations proceeded in the presence of Imperial delegates.

. . . . .

It must be remembered that in 1869 and 1870 the Queen recognized the aboriginal titles in the land theretofore governed by the Hudson's Bay

Company. This was acknowledged by Sir John A. Macdonald himself when he said in the House of Commons on May 2, 1870:

> It is, perhaps, not known to a majority of this House that the old Indian titles are not extinguished over any portion of this country, except for two miles on each side of the Red River and the Assiniboine.

. . . . .

It has been accepted by everyone that the aboriginal rights could not be lost save by the consent of those who enjoyed them. If the Métis people did not give up their aboriginal rights by agreeing to accept the provisions of the *Manitoba Act, 1870* in lieu thereof, then the aboriginal rights of this people must still subsist.

. . . . .

... [T]he federal and provincial legislatures and governments have passed a series of statutes and regulations which were designed to have the effect, and did have the effect, of rendering nugatory the scheme which the Métis representatives had negotiated.

That scheme envisioned the developing of tracts of land *en bloc* to the extent of 1,400,000 acres in Manitoba. The people say they expected to have the land surveyed and allotted in such a way as to enable the half-breeds to continue their way of life which was not to live in isolated square sections, but in communities with community resources, with provision not only for individual cultivation but also for common pasturage and hunting. This point of view was put clearly enough in the negotiations by one of the delegates, Msgr. Ritchot, in the following words as set out in his diary for May 2, 1870:

> We continued to claim 1,500,000 acres and we agreed on the mode of distribution as follows: the land will be chosen throughout the province by each lot and in several different lots and in various places, if it is judged to be proper by the local legislature which ought itself to distribute these parcels of lands to heads of families in proportion to the number of children existing at the time of the distribution; that these lands should then be distributed among the children by their parents or guardians, always under the supervision of the above-mentioned local legislature which could pass laws to ensure the continuance of these lands in the Metis families.

(W. L. Morton, *Manitoba: The Birth of a Province*)

The governments knew well how to allot land in such a way as to enable a community to live as such. They were able to accommodate the Mennonites by the eastern reserve and the western reserve and they were able to accommodate the French-Canadians on Pembina mountain. There, settlers were not given land at random; land was allotted only to persons who shared common values.

Many of the Métis themselves proved how possible it was to allot land in accordance with their customs by themselves setting up settlements on the banks of the Saskatchewan after it became clear to them that the government's understanding of the "treaty" they made was different from theirs. ...

The plaintiffs want court declarations nullifying the laws which, according to them, amended and changed the *Manitoba Act, 1870* in an unconstitutional way.

The *British North America Act, 1871* (now the *Constitution Act, 1871*) was an Imperial Act which confirmed the *Manitoba Act, 1870*. Section 6 of this Act specifically made the Act creating the province unalterable by the Parliament of Canada. An exception was created allowing the provincial legislature to make laws with respect to the qualifications of members of the legislature and elections within the province. The plaintiffs allege that the restrictions imposed on the federal Parliament and the provincial legislature were never adhered to.

The policy of land distribution spelled out in the *Manitoba Act, 1870* was amended by ancillary enactments on at least eleven occasions between 1873 and 1884. According to the plaintiffs, by 1884 the original legislation had been reduced to a hollow shell.

. . . . .

In my opinion, the plaintiffs are suitable persons to assert the claims of the half-breed people and their suit should be allowed to go forward with such suitable amendments as may be sought to conform with the evidence and materials to be introduced in the course of a trial. I would dismiss the application to strike out the statement of claim.

. . . . .

... I think it is important to accept that the claims asserted by the plaintiffs in the present action are justiciable and not merely political. The plaintiffs have status to assert their claims in the Court of Queen's Bench. I am sure the judge assigned to try the case will have a difficult time and will have to be able to adapt the process of the court to suit the nature of the case. But, in the end, in my opinion it is in the development of law to deal with claims of "peoples" that lies the best hope of achieving justice and harmony in a world full of minority groups.

Appeal allowed.

On appeal to the Supreme Court of Canada, the Court unanimously overturned the majority judgment of the Manitoba Court of Appeal. As Justice Wilson explained, according to the test established in *Canada (Attorney General) v. Inuit Tapirisat of Canada*, [1980] 2 S.C.R. 735, 115 D.L.R. (3d) 1, 33 N.R. 304, the outcome of the case was neither "plain and obvious" nor "beyond doubt", therefore the action ought to proceed to trial for determination. As well, she stated that the proper interpretation of the *Manitoba Act, 1870*, the *Constitution Act, 1871* and the impugned ancillary legislation would be better determined at trial once a proper factual basis was established.

What do you think the effect of section 6 of the *Constitution Act, 1871* is on the *Manitoba Act, 1870*? Does section 6 support the claims being made in

Dumont? Can the *Manitoba Act, 1870* be regarded as a treaty, as suggested by O'Sullivan J.A.? Was the Act a unilateral enactment or was it promulgated only after consultation with the Provisional Government of the Red River colony? Can governmental consultation resulting in legislation be termed a treaty? Refer back to the discussion of treaties in Chapter 2.

Some of the controversies emanating from the *Manitoba Act* and the enactments that followed it are canvassed in the following excerpt.

CLEM CHARTIER, "ABORIGINAL RIGHTS AND LAND ISSUES: THE METIS PERSPECTIVE"

in Menno Boldt and J. Anthony Long, eds., in association with Leroy Little
Bear, *The Quest for Justice: Aboriginal Peoples and Aboriginal Rights*
(Toronto: University of Toronto Press, 1988) 54 at 57-60
(references omitted)

The first piece of legislation to refer specifically to the Metis people was the *Manitoba Act, 1870*, which provided for the distribution of lands "towards the extinguishment of the Indian Title to the lands in the Province." By section 31 the government set aside 1,400,000 acres to be divided among the children of the half-breed heads of families residing in Manitoba at the time of the transfer, "in such mode and on such conditions as to settlement or otherwise, as the Governor General in Council may from time to time determine." The government allowed gross injustices to be perpetrated against the half-breed people through the implementation of a grant and scrip system, leaving the half-breeds landless and in abject poverty which persists to this day. In 1879, the *Dominion Lands Act* extended this attempted unilateral extinguishment of rights to the rest of the Northwest Territories, although the provisions were not implemented until the 1885 War of Resistance at Batoche.

. . . . .

A brief overview of the implementation of this form of so-called extinguishment will help in understanding the injustices suffered by the Metis. While treaties with the Indians set apart communal tracts of land and recognized other rights, the scrip issued to the half-breeds was for a specific amount of land which was fully alienable. In addition, by this method of unilateral dealing, the government of Canada also purported to extinguish all aboriginal title rights possessed by the Metis, including the right to hunt. As a consequence of this imposed scrip system, most of the land fell into the hands of speculators.

The Canadian government, in dealing with the Metis, issued land and money scrip. Land scrip was a certificate describing a specified number of acres and naming the person to whom the land was granted. Only that person could register the scrip in exchange for the land selected. Because they lacked information and knowledge about the land scrip system most Metis never registered the scrip; most registrations were done by opportunistic speculators and swindlers, who would appear at the registry office with any aboriginal person who was readily available. To facilitate the transaction, the speculator would have a transfer or quit-claim signed by the unwitting Metis or else would forge his signature, usually an X.

Money scrip was in essence a bearer bond. It was easily negotiable for money, goods, services, or land. Anyone who presented it would be able to redeem it in exchange for dominion land, which at the time was selling at one dollar per acre. Money scrip was introduced after a considerable amount of lobbying by speculators who stood to gain in their dealings with Metis who had no experience or familiarity with such transactions. Both money and land scrip were redeemable at one dollar per acre. After a number of years, however, the price of land and the value of land scrip increased. Thus, money scrip became less desirable.

Both land and money scrip could only be used for dominion lands in surveyed areas. Scrip was only issued to the Metis in what are now the provinces of Manitoba, Saskatchewan, and Alberta, although a limited amount was given to Metis who had moved to the northern United States. This was so even though a portion of Treaty 8 covered the northeast portion of British Columbia. Because scrip could only be applied against surveyed land, a significant number of Metis were immediately at a disadvantage. For example, in the 1906 Treaty 10 area of northern Saskatchewan, 60 per cent of the scrip issued was land scrip. To this day there is virtually no surveyed land in that area. As a consequence, the Metis of northern Saskatchewan were deprived of their land base and their opportunity to acquire ownership of land. With respect to the Northwest Territories, when Treaty 11 was entered into in 1921, the Metis were allotted a cash grant of $240 rather than land or money scrip.

Researchers for the Association of Metis and Non-status Indians of Saskatchewan have documented evidence that of the scrip issued, one-third was land scrip and two-thirds money scrip, for a total of 31,000 certificates or 4,030,000 acres (these figures are based on 80 per cent of the known remaining files). Over 90 per cent of the scrip was delivered into the hands of banks and speculators.

. . . . .

Although scrip was meant to be used for land only, the notes were used for other purposes. Because of the desperate and destitute situation of the Metis, scrip was often sold for cash, bringing the equivalent of twenty-five cents on the dollar or acre in 1878, and rising to five dollars per acre for land scrip in 1908. The majority of scrip, however, was sold for approximately one-third of its face value. Scrip was also exchanged for farm animals, implements, seed, food, and other supplies.

Most of this speculative activity took place outside of the area covered by the *Manitoba Act, 1870*. Therefore, the constitutional implications of section 31 of that act did not apply. Nevertheless, there is a line of thought that holds that all aboriginal peoples in Rupert's Land and the Northwest Territories had their aboriginal title constitutionally entrenched by virtue of section 146 of the *Constitution Act, 1867*. That section provided for the entry into confederation of those two areas, and decreed that "the provisions of any Order-in-Council in that behalf shall have the effect as if they had been enacted by the Parliament of the United Kingdom of Great Britain and Ireland."

On 19 November 1869, the Hudson's Bay Company surrendered its charter to the Crown. Following the negotiations between the provisional government and the Canadian government, the British Parliament passed an order-in-council on 23 June 1870 making Rupert's Land a part of Canada effective 15 July 1870. Section 14 of that order-in-council stated that "any claims of Indians to compensation for lands required for purposes of settlement shall be disposed of by the Canadian Government in communication with the Imperial Government; and the company shall be relieved of all responsibility in respect of them." Also incorporated into the order-in-council were addresses to the Queen by the Senate and the House of Commons. The first one, dated December 1867, asked for the transfer of Rupert's Land to Canada: "Upon the transference of the territories in question to the Canadian Government, the claims of the Indian tribes to compensation for lands required [for] purposes of settlement will be considered and settled in conformity with the equitable principles which have uniformly governed the British Crown in its dealings with the aborigines." The order-in-council does not specifically refer to half-breeds, although it does refer to "aborigines"; it was issued after the *Manitoba Act* expressly recognized the half-breeds' right to land under Indian title.

In the *Paulette* case (1973) Mr. Justice Morrow, then of the Northwest Territories Supreme Court, was of the opinion that the provisions or conditions of the order-in-council had "become part of the Canadian Constitution and could not be removed or altered except by Imperial Statute." But for the provisions found in section 31 of the *Manitoba Act, 1870*, it is clear that the Canadian Parliament is precluded from dealing unilaterally with the aboriginal title of the aboriginal people covered by the order-in-council, that is, those aboriginal people living within the area covered by the Hudson's Bay Company charter. Any doubt about the referential incorporation of that order-in-council under the provisions of section 146 can arguably be laid to rest by the specific inclusion of the order-in-council as the Rupert's Land and the North Western Territory Order under schedule 1 of the *Constitution Act, 1982*.

D. MÉTIS ABORIGINAL RIGHTS

In addition to the controversy surrounding Métis land rights, Métis people face difficulties in attempting to establish the bases of their non-land rights as distinct peoples. While section 35(1) recognizes and affirms existing Aboriginal and treaty rights, it remains to be determined what Métis Aboriginal rights have been recognized and affirmed by section 35(1). The following excerpt from the Royal Commission on Aboriginal Peoples report discusses some of the problems associated with establishing Métis Aboriginal rights.

REPORT OF THE ROYAL COMMISSION ON ABORIGINAL
PEOPLES, PERSPECTIVES AND REALITIES, VOL. 4

(Ottawa: Ministry of Supply & Services, 1996)
at 278-81, 285, 288, 290-2 (references omitted)

Crucial to much of the discussion that follows is the question of whether Métis people are entitled to exercise existing Aboriginal rights. It can confidently be concluded that they are. The evidence from which that conclusion flows is plentiful and persuasive.

Historically, Métis people were closely linked to other Aboriginal peoples. Although the first progeny of Aboriginal mothers and European fathers were genetically both Aboriginal and European, for the most part they followed an Aboriginal lifestyle. Predominant kinship ties also tended to be with the Aboriginal community. In unions between Aboriginal women and Scottish employees of the Hudson's Bay Company, the husbands had a common tendency to treat their "country families" as temporary, to be left behind when they retired to Scotland. The French-Indian families tended to greater permanence, and their lifestyle, at least initially, was closer to Aboriginal patterns than to European ones.

Subsequently, distinctive Métis social patterns of predominantly Aboriginal character evolved in some areas, although not all persons of mixed Aboriginal and European ancestry chose to follow them. ... Métis culture had developed most fully on the prairies, and the situation by the late nineteenth century was described by Alexander Morris thus:

> The Half-breeds in the territories are of three classes — 1st, those who, as at St. Laurent, near Prince Albert, the Qu'Appelle Lakes and Edmonton, have their farms and homes; 2nd, those who are entirely identified with the Indians, living with them and speaking their language; 3rd, those who do not farm, but live after the habits of the Indians, by the pursuit of buffalo and the chase.

Alexander Morris anticipated the complete assimilation of the first and second groups into the European and Aboriginal communities respectively. As for the third group, whom he styled "Métis", he suggested that although they should not be "brought under the treaties", land should be assigned to them and assistance should be provided to them. Other evidence of acceptance that Métis persons could avail themselves of Indian status if they chose to do so is found in documents relating to early western treaties, such as the report of W.M. Simpson concerning Treaty 1:

> During the payment of the several bands, it was found that in some, and most notably in the Indian settlement and Broken Head River Band, a number of those residing among the Indians, and calling themselves Indians, are in reality half-breeds, and entitled to share in the land grant under the provisions of the Manitoba Act. I was most particular, therefore, in causing it to be explained, generally and to individuals, that any person now electing to be classed with Indians, and receiving the Indian pay and gratuity, would, I believed, thereby forfeit his or her right to another grant as a half-breed; and in all cases where it was known that a man was a half-breed, the matter, as it affected himself and his children, was explained to him, and the choice given him to characterize himself. A very few only decided upon taking their grants as half-breeds. The explanation of this apparent sacrifice is found in the fact that the mass of these persons have lived all their lives on

the Indian reserves (so called), and would rather receive such benefits as may accrue to them under the Indian treaty, than wait the realization of any value in their half-breed grant.

Evidence is also found in the transcript of negotiations leading to Treaty 3:

CHIEF — I should not feel happy if I was not to mess with some of my children that are around me — those children that we call the Half-breed, those that have been born of our women of Indian blood. We wish that they should be counted with us, and have their share of what you have promised. We wish you to accept our demands. It is the Half-breeds that are actually living amongst us — those that are married to our women.
GOVERNOR — I am sent here to treat with the Indians. In Red River, where I came from, and where there is a great body of Half-breeds, they must be either white or Indian. If Indians, they get treaty money; if the Half-breeds call themselves white, they get land. All I can do is to refer the matter to the Government at Ottawa, and to recommend what you wish to be granted.

The significance of these observations to the present discussion is threefold:

- They indicate that Métis people were recognized, even at that relatively late date, as being entitled to assert Indian status (and thus entitled to Aboriginal rights).
- They show that the operative method of classifying persons for that purpose at the time was self-identification, regulated, presumably, by community confirmation.
- They confirm that Métis rights had not yet been brought under the treaties.

Until recently, the strongest legal evidence that Métis people were entitled to lay claim to Aboriginal rights, even after a distinctive Métis nation had evolved, was section 31 of the *Manitoba Act, 1870*, a statute of the Parliament of Canada that was subsequently accorded constitutional status by the *Constitution Act, 1871*.

. . . . .

In the present context [s. 31's] importance lies in the fact that it includes an acknowledgement by both Canadian and British parliaments that the people of the Métis Nation were entitled to share Indian title to the land and, it seems clear by implication, all other elements of Aboriginal rights. Further acknowledgement of the existence of Métis Aboriginal rights is found in subsequent legislation, such as the federal *Dominion Lands Act, 1879*, which referred in section 125(e) to Indian title and its extinguishment by grants to Métis people living outside Manitoba on 15 July 1870.

The most recent and conclusive evidence that Aboriginal rights can be exercised by Métis peoples is section 35(2) of the *Constitution Act, 1982*, which explicitly includes the Métis among the Aboriginal peoples whose existing Aboriginal rights are recognized and affirmed by section 35(1).

. . . . .

As to the relationship of Métis to First Nation and Inuit Aboriginal rights, there appear to be two fundamentally different views. The first traces Métis rights to the ancient rights of the peoples from whom Métis peoples derive their Aboriginal ancestry. From that point of view, these rights are older than Métis peoples themselves. The other view is that Métis Aboriginal rights were not derived from those of the ancestral Aboriginal nations but sprang into existence when the Métis themselves were born as a distinct people.

The first approach is more consistent with the meaning of the word "Aboriginal": from the beginning. It is also supported by some of the historical evidence referred to above, such as the linkage of Métis to Indian title in the *Manitoba Act, 1870*; the *Dominion Lands Act*; and the revelation in the documents concerning the early western treaties that Métis people who chose to do so were permitted (and presumably considered entitled) to associate themselves with and exercise the rights of Indian peoples.

The other point of view — that an entirely distinct Aboriginal people came into being as a result of contact between the Indigenous population and Europeans and subsequent socio-economic developments — also finds strong support in history. It is unquestionable, for example, that a unique way of life was forged by Métis people of the North American plains and by the mixed-ancestry communities of Labrador. Morris's book recognized the fact for the prairie Métis and suggested that those Métis who chose to live the distinctive life associated with that culture should not be brought under the treaties. This second approach would not do violence to the dictionary meaning of Aboriginal either, since the word could be read to mean "from the beginning of significant European settlement".

. . . . .

To say that the Aboriginal rights of all Aboriginal peoples are independent and coequal in status does not imply that those rights are necessarily the same for all Aboriginal people.

. . . . .

It makes no sense, therefore, to suggest that Métis Aboriginal rights can be extinguished by a treaty negotiated between the Crown and representatives of other Aboriginal peoples, or that they are in any other way inferior or subordinate to the rights of other Aboriginal peoples.

Although the content of Aboriginal rights is the same, in broad outline, for Métis as for First Nations and Inuit, the details may differ considerably in important ways. ... Métis people may exercise their Aboriginal rights differently from other Aboriginal peoples. Cultural customs of some Métis groups are certainly unique, and there [were] significant historical differences in resource uses as well as in forms of self-government.

. . . . .

Constitutional amendment

Since 17 April 1982, when proclamation of section 35 constitutionalized all unextinguished Aboriginal rights, Parliament has not had the power to extinguish Aboriginal rights by ordinary legislation. Aboriginal rights can now be extinguished only by surrender or by constitutional amendment.

The only constitutional provision purporting to extinguish Aboriginal rights is section 31 of the *Manitoba Act, 1870.* ... Implementation of the *Manitoba Act* was subject to considerable subsequent legislation, both federal and provincial, enacted with a view to clarifying, modifying and supplementing section 31 and other provisions of the *Manitoba Act.* The constitutional validity of some of that supplementary legislation is questionable and is the subject of litigation now before the courts.

· · · · ·

While it is not possible to reach definitive conclusions about all of the aspects of the extinguishment of Métis Aboriginal rights in advance of judicial rulings on certain questions, it seems clear that some of those rights — perhaps most of them — have never been extinguished. Aboriginal rights, therefore, constitute a major source of Métis legal rights.

As illustrated in the above excerpt from the RCAP report, Alexander Morris, Lieutenant-Governor of Manitoba and the North-West Territories and chief negotiator of a number of Crown-Native treaties in the second half of the nineteenth century, revealed the Crown's treaty position regarding the Métis — that "they must be either white or Indian." Further background to this understanding of the Métis, and which underlies the RCAP's conclusions on the points made above, may be found in the following excerpt from Morris' accounts of early Crown-Native treaty-making.

ALEXANDER MORRIS, THE TREATIES WITH THE INDIANS OF MANITOBA AND THE NORTH-WEST TERRITORIES, INCLUDING THE NEGOTIATIONS ON WHICH THEY WERE BASED, AND OTHER INFORMATION RELATING THERETO
(Toronto: Belfords, Clarke, 1880) at 293-5

... I cannot refrain from alluding to the Half-breed population of the North-West Territories. Those people are mainly of French Canadian descent, though there are a few of Scotch blood in the territories. Their influence with the Indian population is extensive. In Manitoba there is a large population of French Metis and Scotch Half-breeds, and they are proud of their mixed blood. This race is an important factor with regard to all North-West questions. His Excellency the Earl of Dufferin, with his keen appreciation of men and facts, astutely seized the position and thus referred to them in his speech at a banquet in his honor, given by the citizens of the whilome hamlet, and now city of Winnipeg, on the occasion of his visit to the Province of Manitoba in the year 1877.

There is no doubt that a great deal of the good feeling thus subsisting between the red men and ourselves is due to the influence and interposition of that invaluable class of men the Half-breed settlers and pioneers of Manitoba, who, combining as they do the hardihood, the endurance and love of enterprise generated by the strain of Indian blood within their veins, with the civilization, the instruction, and the intellectual power derived from their [white] fathers, have preached the Gospel of peace and good will, and mutual respect, with equally beneficial results to the Indian chieftain in his lodge and to the British settler in the shanty. They have been the ambassadors between the east and the west; the interpreters of civilization and its exigencies to the dwellers on the prairie as well as the exponents to the white men of the consideration justly due to the susceptibilities, the sensitive self-respect, the prejudices, the innate craving for justice, of the Indian race. In fact they have done for the colony what otherwise would have been left unaccomplished, and have introduced between the white population and the red man a traditional feeling of amity and friendship which but for them it might have been impossible to establish.

For my own part, I can frankly say, that I always had the confidence, support and active co-operation of the Half-breeds of all origins, in my negotiations with the Indian tribes, and I owe them this full acknowledgment thereof. The Half-breeds in the territories are of three classes — 1st, those who, as at St. Laurent, near Prince Albert, the Qu'Appelle Lakes and Edmonton, have their farms and homes; 2nd, those who are entirely identified with the Indians, living with them, and speaking their language; 3rd, those who do not farm, but live after the habits of the Indians, by the pursuit of the buffalo and the chase.

As to the first class, the question is an easy one. They will, of course, be recognized as possessors of the soil, and confirmed by the Government in their holdings, and will continue to make their living by farming and trading.

The second class have been recognized as Indians, and have passed into the bands among whom they reside.

The position of the third class is more difficult. The loss of the means of livelihood by the destruction of the buffalo, presses upon them, as upon our Indian tribes; and with regard to them I reported in 1876, and I have seen no reason to change my views, as follows:

> There is another class of the population in the North-West whose position I desire to bring under the notice of the Privy Council. I refer to the wandering Half-breeds of the plains, who are chiefly of French descent and live the life of the Indians. There are a few who are identified with the Indians, but there is a large class of Metis who live by the hunt of the buffalo, and have no settled homes. I think that a census of the numbers of these should be procured, and while I would not be disposed to recommend their being brought under the treaties, I would suggest that land should be assigned to them, and that on their settling down, if after an examination into their circumstances, it should be found necessary and expedient, some assistance should be given them to enter upon agricultural operations.

While the terminology used by Morris and the Earl of Dufferin may not meet entirely with modern approval, their sentiments and gratitude towards the Métis appear genuine. More importantly, their statements demonstrate the affection many governmental officials held for the Métis, particularly in the context of the Métis' role as facilitators/conciliators between the Crown and non-Métis Aboriginal peoples.

It was not only the Crown's representatives who held the Métis in high esteem for their contributions to the treaty-making process. The regard held for the Métis' role in the treaty-making process by the Crown was often matched by that emanating from the Aboriginal beneficiaries of those treaties. One example may be seen in the following account relayed by Morris, *ibid.*, at 74 regarding the negotiations for Treaty No. 3:

> CHIEF — "I wish you to understand you owe the treaty much to the Half-breeds."

> GOVERNOR – "I know it. I sent some of them to talk with you, and I am proud that all the Half-breeds from Manitoba, who are here, gave their Governor their cordial support."

While the Métis were valued participants in treaty-making, they could only avail themselves of treaty rights if they chose to be recognized as "Indians". While the Métis' ability to elect Indian status revealed the Crown's recognition of Métis heritage, it also meant that the Métis were forced to reject their own identity in order to obtain treaty benefits. This situation continued, for the most part, in Métis' relations with the Crown until the passage of section 35 of the *Constitution Act, 1982*.

The following commentary speaks to the dichotomy associated with the jurisprudential determination of Métis identity *vis-à-vis* that of "Indians", as defined under section 91(24) of the *Constitution Act, 1867*, and the tension that exists within some Métis communities regarding the issue.

LARRY CHARTRAND, "ARE WE MÉTIS OR ARE WE INDIANS? A COMMENTARY ON *R. v. GRUMBO*"

[1999-2000] 31 Ott. L. Rev. 267 at 274-5, 281 (references omitted)

. . . . .

The Métis people are, without a doubt, a separate and distinct people. This is certainly true historically and culturally. However, from a legal standpoint, there appears to be some doubt. By posing the question, the majority in *Grumbo* [*R. v. Grumbo*, [1998] 4 C.N.L.R. 172, (1998), 159 D.L.R. (4th) 577 (Sask. C.A.)] expressed some doubt that the Métis are indeed separate and unique from Indians.

There has always existed a tension in the Métis community as to our identity with Indians. The potential benefits that affiliation with Indians might provide puts pressure on us to describe ourselves as similar to Indians politically and legally. For instance, if I could receive financial assistance for post-secondary education by identifying more with being Indian, then that is a strong motivating factor to promote such an identity. However, being Métis means that you are distinct from Indians because of a unique history, culture and world view. There is a danger that if we push the "Indian card" too far we may lose our own unique identity. Will we bring dishonour to our grandparents who struggled so hard over the years to maintain our unique and distinctive identity?

The minority [in *Grumbo*] illuminated this dilemma facing the Métis ... The observation was made that if the Métis emphasize their separateness from Indians, they are put in the difficult position of diminishing their claim to inclusion under the term "Indians" as it appears in the NRTA [*Natural Resources Transfer Agreements, 1930*] or in s. 91(24).

Of course, inclusion of the Métis within the term "Indian" in the NRTA and s. 91(24) of the *Constitution Act, 1867* is advantageous in that the Métis may thereby gain certain benefits currently received by Indians. While this may be seen as a positive development, what cost does such a legal strategy of inclusion entail? Should we as the Métis people continue to put forth such arguments? Are they not inconsistent with our history as Métis people distinct from our European and Indian counterparts? Does inclusion of the Métis as Indians not threaten our very identity as a separate and unique Nation?

As a unique Aboriginal Nation, distinct from the European and Indian Nations, we need not deny our difference or our separateness to defend our legal rights. We can claim Aboriginal title and Aboriginal rights that flow from our existence as a separate and distinct Aboriginal People. As a result, we should avoid framing our rights as Indian rights that happen to also belong to the Métis people. Our rights can be and should be Métis rights that belong to the Métis people in and of their own right.

. . . . .

As Métis people, we have struggled too long and have paid a great price to maintain our identity. Let's be careful in choosing the legal strategies and arguments in furthering our rights. The cost in not being careful could be far too great. This, perhaps, is the important underlying message that the Court of Appeal in *Grumbo* is giving us. Are we Métis or are we Indians?

In addition to the preliminary determination made in the *Dumont* case, *supra*, questions about the scope and extent of Métis Aboriginal rights have also been raised in jurisprudence concerning the determination of non-Métis Aboriginal rights in section 35(1). Lamer C.J.C. and L'Heureux-Dubé J. both commented on the definition of Métis Aboriginal rights in their judgments in the Supreme Court of Canada's decision in *R. v. Van der Peet*, below.

R. v. VAN DER PEET

[1996] 4 C.N.L.R. 177, [1996] 9 W.W.R. 1, 23 B.C.L.R. (3d) 1, 50 C.R. (4th) 1, 137 D.L.R. (4th) 289, 109 C.C.C. (3d) 1, 200 N.R. 1 (S.C.C.)

Lamer C.J.C.: — ... I would note that basing the identification of aboriginal rights in the period prior to contact is not inconsistent with the fact that s.

35(2) of the *Constitution Act, 1982* includes within the definition of "aboriginal peoples of Canada" the Métis people of Canada.

Although s. 35 includes the Métis within its definition of "aboriginal peoples of Canada", and thus seems to link their claims to those of other aboriginal peoples under the general heading of "aboriginal rights", the history of the Métis, and the reasons underlying their inclusion in the protection given by s. 35, are quite distinct from those of other aboriginal peoples in Canada. As such, the manner in which the aboriginal rights of other aboriginal peoples are defined is not necessarily determinative of the manner in which the aboriginal rights of the Métis are defined. At the time when this Court is presented with a Métis claim under s. 35 it will then, with the benefit of the arguments of counsel, a factual context and a specific Métis claim, be able to explore the question of the purposes underlying s. 35's protection of the aboriginal rights of Métis people, and answer the question of the kinds of claims which fall within s. 35(1)'s scope when the claimants are Métis. The fact that, for other aboriginal peoples, the protection granted by s. 35 goes to the practices, customs and traditions of aboriginal peoples prior to contact, is not necessarily relevant to the answer which will be given to that question. It may, or it may not, be the case that the claims of the Métis are determined on the basis of the pre-contact practices, customs and traditions of their aboriginal ancestors; whether that is so must await determination in a case in which the issue arises.

. . . . .

L'Heureux-Dubé J.: — ... [W]hen examining the wording of the constitutional provisions regarding aboriginal rights, it appears that the protection should not be limited to pre-contact or pre-sovereignty practices, traditions and customs. Section 35(2) of the *Constitution Act, 1982* provides that the "'aboriginal peoples of Canada' includes the Indian, Inuit and *Métis* peoples of Canada" (emphasis added). Obviously, there were no Métis people prior to contact with Europeans as the Métis are the result of intermarriage between natives and Europeans ... Section 35(2) makes it clear that aboriginal rights are indeed guaranteed to Métis people. As a result, according to the text of the Constitution of Canada, it must be possible for aboriginal rights to arise after British sovereignty, so that Métis people can benefit from the constitutional protection of s. 35(1). The case-by-case application of s. 35(2) of the *Constitution Act, 1982* proposed by the Chief Justice does not address the issue of the interpretation of s. 35(2).

———————

Although *Van der Peet* did consider the issue of Métis Aboriginal rights — in particular, the effect of the Aboriginal rights test it had established upon claims of Métis Aboriginal rights — those rights were not a major focus in that case. Since their early jurisprudential consideration in *Dumont*, Métis rights have been the centre of focus in cases such as *R. v. McPherson*, [1994] 2 C.N.L.R. 137, 111 D.L.R. (4th) 278 (Man. Q.B.); *R. v. Grumbo*, [1998] 4 C.N.L.R. 172, 159 D.L.R. (4th) 577 (Sask. C.A.); *R. v. Powley*, [1999] 1 C.N.L.R. 153 (Ont. Prov. Ct.), var'd (2000), 47 O.R. (3d) 30 (S.C.J.), aff'd

(2001), 196 D.L.R. (4th) 221 (Ont. C.A.) and *R. v. Blais*, [1997] 3 C.N.L.R. 109 (Man. Prov. Ct.), aff'd [1998] 4 C.N.L.R. 103 (Man. Q.B.), aff'd [2001] 3 C.N.L.R. 187 (Man. C.A.). *Powley* and *Blais* were argued before the Supreme Court of Canada on March 17 and 18, 2003, respectively. While, no doubt, the Supreme Court of Canada will add to this existing jurisprudence in its judgments in both *Blais* and *Powley*, these had yet to be released at the time this edition went to press.

As with the definition of "Métis" by Métis groups, there is no single understanding of Métis claims to Métis Aboriginal rights. In its 1990 report, the Manitoba Aboriginal Justice Inquiry compiled the following list of arguments for the determination of Métis rights that have been asserted by Métis people in Manitoba.

THE JUSTICE SYSTEM AND ABORIGINAL PEOPLE: REPORT OF THE ABORIGINAL JUSTICE INQUIRY OF MANITOBA, VOL. 1

(Manitoba: Queen's Printer, 1991)
(Commissioners: A.C. Hamilton and C.M. Sinclair) c. 5 at 197-200
(references omitted)

While there is a general understanding of the foundation of Indian and Inuit claims to Aboriginal and treaty rights, the same cannot be said about either the basis or nature of Metis claims. The different arguments asserted in Manitoba for Metis rights are:

The Metis assert that they have Aboriginal rights by virtue of their share in Indian title.

The *Manitoba Act* and the *Dominion Lands Act* made provision for land grants or scrip for Metis as a response to the "Indian title" of the Metis. This grounds Metis claims on their descent from Indians.

The Metis assert that they have special rights under a treaty between their 1870 Provisional Government and Canada, given force in terms of the *Manitoba Act*.

Louis Riel often referred to the *Manitoba Act* as a treaty and called upon Canada to respect the treaty. Manitoba Metis Federation refers to the Act as The Manitoba Treaty and calls it a bargain between peoples — the Metis and the English-French Confederation.

The Metis argue that they have special rights as Aboriginal people because of the constitutional and statutory provisions applicable to them.

The Metis start with the position that the provisions in the *Manitoba Act* and the *Dominion Lands Act* expressly recognized special rights for them. So they argue that there is no need to go behind the documents to find any other source for their rights.

The Metis claim rights on the basis that they are a distinct people.

This claim is put in terms of natural law. The Metis claim status as a distinct people who were born and developed in the West. They assert that they had an economic base. Their claims to land vis-a-vis the Indians are explained in terms of Indians with traditional rights to the territory having vacated the Red River area, or, alternatively, that the Indians had acquiesced in the Metis presence and their use of the land. The Metis assert they were an "organized society" with established patterns of land use not contested by any other party. They argue, therefore, that they meet the common law tests for possession of Aboriginal title that have been outlined by Canadian courts.

The Metis assert that they are a "people" with a right of self-determination in international law.

The Manitoba Metis Federation [MMF] has argued that the provisions of the *Manitoba Act* recognized the Metis as a people. While the land grants appear to be to individuals or families, the MMF has argued that the fact they are in recognition of "Indian title" means they are in response to a "collective interest."

The Metis assert that they are a founding people, having brought the West into Confederation.

The Metis assert rights as a founding people, who were the ones truly responsible for bringing Manitoba into Confederation. According to this line of reasoning, the *Manitoba Act* was more than an agreement that Canada was to recognize the particular right of the Metis to land. It was a Confederation pact. It was the basis upon which the Metis agreed to join the fledgling state when they held the upper hand in the balance of power in the Prairies.

The Metis argue that the reference to them in the *Constitution Act, 1982* requires that government negotiate with them to settle rights upon them.

The Manitoba Metis Federation [MMF] has argued that the recognition of the Metis in the *Constitution Act, 1982* reflects a need to deal with the Metis. According to Yvon Dumont, the president of the MMF, Canada has an obligation to reach agreement with the Metis regarding their rightful place in the Constitution. This obligation is suggested to be a moral, political and legal one.

Despite these arguments and the apparent validity of the view that as Aboriginal people the Metis must have some type of Aboriginal rights, there is currently no agreement on the part of government that they have any.

. . . . .

The legal system in Manitoba at the moment appears to recognize no rights peculiar to the Metis. Metis may own land, or hold registered traplines, domestic fishing licences or wild rice production licences, but they hold them as individual Manitobans, rather than as Metis.

Practice, however, is different. When the Grand Rapids Dam was constructed and the Chemawawin Indian reserve community was relocated to Easterville, Metis and non-status Indians living in the communities were included in the relocation and were provided with new homes. In the same way, Metis and non-status Indians have been included in the compensation agreements for South Indian Lake and for the Northern Flood Agreement bands. But in all these cases, Metis and non-status Indians have not been included as a party to the negotiations and have been excluded from the community referendums that ratified the final agreement.

This represents a contradictory and inconsistent attitude towards Metis and non-status Indians. They do not have rights on their own, but they can have rights piggybacked on the rights of status Indian communities.

. . . . .

Both the Metis and the non-status Indians are Aboriginal peoples according to section 35(2) of the *Constitution Act, 1982*. Nevertheless, this constitutional recognition has not been translated into respect for their Aboriginal or treaty rights in concrete ways. Instead, both the federal and Manitoba governments have denied that these Aboriginal groups have any such rights, while suggesting that the other level of government is responsible for and should address the social, economic, cultural and political objectives of the Metis and non-status Indians.

While the issue of Métis identity has long been the primary focus of early judicial and academic considerations of Métis issues, the concept of Métis Aboriginal rights, such as those considered by the Manitoba Aboriginal Justice Inquiry, has started to receive more attention. The question of the nature, origins, and scope of these rights has been significantly affected by section 35(1) of the *Constitution Act, 1982*, as well as by the analysis and definition of Aboriginal rights in cases such as *Sparrow* and *Van der Peet*. In the following excerpt, Catherine Bell considers some jurisprudential developments that may have significant impacts upon the judicial recognition of Métis Aboriginal rights.

CATHERINE BELL, "METIS CONSTITUTIONAL RIGHTS IN SECTION 35(1)"

(1997), 36 Alta. L. Rev. 180 at 180-7, 189-92, 194-5 (references omitted)

Prior and subsequent to the explicit constitutional recognition of Metis as Aboriginal, contemporary jurisprudence on the rights of Metis people has focused on their ability to prove Aboriginal title, the continued survival and significance of cultural traits emphasized in judicial constructions of "traditional Indian life," and the Crown's intent to extinguish potential rights founded on occupation and lifestyle. These issues were, and remain, dominant because they are considered crucial to Metis economic and cultural survival and because a substantial amount of Metis rights litigation arises as a result of charges being laid against Metis people asserting rights to hunt and fish. However, conceptual barriers to judicial recognition of Metis rights inevitably arise because of the assumption that Aboriginal constitutional rights recognized and affirmed in s. 35(1) of the *Constitution Act, 1982* can only be enjoyed by those peoples who can prove an exclusive relationship to land sufficient to support a claim to Aboriginal title. As a result of recent rulings by the Supreme Court of Canada, these barriers are no longer insurmountable.

The scope of potential rights and the categories of peoples entitled to exercise them have also been expanded by the introduction of the concept of fiduciary obligation into legal and political analysis of government actions affecting Aboriginal peoples. As the fiduciary principle acquires greater significance in judicial analysis, government obligations to Aboriginal peoples, formerly characterized as political or moral in nature, are being elevated to enforceable, equitable obligations which in turn may generate justiciable, equitable Aboriginal rights. Emphasis on the fiduciary obligations of the British and Canadian governments in their dealings with Aboriginal peoples has also increased the significance of dishonourable and harmful government conduct in the legal analysis of alleged extinguishment. For the Metis, this is another favourable development as twentieth-century federal policy has for the most part denied the existence of Metis Aboriginal rights and, in the alternative, has maintained that whatever rights they may have had were effectively terminated through the scrip distribution system. The application of fiduciary law to the federal-Metis relationship could mean that defects in the implementation of the scrip distribution system nullify extinguishment or generate equitable Metis constitutional rights. This issue is currently the subject of litigation and negotiation.

Despite these developments, Metis may continue to experience difficulty asserting the existence of inherent Metis constitutional rights because of the revival of judicial restraint in Aboriginal rights analysis. Influenced by the potential social, political and economic impact of liberal constructions of Aboriginal constitutional rights, the current Supreme Court may have signalled a retreat to earlier patterns of judicial reasoning which emerged in the context of Aboriginal claims to proprietary interests. Despite the expansion of Aboriginal rights beyond the realm of property law, the elevation of Aboriginal rights to constitutional rights, and the generous and prospective approach to definition that their constitutional status demands, the present Supreme Court has characterized Aboriginal rights in a way that severely limits the significance of their constitutional and contemporary nature. Of particular concern is the recent ruling in *R. v. Van der Peet*, which limits s. 35 Aboriginal rights to the protected exercise of pre-contact Indian activities that were, and continue to be, a central and defining feature of Aboriginal culture. The emergence of this judicial formula suggests that a uniform standard cannot be applied to Indians, Inuit and

Metis if the inclusion of Metis as distinct Aboriginal peoples in s. 35 of the *Constitution Act, 1982* is to be given substantive meaning.

The purpose of this article is to raise some of the special issues faced by Metis people in achieving judicial recognition of their constitutional rights in light of the above developments. In particular, it focuses on the origins of Metis rights and explores the need for a theory of rights which is comprehensive enough to include rights derived from *Indian* or *Inuit* lineage and lifestyle and unique *Metis* rights which inhere to the Metis Nation as a distinct Aboriginal people. The article is influenced by the belief that it is impossible and undesirable to dissect Metis institutions that emerged as a result of cultural blending into functionally distinct Indian, Inuit and European influences. It also argues that the date of imposition, or negotiation, of colonial law and government is the appropriate date to measure the existence of historical Metis institutions upon which a second *sui generis* order of Metis rights can be based. Underlying the argument for a distinct order of Metis rights is a concern that the trend in domestic law to focus on "Aboriginality," without equal emphasis on distinct culture, political organization and national affiliation, fosters judicial assimilation of contemporary rights-bearing Metis collectivities with Indian, Inuit and European ancestral populations. In circumstances where mixed ancestry people identify themselves as "non-treaty" or "non-status" and distinctions based on different cultural institutions are not appropriate, this outcome may not be objectionable. However, for those historical and contemporary people who identify with a distinct Metis culture, judicial assimilation is simply a different manifestation of an old federal policy of non-recognition.

To avoid this result and give substantive meaning to the recognition of Metis as a *distinct* and *contemporary* people, this article argues that Metis constitutional rights can only be understood by looking to various original sources of rights and law which shape the Canadian Aboriginal rights regime.

. . . . .

II. INHERENT, *SUI GENERIS* RIGHTS OF CONTEMPORARY PEOPLES

Section 35(2) of the *Constitution Act, 1982* identifies the Aboriginal peoples as including the Indian, Inuit and Metis peoples. The inclusion of Metis as a distinct Aboriginal people complements the increasing legal relevance of social and political institutions of self-identifying contemporary and historic Aboriginal peoples in the definition of their rights. Also pivotal in the recognition of distinct constitutional and cultural entities is the political atmosphere within which s. 35 was negotiated. Growing activity at the United Nations aimed at ending colonial domination resulted in increased international pressure on nation states to recognize and protect the human

rights of colonized peoples. Within Canada, Aboriginal peoples were asserting the right to self-identify and to be self-determining in the negotiation of their political relationship with Canada. Legal action was also taken
to ensure that amendments to the Canadian Constitution would not proceed without some protection of the Aboriginal and treaty rights of colonized peoples. Although federal and provincial governments rejected the
notion of Aboriginal sovereignty and self-determination, they were prepared to acknowledge the existence of unique cultural rights arising from
original indigenous occupation and social organization. The exact nature,
scope and content of these rights was left open for future negotiation and
litigation. Inclusion of the Metis and Inuit as distinct "peoples" in the constitution, and independent representation of these peoples at subsequent
constitutional conferences ensured that Aboriginal rights, whatever they
were, would be attributable to Aboriginal people of the present, not simply
of the past. However, these rights were qualified by the inclusion of the
term "existing," which effectively reduced the scope of contemporary constitutional Aboriginal rights to those which survived the exercise of federal
powers of termination prior to 17 April 1982 — the date Aboriginal rights
were elevated from common law to constitutional status.

Inclusion in s. 35 also suggests that Metis rights are inherent constitutional rights. Although the concept of inherent rights is commonly used in
legal and political consideration of s. 35(1), it carries with it different
meanings for the various parties affected by its use. For many Aboriginal
people, "inherent" means sourced in the creator. For some politicians it
means Aboriginal rights are no longer dependent on legislative acts of recognition because they are now rooted in the Canadian Constitution. In judicial discourse, the concept is commonly understood to reflect the fact
that prior to the assertion of British sovereignty, Canada was occupied by
Aboriginal societies. As a result of this varied understanding of inherent
rights, judicial emphasis has been placed on the word "aboriginal" in s. 35.
As a corollary of this emphasis, emerging theories on Metis rights have
drawn on genealogical tracing to pre-contact Indian and Inuit society in
the quest for the origins of contemporary Metis constitutional rights. However, if the concept of inherent rights is combined with the *sui generis* nature of those rights, more comprehensive theories on the origin of Metis
rights emerge.

The characterization of Aboriginal rights as *sui generis*, or unique, originally provided Canadian courts the opportunity to avoid principles of international law manipulated to deny the existence of enforceable treaty
obligations and principles of Anglo-Canadian property law that unnecessarily restricted the quality and scope of rights arising from Aboriginal
title. As a tool of judicial interpretation, it has been invoked to distinguish
precedent and to legitimize the consideration of new sources of law to ascertain the nature and content of contemporary Aboriginal rights. The
combined effect of the characterization of Aboriginal constitutional rights
as inherent and *sui generis* is to support theories of rights which arise not
only from the ancestral Indian or Inuit character of Aboriginal rights, but
also the legal origins of the Aboriginal rights regime. A consideration of
both ancestral origins and legal origins takes comprehensive rights analysis beyond rights sourced in racial descent to rights sourced in essential

attributes of "peoplehood or nationhood". Adopting this approach, a proper interpretation of rights in s. 35 is one which places equal emphasis on the words "aboriginal" and "peoples" in assessing the origin, scope and content of Aboriginal rights.

Rights arising from peoplehood are uncertain because the word "peoples" is not defined in Canadian constitutional law and minimal domestic judicial opinion has been rendered on this point. However, it is a term which was used frequently in international political discourse at the time s. 35 was negotiated to distinguish colonized indigenous populations from nation states and ethnic minority immigrant populations within those states. The identification as colonized peoples carried with it potential recognition of land rights sourced in original occupation of colonized territories as well as human rights sourced in existence as a people. The main distinction drawn between the human rights of ethnic minority populations and indigenous peoples was the existence of political rights arising from the injustices perpetrated by the project of colonization. The most fundamental of these political rights are the rights to self-determine membership in, and governmental relations with, nation states, or alternatively, the right to secede. Other human rights attributed to self-determining peoples then and now include: the right to economic, cultural and social development; the right to "maintain and strengthen their distinct identities and characteristics"; the right to "maintain and develop their distinctive spiritual and material relationship with the lands" and the right to restitution for unlawful termination of these rights.

Both the political discourse around s. 35 and the domestication of Aboriginal rights through their incorporation into the Canadian Constitution suggest that the international understanding of peoplehood will be modified if it is used as a domestic tool for legal interpretation. Although Aboriginal peoples assert their rights in international law, the federal and provincial governments have historically denied the sovereign and contemporary self-determining status of Indian, Inuit and Metis peoples. *Sparrow's* recognition of the relevance of political context and Aboriginal perspectives in interpreting s. 35 suggests both of these factors must be considered in reaching a domestic compromise that accommodates Aboriginal and state goals. Pragmatism may also require such modification to meet the needs of peoples who are no longer economically self-sustaining and wish to enjoy the civil, political and economic rights of Canadian citizenship.

A compromise endorsed by numerous legal scholars as well as the Royal Commission on Aboriginal Peoples (RCAP) is an understanding of peoplehood that draws on social science criteria of nationhood. This concept of nationhood is one that emphasizes "a psychological bond joining a people and differentiating them from others, an aversion to being ruled by others, common ideology, common institutions and customs, and a sense of homogeneity." It may involve some qualified form of self-determination within the context of Canadian federalism, but such a right would arguably fall short of a right to secede. The history of the Charlottetown Accord suggests that such a compromise would be more acceptable to Metis, Inuit and Non-treaty Indian peoples than to Treaty Nations. However, it should be noted that the exclusion of certain international norms from the constitutional interpretive framework does not mean Aboriginal peoples were not historically sovereign in status or that they do not have a right to self-determination. Nevertheless, modification does reinforce the position that the recognition of Aboriginal sovereignty and the affirmation of the right of Aboriginal peoples to self-determine outside of the structure of the nation state is not a subject that can be adjudicated within the confines of the Canadian legal and constitutional regime. For this reason, it may be necessary for Aboriginal peoples to continue to lobby domestically and abroad for an international court or some other unique body to adjudicate matters arising from the international Aboriginal-federal relationship.

When incorporated into the interpretation of the word "peoples" in s. 35, this domestic compromise is still an independent source of rights distinct from Indian or Inuit ancestry. It is peoplehood, not lineage, that is the source of rights to self-government and cultural institutions essential to the self-identity and preservation of distinct Aboriginal societies. Therefore, as the Metis Nation emerged as (and remains) a distinct Aboriginal people, their peoplehood, as well as their Aboriginal ancestry, are properly considered sources of constitutional rights. Arguably, emphasis on Aboriginality and peoplehood requires both identification of institutions which, if they did not exist, could "fundamentally alter" *distinct Metis culture* from what it was *and* those institutions that Metis have in common with their pre-contact Indian or Inuit ancestors. This understanding of the duality of Metis constitutional rights has not been expressly articulated by Canadian courts, but must be considered in the context of Metis rights if substantive meaning is to be given to their Aboriginal constitutional rights as Aboriginals *and* autonomous peoples.

. . . . .

In developing a process for the definition of Metis rights which is inclusive of their peoplehood status, the court may have to reconsider the legal relevance of distinguishing between the assertion of sovereignty and the actual historical process of colonization. In the context of Indian and Inuit rights these concepts have been used loosely and interchangeably to identify the date for measuring the original Aboriginal institutions which the Crown had the power to terminate at common law, and which are now protected in s. 35. As Indians and Inuit existed as distinct peoples at the assertion of sovereignty *vis-à-vis* other European nation states and at the time of actual imposition of foreign laws and customs on their communities, the failure to draw the distinction between sovereignty and colonization seems insignificant. However, in the context of Metis rights it is important to draw distinctions. The assertion of sovereignty emerged as a pivotal date to determine rights arising from prior occupation from which, until recently, it was thought all Aboriginal rights must flow. In some cases it is identified through the existence of charters, proclamations, legislative assertion of jurisdiction or treaty-making with other European nations. In others, it is identified as the time of European settlement and the imposition of English law on a particular Aboriginal people. Other opinions point to the cumulative effect of some or all of these events. Although general proclamations, declarations and other imperial actions are relevant in ascertaining England's rights *vis-à-vis* other Europeans, they are irrelevant in ascertaining their rights *vis-à-vis* particular Aboriginal peoples in Canada. After the proclamation of English sovereignty many peoples lived unaffected by English law and customs. It is only through the historical process of colonization which occurred before, during and after assertions of sovereignty that Aboriginal societies became fundamentally altered.

Colonization refers to an actual historic process which occurred before, during and after England asserted sovereignty over various areas in Canada. It refers to the actual dispossession of land, the imposition of one legal system over another, the amalgamation of autonomous political entities and gradual assimilation of the colonized. It is the continual process of "bringing into subjection or subjugation" people who are living in a territory being colonized by Europeans. British colonial law governing this process, and the actual relations between the colonizer and the colonized are the legal basis of Aboriginal rights recognized in s. 35(1). Understood in this context, s. 35(1) does not address injustices arising from a theoretical shift in legal and political regimes that occurs as a result of the assertion of sovereignty but actual injustices suffered by "peoples" as a corollary of British sovereignty through the historical process of colonization. Although the date of colonization varies across the country depending on the historical circumstances of colonization, British colonial law is constant in determining the effects of this process on the survival of distinct Aboriginal social and political constitutions. In spite of sovereignty proclamations and actual colonization, the British recognized that Aboriginal title and distinctive Aboriginal social institutions survived in law unless they were extinguished through defined processes or were inconsistent with the concept of sovereignty or laws that clearly and plainly extinguished them. The issue of selecting the date of colonization in ascertaining the historic and legal origins of Metis rights is discussed in further detail below. The point here is that a distinction should be drawn between the concepts of sovereignty and colonization in order to acquire a full appreciation of the distinct peoplehood rights recognized at common law and protected in s. 35.

If both the concepts of sovereignty and colonization are adopted as key organizational principles for interpreting s. 35, the inclusion of Canada as colonizer is a natural extension of s. 35 analysis. Prior to its emergence as an independent nation state, the Dominion of Canada operated as the colonizing arm of British Imperial government. It assumed the rights and responsibilities of the Imperial colonizer toward Indian and Inuit peoples under s. 91(24) of the *Constitution Act, 1867* and imposed British rule through negotiation, occupation and force. It effectively imposed this rule in Rupert's Land in 1870, after the Riel resistance and as a result of the negotiation of the *Manitoba Act*. There is no doubt that the Metis Nation had emerged as a distinct Aboriginal people by this time. It is this date, the peak of colonization, not some earlier time at which Britain may have declared or acted in accordance with an assumption of sovereignty, that is the relevant date to identify the colonizer, the colonized and the peoplehood rights of the Metis in Manitoba. Different dates may be more appropriate for other Metis such as those living in the Northwest Territories or in Labrador. It may be that other Metis did not emerge as a distinct people before the peak of colonization in their present location and that their rights are limited to those that are Indian or Inuit, rather than peoplehood, in their origins. This will be a question of historical fact in its application to all contemporary self-identifying peoples.

In summation, the inclusion of Metis in s. 35 of the Constitution suggests that their constitutional rights are inherent *sui generis* rights. If equal consideration is given to the characterization of these rights as *sui generis*, the possibility exists for a more comprehensive understanding of Metis rights that extends beyond rights derived from Indian or Inuit ancestry. The *sui generis* nature of these rights provides precedential foundation for Canadian courts to look beyond domestic law for rules to guide in the interpretation of s. 35. In its attempts to understand the significance of the inclusion of the term "peoples," Canadian courts may look to British colonial law or modified norms of international law to develop interpretive tools. Both of these sources of law, as well as the present judicial understanding of the purpose of s. 35, support using the actual pattern and effects of colonization to measure the historical origins of s. 35 rights. In order for substantive meaning to be given to the peoplehood dimensions of Metis constitutional rights, the relevant date for assessing their distinct cultural institutions may have to be pushed forward to the peak of colonization by Canada, rather than the fictional assertion of British sovereignty which, isolated from the subsequent process of colonization, may not be said to have fundamentally altered the legal and political organization of Metis peoples at that time.

. . . . .

Inclusion in s. 35 also speaks to a range of potential constitutional relationships between Metis and other Aboriginal peoples. One possibility is to conceptualize Metis rights as independent from, but the *same as*, and equal in status to, the rights of other Aboriginal peoples. This approach is similar to the constitutional concept of equality adopted in the interpretation of s. 15 of the *Canadian Charter of Rights and Freedoms*. It is based in the assumption that Metis rights are justiciable legal rights derived solely from Aboriginal ancestry and a traditional Indian lifestyle. Because they are situated within the same constitutional space as other Aboriginal people, the term "aboriginal" in s. 35 is not only a defining feature of Metis people as constitutional legal entities, but also a defining feature for the nature and content of their rights. Thus, as a descriptive adjective, "aboriginal" may effectively limit Metis rights to those practices integral to Metis culture that are the *same as*, and are rooted in, their Aboriginal lineage. As discussed above, this notion of formal equality is problematic because it fails to give legal significance to the recognition of the Metis as a distinct people. However, it is a concept that is popular with some legal scholars and lower courts.

. . . . .

It has been argued that because s. 35 Metis rights are rights derived from their Indian and Inuit ancestors, Metis rights are *subordinate* in constitutional status to Inuit and Indian rights. This argument is based in part on the prevalent misunderstanding that all common law Aboriginal rights are derived from Aboriginal title. Aboriginal title is based in occupation prior to the assertion of sovereignty. A familiar western concept of fairness suggests that in the event of competing Aboriginal interests, prior occupants have stronger claims to land than subsequent arrivals. This concept of layered title could mean that Metis land rights are subordinate to Indian and Inuit rights in certain territories, but superior to rights of subsequent European settlers. For example, those Metis claiming land rights as descendants of the Metis Nation may have subordinate land claims to descendants of the Cree, Assiniboine and Salteau, but superior rights to the subsequent French, English and Canadian colonizers. However, this concept of layered possessory title fails to reflect actual landholding patterns of Aboriginal populations in Rupert's Land prior to 1870, the effective date of colonization by Canada. It also assumes that Aboriginal title is similar in nature to Anglo-Canadian possessory title, which arises from exclusive possession. Within that proprietary framework, "first in time, first in right" is an ancient and revered organizing principle. The concept of *sui generis*, discussed above, highlights the fallacies in this reasoning. As mentioned earlier, this concept originated as an analytical tool to allow judges to break free from the confines of the common law of property to assess the characteristics, scope and content of Aboriginal title. Recent acknowledgment by the Supreme Court that Aboriginal rights may exist independently of Aboriginal title also suggests that use of possessory title principles to prioritize potentially competing Aboriginal interests are not appropriately applied to all Aboriginal rights.

If more legal attention is paid to the term "people" in s. 35, it may be that the rights of the Indian, Inuit and Metis will be domestically construed as equal in constitutional status, but *different* in content and origin, from the rights of other Aboriginal peoples. This analysis assumes that s. 35 rights are sourced in Indian and Inuit ancestry and existence as distinct peoples. This peoplehood analysis has been adopted by some judges, but has not been endorsed by the majority of the Supreme Court. Although this issue may be unavoidable in the *Delgamuukw* appeal, the approach to Aboriginal rights in *Van der Peet* suggests that the peoplehood analysis will not be given significant weight in determining the rights of Indian people. Rather, the focus will be on the Indian or Inuit nature of their rights and the continued practice of traditional Indian or Inuit activities. Therefore, if distinct Metis rights are to be realized, it is clear that a different structure for the analysis of their inherent rights will be required. The degree of difference will depend on the willingness of the court to open up the peoplehood debate in the Metis context. On the one hand, a court may be more willing to address peoplehood while interpreting Metis constitutional rights because Metis political organization fits easily into the European constructs and because British colonial law recognized the ability of inhabitants of a colony to form a government *ex necessitate*. To use the words of McEachern C.J., it may not be as easy for a court to conclude that the Metis Nation lived in a "legal and jurisdictional vacuum," particularly if the peak of colonization is used as the effective measure to assess the scope of rights protected in s. 35. On the other hand, the Supreme Court may continue with a uniform emphasis on the Indian or Inuit nature of s. 35

rights in a way that pre-empts the contemporary exercise of distinct Metis practices and reduces the significance of their inclusion in s. 35 to a cunning political tactic on the part of the federal and provincial governments. Even without abandonment of the *Van der Peet* principles by the Supreme Court, Metis constitutional rights will differ substantially in content from the rights of Indian and Inuit peoples. The potential range of distinct Metis rights varies from no rights at all to both Aboriginal ancestral and peoplehood rights. A ruling falling on either extreme of this spectrum would result in their being *different* rather than *equivalent* in origin and scope.

E. CONCLUSION

Métis rights have only recently received the attention that rights belonging to other Aboriginal peoples of Canada have received. The impending *Powley* and *Blais* decisions will be the first substantive Supreme Court of Canada pronouncements on the nature and content of Métis Aboriginal rights. While Métis rights issues will benefit to some extent from the progression in Aboriginal rights jurisprudence in general, they may also suffer from the restrictions imposed on those other rights. There will, of course, be some exceptions: the most obvious of these is the *Van der Peet* test for proof of Aboriginal rights, which cannot logically apply to the Métis in its current form.

While Métis groups aspire towards greater recognition of their rights, the federal government will likely insist that the Métis first resolve issues pertaining to Métis identity. It may well be that the resolution of this issue will have to work in conjunction with the definition of Métis rights in cases such as *Powley* and *Blais*.

CHAPTER 7

FEDERALISM/CONSTITUTIONAL ISSUES

A. INTRODUCTION

In contemporary Canadian Aboriginal rights jurisprudence, when one thinks of constitutional issues pertaining to the Aboriginal peoples of Canada, thoughts generally proceed directly to section 35 of the *Constitution Act, 1982*, being Schedule B to the *Canada Act 1982* (U.K.), 1982, c. 11. Section 35 includes the substantive guarantee of Aboriginal and treaty rights in the Canadian Constitution in subsection (1). The terms of section 35 read as follows:

> 35. (1) The existing aboriginal and treaty rights of the aboriginal peoples of Canada are hereby recognized and affirmed.
>
> (2) In this Act, "aboriginal peoples of Canada" includes the Indian, Inuit, and Métis peoples of Canada.
>
> (3) For greater certainty, in subsection (1) "'treaty rights" includes rights that now exist by way of land claims agreements or may be so acquired.
>
> (4) Notwithstanding any other provision of this Act, the aboriginal and treaty rights referred to in subsection (1) are guaranteed equally to male and female persons.

Section 35 exists as Part II of the *Constitution Act, 1982*. Because of its positioning, section 35 is not subject to the limitation clause in section 1 of the *Canadian Charter of Rights and Freedoms*, Part I of the *Constitution Act, 1982*.

Since other sections of the Charter potentially could have affected section 35 rights — in particular, the equality clause in section 15 — section 25 was included within the Charter to insulate section 35 from the effects of those sections. Section 25 modifies and explains the substantive rights guaranteed in section 35. Section 25 also constitutionally entrenches the rights contained in the *Royal Proclamation, 1763 (U.K.)*, R.S.C. 1985, App. II, No. 1:

> 25. The guarantee in this Charter of certain rights and freedoms shall not be construed so as to abrogate or derogate from any aboriginal, treaty, or other rights or freedoms that pertain to the aboriginal peoples of Canada including
>
> > (*a*) any rights or freedoms that have been recognized by the Royal Proclamation of October 7, 1763; and
> >
> > (*b*) any rights or freedoms that now exist by way of land claims agreement or may be so acquired.

The importance of the constitutionalization of Aboriginal and treaty rights in section 35 was recognized was reasserted by the Supreme Court of Canada in the Quebec Secession Reference: see *Reference re Secession of Quebec*, [1998] 2 S.C.R. 217 at para. 82:

The "promise" of s. 35, as it was termed in *R. v. Sparrow* ... recognized not only the ancient occupation of land by aboriginal peoples, but their contribution to the building of Canada, and the special commitments made to them by successive governments. The protection of these rights, so recently and arduously achieved ... reflects an important underlying constitutional value.

This characterization appropriately posits section 35 as a bridge between the Crown's historic and contemporary relations with the Aboriginal peoples. It also positions section 35 as a blueprint for the future interaction of the parties in a manner that recognizes the importance of their historic relations and the parties' contributions and commitments to each other and the building of Canada.

While sections 25 and 35 of the *Constitution Act, 1982* receive the bulk of attention when focus shifts to constitutional provisions affecting Aboriginal peoples, as seen in previous chapters, they are not the only provisions in the Canadian Constitution that pertain to the Aboriginal peoples of Canada.

Upon the formation of Canada in 1867, there was a legislative division of powers between the federal Parliament and provincial legislatures. This division of powers is seen primarily in sections 91 and 92 of the *British North America Act, 1867* (U.K.), 30 & 31 Vict., c. 3 (now the *Constitution Act, 1867*). Noteworthy in this division of powers was the allocation of exclusive legislative responsibility over "Indians, and Lands reserved for the Indians" to Parliament in section. 91(24) of the *Constitution Act, 1867*. Section 91(24) reads:

> 91. It shall be lawful for the Queen, by and with the Advice and Consent of the Senate and House of Commons, to make Laws for the Peace, Order and good Government of Canada, in relation to all Matters not coming with the Classes of Subjects by this Act assigned exclusively to the Legislatures of the Provinces; and for greater Certainty, but not so as to restrict the Generality of the foregoing Terms of this Section, it is hereby declared that (notwithstanding anything in this Act) the exclusive Legislative Authority of the Parliament of Canada extends to all Matters coming within the Classes of Subjects next hereinafter enumerated; that is to say, —
>
> 24. Indians, and Lands reserved for the Indians.

The federal government used its s. 91(24) power to enact the federal *Indian Act, 1876*, S.C. 1876, c. 18, which consolidated all post-Confederation federal statutes pertaining to "Indians", as defined under the *Indian Act*. The federal government also used this power to engage in treaty negotiations with the Aboriginal peoples. Yet, the *Constitution Act, 1867* had a particular effect on lands surrendered under Crown-Native treaties that had not been foreseen by the federal government at the time it negotiated the treaties.

B. THE IMPLICATIONS OF THE DIVISION OF POWERS ON ABORIGINAL PEOPLES

Until the landmark case of *St. Catherine's Milling & Lumber Co. v. R.* (1888), 14 App. Cas. 46 (reproduced in Chapter 1), little attention was paid to the division of powers in relation to Aboriginal issues. However, the *St. Cath-*

erine's Milling decision profoundly altered previous understandings of the effects of land surrendered under treaties through the Privy Council's interpretation of the effects of sections 91(24) and 109 of the *Constitution Act, 1867*. Section 109 reads as follows:

> 109. All Lands, Mines, Minerals, and Royalties belonging to the several Provinces of Canada, Nova Scotia, and New Brunswick at the Union, and all Sums then due or payable for such Lands, Mines, Minerals, or Royalties, shall belong to the several Provinces of Ontario, Quebec, Nova Scotia, and New Brunswick in which the same are situate or arise, subject to any Trusts existing in respect thereof, and to any Interest other than that of the Province in the same.

Some of the primary effects of the Privy Council's interpretation of sections 91(24) and 109 of the *Constitution Act, 1867* in *St. Catherine's Milling* are summarized in the following excerpt, which also illustrates some of the problems emanating from the judicial interpretation of these sections' effects on lands surrendered under treaties.

LEONARD I. ROTMAN, "PROVINCIAL FIDUCIARY OBLIGATIONS TO FIRST NATIONS: THE NEXUS BETWEEN GOVERNMENTAL POWER AND RESPONSIBILITY"

(1994), 32 Osgoode Hall L.J. 735 at 743-5, 754-8, 760-3 (references omitted)

The *St. Catherine's Milling* decision created a lingering and problematic legacy by juxtaposing the federal Crown's acquisition of Aboriginal lands and "extinguishment" of Aboriginal title by way of treaty to the provincial Crown's acquisition of a beneficial interest in the land once it had been disencumbered of the Aboriginal interest.

. . . . .

The *St. Catherine's Milling* decision centred around a dispute between the Province of Ontario and the Dominion of Canada over the ownership of former Indian lands. The lands had been surrendered under Treaty #3, a post-Confederation treaty signed in 1873, by the Saulteaux Indians. The St. Catherine's Milling and Lumber Company had obtained a licence from the Dominion Crown to cut timber on some of the lands that had been surrendered. The Ontario Crown sought to restrain the lumber company from cutting timber on those lands by claiming that it owned a beneficial interest due to section 109 of the *British North America Act, 1867*. The main issue at bar was which body of the Crown possessed the beneficial interest in the surrendered lands.

. . . . .

[T]he Privy Council found that the federal Crown's section 91(24) power to enter into treaties and obtain surrenders of Indian lands did not give it any interest in the land once its Aboriginal title was extinguished. This conclusion was based upon their Lordships' construction of section 109 and their understanding of that section's effects in the earlier case of *Ontario (A.G.) v. Mercer* [(1883), 8 App. Cas. 767 (P.C.)].

... Section 109 effectively vested the Crown's underlying title to the unsurrendered Indian's lands, which were still subject to Aboriginal title, in the province in which the lands were located. Once those lands were relieved of any Aboriginal interest, the full beneficial interest in those lands became vested in the province.

The Privy Council's finding in *St. Catherine's Milling*, that "the Crown has all along had a present proprietary estate in the land, upon which the Indian title was a mere burden," created a difficult situation. It separated the power to enter into treaties and the power to fulfil the terms of those treaties once they had been concluded. The lasting effect of the decision is to rest exclusive power to obtain a surrender of Indian lands and to create reserves in the federal Crown, and, once a surrender is obtained, to rest exclusive proprietary and administrative rights over the surrendered lands in the provincial Crown.

The practical result of this division of powers is that although only the federal Crown may create a reserve, it cannot use provincial Crown lands (such as those obtained from First Nations by surrender under treaty) for that purpose without the cooperation of the province.

. . . . .

In delivering the judgment in *St. Catherine's Milling* on behalf of the Privy Council, Lord Watson was explicit about Ontario's responsibilities to the treaty signatories. He held that the province was entirely responsible for discharging the annuity obligations incurred under the terms of the treaty:

> Seeing that the benefit of the surrender accrues to her, Ontario must, of course, relieve the Crown, and the Dominion, of all obligations involving the payment of money which were undertaken by Her Majesty, and which are said to have been in part fulfilled by the Dominion government.

. . . . .

The issue of provincial responsibility for treaty obligations arose again in *Seybold* [*Ontario Mining Co. v. Seybold*, [1903] A.C. 73 (P.C.)]. One of the issues in *Seybold* concerned the setting aside and establishment of Indian reserves under the provisions of Treaty #3, the same treaty dealt with in *St. Catherine's Milling*. Out of the lands surrendered under the treaty for the benefit of the treaty signatories, the federal Crown had set aside reserve lands in 1879. It later sold the reserve lands, without the consent of the province, after obtaining their surrender from the Indians. The vital question in *Seybold*, for present purposes, was whether the obligation to set aside reserves under the treaty rightfully belonged to the federal Crown, the Ontario Crown, or both.

At trial, Chancellor Boyd recognized the difficulty created by the *St. Catherine's Milling* decision regarding the establishment of Indian reserves under treaty. He nevertheless determined that the section 91(24) jurisdiction over "Indians, and Lands reserved for the Indians," gave the federal Crown the right to set aside and exercise legislative and administrative jurisdiction over the reserve lands. His ruling directly conflicted with the *St. Catherine's Milling* decision, which had clearly separated the two functions. However, at the conclusion of his judgment — and perhaps in recognition of his contradiction of the *St. Catherine's Milling* precedent — Chancellor Boyd concluded that it would be preferable to have the treaty reserves allocated "with the approval and co-operation of the Crown in its dual character as represented by the general and the provincial authorities."

On appeal to the divisional court, Street J. also recognized the problems in harmonizing the federal Crown's obligation to establish Indian reserves under the terms of the treaty and the precedent established in *St. Catherine's Milling*. To reconcile these incongruous positions, Street J. determined that since only Ontario could set aside the surrendered lands for use as a reserve, it was obliged to do so:

> The surrender was undoubtedly burdened with the obligation imposed by the Treaty to select and lay aside special portions of the tract covered by it for the special use and benefit of the Indians. The Provincial Government could not without plain disregard of justice take advantage of the surrender and refuse to perform the condition attached to it.

A majority decision of the Supreme Court of Canada dismissed the federal Crown's appeal without written reasons. However, Gwynne J., dissenting, insisted that any obligations arising from the treaty must be assumed by Ontario, since it obtained the benefits from the surrender:

> [F]or the benefit so obtained by the province by the treaty of surrender the province alone should in justice bear the burthen of the obligations assumed by Her majesty and the Dominion to obtain the surrender of those lands as was held in the *St. Catherine's Milling & Lumber Co. v. The Queen.*

The Privy Council determined that the federal Crown's actions in setting aside, and later selling, the reserves were *ultra vires*. In delivering the Privy Council's judgment, Lord Davey stated that Ontario had a duty to fulfil the terms of the treaty. That duty, however, did not exist in a strictly legal sense; rather, it only constituted a moral obligation to cooperate with the federal Crown in setting aside reserves under the treaty:

> [T]he Government of the province, taking advantage of the surrender of 1873, came at least under an *honourable engagement* to fulfil the terms on the faith of which the surrender was made, and, therefore, to concur with the Dominion Government in appropriating certain undefined portions of the surrendered lands as Indian reserves. The result, however, is that the choice and location of the lands to be so appropriated could only be effectively made by the joint action of the two Governments. [emphasis added]

Lord Davey's characterization of Ontario's obligations under the treaty is misleading. As a result of the difficulties created by the constitutional division of powers in the *British North America Act, 1867*, the only way to have ensured that the reserve would be set aside was to have held Ontario and the federal Crown jointly responsible for establishing it. This necessitated that Ontario's duty be declared to be legally binding and not merely an "honourable engagement." Otherwise, a guarantee of satisfaction of the treaty promises did not exist, nor did the ability of the Aboriginal signatories to legally enforce the treaty obligations owed to them.

It may be argued that negotiations between Canada and Ontario could resolve this dilemma. Indeed, negotiations between Canada and the provinces have resolved problems surrounding the establishment of Indian reserves under treaty. If Ontario's responsibility under the treaty in the *Seybold* scenario was not legally binding, however, it was not compelled to reach a settlement with Canada. Indeed, it was not obligated to engage in negotiations with Canada on the issue at all.

Lord Davey's characterization of the nature of Ontario's duty had the potential to create further problems if Ontario made unreasonable demands upon Canada for its cooperation in setting aside reserve lands, or simply refused to negotiate altogether. Since Ontario was only under an "honourable engagement" to cooperate with Canada, it was insulated from legal liability for the non-fulfilment of the treaty. Similarly, although legally bound to fulfil the terms of the treaty, Canada could rely upon the constitutional division of powers to protect itself from liability for not discharging the treaty promises.

As a result, even if the Aboriginal signatories to the treaty successfully concluded a legal action that affirmed their right to receive reserves under the treaty, the judiciary would have been unable to enforce that right. A court could neither compel Canada to unilaterally fulfil the treaty, since Canada does not possess the jurisdiction on its own to set aside reserves out of surrendered lands, nor compel Ontario to cooperate with Canada in the setting aside of the reserves, since Ontario was not legally bound by any such obligation.

An analogy may be drawn between this scenario and the proper method of interpreting a statute that explicitly binds *either* the federal *or* a provincial Crown, yet, due to the constitutional division of powers, implicitly binds *both* Crowns in order to effect its intentions. When such a statute would be frustrated or rendered absurd unless it is read to bind both Crowns, the Supreme Court of Canada has held that the statute must be read to bind both by necessity or logical implication. This concept is also consistent with the principles of interpreting treaties and statutes relating to Indians enunciated by the Supreme Court of Canada in *Nowegijick v. R.* [1983] 1 S.C.R. 29].

. . . . .

The issue of provincial responsibility in these cases may have been made clearer had the majority of judges rendering decisions not been adversely affected by the issue of privity. Since the treaties in question had been negotiated and signed by the federal Crown, the judges had difficulty finding that the provinces could be held liable for obligation undertaken by the federal Crown.

. . . . .

The judges' problems with the privity issue are particularly evident in the *Treaty #3 Annuities* case [*Canada v. Ontario*, [1910] A.C. 637 (P.C.)], where Lord Loreburn L.C. stated:

> In making this treaty the Dominion Government acted upon the rights conferred by the Constitution. They were not acting in concert with the Ontario

Government, but on their own responsibility, and it is conceded that the motive was not any special benefit to Ontario, but a motive of policy in the interests of the Dominion as a whole.

Both Idington and Duff JJ. voiced similar concerns in the Supreme Court of Canada's determination of the *Treaty #3 Annuities* case. What the judges failed to consider was that, at the time that the Robinson treaties [the Robinson-Huron and Robinson-Superior Treaties of 1850] and Treaty #3 were signed, the constitutional understanding of the Crown was that it was "one and indivisible" throughout the Commonwealth.

· · · · ·

The fact that the Canadian Crown remained single and indivisible prevented it from escaping its obligations to First Nations by donning a provincial — or federal — Crown "hat" at its convenience. Moreover, the Crown could not escape liability for adequately discharging its fiduciary duties by virtue of jurisdictional problems, such as those surrounding the establishment of Indian reserves from Indian lands surrendered by treaty:

> Each level of government has an independent constitutional role and responsibility. ... Both are, however, subject to the demands of the honour of the Crown, and this must mean, at a minimum, that the aboriginal people to whom the Crown in all its emanations owes an obligation of protection and development, must not lose the benefit of that obligation because of federal-provincial jurisdictional uncertainty.

· · · · ·

Mutual power entails mutual responsibility and it is this mutual responsibility, founded in part upon the sharing of legislative and executive powers by the federal and provincial Crowns, that underlies the Crown's fiduciary obligations to First Nations. If a provincial Crown obtains exclusive proprietary and administrative rights over Indian land surrendered by treaty, then it must, by necessity or logical implication, also obtain a portion of the fiduciary duties owed to the Aboriginal signatories to the treaty. Section 109 of the *British North America Act, 1867* is the conduit by which this transfer is effectuated. Once this transfer takes place, the province is legally bound to cooperate with the federal Crown in fulfilling the terms of the treaty.

In short, the result of the *St. Catherine's Milling* decision on the interplay between sections 91(24) and 109 of the *Constitution Act, 1867* is that only the federal government may legislate in respect of Aboriginal lands unless and until those lands are disencumbered of Aboriginal title. At that point, the lands then fall within the legislative jurisdiction of the province in which they are situated. As Lamer C.J.C. explained in *Delgamuukw v. British Columbia*, [1997] 3 S.C.R. 1010, at 1117:

> Although that provision [s. 109] vests underlying title in provincial Crowns, it qualifies provincial ownership by making it subject to "any Inter-

est other than that of the Province in the same". In *St. Catherine's Milling*, the Privy Council held that aboriginal title was such an interest, and rejected the argument that provincial ownership operated as a limit on federal jurisdiction. The net effect of that decision, therefore, was to separate the ownership of lands held pursuant to aboriginal title from jurisdiction over those lands.

Aside from obligations existing under treaties, the division of powers in the *Constitution Act, 1867* created other uncertainties for the federal and provincial governments regarding the promulgation of laws pertaining to Aboriginal peoples. One such uncertainty was which level of government possessed jurisdiction over Indian reserves. This issue was dealt with by the Supreme Court of Canada in *Cardinal v. Alberta (Attorney General)*, below.

CARDINAL v. ALBERTA (ATTORNEY-GENERAL)

(1973), 40 D.L.R. (3d) 553, [1974] S.C.R. 695,
[1973] 6 W.W.R. 205, 13 C.C.C. (2d) 1
(references omitted)

The judgment of **Fauteux C.J.** and of **Abbott, Martland, Judson, Ritchie** and **Pigeon JJ.** was delivered by

Martland J.:— On December 8, 1970, the appellant, a treaty Indian, at his home on an Indian Reserve, in the Province of Alberta, sold a piece of moose meat to a non-Indian. He was charged with a breach of s. 37 of the *Wildlife Act*, R.S.A. 1970, c. 391, which provides:

> 37. No person shall traffic in any big game or any game bird except as is expressly permitted by this Act or by the regulations.

The trial Judge found that the appellant had trafficked in big game within the meaning of this section. The appellant was acquitted on the ground that the *Wildlife Act* is *ultra vires* of the Alberta Legislature in its application to the appellant as an Indian on an Indian Reserve. A case was stated on this legal issue, which was considered by a Judge of the Supreme Court of Alberta, who held that the decision was correct. An appeal was taken to the Appellate Division of the Supreme Court of Alberta, which allowed the appeal and overruled the judgment of the Court below. The present appeal is brought, with leave, to this Court.

Section 91(24) of the *British North America Act, 1867*, gives to the Parliament of Canada exclusive authority to legislate in respect of:

> 91(24) *Indians*, and Lands reserved for the *Indians*.

An agreement was made between the Government of Canada and the Government of Alberta, dated December 14, 1929, hereinafter referred to as "the Agreement", for the transfer by the former to the latter of the interest of the Crown in all Crown lands, mines and minerals within the Province of Alberta, and the provisions of the *Alberta Act, 1905* (Can.), c. 3, were modified as in the Agreement set out.

Paragraphs 10 to 12 inclusive appear in the Agreement under the heading "Indian Reserves", and it is paras. 10 and 12 which are of importance in considering this appeal. They provide as follows ... :

10. All lands included in Indian Reserves within the Province including those selected and surveyed but not yet confirmed as well as those confirmed, shall continue to be vested in the Crown and administered by the Government of Canada for the purposes of Canada, and the Province will from time to time, upon the request of the Superintendent General of Indian Affairs, set aside, out of the unoccupied Crown lands hereby transferred to its administration, such further areas as the said Superintendent General may, in agreement with the appropriate Minister of the Province, select, as necessary to enable Canada to fulfil its obligations, under the treaties with the Indians of the Province, and such areas shall thereafter be administered by Canada in the same way in all respects as if they had never passed to the Province under the provisions hereof.

12. In order to secure to the Indians of the Province the continuance of the supply of game and fish for their support and subsistence, Canada agrees that the laws respecting game in force in the Province from time to time shall apply to the Indians within the boundaries thereof, provided however, that the said Indians shall have the right, which the Province hereby assures to them, of hunting, trapping and fishing game and fish for food at all seasons of the year on all unoccupied Crown lands and on any other lands to which the said Indians may have a right of access.

This Agreement was approved by the Parliament of Canada and the Legislature of the Province of Alberta and, thereafter, it and also agreements between the Government of Canada and the Provinces of Manitoba, Saskatchewan and British Columbia were confirmed by the *British North America Act, 1930* (U.K.), c. 26. Section 1 of that Act provided:

1. The agreements set out in the Schedule to this Act are hereby confirmed and shall have the force of law notwithstanding anything in the British North America Act, 1867, or any Act amending the same, or any Act of the Parliament of Canada, or in any Order in Council or terms or conditions of union made or approved under any such Act as aforesaid.

Paragraphs 10 and 12 of the Agreement were, therefore, given the force of law, notwithstanding anything in the *British North America Act, 1867*. The question in issue on this appeal is as to whether s. 12 was effective so as to make the provisions of the *Wildlife Act* applicable to the appellant, a treaty Indian, in respect of an act which occurred on an Indian Reserve in the Province of Alberta.

The submission of the appellant is that the Parliament of Canada has exclusive legislative authority to legislate to control the administration of Indian reserves and that provincial laws cannot apply on such a reserve unless referentially introduced through federal legislation. It is contended that the phrase "on all unoccupied Crown lands and on any other lands to which the said Indians may have a right of access" does not include Indian reserve lands and that the only laws to which Indians are subject, while on a reserve, are the laws of Canada. Paragraph 12, it is said, can only have application to Indians in Alberta outside the Indian reserves.

· · · · ·

The present appeal thus raises issues as to the application of para. 12 which have not been considered previously.

As indicated earlier, the appellant starts from the proposition that, prior to the making of the Agreement, Indian reserves were enclaves which were withdrawn from the application of provincial legislation, save by way of reference by virtue of federal legislation. On this premise it is contended that para. 12 should not be construed so as to make provincial game legislation applicable within Indian reserves.

I am not prepared to accept this initial premise. Section 91(24) of the *British North America Act, 1867*, gave exclusive legislative authority to the Canadian Parliament in respect of Indians and over lands reserved for the Indians. Section 92 gave to each Province, in such Province, exclusive legislative power over the subjects therein defined. It is well established, as illustrated in *Union Colliery Company of B.C. v. Bryden*, [1899] A.C. 580, that a Province cannot legislate in relation to a subject-matter exclusively assigned to the Federal Parliament by s. 91. But it is also well established that provincial legislation enacted under a heading of s. 92 does not necessarily become invalid because it affects something which is subject to federal legislation. A vivid illustration of this is to be found in the Privy Council decision a few years after the *Union Colliery* case in *Cunningham v. Tomey Homma*, [1903] A.C. 151, which sustained provincial legislation, pursuant to s. 92(1), which prohibited Japanese, whether naturalized or not, from voting in provincial elections in British Columbia.

A provincial Legislature could not enact legislation in relation to Indians, or in relation to Indian reserves, but this is far from saying that the effect of s. 91(24) of the *British North America Act, 1867*, was to create enclaves within a Province within the boundaries of which provincial legislation could have no application. In my opinion, the test as to the application of provincial legislation within a reserve is the same as with respect to its application within the Province and that is that it must be within the authority of s. 92 and must not be in relation to a subject-matter assigned exclusively to the Canadian Parliament under s. 91. Two of those subjects are Indians and Indian reserves, but if provincial legislation within the limits of s. 92 is not construed as being legislation in relation to those classes of subjects (or any other subject under s. 91) it is applicable anywhere in the Province, including Indian reserves, even though Indians or Indian reserves might be affected by it. My point is that s. 91(24) enumerates classes of subjects over which the federal Parliament has the exclusive power to legislate, but it does not purport to define areas within a Province within which the power of a Province to enact legislation, otherwise within its powers, is to be excluded.

· · · · ·

I now turn to a consideration of the effect of para. 12 of the Agreement.

It has been noted that this section, along with paras. 10 and 11, appears under the heading "Indian Reserves". It begins with the words:

> In order to secure to the Indians of the Province the continuance of the supply of game and fish for their support and subsistence, Canada agrees that the laws respecting game in force in the Province from time to time shall apply to the Indians within the boundaries thereof. ...

The opening words of the paragraph define its purpose. It is to secure to the Indians of the Province a continuing supply of game and fish for their support and subsistence. It is to achieve that purpose that Indians within the boundaries of the Province are to conform to provincial game laws, subject, always, to their right to hunt and fish for food. This being the purpose of the paragraph, it could not have been intended that the controls which would apply to Indians in relation to hunting and fishing for purposes other than for their own food, should apply only to Indians not on reserves.

Furthermore, if the paragraph were to be so restricted in its scope, it would accomplish nothing towards its purpose. Cases decided before the Agreement ... had held that general legislation by a Province, not relating to Indians, *qua* Indians, would apply to them. On their facts, these cases dealt with Indians outside reserves. The point is that the provisions of para. 12 were not required to make provincial game laws apply to Indians off the reserve.

In my opinion, the meaning of para. 12 is that Canada, clothed as it was with legislative jurisdiction over "Indians, and Lands reserved for the Indians", in order to achieve the purpose of the section, agreed to the imposition of provincial controls over hunting and fishing, which, previously, the Province might not have had power to impose. By its express wording, it provides that the game laws of the Province shall apply "to the Indians within the boundaries thereof". To me this must contemplate their application to all Indians within the Province, without restriction as to where, within the Province, they might be.

This view is supported by an examination of the state of the law, in Alberta, at the time the Agreement was made. At that time, s. 69 of the *Indian Act*, R.S.C. 1927, c. 98, provided as follows:

> 69. The Superintendent General may, from time to time, by public notice, declare that, on and after a day therein named, the laws respecting game in force in the province of Manitoba, Saskatchewan or Alberta, or the Territories, or respecting such game as is specified in such notice, shall apply to Indians within the said province or Territories, as the case may be, or to Indians in such parts thereof as to him seems expedient.

The Superintendent General was thus empowered to declare that Alberta laws respecting game should apply to "Indians within the said province" or "in such parts thereof as to him seems expedient". Being a provision of the *Indian Act*, the section must have contemplated the possible exercise of the power with respect to Indians on reserves when it spoke of "Indians within the said province".

When para. 12 was drafted, it stated its general purpose and then went on to provide that the game laws of the Province should apply "to Indians within the boundaries thereof". This is practically the same as the words "Indians within the said province" in s. 69, and, in my opinion, it was intended to have the same meaning and application.

Section 69 ceased to have any effect in Alberta, Saskatchewan and Manitoba after the enactment of the *British North America Act, 1930*, which gave the agreements therein mentioned the force of law, notwithstanding anything in the *British North America Act, 1867*, or any amendments to it, or any Act of the Parliament of Canada. Section 69 disappeared from the *Indian Act* enacted in 1951, c. 29 [S.C. 1951], which then introduced s. 87

(now s. 88) to which reference will be made later ... [s. 88 of the *Indian Act* is discussed in section C of this chapter immediately following this case.]

The appellant places emphasis on the words in the proviso to para. 12 of the Agreement "on any other lands to which the said Indians may have a right of access". The contention is that para. 10 provided for continuance of the vesting of title in Indian reserves in the federal Crown, as well as for the creation of additional reserves, and that, in these lands, the Indians who reside thereon have an interest considerably greater than a mere "right of access". The use of that phrase, it is submitted, is inconsistent with any reference to reserve lands, and therefore, as the proviso, by the terms used, does not apply to Indian reserves, the section, as a whole, must be taken not to have application to them.

I am unable to agree that the broad terms used in the first portion of para. 12 can be limited, inferentially, in this way. In my view, having made all Indians within the boundaries of the Province, in their own interest, subject to provincial game laws, the proviso, by which the Province assured the defined rights of hunting and fishing for food, was drawn in broad terms. The proviso assures the right to hunt and fish for food on Indian reserves, because there can be no doubt that, whatever additional rights Indian residents on a reserve may have, they certainly have the right of access to it.

. . . . .

For these reasons, I am of the opinion that para. 12 of the Agreement made the provisions of the *Wildlife Act* applicable to all Indians, including those on reserves, and governed their activities throughout the Province, including reserves. By virtue of s. 1 of the *British North America Act, 1930*, it has the force of law, notwithstanding anything contained in the *British North America Act, 1867*, any amendment thereto, or any federal statute.

Having reached this conclusion, it is not necessary, in the circumstances of this case, to determine the meaning and effect of s. 88 (formerly s. 87) of the *Indian Act*, R.S.C. 1970, c. I-6.

I would dismiss the appeal.

[The judgment of **Hall**, **Spence** and **Laskin JJ**. was delivered by]

Laskin J. (dissenting):—This appeal raises, for the first time in this Court, the question whether provincial game laws apply to a treaty Indian on an Indian reserve so as to make him liable to their penalties for engaging on the reserve in activities prohibited by the provincial legislation. Although the issue in this case involves Alberta legislation, and hence requires a consideration of the Natural Resources Agreement between Canada and Alberta, as approved respectively by the *Alberta Natural Resources Act, 1930* (Can.), c. 3 and 1930 (Alta.), c. 21, and confirmed by the *British North America Act, 1930* (U.K.), c. 26, it eddies out to sister western Provinces which have like agreements with Canada and, in my opinion, is of equal import to treaty Indians living on reserves in Provinces east of Manitoba.

The Alberta Natural Resources Agreement is part of the constitutional order under which Canada and its respective Provinces exist, and the question arises whether and to what extent it affects and is affected by the distribution of legislative power under ss. 91 and 92 of the *British North America Act, 1867*. The issue in the present case engages, therefore, not only the relevant terms of the Alberta Natural Resources Agreement but also the exclusive federal power under s. 91(24) in relation to *"Indians*, and lands reserved for the *Indians"*. In my opinion, there are parallel questions here of the extent, if any, to which provincial game laws may apply to Indians on a reserve either in the face of the Alberta Natural Resources Agreement (or the Manitoba Natural Resources Agreement or the Saskatchewan Natural Resources Agreement, which have like provisions on the matter in issue) or in the face of unexercised federal legislative power under s. 91(24). In this latter respect, I repeat time-tested words from *Union Colliery Co. of B.C. v. Bryden*, [1899] A.C. 580 ... which express what is now a constitutional axiom:

> The abstinence of the Dominion Parliament from legislating to the full limit of its powers, could not have the effect of transferring to any provincial legislature the legislative power which had been assigned to the Dominion by s. 91 of the Act of 1867.

. . . . .

I propose to deal first with the effect of s. 91(24) upon the reach of provincial game laws. Apart entirely from the exclusive power vested in the Parliament of Canada to legislate in relation to Indians, its exclusive power in relation also to Indian reserves puts such tracts of land, albeit they are physically in a Province, beyond provincial competence to regulate their use or to control resources thereon. This is not because of any title vested in the Parliament of Canada or in the Crown in right of Canada, but because regardless of ultimate title, it is only Parliament that may legislate in relation to reserves once they have been recognized or set aside as such. The issue of title to Indian lands, whether the loosely defined lands referred to in the Royal Proclamation of 1763 or the more precisely defined tracts known as Indian reserves, was considered by the Privy Council in *St. Catherine's Milling and Lumber Co. v. The Queen* ... [discussed in Chapter 1]. The present case involves a reserve in the special sense of lands expressly set aside as such, and it was the result of the *St. Catherine's Milling* case that where such lands are within the limits of a Province, it is only when they are surrendered to the Crown that the full proprietary interest of the Province may be asserted, and that they then become subject to its control and disposition: see also *Ontario Mining Co. v. Seybold*, [1903] A.C. 73.

However, as was noted in *A.-G. Can. v. Giroux* (1916), 30 D.L.R. 123, 53 S.C.R. 172, in the reasons of Duff, J., with whom Anglin, J. concurred, there may be Indian title in a reserve beyond the mere personal and usufructuary interest found to exist in the *St. Catherine's Milling* case. Indians may have the beneficial ownership which is held for them in trust, and if that be so the legislative authority of Parliament under s. 91(24) would remain upon the surrender of the reserve land to the Crown to permit it to effectuate the trust. Surrender would not, in such a case, be to the Crown in right of the Province, as it was in the *St. Catherine's Milling* case where the land in question was unaffected by any trust in favour of the Indians.

. . . . .

Where land in a Province is, as in the present case, an admitted Indian reserve, its administration and the law applicable thereto, so far at least as Indians thereon are concerned, depend on federal legislation. Indian reserves are enclaves which, so long as they exist as reserves, are withdrawn from provincial regulatory power. If provincial legislation is applicable at all, it is only by referential incorporation through adoption by the Parliament of Canada. This is seen in the *Indian Act*.

. . . . .

The significance of the allocation of exclusive legislative power to Parliament in relation to Indian reserves merits emphasis in terms of the kind of enclave that a reserve is. It is a social economic community unit, with its own political structure as well according to the prescriptions of the *Indian Act*. The underlying title (that is, upon surrender) may well be in the Province, but during its existence as such a reserve, in my opinion, is no more subject to provincial legislation than is federal Crown property; and it is no more subject to provincial regulatory authority than is any other enterprise falling within exclusive federal competence.

I do not wish to overdraw analogies. It would strike me as quite strange, however, that when provincial competence is denied in relation to land held by the Crown in right of Canada, or in relation to land upon which a federal service is operated, or in relation to land integral to the operation of a private enterprise that is within exclusive federal competence, there should be any doubt about the want of provincial competence in relation to lands that are within s. 91(24).

. . . . .

The present case concerns the regulation and administration of the resources of land comprised in a reserve, and I can conceive of nothing more integral to that land as such. If the federal power given by s. 91(24) does not preclude the application of such provincial legislation to Indian reserves, the power will have lost the exclusiveness which is ordained by the Constitution.

. . . . .

Since federal power in relation to "lands reserved for the Indians" is independent and exclusive, its content must embrace administrative control and regulatory authority over Indian reserves. Hence, not only provincial game laws but other provincial regulatory legislation can have no application, of its own force, to such reserves, at least where it is sought to subject Indians thereon to such legislation.

. . . . .

I turn now to the Alberta Natural Resources Agreement which deals separately in its paras. 10 and 12 with reserves and with unoccupied Crown lands and other lands to which Indians may have a right of access. The Albert Appellate Division simply mentioned and then completely ignored para. 10 in its reasons in this case, dealing with it as if the only question was whether lands to which Indians had a right of access included Indian reserves as not being dealt with elsewhere in the Agreement. Even in such a frame of reference, I would find it a hardy conclusion to subsume Indian reserves within the phrase "any other lands to which the ... Indians may have a right of access." It would mean federal adoption of provincial laws for reserves without express mention and in a situation where there was already in existence a federal *Indian Act* which itself provided for a limited incorporation of provincial law to operate upon and in the reserves.

But the fact is that Indian reserves were specifically dealt with in the Alberta Natural Resources Agreement as they were expressly dealt with in that of Manitoba and in that of Saskatchewan. The words used in the two paragraphs which are directly of concern here are the same in respect of all three Provinces.

History, which is highly relevant here, denies the equation of Indian reserves with lands to which Indians may have a right of access. Legal logic also denied the equation in a situation where they are separately dealt with as they are here and in the same document. To treat Indian reserves as coming within the description of "lands to which Indians have a right of access", as did the Alberta Appellant Division, is to describe them in terms of their lowest rather than of their highest legal signification. Indians have at least a right of occupancy of reserves, and this is a larger interest than a mere right of access.... I see no justification for enlarging the category of what I may call, for short, access lands beyond lands which strictly fall within that description and have no higher legal quality.

. . . . .

Paragraph 10 of the Alberta Natural Resources Agreement itself negates the view taken by the Court below. All Indian reserves are to continue to be administered by the Government of Canada for the purposes of Canada; there is here no qualification to admit any provincial purpose. Moreover, any further reserves that may be established from unoccupied Crown land transferred to the Province are to be administered by Canada in the same way in all respects as if they had never passed to the Province. That points clearly to the exclusion of reserves from provincial control.

They do not return to that control under para. 12 in respect of the application of provincial game laws. That paragraph deals with a situation unrelated to Indian reserves. It is concerned rather with Indians as such, and with guaranteeing to them a continuing right to hunt, trap and fish for food regardless of provincial game laws which would otherwise confine Indians in parts of the Province that are under provincial administration. Although inelegantly expressed, para. 12 does not expand provincial legislative power but contracts it. Indians are to have the right to take game and fish for food from all unoccupied Crown lands (these would certainly not include reserves) and from all other lands to which they may have a right of access. There is hence, by virtue of the sanction of the *British North America Act, 1930*, a limitation upon provincial authority regardless of whether or not Parliament legislates.

. . . . .

On the facts of this case we are not concerned with the proviso to para. 12 because the accused was not hunting for food, and hence the overriding question is whether provincial game laws apply simply because the reserve where the accused trafficked in big game is in the Province. In my opinion, s. 12 does not, either in its generality or in its proviso, cover "lands reserved for the Indians", which are separately brought under exclusive federal authority under s. 91(24) of the *British North America Act, 1867*, and it does not modify federal power in relation thereto. Even if the words in para. 12, "any other lands to which the said Indians may have a right of access", are taken in a broad general sense as capable, if para. 12 stood alone, of embracing Indian reserves, they must be read to exclude such reserves which are specially dealt with in para. 10. The canon of construction enshrined in the maxim *generalia specialibus non derogant* is particularly apt here.

. . . . .

It is clear from cases ... in which the history of Indian cession treaties is narrated, that Indians who ceded their lands were assured of hunting privileges over them. I need not consider whether such privileges are themselves property interests of a kind which bring them exclusively within federal jurisdiction under s. 91(24) as coming within the phrase "lands reserved for the *Indians*", or whether the jurisdiction attaches because the rights involved are those of Indians. ... What is evident is that the existence of such privileges in such surrendered lands gives subject matter to para. 12 of the Alberta Natural Resources Agreement without compelling the inclusion therein of reserves which are of a different order than lands in respect of which there are only hunting rights or in respect of which hunting rights are assertable by the force of para. 12 alone.

. . . . .

The *Indian Act*, defines "reserve" in s. 2(1) to mean a tract of land, the legal title to which is vested in Her Majesty, that has been set apart by Her Majesty for the use and benefit of an Indian band. Sections 18 and 36 of the Act are as follows:

> 18. (1) Subject to this Act, reserves are held by Her Majesty for the use and benefit of the respective bands for which they were set apart; and subject to this Act and to the terms of any treaty or surrender, the Governor in Council may determine whether any purpose for which lands in a reserve are used or are to be used is for the use and benefit of the band.

(2) The Minister may authorize the use of lands in a reserve for the purpose of Indian schools, the administration of Indian affairs, Indian burial grounds, Indian health projects or, with the consent of the council of the band, for any other purpose for the general welfare of the band, and may take any lands in a reserve required for such purposes, but where an individual Indian, immediately prior to such taking, was entitled to the possession of such lands, compensation for such use shall be paid to the Indian, in such amount as may be agreed between the Indian and the Minister, or, failing agreement, as may be determined in such manner as the Minister may direct.

36. Where lands have been set apart for the use and benefit of a band and legal title thereto is not vested in Her Majesty, this Act applies as though the lands were a reserve within the meaning of this Act.

These, and related provisions which deal with possession by Indians of land within a reserve, reinforce my opinion that provincial regulatory legislation cannot, *ex proprio vigore,* apply to a reserve.

This opinion is unaffected by s. 88 of the *Indian Act* which reads:

88. Subject to the terms of any treaty and any other Act of the Parliament of Canada, all laws of general application from time to time in force in any province are applicable to and in respect of Indians in the province, except to the extent that such laws are inconsistent with this Act or any order, rule, regulation or by-law made thereunder, and except to the extent that such laws make provision for any matter for which provision is made by or under this Act.

This section deals only with Indians, not with reserves, and is, in any event, a referential incorporation of provincial legislation which takes effect under the section as federal legislation. I do not read s. 88 as creating any exception to the operation of federal legislation by making way for otherwise competent provincial legislation. ... If the *Wildlife Act* of Alberta is such an enactment as is envisaged by s. 88, an Indian who violated its terms would be guilty of an offence under federal law and not of an offence under provincial law.

It was contended by the respondent Attorney-General of Alberta that federal power in relation to "Indians" was akin to its power in relation to aliens (s. 91(25)) and that Indians like aliens were subject to provincial laws of general application. I do not pursue the analogy because it breaks down completely when regard is had to the fact that we are dealing here not only with Indians but with "lands reserved for the *Indians*". The fact that s. 88 of the *Indian Act* makes provincial laws of general application "applicable to and in respect of Indians in the province", and hence could be construed as applicable to them on their reserves as well, does not add anything to the case for the application of provincial game laws to Indians on a reserve. Parliament's exercise of its legislative power under s. 91(24) does not enlarge the constitutional scope of provincial legislation that has been adopted by Parliament where the Province seeks to rely on it for its own purposes.

· · · · ·

The conclusion to which I have come does not compel me to rely on the *Indian Act* in order to set aside the conviction of the appellant. I have made it abundantly plain that para. 12 of the Alberta Agreement cannot, in view of para. 10 thereof and in view of s. 91(24) of the *British North America Act, 1867* have the effect of subjecting Indians on a reserve to the Alberta *Wildlife Act*.

Accordingly, I would allow the appeal. ...

Appeal dismissed.

Consider the merits of Justice Laskin's arguments in favour of characterizing Indian reserves as federal enclaves beyond the reach of provincial power. Are his statements consistent with the division of powers envisaged by the *Constitution Act, 1867*? Is the Indian interest in reserve lands a unique, or *sui generis*, interest that differs from the interest that Indians may have in non-reserve lands? If it is not, should it be? In answering these questions, regard should be had to the judgment of Dickson J., as he then was, in *Guerin v. R.* (1984), 13 D.L.R. (4th) 321 at 337 (S.C.C.), in which he stated that the Aboriginal interest in reserve lands and Aboriginal title lands was the same. Note also the commentary upon this characterization in *Osoyoos Indian Band v. Oliver (Town)*, [2001] 3 S.C.R. 746 at paras. 161-4, (excerpted in Chapter 3, *supra*), per Iacobucci J., who stated that it:

> ... simply emphasizes ... the fact that lands to which aboriginal title attaches are also reserve lands protected by the *Indian Act* [but] does not change the aboriginal interest in the land insofar as the right to protection by the Crown as fiduciary is at issue.
> ... [W]here aboriginal title subsisted in lands that are then appropriated to the use of a band as reserve lands, the aboriginal interest in these lands is no different than that found in traditional lands in which there is an unrecognized aboriginal title — at least for the purposes of understanding the existence and the content of a fiduciary obligation.
> I agree with Dickson J. on this point ...
> In sum, this quotation from *Guerin* does not speak to identity of aboriginal title and an interest in reserve land with respect to the origin and termination of the respective interests. Dickson J. was merely comparing reserve lands subject to aboriginal title with non-reserve lands subject to aboriginal title, in context of understanding the existence of the Crown's fiduciary obligation in both cases.

Note also Iacobucci J.'s comments, *ibid.* at para. 41:

> ... when describing the features of the aboriginal interest in reserve land it is useful to refer to this Court's recent jurisprudence on the nature of aboriginal title. Although the two interests are not identical, they are fundamentally similar ... (references omitted).

While the majority decision in *Cardinal* rejected the enclave theory (notwithstanding the vociferous dissent of Laskin J.), there were other questions concerning federal and provincial legislative competency pertaining to Aboriginal peoples that were not expressly dealt with in *Cardinal*. The most important of these questions was whether the federal government's exclusive jurisdiction over "Indians, and lands reserved for the Indians", entailed that it would have to enact *all* laws pertaining to Aboriginal peoples, even if the subject matter of the legislation infringed upon provincial jurisdiction. In order to avoid this difficult situation, what is now section 88 of the federal *Indian Act*, R.S.C. 1985, c. I-5, was created.

C. SECTION 88 OF THE *INDIAN ACT*

To avoid the difficulty of legislating in respect of Aboriginal peoples while navigating the division of powers established in the *Constitution Act, 1867*, the amended *Indian Act*, R.S.C. 1951, c. 29, included a new section, section 87. Upon the renumbering of the *Indian Act* in 1970, section 87 became section 88.

Aside from its numbering, this section has remained unchanged since its inclusion in the 1951 *Indian Act*. It reads:

> Subject to the terms of any treaty and any other Act of the Parliament, all laws of general application from time to time in force in any province are applicable to and in respect of Indians in the province, except to the extent that those laws are inconsistent with this Act or any order, rule, regulation or by-law made thereunder, and except to the extent that those laws make provision for any matter for which provision is made by or under this Act.

While the rules pertaining to the application of section 88 may seem straightforward, the judicial understanding of that section has evolved since the section's first appearance in the *Indian Act*. The application of provincial laws to Aboriginal peoples and the role played by section 88 was the focus of the Supreme Court of Canada's decision in *Dick v. R.*, below.

DICK v. R.

[1985] 2 S.C.R. 309, [1986] 1 W.W.R. 1, 69 B.C.L.R. 184,
[1985] 4 C.N.L.R. 55, 22 C.C.C. (3d) 129, 23 D.L.R. (4th) 33, 62 N.R. 1
(references omitted)

The judgment of the Court was delivered by

Beetz J.: —

I   The facts

The facts are not in dispute. They are summarized by Lambert J.A., dissenting in the British Columbia Court of Appeal ...:

> Arthur Dick is a member of the Alkali Lake Band of the Shuswap people. He lives on the Alkali Lake Reserve in the Chilcotin District of the County of Cariboo. He is a non-treaty Indian. The Alkali Lake Band is comprised of about 10 families, or approximately 350 people, all told. They subsist in large measure by foraging. They catch fish for food and they kill deer and moose for food and other uses.
> The Shuswap word for May is "Pellcwewlemten". It means "time to go fishing". In response to this imperative Arthur Dick and two other band members, with two members of the Canoe Creek Band, set off on May 4, 1980, for Gustafsen Creek, where they intended to catch fish. On the way they passed Holdon Lake. There Arthur Dick killed a deer with a rifle. His purpose was to provide food for the members of the foraging party and for

other band members. The carcass, cut up in pieces, was taken on to Gustaf-sen Creek where a provincial conservation officer and four R.C.M.P. consta-bles found the five Indians in possession of dip nets, a number of rainbow trout, and the deer meat.

One precision should perhaps be added. The killing of the deer oc-curred in the traditional hunting grounds of the Alkali Lake Band but out-side a reserve. I now return to the recital of the facts by Lambert J.A.:

> The *Wildlife Act*, R.S.B.C. 1979, c. 433, said it was a closed season for hunting for deer. So Arthur Dick was charged under the Act with two counts; first, with killing wildlife, to wit; one deer, at a time not within the open season, contrary to s. 3(1); and, secondly, with possession of wildlife that was dead, to wit: parts of one deer, during a closed season, contrary to s. 8. It was also a closed season for fishing in Gustafsen Creek. All five Indi-ans were charged with respect to the fishing.

. . . . .

Leave to appeal was granted by the Court of Appeal but the appeal was dismissed, Lambert J.A. dissenting.

Appellant further appealed to this Court by leave of this Court.

II The issues

Appellant and respondent appear to agree in substance as to the issues raised by this appeal, save one. But they express them differently and I find it preferable to rephrase them as follows:

1. Is the practice of year-round foraging for food so central to the Indian way of life of the Alkali Lake Shuswap that it cannot be restricted by ss. 3(1) and 8(1) of the *Wildlife Act*, R.S.B.C. 1979, c. 433, without im-pairment of their status and capacity as Indians, and invasion of the federal field under s. 91(24) of the *Constitution Act, 1867*?
2. If the answer to the first question is in the affirmative and, conse-quently, the *Wildlife Act* cannot apply *ex proprio vigore* to the appellant, then is this Act a law of general application referentially incorporated into federal law by s. 88 of the *Indian Act*, R.S.C. 1970, c. I-6.

[A third issue, raised only by the respondent, asked whether the appeal raised a question of law alone for the purpose of s. 114 of the *Offence Act*, R.S.B.C. 1979, c. 305. This issue, and the Court's consideration of it, is omitted.]

In addition, a constitutional question was stated by the Chief Justice:

> Are ss. 3(1)(*c*) and 8(1) of the *Wildlife Act*, R.S.B.C. 1979, c. 433, constitution-ally inapplicable in the circumstances of this case on the ground that the re-striction imposed by such sections affects the appellant *qua* Indian and there-fore may only be enacted by the Parliament of Canada pursuant to s. 91(24) of the *Constitution Act, 1867*?

. . . . .

One issue that does not arise is that of Aboriginal Title or Rights. In its factum, the appellant expressly states that he has "not sought to prove or rely on the Aboriginal Title or Rights in the case at bar". As in the *Kruger* case, the issue will accordingly not be dealt with any more than the related or included question whether the Indians' right to hunt is a personal right or, as has been suggested by some learned authors, is a right in the nature of a *profit à prendre* or some other interest in land covered by the expression "Lands reserved for the Indians", rather than the word "Indians" in s. 91(24) of the *Constitution Act, 1867*. No submission was made on this last point and in this Court, as well apparently as in the courts below, the case has been argued as if the Indians' right to hunt were a personal one.

III The first issue

Appellant's main submission which was apparently presented in the Court of Appeal as an alternative argument, is that the *Wildlife Act* strikes at the core of Indianness, that the question stated in the first issue should accordingly be answered in the affirmative and that the *Wildlife Act*, while valid legislation, should be read down so as not to apply to appellant in the circumstances of the case at bar.

. . . . .

The reasons of Lambert J.A., dissenting [in the British Columbia Court of Appeal's decision in *Dick v. R., supra*], are quite elaborate. For the greater part, they expound the similarities and differences between the case at bar and *Kruger* and his understanding of the tests adopted in the latter case to determine whether a law is one of general application, a matter to which I will return in dealing with the second issue. But he used the same tests to answer the question stated in the first issue, namely whether the application of the *Wildlife Act* to appellant would regulate him *qua* Indian. Here is what he wrote.

> ... it seems to me that the same tests as are applied to determine whether the application of a provincial law to a particular group of Indians in a particular activity is the application of a law of general application, should also be applied to determine whether the application of a provincial law to a particular group of Indians in a particular activity is legislation in relation to Indians in their Indianness.
>
> So, subject to the question of referential incorporation, which I will come to next, it is my opinion that the evidence and argument which I have set out in Part III of these reasons require the conclusion that the *Wildlife Act* should be "read down" in order to preserve its constitutionality. That "reading down" would prevent it from applying to Arthur Dick in his activity in this case.

It is well worth quoting substantial parts of the evidence and argument set out in Part III of the reasons of Lambert J.A., which, as I just said, were also relied upon by him to resolve the first issue. He wrote:

> In *Kruger and Manuel v. The Queen, supra*, the two accused were members of the Penticton Indian Band. They shot four deer for food on unoccupied Crown land on the traditional hunting grounds of the Penticton Indian

Band. It was the closed season under the *Wildlife Act* and Kruger and
Manuel did not have a sustenance permit which would have allowed them
to shoot a deer during the closed season.

. . . . .

The evidence in this appeal goes much further than the agreed facts in
Kruger and Manuel v. The Queen. Here there is evidence which indicates that
the line demarking laws of general application from other enactments has
been crossed. In *Kruger and Manuel v. The Queen* the only relevant evidence
was the statement in the agreed facts that the accused had hunted deer
during the closed season on land that was the traditional hunting grounds
of the Penticton Indian Band. There was no evidence that the statutory restrictions on the right to hunt impaired the status and capacities of Kruger
and Manuel as Indians. There was no evidence that the Penticton Indian
Band depended on hunting for their supply of meat. There was no evidence
that it would be impracticable to hunt sufficient meat during the open season. There was no evidence as to the amount of meat obtained through
hunting, the amount of meat needed to feed an Indian family for a year, or
the amount of meat allowed to Indians under the prevailing hunting quotas.
Finally, there was no evidence to indicate that hunting was central to the
way of life of the Penticton Indian Band. There was, in the words of Mr. Justice Dickson, an 'absence of clear evidence' that the provisions in the *Wildlife
Act* crossed the line demarking laws of general application from other enactments.

The situation is entirely different in the present appeal where, in my
opinion, the evidence indicates that the line has been crossed.

Nine members of the Alkali Lake Band and three members of the Canoe
Creek Band gave evidence. They described their lives and the significance of
the rituals of food gathering. They told of their dependence on moose and
deer for food and for traditional and valued items of daily clothing and
ceremonial clothing. Their evidence was placed in its cultural framework by
Dr. Michael Asch, an anthropologist.

In 1980, the year in which Arthur Dick shot the deer at Holdon Lake,
there were 45 active hunters in the Alkali Lake Band. They took 117 deer
and 48 moose in the year. That provided a yield of 65 to 70 pounds of meat
for every man, woman and child in the Band. The meat was shared out
among band members in accordance with the institutional practices of the
Shuswap people.

The times of year for hunting animals and for fishing, the places to hunt,
and the techniques of hunting are taught to young male members of the
band by their fathers and grandfathers.

Some of the meat is smoked, some is salted, some is frozen, and some is
eaten fresh. The preservation of the meat and the preparation of food is
largely done by the women of the band. Women also tan and treat the hides
and make the traditional clothing. The skills and techniques for preserving
food and making clothing are handed down from one generation to the
next.

When the meat supply runs out the hunters go out for more. They go
when it is needed. That happens every spring when the supply of preserved
meat, from animals killed in the fall, comes to an end. The hunters in the Alkali Lake Band do not hunt for trophies; they do not hunt for recreation, nor
do they look on hunting as recreation; they do not leave the carcasses of the
animals they kill in the woods. If they work for wages it is not as an alternative to hunting but in order to acquire the means to hunt for food.

Ricky Dick, a member of the Alkali Lake Band, and one of the foraging
party on May 4, 1980, gave evidence that his own family needs four or five
deer each year for food. But the evidence of the conservation officer at 100

Mile House is that the limit for one hunter in one year from Region 5 is one deer. Of course, if you travel from one region to another, as recreational hunters do, then you can shoot deer in other regions to a total kill of three deer in one year. But, for the hunters of the Alkali Lake Band, the *Wildlife Act* and regulations, if they were to apply, would provide a limit of one deer for each hunter in each year within their hunting grounds.

Dr. Asch drew the relationship between the testimony of the Indian witnesses and the institutions and practices of the traditional way of life of the Alkali Lake Band of the Shuswap people.

In my opinion, it is impossible to read the evidence without realizing that killing fish and animals for food and other uses gives shape and meaning to the lives of the members of the Alkali Lake Band. It is at the centre of what they do and what they are.

In my opinion, this case is distinguishable from *Kruger and Manuel v. The Queen* (1977), 34 C.C.C. (2d) 377, 75 D.L.R. (3d) 434, [1978] 1 S.C.R. 104, because here the appellant has led evidence which, in my opinion, establishes that the *Wildlife Act* in its application to hunting for food impairs the status and capacities of the Alkali Lake Band members and crosses the line demarking laws of general application from other enactments.

And, before concluding ... Lambert J.A. wrote:

> Indeed, I would add that if the facts in this case do not place the killing of the deer within the central core of Indianness, if there is one, or within the boundary that outlines the status and capacities of the Alkali Lake Band, then it is difficult to imagine other facts that would do so.

In *Cardinal v. Attorney General of Alberta* ... it had already been held, apart from any evidence, that provincial game laws do not relate to Indians *qua* Indians. In the case at bar, there was considerable evidence capable of supporting the conclusions of Lambert J.A. to the effect that the *Wildlife Act* did impair the Indianness of the Alkali Lake Band, as well as the opposite conclusions of the courts below.

I am prepared to assume, without deciding, that Lambert J.A. was right on this point and that appellant's submission on the first issue is well taken.

I must confess at being strengthened in this assumption by [the following statement of] Lambert J.A.:

> The question of whether provincial legislation affects Indians as Indians, or Indians in their Indianness, to put it another way, is at the root of both arguments that I have considered in this appeal. I think it is worth adding that I have derived some sense of the nature of Indianness from the fact that the Indians in Alberta, Saskatchewan and Manitoba have the right to hunt and fish for food at all seasons of the year (see the Natural Resources Agreements and the *Constitution Act, 1930*, R.S.C. 1970, Appendix No. 25), and the treaty Indians in British Columbia also have that right: see *R. v. White and Bob* (1965), 52 D.L.R. (2d) 481 *n.*, [1965] S.C.R. vi. I think that those rights are characteristic of Indianness, at least for those Indians, and if for those Indians, why not for the Alkali Lake Band of the Shuswap people?

On the basis of this assumption and subject to the question of referential incorporation which will be dealt with in the next chapter, it follows that the *Wildlife Act* could not apply to the appellant *ex proprio vigore*, and, in order to preserve its constitutionality, it would be necessary to read it down to prevent its applying to appellant in the circumstances of this case.

IV   The second issue

In holding that the tests adopted by this Court in *Kruger* to determine whether a law is one of general application are the same tests which should be applied to determine whether the application of the *Wildlife Act* to appellant would regulate him in his Indianness, Lambert J.A. fell into error, in my respectful opinion. And this error resulted from a misapprehension of what was decided in *Kruger* as to the nature of a law of general application.

The tests which Lambert J.A. applied in reviewing the evidence in his above quoted reasons are perfectly suitable to determine whether the application of the *Wildlife Act* to the appellant would have the effect of regulating him *qua* Indian, with the consequential necessity of a reading down if it did; but, apart from legislative intent and colourability, they have nothing to do with the question whether the *Wildlife Act* is a law of general application. On the contrary, it is precisely because the *Wildlife Act* is a law of general application that it would have to be read down were it not for s. 88 of the *Indian Act*. If the special impact of the *Wildlife Act* on Indians had been the very result contemplated by the Legislature and pursued by it as a matter of policy, the Act could not be read down because it would be in relation to Indians and clearly *ultra vires*.

The *Wildlife Act* does not differ in this respect from a great many provincial labour laws which are couched in general terms and which, taken literally, would apply to federal works and undertakings. So to apply them however would make them regulate such works and undertakings under some essentially federal aspects. They are accordingly read down so as not to apply to federal works and undertakings. ... But it has never been suggested, so far as I know, that, by the same token, those provincial labour laws cease to be laws of general application.

In his reasons for judgment, Lambert J.A. relied on two passages of *Kruger* which he quoted and commented. The first passage is:

> If the law does extend uniformly throughout the jurisdiction the intention and effects of the enactment need to be considered. The law must not be "in relation to" one class of citizens in object and purpose. But the fact that a law may have graver consequence to one person than to another does not, on that account alone, make the law other than one of general application. There are few laws which have a uniform impact. The line is crossed, however, when an enactment, though in relation to another matter, by its effect, impairs the status or capacity of a particular group.

The second passage of *Kruger* quoted by Lambert J.A. is:

> Game conservation laws have as their policy the maintenance of wildlife resources. It might be argued that without some conservation measures the ability of Indians or others to hunt for food would become a moot issue in consequence of the destruction of the resource. The presumption is for the validity of a legislative enactment and in this case the presumption has to mean that in the absence of evidence to the contrary the measures taken by the British Columbia Legislature were taken to maintain an effective resource in the province for its citizens and not to oppose the interests of conservationists and Indians in such a way as to favour the claims of the former. If, of course, it can be shown in future litigation that the province has acted in such a way as to oppose conservation and Indian claims to the detriment

of the latter — to "preserve moose before Indians" in the words of Gordon J.A. in *R. v. Strongquill* (1953), 8 W.W.R. (N.S.) 247 — it might very well be concluded that the effect of the legislation is to cross the line demarking laws of general application from other enactments. It would have to be shown that the policy of such an Act was to impair the status and capacities of Indians. Were that so, s. 88 would not operate to make the Act applicable to Indians. But that has not been done here and in the absence of clear evidence the Court cannot so presume.

Lambert J.A. then emphasized the importance of the effect of the legislation as opposed to its purpose:

> ... evidence about the motives of individual members of the Legislature or even about the more abstract "intention of the legislature" or "legislative purpose of the enactment" is not relevant. What is relevant is evidence about the effect of the legislation. In fact, evidence about its "application".

With all due deference, it seems to me that the correct view is the reverse one and that what Dickson J., as he then was, referred to in *Kruger* when he mentioned laws which had crossed the line of general application were laws which, either overtly or colourably, single out Indians for special treatment and impair their status as Indians. Effect and intent are both relevant. Effect can evidence intent. But in order to determine whether a law is not one of general application, the intent, purpose or policy of the legislation can certainly not be ignored: they form an essential ingredient of a law which discriminates between various classes of persons, as opposed to a law of general application. This in my view is what Dickson J. meant when in the above quoted passage, he wrote:

> It would have to be shown that the policy of such an Act was to impair the status and capacities of Indians.

. . . . .

It has already been held in *Kruger* that on its face, and in form, the *Wildlife Act* is a law of general application. In the previous chapter, I have assumed that its application to appellant would have the effect of regulating the latter *qua* Indian. However, it has not been demonstrated, in my view, that this particular impact has been intended by the provincial legislator. While it is assumed that the *Wildlife Act* impairs the status or capacity of appellant, it has not been established that the legislative policy of the *Wildlife Act* singles out Indians for special treatment or discriminates against them in any way.

I accordingly conclude that the *Wildlife Act* is a law of general application within the meaning of s. 88 of the *Indian Act*.

It remains to decide whether the *Wildlife Act* has been referentially incorporated to federal laws by s. 88 of the *Indian Act*.

In *Kruger*, Dickson J. wrote:

> There is in the legal literature a juridical controversy respecting whether s. 88 referentially incorporates provincial laws of general application or whether such laws apply to Indians *ex proprio vigore*. The issue was considered by this Court in *Natural Parents v. Superintendent of Child Welfare* (1975), 60 D.L.R. (3d) 148, [1976] 2 S.C.R. 751.

This controversy has so far remained unresolved in this Court.

I believe that a distinction should be drawn between two categories of provincial laws. There are, on the one hand, provincial laws which can be applied to Indians without touching their Indianness, like traffic legislation; there are on the other hand, provincial laws which cannot apply to Indians without regulating them *qua* Indians.

Laws of the first category, in my opinion, continue to apply to Indians *ex proprio vigore* as they always did before the enactment of s. 88 in 1951 — then numbered s. 87 (1951 (Can.), c. 29) — and quite apart from s. 88.

I have come to the view that it is to the laws of the second category that s. 88 refers. I agree with what Laskin C.J. wrote in *Natural Parents v. Superintendent of Child Welfare*:

> When s. 88 refers to "all laws of general application from time to time in force in any province" it cannot be assumed to have legislated a nullity but, rather, to have in mind provincial legislation which, *per se*, would not apply to Indians under the *Indian Act* unless given force by federal reference.
>
> I am fully aware of the contention that it is enough to give force to the several opening provisions of s. 88, which, respectively, make the "provincial" reference subject to the terms of any treaty and any other federal Act and subject also to inconsistency with the *Indian Act* and orders, rules, regulations or by-laws thereunder. That contention would have it that s. 88 is otherwise declaratory. On this view, however, it is wholly declaratory save perhaps in its reference to "the terms of any treaty", a strange reason, in my view, to explain all the other provisions of s. 88. I think too that the concluding words of s. 88, "except to the extent that such laws make provision for any matter for which provision is made by or under this Act" indicate clearly that Parliament is indeed effecting incorporation by reference.

I also adopt the suggestion expressed by Professor Lysyk, as he then was:

> Provincial laws of general application will extend to Indians whether on or off reserves. It has been suggested that the constitution permits this result without the assistance of s. 87 of the Indian Act, and that the only significant result of that section is, by expressly embracing *all* laws of general application (subject to the exceptions stated in the section), to contemplate extension of particular laws which otherwise might have been held to be so intimately bound up with the essential capacities and rights inherent in Indian status as to have otherwise required a conclusion that the provincial legislation amounted to an inadmissible encroachment upon s. 91(24) of the British North America Act.

The word "all" in s. 88 is telling but, as was noticed by the late Chief Justice, the concluding words of s. 88 are practically decisive: it would not be open to Parliament in my view to make the *Indian Act* paramount over provincial laws simply because the *Indian Act* occupied the field. Operational conflict would be required to this end. But Parliament could validly provide for any type of paramountcy of the *Indian Act* over other provisions which it alone could enact, referentially or otherwise.

. . . . .

In a supplementary factum, appellant argues that a prospective incorporation into the *Indian Act* of future provincial laws which would regulate the appellant *qua* Indian, involves interdelegation of powers of a type held unconstitutional in *Attorney General of Nova Scotia v. Attorney General of Canada*, [1951] S.C.R. 31. In my opinion, *Attorney General for Ontario v. Scott*, [1956] S.C.R. 137, and *Coughlin v. Ontario Highway Transport Board*, [1968] S.C.R. 569, provide a complete answer to this objection.

I accordingly conclude that, in view of s. 88 of the *Indian Act*, the *Wildlife Act* applies to appellant even if, as I have assumed, it has the effect of regulating him *qua* Indian.

. . . . .

VI The constitutional question

I would answer the constitutional question as follows:

Sections 3(1) and 8(1) of the *Wildlife Act*, R.S.B.C. 1979, c. 433, being laws of general application in the Province of British Columbia, are applicable to the appellant either by referential incorporation under s. 88 of the *Indian Act*, R.S.C. 1970, c. I-6, or of their own force.

VII Conclusions

I would dismiss the appeal and make no order as to costs.

Appeal dismissed.

While the *Dick* case attempted to clarify the application of section 88, the judgment in that case has become the subject of debate itself. Some of the issues emanating from section 88 and its interpretation in *Dick* are illustrated in the following excerpt.

KERRY WILKINS, "STILL CRAZY AFTER ALL THESE YEARS: SECTION 88 OF THE *INDIAN ACT* AT FIFTY"

(2000) 38 Alta. L. Rev. 458 at 465-80, 482-3, 485-7, 497-9, 501-3
(references omitted)

. . . . .

Section 88 displays a clear legislative expectation that provincial laws are to apply, for the most part, to Indians. That much, at least, has always been clear from its phrasing. Initially, though, it was much less clear how s. 88 contributes to realization of that expectation. Is it a mere declaration, for greater certainty, that the kinds of laws specified govern Indians in a province, subject to the restrictions and exceptions it sets out, or does it exist to ensure the application to Indians of those laws (subject, again, to the same exceptions and restrictions) by incorporating them by reference into federal legislation?

... The problems with the "declaratory" view of s. 88 ... were that it left a long and complex statutory provision with very little real work to do, and that, so read, its closing words — "except to the extent that such laws make provision for any matter for which provision is made by or under this Act" — would have to be taken to be suggesting, falsely, that federal and provincial powers are concurrent, not exclusive. The fact that both sets of concerns made sense from a constitutional standpoint was a clear early indication that s. 88 was going to pose problems.

It was only in 1985, in *Dick v. R.*, that the court united behind a single approach to s. 88. That approach takes its shape from a distinction "between two categories of provincial laws[:] ... provincial laws which can be applied to Indians without touching their Indianness, like traffic legislation[, and] provincial laws which cannot apply to Indians without regulating them qua Indians." "[I]t is," the court determined, "to the laws of the second category that s. 88 refers"; "[l]aws of the first category," on the other hand, "continue to apply to Indians *ex proprio vigore*, as they always did before the enactment of s. 88 in 1951 ... and quite apart from s. 88."

We need some background in Canadian constitutional law to understand what the court is saying here. "Indians, and Lands reserved for the Indians" are among the classes of subjects that s. 91 of the Constitution Act, 1867 assigns exclusively to the federal order of government and, by so doing, expressly subtracts from the ambit of provincial authority. This does not mean that Indians are altogether beyond the reach of provincial legislation or executive activity. Generally speaking, valid provincial measures — i.e., those whose primary subject matter is something within the proper scope of provincial authority — apply of their own force (*"ex proprio vigore"*) to Indians, just as they would to anyone else, according to their terms. (Such laws are those in the first category that the Supreme Court identified in *Dick*.) It does mean, though, that there is a certain more limited group of matters over which the provinces, acting as such, may exercise no mandatory control, either directly or indirectly. Each head of federal authority listed in s. 91 has a "basic, minimum and unassailable content": a "core" set of matters from which it takes its definition. As the Supreme Court confirmed in *Dick*, the core of exclusive federal power over "Indians, and Lands reserved for the Indians" includes all matters characteristic of, or unique to, Indians as such: matters relating to "Indianness" or to Indians "qua Indians". Provincial measures that purport to make it their business to govern any such "core" matters are wholly invalid; such laws, altogether without legal force, have no application to anyone. But even otherwise valid provincial measures are "read down" as needed to ensure that they cannot have the effect, even inadvertently, of regulating core federal matters. This last group of provincial laws — those valid but inapplicable, as such, to Indians — are the ones in *Dick*'s second category.

What s. 88 does, then, according to the Supreme Court in *Dick*, is incorporate by reference, and apply as federal law, certain kinds of valid provincial measures ... that, for constitutional reasons, could not otherwise apply to Indians. It leaves undisturbed those provincial laws that apply of their own force to Indians or on Indian lands. Since 1985, the court has reaffirmed repeatedly and unanimously its support for this general proposition.

· · · · ·

Doctrinally speaking, the impact of *Dick* is that s. 88 is irrelevant ... unless and until a court determines that the provincial law at issue is both constitutionally valid in its own right and, at the same time, constitutionally inapplicable, considered as provincial law, to Indians. ...

The problem is that the measures to which s. 88 pertains govern everyone else within their intendment as provincial law but apply only as federal law to Indians. This means, in the first place, that such measures, when applied to Indians, are subject, as a matter of course, to federal procedures, policies, priorities, and discretion but to provincial priorities and procedures when applied to anyone else. This complication is headache enough for those charged with the administration of such measures, especially in the host of easily conjured situations involving both non-Indians and Indians. A second, related complication arises when we try to determine whose task it is to administer these measures. Provincial officials have full power to apply them to everyone else but none, while acting as such, to apply them to Indians. Any capacity such officials have to apply or enforce these laws in respect of Indians is necessarily delegated federal authority. Federal officials are, at best, in the same position, only with roles reversed. There seem to be only two administrative options available: asking officials from different orders of government to apply the same laws to different individuals, sometimes in the same situations, or asking officials from, say, the provincial order of government to operate in accordance with different priorities and policies (the federal and the provincial) in applying these same laws at the same time to Indians and to others. From a functional standpoint, neither option has much to recommend it.

These concerns themselves would be troubling enough, but it gets worse. One cannot always tell at a glance whether a given provincial measure applies, as such, to Indians or whether its application to them depends on s. 88 because its effect is to regulate them "qua Indians". Such determinations are often profoundly difficult. Until they are made, however, there is no way of knowing, at least in difficult cases, which policies and procedures (the federal or the provincial) are to govern the application of these measures to Indians, or, perhaps, which officials (the federal or the provincial) have the power to carry out that aspect of their administration.

Finally, s. 88, by intervening to extend the application of certain provincial measures to Indians, is giving a reach to those measures that the provincial legislature must, for constitutional reasons, be taken to have intended that they not have. There is, at a minimum, room for doubt, in circumstances such as these, whether the federal order has constitutional authority to require that provinces assume the added financial and administrative burden of applying these hybrid measures beyond the permissible range of their application as provincial legislation. The Supreme Court has already held, in somewhat different contexts, that Parliament, acting unilaterally, does not have the power to impose on a province either the cost of federal enforcement activity undertaken within that province (even at the province's request) or the costs of delivering a valid federal program within a province or a municipality. It makes sense to expect the same result in respect of the extra costs that arise when Canada unilaterally extends, by incorporation, the application of a provincial scheme. If, therefore, the federal government contemplates provincial assistance in the administration of federal law and policy in matters beyond provincial legislative competence, it seems reasonable for the provinces to expect it to pay for that help. Efforts to identify the extra costs of administration that s. 88 brings about are complicated substantially, however, by the uncertainty of speculating before the fact whether a given provincial measure applies to Indians (if at all) as provincial or as federal law.

. . . . .

Section 88 ... gives Indian treaties and treaty rights virtually complete protection against the provincial laws to which it applies: better quality protection, in fact, than such rights receive generally from s. 35(1) of the *Constitution Act, 1982*. The problem is that s. 88, as we saw above, incorporates, and applies exclusively to, a limited range of provincial measures. The protection that s. 88 affords to treaty rights, therefore, seems clearly to be available only against the effects of such laws as s. 88 incorporates: provincial laws "of general application" that cannot apply, as such, to Indians. Such rights derive no protection at all from s. 88 against the effects of provincial laws that apply of their own force. As the Supreme Court told us in *Dick*, s. 88 has nothing to do with those.

. . . . .

This would indeed be a troubling result if s. 88 were the only protection — apart from s. 35(1) of the *Constitution Act, 1982* — that treaty rights had against provincial law. There is, however, strong authority buttressed by persuasive considerations of constitutional policy, to the effect that Indian treaty rights are matters integral, and therefore exclusive, to the federal government's constitutional authority over Indians and Indian lands. If this is so, then there is little danger of provincial measures, as such, constraining the exercise of such rights; generally speaking, the provinces simply have no power to do so. Insofar as provincial laws interfere with the terms of such treaties, therefore, they can have no relevant application except pursuant to s. 88. And s. 88, as we saw, insulates the rights preserved, acknowledged, or confirmed in such treaties from the effects of the provincial laws it incorporates.

... Properly understood, s. 88 gives treaty rights no independent protection from provincial activity; all it does is shelter this island of pre-existing incapacity from the current of referential incorporation as federal law for which it is more generally responsible.

B. "... And Any Other Act of the Parliament of Canada, ..."

This phrase ensures that provisions in federal legislation other than the *Indian Act* take precedence, in case of conflict, over measures that s. 88 incorporates into federal law. ...

From some standpoints, it may not be clear why such a provision is useful or necessary; the constitution itself already gives federal measures priority when provincial measures, though valid and applicable, interfere with their operation. What value does this specification in s. 88 contribute in light of existing paramountcy doctrine?

... [T]he phrase is important because the situation that s. 88 addresses differs in two important ways from the standard scenario of federal/provincial conflict. First, as we have seen, s. 88 governs only those provincial laws that cannot apply of their own force to Indians. From a division of powers standpoint, no such laws can give rise, on their own, to questions of paramountcy; true paramountcy issues arise only where provincial and federal laws both apply of their own force. Second, the provincial laws to which s. 88 applies become, upon incorporation, federal legislation, at least in respect of their application to Indians. So understood, such measures no longer give way automatically when they clash with other federal laws; the issue is now one of statutory interpretation, not one of paramountcy. For these reasons, it was not only sensible but important for Parliament to prescribe an explicit hierarchy as between the free-standing federal laws and the s. 88 hybrids. Because of this phrase, the free-standing federal laws will displace the hybrids exactly when and as they would have done apart from s. 88.

Unfortunately, s. 88 does not speak with similar clarity about the relationship between incorporated provincial measures and surviving pre-Confederation legislation including, perhaps most importantly, the Royal Proclamation of 1763. We know as a matter of general law that provinces, acting as such, cannot amend or repeal those parts of the Proclamation that deal with Indians' rights and that those provisions prevail over provincial measures, considered as such, that conflict with them. Once a provincial measure acquires the force of federal law pursuant to s. 88, however, it is from a constitutional standpoint of equal rank with the Proclamation and can operate to curtail the Proclamation's reach. Nothing in s. 88's own text precludes that result. Given the number and the explicitness of the other constraints that s. 88 imposes on the reach of the measures it governs, that omission itself may give courts reason not to protect the Proclamation from the impact of such measures.

C. "... All Laws of General application in Force in Any Province ..."

On its face, this phrasing is broad enough to capture federal, as well as provincial, laws of general application; they too, after all, are "in force in any province." ... The reference, however, is not confined exclusively to laws the provinces have enacted since Confederation; it also includes "any [pre-Confederation] laws which were made a part of the law of a province" as long as those laws count as laws of general application.

But what is a "law of general application"? The Supreme Court, in *Kruger & Manuel*, prescribed two criteria, both of which a provincial law must satisfy to qualify as such a law for purposes of s. 88. The first concerns the territorial reach of the relevant measure. To be "provincial in scope," a law must "extend uniformly throughout the territory"; if it does not, "the inquiry is at an end and the question is answered in the negative." ...

The Supreme Court's second criterion is the one that needs closer examination. It requires attention to "the intention and effects of the enactment" as follows:

> The law must not be "in relation to" one class of citizens in object and purpose. But the fact that a law may have graver consequences to one person than to another does not, on that account alone, make the law other than one of general application. There are few laws which have a uniform impact. The line is crossed, however, when an enactment, though in relation to another matter, by its effect, impairs the status or capacity of a particular group. The analogy may be made to a law which in its effect paralyzes the status and capacities of a federal company. ...

This passage implies that a measure or provision will be "in relation to" a particular class or group, and for that reason will not count as a law of general application, if it has the effect of impairing that group's status or capacity. Later on in the judgment, however, the Supreme Court goes on to say that "[i]t would have to be shown that the policy of the [relevant] Act was to impair the status and capacities of Indians." Relying in part on this latter quotation, it subsequently concluded, in *Dick*, that mere demonstration of such an effect was not sufficient to disqualify a provision or statute from being a law of general application. "Effect and intent," the court said there,

> are both relevant. Effect can evidence intent. But in order to determine whether a law is not one of general application, the intent, purpose or policy of the legislation can certainly not be ignored: they form an essential ingredient of a law which discriminates between various classes of persons, as opposed to a law of general application.

The fact, therefore, that a measure impairs some group's capacity or status will deny it the character of general application if and only if it suffices in all the circumstances to sustain an inference that the measure was enacted to have that effect.

... The only provincial laws, then, even eligible for consideration for federal incorporation pursuant to s. 88 are those whose primary business is not to regulate s. 91(24) lands or Indians (or any other matter within exclusive federal authority) but whose provisions, applied full strength, would nonetheless have the effect of doing so. These are the laws — the only laws — to which s. 88's "general application" requirement has any relevance. For such laws, that requirement serves as one additional eligibility barrier to federal incorporation. ...

D. "... Are Applicable to and in Respect of Indians in the Province ..."

. . . . .

1. Which Indians?

The first of these questions, though important, is fairly easily answered. "Indian" is a term defined within the *Indian Act*, so the only Indians to whom incorporated measures apply are those that satisfy the statutory definition. ... We know, for example, that Inuit cannot be statutory Indians even though they are, indisputably, s. 91(24) Indians. Section 88, therefore, by its own terms, has no impact on the Inuit or on any other s. 91(24) Indians — or others — who do not qualify as statutory Indians. To those in that group, provincial measures either apply of their own force or not at all. It does, on the other hand, apply incorporated provincial measures to all statutory Indians whether or not they are also s. 91(24) Indians.

2. Provincial Laws About Land

The more difficult issue the current phrase poses — especially when read together with the one just preceding it — is what impact, if any, s. 88 has on the application of provincial measures to interests in, and uses of, reserves and other "Lands reserved for the Indians" ("s. 91(24) lands"). On the one hand, s. 88's text provides that "all laws of general application ... are applicable to and in respect of Indians"; nothing it says excludes provincial laws that happen to deal with land uses or interests. On the other hand, those same words say that "all laws of general application ... are applicable to and in respect of Indians in the province"; they say nothing comparably specific to suggest that such laws are also to govern Indian lands. And therein lies the controversy.

. . . . .

... [P]erhaps most important, the land-related provisions in the *Indian Act* and in its subordinate legislation pertain exclusively to the lands that the *Indian Act* has defined as "reserves". For present purposes ... reserves are by no means the only lands that matter. We have known for over a century that "the words actually used [in s. 91(24) of the *Constitution Act, 1867*] are, according to their natural meaning, sufficient to include all lands reserved, upon any terms or conditions, for Indian occupation," not just those lands that qualify under the statute as "reserves". ... In the absence, therefore, of affirmative federal measures concerning them, it is s. 88, as interpreted, that will determine what mainstream legal regime, if any, is going to govern the use, possession, occupation, or disposition of these lands. It will, to take just one example, determine what rights, if any, provincial laws related to matrimonial property disposition can confer on Aboriginal (or other) women residing off reserve on Aboriginal title lands.

. . . . .

In at least some circumstances, therefore, it will matter profoundly whether s. 88 is understood to apply provincial land regimes to Indian lands. We now must return to consider that primary issue. Does s. 88

(subject only to its other exceptions) impose provincial land regulation on
s. 91(24) lands or not?

. . . . .

E.   "... Except to the Extent that Such Laws are Inconsistent with this Act
       or Any Order, Rule, Regulation or By-law Made Thereunder, ..."

Like the earlier phrase "and any other Act of the Parliament of Canada,"
and for the same reasons, this phrase ensures that the *Indian Act*'s own
provisions, and the provisions of any subordinate legislation passed pursuant to it, prevail over any conflicting provincial measures incorporated
as federal law under s. 88. ...

F.   "... And Except to the Extent that such Laws Make Provision for
       Any Matter for Which Provision is Made By or Under This Act."

These are the words that prompted the Supreme Court to conclude, in
Dick, that s. 88 as a whole cannot just declare the terms on which provincial laws will apply, of their own force, to statutory Indians. It is the Constitution, as interpreted, that prescribes when and why provincial laws
must give way in order not to interfere with the operation of federal
schemes. It is not open to Parliament to give its own statutes greater protection from provincial interference than the Constitution already gives
them. ...

These consequences ... clarify that these words do indeed confer on the
Indian Act, and on arrangements enacted under it, extra protection from
the effects of the relevant provincial laws, beyond what would be available
under the usual paramountcy rules. And they confirm that this extra protection is available only against the effects of those provincial laws whose
application to Indians depends on incorporation pursuant to s. 88. It has
nothing to do with any provincial laws that apply, as such, to Indian lands
or to s. 91(24) Indians.

. . . . .

... When federal authorities, or band councils, enact particular schemes
within or pursuant to the *Indian Act*, these words instruct the courts to presume that those schemes are meant to operate to the exclusion of any
overlapping provincial arrangements that s. 88 incorporates; those challenging the provincial arrangement need not offer evidence of that intention, let alone demonstrate it. Any competent "substantive scheme or arrangement" set out in an *Indian Act* provision, regulation, or bylaw, therefore, routinely displaces, to the extent of any overlap, any incorporated
provincial scheme. This means, for example, that permissive band council
bylaws, where authorized by and validly enacted under the *Indian Act*,
will almost always override, on the reserves to which they pertain, any
related prohibitions contained in incorporated provincial measures about
the same matter, unless a bylaw specifically indicates otherwise. Similarly,
administrative or enforcement arrangements that band councils validly

enact to support their own measures will, other things equal, preclude recourse to any alternative mechanisms provided in overlapping incorporated laws. To displace an overlapping measure, all they have to demonstrate is the overlap.

. . . . .

V. Conclusion

Perhaps the greatest irony about s. 88 is that it may well have been intended, at least in part, as what insiders call a "housekeeping amendment". There still exists at least one original copy of Bill 79 that includes, next to some provisions, typewritten marginal notes interleaved with the official explanatory notes included in the printed versions of the bill. Next to s. 87 (now 88) in this copy of the bill is a typewritten note that reads as follows:

> 87. This is new and the effect of this section is to clear a long-standing doubt as to the application of provincial laws to Indians. The present Act is silent on the subject, which has resulted in considerable legal confusion.

Section 88 of the *Indian Act* has been part of our law now for almost exactly half a century: more than enough time to permit a considered appraisal of its contribution. If dispelling doubt and confusion was indeed its purpose, I doubt that very many today would agree that it had succeeded in fulfilling it. By any relevant standard, its contribution has been almost entirely negative.

... [S]. 88 reflects confusion and encourages difference of view about the extent of the provinces' own authority to regulate what Indians do and what happens on and to Indian lands, and about the extent of federal power to facilitate, and to channel and limit, that authority. As might be expected, it has not fit comfortably within the framework the courts have developed more recently for dealing with these constitutional questions. ...

... Understood within the larger constitutional framework, however, the court's solution [in *Dick*] gives rise to unacknowledged, inconvenient, and profoundly difficult problems concerning the powers, costs and mechanisms of enforcement of the provincial standards that measures that s. 88 incorporates. At the same time, it seems, of necessity, to deprive the words "laws of general application" of any meaningful function within the section as a whole, except to screen out measures whose territorial application is not uniform. ...

. . . . .

It is fair to say that s. 88 is now in serious need of legislative reconsideration. ... [I]t has created substantially more legal problems than it has solved. It is ... "of doubtful constitutional validity" when and as it operates to restrict the exercise of existing Aboriginal rights. ... [I]t rests, from a policy standpoint, on contentious and unarticulated assumptions: about which s. 91(24) Indians and which aspects of their lives stand in need of mainstream regulation and by whom; and about when, where, and why such regulation is appropriate. These assumptions, and the questions that they purport to answer, deserve re-examination and reflection in light of contemporary law and experience. ...

The controversy surrounding section 88 continued in *R. v. Côté*, [1996] 3 S.C.R. 139, 202 N.R. 161, 138 D.L.R. (4th) 385, 110 C.C.C. (3d) 122, [1996] 4 C.N.L.R. 26, where Chief Justice Lamer's majority decision contemplated the addition of a *Sparrow*-type justificatory test to section 88. The Chief Justice made the following statements about section 88:

> Originally adopted in 1951, s. 88 has played a pivotal role in our modern federal system by coordinating the interaction of federal and provincial laws in relation to aboriginal peoples. As I understand the intent of the provision, s. 88 presently serves two distinct purposes. First, s. 88 serves an important jurisdictional purpose. Through the operation of the provision, provincial laws which would otherwise not apply to Indians under the federal and provincial division of powers are made applicable as incorporated federal law: *R. v. Dick*, [1985] 2 S.C.R. 309. Second, s. 88 accords federal statutory protection to aboriginal treaty rights. The application of such generally applicable provincial laws through federal incorporation is expressly made "[s]ubject to the terms of any treaty". Section 88 accords a special statutory protection to aboriginal treaty rights from contrary provincial law through the operation of the doctrine of federal paramountcy.
>
> . . . . .
>
> This second purpose, of course, has become of diminished importance as a result of the constitutional entrenchment of treaty rights in 1982. But I note that, on the face of s. 88, treaty rights appear to enjoy a broader protection from contrary provincial law under the *Indian Act* than under the *Constitution Act, 1982*. Once it has been demonstrated that a provincial law infringes 'the terms of [a] treaty', the treaty would arguably prevail under s. 88 even in the presence of a well-grounded justification. The statutory provision does not *expressly* incorporate a justification requirement analogous to the justification stage included in the *Sparrow* framework. But the precise boundaries of the protection of s. 88 remains a topic for future consideration. I know of no case which has authoritatively discounted the potential existence of an *implicit* justification stage under s. 88. In the near future, Parliament will no doubt feel compelled to re-examine the existence and scope of this statutory protection in light of these uncertainties and in light of the parallel constitutionalization of treaty rights under s. 35(1).[1]

The Chief Justice ultimately found that section 88 was not engaged in the matter before him and therefore did not need to consider whether section 88 was subject to a *Sparrow*-type justificatory test. Should section 88 be made subject to such a test?

In *R. v. Alphonse* (1993), 83 C.C.C. (3d) 417, [1993] 5 W.W.R. 401, 80 B.C.L.R. (2d) 17, 4 C.N.L.R. 19 (C.A.), the majority judgment of the British Columbia Court of Appeal considered this argument, but held that, insofar as section 88 does not, itself, infringe Aboriginal rights, it did not require justification under the *Sparrow* test. Rather, the court held that if the referentially incorporated provincial laws were found to have infringed section

35(1) rights, they, and not section 88, would need to be justified under the *Sparrow* test.

In criticizing this approach, McNeil stated that the *Alphonse* decision:

> ... seems to place the burden of justification on the provinces, when in fact they are not responsible for the application of these referentially incorporated laws to Indians. If the British Columbia Court of Appeal's approach in these cases is correct, then Parliament, through the mechanism of s. 88, has succeeded in casting responsibility onto the provinces without their participation or consent, and has also been able to wash its hands of the matter without justifying this abdication of responsibility to the Aboriginal peoples whose rights are affected. This state of affairs cannot be right if the constitutional principles of division of powers and federal responsibility for s. 91(24) "Indians" have any meaning in this context.[2]

See also K. Wilkins, "Of Provinces and Section 35 Rights" (1999) 22 Dal. L.J. 185, where the author states:

> If Canada had chosen ... to enact, one by one, its own measures duplicating, for Indians, the effects of selected existing provincial laws, no one would suggest that any s. 35 inquiry should focus exclusively — or at all — on the inapplicable provincial prototypes. In one respect, s. 88 does exactly that, only by different means.

See also *ibid.* at 230: "An inquiry into s. 88's own justifiability ... must be independent of any possible inquiry into the merits of any of the provincial laws it incorporates.[3]

Wilkins suggests, in opposition to *Alphonse*, that section 88 ought to require justification; further, he expresses doubt as to whether that is possible, even assuming that its underlying objectives are "compelling and substantial."[4] He further maintains that section 88 neither meets *Sparrow*'s requirements that there be "as little infringement as possible in order to effect the desired result", nor that there be "sensitivity to and respect for the rights of aboriginal peoples".[5] This is so because, as he states, section 88 "makes no allowance whatever for aboriginal rights, either by according them some statutory priority (as it did for treaty rights), or by requiring some prior review of incorporated statutes to ensure some threshold of sensitivity or of proportionality".[6]

In addition to addressing the application of the *Sparrow* test to section 88, the court in *Alphonse* considered the constitutional validity of section 88 in light of the protections existing in section 35(1) of the *Constitution Act, 1982*. It determined that section 88 remained valid in the face of section 35(1). Academic commentary has largely come to the opposite conclusion. As Brian Slattery has suggested:

> ... [T]he Federal Parliament cannot subvert the overall constitutional scheme by enacting legislation for Aboriginal peoples that referentially incorporates a wide range of Provincial statutes that could not otherwise apply to First Nations under the division of powers. Such Federal legislation, it is submitted, would seriously affect the Aboriginal right of self-government under section 35 of the *Constitution Act, 1982* and cannot meet the *Sparrow* standard of justification. So, section 88 of the current *Indian Act*, which referentially makes applicable to Indians 'all laws of general application from time to time in force in any province' is of doubtful constitutional validity.[7]

In response to the above argument, Kent McNeil stated in "Aboriginal Title and Section 88 of the Indian Act" (2000) 34 U.B.C. L. Rev. 159 at para. 12, that:

> ... Slattery's argument appears to relate only to provincial laws that infringe the rights protected by s. 35(1). Are there provincial laws of general application that could be referentially incorporated by s. 88 without infringing those rights? The answer depends upon whether the "core of Indianness at the heart of s. 91(24)" is limited to matters relating to Aboriginal and treaty rights, or is broader than that. While Chief Justice Lamer did not fully define the extent of the core of federal jurisdiction in *Delgamuukw*, earlier case law indicates that it does include exclusive jurisdiction over the status and capacity of Indians, whether or not Aboriginal or treaty rights are involved. The case law therefore suggests that the core of federal jurisdiction under s. 91(24), to which the doctrine of interjurisdictional immunity applies, extends beyond those rights. If so, then there is some room for s. 88 to operate without infringing Aboriginal or treaty rights. In that case, if Slattery is correct (as I think he is) that federal authorization of provincial infringements of those rights is unconstitutional, then s. 88 would not be invalid, but would have to be read down in order for referential incorporation to exclude provincial laws having that effect.[8]

McNeil summarizes the situation as follows:

> ... [T]he constitutional validity of s. 88 really depends on whether it incorporates any provincial laws that do not infringe Aboriginal rights. If it does, as the pre-*Delgamuukw* jurisprudence suggests, then it is still valid, but should be read down to limit its application to the incorporation of those laws. However, if the only laws incorporated by it are laws that infringe Aboriginal rights, for the reasons outlined above it should be struck down because it violates s. 35(1). This approach would eliminate the discrepancy in the treatment of Aboriginal and treaty rights under s. 88, the historical justification for which disappeared when Aboriginal rights were acknowledged by the Supreme Court. It would also be more consistent, in the words of Lord Watson, with the "plain policy" of Canada's Constitution, whereby, "in order to ensure uniformity of administration ... Indian affairs generally [were placed] under the legislative control of one central authority." As a result, "the government vested with primary constitutional responsibility for securing the welfare of Canada's aboriginal peoples" would no longer be able to use s. 88 to avoid its fiduciary obligation to respect Aboriginal rights.[9]

The most recent Supreme Court of Canada considerations of the federal government's legislative power over "Indians" under section 91(24) of the *Constitution Act, 1867* and the effects of section 88 upon that power may be seen in *Delgamuukw v. British Columbia*, [1997] 3 S.C.R. 1010 and in *Kitkatla Band v. British Columbia (Minister of Small Business, Tourism and Culture)*, 2002 SCC 31, both of which are excerpted below.

DELGAMUUKW v. BRITISH COLUMBIA

[1997] 3 S.C.R. 1010

Cory, McLachlin and Major JJ. concur with

Lamer C.J.C.: — The extent of federal jurisdiction over Indians has not been definitively addressed by this Court. We have not needed to do so because the *vires* of federal legislation with respect to Indians, under the division of powers, has never been at issue. The cases which have come before the Court under s. 91(24) have implicated the question of jurisdiction over Indians from the other direction — whether provincial laws which on their face apply to Indians intrude on federal jurisdiction and are inapplicable to Indians to the extent of that intrusion. As I explain below, the Court has held that s. 91(24) protects a "core" of Indianness from provincial intrusion, through the doctrine of interjurisdictional immunity.[10]

It follows, at the very least, that this core falls within the scope of federal jurisdiction over Indians. That core, for reasons I will develop, encompasses aboriginal rights, including the rights that are recognized and affirmed by s. 35(1). Laws which purport to extinguish those rights therefore touch the core of Indianness which lies at the heart of s. 91(24), and are beyond the legislative competence of the provinces to enact. The core of Indianness encompasses the whole range of aboriginal rights that are protected by s. 35(1). Those rights include rights in relation to land; that part of the core derives from s. 91(24)'s reference to "Lands reserved for the Indians". But those rights also encompass practices, customs and traditions which are not tied to land as well; that part of the core can be traced to federal jurisdiction over "Indians". Provincial governments are prevented from legislating in relation to both types of aboriginal rights.

(3) *Provincial Laws of General Application*

The vesting of exclusive jurisdiction with the federal government over Indians and Indian lands under s. 91(24), operates to preclude provincial laws in relation to those matters. Thus, provincial laws which single out Indians for special treatment are *ultra vires*, because they are in relation to Indians and therefore invade federal jurisdiction: see *R. v. Sutherland*, [1980] 2 S.C.R. 451. However, it is a well established principle that (*Four B Manufacturing Ltd.*, *supra*, at p. 1048):

> The conferring upon Parliament of exclusive legislative competence to make laws relating to certain classes of persons does not mean that the totality of these persons' rights and duties comes under primary federal competence to the exclusion of provincial laws of general application.

In other words, notwithstanding s. 91(24), provincial laws of general application apply *proprio vigore* to Indians and Indian lands. Thus, this Court has held that provincial labour relations legislation (*Four B*) and motor vehicle laws (*R. v. Francis*, [1988] 1 S.C.R. 1025), which purport to apply to all persons in the province, also apply to Indians living on reserves.

What must be answered, however, is whether the same principle allows provincial laws of general application to extinguish aboriginal rights. I have come to the conclusion that a provincial law of general application could not have this effect, for two reasons. First, a law of general application cannot, by definition, meet the standard which has been set by this Court for the extinguishment of aboriginal rights without being *ultra vires* the province. That standard was laid down in *Sparrow* ... as one of "clear and plain" intent. In that decision, the Court drew a distinction between laws which extinguished aboriginal rights, and those which merely regulated them. Although the latter types of laws may have been "necessarily inconsistent" with the continued exercise of aboriginal rights, they could not extinguish those rights. While the requirement of clear and plain intent does not, perhaps, require that the Crown "use language which refers expressly to its extinguishment of aboriginal rights" ... the standard is still quite high. My concern is that the only laws with the sufficiently clear and plain intention to extinguish aboriginal rights would be laws in relation to Indians and Indian lands. As a result, a provincial law could never, *proprio vigore*, extinguish aboriginal rights, because the intention to do so would take the law outside provincial jurisdiction.

Second, as I mentioned earlier, s. 91(24) protects a core of federal jurisdiction even from provincial laws of general application, through the operation of the doctrine of interjurisdictional immunity. That core has been described as matters touching on "Indianness" or the "core of Indianness" (*Dick*, *supra*, at pp. 326 and 315; also see *Four B*, *supra* at p. 1047 and *Francis*, *supra*, at pp. 1028-29). The core of Indianness at the heart of s. 91(24) has been defined in both negative and positive terms. Negatively, it has been held to not include labour relations (*Four B*) and the driving of motor vehicles (*Francis*). The only positive formulation of Indianness was offered in *Dick*. Speaking for the Court, Beetz J. assumed, but did not decide, that a provincial hunting law did not apply *proprio vigore* to the members of an Indian band to hunt and because those activities were "at the centre of what they do and who they are" (*supra*, at p. 320). But in *Van der Peet*, I described and defined the aboriginal rights that are recognized and affirmed by s. 35(1) in a similar fashion, as protecting the occupation of land and the activities which are integral to the distinctive aboriginal culture of the group claiming the right. It follows that aboriginal rights are part of the core of Indianness at the heart of s. 91(24). Prior to 1982, as a result, they could not be extinguished by provincial laws of general application.

(4) *Section 88 of the Indian Act*

Provincial laws which would otherwise not apply to Indians *proprio vigore*, however, are allowed to do so by s. 88 of the *Indian Act*, which incorporates by reference provincial laws of general application ... However, it is important to note, in Professor Hogg's words, that s. 88 does not "invigorate" provincial laws which are invalid because they are in relation to Indians and Indian lands (*Constitutional Law of Canada* (3rd ed. 1992), at p. 676 ... What this means is that s. 88 extends the effect of provincial laws of general application which cannot apply to Indians and Indian lands because they touch on the Indianness at the core of s. 91(24). For example, a provincial law which regulated hunting may very well touch on this core. Although such a law would not apply to aboriginal people *proprio vigore*, it would still apply through s. 88 of the *Indian Act*, being a law of general application. Such laws are enacted to conserve game and for the safety of all.

The respondent B.C. Crown argues that since such laws are *intra vires* the province, and applicable to aboriginal persons, s. 88 could allow provincial laws to extinguish aboriginal rights. I reject this submission, for the simple reason that s. 88 does not evince the requisite clear and plain intent to extinguish aboriginal rights. ... I see nothing in the language of the provision which even suggests the intention to extinguish aboriginal rights. Indeed, the explicit reference to treaty rights in s. 88 suggests that the provision was clearly not intended to undermine aboriginal rights.

In the *Kitkatla* case, below, the Supreme Court was faced with determining whether British Columbia heritage object legislation that permitted, *inter alia*, the issuing of permits to "damage, alter, cover, or move" Aboriginal cultural objects was *intra vires* the province or, alternatively, whether the legislation could be validated by section 88.

KITKATLA BAND v. BRITISH COLUMBIA (MINISTER OF SMALL BUSINESS, TOURISM AND CULTURE)

2002 SCC 31

Le Bel J.: — This case concerns a constitutional challenge to the application of provincial legislation on the protection of cultural heritage property. The dispute relates to culturally modified trees or CMTs. These trees have often been altered by aboriginal people as part of their traditional use and have cultural, historical and scientific importance for a number of First Nations in British Columbia. ...

II. The Origins of the Case

The dispute arose during the process of administrative review and authorization of logging operations in British Columbia. The respondent, International Forest Products Limited ("Interfor"), had long held a forest licence over land in the central coast of British Columbia which included an area known as the Kumealon. Provincial forestry legislation required Interfor, as the holder of a forest licence, to propose sequential forest development plans. The legislation also granted the public some participatory rights in the creation of these plans. Interfor provided direct notification of its development plans to the appellant Kitkatla Band ("the Band") since early 1994, but these plans never specifically identified the Kumealon area. The appellants claimed aboriginal rights in this area and had been engaged in treaty negotiations with the province. In early 1998, aware of its obligations under the Act, Interfor hired a firm of archaeologists in order to report on the impact of future logging operations in an area that included the Kumealon. Coincidentally, it appears, the appellants expressed an interest in the Kumealon at roughly the same time. Interfor was alerted to this claim, and, shortly thereafter, the firm it hired contacted the Band in order to ascertain their views. The Band designated two persons for this purpose. Interfor was concerned with the possible presence of native heritage sites and objects including CMTs in the area to be harvested. The archaeologist eventually reported the presence of a significant number of these trees in seven cutblocks Interfor intended to harvest.

Meanwhile, Interfor applied to the respondent, the Minister of Small Business, Tourism and Culture ("the Minister"), for a site alteration permit under s. 12 of the Act, to authorize the cutting and processing of CMTs during logging operations. The Minister forwarded Interfor's application to the Band, along with a cover letter requesting its written submissions on the application. No submissions were received by the deadline. One week later, on March 31, 1998, and without having considered a single archaeological report, the Minister issued a site alteration permit.

At this stage, the Band commenced proceedings to challenge the legality of the permit. They began judicial review proceedings. These proceedings raised administrative law arguments asserting that the Minister had failed to address all relevant issues — and had violated his fiduciary obligations towards the appellants by failing to provide them with proper notification and the opportunity to consult — before issuing the permit. The Band also challenged the Act as being *ultra vires* the province.

The administrative law challenge succeeded. A judgment of the British Columbia Supreme Court ordered the Minister to reconsider the part of its decision which affected the CMTs, after giving the Band an adequate opportunity to be consulted and to make representations. At the same time, the trial court dismissed the constitutional challenge.

The Minister went through the reconsideration process. During this process, the Band asserted a claim of aboriginal rights in the continued existence of the CMTs. It petitioned for an order in the nature of prohibition, to restrain the Minister from granting the site alteration permit. The Minister took the position that this issue fell outside the scope of the permit granting procedure and should be left to the courts. Wilson J. agreed with the Minister and dismissed the petition. In the end, the Minister issued a site alteration permit in accordance with the CMTs management plan proposed by Interfor which provided that all fallen CMTs should be preserved together with 76 of 116 trees still standing in the cutblocks. This led to the present appeal. Meanwhile, the Band launched another judicial review application on the basis that the Minister should have considered native rights in the permit granting procedure. This new challenge also failed.

. . . . .

V. Constitutional Questions

On January 22, 2001, the Chief Justice stated the following constitutional questions:

(1) Is s. 12(2)(*a*) in respect of the subject matter of s. 13(2)(*c*) and (*d*) of the *Heritage Conservation Act* in pith and substance law in relation to Indians or Lands reserved for the Indians, or alternatively, is the law in relation to property, and, therefore, within the exclusive legislative competence of the Province under s. 92(13) of the *Constitution Act, 1867*?

(2) If the impugned provisions of the *Heritage Conservation Act* are within provincial jurisdiction under s. 92(13) of the *Constitution Act, 1867* do they apply to the subject matter of s. 13(2)(*c*) and (*d*) of the *Heritage Conservation Act*?

(3) If the impugned provisions do not apply to the appellants *ex proprio vigore*, do they nonetheless apply by virtue of s. 88 of the *Indian Act*?

VI. The Issues

. . . . .

The Court must first consider the pith and substance of the legislation. Three sub-questions must be discussed in this respect. First, do ss. 12(2)(*a*) and 13(2)(*c*) and (*d*) intrude into a federal head of power, and to what extent? Then, if they do intrude, are they nevertheless part of a valid legislative scheme? At the next step of the analysis, it should be considered whether the impugned provisions are sufficiently integrated with the scheme. If the answer is yes, we may turn to consider the doctrine of interjurisdictional immunity and, if need be, s. 88 of the *Indian Act*. Before I move on to these, I will review the heritage conservation scheme adopted by the province of British Columbia and discuss some evidentiary issues relevant to the rights claimed by the appellants.

C. *Heritage Conservation Legislation in British Columbia*

The *Heritage Conservation Act* is designed to grant a broad protection to the cultural heritage of British Columbia in a very comprehensive manner. The history of the province means that its cultural heritage is in the vast majority of cases an aboriginal one, often going back to pre-contact times and prior to the establishment of the first non-native settlements and the creation of the British colonies on Vancouver Island and on the mainland. The Act was adopted to conserve and protect all forms of cultural property, objects and artifacts as well as sites in British Columbia which have heritage value to the province as a whole, to a community or to an aboriginal people, as appears for example in the definition of "heritage object" in the Act: "heritage object, means, whether designated or not, personal property that has heritage value to British Columbia, a community or an aboriginal people".

The Act attempts to address the importance of the cultural heritage of First Nations in various ways. Section 4 provides for agreements with First Nations with respect to the preservation of aboriginal sites and artifacts. Section 8 states a key interpretive principle in the interpretation and implementation of the Act which is designed to protect aboriginal and treaty rights of First Nations:

> For greater certainty, no provision of this Act and no provision in an agreement entered into under section 4 abrogates or derogates from the aboriginal and treaty rights of a first nation or of any aboriginal peoples.

Native concerns must be weighed at most steps of the administrative procedures created for the application of the Act. For example, prior to the designation of lands as a heritage site, notice must be given to the First Nations within whose traditional territory they lie. Section 13 grants broad protection against any alteration of sites or things in use before 1846, which will usually be part of the cultural heritage of First Nations in British Columbia (see s. 13(2)(*d*)).

The Act considers First Nations' culture as part of the heritage of all residents of British Columbia. It must be protected, not only as an essential part of the collective material memory which belongs to the history and identity of First Nations, but also as part of the shared heritage of all British Columbians. The Act grants protection where none existed before. At the same time, heritage conservation schemes such as the Act here must strike a balance between conservation and other societal interests, which may require the destruction of heritage objects or sites after a careful review by the Minister. Time and nature, as well as mishaps and unforeseen events, may destroy or render the conservation of a site or thing an impossibility. Other needs and concerns may arise and require an assessment of the nature and importance of a site or cultural object. Conservation schemes must thus also provide for removal and destruction. This is what is at issue here. Is the power to order the alteration or even destruction of a cultural object beyond provincial powers when it affects native cultural objects?

D. *Evidentiary Problems*

Constitutional questions should not be discussed in a factual vacuum. Even in a division of powers case, rights must be asserted and their factual underpinnings demonstrated. In this case, the appellants assert that the importance of the CMTs goes to the core of their cultural values and identity. This assertion grounds their claim that the impugned provisions of the Act impinge on a federal head of power. Because of this assertion, the nature and quality of the evidence offered will have to be assessed and discussed. Even if this case remains a division of powers case, the comments of McLachlin C.J. on evidentiary standards and problems in aboriginal law cases in *Mitchell v. M.N.R.*, [2001] 1 S.C.R. 911, 2001 SCC 33, remain highly apposite. In such cases, oral evidence of aboriginal values, customs and practices is necessary and relevant. It should be assessed with understanding and sensitivity to the traditions of a civilization which remained an essentially oral one before and after the period of contact with Europeans who brought their own tradition of reliance on written legal and archival records. Nevertheless, this kind of evidence must be evaluated like any other. Claims must be established on a balance of probabilities, by persuasive evidence (*Mitchell, supra,* at para. 39, *per* McLachlin C.J.). "Sparse, doubtful and equivocal evidence cannot serve as the foundation for a successful claim . . ." (*Mitchell,* at para. 51, *per* McLachlin C.J.).

These comments on the use of evidence must be kept in mind during a review of the evidence in this case. The appellants attempted to downplay the importance and relevance of this issue by stressing that this Court was not faced with a claim of aboriginal rights or title. As stated above, facts must be established in order to demonstrate in this case that there exists a conflict between federal and provincial legislative powers. In this respect, the factual basis of the claim looks weak.

The appellants' claim in this case is concerned with what archaeologists refer to as culturally modified trees (CMTs). From the evidence, large numbers of CMTs are found in British Columbia. Thousands are reported and registered every year in British Columbia in the archaeology branch of the ministry. For ministry purposes, CMTs are trees which bear the marks of past aboriginal intervention occurring as part of traditional aboriginal use. Bark may have been stripped from them. Pieces or chunks of wood may have been removed from the trees to make tools or build canoes. Sap or pitch may have been collected from the trees. It would appear that the identification of CMTs is an involved process. Sometimes, the modifications found on trees result from the work of nature. On the other hand, modifications may have been made by non-native persons. Therefore, in order to identify true CMTs, archaeologists have developed complex "field" guidelines. In certain cases, these guidelines will prove incapable to the task, and it will be necessary to take a sample or even fell a particular tree to determine whether it is a CMT. In this appeal, the CMTs that the archaeologists were able to identify were generally categorized as either "bark-stripped trees" or "aboriginally-logged trees".

In addition, there is one matter that, as of now, lies beyond the ken from any archaeological expert. Even if there is evidence of native intervention, it is next to impossible to tell which aboriginal group modified them (see Braidwood J.A., at para. 30). In this case, in particular, the trees are found in an area covered by the conflicting claims of the Band and another group, the Lax Kw'alaams, which, like the appellants, also belong to the Tsimshian Tribal Council. This second group has agreed with the forestry management plan proposed by Interfor, and approved by the Minister.

The appellants, in support of their claim, assert that the preservation of the CMTs as living trees is required in order to safeguard evidence of their cultural heritage including the work, activities and endeavours of their forebears. Indeed, they argue that the CMTs constitute the only physical record of their heritage. Unfortunately, the evidence supporting these claims is sparse. Aside from an affidavit sworn by the appellant Chief Hill, there is very little evidence as to the extent to which these trees in the Kumealon had been related to or incorporated into the culture of the Band. In this respect, according to other evidence, the firm of archeologists hired by Interfor identified these CMTs and brought their existence to the attention of the appellants. The constitutional questions must be reviewed in the context of this factual record, with its particular weaknesses. I will now turn to the constitutional issues.

E. *The Division of Powers Issue*

The constitution of Canada does not include an express grant of power with respect to "culture" as such. Most constitutional litigation on cultural issues has arisen in the context of language and education rights. However, provinces are also concerned with broader and more diverse cultural problems and interests. In addition, the federal government affects cultural activity in this country through the exercise of its broad powers over communications and through the establishment of federally funded cultural institutions. Consequently, particular cultural issues must be analyzed in their context, in relation to the relevant sources of legislative power. In this case, the issues raised by the parties concern the use and protection of property in the province. The Act imposes limitations on property rights in the province by reason of their cultural importance. At first blush, this would seem to be a provincial matter falling within the scope of s. 92(13) of the *Constitution Act, 1867*. This view will have to be tested through a proper pith and substance analysis, in order to establish the relationship between the impugned provisions and the federal power on Indian affairs.

F. *The Pith and Substance of the Provisions of the Heritage Conservation Act*

The beginning of any division of powers analysis is a characterization of the impugned law to determine the head of power within which it falls. This process is commonly known as "pith and substance analysis" ... By thus categorizing the impugned provision, one is able to determine whether the enacting legislature possesses the authority under the constitution to do what it did.

A pith and substance analysis looks at both (1) the purpose of the legislation as well as (2) its effect. First, to determine the purpose of the legislation, the Court may look at both intrinsic evidence, such as purpose clauses, or extrinsic evidence, such as Hansard or the minutes of parliamentary committees.

Second, in looking at the effect of the legislation, the Court may consider both its legal effect and its practical effect. In other words, the Court looks to see, first, what effect flows directly from the provisions of the statute itself; then, second, what "side" effects flow from the application of the statute which are not direct effects of the provisions of the statute itself ... Iacobucci J. provided some examples of how this would work in *Global Securities Corp. v. British Columbia (Securities Commission)*, [2000] 1 S.C.R. 494, 2000 SCC 21, at para. 23:

> The effects of the legislation may also be relevant to the validity of the legislation in so far as they reveal its pith and substance. For example, in *Saumur v. City of Quebec*, [1953] 2 S.C.R. 299, the Court struck down a municipal by-law that prohibited leafleting because it had been applied so as to suppress the religious views of Jehovah's Witnesses. Similarly, in *Attorney-General for Alberta v. Attorney-General for Canada*, [1939] A.C. 117, the Privy Council struck down a law imposing a tax on banks because the effects of the tax were so severe that the true purpose of the law could only be in relation to banking, not taxation. However, merely incidental effects will not disturb the constitutionality of an otherwise *intra vires* law.

There is some controversy among the parties to this case as to the appropriate approach to the pith and substance analysis where what is challenged is not the Act as a whole but simply one part of it. The appellants tend to emphasize the characterization of the impugned provisions outside the context of the Act as a whole. The respondents and interveners take the opposite view, placing greater emphasis on the pith and substance of the Act as a whole. The parties also disagree as to the order in which the analysis should take place: the appellants favour looking at the impugned provisions first, while the respondents and interveners tend to prefer to look at the Act first.

In my opinion, the proper approach to follow in a case such as this is to look first to the challenged provisions. Such a rule is stated in the dictum of Dickson J. (as he then was) in *Attorney General of Canada v. Canadian National Transportation Ltd.*, [1983] 2 S.C.R. 206, at p. 270 (quoted by Dickson C.J. in *General Motors of Canada Ltd. v. City National Leasing*, [1989] 1 S.C.R. 641, at p. 665):

> It is obvious at the outset that a constitutionally invalid provision will not be saved by being put into an otherwise valid statute, even if the statute comprises a regulatory scheme under the general trade and commerce branch of s. 91(2). The correct approach, where there is some doubt that the impugned provision has the same constitutional characterization as the Act in which it is found, is to start with the challenged section rather than with a demonstration of the validity of the statute as a whole. I do not think, however, this means that the section in question must be read in isolation. If the claim to constitutional validity is based on the contention that the impugned provision is part of a regulatory scheme it would seem necessary to read it in its context. If it can in fact be seen as part of such a scheme, attention will then shift to the constitutionality of the scheme as a whole.

Laskin C.J. took the same view but put it in somewhat different words in referring to the appropriate analysis of a section of the *Trade Marks Act* in an earlier case, *MacDonald v. Vapor Canada Ltd.*, [1977] 2 S.C.R. 134 at p. 159 (quoted by Dickson C.J. in *General Motors of Canada Ltd., supra*, at p. 665):

> If [the impugned provision] can stand alone, it needs no other support; if not, it may take on a valid constitutional cast by the context and association in which it is fixed as complementary provision [*sic*] serving to reinforce other admittedly valid provisions.

Dickson C.J. set out in *General Motors of Canada Ltd., supra*, at pp. 666-69, a three-part test for determining the pith and substance of an impugned provision. ... In my view, Dickson C.J.'s test could be re-stated in the following form:

1. Do the impugned provisions intrude into a federal head of power, and to what extent?

2. If the impugned provisions intrude into a federal head of power, are they nevertheless part of a valid provincial legislative scheme?

3. If the impugned provisions are part of a valid provincial legislative scheme, are they sufficiently integrated with the scheme?

In the rest of this section, I will consider these questions and apply the test in the context of this appeal.

G. *Purpose of the Provisions Test*

The first stage of the analysis requires a characterization of the impugned provisions in isolation, looking at both their purpose and effect. For convenience, I reproduce here ss. 12(2)(*a*) and 13(2)(*c*) and (*d*):

12...

(2)   The minister may

(a)   issue a permit authorizing an action referred to in section 13, ...

13...

(2)   Except as authorized by a permit issued under section 12 or 14, or an order issued under section 14, a person must not do any of the following:

. . . . .

(c)   damage, alter, cover or move an aboriginal rock painting or aboriginal rock carving that has historical or archaeological value;

(d)   damage, excavate, dig in or alter, or remove any heritage object from, a site that contains artifacts, features, materials or other physical evidence of human habitation or use before 1846; . . .

Paragraphs (c) and (d) of s. 13(2) have as their purpose the protection of certain aboriginal heritage objects from damage, alteration, or removal. In other words, the purpose of these paragraphs is heritage conservation, specifically the heritage of the aboriginal peoples of British Columbia. The protection extends to all aboriginal rock paintings or aboriginal rock carvings that have historical or archaeological value, as well as to heritage objects, including artifacts, features, materials or other physical evidence of human habitation or use before 1846, which in effect consists almost entirely of aboriginal cultural artifacts.

Paragraph (a) of s. 12(2), on the other hand, provides the minister responsible for the operation of the Act as a whole with the discretion to grant a permit authorizing one of the actions prohibited under s. 13(2)(c) and (d). In other words, this paragraph provides a tempering of the absolute protection otherwise provided by s. 13(2)(c) and (d).

The purpose of such a provision seems obvious when one considers the nature of heritage conservation legislation generally and its specific application in the context of British Columbia. No heritage conservation scheme can provide absolute protection to all objects or sites that possess some historical, archaeological, or cultural value to a society. To grant such an absolute protection would be to freeze a society at a particular moment in time. It would make impossible the need to remove, for example, buildings or artifacts of heritage value which, nevertheless, create a public health hazard or otherwise endanger lives. In other cases, the value of preserving an object may be greatly outweighed by the benefit that could accrue from allowing it to be removed or destroyed in order to accomplish a goal deemed by society to be of greater value. It cannot be denied that ss. 12(2)(a) and 13(2)(c) could sometimes affect aboriginal interests. As will be seen below, these provisions form part of a carefully balanced scheme. As recommended by the Court in *Delgamuukw, supra*, it is highly sensitive to native cultural interests. At the same time, it appears to strike an appropriate balance between native and non-native interests. Native interests must be carefully taken into account at every stage of a procedure under the Act. The Act clearly considers them as an essential part of the interests to be preserved and of the cultural heritage of British Columbia as well as of all First Nations.

Consequently, any heritage conservation scheme inevitably includes provisions to make exceptions to the general protection the legislation is intended to provide. Such a permissive provision strikes a balance among competing social goals.

H. *Effect of the Provisions*

Having looked at the purpose of these provisions, I turn now to consider their effects. Sections 12(2)(*a*) and 13(2)(*c*) and (*d*) grant the Minister a discretion to allow the alteration or removal of aboriginal heritage objects. We have no evidence before us with respect to the total number of aboriginal heritage objects which may be covered by this legislation. Nor do we have any evidence as to how often the Minister has exercised the discretion to permit the removal or destruction of aboriginal heritage objects of whatever type. We know only that, in the present case, the permit granted to the respondent Interfor allowed it to cut 40 out of about 120 standing CMTs within seven identified cutblocks. Thus, the practical effect, in this case anyway, is to permit the destruction of what are alleged to be Kitkatla heritage objects (although there is no specific proof here that the 40 CMTs in question were indeed the products of Kitkatla ancestors) while protecting 80 CMTs from alteration and removal. In addition, all CMTs allowed to be logged must be catalogued and an archival record of them must be retained. In other words, the effect here is the striking of a balance between the need and desire to preserve aboriginal heritage with the need and desire to promote the exploitation of British Columbia's natural resources.

I. *Effect on Federal Powers*

Given this analysis of the purpose and effect of the legislation in order to characterize the impugned provisions, the Court must then determine whether the pith and substance of ss. 12(2)(*a*) and 13(2)(*c*) and (*d*) fall within a provincial head of power or if, rather, they fall within a federal head of power. If the Court characterizes these provisions as a heritage conservation measure that is designed to strike a balance between the need to preserve the past while also allowing the exploitation of natural resources today, then they would fall squarely within the provincial head of power in s. 92(13) of the *Constitution Act, 1867* with respect to property and civil rights in the province.

On the other hand, one cannot escape the fact that the impugned provisions directly affect the existence of aboriginal heritage objects, raising the issue of whether the provisions are in fact with respect to Indians and lands reserved to Indians, a federal head of power under s. 91(24) of the *Constitution Act, 1867*. In considering this question, the Court must assess a number of factors. First, the Court must remember the basic assumption that provincial laws can apply to aboriginal peoples; First Nations are not enclaves of federal power in a sea of provincial jurisdiction: see *Cardinal v. Attorney General of Alberta*, [1974] S.C.R. 695. The mere mention of the word "aboriginal" in a statutory provision does not render it *ultra vires* the province.

Second, it is clear that legislation which singles out aboriginal people for special treatment is *ultra vires* the province ... For example, a law which purported to affect the Indian status of adopted children was held to be *ultra vires* the province: see *Natural Parents v. Superintendent of Child Welfare*, [1976] 2 S.C.R. 751. Similarly, laws which purported to define the extent of Indian access to land for the purpose of hunting were *ultra vires* the provinces because they singled out Indians: see *Sutherland, supra; Moosehunter v. The Queen*, [1981] 1 S.C.R. 282. Further, provincial laws must not impair the status or capacity of Indians: see *Kruger v. The Queen*, [1978] 1 S.C.R. 104, at p. 110; *Dick, supra*, at pp. 323-24.

Nevertheless, "singling out" should not be confused with disproportionate effect. Dickson J. (as he then was) said in *Kruger, supra*, at p. 110, that "the fact that a law may have graver consequence to one person than to another does not, on that account alone, make the law other than one of general application".

In the present case, the impugned provisions cannot be said to single out aboriginal peoples, at least from one point of view. The provisions prohibit everyone, not just aboriginal peoples, from the named acts, and require everyone, not just aboriginal peoples, to seek permission of the Minister to commit the prohibited acts. In that respect, the impugned provisions treat everyone the same. The impugned provisions' disproportionate effects can be attributed to the fact that aboriginal peoples have produced by far the largest number of heritage objects in British Columbia. These peoples have been resident in British Columbia for thousands of years; other British Columbians arrived in the last two hundred years.

A more serious objection is raised with respect to the issue of whether permitting the destruction of aboriginal heritage objects impairs the status or capacity of Indians. The appellants' submission seeks to situate these cultural interests, along with aboriginal rights, at the "core of Indianness", *Delgamuukw, supra*, at para. 181. However, as pointed out above, little evidence has been offered by the appellants with respect to the relationship between the CMTs and Kitkatla culture in this area. The appellants argue that aboriginal heritage objects constitute a major portion of their identity and culture in a way that non-aboriginal heritage objects do not go to the centre of non-aboriginal identity. Consequently, they argue, aboriginal people are singled out for more severe treatment. I would reject this argument. Because British Columbia's history is dominated by aboriginal culture, fewer non-aboriginal objects and sites receive protection than aboriginal objects and sites. The Act provides a shield, in the guise of the permit process, against the destruction or alteration of heritage property. When one considers the relative protection afforded aboriginal and non-aboriginal heritage objects, the treatment received by both groups is the same, and indeed is more favourable, in one sense to aboriginal peoples.

In any case, it should be remembered that the Act cannot apply to any aboriginal heritage object or site which is the subject of an established aboriginal right or title, by operation of s. 35(1) of the *Constitution Act, 1982* and by operation of s. 8 of the *Heritage Conservation Act* (and, by implication, s. 12(7) of that Act which states that a permit does not grant a right to alter or remove an object without the consent of the party which has title to the object or site on which the object is situated). The Act is tailored, whether by design or by operation of constitutional law, to not affect the established rights of aboriginal peoples, a protection that is not extended to any other group. On the whole, then, I am of the opinion that ss. 12(2)(*a*) and 13(2)(*c*) and (*d*) of the Act are valid provincial law and that they do not single out aboriginal peoples or impair their status or condition as Indians.

It should be noted that the Attorney General of Canada intervened in support of British Columbia in this case. Dickson C.J. in *OPSEU v. Ontario (Attorney General)*, [1987] 2 S.C.R. 2, at pp. 19-20, commented on the significance of such an intervention in constitutional litigation with respect to the distribution of legislative powers.

> I think it is important to note, and attach some significance to, not only the similar federal legislation but also the fact that the federal government intervened in this appeal to support the Ontario law. The distribution of powers provisions contained in the Constitution Act, 1867 do not have as their exclusive addressees the federal and provincial governments. They set boundaries that are of interest to, and can be relied upon by, all Canadians. Accordingly, the fact of federal-provincial agreement on a particular boundary between their jurisdictions is not conclusive of the demarcation of that boundary. Nevertheless, in my opinion the Court should be particularly cautious about invalidating a provincial law when the federal government does not contest its validity or, as in this case, actually intervenes to support it and has enacted legislation based on the same constitutional approach adopted by Ontario. [Emphasis deleted.]

That is essentially the situation in this case: the Attorney General of Canada has intervened in support of the view of the British Columbia government with respect to the latter's right to legislate in this area. While this is not determinative of the issue, as Dickson C.J. said, it does invite the Court to exercise caution before it finds that the impugned provisions of the Act are *ultra vires* the province.

J. *Paramountcy and Federal Powers*

The doctrine of paramountcy does not appear applicable in this case, as no valid federal legislation occupies the same field. There are provisions in the *Indian Act* with respect to aboriginal heritage conservation, but they are confined to objects on reserve lands. As I noted above, the *Heritage Conservation Act* does not apply to aboriginal heritage objects or sites which are the subject of an established aboriginal right or title by virtue both of s. 35(1) of the *Constitution Act, 1982* and s. 8 of the Act itself, which is declaratory of that fact. In any case, the CMTs in question in this case are not located on an Indian reserve but on Crown land.

I thus find that there is no intrusion on a federal head of power. It has not been established that these provisions affect the essential and distinctive core values of Indianness which would engage the federal power over native affairs and First Nations in Canada. They are part of a valid provincial legislative scheme. The legislature has made them a closely integrated part of this scheme. The provisions now protect native interests in situations where, before, land owners and business undertakings might have disregarded them, absent evidence of a constitutional right.

The Act purports to give the provincial government a means of protecting heritage objects while retaining the ability to make exceptions where economic development or other values outweigh the heritage value of the objects. In the British Columbia context, this generally means that the provincial government must balance the need to exploit the province's natural resources, particularly its rich abundance of lumber, in order to maintain a viable economy that can sustain the province's population, with the need to preserve all types of cultural and historical heritage objects and sites within the province. Given the overwhelming prevalence of aboriginal heritage objects in the province and, in this particular case, the ubiquitous nature of CMTs, legislation which sought to permit the striking of this balance but which did not attempt to extend this to aboriginal heritage objects and sites would inevitably fall very far short of its goal, if in fact it would not in most respects gut the purposes of the *Act*.

Given this conclusion, it will not be useful to discuss the doctrine of interjurisdictional immunity. It would apply only if the provincial legislation went to the core of the federal power. … In these circumstances, no discussion of the principle governing the application of s. 88 of the *Indian Act* would be warranted.

VII. Conclusion and Disposition

Heritage properties and sites may certainly, in some cases, turn out to be a key part of the collective identity of people. In some future case, it might very well happen that some component of the cultural heritage of a First Nation would go to the core of its identity in such a way that it would affect the federal power over native affairs and the applicability of provincial legislation. This appeal does not raise such issues, based on the weak evidentiary record and the relevant principles governing the division of powers in Canada. In the circumstances of this case, the overall effect of the provision is to improve the protection of native cultural heritage and, indeed, to safeguard the presence and the memory of the cultural objects involved in this litigation, without jeopardizing the core values defining the identity of the appellants as Indians. For these reasons, I would dismiss the appeal, without costs. The constitutional questions should be answered as follows:

1. Is s. 12(2)(*a*) in respect of the subject matter of s. 13(2)(*c*) and (*d*) of the *Heritage Conservation Act* in pith and substance law in relation to Indians or Lands reserved for the Indians, or alternatively, is the law in relation to property, and, therefore, within the exclusive legislative competence of the Province under s. 92(13) of the *Constitution Act, 1867*?

Answer: Section 12(2)(*a*) in respect of the subject matter in s. 13(2)(*c*) and (*d*) of the *Heritage Conservation Act* is in pith and substance law within the legislative competence of the Province under s. 92(13) of the *Constitution Act, 1867*.

2. If the impugned provisions of the *Heritage Conservation Act* are within provincial jurisdiction under s. 92(13) of the *Constitution Act, 1867* do they apply to the subject matter of s. 13(2)(*c*) and (*d*) of the *Heritage Conservation Act*?

Answer: Yes.

3. If the impugned provisions do not apply to the appellants *ex proprio vigore*, do they nonetheless apply by virtue of s. 88 of the *Indian Act*?

Answer: No need to answer.

Appeal dismissed.

D. ABROGATING OR DEROGATING FROM ABORIGINAL AND TREATY RIGHTS

Section 88 is not the only controversial enactment or activity engaged in by the federal government that has significantly affected Aboriginal peoples. In 1916, Great Britain (on behalf of Canada) entered into a convention with the United States to protect migratory birds. The *Migratory Birds Convention Act, 1917*, S.C. 1917, c. 18 [now R.S.C. 1994, c. 22] implemented the convention into Canadian domestic law. Under the convention, the ability to hunt migratory birds was restricted, with limited exceptions being made for hunting by Aboriginal peoples. When Treaty No. 11 was signed in 1921, the Aboriginal signatories were assured that their rights to hunt would be protected. No mention was made about the effect, if any, of the Migratory Birds Convention on those rights. This issue came to a head in the case of *R. v. Sikyea*, below, when a charge was laid against a Treaty No. 11 Indian who had shot a migratory bird out of season.

R. v. SIKYEA

(1964), 43 D.L.R. (2d) 150, 43 C.R. 83, 46 W.W.R. 65, [1964] 2 C.C.C. 325
(N.W.T. C.A.), aff'd. [1964] S.C.R. 642, 44 C.R. 266, 49 W.W.R. 306,
[1965] 2 C.C.C. 129, 50 D.L.R. (2d) 80

The judgment of the Court was delivered by

Johnson J.A.: — The respondent in this case was convicted by a Magistrate at Yellowknife upon a charge of unlawfully killing a migratory bird in an area described in Schedule A, Part XI, of the *Migratory Bird Regulations* P.C. 1958 1070, SOR/58-308, at a time not during an open season for that bird in the area, in violation of s. 5(1)(a) of the *Migratory Bird Regulations*. He was fined $10 and costs.

. . . . .

The respondent is an Indian and a member of Band Number 84 under Treaty 11. ... [H]e was on his way out to the bush to see if he was able to do his customary work. He had taken his tent, gun and muskrat traps and was planning to trap muskrats. He expected to be away two or three weeks. He had taken no food, expecting to shoot game. He shot this duck for food.

The right of Indians to hunt and fish for food on unoccupied Crown lands has always been recognized in Canada — in the early days as an incident of their "ownership" of the land, and later by the treaties by which the Indians gave up their ownership right in these lands.

. . . . .

It was not until 1921 that the Indian rights in that part of the Northwest Territories that includes Yellowknife were surrendered by Treaty 11. As part of the consideration for surrendering their interest in the lands covered by the treaty, the Indians received the following covenant:

> And his Majesty the King hereby agrees with the said Indians that they shall have the right to pursue their usual vocations of hunting, trapping and fishing throughout the tract surrendered as heretofore described, subject to such regulations as may from time to time be made by the Government of the Country acting under the authority of His Majesty, and saving and excepting such tracts as may be required or taken up from time to time for settlement, mining, lumbering, trading or other purposes.

. . . . .

... [I]t is, I think, obvious that while the Government hoped that the Indians would ultimately take up the white man's way of life, until they did, they were expected to continue their previous mode of life with only such regulations and restrictions as would assure that a supply of game for their own needs would be maintained. The regulations that "the Government of the Country" were entitled to make under the clause of the treaty which I have quoted, were, I think, limited to this kind of regulation. Certainly the Commissioners who represented the Government at the signing of the treaties so understood it. For example, in the report of the Commissioners who negotiated Treaty 8, this appears:

> Our chief difficulty was the apprehension that the hunting and fishing privileges were to be curtailed. The provision in the treaty under which ammunition and twine is to be furnished went far in the direction of quieting the fears of the Indians, for they admitted that it would be unreasonable to furnish the means of hunting and fishing if laws were to be enacted which would make hunting and fishing so restricted as to render it impossible to make a livelihood by such pursuits. But over and above the provisions, we had to solemnly assure them that only such laws as to hunting and fishing as were in the interests of the Indians and were found necessary in order to protect the fish and fur-bearing animals would be made, and that they would be as free to hunt after the treaty as they would be if they never entered into it.

These Indians, as well as all others, would have been surprised indeed if in the face of such assurances, the clause in their treaty which purported to continue their rights to hunt and fish could be used to restrict their right to shoot game birds to one and a half months each year. I agree with the view of McGillivray, J.A., in the *Wesley* case where he says [p. 789 D.L.R., p. 284 C.C.C., p. 45 A.L.R.]:

> It is true that Government regulations in respect of hunting are contemplated in the Treaty but considering that Treaty in its proper setting I do not think that any of the makers of it could by any stretch of the imagination be deemed to have contemplated a day when the Indians would be deprived of an unfettered right to hunt game of all kinds for food on unoccupied Crown land.

Discussing the nature of the rights which the Indians obtained under the treaties, Lord Watson, speaking for the Judicial Committee in *A-G. Can. v. A.-G. Ont., A-G. Que. v. A-G. Ont.*, [1897] A. C. 199 at p. 213, said:

> Their Lordships have had no difficulty in coming to the conclusion that, under the treaties, the Indians obtained no right to their annuities, whether original or augmented, beyond a promise and agreement, which was nothing more than a personal obligation by its governor, as representing the old province, that the latter should pay the annuities as and when they became due. ...

While this refers only to the annuities payable under the treaties, it is difficult to see that the other covenants in the treaties, including the one we are here concerned with, can stand on any higher footing. It is always to be kept in mind that the Indians surrendered their rights in the territory in exchange for these promises. This "promise and agreement", like any other, can, of course, be breached, and there is no law of which I am aware that would prevent Parliament by legislation, properly within s. 91 of the *B.N.A. Act*, from doing so.

The Government in dealing with the Indians, has, on the whole, treated its obligations under these treaties seriously. This was probably not always the case if we may judge from the remarks of John Beverley Robinson, Attorney-General for Upper Canada, in 1824, as quoted in *Sero v. Gault* (1921), 64 D.L.R. 327 at p. 330, 50 O.L.R. 27 at pp. 31-2:

> To talk of treaties with the Mohawk Indians, residing in the heart of one of the most populous districts of Upper Canada, upon lands purchased for them and given to them by the British Government, is much the same, in my humble opinion, as to talk of making a treaty of alliance with the Jews in Duke street or with the French emigrants who have settled in England: Canadian Archives, Q. 337, pt. II., pp. 367, 368.

In refreshing contrast is a speech of Lieutenant-Governor Morris to the Indians during the negotiation of the Qu'Appelle Treaty as reported in his book [*The Treaties of Canada with the Indians of Manitoba and the North-West Territories* (Toronto: Belfords, Clarke, 1880) at 96]:

> Therefore, the promises we have to make to you are not for today only but for to-morrow, not only for you but for your children born and unborn, and the promise we make will be carried out as long as the sun shines above and the water flows in the ocean.

It is interesting to note that when the Government of Canada transferred the natural resources within the Province of Alberta to that Province in 1930 [*Alberta Natural Resources Act*, 1930 (Alta.), c. 21], the agreement contained the following paragraph:

> 12. In order to secure to the Indians of the Province the continuance of the supply of game and fish for their support and subsistence, Canada agrees that the laws respecting game in force in the Province from time to time shall apply to the Indians within the boundaries thereof, provided, however that the said Indians shall have the right, which the Province hereby assures to them, of hunting, trapping, and fishing game and fish for food at all seasons of the year on all unoccupied Crown lands and on any other lands to which the said Indians may have a right of access.

Because of the Government's concern with the Indians' right to pursue "their usual vocations of hunting, trapping and fishing", and that its obligations under the treaties should be performed, it is difficult to understand why these treaties were not kept in mind when the Migratory Birds Convention was negotiated and when its terms were implemented by the *Migratory Birds Convention Act*, R.S.C. 1952, c. 179, and the Regulations made under that Act.

That Convention was entered into by Great Britain (on behalf of Canada), with the United States in August, 1916 and ratified by both Governments in December of that year.

. . . . .

Article I defines the birds covered by the Convention and among the migratory birds are "wild ducks".

. . . . .

[T]he purpose of the Convention was to save migratory birds "from indiscriminate slaughter" and to assure their preservation. This, it seems to me, would have allowed for exceptions or reservations in favour of the Indians, for there can be no doubt that the amount of game birds taken by the Indians for food during the close season would not have resulted in "indiscriminate slaughter" of birds nor would the preservation of those birds have been threatened. We are told that the treaty between the United States and Mexico negotiated in 1936 permits indigent persons in Mexico to take these types of birds for food.

The *Migratory Birds Convention Act*, 1917 (Can.), c. 18, "sanctioned, ratified and confirmed" the Convention.

. . . . .

Section 5(1) and (2) of the present Regulations provides:

> 5(1) Unless otherwise permitted under these Regulations to do so, no person shall

(*a*) in any area described in Schedule A, kill, hunt, capture, injure, take or molest a migratory bird at any time except during an open season specified for that bird and that area in Schedule A, or

(*b*) from any area described in Schedule A, kill, hunt, capture, injure, take or molest a migratory bird at any time in another area described in Schedule A except during an open season specified for that bird and both those areas in Schedule A.

(2) Indians and Eskimos may take auks, auklets, guillemots, murres, puffins and scoters and their eggs at any time for human food or clothing, but they shall not sell or trade or offer to sell or trade birds or eggs so taken and they shall not take such birds or eggs within a bird sanctuary.

The "scoter" mentioned in this section and in the Convention is defined in Murray's New English Dictionary:

Scoter. [Of obscure origin.] A duck of the genus *Oedemia*, esp. *Oedemia nigra*, a native of the Arctic regions and common in the seas of Northern Europe and America. Also *scoter-duck*.

There is no evidence that there are any of these ducks in the Yellowknife area which is several hundred miles from the sea.

The open season under these Regulations for mallard ducks in the Yellowknife area is from September 1st to October 15th.

. . . . .

I have quoted s. 5(1) of the Regulations which says that "no person shall ... kill ... a migratory bird at any time except during an open season ...". It is difficult to see how this language admits of any exceptions. When, however, we find that reference in both the Convention and in the Regulations to what kind of birds an Indian and Eskimo may "take" at any time for food, it is impossible for me to say that the hunting rights of the Indians as to these migratory birds, have not been abrogated, abridged or infringed upon.

It is, I think, clear that the rights given to the Indians by their treaties as they apply to migratory birds have been taken away by this Act and its Regulations. How are we to explain this apparent breach of faith on the part of the Government, for I cannot think it can be described in any other terms? This cannot be described as a minor or insignificant curtailment of these treaty rights, for game birds have always been a most plentiful, a most reliable and a readily obtainable food in large areas of Canada. I cannot believe that the Government of Canada realized that in implementing the Convention they were at the same time breaching the treaties that they had made with the Indians. It is much more likely that these obligations under the treaties were overlooked — a case of the left hand having forgotten what the right hand had done. The subsequent history of the Government's dealing with the Indians would seem to bear this out. When the treaty we are concerned with here was signed in 1921, only five years after the enactment of the *Migratory Birds Convention Act*, we find the Commissioners who negotiated the treaty reporting:

The Indians seemed afraid, for one thing, that their liberty to hunt, trap and fish would be taken away or curtailed, but were assured by me that this would not be the case, and the Government will expect them to support themselves in their own way, and, in fact, that more twine for nets and more ammunition were given under the terms of this treaty than under any of the preceding ones; this went a long way to calm their fears. I also pointed out that any game laws made were to their advantage, and, whether they took treaty or not, they were subject to the laws of the Dominion.

and there is nothing in this report which would indicate that the Indians were told that their right to shoot migratory birds had already been taken away from them. ... It is of some importance that while the Indians in the Northwest Territories continued to shoot ducks at all seasons for food, it is only recently that any attempt has been made to enforce the Act.

I can come to no other conclusion than that the Indians, notwithstanding the rights given to them by their treaties, are prohibited by this Act and its Regulations from shooting migratory birds out of season. Unless one or other of the matters mentioned in the learned trial Judge's reasons for judgment or raised by the respondent's counsel at the hearing of the appeal is a defence to the charge, the appeal must be allowed and the conviction sustained.

. . . . .

In coming to this conclusion, I regret that I cannot share the satisfaction that was expressed by McGillivray, J.A., in *R. v. Wesley*, [1932] 4 D.L.R. at p. 790, 58 C.C.C. at p. 285, 26 A.L.R. at p. 451, when he was writing his judgment dismissing the appeal in that case:

> It is satisfactory to be able to come to this conclusion and not to have to decide that "the Queen's promises" have not been fulfilled. It is satisfactory to think that legislators have not so enacted but that the Indians may still be "convinced of our justice and determined resolution to remove all reasonable cause of discontent."

Appeal allowed.

The *Sikyea* case was appealed to the Supreme Court of Canada, where it was dismissed. In dismissing the appeal, the Court held that Johnson J.A. "dealt with the important issues fully and correctly in their historical and legal settings". The Supreme Court did not address the issue raised by Johnson J.A. as to whether the curtailment of the Treaty No. 11 Indians' hunting rights pursuant to the furtherance of Canada's obligations under the *Migratory Birds Convention* was "a case of the left hand having forgotten what the right hand had done".

As discussed in Chapter 2, and emphasized by Johnson J.A. in *Sikyea*, there was nothing prohibiting the federal government from unilaterally infringing upon treaty rights at that time. Of course, section 35(1) of the *Constitution Act, 1982* would no longer allow such activity. It is open to question, however, whether the Crown's actions documented in *Sikyea* constituted a breach of either its treaty or fiduciary obligations to the Treaty No. 11 Indians, especially in light of Commissioner H.A. Conroy's assurances to them, as documented in the *Sikyea* case (quoted from in Chapter 2, *supra*). Could such an argument be made today?

In the cases of *R. v. Horseman*, [1990] 1 S.C.R. 901 and *R. v. Badger* (1996), 133 D.L.R. (4th) 324 (S.C.C.) excerpted below, similar situations to that in *Sikyea* arose in relation to the Alberta *Natural Resources Transfer Agreement, 1930*, S.C. 1930, c. 3 (hereinafter "NRTA"), which had been expressly referred to by Johnson J.A. in his judgment.

There was not one, but three NRTAs, one for each of Manitoba, Saskatchewan, and Alberta, although their content was the same. The purpose of the NRTAs was to grant those provinces the same administration and control over Crown lands and natural resources existing within their jurisdictional boundaries as that held by other Canadian provinces. The NRTAs were, essentially, re-enactments of s. 109 of the *Constitution Act, 1867* applied to Manitoba, Saskatchewan, and Alberta.

In addition, the NRTAs ensured that land would be made available by those provinces to fulfil the federal Crown's outstanding treaty land entitlements (promises of land made to Aboriginal groups in treaties) — and thus avoid the problem discussed in the Rotman excerpt earlier in this chapter — and provided for the application of provincial game laws to the Aboriginal peoples residing in those provinces. These provisions, taken from the Alberta NRTA, read as follows:

> 10. All lands included in Indian reserves within the Province, including those selected and surveyed but not yet confirmed, as well as those confirmed, shall continue to be vested in the Crown and administered by the Government of Canada for the purposes of Canada, and the Province will from time to time, upon the request of the Superintendent General of Indian Affairs, set aside, out of the unoccupied Crown lands hereby transferred to its administration, such further areas as the said Superintendent General may, in agreement with the appropriate Minister of the Province, select as necessary to enable Canada to fulfil its obligations under the treaties with the Indians of the Province, and such areas shall thereafter be administered by Canada in the same way in all respects as if they had never passed to the Province under the provisions hereof.
>
> . . . . .
>
> 12. In order to secure to the Indians of the Province the continuance of the supply of game and fish for their support and subsistence, Canada agrees that the laws respecting game in force in the Province from time to time shall apply to the Indians within the boundaries thereof, provided however, that the said Indians shall have the right, which the Province hereby assures to them, of hunting, trapping and fishing game and fish for food at all seasons of the year on all unoccupied Crown lands and on any other lands to which the said Indians may have a right of access.

In *Horseman*, the Supreme Court of Canada had to consider the effects of the NRTA on the hunting rights guaranteed by Treaty No. 8, signed in 1899.

R. v. HORSEMAN

[1990] 1 S.C.R. 901, [1990] 4 W.W.R. 97, 73 Alta. L.R. (2d) 193, 55 C.C.C.
(3d) 353, 108 N.R. 1, [1990] 3 C.N.L.R. 95

The judgment of **Lamer, La Forest, Gonthier,** and **Cory JJ.** was delivered by

Cory J.: — At issue on this appeal is whether the provisions of s. 42 and s.
1(*s*) of the *Wildlife Act*, R.S.A. 1980, c. W-9, apply to the appellant, whose
forebears were members of one of the Indian Bands party to Treaty No. 8
signed in 1899 which guaranteed substantive hunting rights to certain Indian people.

Factual Background

The facts are not in dispute and were agreed upon at trial. Mr. Bert
Horseman is an Indian within the meaning of the *Indian Act*, R.S.C. 1970, c.
I-6. He is a descendant of the Indian people who were parties to Treaty
No. 8.

. . . . .

In the spring of 1983 the appellant went moose hunting in the territory
north of his Reserve in order to feed himself and his family. This he was
entitled to do pursuant to the provisions of Treaty No. 8. He was successful in his hunt. He shot a moose, cut it and skinned it. The moose was too
large for the appellant to bring back to the Reserve. He therefore hurried
home to obtain the assistance of other Band members to haul it out of the
bush. When they arrived at the carcass the appellant and his friends were
unpleasantly surprised to find that a grizzly bear had appropriated the
moose. The arrival of the appellant was even more unpleasant and upsetting for the bear, which by this time clearly believed it had acquired a
valid possessory title to the moose. Faced with the conflicting claim, the
bear charged the appellant. Bert Horseman displayed cool courage and
skill under attack. He shot and killed the bear, skinned it and took the
hide.
    ... Horseman did not have a licence under the *Wildlife Act* to hunt grizzly bears or sell their hides. This omission ordinarily could be readily excused for neither the presence of the bear nor its attack could have been
foreseen.
    One year later, in the spring of 1984, the appellant found himself in the
unfortunate position of being out of work and in need of money to support
his family. In these straitened circumstances he decided to sell the grizzly
hide. On or about April 19th he applied for and was issued a grizzly bear
licence under s. 18 of the *Wildlife Act*. This licence entitled him to hunt and
kill one bear and sell the hide to a licensed dealer as provided by the
regulations passed pursuant to that Act. The appellant made use of this
licence to sell the hide of his adversary of the year before to a licensed
dealer for a price of $200. This isolated sale, which was clearly not part of
any organized commercial transaction, took place between April 19th and
May 22nd.

There can be no doubt of the financial needs of the appellant nor of his good faith. He certainly made efforts to stay within the spirit of the law. Nevertheless, an information was laid against him in July of 1984 charging him with trafficking in wildlife.

. . . . .

The sole defence raised on behalf of Horseman was that the *Wildlife Act* did not apply to him and that he was within his Treaty 8 rights when he sold the bear hide. Nothing is to turn on the killing of the bear in self-defence. Nor is it argued that Horseman was induced into a mistake of the law by the words of an official of the Government. Rather, it is the appellant's position that he can, at any time, on Crown lands or on lands to which Indians have access, kill a grizzly bear for food. Further, it is said that he can sell the hide of any grizzly bear he kills in order to buy food.

. . . . .

Applicable Legislation

Treaty No. 8, 1899:

> And Her Majesty the Queen HEREBY AGREES with the said Indians that they shall have right to pursue their usual vocations of hunting, trapping and fishing throughout the tract surrendered as heretofore described, subject to such regulations as may from time to time be made by the Government of the country, acting under the authority of Her Majesty, and saving and excepting such tracts as may be required or taken up from time to time for settlement, mining, lumbering, trading or other purposes.

Constitution Act, 1930:

> **1.** The agreements set out in the Schedule to this Act are hereby confirmed and shall have the force of law notwithstanding anything in the Constitution Act, 1867, or any Act amending the same, or any Act of the Parliament of Canada, or in any Order in Council or terms or conditions of union made or approved under any such Act as aforesaid.

Natural Resources Transfer Agreement, 1930 (Alberta):

> **12** In order to secure to the Indians of the Province the continuance of the supply of game and fish for their support and subsistence, Canada agrees that the laws respecting game in force in the Province from time to time shall apply to the Indians within the boundaries thereof, provided, however, that the said Indians shall have the right, which the Province hereby assures to them, of hunting, trapping and fishing game and fish for food at all seasons of the year on all unoccupied Crown lands and on any other lands to which the said Indians may have a right of access.

Wildlife Act, R.S.A. 1980, c. W-9:

> **42** No person shall traffic in any wildlife except as is expressly permitted by this Act or by the regulations.

1...

(s) "traffic" means any single act of selling, offering for sale, buying, bartering, soliciting or trading;

Treaty and Hunting Rights

An examination of the historical background leading to the negotiations for Treaty No. 8 and the other numbered treaties leads inevitably to the conclusion that the hunting rights reserved by the Treaty included hunting for commercial purposes. ... It can be seen that the Indians ceded title to the Treaty 8 lands on the condition that they could reserve exclusively to themselves "their usual vocations of hunting, trapping and fishing throughout the tracts surrendered".

The economy of the Indian population at the time of the Treaty had clearly evolved to such a degree that hunting and fishing for commercial purposes was an integral part of their way of life. In his *Commentary on Economic History of Treaty 8 Area* (unpublished; June 13, 1985), Professor Ray notes:

> [C]ommercial provision hunting was an important aspect of the commercial hunting economy of the region from the onset of the fur trade in the late 18th century. However, no data exists that makes it possible to determine what proportion of the native hunt was intended to obtain provisions for domestic use as opposed to exchange.
>
> Furthermore, in terms of economic history, I am not sure any attempts to make such distinctions would be very meaningful in that Indians often killed animals, such as beaver, primarily to obtain pelts for trade. However, the Indians consumed beaver meat and in many areas it was an important component of the diet. Conversely, moose, caribou and wood buffalo were killed in order to obtain meat for consumption and for trade. Similarly, the hides of these animals were used by Indians and they were traded. For these reasons, differentiating domestic hunting from commercial hunting is unrealistic and does not enable one to fully appreciate the complex nature of the native economy following contact.

The report of the Commissioners who negotiated Treaty No. 8 on behalf of the government of Canada lends further support to this conclusion [see the Treaty No. 8 Commissioners' Report in Chapter 2.]

. . . . .

I am in complete agreement with the finding of the trial judge that the original Treaty right clearly included hunting for purposes of commerce. The next question that must be resolved is whether or not that right was in any way limited or affected by the Transfer Agreement of 1930.

The Effect of the 1930 Transfer Agreement

At the outset two established principles must be borne in mind. First, the onus of proving either express or implicit extinguishment lies upon the Crown. See *Simon v. The Queen*, [1985] 2 S.C.R. 387; *Calder v. Attorney-General of British Columbia*, [1973] S.C.R. 313. Secondly, any ambiguities in the wording of the Treaty or document must be resolved in favour of the Native people.

. . . . .

The appellant argues that the Transfer Agreement of 1930 was not signed by the Indians. Since they were not a party to it, they could not have agreed to any restriction of their hunting and fishing rights and that these rights could not have been lost as a result of the operation of what has been called the "merger and consolidation" theory.

The Crown on the other hand states that it is clear from the wording of para. 12 itself that the hunting rights were limited by the Agreement.

. . . . .

The Crown argues that the rights granted to the Indians by the Treaty of 1899 were "merged and consolidated" in the 1930 Transfer Agreement.

. . . . .

The merger and consolidation theory was first put forward by McNiven J.A. in *R. v. Strongquill* (1953), 8 W.W.R. (N.S.) 247 (Sask. C.A.).

. . . . .

In later decisions Dickson J., as he then was, adopted this approach. It was his view that the Transfer Agreement operated so as to cut down the scope of Indian hunting rights. In *Frank v. The Queen, supra,* at p. 100, he commented:

> It would appear that the overall purpose of the para. 12 of the Natural Resources Transfer Agreement was to effect a merger and consolidation of the treaty rights theretofore enjoyed by the Indians but of equal importance was the desire to re-state and reassure to the treaty Indians the continued enjoyment of the right to hunt and fish for food.

. . . . .

The appellant contends that these authorities should not be followed. The position is three-fold. Firstly, it is argued that when it is looked at in its historical context, the 1930 Transfer Agreement was meant to protect the rights of Indians and not to derogate from those rights. Secondly, and most importantly, it is contended that the traditional hunting rights granted to Indians by Treaty No. 8 could not be reduced or abridged in any way without some form of approval and consent given by the Indians, the parties most affected by the derogation, and without some form of compensation or *quid pro quo* for the reduction in the hunting rights. Thirdly, it is said that on policy grounds the Crown should not undertake to unilaterally change and derogate the Treaty rights granted earlier. To permit such a course of action could only lead to the dishonour of the Crown. It is argued that there rests upon the Crown an obligation to uphold the original Native interests protected by the Treaty. That is to say, the Crown should be looked upon as a trustee of the Native hunting rights.

· · · · ·

It is ... clear that the Transfer Agreements were meant to modify the division of powers originally set out in the *Constitution Act, 1867* (formerly the *British North America Act, 1867*). Section 1 of the *Constitution Act, 1930* is unambiguous in this regard: "The agreements ... shall have the force of law notwithstanding anything in the *Constitution Act, 1867* ...".

In addition, there was in fact a *quid pro quo* granted by the Crown for the reduction in the hunting right. Although the Agreement did take away the right to hunt commercially, the nature of the right to hunt for food was substantially enlarged. The geographical areas in which the Indian people could hunt was widely extended. Further, the means employed by them in hunting for their food was placed beyond the reach of provincial governments. For example, they may hunt deer with night lights and with dogs, methods which are or may be prohibited for others. Nor are the Indians subject to seasonal limitations as are all other hunters. ... Indians are [also] not limited with regard to the type of game they may kill. ... It can be seen that the *quid pro quo* was substantial. Both the area of hunting and the way in which the hunting could be conducted was extended and removed from the jurisdiction of provincial governments.

· · · · ·

It is thus apparent that although the Transfer Agreement modified the Treaty rights as to hunting, there was a very real *quid pro quo* which extended the Native rights to hunt for food. In addition, although it might well be politically and morally unacceptable in today's climate to take such a step as that set out in the 1930 Agreement without consultation with and concurrence of the Native peoples affected, nonetheless the power of the Federal Government to unilaterally make such a modification is unquestioned and has not been challenged in this case.

· · · · ·

[A]t the time the Treaty was made only the Federal Government had jurisdiction over the territory affected and it was the only contemplated "government of the country". The Transfer Agreement of 1930 changed the governmental authority which might regulate aspects of hunting in the interests of conservation. This change of governmental authority did not contradict the spirit of the original Agreement as evidenced by federal and provincial regulations in effect at the time. Even in 1899 conservation was a matter of concern for the governmental authority.

... [T]he hunting rights granted by the 1899 Treaty were not unlimited. Rather they were subject to governmental regulation. The 1930 Agreement widened the hunting territory and the means by which the Indians could hunt for food thus providing a real *quid pro quo* for the reduction in the right to hunt for purposes of commerce granted by the Treaty of 1899. The right of the Federal Government to act unilaterally in that manner is unquestioned. I therefore conclude that the 1930 Transfer Agreement did alter the nature of the hunting rights originally guaranteed by Treaty No. 8.

Section 42 of the Wildlife Act

At the outset it must be recognized that the *Wildlife Act* is a provincial law of general application affecting Indians not *qua* Indians but rather as inhabitants of the Province. It follows that the Act can be applicable to Indians pursuant to the provisions of s. 88 of the *Indian Act* so long as it does not conflict with a treaty right. ... The courts below correctly found that the sale of the bear hide constituted a hunting activity that had ceased to be that of hunting "for food" but rather was an act of commerce. As a result it was no longer a right protected by Treaty No. 8, as amended by the 1930 Transfer Agreement. Thus the application of s. 42 to Indians who are hunting for commercial purposes is not precluded by s. 88 of the *Indian Act*.

The fact that a grizzly bear was killed by the appellant in self-defence must engender admiration and sympathy, but it is unfortunately not relevant to a consideration of whether there has been a breach of s. 42 of the *Wildlife Act*. ... [T]he prohibition against trafficking in bear hides without a licence cannot admit of any exceptions.

Neither, regrettably, can it be relevant to the breach of s. 42 that the appellant in fact obtained a grizzly bear hunting permit after he was in the possession of a bear hide. The granting of a permit does not bring a hunter any guarantee of success but only an opportunity to legitimately slay a bear. The evidence presented at trial indicated that the limitations placed upon obtaining a licence and the limited chance of success in a bear hunt resulted in the success rate of between 2 and 4 per cent of the licence holder. This must be an important factor in the management of the bear population. Wildlife administrators must be able to rely on the success ratio and proceed on the assumption that those applying for a permit have not already shot a bear. The success ratio will determine the number of licences issued in any year. The whole management scheme which is essential to the survival of the grizzly bear would be undermined if a licence were granted to an applicant who had already completed a successful hunt.

As well, s. 42 of the *Wildlife Act* is consistent with the very spirit of Treaty No. 8, which specified that the right to hunt would still be subject to government regulations. The evidence indicates that there remain only 575 grizzly bears on provincial lands. ... Trafficking in bear hides, other than pursuant to the provisions of the *Wildlife Act*, threatens the very existence of the grizzly bear. The bear may snarl defiance and even occasionally launch a desperate attack upon man, but until such time as it masters the operation of firearms, it cannot triumph and must rely on man for protection and indeed for survival. That protection is provided by the *Wildlife Act*, but if it is to succeed it must be strictly enforced.

Section 42 of the *Wildlife Act* is valid legislation enacted by the government with jurisdiction in the field. It reflects a *bona fide* concern for the preservation of a species. It is a law of general application which does not infringe upon the Treaty 8 hunting rights of Indians as limited by the 1930 Transfer Agreement.

Disposition

In the result, I would dismiss the appeal. The constitutional question posed should be answered as follows:

Question:

Between February 1, 1984 and May 30, 1984, was s. 42 of the *Wildlife Act*, R.S.A. 1980, c. W-9, constitutionally applicable to Treaty 8 Indians in virtue of the hunting rights granted to them under the said Treaty? In particular, were the hunting rights granted by Treaty No. 8 of 1899 extinguished, reduced or modified by para. 12 of the Alberta Natural Resources Transfer Agreement, as confirmed by the *Constitution Act, 1930*?

Answer:

The answer to both queries framed in the Question should be in the affirmative.

The *Wildlife Act* applied to the appellant and Horseman is guilty of violating s. 42 of the Act. Nonetheless he did not seek out the bear and shot it only in self-defence. The trial judge found that he acted in good faith when he obtained the licence to hunt bear. He was in financial difficulties when he sold the bear hide in an isolated transaction. He has provided the means whereby the application of the *Wildlife Act* to Indians was explored. If it were not for statutory requirement of a minimum fine, in the unique circumstances of the case, I would vary the sentence by waiving the payment of the minimum fine. Nevertheless, in light of the circumstances of the case, and the time that has elapsed, I would order a stay of proceedings.

The reasons of **Dickson C.J.** and **Wilson** and **L'Heureux-Dubé JJ.** were delivered by

Wilson J. (dissenting): — I have had the advantage of reading the reasons of my colleague Justice Cory and must respectfully disagree with his conclusion that the appellant's conduct is caught by s. 42 of the *Wildlife Act*, R.S.A. 1980, c. W-9.

... I believe it is important to emphasize that all parties were agreed and the trial judge so found that Mr. Horseman was legitimately engaged in hunting moose for his own use in the Treaty 8 area when he killed the bear in self-defence. Mr. Horseman did not kill the bear with a view to selling its hide although he was eventually driven to do so a year later in order to feed himself and his family. The sale of the bear hide was an isolated act and not part of any planned commercial activity. None of this is in dispute.

The narrow question before us in this appeal then is whether the isolated sale for food of a bear hide obtained by the appellant fortuitously as the result of an act of self-defence is something that the government of Alberta is entitled to penalize under the *Wildlife Act*. In my view, the answer to this question requires a careful examination of the terms of Treaty No. 8 and the wording of para. 12 of the Natural Resources Transfer Agreement, 1930 (Alberta) (the "Transfer Agreement").

Interpreting Indian Treaties

This Court has already established a number of important guidelines for the interpretation of Indian treaties. [The discussion of treaty interpretation is omitted; see the discussion of treaty interpretation in Chapter 2]

. . . . .

Any assessment of the impact of the Transfer Agreement on the rights that Treaty 8 Indians were assured in the treaty would continue to be protected cannot ignore the fact that Treaty No. 8 embodied a "solemn engagement". Accordingly, when interpreting the Transfer Agreement between the federal and provincial governments we must keep in mind the solemn commitment made to the Treaty 8 Indians by the federal government in 1899. We should not readily assume that the federal government intended to renege on the commitment it had made. Rather we should give it an interpretation, if this is possible on the language, which will implement and be fully consistent with that commitment.

. . . . .

Treaty No. 8 and Indian Hunting Rights

In his *Commentary on Economic History of Treaty 8* Area (unpublished; June 13, 1985, at p. 8), Professor Ray warns of the dangers involved in trying to understand the hunting practices of Indians in the Treaty 8 area by drawing neat distinctions between hunting for domestic use and hunting for commercial purposes. ... They hunted beaver, moose, caribou and wood buffalo with a view to consuming some portions of their catch and exchanging other portions. "For these reasons, differentiating domestic hunting from commercial hunting is unrealistic and does not enable one to fully appreciate the complex nature of the native economy following contact" (p. 9).

. . . . .

In my view, it is important to bear in mind this picture of the Treaty 8 Indians' way of life prior to 1899 when considering the context in which they consented to Treaty No. 8.

. . . . .

[T]he Indians were especially concerned that the most important aspect of their way of life, their ability to hunt and fish, not be interfered with. ...

[T]he Commissioners repeatedly sought to assure the Indians that they would continue to be free to pursue these activities as they always had. [See the Treaty No. 8 Commissioners' Report in Chapter 2.] ...

. . . . .

Interviews with Indian elders of the Lesser Slave Lake area confirm the archival evidence with respect to the critical role played by the promise with respect to hunting and fishing rights. James Cornwall, who was present at the treaty negotiations at Lesser Slave Lake, signed an affidavit in 1937 ... in which he stated:

> Much stress was laid on one point by the Indians, as follows: They would not sign under any circumstances, unless their right to hunt, trap and fish was guaranteed and it must be understood that these rights they would never surrender.

More recent interviews with William Okeymaw of the Sucker Creek Reserve and Felix Gobot of Fort Chipewyan confirm that the treaty was to "be in effect as long as the sun shines and the rivers flow" (see: p. 151 of Peter O'Chiese *et al.*, "Interviews with Elders", in *The Spirit of the Alberta Indian Treaties* ... at pp. 113-60). Lynn Hickey, Richard L. Lightning and Gordon Lee, who have conducted numerous interviews with elders in the Treaty 8 area, summarize the result of their findings as follows, in "T.A.R.R. Interview with Elders Program", in *The Spirit of the Alberta Indian Treaties*, pp. 103-12 (at p. 106):

> It is agreed that the treaty involved surrendering land, though a few people express this as an agreement to share land or surrender the surface only. Land is the only thing that was given up, however. *The main discussion of the treaty by most elders concerns hunting, fishing, and trapping and how rights to pursue their traditional livelihood were not given up and were even strongly guaranteed in the treaty to last forever. Giving up the land would not interfere with the Indian's pursuit of his livelihood, and the Indians only signed the treaty on this condition.* [Emphasis added.]

While one must obviously be sensitive to the fact that contemporary oral evidence of the meaning of provisions of Treaty No. 8 will not necessarily capture the understanding of the treaty that the Indians had in 1899, in my view such evidence is relevant where it confirms the archival evidence with respect to the meaning of the treaty. Indeed, it seems to me to be of particular significance that the Treaty 8 Commissioners, historians who have studied Treaty No. 8, and Treaty 8 Indians of several different generations unanimously affirm that the government of Canada's promise that hunting, fishing and trapping rights would be protected forever was the *sine qua non* for obtaining the Indians' agreement to enter into Treaty No. 8. Hunting, fishing and trapping lay at the centre of their way of life. Provided that the source of their livelihood was protected, the Indians were prepared to allow the government of Canada to "have title" to the land in the Treaty 8 area.

In my view, it is in light of this historical context, one which did not, from the Indians' perspective, allow for simple distinctions between hunting for domestic use and hunting for commercial purposes and which involved a solemn engagement that Indians would continue to have un-limited access to wildlife, that one must understand the provision in Treaty No. 8 [which is reproduced in **Cory J.**'s judgment.]

. . . . .

If we are to remain faithful to the interpretive principles set out in *Nowegijick* and *Simon*, then we must not only be careful to understand that the language of Treaty No. 8 embodied a solemn engagement to Indians in the Treaty 8 area that their livelihood would be respected, but we must also recognize that in referring to potential "regulations" with respect to hunting, trapping and fishing the government of Canada was promising that such regulations would always be designed so as to ensure that the Indians' way of life would continue to be respected. To read Treaty No. 8 as an agreement that was to enable the government of Canada to regulate hunting, fishing and trapping in any manner that it saw fit, regardless of the impact of the regulations on the "usual vocations" of Treaty 8 Indians, is not credible in light of oral and archival evidence that includes a Commissioners' report stating that a solemn assurance was made that only such laws "as were in the interest of the Indians and were found necessary in order to protect the fish and fur-bearing animals would be made".

. . . . .

Natural Resources Transfer Agreement

. . . . .

The proposition that para. 12 of the Transfer Agreement was formulated with a view to protecting Treaty 8 rights and that it is therefore quite proper to look at Treaty No. 8 in order to understand the meaning of para. 12 of the Transfer Agreement has been emphasized on a number of occasions. [A discussion of cases is omitted.]

. . . . .

[T]o the extent that it is possible, one should view para. 12 of the Transfer Agreement as an attempt to respect the solemn engagement embodied in Treaty No. 8, not as an attempt to abrogate or derogate from that treaty. While it is clear that para. 12 of the Transfer Agreement adjusted the areas within which Treaty 8 Indians would thereafter be able to engage in their traditional way of life, given the oral and archival evidence with respect to the negotiation of Treaty No. 8 and the pivotal nature of the guarantee concerning hunting, fishing and trapping, one should be extremely hesi-tant about accepting the proposition that para. 12 of the Transfer Agree-ment was also designed to place serious and invidious restrictions on the range of hunting, fishing and trapping related activities that Treaty 8 Indi-ans could continue to engage in. In so saying I am fully aware that this Court has stated on previous occasions that it is not in a position to ques-tion an unambiguous decision on the part of the federal government to modify its treaty obligations: *Sikyea v. The Queen*, [1964] S.C.R. 642, *R. v. George*, [1966] S.C.R. 267, and *Moosehunter v. The Queen*, [1981] 1 S.C.R. 282, at p. 293. We must, however, be satisfied that the federal government did make an "unambiguous decision" to renege on its Treaty 8 obligations when it signed the 1930 Transfer Agreement.

The respondent in this appeal has not pointed to any historical evidence in support of its claim that para. 12 of the Transfer Agreement was intended to limit the Indians' traditional right to hunt and fish (which included a right of exchange) to one confined to hunting and fishing for personal consumption only. Absent such evidence, and in view of the implications of bad faith on the part of the federal government which would arise from it, I am not prepared to accept that this was the legislature's intent.

. . . . .

[T]he respondent argues that the use of the words "for food" in para. 12 of the Transfer Agreement ... demonstrate ... an intention on the part of the legislature to place substantial limits on the range of hunting related activities that Treaty 8 Indians can pursue free from provincial regulation. The respondent submits that Treaty 8 Indians can only derive protection from para. 12 if the purpose for which they are hunting is to feed themselves or their families and that because Mr. Horseman did not kill the bear with this purpose in mind his act falls outside the ambit of para. 12.

... I am of the view that this Court's previous decisions with respect to the language of para. 12 (and its equivalent in other Transfer Agreements) do not require the Court to construe the term "for food" in such a narrow and restricted manner. Given that Treaty No. 8 embodied a solemn engagement on the part of the government of Canada to respect a way of life that was built around hunting, fishing and trapping [and] given that our courts have on a number of occasions emphasized that we should seek to give meaning to the language used in para. 12 by looking to Treaty No. 8 ... it seems to me that we should be very reluctant to accept any reading of the term "for food" that would constitute a profound inroad into the ability of Treaty 8 Indians to engage in the traditional way of life which they believed had been secured to them by the treaty.

. . . . .

[I]f we are to give para. 12 the "broad and liberal" construction ... that reflects the principle enunciated in *Nowegijick* and *Simon* that statutes relating to Indians must be given a "fair, large and liberal construction", then we should be prepared to accept that the range of activity encompassed by the term "for food" extends to hunting for "support and subsistence", i.e. hunting not only for direct consumption but also hunting in order to exchange the product of the hunt for other items as was their wont, as opposed to purely commercial or sport hunting.

... The whole emphasis of Treaty No. 8 was on the preservation of the Indian's traditional way of life. But this surely did not mean that the Indians were to be forever consigned to a diet of meat and fish and were to have no opportunity to share in the advances of modern civilization over the next one hundred years. Of course, the Indians' hunting and fishing rights were to be preserved and protected ... [b]ut this cannot mean that in 1990 they are to be precluded from selling their meat and fish to buy other items necessary for their sustenance and the sustenance of their children. Provided the purpose of their hunting is either to consume the meat or to exchange or sell it in order to support themselves and their families, I fail to see why this is precluded by any common sense interpretation of the words "for food". It will, of course, be a question of fact in each case whether a sale is made for purposes of sustenance or for purely commercial profit.

. . . . .

When the phrase "for food" is read in this way para. 12 of the Transfer Agreement remains faithful to the Treaty 8 Commissioners' solemn engagement that the government of Canada would only enact "such laws as to hunting as were in the interest of the Indians and were found necessary in order to protect the fish and fur-bearing animals" and that Treaty 8 Indians "would be free to hunt and fish after the treaty as they would be if they never entered into it". ... What is not consistent with the spirit and language of Treaty No. 8 is to restrict the ability of the Indians to hunt for "support and subsistence" unless this restriction also is required for the preservation of species threatened with extinction.

. . . . .

I have difficulty in accepting my colleague's conclusion that the Transfer Agreement involved some sort of expansion of these hunting rights. Moreover, it seems to me somewhat disingenuous to attempt to justify any unilateral "cutting down of hunting rights" by the use of terminology connoting a reciprocal process in which contracting parties engage in a mutual exchange of promises. Be that as it may, I see no evidence at all that the federal government intended to renege in any way from the solemn engagement embodied in Treaty No. 8.

The Case at Bar

The learned trial judge found as a fact that the appellant killed the bear in self-defence and not with a view to selling, exchanging or bartering its hide. It is difficult therefore to describe Mr. Horseman's act as hunting for commerce or sport. Indeed, it is difficult to describe Mr. Horseman's act as "hunting" at all. It would be passing strange if the government of Canada in enacting the Transfer Agreement of 1930 intended to put Treaty 8 Indians in the absurd position of being penalized for defending themselves against attack by wild animals. ...

Section 42 of the *Wildlife Act* states that "no person shall traffic in any wildlife except as is expressly permitted by this Act or by the regulations". I have already suggested that while the federal government may have the power to regulate trafficking in wildlife provided that such regulation is in the interest of the Indians, the provincial government has no power to regulate Indian practices that fall within the Indians' traditional way of life and that are linked to their support and subsistence. In so far as Treaty 8 Indians are concerned, the government of Alberta is limited to regulation of purely commercial and sport hunting.

... While the province may be able to limit the Indians' right to traffic in hides where such trafficking forms part of a commercial venture or is the result of sport hunting, it does not, in my view, have the power to regulate an isolated sale that is the result of an act of self-defence. All the more so when the hide was sold by Mr. Horseman, as the trial judge found on the facts, not for commercial profit but to buy food for his family.

I would allow the appeal, set aside the order of the Court of Appeal, and restore the acquittal. I would answer the constitutional question as follows:

Question:

Between February 1, 1984 and May 30, 1984, was s. 42 of the *Wildlife Act*, R.S.A. 1980, c. W-9, constitutionally applicable to Treaty 8 Indians in virtue of the hunting rights granted to them under the said Treaty? In particular, were the hunting rights granted by Treaty No. 8 of 1899 extinguished, reduced or modified by para. 12 of the Alberta Natural Resources Transfer Agreement, as confirmed by the *Constitution Act, 1930*?

Answer:

Section 42 of the *Wildlife Act* was applicable to Treaty 8 Indians only to the extent that they were engaged in commercial or sport hunting. The Treaty 8 hunting rights were neither extinguished nor reduced by para. 12 of the Alberta Natural Resources Transfer Agreement. The territorial limits within which they could be exercised were, however, modified by para. 12.

Appeal dismissed.

The majority decision in *Horseman* held that the NRTA unilaterally superseded the terms of Treaty No. 8, thereby extinguishing the rights contained in the latter. Is such a finding consistent with the sanctity of Aboriginal treaties? Is it consistent with the notion of treaties as negotiated compacts? Refer back to the discussion of treaties in Chapter 2. Do the Crown's actions in promulgating the NRTA, assuming it has this effect on treaty rights, implicate its fiduciary obligations to the Aboriginal peoples? See the discussion of Crown-Native fiduciary relations in Chapter 3.

The *Horseman* decision was reconsidered in the Supreme Court of Canada's judgment in *R. v. Badger*, below (which is also discussed in Chapter 2, for its consideration of treaty interpretation). Unlike in the *Horseman* decision, the Court in *Badger* considered the application of section 35(1) of the *Constitution Act, 1982* and its protection of existing treaty rights. The following excerpt from the *Badger* case relates to the Court's discussion of the effect of the Alberta NRTA on hunting rights protected by Treaty No. 8.

R. v. BADGER

(1996), 133 D.L.R. (4th) 324, [1996] 4 W.W.R. 457, 37 Alta. L.R. (3d) 153, 195 N.R. 1, 105 C.C.C. (3d) 289 (S.C.C.)

[The facts of the case are set out in the discussion of the case in Chapter 2.]

Sopinka J. (Lamer C.J.C. concurring): — I have had the benefit of reading the reasons for judgment prepared in this appeal by my colleague, Justice Cory, and I am in agreement with his disposition of the appeal and with his reasons with the exception of his exposition of the relationship between Treaty No. 8, the *Natural Resources Transfer Agreement, 1930* [*Constitution Act, 1930,* Schedule 2] (NRTA), and s. 35 of the *Constitution Act, 1982.*

In my view, the rights of Indians to hunt for food provided in Treaty No. 8 were merged in the NRTA which is the sole source of those rights. While I agree that the impugned provision of the *Wildlife Act,* S.A. 1984, c. W-9.1, infringes the constitutional right of Indians to hunt for food, I disagree that this constitutional right is one covered by s. 35(1) of the *Constitution Act, 1982.* I agree, however, that the constitutional right to hunt for food must be balanced against the right of the province to pass laws for the purpose of conservation and that this balancing may be carried out on the basis of the principles set out in *R. v. Sparrow,* [1990] 1 S.C.R. 1075.

There is no disagreement that the NRTA:

(a) duplicated the right of Indians to hunt for food which was contained in Treaty No. 8;
(b) widely extended the geographical area to include the whole of the province rather than being limited to the tract of land surrendered;
(c) shifted responsibility for passing game laws from the federal government to the provinces;
(d) eliminated the right to hunt for commercial purposes;
(e) is a constitutional document and the Treaty is not, although the Treaty receives constitutional protection by virtue of s. 35(1) of the *Constitution Act, 1982.*

In these circumstances, I am of the view that it was clearly the intention of the framers to merge the rights in the treaty in the NRTA. To characterize the NRTA as modifying the treaty is to treat it as an amending document to the treaty. This clearly was not the intent of the NRTA. In enlarging the area in which hunting for food was permitted to extend to the whole of the province, it could not be suggested that the NRTA extended the treaty to all of the province. Rather, the right to hunt for food was extended by the NRTA to the whole of the province, including the area covered by the treaty. An Indian hunting on land outside the treaty lands could not claim to be covered by the treaty. If the NRTA merely modified the treaty, an Indian hunting on treaty lands could claim the right under the treaty while an Indian hunting in other parts of the province could claim only under the NRTA. This would invite bifurcation of the rights of Indians hunting for food in the province.

Similarly, the provisions which transferred to the province the power to pass gaming laws for the purpose of conservation could not have been intended simply to amend the treaty. As an amendment to the treaty, this provision would have no constitutional force and could not alter the constitutionally entrenched division of powers. It might be suggested that the NRTA both amended the treaty and, as an independent constitutional document, amended the Constitution. If this were the intent, it is difficult to understand why all the terms of the treaty relating to the right to hunt for food were replicated in NRTA. It must have been the intention to merge these rights in the NRTA so that they could be balanced with the power of the provinces to legislate for conservation purposes. In order to achieve a reasonable balance between them, it was important that they both appear in one document having constitutional status.

I can suggest no reason why the framers of the NRTA would have wanted to maintain any aspects of the treaty except as an interpretative tool. They surely did not do so in order to allow these rights to be recognized under s. 35(1) of the *Constitution Act, 1982* which appears to be the sole present justification for preserving the treaty. However, even that justification loses any force when considered in light of the fact that the NRTA is itself a constitutional document and recognition under s. 35(1) is unnecessary for the protection of these important Indian rights.

From the foregoing, I conclude that it was the intention of the framers of para. 12 of the NRTA to effectuate a merger and consolidation of the treaty rights.

. . . . .

If this was the intention, and I conclude that it was, then the proper characterization of the relationship between the NRTA and the treaty rights is that the sole source for a claim involving the right to hunt for food is the NRTA. The treaty rights have been subsumed in a document of a higher order. The treaty may be relied on for the purpose of assisting in the interpretation of the NRTA, but it has no other legal significance.

The fact that the source of the appellants' rights to hunt and fish for sustenance is found within the provisions of the NRTA does not alter the analysis that has previously been employed in the interpretation of treaty rights. ... [I]t was through the enactment of the NRTA that the "federal government attempted to fulfil their treaty obligations": see *Moosehunter v. The Queen*, [1981] 1 S.C.R. 282, at p. 293.

Validity of the provisions of the Wildlife Act

... [A]t the time the treaties were signed and, even more so, at the time that the NRTA was agreed to by the provinces and the federal government, it would have been clearly understood that the rights of Indians pursuant to either document would be subject to governmental regulation for conservation purposes. The rights protected by the NRTA thus cannot be viewed as being constitutional rights of an absolute nature for which governmental regulation is prohibited.

How, then, is the governmental regulation permitted by the NRTA, and the extent of the protection of the appellants' rights in the face of such regulation, to be assessed? ... Section 35(1) was intended to provide constitutional protection for aboriginal rights and treaty rights that did not enjoy such protection. It cannot have been intended to be redundant and provide constitutional protection for rights that already enjoyed constitutional protection. Moreover, para. 12 of the NRTA is a constitutional provision and, as such, s. 35(1) has no direct application to it. Infringements of constitutional rights cannot be remedied by the application of a different constitutional provision.

. . . . .

That is not to say, however, that the principles underlying the interpretation of s. 35(1) have no relevance to the determination of whether a particular legislative enactment has an acceptable purpose and whether it constitutes an acceptable limitation on the rights granted by the NRTA. There is no method provided in the NRTA whereby government measures that may impinge upon the rights the same document grants to Indians can be scrutinized. It is clear, however, that the NRTA does require a balancing of rights. The right of the province to legislate with respect to conservation must be balanced against the right granted to the Indians to hunt for food. ... Although the *Sparrow* test was developed in the context of s. 35(1), the basic thrust of the test, to protect aboriginal rights but also to permit governments to legislate for legitimate purposes where the legislation is a justifiable infringement on those protected rights, applies equally well to the regulatory authority granted to the provinces under para. 12 of the NRTA as to federal power to legislate in respect of Indians.

In this way, the *Sparrow* test is applied to the NRTA by analogy, with the result that the Court will have a means by which to ensure that the rights in the NRTA are protected, but that provincial governments are also provided with some flexibility in terms of their ability to affect those rights for the purpose of legislating in relation to conservation.

. . . . .

I agree with Cory J. that, in the absence of evidence with respect to justification, there must be a new trial and I would dispose of the appeal as suggested by him.

The constitutional question and answers are as follows:

> If Treaty 8 confirmed to the Indians of the Treaty 8 Territory the right to hunt throughout the tract surrendered, does the right continue to exist or was it extinguished and replaced by paragraph 12 of the Natural Resources Transfer Agreement, 1930 (*Constitution Act, 1930*, 20-21 George V, c. 26 (U.K.)), and if the right continues to exist, could that right be exercised on the lands in question and, if so, was the right impermissibly infringed upon by s. 26(1) or s. 27(1) of the *Wildlife Act*, S.A. 1984, c. W-9.1, given Treaty 8 and s. 35(1) of the *Constitution Act, 1982*?

The right to hunt for food referred to in Treaty No. 8 was merged in the NRTA which is the sole source of the right.

Sections 26(1) and 27(1) of the *Wildlife Act* did not infringe the constitutional rights of Mr. Badger or Mr. Kiyawasew to hunt for food.

Mr. Ominayak was exercising his constitutional right to hunt for food. Section 26(1) of the *Wildlife Act* is a *prima facie* infringement of his right to hunt for food under NRTA and is invalid unless justified.

[The judgment of **La Forest, L'Heureux-Dubé, Gonthier, Cory** and **Iacobucci JJ.** was delivered by]

Cory J.: — Three questions must be answered on this appeal. First, do Indians who have status under Treaty No. 8 have the right to hunt for food on privately owned land which lies within the territory surrendered under that treaty? Secondly, have the hunting rights set out in Treaty No. 8 been extinguished or modified as a result of the provisions of para. 12 of the *Natural Resources Transfer Agreement, 1930 (Constitution Act, 1930,* Sch. 2)? Thirdly, to what extent, if any, do s. 26(1) and s. 27(1) of the *Wildlife Act,* S.A. 1984, c. W-9.1, apply to the appellants?

. . . . .

Constitutional question

The constitutional question stated by this Court on May 2, 1994 is as follows:

> If Treaty 8 confirmed to the Indians of the Treaty 8 Territory the right to hunt throughout the tract surrendered, does the right continue to exist or was it extinguished and replaced by paragraph 12 of the Natural Resources Transfer Agreement, 1930 *(Constitution Act, 1930,* 20-21 George V, c. 26 (U.K.)), and if the right continues to exist, could that right be exercised on the lands in question and, if so, was the right impermissibly infringed upon by s. 26(1) or s. 27(1) of the *Wildlife Act,* S.A. 1984, c. W-9.1, given Treaty 8 and s. 35(1) of the *Constitution Act, 1982*?

. . . . .

Impact of Paragraph 12 of the NRTA

Principles of Interpretation

. . . . .

[Cory J. discussed the principles of treaty interpretation, which are excerpted in Chapter 2.]

Interpreting the NRTA

The issue at this stage is whether the NRTA extinguished and replaced the Treaty No. 8 right to hunt for food. It is my conclusion that it did not.

. . . . .

This Court most recently considered the effect the NRTA had upon treaty rights in *Horseman, supra*. There, it was held that para. 12 of the NRTA evidenced a clear intention to extinguish the treaty protection of the right to hunt *commercially*. However, it was emphasized that the right to hunt *for food* continued to be protected and had in fact been expanded by the NRTA. ... I might add that *Horseman, supra*, is a recent decision which should be accepted as resolving the issues which it considered. The decisions of this Court confirm that para. 12 of the NRTA did, to the extent that its intent is clear, modify and alter the right to hunt for food provided in Treaty No. 8.

Pursuant to s. 1 of the *Constitution Act, 1930*, there can be no doubt that para. 12 of the NRTA is binding law. It is the legal instrument which currently sets out and governs the Indian right to hunt. However, the existence of the NRTA has not deprived Treaty No. 8 of legal significance. Treaties are sacred promises and the Crown's honour requires the Court to assume that the Crown intended to fulfil its promises. Treaty rights can only be amended where it is clear that effect was intended. It is helpful to recall that Dickson J. in *Frank, supra* [*Frank v. R.* (1977), [1978] 1 S.C.R. 95, [1977] 4 W.W.R. 294, 34 C.C.C. (2d) 209, 4 A.R. 271, 15 N.R. 487, 75 D.L.R. (3d) 481], observed at p. 100 that, while the NRTA had partially amended the scope of the treaty hunting right, "*of equal importance* was the desire to re-state and reassure to the treaty Indians the continued enjoyment of the right to hunt and fish for food" (emphasis added). I believe that these words support my conclusion that the Treaty No. 8 right to hunt has *only* been altered or modified by the NRTA *to the extent that* the NRTA evinces a clear intention to effect such a modification. This position has been repeatedly confirmed in the decisions referred to earlier. Unless there is a direct conflict between the NRTA and a treaty, the NRTA will not have modified the treaty rights. Therefore, the NRTA language which outlines the right to hunt for food must be read in light of the fact that this aspect of the treaty right continues in force and effect.

. . . . .

[T]he solemn promises made in the treaty should be altered or modified as little as possible. The NRTA clearly intended to modify the right to hunt. It did so by eliminating the right to hunt commercially and by preserving and extending the right to hunt for food. The treaty right thus modified pertains to the right to hunt for food which prior to the treaty was an aboriginal right.

. . . . .

Treaty No. 8 represents a solemn promise of the Crown. For the reasons set out earlier, it can only be modified or altered to the extent that the NRTA clearly intended to modify or alter those rights. The federal government, as it was empowered to do, unilaterally enacted the NRTA. It is unlikely that it would proceed in that manner today. The manner in which the NRTA was unilaterally enacted strengthens the conclusion that the right to hunt which it provides should be construed in light of the provisions of Treaty No. 8.

. . . . .

This Court has held on numerous occasions that there can be no limitation on the method, timing and extent of Indian hunting under a treaty. I would add that a treaty as amended by the NRTA should be considered in the same manner.

. . . . .

Justification

In my view justification of provincial regulations enacted pursuant to the NRTA should meet the same test for justification of treaty rights that was set out in *Sparrow, supra*. The reason for this is obvious. The effect of para. 12 of the NRTA is to place the provincial government in exactly the same position which the federal Crown formerly occupied. Thus the provincial government has the same duty not to infringe unjustifiably the hunting right provided by Treaty No. 8 as modified by the NRTA. Paragraph 12 of the NRTA provides that the province may make laws for a conservation purpose, subject to the Indian right to hunt and fish for food. Accordingly, there is a need for a means to assess which conservation laws will if they infringe that right, nevertheless be justifiable. The *Sparrow* analysis provides a reasonable, flexible and current method of assessing conservation regulations and enactments.

. . . . .

In the present case, the government has not led any evidence with respect to justification. In the absence of such evidence, it is not open to this Court to supply its own justification. Section 26(1) of the *Wildlife Act* constitutes a *prima facie* infringement of the appellant Mr. Ominayak's treaty right to hunt. Yet, the issue of conservation is of such importance that a new trial must be ordered so that the question of justification may be addressed.

Conclusion

The constitutional question posed before this Court was:

> If Treaty 8 confirmed to the Indians of the Treaty 8 Territory the right to hunt throughout the tract surrendered, does the right continue to exist or was it extinguished and replaced by paragraph 12 of the Natural Resources Transfer Agreement, 1930 (*Constitution Act, 1930,* 20-21 George V, c. 26 (U.K.)), and if the right continues to exist, could that right be exercised on the lands in question and, if so, was the right impermissibly infringed upon

by s. 26(1) or s. 27(1) of the *Wildlife Act*, S.A. 1984, c. W-9.1, given Treaty 8 and s. 35(1) of the *Constitution Act, 1982*?

It is evident from these reasons that the constitutional question should be answered as follows. The hunting rights confirmed by Treaty No. 8 were modified by para. 12 of the NRTA to the extent indicated in these reasons. Paragraph 12 of the NRTA provided for a continuing right to hunt for food on unoccupied land.

Mr. Badger and Mr. Kiyawasew were hunting on occupied land to which they had no right of access under Treaty No. 8 or the NRTA. Accordingly, ss. 26(1) and 27(1) of the *Wildlife Act* do not infringe their constitutional right to hunt for food.

However, Mr. Ominayak was exercising his constitutional right on land which was unoccupied for the purposes of this case. Section 26(1) of the *Wildlife Act* constitutes a *prima facie* infringement of his treaty right to hunt for food. As a result of their conclusions, the issue of justification was not considered by the courts below. Therefore, in his case, a new trial must be ordered so that the issue of justification may be addressed.

Disposition

The appeals of Mr. Badger and Mr. Kiyawasew are dismissed.

The appeal of Mr. Ominayak is allowed and a new trial directed so that the issue of the justification of the infringement created by s. 26(1) of the *Wildlife Act* and any regulations passed pursuant to that section may be addressed.

From Cory J.'s decision in *Badger*, it may be seen that treaty rights are no longer deemed to be extinguished or replaced by the NRTA, as had been held in *Horseman* and previous decisions. Rather, treaty rights will be modified where they come into conflict with the NRTA. Meanwhile, the treaties are to be used to assist in the interpretation of the NRTA. As Cory J. explained at p. 348 [133 D.L.R. (4th)], citing *R. v. Smith*, [1935] 3 D.L.R. 703, at p. 705, [1935] 2 W.W.R. 433, 64 C.C.C. 131 (Sask. C.A.): "'[I]t is proper to consult th[e] treaty in order to glean from it whatever may throw some light on the meaning to be given to the words' in the NRTA." How can a treaty that states that existing treaty hunting rights are to be preserved (albeit subject to future, unspecified regulation) and a corresponding Treaty Commissioners' report that repeatedly highlights the commissioners' assurances to the Aboriginal peoples that "the same means of earning a livelihood would continue after the treaty as existed before it",[11] help to interpret a unilateral constitutional enactment that extinguishes a principal element of the treaty signatories' hunting practices (as demonstrated by Arthur Ray's report, cited by both Cory and Wilson JJ. in *Horseman*)?

Despite Justice Cory's finding that treaty rights will not be extinguished by the NRTA but will only be modified where they come into conflict with the NRTA, the conflict between Treaty No. 8 and the NRTA over the scope of the treaty right to hunt resulted in commercial hunting rights being extinguished. Is the complete extinguishment of the Treaty No. 8 right to commercially hunt, a right that had been found to exist (at least prior to the NRTA) in *Horseman*, consistent with a "modification" of that right? Alternatively, is this result in *Badger* more consistent with the judgment rendered in that case by Justice Sopinka or with Cory J.'s judgment in *Horseman*?

E. THE CHARTER AND ABORIGINAL PEOPLES

As explained earlier, the Aboriginal and treaty rights existing in section 35(1) of the *Constitution Act, 1982* exist outside of the Charter and are, therefore, not affected by it. That does not entail, however, that Aboriginal peoples are not affected by the Charter, although the Charter's application to Aboriginal peoples and governments has been a controversial issue. As indicated in *Lovelace v. Ontario*, [2000] 1 S.C.R. 950, a case concerning the Ontario government's plan for distributing profits from one of its casinos to certain Aboriginal bands in the province, the Charter may be used by Aboriginal peoples as a means to protect their interests against government action (even though the action in *Lovelace* was ultimately unsuccessful). This ability exists separate and apart from, or in addition to, the ability of Aboriginal peoples to enforce their rights under section 35(1).

LOVELACE v. ONTARIO

[2000] 1 S.C.R. 950

The judgment of the Court was delivered by

Iacobucci J.: —

I. Introduction

In 1993, the Province of Ontario and representatives from Ontario's First Nations entered into a process of negotiations with the goal of partnering in the development of the province's first reserve-based commercial casino, which was to become Casino Rama. Profits from the casino were to be shared among Ontario's First Nations. ... Casino Rama opened its doors to the public in the summer of 1996. Meanwhile, the province and representatives of the Chiefs of Ontario had begun a process of negotiating the terms for distributing the casino's proceeds ("First Nations Fund") to the First Nations communities. In the spring of 1996, the province informed the appellant aboriginal communities that the First Nations Fund was to be distributed only to Ontario First Nations communities registered as bands under the *Indian Act*, R.S.C., 1985, c. I-5.

· · · · ·

In basic terms, this appeal requires a determination of the constitutionality of the exclusion of non-band aboriginal communities from sharing in the proceeds, and from negotiating the distribution terms for the First Nations Fund. Specifically, the question is whether the First Nations Fund's underinclusiveness violates the appellants' equality rights as guaranteed by s. 15 of the *Canadian Charter of Rights and Freedoms*. We must also determine whether the province's decision to exclude the appellants on the basis that they are not bands under the *Indian Act* was *ultra vires* its jurisdiction under the *Constitution Act, 1867*.

. . . . .

This appeal also raises the question of the proper interpretation of s. 15(2) of the *Charter*. ...

With respect to s. 15(1), in my view the exclusion of the non-band aboriginal communities from the First Nations Fund does not violate s. 15 of the *Charter*. I reach this conclusion despite a recognition that, regrettably, the appellant and respondent aboriginal communities have overlapping and largely shared histories of discrimination, poverty, and systemic disadvantage that cry out for improvement.

In my opinion, a contextual analysis reveals an almost precise correspondence between the casino project and the needs and circumstances of the First Nations bands. The casino project was undertaken by the province of Ontario in order to further develop a partnership or a "government-to-government" relationship with Ontario's First Nations band communities. It is a project that is aimed at supporting the journey of these aboriginal groups towards empowerment, dignity, and self-reliance. It is not, however, designed to meet similar needs in the appellant aboriginal communities, but its failure to do so does not amount to discrimination under s. 15.

Finally, I conclude that the province did not act *ultra vires* in partnering the casino initiative with *Indian Act* registered aboriginal communities. The exclusion of non-registered aboriginal communities did not act to define or impair the "Indianness" of the appellants since the province simply exercised its constitutional spending power in making the casino arrangements.

. . . . .

... [T]o invoke s. 15(2) a court need only be satisfied that the target of the program was a disadvantaged group, and the purpose of the program was to ameliorate these conditions. ...

... Since s. 15(2) affirms government initiatives directed at redressing disadvantage, these programs should be shielded to the extent that they address a specific disadvantage. In short, in underinclusive situations, one can find discrimination only if a distinction is made resulting in the denial of a benefit to a member of the group targeted by the program. As a result, the key to the s. 15(2) analysis is properly characterizing the object or the purpose of the program in order to determine whether the claimants are within a group targeted by that program's objects. ...

. . . . .

The ameliorative purpose of the overall casino project and the related First Nations Fund has clearly been established. In particular, the First Nations Fund will provide bands with resources in order to ameliorate specifically social, health, cultural, education, and economic disadvantages. It is anticipated that the bands will be able to target the allocation of these monies within these specified areas, thereby increasing the fiscal autonomy of the bands. This aspect of the First Nations Fund is consistent with the related ameliorative purpose of supporting the bands in achieving self-government and self-reliance. Without a doubt, this program has been designed to redress historical disadvantage and contribute to enhancing the dignity and recognition of bands in Canadian society. Furthermore, both of the above ameliorative objectives can be met while, at the same time, ensuring that on-reserve commercial casino gaming is undertaken in compliance with the strict regulations applicable to the supervision of gaming activities. The First Nations Fund has, therefore, a purpose that is consistent with s. 15(1) of the *Charter* and the exclusion of the appellants does not undermine this purpose since it is not associated with a misconception as to their actual needs, capacities and circumstances.

. . . . .

I would answer the constitutional questions as follows:

Question 1: Does the exclusion of the appellant aboriginal groups from the First Nations Fund, and from the negotiations on the establishment and operation of the Fund, set up pursuant to s. 15(1) of the *Ontario Casino Corporation Act, 1993*, S.O. 1993, c. 25, on the grounds that they are not aboriginal groups registered as *Indian Act* bands under the *Indian Act*, R.S.C., 1985, c. I-5, violate s. 15 of the *Canadian Charter of Rights and Freedoms*?

Answer: No.

Question 2: If the answer to question No. 1 is yes, is the violation demonstrably justified under s. 1 of the *Canadian Charter of Rights and Freedoms*?

Answer: In view of the answer to Question 1, it is not necessary to answer this question.

Question 3: Is the exclusion of the appellant aboriginal groups from the First Nations Fund of the Casino Rama Project, and from the negotiations on the establishment and operation of the Fund on the grounds that they are not aboriginal groups registered as *Indian Act* bands under the *Indian Act*, R.S.C., 1985, c. I-5, *ultra vires* the power of the province under the *Constitution Act, 1867*?

Answer: No.

Appeal dismissed.

While the Supreme Court of Canada held that Ontario was not bound to include non-registered bands in its casino revenue redistribution, should it have included them? Why do you think that it did not include them? Can you think of reasons for distinguishing among bands on the basis of *Indian Act* registration?

In addition to the *Lovelace* decision, the Supreme Court of Canada considered the application of section 15(1) to Aboriginal peoples in *Corbiere v. Canada (Minister of Indian and Northern Affairs)*, [1999] 2 S.C.R. 203. The controversy in that case surrounded section 77(1) of the *Indian Act*, R.S.C. 1985, c. I-5, which held that only those status Indians "ordinarily resident on a reserve" could vote in band council elections, while those who were band members, but resident off-reserve, could not vote in those elections. The Supreme Court of Canada held that a status Indian's place of residence constituted an analogous form of discrimination in the context of determining who was entitled to vote in band council elections. As a result, the phrase "ordinarily resident on a reserve", was declared inconsistent with section 15(1) of the Charter and struck down, although implementation of the change was suspended for 18 months. The *Corbiere* case is excerpted in Chapter 8, *infra*.

F. CONSTITUTIONAL AMENDMENT AND ABORIGINAL PEOPLES

In the draft text of the Charlottetown Accord, which was defeated by a national referendum on October 26, 1992, a number of constitutional amendments were proposed that pertained directly to Aboriginal peoples. Although the Accord was defeated, these proposals may serve as prototypes for future negotiations between the Crown and Aboriginal peoples, if not for future attempts at constitutional amendment. In your contemplation of these amendments, consider how these measures, had they been implemented into Canadian constitutional law, would have affected existing understandings of Aboriginal and treaty rights.

DRAFT LEGAL TEXT OF THE CHARLOTTETOWN ACCORD,

October 9, 1992

25.   Section 25 of the said Act is amended by striking out the word "and" at the end of paragraph (b) thereof and by adding thereto the following paragraph:

"(c)   any rights or freedoms relating to the exercise or protection of their languages, cultures or traditions"

26.   Subsection 32(1) of the said Act is amended by striking out the word "and" at the end of paragraph (a) thereof, by adding the word "and" at the end of paragraph (b) thereof and by adding thereto the following paragraph:

"(c)   to all legislative bodies and governments of the Aboriginal peoples of Canada in respect of all matters within the authority of their respective legislative bodies."

27.   The said Act is further amended by adding thereto, immediately after section 33 thereof, the following section:

Application of section 33 to aboriginal legislative bodies

"33.1   Section 33 applies to legislative bodies of the Aboriginal peoples of Canada with such modifications, consistent with the purposes of the requirements of that section, as are appropriate to the circumstances of the Aboriginal peoples concerned."

28.   (1)   Subsection 35(1) of the English version of the said Act is amended by substituting the expression "Aboriginal peoples of Canada" for the expression "aboriginal peoples of Canada".

(2)   Subsection 35(2) of the said Act is repealed and the following substituted therefor:

Definition of "Aboriginal peoples of Canada"

"(2)   In the Constitution of Canada, "Aboriginal peoples of Canada" includes the Indian, Inuit and Métis peoples of Canada."

(3)   Subsection 35(4) of the said Act is repealed and the following substituted therefor:

Access by all Aboriginal peoples

"(4)   For greater certainty, all the Aboriginal peoples of Canada have access to the aboriginal and treaty rights recognized and affirmed in this Part that pertain to them."

29.   Section 35.1 of the said Act is repealed and the following substituted therefor:

Inherent right of self-government

"35.1   (1)   The Aboriginal peoples of Canada have the inherent right of self-government within Canada.

Three orders of government

(2) The right referred to in subsection (1) shall be interpreted in a manner consistent with the recognition of the governments of the Aboriginal peoples of Canada as constituting one of three orders of government in Canada.

Contextual statement

(3) The exercise of the right referred to in subsection (1) includes the authority of duly constituted legislative bodies of the Aboriginal peoples, each within its own jurisdiction.

    1. to safeguard and develop their languages, cultures, economies, identities, institutions and traditions, and

    2. to develop, maintain and strengthen their relationship with their lands, waters and environment,

so as to determine and control their development as peoples according to their own values and priorities and to ensure the integrity of their societies.

Issues before court or tribunal

(4) Where an issue arises in any proceedings in relation to the scope of the inherent right of self-government, or in relation to an assertion of that right, a court or tribunal

    (a) before making any final determination of the issue, shall inquire into the efforts that have been made to resolve the issue through negotiations under section 35.2 and may order the parties to take such steps as may be appropriate in the circumstances to effect a negotiated resolution; and

    (b) in making any final determination of the issue, shall take into account subsection (3).

Land

(5) Neither the right referred to in subsection (1) nor anything in subsection 35.2(1) creates new aboriginal rights to land or abrogates or derogates from ex-

isting aboriginal or treaty rights to land, except as otherwise provided in self-government agreements negotiated under section 35.2.

Commitment to negotiate

35.2 (1) The government of Canada, the provincial and territorial governments and the Aboriginal peoples of Canada, including the Indian, Inuit and Métis peoples of Canada, in the various regions and communities of Canada shall negotiate in good faith the implementation of the right of self-government, including issues of

    (a)   jurisdiction,

    (b)   lands and resources, and

    (c)   economic and fiscal arrangements

with the objective of concluding agreements elaborating relationships between governments of Aboriginal peoples and the government of Canada and provincial or territorial governments.

Process of negotiation

(2) Negotiations referred to in subsection (1) may be initiated only by the representatives or governments of the Aboriginal peoples concerned, and shall, unless otherwise agreed by the parties to the negotiations, be conducted in accordance with the process for negotiations outlined in an accord entered into by the government of Canada, the provincial and territorial governments and representatives of the Aboriginal peoples.

Equitable access

(3) All the Aboriginal peoples of Canada shall have equitable access to negotiations referred to in subsection (1).

Agreements may allow participation of all residents

(4) An agreement negotiated under this section may provide for bodies or institutions of self-government that are open to the participation of all residents of the region to which the agreement relates as determined by the agreement.

Different circum-stances		(5)	The parties to negotiations referred to in subsection (1) shall have regard to the different circumstances of the various Aboriginal peoples of Canada.

Where rights are treaty rights

(6) Where an agreement negotiated under this section

    (a) is set out in a treaty or land claims agreement, or in an amendment to a treaty including a land claims agreement, or

    (b) contains a declaration that the rights of the Aboriginal peoples set out in the agreement are treaty rights,

the rights of the Aboriginal peoples set out in the agreement are treaty rights under subsection 35(1).

Non-dero-gation

(7) Nothing in this section abrogates or derogates from the rights referred to in section 35 or 35.1, or from the enforceability thereof, and nothing in subsection 35.1(3) or in this section makes those rights contingent on the commitment to negotiate under this section.

Delay of justiciabil-ity   35.3   (1) Except in relation to self-government agreements concluded after the coming into force of this section, section 35.1 shall not be made the subject of judicial notice, interpretation or enforcement for five years after that section comes into force.

For greater certainty

(2) For greater certainty, nothing in subsection (1) prevents the justiciability of disputes in relation to

    (a) any existing rights that are recognized and affirmed in subsection 35(1), including any rights relating to self-government, when raised in any court; or

    (b) the process of negotiation under section 35.2.

Idem

(3) Nothing in subsection (1) abrogates or derogates from section 35.1 or renders section 35.1 contingent on the happening of any future event, and subsection (1) merely de-

lays for five years judicial notice, interpretation or enforcement of that section.

Application of laws   35.4   (1)   Except as otherwise provided by the Constitution of Canada, the laws of Canada and the laws of the provinces and territories continue to apply to the Aboriginal peoples of Canada, subject nevertheless to being displaced by laws enacted by legislative bodies of the Aboriginal peoples according to their authority.

Peace, order and good government in Canada   (2)   No aboriginal law or any other exercise of the inherent right of self-government under section 35.1 may be inconsistent with federal or provincial laws that are essential to the preservation of peace, order and good government in Canada.

Legislative authority not extended   (3)   For greater certainty, nothing in this section extends the legislative authority of the Parliament of Canada or the legislatures of the provinces or territories.

Affirmative action   35.5   (1)   Subsections 6(2) and (3) of the *Canadian Charter of Rights and Freedoms* do not preclude a legislative body or government of the Aboriginal peoples of Canada from exercising authority pursuant to this Part through affirmative action measures that have as their object the amelioration of conditions of individuals or groups who are socially or economically disadvantaged or the protection and advancement of aboriginal languages and cultures.

For greater certainty   (2)   For greater certainty, nothing in this section abrogates or derogates from section 15, 25, or 28 of the *Canadian Charter of Rights and Freedoms* or from section 35.7 of this Part.

Interpretation of treaty rights   35.6   (1)   The treaty rights referred to in subsection 35(1) shall be interpreted in a just, broad and liberal manner taking into account their spirit and intent and the context of the specific treaty negotiations relating thereto.

Commitment to processes to clarify, implement or rectify treaties	(2)	The government of Canada is committed to establishing treaty processes to clarify or implement treaty rights and, where the parties agree, to rectify terms of the treaties, and is committed, where requested by the Aboriginal peoples of Canada concerned, to participating in good faith in the process that relates to them.
Participation of provinces and territories	(3)	The governments of the provinces and territories are committed, to the extent that they have jurisdiction, to participating in good faith in the processes referred to in subsection (2), where jointly invited by the government of Canada and the Aboriginal peoples of Canada concerned or where it is specified that they will do so under the terms of the treaty concerned.
Spirit and intent	(4)	The participants in the processes referred to in subsection (2) shall have regard to, among other things and where appropriate, the spirit and intent of the treaties, as understood by the Aboriginal peoples concerned.
Equitable access	(5)	For greater certainty, all those Aboriginal peoples of Canada who have treaty rights shall have equitable access to the processes referred to in this section.
Non-derogation	(6)	Nothing in this section abrogates or derogates from any rights of the Aboriginal peoples of Canada who are not parties to a particular treaty.
Rights of the Aboriginal peoples of Canada guaranteed equally to both sexes	35.7	Notwithstanding any other provision of this Act, the rights of the Aboriginal peoples of Canada referred to in this Part are guaranteed equally to male and female persons.

Commit-   [35.8*   The government of Canada and the
ment to   provincial governments are committed
participate   to the principle that, before any
in constitu-   amendment *described in section 45.1* is
tional con-   made,
ference

(a)   a constitutional conference that includes in its agenda an item relating to the proposed amendment, composed of the Prime Minister of Canada and the first ministers of the provinces, will be convened by the Prime Minister of Canada; and

* The final wording of this provision (based on existing s. 35.1 added in 1984) is to be revisited when the consent mechanism is finalized for s. 45.1, at which time concerns will be addressed in respect of amendments directly referring to Aboriginal peoples in some but not all regions of Canada.

(b)   the Prime Minister of Canada will invite representatives of the Aboriginal peoples of Canada to participate in the discussions on that item.]

Constitutional   35.9   (1)   At least four constitutional con-
conferences   ferences on aboriginal issues composed of the Prime Minister of Canada, the first ministers of the provinces, representatives of the Aboriginal peoples of Canada and elected representatives of the governments of the territories shall be convened by the Prime Minister of Canada, the first to be held no later than 1996 and the three subsequent conferences to be held once every two years thereafter.

Agenda   (2)   Each conference convened under subsection (1) shall have included in its agenda such items as are proposed by the representatives of the Aboriginal peoples of Canada.

Powers of   35.91   For greater certainty, nothing in this
territories   Part extends the powers of the legislative authorities or governments of the territories."

G. CONCLUSION

While this chapter has highlighted some of the federalism/constitutional issues that affect Aboriginal peoples, the key element of such a discussion, whether explicitly or implicitly, is section 35(1) of the *Constitution Act, 1982*. Section 35 is both a recognition and an affirmation of existing Aboriginal and treaty rights. As a constitutional enactment, it is the primary basis for protecting the special rights belonging to Aboriginal peoples. At present, however, section 35 has yet to be sufficiently elaborated upon to provide a better indication of exactly what it is designed to protect and what form of protection it provides to the rights contained within it.

Chapter 4 illustrated the Supreme Court of Canada's most significant discussions of the scope of section 35(1) in *R. v. Sparrow*, [1990] 1 S.C.R. 1075, [1990] 4 W.W.R. 410, 46 B.C.L.R. (2d) 1, 56 C.C.C. (3d) 263, 70 D.L.R. (4th) 385, 111 N.R. 241, [1990] 3 C.N.L.R. 160 and *R. v. Van der Peet*, [1996] 9 W.W.R. 1, 23 B.C.L.R. (3d) 1, 50 C.R. (4th) 1, 137 D.L.R. (4th) 289, 109 C.C.C. (3d) 1, 200 N.R. 1, [1996] 4 C.N.L.R. 177 (S.C.C.). After these cases, there are still many unresolved issues surrounding section 35(1). Indeed, as mentioned in Chapter 4, those cases, in particular *Van der Peet*, raise many more questions than they answer.

Section 35(1) is a unique provision within the Canadian constitution because it recognizes the special relationship between the Crown and Aboriginal peoples in Canada. In the following excerpt, Noel Lyon explains some of the reasons for a relationship-based understanding of the purpose and scope of section 35(1).

NOEL LYON, "A PERSPECTIVE ON THE APPLICATION OF THE CRIMINAL CODE TO ABORIGINAL PEOPLES IN LIGHT OF THE JUDGMENT OF THE SUPREME COURT OF CANADA IN R. V. SPARROW"

(1992), U.B.C. L. Rev. Special Edition on Aboriginal Justice 306 at 306-11
(references omitted)

Section 35 of the *Constitution Act, 1982* is a unique provision. Unlike other constitutional enactments, it is not an attempt to express in writing some shared value from which we can deduce a "meaning". Rather, it is a hastily-constructed letter of intent through which we have agreed to mediate an historically-defined relationship.

. . . . .

This is part of a larger learning process that began in 1982, when we altered our constitution in ways so fundamental that the required changes in thinking are slow to come.

. . . . .

Before 1982, we had a written constitution, but we did not have the legal mindset that goes with constitutionalism. The Canadian legal profession clung tenaciously to a model of constitutional law built on the doctrine of parliamentary supremacy, and the values of the common law served by default as the shared values of Canadian society. The *Canadian Charter of Rights and Freedoms*, s. 35, and, above all, the supremacy clause of the 1982 Constitution created a sharp discontinuity in legal thinking that we have been scrambling to overcome for nearly a decade.

. . . . .

Section 35 not only permits this change in thinking, it requires it. The rest of the 1982 Constitution is anchored in the past, in the institutions, practices and values of Euro-Canadian society. New directions required by the *Charter* build on that historic base: not so with s. 35. Its mandate is directed to a future resolution because the historic base is unacceptable as a foundation to build on.

. . . . .

The unique character of s. 35 ... requires that we learn from it before we can properly give effect to it. Like other key features of the law of aboriginal peoples, it is *sui generis*, and it takes time to acquire the new modes of thinking that are needed to avoid dealing this wild card back into the deck and treating it in the same way as the rest of the deck.

The term *"sui generis"* has become prominent in judgments of the Supreme Court of Canada on aboriginal claims. It is the Court's way of signalling that a distinct body of doctrine and interpretive principles is required for aboriginal rights. We now understand that English property law does not respond to aboriginal land claims and that treaties are not simply a special form of contract. One way to absorb what the Court is saying is to think of general law, on the one hand, and the law of aboriginal rights, on the other, as the legal equivalents of the two rows of beads in the two-row wampum [see the discussion of the two-row wampum in Chapter 2]. Each group is to travel its own path, neither imposing its own ways on the other, and the Supreme Court has the delicate task of making space for a second row, the *sui generis* body of law, and giving it shape by listening to a narrative tradition that is foreign to all of the judges.

. . . . .

The failure of the Constitutional Conferences of 1983 to 1987 has left the Supreme Court of Canada with the task of explaining s. 35, and the Court made an impressive beginning in 1990 with the judgments in *Sparrow* and *Sioui*. The essence of those judgments is that s. 35 is an expression of the special relationship between the Crown and aboriginal peoples. That relationship was established both by treaties and by the *Royal Proclamation of 1763*. ... The *Sparrow* decision may be the beginning of a judicial awareness that the fundamental rights of aboriginal peoples cannot be secured within a constitutional model that is closed to the ultimate basis of those rights, which is the falsity of the claim of discovery on which Canada bases its legitimacy in imposing its will on aboriginal peoples.

. . . . .

Blocked by their own complicity in the imperial exercise from making an independent, impartial determination of the matters in issue in *Sparrow* and *Sioui*, the judges did the next best thing: they converted governmental claims of absolute power into a fiduciary relationship that transforms our constitutional law in a way that we are only beginning to understand. The result is a trust-like mandate that attaches to both legislative and executive powers and which has no parallel in our constitutional law.

. . . . .

Before *Sparrow*, it was possible to define the Crown's special relationship simply in terms of the right to go on the land to hunt and fish. Now we have both *Sparrow* and *Sioui* to tell us that our understanding of aboriginal rights has been built on a misreading of history and a persistent failure of governments to honour their commitments. The government's duty is to protect a way of life, not just certain activities.

————————

As Lyon suggests, section 35(1) ought to be regarded as a promise to the Aboriginal peoples that their rights will be respected. Recall his commentary, adopted with approval in *R. v. Sparrow* (1990), 70 D.L.R. (4th) 385 (S.C.C.) at 406:

> Professor Lyon in "An Essay on Constitutional Interpretation" (1988), 26 Osgoode Hall L.J. 95, says the following about s. 35(1), at p. 100:
>
> . . . the context of 1982 is surely enough to tell us that this is not just a codification of the case law on aboriginal rights that had accumulated by 1982. Section 35 calls for a just settlement for aboriginal peoples. It renounces the old rules of the game under which the Crown established courts of law and denied those courts the authority to question sovereign claims made by the Crown.

Note, however, the comments made by Binnie J. in *Mitchell v. M.N.R.*, [2001] 1 S.C.R. 911 (as excerpted in Chapter 9), where he said that "... The *Constitution Act, 1982* ushered in a new chapter but it did not start a new book." Refer back to the commentary on this point in Chapter 4, *supra*.

The purposive nature of section 35(1), as indicated by the Supreme Court of Canada in *Sparrow*, *supra*, imposes a constitutional responsibility upon government to act in a manner consistent with the furtherance of those rights. Combining the purposive nature of section 35(1) with the Crown's fiduciary and treaty obligations to the Aboriginal peoples requires that the Crown take positive action to give greater shape and content to Aboriginal and treaty rights and to facilitate timely and equitable settlements of aboriginal and treaty rights disputes. As the Federal Court, Trial Division explained in *Pacific Fishermen's Defence Alliance v. Canada*, [1987] 3 F.C. 272 at 280-1 (T.D.):

> Subsection 35(1) of the *Constitution Act, 1982* recognizes and affirms the existing aboriginal and treaty rights of the aboriginal peoples of Canada. It is, therefore, the duty of the federal government to negotiate with Indians in an attempt to settle those rights. ... The government's task is to determine, define, recognize and affirm whatever aboriginal rights existed.[12]

ENDNOTES

1. *R. v. Coté*, [1996] 4 C.N.L.R. 26 at 60, [1996] 3 S.C.R. 139.
2. See K. McNeil, "Aboriginal Title and Section 88 of the Indian Act" (2000) 34 U.B.C. L. Rev. 159 at para. 13.
3. K. Wilkins, "Of Provinces and Section 35 Rights" (1999) 22 Dal. L.J. 185 at 229.
4. *Ibid.* at 232.
5. *Ibid.*
6. *Ibid.* at 233.
7. B. Slattery, "First Nations and the Constitution: A Question of Trust" (1992) 71 Can. Bar Rev. 261 at 285-6.
8. K. McNeil, *supra* note 2, at para. 12. See also *ibid.* at n. 30, modifying McNeil, "Aboriginal Title and the Division of Powers: Rethinking Federal and Provincial Jurisdiction" (1998) 61 Sask. L. Rev. 431 at 440-1:

> How would th[e] honour of the Crown [which is intimately connected with the Crown's fiduciary obligations] be upheld by Parliamentary delegation of authority to the provinces to infringe Aboriginal rights through the mechanism of referential incorporation? Would this not be a dishonourable abdication of the responsibility that was placed primarily on the federal government by s. 91(24) of the Constitution Act, 1867?

9. McNeil, *supra* note 2, at para. 19.
10. The doctrine of interjurisdictional immunity protects the jurisdiction of either the federal or provincial levels of government from otherwise valid laws promulgated by the other level of government. While the doctrine has been applied only to provincial laws that purport to affect matters of federal jurisdiction, there is nothing inherent in the doctrine that necessitates that it cannot work to immunize provincial areas of jurisdiction from the effect of federal laws. A summary of existing jurisprudence indicates that the doctrine applies where an otherwise-valid provincial law impairs, paralyzes, or sterilizes a federal undertaking or it directly affects a vital part of the management or operation of that undertaking. In these situations, the provincial laws are deemed to be invalid in their application to the federal undertaking in question.
11. *Treaty No. 8 Made June 21, 1899 and Adhesions, Reports, etc.* (Ottawa: Queen's Printer, 1966) at 5.
12. Note also the comments by Lamer C.J.C. in *Delgamuukw v. British Columbia*, [1997] 3 S.C.R. 1010, at para. 186 where, in relation to his exhortation that negotiation of the Gitksan and Wet'suwet'en claims should also involve other Aboriginal nations with stakes in the territory being claimed, he stated that the "Crown is under a moral, if not a legal, duty to enter into and conduct those negotiations in good faith".

CHAPTER 8

ABORIGINAL WOMEN

A. INTRODUCTION

Aboriginal women have encountered significant discrimination in their dealings with the Canadian state. They have not only been disadvantaged because of their race, but have also been discriminated against because of their gender. This discrimination is often contrary to the traditional values of many communities which were matrilineal or matrilocal in nature, or which enjoyed a greater degree of equality between the sexes than was the case in many non-native societies. The *Indian Act* [now R.S.C. 1985, c. I-5] played a large part in perpetuating detrimental stereotypes and denying Indian women a significant role within their communities. The destructive influence of the Act is explored in this chapter. A study of these issues is an investigation into how the law implements colonialism and sexism, and reproduces its effects within native communities. This chapter reveals that the destructive impact of colonialism is most devastatingly effective when its ideologies are replicated within the group it seeks to legislate. This issue is investigated by studying the legal structures which deny many Aboriginal women matrimonial property, community membership and political representation. Also examined in this chapter are the small steps that have been taken to reverse the exclusion aboriginal women encounter in Canada.

"ABORIGINAL WOMEN"

in A.C. Hamilton and C.M. Sinclair, The Justice System and Aboriginal People: Report of the Aboriginal Justice Inquiry of Manitoba, Vol. 1 (Winnipeg: Queen's Printer, 1991) at 475-487 (references omitted)

Introduction

Aboriginal women and their children suffer tremendously as victims in contemporary Canadian society. They are the victims of racism, of sexism and of unconscionable levels of domestic violence. The justice system has done little to protect them from any of these assaults. At the same time, Aboriginal women have an even higher rate of over-representation in the prison system than Aboriginal men. In community after community, Aboriginal women brought these disturbing facts to our attention. We believe the plight of Aboriginal women and their children must be a priority for any changes in the justice system. In addition, we believe that changes must be based on the proposals that Aboriginal women presented to us throughout our Inquiry.

Women in Traditional Aboriginal Society

Women traditionally played a central role within the Aboriginal family, within Aboriginal government and in spiritual ceremonies. Men and women enjoyed considerable personal autonomy and both performed functions vital to the survival of Aboriginal communities. The men were responsible for providing food, shelter and clothing. Women were responsible for the domestic sphere and were viewed as both life-givers and the caretakers of life. As a result, women were responsible for the early socialization of children.

Traditional Aboriginal society experienced very little family breakdown. Husbands and wives were expected to respect and honour one another, and to care for one another with honesty and kindness. In matriarchal societies, such as of the Mohawk, women were honoured for their wisdom and vision. Aboriginal men also respected women for the sacred gifts which they believed the Creator had given to them. In Aboriginal teachings, passed on through the oral histories of the Aboriginal people of this province from generation to generation, Aboriginal men and women were equal in power and each had autonomy within their personal lives.

Women figured centrally in almost all Aboriginal creation legends. In Ojibway and Cree legends, it was a woman who came to earth through a hole in the sky to care for the earth. It was a woman, Nokomis (grandmother), who taught Original Man (Anishinabe, an Ojibway word meaning "human being") about the medicines of the earth and about technology. When a traditional Ojibway person prays, thanks is given and the pipe is raised in each of the four directions, then to Mother Earth as well as to Grandfather, Mishomis, in the sky.

To the Ojibway, the earth is woman, the Mother of the people, and her hair, the sweet-grass, is braided and used in ceremonies. The Dakota and Lakota (Sioux) people of Manitoba and the Dakotas tell how a woman — White Buffalo Calf Woman — brought the pipe to their people. It is through the pipe that prayer is carried by its smoke upwards to the Creator in their most sacred ceremonies.

The strength that Aboriginal peoples gain today from their traditional teachings and their cultures comes from centuries of oral tradition and Aboriginal teachings, which emphasized the equality of man and woman and the balanced roles of both in the continuation of life. Such teachings hold promise for the future of the Aboriginal community as a whole. We have been told that more and more young Aboriginal people are turning to the beliefs and values of Aboriginal traditions to find answers for the problems which they are facing in this day and age.

Aboriginal author Paula Gunn Allen points out:

> Since the coming of the Anglo-Europeans beginning in the fifteenth century the fragile web of identity that long held tribal people secure has gradually been weakened and torn. But the oral tradition has prevented the complete destruction of the web, the ultimate disruption of tribal ways. The oral tradition is vital: it heals itself and the tribal web by adapting to the flow of the present while never relinquishing its connection to the past.

This revival is necessitated, in large measure, by the assault that Aboriginal culture has experienced during the last century.

The Attack on Aboriginal Culture

Women were never considered inferior in Aboriginal society until Europeans arrived. Women had few rights in European society at the time of first contact with Aboriginal people. Men were considered their social, legal and political masters. Any rights which women had were those derived through their husbands. The law of England, for example, held that women did not have the right to vote, to own property or to enter into contracts. This attitude was ultimately reflected in the *Indian Act*, which blatantly discriminated against women.

This attitude toward women continued until relatively recently in Canada. Women had to fight battles in this century to win the right to vote and to be recognized as legal persons, and it was only within the past few decades that the final legal restrictions upon their right to contract and own property were lifted. ...

Economic factors served as the initial catalyst for change within Aboriginal societies. Aboriginal people were first directed away from hunting into the economic order of the fur trade society. Gradually, more and more of them became removed from the land and went into settlements with a welfare economy. These changes to Aboriginal lifestyle distorted the traditional Aboriginal male and female roles.

> [W]ith the loss of Indian male roles and as a result of being reduced to a state of powerlessness and vulnerability which their own culture deemed highly inappropriate, Indian men came to experience severe role strain.

Cultural changes resulting from the economic factors at play had their greatest impact on the role of Aboriginal women.

Cultural Changes — The Impact upon Aboriginal Women

For Aboriginal women, European economic and cultural expansion was especially destructive. Their value as equal partners in tribal society was undermined completely.

It is only in the past decade that writers have acknowledged the very important role Aboriginal women played in the first centuries of contact with Europeans and their descendants. Yet, while [women's] role within Aboriginal society remained relatively stable for some time after contact, all that changed completely with the advent of the residential school system.

The victimization of Aboriginal women accelerated with the introduction after Confederation of residential schools for Aboriginal children. Children were removed from their families and homes at a young age, some to return eight to 10 years later, some never to return. The ability to speak Aboriginal languages and the motivation to do so were severely undermined. Aboriginal students were taught to devalue everything Aboriginal and value anything Euro-Canadian.

Many Aboriginal grandparents and parents today are products of the residential school system. The development of parenting skills, normally a significant aspect of their training as children within Aboriginal families, was denied to them by the fact that they were removed from their families and communities, and by the lack of attention paid to the issue by residential schools. Parenting skills neither were observed nor taught in those institutions. Aboriginal children traditionally learned their parenting skills from their parents through example and daily direction. That learning process was denied to several generations of Aboriginal parents. In addition to the physical and sexual abuse that Canadians are now hearing took place in residential schools, emotional abuse was the most prevalent and the most severe.

Not only did residential schools not support the development of traditional parental roles among the children, but they taught the children that they were "pagan" — an inferior state of being — and should never use their language or honour their religious beliefs. These messages were imparted to Aboriginal children in a sometimes brutal manner. Several presenters also pointed out that residential schools not only removed children from their families, but they also prevented any closeness, even contact, from occurring between siblings and relatives at the same school.

The damage done by residential schools is evident today as Aboriginal people, long deprived of parenting skills, struggle with family responsibilities and attempt to recapture cultural practices and beliefs so long denied. Grand Chief Dave Courchene Sr. put the experience succinctly:

> Residential schools taught self-hate. That is child abuse. ... Too many of our people got the message and passed it on. It is their younger generations that appear before you (in court).

We believe the breakdown of Aboriginal cultural values and the abuse suffered by Aboriginal children in the schools contributed to family breakdown. This began a cycle of abuse in Aboriginal communities, with women and children being the primary victims. The Canadian government also undermined equality between Aboriginal men and women with the legalization of sexist and racist discrimination in successive pieces of legislation. In 1869 it introduced the concept of enfranchisement, whereby Indian people would lose their status as Indians and be treated the same as other Canadians. For Aboriginal women, this process of enfranchisement had particularly devastating consequences, because the role assigned to Canadian women was one of inferiority and subjugation to the male.

Upon becoming enfranchised, Aboriginal people lost their status under the *Indian Act.* An Indian woman lost her status automatically upon marrying a man who was not a status Indian. This was not true for Indian men, whose non-Indian wives gained status as Indians upon marriage. Under subsequent *Indian Acts*, Indian agents could enfranchise an Indian if he were deemed "progressive." In cases where a man became enfranchised, his wife and children automatically lost their status, as well.

While Bill C-31 (1985) [*An Act to Amend the Indian Act*, S.C. 1985, c. 27] addressed many of these problems, it created new ones in terms of the differential treatment of male and female children of Aboriginal people. Under the new Act, anomalies can develop where the children of a status Indian woman can pass on status to their children only if they marry registered Indians, whereas the grandchildren of a status male will have full status, despite the fact that one of their parents does not have status.

Aboriginal women traditionally played a prominent role in the consensual decision-making process of their communities. The *Indian Act* created the chief and council system of local government. The local Indian agent chaired the meetings of the chief and council, and had the power to remove the chief and council from office. Aboriginal women were denied any vote in the new system imposed by the Indian Affairs administration. As a result, they were stripped of any formal involvement in the political process.

The segregation of Aboriginal women, both from wider society and from their traditional role as equal and strong members of tribal society, continues to the present day. This is due partly to the fact that the effects of past discrimination have resulted in the poor socio-economic situation applicable to most Aboriginal women, but it is also attributable to the demeaning image of Aboriginal women that has developed over the years. North American society has adopted a destructive and stereotypical view of Aboriginal women.

The Changing Image of Aboriginal Women

The demeaning image of Aboriginal women is rampant in North American culture. School textbooks have portrayed Aboriginal woman as ill-treated at the hands of Aboriginal men, almost a "beast of burden." These images are more than symbolic — they have helped to facilitate the physical and sexual abuse of Aboriginal women in contemporary society. Emma LaRocque, a Métis woman and professor of Native Studies at the University of Manitoba, wrote to the Inquiry about such demeaning images.

> The portrayal of the squaw is one of the most degraded, most despised and most dehumanized anywhere in the world. The "squaw" is the female counterpart to the Indian male "savage" and as such she has no human face; she is lustful, immoral, unfeeling and dirty. Such grotesque dehumanization has rendered all Native women and girls vulnerable to gross physical, psychological and sexual violence. ... I believe that there is a direct relationship between these horrible racist/sexist stereotypes and violence against Native women and girls. I believe, for example, that Helen Betty Osborne was murdered in 1972 by four young men from The Pas, because these youths grew up with twisted notions of "Indian girls" as "squaws" ... Osborne's attempts to fight off these men's sexual advances challenged their racist expectations that an "Indian squaw" should show subservience ... [causing] the whites ... to go into a rage and proceed to brutalize the victim. ...

Our Inquiry was told by the Canadian Coalition for Equality and by the Manitoba Women's Directorate that the media today continue to employ stereotypical images of women. Both presentations compared lurid newspaper coverage of the Helen Betty Osborne murder in The Pas to the more straightforward and sympathetic coverage of the killing of a young non-Aboriginal woman in Winnipeg.

We consider societal attitudes to be an issue that this Inquiry must address. There is a perception among women's groups, both Aboriginal and non-Aboriginal, that abuse of Aboriginal women is more acceptable to the courts than abuse of non-Aboriginal women. While we do not subscribe to the view that there is differential treatment, we are disturbed enough by the perception to suggest that it needs to be addressed. At the heart of the problem is the belief that, fundamentally, justice authorities do not understand, and do not wish to understand, the unique issues facing Aboriginal women.

In order to address the underlying problems that give rise to this perception, the public generally, and those within the justice system specifically, need to be educated about those issues by Aboriginal women. Elsewhere in this report we have recommended that cross-cultural training be provided to a variety of individuals involved in the justice system. We would like to make it clear that Aboriginal women must play a central role in the development and delivery of those programs.

Unfortunately, Aboriginal men, over the centuries, have adopted the same attitude toward women as the European. As a result, the cultural and social degradation of Aboriginal women has been devastating.

According to the Manitoba Women's Directorate, the average annual income for Manitoba's Aboriginal women is less than 75% of that for other women. The labour force participation rate for Aboriginal women is 40%, while 72% of Aboriginal women do not have a high school diploma.

The status of Aboriginal women in the city of Winnipeg is particularly disturbing. Forty-three per cent of Aboriginal families are headed by single women, compared to 10% of non-Aboriginal families. In her presentation on behalf of the Women's Directorate, Janet Fontaine said:

> Poverty is an unmistakable factor in the lives of Manitoba Native women and children. Poverty has been shown to be positively correlated with conflict with the law, low levels of education, decreased opportunity for employment, and a low level of health.

The Abuse of Women and Children

The presentations of Aboriginal women were blunt and direct. Violence and abuse in Aboriginal communities has reached epidemic proportions.

This violence takes a number of forms. Sometimes it involves physical assaults between adult males. More often — and more disturbingly — it involves the victimization of the least powerful members of the community: women and children.

The Manitoba Women's Directorate submitted to our Inquiry a document entitled "Native Perspective on Rape." According to one of the women interviewed for the study:

- Rape is a common and widespread experience.
- Rape extends back many generations.
- People treat rape as a personal, private pain and do not talk about it unless there is an unavoidable crisis.
- The individual who is raped comes to view violence as [the norm].

The victimization of Aboriginal women has not only been manifested in their abuse, but also in the manner in which Aboriginal female victims are treated. Women victims often suffer unsympathetic treatment from those who should be there to help them. We heard one example of such treatment from the Aboriginal mother of a 16-year-old rape victim. She told of how the police came to her home after her daughter had reported being raped and had undergone hospital examination and police questioning.

The police told the mother that her daughter was lying and should be charged with public mischief. According to the mother, the officer added, "Didn't you want it when you were 16?" ...

Spousal Abuse

One study presented to our Inquiry stated that while one in 10 women in Canada is abused by her partner, for Aboriginal women the figure is closer to one in three. The most recent study of Aboriginal women by Aboriginal women, a survey conducted by the Ontario Native Women's Association in 1989, found that 80% of Aboriginal women had personally experienced family violence. Fifty-three per cent of Aboriginal women who responded to a survey conducted for us by the Indigenous Women's Collective indicated they had been physically abused. Seventy-four per cent of those women indicated they did not seek help.

The Thompson Crisis Centre stated that, generally, women are abused at least 20 times before seeking help. A March 1991 study by the Manitoba Association of Women and the Law found that the statistics of a 1980 federal study, Wife Battering in Canada: A Vicious Circle, still held: "women endure anywhere from 11 to 39 episodes of abuse before seeking help, and then they seek help more often from a shelter than from police. The Manitoba government Family Disputes Services branch says that abuse occurs at least 35 times before any outside assistance is sought. ..."

According to the 1991 report of the Manitoba Association of Women and the Law, some improvements have been made since 1983. Nevertheless, over 30% of domestic assault charges are stayed at some stage before trial. The percentage of those sentenced has increased from 48% in 1983 to 64% in 1986. However, only 7% of those sentenced in 1987 were sentenced to a term in jail. While we agree that certain cases need to be prosecuted to the full extent of the law, it does not appear that that avenue has been very effective to date.

Aboriginal women surveyed by the Indigenous Women's Collective indicated that the police response received by others discouraged them from going to the police for help. They complained of the lack of understanding of the problem by officers, and their lack of sensitivity. They believe the police do not understand the situation of the abused woman and the needs of children.

More than one woman who spoke to us told of complaining to the police, only to become the one removed from the home. This happened in spite of the fact that young children were left in the care of an intoxicated father. Others told of situations where police attended in the home, saw the situation was calm when they were there and told the woman everything would be all right. When the police left, the violence became worse than before. With such lack of support from police authorities, it is not surprising that women suffer in silence.

From this information, it is clear that women in abusive situations, particularly in isolated communities in northern Manitoba, do not feel confident in turning to the justice system. We were told that many abused Aboriginal women did not feel safe enough even to bring their personal stories before the inquiry.

Testimony presented to us by the Manitoba Action Committee on the Status of Women in Thompson made it clear why this was the case:

> A man who beat his sister with a length of wood and who had a record of previous convictions for violent acts, was sentenced to seven months. A man who severely beat his common law wife, smashing her face against a fence, kicking her in the face, and slamming her face against the wall, before dragging her into a house, was sentenced to five months in jail, to be followed by probation after his release.

Both these offenders were going to return to their home communities after serving their sentences. Offenders are returned to their community without notice to the victim — and without treatment — and, as a result, their victims were at risk upon their release. Reporting the crime to police authorities provides a temporary respite at best if the causes of abuse are not dealt with. ...

Women's groups expressed concern about the whole criminal justice system, from police to Crown attorneys, judges and correctional institutions. Crisis shelter workers affirmed the experience Aboriginal women have in dealing with the justice system:

> ... indifference/arrogance of lawyers; long police response time; insensitive response of police to spousal abuse; humiliating questioning; failure of police to protect victims; failure of police to take spousal abuse as a serious crime; difficulties obtaining peace bonds; lack of supports to witnesses and treatment of witnesses as criminals; difficulties obtaining protection or getting away from abusive partners in small communities.

In northern, isolated reserve communities, the abused woman is placed in a more difficult situation when the question of calling the police arises. If she calls the police, it may take a day or longer for them to arrive. If they arrive while a party is going on, they may refuse to remove the offender or may simply drive him down the road, from where he can return again, only angrier. There is a lack of housing for families in isolated communities and no "safe house" available for women and children trying to escape an abusive man. They may be forced to spend the night in the bush, or be forced to leave the reserve entirely.

Professor LaRocque points out that women move to urban centres to escape family or community problems. Men, on the other hand, cite employment as the reason for moving. In the new setting Aboriginal women experience personal, systemic, subtle and overt racial discrimination. What they are forced to run to is often as bad as what they had to run from. Why they feel they have to leave is a matter worthy of comment. Most chiefs and council members are male and often exhibit bias in favour of the male partner in a domestic abuse situation. This can effectively chase the woman from her home and community.

The unwillingness of chiefs and councils to address the plight of women and children suffering abuse at the hands of husbands and fathers is quite alarming. We are concerned enough about it to state that we believe that the failure of Aboriginal government leaders to deal at all with the problem of domestic abuse is unconscionable. We believe that there is a heavy responsibility on Aboriginal leaders to recognize the significance of the problem within their own communities. They must begin to recognize, as well, how much their silence and failure to act actually contribute to the problem.

Aboriginal leaders must speak out against abuse within their communities to their own community members, and they must take steps within their own spheres of community influence to assist the true victims. Women and children who report abuse should never feel they have to leave their communities in order to feel safe. Aboriginal communities and their leaders must do what is possible to make the home communities of abused women and children havens from abuse. The problem of abuse is dealt with presently by women either staying on the reserves and putting up with the abuse, or leaving their communities to live elsewhere, just to escape from it. It is clear, however, that most would prefer to stay in their home communities if they could be protected. ...

There is no equal division of property upon marriage breakdown recognized under the *Indian Act*. This has to be rectified. While we recognize that amending the *Indian Act* is not a high priority for either the federal government or the Aboriginal leadership of Canada we do believe that this matter warrants immediate attention. The Act's failure to deal fairly and equitably with Aboriginal women is not only quite probably unconstitutional, but also appears to encourage administrative discrimination in the provision of housing and other services to Aboriginal women by the Department of Indian Affairs and local governments.

B. MATRIMONIAL PROPERTY

One of the many forms of discrimination and abuse that Indian women face as a result of the *Indian Act* is an inability to effectively access and control property upon marital breakdown. Under the *Indian Act*, title to individual property is often held as a certificate of possession issued by the band council. On many Canadian reserves a strong trend has developed of issuing these certificates in the man's name in a marriage relationship, despite the matrilineal traditions that existed in some communities. Such a practice represents the extension of the patriarchal assumptions underlying the *Indian Act* that unequally distributed Indian status, political power, and property to men. The issue of the division of property upon marital breakdown on a reserve was dealt with in the following case.

DERRICKSON v. DERRICKSON

[1986] 1 S.C.R. 285, 26 D.L.R. (4th) 175

The judgment of the Court was delivered by

Chouinard J.: — The constitutional question stated in this appeal is as follows:

> Whether the provisions of Part 3 of the *Family Relations Act*, R.S.B.C. 1979, c. 121, dealing with the division of family assets, are constitutionally applicable to lands in a reserve held by an Indian, in view of the *Indian Act*, R.S.C. 1970, c. I-6?

The factual background is summarized by Hinkson J.A., who wrote the unanimous judgment of the Court of Appeal of British Columbia, [1984] 2 W.W.R. 754 at p. 755:

> The appellant wife and the respondent husband are members of the Westbank Indian Band. Each of them holds certificates of possession issued to them pursuant to the provisions of the *Indian Act*, R.S.C. 1970, c. I-6.
>
> The wife brought a petition for divorce and for other relief including a division of family assets pursuant to the provisions of the *Family Relations Act*, R.S.B.C. 1979, c. 121.
>
> At trial, the trial judge raised with counsel the question of whether the provisions of the *Family Relations Act* applied to lands alloted to the spouses by the Westbank Indian Band and for which they held certificates or possession issued pursuant to s. 20 of the *Indian Act*.
>
> The wife sought a declaration pursuant to Pt. 3 of the *Family Relations Act* that she was entitled to an undivided one-half interest in the properties for which her husband held certificates of possession. The husband resisted that claim for relief on the basis that if the lands in question were family assets as defined in the *Family Relations Act*, then that Act had no application to the lands because they were Indian lands. ...

The Interveners

Before this court, the Attorney General of British Columbia and the Attorney General of Ontario intervened in support of the appellant, the Attorney General of Canada in support of the respondent.

The Issues

In the case at bar it is common ground that the *Family Relations Act* is valid provincial legislation of general application. Beyond that the arguments developed in this Court were many and varied, and not always congruent even when supporting the same conclusions.

With respect, however, this appeal can in my view be resolved by consideration of the three following issues:

1. Are the provisions of the *Family Relations Act* applicable of their own force to lands reserved for the Indians?
2. Is the *Family Relations Act* referentially incorporated in the *Indian Act* by the application of s. 88 of the latter Act?
   This issue in turn breaks down into two:

   (a) Does s. 88 of the *Indian Act* apply to lands reserved for the Indians?
   (b) In the affirmative, do the provisions of the *Family Relations Act* fall within one of the exceptions in s. 88?

3. Can an order for compensation be made in accordance with s. 52(2)(c) of the *Family Relations Act* with respect to lands on a reserve in lieu of an order directing division of property?

1. Are the Provisions of the Family Relations Act Applicable of Their Own Force to Lands Reserved for the Indians?

Section 91(24) of the *Constitution Act, 1867* confers exclusive legislative authority on the Parliament of Canada in "all Matters" coming within the subject "Indians, and lands reserved for the Indians".

Title to reserve lands is vested in the Crown, federal or provincial. So long as they remain such, reserve lands are administered by the federal government and Parliament has exclusive legislative authority over them. The *Indian Act*, enacted under that authority, provides in s. 18(1):

> **18**(1) Subject to this Act, reserves are held by Her Majesty for the use and benefit of the respective bands for which they were set apart; and subject to this Act and to the terms of any treaty or surrender, the Governor in Council may determine whether any purpose for which lands in a reserve are used or are to be used is for the use and benefit of the band.

The purpose of the above subsection is to ensure that lands reserved for Indians are and remain used for the use and benefit of the band.

Under s. 20 ... possession of lands in a reserve is allotted to individual members of the band by the band council with the approval of the Minister of Indian Affairs and Northern Development who issues a certificate of possession.

By virtue of s. 24 cited above, a member of the band may transfer his right to possession only to the band or to another member of the band but no such transfer is effective until it is approved by the Minister.

I turn now to the provisions of the *Family Relations Act*.

Section 43 declares that each spouse is entitled to an undivided half-interest in each family asset upon the occurrence of certain events, in this case an order for dissolution of marriage.

Section 45 defines as a family asset property used for a family purpose.

Sections 48 and 49 deal with the effect of marriage and separation agreements upon family assets and provide for the filing, in the land title office, of a notice setting out the provisions of the marriage or separation agreement relating to the land in question.

Section 50 provides for the enforceability of a spouse's interest in matrimonial property.

Section 51 deals with judicial reapportionment of matrimonial property where the division under s. 43 or a marriage agreement would be unfair.

Section 52, already reproduced, governs the determination of the ownership, possession or division of matrimonial property.

Section 53 allows the court to make interim orders in respect of matrimonial property.

The appellant argues that the pith and substance of the *Family Relations Act* is the division of matrimonial property, not the use of Indian lands. She further argues that it in no way encroaches on the exclusive federal jurisdiction as to the use of Indian lands. She is supported in these views by the Attorney-General of British Columbia and the Attorney-General of Ontario.

With respect I do not accept the latter proposition where Indian lands are involved.

The various orders that can be made under s. 52(2) deal, inter alia, with ownership, right of possession, transfer of title, partition or sale of property, severance of joint tenancy. ...

The right to possession of lands on an Indian reserve is manifestly of the very essence of the federal exclusive legislative power under s. 91(24) of the *Constitution Act, 1867*. It follows that provincial legislation cannot apply to the right of possession of Indian reserve lands.

When otherwise valid provincial legislation, given the generality of its terms, extends beyond the matter over which the legislature has jurisdiction and over a matter of federal exclusive jurisdiction, it must, in order to preserve its constitutionality, be read down and given the limited meaning which will confine it within the limits of the provincial jurisdiction.

It follows that the provisions of the *Family Relations Act* dealing with the right of ownership and possession of immovable property, while valid in respect of other immovable property, cannot apply to lands on an Indian reserve.

2. Is the Family Relations Act Referentially Incorporated in the Indian Act by the Application of s. 88 of the Latter Act?

With respect to Indians, valid provincial legislation of general application which would normally have to be read down in order to preserve its constitutionality, may be made applicable to Indians by referential incorporation in the *Indian Act* through the operation of s. 88 of the Act, subject to the exceptions stated in the section.

Section 88 of the *Indian Act* reads:

> 88. Subject to the terms of any treaty and any other Act of the Parliament of Canada, all laws of general application from time to time in force in any province are applicable to and in respect of Indians in the province, except to the extent that such laws are inconsistent with this Act or any order, rule, regulation or by-law made thereunder, and except to the extent that such laws make provision for any matter for which provision is made by or under this Act.

It is now settled that the provincial laws of general application to which s. 88 refers are those laws which could not apply to Indians without regulating them *qua* Indians. It is also settled that those laws that are made applicable to Indians by the operation of s. 88 are not applicable to them *ex proprio vigore* but are so made applicable by referential incorporation in the *Indian Act*: see *Dick v. The Queen*, [1985] 2 S.C.R. 309. ...

It is far from settled, however, that s. 88 contemplates referential incorporation with respect to lands reserved for the Indians.

It follows that the provisions of the *Family Relations Act* at issue will be found not to be referentially incorporated in the *Indian Act* if s. 88 does not apply to lands reserved for the Indians.

If it were found that s. 88 does apply to Indian lands, the provisions of the *Family Relations Act* would still not be referentially incorporated if they fall within one of the exceptions provided for in that section. Hence the two following questions.

(a) Does s. 88 of the Indian Act Apply to Lands Reserved for the Indians?

... The submission that s. 88 does not apply to lands reserved for Indians is quite simple. It is to the effect that not one but two subject-matters are the object of s. 91(24) of the *Constitution Act, 1867*, namely: "Indians" and "Lands reserved for the Indians". Since only Indians are mentioned in s. 88, that section would not apply to lands reserved for the Indians. ...

Be that as it may, it is not essential for the resolution of this case to determine the issue if we find, as I think we must, that even assuming that s. 88 applies to lands reserved for the Indians, the impugned provisions of the *Family Relations Act* are not referentially incorporated in the *Indian Act* since they are excluded by the application of the federal paramountcy set out in the section.

(b) Do the Provisions of the Family Relations Act Fall Within One of the Exceptions in s. 88?

In P.W. Hogg, *Constitutional Law of Canada* (2nd ed. 1985), it is stated at pp. 561-62:

> The Importance of s. 88 lies in its definition of the laws that *do not* apply to Indians. The section is explicitly "subject to the terms of any treaty", which means that any conflict between a treaty made with the Indians and a provincial law of general application has to be resolved in favour of the treaty provision, thus reversing the normal rule for such conflicts.
>
> The section is also subject to "any other act of the Parliament of Canada", so that any conflict between a federal statute and a provincial law has to be resolved in favour of the federal statute. A provincial law is also inapplicable where it is "inconsistent with this Act or any order, rule, regulation or by-law made thereunder". These two parts of the section seem to be intended to make clear that the paramountcy doctrine applies to provincial laws, notwithstanding their adoption by a federal statute. However, the closing language of the section goes on to provide that the provincial laws are applicable "except to the extent that such laws make provision for any matter for which provision is made by or under this Act". This language in its context seems to contemplate that a provincial law which makes provision for any matter for which provision is made by (or under) the *Indian Act* must yield to the provisions of the *Indian Act*. The doctrine of paramountcy, on the other hand, at least as it has been interpreted recently, applies only where there is an express contradiction between a federal and a provincial law. It does not apply where the federal and provincial laws, while not in direct conflict, are merely occupying the same field, or in other words making provision for the same matters. It seems probable therefore that the closing words of s. 88 go further than the paramountcy doctrine and will render inapplicable to Indians some provincial laws which would have been applicable under the general law.

... With respect, in my view, the impugned provisions of the *Family Relations Act* do conflict with the *Indian Act*.

Section 18 of the *Indian Act* provides that reserves are held by Her Majesty for the use and benefit of the bands.

Section 20 provides that the possession by an individual Indian can only come through allotment by the council together with the approval of the Minister. ...

Provisions such as are made in s. 52 of the *Family Relations Act* for orders dealing with ownership, right of possession, transfer of title, partition or sale of property, severance of joint tenancy are, in my view, in "actual conflict" with the above provisions of the *Indian Act*.

Were the provisions of both Acts to be applied at once as was sought in this case, the husband by virtue of his Certificate of Possession issued by the Minister following an allotment by the band council would be entitled to the sole possession of the land while the wife by virtue of an order of the court would be entitled to a half interest in the Certificate of Possession and the rights flowing therefrom.

In my respectful view, to make the order conditional on the approval of the Minister would not change the situation. ...

In the result, even assuming that s. 88 of the *Indian Act* applies to lands reserved for the Indians, the provisions of the *Family Relations Act* would, in my opinion, fall within that exception of s. 88 and would not be applicable to lands reserved for the Indians.

In reaching this conclusion I am not unmindful of the ensuing consequences for the spouses, arising out of the laws in question, according as real property is located on a reserve or not. In this respect I borrow the following sentence, albeit in a different context, from P. W. Hogg, *op. cit.*, at p. 554:

> Whether such laws are wise or unwise is of course a much-controverted question, but it is not relevant to their constitutional validity.

3. Can an Order for Compensation be Made in Accordance With s. 52(2)(c) of the Family Relations Act with Respect to Lands on a Reserve in Lieu of an Order Directing Division of Property?

Section 52(2)(c) of the *Family Relations Act* provides that the court may "order a spouse to pay compensation to the other spouse where property has been disposed of, or for the purpose of adjusting the division". ...

In this respect the trial judge held:

> As there can be no division of the reserve lands under Section 43 then there can be no determination of what "would be unfair". I, therefore, cannot make a substitution of compensation under Section 52(2)(c) for an "unfair division" under Sections 43 or 51.

Reversing on this point the Court of Appeal wrote, at p. 761:

> If the court is unable to award the wife an interest in the Indian reserve lands then the court may make an order for compensation for the purpose of adjusting the division of family assets between the spouses.

The Court of Appeal accordingly ordered that the matter be remitted to the trial judge in order that he may complete the disposition of the family assets involved in this proceeding by awarding compensation for the purpose of adjusting the division of family assets between the spouses.

With this I agree. If the court may make an order for compensation because division is not possible where property has been disposed of, surely it must be empowered to make such an order "for the purpose of adjusting the division", where property exists but cannot be divided because no division can be made of reserve lands.

The rule under s. 43 is that each spouse is entitled to an undivided half interest in all family assets, not immovable property only. Where having regard to the factors listed in s. 51 the division would be unfair, the court may fix different shares. With this we are not concerned here. Section 52(2)(c) provides for a compensation order "for the purpose of adjusting the division". All family assets having been taken into account, where an equal division is not possible because some assets, in this case lands on a reserve, cannot be divided, I fail to see why a compensation order could not be had.

Compensation in lieu of a division of property is not a matter for which provision is made under the *Indian Act* and in my view there is no inconsistency or "actual conflicts" between such a provision for compensation between spouses and the *Indian Act*.

I would answer the constitutional question as follows:

Question: Whether the provisions of Part 3 of the *Family Relations Act*, R.S.B.C. 1979, c. 121, dealing with the division of family assets, are constitutionally applicable to lands in a reserve held by an Indian, in view of the *Indian Act*, R.S.C. 1970, c. I-6?

Answer: No.

I would dismiss the appeal. No order as to costs was made by the Supreme Court nor by the Court of Appeal. I would likewise make no order as to costs.

Appeal dismissed.

MARY-ELLEN TURPEL, "HOME/LAND"

(1991), 10 Canadian Journal of Family Law 17 at 30 (references omitted)

The decisions in *Derrickson* and *Paul*, particularly at the Supreme Court of Canada level, project an image of a perfunctory division of powers conflict resolved by application of the constitutional doctrine of exclusivity of federal jurisdiction over Indians and lands reserved for the Indians. This style of reasoning masks the political complexity of the conflict(s) which were at the basis of *Derrickson* and *Paul*. The complexity stems from what can be called the "aboriginal dimension" of the legal dispute. This refers to the fact that the disputes that have arisen in these cases stem directly from the legacy of a colonial regime that continues to be imposed on aboriginal people by decontextualizing these conflicts and ignoring the impact of the law on aboriginal peoples' lives. To do otherwise would demand critical reflection on the inadequacy and oppressive nature of the colonial regime established by the *Constitution Act, 1867* and the *Indian Act*.

The chosen legal issue in *Derrickson* and *Paul* is which branch of the state should control which aspects of aboriginal life, not the very matter of state control itself. The state control of aboriginal life is the central political issue in these cases. Framing the issue in constitutional division of powers doctrine is an effective strategy for depoliticizing the cases and silencing any questioning of the overwhelming state control of (jurisdiction over) aboriginal peoples. The court, as an emanation of the colonial political regime for aboriginal peoples, is blinded to its role and to the political nature of the law it applies in this context.

Insensitivity to Aboriginal Conceptions of Property

The consequence of the *Derrickson* and *Paul* decisions is that an aboriginal woman who resides in a home on a reserve with her spouse cannot make an application under provincial family legislation for occupation or possession of the home upon marriage breakdown or in the event of physical and emotional abuse from her spouse. There is no federal family legislation to govern these conflicts. ...

Even if an aboriginal woman holds a certificate of possession jointly with her spouse under the *Indian Act*, she will have no recourse under provincial family law (the only family law) for access to her home. Moreover, the situation on Indian reserves is such that the certificates of possession are invariably issued to male band members so an appeal to the Department of Indian Affairs or the band council would be equally futile in most, if not all, cases. The practice of issuing certificates to men is a carry-over from the late nineteenth century practice of issuing location tickets to males, an extension of Anglo-European patriarchal notions of land holding and succession. It was this same philosophy that infused the gender discrimination provisions in relation to Indian status.

The *Indian Act* requirement of ministerial approval for any transfer of reserve land likely forecloses the possibility of successfully pursuing a remedy for the situation at common law ... Essentially, an aboriginal woman has no legally recognizable interest in her matrimonial home, unless she solely holds the certificate of possession. Even if this is the case, gaining an interim order for exclusive possession will be impossible as there is no legislation which will apply in this context. While this is an obvious injustice, there is another layer here which makes the injustice particularly cruel and oppressive: that is the cultural significance of property from an aboriginal perspective.

For aboriginal women, it is not the commodity character of property which is vital to her survival. ... The significance of matrimonial property must be understood in the context of what the reserve represents: it is a home of a distinct cultural and linguistic people. It is a community of extended families, tightly connected by history, language and culture. It is often the place where children can be educated in their language and culturally appropriate pedagogies. ... The economic value of the land is secondary to its value as shelter within a larger homeland — the homeland of her people, her family.

The second aspect of matrimonial property theory that infuses this area, the notion of equality of the spouses, is, similarly, not entirely applicable in the aboriginal matrimonial context. In most aboriginal communities, the belief is that women, children and elders come before men and the responsibility of the men is to live life as a good helper toward women, children and elders. Traditional tribal control of property did not lead to the victimization of aboriginal women. As one Mohawk lawyer suggests of property customs in the Iroquois Confederacy:

> The Iroquois woman's rights to the family property was based on political influence via the control over the economic wealth of the family ... she had real property rights even superior to those of her husband ... The property situation of the modern day Iroquois woman is vastly different from her historical sister prior to European contact. Traditionally she had the control of the family assets and family life. There has been a complete demotion. If she is not the legal owner of the family asset situated on an Indian reserve, then upon marriage dissolution she has no possibility of real property rights ... She is truly the forgotten victim in a matrimonial dissolution. Her situation is equivalent to that under the "separate as to property regime" which was remedied by provincial matrimonial legislation in the common law provinces. She has recourse only under common law trust doctrines and provincial compensation schemes. She no longer has her traditional real property rights over family assets.

The decisions in *Derrickson* and *Paul* sanction a situation which is completely opposite to that of the customs of many tribes. There are no obligations on aboriginal men now recognized at law to provide shelter for women, children or elders. Indeed, customary law has no place in matrimonial property disputes as Canadian law will not recognize it — it is the federal or provincial government which exercises jurisdiction over Indians upon marriage breakdown. The impact of this oppression of aboriginal custom on communities cannot be underestimated. When men no longer have to fulfill their responsibilities to women, children and elders, the social control network of the community disintegrates and respect for social responsibilities is lost.

Disregard For the Violence Aboriginal Women Endure

The cultural and spiritual conceptions of property held by aboriginal peoples find no recognition in the cases on matrimonial property. The social reality for aboriginal peoples also does not enter into the discourse of division of powers which has been seized upon by all levels of courts in these cases. The appellants had to structure their arguments into claims based upon alien property notions and legal doctrines foreign to the customs of their communities. Could a claim have been made on the basis of customary law (that is, the aboriginal) practice of the community? Undoubtedly, this was the farthest thing in the minds of lawyers advising the appellants in *Derrickson* and *Paul*, or the court in examining the legitimacy of their claims under Canadian (*i.e.* federal or provincial) law. Moreover, it would be difficult, if not impossible, according to Canadian constitutional law.

The Canadian legal system is revealed, once again, as a thoroughly colonial regime. It is too busy trying to categorize jurisdictional matters between federal and provincial governments to step back and realize the oppressive and presumptuous nature of its exercise. To expect it to do so is to expect too much given that this branch of the state is an emanation and expression of a colonial state. In fact, the role of the judicial branch of the state is going to be, in such a regime, to justify the colonial mentality using legal doctrine. It is little wonder that the legal system enjoys a low level of respect from aboriginal peoples who see this exercise. The actors within the system and, even most academic commentators, often fail to see the violence this situation foists on aboriginal peoples. Aboriginal peoples have nowhere to turn to voice their grievances — taking them to court means accepting an alien system. Doing nothing has only meant continued oppression and an implosion of violence and social upheaval in communities. The violence of silence is difficult to endure, and it is violence. ...

The complete silencing of aboriginal women's experiences and indeed of the aboriginal dimension of *Derrickson* and *Paul*, exposes the deleterious colonial character of Canadian constitutional law. The reasoning employed in the two decisions demonstrates the role played by the Canadian legal system in camouflaging the social and political aspects of aboriginal peoples' conflicts. Courts have been unable to grasp the impact of aboriginal treatment by a colonial legal system because this would require its dismantling and a critical examination of the function of the courts and law in perpetuating the oppression. Dismantling it would require recognizing aboriginal peoples' presence as political communities in Canada with distinct cultural linguistic and social systems. It would require ending bureaucratic regulation of Indian life through the *Indian Act*. No court has been honest or reflective enough to acknowledge the colonial character of the regulation of aboriginal life in Canada. Meanwhile aboriginal peoples have had to endure the violence of a colonial regime which silences aboriginal reality and displays disregard for aboriginal peoples' suffering.

C. DENIAL OF STATUS UNDER THE INDIAN ACT

The *Indian Act*'s discriminatory provisions extend far beyond the denial of property to women in cases of marital breakdown. Another example of the inequality built into the Act is found in its provisions relating to Indian status. For many years, Indian women who married non-Indian men automatically lost their status under the *Indian Act*. If an Indian man married a non-Indian women, no such disability was incurred. The disparate impact of these provisions reflected the patrilineal assumptions that underlie the Act. Once a woman lost her status she could no longer reside on the reserve, secure treaty promises and policy initiatives designed to assist Indians, or participate in the political and social life of the community. The effect of these provisions was to fracture extended families and exile women from their homes and culture. This legislation sent women from the reserves and undermined their influence and position within their communities. In the last few decades this negative change in gender relations created a drive to reconstruct Indian communities and restore the dignity and respect Indian women once enjoyed. The effort to reinstate this dignity was undertaken by some very courageous women who worked hard against the discrimination they faced. Reform of the provisions of the *Indian Act* that concerned the discriminatory effects of Indian status is explored below through a review of the Act's history, and the efforts of aboriginal women who brought important cases in the domestic and international realm to challenge its provisions.

REPORT OF THE ROYAL COMMISSION ON ABORIGINAL PEOPLES, PERSPECTIVES AND REALITIES, VOL. 4

(Ottawa: Ministry of Supply and Services, 1996) at 24-33
(references omitted)

Policy Development and its impact on First Nations Women

The First 100 Years: 1850 – 1950

> Historically the Indian Act has thoroughly brainwashed us. Since 1869 Indian women already were legislated as to who she should be. Six times the Indian Act changed on Indian women. But each time she lost a little bit of her rights as an Indian.

> Nellie Carlson
> Indian Rights for Indian Women
> Edmonton, Alberta, 11 June 1992

The earliest laws dealing directly and explicitly with Indian people date from the middle of the nineteenth century and were enacted as part of the reserve policy of imperial and colonial governments to protect reserve lands from encroachment by non-Indian settlers. Once protected lands had been set aside for exclusive Indian use and occupation, it became necessary to define who was Indian.

The first statutory definition of "Indian" is found in *An Act for the better protection of the Lands and Property of the Indians in Lower Canada*, passed in 1850. The definition is quite inclusive. It includes all those of Indian blood and their descendants, non-Indians who have married Indians living on the designated lands, and even persons adopted in infancy by Indians. Within one year, this definition became more restrictive as a result of amending legislation that denied non-Indian men who married Indian women the right to acquire Indian status, but Indian status could still be gained by non-Indian women who married Indian men.

The descendants of all intermarriages who actually resided on a reserve would nonetheless still be considered Indians irrespective of the status of one of the spouses, since they would fall within that part of the definition of Indian that referred to Indian blood. However, it is obvious that the same rule did not apply to men and women in mixed marriages as it had under the earlier legislation. For the first time, Indian status began to be associated with the male line of descent.

The concept of enfranchisement was introduced in 1857 through *An Act to encourage the gradual Civilization of the Indian Tribes in the Province, and to amend the Laws respecting Indians*. The act applied to both Upper and Lower Canada, and its operating premise was that by removing the legal distinctions between Indians and non-Indians through enfranchisement and by facilitating the acquisition of individual property by Indians, it would be possible in time to absorb Indians fully into colonial society. An enfranchised Indian was, in effect, actually renouncing Indian status and the right to live on protected reserve land in order to join non-Aboriginal colonial society. The modern department of Indian affairs describes the nature and effect of the *Gradual Civilization Act* as follows:

> [The Act]...contained property and monetary inducements to encourage Indians to leave tribal societies and seek enfranchisement. An enfranchised person could receive land and a sum of money equal to the principal of the annuities and other yearly revenues received by the band. The intent of this legislation was that enfranchised Indians would continue to reside in the Native community but would have the same rights as non-Indian citizens.

The Act applied only to adult male Indians. Under s. 3 of the act, to be enfranchised an Indian had to be male, over age 21, able to read and write either English or French, reasonably well educated, free of debt, and of good moral character as determined by a commission of examiners. The right to exercise the franchise depended upon meeting the requirements in federal and provincial legislation in terms of property ownership. Thus, there was no automatic right to vote. Indians were given a three-year qualifying period to acquire these attributes.

Women were not to be enfranchised independently. Yet if an Indian man was enfranchised, his wife and children were automatically enfranchised along with him, regardless of their wishes; willingly or not, they lost their Indian status. From a woman's perspective, this act perpetuated the notion of a wife and children as the husband's property, his chattels. Unlike her husband, the enfranchised woman did not receive a share of reserve lands, because by this time, in keeping with prevailing Victorian notions, maleness and the right to possess and live on reserve lands were becoming fixtures of Indian policy.

If an enfranchised man died, for example, his children of lineal descent were given precedence to inherit the estate and to live on his land. His wife would inherit the estate and land allotted to him if and only if there were no children of lineal descent. She would then have the right to use it only until her re-marriage or death, at which point it would revert to Crown ownership.

In the pre-Confederation period, concepts were introduced that were foreign to Aboriginal communities and that, wittingly or unwittingly, undermined Aboriginal cultural values. In many cases, the legislation displaced the natural, community-based and self-identification approach to determining membership — which included descent, marriage, residency, adoption and simple voluntary association with a particular group — and thus disrupted complex and interrelated social, economic and kinship structures. Patrilineal descent of the type embodied in the *Gradual Civilization Act*, for example, was the least common principle of descent in Aboriginal societies, but through these laws, it became predominant. From this perspective, the *Gradual Civilization Act* was an exercise in government control in deciding who was and was not an Indian.

At Confederation, the secretary of state became the superintendent general of Indian affairs and, in 1868, acquired control over Indian lands and funds through federal legislation. The definition of "Indian" was finalized on a patrilineal model, excluding non-Indian men who married Indian women but including non-Indian women who married Indian men.

The first important piece of post-Confederation legislation, the *Gradual Enfranchisement Act*, was passed in 1869. This act went further than previous legislation in its "civilizing" and assimilative purposes and in marginalizing Indian women: for the first time, Indian women were accorded fewer legal rights than Indian men in their home communities. The prevailing Victorian social and political norms were now extended to include reserve communities. For example, Indian women were denied the right to vote in band elections; voting was now restricted to adult men, as it was in Canadian society generally. As well, a new provision was added to the provisions carried over from the *Gradual Civilization Act*. Now a woman who married an Indian man from another band lost membership in her home community, as did her children, and she became a member of her husband's band.

In the eyes of Aboriginal women, the most damaging aspects of this legislation were the new provisions that penalized women who married non-Indian men. Under the earlier *Gradual Civilization Act*, there had been no penalty for such a marriage beyond the fact that the non-Indian husband did not gain Indian status upon marriage. Under this new legislation, by contrast, the Indian wife was legally stripped of her recognized Indian identity, and she and the children of the marriage lost the rights that flowed from Indian status. They were no longer entitled to treaty payments, for example, unless the band council agreed to continue them. No similarly disadvantageous provisions applied to Indian men who married non-Indian women. Aside from the inherent unfairness of this policy, there were other potentially damaging consequences for women. A woman could be compelled to leave the reserve — her home community — since her non-Indian husband could be summarily ejected by the superintendent general.

From the perspective of the twentieth century, one may well wonder how such a policy could make its way into federal legislation. The official explanation at the time focused on concerns about control over reserve lands and the need to prevent non-Indian men from gaining access to them. Thus, in 1869 the secretary of state wrote to the Mohawks of Kahnawake regarding the marrying out provisions of the new legislation, stressing that the goal was "preventing men not of Indian Blood having by marrying Indian women either through their Wives or Children any pretext for Settling on Indian lands". The *Gradual Enfranchisement Act* permitted reserves to be subdivided into lots; the superintendent general could then issue "location tickets" allocating specific lots to individual Indian men or women. In the earlier *Gradual Civilization Act*, the fear had been that non-Indian men might gain control over Indian lands; hence the need to exclude them from Indian status and reserve residency rights. In the *Gradual Enfranchisement Act*, that same rationale was extended to justify the exclusion of women from their own communities. Moreover, given the social values of the day, it also seems to have been assumed that Indian women who married non-Indians would be protected by them and would acquire property rights under Canadian law through their non-Indian spouse, thus rendering unnecessary the protection that came from Indian status and the property rights they might have as members of an Indian community on protected reserve lands.

In the relatively short period between the 1850 Lower Canada legislation and the 1863 *Gradual Enfranchisement Act*, it seems apparent that

Indian women were singled out for discriminatory treatment under a policy that made their identity as Indian people increasingly dependent on the identity of their husbands. They were subject to rules that applied only to them as women and that can be summarized as follows: they could not vote in band elections; if they married an Indian man from another band, they lost membership in their home communities; if they married out by wedding a non-Indian man, they lost Indian status, membership in their home communities, and the right to transmit Indian status to the children of that marriage; if they married an Indian man who became enfranchised, they lost status, membership, treaty payments and related rights and the right to inherit the enfranchised husband's lands when he died. Despite strong objections, these discriminatory provisions were carried forward into the first *Indian Act* in 1876.

1876: The first Indian Act

In its 100 sections, the 1876 *Indian Act* consolidated and expanded previous Indian legislation, carrying forward the provisions that put Indian women at a disadvantage compared to Indian men. Commenting on these provisions, historian J.R. Miller highlights the irony of the official justification that these measures were necessary to protect Indian lands and social structures:

> The *Indian Act's* tracing of Indian descent and identity through the father was the unthinking application of European patrilineal assumptions by a patriarchal society; but it accorded ill with those Indian societies, such as the Iroquoian, in which identity and authority flowed through the female side of the family. All these attempts at cultural remodelling also illustrate how the first step on the path of protection seemed always to lead to the depths of coercion.

As we will see, a large share of the effects of this coercion was borne by Indian women.

The *Indian Act* went through a number of changes as amendments were introduced and adopted over the years, usually in response to unanticipated administrative problems or to strengthen the assimilative thrust of federal Indian policy. Although most of the provisions that discriminated against women were simply carried forward from earlier legislation, additional measures of the same nature were also adopted. Thus, in 1884, an amendment permitted the wife of an Indian man who held reserve land by location ticket to receive one-third of her husband's estate, if he died without a will. But the amendment stated that the widow might receive it only if she were living with him at the time of death and was "of good moral character" as determined by federal authorities. This amendment applied standards to women that were not applied to men, standards that were, moreover, ambiguous and that could be interpreted arbitrarily by officials outside Indian communities.

Amendments in 1920 increased the power of the superintendent general at the expense of the band council. Until this time, councils had the authority to decide whether an Indian woman who married out would continue to receive treaty annuity payments and band money distributions, or whether she would get a lump sum settlement. Many bands allowed these women to continue receiving payments and distributions so they could retain some link to the home community. The 1920 amendments removed this power from the band and lodged it in the hands of the superintendent general of Indian affairs. The official rationale for this provision was set out in a letter from Deputy Superintendent General Duncan Campbell Scott:

> When an Indian woman marries outside the band, whether a non-treaty Indian or a white man, it is in the interest of the Department, and in her interest as well, to sever her connection wholly with the reserve and the Indian mode of life, and the purpose of this section was to enable us to commute her financial interests. The words "with the consent of the band" have in many cases been effectual in preventing this severance ... The amendment makes in the same direction as the proposed Enfranchisement Clauses, that is it takes away the power from unprogressive bands of preventing their members from advancing to full citizenship.

Importantly, in that same set of amendments were new enfranchisement provisions that allowed the governor in council, on the recommendation of the superintendent general, forcibly to enfranchise any Indian, male or female, if found to be "fit for enfranchisement", along with his or her children."

The 1951 amendments to the Indian Act

The *Indian Act* was completely revised in 1951. A number of provisions were introduced that would affect Indian women. The provisions dealing with status, membership and enfranchisement were significantly modified in a way that further disadvantaged women and their children. The status provisions became vastly more elaborate and spelled out in great detail who was and was not entitled to be registered as an Indian for federal government purposes.

The mention of Indian blood, a feature of the definition of "Indian" since 1876, was replaced by the notion of registration, with a strong emphasis on the male line of descent. The new rules dealt with acquisition and loss of Indian status, referring to persons who were "entitled to be registered" as "Indian". Only they would be recognized as Indian by federal authorities. The result was that many people of Indian ancestry and culture who had been involuntarily enfranchised, who had been deleted from treaty or band lists accidentally. ...

Before these new provisions were introduced in 1951, women who had lost their Indian status through marrying out had often been able to retain their links to their communities. Some Indian agencies would issue an informal identity card known as a "red ticket" identifying such women as entitled to share in band treaty moneys and, in many cases, to continue to live on the reserve. Because they were no longer legally Indians but remained members of the reserve community by virtue of band practice and their red tickets, the precise status in law of such women was unclear to Indian affairs officials and the general Canadian public. With forced enfranchisement upon marrying out, there could no longer be doubt in anyone's mind that they were not Indian and, moreover, not part of any Indian community.

Nonetheless, Indian women who had married out before the 1951 changes were permitted to keep their red ticket status if they did not accept a lump sum settlement in exchange for their treaty payments. However, an amendment to the Indian Act in 1956 stopped this practice. After 1956, "red ticket" women were paid a lump sum of 10 times the average annual amount of all payments paid over the preceding 10 years. These women were put in the same unfavourable position as Indian women who married out after the 1951 revision. The children of mixed marriages were not mentioned in the 1951 legislation. Despite the lack of legal authority for it, enfranchisement was forced on them too, under subsection 108(2). To correct this injustice, in 1956 Indian status was restored to these children. But the 1956 *Indian Act* amendments also allowed the governor in council "by order [to] declare that all or any of her children are enfranchised as of the date of the marriage or any such other date as the order may specify". While there do not appear to be any common or consistent criteria regarding how the discretion of the governor in council was to be exercised, the usual practice was that off-reserve children were enfranchised but children living on-reserve were allowed to keep their status.

None of these provisions applied to Indian men. They could not be enfranchised against their will after 1951 except through a stringent judicial inquiry procedure as prescribed in the revised *Indian Act*. This difference in treatment created a huge imbalance between the number of enfranchised men and the number of involuntarily enfranchised women. Between 1955 and 1975 (when forced enfranchisement of women stopped), 1,576 men became enfranchised (along with 1,090 wives and children), while 8,537 women (as well as 1,974 of their children) were forcibly enfranchised and lost their status. From 1965 to 1975, only five per cent of enfranchisements were voluntary; 95 per cent were involuntary, and the great majority of these involved women.

Post-1951 to pre-1985: Growing awareness, growing tension

Between 1951 and 1985, equality and civil rights movements were a prominent feature of the socio-political landscape in North America. Aboriginal voices were being raised, and there was growing awareness of the concerns of Aboriginal people, including the concerns of Indian women. The governments of the day were making some effort to consult Aboriginal people about issues affecting them, but there was little change in the *Indian Act* until the early 1980s.

The status provisions of the *Indian Act* and the exclusion of women who married out were of great concern to the Aboriginal women's groups that sprang up during this period. In 1970, the Royal Commission on the Status of Women tabled its final report. The commission was particularly concerned that the "special kind of discrimination under the terms of the *Indian Act* ... the loss of Indian status, or enfranchisement, implies that rights and privileges given to a member of a band ... will be denied to that person ... Enfranchisement or deletion of the name of an Indian from the Indian Registry is much more frequent for women than for men". The commission recommended that the act be amended to allow an Indian woman upon marriage to a non-Indian to "(a) retain her Indian status and (b) transmit her Indian status to her children". Two important court cases challenged this inequality head on. Jeannette Corbiere Lavell, an Ojibwa woman and member of the Wikwemikong band on Manitoulin Island in Ontario, had married a non-Indian in 1970. She was living in Toronto when she brought the action in 1971, charging that subsection 12(l)(b) violated the equality clause in the 1960 *Canadian Bill of Rights* on the grounds of discrimination by reason of sex. ... Yvonne Bedard, from the Six Nations Reserve in southern Ontario, lost her status when she married out in 1964. ... Her case was argued on the same grounds as the *Lavell* case. ...

Significantly, both Lavell and Bedard pursued their cases without any support — moral or otherwise — from their communities, band councils, or Indian political organizations. On the contrary, they were actively opposed, not only by the government of Canada but also by their own communities.

CANADA (ATTORNEY GENERAL) v. LAVELL

[1974] S.C.R. 1349, 38 D.L.R. (3d) 481

The judgment of **Fauteux C.J.**, and **Martland**, **Judson** and **Ritchie JJ.** was delivered by

Ritchie J.: — I have had the advantage of reading the reasons for judgment prepared for delivery by my brother Laskin.

These appeals, which were heard together, are from two judgments holding that the provisions of s. 12(1)(*b*) of the *Indian Act*, R.S.C. 1970, c. I-6, are rendered inoperative by s. 1(*b*) of the *Canadian Bill of Rights*, 1960 (Can.), c. 44, as denying equality before the law to the two respondents.

Both respondents were registered Indians and "Band" members within the meaning of s. 11(*b*) of the *Indian Act* when they elected to marry non-Indians and thereby relinquished their status as Indians in conformity with the said s. 12(1)(b) which reads as follows:

> **12.** (1) The following persons are not entitled to be registered, namely,
>
> (*b*) a woman who married a person who is not an Indian, unless that woman is subsequently the wife or widow of a person described in section 11.

It is contended on behalf of both respondents that s. 12(1)(b) of the Act should be held to be inoperative as discriminating between Indian men and women and as being in conflict with the provisions of the *Canadian Bill of Rights* and particularly s. 1 thereof which provides:

> **1.** It is hereby recognized and declared that in Canada there have existed and shall continue to exist without discrimination by reason of race, national origin, colour, religion or sex, the following human rights and fundamental freedoms, namely, ...
>
> (*b*) the right of the individual to equality before the law and the protection of the law; ...

I think it desirable at the outset to outline the facts concerning the two respondents separately.

1. *Mrs. Lavell* — This woman was a member of the Wikwemikong Band of Indians who married a non-Indian and whose name was deleted from the Indian Register by the Registrar in charge thereof pursuant to the provisions of section 12(1)(b) of the Act. An appeal was taken from the Registrar's decision and was heard before His Honour Judge Grossberg, acting as *persona designata* under the *Indian Act* before whom evidence was taken which disclosed that at the time of the hearing and for some nine years before her marriage Mrs. Lavell had not lived on any Reserve except for sporadic visits to her family, and the learned judge declined to accept the suggestion that she could not visit her family on the Reserve whenever she wished. Mrs. Lavell did not claim to have been deprived of any property rights on the Reserve except those incidental to the right as a Band member.

Judge Grossberg having found that in his opinion section 12(1)(*b*) of the *Indian Act* was not rendered inoperative by the *Bill of Rights*, an appeal was taken from his judgment to the Federal Court of Appeal where a judgment was rendered by Mr. Justice Thurlow who concluded his opinion by saying of section 12(1)(*b*) of the *Indian Act*:

> These provisions are thus laws which abrogate, abridge and infringe the right of an individual Indian woman to equality with other Indians before the law. Though this is not a situation in which an act is made punishable at law on account of race or sex, it is one in which under the provisions here in question the consequences of the marriage of an Indian woman to a person who is not an Indian are worse for her than for other Indians who marry non-Indians and than for other Indians of her band who marry persons who are not Indians. *In my opinion this offends the right of such an Indian woman as an individual to equality before the law* and the *Canadian Bill of Rights* therefore applied to render the provisions in question inoperative.

(The italics are my own.)

It is from this judgment that the Crown now appeals.

2. *Mrs. Bédard* — In this case the respondent sought an injunction restraining the members of the Six Nations Council from expelling her and her two infant children from the home she occupied on the Six Nations Indian Reserve in the County of Brant, and an order setting aside a resolution passed by the Council ordering her to dispose of such property. By agreement an additional claim was added for a declaratory judgment concerning the respective rights of the parties.

Mrs. Bédard was born on the Six Nations Indian Reserve of Indian parents and she married a non-Indian in May, 1964, by whom she had two children and with whom she resided off the Reserve until June 23, 1970 when, having separated from her husband, she returned to the Reserve to live in a house on a property to which her mother had held a Certificate of Possession under s. 20 of the *Indian Act* and which had been bequeathed to her under her mother's will which had been approved by the Council of the Six Nations and on behalf of the Minister of Indian Affairs as required by the *Indian Act*, (section 45(3)) on August 7, 1969.

When Mrs. Bédard returned to the Reserve with her children in 1970 to occupy her mother's house, the Council passed a series of resolutions giving her permission to reside on the Reserve for a period of six months during which she was to dispose of the property, and extending this permission for a further eight months, after which any further requests for her continued residence would be denied. In accordance with these resolutions this respondent conveyed her interest in the property in question to her brother who was a registered member of the Six Nations Band, and to whom a Certificate of Possession of the property was granted on March 15, 1971 by the Minister. Her brother, however, permitted Mrs. Bédard and her infant children to continue occupying the premises without rent, but the Band Council passed a further resolution on September 15, 1971 by which it was resolved that the Brant District Supervisor should be requested to serve a notice to quit the Reserve upon this respondent. It should be noted that the writ instituting this action was issued on September 14, 1971, more than a year after the brother had obtained his Certificate of Possession and that no notice to quit has been served on Mrs. Bédard pursuant to the resolution which was passed after the writ was issued.

Mrs. Bédard's case was heard by Mr. Justice Osler in the Supreme Court of Ontario where it was contended that the Council's request to the District Supervisor and any action taken by the Supervisor pursuant to such request, and the removal of her name from the Band list simply because of her marriage to a non-Indian, are actions that discriminate against her by reason of her race and sex and deny her "equality before the law". Mr. Justice Osler, basing his decision on the judgment of the Federal Court of Appeal in the *Lavell* case, concluded that:

> Section 12(1)(*b*) of the Act is ... inoperative and all acts of the Council Band and of the District Supervisor purporting to be based on the provisions of that section can be of no effect.

Leave to appeal from this judgment was granted by order of this Court on January 25, 1972.

The contention which formed the basis of the argument submitted by both respondents was that they had been denied equality before the law *by reason of sex*, and I propose to deal with the matter on this basis. ...

In my opinion the exclusive legislative authority vested in Parliament under s. 91(24) could not have been effectively exercised without enacting laws establishing the qualifications required to entitle persons to status as Indians and to the use and benefit of Crown "lands reserved for Indians". The legislation enacted to this end was, in my view, necessary for the implementation of the authority so vested in Parliament under the constitution.

To suggest that the provisions of the *Bill of Rights* have the effect of making the whole *Indian Act* inoperative as discriminatory is to assert that the Bill has rendered Parliament powerless to exercise the authority entrusted to it under the constitution of enacting legislation which treats Indians living on Reserves differently from other Canadians in relation to their property and civil rights. The proposition that such a wide effect is to be given to the *Bill of Rights* was expressly reserved by the majority of this Court in the case of *The Queen v. Drybones* [[1970] S.C.R. 282], at 298, to which reference will hereafter be made, and I do not think that it can be sustained.

What is at issue here is whether the *Bill of Rights* is to be construed as rendering inoperative one of the conditions imposed by Parliament for the use and occupation of Crown lands reserved for Indians. These conditions were imposed as a necessary part of the structure created by Parliament for the internal administration of the life of Indians on Reserves and their entitlement to the use and benefit of Crown lands situate thereon, they were thus imposed, in discharge of Parliament's constitutional function under s. 91(24) and in my view can only be changed by plain statutory language expressly enacted for the purpose. It does not appear to me that Parliament can be taken to have made or intended to make such a change by the use of broad general language directed at the statutory proclamation of the fundamental rights and freedoms enjoyed by all Canadians, and I am therefore of opinion that the *Bill of Rights* had no such effect....

The contention that the *Bill of Rights* is to be construed as overriding all of the special legislation imposed by Parliament under the *Indian Act* is, in my view, fully answered by Pigeon J. in his dissenting opinion in the *Drybones* [[1970] S.C.R. 282] case where he said, at p. 304:

> If one of the effects of the *Canadian Bill of Rights* is to render inoperative all legal provisions whereby Indians as such are not dealt with in the same way as the general public, the conclusion is inescapable that Parliament, by the enactment of the *Bill*, has not only fundamentally altered the status of the Indians in that indirect fashion but has also made any future use of federal legislative authority over them subject to the requirement of expressly declaring every time 'that the law shall operate notwithstanding the *Canadian Bill of Rights*'. I find it very difficult to believe that Parliament so intended when enacting the *Bill*. If a virtual suppression of federal legislation over Indians as such was meant, one would have expected this important change to be made explicitly not surreptitiously so to speak.

That it is membership in the Band which entitles an Indian to the use and benefit of lands on the Reserve is made plain by the provisions of ss. 2 and 18 of the *Indian Act*; Section 2(1)(*a*) reads as follows:

> **2.**(1) In this Act 'band' means a body of Indians
>
> (*a*) for whose use and benefit in common, lands the legal title to which is vested in Her Majesty, have been set apart before, on or after the 4th day of September 1951,
>
>   . . . . .

Section 18 reads as follows:

> **18.** (1) Subject to this Act, reserves are held by Her Majesty for the use and benefit of the respective bands for which they were set apart; and subject to this Act and to the terms of any treaty or surrender, the Governor in Council may determine whether any purpose for which lands in a reserve are used or are to be used is for the use and benefit of the band... .

The opening words of s. 2 of the *Bill of Rights* are, in my view, determinative of the test to be applied in deciding whether the section here impugned is to be declared inoperative. The words to which I refer are:

2. Every law of Canada shall, unless it is expressly declared by an act of the Parliament of Canada that it shall operate notwithstanding *the Canadian Bill of Rights*, be so construed and applied as not to abrogate, abridge or infringe or authorize the abrogation, abridgement [or] infringement of the freedoms herein recognized and declared ...

In the course of the reasons for judgment rendered on behalf of the majority of this Court in *The Queen v. Drybones, supra,* this language was interpreted in the following passage at p. 294:

It seems to me that a more realistic meaning must be given to the words in question and they afford, in my view, the clearest indication that s. 2 is intended to mean and does mean that if a law of Canada cannot be "sensibly construed and applied' so that it does not abrogate, abridge or infringe one of the rights and freedoms, recognized and declared by the Bill, then such law is inoperative 'unless it is expressly declared by an Act of the Parliament of Canada that it shall operate notwithstanding the *Canadian Bill of Rights*".

Accordingly, in my opinion, the question to be determined in these appeals is confined to deciding whether the Parliament of Canada in defining the prerequisites of Indian status so as not to include women of Indian birth who have chosen to marry non-Indians, enacted a law which cannot be sensibly construed and applied without abrogating, abridging or infringing the rights of such women to equality before the law.

In my view the meaning to be given to the language employed in the *Bill of Rights* is the meaning which it bore in Canada at the time when the Bill was enacted, and it follows that the phrase "equality before the law" is to be construed in light of the law existing in Canada at that time.

In considering the meaning to be attached to "equality before the law" as those words occur in section 1(*b*) of the Bill, I think it important to point out that in my opinion this phrase is not effective to invoke the egalitarian concept exemplified by the 14th Amendment of the U.S. Constitution as interpreted by the courts of that country. (See *Smythe v. The Queen* [[1971] S.C.R. 680] per Fauteux C.J. at pp. 683 and 686). I think rather that, having regard to the language employed in the second paragraph of the preamble to the *Bill of Rights*, the phrase "equality before the law" as used in s. 1 is to be read in its context as a part of "the rule of law" to which overriding authority is accorded by the terms of that paragraph.

In this connection I refer to *Stephens Commentaries on the Laws of England*, 21st Ed. 1950, where it is said in Vol. III at p. 337:

Now the great constitutional lawyer Dicey writing in 1885 was so deeply impressed by the absence of arbitrary governments present and past, that he coined the phrase "the rule of law" to express the regime under which Englishmen lived; and he tried to give precision to it in the following words which have exercised a profound influence on all subsequent thought and conduct.

"That the 'rule of law' which forms a fundamental principle of the constitution has three meanings or may be regarded from three different points of view ...."

The second meaning proposed by Dicey is the one with which we are here concerned and it was stated in the following terms:

It means again equality before the law or the equal subjection of all classes to the ordinary law of the land administered by the ordinary courts; the "rule of law" in this sense excludes the idea of any exemption of officials or others from the duty of obedience to the law which governs other citizens or from the jurisdiction of the ordinary courts.

"Equality before the law" in this sense is frequently invoked to demonstrate that the same law applies to the highest official of government as to any other ordinary citizen, and in this regard Professor F.R. Scott, in delivering the Plaunt Memorial Lectures on Civil Liberties and Canadian Federalism in 1959, speaking of the case of *Roncarelli v. Duplessis* [[1959] S.C.R. 121], had occasion to say:

It is always a triumph for the law to show that it is applied equally to all without fear or favour. This is what we mean when we say that all are equal before the law.

The relevance of these quotations to the present circumstances is that "equality before the law" as recognized by Dicey as a segment of the rule of law, carries the meaning of equal subjection of all classes to the ordinary law of the land *as administered by the ordinary courts*, and in my opinion the phrase "equally before the law" as employed in section 1(*b*) of the *Bill of Rights* is to be treated as meaning equality in the administration or application of the law by the law enforcement authorities and the ordinary courts of the land. This construction is, in my view, supported by the provisions of subsections (*a*) to (*g*) of s. 2 of the Bill which clearly indicate to me that it was equality in the administration and enforcement of the law with which Parliament was concerned when it guaranteed the continued existence of "equality before the law".

Turning to the *Indian Act* itself, it should first be observed that by far the greater part of that Act is concerned with the internal regulation of the lives of Indians on Reserves and that the exceptional provisions dealing with the conduct of Indians off Reserves and their contacts with other Canadian citizens fall into an entirely different category.

It was, of course necessary for Parliament, in the exercise of section 91(24) authority, to first define what Indian meant, and in this regard s. 2(1) of the Act provides that:

"Indian" means a person who pursuant to this Act is registered as an Indian or is entitled to be registered as an Indian.

It is therefore clear that registration is a necessary prerequisite to Indian status...

The *Drybones* case can, in my opinion, have no application to the present appeals as it was in no way concerned with the internal regulation of the lives of Indians on Reserves or their right to the use and benefit of Crown lands thereon, but rather deals exclusively with the effect of the *Bill of Rights* on a section of the *Indian Act* creating a crime with attendant penalties for the conduct by Indians off a Reserve in an area where non-Indians, who were also governed by federal law, were not subject to any such restriction.

The fundamental distinction between the present case and that of *Drybones*, however, appears to me to be that the impugned section in the latter case could not be enforced without denying equality of treatment in the administration and enforcement of the law before the ordinary courts of the land to a racial group, whereas no such inequality of treatment between Indian men and women flows as a necessary result of the application of s. 12(1)(*b*) of the *Indian Act*.

To summarize the above, I am of opinion:

1. That the *Bill of Rights* is not effective to render inoperative legislation, such as s. 12(1)(*b*) of the *Indian Act*, passed by the Parliament of Canada in discharge of its constitutional function under s. 91(24) of the *B.N.A. Act*, to specify how and by whom Crown lands reserved for Indians are to be used;

2. that the *Bill of Rights* does not require federal legislation to be declared inoperative unless it offends against one of the rights specifically guaranteed by section 1, but where legislation is found to be discriminatory, this affords an added reason for rendering it ineffective;

3. that equality before the law under the *Bill of Rights* means equality of treatment in the enforcement and application of the laws of Canada before the law enforcement authorities and the ordinary courts of the land, and no such inequality is necessarily entailed in the construction and application of s. 12(1)(*b*).

I would allow the appeal of the *Attorney General of Canada against J.V. Corbiere Lavell*, reverse the judgment of the Federal Court of Appeal and restore the decision of Judge B.W. Grossberg. In accordance with the terms of the order of the Federal Court of Appeal granting leave to appeal to this Court, the appellant will pay to the respondent her solicitor and client costs of the appeal and the application for leave. There should be no further order as to costs.

On the appeal of *Richard Isaac and others v. Yvonne Bédard*, a question was raised in this Court as to the jurisdiction of the trial court. In view of the conclusion reached on the merits, no decision is now necessary on that question. The appeal to this Court should be allowed, the judgment at trial should be reversed and the action dismissed. Under the circumstances, there should be no order as to costs in that case in any court.

Abbott J. (dissenting): ... I would dismiss both appeals with costs.

The judgment of **Hall, Spence** and **Laskin JJ.** (dissenting) was delivered by

J. Laskin J. (dissenting) ... In my opinion, unless we are to depart from what was said in *Drybones*, both appeals now before us must be dismissed. I have no disposition to reject what was decided in *Drybones*; and on the central issue of prohibited discrimination as catalogued in s. 1 of the *Canadian Bill of Rights*, it is, in my opinion, impossible to distinguish *Drybones* from the two cases in appeal. If, as in *Drybones*, discrimination by reason of race makes certain statutory provisions inoperative, the same result must follow as to statutory provisions which exhibit discrimination by reason of sex. ...

The *Drybones* case decided two things. It decided first-hand this decision was a necessary basis for the second point in it — that the *Canadian Bill of Rights* was more than a mere interpretation statute whose terms would yield to a contrary intention; it had paramount force when a federal enactment conflicted with its terms, and it was the incompatible federal enactment which had to give way. ... The second thing decided by *Drybones* was that the accused in that case, an Indian under the *Indian Act*, was denied equality before the law, under s. 1(*b*) of the *Canadian Bill of Rights*, when it was made a punishable offence for him, on account of his race, to do something which his fellow Canadians were free to do without being liable to punishment for an offence. ...

It would be unsupportable in principle to view the *Drybones* case as turning on the fact that the challenged s. 94 of the *Indian Act* created an offence visited by punishment. The gist of the judgment lay in the legal disability imposed upon a person by reason of his race when other persons were under no similar restraint. If for the words "on account of race" there are substituted the words "on account of sex" the result must surely be the same where a federal enactment imposes disabilities or prescribes disqualifications for members of the female sex which are not imposed upon members of the male sex in the same circumstances.

It is said, however, that although this may be so as between males and females in general, it does not follow where the distinction on the basis of sex is limited as here to members of the Indian race. This, it is said further, does not offend the guarantee of "equality before the law" upon which the *Drybones* case proceeded. I wish to deal with these two points in turn and to review, in connection with the first point, the legal consequences for an Indian woman under the *Indian Act* when she marries a non-Indian.

It appears to me that the contention that a differentiation on the basis of sex is not offensive to the *Canadian Bill of Rights* where that differentiation operates only among Indians under the *Indian Act* is one that compounds racial inequality even beyond the point that the Drybones case found unacceptable. ...

Section 12(1)(*b*) effects a statutory excommunication of Indian women from this society but not of Indian men. Indeed, as was pointed out by counsel for the Native Council of Canada, the effect of ss. 11 and 12(1)(*b*) is to excommunicate the children of a union of an Indian woman with a non-Indian. There is also the invidious distinction, invidious at least in the light of the *Canadian Bill of Rights*, that the *Indian Act* creates between brothers and sisters who are Indians and who respectively marry non-Indians. The statutory banishment directed by s. 12(1)(*b*) is not qualified by the provision in s. 109(2) for a governmental order declaring an Indian woman who has married a non-Indian to be enfranchised. Such an order is not automatic and no such order was made in relation to Mrs. Bédard; but when made the woman affected is, by s. 110, deemed not to be an Indian within the *Indian Act* or any other statute or law. It is, if anything, an additional legal instrument of separation of an Indian woman from her native society and from her kin, a separation to which no Indian man who marries a non-Indian is exposed. ...

In my opinion, the appellants' contentions gain no additional force because the *Indian Act*, including the challenged s. 12(1)(*b*) thereof, is a fruit of the exercise of Parliament's exclusive legislative power in relation to "Indians, and Lands reserved for the Indians" under s. 91(24) of the *British North America Act*. Discriminatory treatment on the basis of race or colour or sex does not inhere in that grant of legislative power. The fact that its exercise may be attended by forms of discrimination prohibited by the *Canadian Bill of Rights* is no more a justification for a breach of the *Canadian Bill of Rights* than there would be in the case of the exercise of any other head of federal legislative power involving provisions offensive to the *Canadian Bill of Rights*. The majority opinion in the *Drybones* case dispels any attempt to rely on the grant of legislative power as a ground for escaping from the force of the *Canadian Bill of Rights*. The latter does not differentiate among the various heads of legislative power; it embraces all exercises under whatever head or heads they arise. Section 3 which directs the Minister of Justice to scrutinize every Bill to ascertain whether any of its provisions are inconsistent with ss. 1 and 2 is simply an affirmation of this fact which is evident enough from ss. 1 and 2.

Pigeon J.: — I agree in the result with **Ritchie J.**

----

1. What justifies the government being involved with the internal affairs of Indians according to the majority in this case?
2. Justice Ritchie wrote that: "no inequality of treatment between Indian men and Indian women flows as a necessary result of the application of s. 12(1)(*b*) of the *Indian Act*". Do you agree? How did Justice Ritchie arrive at this conclusion?
3. Do you think the *Lavell and Bédard* case would be decided differently under the Charter?
4. Justice Ritchie characterizes the case as follows: "what is at issue here is rendering inoperative conditions imposed by parliament". Do you agree?

The case of *Lavell and Bédard* illustrates the difficulties Aboriginal women encountered in challenging the *Indian Act* before the Canadian courts. The Supreme Court's deference to federal legislative power and its adherence to select notions of formal equality stood as significant barriers to remedying the inequality of Aboriginal women within their communities. Having exhausted their avenues of appeal within Canada, Aboriginal women continued their efforts to reform the *Indian Act* before the international community. The following case and commentary from Sandra Lovelace demonstrates the importance of international legal instruments and domestic advocacy in fighting discrimination in Canada.

LOVELACE v. CANADA

36 U.N. GOAR Supp. (No. 40) Annex XVIII; U.N. Doc. A/36/40 (1981)

Views of the Human Rights Committee under Article 5(4) of the Optional Protocol of the International Covenant on Civil and Political Rights concerning

Communication No. R.6/24

Submitted by: Sandra Lovelace
Date of communication: 29 December 1977

The Human Rights Committee established under article 28 of the *International Covenant on Civil and Political Rights*

Meeting on 30 July 1981; — having concluded its consideration of communication No. R.6/24 submitted to the Committee by Sandra Lovelace under the Optional Protocol to the *International Covenant on Civil and Political Rights*; — having taken into account the written information made available to it by the authors of the communication and by the state party concerned; adopts the following:

VIEWS UNDER ARTICLE (4) Of THE OPTIONAL PROTOCOL

1. The author of the communication dated 29 December 1977 and supplemented by letters of 17 April 1978, 28 November 1979 and 20 June 1980, is a 32 year old woman, living in Canada. She was born and registered as "Maliseet Indian" but has lost her rights and status as an Indian in accordance with section 12(1)(b) of the *Indian Act*, after having married a non-Indian on 23 May 1970. Pointing out that an Indian man who marries a non-Indian woman does not lose his Indian status, she claims that the Act is discriminatory on the grounds of sex and contrary to articles 2(1), 3, 23(1) and (4), 26 and 27 of the Covenant. As to the admissibility of the communication she contends that she was not required to exhaust local remedies since the Supreme Court of Canada, in *The Attorney General of Canada v. Jeanette Lavell, Richard Isaac et al. v. Yvonne Bedard* (1974) S.C.R. 1349, held that section 12(1)(b) was fully operative, irrespective of its inconsistency with the *Canadian Bill of Rights* on account of discrimination based on sex.

. . . . .

5. In its submission under article 4(2) of the Optional protocol concerning the merits of the case, dated 4 April 1980, the state party recognized that "many of the provisions of the ... *Indian Act*, including section 12(l)(b), require serious reconsideration and reform". The government further referred to an earlier public declaration to the effect that it intended to put a reform bill before the Canadian Parliament. It none the less stressed the necessity of the *Indian Act* as an instrument designed to protect the Indian minority in accordance with article 27 of the Covenant. A definition of the Indian was inevitable in view of the special privileges granted to the Indian communities, in particular their right to occupy reserve lands. Traditionally, patrilineal family relationships were taken into account for determining legal claims. Since, additionally, in the farming societies of the nineteenth century, reserve land was felt to

be more threatened by non-Indian men than by non-Indian women, legal enactments as from 1869 provided that an Indian woman who married a non-Indian man would lose her status as an Indian. These reasons were still valid. A change in the law could only be sought in consultation with the Indians themselves who, however, were divided on the issue of equal rights. The Indian community should not be endangered by legislative changes. Therefore, although the government was in principle committed to amending section 12(1)(b) of the *Indian Act*, no quick and immediate legislative action could be expected.

6. The author of the communication, in her submission of 20 June 1980, disputes the contention that legal relationships within Indian families were traditionally patrilineal in nature.

. . . . .

9.2 It emerges from statistics provided by the state party that from 1965 to 1978, on an average, 510 Indian women married non-Indian men each year. Marriages between Indian women and Indian men of the same band during that period were 390 on the average each year; between Indian women and Indian men of a different band 422 on the average each year; and between Indian men and non-Indian women 448 on the average each year.

. . . . .

9.6 As to Mrs. Lovelace's place of abode prior to her marriage, both parties confirm that she was at that time living on the Tobique Reserve with her parents. Sandra Lovelace adds that as a result of her marriage, she was denied the right to live on an Indian reserve. As to her abode since then, the state party observes:

> Since her marriage and following her divorce, Mrs. Lovelace has, from time to time, lived on the reserve in the home of her parents, and the band Council has made no move to prevent her from doing so. However, Mrs. Lovelace wishes to live permanently on the reserve and to obtain a new house. To do so, she has to apply to the Band Council. Housing on reserves is provided with money set aside by Parliament for the benefit of registered Indians. The Council has not agreed to provide Mrs. Lovelace with a new house. It considers that in the provision of such housing priority is to be given to registered Indians.

. . . . .

9.9 On behalf of Sandra Lovelace the following is submitted in this connection:

All the consequence of loss of status persist in that they are permanent and continue to deny the complainant of the right she was born with.

A person who ceases to be an Indian under the *Indian Act* suffers from the following consequences:

1. Loss of the right to possess or reside on lands on a reserve (ss. 25 and 28(1)). This includes loss of the right to return to the reserve after leaving, the right to inherit possessory interest in land from parents and others, and the right to be buried on a reserve;

2. An Indian without status cannot receive loans from the Consolidated Revenue Fund for the purposes set out in section 70;

3. An Indian with benefit cannot benefit from instruction in farming… (see s. 71);

4. An Indian without status cannot benefit from medical treatment and health services under section 73(1)(g);

5. An Indian without status cannot reside on tax exempt lands (See section 87);

6. A person ceasing to be an Indian loses the right to borrow money for housing from the Band Council (Consolidated Regulations of Canada 1978, c. 949);

7. A person ceasing to be an Indian loses the right to cut timber free of dues on an Indian reserve…

8. A person ceasing to be an Indian loses traditional hunting and fishing rights that may exist;

9. The major loss to a person ceasing to be an Indian is the loss of cultural benefits of living in an Indian community, the emotional ties to home, family, friends and neighbours, and the loss of identity.

10. The Human Rights Committee, in the examination of the communication before it, has to proceed from the basic fact that Sandra Lovelace married a non-Indian on 23 May 1970 and consequently lost her status as a Maliseet Indian under section 12(l)(b) of the *Indian Act*. This provision was — and still is — based on a distinction de jure on the ground of sex. However, neither its application to her marriage as the cause of her loss of Indian status nor its effects could at that time amount to a violation of the Covenant, because this instrument did not come into force for Canada until 19 August 1976. Moreover, the Committee is not competent, as a rule, to examine allegations relating to events having taken place before the entry into force of the Covenant and the Optional protocol. Therefore, as regards Canada, it can only consider alleged violations of human rights occurring on or after 19 August 1976. …

11. The Committee recognizes, however, that the situation may be different if the alleged violations, although relating to events occurring before 19 August 1976, continue, or have effects which themselves constitute violations, after that date. In examining the situation of Sandra Lovelace in this respect, the Committee must have regard to all relevant provisions of the Covenant. It has considered, in particular, the extent to which the general provisions in articles 2 and 3 as well as the rights in articles 12(1), 17(1), 23(1), 44, 26 and 27, may be applicable to the facts of her present situation.

12. The Committee first observes that from 19 August 1976 Canada had undertaken under article 2(1) and (2) of the Covenant to respect and ensure to all individuals within its territory and subject to its jurisdiction, the rights recognized in the Covenant without distinction of any kind such as sex, and to adopt the necessary measures to give effect to these rights. Further, under article 3, Canada undertook to ensure the equal right of

men and women to the enjoyment of these rights. These undertakings apply also to the position of Sandra Lovelace. The Committee considers, however, that it is not necessary for the purposes of her communication to decide their extent in all aspects. The full scope of the obligation of Canada to remove the effects or inequalities caused by the application of existing laws to past events, in particular as regards such matters as civil or personal status, does not have to be examined in the present case, for the reasons set out below.

13.1 The Committee considers that the essence of the present complaint concerns the continuing effect of the *Indian Act*, in denying Sandra Lovelace legal status as an Indian, in particular because she cannot for this reason claim a legal right to reside where she wishes to, on the Tobique Reserve. This fact persists after the entry into force of the Covenant, and its effects have to be examined, without regard to their original cause. Among the effects referred to on behalf of the author (quoted in paragraph 9.9, above, and listed (1) to (9)), the greater number, ((1) to (8)), relate to the *Indian Act* and other Canadian rules in fields which do not necessarily adversely affect the enjoyment of rights protected by the Covenant. In this respect the significant matter is her last claim, that "the major loss to a person ceasing to be an Indian is the loss of the cultural benefits of living in an Indian community, the emotional ties to home, family, friends and neighbours, and the loss of identity".

13.2 Although a number of provisions of the Covenant have been invoked by Sandra Lovelace, the Committee considers that the one which is most directly applicable to this complaint is article 27, which reads as follows:

> In those states in which ethnic, religious or linguistic minorities exist, persons belonging to such minorities shall not be denied the right, in community with other members of their group, to enjoy their own culture, to profess and practice their own religion, or to use their own language.

It has to be considered whether Sandra Lovelace, because she is denied the legal right to reside on the Tobique Reserve, has by that fact been denied the right guaranteed by article 27 to persons belonging to minorities, to enjoy their own culture and to use their own language in community with other members of their group.

14. The rights under article 27 of the Covenant have to be secured to "persons belonging" to the minority. At present Sandra Lovelace does not qualify as an Indian under Canadian legislation. However, the *Indian Act* deals primarily with a number of privileges which, as stated above, do not as such come within the scope of the Covenant. Protection under *the Indian Act* and protection under article 27 of the Covenant therefore have to be distinguished. Persons who are born and brought up on a reserve, who have kept ties with their community and wish to maintain these ties must normally be considered as belonging to that minority within the meaning of the Covenant. Since Sandra Lovelace is ethnically a Maliseet Indian and has only been absent from her home reserve for a few years during the existence of her marriage, she is, in the opinion of the Committee, entitled to be regarded as "belonging" to this minority and to claim the benefits of article 27 of the Covenant. The question whether these benefits have been denied to her, depends on how far they extend.

15. The right to live on a reserve is not as such guaranteed by article 27 of the Covenant. Moreover, the *Indian Act* does not interfere directly with the functions which are expressly mentioned in that article. However, in the opinion of the Committee the right of Sandra Lovelace to access to her native culture and language "in community with the other members" of her group, has in fact been, and continues to be interfered with, because there is no place outside the Tobique Reserve where such a community exists. ...

16. In this respect, the Committee is of the view that statutory restrictions affecting the right to residence on a reserve of a person belonging to the minority concerned, must have both a reasonable and objective justification and be consistent with the other provisions of the Covenant. Read as a whole, Article 27 must be construed and applied in the light of the other provisions mentioned above, such as articles 12, 17 and 23 insofar as they may be relevant to the particular case, and also the provisions against discrimination, such as articles 2, 3 and 26, as the case may be. It is not necessary, however, to determine in any general manner which restrictions may be justified under the Covenant, in particular as a result of marriage, because the circumstances are special in the present else.

17. The case of Sandra Lovelace should be considered in the light of the fact that her marriage to a non-Indian has broken up, it is natural that in such a situation she wishes to return to the environment in which she was born, particularly as after the dissolution of her marriage her main cultural attachment again was to the Maliseet band. Whatever may be the merits of the *Indian Act* in other respects, it does not seem to the Committee that to deny Sandra Lovelace the right to reside on the reserve is reasonable, or necessary to preserve the identity of the tribe. The Committee therefore concludes that to prevent her recognition as belonging to the band is an unjustifiable denial of her rights under article 27 of the Covenant, read in the context of the other provisions referred to.

18. In view of this finding, the Committee does not consider it necessary to examine whether the same facts also show separate breaches of the other rights invoked. ...

19. Accordingly, the Human Rights Committee, acting under article 5(4) of the Optional protocol to *the International Covenant on Civil and Political Rights*, is of the view that the facts of the present case, which establish that Sandra Lovelace has been denied the legal right to reside on the Tobique Reserve, disclose a breach by Canada of article 27 of the Covenant.

Do you agree with the Committee's decision to treat Sandra Lovelace's case as a violation of Article 27 (minority rights) of the *International Covenant on Civil and Political Rights,* rather than a violation of Articles 2 and 3 (equality rights) of the *Covenant*?

Should Aboriginal peoples more frequently turn to International Law in dealing with Aboriginal rights in Canada? What are the weaknesses and strengths of this system?

As you consider the success of the *Lovelace* case, it is important to remember that cases such as this are not launched in a vacuum. Intense personal and community decisions and much hard work often lie behind each action. As you read the following excerpt ask yourself: How important to the success of a legal action are the people behind the written decisions?

"RETROSPECTIVE", ENOUGH IS ENOUGH: ABORIGINAL WOMEN SPEAK OUT

(Toronto: The Women's Press, 1987) at 293-245

SANDRA LOVELACE SAPPIER AND KAREN PERLEY

SANDRA: We got into a lot of arguments with the chiefs about the reinstatement issue. They said things like, "You've made your bed, now sleep in it"; "My (white) wife is an Indian because the law says she is."

KAREN: They *believed*, the government says you're Indian, so you're Indian. Therefore the government tell us we're not Indian, so we're not Indians.

SANDRA: Then we'd start arguing. Heavy arguments! (laughter) "I was born an Indian," that's what I'd tell them.

KAREN: If they believed that, where is the reason in all of it! Sometimes your own flesh and blood would say, "You're not an Indian any more. That's the law; that's the *Indian Act*." See how law abiding Native Indian people are! (laughter) So we'd have these chiefs telling us, "It's our *right* to discriminate."

SANDRA: A few chiefs supported us. Davey, of course. But most of them are chauvinist. They'd say, "You're only a woman, so what do you know! Go watch your babies, clean your house." That's the attitude.

KAREN: Maybe the men will start changing now that the law has changed, though I don't think some of them realize yet that it has really changed. The other day a guy from here wanted to register his white bride. The band office said, "No way," and was he mad. See, that's how "aware" they are. The guy kept arguing, still trying to make her an Indian. What nerve!

SANDRA: Another argument our so-called leaders used against us was, giving women their status back would "dilute the Indian culture." How could it! I teach my children my Indian culture; the white women teach their kids their white culture, because the men are out working. It's mostly the mothers that teach the kids. My children are surrounded by my culture, my language, so how can we dilute it! I think Indian women coming back will *improve* it.

When you hear some of those guys, you get really angry. Then you go out there even if it means scraping together your welfare pennies to do it. If they are going to treat my child different from theirs, that makes me angry. Plus, I have two daughters and I don't want them to have to go through the same thing.

All that lobbying we did! The most devastating experience for me was when Joe Clark's government fell in late 1979. That was disgusting because we knew we were so close; Clark had promised the change. We were so sure. Then we had to start from square one with the Liberals all over again, and we already knew what asses the Liberals are. (laughter) They listen to men.

KAREN: There were so many frustrating experiences, I can't think of which was the worst. The Liberals, Indian Affairs. The Union (of New Brunswick Indians) so much against us, telling the media, "If there is reinstatement, there's going to be violence" — well, there hasn't been any violence yet.

SANDRA: Graydon, the Union president, told the media there was going to be violence if the women were reinstated. Who is going to do the violence? The Union? He said people would burn any houses non-status get. I doubt it. I don't think anyone would dare do that here, because the women would stick together.

KAREN: It was so frustrating when those guys talked so nice to our face, then went against us behind our back; also when the Native Women's Association of Canada wouldn't fight for the same things as us, when it should have been their fight too.

One thing I wish didn't happen was all the tension and bad feeling right here at home during the occupations. God, it was awful. You could feel the hate. Honest, it is just this year I started talking to some of those people — and it is an election year! (laughter) I won't be talking to them for long; things start getting dug up again.

SANDRA: The really painful stuff was right here at home. Plus strain on marriages and relationships because we were always gone lobbying. Especially towards the end, it started happening to all of us — "Gee, you're going *again*!" But we'd all go. (laughter) Because we knew it was important. We had to get it done and reinstatement was so close.

KAREN: I think we came up with some good strategies along the way, like getting white women's groups involved, writing letters and sending petitions to Ottawa. Some of those organizations were really big, like the United Church and NAC. The women's walk to Ottawa because it was women and children — we knew that would get to people. Getting to know the women M.P.s and senators. They did a lot of lobbying for us. Flora MacDonald, Lynn McDonald. Like in 1981 the women in parliament and senate from all the parties held a press conference and issued a joint statement calling for an end to 12(l)(b).

Then there were the strategies here at home. The petitions. Ninety-five percent of band members signed in favour of reinstatement, and we could tell people outside about that. Another good strategy was near election time when we thought, who can we get in here for chief that would support us! That's when we came up with Dave Perley.

SANDRA: At first he wasn't interested, but then individual people talked to him, "Come on, Davey, go for it." He did and after that, it always helped to tell the media, "Our chief supports us. He backs us up and accepts us." I always made sure I mentioned it, because it would make the other chiefs look bad for not supporting their women.

KAREN: Another thing, I think Glenna and Caroline were talking about, and honestly, I was just waiting for it to happen; having all of our sons marry the non-status women just so they could become status again. We were going to plan a mass wedding, like my son would marry Mavis or Pearl, and so on. (laughter) It sure would have gotten a lot of press!

I was kind of looking forward to that. But we didn't have to go that far.

Another effective strategy was Sandra's case to the United Nations. That's what got the media attention. I mean, it's *history*; it will be in history books, "Sandra Lovelace." (laughter) Once when we were at one of those cocktail parties in Ottawa, Sandra said, "I'd better take it easy. Tomorrow it might be in the papers, 'Sandra Lovelace fell on her face'." (laughter) All those trips to Ottawa.

KAREN: With me, I was still kind of nervous when it came to talking with people; I was always afraid I'd say the wrong thing, or I wouldn't understand what they were saying. (laughter) I never had to go through being interviewed for the press. I never said too much. I would tell Caroline, "Why should I go! I never really say anything." She'd say, "Yes, but you're very good at remembering things and writing stuff down."

SANDRA: There have to be people who watch and take notes.

KAREN: That's right. You sit and watch what's going on in the background while the other person is busy talking, and you learn a lot of things.

SANDRA: Even if we went and relaxed over a drink, we'd talk about it all the time; going over what had just happened, deciding what to do the next day. That's how we lived — it was our life.

KAREN: Another time, way back during the walk, somebody — Glenna, I think — called a cab. It was her first time in Ottawa, and she didn't know where anything was. We were on Parliament Hill and she told the cab driver where we wanted to go. A bunch of us women climbed in, and the guy drove around the corner and stopped. (laughter) The place was right there.

SANDRA: We had our disagreements, but we never disagreed on the most important issue. Our goal was reinstatement and we all agreed to that.

KAREN: If a couple of us disagreed over something, we'd just stay away from each other for a while, and by the next meeting everything would be all right. We never let anything break us up or stand in our way.

I think we were the first group of women to ever stand up to a chief and council on a reserve. We are amongst the reserves I know of. Maybe — I hope — some are doing it now. Why us!

SANDRA: Strong women. Stubborn, too.

KAREN: Strong, political-minded people, I think. Like Glenna is a very strong woman. Gookum. They were the two that started it. My mother was politically minded. When election time came around, she got into it — on the reserve and federal elections, too. We were exposed to politics at an early age.

Another thing is that we all lived in the States and travelled a lot. Maybe if you stay on the reserve all your life, you don't see anything. I mean, you live in a small, little world. But when you leave, and then come back, you see the difference.

SANDRA: You start asking, how come things are happening here that aren't happening anywheres else!

KAREN: And the ones who haven't been anywheres else were the hardest ones to try and convince to change.

Another thing with Tobique is that we've kept our language, whereas other reserves around here haven't so much. Maybe some of the matrilineal stuff and the strength of the women has been passed on, too.

SANDRA: A long time ago, before Christianity got in here, I think the men and women lived together equally. There was no discrimination. It was the women who chose their leader traditionally, because they were the ones raising the children; they knew who was strong.

When the men argued that they didn't want reinstatement for fear of the white men coming in and taking over, I think it's really us women they were afraid of. I think that is the main reason the chiefs opposed us so much. They know we are persistent. If we believe in something, we will fight, we'll keep at it until something comes of it. Maybe the men are afraid of the competition. (laughter)

That's why they want self-government without sexual equality. I never wanted self-government before the women got their rights back. The men have to work with the women to accomplish anything, and the sooner they learn that, the better everybody will be. I told a guy in Ottawa, "Listen, if you men would only work with us in unity." See, they were the ones always talking about "unity", but they didn't even want me back on the reserve and I was born here. I said, "If we all worked together we could have a lot of things accomplished. We could get Indian self-government, but we have to work together and be equal." He said, "You're right." But do you think they would do it! Not yet.

D.   AMENDMENTS TO THE INDIAN ACT: BILL C-31 AND ITS EFFECTS

The *Lovelace* decision caused Canada considerable international embarrassment and was regarded by many Indian women as a significant step towards their reinstatement as Indians and their restoration to their communities. Following the *Lovelace* case and a series of Constitutional conferences under s. 37 of the *Constitution Act, 1982* [being Schedule B of the *Canada Act 1982* (U.K.), 1982, c. 11], the federal government acted to amend the *Indian Act* and remove some of its offending provisions. These amendments, hereinafter referred to as Bill C-31 *(An Act to amend the Indian Act*, R.S.C. 1985, c. 32 (1st Supp.)), remedied some of the discrimination on the basis of sex found in the Act. The effects of these amendments are recounted in the following excerpt.

REPORT OF THE ROYAL COMMISSION ON ABORIGINAL PEOPLES, PERSPECTIVES AND REALITIES, VOL. 4

(Ottawa: Ministry of Supply and Services, 1996) at 33-36
(references omitted)

Bill C-31

The 1982 amendment of the constitution, incorporating the *Canadian Charter of Rights and Freedoms*, included the provision, in section 15, that "every individual is equal before and under the law and has the right to the equal protection and benefit of the law without discrimination based on race, national or ethnic origin, colour, religion, sex, age, or mental or physical disability". Section 15 of the *Charter* came into effect on 17 April 1985. The *Charter* accomplished overnight what the *Canadian Bill of Rights* and the *Canadian Human Rights Act* had been unable to do — motivating the government to eliminate provisions of the *Indian Act* that had been criticized for discriminating against Indian women. Some influence was also exerted by the case of *Lovelace v. Canada*, in which Canada's treatment of Indian women under the *Indian Act* was strongly criticized by the United Nations Human Rights Committee.

Bill C-31 Provisions

This led to the passage of Bill C-31 in 1985. The bill amended various sections of the *Indian Act*, in particular the status and band membership provisions. While Indian status would continue to be determined by the federal government, status was restored to those who lost it under subsection 12(1)(b) and other similarly discriminatory sections of the status and membership provisions. The general rule was that in future Indian status would be granted to those with at least one parent with status. The concept of enfranchisement, voluntary or otherwise, was totally abolished, and those who lost status through enfranchisement had their status restored. First-generation children of restored persons were granted first-time status. Band membership was guaranteed for some classes of persons restored to status or admitted to status for the first time. Not all were guaranteed automatic band membership, however.

Legal status as an Indian and band membership were formally separated in the act, with the former remaining under federal control. A band may now take control of its own membership from the department of Indian affairs by following the procedures set our in Bill C-31. Once a band has taken control of its membership, persons may be added to or deleted from the list of members according to the rules established by the band in a membership code. In short, the department of Indian affairs will no longer maintain the membership list for that particular band and will no longer have a say in how band membership decisions are made. ...

The amendments concerning restoration of Indian status and band control of membership would be a source of conflict when it came time to implement Bill C-31. There was concern that some bands might reject persons who had acquired or re-acquired Indian status through Bill C-31, whether because of sex discrimination or because of concerns that resources needed to accommodate new members might not be forthcoming from the federal government. To forestall this possibility, subsection 10(4) of the 1985 *Indian Act* included a provision that prohibited First Nations from excluding certain classes of persons from their membership lists. ...

The Impact of Bill C-31

The impact of Bill C-31 was enormous and profound. ... By June 1990, 75,761 applications had been made, representing 133,134 persons. The status Indian population grew by 19 per cent in five years because of Bill C-31 alone and, when natural growth was included, by a total of 33 per cent. ... As of 30 June 1995, Bill C-31 had added 95,429 persons to the status Indian population in Canada, more than half of them (57.2 per cent, 54,589) female.

Despite the amendments to the *Indian Act* that reinstated Aboriginal women to Indian status, many still continue to experience discrimination in their communities. The enormous increase in the status Indian population did not result in an equal increase in the population of reserve communities. This is largely because most persons restored to Indian status or with first-time status under Bill C-31 still live off-reserve. Although most Bill C-31 registrants continue to live off-reserve, it is not always by choice, since it has been difficult for some of them to get reserve residency rights even as band members. Some bands experienced significant population increases from Bill C-31 registrants while others had none. The average band increased in size by 19 per cent, although 80 per cent of the bands had fewer than 15 Bill C-31 registrants living on-reserve.

REPORT OF THE ROYAL COMMISSION ON ABORIGINAL PEOPLES, PERSPECTIVES AND REALITIES, VOL. 4

(Ottawa: Ministry of Supply and Services, 1996) at 36-37, 39-42
(references omitted)

Clearly, the full impact of Bill C-31 on reserve communities has yet to be felt. Some band leaders and community members are concerned about the possibility of crowding and disruption and have been resistant to inclusion of new band members in their communities. Services that could be affected by a population increase include housing, health and post-secondary education.

Indian women have their own concerns about Bill C-31. Women make up the majority of people reinstated under the bill, and fully three-quarters of those whose Indian status was restored — as opposed to those who gained status for the first time — are women. Despite its avowed attempt of bringing about sexual equality in the status and membership provisions of the *Indian Act*, Bill C-31 is nonetheless seen by many Aboriginal women as a continuation of the sexist policies of the past. ...

The bill created two main categories of status Indians. Under subsection 6(1), legal status is assigned to all those who had status before 17 April 1985, all persons who are members of new bands created since 17 April 1985 ... and all individuals who lost status through the discriminatory provisions of the *Indian Act*. ... Subsection 6(2) covers people with only one parent who is or was a status Indian under any part of section 6(1). ... The consequences [for future generations of First Nations people for] falling within subsection 6(1) or subsection 6(2) are felt by the woman's children and grandchildren. For these descendants the way their parents and grandparents acquired status will be important determinants of whether they will have Indian status and, if they do, whether and to what extent they will be able to pass it on to their children. ...

An example helps illustrate the inequality that results from these rules. The following is taken from the *Report of the Aboriginal Justice Inquiry of Manitoba* (which recommended that this form of discrimination cease):

> John and Joan, a brother and sister were both registered Indians. Joan married a Metis man before 1985 so she lost her Indian status under section 12(1)(b) of the former Act. John married a white woman before 1985 and she automatically became a status Indian. Both John and Joan have had children over the years. Joan now is eligible to regain her status under section 6(1)(c) and her children will qualify under section 6(2). They are treated as having only one eligible parent, their mother, although both parents are aboriginal. John's children gained status at birth as both parents were Indian legally, even though one was an aboriginal person.
>
> Joan's children can pass on status to their offspring only if they also marry registered Indians. If they marry unregistered aboriginal people or non-aboriginal people, then no status will pass to their children. All John's grandchildren will be status Indians, regardless of who his children marry. Thus, entitlement to registration for the second generation has nothing to do with racial or cultural characteristics. The Act has eliminated the discrimination faced by those who lost status, but has passed it on to the next generation.

The establishment of categories for Indian status was a concoction of the federal government, and instead of devising a bill that would truly repair the situation, it created a "paper blood system" that denied thousands of individuals the opportunity to claim or reclaim their heritage. ... The categorization of Indian status under Bill C-31 has implications for the entire aboriginal population in the coming generations. At present rates of marriage outside the 6(1) and 6(2) categories, status Indians will begin to disappear from the Indian register if the rules are not changed. One report of the problem supports this conclusions in the strongest or terms, noting that Bill C-31 "is the gateway to a world in which some Indians are more equal than others" because the 6(1)/ 6(2) distinction "creates two classes of Indian: *full* Indians and *half* Indians." Moreover, the report concludes, "In the long run these rules will lead to the extinction of First Nations".

While the cause of this discrimination can rightly be found to have originated in and been perpetrated by the *Indian Act*, some women are now experiencing adverse treatment from members within their communities. What is disturbing about this new form of discrimination is that, at times, it seems to be represented and perpetrated by the leadership within certain communities. Furthermore, recent issues of discrimination raise questions about who should participate in a share of the community's resources, be considered as part of the culture, and have a right to define what are acceptable grounds for determining citizenship. The following case, *Sawridge Band v. Canada (T.D.)*, [1996] 1 F.C. 3, [1995] 4 C.N.L.R. 121 (T.D.) raises the issue of the continued discrimination that First Nations women still appear to be encountering under the *Indian Act*.

SAWRIDGE BAND v. CANADA (T.D.)

[1996] 1 F.C. 3, [1995] 4 C.N.L.R. 121 (T.D.)

Muldoon J.: — This is a constitutional case, in which the plaintiffs sue for a declaration that key provisions of an Act of Parliament are inconsistent with parts of Section 35 of the Constitution of Canada, and in particular, as enacted by the *Constitution Act, 1982*, Schedule B, *Canada Act 1982*, 1982, c. 11 (U.K.). ...

The Legislation

The plaintiffs' grievance is stated to reside in an Act of Parliament: 33-34 Elizabeth II, *An Act to amend the Indian Act*, S.C. 1985, c. 27 (the 1985 amendment). Section 4 of that 1985 amendment is particularly noticed in enacting new Sections 8, 9, 10, 11 and 12 in the *Indian Act*, R.S.C. 1985, c. I-5. ...

The matters in issue focus primarily on the 1985 amendments' Sections 11 and 12, by contrast with their repealed predecessors...

The Pleadings

Paragraph 13 of the amended statement of claim alleges that the statutes of Parliament prior to the recognition and affirmation of existing Aboriginal and treaty rights on April 17, 1982 (with a few unstated limited exceptions) confirmed Indians' rights to determine their bands' members and did not impose additional members on the bands. The Attorney General's defence, however, denies all that, and avers those allegations are contrary to the explicit provisions of the successive Indian Acts and to the executive decisions made pursuant to that legislation. ...

Paragraph 14 of the statement of claim alleges as follows:

> 14. With the enactment of an Act entitled An Act to Amend the *Indian Act*, S.C. 1985, c.27 (the "1985 Amendment") Parliament attempted unilaterally to require Indian bands to admit certain persons to membership. The 1985 Amendment imposes members on a band without the necessity of consent by the council of the band or the members of the band itself and, indeed, imposes such persons on the band even if the council of the band or the membership objects to the inclusion of such persons in the band. This exercise of power by Parliament was unprecedented in the predecessor legislation.

The defendant avers in answer to the effect that he denies the allegation expressed in the last sentence and asserts that the 1985 amendment speaks for itself and further regarding the plaintiffs' paragraph 14, that section 91 head 24 of the *Constitution Act, 1867* ... accords Parliament exclusive authority to legislate, and it did legislate the criteria and conditions of band membership, as well as the circumstances in which entitlement can be acquired, held, lost, revoked, regained or restored without the consent of bands or band councils.

To the defendant's statements, the plaintiffs replied and joined issue (certified record: tab 4, page 2, paragraphs 2):

> 2. With respect to paragraphs 5(b), 11, 12 and 14 the Plaintiffs say that their existence as Indians, Tribes and Bands, living in organized societies, long

preceded any statute of the Parliament of Canada or treaty and that no such statute or treaty extinguished the right of such societies to determine their own membership. ...

Concerns About 1985 Amendments in Testimony

The foregoing review of the pleadings on how the 1985 amendment operated or was foreseen to operate, was reflected in the testimony of various witnesses. Perhaps the Court ought not to have permitted such speculative testimony, but it was not wholly inappropriate to hear from an elderly Aboriginal witness who was called and permitted to give "oral history", despite the rule against hearsay. Sophie Makinaw testified through the very excellent oral interpretation services of Harold Cardinal whom the Court praises and thanks for his manifestly first-rate, proficient and dedicated services. Mrs. Makinaw's testimony here is taken not for predictive accuracy, but for the purpose of demonstrating the plaintiffs' worst fears about the practical operation of the 1985 amendments. ...

> Now, when we look at this situation, it's got to be clear that we're not talking about only the woman who left our reserve [since 1951] returning to our communities. Those women now have their children, and in some cases they have their grandchildren. And in many cases if they return to our reserves, they will want to come back with their husbands; they will want their husbands to return with them.
>
> I want to talk specifically about the white husband in this instance. It is not clear that the white husband is going to be able to accept our ways and live the way we are. It may be that the white man who comes to live on our reserve will want to impose his own values, his ways which he is familiar with on us, on our communities, and I haven't really thought yet, I haven't had time to really try and determine what all the consequences of this possibility might be.
>
> One of the problems that we're even now encountering and that's going to be aggravating if large numbers of people come back to our reserves is the fact that even now our reserves are getting over populated. ...
>
> The question of who should live on our reserve is really a matter that should be decided by us as people who own and live on the land. That is a decision that should not be taken elsewhere or by someone else for us. ...
>
> The decision on who is a member of our band or not, or who is entitled, should be made by us. We already share ... as Cree people we already share a lot of land with, with the white people. All we retained for ourselves is what we have now in our reserves. If the white people want to give more land, more services, then they should take part of the land that was shared with them because they have an abundance of land to provide these things to these people, if that is what they want to do. ...
>
> We ... my difficulty is with non-Cree people or non-Cree persons because whether we're talking about a white person or a Métis, they are not familiar with our culture, they are not familiar with our ways, and when they come and live with us, they are aggressive, they want to control us. They live in a way that's different from us and often they're not honest, and that's what ... that's a difficulty I have. ...

The Constitution's Textual Provisions

One should return to the theme of the plaintiffs' apprehensions about the 1985 amendment which they allege to be unconstitutional and *ultra vires* of

Parliament. What makes it unconstitutional and *ultra vires*, the plaintiffs say, is the existence and operation of s. 35 of the *Constitution Act, 1982.* ...

About one year and two months after s. 35, above recited, came into force, it was amended as is reflected in the *Constitution Amendment Proclamation, 1983* which added the following two subsections:

> (3) For greater certainty in subsection (1) "treaty rights" includes rights that now exist by way of land claims agreements or may be so acquired.
>
> (4) Notwithstanding any other provision of this Act, the aboriginal and treaty rights referred to in subsection (1) are guaranteed equally to male and female persons.

Subsection 35(4) is Conclusive

Given the nature and main substance of the plaintiffs' complaints (earlier above related), as understood and appreciated by the nature and main substance of the interveners' complaints against the state of the law which existed before the 1985 amendment (described in the testimony of Mary Two-Axe Early — TT48), subsection 35(4) appears to be conclusive. Without going into the plaintiffs' case further, it can be clearly seen that the marital custom, the so-called Aboriginal and treaty rights which permit an Indian husband to bring his non-Indian wife into residence on a reserve, but which forbid an Indian wife from so bringing her non-Indian husband are extinguished utterly by subsection 35(4).

The plaintiffs are firmly caught by the provisions of s. 35 of the *Constitution Act* which they themselves invoke. The more firmly the plaintiffs bring themselves into and under subsection 35(1) the more surely subsection 35(4) acts upon their alleged rights pursuant to subsection 35(1) which, therefore are modified so as to be guaranteed equally to the whole collectivity of Indian men and Indian women.

If ever there was or could be a clear extinguishment of any alleged Aboriginal or treaty right to discriminate within the collectivity of Indians and more particularly against Indian women, subsection 35(4) of the *Constitution Act* is that; and it works that extinguishment, very specifically, absolutely, and imperatively. It operates "notwithstanding any other provision of this Act", that is, the *Constitution Act, 1982.*

The hardship and heartache of those women who were in effect expelled from their homes and home reserves, and even expelled from Indian status, and their grievous sense of injustice of becoming non-Indians while at the same time the "white ladies" who married male band members, became Indians, was well illustrated in the testimony of the interveners' witnesses. Subsection 35(4) is aimed at providing their relief.

That constitutional provision exacts equality of rights between male and female persons, no matter what rights or responsibilities may have pertained in earlier times. On this basis alone, the plaintiffs' action is dismissed. It is the supreme law of Canada which speaks, to end the inequality of marital status of Indian women who are subject to it. The impugned legislation could surely be supported by section 15 of the *Canadian Charter of Rights and Freedoms*, too, were it not perhaps for section 25, but subsection 35(4) of the *Constitution Act* along with the other subsections of the whole of section 35 is in effect an "Indian provision" in an otherwise largely anti-racist constitution, and it speaks deliberately and specifically to the diminution of past inequalities between Indian men and women. Thus the 1985 amendment is doubly validated by maybe section 15 and absolutely by subsection 35(4); and there is no doubt that it is within Parliament's legislative jurisdiction in regard to Indians. So, section 35(4) operates and commands whether pleaded or not; it cannot be evaded. ...

The plaintiffs put forth several other arguments in support of their position, and in justice, the Court ought to consider them all, for some are quite cogent. ...

English and British Sovereignty

The King of England, Charles II, acting in right of England (and apparently not in right of Scotland) by executive act incorporated a trading company of considerable corporate jurisdiction: "The Governor and Company of Adventurers of England Trading into Hudson's Bay", hereinafter HBC. That considerable corporate jurisdiction is, for example, described in that statute of the U.K. known as the *Rupert's Land Act*, 1868, 31-32 Vict., c. 105 (U.K.) refers to the HBC's "lands and territories, rights of government, and other rights, privileges, liberties, franchises, powers and authorities". The HBC's incorporation was effected by means of the king's letters patent often referred to as the company's Royal Charter, granted on May 2, 1670. ...

The Court finds that the assertion of English sovereignty, later to become British sovereignty, was first formally expressed in the HBC Charter, May 2, 1670. Any rights which the plaintiffs can successfully establish must have been exerted before that day, and must not have been extinguished before the coming into force of s-s. 35(1) of the *Constitution Act, 1982* and must withstand Subsection 35(4) thereof. It must be left to others at another time to explain how the revisionists who settled upon Subsection 35(2) thought that they could honestly characterize Metis people as Aboriginal people, wielding Aboriginal rights. Nature has special blessings for hybrid people, the offspring of interracial procreation, as was correctly asserted by the plaintiff Wayne Roan in his testimony, TT8, at p. 837. Only some determined revisionist would seek to regard Metis as being exemplars of only one of their inherently dual lines of ancestors. It will be seen, however, that conduct and lifestyle will be noted in terms of "half-breeds living the 'Indian way of Life'," in this dismally racist subject of litigation.

The Plaintiffs' View of Merger or Subsumption of Aboriginal Rights Under and into Treaty Rights

... The diminution of Aboriginal rights is no doubt true, but the plaintiffs pleaded, and the Court accepts, that the Aboriginal rights so diminished must be rights specified in the treaty, of course, and not all Aboriginal rights at large. The treaties, along with the various versions of the *Indian Act* which preceded the treaties here considered, all bore upon and diminished Aboriginal rights and Aboriginal lifestyle. Even the assertion of sovereignty made the Aboriginal peoples subject to laws of general application in regard to crime, property, civil administration and tort which came into force as English and British sovereignty was secured. To the extent that those general laws impinged on or extinguished Aboriginal rights to such extent they were diminished. The Aboriginal peoples are not "foreigners", but from the time of assertion of sovereignty have been subjects of the sovereign. In that regard, section 88 of the *Indian Act* states, almost redundantly, the evident truth of general status consequent upon the subtraction therefrom of the Indians' special status. It confirms the Aboriginal peoples' status as subjects of the Crown both specially and generally in defining the profile of the boundary between the two.

Like others, no matter how much some judges and public servants seek paternally to patronize them, the western Indians are obliged to obey the laws of [the] land, even if such laws were unknown to their distant ancestors, so long as the law of the land does not abrogate surviving Aboriginal rights, as stated in Subsection 35(1) of the *Constitution Act, 1982*. Before Subsection 35(1) came into force, the law of the land as enacted by Parliament could indeed extinguish Aboriginal rights, but to be clear and unambiguous about such extinguishment or abrogation, the law did not need to state that "such Aboriginal rights as conflict with this law, to wit..., are, to such extent, extinguished". A law which had that clear effect even without those clear words was valid, if enacted in conformity with the wide purview of section 91, head 24 of the *Constitution Act, 1867*. So it was said by the Supreme Court of Canada in regard to treaty rights and State obligations thereto in *Sikyea v. The Queen*, [1964] S.C.R. 642; *The Queen v. George*, [1966] S.C.R. and *The Queen v. Moosehunter*, [1981] 1 S.C.R. 282.

The Treaties

In order to discover which Aboriginal rights were and are truly subsumed into and accordingly extinguished by the treaties, it is necessary to analyze the treaties carefully.

Thereafter, if the particular Aboriginal rights which the plaintiffs contend are theirs unto this very day remain untouched by the treaties, it will be necessary to enquire whether that which the plaintiffs assert be truly an Aboriginal right is indeed such as they assert.

In effect the plaintiffs assert two Aboriginal rights. The first has to do with the plaintiffs' principal but narrower grievance, about permitting Indian women who married non-Indians to live either by remaining in or returning to the women's own reserves of residence, inevitably their natal reserves with membership retained in their natal bands. The plaintiffs claim that their present expression of the Aboriginal right which they assert stems from the Aboriginal principle and practice that, upon marriage the woman followed the man to reside in or at his ordinary residence within his tribal group, not hers. From that narrow principle, the plaintiffs assert more globally that from Aboriginal times Indian groups or encampments controlled their own membership and that such an Aboriginal right either survived the treaty making, or is enshrined in the treaties. The plaintiffs triumphantly state that control of membership is an inevitable incident of their ancestors' "organised societies", which the defendant admitted orally by counsel at trial. These are matters for subsequent analysis.

Basis for the Treaties

The racial and religious hatreds of the historical past provide only a sterile and hopeless basis for nurturing those hatreds into the present and the future. That proposition is a stunningly, obviously, eternal verity as was clear, at least until recent days, in Ireland and is still evident in the present murderous stupidities among the South Slavs in Europe and between the Hutus and Tutsi in Africa. North America was surely going to be occupied and dominated by Europeans because of historical and economic processes which were unavoidable. There is no use in mourning that fact of destiny. The only question was whether the dominant Europeans would be the French, the British or the Spanish, and in the nineteenth century it was as between the Canadians and Americans. ...

There is no doubt that, in entering into the treaties they sought the protection of — and perhaps ill-advisedly — the dependence on, the Crown, as represented by Ottawa's Treaty Commissioners. Those commissioners, unlike General Custer and his government, did have the authority and ability to allow the Indians to live in peace, and to protect them from the Americans — 7th Cavalry and whiskey traders alike.

Among the other important factors of those days inducing the Indians to seek the treaties were: disease and famine and the clearly-to-be-seen demise of the huge natural herds of bison, called buffalo, upon which the Plains Indians depended for food, hides, sinew, bones and horns to maintain their unique pre-industrial life style. Quite possibly the introduction by the Spanish of the horse which quickly became widespread, and the introduction by all the Europeans of the rifle and other firearms, must have contributed to the diminution of the herds. No doubt the introduction of Euro-settlers also contributed greatly to the buffaloes' disappearance. ...

So there was a quid pro quo inherent in Treaties 6, 7 and 8. The Canadian government wanted to open the Prairies to eastern Canadian settlement — expansionism Canadian style, kept non-murderous with the help of the mounted police — and the Indians, in their straitened circumstances of that different world, wanted the protection from the settlers *inter alia* and wanted the dependent status into which they bargained themselves, seemingly "forever". ... The government's payments work another evil, too. They are an eternal charge on the country's taxpayers, even although the dolorous conditions of the last century lie dead in the past along with its glory, if any, which cannot be now restored. ...

Statutes

Apart from social and economic conditions above mentioned as the basis for the treaties were the various statutes which can be regarded as the historical continuum of the *Indian Act*. That Act precedes the treaties which are under consideration in this litigation. ...

The plaintiffs' asserted right to control their own membership of their "bands" (a wholly statutory term) was emphatically extinguished by the *Indian Act, 1876*. Complete control was taken by Parliament in the enactment of that statute and its predecessors. Even if control of hunting and social groups' or encampments' membership had been a real Aboriginal right it was extinguished by most clear and unambiguous legislation before Treaties 6, 7 and 8 ever came into being. ...

Negotiations

... an Aboriginal right of control of membership it was conclusively extinguished at treaty time and as a condition of concluding the treaty. Governor Morris certainly asserted control over membership by the Canadian government and in consonance with the provisions of the *Indian Act 1876* and preceding legislation enacted by the Parliament of Canada. Other sources of the same historic assertion of control are exhibit 1(4), pp. 36 to 39, and of course the plaintiffs' counsel's reading of the passages into the record in trial transcript (TT) 2, pp. 81 and 82. The government's assertion of control over band membership on reserves, and off, was unambiguously stated by statute and by Alexander Morris, the government's treaty commissioner. ...

Clearly, a people who were experiencing the setting-up of false, puppet chiefs and social granulation "into little parties" due to the influence of traders, cannot be believed to be controlling its own membership. A people which sought governmental establishment of its own "chiefships" in order to have the State make its political and social officers have official recognition in order to avoid that people's willy-nilly granulation at the whim and commercial greed of traders, cannot be held to be controlling its own membership. If such control were truly an Aboriginal practice, then the Indians themselves lost it without any push by the government of Canada which truly asserted and exercised such control. Was this conclusion understood then by the Indians as this Court now understands it? It was they who first acknowledged loss (or absence) of control in the first place; and it was they who requested the government to assert control, for and on their behalf, as in the statutes, so in the treaties.

There is an underlying, sometimes articulated premise in the jurisprudence and among certain cynical activists that the "pitiable Indians" were easy dupes for superior Euro-Canadians and needing protections which applied not only to 19th Century Indians, but also to contemporary Indians, born in the mid-20th Century. This Court finds nothing inferior, genetic, social or intellectual *inter alia* about those Indians who entered into the treaties, nor their descendants today. This Court rejects all stated or implied notions of any inferiority of Indians, whatever. That is why the Court leans against the alleged need, over a century later, of special State protection of Indians, which protection often appears to be excessive and degrading to Indians in comparison with all the other "visible" (and not so "visible") peoples who make up the tax-paying and general population of Canada. Certainly the Morris record (pp. 219-28, 270-71) reveals instances of hard-bargaining and excessive demands beyond the Canadian government's Commissioners' power to yield. There is even at least one instance in which the Commissioners exceeded their authority because of the Indians' persuasion acknowledged that they were taking a risk in hoping to have their so yielding subsequently ratified by Ottawa. The Courts, too, often and too much pretend that the Indians did not understand their bargained treaties. ...

Peoples found to be in a more primitive (i.e. hunting) state of development than the others' state (i.e. industrial or post-industrial) are emphatically not inferior peoples. Their state of development might be likened by analogy to "adolescent" compared with the others' (non-Indians') "adult" state of development. But the law and treaties have protected Indians from "spreading their wings" as may non-Indian adolescents who do and always have made "improvident transactions" until a majority learned not to do so, but to conduct themselves prudently. ...

It is surely apparent that it is not eternal dependence with apartheid, but equal self-reliance, (including Canada's so-called "social safety net" for such as it is and will be) which promote the equal human dignity of all Canadians. It is difficult to understand why the Courts in recent years have promoted dependence. The so-called "honour of the Crown" is surely nothing more than a transparent semantic membrane for wrapping together Indian reserve apartheid and perpetual dependence on Canadian taxpayers. This melancholy situation, being authentically historic, does nothing to support the plaintiffs' claim to control their own membership as is already demonstrated herein. It has contributed to the depression and poverty of many Indians over time. ...

Treaty Text

Taken all-in-all with the Act and the negotiations, no treaty right of Indians to control their band and reserve membership can be discerned. They understood that to be so. The disputed matter of hunting trapping and fishing being subject to governmental regulation is shown in the version reported. As in Treaties 6 and 7, Treaty 8 foresees ever diminishing territory for hunting, trapping and fishing because it was agreed that such activities could be pursued there "saving and excepting such tracts as may be required or taken up from time to time for settlement, mining, lumbering, trading or other purposes."

It was quite obvious and well understood by the Indian parties to all three treaties that the Government of Canada was thereafter to control their band and reserve membership, because the government was committed to pay Indians forever as an eternal charge on taxpayers. Clearly the government was committed also to control who was to be paid individually, and who was not entitled to be paid individually. The Indians were neither simpletons nor crazy. They well understood that "money talks" and that "whoever pays the piper, calls the tune". ...

Woman Follows Man

... It is well known that legislation enacted contrary to the Constitution's provisions is, to the extent of any inconsistency, of no force or effect. Remembering the words of Mr. Justice La Forest in *Mitchell v. Peguis* ... it must be observed that a constitutional recognition and affirmation does not constitutionalize ordinary legislation such as the women's-loss-of-membership-on-marriage-out provisions of previous, successive *Indian Acts*. ...

The plaintiffs assert that the marital régime for which they contend is an Aboriginal right; and that Aboriginal rights are collective rights. Surely, however, the notion of "woman follows man", and is unable to confer her status upon her non-Indian husband, represent a collective right only for men. It was and is not a right for women. If one is going to elevate Aboriginal practices into constitutional imperatives, then the Aboriginal practices of no individual identity for women, and no voice in the encampments' affairs should need constitutional recognition and affirmation, too! It is nonsense to try to keep women silent and invisible. ...

In no time at all historical stories, if ever accurate, soon become mortally skewed propaganda, without objective verity. Since the above mentioned pejorative characteristics, and more, are alas common to humanity they must have been verily evinced by everybody's ancestors, as they are by the present day descendants, but no one, including oral historians wants to admit that. Each tribe or ethnicity in the whole human species raises its young to believe that they are "better" than everyone else. Hence, the wars which have blighted human history. So ancestor advocacy or ancestor worship is one of the most counter-productive, racist, hateful and backward-looking of all human characteristics, or religion, or what passes for thought. People are of course free to indulge in it — perhaps it is an aspect of human nature — but it is that aspect which renders oral history highly unreliable. So saying, the Court is most emphatically not mocking or belittling those who assert that, because their ancestors never developed writing, oral history is their only means of keeping their history alive. It would always be best to put the stories into writing at the earliest possible time in order to avoid some of the embellishments which render oral history so unreliable. ...

The Court finds that in Aboriginal times and up to the making of the treaties, all of the plaintiffs' predecessors had no custom of controlling their groups' or chiefs' peoples' membership. Quite the contrary. The chiefs' stature depended on how many individuals or families attached themselves to the respective chiefs. Even those born into a chief's people were free simply to walk out of the chief's encampment and attach themselves to another. No questions asked. One chief's loss was another's gain. If this freedom to join and depart were an Aboriginal custom, it was the diametric opposite of "control" of membership. ...

If the bands with membership codes think that provisions about "blood quantum" will do what they think "repute" should have done for them, they are calling down untold agonies on themselves and their people. In the first place there is human verity in the old adage: "It's a wise child who knows his own father." There was a sad afternoon at trial herein when one of the plaintiffs' counsel insensitively sought to enlist a witness in his effort to prove that the witness was a so-called illegitimate child. As if any human being can be considered illegitimate! The person being conceived, after all, does not know who are doing it. "Blood quantum" is a highly fascist and racist notion, and puts its practitioners on the path of the Nazi Party led by the late, most unlamented Adolf Hitler. It will bring heartache, for example, to the mother of children sired by different fathers, say an Indian and a non-Indian, who may be required to go into exile rather than to exile some of her children from their siblings. The Court heard testimony to the effect that the Sarcee (Tsuu T'ina) are conjuring with the practice of "blood quantum". One hopes that people who characterize themselves as generous, hospitable and living in tune with Mother Earth and all nature, will not set out to turn some unfortunates among their number against their own grandparents. ...

SAWRIDGE BAND v. CANADA

[1997] 3 F.C. 583 (C.A.)

Isaac C.J., Strayer and **Linden JJ.A.:—**

Introduction

On June 3, 1997 this Court, having heard argument on the first ground of appeal that there was a reasonable apprehension of bias on the part of the Trial Judge, was obliged to dispose of that ground before hearing the remainder of the argument. As a result the Court allowed the appeal on that ground, for reasons to follow. These are those reasons. As will be apparent, they do not address the substance of the Judge's decision.

Facts

This appeal involves an action commenced in 1986 for declarations that certain sections of the *Indian Act* are invalid. These sections were added by an amendment in 1985. Briefly put, this legislation, while conferring on Indian bands the right to control their own band lists, obliged bands to include in their membership certain persons who became entitled to Indian status by virtue of the 1985 legislation. Such persons included: women who had become disentitled to Indian status through marriage to non-Indian men and the children of such women; those who had lost status because their mother and paternal grandmother were non-Indian and had gained Indian status through marriage to an Indian; and those who had lost status on the basis that they were illegitimate offspring of an Indian woman and a non-Indian man. Bands assuming control of their band lists would be obliged to accept all these people as members. Such bands would also be allowed, if they chose, to accept certain other categories of persons previously excluded from Indian status. ...

The trial of this action occupied some seventy-five days commencing September 20, 1993 and ending April 25, 1994. Reasons were issued on July 6, 1995 [[1996] 1 F.C. 3]. ... The Trial Judge dismissed the action for the declarations. ...

The plaintiffs appealed this judgment. ... The two appeals A-779-95 and A-807-95 filed in respect of this matter (the former on behalf of the Ermineskin Band and the latter on behalf of the Sawridge Band and the Sarcee Band, now known as the Tsuu T'ina First Nation) were ordered joined for the hearing of the appeal. These reasons apply to both appeals.

As noted earlier, the first ground of appeal raised by the appellants Sawridge and Sarcee bands was that the record disclosed the basis for a reasonable apprehension of bias on the part of the Trial Judge against the appellants. ...

Counsel for all of the appellants then proceeded to present to the Court, from the trial record, comments or conduct during the trial by the Trial Judge, and passages in his reasons, to support their assertion of a reasonable apprehension of bias. ...

The Court was obliged to dispose of this ground of appeal before proceeding. In allowing the appeal on this basis, with reasons to be delivered later, the Court indicated that it had concluded that there was material in the record upon which a reasonable apprehension of bias could be found.

Analysis

It is first important to underline that no actual bias has been alleged on the part of the Trial Judge, nor does this Court find such bias. ...

We do think, however, that a reasonable observer would have formed the impression that the Trial Judge was strongly opposed to a special regime for some or all Aboriginal peoples different from the system of rights and responsibilities applying to other Canadians. If this apprehension were formed, it could have led such an observer to think that the Trial Judge was thereby influenced in his conclusion that no Aboriginal right had existed for the plaintiff bands to control their own membership or if it had, the right had been extinguished prior to the adoption of section 35 of the *Constitution Act, 1982*.

Such an observer might well have reflected on the fact that, ever since the adoption of the *Constitution Act, 1867* [30 & 31 Vict., c. 3 (U.K.) (as am. by *Canada Act 1982*, 1982, c. 11 (U.K.), Schedule to the *Constitution Act, 1982*, Item 1) [R.S.C., 1985, Appendix II, No. 5]], section 91(24) thereof has given Parliament the power and responsibility to make special laws for Indians in distinction from other persons. This power and responsibility, of necessity, has always required some criteria for defining Indians in order to distinguish them from other Canadians as subjects of legislation. He would further recall that other constitutional documents, treaties and court decisions have distinguished between Aboriginal peoples and others, and section 35 of the *Constitution Act, 1982* has now guaranteed existing Aboriginal rights as rights pertaining to Indians, Inuit, and Métis. The existence of special status for Aboriginal peoples is, therefore, enshrined in our Constitution. It was not for the Trial Judge to dispute this aspect of Canada's constitutional law.

Regrettably, there are a number of passages in the trial transcript and in the Judge's reasons which convey a very negative view of Aboriginal rights or special status for all or some Aboriginal peoples. ...

Conclusions

We believe the foregoing would indeed create in the mind of a fair-minded and reasonably well-informed observer the belief that the Trial Judge held certain views during the trial, which were confirmed in his reasons, that Aboriginal rights are "racist" and a form of "apartheid". Having ascribed these pejorative terms to a system which is recognized in the history, the common law, and the Constitution of Canada, he might well be expected to give the narrowest possible interpretation to, or reject, any newly claimed Aboriginal right asserted by the plaintiffs to have existed in 1982.

He might also be taken to assume that this alleged right — the right of bands to control their own membership — would be used to promote racism and apartheid and should therefore not be recognized. ...

Nevertheless, for the reasons indicated earlier we found it necessary to set aside the judgment and order a new trial notwithstanding the great cost and inconvenience which this may cause. It is possible that this situation might have been avoided had counsel for the plaintiffs objected in a clear and timely manner to the Trial Judge's interventions, to make him aware of the unfortunate impression he seems to have given that he had some fixed views on the matters in dispute.

Needless to say, this disposition is in no way a finding that the conclusions of the Judge on the facts and the law were incorrect. These matters remain for determination at the new trial if it proceeds.

Disposition

It is for these reasons that the Court held that the record disclosed a basis for finding a reasonable apprehension of bias, the appeal was allowed, and a new trial ordered with costs to the appellants both here and below and no costs to the interveners either here or below.

---

1. If, as Justice Muldoon held, section 35(4) was conclusive of the matter before him, was it proper for him to consider and comment on issues of English and British sovereignty, treaties, statutes and negotiations, as he did in the remainder of his judgment?
2. Was Justice Muldoon right to characterize this case as being a "dismally racist subject of litigation"? As we have seen, rarely do courts talk about race and racism in the context of Aboriginal rights. Why did Justice Muldoon invoke this language in this particular case? Why was the language of racism not taken up by the Court of Appeal? Why has the language of racism not been taken up in the other cases you have read? What is the place, if there is any at all, of the language of racism in the law dealing with Aboriginal peoples?
3. Could Justice Muldoon draw upon any legal authority in making the statement: "North America was surely going to be occupied and dominated by Europeans because of historical and economic processes which were unavoidable"?
4. Justice Muldoon described treaty annuities as being "an eternal charge on the country's taxpayers". What is wrong with the government having to live up to its promises, and make payments in perpetuity for the use of lands used formerly and exclusively by the Indians? What would be your reaction to an Aboriginal person stating: "Non-Aboriginal peoples' use of our land is an eternal charge on our governments"?
5. Aboriginal leader Sharon McIvor has written (in "Self-Government and Aboriginal Women", *Scratching the Surface: Canadian Anti-Racist Feminist Thought*, E. Dua and A. Robertson, eds., 167):

As with other existing Aboriginal rights, women's civil and political rights are foundational and do not derive from documents or treaties. The right of Aboriginal women to establish and maintain their civic and political role within the context of Aboriginal self-government has always existed. The regulation of women's political rights through successive Indian Acts did not extinguish their fundamental civil and political rights. Even if the suppression of women's rights was so oppressive it led to their banishment from Aboriginal communities, this, in itself, did not lead to the extinguishment of their rights. There is no extinguishment by regulation in the Aboriginal field ...[Aboriginal women's] rights are part of the inherent right to self-government, of customary laws of Aboriginal people.

Is Ms. McIvor's statement congruent with Justice Muldoon's observation?

6. Is the following statement of Justice Muldoon true?: "Surely, however, the notion of 'woman follows man', and is unable to confer her status upon her non-Indian husband, represents a collective right only for men."

7. The Supreme Court of Canada's decision in *Corbiere v. Canada* (reproduced in part below) delivered May 20, 1999, made residence a ground of discrimination under section 15 of the *Charter of Rights and Freedoms*. The issue in *Corbiere* was whether section 77(1) of the *Indian Act* was discriminatory because it restricted the right to vote to band members living on reserve. This provision arguably had the effect of disenfranchising those members who lived off the reserve.

CORBIERE v. CANADA (MINISTER OF INDIAN AND NORTHERN AFFAIRS)

[1999] 2 S.C.R. 203

McLachlin and **Bastarache JJ. (Lamer C.J.C., Cory, Major JJ.)** –

. . . . .

[3] The narrow issue raised in this appeal is whether the exclusion of off-reserve members of an Indian band from the right to vote in band elections pursuant to s. 77(1) of the *Indian Act*, R.S.C., 1985, c. I-5, is inconsistent with s. 15(1) of the *Canadian Charter of Rights and Freedoms*.

. . . . .

[Note from Justice L'Heureux-Dubé's statement of facts:

[30] The number of Batchewana Band members has risen dramatically since 1985, and at the same time the percentage of band members living on the reserves has dramatically fallen. In 1985, 71.1 percent of the 543 registered members of the band lived on-reserve. In 1991, only 32.8 percent of the 1,426 registered members lived on the reserves. The parties agree that this trend is continuing. This dramatic increase in the number of off-reserve members occurred largely because of the passage of *An Act to*

amend the Indian Act, S.C. 1985, c. 27 ("Bill C-31"), by Parliament. This legislation restored Indian status to most of those who had lost this status because of the operation of certain sections of the *Indian Act*, as well as to the descendants of such people. Prior to this legislation, women with Indian status who married non-Indian men lost their status, and their children did not get status, though men who married non-Indian women, and their children, maintained Indian status. Registered Indians who voluntarily "enfranchised" also lost Indian status. For the Batchewana Band, approximately 85 percent of the growth in band membership consisted of people who were reinstated to Indian status and band membership because of Bill C-31. Similar trends may be seen in many other bands.]

[6] We agree with L'Heureux-Dubé J. that Aboriginality-residence (off-reserve band member status) constitutes a ground of discrimination analogous to the enumerated grounds.

. . . . .

[14] L'Heureux-Dubé J. ultimately concludes that "Aboriginality-residence" as it pertains to whether an Aboriginal band member lives on or off the reserve is an analogous ground. We agree. L'Heureux-Dubé J.'s discussion makes clear that the distinction goes to a personal characteristic essential to a band member's personal identity, which is no less constructively immutable than religion or citizenship. Off-reserve Aboriginal band members can change their status to on-reserve band members only at great cost, if at all.

[15] Two brief comments on this new analogous ground are warranted. First, reserve status should not be confused with residence. The ordinary "residence" decisions faced by the average Canadians should not be confused with the profound decisions Aboriginal band members make to live on or off their reserves, assuming choice is possible. The reality of their situation is unique and complex. Thus no new water is charted, in the sense of finding residence, in the generalized abstract, to be an analogous ground. Second, we note that the analogous ground of off-reserve status or Aboriginality-residence is limited to a subset of the Canadian population, while s. 15 is directed to everyone. In our view, this is no impediment to its inclusion as an analogous ground under s. 15. Its demographic limitation is no different, for example, from pregnancy, which is a distinct, but fundamentally interrelated form of discrimination from gender. "Embedded" analogous grounds may be necessary to permit meaningful consideration of intra-group discrimination.

[16] Having concluded that the distinction made by the impugned law is made on an analogous ground, we come to the final step of the s. 15(1) analysis: whether the distinction at issue in this case in fact constitutes discrimination. In plain words, does the distinction undermine the presumption upon which the guarantee of equality is based — that each individual is deemed to be of equal worth regardless of the group to which he or she belongs?

[17] Applying the applicable *Law* factors to this case — pre-existing disadvantage, correspondence and importance of the affected interest — we conclude that the answer to this question is yes. The impugned distinction

perpetuates the historic disadvantage experienced by off-reserve band members by denying them the right to vote and participate in their band's governance. Off-reserve band members have important interests in band governance which the distinction denies. They are co-owners of the band's assets. The reserve, whether they live on or off it, is their and their children's land. The band council represents them as band members to the community at large, in negotiations with the government, and within Aboriginal organizations. Although there are some matters of purely local interest, which do not as directly affect the interests of off-reserve band members, the complete denial to off-reserve members of the right to vote and participate in band governance treats them as less worthy and entitled, not on the merits of their situation, but simply because they live off-reserve. The importance of the interest affected is underlined by the findings of the Royal Commission on Aboriginal Peoples, *Report of the Royal Commission on Aboriginal Peoples* (1996), vol. 1, *Looking Forward, Looking Back*, at pp. 137-91. The Royal Commission writes in vol. 4, *Perspectives and Realities*, at p. 521:

> Throughout the Commission's hearings, Aboriginal people stressed the fundamental importance of retaining and enhancing their cultural identity while living in urban areas. Aboriginal identity lies at the heart of Aboriginal peoples' existence; maintaining that identity is an essential and self-validating pursuit for Aboriginal people in cities.

And at p. 525:

> Cultural identity for urban Aboriginal people is also tied to a land base or ancestral territory. For many, the two concepts are inseparable. . . . Identification with an ancestral place is important to urban people because of the associated ritual, ceremony and traditions, as well as the people who remain there, the sense of belonging, the bond to an ancestral community, and the accessibility of family, community and elders.

[18] Taking all this into account, it is clear that the s. 77(1) disenfranchisement is discriminatory. It denies off-reserve band members the right to participate fully in band governance on the arbitrary basis of a personal characteristic. It reaches the cultural identity of off-reserve Aboriginals in a stereotypical way. It presumes that Aboriginals living off-reserve are not interested in maintaining meaningful participation in the band or in preserving their cultural identity, and are therefore less deserving members of the band. The effect is clear, as is the message: off-reserve band members are not as deserving as those band members who live on reserves. This engages the dignity aspect of the s. 15 analysis and results in the denial of substantive equality.

[19] The conclusion that discrimination exists at the third stage of the *Law* test does not depend on the composition of the off-reserve band members group, its relative homogeneity or the particular historical discrimination it may have suffered. It is the present situation of the group relative to that of the comparator group, on-reserve band members, that is relevant. All parties have accepted that the off-reserve group comprises persons who have chosen to live off-reserve freely, persons who have been forced to leave the reserve reluctantly because of economic and social considerations, persons who have at some point been expelled then restored

to band membership through Bill C-31 (*An Act to amend the Indian Act*, S.C. 1985, c. 27), and descendants of these people. It is accepted that off-reserve band members are the object of discrimination and constitute an under-privileged group. It is also accepted that many off-reserve band members were expelled from the reserves because of policies and legal provisions which were changed by Bill C-31 and can be said to have suffered double discrimination. But Aboriginals living on reserves are subject to the same discrimination. Some were affected by Bill C-31. Some left the reserve and returned. The relevant social facts in this case are those that relate to off-reserve band members as opposed to on-reserve band members. Even if all band members living off-reserve had voluntarily chosen this way of life and were not subject to discrimination in the broader Canadian society, they would still have the same cause of action. They would still suffer a detriment by being denied full participation in the affairs of the bands to which they would continue to belong while the band councils are able to affect their interests, in particular by making decisions with respect to the surrender of lands, the allocation of land to band members, the raising of funds and making of expenditures for the benefit of all band members. The effect of the legislation is to force band members to choose between living on the reserve and exercising their political rights, or living off-reserve and renouncing the exercise of their political rights. The political rights in question are related to the race of the individuals affected, and to their cultural identity. As mentioned earlier, the differential treatment resulting from the legislation is discriminatory because it implies that off-reserve band members are lesser members of their bands or persons who have chosen to be assimilated by the mainstream society.

. . . . .

[21] Having found that s. 77(1) is discriminatory, we must address the s. 1 argument of the appellants. ... We are satisfied that the restriction on voting is rationally connected to the aim of the legislation, which is to give a voice in the affairs of the reserve only to the persons most directly affected by the decisions of the band council. It is admitted that although all band members are subject to some decisions of the band council, most decisions would only impact on members living on the reserve. The restriction of s. 15 rights is however not justified under the second branch of the s. 1 test; it has not been demonstrated that s. 77(1) of the *Indian Act* impairs the s. 15 rights minimally. Even if it is accepted that some distinction may be justified in order to protect legitimate interests of band members living on the reserve, it has not been demonstrated that a complete denial of the right of band members living off-reserve to participate in the affairs of the band through the democratic process of elections is necessary. Some parties and interveners have mentioned the possibility of a two-tiered council, of reserved seats for off-reserve members of the band, of double-majority votes on some issues. The appellants argue that there are important difficulties and costs involved in maintaining an electoral list of off-reserve band members and in setting up a system of governance balancing the rights of on-reserve and off-reserve band members. But they present no evidence of efforts deployed or schemes considered and costed, and no

argument or authority in support of the conclusion that costs and administrative convenience could justify a complete denial of the constitutional right. Under these circumstances, we must conclude that the violation has not been shown to be demonstrably justified.

[22] With regard to remedy, the Court of Appeal was of the view that it would be preferable to grant the Batchewana Band a permanent constitutional exemption rather than to declare s. 77(1) of the *Indian Act* to be unconstitutional and without effect generally. With respect, we must disagree. The remedy of constitutional exemption has been recognized in a very limited way in this Court, to protect the interests of a party who has succeeded in having a legislative provision declared unconstitutional, where the declaration of invalidity has been suspended. ...We do not think this is a case where a possible expansion of the constitutional exemption remedy should be considered. There is no evidence of special circumstances upon which this possibility might be raised. The evidence before the Court is that there are off-reserve members of most if not all Indian bands in Canada that are affected by s. 77(1) of the *Indian Act*, and no evidence of other rights that may be relevant in examining the effect of s. 77(1) with regard to any band other than the Batchewana Band. If another band could establish an Aboriginal right to restrict voting, as suggested by the Court of Appeal, that right would simply have precedence over the terms of the *Indian Act*; this is not a reason to restrict the declaration of invalidity to the Batchewana Band.

[23] Where there is inconsistency between the *Charter* and a legislative provision, s. 52 of the *Constitution Act, 1982* provides that the provision shall be rendered void to the extent of the inconsistency. We would declare the words "and is ordinarily resident on the reserve" in s. 77(1) of the *Indian Act* to be inconsistent with s. 15(1) but suspend the implementation of this declaration for 18 months. We would not grant a constitutional exemption to the Batchewana Band during the period of suspension, as would normally be done according to the rule in *Schachter*. The reason for this is that in the particular circumstances of this case, it would appear to be preferable to develop an electoral process that will balance the rights of off-reserve and on-reserve band members. We have not overlooked the possibility that legislative inaction may create new problems. Such claims will fall to be dealt with on their merits should they arise.

[24] We would therefore dismiss the appeal and modify the remedy by striking out the words "and is ordinarily resident on the reserve" in s. 77(1) of the *Indian Act* and suspending the implementation of the declaration of invalidity for 18 months, with costs to the respondents. We would answer the restated constitutional questions as follows:

1. Do the words "and is ordinarily resident on the reserve" contained in s. 77(1) of the *Indian Act*, R.S.C., 1985, c. I-5, contravene s. 15(1) of the *Canadian Charter of Rights and Freedoms*, either generally or with respect only to members of the Batchewana Indian Band?

   Yes, in their general application.

2. If the answer to question 1 is in the affirmative, is s. 77(1) of the *Indian Act* demonstrably justified as a reasonable limit pursuant to s. 1 of the *Canadian Charter of Rights and Freedoms*?

   No.

L'Heureux-Dubé, Gonthier, Iacobucci and **Binnie JJ.** (concurring in the result).

---

1. Did the Supreme Court inappropriately "duck" the issue of sexual inequality that structured the factual background of the *Corbiere* case? Remember, Justice L'Heureux-Dubé's factual recitation noted that 85 per cent of the growth in band membership in these communities consisted of people who were reinstated to Indian status and band membership because of Bill C-31 (a majority of those reinstated would have been women). Why didn't this issue figure more prominently in the Court's reasons?
2. The *Indian Act* voting regulations were amended to comply with the *Corbiere* case on October 20, 2000. These regulations apply to votes held on or after November 20, 2000. The *Indian Band Election Regulations and the Indian Referendum Regulations* were published in the Canada Gazette, Part II in October of 2000. As a result of these amendments, the following deadlines apply to Indian band elections held on or after January 8, 2001:

    *   voters must register at least 79 days prior to the election date;
    *   the voters list must be provided to the Electoral Officer 79 days before the election;
    *   mail-in ballots will be sent to registered off-reserve voters 35 days before election day;
    *   the nomination meeting for Chief and Council will be held 42 days before election day; and
    *   a notice of the nomination meeting will be posted on the reserve and mailed to electors residing off reserve at least 30 days before the nomination meeting.

    Do you think these provisions help overcome the legacy of sex discrimination under the *Indian Act*?
3. More than 300 First Nations hold elections according to custom election codes, following the traditions of the individual First Nation community. Many of these custom election codes allow off-reserve members to vote in Band elections and on certain key decisions involving lands and money. Although the *Corbiere* decision does not specifically address bands holding elections under custom processes, custom bands have been analyzing their procedures in light of the *Corbiere* decision.

E. ABORIGINAL WOMEN'S ORGANIZATIONS

Aboriginal women formed political organizations to cope with the discrimination that they continued to encounter, and worked for social and legislative reform. These organizations have been influential in affecting the debate and changing law and policy concerning Aboriginal women. While these interventions have sometimes been fractious for Aboriginal icommunities, at the same time they have served to deepen the level of understanding on the issues in question. The development of the contemporary political and legal landscape regarding Aboriginal peoples cannot be fully understood without taking account of these forces. The following commentary and case describe the role of Aboriginal women's organizations in Canada.

REPORT OF THE ROYAL COMMISSION ON ABORIGINAL PEOPLES, PERSPECTIVES AND REALITIES, VOL. 4

(Ottawa: Ministry of Supply and Services, 1996) at 68-71
(references omitted)

THE RISE OF ABORIGINAL WOMEN'S ORGANIZATIONS

During the period 1951-1970, Aboriginal people became more aware of their legal rights and as a result organized to address their concerns. Aboriginal women's organizations came into being and took on a range of issues, including the development of women in leadership roles and the resolution of health and social problems in their communities. This was a far cry from the first organizations started in 1937 by the Indian affairs department with the stated goal of assisting Indian women "to acquire sound and approved practices for greater home efficiency".

First instituted and promoted by the department during the Depression, Indian homemakers' associations formed on reserves across Canada between 1930 and 1960. In the 1960s, most of these groups underwent a transformation from clubs focusing on home economics to clubs involved in public affairs, tackling issues such as housing standards, living conditions, Aboriginal rights and women's rights. The Indian Homemakers' Association of British Columbia was formed in 1965 to amalgamate clubs throughout the province. Incorporated in 1969, it has the distinction of being the country's oldest provincial Aboriginal women's organization in operation today. Other associations, chapters and locals regrouping Aboriginal women were established across Canada, on reserves, in rural communities and in urban centres.

The idea of a national body to represent Aboriginal women emerged at a 1970 international conference of Aboriginal women in Albuquerque, New Mexico, and in March 1971 the first National Native Women's Conference was held in Canada. In August 1974, the Native Women's Association of Canada (NWAC) convened its first annual assembly in Thunder Bay, Ontario. Until the early 1980s, NWAC spoke on behalf of First Nations, Inuit and Métis women.

In 1984, because of major differences in language, culture, and circumstances, Inuit women felt a need to create their own organization — Pauktuutit. Its mandate is to foster a greater awareness of the needs of Inuit women and to encourage their participation in community, regional and national concerns in relation to social, cultural and economic development.

In 1992, the Métis National Council of Women was incorporated as a federation of six independent provincial and territorial Métis women's organizations: British Columbia, Alberta, Northwest Territories, Saskatchewan, Manitoba and Ontario.

Although stated differently, the goals and objectives of each Aboriginal women's organization are similar: improving the quality of life for Aboriginal women and their children by achieving equal participation in the social, economic, cultural and political life not only of their communities but of Canadian society as a whole.

Throughout the 1970s and '80s, the discriminatory provisions in the *Indian Act* were a central focus of concern. Women such as Yvonne Bedard, Jeannette Corbiere-Lavell, Mary Two Axe Early and Sandra Lovelace instituted legal proceedings challenging the loss of Indian status and rights. Aboriginal women wanted to see major changes in their lives and communities, and they were determined to take action locally, regionally, nationally and internationally.

> In 1981, Sandra Lovelace took her case to the United Nations Human Rights Committee. It held that Canada was in contravention of article 27 of the *International Covenant on Civil and Political Rights*. The committee ruled that the cultural rights guaranteed by article 27 of the Covenant were denied because she was forced to be separate from her community. Only after this decision did the Canadian government try to correct the situation, finally enacting Bill C-31 in 1985. ... This could not have happened if it were not for the Aboriginal women speaking out. ...
>
> Kathy Martin, The Pas, Manitoba 20 May 1992

Although the discriminatory provisions of the *Indian Act* were important, a wide range of other concerns captured the attention of Aboriginal women's organizations. They were also placing increased emphasis on their participation in the decision-making processes of other national Aboriginal organizations.

Discussions on the patriation of the constitution had been occurring for a number of years, but it was not until 1981 that representatives of three national Aboriginal groups — the Assembly of First Nations (AFN), the Inuit Committee on National Issues (ICNI, predecessor of Inuit Tapirisat), and the Native Council of Canada (NCC) — became more involved. A first ministers conference, convened in November 1981, produced a political accord on constitutional reform supported by the federal government and nine provinces. This accord had one glaring omission: Aboriginal rights. The Aboriginal Rights Coalition, led by NCC, ICNI, NWAC, the Dene Nation, the Council for Yukon Indians, the Nisga'a Tribal Council and the National Association of Friendship Centres, initiated a series of public protests. With the support of Canadian women concerned about sexual equality and a support network of Canadian church organizations through Project North, they were able to have Aboriginal and treaty rights — albeit qualified as 'existing' Aboriginal and treaty rights — recognized in section 35(1) of the *Constitution Act, 1982*.

During the first ministers conferences held between 1983 and 1987, NWAC continued to be involved in meetings of AFN's constitutional working group and the Native Council of Canada's constitutional process. During the 1983 first ministers conference, NWAC was instrumental in gaining a further amendment to section 35 of the Act: "Notwithstanding any other provision of this Act, the aboriginal and treaty rights referred to in subsection (1) are guaranteed equally to male and female persons."

NWAC was not a formal participant in these conferences, however. It did not have its own seat at the table, nor was it given equitable funding. During the constitutional talks in 1992, NWAC launched a court case to gain equal participation and funding. In March 1992, the Native Women's Association of Canada put forward legal arguments that the *Charter* rights of Aboriginal women had been infringed by the government of Canada. ...NWAC...made the point that Aboriginal women want a say in the decisions that will affect their future. At the July 1993 intergovernmental conference of federal, provincial and territorial ministers responsible for Aboriginal affairs, held in Inuvik, Northwest Territories, the Native Women's Association of Canada was officially invited to participate. NWAC also had its own seat at a similar conference in Toronto in February 1994. The case that brought Aboriginal women to the table is:

NATIVE WOMEN'S ASSN. OF CANADA v. CANADA

[1994] 3 S.C.R. 627

The judgment of **Lamer C.J.C.** and **La Forest, Sopinka, Gonthier, Cory, Iacobucci** and **Major JJ**. was delivered by

Sopinka J.: — This case raises the issue of the extent to which the freedom of expression and equality provisions of the *Canadian Charter of Rights and Freedoms* require that government funding be provided to various groups in order to promote the representation of certain interests at constitutional reform discussions. Specifically, where the Government of Canada provides funding to certain Aboriginal groups, alleged to be male-dominated, does s. 2(b) in combination with s. 28 of the *Charter* oblige the Government of Canada to provide equal funding to an association claiming to represent the interests of female Aboriginal persons so that they may also express their views at the constitutional discussions? Alternatively, is this result mandated by s. 15 of the *Charter* or s. 35 of the *Constitution Act, 1982*? This case also invites consideration of whether there is any violation of the *Charter* if the Government of Canada refuses to extend an invitation to a group representing the interests of Aboriginal women to come to the table to discuss possible constitutional reform. ...

Following a review of the facts, I will ... embark on a discussion of the main focus of this appeal regarding the alleged violations of the *Charter*. In light of my conclusion that there was no *Charter* violation in this case, it will be unnecessary to address the issue concerning justiciability. Therefore, for the purposes of this appeal, I will assume that the matters raised herein are justiciable.

I. Facts

The respondent Gail Stacey-Moore is the chief elected officer of the respondent Native Women's Association of Canada ("NWAC"). In 1990, she was elected National Speaker of NWAC. The respondent Sharon Donna

McIvor was elected as the executive member for the West Region of NWAC in 1988. She was also the NWAC representative to the Assembly of First Nations Constitutional Commission which participated in the Canada Round of constitutional discussions. Both individuals have been actively involved in advancing the rights of Aboriginal women across Canada.

This case arises in the context of the constitutional discussions known as the Canada Round which eventually led to the completion of the Charlottetown Accord. On September 24, 1991, the Government of Canada set out 28 proposals for constitutional reform in a document entitled Shaping Canada's Future Together — Proposals. One proposal was to amend the *Constitution* to entrench a general justiciable right to Aboriginal self-government. A Special Joint Committee of the Senate and the House of Commons (the "Beaudoin-Dobbie Committee") was appointed to inquire into and make recommendations to Parliament regarding the above proposals.

During this time, it was decided that a parallel process of consultation should take place within the Aboriginal community of Canada. The Government of Canada provided funding to four national Aboriginal organizations: the Assembly of First Nations ("AFN"), the Native Council of Canada ("NCC"), the Metis National Council ("MNC") and the Inuit Tapirisat of Canada ("ITC"). The Government entered into Contribution Agreements with each of the four Aboriginal organizations in order to provide $10 million to fund participation through the Aboriginal Constitutional Review Program of the Department of the Secretary of State.

NWAC was not specifically included in the Government of Canada funding. However, pursuant to the Contribution Agreements, it was required that part of the $10 million in funding be earmarked for women's issues. As a result, AFN and NCC each paid $130,000 to the respondent NWAC. A further $300,000 was later received by NWAC directly from the Government of Canada under a separate Contribution Agreement entered into on February 4, 1992, in order to fund a study of the *Charter*. The entire funding received by NWAC amounted to 5 per cent of the total funding received by Aboriginal groups for constitutional purposes. The Secretary of State also contributed approximately $457,000 per year to NWAC for the purpose of "core funding" of its operations, although none of this money covered constitutional matters.

On March 12, 1992, the Minister Responsible for Constitutional Affairs announced that representatives of the four national Aboriginal organizations (AFN, NCC, ITC and MNC) were invited to participate in a multilateral process of constitutional discussions regarding the Beaudoin-Dobbie Committee Report. The purpose of these meetings was to prepare constitutional amendments that could be presented to Canada as a consensus package. NWAC was not invited to participate in these meetings which took place subsequent to March 12, 1992.

NWAC was concerned that their exclusion from direct funding for constitutional matters and from direct participation in the discussions threatened the equality of Aboriginal women. In particular, NWAC was concerned that the proposals advanced for constitutional amendment would not include the requirement that the *Charter* be made applicable to any form of Aboriginal self-government which might be negotiated. This fear was based on NWAC's perception that the national Aboriginal organizations, and in particular the AFN, are male-dominated so that there was little likelihood that the male majority would adopt the pro-Charter view of NWAC.

As a result, in a letter written February 12, 1992 to the Right Honourable Joe Clark, Minister Responsible for Constitutional Affairs, NWAC made a request for funding and participation equal to the other four national Aboriginal organizations. On March 2, 1992, the Minister responded that the national associations represent both men and women and he encouraged NWAC to work within the Aboriginal communities to ensure its views are heard and represented. The Minister also noted that, in recognition of the need for funding, the Contribution Agreements required that the national organizations specifically direct portions of their funding to Aboriginal women's issues. Furthermore, he stated that the concerns of NWAC would not be rectified through the addition of another seat to the constitutional table.

Despite the fact that NWAC participated in the parallel process set up by the four national Aboriginal organizations, as demonstrated by the letter of February 12, 1992 to the Right Honourable Joe Clark, NWAC remained fearful that it would be unsuccessful at putting forward its view that the *Charter* must apply to any form of Aboriginal self-government. Primarily, NWAC was worried that AFN would strongly contest the application of the *Charter* to Aboriginal self-government.

On March 18, 1992, NWAC commenced proceedings in the Federal Court, Trial Division against the Government of Canada, seeking an order of prohibition to prevent any further disbursements of funds to the four Aboriginal organizations, under the 1991 Contribution Agreements until NWAC was provided with equal funding as well as the right to participate in the constitutional review process on the same terms as the four recipient groups. ITC, MNC and NCC intervened in the proceedings. AFN did not intervene until the appeal to this Court.

The substance of the complaint is that by financing the four recipient Aboriginal groups with respect to the constitutional renewal discussions, the Government of Canada assisted the propagation of the view that the *Charter* should not apply to Aboriginal self-government. The respondents allege that by funding male-dominated groups and failing to provide equal funding to NWAC, the Government of Canada violated their freedom of expression and right to equality. The respondents' application was dismissed by the Federal Court, Trial Division: [1992] 2 F.C. 462, 53 F.T.R. 194, 90 D.L.R. (4th) 394, [1992] 4 C.N.L.R. 59. The Federal Court of Appeal also refused to issue an order of prohibition. However, the court made a declaration that the Government of Canada restricted the freedom of expression of Aboriginal women in a manner that violated ss. 2(b) and 28 of the *Charter*: [1992] 3 F.C. 192, 146 N.R. 40, 95 D.L.R. (4th) 106, [1992] 4 C.N.L.R. 71, 10 C.R.R. (2d) 268.

. . . . .

IV. Issues

I will deal with the following issues: ...

2. Did the Government of Canada violate the freedom of expression of the individual respondents or of Aboriginal women represented by the respondent NWAC, as guaranteed by s. 2(b) read together with s. 28 of the *Canadian Charter of Rights and Freedoms*, by funding the four Aboriginal organizations and permitting their participation in the constitutional discussions while not providing an equal right of participation and funding to NWAC?

3. Did the Government of Canada violate the equality rights of the individual respondents or of Aboriginal women represented by NWAC, as guaranteed by s. 15(1) of the *Canadian Charter of Rights and Freedoms*, by funding the four Aboriginal organizations and permitting their participation in the constitutional discussions while not providing an equal right of participation and funding to NWAC?

4. Did the Government of Canada violate s. 35 of the *Constitution Act, 1982* by failing to recognize existing Aboriginal and treaty rights, which are guaranteed equally to male and female persons?

V. Analysis

A. Preliminary Issues

(1) Mootness

The respondents brought an application returnable on the opening of the appeal to declare the case moot. It was submitted that since the constitutional process out of which these proceedings arose had run its course, the matter was academic. The appellant, however, pointed out that an action is outstanding against the Crown for six million dollars based on the judgment of the Court of Appeal. The application to declare the appeal moot was dismissed at the conclusion of submissions on this point.

. . . . .

B. Constitutional Issues

(1) The Applicability of the Charter

The appellant argues that the constitutional violation found by the Court of Appeal did not flow from the Government of Canada's decision to provide funding to the four Aboriginal groups. Rather any *Charter* breach was caused by the subsequent actions of the recipients in failing to equally include NWAC. Therefore, it is argued that the *Charter* does not apply since any violation resulted from the actions of private parties.

This argument misapprehends the nature of the claim of the respondents. It is their contention that the decision of the Government of Canada not to directly fund NWAC to the same extent as AFN, ITC, MNC and NCC and not to invite NWAC to the constitutional discussions violated their rights. I would not, therefore, give effect to this submission.

(2)   Sections 2(b) and 28 of the *Charter*: Freedom of Expression Guaranteed Equally to Male and Female Persons

The main contention of the respondents is that the Government's provision of funding to NCC, ITC, AFN and MNC, along with the opportunity to participate in the constitutional discussions, required the Government to bestow upon NWAC an equal chance for expression of its views. ...

It cannot plausibly be contended that the governmental action in question here had as its purpose the restriction of the respondents' freedom of expression. In fact, it could be said that the decision to provide funding to the AFN, NCC, ITC and MNC and invite the four national Aboriginal groups to the constitutional table had as its very purpose the encouragement of free expression and the exchange of ideas. Therefore, the respondents' position must rely on the effect of the decision of the Government. In this regard, their argument is summarized by the Court of Appeal as follows (at p. 211):

> The [respondents] argue that, by funding and thereby supporting male-dominated aboriginal organizations in that activity, the Canadian government has enhanced their ability to communicate their anti-*Charter* positions to the virtual exclusion of NWAC's pro-*Charter* position. Government action has given the male-dominated organizations an ability to communicate effectively which has been denied aboriginal women, thereby abridging the guarantee of section 28 that freedom of expression is equally the freedom of male and female persons.

The respondents argued that the four Aboriginal groups were given something extra from which NWAC was excluded. While it is conceded that s. 2(b) does not include the right to any particular means of expression, the respondents contend that if the Government chooses to fund and to offer a voice to anti-*Charter*, male-led Aboriginal organizations, it is under a constitutional duty to do so equitably and in accordance with the *Charter*. Therefore, the Government must also fund and invite participation by NWAC. It is submitted that such a result is mandated by the decision of this Court in *Haig v. Canada*, [1993] 2 S.C.R. 995, as well as by s. 28 of the *Charter* which guarantees the rights and freedoms of the *Charter* equally to male and female persons.

In order to determine whether the assertions of the respondents are valid, it is necessary to consider the scope of the freedom of expression as guaranteed by s. 2(b) of the *Charter*. In particular, it must be determined whether there is any positive duty on the Government to provide funding to NWAC in these circumstances. This case does not involve the typical situation of government action restricting or interfering with freedom of expression in the negative sense. Rather, the respondents claim that the *Charter* requires the Government of Canada to provide them with a forum for expression equal to that of the other Aboriginal organizations. In this light, I must also consider whether there is any evidence to support the argument that the funded groups were any less representative of Aboriginal women's views regarding the Constitution such that NWAC was constitutionally entitled to participate in the funding. The argument under ss. 2(b) and 28 of the *Charter* depends on a finding that the funding of and participation by NWAC was necessary to provide an equal voice for the rights of women.

(a) The Scope of Section 2(b)

It is beyond dispute that freedom of expression is a guaranteed right and a value of fundamental importance to our society. The essential nature of freedom of expression in a democratic society has been discussed by this Court in numerous cases. ...

Traditionally, the cases involving s. 2(b) of the *Charter* have dealt with situations whereby the government has attempted, in some way, to limit or interfere with one's freedom of expression. In the present situation, the respondents are requesting the Court to consider whether there may be a positive duty on governments to facilitate expression in certain circumstances.

Whether freedom of expression includes a positive right to be provided with specific means of expression was recently considered for the first time by this Court in *Haig*. ...

The conclusions reached in Haig have application to the case at bar. Similar to a referendum, the Government of Canada was engaging in a consultative process to secure the public opinion with respect to potential constitutional amendments. To further this goal, a parallel process of consultation was established within the Aboriginal community. It cannot be claimed that NWAC has a constitutional right to receive government funding aimed at promoting participation in the constitutional conferences. The respondents conceded as much in paragraph 91 of their factum as well as in oral argument. Furthermore, the provision of funding and the invitation to participate in constitutional discussions facilitated and enhanced the expression of Aboriginal groups. It did not stifle expression.

However, the respondents rely on *Haig* for the proposition that the Government cannot provide a platform of expression in a discriminatory fashion or in a way which otherwise violates the *Charter*. They state that this result is clearly mandated by s. 28 of the *Charter*. ...

Haig establishes the principle that generally the government is under no obligation to fund or provide a specific platform of expression to an individual or a group. However, the decision in *Haig* leaves open the possibility that, in certain circumstances, positive governmental action may be required in order to make the freedom of expression meaningful. Furthermore, in some circumstances where the government does provide such a platform, it must not do so in a discriminatory fashion contrary to the *Charter*. It is this last proposition upon which the respondents rely in conjunction with s. 28 of the *Charter* to support their position that their rights under s. 2(b) of the *Charter* were violated in that they did not receive an equal platform to express their views.

At this point, I should add that it cannot be said that every time the Government of Canada chooses to fund or consult a certain group, thereby providing a platform upon which to convey certain views, that the Government is also required to fund a group purporting to represent the opposite point of view. Otherwise, the implications of this proposition would be untenable. For example, if the Government chooses to fund a women's organization to study the issue of abortion to assist in drafting proposed legislation, can it be argued that the Government is bound by the Constitution to provide equal funding to a group purporting to represent the rights of fathers? If this was the intended scope of s. 2(b) of the *Charter*, the ramifications on government spending would be far reaching indeed. ...

Therefore, while it may be true that the Government cannot provide a particular means of expression that has the effect of discriminating against a group, it cannot be said that merely by consulting an organization, or organizations, purportedly representing a male or female point of view, the Government must automatically consult groups representing the opposite perspective. It will be rare indeed that the provision of a platform or funding to one or several organizations will have the effect of suppressing another's freedom of speech. ...

There is no question here of the Government of Canada attempting to suppress NWAC's expression of its point of view with respect to the *Constitution*. The s. 2(b) argument advanced is dependent on a finding that the funding of and participation by NWAC were essential to provide an equal voice for the rights of women. A corollary to this submission is that the funded groups are not representative of Native women because they advocate a male-dominated aboriginal self-government. This is the submission that was accepted by the Court of Appeal and is the foundation of its judgment. A review of the factual record reveals that there was no evidence to support the contention that the funded groups were less representative of the viewpoint of women with respect to the *Constitution*. Nor was there any evidence with respect to the level of support of NWAC by women as compared to the funded groups. As well, the evidence does not support the contention that the funded groups advocate a male-dominated form of self-government. At this point, a closer examination of the evidence is necessary in order to illustrate my conclusion.

(b) The Absence of Evidence Supporting a Violation of Section 2(b) of the Charter

As the contention of the respondents hinges on the fact that the four funded Aboriginal groups represented a male-dominated point of view and did not represent Aboriginal women, it is necessary to explore the background of AFN, NCC, MNC and ITC as well as NWAC, as revealed by the record. This will assist in determining whether NWAC's position is supportable.

NWAC is a non-profit organization incorporated in 1974. It has a board of directors consisting of the National Speaker, four Regional Executive Leaders, four Regional Youth Representatives and thirteen Regional Representatives. The respondent Stacey-Moore deposes in her affidavit that among the objectives of NWAC is to be the national voice for Aboriginal women and address issues concerning Native women. It is the position of NWAC that the retention of the *Charter* to any form of Aboriginal self-government is essential to the interests of Aboriginal women in striving for equality.

NCC was founded in 1972 as a non-profit organization with the object of advancing the rights and interests of Métis, non-status Indians and off-reserve registered Indians throughout Canada. The affidavit of Ron George, president of NCC, states that it is a national organization consisting of organizations in the provinces and territories. NCC has participated in the process of constitutional review in order to ensure that the Aboriginal and treaty rights of all Métis and Indians are protected under any proposed amendments. In his affidavit, Ron George further states that NCC participated in the First Minister's discussions between 1985 and 1987 to develop draft constitutional amendments that would ensure sexual equality and "in particular to ensure that *Charter* equality guarantees would be provided for under laws passed by aboriginal government institutions operating under a proposed new provision". NCC also worked actively to remove discrimination against women contained in the *Indian Act*, R.S.C., 1985, c. I-5 (formerly R.S.C. 1970, c. I-6). Finally, the president of NCC states that it "has not advocated and does not support any lessening of the rights enjoyed by all Indian and Métis people, male and female, under the *Canadian Charter of Rights and Freedoms*". However, it is the opinion of NCC that under self-government the application of the *Charter* should be a matter left to each Aboriginal nation to decide.

MNC was incorporated in 1985 with the object of determining and expressing the rights and aspirations of the Métis people of Canada as they relate to the *Constitution*. MNC consists of a federation of provincial and territorial organizations representing the Métis people of those regions. According to Ron Rivard, the Executive Director of MNC, it supports the retention of the Charter with respect to Aboriginal self-government. MNC also supported the entrenchment of gender equality between Aboriginal men and women contained in s. 35(4) of the *Constitution Act, 1982*. To the best of Ron Rivard's knowledge, NWAC does not speak for, nor represent the Métis women of Canada.

The president of ITC, Rosemarie Kuptana, took office in 1991. She deposes in her affidavit that ITC is a national organization representing Inuit from the Northwest Territories, northern Quebec and Labrador. Furthermore, NWAC does not represent Inuit women, rather they are represented by their own organization called Pauktuutit. She denies that ITC is a male-dominated organization and points to the fact that the Inuit Committee on Constitutional Issues directing the representation of Inuit interests in the constitutional discussions is composed of seven members, three of whom are women. The president of Pauktuutit is a full participating member of the Committee. ITC is willing to consider the implementation of the *Charter* to any future Inuit self- government. The Vice President of Pauktuutit, Martha Greig, deposes that Inuit women will have a full opportunity to express their views on constitutional reform and Inuit self- government through the ITC Committee on Constitutional Issues and with financial assistance provided by ITC.

AFN did not intervene at the Federal Court of Appeal and so there is no evidence from AFN as to its structure or objectives. However, the respondent Stacey-Moore deposes in her affidavit that AFN is comprised of all the Chiefs of Indian Bands in Canada. Of the 633 Member Chiefs, only 60 are women. She also deposes that AFN was strongly opposed to the application of the Charter to Aboriginal self-government. AFN denies that it was unalterably opposed to the application of the *Charter* to Native self-governments. Rather, AFN rejected "the undemocratic, non-consensual imposition of the *Charter*, without protection for First Nations' languages, cultures, and traditions". The respondents also allege that AFN did not support their goal of repealing s. 12(1)(b) of the *Indian Act*, R.S.C. 1970, c. I-6, in order to eliminate the sexual discrimination of that provision. However, the evidence does not support this contention. The Minutes of Proceedings and Evidence of the Standing Committee on Indian Affairs and Northern Development, September 20, 1982 (exhibit M to the affidavit of the respondent Stacey-Moore), reveals that AFN favoured the end to all discriminatory aspects of the *Indian Act* and not merely those relating to the sexual discrimination found in s. 12(1)(b).

I am in complete agreement with the intervener AFN's submissions that there was no evidence before the Federal Court of Appeal, nor before this Court, that AFN or the other funded groups advocated "male-dominated Aboriginal self-governments". Nor was there any evidence to suggest that AFN, NCC, ITC or MNC were less representative of the viewpoint of women with respect to the Constitution. The main argument of NWAC in this regard is that only they were advocating the inclusion of the *Charter* in any negotiated form of Aboriginal self-government. The evidence clearly discloses that of the four funded groups at least MNC also supported its inclusion. Furthermore, NCC did not oppose application of the *Charter*, rather it desired that each Aboriginal self-government be free to determine the issue for itself. ITC was also willing to consider application of the *Charter*. Thus, it was not exclusively the position of NWAC that the *Charter* be maintained.

Furthermore, in a letter dated March 2, 1992 (exhibit A to the supplementary affidavit of Gail Stacey-Moore), the Minister Responsible for Constitutional Affairs wrote the following:

> The national Aboriginal associations do represent both men and women from their communities. I encourage you to work within your communities to ensure your views are heard and represented through those associations.

Thus, in the opinion of the Government of Canada as well, the funded organizations were not perpetuating only a male-dominated point of view. Although this is certainly not determinative, it is indicative that a minister of the Crown who was familiar with the position and views advanced by them regarded the four national organizations as *bona fide* representatives of Aboriginal persons.

It is evident from the record that NWAC had the opportunity to express its ideas both directly to the Government as well as through the four Aboriginal representative organizations. ...

The evidence is also indicative of the fact that Aboriginal women, including members of NWAC, did have a direct voice regarding the position of the funded groups with respect to the constitutional discussions. NWAC participated in the parallel process set up by the four national Aboriginal organizations to discuss constitutional reform. For example, the respondent Stacey-Moore and other women secured positions on the Constitutional Working Group of the AFN. The respondent McIvor was the NWAC representative to the AFN Constitutional Commission, while Jane Gottfriedson, President of the British Columbia Native Women's Society (affiliated with NWAC) was appointed to the NCC Constitutional Commission. As well, on March 13, 14 and 15, 1992, an Aboriginal Conference on the Constitution was held in Ottawa. After a sustained effort, NWAC secured eight official seats and four observers out of a total of 184 delegates.

Furthermore, NWAC also received some of the Government funding under the Contribution Agreements, as all four groups were required to direct a portion of the funds received specifically to address women's issues. AFN and NCC each supplied $130,000 to NWAC. ITC contributed $170,000 to its women's organization, Pauktuutit, for research and other work related to constitutional affairs and more funding was expected. Pauktuutit, as the representative of Inuit women, was actively involved in the constitutional process.

Rather than illustrate that the funded groups advocated male-dominated Aboriginal self-government, the evidence discloses that the four funded groups made efforts to include the viewpoint of women. As well, there was no evidence to suggest that NWAC enjoyed any higher level of support amongst Aboriginal women as compared to the funded Aboriginal groups.

(c) Conclusions on Sections 2(b) and 28 of the Charter

The freedom of expression guaranteed by s. 2(b) of the *Charter* does not guarantee any particular means of expression or place a positive obligation upon the Government to consult anyone. The right to a particular platform or means of expression was clearly rejected by this Court in *Haig*. The respondents had many opportunities to express their views through the four Aboriginal groups as well as directly to the Government, for example, through the Beaudoin-Dobbie Commission. NWAC even took the opportunity to express its concerns directly to the Minister Responsible for Constitutional Affairs and received a response, albeit one that did not satisfy NWAC. ...

Even assuming that in certain extreme circumstances, the provision of a platform of expression to one group may infringe the expression of another and thereby require the Government to provide an equal opportunity for the expression of that group, there was no evidence in this case to suggest that the funding or consultation of the four Aboriginal groups infringed the respondents' equal right of freedom of expression. The four Aboriginal groups invited to discuss possible constitutional amendments are all *bona fide* national representatives of Aboriginal people in Canada and, based on the facts in this case, there was no requirement under s. 2(b) of the *Charter* to also extend an invitation and funding directly to the respondents.

Although I would hope that it is evident from these reasons, I wish to stress that nothing stated in them is intended to detract in any way from any contention by or on behalf of Aboriginal women that they face racial and sexual discrimination which impose serious hurdles to their equality.

(3) Section 15(1) of the *Charter*: Equality Rights

It seems that the respondents' contentions regarding ss. 2(b) and 28 of the *Charter* are better characterized as a s. 15 *Charter* argument. As L'Heureux-Dubé, J. stated in *Haig, supra,* the allegations that a platform of expression has been provided on a discriminatory basis are preferably dealt with under s. 15.

The respondents contend that the refusal to fund NWAC and invite them to be equal participants at the round of constitutional discussions violated their rights under s. 15(1) of the *Charter* due to the under-inclusive nature of the Government's decision. Again relying on Haig in their factum, the respondents submit that an equality claim may involve the provision of means of expression to certain groups or individuals.

I have concluded that the arguments of the respondents with respect to s. 15 must also fail. The lack of an evidentiary basis for the arguments with respect to ss. 2(b) and 28 is equally applicable to any arguments advanced under s. 15(1) of the *Charter* in this case. I agree with the Court of Appeal that s. 15(1) is of no assistance to the respondents.

(4) Section 35 of the *Constitution Act, 1982*: Existing Aboriginal and Treaty Rights

I also agree with the conclusions of the Court of Appeal with respect to the inapplicability of s. 35 of the *Constitution Act, 1982* to the present case. The right of the Aboriginal people of Canada to participate in constitutional discussions does not derive from any existing Aboriginal or treaty right protected under s. 35. Therefore, s. 35(4) of the *Constitution Act, 1982*, which guarantees Aboriginal and treaty rights referred to in s. 35(1) equally to male and female persons, is of no assistance to the respondents.

VI. Disposition

I respectfully disagree with the conclusion of the Federal Court of Appeal that the failure to provide funding to the respondents and invite them as equal participants in the constitutional discussions violated their rights under ss. 2(b) and 28 of the *Charter*. I am, however, in agreement with the Federal Court of Appeal that s. 15(1) of the *Charter* and s. 35 of the *Constitution Act, 1982* have no application in this case. Therefore, I would allow the appeal, set aside the declaration made by the Federal Court of Appeal and restore the judgment of Walsh D.J. with costs to the appellant both here and in the Court of Appeal if demanded.

F. CONCLUSION

This rise and struggle of Aboriginal women's organizations have left their mark on the legal and political community. They have raised important questions that both challenge and clarify critical issues in discussions about self-government. It is clear from their message that Aboriginal women will not accept discrimination in their communities. While this chapter has demonstrated the continued discrimination Aboriginal women encounter in society, it has also reviewed the significant steps that have been taken to counter this challenge. This examination has shown that, in the past 25 years, Aboriginal women have not always been passive objects of colonial policy but often have been active subjects, influencing and creating the contours of law and policy dealing with Aboriginal rights. Many strong and courageous women have made a difference through their efforts. People like Mary-Two Axe Early, Jeanette Corbière, Yvonne Bédard, Sandra Lovelace, and others, have been influential in changing Canada's law concerning Aboriginal people. As a result, many have begun to rectify the injustice perpetrated by the *Indian Act* and have strengthened their identity, have reunited with their communities, and have had their status reinstated. At the same time, other Aboriginal women continue to experience the double discrimination of racism and sexism. Cases like *Derrickson*, *Sawridge* and *Corbiere* illustrate such issues that still require resolution. The imposition of the *Indian Act* over the past 120 years has been destructive. The role of Aboriginal women in nation building and their expressions of justice cannot be ignored. These visions must guide the development of law in Canada for Aboriginal Nations to become healthy, vibrant and strong.

CHAPTER 9

GOVERNANCE

A. INTRODUCTION

Aboriginal peoples exercised powers of governance for millennia prior to the arrival of Europeans and others in North America. These powers of governance varied according to clan and nation, and were suited to the varieties of languages and cultures represented on the continent. There were alliances, confederacies, powerful families, democracies and empires. Traditions of governance were often closely connected to land and family, and many emphasized the connection of the spiritual, familial, economic and political spheres.

The arrival of others challenged the governing structures of Aboriginal nations and tested their ability to perpetuate their institutions. These challenges were both internal and external. Internally, the appearance of alternative values and options for governance provided a greater range of choice to individuals and communities. Some chose to depart from or alter their traditions in response to these influences and, in the process, severely weakened the fabric of their governing structures. Others had little choice in the matter and were forced to surrender their traditional ways. Externally, the coercive implementation of the *Indian Act* [now R.S.C. 1985, c. I-5] and the associated onslaught of "civilizing" programs such as residential school and child welfare policies tested the ability of Aboriginal people to perpetuate their traditional governance. Today, despite these difficulties, many Aboriginal people continue to be guided by their ancient practices and traditions in their approaches to governance.

The materials that follow explore the legal principles relevant to Aboriginal governance in Canada today.

B. ABORIGINAL VIEWS ON GOVERNANCE

REPORT OF THE ROYAL COMMISSION ON ABORIGINAL PEOPLES: RESTRUCTURING THE RELATIONSHIP, VOL. 2

(Ottawa: Ministry of Supply and Services, 1996) at 105-6, 108-14
(references omitted)

CONCEPTS AND TRADITIONS OF GOVERNANCE

IN THE TIME BEFORE there were human beings on Earth, the Creator called a great meeting of the Animal People.

During that period of the world's history, the Animal People lived harmoniously with one another and could speak to the Creator with one mind.

They were very curious about the reason for the gathering. When they had all assembled together, the Creator spoke.

"I am sending a strange new creature to live among you," he told the Animal People. "He is to be called Man and he is to be your brother.

"But unlike you he will have no fur on his body, will walk on two legs and will not be able to speak with you. Because of this he will need your help in order to survive and become who I am creating him to be. You will need to be more than brothers and sisters, you will need to be his teachers.

"Man will not be like you. He will not come into the world like you. He will not be born knowing and understanding who and what he is. He will have to search for that. And it is in the search that he will find himself.

"He will also have a tremendous gift that you do not have. He will have the ability to dream. With this ability he will be able to invent great things and because of this he will move further and further away from you and will need your help even more when this happens.

"But to help him I am going to send him out into the world with one very special gift. I am going to give him the gift of the knowledge of Truth and Justice. But like his identity it must be a search, because if he finds this knowledge too easily he will take it for granted. So I am going to hide it and I need your help to find a good hiding-place. That is why I have called you here."

A great murmur ran through the crowd of Animal People. They were excited at the prospect of welcoming a new creature into the world and they were honoured by the Creator's request for their help. This was truly an important day.

One by one the Animal People came forward with suggestions of where the Creator should hide the gift of knowledge of Truth and Justice.

"Give it to me, my Creator," said the Buffalo, "and I will carry it on my hump to the very centre of the plains and bury it there."

"A good idea, my brother," the Creator said, "but it is destined that Man should cover most of the world and he would find it there too easily and take it for granted."

"Then give it to me," said the Salmon, "and I will carry it in my mouth to the deepest part of the ocean and I will hide it there."

"Another excellent idea," said the Creator, "but it is destined that with his power to dream, Man will invent a device that will carry him there and he would find it too easily and take it for granted."

"Then I will take it," said the Eagle, "and carry it in my talons and fly to the very face of the Moon and hide it there."

"No, my brother," said the Creator, "even there he would find it too easily because Man will one day travel there as well."

Animal after animal came forward with marvellous suggestions on where to hide this precious gift, and one by one the Creator turned down their ideas. Finally, just when discouragement was about to invade their circle, a tiny voice spoke from the back of the gathering. The Animal People were all surprised to find that the voice belonged to the Mole.

The Mole was a small creature who spent his life tunnelling through the earth and because of this had lost most of the use of his eyes. Yet because he was always in touch with Mother Earth, the Mole had developed true spiritual insight.

The Animal People listened respectfully when Mole began to speak.

"I know where to hide it, my Creator," he said. "I know where to hide the gift of the knowledge of Truth and Justice."

"Where then, my brother?" asked the Creator. "Where should I hide this gift?"

"Put it inside them," said the Mole. "Put it inside them because then only the wisest and purest of heart will have the courage to look there."

And that is where the Creator placed the gift of the knowledge of Truth and Justice.

. . . . .

1. Aboriginal Perspectives

1.1 Basic Concepts

... [H]uman beings are born with the inherent freedom to discover who and what they are. For many Aboriginal people, this is perhaps the most basic definition of sovereignty — the right to know who and what you are. Sovereignty is the natural right of all human beings to define, sustain and perpetuate their identities as individuals, communities and nations.

Many Aboriginal people see sovereignty as much as a human right as a political and legal one. Seen in this way, sovereignty is an inherent human attribute that cannot be surrendered or taken away.

> What is sovereignty? Sovereignty is difficult to define because it is intangible, it cannot be seen or touched. It is very much inherent, an awesome power, a strong feeling or the belief of a people. What can be seen, however, is the exercise of Aboriginal powers. For our purposes, a working definition of sovereignty is the ultimate power from which all specific political powers are derived.

> Roger Jones, Councillor and Elder
> Shawanaga First Nation
> Sudbury, Ontario, 1 June 1993*

As an inherent human quality, sovereignty finds its natural expression in the principle of self-determination. Self-determining peoples have the freedom to choose the pathways that best express their identity, their sense of themselves and the character of their relations with others. Self-determination is the power of choice in action.

> Self-determination is looking at our desires and our aspirations of where we want to go and being given the chance to attain that ... for life itself, for existence itself, for nationhood itself ... .

> René Tenasco, Councillor
> Kitigan Zibi Anishinabeg Council
> Maniwaki, Quebec, 2 December 1992

Self-government is one path Aboriginal people may take in putting the principle of self-determination into effect. Self-government flows from the principle of self-determination. In its most basic sense, it is the ability to assess and satisfy needs without outside influence, permission or restriction. In a study prepared for the Commission, the Metis Family and Community Justice Services of Saskatchewan asserts the following:

> The political movement towards Métis self-government may be understood as a viable alternative to a mainstream political and administrative system that has consistently failed to address our goals and needs. Our desire to control our own affairs should be viewed as a positive step, as an expression of nationhood, built upon a history in which the right to self-determination was never relinquished, in which the governing apparatus will have legitimacy in the eyes of its citizens.

Of course, self-government may take a variety of forms. For some peoples, it may mean establishing distinct governmental institutions on an 'exclusive' territory. For others, it may mean setting up a public government generally connected with modern treaties or land claims agreements. Alternatively, self-government may involve sharing power in joint governmental institutions, with guaranteed representation for the nations and peoples involved. In other instances, it may involve setting up culturally specific institutions and services within a broader framework of public government. ...

While the terms sovereignty, self-determination and self-government have distinct meanings, they are versatile concepts, with meanings that overlap one another. They are used by different peoples in different ways.

. . . . .

Sovereignty, in the words of one brief, is "the original freedom conferred to our people by the Creator rather than a temporal power." As a gift from the Creator, sovereignty can neither be given nor taken away, nor can its basic terms be negotiated. This view is shared by many Aboriginal people, whose political traditions are infused with a deep sense of spirituality and a sense of the inter-connectedness of all things. Such concepts as sovereignty, self-government and the land, which for some Canadians have largely secular definitions, all retain a spiritual dimension in contemporary Aboriginal thinking. Dave Courchene, Jr. alluded to this point in his testimony to the Commission:

> The underlying premise upon which all else was based was to recognize and fulfil the spirit of life within oneself and with all others in the circle of individuals, relationship or community and the land. This was achieved through concerted effort on developing the spirit through prayer, meditation, vision quests, fasting, ceremony, and in other ways of communicating with the Creator.
>
> Dave Courchene, Jr.
> Fort Alexander, Manitoba
> 30 October 1992

From this perspective, sovereignty is seen as an inherent attribute, flowing from sources within a people or nation rather than from external sources such as international law, common law or the Constitution. Herb George of the Gitksan and Wet'suwet'en stated:

> What is required here is not an inquiry of the current law or international law to determine the source of our rights. What is required here is the recognition that our rights exist in spite of what international law says, in spite of what the common law says, and in spite of what have been the policies of this government to the present day.
>
> If this issue is to be dealt with in a fair way, then what is required is a strong recommendation from this Commission to government that the source of our rights, the source of our lives and the source of our government is from us. That the source of our lives comes from Gitksan-Wet'suwet'en law.
>
> Herb George
> Gitksan-Wet'suwet'en Government
> Commission on Social Development
> Kispiox, British Columbia, 16 June 1992

While Aboriginal sovereignty is inherent, it also has an historical basis in the extensive diplomatic relations between Aboriginal peoples and European powers from the early period of contact onward. In the eyes of many treaty peoples, the fact that the French and British Crowns concluded alliances and treaties with First Nations demonstrates that these nations were sovereign peoples capable of conducting international relations. The president of the Union of Nova Scotia Indians said to the Commission:

> We see our right of self-government as an inherent right which does not come from other governments. It does not originate in our treaties. The right of self-government and self-determination comes from the Mi'kmaq people themselves. It is through their authority that we govern. The treaties reflect the Crown's recognition that we were, and would remain, self-governing, but they did not create our nationhood ... .In this light, the treaties should be effective vehicles for the implementation of our constitutionally protected right to exercise jurisdiction and authority as governments. Self-government can start with the process of interpreting and fully implementing the 1752 Treaty, to build onto it an understanding of the political relationship between the Mi'kmaq people and the Crown.

> Alex Christmas
> Eskasoni, Nova Scotia
> 6 May 1992

Some interveners spoke of the need for caution in using the term sovereignty. They noted that the word has roots in European languages and political thought and draws on attitudes associated with the rise of the unitary state, attitudes that do not harmonize well with Aboriginal ideas of governance. For example, in some strands of European thought, sovereignty is coloured by theories suggesting that absolute political authority is vested in a single political office or body, which has no legal limits on its power. The classic notion of the sovereignty of Parliament as developed in British constitutional thought reflects such an approach.

This understanding of sovereignty is very different from that held by most Aboriginal people.

> I don't even like the word sovereignty because ... it denotes the idea that there's a sovereign, a king, or a head honcho, whatever. I don't think that native people govern themselves that way ... .I think native peoples' government was more of a consultative process where everyone was involved — women, men and children.

> Greg Johnson
> Eskasoni, Nova Scotia
> 6 May 1992

Gerald Alfred makes similar observations in a study dealing with the meaning of self-government among the Mohawk people of Kahnawake:

> The use of the term 'sovereignty' is itself problematic, as it skews the terms of the debate in favour of a European conception of a proper relationship. In adopting the English language as a means of communication, Aboriginal peoples have been compromised to a certain degree in that accepting the language means accepting basic premises developed in European thought and reflected in the debate surrounding the issues of sovereignty in general and Aboriginal or Native sovereignty in particular.

A better term for political authority, Alfred suggests, is the Mohawk word tewatatowie, which means 'we help ourselves'. Tewatatowie is linked to philosophical concepts embodied in the Iroquois Kaianerekowa, or Great Law of Peace. It is understood not only in terms of interests and boundaries, but also in terms of land, relationships and spirituality. The essence of Mohawk sovereignty is harmony, achieved through balanced relationships. This requires respect for the common interests of individuals and communities, as well as for the differences that require them to maintain a measure of autonomy from one another. For the Mohawk, as for many other Aboriginal peoples, sovereignty does not mean establishing an all-powerful government over a nation or people. It means that the people take care of themselves and the lands for which they are responsible. It means using political power to express the people's will.

Commissioners heard differing views about what Aboriginal sovereignty means for the relationship between Aboriginal peoples and Canada. Some Aboriginal people spoke about degrees of sovereignty and joint jurisdiction. A number of treaty nations used the term 'shared sovereignty' and maintained that their treaties created a confederal relationship with the Crown, or a form of treaty federalism. For example, the Federation of Saskatchewan Indian Nations outlined a vision of shared but equal sovereignties, affirmed by treaties between First Nations and the Crown. This view envisages relations among First Nations governments, provincial governments and the federal government that are based on principles of coexistence and equality.

Others adopt a more autonomous stance. For example, the Mohawk people draw a clear distinction between co-operating with Canada at an administrative level and surrendering sovereignty. They hold that the first does not necessarily involve the second. They consider the freedom to make associations an essential element of self-determination and self-government. The point is elaborated in a joint statement by the Mohawk Council of Akwesasne, Kahnawake and Kanesatake:

> We see self-determination and governance as discrete concepts. But by believing that our Nation constitutes a sovereign power, we are not precluding political or economic cooperation with Canada. Self-determination is a right we have and which must be respected, but we recognize that it is a right which operates within the context of a political and economic reality. From our perspective, our right to self-determination is not detrimentally affected by the arrangements and agreements we reach with Canada for the mutual benefit of our peoples. Our position with respect to any agreement must be based upon our assessment of our current capabilities to govern and administer, it in no way derogates from the unlimited right to change those arrangements in the future upon reflection.

The right of self-determination is also a basic concept for Inuit. This right is grounded in their identity as a distinct people, the strong bonds they have with their homelands, and the fact that they have governed themselves on those lands for thousands of years. They call for their rights to be viewed within a human rights framework as opposed to an ethnic rights framework:

> If more emphasis was placed on examining the self-government question from a human rights perspective, the dominating principles would be the

universality of human rights and the equality of all peoples. This would lead to a recognition of the right of aboriginal peoples, like other peoples, to self-determination. Self-determination is not defined as an ethnic right internationally. It is a fundamental human right of peoples, not of ethnic groups.

In the eyes of Inuit, self-determination has both international and domestic aspects. Nevertheless, they have clearly indicated that they wish to exercise their right of self-determination mainly through constitutional reform and the negotiation of self-government agreements. Rosemarie Kuptana, former president of Inuit Tapirisat of Canada, has expressed this position as follows:

> The implementation of our right to self-determination will be pursued in a cooperative and practical manner with all Arctic States including Canada, but the Inuit agenda is first and foremost premised upon our recognition as a people. We are a people who have been subjected to the sovereignty of Canada without our consent, without recognition of our collective identity as a people and in violation of our right to self-determination under international law. This must be rectified by several initiatives: the negotiation of regional self-government agreements, constitutional entrenchment of the inherent right of self-government, and the full recognition of the right of indigenous peoples to self-determination, under international human rights standards.

Métis people also maintain that they have a right of self-determination as a distinct people. This right forms the background to their assertion of the right to govern themselves and, more generally, to control their own social, cultural and economic development. The Métis right of self-determination arises from their distinctive political history, which has taken different forms in different parts of Canada. For example, the political consciousness of Métis people in western Canada is rooted in the unique character and status of the Métis Nation, which emerged in the prairies during the eighteenth and nineteenth centuries in the course of activities centred on the fur trade and buffalo hunting. The historical dimensions of self-determination are emphasized in a study by the Metis Society of Saskatchewan:

> At the outset, it is important to note that our self-determination objectives, through self-government, are not new. Metis history bears witness to a lengthy legacy of struggles aimed at asserting our fundamental right to control our own destiny. In what is now the province of Saskatchewan, for example, ever escalating political, economic, social and cultural disputes between the Metis and the European settlers culminated in the well known Metis resistance to Ottawa in 1885. Other sites in nineteenth century Western Canada were also scenes of conflict over many of the same issues. As might be expected, while the military conflicts that sometimes erupted were relatively short-lived, the political struggle to protect Metis economic, social and cultural values and goals has persisted.

> This enduring theme in our Metis history — that we as a people have struggled against often overwhelming odds to reclaim our traditional Homeland and assert our sense of nationhood — lies behind much of the current drive towards self-government.

Métis people in eastern and central Canada also point to their long-standing and unique history, their position as mediators between First

Nations and incoming Europeans and their involvement in the earliest treaties of peace and friendship. They also emphasize the continuity between their own traditions and those of other Aboriginal people.

While they ground their right of self-determination in international law, Métis people see Canada as the main venue for exercising that right.

The Métis Nation, while believing that it possesses the right of self-determination in the context of international law, has consistently pursued the recognition of its autonomy within the confines of the Canadian state and has vigorously advocated the need to negotiate self-government arrangements.

Métis organizations have urged Canadian governments to ratify a Métis Nation accord, similar to the Charlottetown Accord of 1992. They have also called for the explicit entrenchment of the inherent right of Métis self-government in the Canadian constitution. Such measures would allow Métis people to negotiate self-government agreements as a "nation within a nation".

In summary, while Aboriginal people use a variety of terms to describe their fundamental rights, they are unanimous in asserting that they have an inherent right of self-determination arising from their status as distinct or sovereign peoples. This right entitles them to determine their own governmental arrangements and the character of their relations with other people in Canada. As Elder Moses Smith of the Nuu-chah-nulth Nation told Commissioners:

> What we have — the big thing within our system ... Ha Houlthee. That is the very basic of our political setup, is Ha Houlthee, which is, we might say, putting it in English, that is true sovereignty ... .That is absolutely the key, the key of why we are today now, is that we have always been. That was never taken away from us.

C. THE COURT'S VIEW ON GOVERNANCE: HISTORICAL RECOGNITION

Historically, Aboriginal peoples often expressed their powers of governance through relations with others. As Chapter 2 demonstrated, these agreements were originally carried on with attention to Aboriginal protocol, and were respected by non-Aboriginal nations because of the power Aboriginal nations exercised. The Supreme Court of Canada has recognized the autonomy and independence of Aboriginal peoples in early North American relations and has provided contemporary protection for treaties formed in this period. The case of *R. v. Sioui*, below, illustrates the inherent nature of Aboriginal governance powers that provided them with authority to enter into nation-to-nation agreements with France and Great Britain.

R. v. SIOUI

[1990] 1 S.C.R. 1025, 70 D.L.R. (4th) 427

[Four members of the Huron nation were charged with cutting trees, camping and making fires in a provincial park, contrary to provincial regulations in Quebec. The Huron admitted performing the acts for which they were charged, but claimed they were practising ancestral customs and religious rites guaranteed by a treaty with the British in 1760. In resolving this appeal in favour of the Huron, the Supreme Court considered the unique relationship of First Nations to European powers at the time the treaty was signed, and commented on the independence of the Huron at this date.]

Lamer J. (Dickson C.J.C., Wilson, La Forest, L'Heureux-Dubé, Sopinka, Gonthier, Cory and **McLachlin JJ.** concurring):

[62] ... On September 5, 1760, France and England were engaged in a war begun four years earlier, which ended with the Treaty of Paris signed on February 10, 1763. About a year earlier, the battle of the Plains of Abraham had allowed the British to take control of Quebec City and the surrounding area. During the year following this victory, British troops had worked to consolidate their military position in Canada and to solve the supply and other practical problems engendered by the very harsh winter of 1759.

[63] ... General Murray at that time invited French soldiers to surrender and Canadians to lay down their arms. He had made it widely known that he would pardon those who surrendered and allow them to keep their land. He had also promised them that he would make larger grants of land and protect them. He gave those who responded to his appeal and took the oath of allegiance to the British Crown safe conducts to return to their parishes. Steps were also taken to inform the Indians who were allies of the British of these changes of allegiance so as to ensure that they would not be attacked on the way back.

[64] As the advantageous position and strength of the British troops became more and more apparent, several groups did surrender and it appears that this movement accelerated in the days preceding that on which the document at issue was signed. In his Historical Journal, at the entries for September 1, 2 and 3, 1760, Knox indicates that:

> The whole parish of Varenne have surrendered, delivered up their arms, and taken the oaths; their fighting-men consisted of five companies of militia: two other parishes, equally numerous, have signified their intentions of submitting to-morrow.

. . . . .

> The Canadians are surrendering every-where; they are terrified at the thoughts of Sir William Johnson's Indians coming among them, by which we conjecture they are near at hand.

. . . . .

[65] In fact, the total defeat of France in Canada was very near: the Act of Capitulation of Montreal, by which the French troops stationed in

Canada laid down their arms, was signed on September 8, 1760 and signaled the end of France's de facto control in Canada.

[66] Great Britain's *de jure* control of Canada took the form of the Treaty of Paris of February 10, 1763.... Some months later, the *Royal Proclamation* of October 7, 1763 organized the territories recently acquired by Great Britain and reserved two types of land for the Indians: that located outside the colony's territorial limits and the establishments authorized by the Crown inside the colony...

[68] I consider that ... we can conclude from the historical documents that both Great Britain and France felt that the Indian nations had sufficient independence and played a large enough role in North America for it to be good policy to maintain relations with them very close to those maintained between sovereign nations.

[69] The mother countries did everything in their power to secure the alliance of each Indian nation and to encourage nations allied with the enemy to change sides. When these efforts met with success, they were incorporated in treaties of alliance or neutrality. This clearly indicates that the Indian nations were regarded in their relations with the European nations which occupied North America as independent nations. The papers of Sir William Johnson (The Papers of Sir William Johnson, 14 vol.), who was in charge of Indian affairs in British North America, demonstrate the recognition by Great Britain that nation-to-nation relations had to be conducted with the North American Indians. As an example, I cite an extract from a speech by Sir Johnson at the Onondaga Conference held in April 1748, attended by the Five Nations:

> Brethren of the five Nations I will begin upon a thing of a long standing, our first *Brothership*. My Reason for it is, I think there are several among you who seem to forget it; It may seem strange to you how I a *Foreigner* should know this, But I tell you I found out some of the old Writings of our Forefathers which was thought to have been lost and in this old valuable Record I find, that our first *Friendship* Commenced at the Arrival of the first great Canoe or Vessel at Albany . . . (Emphasis added.) (The Papers of Sir William Johnson, vol. I, 1921, at pp. 157-58.)

[70] As the Chief Justice of the United States Supreme Court said in 1832 in *Worcester v. State of Georgia*, 31 U.S. (6 Pet.) 515 (1832), at pp. 548-49, about British policy towards the Indians in the mid-eighteenth century:

> Such was the policy of Great Britain towards the Indian nations inhabiting the territory from which she excluded all other Europeans; such her claims, and such her practical exposition of the charters she had granted: *she considered them as nations capable of maintaining the relations of peace and war; of governing themselves, under her protection; and she made treaties with them, the obligation of which she acknowledged.* (Emphasis added.)

[71] Further, both the French and the English recognized the critical importance of alliances with the Indians, or at least their neutrality, in determining the outcome of the war between them and the security of the North American colonies.

[72] Following the crushing defeats of the English by the French in 1755, the English realized that control of North America could not be acquired without the co-operation of the Indians. Accordingly, from then on they made efforts to ally themselves with as many Indian nations as possi-

ble. The French, who had long realized the strategic role of the Indians in the success of any war effort, also did everything they could to secure their alliance or maintain alliances already established. ...

[73] England also wished to secure the friendship of the Indian nations by treating them with generosity and respect for fear that the safety and development of the colonies and their inhabitants would be compromised by Indians with feelings of hostility. One of the extracts from Knox's work which I cited above reports that the Canadians and the French soldiers who surrendered asked to be protected from Indians on the way back to their parishes. Another passage from Knox, also cited above, relates that the Canadians were terrified at the idea of seeing Sir William Johnson's Indians coming among them. This proves that in the minds of the local population the Indians represented a real and disturbing threat. The fact that England was also aware of the danger the colonies and their inhabitants might run if the Indians withdrew their co-operation is echoed in the...documents...and by analogy Governor Murray's *Journal of the Siege of Quebec*, entry of December 31, 1759, at pp. 15-16.

[74] This "generous" policy which the British chose to adopt also found expression in other areas. The British Crown recognized that the Indians had certain ownership rights over their land, it sought to establish trade with them which would rise above the level of exploitation and give them a fair return. It also allowed them autonomy in their internal affairs, intervening in this area as little as possible.

[Drawing on this historical context and noting the need to reconcile the independence of the Huron with the colonial aspirations of the British, the Court found that the Hurons exercised their autonomy in the period in question by entering into a treaty to protect their religious liberties and customs. They further found that this treaty was still valid, that the acts protected by its terms were not incompatible with Crown suzerainty and that, therefore, the treaty provided an effective defence against the acts for which the Huron were charged.]

The early history of Aboriginal/Crown relations in eastern North America demonstrates that the Crown often recognized the autonomy of Aboriginal Nations. Practices and principles were developed to affirm this fact and to facilitate productive relations between the parties. *The Royal Proclamation of 1763* [R.S.C. 1985, App. II, No. 1] figured prominently in the *Sioui* decision as evidence of a policy of peaceful alliance the Crown pursued with Indians. The *Royal Proclamation* and its associated history have significant implications for the recognition of Aboriginal self-government in contemporary affairs.

The *Royal Proclamation* was declared to delineate boundaries and define jurisdiction between Aboriginal people and the Crown. The Proclamation attempted to convince Indians that the British would respect existing political and territorial jurisdiction by incorporating Aboriginal understandings of this relationship in the document. The Proclamation does this by implying that no lands would be taken from Indians without their consent.

However, in order to consolidate the Crown's position in North America, words were also placed in the document that did not accord with Aboriginal viewpoints. For example, the British inserted statements in the Proclamation that claimed "Dominion" and "Sovereignty" over the territories that First Nations occupied. In placing these divergent notions within the Proclamation the British were trying to convince Native people that they had nothing to fear from the colonists, while at the same time trying to increase their own political and economic power. The British perceptively realized that alleviating Indian discontent required Native people to believe that their jurisdiction and territory were protected. However, the British also realized that the colonial enterprise required an expansion of the Crown's sovereignty and dominion over Indian lands. Thus, while the Proclamation seemingly reinforced Indian preferences that their territories remain free from European settlement, it also opened the door for the erosion of these same preferences. *The Royal Proclamation* uncomfortably straddles contradictory aspirations.

JOHN BORROWS, "WAMPUM AT NIAGARA: THE ROYAL PROCLAMATION, CANADIAN LEGAL HISTORY AND SELF-GOVERNMENT"

In Michael Asch, ed., *Aboriginal and Treaty Rights in Canada: Essays on Law, Equality and Respect for Difference*
(Vancouver: U.B.C. Press, 1997) 155 at 161-65, 168-69

The Treaty of Niagara

Since the wording of the [Royal] Proclamation is contradictory in describing the autonomy and jurisdiction of First Nations, and since the Proclamation was drafted under the control and preference of the colonial power, the spirit and intent of the Royal Proclamation can best be discerned by reference to a treaty with First Nations representatives at Niagara in 1764. At this gathering a nation-to-nation relationship between settler and First Nation peoples was renewed and extended, and the Covenant Chain of Friendship, a multination alliance in which no member gave up their sovereignty, was affirmed. The Royal Proclamation became a treaty at Niagara because it was presented by the colonialists for affirmation, and was accepted by the First Nations. However, when presenting the Proclamation, both parties made representations and promises through methods other than the written word, such as oral statements and belts of wampum. It is significant to note that Sir William Johnson, superintendent of Indian affairs, had earlier agreed to meet with the First Nations and reassert their mutual relationship through requirements prescribed by the Aboriginal peoples, which involved the giving and receiving of wampum belts. Some principles that were implicit in the written version of the Proclamation were made explicit to First Nations in these other communications. For example, First Nation peoples approved terms of the Proclamation that encompassed more than a system of land allotment, including express guarantees of First Nations sovereignty.

In the winter after the Royal Proclamation was issued, First Nation leaders throughout the northeast, mid-east, and mid-west of North America were invited to attend a conference to be held the following summer to discuss the formation of principles that would govern their relationship with the Crown. The people of the Algonquin and Nipissing nations met with the British superintendent of Indian affairs at Oswegatchie and were persuaded to be messengers in inviting other First Nations to attend a peace council at Niagara in the summer of 1764. Representatives of these two nations travelled throughout the winter of 1763-4 with a printed copy of the Royal Proclamation, and with various strings of wampum, in order to summons the various First Nations to a council with the British.

William Johnson described the purpose of the intended meeting at Niagara as a "Treaty of Offensive and Defensive Alliance" that would include British promises to assure them of a Free Fair & Open trade, at the principal Posts, & a free intercourse, & passage into our Country, That we will make no Settlements or Encroachments contrary to Treaty, or without their permission. That we will bring to justice any persons who commit Robberys or Murders on them & that we will protect & aid them against their & our Enemys, & duly observe our Engagements with them." It is clear that, in conjunction with their issuance of the Proclamation, the British proposed that a treaty be entered into to negotiate and formalize the principles upon which their relationship would be based. The invitation to treaty, with the accompanying promises that were to govern the parties' relationship, demonstrates the intent of the British to enter into momentous negotiations with the First Nations of North America. Johnson further proposed, on behalf of the British, that: at this treaty ... we should tie them down (in the Peace) according to their own forms of which they take the most notice, for example by exchanging a very large belt with some remarkable & intelligible figures thereon. Expressive of the occasion which should always be shown to remind them of their promises." Thus, the treaty at Niagara was to be recorded in the manner that the First Nations were familiar with. Wampum belts were to be exchanged which would communicate the promises exchanged, and which would form the record of the agreement.

The treaty at Niagara was entered into in July and August 1764, and was regarded as "the most widely representative gathering of American Indians ever assembled," as approximately two thousand chiefs attended the negotiations. There were over twenty-four Nations gathered with "representative nations as far east as Nova Scotia, and as far west as Mississippi, and as far north as Hudson Bay." It is also possible that representatives from even further afield participated in the treaty as some records indicate that the Cree and Lakota (Sioux) nations were also present at this event. It is obvious that a substantial number of First Nations people attended the gathering at Niagara. Aboriginal people throughout the Great Lakes and northern, eastern, and western colonial regions had travelled for weeks and months to attend this meeting.

When everyone was assembled, William Johnson presented the terms of what he hoped would prove a Pax Britannica for North America." Johnson read the terms of the Royal Proclamation to representatives of the nations and a promise of peace was given by Aboriginal representatives and a state of mutual non-interference established. Presents were exchanged to certify the binding nature of the promises being exchanged. Johnson then presented the Covenant Chain and wampum belts and stated:

> Brothers of the Western Nations, Sachems, Chiefs and Warriors; You have now been here for several days, during which time we have frequently met to renew and Strengthen our Engagements and you have made so many Promises of your Friendship and Attachment to the English that there now remains for us only to exchange the great Belt of the Covenant Chain that we may not forget out mutual Engagements.
>
> I now therefore present you the great Belt by which I bind all your Western Nations together with the English, and I desire that you will take fast hold of the same, and never let it slip, to which end I desire that after you have shewn this Belt to all Nations you will fix one end of it with the Chipeweighs at St. Marys [Michilimackinac] whilst the other end remains at my house, and moreover I desire that you will never listen to any news which comes to any other Quarter. If you do it, it may shake the Belt.

By this speech, and an exchange of presents and wampum, a treaty of alliance and peace was established between the parties. When Johnson had finished speaking, a two-row wampum belt was used by First Nation peoples to reflect their understanding of the treaty of Niagara and the words of the Royal Proclamation.

The two-row wampum belt reflects a diplomatic convention that recognizes interaction and separation of settler and First Nation societies. This agreement was first struck by the Haudonosaunee (Iroquois) upon contact with the Europeans, and the principles it represents were renewed in 1764. The symbolism of the two-row wampum belt has been commented on by a leading Native legal academic, Robert A. Williams, Jr.:

> When the Haudenosaunee first came into contact with the European nations, treaties of peace and friendship were made. Each was symbolized by the Gus-Wen-Tah, or Two Row Wampum. There is a bed of white wampum which symbolizes the purity of the agreement. There are two rows of purple, and those two rows have the spirit of your ancestors and mine. There are three beads of wampum separating the two rows and they symbolize peace, friendship and respect. These two rows will symbolize two paths or two vessels, travelling down the same river together. One, a birch bark canoe, will be for the Indian people, their laws, their customs and their ways. The other, a ship, will be for the white people and theirs laws, their customs, and their ways. We shall each travel the river together, side by side, but in our own boat. Neither of us will try to steer the other's vessel.

The two-row wampum belt illustrates a First Nation/Crown relationship that is founded on peace, friendship, and respect, where each nation will not interfere with the internal affairs of the other. An interpretation of the Proclamation using the Treaty of Niagara discredits the claims of the Crown to exercise sovereignty over First Nations. In fact, Sir William Johnson indicated as much when he commented on a questionable treaty in 1865:

> These people had subscribed to a Treaty with me at Niagara in August last, but by the present Treaty I find, they make expressions of subjection, which must either have arisen from the ignorance of the Interpreter, or from some mistake; for I am well convinced, they never mean or intend anything like it, and that they can not be brought under our laws, for some Centuries, nei-

ther have they any word which can convey the most distant idea of subjection, and should it be fully explained to them, and the nature of subordination punishment ettc [sic], defined, it might produce infinite harm ... and I dread its consequences, as I recollect that some attempts towards Sovereignty not long ago, was one of the principal causes of all our troubles.

One can see that Sir William Johnson did not regard the extension of the Royal Proclamation and the Treaty at Niagara as an assertion of sovereignty over the First Nations. Records such as the two-row wampum belt, and statements such as Johnson's, further allow First Nations to assert that their jurisdiction cannot be molested or disturbed without Aboriginal consent.

The evidence surrounding the Treaty of Niagara demonstrates that the written text of the Proclamation, while it contains a partial understanding of the agreement at Niagara, does not fully reflect the consensus of the parties. The concepts found in the Proclamation have different meanings when interpreted in accord with the wampum belt. For example, the belt's denotation of each nation pursuing its own path while living beside one another in peace and friendship casts new light on the Proclamation's wording "The several Nations ... with whom we are connected ... should not be molested or disturbed." These words, read in conjunction with the two row wampum, demonstrate that the connection between the nations spoken of in the Proclamation is one that mandates colonial noninterference in the land use and governments of First Nations. Therefore, First Nations regarded the agreement, represented by the Proclamation and the two-row wampum, as one that affirmed their powers of self-determination in, among other things, allocating land. This agreement, at the start of the formal relationship between the British and the First Nations of Canada, demonstrates the foundation-building principles of peace, friendship, and respect agreed to between the parties.

Conclusion

The promises made at Niagara and echoed in the Royal Proclamation have never been abridged, repealed, or rendered nugatory. Since Aboriginal rights are presumed to continue until the contrary is proven, the supposed "increasing weight" of colonial history and its disregard of the Treaty of Niagara does not render void the Aboriginal rights under its protection. Furthermore, since the Proclamation is not a unilateral declaration of the Crown but part of a treaty into which First Nations had considerable input, it therefore must be interpreted as it would be "naturally understood" by them. A "natural understanding" of the Proclamation by First Nations prompts an interpretation that includes the promises made at Niagara. These promises are: a respect for the sovereignty of First Nations, the creation of an alliance ("The several Nations ... with whom we are connected"), free and open trade and passage between the Crown and First Nations ("Shall not be molested or disturbed"), permission or consent needed for settlement of First Nations territory ("Same shall be purchased for use ... at some public meeting or assembly of Indians"), the English provision of presents to First Nations, mutual peace, friendship, and respect ("That the Indians may be convinced of our Justice and determined resolution to remove all reasonable cause of discontent"). The promises made at Niagara, and their solemnization in proclamation and treaty, demonstrate that there was from the outset considerable doubt about the Crown's assertion of sovereignty and legislative power over Aboriginal rights. The securing of these significant promises demonstrates that First Nations treated with the Crown as active and powerful partners in making provisions for the future relationship between the parties.

By examining Aboriginal perspectives on the meaning of the right to governance, there is evidence in the historic period that many Aboriginal people did not intend to surrender this power. They intended to continue living according to ancient customs, practices, and laws. In short, they desired to live by the systems and values that had organized their conduct for generations. While they encountered great resistance in following these ways, the sovereignty and autonomy of Aboriginal governance found some limited recognition in early Canadian case law. The following excerpt describes one such instance.

REPORT OF THE ROYAL COMMISSION ON ABORIGINAL PEOPLES, RESTRUCTURING THE RELATIONSHIP, VOL. 2

(Ottawa: Ministry of Supply and Services, 1996) at 186-190
(references omitted)

In about 1802, a young Quebec lad by the name of William Connolly left his home near Montreal and went west to seek his fortune in the fur trade with the North-West Company. A year or so later, William married a young woman of the Cree Nation, Suzanne by name. Suzanne had an interesting background. She was born of a Cree mother and a French-Canadian father and was the stepdaughter of a Cree chief at Cumberland House, located west of Lake Winnipeg. The union between William and Suzanne was formed under Cree law by mutual consent, with a gift probably given to Suzanne's stepfather. It was never solemnized by a priest or minister. Marriages of this kind were common in the fur trade during that era.

William and Suzanne lived happily together for nearly 30 years and had six children, one of whom later became Lady Amelia Douglas, the wife of the first governor of British Columbia. William Connolly prospered in the fur trade. He was described by a contemporary as "a veritable *bon garçon*, and an Emeralder of the first order." When the North-West Company merged with the Hudson's Bay Company, he continued on as a chief trader and was later promoted to the position of chief factor.

In 1831, William left the western fur trade and returned to the Montreal area with Suzanne and several of their children. Not long after, however, William decided to treat his first marriage as invalid and he married his well-to-do second cousin, Julia Woolrich, in a Catholic ceremony. Suzanne eventually returned west with her younger children and spent her final years living in the Grey Nuns convent at St. Boniface, Manitoba, where she was supported by William and later by Julia. When William died in the late 1840s, he willed all his property to Julia and their two children, cutting Suzanne and her children out of the estate.

Several years after Suzanne's death in 1862, her eldest son, John Connolly, sued Julia Woolrich for a share of his father's estate. This famous case, *Connolly v. Woolrich*, was fought through the courts of Quebec and was eventually appealed to the privy council in Britain before being settled out of court. The judgement delivered in the case sheds a remarkable light on the constitutional status of Aboriginal nations and their relations with incoming French and English settlers.

In support of his claim, John Connolly argued that the marriage between his mother and William Connolly was valid under Cree law and that the couple had been in 'community of property', so that each partner to the marriage was entitled to one-half of their jointly owned property. When William died, only his half-share of the property could be left to Julia, with the other half passing automatically to Suzanne as his lawful wife. On Suzanne's death, her children would be entitled to inherit her share of the estate, now in the hands of Julia.

The initial question for the Quebec courts was whether the Cree marriage between Suzanne and William was valid. The lawyer for Julia Woolrich argued that it was not valid. He maintained that English common law was in force in the northwest in 1803 and that the union between Suzanne and William did not meet its requirements. Moreover, he said, in an argument that catered to the worst prejudices of the times, the marriage customs of so-called uncivilized and pagan nations could not be recognized by the court as validating a marriage even between two Aboriginal people, much less between an Aboriginal and a non-Aboriginal person.

The Quebec Superior Court rejected Julia Woolrich's arguments. It held that the Cree marriage between Suzanne and William was valid and that their eldest son was entitled to his rightful share of the estate. This decision was maintained on appeal to the Quebec Court of Queen's Bench.

In his judgement, Justice Monk of the Superior Court stated that he was prepared to assume, for the sake of argument, that the first European traders to inhabit the northwest brought with them their own laws as their birthright. Nevertheless, the region was already occupied by "numerous and powerful tribes of Indians; by aboriginal nations, who had been in possession of these countries for ages". Assuming that French or English law had been introduced in the area at some point, "will it be contended that the territorial rights, political organization, such as it was, or the laws and usages of the Indian tribes, were abrogated; that they ceased to exist, when these two European nations began to trade with the aboriginal occupants?" Answering his own question in the negative, Justice Monk wrote: "In my opinion, it is beyond controversy that they did not, that so far from being abolished, they were left in full force, and were not even modified in the slightest degree, in regard to the civil rights of the natives."

Justice Monk supported this conclusion by quoting at length from *Worcester v. Georgia*, a landmark case decided in 1832 by the United States Supreme Court under Chief Justice Marshall. Justice Marshall, describing the policy of the British Crown in America before the American Revolution, states:

Certain it is, that our history furnishes no example, from the first settlement of our country, *of any attempt on the part of the Crown to interfere with the internal affairs of the Indians*, farther than to keep out the agents of foreign powers, who, as traders or otherwise, might seduce them into foreign alliances. The king purchased their lands when they were willing to sell, at a price they were willing to take; but never coerced a surrender of them. *He also purchased their alliance and dependence by subsidies; but never intruded into the interior of their affairs, or interfered with their self-government, so far as respected themselves only.* [emphasis supplied by Justice Monk]

According to this passage, the British Crown did not interfere with the domestic affairs of its Indian allies and dependencies, so that they remained self-governing in internal matters. Adopting this outlook, Justice Monk concluded that he had no hesitation in holding that "the Indian political and territorial right, laws, and usages remained in full force" in the northwest at the relevant time. This decision portrays Aboriginal peoples as autonomous nations living within the protection of the Crown but retaining their territorial rights, political organizations and common laws.

A number of lessons can be drawn from *Connolly v. Woolrich*. First, the sources of law and authority in Canada are more diverse than is sometimes assumed. They include the common laws and political systems of Aboriginal nations in addition to the standard range of Euro-Canadian sources.

Second, in earlier times, the history of Canada often featured close and relatively harmonious relations between Aboriginal peoples and newcomers. The fur trade, which played an important role in the economy of early Canada, was based on long-standing alliances between European fur traders and Aboriginal hunters and traders. At the personal level, these alliances resulted in people of mixed origins, who sometimes were assimilated into existing groups but in other cases coalesced into distinct nations and communities, as with the Métis of Red River.

Connolly v. Woolrich demonstrates that newcomers have sometimes found it convenient to forget their early alliances and pacts with Aboriginal peoples and to construct communities that excluded them and suppressed any local roots. Despite these efforts, however, the courts have periodically upheld the original relationship between newcomers and Aboriginal peoples and enforced the rights it embraced. Among these was the right of Aboriginal peoples to conduct their affairs under their own laws, within a larger constitutional framework linking them with the Crown.

The decision in *Connolly v. Woolrich* stands in contrast, then, to the common impression that Aboriginal peoples do not have any general right to govern themselves. It is often thought that all governmental authority in Canada flows from the Crown to Parliament and the provincial legislatures, as provided in the constitution acts — the basic enactments that form the core of our written constitution. According to this view, since the constitution acts do not explicitly recognize the existence of Aboriginal governments, the only governmental powers held by Aboriginal peoples are those delegated to them by Parliament or the provincial legislatures, under such statutes as the *Indian Act* and the Alberta *Metis Settlements Act*.

This outlook assumes that all law is found in statutes or other written legal instruments. Under this view, if a right has not been enshrined in such a document, it is not a legal right. At best, it is regarded as only a moral or political right, which does not have legal status and so cannot be enforced in the ordinary courts. Since the constitution acts do not explicitly acknowledge an Aboriginal right of self-government, such a right does not exist as a matter of Canadian law.

However, this view overlooks important features of our legal system. The laws of Canada spring from a great variety of sources, both written and unwritten, statutory and customary. It has long been recognized, for example, that the written constitution is based on fundamental unwritten principles, which govern its status and interpretation. In Quebec, the general laws governing the private affairs of citizens trace their origins in large part to a body of French customary law, the *Coûtume de Paris*, which was imported to Canada in the 1600s and embodied in the *Civil Code of Lower Canada* in 1866. In the other provinces, the foundation of the general private law system is English common law, a body of unwritten law administered by the courts, with its roots in the Middle Ages. English common law has never been reduced to statutory form, except in partial and fragmentary ways. Over the years, it has become a supple legal instrument, capable of being adapted by the courts to suit changing circumstances and social conditions.

Given the multiple sources of law and rights in Canada, it is no surprise that Canadian courts have recognized the existence of a special body of 'Aboriginal rights'. These are not based on written instruments such as statutes, but on unwritten sources such as long-standing custom and practice. In the *Sparrow* case, for example, the Supreme Court of Canada recognized the Aboriginal fishing rights of the Musqueam people on the basis of evidence "that the Musqueam have lived in the area as an organized society long before the coming of European settlers, and that the taking of salmon was an integral part of their lives and remains so to this day." The court went on to hold that government regulations governing the Aboriginal fishing right were incapable of delineating the content and scope of the right.

Aboriginal rights include rights to land, rights to hunt and fish, special linguistic, cultural and religious rights, and rights held under customary systems of Aboriginal law. Also included is the right of self-government. This broad viewpoint is reflected in the words of John Amagoalik, speaking for the Inuit Committee on National Issues in 1983:

> Our position is that aboriginal rights, aboriginal title to land, water and sea ice flow from aboriginal rights; and all rights to practise our customs and traditions, to retain and develop our languages and cultures, and the rights to self-government, all these things flow from the fact that we have aboriginal rights ... .In our view, aboriginal rights can also be seen as human rights, because these are the things that we need to continue to survive as distinct peoples in Canada.

This point was echoed by Clem Chartier, speaking on behalf of the Métis National Council:

What we feel is that aboriginal title or aboriginal right is the right to collective ownership of land, water, resources, both renewable and nonrenewable. It is a right to self-government, a right to govern yourselves with your own institutions ... .

A similar view underlies a resolution passed by the Quebec National Assembly in 1985. This recognizes the existing Aboriginal rights of the indigenous nations of Quebec. It also urges the government of Quebec to conclude agreements with indigenous nations guaranteeing them

(a) the right to self-government within Quebec;

(b) the right to their own language, culture and traditions;

(c) the right to own and control land;

(d) the right to hunt, fish, trap, harvest and participate in wildlife management; and

(e) the right to participate in, and benefit from, the economic development of Quebec ... [translation]

The doctrine of Aboriginal rights is not a modern innovation, invented by courts to remedy injustices perpetrated in the past. The doctrine was reflected in the numerous treaties of peace and friendship concluded in the seventeenth and eighteenth centuries between Aboriginal peoples and the French and British Crowns. Aboriginal rights are also apparent in the *Royal Proclamation of 1763* and other instruments of the same period, and in the treaties signed in Ontario, the west, and the northwest during the late nineteenth and early twentieth century. These rights are also considered in the many statutes dealing with Aboriginal matters from earliest times and in a series of judicial decisions extending over nearly two centuries. As such, the doctrine of Aboriginal rights is one of the most ancient and enduring doctrines of Canadian law.

The principles behind the decision in *Connolly* v. *Woolrich* form the core of the modern Canadian law of Aboriginal rights. This body of law provides the basic constitutional context for relations between Aboriginal peoples and the Crown and oversees the interaction between general Canadian systems of law and government and Aboriginal laws, government institutions and territories.

D. THE CHALLENGE TO ABORIGINAL GOVERNANCE

The vision of Aboriginal sovereignty and governance reflected in the early agreements and case law has not received the high level of judicial recognition foreshadowed by these earlier events. In fact, encroachments on Aboriginal governments have occurred time and again throughout Canadian history. On the west coast the Potlatch, a central governing institution of the Indians, was outlawed under the provisions of the *Indian Act*. The Sun Dance on the Prairies suffered a similar fate. In Ontario, the case of the Haudenosaunee Confederacy (Iroquois) is a particularly striking example of the disregard for Aboriginal governance.

The Haudenosaunee Confederacy has consistently insisted on its independent governmental status. It draws this independence from the agreements it entered into throughout its history. Treaties such as the covenant chain of friendship and the two-row wampum are examples of this status. There are numerous expressions of Haudenosaunee sovereignty. For example, in 1876, the year the first consolidated *Indian Act* was passed, 33 Onondaga Chiefs wrote, from the Oshweken Council House of the Six Nations Indians on 17 August 1876:

> To the Honourable Mr. D. Laird Superintendent of Indian Affairs:
>
> We the undersigned Chiefs & Members of the Six United Nation Indian Allies to the British Government residing on the Grand River, Township of Tuscarora, Onondaga and Oneida, in the counties of Brant and Haldimand Ont., to your Honourable our Brother by the treaty of Peace we thought it is fit and proper to bring a certain thing under your Notice which is a very great hindrance and grievance in our council for we believe in this part it is your duty to take it into consideration with your government to have this great hindrance and grievance to be removed in our council and it is this, one says we are subjects to the British Government and ought to be controled under those Laws which was past in the Dominion Parliament by your Government you personally and the others (That is us) says we are not subjects but we are Allies to the British Government; and to your Honourable our Brother we will now inform you and your Government, personally, that we will not deny to be Allies but we will be Allies to the British Government as our forefathers were; we will further inform your Honourable our Brother and to your Government that we do now seprate from them henceforth we will have nothing to do with them anymore as they like to be controled under your Laws we now let them go to become as your own people, but us we will follow our Ancient Laws and Rules, and we will not depart from it.
>
> Source: NAC RGIO, Red Series, volume 1995, file 6897, MR C11130, 17 August 1876 [original spelling and punctuation preserved]; cited in The *Report of the Royal Commission on Aboriginal Peoples, Looking Forward, Looking Back, Vol. 1* (Ottawa: Supply and Services, 1996), at 182.

Despite these repeated agreements, and their strong assertions of independence, the Confederacy's government has been disregarded in law. In the 1920s the Chiefs prepared a case and sent their leaders to London, England and Geneva, Switzerland to secure recognition of their sovereignty before the international community (Appeal of the Six Nations to the League, *League of Nations Official Journal*, June 24, 1924, 829-837). They were unsuccessful in their attempts but their efforts created considerable anxiety within the Canadian government. As a result the deputy superintendent general of Indian Affairs, Duncan Campbell Scott, secured approval from the federal Cabinet to displace the confederacy council and replace it with an elected one under the *Indian Act*. Without prior notice to the chiefs, they were removed from office by an order-in-council on the morning of October 7, 1924. The Royal Canadian Mounted Police seized the wampum used to sanction council proceedings, and posted a proclamation on the doors of the council house announcing the date and procedures for an elected government on the Six Nations reserve. The following case represents Canadian law's treatment of the Confederacy.

LOGAN v. STYRES

(*sub nom. Logan v. Canada (Attorney General)*

(1959), 20 D.L.R. (2d) 416, [1959] O.W.N. 361 (H.C.)

King J.: — In the statement of claim the plaintiff is described as a member of the Six Nations Indian Band residing upon the Six Nations Indian Reserve near Brantford, Ontario, and the wife of Joseph Logan, Jr., a Mohawk Chief of the Six Nations Indians. The constituent members of the said Six Nations Indians are the Mohawk, the Oneida, the Onondaga, the Cayuga, the Seneca and the Tuscarora.

In the course of her evidence the plaintiff stated that she was nominated to bring the action on behalf of the hereditary Chiefs of the Six Nations Indian Band and although the defendants submitted that the plaintiff, as an individual member of the Six Nations Indian Band, had no status to maintain the action for the relief claimed, I have nevertheless allowed the action to proceed.

The defendant, Clifford E. Styres, is chief councillor of the elected council of the said Six Nations Indian Band and the defendant R.J. Stallwood is superintendent of the Six Nations Indian Agency at Brantford, Ontario.

The Six Nations Indian Reserve at Brantford consists of slightly more than 45,000 acres of land set aside for the use and benefit of the Six Nations Band.

The present action is for an injunction to restrain the defendants from taking any steps to facilitate the surrender of 3.05 acres of land being a part of the said Reserve and for a declaration that Order in Council P.C. 1629 dated September 17, 1924 and Order in Council P.C. 6015 [[1951] S.O.R. 528] dated November 12, 1951 are *ultra vires* the powers of His Excellency the Governor-General of Canada acting for and with the advice and consent of the Queen's Privy Council for Canada.

Briefly, the position taken by the plaintiff is that the Six Nations Indians in the latter part of the eighteenth century and subsequently were the faithful allies of the British Crown and that they continue to the present day to be such faithful allies and that they never were and are not today subjects of the Crown. The plaintiff then takes the further position that the Six Nations Indians, not being subjects of the Crown, it was *ultra vires* the powers of the Parliament of the United Kingdom to enact section 91(24) of the *B.N.A. Act*, whereby the legislative authority of the Parliament of Canada is made to extend to all matters coming within the classification Indians, and Lands reserved for the Indians" insofar as the said Six Nations Indians are concerned. If this be so the plaintiff then states that it is *ultra vires* the powers of the Parliament of Canada to enact the *Indian Act*, R.S.C. 1952, c. 149, insofar as the said Six Nations Indians are concerned and that likewise the Orders in Council already referred to and made pursuant to the *Indian Act* are likewise *ultra vires* insofar as the Six Nations Indians are concerned.

If the plaintiff is able to establish the above then I am of the opinion that judgment should be given for the relief asked but of course it is a formidable task that the plaintiff has undertaken.

The difficulties would appear to have arisen with the Orders in Council already referred to. Almost from time immemorial the Indian Bands which formed, first the Five Nations Confederacy, and later the Six Nations Confederacy were governed by their hereditary Chiefs. I have used the term "Hereditary Chiefs" to describe the system whereby the Clan Mothers designated a Chief from among the male members of certain families within the Clan. The Orders in Council to which objection is taken set up a system whereby elected Councillors would supplant the [hereditary] Chiefs among other matters in dealing with the surrender of Reserve lands. It would appear that many of the Six Nations Indians, a great majority in fact, do not recognize the authority of the Parliament of Canada to provide for elected Councillors or to provide for the surrender of Reserve lands by means of a vote. Such members of the Six Nations Indians, it would appear, simply refrain from voting at all and in the proposed surrender of the lands in question when a vote was held on July 27, 1957, only 53 votes were cast out of which 30 voted for surrender and 23 against surrender and this out of about, 3,600 eligible voters. It is the elected Councillors who negotiate the terms of surrender. ...

It should be remembered that the *Indian Act* provides in ss. 39 and 40 that the Governor in Council may accept or refuse a surrender of land so that it is still quite possible for the Governor in Council to take the position that the surrender of the land in question in this action should be refused. From the evidence given at the trial it is difficult to see what advantage would accrue to the Six Nations Indians by surrendering the land in question.

Before turning to the evidence in this action I should say that in my opinion all of the witnesses were honest witnesses who were endeavoring to tell the truth. Indeed, there is no dispute about any facts of any consequence. I should say, however, that the plaintiff was given some leeway in presenting the historical background of the plaintiff's claim and in putting forward the merits of the hereditary system of Chiefs as opposed to the elective system of Councillors. The defendants did not consider it necessary to present any evidence with respect to the merits of the hereditary system as opposed to the elective system so that only one side of this matter was before the Court.

A start has to be made at some stage and I believe a satisfactory point at which to begin is with the Haldimand Deed dated October 25, 1784, which followed the conclusion of the American Revolution and which in its recitals sets out a sufficient background. It is as follows:

Frederick Haldimand Captain General and *Governor in chief* of the province of *Quebec* and *Territories* depending thereon *etc etc etc General* and *Commander in Chief* of His Majesty's Forces in said province and the Frontiers thereof — etc — etc — etc —

Whereas His Majesty having been pleased to direct that in consideration of the early attachment to his cause manifested by the *Mohawk Indians* and of the loss of their settlement which they thereby sustained — that a convenient tract of land under his protection should be chosen as a safe and comfortable retreat for them and others of the *Six Nations*, who have either lost their settlements within the *Territory* of the *American States*, or wish to retire from them to the British — I have at the earnest desire of many of these *His Majesty's Faithful allies* purchased a tract of land from the *Indians* situated between the *Lakes Ontario, Erie* and *Huron,* and I do hereby in His Majesty's name authorize and permit the said *Mohawk Nation* and such others of the *Six Nation Indians* as wish to settle in that quarter to take possession of and settle upon the Banks of the *River* commonly called *Ouse* or *Grand River,* running into *Lake Erie,* allotting to them for that purpose *six miles deep* from *each side* of the river beginning at Lake Erie and extending *in that proportion to the head of the said river* which them and their posterity are to enjoy for ever.

Given under my hand and seal at arms at the *Castle of St. Lewis* at *Quebec* this *twenty-fifth* day of *October* one thousand seven hundred and *eighty-four* and in the *twenty-fifth* year of the reign of our Sovereign *Lord George The Third* by the Grace of *God* of Great Britain, France and Ireland *King* Defender of the *Faith* and *so forth.* ...

(Emphasis in original)

However, there is another document upon which the Six Nations Indians rely and it is known as the "Simcoe Deed" dated January 14, 1793, and it is as follows:

John Graves Simcoe
(Great Seal of Canada)
George the Third, by the Grace of God, King of Great Britain, France and Ireland, Defender of the Faith, and so forth. To all to whom these presents shall come, Greeting!

Know ye, that whereas the attachment and fidelity of the Chiefs, Warriors, and people of the Six Nations, to Us and Our Government has been made manifest on divers Occasions by their spirited and zealous Exertions, and by the Bravery of their Conduct, and We being desirous of showing Our Approbation of the same and in recompense of the Losses they may have sustained of providing a convenient Tract of Land under Our protection for a safe and suitable Retreat for them and their Posterity, Have of Our Special Grace, certain Knowledge and mere motion, given and granted and by these Presents Do Give and Grant to the Chiefs, Warriors, Women and People of the said Six Nations and their Heirs forever, All that District or Territory of Land, being Parcel of a certain District ... To have and to Hold the said District or Territory of Land so bounded as aforesaid of Us, Our Heirs and Successors, to them the Chiefs, Warriors, Women and People of the Six Nations, and to and for the sole use and Behoof of them and their Heirs for ever, Freely and Clearly of and from, all, and all manner of rents, fines, and services whatever to be rendered by them or any of them to Us or Our Successors for the same, and of and from all conditions, stipulations and agreements whatever, except as hereinafter by Us expressed and declared. Giving and granting, and by these Presents confirming to the said Chiefs, Warriors, Women, and People of the said Six Nations and their Heirs, the full and entire possession, use, benefit and advantage of the said district or territory, to be held and enjoyed by them in the most free and ample manner, and according to the several customs and usages of them the said Chiefs, Warriors, Women, and People of the said Six Nations; Provided always, and be it understood to be the true intent and meaning of these Presents, that, for the purpose of assuring the said lands, as aforesaid to the said Chiefs, Warriors, Women, and People of the Six Nations, and their Heirs, and of securing to them the free and undisturbed possession and enjoyment of the same, it is Our Royal will and pleasure that no transfer, alienation, conveyance, sale, gift, exchange, lease, property or possession, shall at any time be had, made, or given of the said district or territory, or any part or parcel thereof, by any of the said Chiefs, Warriors, Women or People, to any other nation or body of people, person, or persons whatever, other than among themselves the said Chiefs, Warriors, Women and People, but that any such transfer, alienation, conveyance, sale, gift, exchange, lease or possession shall be null and void, and of no effect whatever, and that no person or persons shall possess or occupy the said district or territory or any part or parcel thereof, by or under pretence of any such alienation, title or conveyance as aforesaid, or by or under any pretence whatever, upon pain of Our severe displeasure.

And that in case any person or persons other than them, the said Chiefs, Warriors, Women and People of the said Six Nations, shall under pretence of any such title as aforesaid presume to possess or occupy the said district or territory or any part or parcel thereof, that it shall and may be lawful for Us, Our heirs and successors, at any time hereafter, to enter upon the lands so occupied and possessed by any person or persons other than the people of the said Six Nations, and them the said intruders thereof and therefrom, wholly to dispossess and evict, and to resume the part or parcel so occupied to Ourselves, Our heirs and successors; Provided, always, that if at any time the said Chiefs, Warriors, Women and People of the said Six Nations should be inclined to dispose of and surrender their use and interest in the said district or territory or any part thereof, the same shall be purchased for Us, Our heirs and successors, at some public meeting or assembly of the Chiefs, Warriors, and People of the said Six Nations, to be holden for that purpose by the Governor, Lieutenant-Governor, or person administering Our Government in Our Province of Upper Canada. ...

(Signed) Wm. Jarvis, Secretary. Recorded February 20th, 1837...

The purpose of the Simcoe Deed would seem to be to confirm the grant already made by the Haldimand Deed. In each of these deeds it is made clear that those of the Six Nations Indians settling on the lands therein described do so under the protection of the Crown. In my opinion, those of the Six Nations Indians so settling on such lands, together with their posterity, by accepting the protection of the Crown then owed allegiance to the Crown and thus became subjects of the Crown. Thus, the said Six Nations Indians from having been the faithful allies of the Crown became, instead, loyal subjects of the Crown.

The position which the Six Nations Indians have taken throughout the years is perhaps best stated in their own words in the submission made by them to the representatives of the United Nations at San Francisco, California, U.S.A., on April 13, 1945 and which was as follows:

On behalf of the people of the Six Nations Indians settled upon part of the territory granted to them pursuant to the pledge given by the British Crown and granted under the terms of the Haldimand Treaty of March 1784, we, the representatives of the above named people of the Six Nations Indians, appeal to the conscience of the democratic nations for action to correct the deep injustice under which we are suffering.

In accord with the terms of the proposal made to us by representatives of the English Crown, we as a sovereign people accepted the terms of the Haldimand Treaty and settled upon the territory thereby granted to us. A few years after our occupation of the territory and before it was fully settled a large part of the territory was alienated from us by methods and on terms which did a deep injustice to our people and all their descendents. One, Joseph Brant, using an alleged power of attorney from the Six Nations Indians dated November 2, 1796, leased large sections of our territory to white people. No revenue whatsoever accrued to the people of the Six Nations Indians for such leases and until now we have been unable to secure either restoration of the property which was granted to us and our descendents and friends in perpetuity, nor to secure compensation for its alienation.

Our claim for abrogation of the so-called leases under which this property was alienated from us or, failings such abrogation, compensation for such alienation or revenues from all such lands, is based upon the fact that, according to the terms of the India Act (which deny to Indians the legal status of a person) and the terms under which the land was granted to us, the methods by which the above named Brant disposed of said lands were illegal and cannot be justified either in the eyes of the law or by the conscience of governments.

We appeal to the representatives of the governments and peoples of the United Nations gathered here in this historic conference at San Francisco to aid the people of the Six Nations Indians in securing these fundamental rights. Our appeal for restoration of the property rights guaranteed to us in 1784 is based first of all upon our duty, as parents, to protect the rights and the futures of our children, but it is based also upon our solemn obligation to protect the rights of our people as a whole. We, the people of the Six Nations Indians, who fought as allies of the British Crown during the American revolutionary war, accepted the grant of lands described in the Haldimand Treaty and came to Canada from the United States to settle on those lands in the spirit and in the understanding that we were doing so as a sovereign people. As a nation we now appeal to the conscience of the nations of the world. We appeal for the restoration of those lands which the terms of the Haldimand Treaty guaranteed the people of the Six Nations and their posterity are to enjoy forever.

Verification of all the above statements is to be found in the copy of Sessional Paper No. 151 tabled in the House of Commons Canada on April 5th, 1945, which is attached.

ON BEHALF Of the people of the Six Nations Indians on the Grand River at Brantford, Ontario ...

From the evidence before me however it would appear the strongest case for the Six Nations Indians should be based upon the submission that Parliament should not make the Order in Council to which objection is taken applicable to the Six Nations Indians rather than that Parliament cannot make such Orders in Council applicable. It seems to me much might be said on that score.

I am of the opinion that the Six Nations Indians are entitled to the protection of the laws of the land duly made by competent authority and at the same time are subject to such laws. While it might be unjust or unfair under the circumstances for the Parliament of Canada to interfere with their system of internal Government by hereditary Chiefs, I am of the opinion that Parliament has the authority to provide for the surrender of Reserve land, as has been done herein, and that Privy Council Order P.C. 6015 is not *ultra vires*. It should be noted that P.C. 1629 has been revoked by P.C. 6015, so it is not necessary to consider P.C. 1629 further.

In my opinion, therefore, the plaintiff is not entitled to an injunction and is not entitled to the declaration asked for.

The plaintiff's action is therefore dismissed but, under the circumstances, without costs.

Action dismissed.

"THE LAST SPEECH OF DES-KA-HEH"

March 10, 1925

[Deskaheh (1873-1925), or Hi-wyi-iss, Levi General, was a Cayuga chief of the Younger Bear Clan of the Six Nations Indians. In 1923, as the government was taking steps to replace the traditional Six Nations government at the Grand River with an *"Indian Act"* elective system; Deskaheh, who opposed the change, travelled to London and Geneva to make his case before the British government and the League of Nations. Returning to Canada he felt his freedom was threatened, and he therefore spent the rest of his days in exile south of the border. His last speech, part of which follows, was made over the radio in Rochester, New York, on 10 March 1925.]

My home is on the Grand River. Until we sold off a large part, our country extended down to Lake Erie, where, 140 winters ago, we had a little sea-shore of our own and a birch-bark navy. You would call it Canada. We do not. We call the little ten-miles square we have left the "Grand River Country." We have the right to do that. It is ours. We have the written pledge of George III that we should have it forever as against him or his successors and he promised to protect us in it. We didn't think we would ever live long enough to find that a British promise was not good. An enemy's foot is on our country and George V knows it for I told him so but he will not lift his finger to protect us nor will any of his ministers ...

In some respects we are just like you. We like to tell our troubles. You do that. You told us you were in great trouble a few winters ago because a great big giant with a big stick was after you. We helped you whip him. Many of our young men volunteered and many gave their lives for you. You were willing to let them fight in the front ranks in France. Now we want to tell our troubles to you — I do not mean that we are calling on your governments. We are tired of calling on the governments of pale-faced peoples in America and Europe. We have tried that and found it was no use. They deal only in fine words ... We have a little territory left — just enough to live and die on. Don't you think your governments ought to be ashamed to take that away from us by pretending it is part of theirs? You ought to be ashamed if you let them. Before it is all gone we mean to let you know what your governments are doing. If you are a free people you can have your own way. The governments at Washington and Ottawa have a silent partnership of policy — It is aimed to break up every tribe of Red-men so as to dominate every acre of their territory. Your high officials are the nomads today — not the Red People. Your officials won't stay at home. Over in Ottawa they call that policy "Indian Advancement". Over in Washington they call it "Assimilation." We, who would be the helpless victims, say it is tyranny ...

We want none of your laws or customs that we have not willingly adopted for ourselves. We have adopted many. You have adopted some of ours — votes for women for instance — We are as well behaved as you and you would think so if you knew us better. We would be happier to-day, left alone, than you who call yourselves Canadians and Americans. We have no jails and do not need them. You have many jails, but do they hold all the criminals you convict? And do you convict or prosecute all your violators of the thousands of laws you have?

Your governments have lately resorted to new practices in their Indian policies. In the old days they often bribed our chiefs to sign treaties to get our lands. Now they know that our remaining territory can easily be gotten away from us by first taking our political rights away in forcing us into your citizenship, so they give jobs in their Indian offices to the bright young people among us who will take them and who, to earn their pay, say that our people wish to become citizens with you and that we are ready to have our tribal life destroyed and want your governments to do it. But that is not true. Your governments of today learned that method from the British. The British have long practiced it on weaker peoples in carrying out their policy of subjugating the world, if they can, to British Imperialism. Under cover of it, your law-makers now assume to govern other peoples too weak to resist your courts. There are no three-mile limits or twelve-mile limits to strong governments who wish to do that. About three winters ago the Canadian government set out to take mortgages on farms of our returned soldiers to secure loans made to them intending to use Canadian courts to enforce those mortgages in the name of Canadian authority within our country. When Ottawa tried that our people resented it. We knew that would mean the end of our own government. Because we did so the Canadian government began to enforce all sorts of Dominion and Provincial laws over us and quartered armed men among us to enforce Canadian laws and customs upon us. We appealed to Ottawa in the name of our right as a separate people and by right of our treaties and the door was closed in our faces. We then went to London with our treaty and asked for the protection it promised and got no attention. Then we went to the League of Nations at Geneva with its covenant to protect little peoples and to enforce respect for treaties by its members and we spent a whole year patiently waiting but got no hearing.

To punish us for trying to preserve our rights, the Canadian government has now pretended to abolish our government by Royal Proclamation and has pretended to set up a Canadian-made government over us, composed of the few traitors among us who are willing to accept pay from Ottawa and do its bidding. Finally Ottawa officials, under pretence of a friendly visit, asked to inspect our precious wampum belts, made by our Fathers centuries ago as records of our history, and when shown to them those false-faced officials seized and carried away those belts as bandits take your precious belongings ... The Ottawa government thought that with no wampum belts to read in the opening of our Six Nations Councils, we would give up our home rule and self-government, the victims of superstition. Any superstition of which the Grand River People have been victims are not in reverence for wampum belts but in their trust in the honor of governments who boast of a higher civilization ...

We are not as dependent in some ways as we were in the early days. We do not need interpreters now. We know your language and can understand your words for ourselves and we have learned to decide for ourselves what is good for us. It is bad for any people to take the advice of an alien people as to that.

You Mothers, I hear, have a good deal to say about your government. Our Mothers have always had a hand in ours. Maybe you can do something to help us now. If you white mothers are hard-hearted and will not, perhaps you boys and girls who are listening and who have loved to read stories about our people — the true ones, I mean — will help us when you grow up if there are any of us left then to be helped. If you are bound to treat us as though we were citizens under your government then those of your people who are land hungry will get our farms away from us by hooks and crooks under your property laws and in your courts that we do not understand and do not wish to learn. We would then be homeless and have to drift into your big cities to work for wages, to buy bread and have to pay rent, as you call it, to live on this earth and to live in little rooms in which we would suffocate. We would then be scattered and lost to each other and lost among so many of you. Our boys and girls would then have to intermarry with you or not at all. If consumption took us off or if we brought no children into the world or our children mixed with the ocean of your blood then there would be no Iroquois left ...

Boys — think this over. Do it before your minds lose the power to grasp the idea that there are other peoples in this world beside your own and with an equal right to be here. You see that a people as strong as yours is a great danger to other peoples near you. Already your will comes pretty near being law in this world where no one can whip you, think then what it will mean if you grow up with a will to be unjust to other peoples; to believe that whatever your government does to other peoples is no crime however wicked. I hope the Irish-Americans hear that and will think about it — they used to when that shoe pinched their foot.

This is the story of the Mohawks, the story of the Oneidas, of the Cayugas — I am a Cayuga — of the Onondagas, the Senecas and the Tuscaroras. They are the Iroquois. Tell it to those who have not been listening. Maybe I will be stopped from telling it. But if I am prevented from telling it over, as I hope to do, the story will not be lost. I have already told it to thousands of listeners in Europe — it has gone into the records where your children can find it when I may be dead or be in jail for daring to tell the truth — I have told this story in Switzerland. They have free speech in little Switzerland. One can tell the truth over there in public even if it is uncomfortable for some great people.

This story comes straight from Des-ka-heh, one of the Chiefs of the Cayugas. I am the speaker of the Council of the Six Nations, the oldest League of Nations now existing. It was founded by Hiawatha. It is a League which is still alive and intends, as best it can, to defend the rights of the Iroquois to live under their own laws in their own little countries.

E. CONTEMPORARY CASES: LITIGATING GOVERNANCE

Contemporary Canadian jurisprudence has only recently started to address the issue of Aboriginal rights to self-government raised in these earlier cases. This more current case law has defined Aboriginal powers of governance in a much narrower manner than historic practice might warrant, or Aboriginal people may desire. This reduction in Aboriginal rights to governance simultaneously vests ever-widening powers of governance in non-Aboriginal institutions. The courts closely and carefully scrutinize

Aboriginal expressions of governance, while at the same time allowing broad assertions of Crown sovereignty to go unchallenged. The unequal application of Aboriginal and non-Aboriginal sovereignty has not yet been adequately explained. The following cases of *R. v. Pamajewon*, and *Delgamuukw v. British Columbia*, provide an indication of the court's current interpretation of Aboriginal governance rights.

R. v. PAMAJEWON

[1996] 2 S.C.R. 821, 138 D.L.R. (4th) 204

[Pamajewon and his co-accused, each a member of either the Shawanaga First Nation or Eagle Lake Band, were convicted of keeping a common gaming house contrary to section 201 of the *Criminal Code*. The gaming activities were conducted on reserves, though many of the participants were non-natives. On appeal the Band members argued, *inter alia*, that the activities in question were protected as an Aboriginal right under section 35(1) or as an incident of the inherent right of self-government claimed by the two First Nations. The Ontario Court of Appeal and the Supreme Court of Canada dismissed the appeals.]

Lamer C.J.C. (La Forest, Sopinka, Gonthier, Cory, McLachlin, Iacobucci and Major JJ. concurring): ...

[1]   This appeal raises the question of whether the conduct of high stakes gambling by the Shawanaga and Eagle Lake First Nations falls within the scope of the aboriginal rights recognized and affirmed by s. 35(1) of the *Constitution Act, 1982*.

. . . . .

[21]   The appellants appealed on the basis that the Court of Appeal erred in restricting aboriginal title to rights that are activity and site specific and in concluding that self-government only extends to those matters which were governed by ancient laws or customs. The appellant argued further that the Court of Appeal erred in concluding that the *Code* extinguished self-government regarding gaming and in not addressing whether the *Code*'s gaming provisions unjustifiably interfered with the rights recognized and affirmed by s. 35(1) of the *Constitution Act, 1982*.

. . . . .

[23]   The resolution of the appellants' claim in this case rests on the application of the test, laid out by this Court in *R. v. Van der Peet*, [1996] 2 S.C.R. 507, for determining the aboriginal rights recognized and affirmed by s. 35(1) of the *Constitution Act, 1982*. The appellants in this case are claiming that the gambling activities in which they took part, and their respective bands' regulation of those gambling activities, fell within the scope of the aboriginal rights recognized and affirmed by s. 35(1). *Van der Peet, supra*, lays out the test for determining the practices, customs and tra-

ditions which fall within s. 35(1) and, as such, provides the legal standard against which the appellants' claim must be measured.

[24] The appellants' claim involves the assertion that s. 35(1) encompasses the right of self-government, and that this right includes the right to regulate gambling activities on the reservation. Assuming without deciding that s. 35(1) includes self-government claims, the applicable legal standard is nonetheless that laid out in *Van der Peet, supra.* Assuming s. 35(1) encompasses claims to aboriginal self-government, such claims must be considered in light of the purposes underlying that provision and must, therefore, be considered against the test derived from consideration of those purposes. This is the test laid out in *Van der Peet, supra.* In so far as they can be made under s. 35(1), claims to self-government are no different from other claims to the enjoyment of aboriginal rights and must, as such, be measured against the same standard.

[25] In *Van der Peet, supra,* the test for identifying aboriginal rights was said to be as follows, at para. 46:

> ... In order to be an aboriginal right an activity must be an element of a practice, custom or tradition integral to the distinctive culture of the aboriginal group claiming the right.

In applying this test the Court must first identify the exact nature of the activity claimed to be a right and must then go on to determine whether, on the evidence presented to the trial judge, and on the facts as found by the trial judge, that activity could be said to be (*Van der Peet,* at para. 59) "a defining feature of the culture in question" prior to contact with Europeans.

[26] I now turn to the first part of the *Van der Peet* test, the characterization of the appellants' claim. In *Van der Peet, supra,* the Court held at para. 53 that:

> To characterize an applicant's claim correctly, a court should consider such factors as the nature of the action which the applicant is claiming was done pursuant to an aboriginal right, the nature of the governmental regulation, statute or action being impugned, and the practice, custom or tradition being relied upon to establish the right.

When these factors are considered in this case it can be seen that the correct characterization of the appellants' claim is that they are claiming the right to participate in, and to regulate, high stakes gambling activities on the reservation. The activity which the appellants organized, and which their bands regulated, was high stakes gambling. The statute which they argue violates those rights prohibits gambling subject only to a few very limited exceptions (laid out in s. 207 of the *Code*). Finally, the applicants rely in support of their claim on the fact that the "Ojibwa people ... had a long tradition of public games and sporting events, which pre-dated the arrival of Europeans". Thus, the activity in which the appellants were engaged and which their bands regulated, the statute they are impugning, and the historical evidence on which they rely, all relate to the conduct and regulation of gambling. As such, the most accurate characterization of the appellants' claim is that they are asserting that s. 35(1) recognizes and affirms the rights of the Shawanaga and Eagle Lake First Nations to participate in, and to regulate, gambling activities on their respective reserve lands.

[27] The appellants themselves would have this Court characterize their claim as to "a broad right to manage the use of their reserve lands". To so characterize the appellants' claim would be to cast the Court's inquiry at a level of excessive generality. Aboriginal rights, including any asserted right to self-government, must be looked at in light of the specific circumstances of each case and, in particular, in light of the specific history and culture of the aboriginal group claiming the right. The factors laid out in *Van der Peet*, and applied, *supra*, allow the Court to consider the appellants' claim at the appropriate level of specificity; the characterization put forward by the appellants would not allow the Court to do so.

[28] I now turn to the second branch of the *Van der Peet* test, the consideration of whether the participation in, and regulation of, gambling on the reserve lands was an integral part of the distinctive cultures of the Shawanaga or Eagle Lake First Nations. The evidence presented at both the Pamajewon and Gardner trials does not demonstrate that gambling, or that the regulation of gambling, was an integral part of the distinctive cultures of the Shawanaga or Eagle Lake First Nations. In fact, the only evidence presented at either trial dealing with the question of the importance of gambling was that of James Morrison, who testified at the Pamajewon trial with regards to the importance and prevalence of gaming in Ojibwa culture. While Mr. Morrison's evidence does demonstrate that the Ojibwa gambled, it does not demonstrate that gambling was of central significance to the Ojibwa people. Moreover, his evidence in no way addresses the extent to which this gambling was the subject of regulation by the Ojibwa community. His account is of informal gambling activities taking place on a small-scale; he does not describe large-scale activities, subject to community regulation, of the sort at issue in this appeal.

[29] I would note that neither of the trial judges in these cases relied upon findings of fact regarding the importance of gambling to the Ojibwa; however, upon review of the evidence I find myself in agreement with the conclusion arrived at by Osborne J.A. when he said first, at p. 400, that there "is no evidence to support a conclusion that gambling generally or high stakes gambling of the sort in issue here, were part of the First Nations' historic cultures and traditions, or an aspect of their use of their land" and, second, at p. 400, that "there is no evidence that gambling on the reserve lands generally was ever the subject matter of aboriginal regulation". I also agree with the observation made by Flaherty Prov. Ct. J. in the Gardner trial when he said that

> commercial lotteries such as bingo are a twentieth century phenomena and nothing of the kind existed amongst aboriginal peoples and was never part of the means by which those societies were traditionally sustained or socialized.

[30] Given this evidentiary record, it is clear that the appellants have failed to demonstrate that the gambling activities in which they were engaged, and their respective bands' regulation of those activities, took place pursuant to an aboriginal right recognized and affirmed by s. 35(1) of the *Constitution Act, 1982*.

[L'Heureux-Dube J. concurred in separate reasons.]

Appeal dismissed.

DELGAMUUKW v. BRITISH COLUMBIA
[1997] 3 S.C.R. 1010

. . . . .

D. Has a claim to self-government been made out by the appellants?

In the courts below, considerable attention was given to the question of whether s. 35(1) can protect a right to self-government, and if so, what the contours of that right are. The errors of fact made by the trial judge, and the resultant need for a new trial, make it impossible for this Court to determine whether the claim to self-government has been made out. Moreover, this is not the right case for the Court to lay down the legal principles to guide future litigation. The parties seem to have acknowledged this point, perhaps implicitly, by giving the arguments on self government much less weight on appeal. One source of the decreased emphasis on the right to self-government on appeal is this Court's judgment in *Pamajewon*. There, I held that rights to self-government, if they existed, cannot be framed in excessively general terms. The appellants did not have the benefit of my judgment at trial. Unsurprisingly, as counsel for the Wet'suwet'en specifically concedes, the appellants advanced the right to self-government in very broad terms, and therefore in a manner not cognizable under s. 35(1).

The broad nature of the claim at trial also led to a failure by the parties to address many of the difficult conceptual issues which surround the recognition of aboriginal self-government. The degree of complexity involved can be gleaned from the *Report of the Royal Commission on Aboriginal Peoples*, which devotes 277 pages to the issue. That report describes different models of self-government, each differing with respect to their conception of territory, citizenship, jurisdiction, internal government organization, etc.. We received little in the way of submission that would help us grapple with these difficult and central issues. Without assistance from the parties, it would be imprudent for the Court to step into the breach. In these issues, the issue of self-government will fall to be determined at trial.

In its brief two-paragraph examination of self-government, the Supreme Court of Canada revealed the effects of its unreflective acceptance of Crown sovereignty on its comprehension of the issues before it. After relying on assertions of Crown sovereignty to ground Crown rights throughout the judgment (see *Delgamuukw* in Chapter one), the Court did not extend to Aboriginal peoples equivalent generous treatment concerning the effects of Aboriginal sovereignty. Relying on its earlier judgment in *R. v. Pamajewon*, the Court reasserted that Aboriginal rights to self-government, if they existed, cannot be framed in excessively general terms. This contrast in the Court's treatment of Crown and Aboriginal sovereignty could not be more profound. The Court was quite willing to frame Crown rights to self-government in the most excessive and general of terms — simple utterances were sufficient to grant the Crown the widest possible range of entitlements to other's ancient rights. On the other hand, detailed evidence concerning Gitksan and Wet'suwet'en sovereignty (houses, clans, chiefs, feasts, crests, poles, laws, etc.) over specific people and territory was too broad to "lay down the legal principles to guide future litigation". As a result the Court held that the advancement of the Aboriginal right to self-government in the supposedly very broad terms in the case before it was not cognizable under section 35(1) of the Constitution. Is the Crown's assertion of broad rights of Crown sovereignty any more cognizable given its unexamined extension and unquestioned acceptance by the Court in this case?

It would be interesting to subject the Court's treatment of Crown sovereignty to the same standards it expects for evidence of Aboriginal self-government. If this approach was followed could it not also be said of Crown sovereignty, as the Court wrote of Aboriginal sovereignty:

> The broad nature of the claim at trial also led to a failure by the parties to address many of the difficult conceptual issues which surround the recognition of [Crown] self-government. ... We received little in the way of submissions that would help us to grapple with these difficult and central issues. Without assistance from the parties it would be imprudent for the Court to step into the breach. In these circumstances the issue of [Crown] self-government will fall to be determined at trial.

The implications of the assertion of Crown sovereignty need to be more carefully scrutinized to assess the justice of colonialism in British Columbia. Without such an examination, the unequal treatment of Aboriginal and Crown sovereignty perpetuates historical injustices and therefore fails to respect the distinctive cultures of pre-existing Aboriginal societies in contemporary Canadian society.

When British Columbia entered Confederation in 1871, Indians composed a majority of people within the province, yet did not participate in its creation. Most continued to live within their own governments on their lands as they had done for centuries, with little or no thought for British assertions of sovereignty. As stated by former United States Supreme Court Justice John Marshall in *Worcester v. Georgia*, 31 U.S. (6 Pet.) 515, 8 L.Ed. 483 (U.S.S.C. 1832):

> It is difficult to comprehend the proposition that the inhabitants of the globe could have rightful original claims of dominion over the inhabitants of the other, or over the lands they occupied; or that the discovery of either by the other should give the discoverer rights in the country discovered which annulled the pre-existing rights of its ancient possessions.

It should be asked how, then, under such circumstances did the Indians become "subject to the legislative authority of Canada" as the Court of Appeal suggested in its reasons? Is it because they "became a conquered people, not by force of arms, for that was not necessary, but by an invading culture and a relentless energy with which they would not, or could not compete", as the trial judge, MacEachern J., suggested in his judgment in *Delgamuukw v. The Queen*, [1991] reasons for judgment of the Honourable Chief Justice Allen McEachern in Supreme Court of B.C. Number 0843, Smithers Registry, at 129. Or did this subjection come about by the assertion of British sovereignty through unjust and discriminatory laws? In 1881, 10 years after union, Indians were still the majority population in British Columbia: there were 28,704 Indians, 4,195 Chinese and 19,069 settlers of European origin. Yet in 1872, a year after union, when the Indian population was closer to 40,000 and the settler population was smaller still, one of the new province's first legislative acts was to remove voting rights from the Indians. This same government continued to uphold laws that denied Indians fee simple title to pre-empted lands taken up through settlement, a right freely granted to non-Aboriginal people in British Columbia. Furthermore, this government only allowed for the surveying of extremely small reserves for Indians, and would not recognize any Aboriginal title to land. When Aboriginal peoples in British Columbia tried to dispute this mistreatment the province responded by further diminishing their land and political rights, and the federal government eventually followed suit by amending the *Indian Act* and making it virtually illegal to raise these matters before the courts.

"Taking the perspective of the aboriginal people themselves, on the meaning of the rights at stake" it should be asked whether the authority of an imposed, obstructionist and unrepresentative government, should be recognized as legally infringing or extinguishing any "Aboriginal legislative or other jurisdiction" which Aboriginal people possess. In these circumstances, is the assertion of British sovereignty over Aboriginal peoples in British Columbia a "morally and politically defensible conception of aboriginal rights"? Does it "perpetuate historical injustice suffered by aboriginal peoples at the hands of the colonizers"? Is it consistent with the "noble and prospective purpose of the Constitutional entrenchment of aboriginal and treaty rights in the Constitution"? If assertions of sovereignty operate as they have done throughout Western European legal thought, should we ask whether "an unjust and discriminatory doctrine of that kind can any longer be accepted"?

F. NEGOTIATING GOVERNANCE AGREEMENTS

Negotiation is an alternative to litigating the issue of Aboriginal governance. While negotiation can be a promising option, relatively few agreements include the Aboriginal right to governance. The Cree, Naskapi and Inuit of Northern Quebec have some elements of governance protected in the 1975 *James Bay and Northern Québec Agreement* and the 1978 *Northeastern Québec Agreement*; the Sechelt Indian Band of British Columbia has a measure of delegated governance under the 1986 *Sechelt Indian Band Self-Government Act*; and seven Yukon First Nations have sections dealing with self-government pursuant to a 1993 Umbrella Final Agreement. None of these pre-1995 self-government arrangements is explicitly "covered" by section 35 of the *Constitution Act, 1982*.

Other comprehensive land claim agreements concluded prior to 1995 under section 35 do not include self-governance provisions (such as the 1993 *Nunavut Land Claims Agreement*, the 1992 *Gwich'in Comprehensive Land Claim Agreement* and the 1994 *Sahtu Dene and Metis Comprehensive Land Claim Agreement*). Nunavut has a public model of governance rather than an Inuit-exclusive government structure that does not benefit from protection under section 35.

In January 1998, the federal government released *Gathering Strength — Canada's Aboriginal Action Plan* to deal with the issue of Aboriginal governance. In the document the government said it:

- was "open to further discussions on the departmental and institutional arrangements that could improve existing systems";
- would "consult with Aboriginal organizations and the provinces and territories on appropriate instruments to recognize Aboriginal governments";
- would focus on improving the capacity of First Nations to negotiate and implement self-government;
- would work with Treaty First Nations to achieve self-government within the context of the treaty relationship.

The 1995 inherent right policy was directly implemented for the first time with the 1998 *Nisga'a Final Agreement*. This Agreement came into effect on 11 May 2000 after being ratified by the Nisga'a, the B.C. Legislative Assembly and federal Parliament.

The Nisga'a Treaty is the first modern-day treaty in B.C. and is the fourteenth modern treaty in Canada to be negotiated since 1976.

CHIEF GOSNELL'S HISTORIC SPEECH TO THE BRITISH COLUMBIA LEGISLATURE

Official Report of the Legislative Assembly (B.C. *Hansard*), Wednesday December 2, 1998, Vol. 12, No. 17

Madame Speaker, Honourable Members, ladies and gentlemen.

Today marks a turning point in the history of British Columbia. Today, aboriginal and non-aboriginal people are coming together to decide the future of this province.

I am talking about the Nisga'a Treaty — a triumph for all British Columbians — and a beacon of hope for aboriginal people around the world.

A triumph, I believe, which proves to the world that reasonable people can sit down and settle historical wrongs. It proves that a modern society can correct the mistakes of the past. As British Columbians, as Canadians, we should all be very proud.

A triumph because, under the Treaty, the Nisga'a people will join Canada and British Columbia as free citizens — full and equal participants in the social, economic and political life of this province, of this country.

A triumph because, under the Treaty, we will no longer be wards of the state, no longer beggars in our own lands.

A triumph because, under the Treaty, we will collectively own about 2,000 square kilometres of land, far exceeding the postage-stamp reserves set aside for us by colonial governments. We will once again govern ourselves by our own institutions, but within the context of Canadian law.

It is a triumph because, under the Treaty, we will be allowed to make our own mistakes, to savor our own victories, to stand on our own feet once again.

A triumph because, clause by clause, the Nisga'a Treaty emphasizes self-reliance, personal responsibility and modern education. It also encourages, for the first time, investment in Nisga'a lands and resources, and allows us to pursue meaningful employment from the resources of our own territory, for our own people.

To investors, it provides economic certainty and gives us a fighting chance to establish legitimate economic independence — to prosper in common with our non-aboriginal neighbors in a new and proud Canada.

A triumph, Madame Speaker and Honorable Members, because the Treaty proves, beyond all doubt, that negotiations — not lawsuits, not blockades, not violence — are the most effective, most honorable way to resolve aboriginal issues in this country.

A triumph that signals the end of the *Indian Act* — the end of more than a century of humiliation, degradation and despair.

In 1887, my ancestors made an epic journey from the Nass River here to Victoria's inner harbor.

Determined to settle the Land Question, they were met by a Premier who barred them from the Legislature.

He was blunt. Premier Smithe rejected all our aspirations to settle the Land Question. Then he made this pronouncement, and I quote: "When the white man first came among you, you were little better than wild beasts of the field."

Wild beasts of the field! Little wonder then, that this brutal racism was soon translated into narrow policies which plunged British Columbia into a century of darkness for the Nisga'a and other aboriginal people.

Like many colonists of the day, Premier Smithe did not know, or care to know, that the Nisga'a is an old nation, as old as any in Europe.

From time immemorial, our oral literature, passed down from generation to generation, records the story of the way the Nisga'a people were placed on earth, entrusted with the care and protection of our land.

Through the ages, we lived a settled life in villages along the Nass River. We lived in large, cedar-planked houses, fronted with totem poles depicting the great heraldry and the family crests of our nobility. We thrived from the bounty of the sea, the river, the forest and the mountains.

We governed ourselves according to Ayuukhl Nisga'a, the code of our own strict and ancient laws of property ownership, succession, and civil order.

Our first encounters with Europeans were friendly. We welcomed these strange visitors, visitors who never left.

The Europeans also valued their encounters with us. They thought we were fair and tough entrepreneurs, and no doubt today, negotiators. In

1832, traders from the Hudson Bay Company found us living, in their words, in "two story wooden houses the equal of any in Europe." For a time, we continued to prosper.

But there were dark days to come.

Between the late 1700s and the mid-1800s, the Nisga'a people, like so many other coastal nations of the time, were devastated by European diseases, such as smallpox, measles and fevers. Our population, once 30,000, dwindled to about 800 people. Today, I am pleased to report, our population is growing again. Today, we number 5,500 people.

We took to heart the promises of King George III, set out in the Royal Proclamation of 1763, that our lands would not be taken without our permission, and that treaty-making was the way the Nisga'a would become part of this new nation.

We continued to follow our ayuukhl, our code of laws. We vowed to obey the white man's laws, too, and we expected him to obey his own law — and to respect ours.

But the Europeans would not obey their own laws, and continued to trespass on our lands. The King's governments continued to take our lands from us, until we were told that all of our lands had come to belong to the Crown, and even the tiny bits of land that enclosed our villages were not ours, but belonged to the government.

Still, we kept faith that the rule of law would prevail one day, that justice would be done. That one day, the Land Question would be settled fairly and honorably.

In 1913, the Nisga'a Land Committee drafted a Petition to London. The Petition contained a declaration of our traditional land ownership and governance and it contained the critical affirmation that, in the new British colony, our land ownership would be respected. In part the Petition said quote:

> We are not opposed to the coming of the white people into our territory, provided this be carried out justly and in accordance with the British principles embodied in the Royal Proclamation. If therefore as we expect the aboriginal rights which we claim should be established by the decision of His Majesty's Privy Council, we would be prepared to take a moderate and reasonable position. In that event, while claiming the right to decide for ourselves, the terms upon which we would deal with our territory, we would be willing that all matters outstanding between the province and ourselves should be finally adjusted by some equitable method to be agreed upon which should include representation of the Indian Tribes upon any Commission which might then be appointed.

The above statement was unanimously adopted at a meeting of the Nisga'a Nation or Tribe of Indians held at the village of Kincolith on the 22nd day of January, 1913.

Sadly, this was not to be the case.

Also in 1913, Duncan Campbell Scott became deputy superintendent of Indian Affairs. His narrow vision of assimilation dominated federal aboriginal policy for years and years to come and was later codified as the *Indian Act*.

Mr. Scott said, I want to get rid of the Indian problem. "Our objective is to continue until there is not a single Indian in Canada that has not been absorbed into the body politic and there is no Indian question."

One of this man's earliest efforts was to undermine the influence of the Nisga'a Petition to London and to deflect attention away from political action.

But these men, Smithe and Scott failed; and are now deservedly only dusty footnotes in history.

Still, the situation of the Nisga'a worsened. In 1927, Canada passed a law to prevent us from pursuing our land claims, from hiring lawyers to plead our case.

At the same time, our central institution of tribal government, the potlatch system (yuukw), was outlawed by an Act of Parliament. It was against the law for us to give presents to one another during our ceremonies, which our laws instructed us to do. It was even made illegal for us to sing, to dance.

But still, we never gave up. And then finally, under the leadership of President Emeritus Frank Calder, the Nisga'a Land Committee was reborn as the Nisga'a Tribal Council in 1955. In 1968, we took our Land Question to the B.C. Supreme Court. We lost but appealed to the Supreme Court of Canada, where in 1973 — in what is now known as the *Calder Case* — the judges ruled that aboriginal title existed prior to Confederation. This initiated the modern day process of land claims negotiations.

The government of Canada agreed it was best to negotiate modern-day treaties. Canada agreed it was time to build a new relationship, based on trust, respect, and the rule of law.

In time, as you well know Madame Speaker, the Province of British Columbia came to the negotiating table as well. For the past twenty-five years, in good faith, the Nisga'a struggled to negotiate this Treaty and finally, it was initialed in August in our village of New Aiyansh.

How the world has changed. Two days ago and one hundred and eleven years after Smithe's rejection, I walked up the steps of this Legislature as the sound of Nisga'a drumming and singing filled the rotunda. To the Nisga'a people, it was a joyous sound, the sound of freedom.

What does "Freedom" mean? I looked it up in the dictionary. It means The state or condition of being free, the condition of not being under another's control; the power to do, say, or think as one pleases."

Our people have enjoyed the hospitality and warmth of this Legislature, this capital city, its sights and its people — in churches, schools, malls, streets and public places. Our people have been embraced, welcomed and congratulated by the people of British Columbia, Madame Speaker.

People sometimes wonder why we have struggled so long to sign a Treaty.

Why, we are asked, did our elders and elected officials dedicate their lives to a resolution of the Land Question? What is it about a Treaty?

To us, a Treaty is a sacred instrument. It represents an understanding between distinct cultures and shows respect for each other's way of life. We know we are here for a long time together. A Treaty stands as a symbol of high idealism in a divided world. That is why we have fought so long, and so hard.

I have been asked, has it been worth it? Yes, a resounding yes. But, believe me, it has been a long and hard-fought battle. Some may have heard us say that a generation of Nisga'a men and women has grown old at the negotiating table. Sadly, it is very, very true.

Let me share some personal history. When I began this process I was a young man. When I first became involved in our Tribal Council, I was 25 years old. Now I am 63. Today, my hair is grey. The terms of six Prime Ministers chart the years I have grown old at the negotiating table:

The Right Honourable Pierre Trudeau,

Joe Clark,

John Turner,

Brian Mulroney,

Kim Campbell, and

Jean Chretien.

And five British Columbia Premiers:

Bill Bennett,

William Vander Zalm,

Rita Johnson,

Mike Harcourt, and

Glen Clark.

I will spare you the list of deputy ministers, senior bureaucrats and other officials we have met across the table during the past quarter century. Their names would paper the walls of this Chamber. At least twice, I'd bet.

We are not naive. We know that some people do not want this Treaty. We know there are naysayers, some sitting here today. We know there are some who say Canada and B.C. are "giving" us too much. And a few who want to re-open negotiations in order to "give" us less.

Others — still upholding the values of Smithe and Scott — are practising a willful ignorance. This colonial attitude is fanning the flames of fear and ignorance in this province and re-igniting a poisonous attitude so familiar to aboriginal people.

But these are desperate tactics — doomed to fail. By playing politics with the aspirations of aboriginal people these naysayers are blighting the promise of the Nisga'a Treaty — not only for us, but for non-aboriginal people as well.

Because, Madame Speaker, this is about people. We are not numbers. In this Legislative debate, you will be dealing with the lives of our people; with the futures of our individual people. This is about the legitimate aspirations of people no longer willing to step aside or be marginalized.

We intend to be free and equal citizens, Madame Speaker. Witness the flags that have been waved in this Chamber over the past two days — by the Nisga'a people of British Columbia, the Nisga'a people of Canada.

Now, on the eve of the 50th anniversary of the Declaration of Human Rights, this Legislature embarks on a great debate about aboriginal rights. The Nisga'a people welcome that debate — one of the most important in the modern history of British Columbia.

And we have every confidence that elected members of this Legislature will look beyond narrow politics to correct a shameful and historic wrong. I ask every honorable member to search their hearts deeply and to allow the light of our message to guide their decision.

We have worked for justice for more than a century. Now, it is time to ratify the Nisga'a Treaty, for aboriginal and non-aboriginal people to come together and write a new chapter in the history of our Nation, our province, our country and indeed, the world.

The world is our witness.

Be strong. Be steadfast. Be true.

The Preamble to the Nisga'a Final Agreement reads as follows:

WHEREAS the Nisga'a Nation has lived in the Nass Area since time immemorial;

WHEREAS the Nisga'a Nation is an aboriginal people of Canada;

WHEREAS section 35 of the *Constitution Act, 1982* recognizes and affirms the existing aboriginal and treaty rights of the aboriginal peoples of Canada, which the Courts have stated include aboriginal title;

WHEREAS the Nisga'a Nation has never entered into a treaty with Canada or British Columbia;

WHEREAS the Nisga'a Nation has sought a just and equitable settlement of the land question since the arrival of the British Crown, including the preparation of the Nisga'a Petition to His Majesty's Privy Council, dated 21 May, 1913, and the conduct of the litigation that led to the decision of the Supreme Court of Canada in *Calder v. the Attorney-General of British Columbia* in 1973, and this Agreement is intended to be the just and equitable settlement of the land question;

WHEREAS Canadian courts have stated that the reconciliation between the prior presence of aboriginal peoples and the assertion of sovereignty by the Crown is best achieved through negotiation and agreement, rather than through litigation or conflict;

WHEREAS the Parties intend that this Agreement will result in this reconciliation and establish a new relationship among them;

WHEREAS this Agreement sets out Nisga'a section 35 rights inside and outside of the area that is identified in this Agreement as Nisga'a Lands;

WHEREAS the Parties acknowledge the ongoing importance to the Nisga'a Nation of the *Simgigat* and *Sigidimhaanak* (hereditary chiefs and matriarchs) continuing to tell their *Adaawak* (oral histories) relating to their *Ango'oskw* (family hunting, fishing, and gathering territories) in accordance with the *Ayuuk* (Nisga'a traditional laws and practices);

WHEREAS the Parties intend their relationship to be based on a new approach to mutual recognition and sharing, and to achieve this mutual recognition and sharing by agreeing on rights, rather than by the extinguishment of rights; and

WHEREAS the Parties intend that this Agreement will provide certainty with respect to Nisga'a ownership and use of lands and resources, and the relationship of federal, provincial and Nisga'a laws, within the Nass Area.

Chapter 2 of the Agreement, outlining its General Provisions begins:

This Agreement is a treaty and a land claims agreement within the meaning of sections 25 and 35 of the *Constitution Act, 1982.*

DOUGLAS SANDERS, "WE INTEND TO LIVE HERE FOREVER: A PRIMER ON THE NISGA'A TREATY"

(1999) 33 U.B.C. Law Rev. 103-128

At the signing of the Nisga'a Treaty in New Aiyansh in August 1998, Chief Joseph Gosnell said: "Look around you. Look at our faces. We are the survivors of a long journey. We intend to live here forever. And, under the Nisga'a Treaty, we will flourish." For the governments of Canada and British Columbia, the Nisga'a Treaty is the first agreement to define both aboriginal resource rights and self-government powers. In the years ahead, Canada and British Columbia anticipate fifty-one additional agreements with First Nations in the province.

Still, the Nisga'a Treaty has generated a level of controversy in British Columbia that is reminiscent of the debates over the Meech Lake and Charlottetown Accord packages of constitutional amendments. What are the elements of this public debate?

Supporters of the Treaty argue that it will move us away from the old, paternalistic system under the *Indian Act*, toward Nisga'a self-government based on constitutionally protected treaty rights. The government of Canada was determined to extricate itself from the burdens and obligations of paternalism. To this end, Nisga'a lands will no longer fall under federal jurisdiction nor will they be governed under the *Indian Act*. Secondly, the Treaty settles land claims in the Nass River Valley by a compromise that gives a portion to the Nisga'a, while leaving most of the land and resources under the dominant legal system. The government of British Columbia wanted a treaty in order to bring investment certainty to the province's resource-based economy and to stop recurring confrontations and court challenges. Thirdly, the Nisga'a government will be both recognized and integrated into the constitutional system of Canada, with most parts of federal and provincial laws applying to the Nisga'a and their lands.

Public criticism of the Treaty has been dominated by non-Indian voices. These critics argue that the Treaty establishes a system of rights and self-government that are "race-based" and, therefore, comparable to apartheid. Secondly, they argue that a constitutionally protected self-government system is a permanent and dramatic shift in Canadian constitutional architecture and, as such, either requires or deserves a public referendum. Thirdly, it has been said, that non-Nisga'a living on Nisga'a lands will become second-class citizens, denied the right to vote or hold public office in the local government that affects parts of their lives.

Phil Fontaine, [former] National Chief of the Assembly of First Nations, supports the Treaty on the basis that it represents what the Nisga'a people want. Support, on those terms, has also come from various tribal councils in British Columbia and from the First Nations Summit. But in general, First Nations people are critical of the Treaty. The sharpest Indian critics call it a "custodial agreement" or the "B.C. *Indian Act.*" Some Indian critics say that the Treaty gives the Provincial government a much stronger constitutional role than in the past, in spite of historic treaties that have directly affected the relationship between Canada and its First Nations. The Treaty is also criticized for creating only a limited self-government. Accordingly, the powers involved are said to be modest and said to be "municipal" in character. The Treaty does not address, much less settle, issues surrounding Indian sovereignty. It is also said to represent a settlement but not a new relationship; that is, it is not a commitment to Indian survival, development, or achievement within the Canadian system, because it gives Indians too little and involves too much outside control. Others among the critics say that they will never agree to such provisions as the ending of tax exemptions under the *Indian Act.*

Four court challenges to the Treaty and its the process have been filed. In 1997, some of the Nisga'a community went to court with the claim that their leaders did not have the authority to sign the Treaty. They failed, however, because they could not demonstrate significant support for their position and were refused a pre-trial injunction. One court challenge is based on a border dispute between the Gitanyow and the Nisga'a. Another, by Reform MP John Cummins and the Fisheries Survival Coalition (a group that has actively protested Indian fishing rights for a number of years), has been brought. However, the leading challenge is that of the provincial Liberal party — the official opposition party in British Columbia. The Liberal party's case focuses primarily on the self-government provisions of the Treaty.

The decision dismissing the Liberal party of British Columbia's challenge to the Nisga'a treaty is found in *Campbell v. British Columbia (Attorney General)* (2000), 189 D.L.R. (4th) 333 (B.C.S.C.). The main issue in the *Campbell* case was whether the Nisga'a Treaty was inconsistent with the division of powers granted to Parliament and the Legislative Assemblies of the Provinces by sections 91 and 92 of the *Constitution Act, 1867*. The Liberal party argued the Agreement was of no force or effect, *to the extent* that it purports to provide the Nisga'a government with legislative jurisdiction, or provides that the Nisga'a government may make laws that prevail over federal and provincial laws. Justice Williamson, of the British Columbia Supreme Court, ruled against the challenge, finding that self-government was a constitutionally protected right within the Nisga'a Agreement. His reasons for decision are as follows:

CAMPBELL v. BRITISH COLUMBIA (ATTORNEY GENERAL)

(2000), 189 D.L.R. (4th) 333 (B.C.S.C.)

Williamson J.: —

. . . . .

THE NISGA'A TREATY

[34] The Nisga'a Final Agreement, now a "treaty", is a complex tripartite agreement which purports to define in an exhaustive way the treaty rights of the Nisga'a Nation. Counsel for the plaintiffs have characterized the Treaty as having four basic components. The first is the substitution for aboriginal title with a grant of a fee simple to the Nisga'a Nation of just under 2,000 square kilometres of land in the Nass Valley. This would, to use the word in the Treaty, "modify" the existing aboriginal title. It is an area much smaller than that originally claimed by the Nisga'a.

[35] Second, the Treaty defines existing hunting, fishing and trapping rights in the Nisga'a lands, but also permits participation in wildlife and fisheries management over a much larger area known as the Nass Wildlife Area. Thus, it is important to note that there are two areas of land involved. The first is the smaller fee simple area owned by the Nisga'a Nation and over which it has defined legislative power. The second is the larger area in which the Nisga'a have certain specified hunting, fishing and trapping rights.

[36] The third basic component is the payment of money over a period of years which can be seen as compensation for what the Nisga'a have given up or possibly for the negative impact upon the Nisga'a which followed upon the arrival of Europeans.

[37] The fourth component is described by the plaintiffs as "a new order of government", a government with certain legislative jurisdiction specified in Chapter 11 of the Treaty. I have put the words "a new order of government" in quotation marks as there is some dispute about whether this government can be called new, except as to its structure.

[38] The Nisga'a government is divided into two groups: the Nisga'a Lisims Government and the Nisga'a Village Governments, intended to govern the Nisga'a Nation and the Nisga'a villages respectively. The Nisga'a Lisims Government is responsible for intergovernmental relations between the Nisga'a Nation and Canada or British Columbia. Each of these governments is a separate legal entity which can enter into contracts and agreements, acquire and hold property, raise and spend money, sue and be sued, and do those things ancillary to the exercise of its powers. The Agreement provides for the creation, continuation, amalgamation, or dissolution of Nisga'a villages.

[39] The Treaty provides for a Nisga'a Constitution which must, however, be consistent with the Treaty.

[40] The Treaty also provides for the creation of Nisga'a Urban Locals, a provision designed to ensure that the Nisga'a who live away from the Nass Valley in three specified areas (Greater Vancouver, Terrace and

Prince Rupert/Port Edward) will be able to participate in the Nisga'a Lisims Government.

[41] The *Canadian Charter of Rights and Freedoms* is stated expressly to apply to Nisga'a government "in respect of all matters within its authority, bearing in mind the free and democratic nature of Nisga'a Government" as set out in the Treaty.

[42] Nisga'a citizenship, or enrolment under the agreement, is the subject of detailed provisions. Individuals are eligible to be enrolled if they are of Nisga'a ancestry and if their mother was born into one of the Nisga'a tribes, as are descendants and adopted children of such individuals. An "enrolment committee" is established to consider applications for enrolment under the Treaty.

[43] Another provision in the Treaty allows other Aboriginal Canadians who marry a Nisga'a citizen, and are adopted into one of the four Nisga'a tribes in accordance with the *Ayuuk̲hl Nisga'a* (that is, traditional Nisga'a law), to apply for enrolment. In regards to non-Nisga'a citizens resident on Nisga'a lands, the Agreement requires the Nisga'a government to consult with them concerning decisions which "directly and significantly affect them".

[44] … [t]he plaintiffs do not challenge the transfer to the Nisga'a Nation of fee simple title to the Nisga'a lands, the confirmation of hunting, fishing and trapping rights, or the payment of compensation. They limit their constitutional challenge to what they submit is the establishment of a new order of government. I will therefore survey briefly the legislative powers of the Nisga'a nation as set out in the Treaty.

LEGISLATIVE POWERS OF THE NISGA'A GOVERNMENT

[45] The Nisga'a Government has power to make laws in a number of different areas which can be divided generally into two groupings. In the first category, when Nisga'a law conflicts with federal or provincial law, the Nisga'a law will prevail, although in many cases only if it is consistent with comparable standards established by Parliament, the Legislative Assembly, or relevant administrative tribunals.

[46] Generally speaking, the subjects in this category are matters which concern the identity of the Nisga'a people, their education, the preservation of their culture, the use of their land and resources, and the means by which they will make decisions in these areas. As noted, however, some of these areas remain subject to comparable provincial standards. For example, adoption laws must provide for the best interests of the child, just as does the *Adoption Act*, R.S.B.C. 1996, c. 5. The provision for Nisga'a control of education is subject to various comparable provincial educational standards.

[47] Other jurisdictions of the Nisga'a government in this category have specific matters carved out and reserved to the Crown, or to laws generally applicable in the subject area. For example, the right to regulate the use and development of Nisga'a Lands rests with the Nisga'a, but rights of way held or required by the Crown are subject to special provisions. The right to regulate businesses, professions and trades on Nisga'a lands rests

with the Nisga'a, but it is subject to provincial laws concerning accreditation, certification and regulation of the conduct of professions and trades.

[48] In the second classification of jurisdiction, when a Nisga'a law conflicts with federal or provincial law, the federal or provincial law will prevail.

[49] The Treaty permits the Nisga'a to establish police services and a police board. Any regimes established pursuant to these provisions require the approval of the provincial cabinet. If the Attorney General of the province is of the opinion that "effective policing in accordance with standards prevailing elsewhere in British Columbia" is not in place, she or he may provide or reorganize policing on the Nisga'a lands, appointing constables or using the provincial police (the R.C.M.P.) as a police force.

[50] The Treaty also provides that the Nisga'a Lisims Government may decide to establish a Nisga'a Court. But again, if that course is followed, its structure and procedures, and the method of selecting judges, must be approved by the provincial cabinet. Further, an appeal from a final decision of the Nisga'a Court lies to the Supreme Court of British Columbia. The Court section of the Treaty includes a number of references to the requirement that any Nisga'a court system must operate in accordance with generally accepted principles. For example, a Nisga'a Court and its judges must comply with "generally recognized principles in respect of judicial fairness, independence and impartiality".

[51] The Nisga'a Government has no authority to make criminal law (that power remains with Parliament). Importantly, a person accused of any offence for which he or she may be imprisoned under Nisga'a law has the right to elect to be tried in the Provincial Court of British Columbia rather than a Nisga'a Court. Any provincial court proceedings would be subject to rights of appeal to the Supreme Court of British Columbia or the Court of Appeal.

[52] Labour relations law, or what in the Agreement is called industrial relations, is governed by federal and provincial laws. However, the Nisga'a Lisims Government has a right in some instances to make representations concerning the effect of a particular aspect of labour relations law upon Nisga'a culture.

[53] While the Treaty defines the right of the Nisga'a to harvest fish and aquatic plants in Nisga'a fisheries areas, all the fisheries rights of the Nisga'a are expressly subject to measures that are necessary for conservation and to legislation enacted for the purposes of public health or safety. Nisga'a peoples' harvest of fish is subject to limits set by the federal Minister of Fisheries. Any laws made by the Nisga'a government concerning fish or aquatic plants harvested by the Nisga'a are subject to relevant federal or provincial laws.

[54] The Nisga'a government may make laws concerning assets the Nisga'a Nation, a Nisga'a village or Nisga'a corporation may hold off Nisga'a lands, but in the event of a conflict between such laws and federal or provincial laws of general application, the latter prevail.

[55] Similarly, while the Nisga'a may make laws concerning the sale and consumption of alcohol (intoxicants) on Nisga'a lands, they are subject to federal and provincial laws in the area in the event of conflict.

[56] British Columbia retains the right to licence or approve gambling or gaming facilities on Nisga'a lands, but the Agreement provides that the

province will not do so except in accordance with terms established by the Nisga'a government. Such terms, however, must not be inconsistent with federal and provincial laws.

[57] The above paragraphs do not list every jurisdiction and every rule set out in this lengthy and complex agreement about which law will prevail. This review, however, is enough to show that the legislative powers of the Nisga'a Government are significantly limited by the Treaty itself, without considering the effect of s. 35 of the *Constitution Act, 1982*.

[58] Recognizing these restrictions, the plaintiffs submit that it is only those portions of the Treaty which allocate legislative power in the Nisga'a Government, and which provide that in the event of a conflict with federal or provincial law Nisga'a law will prevail, which are unconstitutional.

[59] The heart of this argument is that any right to such self-government or legislative power was extinguished at the time of Confederation. Thus, the plaintiffs distinguish aboriginal title and other aboriginal rights, such as the right to hunt or to fish, from the right to govern one's own affairs. They say that in 1867, when the then *British North America Act* (now called the *Constitution Act, 1867*) was enacted, although other aboriginal rights including aboriginal title survived, any right to self-government did not. All legislative power was divided between Parliament and the legislative assemblies. While they concede that Parliament, or the Legislative Assembly, may delegate authority, they say legislative bodies may not give up or abdicate that authority. To do so, they argue, is unconstitutional.

[60] For this reason, they ask this court to strike down those provisions of the Nisga'a Treaty which so provide.

. . . . .

SECTIONS 91 AND 92: THE DIVISION OF POWERS

[62] I turn first to the significance of the division of powers between the federal and provincial governments originally set out in 1867 by the Parliament of the United Kingdom in ss. 91 and 92 of the *British North America Act*. It is necessary to ask whether the passage of the *British North America Act* effectively concentrated all law making power in Parliament and the Legislative Assemblies. ...

[64] These sections, in view of the submissions of the plaintiffs, lead to at least two related questions. First, when the Parliament of the United Kingdom enacted the *British North America Act* in 1867 was all legislative power distributed through Sections 91 and 92? Second, is the legislative power granted to the Nisga'a Nation a new order of government? I have concluded the answer to both of these questions is "no".

THE PREAMBLE TO THE CONSTITUTION ACT, 1867

[65] The argument that Sections 91 and 92 exhaustively distribute all legislative power does not sufficiently consider the preamble to the *Act*. That opening statement provides that the intention of the statute is to endow Canada "with a Constitution similar in Principle to that of the United Kingdom". In considering this Preamble, the Supreme Court of Canada

has recognized that there are a number of constitutional principles and powers not set out in writing in the *Constitution Act, 1867* which nevertheless are fundamental to the Constitution.

[66] In *Reference re Remuneration of Judges of the Provincial Court of Prince Edward Island (the Provincial Court Judges Reference)*, [1997] 3 S.C.R. 3 at 75, the Chief Justice, speaking for the court...wrote:

> ... the preamble is not only a key to construing the express provisions of the *Constitution Act, 1867* but also invites the use of those organizing principles to fill out gaps in the express terms of the constitutional scheme. It is the means by which the underlying logic of the Act can be given the force of law.

[67] Some two years later in *Reference Re Secession of Quebec*, [1998] 2 S.C.R. 217, the Court referred to the *Provincial Court Judges Reference* and again affirmed, at page 239, that the Constitution "embraces unwritten as well as written" rules.

[68] British imperial policy, reflected in the instructions given to colonial authorities in North America prior to Confederation, recognized a continued form, albeit diminished, of aboriginal self-government after the assertion of sovereignty by the Crown. This imperial policy, through the preamble to the *Constitution Act, 1867*, assists in filling out "gaps in the express terms of the constitutional scheme".

[69] The history of the negotiation of treaties by the executive branch after Confederation indicates that the distribution of power in Sections 91 and 92, and in particular the designation of "Indians, and Lands reserved for the Indians" as a parliamentary responsibility in Section 91(24), did not interfere with the royal or executive prerogative to negotiate treaties with aboriginal nations.

[70] Nor did the distribution of power in Sections 91 and 92 terminate the development of the common law, law binding upon citizens and enforceable by the courts. And until the *Statute of Westminster* was passed in 1931, 64 years after Confederation, all legislation enacted in Canada was subject to the overriding powers of the Parliament of the United Kingdom. In short, long before the 1982 enactment of s. 35, aboriginal rights formed part of the unwritten principles underlying our constitution.

DO SECTIONS 91 AND 92 EXHAUST LEGISLATIVE POWER?

[71] The plaintiffs argue that all legislative power in Canada is "exhaustively" distributed between Parliament and the legislative assemblies by virtue of the *Constitution Act, 1867*. Consequently, they submit, an amendment to the constitution would be required to allow aboriginal governments, such as the Lisims Government of the Nisga'a Nation established by the Treaty, the power to make laws which prevail over federal or provincial laws. ...For example, in *A.G. Ont. v. A.G. Canada*, [1912] A.C. 571, a case which did not concern aboriginal rights but which was considered in detail by the Court of Appeal in *Delgamuukw*, the Privy Council, while discussing the *British North America Act*, said at p. 581:

> Now, there can be no doubt that under this organic instrument the powers distributed between the Dominion on the one hand and the provinces on the

other hand cover the whole area of self-government within the whole area of Canada.

[72] This is the heart of the plaintiffs' argument. If the powers granted to Parliament and the legislatures combined "cover the whole area of self-government" within Canada, there can be no legislative power left to aboriginal peoples.

[73] The flaw in this submission, however, becomes evident when one considers what the Privy Council said in the same judgment three pages on at p. 584:

> For whatever belongs to self-government in Canada belongs either to the Dominion or to the provinces, *within the limits* of the British North America Act. (emphasis added)

[74] What are "the limits of the British North America Act"?

[75] In *R. v. Secretary of State for Foreign and Commonwealth Affairs, ex parte Indian Association of Alberta and others*, [1982] 2 All E.R. 118, the English Court of Appeal dealt with the question of whether after Canada obtained independence obligations owed by the Crown to aboriginal peoples remained with the Crown in right of the United Kingdom or became the responsibility of the Crown in right of Canada. The court found that such obligations had become the responsibility of the Crown in right of Canada. In his reasons, May L.J. quoted with approval the following passage from the decision of Watson J. in *Liquidators of the Maritime Bank of Canada v. Receiver-General of New Brunswick*, [1892] A.C. 437 at 441-2:

> The object of the [*British North America Act*] ... was accomplished by distributing between the Dominion and the provinces, all powers executive and legislative, and all public property and revenues *which had previously belonged to the provinces;* so that the Dominion government should be vested with such of these powers, property, and revenues as were necessary for the due performance of its constitutional functions, and that the remainder should be retained by the provinces for the purposes of provincial government. (emphasis added)

[76] Thus, what was distributed in ss. 91 and 92 of the *British North America Act* was all of (but no more than) the powers which until June 30, 1867 had belonged to the colonies. Anything outside of the powers enjoyed by the colonies was not encompassed by ss. 91 and 92 and remained outside of the power of Parliament and the legislative assemblies just as it had been beyond the powers of the colonies.

[77] In the *Quebec Secession Reference*, the Supreme Court of Canada reviewed the historical context of the events leading to Confederation. The Court observed, at pp. 244-5, that:

> Federalism was a legal response to the underlying political and cultural realities that existed at Confederation and continue to exist today. At Confederation, political leaders told their respective communities that the Canadian union would be able to reconcile diversity with unity.
>
> . . . . .
>
> The federal-provincial division of powers was a legal recognition of the diversity that existed among the initial members of Confederation, and manifested a concern to accommodate that diversity within a single nation ...

Federalism was the political mechanism by which diversity could be reconciled with unity.

[78] This demonstrates that the object of the division of powers in ss. 91 and 92 between the federal government and the provinces was not to extinguish diversity (or aboriginal rights), but to ensure that the local and distinct needs of Upper and Lower Canada (Ontario and Quebec) and the maritime provinces were protected in a federal system.

[79] Several pages on in the same judgment, at para. 82, the Court spoke of the explicit protection for aboriginal and treaty rights in ss. 25 and 35 of the *Constitution Act, 1982,* as being consistent with a tradition of respect for minority rights reflecting "an important underlying constitutional value".

[80] The unique relationship between the Crown and aboriginal peoples, then, is a underlying constitutional value. In *Mitchell v. Peguis Indian Band* [1990] 2 S.C.R. 85 both Dickson C.J.C. and La Forest J. discussed this "unique historical relationship". After discussing *Guerin v. The Queen,* [1984] 2 S.C.R. 335; 13 D.L.R. (4th) 321 (S.C.C.), the Chief Justice wrote at pp. 108-9 that since 1867:

> ... the Crown's role has been played, as a matter of the federal division of powers, by Her Majesty in right of Canada, with the *Indian Act* representing a confirmation of the Crown's historic responsibility for the welfare and interests of these peoples. However, the Indians' relationship with the Crown or sovereign has never depended on the particular representatives of the Crown involved. From the aboriginal perspective, any federal-provincial divisions that the Crown has imposed on itself are internal to itself and do not alter the basic structure of Sovereign-Indian relations.

[81] A consideration of these various observations by the Supreme Court of Canada supports the submission that aboriginal rights, and in particular a right to self-government akin to a legislative power to make laws, survived as one of the unwritten "underlying values" of the Constitution outside of the powers distributed to Parliament and the legislatures in 1867. The federal-provincial division of powers in 1867 was aimed at a different issue and was a division "internal" to the Crown.

. . . . .

RECOGNITION OF ABORIGINAL LAW AFTER CONFEDERATION

[84] ... The common law has long recognized "customs" or rules that have obtained the force of law in a particular locality. Agreements such as treaties negotiated and entered into by exercise of executive prerogative will be enforced by the courts.

[85] History, and a review of the authorities, persuades me that the aboriginal peoples of Canada, including the Nisga'a, had legal systems prior to the arrival of Europeans on this continent and that these legal systems, although diminished, continued after contact. Aboriginal laws did not emanate from a central print oriented law-making authority similar to a legislative assembly, but took unwritten form. Lord Denning, in *R. v. Secretary of State For Foreign and Commonwealth Affairs* at p. 123 likened aboriginal laws to "custom":

These customary laws are not written down. They are handed down by tradition from one generation to another. Yet beyond doubt they are well established and have the force of law within the community.

[86] The continued existence of indigenous legal systems in North America after the arrival of Europeans was articulated as early as the 1820s by the Supreme Court of the United States. But the most salient fact, for the purposes of the question of whether a power to make and rely upon aboriginal law survived Canadian Confederation, is that since 1867 courts in Canada have enforced laws made by aboriginal societies. This demonstrates not only that at least a limited right to self-government, or a limited degree of legislative power, remained with aboriginal peoples after the assertion of sovereignty and after Confederation, but also that such rules, whether they result from custom, tradition, agreement, or some other decision making process, are "laws" in the Dicey constitutional sense.

[A review of historic and contemporary cases recognizing Aboriginal governance and law-making power is omitted.]

THE FRAMEWORK

[167] The Supreme Court of Canada has referred to s. 35 as a "framework" for reconciling the prior existence of aboriginal peoples with the sovereignty of the Crown. In *Van der Peet*, Lamer C.J.C. wrote at pp. 533-9:

> In my view, the doctrine of aboriginal rights exists, and is recognized and affirmed by s. 35 (1), because of one simple fact: when Europeans arrived in North America, aboriginal peoples, <u>were already here</u>, living in communities on the land, and participating in distinctive cultures, as they had done for centuries. It is this fact, and this fact above all others, which separates aboriginal peoples from all other minority groups in Canadian society and which mandates their special legal, and now constitutional, status.
>
> More specifically, what s. 35(1) does is provide the constitutional framework through which the fact that aboriginals lived on the land in distinctive societies, with their own practices, traditions and cultures, is acknowledged and reconciled with the sovereignty of the Crown. The substantive rights which fall within the provision must be defined in light of this purpose; ... [underlining in original]

[168] That the purpose of s. 35(1) is to provide a framework within which the prior existence of aboriginal peoples may be reconciled with the sovereignty of the Crown can mean nothing other than that there are existing aboriginal rights which have not yet been so reconciled. In much of Canada, these rights were reconciled through the negotiation of treaties. In most of British Columbia they were not.

[169] There are two ways to achieve the definition of "the substantive rights" which fall within s. 35(1): by resort to the courts, or by the negotiation of treaties. The Supreme Court of Canada, as have other courts, has stated a number of times that negotiation is the preferred method.

. . . . .

[171] Section 35(1), then, provides the solid constitutional framework within which aboriginal rights in British Columbia may be defined by the negotiation of treaties in a manner compatible with the sovereignty of the Canadian state. I conclude that what Canada, British Columbia and the Nisga'a have achieved in the Nisga'a Final Agreement is consistent both with what the Supreme Court of Canada has encouraged, and consistent with the purpose of s. 35 of the *Constitution Act, 1982.*

[172] The idea that treaties could be the vehicle to define rights to be given constitutional protection by s. 35 is supported by a consideration of the records of meetings of the framers of s. 35, and a consideration of a temporary provision in the *Constitution Act, 1982,* s. 37, the provision which mandated a first ministers' conference within one year of the passage of that *Act.*

[173] The meeting required by this section took place in March of 1983. It was at this conference that the First Ministers agreed to add s. 35(3) to the Constitution. They also agreed to add s. 37(2) which stated that a future conference would include in the agenda

> ... an item respecting constitutional matters that directly affect the aboriginal peoples of Canada, including the identification and definition of the rights of those peoples to be included in the Constitution of Canada ...

[174] At the 1983 conference, transcripts of which are in evidence, the then Prime Minister said that one matter for the meeting was the "the identification of rights" to be included in s. 35. He went on to say that:

> ... the heart of the matter, the crux of our efforts to improve the condition of our aboriginal peoples and strengthen their relationships with other Canadians, is found within the set of issues concerning aboriginal government.

[175] Twelve years later in December of 1995, in another document in evidence, the federal government published a policy statement entitled *Aboriginal Self-Government: the Government of Canada's Approach to Implementation of the Inherent Right and the Negotiation of Aboriginal Self-Government.* That policy statement said, at p. 3, that:

> The Government of Canada recognizes the inherent right of self-government as an existing aboriginal right under section 35 of the *Constitution Act, 1982.* It recognizes, as well, that the inherent right may find expression in treaties...

[176] These extrinsic documents are evidence that the framers of s. 35(3) considered that a form of self-government yet to be defined was to be included in the bundle of rights protected by that section, and that the Crown in right of Canada accepted treaties as a method of defining such rights as part of its policy.

[177] The Supreme Court of Canada recognized in 1990 that the rights guaranteed by s. 35 required definition. In *Sparrow* at p. 1108, the Court wrote of s. 35 as a "solemn commitment that must be *given meaningful content*" (emphasis added). The Nisga'a Final Agreement provides, with respect to the Nisga'a, that content.

. . . . .

SUMMARY

[179] For the reasons set out above, I have concluded that after the assertion of sovereignty by the British Crown, and continuing to and after the time of Confederation, although the right of aboriginal people to govern themselves was diminished, it was not extinguished. Any aboriginal right to self-government could be extinguished after Confederation and before 1982 by federal legislation which plainly expressed that intention, or it could be replaced or modified by the negotiation of a treaty. Post-1982, such rights cannot be extinguished, but they may be defined (given content) in a treaty. The Nisga'a Final Agreement does the latter expressly.

[180] I have also concluded that the *Constitution Act, 1867* did not distribute all legislative power to the Parliament and the legislatures. Those bodies have exclusive powers in the areas listed in Sections 91 and 92 (subject until 1931 to the Imperial Parliament). But the *Constitution Act, 1867*, did not purport to, and does not end, what remains of the royal prerogative or aboriginal and treaty rights, including the diminished but not extinguished power of self-government which remained with the Nisga'a people in 1982.

[181] Section 35 of the *Constitution Act, 1982*, then, constitutionally guarantees, among other things, the limited form of self-government which remained with the Nisga'a after the assertion of sovereignty. The Nisga'a Final Agreement and the settlement legislation give that limited right definition and content. Any decision or action which results from the exercise of this now-entrenched treaty right is subject to being infringed upon by Parliament and the legislative assembly. This is because the Supreme Court of Canada has determined that both aboriginal and treaty rights guaranteed by s. 35 may be impaired if such interference can be justified and is consistent with the honour of the Crown.

[182] The Nisga'a Final Agreement, negotiated in full knowledge of the limited effect (a fact accepted by the Nisga'a Nation in these proceedings) of the constitutional promise of s. 35, itself limits the new Nisga'a governments' rights to legislate. In addition, it specifies that in a number of areas, should there be any conflict between Nisga'a laws and federal or provincial laws, federal or provincial laws will prevail.

[183] Thus, the Nisga'a government, subject as it is to both the limitations set out in the treaty itself and to the limited guarantee of s. 35 of the *Constitution Act, 1982*, does not have absolute or sovereign powers.

[184] As set out above, the submission that the Nisga'a Treaty impinges improperly upon the offices of the Governor General and the Lieutenant Governor is answered by a plain reading of s. 55 of the *Constitution Act, 1867*. The challenges based upon the *Canadian Charter of Rights and Freedoms* are answered by s. 25 of the *Charter*.

RESULT

[185] In the result, I find the Nisga'a Final Agreement, and the settlement legislation passed by Parliament and the Legislative Assembly of the Province of British Columbia, establish a treaty as contemplated by Section 35 of the *Constitution Act, 1982*. The legislation and the Treaty are

constitutionally valid. The application for a declaration that the settlement legislation and the Treaty are in part void and of no effect is dismissed.

G. GOVERNANCE ISSUES UNDER THE INDIAN ACT

As noted above, one way in which new legal understandings of Aboriginal governance have emerged is through negotiated self-government agreements, such as the Cree-Naskapi (see *Cree-Naskapi (of Quebec) Act*, S.C. 1984, c. 18), the Sechelt Indians on the Sunshine Coast of British Columbia (see *Sechelt Indian Band Self-Government Act*, S.C. 1986, c. 27), *the Champagne and Aishihik Self-Government Agreement* (Yukon), Nunavut (Eastern Arctic) pursuant to the *Nunavut Land Claims Agreement Act*, S.C. 1993, c. 29, and the Nisga'a Treaty (British Columbia). Other nations have proceeded with self-government initiatives through sectoral agreements in education, health, resources management, etc. These smaller agreements allow communities to gain experience in areas of strategic importance to a First Nation.

The *Report of the Royal Commission on Aboriginal Peoples*, Vol. 2, Restructuring the Relationship (Ottawa: Ministry of Supply and Services, 1996), at 215 suggested that Aboriginal people are free to implement their inherent right to self-government through self-starting initiatives, without the need for agreements with federal or provincial governments. These initiatives can occur in what the commission called "core" areas of Aboriginal jurisdiction. While they considered it preferable for governance to be negotiated, to minimize the potential for misunderstanding by creating mechanisms for reciprocal recognition, the commission defined the core to include all matters that:

- are of vital concern to the life and welfare of a particular Aboriginal people, its culture and identity;
- do not have a major impact on adjacent jurisdictions; and
- are not otherwise the object of transcendent federal or provincial concern.

The commission then defined a "periphery" of Aboriginal jurisdiction which "takes up the remainder of inherent Aboriginal jurisdiction."

In 1995 the federal government issued a policy guide, entitled *Aboriginal Self-Government*, often referred to as the inherent rights policy. This policy lists the areas of governance the federal government thinks Aboriginal peoples have within the scope of their jurisdiction. It views Aboriginal jurisdiction as extending to "matters that are internal to the group, integral to its distinct Aboriginal culture, and essential to its operation as a government". These areas include: internal constitutions, elections, membership, marriage, adoption and child welfare, language, culture, education, health, social services, administration and enforcement of Aboriginal laws, policing, internal land management, agriculture, taxation of members, housing, transportation, and licensing of local businesses.

Aside from their relationship with the Canadian government, another important issue of Aboriginal governance is the nature and scope of governance under the *Indian Act*. While many bands argue that the *Indian Act* did not extinguish inherent rights of governance, there is no doubt that the Act has had a great influence on the exercise of their powers. This is especially true when competing visions of governance emerge within the community.

Recently, there has been some heated debate about whether the *Indian Act* should be supplemented by a *First Nations Governance Act* (FNGA) to deal with these issues. The purported purpose of the FNGA is to provide bands operating under the *Indian Act* with more effective governance tools until self-government arrangements are negotiated and implemented. The Minister of Indian Affairs says the FNGA is not designed to replace the *Indian Act* though, if passed, some sections would disappear and new provisions would replace other sections. At the heart of the proposed FNGA are provisions requiring a band to develop and implement codes for leadership selection, government administration, and financial management/accountability. If a band does not develop and pass its own codes the Governor in Council (Cabinet) would impose a default code on it through regulation.

The Act states that each code needs to be in writing and ratified by a secret ballot vote. All members 18 years and older, residing on or off the reserve, are provided an opportunity to participate. In order to be ratified, a code needs the support of a majority of the eligible electors who vote, which must represent at least 25 per cent of all members eligible to vote.

1. Leadership Selection Codes

According to the Act, the Leadership Selection Codes would need to include at least the following elements:

- size and composition of the council;
- mode of selection (a majority of the council members at least would have to be elected);
- term of office (not exceeding five years);
- procedure for selection of members (secret ballot vote for elected members);
- qualifications to vote, run for office and nominate candidates;
- manner of filling vacancies;
- an appeal mechanism;
- policy for removal from office of elected and non-elected members of the council;
- definition of corrupt electoral practices; and
- an amending formula.

If a band operates according to "custom" the Act would also apply, though a few modifications are permitted.

2. Administration of Government Codes

Codes for the governmental administration need to include, at least:

- rules for meetings of the members of the band, including frequency of meetings (at least one per calendar year), procedures to call and publicize meetings, participation of members in meetings and keeping of minutes of proceedings accessible to members;
- rules for meetings of the council, including one meeting open to the band members at least once each calendar year, procedures to call and publicize meetings, manner of making decisions and exercising powers, and record of decisions of the council accessible to members;
- rules and procedures for the development, making and registration of band laws, including reasonable public notice to enable band members and residents to comment before a law is passed, procedure for making laws, and maintenance of a band registry;
- role and authorities of the band administration and its relationship to the council;
- conflict of interest rules for council members and band employees;
- rules relating to access to information under the control of the band, protection of personal information under its control and access by individuals to information about themselves; and
- an amending procedure.

3. Financial Management and Accountability Codes

In designing Financial Management and Accountability Codes a band would need to include at least rules with respect to:

- the preparation of an annual budget (adopted by the council and presented to members of the band);
- the control of expenditures, including signing authorities;
- internal financial control on deposits, assets management, and the purchase of goods and services, including tenders for contracts;
- loans to band members, loans or guarantees to others, and repayment and collection of loans;
- the remuneration of members of council and band employees;
- debt and debt management;
- deficit management and limitations; and
- an amending procedure.

There are also principles for redress in the FNGA if a party is aggrieved because of the violation of a code. The council is required to authorize (through a band by-law) an impartial decision-maker to consider complaints for the breach of a code. This person could order the council or employee to take any measures necessary to rectify the breach or to reconsider the decision. The determination needs to be in writing and a person who has a conflict of interest in relation to the complaint cannot consider a complaint.

Furthermore, if passed, the FNGA will replace sections 81 and 85.1 of the *Indian Act* and give bands the following law-making powers:

- health of residents and prevention of injury to persons;
- prevention of damage to property;
- activities in public places;
- provision of services by or on behalf of the band;
- local works, public utilities and waste management;
- zoning, use and development of land and buildings on reserve;
- nuisances, including unsightly property;
- construction, maintenance, repair, alteration, removal, demolition and abandonment of buildings, other structures and infrastructure, and their use;
- residential tenancies, including powers of eviction;
- traffic;
- regulation of business activities;
- keeping of wild and domestic animals, except fish, and related activities;
- observance of law and order;
- prohibition of sale, exchange, supply, manufacture, possession or use of liquids, preparations or mixtures capable of human consumption that can cause inebriation;
- issuance of licences or permits for a fee, for the purposes of band laws; and
- matters related to the exercise of powers under this section.

Moreover, if passed, the council may adopt laws for band purposes with respect to:

- protection, conservation of natural resources within the reserve and the disposition, for personal and commercial use, of those resources, other than wildlife and fish or resources that can only be disposed of by surrender under the *Indian Act*;
- protection, conservation and management of wildlife and fish on the reserve;
- preservation of culture and language of the band;
- trespassing on the band's reserve or frequenting it for prohibited purposes;
- residence of members of the band and other persons on the reserve;
- survey and allotment of reserve lands among members of the band and establishment of a register of certificates of possession and certificates of occupation relating to allotments and the setting apart of reserve lands for common use, if authority has been granted under section 60 of the *Indian Act*;
- rights of spouses or common law partners and children who reside with members of the band on reserve with respect to any matter in relation to which council may make laws in respect of members;
- authority of Minister to make payments out of capital or revenue moneys to persons whose names were deleted from the band list;

- bringing section 64.1(2) of the *Indian Act* into effect in respect of the band;
- issuance of licences or permits for a fee, for the purposes of band laws;
- the establishment of bodies, their composition, powers and duties;
- the delegation of council's powers and authorities under the FNGA or the *Indian Act*, other than its powers under this section;
- council elections;
- conflicts of interest;
- access to information under the control of the band; protection of personal information under its control and access by individuals to information about themselves;
- conditions under which council may enter into transactions; and
- matters related to the exercise of powers under this section.

Finally, the FNGA would strengthen bands' capacity to enforce laws by providing authority to:

- set the maximum fine amount payable at $10,000, or a term of imprisonment not exceeding three months, or both, except when it is a contravention of a band law that is intended to prevent adverse effects on the environment where the maximum fine amount would be $300,000, or a term of imprisonment not exceeding six months, or both;
- establish a ticketing scheme for infractions of band laws and allow bands to directly collect fines; and
- designate band enforcement officers to:
  - issue notices of violation requiring the accused to pay a fine;
  - inspect at all reasonable times and on any property subject to the law to determine whether the requirements of that law are being observed; and
  - search and seize evidence related to the breach of a band law.

There have been many critiques of the *First Nations Governance Act*. The following article outlines some of these problems.

"HARVARD STUDY GROUP FINDS FAULT WITH FNGA"

By Paul Barnsley
Windspeaker, Canada's National Aboriginal Newspaper, February 2003

The team of academics that conducted the highly-respected Harvard University study of Native American governance and economic development has examined the *First Nations Governance Act* (FNGA) and found it lacking.

The Harvard Project on American Indian Economic Development produced conclusions about what works — and what doesn't — in Native American communities in regards to governance and self-sufficiency ...

Dr. Stephen Cornell, professor of sociology and public administration and policy at the University of Arizona, is also the director of the school's

Udall Center for Studies in Public Policy. He and Dr. Joseph P. Kalt were the co-directors of the Harvard Project. Dr. Miriam Jorgenson and Dr. Manley Begay were the other team members.

Windspeaker reached Cornell at his office in Arizona. He began by making the limitations of the team's FNGA report quite clear. ...

The report concluded that there are three central requirements that are essential for sustainable economic development:

1. Practical sovereignty, meaning genuine decision-making power over internal affairs, governance, resources, institutions, and development strategies;
2. Capable governing institutions, which exercise power effectively, responsibly, and reliably; and
3. Cultural match-formal institutions of government that match Indigenous conceptions of how authority should be organized and exercised.

... "Part of our criticism of the act is that it says that it respects First Nations' right to self-governance, but it seems to have a very modest conception of self-governance. The act then goes on to specify all sorts of things about First Nations government that First Nations have to or should adopt. Our research suggests that a crucial piece of self-government is having some control over how you're governed. If some outsider is going to specify how you govern yourself, that doesn't look much like self-governance to us."

The United States has legislated a form of Native sovereignty, but it appears to Cornell and his fellow researchers that Canada doesn't want to go down the road of sovereignty, even dependant sovereignty, and that shows through clearly in the act.

"The act to us doesn't address issues of jurisdiction. The U.S. research says that issues of jurisdiction are critical. And when I talk about jurisdiction what I really mean is, who is calling the shots? Who's deciding what governmental form will look like? Who's deciding how resources will be used? Who's deciding what development priorities will be? Who's deciding how internal affairs shall operate? The research from the U.S. shows very decidedly that where outsiders are making those decisions, you shouldn't expect to see much in the way of sustainable development," he said.

"When First Nations are making those decisions, it's no guarantee of development, but it does open the door to development. In other words, moving significant jurisdiction ... into the hands of Native nations tends to open up the possibility of sustainable development. One of the concerns about the act is that it doesn't address jurisdictional issues and in fact the act itself constitutes a kind of an imposition of particular governmental models on Native nations which seems to be the opposite of substantive jurisdiction."

Minister Robert Nault's public comments about the bill and the bill itself emphasize improved accountability for First Nation governments. Cornell said there's an important element of accountability that's missing from the FNGA.

"I'm an American Indian nation and I get some money from Washington to run a program that's designed in Washington, reflects Washington bureaucrats concerns and interests, reflects their need to justify what they do to the U.S. Congress or to higher ups within their agencies. It reflects their needs for certain budgetary procedures and concerns," he explained. "Yet I am told that I am accountable for whether or not this program actually works and or whether or not it meets their expectations of how it should perform. Furthermore, I know that is probably the only source of significant resources that I'm going to receive to address a serious problem.

"So I'm being held accountable for whether or not this program I did not design that reflects somebody else's interests, solves my problem. Now I think accountability is critical. But I don't know why the Indian nation in that case should be held accountable for the performance of the program. They had no decision-making power. If they designed the program, then I think they should be held absolutely accountable. And I fully understand that they should have some accountability for how funds are used. I'm not saying we should hand out money and just say, 'Do what you want.' But there is a big range between my giving you money and saying you don't have to account for it and my demanding absolute accountability for you but retaining decision-making power in my own hands."

And there is a second issue related to accountability, he said.

"We are not critical of the concern with accountability, although we think there's a second issue with accountability other than the decision-making power link and that is: to whom are you being accountable? I firmly believe in accountability upwards but we also have to think about accountability downwards and sometimes those two get into conflict," he said. "If I'm a First Nations government, I'm trying to be accountable to my own citizens, I'm trying to be accountable to funders because of the regulations under which I'm operating. And there are times when those things conflict. My citizens are going to be saying to me, 'Why are you running a program like this? It doesn't make sense.'" Accountability is a great buzzword, but it is a complicated business and it has links to other things. And the idea that you can keep decision-making power in your hands and make somebody else accountable, that's simply escaping responsibility. ...

The report also stated that Canada has tried to fit all First Nations into the same box. Cornell said that can be very harmful.

"I think this is something that often the mainstream part of a large society like the United States or like Canada has some difficulty in recognizing. There's enormous diversity out there. People think, 'Oh sure, there's diversity. These guys do this kind of dance and these guys do that kind of ceremony.' We're talking about a more fundamental kind of diversity than that, which is that the citizens of these nations see themselves as peoples. They have distinctive ways of life. They make, in some cases, different assumptions about things. Culture can reach fairly deeply. It's not just a matter of what kind of ceremonies you put on or what kind of art you like," he said. "There's a critical challenge for any government. The people you are governing have to have some fundamental faith in the institutions by which they're being governed. They've got to believe that these institutions resonate somehow with their own sense of what is an appropriate way to govern. In the United States, there's a lot of diversity in those values and in that sense of how it's appropriate to govern. A lot of governing institutions become the objects of rip-off artists and corruption and so forth because people don't believe in them. People think, 'These aren't our institutions, why should we respect them? We didn't plan these institutions.'"

Accommodating diversity is essential for success, he added.

"In the United States we see successful Indian nations governing themselves in radically — and I mean radically — different ways. From traditional pueblos in the American Southwest who have no written constitutions and no electoral codes, not even any elections, but who are doing a very professional and productive job of economic development. They may not have written constitutions and elections codes but they have deeply imbedded cultural rules that manage people's behavior and the people in the community believe in those rules and treat them with respect," he said. "And we have successful Indian nations whose governing institutions look like they came out of my high school civics textbook. What these nations have in common is that in each case the people have respect for the institutions by which they're being governed.

"The danger in a one-size-fits-all solution to these governing problems is that you go out there and impose, fundamentally, a single template of how to govern, paying very little attention to whether or not this template resonates with the Indigenous conception of what government ought to look like. And where it doesn't resonate, I think what you're buying is a whole lot of trouble because within that community what you're effectively going to do is reduce respect for government. You're going to frustrate people who feel, 'We're supposed to be governing ourselves, but we cannot do it in our own ways.' It can lead to kinds of problems where if people don't respect the institutions, they'll use them to their own advantage."

So the corruption [that some people] point to as evidence that First Nations can't govern themselves can be explained by a lack of respect for diversity? Windspeaker asked.

"It is certainly a factor in corruption. I don't think it's the only factor. I mean, the City of Chicago when I was living there, had it. You know, name the community. But this is one of the factors that leads in that direction," he said. "It's a classic mistake that decentralizers make. They say, 'Oh yeah, you guys can govern yourselves. Here's the model that you all have to use.' That's fine if we're all on the same cultural wavelength. I think the First Nations governance act seems to make this assumption that we're all Canadians, we all share the same values, we all look at the world the same way so, of course, this form of government is just perfect for everybody. That's a pipe dream. It's just not true. There are a lot of First Nations out there that might find it perfectly congenial, but there are a lot of First Nations that might scratch their heads and say, 'We have to operate this way? Who came up with this? This isn't us.' So if you pull it out over the long run, the one-size-fits-all approach to the diverse situation is going to buy you inefficiencies, probably increased costs, lots of frustrations. I don't think it's in the government of Canada's interest."

The following case, *Boyer v. Canada*, demonstrates the problems Aboriginal people encounter when governing under the individualistic assumptions motivating certain interpretations of the *Indian Act*. In the *Boyer* case the Court interprets the *Indian Act* such that it incorporates Western ideas of the rule of law and individual autonomy that overturn ancient principles of community stewardship. It raises important questions of how Aboriginal Nations will deal with significant issues concerning their representation in the context of individual rights and collective exercises of governance. It illustrates the continued challenge that the *Indian Act* poses for contemporary First Nations' governance, and foreshadows potential problems with legislation like the FNGA.

BOYER v. CANADA

[1986] 4 C.N.L.R. 53, [1986] 2 F.C. 396 (C.A.); leave to appeal
to S.C.C. refused (1986), 72 N.R. 365*n*

Marceau J.: — This appeal arises from a judgment of the Trial Division ... which dismissed an application, brought by an Indian Chief and the other members of his Band, for a declaration that a lease of reserve land entered into between Her Majesty and an Ontario Corporation, purportedly under the authority of the *Indian Act*, R.S.C. 1970, c. I-6, was void and of no effect. Its scope and difficulty are not immediately apparent, since it presents no real problem as to the facts and involves the construction of only one short subsection of the Act. It so happens, however, that provision contained in that subsection is not only fundamental from a practical point of view, but it concerns one of the features of the legislative scheme adopted in the Act and quite surprisingly it has, apparently, never been scrutinized yet by any judicial authority.

This provision of the Act, on the proper understanding of which the solution of the whole controversy herein depends, is contained in section 58(3). ...

John Corbiere is a member of the Batchewana Indian Band for the benefit of which Rankin Location Indian Reserve No. 15A was set apart. He has been the Chief of the Band for many years and it is said that under his leadership, conditions on the reserve have considerably improved. Corbiere is in lawful possession" of a piece of land located within the reserve. It was allotted to him, in 1973, by the Band Council with the approval of the Minister, and a certificate of possession was then issued confirming his rights thereon. At the time of the allotment, the land was wild and swampy, but its location alongside the St. Mary's River was ideal for development. This indeed was the intention of Corbiere from the outset, and, in 1980, he applied to the Band Council for permission to lease the land, for purpose of development, to a corporation in which he and his wife owned all the outstanding shares. That corporation, the numbered company respondent herein, had been formed by him in order to facilitate financing. A resolution granting permission was adopted at the time; however, Corbiere's project was still vague and a lot had to be done before it could proceed. Various feasibility and other studies were required, financing had to be arranged, decisions had to be made as to the extent and type of development. For the next two years, Corbiere worked on his project, keeping in constant contact with officials of the Department of Indian Affairs (hereinafter sometimes referred to as "The Department"), and, finally, in April 1982, feeling he was at last ready, he applied to the Minister for a lease of the land to his company pursuant to s. 58(3) of the Act. A lease was drafted and sent to the Band Council for comment. The Band responded by disputing the Minister's authority to enter into such a lease without its formal consent, adding a few objections regarding some aspects of the development of the project. Corbiere decided thereupon to modify his plans by replacing a housing complex with a full service marina, and in September 1983, a revised lease giving effect to the new plans was sent to the Band Council, with a request that further comment, if any, be made before December 1. On November 24, the Council passed a resolution again disputing the Minister's authority and formally disapproving the lease and then through its solicitor, it requested a further extension of time in which to respond. The Department felt it was not proper to delay any longer and the lease was executed on December 9, 1983. It was in April 1984 that the proceedings herein were commenced.

As I indicated at the outset, the relief sought in the action is a declaration that the lease entered into, on December 4, 1983, between Her Majesty the Queen as represented by the duly authorized representative of the Minister of Indian Affairs and Northern Development and 488619 Ontario Inc., a corporation carrying on business as Alcor Developments, is void and of no effect. The lease would be so void and of no effect, in the plaintiffs-appellant's submission, because neither the Band nor the Band Council has consented to it. The defendants-respondents dispute the contention that consent was required and in the alternative argue that such consent was, in any event, given.

It may be appropriate, so as to focus on the real issue, to dispose immediately of this alternative position taken by the respondent that consent was in fact given. It is, of course, the 1980 resolution passed by the Band Council purporting to give Corbiere, then still Chief of the Band, permission to lease his land to his company, which is invoked and relied upon. The position, in my view, is untenable. This 1980 resolution was, at the most, one of principle, which may be taken as a sort of consent to the land being leased, but obviously not a consent to a particular lease. If a consent is required, it can certainly not be one limited to principle, it must be an inferred and particularized one. The 1980 resolution cannot be seen as an approval of the lease executed on December 4, 1983. I have no doubt that the only question that has to be determined in order to dispose of the case is whether or not the validity of this lease depended on the consent of the Band or its Council.

In support of their contention that consent was indeed required, the appellants advance two alternative arguments which must be considered in turn.

(1) Their first argument is that the only provision of the Act under which a lease such as the one here in question can be executed by the Minister is that contained in s. 58(1)(*b*), which makes the consent of the

Band a formal and express requirement. Section 58(3) pursuant to which the Minister purported to be acting in fact had no application.

For convenience, I reproduce again the relevant portions of section 58:

> **58.**(1) Where land in a reserve is uncultivated or unused, the Minister may, with the consent of the council of the band,
>
> . . . . .
>
> (b)   where the land is in the lawful possession of any individual, grant lease of such land for agricultural or grazing purposes or for any purpose that is for the benefit of the person in possession; and
>
> . . . . .
>
> (3) The Minister may lease for the benefit of any Indian upon his application for that purpose, the land of which he is lawfully in possession without the land being surrendered.

Paragraph 58(1)(*b*) and not subsection 58(3) would be the operative provision, according to the argument, because the land to be leased was unused and subsection 58(3), by a sort of negative inference, only applies to developed and used land. I fully agree that the land was unused; I do not share the view of the learned Trial Judge that the clearing work done on part of the land and the feasibility studies conducted thereon constituted use within the meaning of the section; I understand the word use" therein as implying occupation or utilization or exploitation of some sort. However, I see no reason here to resort to such an extraordinary means of interpretation as a so-called negative inference. There is absolutely no need to look behind the words to find the respective sphere of application of the two provisions. Indeed, subsection 58(3) only governs when there is a request by the Indian who is in lawful possession of the land, while paragraph 58(1)(*b*) is obviously concerned exclusively with situations where the lawful possessor of the land is indifferent to its use, which is why subsection 58(2) on the one hand contemplates the possibility that improvements on the land be made by the Minister himself and on the other provides that in all cases only part of the proceeds, to be calculated on the basis of a reasonable rent, will go to the Indian in lawful possession. I have no hesitation in saying that paragraph 58(1)(*b*) was not applicable here: the lease could only be executed under subsection 58(3).

The second argument relied on by the appellants in the event that s. 58(3) would be found to be applicable is twofold: consent is required under that provision, they say, either by necessary implication resulting from the context or as an effect of the fiduciary obligation of the Crown toward the Band.

(a) In the first branch of this second argument, the appellants again plead for a construction of the provision that would disregard the apparent meaning of Parliament's words. There are, it is true, in the cases, a few examples where a court has taken upon itself to correct the wording of a provision by reading into it something missing or deleting something redundant. But these examples are quite rare and present instances where the drafting mistakes were quite obvious and the context made it clear that the words used did not convey accurately or completely what was intended ... There is nothing to suggest that drafting mistake may have been made here. If one looks at the strict context in which the provision was enacted, one is certainly not easily led to believe that failure to refer to the consent of the Band in subsection 58(3) was due to an oversight. As noted above, three of the four subsections of section 58 deal with various situations where the Minister is empowered to enter into agreements affecting reserve lands, the first, third and fourth, the second being only an addition to the first, and a reference to the consent of the Band is made in two of them: the contrast is so striking that it could not have passed unnoticed. And if one looks at the broader context there is, in my view, no more reason to think that the provision, taken as it is, does not fit into the scheme of the Act, which leads me to the appellants' main point.

Under the scheme of the *Indian Act*, say the appellants, the interest of a locatee, such as Corbiere, in his or her parcel of reserve land, is subordinate to the communal interest of the Band itself, and the allocation of possessory rights to Band members does not suppress the recognized interest of the Band in the development of allotted lands; besides, the rule is that non-Indians cannot have possession of reserve lands unless these lands have been surrendered by the Band and except for a few limited purposes set out in the Act, the Minister is unable to authorize non-Indian use or occupation of reserve land without consent of the Band or its Council. If, they say, subsection 58(3) was construed literally and made applicable to any land developed or undeveloped, those principles could be disregarded and the scheme of the Act itself would thereby be defeated, which is precisely the case here, since the lease is made in favour of a corporation, which is a non-Indian entity notwithstanding the status of its shareholders.

I am afraid my understanding of the scheme of the *Indian Act* does not correspond totally with that of the appellants. I have already referred to a few sections of the Act where the words and expressions used in subsection 58(3) are defined. It is in fact in these sections and a few others that the basic features of the legislation, with respect to reserve lands, are to be found. I see them as follows. The Band for whose use and benefit a "tract of land" has been set apart by Her Majesty no doubt has an interest in these lands, since it has the right to occupy and possess them. It is an interest which belongs to the Band as a collectivity, and the right to occupy and possess, of which it is comprised, a collective right. This interest can be extinguished by a voluntary surrender by the Band to the Crown or by expropriation for a public purpose, but it cannot be alienated. The Band, however, acting through its Council, has the power to allot, with the approval of the minister, parcels of land in its reserve to Band members. The right of a Band member in the piece of land which is allotted to him and of which he has "lawful possession", although in principle irrevocable, is nevertheless subject to many formal limitations. The member is not entitled to dispose of his right to possession or lease his land to non-member (section 28), nor can he mortgage it, the land being immune from seizure under legal process (section 29), and he may be forced to dispose of his right, if he ceases to be entitled to reside on the reserve (section 25). These are all undoubtedly limitations which make the right of the Indian in lawful possession very different from that of a common law owner in fee simple. But it must nevertheless be carefully noted that all of those limitations have the same goal: to prevent the purpose for which the lands have been set apart, i.e., the use of the Band and its members, from being defeated. None of them concerns the use to which the land may be put or the benefit that can be derived from it. The land being in the reserve, its use will, of course, always remain subject to provincial laws of general application and the zoning bylaws enacted by the Band Council, as for any land in any municipality where zoning bylaws are in force, but otherwise I do not see how or why the Indian in lawful possession of land in a reserve could be prevented from developing it as he wishes. There is nothing in the legislation that could be seen as "subjugating" his right to another right of the same type existing simultaneously in the Band Council. To me, the "allotment" of a piece of land in a reserve shifts the right to the use and benefit thereof from being the collective right of the Band to being the individual and personalized right of the locatee. The interest of the Band, in the technical and legal sense, has disappeared or is at least suspended. This being my understanding of the scheme of the Act, not only do I disagree with the contention that the principles embodied therein require that the words "with the consent of the Band" be read into the provision of subsection 58(3), I think that those principles would be frustrated by doing so. ...

(b) In the second branch of their argument the consent of the Band was required for a lease under subsection 58(3), the appellants speak of an incident of the Crown's fiduciary obligations arising out of the inherent nature of Indian title", and they quote the Supreme Court decision in *Guerin v. Canada*, [1984] 2 S.C.R. 335; 55 N.R. 161 [*sub nom. Guerin v. The Queen*, [1985] 1 C.N.L.R 120], as their authority.

I will say first that I have some difficulty in understanding how that submission can have a real role to play in the context of the action as instituted. The relief sought is not damages but a declaration that the lease is null and of no effect. I fail to see how the breach of a fiduciary duty on the part of the Minister in entering into a contract could have the effect of nullifying the contract itself when all legal requirements for its execution have been complied with. But in any event, I simply do not think that the Crown, when acting under subsection 58(3), is under any fiduciary obligation to the Band. When a lease is entered into pursuant to subsection 58(3), the circumstances are different [from *Guerin*] altogether: no alienation is contemplated, the right to be transferred temporarily is the right to use which belongs to the individual Indian in possession and no interest of the Band can be affected (I repeat that of course I am talking about interest in a technical and legal sense; it is obvious that morally speaking the Band may always be concerned by the behaviour and attitude of its members). In my view, when he acts under subsection 58(3), the duty of the Minister is, so to speak, only toward the law: he cannot go beyond the power granted to him, which he would do if, under the guise of a lease, he was to proceed to what would be, for all practical purposes, an alienation of the land (certainly not the case here, the lease being for a term of 21 years with no special renewal clause); and he cannot let extraneous consideration enter into the exercise of his discretion, which would be the case if he was to take into account anything other than the benefit of the Indian in lawful possession of the land and at whose request he is acting. The duty of the Minister is simply not towards the Band.

The conclusion to me is clear. Bearing in mind the structure of the *Indian Act* and the clear wording of subsection 58(3) thereof, there is no basis for thinking that the Minister is required to secure the consent of the Band or the Band Council before executing a lease such as the one here in question. It seems that the Act which has been so much criticised for its paternalistic spirit has nevertheless seen fit to give the individual member of a Band a certain autonomy, relative independence from the dictates of his Band Council, when it comes to the exercise of his entrepreneurship and the development of his land.

This appeal has, in my view, no merit and should be dismissed with costs.

MacGuigan J.: — I agree with the disposition of this appeal proposed by my colleague, Mr. Justice Marceau, and also with his reasons for that disposition. My comments are therefore of a supplementary nature.

This case embodies a new version of the age-old problem of the person and the state, as particularized in the microcosm of an Indian community under the *Indian Act* ("The Act"). ...

In the absence of any clear guide from statute or precedent, a court must I believe look for guidance to the words in the preamble of the *Constitution Act, 1867* that Canada is to have a "Constitution similar in principle to that of the United Kingdom".

Rand J., made bold to say in *Saumur v. City of Quebec and Attorney-General for Quebec*, [1953] 2 S.C.R. 299, 329, that:

> Strictly speaking, civil rights arise from positive law; but freedom of speech, religion and the inviolability of the person, are original freedoms which are at once the necessary attributes of self-expression of human beings and the primary conditions of their community life within a legal order. It is in the circumscription of these liberties by the creation of civil rights in persons who may be injured by their exercise, and by the sanctions of public law, that the positive law operates. What we realize is the residue inside that periphery.

Abbott J., went further *in obiter dicta* in *Switzman v. Elbling and Attorney-General of Quebec*, [1957] S.C.R. 285, 328:

> Although it is not necessary, of course, to determine this question for purposes of the present appeal, the Canadian Constitution being declared to be similar in principle to that of the United Kingdom, I am also of opinion that as our constitutional Act now stands, Parliament itself could not abrogate this right of discussion and debate.

This is similar in approach to the Western tradition succinctly expressed by the French philosopher Jacques Maritain, in *Man and the State* (Chicago, University of Chicago Press, 1951), at p. 13, "...man is by no means for the State. The State is for man".

However, even the more traditional and much more limited view of liberty espoused by A.V. Dicey would in this instance lead to the same result. Although for Dicey the extent of liberty depends upon what is left permissible by law, what is characteristic of the English Constitution is the way in which the Courts maintain the traditional sphere of freedom, *Introduction to the Study of the Law of the Constitution* (10th Ed. 1959) (E.C.S. Wade), p. 201:

Where ... [as in England] the right to individual freedom is part of the constitution because it is inherent in the ordinary law of the land, the right is one which can hardly be destroyed without a thorough revolution in the institutions and manners of the nation.

Even on this interpretation, the freedom of the individual person in Canada, with the constitution similar in principle to that of the United Kingdom, is prior to the exigencies of the community.

In fact, where group rights are, exceptionally, given priority, the Canadian Constitution so provides specifically. ... *The Charter of Rights and Freedoms* is itself a fundamental affirmation of the rights and freedoms of the individual person. In sum, in the absence of legal provisions to the contrary, the interests of individual persons will be deemed to have precedence over collective rights. In the absence of law to the contrary, this must be as true of Indian Canadians as of others.

The appellants' final argument was that the *Indian Act* must be interpreted in the light of the preference of Indian culture for group rights. Unfortunately for this contention, there is no evidence in the record to establish it or indeed with respect to Indian culture at all, and it is not a matter of which a court could simply take judicial notice.

Finally, it is highly material that the valid concerns of the Indian community against adverse land use are well protected by its powers under paragraph 81(g). The fact that the band council did not choose to exercise its zoning powers and probably cannot now do so retroactively is no reason to create a broader alternative right.

H. CONCLUSION

The question of how to facilitate and implement Aboriginal governance more fully is just now beginning to unfold. Respect for and acceptance of Aboriginal governance will not be easy to accomplish, even though historic precedent would allow it, and contemporary instruments in domestic and international law can accommodate it. For many who struggle from day to day under intolerable conditions the pace of change is painstakingly slow. Thirty years have now passed since Prime Minister Trudeau attempted to eliminate Indian rights in Canada. At the time, Harold Cardinal wrote an influential book entitled *The Unjust Society* to refute this drive. He described the denial of Indian citizenship and governance rights that faced Aboriginal people at that time. His message captured the feelings of Aboriginal people everywhere. He chronicled a disturbing tale of how Indians were marginalized in Canada through bureaucratic neglect, political indifference and societal ignorance. He labelled Canada's treatment of Indians as "cultural genocide", and in the process gave widespread literary presence to the absence of Indian rights. In convincing tones he outlined thoughtful solutions to overcome threats to Aboriginal governance, organized around the central theme of Indian control of Indian affairs. His work in proposing the contours for Aboriginal governance was groundbreaking. He advocated the strengthening of Indian organizations, the abolition of the Department of Indian Affairs, educational reform, restructured social institutions, broad-based economic development and the "immediate recognition of all Indian rights for the re-establishment, review and renewal of all existing Indian treaties". Cardinal's ideas resonated within Indian country and parallel proposals became the mainstay of Indian political discourse for the next three decades.

Three decades later the massive five-volume *Report of the Royal Commission on Aboriginal Peoples* was released. It contained many of the same ideas Cardinal had put forward a generation earlier. The Commission provided an account of the violation of Aboriginal rights, and called for their immediate recognition and renewal. The Report recorded the continued diminishment of Aboriginal control over their affairs of life and governance. It demonstrated that the problems Cardinal profiled stubbornly remain. Despite some notable achievements in the intervening years, such as the recognition and affirmation of Aboriginal rights in the Constitution, it illustrated how indigenous citizenship with the land is increasingly tenuous. In their broad outlines, Cardinal and the Commission's messages are notable for their similarity. Aboriginal people are suffering, their rights are being abrogated, and the answer to this challenge is Aboriginal control of Aboriginal affairs. Like Cardinal, though more elaborately and expansively, the Commission recommended a series of legislative and policy goals: such as the strengthening of Aboriginal nations, the abolition of the Department of Indian Affairs, educational reform, restructured social institutions, broad-based economic development, and the immediate recognition of all Aboriginal rights for the re-establishment, review, renewal and creation of treaties.

While many efforts have been put forward over the years to strengthen Aboriginal governance, as this chapter has demonstrated it is still the case that contemporary dynamics of legal, political, economic and social power place non-Aboriginal governments in a domineering position relative to Aboriginal governments. It will continue to be a great challenge to unburden Aboriginal governance from the constrictions and obstacles they encounter. The traditional laws, values and principles that guided Aboriginal people in their past, and which still have a great presence in many communities today, are stifled by alien institutions and ideologies. The acceptance of these laws is also restrained by bias and prejudice that discounts the authenticity and utility of these ancient legal genealogies. Yet First Nations legal traditions are strong, dynamic and can be interpreted flexibly to deal with the pressing issues these communities encounter. Their principles can be drawn from ancient stories, customs and codes, historic agreements with the Crown, Canadian common law, constitutional law, and contemporary international instruments. They can be implemented through proclamation, direct action, litigation, and negotiation. The framework of the *Indian Act* does not provide a good base on which to build healthy and productive communities. The *Boyer* case illustrates the problems encountered in trying to structure relations under this model. Cooperation, imagination and political will are needed to make progress in facilitating Aboriginal governance. Aboriginal law and philosophies can be given a more central place within the communities. Historic agreements could be recognized and affirmed as a base upon which contemporary relations can be forged. Section 35(1) of the *Constitution Act* could be interpreted in a broad and generous way to recognize and affirm an inherent jurisdictional base for governance. This chapter has introduced these issues in the hope that further critical and constructive inquiry can illuminate the path for the achievement of effective Aboriginal governance.

CHAPTER 10

TAXATION

A. INTRODUCTION

Taxation raises fundamental issues of representation, participation and citizenship. As such, the development of the Canadian tax structure has been substantially influenced by constitutional considerations. As earlier chapters have demonstrated, however, Aboriginal peoples have not always received fair treatment within Canada's constitutional structure. This has created considerable tension between Aboriginal peoples and the Crown. Taxation is a significant factor in wealth creation and redistribution, yet materially Aboriginal peoples remain among the poorest group in Canada. This has also generated conflict as Aboriginal people seek to use taxation to produce and retain wealth within their own communities. This chapter explores the history and treatment of Indian taxation in Canada. It provides examples of how the law has interpreted provisions for customs and excise taxes, incomes taxes, sales taxes and corporate income taxes relative to Indians.

B. HISTORY

RICHARD H. BARTLETT, INDIANS AND TAXATION IN CANADA, 3RD ED.

(Saskatoon: Native Law Centre, 1992) 1-14 (references omitted)

Historical Overview

1. Canadian Indian Legislation, Policy and Interpretation

Historically Canadian Indian policy as contained in the *Indian Act* of Canada has been described as possessing two components. Firstly, "'civilizing' the Indian population and achieving assimilation and integration as soon as possible," and secondly, "[p]rotection of the Indians and their land from abuse and imposition ... until such time, as being 'civilized,' such protection was superfluous." Such a protection from "abuse and imposition" was considered to require an exemption from taxation of Indians and their lands. In 1850 the Province of Canada *passed An Act for the protection of the Indians in Upper Canada from imposition, and the property occupied or enjoyed by them from trespass and injury*. Section 4 provided:

IV. That no taxes shall be levied or assessed upon any Indian or any person intermarried with any Indian for or in respect of any of the said Indian lands, nor shall any taxes or assessments whatsoever be levied or imposed upon any Indian or any person inter-married with any Indian so long as he, she or they shall reside on Indian lands not ceded to the Crown, or which having been so ceded may have been again set apart by the Crown for the occupation of Indians.

Nor could taxation be assessed with respect to lands "held by Her Majesty or any other person or body corporate in trust for or for the use of any tribe or body of Indians."

The 1857 *Act to Encourage the Gradual Civilization of Indian Tribes* afforded an explicit statement of the policy of assimilation in providing for the enfranchisement of Indians of a "sufficiently advanced" education or "sufficiently intelligent to be capable of managing their own affairs. Enfranchisement removed the disabilities and distinctions imposed upon the Indian people for their protection. In particular, section 14 provided:

14. Lands allotted under this Act to an Indian enfranchised under it shall be liable to taxes and all other obligations and duties under the Municipal and School Laws of the section of the Province in which such land is situated, as he shall also be in respect of them and of his other property.

The exemption from taxation declared in the 1850 legislation remained unchanged until the first consolidation of Canadian Indian legislation provided in the *Indian Act* of 1876. It appears that until that time the exemption from taxation outside Upper Canada was assumed, rather than declared, to apply. The need for consolidation of Indian legislation became apparent with the settlement of the Northwest Territories and the establishment of treaty relations with Indians inhabiting the area. The 1876 Act did not contain substantial changes from previously established legislative policy, but the ambit of the exemption from taxation was altered. Sections 64 and 65 provided:

64. No Indian or non-treaty Indian shall be liable to be taxed for any real or personal property, unless he holds real estate under lease or in fee simple, or personal property, outside of the reserve or special reserve, in which case he shall be liable to be taxed for such real or personal property at the same rate as other persons in the locality in which it is situated.
65. All land vested in the Crown, or in any person or body corporate, in trust for or for the use of any Indian or non-treaty Indian, or any band or irregular band of Indians or non-treaty Indians, shall be exempt from taxation.

Section 88 declared that upon enfranchisement "the provisions of this Act and of any Act or law making any distinction between the legal rights, privileges, disabilities and liabilities of Indians and those of Her Majesty's other subjects shall cease to apply." The exemption from taxation contained in the *Indian Act* of 1876 is significantly different from that of the legislation of 1850. The wording of the 1850 legislation ruled out taxation upon Indian lands and Indians resident thereon. The 1876 statute explicitly exempts the real or personal property of an Indian situated on a reserve, but does not expressly extend to the person. The exemption remained almost unaltered until 1951. The only two changes in that entire period consisted in an amendment in 1884, which sought to continue the exemption upon lands allotted to enfranchised Indians until declared taxable by proclamation, and an amendment in 1888, which clarified the liability to taxation of surrendered lands.

In 1951 the exemption was rewritten and is now embodied in sections 87 and 90 of the *Indian Act* ...:

In *Mitchell v. Peguis Indian Band*, La Forest J. in the Supreme Court of Canada pointed to the "historical record" of section 87 and concluded that it constituted part of a legislative "package" which bears the impress of an obligation to Native peoples which the Crown has recognized at least since the signing of the Royal Proclamation of 1763. From that time on, the Crown has always acknowledged that it is honour-bound to shield Indians from any efforts by non-Natives to dispossess Indians of the property which they hold qua Indians, i.e. their land base and the chattels on that land base. ...

2. Indian Tradition and the Treaties

... The written terms of the treaties nowhere refer to taxation. Oral assurances and promises are recorded which intimated that the Indians should be prepared to adopt changes in their way of life and yet suggested that no compulsion to do so would be exerted. Thus in 1876 the Treaty Commissioner for Treaty No. 6 observed:

> I accordingly shaped my address, so as to give them confidence in the intentions of the Government, and to quiet their apprehensions. I impressed strongly on them the necessity of changing their present mode of life, and commencing to make homes and gardens for themselves, so as to be prepared for the diminution of the buffalo and other large animals, which is going on so rapidly.
> ... I then fully explained to them the proposals I had to make, that we did not wish to interfere with their present mode of living, but would assign them reserves and assist them as was being done elsewhere, in commencing to farm.
> ... [W]hat was offered was a gift as they still had their old mode of living.

The only specific reference to taxation in the oral assurances recorded at the time of the treaties is contained in the report of the Treaty Commissioner in respect of Treaty No. 8 in 1899:

> There was expressed at every point the fear that the making of the treaty would be followed by the curtailment of the hunting and fishing privileges, and many were impressed with the notion that the treaty would lead to taxation and enforced military service.
> We assured them that the treaty would not lead to any forced interference with their mode of life, that it did not open the way to the imposition of any tax, and that there was no fear of enforced military service.

In modern times agreements have been signed with respect to Northern Quebec (the James Bay (1975) and Northeastern Quebec (1978) Agreements), the Western Arctic (1984), the Yukon (1991), and the Eastern Arctic (1991). The *James Bay Agreement* (cl. 2.11) preserved the exemptions conferred by the *Indian Act*. The agreements in the Yukon and Northwest Territory have sought to eliminate or restrict the application of the exemptions. This pattern reflects a history of the North in which reserves were not established and accordingly no tax exemption, focused on situs on a reserve, was recognized. A factor in the refusal of the Dene-Metis in 1990 to ratify the agreement in the western half of the Northwest Territory was the attempt to similarly restrict the exemption in that region.

3. Indian Powers of Taxation under the *Indian Act*

Federal legislation has acknowledged only the most limited Indian power to levy taxes. In 1884 the *Indian Advancement Act* which sought to replace government by chiefs in council with government by council, provided that bands considered "advanced," and accordingly "fit," might assess and tax "lands of Indians enfranchised, or in possession of lands by location ticket in the reserve" subject to the approval and confirmation of the Superintendent General. The assessment was subject to one half of a maximum of one percent of the assessed value of the land. The revenue might only be expended on matters in respect of which the council might pass by-laws. The provision remained unchanged until 1951. No Indian band in Western Canada was considered "fit" to exercise the power first conferred in 1884. In 1951 the modern form of the taxation power was introduced along with the power to license businesses. In June 1988 the "Kamloops" amendment to the *Indian Act* sought by Chief Manny Jules of the Kamloops Indian Band received Royal Assent. It clarified and consolidated the power of band councils to levy taxes on reserve lands leased to non-Indians, but also limited the power of band councils to raise money by licensing. It also removed the requirement that in order to exercise the power to levy taxes and raise money the Governor in Council must have declared that the band had reached an "advanced stage of development. ..."

4. The Franchise and Taxation

The principle form of revenue of the founding colonies of Confederation in 1867 was customs and excise. It was accordingly determined that as the federal government was to assume the more burdensome expenditures it should be accorded unlimited powers of taxation, including the tariff. Provincial powers were restricted to direct taxation and thereby provided for municipal real property taxation. ...

Necessity, however, required that the provinces utilize their powers of taxation, and accordingly British Columbia in 1876, and Prince Edward Island in 1894, levied personal income taxes. The expenses of World War I caused the imposition of a federal income tax in 1917, and shortly thereafter the federal sales tax was introduced. Heavy capital expenditures after the war compelled the provinces to devise new methods of taxation; gasoline taxes and liquor control "were to build many a road and school." Provincial sales taxes were not introduced until the Depression. By 1940 there were provincial retail taxes in Saskatchewan and Quebec, and municipal sales taxes in Montreal and Quebec City. Today the only province in which no sales tax is levied is Alberta.

The early reliance of provincial governments upon real property taxation effectively disenfranchised Indians resident upon reserves. The Indian interest in reserved lands was not entered upon the assessment list upon which the right to vote depended. Thus section 4 of the *Election Act* of the Province of Ontario passed in 1876 provided:

> To remove doubts, it is hereby declared that all Indians, or persons with part Indian blood, who have been duly enfranchised, and all Indians or persons with part Indian blood, who do not reside among Indians, though they participate in the annuities, interest moneys and rents of a tribe, band or body of Indians, shall be entitled to vote, subject to the same qualifications in other respects, and to the same provisions and restrictions, as other persons in the electoral district.

The section recognized the right to vote of enfranchised Indians who had been allotted sufficiently valuable land or those Indians, albeit not enfranchised, who had left the reserve and managed to acquire sufficient real property so as to be eligible to vote.

Until 1885 federal elections were governed by existing provincial statutes. In 1885 the Conservative government of Sir John A. Macdonald passed the *Electoral Franchise Act* to provide for federal elections. The franchise was extended to Indians in the east possessed of real property on reserve valued in excess of one hundred and fifty dollars and not otherwise qualified. The Six Nations Indians expressed concern as to the implications of the extension of the franchise. Chief Jones wrote to Macdonald:

> Many of the Indians on the Grand River Reservation have been told, that in case they received the right to vote, then Treaty Rights with the Government would not be able to compel the Government to observe and carry out the treaties. ...

Macdonald wrote to Chief Johnson of Desoranto as follows:

> I am informed that you are under the impression that if an Indian on a reserve should exercise the franchise under the late act it would render him liable to pay additional taxes. This is altogether a mistake. The Grits who did all they could to deprive the Indians of the right of voting are spreading that falsehood in order to prevent the original proprietors of the soil of this country from standing on a footing of equality with the white men who have come into it. I can assure you that an Indian will not increase his liability, his burdens, or his duties as a subject or citizen by voting at the election. He will stand exactly in the same position in all respects the hour after he may vote as he stood the hours before he voted.

The Grits [Liberals] were returned to power in 1896 and the *Franchise Act* of 1898 eliminated the separate federal franchise. In 1920 the federal franchise was re-established but excluded:

> ... an Indian ordinarily resident on an Indian reservation, (d) provided, however, that any Indian who has served in the naval, military or air forces of Canada in the war declared by His Majesty on the fourth day of August, one thousand nine hundred and fourteen, against the Empire of Germany and subsequently, against other powers, shall be qualified to vote ...

In 1944 the franchise was extended to the Indians who fought in World War II, and in 1948 to the spouses of those who had served in the two World Wars. The anxiety of the Six Nations, expressed sixty-five years before, proved well-founded when in 1950 the franchise was extended to those Indians who,

... executed a waiver, in a form prescribed by the Minister of Citizenship and Immigration, of exemptions under the *Indian Act* from taxation on and in respect of personal property, and subsequent to the execution of such waiver a writ has issued ordering an election in any electoral district.

The Minister of Citizenship and Immigration, who moved second reading of the amendment in the House of Commons observed:

> The exemption from taxation of real personal property held by Indians on reserves has been modified so that it will not apply to the personal property of Indians ordinarily resident on reserves, other than veterans of the first and second great wars, and their wives, who execute a waiver under an amendment to *the Dominion Elections Act*, 1938; otherwise the exemption from taxation stands as it has stood since this provision was enacted in 1876. It is proposed to apply this only to personal property; the real property on the reserve is held in trust by the Crown and does not belong to the individual Indian, but is held for the use and benefit of the band or community as a whole, and it is felt that such property should not be taxed, as the individual Indian has only an occupational interest in the land. ...

A member of the House of Commons responded:

> And yet at least in my opinion,... we ask the Indian to barter his right to the exemption for the privilege of voting in a federal election. That is something which I feel is fundamentally and basically wrong.
> We inquire why this is done, and the minister says he does not want to set up a special category of Indians. It seems to me there are about one hundred Indians in reserves in Canada — and I give that figure only as a rough guess — who are earning taxable incomes, or incomes that would be exempt under our present legislation. I would be very pleased to have the minister correct me if I am wrong. In other words we are disfranchising about 125,000 people, or at least making it difficult for them, and asking them to waive some of their rights, in order that the Department of National Revenue here in Ottawa may collect some revenue from about one hundred Indians.

The franchise granted to the Eskimos in that year was not subject to any conditions. The Minister of Citizenship and Immigration explained that "[t]he Eskimo, not being exempt from taxation, may vote." In 1951 the franchise was extended to those Indians and their spouses who served in the Korean War. It was not until 1960 that the federal franchise was finally extended to Indians upon the same conditions as other citizens of Canada. The restriction upon the franchise requiring a waiver of the taxation exemption was repealed. The Minister of Citizenship and Immigration expressed a dramatically different view from that of nine years previously and reiterated the remarks of Sir John A. Macdonald nearly a century before:

> The proposal now before the house is that the restriction which applies to the Indian living on reserves be abolished so that all Indians will have the right to vote on the same basis as other citizens. Many reasons can be forwarded in support of this proposal. Foremost is the fact that it is not in keeping with our democratic principles that there should be citizens — and all Indians are citizens — who are restricted in the exercise of one of the fundamental rights of a democracy, the right to participate in the election of their representatives in parliament. ...

C. CUSTOMS AND EXCISE

Aboriginal perspectives on Indian taxation usually begin with the idea that they are not merely "exempt" from taxation, but "immune" from its application because of their unique citizenship within Canada. The claim for tax immunity stems from the idea that Indians retain a measure of sovereignty that absolves them from Canadian taxation and obligates them to contribute to their own governments. The United States Supreme Court has taken this approach and recognized a wide range of immunities against state and federal taxation for Indigenous peoples in that country. No Canadian court has pursued the issue of taxation from this perspective or recognized statutory Indian taxation provisions as an immunity from taxation. Despite these rulings, many Aboriginal people continue to claim these immunities.

FRANCIS v. CANADA

[1956] S.C.R. 618, 3 D.L.R. (2d) 641

The judgment of **Kerwin C.J., Taschereau** and **Fauteux JJ.** was delivered by:

The Chief Justice: — This is an appeal against a decision of the Exchequer Court dismissing the Petition of Right of the suppliant (an Indian resident in a reserve in Canada) and the question is whether three articles, a washing machine, a refrigerator and an oil heater, brought by him into Canada from the United States of America are subject to duties of customs and sales tax under the relevant statutes of Canada. None was paid and in fact the articles were not brought into this country at a port of entry; they were subsequently placed under customs detention or seizure and in order to obtain their release, the appellant, under protest, paid the sum demanded by the Crown. The Petition of Right claims the return of this money and a declaration that no duties or taxes were payable by the appellant with respect to the goods. ...

The appellant falls within the definition of "Indian" in s. 2(1)(g) of R.S.C. 1951, c. 29 and at all relevant times he resided on the St. Regis Indian Reserve in St. Regis village in the westerly part of the Province of Quebec, which adjoins an Indian reserve in the State of New York in the United States of America, the residents of both reserves belonging to the St. Regis Tribe of Indians. The articles were brought into Canada in the manner already described in order to lay the foundation for the present proceeding as a test case.

The first claim advanced on behalf of the appellant is that these imposts need not be paid because of the following provisions of Article III of the Treaty of Amity, Commerce and Navigation, between His Britannic Majesty and the United States of America signed on November 19, 1794, and generally known as the *Jay Treaty*: —

> No Duty on Entry shall ever be levied by either Party on Peltries brought by Land, or Inland Navigation into the said Territories respectively, nor shall the Indians passing or re-passing with their own proper Goods and Effects of whatever nature, pay for the same any Impost or Duty whatever. But

Goods in Bales or other large Packages unusual among Indians shall not be considered as Goods belonging *bona fide* to Indians.

In view of the conclusion at which I have arrived, it is unnecessary to deal with the question raised by the respondent that the articles imported by the appellant were not his "own proper goods and effects".

The *Jay Treaty* was not a Treaty of Peace and it is clear that in Canada such rights and privileges as are here advanced of subjects of a contracting party to a treaty are enforceable by the Courts only where the treaty has been implemented or sanctioned by legislation. ...

I agree with Mr. Justice Cameron that clause (*b*) of s. 86 of *The Indian Act* does not apply, because customs duties are not taxes upon the personal property of an Indian situated on a Reserve but are imposed upon the importation of goods into Canada. ...

The appeal should be dismissed with costs.

Rand J. (Cartwright J. concurring): — ... The claim is based first on that clause of art. 3 of the Jay Treaty between Great Britain and the United States of 1794 ... and on the 9th article of the *Treaty of Ghent*, 1815, between the same states. ...

... Following [early treaties] large-scale transfers of Indians belonging to the Six Nations and more western tribes took place from the United States to lands north of Lake Erie. ...

In 1794 European settlement of North America was in its early stages. In 1768 a treaty had been made with the Indians that had placed the western boundary of the advance south of the Great Lakes at the Ohio river. The lands to the north and west of those lakes were within the charter granted to the Hudson's Bay Company. The section of the international boundary from the Lake of the Woods to the Rocky Mountains was not fixed until 1818 and that beyond to the Pacific ocean until 1846. Confederation succeeded in 1867 and a few years later drew within its orbit all the territory reaching to the Pacific and the far north. Government in relation to the Indians was thus greatly extended. ...

Indian affairs generally ... have for over a century been the subject of expanding administration throughout what is now the Dominion, superseding the local enactments following the treaty designed to meet an immediate urgency. ... There followed the slow but inevitable march of events ... and today there remain along the border only fragmentary reminders of that past. The strife that had waged over the free and ancient hunting grounds and their fruits, lands which were divided between two powers, but that life in its original mode and scope has long since disappeared.

These considerations seem to justify the conclusion that both the Crown and Parliament of this country have treated the provisional accommodation as having been replaced by an exclusive code of new and special rights and privileges. Appreciating fully the obligation of good faith toward these wards of the state, there can be no doubt that the conditions constituting the raison d'être of the clause were and have been considered such as would in foreseeable time disappear. That a radical change of this nature brings about a cession of such a treaty provision appears to be supported by the authorities available: McNair, *The Law of Treaties*, 378-381.

Assuming that art. 9 of the *Treaty of Ghent* extended to the exemption, it was only an "engagement" to restore which, by itself, could do no more than to revive the clause in its original treaty effect, and supplementary action was clearly envisaged. Whether, then, the time of its expiration has been reached or not it is not here necessary to decide; it is sufficient to say that there is no legislation now in force implementing the stipulation. ...

The appeal must therefore be dismissed and with costs if demanded.

Unlike Canada, the United States recognized that the *Jay Treaty* provided authority for some differential treatment for Indians, in *Karnuth v. United States* (1929), 23 Am. J. Intl. L. (U.S.S.C.); *U.S. v. Garrow*, 88 F.2d 318 (C.C.P.A. 1937). The issue addressed in *Francis* is still not settled in the minds of many Aboriginal people in Canada. It is difficult for some to accept some of the reasons upon which the judgment rests, that "There followed the slow but inevitable march of events ... and today there remain along the border only fragmentary reminders of [the Aboriginal] past. The strife ... waged over the free and ancient [Aboriginal] hunting grounds and their fruits, [the land] divided between two powers" and the Aboriginal mode of life has long since disappeared. Aboriginal people believe that such justifications amount to an erasure of their continuing presence as contemporary political powers. They are gravely concerned when treaty and other rights are abrogated on the assumption that the development of Canada and the United States inevitably fragmented their rights and way of life such that any justification for the protection of these rights has "long since disappeared".

As a result of dissatisfaction with the Canadian interpretation of the Jay Treaty, Grand Chief Mitchell of the Mohawks of Akwesasne brought the case of *Mitchell v. M.N.R.*, below. In this challenge, however, instead of framing the issue under the Treaty, Chief Mitchell asserted that the Mohawk possessed an existing Aboriginal right to cross the border free of customs and excise taxes.

MITCHELL v. M.N.R.

(2001), 199 D.L.R. (4th) 385 (S.C.C.)

McLachlin C.J.C. (Gonthier, Iacobucci, Arbour and LeBel JJ.): —

Introduction

This case raises the issue of whether the Mohawk Canadians of Akwesasne have the right to bring goods into Canada from the United States for collective use and trade with other First Nations without paying customs duties. Grand Chief Michael Mitchell claims that his people have an aboriginal right that ousts Canadian customs law. The government replies that no such right exists, first because the evidence does not support it and second because such a right would be fundamentally contrary to Canadian sovereignty. At the heart of the case lies the question of the evidence that must be adduced to establish an aboriginal right.

Chief Mitchell is a Mohawk of Akwesasne, a Mohawk community located just west of Montreal, and a descendant of the Mohawk nation, one of the polities comprising the Iroquois Confederacy prior to the arrival of Europeans. On March 22, 1988, Chief Mitchell crossed the international border from the United States into Canada, arriving at the Cornwall customs office. He brought with him some blankets, bibles, motor oil, food, clothing, and a washing machine, all of which had been purchased in the United States. He declared the goods to the Canadian customs agents but asserted that he had aboriginal and treaty rights which exempted him from paying duty on the goods. After some discussion, the customs agents notified Chief Mitchell that he would be charged $142.88 in duty, and they permitted him to continue into Canada. Chief Mitchell, along with other Mohawks of Akwesasne, presented everything but the motor oil to the Mohawk community of Tyendinaga. The gifts were intended to symbolize the renewal of the historic trading relationship between the two communities. The oil was taken to a store in Akwesasne territory for resale to members of that community. In September of 1989, Chief Mitchell was served with a Notice of Ascertained Forfeiture claiming $361.64 for unpaid duty, taxes and penalties.

I conclude that the aboriginal right claimed has not been established. The sparse and tenuous evidence advanced in this case to prove the existence of pre-contact Mohawk trading north of the Canada-United States boundary simply cannot support the claimed right. Even if deference is paid to the trial judge on this finding, any such trade was clearly incidental, and not integral, to the Mohawk culture. As a result, Chief Mitchell must pay duty on the goods he imported to Canada. ...

What is the Nature of Aboriginal Rights?

... European settlement did not terminate the interests of aboriginal peoples arising from their historical occupation and use of the land. To the contrary, aboriginal interests and customary laws were presumed to survive the assertion of sovereignty, and were absorbed into the common law as rights, unless (1) they were incompatible with the Crown's assertion of sovereignty, (2) they were surrendered voluntarily via the treaty process, or (3) the government extinguished them: see B. Slattery, "Understanding Aboriginal Rights" (1987), 66 Can. Bar Rev. 727. Barring one of these exceptions, the practices, customs and traditions that defined the various aboriginal societies as distinctive cultures continued as part of the law of Canada. ...

The common law status of aboriginal rights rendered them vulnerable to unilateral extinguishment, and thus they were "dependent upon the good will of the Sovereign": see *St. Catherine's Milling and Lumber Co. v. The Queen* (1888), 14 App. Cas. 46 (P.C.), at p. 54. This situation changed in 1982, when Canada's constitution was amended to entrench existing aboriginal and treaty rights. ...

[T]he issue is whether the act which gave rise to the case at bar is an expression of [an Aboriginal] right. Aboriginal rights are not frozen in their pre-contact form: ancestral rights may find modern expression. The question is whether the impugned act represents the modern exercise of an ancestral practice, custom or tradition.

What is the Aboriginal Right Claimed?

... Chief Mitchell characterizes his claim as the right to enter Canada from the United States with personal and community goods, without paying customs or duties, and the right to trade these goods with other First Nations. On the strength of this claimed right, he crossed the Canada-United States boundary with personal and community goods, the action giving rise to the case at bar. Although the motor oil was the only item transported by Chief Mitchell that was destined for resale, it can only be concluded that Chief Mitchell's actions — and his case — focused in fact on trade. The claimants asserted that "trade and commerce [is] central to their soul". Witness after witness was asked to describe historical Mohawk trading practices. Furthermore, when Chief Mitchell exercised his alleged right, all of the goods brought into Canada were trade-related: they were intended as gifts to seal a trade agreement with Tyendinaga and to signify renewed trading relations, in accordance with customary practice. Therefore the first factor, the action claimed as an exercise of an aboriginal right, suggests that the heart of the claim is the right to bring goods across the Canada-United States border for purposes of trade.

The second factor, the nature of the conflict between the claimed right and the relevant legislation, while more neutral, does not displace this conclusion. The law in conflict with the alleged right is the Customs Act. It applies both to personal goods and goods for trade.

The third factor to be considered in characterizing the claim is the relevant traditions and practices of the aboriginal people in question. The ancestral aboriginal practices upon which the claimant relies provide a strong indication of the nature and scope of the right claimed. In this case, the claimants emphasize their ancestral trading practices; indeed these practices and the alleged limitations on them raised by the appellant, lie at the heart of the case. As noted, the claimants assert that historically "trade and commerce [is] central to their soul". One of the claimant's expert witnesses testified that trade "came as easily to the Iroquois as living and breathing". The government, while not denying that the Mohawks traditionally traded, asserts that such trade did not exterd north into what is now Canada and that, in any event, the Mohawks traditionally accepted the custom of paying tributes and duties to cross boundaries established by other polities.

I conclude that the *Van der Peet* factors of the impugned action, the governmental action or legislation with which it conflicts, and the ancestral practice relied on, all suggest the claim here is properly characterized as the right to bring goods across the Canada-United States boundary at the St. Lawrence River for purposes of trade. ...

Has the Claimed Aboriginal Right Been Established?

Van der Peet set out the test for establishing an aboriginal right protected under s. 35(1). Briefly stated, the claimant is required to prove: (1) the existence of the ancestral practice, custom or tradition advanced as supporting the claimed right; (2) that this practice, custom or tradition was "integral" to his or her pre-contact society in the sense it marked it as distinctive; and (3) reasonable continuity between the pre-contact practice and the contemporary claim. I will consider each of these elements in turn. First, however, it is necessary to consider the evidence upon which claims may be proved, and the approach courts should adopt in interpreting such evidence.

Evidentiary Concerns — Proving Aboriginal Rights

Aboriginal right claims give rise to unique and inherent evidentiary difficulties. Claimants are called upon to demonstrate features of their pre-contact society, across a gulf of centuries and without the aid of written records. Recognizing these difficulties, this Court has cautioned that the rights protected under s. 35(1) should not be rendered illusory by imposing an impossible burden of proof on those claiming this protection. ...

The Interpretation of Evidence in Aboriginal Rights Claims

[After discussing the admissibility and interpretation of evidence in Aboriginal rights claims Chief Justice McLachlin wrote] ... it must be emphasized that a consciousness of the special nature of aboriginal claims does not negate the operation of general evidentiary principles. While evidence adduced in support of aboriginal claims must not be undervalued, neither should it be interpreted or weighed in a manner that fundamentally contravenes the principles of evidence law, which, as they relate to the valuing of evidence, are often synonymous with the "general principles of common sense" (Sopinka and Lederman, *supra*, at p. 524). ...

There is a boundary that must not be crossed between a sensitive application and a complete abandonment of the rules of evidence. As Binnie J. observed in the context of treaty rights, "[g]enerous rules of interpretation should not be confused with a vague sense of after-the-fact largesse" (*R. v. Marshall*, [1999] 3 S.C.R. 456, at para. 14). In particular, the *Van der Peet* approach does not operate to amplify the cogency of evidence adduced in support of an aboriginal claim. Evidence advanced in support of aboriginal claims, like the evidence offered in any case, can run the gamut of cogency from the highly compelling to the highly dubious. Claims must still be established on the basis of persuasive evidence demonstrating their validity on the balance of probabilities. Placing "due weight" on the aboriginal perspective, or ensuring its supporting evidence an "equal footing" with more familiar forms of evidence, means precisely what these phrases suggest: equal and due treatment. While the evidence presented by aboriginal claimants should not be undervalued "simply because that evidence does not conform precisely with the evidentiary standards that would be applied in, for example, a private law torts case" (*Van der Peet*, *supra*, at para. 68), neither should it be artificially strained to carry more weight than it can reasonably support. If this is an obvious proposition, it must nonetheless be stated.

With these principles in mind, I turn now to the consideration of whether the evidence offered in the present case in fact supports an aboriginal right to bring goods across the St. Lawrence River for the purposes of trade.

Does the Evidence Show an Ancestral Mohawk Practice of Trading North of the St. Lawrence River?

While the ancestral home of the Mohawks lay in the Mohawk Valley of present-day New York State, the evidence establishes that, before the arrival of Europeans, they travelled north on occasion across the St. Lawrence River. We may assume they travelled with goods to sustain themselves. There was also ample evidence before McKeown J. to support his finding that trade was a central, distinguishing feature of the Iroquois in general and the Mohawks in particular. This evidence indicates the Mohawks were well situated for trade, and engaged in small-scale exchange with other First Nations. A critical question in this case, however, is whether these trading practices and northerly travel coincided prior to the arrival of Europeans; that is, does the evidence establish an ancestral Mohawk practice of transporting goods across the St. Lawrence River for the purposes of trade? Only if this ancestral practice is established does it become necessary to determine whether it is an integral feature of Mohawk culture with continuity to the present day.

With respect, the trial judge's affirmative response to this question finds virtually no support in the evidentiary record. ...

[C]laims must be proven on the basis of cogent evidence establishing their validity on the balance of probabilities. Sparse, doubtful and equivocal evidence cannot serve as the foundation for a successful claim. With respect, this is exactly what has occurred in the present case. The contradiction between McKeown J.'s statement that little direct evidence supports a cross-river trading right and his conclusion that such a right exists suggests the application of a very relaxed standard of proof (or, perhaps more accurately, an unreasonably generous weighing of tenuous evidence). The *Van der Peet* approach, while mandating the equal and due treatment of evidence supporting aboriginal claims, does not bolster or enhance the cogency of this evidence. The relevant evidence in this case — a single knife, treaties that make no reference to pre-existing trade, and the mere fact of Mohawk involvement in the fur trade — can only support the conclusion reached by the trial judge if strained beyond the weight they can reasonably hold. Such a result is not contemplated by *Van der Peet* or s. 35(1). While appellate courts grant considerable deference to findings of fact made by trial judges, I am satisfied that the findings in the present case represent a "palpable and overriding error" warranting the substitution of a different result (*Delgamuukw, supra*, at paras. 78-80). I conclude that the claimant has not established an ancestral practice of transporting goods across the St. Lawrence River for the purposes of trade. ...

In view of the paucity of evidence of Mohawk trade north of the St. Lawrence River, I need not consider the argument that, even if it were established, any Mohawk trading right should be characterized as inherently subject to border controls, tolls and duties imposed by other peoples, as recognized by ancestral aboriginal custom. ...

I would allow the appeal. Chief Mitchell must pay the duty claimed by the government. I note that the government has undertaken to pay Chief Mitchell's costs.

Binnie J. (**Major J.** concurring): — I have read the reasons of the Chief Justice and I concur in the result and with her conclusion that even if Mohawks did occasionally trade goods across the St. Lawrence River with First Nations to the north, this practice was not on the evidence a "defining feature of the Mohawk culture" (para. 54) or "vital to the Mohawk's collective identity" (para. 60) in pre-contact times. There are, however, some additional considerations that have led me to conclude that the appeal must be allowed. ...

It has been almost 30 years since this Court emphatically rejected the argument that the mere assertion of sovereignty by the European powers in North America was necessarily incompatible with the survival and continuation of aboriginal rights: *Calder v. Attorney-General of British Columbia*, [1973] S.C.R. 313. Because not all customs and traditions of aboriginal First Nations are incompatible with Canadian sovereignty, however, does not mean that none of them can be in such conflict. The Chief Justice refrains from addressing the sovereignty issue (para. 64) but she holds, correctly in my view, that "any finding of a trading right would also confirm a mobility right" (para. 22 (emphasis added)). ...

[H]owever, we are left with [the] court's legitimate concern about the sovereignty implications of the international trading/mobility right claimed by the respondent. ...

Counsel for the respondent does not challenge the reality of Canadian sovereignty, but he seeks for the Mohawk people of the Iroquois Confederacy the maximum degree of legal autonomy to which he believes they are entitled because of their long history at Akwesasne and elsewhere in eastern North America. This asserted autonomy, to be sure, does not presently flow from the ancient Iroquois legal order that is said to have created it, but from the *Constitution Act, 1982*. Section 35(1), adopted by the elected representatives of Canadians, recognizes and affirms existing aboriginal and treaty rights. If the respondent's claimed aboriginal right is to prevail, it does so not because of its own inherent strength, but because the *Constitution Act, 1982* brings about that result. ...

In terms of traditional aboriginal law, the issue, as I see it, is whether trading/mobility activities asserted by the respondent not as a Canadian citizen but as an heir of the Mohawk regime that existed prior to the arrival of the Europeans, created a legal right to cross international boundaries under succeeding sovereigns. This aspect of the debate, to be clear, is not at the level of fact about the effectiveness of border controls in the 18th century. (Nor is it about the compatibility of internal aboriginal self-government with Canadian sovereignty.) The issue is at the level of law about the alleged incompatibility between European (now Canadian) sovereignty and mobility rights across non-aboriginal borders said by the trial judge to have been acquired by the Mohawks of Akwesasne by reason of their conduct prior to 1609. ...

The Sovereignty Objection

... The *Constitution Act, 1982* ushered in a new chapter but it did not start a new book. Within the framework of s. 35(1) regard is to be had to the common law ("what the law has historically accepted") to enable a court to determine what constitutes an aboriginal right. ...

Fundamentally, the respondent views his aboriginal rights as a shield against non-aboriginal laws, including what he sees as the imposition of a border that "wasn't meant for [the] Kanienkehaka or the Mohawk Nation or any of the Six Nations". He thus testified at trial:

> Even though my grandfather didn't speak any English he was able to explain to me, as other elders have, that the promises made by the English to the Haudenosaunee that they would continue to recognize our nation as free and independent peoples. At one meeting they would recite it, what exactly were those words and the gist that we had to understand it.
>
> So, when our people in Akwesasne today say this border was not intended for us, they have an understanding in historical terms of the interpretation of those promises. In our language and the way it is passed down, the line of what is now known as the International Border belongs to somebody else. It wasn't meant for Kanienkehaka or the Mohawk Nation or any of the Six Nations. We understand that much.

In this testimony the respondent refers to "promises made by the English to the Haudenosaunee", but his claim to base a trading/mobility right and tax exemptions on an existing treaty right was rejected by the trial judge and has not been appealed to this Court. His contention here is that whether or not the British made a treaty promise to that effect, the Mohawks were in fact free under the Mohawk legal regime "to pass and repass ... across what is now the Canada-United States boundary" with goods for trade and this freedom should now receive s. 35 protection.

The claim to trade and mobility across international boundaries as a citizen of Haudenosaunee engages the sovereignty issue. ...

The Substance of the Claim Disclosed by the Evidence

... [T]he respondent's claim ... is not just about physical movement of people or goods in and about Akwesasne. It is about pushing the envelope of Mohawk autonomy within the Canadian Constitution. It is about the Mohawks' aspiration to live as if the international boundary did not exist. Whatever financial benefit accrues from the ability to move goods across the border without payment of duty is clearly incidental to this larger vision. ...

In the constitutional framework envisaged by the respondent, the claimed aboriginal right is simply a manifestation of the more fundamental relationship between the aboriginal and non-aboriginal people. In the Mohawk tradition this relationship is memorialized by the "two-row" wampum ... described in the Haudenosaunee presentation to the Parliamentary Special Committee on Indian Self-Government in 1983 as follows:

> When the Haudenosaunee first came into contact with the European nations, treaties of peace and friendship were made. Each was symbolized by the Gus-Wen-Tah or Two Row Wampum. There is a bed of white wampum which symbolizes the purity of the agreement. There are two rows of pur-

ple, and those two rows have the spirit of your ancestors and mine. There are three beads of wampum separating the two rows and they symbolize peace, friendship and respect.

These two rows will symbolize two paths or two vessels, travelling down the same river together. One, a birch bark canoe, will be for the Indian people, their laws, their customs and their ways. The other, a ship, will be for the white people and their laws, their customs and their ways. We shall each travel the river together, side by side, but in our own boat. Neither of us will try to steer the other's vessel. (Indian Self-Government in Canada: Report of the Special Committee (1983), back cover)

Thus, in the "two-row" wampum there are two parallel paths. In one path travels the aboriginal canoe. In the other path travels the European ship. The two vessels co-exist but they never touch. Each is the sovereign of its own destiny.

The modern embodiment of the "two-row" wampum concept, modified to reflect some of the realities of a modern state, is the idea of a "merged" or "shared" sovereignty. "Merged sovereignty" asserts that First Nations were not wholly subordinated to non-aboriginal sovereignty, but over time became merger partners. The final Report of the Royal Commission on Aboriginal Peoples, vol. 2 (Restructuring the Relationship (1996)), at p. 214, says that "Aboriginal governments give the constitution [of Canada] its deepest and most resilient roots in the Canadian soil." This updated concept of Crown sovereignty is of importance. Whereas historically the Crown may have been portrayed as an entity across the seas with which aboriginal people could scarcely be expected to identify, this was no longer the case in 1982 when the s. 35(1) reconciliation process was established. The Constitution was patriated and all aspects of our sovereignty became firmly located within our borders. If the principle of "merged sovereignty" articulated by the Royal Commission on Aboriginal Peoples is to have any true meaning, it must include at least the idea that aboriginal and non-aboriginal Canadians together form a sovereign entity with a measure of common purpose and united effort. It is this new entity, as inheritor of the historical attributes of sovereignty, with which existing aboriginal and treaty rights must be reconciled. ...

On this view, to return to the nautical metaphor of the "two-row" wampum, "merged" sovereignty is envisaged as a single vessel (or ship of state) composed of the historic elements of wood, iron and canvas. The vessel's components pull together as a harmonious whole, but the wood remains wood, the iron remains iron and the canvas remains canvas. Non-aboriginal leaders, including Sir Wilfrid Laurier, have used similar metaphors. It represents, in a phrase, partnership without assimilation. ...

In the earlier years of the century the federal government occasionally argued that Parliament's jurisdiction under s. 91(24) of the *Constitution Act, 1867* ("Indians, and Lands reserved for the Indians") was plenary. Indians were said to be federal people whose lives were wholly subject to federal "regulation". This was rejected by the courts, which ruled that while an aboriginal person could be characterized as an Indian for some purposes including language, culture and the exercise of traditional rights, he or she does not cease thereby to be a resident of a province or territory. For other purposes he or she must be recognized and treated as an ordinary member of Canadian society. In a decision handed down soon after the coming into force of the *Constitution Act, 1982*, in *Nowegijick v. The Queen*, a tax case, Dickson J. (as he then was) wrote at p. 36, "Indians are citizens and, in affairs of life not governed by treaties or the Indian Act, they are subject to all of the responsibilities ... of other Canadian citizens". ... The constitutional objective is reconciliation not mutual isolation.

The Royal Commission ... recognized the challenge aboriginal self-government poses to the orthodox view that constitutional powers in Canada are wholly and exhaustively distributed between the federal and provincial governments. ... What is significant is that the Royal Commission itself sees aboriginal peoples as full participants with non-aboriginal peoples in a shared Canadian sovereignty. Aboriginal peoples do not stand in opposition to, nor are they subjugated by, Canadian sovereignty. They are part of it.

With this background I return to the point that the respondent does not base his mobility rights in this test case as a Canadian citizen. ...

The respondent's claim thus presents two defining elements. He asserts a trading and mobility right across the international boundary and he attaches this right to his current citizenship not of Canada but of the Haudenosaunee Confederacy with its capital in Onondaga, New York State.

The Legal Basis of the Respondent's Claim

The respondent initially asserted both a treaty right and an aboriginal right but the conceptual distinction between these two sources of entitlement is important. A treaty right is an affirmative promise by the Crown which will be interpreted generously and enforced in a way that upholds the honour of the Crown. ... A treaty right is itself an expression of Crown sovereignty.

In the case of aboriginal rights, there is no historical event comparable to the treaty-making process in which the Crown negotiated the right or obligation sought to be enforced. The respondent's claim is rooted in practices which he says long preceded the Mohawks' first contact with Europeans in 1609. ...

Reference has already been made to the fact that one of several sources of the concept of aboriginal rights, now significantly modified by the more generous principles of constitutional interpretation, is traditional British colonial law. Many of the cases decided by the Judicial Committee of the Privy Council were concerned with rights of property created under a former regime. In *Amodu Tijani v. Southern Nigeria (Secretary)*, [1921] 2 A.C. 399, at p. 407, it was confirmed that "A mere change in sovereignty is not to be presumed as meant to disturb rights of private owners" (emphasis added). More recently, Lord Denning, speaking for the Privy Council in *Oyekan v. Adele*, [1957] 2 All E.R. 785, at p. 788, said: "In inquiring ... what rights are recognised, there is one guiding principle. It is this: The courts will assume that the British Crown intends that the rights of property of the inhabitants are to be fully respected" (emphasis added). As with the modern law of aboriginal rights, the law of sovereign succession was intended to reconcile the interests of the local inhabitants across the empire to a change in sovereignty. ...

The root of the respondent's argument nevertheless is that the Mohawks of Akwesasne acquired under the legal regimes of 18th century North America, a positive legal right as a group to continue to come and go across any subsequent international border dividing their traditional homelands with whatever goods they wished, just as they had in pre-contact times. In other words, Mohawk autonomy in this respect was continued but not as a mere custom or practice. It emerged in the new European-based constitutional order as a legal trading and mobility right. By s. 35(1) of the *Constitution Act, 1982*, it became a constitutionally protected right. That is the respondent's argument.

The Limitation of "Sovereign Incompatibility"

Care must be taken not to carry forward doctrines of British colonial law into the interpretation of s. 35(1) without careful reflection. ...

The subject matter of the constitutional provision is "existing" aboriginal and treaty rights and they are said to be "recognized and affirmed" not wholly cut loose from either their legal or historical origins. One of the defining characteristics of sovereign succession and therefore a limitation on the scope of aboriginal rights, as already discussed, was the notion of incompatibility with the new sovereignty. ...

Prior to *Calder, supra*, "sovereign incompatibility" was given excessive scope. The assertion of sovereign authority was confused with doctrines of feudal title to deny aboriginal peoples any interest at all in their traditional lands or even in activities related to the use of those lands. To acknowledge that the doctrine of sovereign incompatibility was sometimes given excessive scope in the past is not to deny that it has any scope at all, but it is a doctrine that must be applied with caution. ...

In my opinion, sovereign incompatibility continues to be an element in the s. 35(1) analysis, albeit a limitation that will be sparingly applied. For the most part, the protection of practices, traditions and customs that are distinctive to aboriginal cultures in Canada does not raise legitimate sovereignty issues at the definitional stage.

The Alleged Incompatibility Between the Aboriginal Right Disclosed by the Evidence and Canadian Sovereignty

... The question is whether the asserted legal right to the autonomous exercise of international trade and mobility was compatible with the new European (now Canadian) sovereignty and the reciprocal loss (or impairment) of Mohawk sovereignty.

In the resolution of this legal issue, as stated, we are addressing legal incompatibility as opposed to factual incompatibility. The latter emerged more slowly as assertions of sovereignty gave way to colonisation and progressive occupation of land. ...

Control over the mobility of persons and goods into one country is, and always has been, a fundamental attribute of sovereignty. ...

In other words, not only does authority over the border exist as an incident of sovereignty, the state is expected to exercise it in the public interest. The duty cannot be abdicated to the vagaries of an earlier regime whose sovereignty has been eclipsed (Cain, *supra*, at pp. 545-46).

The legal situation is further complicated by the fact, previously mentioned, that the respondent attributes his international trading and mobility right not to his status as a Canadian citizen but as a citizen of the Haudenosaunee (Iroquois Confederacy) based at Onondaga, New York. Border conditions in the modern era are vastly different from those in the 18th century. Nevertheless, as stated, borders existed among nations, including First Nations. They were expressions of sovereign autonomy and then, as now, compelled observance. ...

In my view, therefore, the international trading/mobility right claimed by the respondent as a citizen of the Haudenosaunee (Iroquois) Confederacy is incompatible with the historical attributes of Canadian sovereignty.

The question that then arises is whether this conclusion is at odds with the purpose of s. 35(1), i.e. the reconciliation of the interests of aboriginal peoples with Crown sovereignty? In addressing this question it must be remembered that aboriginal people are themselves part of Canadian sovereignty as discussed above. I agree with Borrows, *supra*, at p. 40, that accommodation of aboriginal rights should not be seen as "a zero-sum relationship between minority rights and citizenship; as if every gain in the direction of accommodating diversity comes at the expense of promoting citizenship" (quoting W. Kymlicka and W. Norman, eds., Citizenship in Diverse Societies (2000), at p. 39). On the other hand, the reverse is also true. Affirmation of the sovereign interest of Canadians as a whole, including aboriginal peoples, should not necessarily be seen as a loss of sufficient "constitutional space for aboriginal peoples to be aboriginal" (Greschner, *supra*, at p. 342). ...

In terms of sovereign incompatibility, it is a conclusion that the respondent's claim relates to national interests that all of us have in common rather than to distinctive interests that for some purposes differentiate an aboriginal community. In my view, reconciliation of these interests in this particular case favours an affirmation of our collective sovereignty.

Implications for Internal Aboriginal Self-Government

In reaching that conclusion, however, I do not wish to be taken as either foreclosing or endorsing any position on the compatibility or incompatibility of internal self-governing institutions of First Nations with Crown sovereignty, either past or present. I point out in this connection that the sovereign incompatibility principle has not prevented the United States (albeit with its very different constitutional framework) from continuing to recognize forms of internal aboriginal self-government which it considers to be expressions of residual aboriginal sovereignty. ...

The United States has lived with internal tribal self-government within the framework of external relations determined wholly by the United States government without doctrinal difficulties since *Johnson v. M'Intosh*, 21 U.S. (8 Wheat.) 543 (1823), was decided almost 170 years ago.

The question under consideration here is ... whether the claimed international trading and mobility right could, as a matter of law, have arisen in the first place.

It was, of course, an expression of sovereignty in 1982 to recognize existing aboriginal rights under s. 35(1) of the *Constitution Act, 1982*. However, if the claimed aboriginal right did not survive the transition to non-Mohawk sovereignty, there was nothing in existence in 1982 to which s. 35(1) protection of existing aboriginal rights could attach. It would have been, of course, quite within the sovereign's power to confer specific border privileges by treaty, but the respondent's claim to a treaty right was dismissed.

In my respectful view the claimed aboriginal right never came into existence and it is unnecessary to consider the Crown's argument that whatever aboriginal rights in this respect may have existed were extinguished by border controls enforced by Canada prior to April 17, 1982.

---

1. Is Justice Binnie's concurring decision in *Mitchell* reminiscent of Justice Rand's decision in *Francis*?
2. In *Mitchell*, Justice Binnie wrote: "The *Constitution Act, 1982* ushered in a new chapter but it did not start a new book." Can you reconcile this statement with the Supreme Court's approach in *R. v. Sparrow*, [1990] 1 S.C.R. 1075 at 1106, where the Court wrote: "the context of 1982 is surely enough to tell us that this is not just a codification of the case law on aboriginal rights that had accumulated by 1982. Section 35 calls for a just settlement for aboriginal peoples. It renounces the old rules of the game under which the Crown established courts of law and denied those courts the authority to question sovereign claims made by the Crown."
3. Is it appropriate for Justice Binnie to re-interpret the Two-Row Wampum as he did? See Gordon Christie, "The Court's Exercise of Plenary Power: Rewriting the Two-row Wampum" (2002), 16 S.C.L.R. (2d), at pp. 285-301.
4. If ever accepted as the majority position, does Justice Binnie's theory of sovereign incompatibility herald an expansion or contraction of Aboriginal rights and jurisdiction? Can you develop arguments on both sides of the issue? It may be said that a theory of sovereign incompatibility could severely constrain Aboriginal jurisdiction because — whenever it tried to "push back" Crown interference — an Aboriginal community's every action could be challenged as being incompatible with the Crown's sovereignty. On the other hand, modern theories of federalism have strained to allow coordinate, overlapping spheres between the federal and provincial governments. As a result, each level of government can act in relation to the other's power and not have their actions characterized as being incompatible with the other (*Ross v. Ontario (Registrar of Motor Vehicles)*, [1975] 1 S.C.R. 5; *Multiple Access Ltd. v. McCutcheon*, [1982] 2 S.C.R. 161). Could a theory of sovereign incompatibility dealing with Aboriginal peoples take on this approach and actually expand Aboriginal jurisdiction?

D. PERSONAL INCOME TAX

The issue of immunity or exemption from taxation also arises in the field of income tax. The courts have found that Indian property that is not situated on reserve land is subject to taxation. Likewise, they have exempted property that is "situate on reserve" as a result of s. 87 of the *Indian Act* [R.S.C. 1985, c. I-5]. The following commentary, and the reproduction of three landmark cases (*R. v. Nowegijick*, [1983] 1 S.C.R. 29, 144 D.L.R. (3d) 193, *Mitchell v. Peguis Indian Band*, [1990] 2 S.C.R. 85, [1990] 3 C.N.L.R. 46 and *Williams v. Canada*, [1992] 1 S.C.R. 877) demonstrates the court's treatment of income tax under these circumstances.

RICHARD BARTLETT, INDIANS AND TAXATION IN CANADA, 3RD ED.

(Saskatoon: Native Law Centre, 1992) at 47-56 (references omitted)

The exemption conferred by section 87 of the *Indian Act* applies "notwithstanding any other Act of the Parliament of Canada or any Act of the legislature of a province". ... But the collection arrangements make clear that income tax levied for provincial purposes is imposed under provincial jurisdiction, rather than by a "renting" of that power to the federal government, and accordingly the provincial tax is subject to being treaty barred under section 88 of the *Indian Act*.

1. 1972 Departmental Practice

In 1972 the Department of National Revenue announced its practice in the collection of federal and provincial income tax to be as follows:

> 5. While the exemption in the *Indian Act* refers to "property" and the tax imposed under the *Income Tax Act* is a tax calculated on the income of a person rather than a tax in respect of his property, it is considered that the intention of the *Indian Act* is not to tax Indians on income earned on a reserve. Income earned by an Indian off a reserve, however, does not come within this exemption, and is therefore subject to tax under the *Income Tax Act*.

... In the first part of this century the Department placed some emphasis on the residence of the income earner. Judicial support for an exemption from taxation of Indians residing upon a reserve is evident in the 1924 decision of the British Columbia Court of Appeal in *Armstrong Growers Association v. Harris*. A creditor sought to attach moneys owing to an Indian reserve farmer by an off-reserve purchaser of wheat, and the court held that the income was not subject to charge. Macdonald J.A. declared:

> The wheat while on the Reserve, would not, I think, be subject to taxation, nor to process of execution, and I am of opinion that the language of the Act does not render the proceeds of it subject to taxation. It might, I do not say it would, be different where the Indian received the proceeds and deposited it, say in a bank outside the Reserve, but here, the debtor was obliged to seek his creditor at home on the reserve and pay him there. But even apart from this technical rule, I think there is a clear intention shewn in the Act to exempt from taxation such a chose in action as we have here.

The Department of Justice had immediately adopted the analysis suggested in *Armstrong*. The Deputy Minister opened in 1925 that wages earned off the reserve by an Indian residing on a reserve were situated on the reserve and accordingly exempt:

> I understand the circumstances of the present case to be that a creditor has attempted to attach moneys due from a person outside the reserve to an Indian resident upon a reserve, such moneys being wages for labour performed outside. The property of the Indian in this case is to a right to have paid to him the wages due and ordinarily he is entitled to have his creditor come to him with such payment. It would appear that this property in the case cited of an Indian residing on a reserve should be held personal property within the reserve and not subject to execution or attachment?

In 1929 the Department of Indian Affairs advised its regional offices that "pursuant to the 105th Section of the *Indian Act*, the income of an Indian who resides on a reserve cannot be taxed no matter from what source it is derived."

The Department of National Revenue did not, however, follow such advice and declared:

> You are advised that it has been a long standing ruling of this Division that real or personal property of Indians residing on a Reserve is exempt from taxation, but Indians not residing on a Reserve are liable to taxation as are any other persons ordinarily resident in Canada. Further, if an Indian earns his income outside of the Reserve, then he is liable to taxation in respect of such income even although he may subsequently return and reside on the reserve.

The Department of National Revenue thereby adopted the requirement of the residence on the reserve, suggested by Armstrong, and the requirement that the income be earned on the reserve.

In 1967 the Department of National Revenue abandoned any concern with the residence of an Indian and forsook any connection between the exemption from taxation and government by Indian bands of residents of their lands. It did so on account of the inconsistency between the reasoning employed in Armstrong with that of *Petersen v. Cree and Canadian Pacific Express Company*. ...

2. The Indian Exemption from Income Taxation: *Nowegijick*

In the late 1970s the arguments of Indian organizations and the practice of the Department of National Revenue were fundamentally questioned by the Federal Court of Appeal. On April 19, 1979 in *Snow v. The Queen* the court declared that income taxation was not subject to the exemption of section 87. ...

In 1972 Russell Snow, a member of the Caughnawaga Indian Band challenged the imposition of taxation upon income earned off the reserve. Roland St. Onge, Q.C., in November 1974, for the Tax Review Board suggested that there was no exemption from income taxation conferred by section 87 irrespective of where the income was earned:

> Because the *Income Tax Act* taxes all the residents of Canada and does not exclude the Indian as an actual taxpayer, and as the *Indian Act* is completely silent on this important matter of income tax it is self-evident that an Indian

falls under the *Income Tax Act*, especially when his income is earned outside the Reserve.

In *The Queen v. National Indian Brotherhood* decided four months later, A.J. Frost for the Tax Review Board applied the exemption of section 87 to income taxation and offered his explanation of his resolution of the dilemma:

> Statutory law exempting Indians from taxation preceded, by many years, the *Income Tax Act*, and established the broad principle that all property of an Indian situated on a reserve is exempt from taxation, thereby raising a presumption in law that the *Income Tax Act* cannot be taken to apply to the property of Indians on a reserve unless it is spelled out in clear unambiguous language and there is no conflict. Although the language of the *Indian Act* and the *Income Tax Act* appear to be repugnant in respect to taxation, it cannot be supposed that Parliament intended to contradict itself by exempting Indians under the earlier legislation and then tearing up the earlier statutes by imposing liabilities on them under the *Income Tax Act*. Besides the question of repugnancy, the *Indian Act* is a special Act which tends to be derogatory of the *Income Tax Act*, which is a general taxing Act. To avoid collision between these two statutes, the logical construction is simply that the *Income Tax Act* as a general statute applies to Indians only in respect of those areas of taxation wherein the *Indian Act* is silent. The *Indian Act*, however, is not silent but speaks with rather a loud voice, on the subject of taxability of Indians. The appropriate sections read as follows: [sections 87 and 90 are recited].
> The language of the above provisions is broad and speaks to exclude all other tax legislation, and thereby constitutes special legislation overriding the *Income Tax Act*. It is only where the *Indian Act* is silent that other statutes can affect the rights of unenfranchised Indians.

Upon appeal of both cases to the Federal Court Trial Division argument was confined to the question of situs of the income and the court was able, in the language of Thurlow A.C.J. in *The Queen v. National Indian Brotherhood*, to "[assume] that the taxation imposed by the *Income Tax Act* is taxation of individuals in respect of property and that a salary or a right of salary is property." Shortly prior thereto a fellow judge of the Trial Division had found that a scholarship did constitute "property" within the exemption conferred by section 87, in the face of argument that "the *Income Tax Act* levies a tax on persons, not on property." Mahoney J. in *Greyeyes v. The Queen* refused to accept the soundness of the Crown's position in citing *Sura v. M.N.R.* wherein Mr. Justice Taschereau for the Supreme Court of Canada observed:

> Nothing in subsequent amendments of the (*Income Tax*) *Act* has changed the principle that it is not ownership of a thing which is taxable, but that tax is imposed on a taxpayer ... As Mignault J. in *McLeod v. Minister of Customs and Excise*, [1917-27] C.T.C. 290 at p. 296: "All of this is in accord with the general policy of the Act which imposes the income tax on the person and not on the property."

The Federal Court of Appeal was not as reticent as the Trial Division. In *M.N.R. v. Iroquois of Caughnawaga* Chief Justice Jackett (Pratte J. and Hyde D.J. concurring on this matter) declared that the obligation of an employer to pay statutory unemployment insurance premiums was not "taxation on 'property' within the ambit of section 87." The Chief Justice commented:

From one point of view, all taxation is directly or indirectly taxation on property; from another point of view, all taxation is directly or indirectly taxation on persons. It is my view, however, that when section 87 exempts "personal property of an Indian or band situated on a reserve" from "taxation," its effect is to exempt what can properly be classified as direct taxation on property. The courts have had to develop jurisprudence as to when taxation is taxation on property and when it is taxation on persons for the purposes of subsection 92(2) of the *British North America Act, 1867*, and there would seem to be no reason why such jurisprudence should not be applied to the interpretation of section 87 of the *Indian Act*....

The Chief Justice asserted that the exemption conferred by section 87 should be confined to indirect taxation. ...

Doubts as to the soundness of the rationale offered by the Chief Justice may explain the sparseness of the judgment of the Federal Court of Appeal in *Snow v. The Queen*. In a stunningly brief judgment Le Dain J. observed:

We are all of the view that the appeal must be dismissed on the ground that the tax imposed on the appellant under the *Income Tax Act* ... is not taxation in respect of personal property within the meaning of section [87] of the *Indian Act* ... In our opinion section [87] contemplates taxation in respect of specific personal property qua property and not taxation in respect of taxable income as defined by the *Income Tax Act*, which, while it may reflect items that are personal property, is not itself personal property but an amount to be determined as a matter of calculation by application of the provisions of the Act.

Five months later the Federal Court of Appeal reversed the trial court decision in *Nowegijick* "for the reasons given in the Snow case".

In January 1983 the Supreme Court of Canada rendered its landmark decision in *Nowegijick v. R.* and rejected the analysis of the Federal Court of Appeal.

R. v. NOWEGIJICK

[1983] 1 S.C.R. 29, [1983] 2 C.N.L.R. 89, 144 D.L.R. (3d) 193

The judgment of the Court was delivered by

Dickson J.:— The question is whether the appellant, Gene A. Nowegijick, a registered Indian can claim by virtue of the *Indian Act*, R.S.C. 1970, c. I-6, an exemption from income tax for the 1975 taxation year.

The Facts

The facts are few and not in dispute. Mr. Nowegijick is an Indian within the meaning of the *Indian Act* and a member of the Gull Bay (Ontario) Indian Band. During the 1975 taxation year Mr. Nowegijick was an employee of the Gull Bay Development Corporation, a company without share capital, having its head office and administrative offices on the Gull Bay Reserve. All the directors, members and employees of the Corporation live on the Reserve and are registered Indians.

During 1975 the Corporation in the course of its business conducted a logging operation 10 miles from the Gull Bay Reserve. Mr. Nowegijick was employed as a logger and remunerated on a piece-work basis. He was paid bi-weekly by cheque at the head office of the Corporation on the Reserve.

During 1975, Mr. Nowegijick maintained his permanent dwelling on the Gull Bay Reserve. Each morning he would leave the Reserve to work on the logging operations, and return to the Reserve at the end of the working day.

Mr. Nowegijick earned $11,057.08 in such employment. His assessed taxable income for the 1975 taxation year was $8,698 on which he was assessed tax of $1,965.80. By Notice of Objection he objected to the assessment on the basis that the income in respect of which the assessment was made is the "personal property of an Indian ... situated on a reserve" and thus not subject to taxation by virtue of s. 87 of the *Indian Act*. ....

The Legislation

Mr. Nowegijick, in his claim for exemption from income tax relies upon s. 87 of the *Indian Act*...

Stripped to relevant essentials s. 87 reads:

Notwithstanding any other Act of the Parliament of Canada ... the following property is exempt from taxation, namely:
(a) the interest of an Indian or a band in reserve or surrendered lands; and
(b) the personal property of an Indian or band situated on a reserve; and no Indian or band is subject to taxation in respect of the ownership, occupation, possession or use of any property mentioned in paragraph (a) or (b) or is otherwise subject to taxation in respect of any such property ...

The short but difficult question to be determined is whether the tax sought to be imposed under the *Income Tax Act*, 1970-71-72 (Can.), c. 63 upon the income of Mr. Nowegijick can be said to be "in respect of" "any" personal property situated upon a reserve . ....

Construction of section 87 of the Indian Act

Indians are citizens and, in affairs of life not governed by treaties or the *Indian Act*, they are subject to all of the responsibilities, including payment of taxes, of other Canadian citizens.

It is legal lore that, to be valid, exemptions to tax laws should be clearly expressed. It seems to me, however, that treaties and statutes relating to Indians should be liberally construed and doubtful expressions resolved in favour of the Indians. If the statute contains language which can reasonably be construed to confer tax exemption that construction, in my view, is to be favoured over a more technical construction which might be available to deny exemption. In *Jones v. Meehan*, 175 U.S. 1 (1899), it was held that Indian treaties "must ... be construed, not according to the technical meaning of [their] words ... but in the sense in which they would naturally be understood by the Indians".

There is little in the cases to assist in the construction of s. 87 of the *Indian Act*. In *R. v. National Indian Brotherhood, supra*, the question was as to situs, an issue which does not arise in the present case. The appeal related to the failure of the National Indian Brotherhood to deduct and pay over to the Receiver General for Canada the amount which the defendant was required by the *Income Tax Act* and regulations to deduct from the salaries of its Indian employees. The salaries in question were paid to the employees in Ottawa by cheque drawn on an Ottawa bank. Thurlow A.C.J. said (at pp. 108-09):

> I have already indicated that it is my view that the exemption provided for by section 87 does not extend beyond the ordinary meaning of the words and expressions used in it. There is no legal basis, notwithstanding the history of the exemption, and the special position of Indians in Canadian society, for extending it by reference to any notional extension of reserves or of what may be considered as being done on reserves. The issue, as I see it, assuming that the taxation imposed by the *Income Tax Act* is taxation of individuals in respect of property and that a salary or a right to salary is property, is whether the salary which the individual Indian received or to which he was entitled was "personal property" of the Indian "situated on a reserve".

The other case is *Greyeyes v. The Queen*, [1978] 2 F.C. 385. The question was whether an education scholarship paid by the federal government to a status Indian was taxable in the Indian's hands. Mahoney J. held that it was not taxable, by reason of s. 87 of the *Indian Act*. ...

The prime task of the Court in this case is to construe the words "no Indian ... is ... subject to taxation in respect of any such [personal] property". Is taxable income personal property? The Supreme Court of Illinois in the case of *Bachrach v. Nelson*, 182 N.E. 909 (1932) considered whether "income" is "property" and responded (at p. 914):

> The overwhelming weight of judicial authority holds that it is. The cases of *Eliasberg Bros. Mercantile Co. v. Grimes*, 204 Ala. 492, 86 So. 56, 11 A.L.R. 300, *Tax Commissioner v. Putnam*, 227 Mass. 522, 116 N.E. 904, L.R.A. 1917F, 806, *Stratton's Independence v. Howbert*, 231 U.S. 399, 34 S. Ct. 136, 58 L. Ed. 285, *Doyle v. Mitchell Bros. Co.*, 247 U.S. 179, 38 S. Ct. 467, 62 L. Ed. 1054, *Board of Revenue v. Montgomery Gaslight Co.*, 64 Ala. 269, *Greene v. Knox*, 175 N.Y. 432, 67 N.E. 910, *Hibbard v. State*, 65 Ohio St. 574, 64 N.E. 109, 58 L.R.A. 654, *Ludlow-Saylor Wire Co. v. Wollbrinck*, 275 Mo. 339, 205 S.W. 196, and *State v. Pinder*, 7 Boyce (30 Del.) 416, 108 A. 43, define what is personal property and in substance hold that money or any other thing of value acquired as gain or profit from capital or labour is property, and that, in the aggregate, these acquisitions constitute income, and, in accordance with the axiom that the whole includes all of its parts, income includes property and nothing but property, and therefore is itself property.

I would adopt this language. A tax on income is in reality a tax on property itself. If income can be said to be property I cannot think that taxable income is any less so. Taxable income is by definition, s. 2(2) of the *Income Tax Act*, "his income for the year minus the deductions permitted by Division C". Although the Crown in paragraph 14 of its factum recognizes that "salaries" and "wages" can be classified as "personal property" it submits that the basis of taxation is a person's "taxable" income and that such taxable income is not "personal property" but rather a "concept", that results from a number of operations. This is too fine a distinction for my liking. If wages are personal property it seems to me difficult to say that a person taxed "in respect of" wages is not being taxed in respect of personal property. It is true that certain calculations are needed in order to determine the quantum of tax but I do not think this in any way invalidates the basic proposition. The words "in respect of" are, in my opinion, words of the widest possible scope. They import such meanings as "in relation to", "with reference to" or "in connection with". The phrase "in respect of" is probably the widest of any expression intended to convey some connection between two related subject matters.

Crown counsel submits that the effect of s. 87 of the *Indian Act* is to exempt what can properly be classified as "direct taxation on property" and the judgment of Jackett C.J. in *Minister of National Revenue v. Iroquois of Caughnawaga*, [1977] 2 F.C. 269 is cited. The question in that case was whether the employer's share of unemployment insurance premiums was payable in respect of persons employed by an Indian band at a hospital operated by the band on a reserve. It was argued that the premiums were "taxation" on "property" within s. 87 of the *Indian Act*. Chief Justice Jackett held that even if the imposition by statute on an employer of liability to contribute to the cost of a scheme of unemployment insurance were "taxation" it would not, in the view of the Chief Justice, be taxation on "property" within the ambit of s. 87. The Chief Justice continued (at p. 271):

> From one point of view, all taxation is directly or indirectly taxation on property; from another point of view, all taxation is directly or indirectly taxation on persons. It is my view, however, that when section 87 exempts "personal property of an Indian or band situated on a reserve" from "taxation", its effect is to exempt what can properly be classified as direct taxation on property. The courts have had to develop jurisprudence as to when taxation is taxation on property and when it is taxation on persons for the purposes of section 92(2) of *The British North America Act, 1867*, and there would seem to be no reason why such jurisprudence should not be applied to the interpretation of section 87 of the *Indian Act*. See, for example, with reference to section 92(2), Provincial Treasurer of *Alberta v. Kerr*, [1933] A.C. 710. ...

With respect, I do not agree with Chief Justice Jackett that the effect of s. 87 of the *Indian Act* is only to exempt what can properly be classified as direct taxation on property. Section 87 provides that "the personal property of an Indian ... on a reserve" is exempt from taxation; but it also provides that "no Indian ... is ... subject to taxation in respect of any such property". The earlier words certainly exempt certain property from taxation; but the latter words also exempt certain persons from taxation in respect of such property. As I read it, s. 87 creates an exemption for both persons and property. It does not matter then that the taxation of employment income may be characterized as a tax on persons, as opposed to a tax on property.

We must, I think, in these cases, have regard to substance and the plain and ordinary meaning of the language used, rather than to forensic dialectics. I do not think we should give any refined construction to the section. A person exempt from taxation in respect of any of his personal property would have difficulty in understanding why he should pay tax in respect of his wages. And I do not think it is a sufficient answer to say that the conceptualization of the *Income Tax Act* renders it so.

I conclude by saying that nothing in these reasons should be taken as implying that no Indian shall ever pay tax of any kind. Counsel for the appellant and counsel for the interveners do not take that position. Nor do I. We are concerned here with personal property situated on a reserve and only with property situated on a reserve.

I would allow the appeal, set aside the judgment of the Federal Court of Appeal and reinstate the judgment in the Trial Division of that Court. Pursuant to the arrangement of the parties the appellant is entitled to his costs in all courts to be taxed as between solicitor and client. There should be no costs payable by or to the interveners.

Appeal allowed with costs.

MITCHELL v. PEGUIS INDIAN BAND

[1990] 2 S.C.R. 85, [*sub nom. Mitchell v. Sandy Bay Indian Band*]
[1990] 3 C.N.L.R. 46, 67 Man. R. (2d) 81

La Forest J. (**Sopinka** and **Gonthier JJ.** concurring): — I have had the advantage of reading the reasons of the Chief Justice. I agree with his proposed disposition of this case, but I do so for quite different reasons. With respect, I am unable to agree with his approach and, in particular, with his adoption of the trial judge's interpretation of s. 90(1)(*b*) of the *Indian Act*, R.S.C. 1970, c. I-6. The Chief Justice has summarized the facts and the judicial history and I need not repeat them. In broad terms, the issue to be determined involves funds in the hands of the Government of Manitoba, which it agreed to pay to the respondent Indians in settlement of a claim for the return of taxes paid by the Indians to Manitoba Hydro in respect of sales of electricity on reserves. The question is whether those funds may be garnisheed by the appellants who are suing the Indians for fees for representing the Indians in negotiating the settlement.

Both the trial judge and the Court of Appeal held the funds were not subject to garnishment. These decisions, as the Chief Justice has noted, were based on the interpretation given by those courts to s. 90(1)(*b*) of the *Indian Act*. In my respectful view, this interpretation not only goes beyond the clear terms and purposes of the Act, but flies in the face of the historical record and has serious implications for Indian policy that are harmful both for government and native people. ...

As is clear from the comments of the Chief Justice in *Guerin v. The Queen*, [1984] 2 S.C.R. 335, at p. 383, these legislative restraints on the alienability of Indian lands are but the continuation of a policy that has shaped the dealings between the Indians and the European settlers since the time of the *Royal Proclamation of 1763*. The historical record leaves no doubt that native peoples acknowledged the ultimate sovereignty of the British Crown, and agreed to cede their traditional homelands on the understanding that the Crown would thereafter protect them in the possession and use of such lands as were reserved for their use; see the comments of Professor Slattery in his article "Understanding Aboriginal Rights" (1987), 66 Can. Bar Rev. 727, at p. 753. The sections of the *Indian Act* relating to the inalienability of Indian lands seek to give effect to this protection by interposing the Crown between the Indians and the market forces which, if left unchecked, had the potential to erode Indian ownership of these reserve lands. This Court, in its recent decision of *Canadian Pacific Ltd. v. Paul*, [1988] 2 S.C.R. 654, alluded to this point when it noted, at p. 677, that the feature of inalienability was adopted as a protective measure for the Indian population lest it be persuaded into improvident transactions. I take it to be obvious that the protections afforded against taxation and attachment by ss. 87 and 89 of the *Indian Act* go hand-in-hand with these restraints on the alienability of land. I noted above that the Crown, as part of the consideration for the cession of Indian lands, often committed itself to giving goods and services to the natives concerned. Taking but one example, by terms of the "numbered treaties" concluded between the Indians of the prairie regions and part of the Northwest Territories, the Crown undertook to provide Indians with assistance in such matters as education, medicine and agriculture, and to furnish supplies which Indians could use in the pursuit of their traditional vocations of hunting, fishing, and trapping. The exemptions from taxation and distraint have historically protected the ability of Indians to benefit from this property in two ways. First, they guard against the possibility that one branch of government, through the imposition of taxes, could erode the full measure of the benefits given by that branch of government entrusted with the supervision of Indian affairs. Secondly, the protection against attachment ensures that the enforcement of civil judgments by non-natives will not be allowed to hinder Indians in the untrammelled enjoyment of such advantages as they had retained or might acquire pursuant to the fulfillment by the Crown of its treaty obligations. In effect, these sections shield Indians from the imposition of the civil liabilities that could lead, albeit through an indirect route, to the alienation of the Indian land base through the medium of foreclosure sales and the like; see Brennan J.'s discussion of the purpose served by Indian tax immunities in the American context in *Bryan v. Itasca County*, 426 U.S. 373 (1976), at p. 391.

In summary, the historical record makes it clear that ss. 87 and 89 of the *Indian Act*, the sections to which the deeming provision of s. 90 applies, constitute part of a legislative "package" which bears the impress of an obligation to native peoples which the Crown has recognized at least since the signing of the *Royal Proclamation of 1763*. From that time on, the Crown has always acknowledged that it is honour-bound to shield Indians from any efforts by non-natives to dispossess Indians of the property which they hold qua Indians, i.e., their land base and the chattels on that land base.

It is also important to underscore the corollary to the conclusion I have just drawn. The fact that the modern-day legislation, like its historical counterparts, is so careful to underline that exemptions from taxation and distraint apply only in respect of personal property situated on reserves demonstrates that the purpose of the legislation is not to remedy the economically disadvantaged position of Indians by ensuring that Indians may acquire, hold, and deal with property in the commercial mainstream on different terms than their fellow citizens. An examination of the decisions bearing on these sections confirms that Indians who acquire and deal in property outside lands reserved for their use, deal with it on the same basis as all other Canadians. ...

In summary, I conclude that an interpretation of s. 90(1)(*b*), which sees its purpose as limited to preventing non-natives from hampering Indians from benefitting in full from the personal property promised Indians in treaties and ancillary agreements, is perfectly consistent with the tenor of the obligations that the Crown has always assumed vis-a-vis the protection of native property.

Section 90(1)(b) as including the Provincial Crowns

I turn next to the second of the two alternative readings of "Her Majesty" in s. 90(1)(*b*). If this term is meant to include the provincial Crowns, the exemptions and privileges of ss. 87 and 89 will apply to a much wider range of personal property. In effect, it would follow inexorably that the notional situs of s. 90(1)(*b*) will extend these protections to any and all personal property that could enure to Indians through the whole range of agreements that might be concluded between an Indian band and Her Majesty in right of a province.

As I see it, if one is to reject the interpretation advanced above, that s. 90(1)(*b*) refers solely to property which inures to Indians from the federal Crown through operation of the treaties and ancillary agreements, there is no basis in logic for the further assumption that some, but not all agreements, between Indian bands and Provincial Crown would be contemplated by the provision. Section 90(1)(*b*) does not qualify the term "agreement", and if one interprets "Her Majesty" as including the provincial Crown, it must follow as a matter of due course that s. 90(1)(*b*) takes in all agreements that could be concluded between an Indian band and a provincial Crown.

It follows inexorably that if an Indian band, pursuant to a purely commercial agreement with a provincial Crown, acquires personal property, that property will be exempt from taxation and distraint, regardless of its situs. Moreover, the protections of ss. 87 and 89 would apply in respect of any subsequent dealings by the Indian band respecting that property, even if those dealings were confined to ordinary commercial matters. This would have broad ramifications, and I cannot accept the notion that Parliament, in fulfilling its constitutional responsibility over Indian affairs, intended that the protective envelope of ss. 87 and 89 should apply on such a broad scale.

My conclusion rests on the fact that such a result cannot be reconciled with the scope of the protections that the Crown has traditionally extended to the property of natives. As I stated earlier, a review of the obligations that the Crown has assumed in this area shows that it has done no more than seek to shield the property of Indians that has an immediate and discernible nexus to the occupancy of reserve lands from interference at the hands of non-natives. The legislation has always distinguished between property situated on reserves and property Indians hold outside reserves. There is simply no evidence that the Crown has ever taken the position that it must protect property simply because that property is held by an Indian as opposed to a non-native. Indeed, unless one were to take the view that there exist two laws of contract, one applying to Indians and one to non-Indians, it would be difficult to rationalize a result that saw exemptions against taxation and distraint apply in respect of property simply because the person acquiring it happened to be an Indian. But, as I have intimated above, the interpretation of s. 90(1)(*b*) advanced by the trial judge and affirmed by the Chief Justice must, in logic, lead precisely to this result.

When Indian bands enter the commercial mainstream, it is to be expected that they will have occasion, from time to time, to enter into purely commercial agreements with the provincial Crowns in the same way as with private interests. The provincial Crowns are, after all, important players in the marketplace. If, then, an Indian band enters into a normal business transaction, be it with a provincial Crown, or a private corporation, and acquires personal property, be it in the form of chattels or debt obligations, how is one to characterize the property concerned? To my mind, it makes no sense to compare it with the property that enures to Indians pursuant to treaties and their ancillary agreements. Indians have a plenary entitlement to their treaty property; it is owed to them qua Indians. Personal property acquired by Indians in normal business dealings is clearly different; it is simply property anyone else might have acquired, and I can see no reason why in those circumstances Indians should not be treated in the same way as other people.

There can be no doubt, on a reading of s. 90(1)(b), that it would not apply to any personal property that an Indian band might acquire in connection with an ordinary commercial agreement with a private concern. Property of that nature will only be protected once it can be established that it is situated on a reserve. Accordingly, any dealings in the commercial mainstream in property acquired in this manner will fall to be regulated by the laws of general application. Indians will enjoy no exemptions from taxation in respect of this property, and will be free to deal with it in the same manner as any other citizen. In addition, provided the property is not situated on reserve lands, third parties will be free to issue execution on this property. I think it would be truly paradoxical if it were to be otherwise. As the Chief Justice has pointed out in *Nowegijick v. The Queen*, [1983] 1 S.C.R. 29, at p. 36:

> Indians are citizens and, in affairs of life not governed by treaties or the Indian Act, they are subject to all of the responsibilities, including payment of taxes, of other Canadian citizens.

But, in my respectful view, the implications flowing from the interpretation the trial judge advanced of s. 90(1)(b) go counter to this statement, for as I have pointed out earlier, as a logical consequence of that interpretation, any time Indians acquired personal property in an agreement with a provincial Crown, even one of a purely commercial character, the exemptions and protections of ss. 87 and 89 would apply in respect of that particular asset, regardless of situs.... As I see it, if Parliament had intended to cast aside these traditional constraints on the Crown's obligations to protect the property of Indians, it would have expressed this in the clearest of terms. I am loathe to conclude that this result can be made to rest on the strength of a supposed ambiguity in s. 90(1)(b), which, as I have suggested above, can only arguably be an ambiguity if one turns a blind eye to compelling historical and textual arguments.

To reiterate, I simply cannot reconcile the implications that flow from reading the term "Her Majesty" in s. 90(1)(b) as including the provincial Crowns with the scope of the protections that the Crown has accorded Indian property to date. The historical record that so clearly reveals a cogent rationale for protecting the personal property that enures to Indians by operation of treaty obligations regardless of situs, is silent as to any reason why personal property that Indian bands acquire from the provincial Crowns should receive the same extraordinary level of protection.

Moreover, an examination of s. 90(2) confirms that it is fallacious to interpret s. 90(1)(*b*) as intended to expand on the scope of the protections that the Crown has traditionally assumed with regard to the protection of native property. Section 90(2) provides that the Minister of Indian Affairs must approve any transaction purporting to transfer title or any interest in any property to which s. 90(1)(*b*) applies:

> 90.(2) Every transaction purporting to pass title to any property that is by this section deemed to be situated on a reserve, or any interest in such property, is void unless the transaction is entered into with the consent of the Minister or is entered into between members of a band or between the band and a member thereof.

A reading of the *Indian Act* shows that this provision is but one of a number of sections which seek to protect property to which Indians may be said to have an entitlement by virtue of their right to occupy the lands reserved for their use. In addition to the protections relating to Indian lands to which I have already drawn attention, the range of property protected runs from crops raised on reserve lands to deposits of minerals; see ss. 32, 91, 92, 93. These sections restrict the ability of non-natives to acquire the particular property concerned by requiring that the Minister approve all transactions in respect of it. As is the case with the restrictions on alienability to which I drew attention earlier, the intent of these sections is to guard against the possibility that Indians will be victimized by "sharp dealing" on the part of non-natives and dispossessed of their entitlements....

I conclude that the statutory notional situs of s. 90(1)(*b*) is meant to extend solely to personal property which enures to Indians through the discharge by "Her Majesty" of her treaty or ancillary obligations. Pursuant to s. 91(24) of the *Constitution Act, 1867*, it is of course "Her Majesty" in right of Canada who bears the sole responsibility for conferring any such property on Indians, and I would, therefore, limit application of the term "Her Majesty" as used in s. 90(1)(*b*) to the federal Crown.

Nowegijick v. The Queen

While the textual and historical arguments to be made for limiting the meaning of "Her Majesty" in s. 90(1)(*b*) to the federal Crown appear to me to be irrefutable, I recognize that it is necessary to ask whether the canons of construction generic to the interpretation of statutes relating to Indians change this result. These canons are, of course, those set out by the Chief Justice in *Nowegijick, supra*, at p. 36.

I note at the outset that I do not take issue with the principle that treaties and statutes relating to Indians should be liberally construed and doubtful expressions resolved in favour of the Indians. In the case of treaties, this principle finds its justification in the fact that the Crown enjoyed a superior bargaining position when negotiating treaties with native peoples. From the perspective of the Indians, treaties were drawn up in a foreign language, and incorporated references to legal concepts of a system of law with which Indians were unfamiliar. In the interpretation of these documents it is, therefore, only just that the courts attempt to construe various provisions as the Indians may be taken to have understood them.

But as I view the matter, somewhat different considerations must apply in the case of statutes relating to Indians. Whereas a treaty is the product of bargaining between two contracting parties, statutes relating to Indians are an expression of the will of Parliament. Given this fact, I do not find it particularly helpful to engage in speculation as to how Indians may be taken to understand a given provision. Rather, I think the approach must be to read the Act concerned with a view to elucidating what it was that Parliament wished to effect in enacting the particular section in question. This approach is not a jettisoning of the liberal interpretative method. As already stated, it is clear that in the interpretation of any statutory enactment dealing with Indians, and particularly the *Indian Act*, it is appropriate to interpret in a broad manner provisions that are aimed at maintaining Indian rights, and to interpret narrowly provisions aimed at limiting or abrogating them. Thus if legislation bears on treaty promises, the courts will always strain against adopting an interpretation that has the effect of negating commitments undertaken by the Crown; see *United States v. Powers*, 305 U.S. 527 (1939), at p. 533.

At the same time, I do not accept that this salutary rule that statutory ambiguities must be resolved in favour of the Indians implies automatic acceptance of a given construction simply because it may be expected that the Indians would favour it over any other competing interpretation. It is also necessary to reconcile any given interpretation with the policies the Act seeks to promote.

It is consideration of this factor that leads me to reject the interpretation the trial judge would give to s. 90(1)(*b*). The provincial Crowns bear no responsibility to provide for the welfare and protection of native peoples, and I am not prepared to accept that Parliament, in enacting s. 90(1)(*b*), intended that the privileges of ss. 87 and 89 exempt Indian bands from taxation and civil process in respect of all personal property that they may acquire pursuant to all agreements with that level of government, regardless of where that property is located. This interpretation is simply too broad. As I have attempted to show, it would take in any agreement relating to purely commercial dealings Indian bands might conclude with the provincial Crowns when competing in the economic mainstream of society. To my mind, such an interpretation takes one beyond the liberal and the generous and subverts the very character of the commitments that the Crown has historically undertaken *vis-à-vis* the protection of native property. ...

In arriving at his conclusion that the trial judge was correct in interpreting "Her Majesty" in s. 90(1)(*b*) as including the provincial Crowns, the Chief Justice sets considerable store on what he takes to be the aboriginal perception of "Her Majesty". With deference, I question his conclusion that it is realistic, in this day and age, to proceed on the assumption that from the aboriginal perspective, any federal-provincial divisions that the Crown has imposed on itself are simply internal to itself, such that the Crown may be considered what one might style an "indivisible entity". But even accepting that assumption, it does not follow that fairness requires one to proceed on the basis that Indians would be justified in concluding that all property they may acquire pursuant to agreements with that "indivisible entity" should be automatically protected, regardless of situs, by the exemptions and privileges conferred by ss. 87 and 89 of the *Indian Act*. I have no doubt that Indians are very much aware that ordinary commercial dealings constitute "affairs of life" that do not fall to be governed by their treaties or the *Indian Act*. Thus I take it that Indians, when engaging in the cut and thrust of business dealings in the commercial mainstream are under no illusions that they can expect to compete from a position of privilege with respect to their fellow Canadians. This distinction, it is fair to say, will be driven home every time Indians do business off their reserve lands. Professor Slattery puts the matter plainly when he notes, *supra*, at p. 776, that the purchases made by Indians in a normal drugstore are governed by laws of general application.

The conclusion I draw is that it is entirely reasonable to expect that Indians, when acquiring personal property pursuant to an agreement with that "indivisible entity" constituted by the Crown, will recognize that the question whether the exemptions of ss. 87 and 89 should apply in respect of that property, regardless of situs, must turn on the nature of the property concerned. If the property in question simply represents property which Indians acquired in the same manner any other Canadian might have done, I am at a loss to see why Indians should expect that the statutory notional situs of s. 90(1)(*b*) should apply in respect of it. In other words, even if the Indians perceive the Crown to be "indivisible", it is unclear to me how it could be that Indians could perceive that s. 90(1)(*b*) is meant to extend the protections of ss. 87 and 89 in an "indivisible" manner to all property acquired by them pursuant to agreements with that entity, regardless of where that property is held. What if the property concerned is property held off the reserve, and was acquired by the Indian band concerned simply with a view to further business dealings in the commercial mainstream?...

Moreover, I would question the conclusion that interpreting "Her Majesty" as including the provincial Crowns in the context of s. 90(1)(*b*) is tantamount to resolving the ambiguity of the meaning of this term in favour of the Indians. Sections 87 and 89, as I have shown above, have been crafted so as to place obstacles in the way of non-natives who would presume to dispossess Indians of personal property that is situated on reserves. But when Indians deal in the general marketplace, the protections conferred by these sections have the potential to become powerful impediments to their engaging successfully in commercial matters. Access to credit is the lifeblood of commerce, and I find it very difficult to accept that Indians would see any advantage, when seeking credit, in being precluded from putting forth in pledge property they may acquire from provincial Crowns. Indians, I would have thought, would much prefer to have free rein to conduct their affairs as all other fellow citizens when dealing in the commercial mainstream.

To elaborate, if Indians are to be unable to pledge or mortgage such personal property as they acquire in agreements with provincial Crowns, businessmen will have a strong incentive to avoid dealings with Indians. This is simply because the fact that Indians will be liable to be distrained in respect of some classes of property, and not in respect of others, will introduce a level of complexity in business dealings with Indians that is not present in other transactions. I think it safe to say that businessmen place a great premium on certainty in their commercial dealings, and that, accordingly, the greatest possible incentive to do business with Indians would be the knowledge that business may be conducted with them on exactly the same basis as with any other person. Any special considerations, extraordinary protections or exemptions that Indians bring with them to the marketplace introduce complications and would seem guaranteed to frighten off potential business partners.

In summary, while I of course endorse the applicability of the canons of interpretation laid down in Nowegijick, it is my respectful view that the interpretation proposed in this particular instance takes one beyond the confines of the fair, large and liberal, and can, in fact, be seen to involve the resolution of a supposed ambiguity in a manner most unfavourable to Indian interests. ...

Disposition

I would dismiss the appeal with costs throughout.

Lamer, **Wilson** and **L'Heureux-Dubé JJ.** (concurring), **Dickson C.J.C.** (concurring in the result but differing on the interpretation of "Her Majesty")

In the *Mitchell v. Peguis* case, Justice La Forest was called upon to decide how courts should interpret statutes relating to Indians. Remember, he had to contend with Justice Dickson's point from *Nowegijick* "that treaties and statutes relating to Indians should be liberally construed and doubtful expressions resolved in favour of the Indians". In analyzing this interpretive provision Justice La Forest wrote, "that statutes relating to Indians are an expression of the will of Parliament. Given this fact, I do not find it particularly helpful to engage in speculation as to how Indians may be taken to understand a given provision".

1. Do you agree with Justice La Forest's re-interpretation of *Nowejigick*? What are the implications of this approach?
2. If Justice La Forest does not "find it helpful to engage in speculation as to how Indians may be taken to understand a given provision", how should one deal with his point that "Indians, I would have thought, would much prefer to have free rein to conduct their affairs as all other fellow citizens when dealing in the commercial mainstream". Similarly, if Justice La Forest does not regard it as helpful to speculate on how Indians understand statutory provisions relating to them, how should one read his point that: "I have no doubt that Indians are very much aware that ordinary commercial dealings constitute 'affairs of life' that do not fall to be governed by their treaties or the *Indian Act*. Thus I take it that Indians, when engaging in the cut and thrust of business dealings in the commercial mainstream are under no illusions that they can expect to compete from a position of privilege with respect to their fellow Canadians".

WILLIAMS v. CANADA

[1992] 1 S.C.R. 877

The judgment of the Court was delivered by

Gonthier J.:— At issue in this case is the situs of unemployment insurance benefits received by an Indian for the purpose of the exemption from taxation provided by s. 87 of the *Indian Act*, R.S.C. 1970, c. I-6 (now R.S.C., 1985, c. I-5).

I — Facts and Procedural History

The appellant received a notice of assessment by the Minister of National Revenue which included in his income, for the taxation year 1984, certain unemployment insurance benefits. The appellant contested the assessment. His objection was overruled by the Minister of National Revenue. The appellant appealed to the Federal Court, Trial Division: [1989] 2 F.C. 318, 24 F.T.R. 169, 24 C.C.E.L. 119, 89 D.T.C. 5032, [1989] 1 C.T.C. 117, [1989] 1 C.N.L.R. 184. The appeal proceeded on the basis of an agreed statement of facts.

At all material times, the appellant was a member of the Penticton Indian Band and resided on the Penticton Indian Reserve No. 1. In 1984 he received regular unemployment insurance benefits for which he qualified because of his former employment with a logging company situated on the reserve, and his employment by the Band in a "NEED Project" on the reserve. In both cases, the work was performed on the reserve, the employer was located on the reserve, and the appellant was paid on the reserve. During his employment, contributions to the unemployment insurance scheme were paid both by the appellant and his employers.

All of the regular unemployment insurance benefits were paid by federal government cheques mailed from the Canada Employment and Immigration Commission's regional computer centre in Vancouver. (While the instruments of payment may not technically have been cheques, this is of no consequence in this appeal.)

In addition to regular benefits, the appellant also received "enhanced" unemployment insurance benefits paid in respect of a job creation project administered on the reserve by the Band, pursuant to a written agreement between the Band and the Commission. The appellant was employed pursuant to this project in work which took place on the reserve, during a time in which he would otherwise have received regular benefits. The Band paid the appellant $60 per week during the program. The enhanced benefits constituted the bulk of the appellant's remuneration for his work in this program.

Section 38 of the *Unemployment Insurance Act, 1971*, S.C. 1970-71-72, c. 48, authorized the creation of such programs on a general basis, without any limitation to Indians. The enhanced unemployment insurance benefits were also paid by the Commission's regional computer centre in Vancouver.

The issue at trial was whether the unemployment insurance benefits received by the appellant were exempt from taxation pursuant to s. 87 of the *Indian Act*. With regard to the requirements of that section, the disputed issue was whether the benefits received by the appellant were "situated" on a reserve....

III — Framing the Issues

In order to decide the basis upon which a situs is to be assigned to the unemployment insurance benefits in this case, it is necessary to explore the purposes of the exemption from taxation in s. 87 of the *Indian Act*, the nature of the benefits in question, and the manner in which the incidence of taxation falls upon the benefits to be taxed.

A — The Nature and Purpose of the Exemption from Taxation

The question of the purpose of ss. 87, 89 and 90 has been thoroughly addressed by La Forest J. in the case of *Mitchell v. Peguis Indian Band*, [1990] 2 S.C.R. 85. La Forest J. expressed the view that the purpose of these sections was to preserve the entitlements of Indians to their reserve lands and to ensure that the use of their property on their reserve lands was not eroded by the ability of governments to tax, or creditors to seize. The corollary of this conclusion was that the purpose of the sections was not to confer a general economic benefit upon the Indians (at pp. 130-31):

> ... In summary, the historical record makes it clear that ss. 87 and 89 of the *Indian Act*, the sections to which the deeming provision of s. 90 applies, constitute part of a legislative "package" which bears the impress of an obligation to native peoples which the Crown has recognized at least since the signing of the *Royal Proclamation of 1763*. From that time on, the Crown has always acknowledged that it is honour-bound to shield Indians from any efforts by non-natives to dispossess Indians of the property which they hold qua Indians, i.e., their land base and the chattels on that land base.
> It is also important to underscore the corollary to the conclusion I have just drawn. The fact that the modern-day legislation, like its historical counterparts, is so careful to underline that exemptions from taxation and distraint apply only in respect of personal property situated on reserves demonstrates that the purpose of the legislation is not to remedy the economically disadvantaged position of Indians by ensuring that Indians may acquire, hold, and deal with property in the commercial mainstream on different terms than their fellow citizens. An examination of the decisions bearing on these sections confirms that Indians who acquire and deal in property outside lands reserved for their use, deal with it on the same basis as all other Canadians.

La Forest J. also noted that the protection from seizure is a mixed blessing, in that it removes the assets of an Indian on a reserve from the ordinary stream of commercial dealings (at pp. 146-47).

Therefore, under the *Indian Act*, an Indian has a choice with regard to his personal property. The Indian may situate this property on the reserve, in which case it is within the protected area and free from seizure and taxation, or the Indian may situate this property off the reserve, in which case it is outside the protected area, and more fully available for ordinary commercial purposes in society. Whether the Indian wishes to remain within the protected reserve system or integrate more fully into the larger commercial world is a choice left to the Indian.

The purpose of the situs test in s. 87 is to determine whether the Indian holds the property in question as part of the entitlement of an Indian qua Indian on the reserve. Where it is necessary to decide amongst various methods of fixing the location of the relevant property, such a method must be selected having regard to this purpose.

B — Nature of Benefit and the Incidence of Taxation

Section 56 of the *Income Tax Act* is the section which taxes income from unemployment insurance benefits. That section specifies that unemployment insurance benefits which are "received by the taxpayer in the year" are to be included in computing the income of a taxpayer. The parties have approached this question on the basis that what is being taxed is a debt owing from the Crown to the taxpayer on account of unemployment insurance which the taxpayer has qualified for. This is not precisely true, since the liability for taxation arises not when the debt (if that is what it is) arises, but rather when it is paid, and the money is received by the taxpayer. However, it is true that the taxation does not attach to the money in the hands of the taxpayer, but instead to the receipt by the taxpayer of the money. Thus, the incidence of taxation in the case of unemployment insurance benefits is on the taxpayer in respect of the transaction, that is, the receipt of the benefit.

This Court's decision in *Nowegijick v. The Queen*, [1983] 1 S.C.R. 29, stands for the proposition that the receipt of salary income is personal property for the purpose of the exemption from taxation provided by the *Indian Act*. I can see no difference between salary income and income from unemployment insurance benefits in this regard, therefore I hold that the receipt of income from unemployment insurance benefits is also personal property for the purposes of the *Indian Act*.

Nowegijick also stands for the proposition that the inclusion of personal property in the calculation of a taxpayer's income gives rise to a tax in respect of that personal property within the meaning of the *Indian Act*, despite the fact that the tax is on the person rather than on the property directly.

Therefore, most of the requirements of s. 87 of the *Indian Act* have clearly been met in this case. The receipt of unemployment insurance benefits is personal property. That property is owned by an Indian. The Indian is being taxed in respect of that property, since it is being included in his income for the purpose of income taxation. The remaining question is whether the property in question is situated on a reserve.

Since it is the receipt of the benefit that is taxed, the simplest argument would be that the situs of the receipt of the benefit is where it is received, which would generally be the residence of the taxpayer. However, the *Income Tax Act* qualifies "received" by "in the year". This suggests that the notion of "receipt" in the *Income Tax Act* has more to do with when the income is received, rather than where. Thus, aside from the fact that the incidence of taxation falls upon the transaction itself, rather than the money in the hands of the employer or the taxpayer, little ought to be made of the notion of receipt in this context.

C — Comments on the "Residence of the Debtor" Test

The factor identified in previous cases as being of primary importance to determine the situs of this kind of property is the residence of the debtor, that is, the person paying the income. This was clearly stated by Thurlow A.C.J. in *The Queen v. National Indian Brotherhood*, [1979] 1 F.C. 103 (T.D.), at p. 109:

> A chose in action such as the right to a salary in fact has no situs. But where for some purpose the law has found it necessary to attribute a situs, in the absence of anything in the contract or elsewhere to indicate the contrary, the situs of a simple contract debt has been held to be the residence or place where the debtor is found. See Cheshire, *Private International Law*, seventh edition, pp. 420 et seq.

This conclusion was cited with approval by this Court in *Nowegijick v. The Queen, supra*, at p. 34:

> The Crown conceded in argument, correctly in my view, that the situs of the salary which Mr. Nowegijick received was sited on the reserve because it was there that the residence or place of the debtor, the Gull Bay Development Corporation, was to be found and it was there that the wages were payable. See Cheshire and North, *Private International Law* (10th ed., 1979) at pp. 536 et seq. and also the judgment of Thurlow A.C.J. in *R. v. National Indian Brotherhood*, [1979] 1 F.C. 103 particularly at pp. 109 et seq.

The only justification given in these cases for locating the situs of a debt at the residence of the debtor is that this is the rule applied in the conflict of laws. The rationale for this rule in the conflict of laws is that it is at the residence of the debtor that the debt may normally be enforced. Cheshire and North, *Private International Law* (11th ed. 1987), quote Atkin L.J. to this effect in *New York Life Insurance Co. v. Public Trustee*, [1924] 2 Ch. 101 (C.A.), at p. 119. ...This may be reasonable for the general purposes of conflicts of laws. However, one must inquire as to its utility for the purposes underlying the exemption from taxation in the *Indian Act*.

. . . . .

In resolving this question, it is readily apparent that to simply adopt general conflicts principles in the present context would be entirely out of keeping with the scheme and purposes of the *Indian Act* and *Income Tax Act*. The purposes of the conflict of laws have little or nothing in common with the purposes underlying the *Indian Act*. It is simply not apparent how the place where a debt may normally be enforced has any relevance to the question whether to tax the receipt of the payment of that debt would amount to the erosion of the entitlements of an Indian qua Indian on a reserve. The test for situs under the *Indian Act* must be constructed according to its purposes, not the purposes of the conflict of laws. Therefore, the position that the residence of the debtor exclusively determines the situs of benefits such as those paid in this case must be closely reexamined in light of the purposes of the *Indian Act*. It may be that the residence of the debtor remains an important factor, or even the exclusive one. However, this conclusion cannot be directly drawn from an analysis of how the conflict of laws deals with such an issue.

IV — The Proper Test

Because the transaction by which a taxpayer receives unemployment insurance benefits is not a physical object, the method by which one might fix its situs is not immediately apparent. In one sense, the difficulty is that the transaction has no situs. However, in another sense, the problem is that it has too many. There is the situs of the debtor, the situs of the creditor, the situs where the payment is made, the situs of the employment which created the qualification for the receipt of income, the situs where the payment will be used, and no doubt others. The task is then to identify which of these locations is the relevant one, or which combination of these factors controls the location of the transaction.

The appellant suggests that in deciding the situs of the receipt of income, a court ought to balance all of the relevant "connecting factors" on a case by case basis. Such an approach would have the advantage of flexibility, but it would have to be applied carefully in order to avoid several potential pitfalls. It is desirable, when construing exemptions from taxation, to develop criteria which are predictable in their application, so that the taxpayers involved may plan their affairs appropriately. This is also important as the same criteria govern an exemption from seizure.

Furthermore, it would be dangerous to balance connecting factors in an abstract manner, divorced from the purpose of the exemption under the *Indian Act*. A connecting factor is only relevant in so much as it identifies the location of the property in question for the purposes of the *Indian Act*. In particular categories of cases, therefore, one connecting factor may have much more weight than another. It would be easy in balancing connecting factors on a case by case basis to lose sight of this.

However, an overly rigid test which identified one or two factors as having controlling force has its own potential pitfalls. Such a test would be open to manipulation and abuse, and in focusing on too few factors could miss the purposes of the exemption in the *Indian Act* as easily as a test which indiscriminately focuses on too many.

The approach which best reflects these concerns is one which analyzes the matter in terms of categories of property and types of taxation. For instance, connecting factors may have different relevance with regard to unemployment insurance benefits than in respect of employment income, or pension benefits. The first step is to identify the various connecting factors which are potentially relevant. These factors should then be analyzed to determine what weight they should be given in identifying the location of the property, in light of three considerations: (1) the purpose of the exemption under the *Indian Act*; (2) the type of property in question; and (3) the nature of the taxation of that property. The question with regard to each connecting factor is therefore what weight should be given that factor in answering the question whether to tax that form of property in that manner would amount to the erosion of the entitlement of the Indian qua Indian on a reserve.

This approach preserves the flexibility of the case by case approach, but within a framework which properly identifies the weight which is to be placed on various connecting factors. Of course, the weight to be given various connecting factors cannot be determined precisely. However, this approach has the advantage that it preserves the ability to deal appropriately with future cases which present considerations not previously apparent.

A — The Test for the Situs of the Unemployment Insurance Benefits

Unemployment insurance benefits are income replacement insurance, paid when a person is out of work under certain qualifying conditions. While one often refers to unemployment insurance "benefits", the scheme is based on employer and employee premiums. These premiums are themselves tax-deductible for both the employer and employee.

There are a number of potentially relevant connecting factors in determining the location of the receipt of unemployment insurance benefits. The following have been suggested: the residence of the debtor, the residence of the person receiving the benefits, the place the benefits are paid, and the location of the employment income which gave rise to the qualification for the benefits. One's attention is naturally first drawn to the traditional test, that of the residence of the debtor. The debtor in this case is the federal Crown, through the Canada Employment and Immigration Commission. The Commission argues that the residence of the debtor in this case is Ottawa, referring to s. 11 of the *Employment and Immigration Department and Commission Act*, S.C. 1976-77, c. 54 (now R.S.C., 1985, c. E-5, s. 17), which mandates that the head office of the Commission be located in the National Capital Region.

There are, however, conceptual difficulties in establishing the situs of a Crown agency in any particular place within Canada. For most purposes, it is unnecessary to establish the situs of the Crown. The conflict of laws is interested in situs to determine jurisdictional and choice of law questions. With regard to the Crown, no such questions arise, since the Crown is present throughout Canada and may be sued anywhere in Canada. Unemployment insurance benefits are also available anywhere in Canada, to any Canadian who qualifies for them. Therefore, the purposes behind fixing the situs of an ordinary person do not apply to the Crown, and in particular do not apply to the Canada Employment and Immigration Commission in respect of the receipt of unemployment insurance benefits.

This does not necessarily mean that the physical location of the Crown is irrelevant to the purposes underlying the exemption from taxation provided by the *Indian Act*. However, it does suggest that the significance of the Crown being the source of the payments at issue in this case may lie more in the special nature of the public policy behind the payments, rather than the Crown's situs, assuming it can be fixed. Therefore, the residence of the debtor is a connecting factor of limited weight in the context of unemployment insurance benefits. For similar reasons, the place where the benefits are paid is of limited importance in this context.

This leaves two factors to be considered: the residence of the recipient of the benefits, and the location of the employment income which was the basis of the qualification for the benefits. ...

The general scheme of taxation with regard to unemployment insurance premiums and benefits bears further examination in this regard. As noted above, unemployment insurance is premium based. The intent of the scheme is that the premiums received will, overall, largely equal the benefits paid out. This is not to say that the scheme is completely self-financing. However, it is more accurate to characterize an unemployment insurance benefit as something paid for through the premiums of employed persons than to characterize it as a benefit granted by the government out of its general revenues.

This becomes important in analyzing the tax implications of the unemployment insurance benefit scheme. The treatment of premiums and benefits for the purposes of taxation is that the premiums paid by employed persons are deductible from their taxable income, whereas the benefits paid to unemployed persons must be included in their taxable income. By allowing premiums to be deducted from taxable income, and mandating that benefits be included in taxable income, the effect of the unemployment insurance scheme on general tax revenue is minimized. The tax revenues lost by the government due to the deductibility of premiums are offset by the revenues gained by the taxation of the benefits. This is not to say that the unemployment insurance scheme has no effect on taxation revenues, since premiums may not precisely equal benefits overall, and the effect of different rates of taxation cannot be ignored. However, it is clear that the scheme established by Parliament was intended, in principle, to minimize the tax implications of unemployment insurance.

Since unemployment insurance benefits are based on premiums arising out of previous employment, not general tax revenue, the connection between the previous employment and the benefits is a strong one. The manner in which unemployment insurance benefits are treated for the purposes of taxation further strengthens this connection, as there is a symmetry of treatment in the taxation of premiums and benefits, since premiums are tax-deductible and benefits are taxed, thereby minimizing the influence of the unemployment insurance scheme on general tax revenues.

The location of the qualifying employment income is therefore an important factor in establishing whether the taxation of subsequent benefits would erode the entitlements of an Indian qua Indian on the reserve. For in the case of an Indian whose qualifying employment income was on the reserve, the symmetry in the tax implications of premiums and benefits breaks down. For such an Indian, the original employment income was tax-exempt. The taxation paid on the subsequent benefits therefore does more than merely offset the tax saved by virtue of the premiums. Instead, it is an erosion of the entitlements created by the Indian's employment on the reserve.

Furthermore, since the duration and extent of the benefits are tied to the terms of employment during a specified period, it is the location of the qualifying employment income during that period that is relevant.

Having regard to the importance of the location of the qualifying employment income as a factor in identifying the location of the unemployment insurance benefits, the remaining factor of the residence of the recipient of the benefits at the time of their receipt is only potentially significant if it points to a location different from that of the qualifying employment.

B — *The Situs of the Appellant's Unemployment Insurance Benefits*

In the present case, the residence of the appellant when he received the benefits was on the reserve.

It has been assumed by the parties that the previous employment of the appellant which gave rise to the qualification for unemployment insurance benefits was also located on the reserve, since the two employers in question were located on the reserve. This question must be reexamined in light of our determination that this conclusion cannot safely be drawn from the principles of the conflicts of laws.

However, this would not be an appropriate case in which to develop a test for the situs of the receipt of employment income. All the potential connecting factors with respect to the qualifying employment of the appellant point to the reserve. The employer was located on the reserve, the work was performed on the reserve, the appellant resided on the reserve, and he was paid on the reserve. A test for the situs of employment income could therefore only be developed in an abstract vacuum in this case, since there is no real controversy of relevant factors pulling in opposite directions. The same would be true of any consideration of the weight, if any, to be given to the residence of the appellant upon receipt of the benefits as this was also on the reserve.

Furthermore, as can be seen from our discussion of the test for the situs of unemployment insurance benefits, the creation of a test for the location of intangible property under the *Indian Act* is a complex endeavour. In the context of unemployment insurance we were able to focus on certain features of the scheme and its taxation implications in order to establish one factor as having particular importance. It is not clear whether this would be possible in the context of employment income, or what features of employment income and its taxation should be examined to that end.

Therefore, for the purposes of the present appeal, we merely note that the employment of the appellant by which he qualified for unemployment insurance benefits was clearly located on the reserve, no matter what the proper test for the situs of employment income is determined to be. Because the qualifying employment was located on the reserve, so too were the benefits subsequently received. The question of the relevance of the residence of the recipient of the benefits at the time of receipt does not arise in this case since it was also on the reserve.

C — *The Situs of the Enhanced Unemployment Insurance Benefits*

According to s. 38(3) of *the Unemployment Insurance Act, 1971* enhanced benefits are to be considered unemployment insurance benefits for the purpose of the *Income Tax Act*. ...

This is also the manner in which enhanced benefits should be characterized for the purpose of the exemption from taxation in the *Indian Act*, since this only reflects the reality of the situation. The appellant only qualified for participation in the job creation program because he had been receiving regular unemployment insurance benefits, that is, because of his prior employment that had ceased. The benefits which he continued to receive would not have ceased had he quit his employment with the program. The program itself was located on the reserve. Therefore, the conclusion that the unemployment insurance benefits received by the appellant were situated on the reserve applies to both the regular and enhanced benefits.

V — Conclusion

Determining the situs of intangible personal property requires a court to evaluate various connecting factors which tie the property to one location or another. In the context of the exemption from taxation in the *Indian Act*, there are three important considerations: the purpose of the exemption; the character of the property in question; and the incidence of taxation upon that property. Given the purpose of the exemption, the ultimate question is to what extent each factor is relevant in determining whether to tax the particular kind of property in a particular manner would erode the entitlement of an Indian qua Indian to personal property on the reserve.

With regard to the unemployment insurance benefits received by the appellant, a particularly important factor is the location of the employment which gave rise to the qualification for the benefits. In this case, the location of the qualifying employment was on the reserve, therefore the benefits received by the appellant were also located on the reserve. The question of the relevance of the residence of the recipient of the benefits at the time of receipt does not arise in this case.

The appeal is therefore allowed and the cross-appeal dismissed, with costs throughout. The matter is referred back to the Minister of National Revenue to be reassessed on the basis that all of the unemployment benefits in question are exempt from taxation.

After the Supreme Court of Canada's ruling in *Williams*, Revenue Canada developed interpretive guidelines to apply the "connecting factors" test for determining whether property was situate on reserve and thus exempt from taxation. These guidelines have been the subject of extensive protests and litigation by Indians. There is concern that they are interpreted too strictly, ignoring Gonthier J.'s caution in *Williams* that "it would be dangerous to balance connecting factors in an abstract manner, divorced from the purpose of the exemption under the *Indian Act*." Gonthier J. further noted [at p. 892]:

> [a] connecting factor is only relevant in so much as it identifies the location of the property in question for the purposes of the *Indian Act*... In particular categories of cases, therefore, one connecting factor may have much more weight than another. It would be easy in balancing connecting factors on a case by case basis to lose sight of this.
>
> However, an overly rigid test which identified one or two factors as having controlling force has its own potential pitfalls. Such a test would be open to manipulation and abuse, and in focusing on too few factors could miss the purposes of the exemption in the Indian Act as easily as a test which indiscriminately focuses on too many.

This brief excerpt from the *Folster* case illustrates limitations the Court finds in Revenue Canada's guidelines applying the test found in *Williams*.

FOLSTER v. CANADA

[1997] 3 F.C. 269, 148 D.L.R. (4th) 314 (C.A.)

Isaac C.J. and **Pratte** and **Linden JJ.**

The judgment of the Court was delivered by

Linden J.: — ... Gonthier J. crafted a new test based on the foundation of La Forest J.'s purposive analysis in *Mitchell*. He recognized that, although there are necessarily many factors which may be of assistance in determining the situs of intangible property such as unemployment insurance or employment income, the relevance of these "connecting factors" must be assessed on the basis of their ability to further the purpose of section 87. Further, the weight to be given to each factor may change from case to case. ...

This new test was not designed to extend the tax exemption benefit to all Indians. Nor was it aimed at exempting all Indians living on reserves. Rather, in suggesting reliance on a range of factors which may be relevant to determining the situs of the property, Gonthier J. sought to ensure that any tax exemption would serve the purpose it was meant to achieve, namely, the preservation of property held by Indians qua Indians on reserves so that their traditional way of life would not be jeopardized. ...

... Following the Supreme Court's decision in *Williams*, Revenue Canada issued four guidelines intended to assist in the interpretation of section 87 of the Act according to the connecting factors test. These guidelines are as follows (Indian Act Exemption for employment income, Guidelines, June 1994, Revenue Canada, at 2-8).

> When at least 90% of the duties of an employment are performed on a reserve, all of the income of an Indian from that employment will usually be exempt from income tax...When less than 90% of the duties of an employment are performed on a reserve and the employment income is not exempted by another guideline, the exemption is prorated. The exemption will apply to the portion of the income related to the duties performed on the reserve....
> When: (i) the employer is resident on the reserve; and (ii) the Indian lives on a reserve; all of the income of an Indian from an employment will usually be exempt from income tax...
> When: (i) more than 50% of the duties of an employment are performed on a reserve; and (ii) the employer is resident on a reserve, or the Indian lives on a reserve; all of the income of an Indian from an employment will usually be exempt from income tax...When: (i) the employer is resident on a reserve; and (ii) the employer is: (a) an Indian band which has a reserve, or a tribal council representing one or more Indian bands which have reserves, or (b) an Indian organization controlled by one or more such bands or tribal councils, if the organization is dedicated exclusively to the social, cultural, educational, or economic development of Indians who for the most part live on reserves; and (iii) the duties of the employment are in connection with the employer's non-commercial activities carried on exclusively for the benefit

of Indians who for the most part live on the reserves; all of the income of an Indian from an employment will usually be exempt from income tax.

As is evident, the guidelines understandably are based largely on the residence of the employer and the location where the duties of the employee are performed. While these factors may be useful for the determination of whether employment income falls within section 87, a central premise of *Williams* is that, in the final analysis, the relative weighting of connecting factors must proceed on a case-by-case basis. Consequently, although guidelines may assist in routine cases, it is not possible to establish, in advance, the precise formula by which employment income is to be assessed in all cases.

In *Shilling v. Canada M.N.R.*, 2001 FCA 178, a status Indian was assessed income tax by the Minister of National Revenue. Ms. Shilling had in the past resided on the Rama reserve and in the present maintained substantial connections with her family and community on the reserve. She had, however, lived and worked in Toronto during the period that she earned the employment income at issue in the case. While her salary was earned off the reserve, it was paid by a person residing on and carrying on business on the reserve (a native employee leasing service). Ms. Shilling's salary payments took the form of transfers of funds from her employer's bank account on the reserve to her bank account on the reserve. The Federal Court, Trial Division determined ([1999] 4 F.C. 178 (T.D.)) that Ms. Shilling's employment income was tax-exempt as the property of an Indian situated on a reserve. The Crown's appeal to the Federal Court of Appeal was allowed. The Court applied the connecting factors test from *Williams* and held that the employer's head office location was the only factor connecting Ms. Shilling's employment income to a reserve. It held that this was not sufficient to find the *situs* of the employment income to be on the reserve. The fact that Ms. Shilling was employed by a business with its head office and bank account on-reserve was not, in the Court's view, sufficient to make her employment "integral to the life of the reserve". The Court wrote (paragraphs 65-66):

> Ms. Shilling's employment is to be regarded as in the "commercial mainstream". This conclusion may appear counter-intuitive when applied to a Native person who identifies with her Band and First Nation, and is working with a social agency delivering programmes to assist Native people, in large part through reconnecting them with their culture and traditions.
>
> However, in the context of determining the location of intangible property for the purpose of section 87, "commercial mainstream" is to be contrasted with "integral to the life of a reserve": *Folster, supra*, at paragraph 14. …The purpose of the tax exemption in paragraph 87(1)(*b*) is not to address the general economically disadvantaged position of Indians in Canada.

Hence, Ms. Shilling's employment income earned while working in Toronto was not situated on a reserve, and was not exempt from taxation under the *Indian Act*. Leave to appeal to the Supreme Court of Canada was denied (2002).

In *Canada v. Monias*, 2001 FCA 239, leave to appeal to S.C.C. denied (2002), a number of Indians were employed by the Awasis Agency of Northern Manitoba ("Awasis") and assessed taxation. Awasis received its funding from Indian and Northern Affairs Canada pursuant to a series of comprehensive funding arrangements between it and the federal Crown. While the work performed by the taxpayers was mostly for the benefit of people on the reserve, it generally was performed off of the reserve and the taxpayers themselves did not reside on a reserve. The Minister denied the *Indian Act* exemption. The Tax Court allowed the appeals on the basis that the taxpayers' employment was intimately connected with various Indian communities all located on a reserve. The Crown appealed to the Federal Court of Appeal. The Federal Court of Appeal first considered the purpose of the *Indian Act* exemption. Considering the purpose and the facts in the case, the Court concluded the factors connecting the income to a reserve were not sufficient to determine that the income was situated on a reserve. Further, while the taxpayers' work might have helped to maintain and enhance the quality of life on the reserves for members of the Bands living there, it did not necessarily connect the acquisition or use of their employment income to the reserves as physical locations. The Federal Court of Appeal wrote (paragraph 66):

> That the work from which employment income is earned benefits Indians on reserves, and indeed may be integral to maintaining the reserves as viable social units, is not in itself sufficient to situate the employment income there. It is not the policy of paragraph 87(1)(*b*) to provide a tax subsidy for services provided to and for the benefit of reserves. Rather, it is to protect from erosion by taxation the property of individual Indians that they acquire, hold and use on a reserve, although in the case of an intangible, such as employment income, it is the *situs* of its *acquisition* that is particularly important.

To summarize *Monias*: the fact that the work from which employment income is earned benefits Indians on reserves (and may even be integral to maintaining the reserves as viable social units) is not in itself sufficient to situate the employment income on the reserve. The taxpayers, therefore, were not entitled to the exemption claimed.

Investment income is treated in a manner similar to personal income. The connecting factors test gives a great deal of discretion to judges in determining whether income falls within section 87's exemption. In *Recalma v. Canada* (1998) (see below), notice how the Court treats the purpose of the connecting factors test where the amounts earned are very large, and the income is earned in what the Court considers to be "the commercial mainstream". It states that "[i]n evaluating the various factors the Court must decide where it 'makes the most sense' to locate the personal property in issue in order to avoid the 'erosion of property held by Indians qua Indians' so as to protect the traditional Native way of life". It further observes that in making this judgment, "the primary reasoning exercise is to decide, looking at all the connecting factors and keeping in mind the purpose of the section, where the property is situated, that is, whether the income earned was 'integral to the life of the Reserve', whether it was 'intimately connected' to that life, and whether it should be protected to prevent the erosion of the property held by Natives quo Natives". In casting the test in these terms is the Court suggesting there are integrally "native (*qua* native)" and "non-native" ways of earning income? Are you comfortable with what the Court considers to be integral and intimately connected as "the traditional Native way of life"? By stating the test in this way, did the Court in *Recalma* properly characterize and apply the *Williams* test and give appropriate weight to the connecting factors?

RECALMA v. CANADA

[1998] F.C.J. No. 433 (Fed. C.A.), application for leave to appeal to
S.C.C. refused, [1998] 2 C.T.C. 403

[1] **Linden J.A.:** — The issue in these cases is whether certain investment income earned in 1991 by the appellants is exempt from income taxation by virtue of section 87 of the *Indian Act* because it is "personal property ... situated on a reserve". ...

[2] The Recalma family is a successful and community-oriented Native family, members of the Qualicum Band, living on the Qualicum Indian Reserve on Vancouver Island. The two male appellants have been elected chief of their band at different times. They, along with the female appellant, operate a fishing business through various corporations which has been very successful over the years yielding for them in the 1991 taxation year alone (which was not atypical) over $1,000,000.00 in income.

[3] Some of the Recalmas' accumulated wealth, over $4,000,000.00, was invested in certain financial investments called Bankers' Acceptances and Mutual Funds. A Bankers' Acceptance is a short-term note issued by a third party which the bank selling the note is primarily responsible for (or guarantees) repayment. They are sold at a discount and are redeemed at face value, the money being paid directly into the customer's accounts. The units of the Mutual Funds purchased were part of the First Canadian Money Market Fund, which invests in short-term debts issued by Canadian governments and corporations and in the First Canadian Mortgage Fund, which invests in mortgages. Upon redemption, these proceeds are deposited in the investors' accounts or as directed. These investments are very different from ordinary bank deposits in reserve banks which yield interest, income from which, until recently at least, have not been taxed by the Minister. These investments in Bankers' Acceptances and Mutual Funds yielded for the Recalmas in the 1991 taxation year, over $170,000.00 the tax on which is here being disputed. In other years, similar amounts were earned but these are not relevant here.

[4] This money had been invested in these securities through a Bank of Montreal branch located on rented premises in a shopping centre called Park Royal on a Squamish Band Reserve in West Vancouver. The purpose of using this branch, it was said, was both to support Native economic advancement as well as to obtain certain tax advantages.

[5] There is, of course, nothing wrong with Canadians arranging their affairs in order to minimize their tax burden. This is no less so for Natives than it is for other entrepreneurs who arrange mergers and offshore vehicles to reduce their tax burdens. Same efforts made to save taxes are successful and others are not. We must decide whether this one succeeded or whether it has failed. In our view, it has not succeeded.

[6] It is common ground that this case involves personal property, owned by Indians who are being taxed in respect of that property. What is at issue is whether this personal property is situated on the reserve, a question that has become extremely complicated in recent years.

[7] Our Court approaches the interpretation of section 87 with a keen eye on its purpose, which was designed to "shield Indians from any efforts by non-natives to dispossess Indians of the property which they hold quo Indians". but "not to remedy the economically disadvantaged position of Indians by ensuring that Indians may acquire, hold and deal with property in the commercial mainstream on different terms than their fellow citizens." (See La Forest, J. in *Mitchell v. Peguis Indian Band*, [1990] 2 S.C.R. 85 at page 131.)

[8] Building on *Mitchell*, the Supreme Court of Canada has developed a complex test involving the analysis of certain connecting factors in order to determine whether various types of personal property are so linked to a reserve as to be considered as "situated" there. ...

[9] In evaluating the various factors the Court must decide where it "makes the most sense" to locate the personal property in issue in order to avoid the "erosion of property held by Indians qua Indians" so as to protect the traditional Native way of life. It is also important in assessing the different factors to consider whether the activity generating the income was "intimately connected to" the Reserve, that is, an "integral part" of Reserve life, or whether it was more appropriate to consider it a part of "commercial mainstream" activity (see *Folster v. The Queen* (1997), 97 D.T.C. 5315 (F.C.A.)). We should indicate that the concept of "commercial mainstream" is not a test for determining whether property is situated on a reserve; it is merely an aid to be used in evaluating the various factors being considered. It is by no means determinative. The primary reasoning exercise is to decide, looking at all the connecting factors and keeping in mind the purpose of the section, where the property is situated, that is, whether the income earned was "integral to the life of the Reserve", whether it was "intimately connected" to that life, and whether it should be protected to prevent the erosion of the property held by Natives quo Natives.

[10] It is plain that different factors may be given different weights in each case. Extremely important, particularly in this case, is the type of income being considered as attracting taxation. Where the income is employment or salary income, the residence of the taxpayer, the type of work being performed, the place where the work was done and the nature of the benefit to the Reserve are given great weight. (See *Folster, supra*). Where the income is unemployment insurance benefits, the most weighty factor is where the qualifying work is performed. (See *Williams, supra*) Where business income is involved, most weight was placed on where the work was done and where the source of the income was situated. (See *Southwind v. The Queen*, January 14, 1998, Docket No. A-760-95 (F.C.A.)).

[11] So too, where investment income is at issue, it must be viewed in relation to its connection to the Reserve, its benefit to the traditional Native way of life, the potential danger to the erosion of Native property and the extent to which it may be considered as being derived from economic mainstream activity. In our view, the Tax Court Judge correctly placed

considerable weight on the way the investment income was generated, just as the Courts have done in cases involving employment, U.I. benefits and business income. Investment income, being passive income, is not generated by the individual work of the taxpayer. In a way, the work is done by the money which is invested across the land. The Tax Court Judge rightly placed great weight on factors such as the residence of the issuer of the security, the location of the issuer's income generating operations, and the location of the security issuer's property. While the dealer in these securities, the local branch of the Bank of Montreal, was on a Reserve, the issuers of the securities were not; the corporations which offered the Bankers' Acceptances and the managers of the Mutual Funds in question were not connected in any way to a Reserve. They were in the head offices of the corporations in cities far removed from any reserve. Similarly, the main income generating activity of the issuers was situated in towns and cities across Canada and around the world, not on Reserves. In addition, the assets of the issuers of the securities in question were predominantly off Reserves, which in case of default would be most significant.

[12] Less weight was properly accorded by the Tax Court Judge, in this case of investment income, to factors such as the residence of the taxpayer, the source of the capital with which the security was bought, the place where the security was purchased and the income received, the place where the security document was held and where the income was spent. We can find no fault with the reasoning of the Tax Court Judge in the way he balanced the various connecting factors involved in this case in the light of the purpose of the legislation.

[13] Thus, in our view, taking a purposive approach, the investment income earned by these taxpayers cannot be said to be personal property "situated on a reserve" and, hence, is not exempt from income taxation.

[14] To hold otherwise would open the door to wealthy Natives living on reserves across Canada to place their holdings into banks or other financial institutions situated on reserves and through these agencies invest in stocks, bonds and mortgages across Canada and the world without attracting any income tax on their profits. We cannot imagine that such a result was meant to be achieved by the drafters of section 87. The result may, of course, be otherwise in factual circumstances where funds invested directly or through banks on reserves are used exclusively or mainly for loans to Natives on reserves. When Natives, however worthy and committed to their traditions, choose to invest their funds in the general mainstream of the economy, they cannot shield themselves from tax merely by using a financial institution situated on a reserve to do so.

[15] The argument of the appellant in relation to subsection 87(2), which was not properly pleaded, is unpersuasive on its merits in any event and, therefore, cannot succeed.

[16] This appeal should be dismissed with costs.

––––––––––

The reasoning in the *Recalma* case has been followed in subsequent cases: *Lewin v. Canada*, [2001] 2 C.T.C. 2560 (T.C.C.), upheld 2002 FCA 461; *Sero v. Canada*, 2001 D.T.C. 575 (T.C.C.). These cases deal with the issue of whether interest paid in respect on an Indian's account at a branch of a financial institution on reserve is exempt from tax.

1. In *Lewin*, the issue was whether interest paid to a status Indian who did not live on a reserve, and did not earn the invested income on a re-serve from a *caisse-populaire* situated on a reserve, was exempt from tax. Mr. Lewin resided off reserve, but was a member of the Huron Wendat Nation and had his name on a waiting list to live on the re-serve. He deposited funds in an account with the Caisse Populaire Desjardins du Village Huron, a financial institution with its head office and main business location on the reserve. Mr. Lewin was assessed in-come tax in respect of interest paid on the deposit account at the Caisse. The majority of financial activities that enabled the interest to be paid to Lewin occurred off-reserve. The Court denied the exemp-tion on the basis that "[w]here the only thing Indian about a credit union is the location of part of its operations, the fact that property in-come has gone through the credit union does not make it non-taxable". Based on this fact, the Tax Court concluded that the use of the princi-pal invested by Mr. Lewin was similar to the situation in *Recalma*. The Court wrote (paragraphs 60-64):

> [60] In the case at bar, the appellant lived off the reserve; his way of life and habits were similar and comparable to those of all Canadians. In the context of his everyday activities, he saved money. He decided to deposit his savings to the credit union, a financial institution with operating rules as all those other similar institutions known as credit unions.
>
> [61] In fact, there was just one distinctive characteristic: the credit union was situated on a reserve. It was not owned by an Indian or the Indian community, although the vast majority of its members were Indians; however, any non-Indian could have been a member and, in theory, it would have been possible for non-Indians to control and run it, although its *situs* did not lend itself to this.
>
> [62] The interest paid to the appellant by the credit union was paid pur-suant to a loan agreement under which the appellant was the lender and the credit union the debtor; the *situs* of the agreement that generated the interest was, physically, the location of the credit union's place of busi-ness, namely the reserve, and there is no doubt about this in the instant case.
>
> [63] Can this fact alone make the interest that was paid tax-exempt in the hands of the appellant, an Indian who was not a resident of the reserve? My answer is no, mainly for the following reasons:
>
> - The capital used for the appellant's investment at the credit union was put together mainly through off-reserve work and economic activities.
> - The vast majority of the economic and financial activities that enabled interest to be paid to the appellant were carried on off the reserve.
> - The interest paid to the appellant did not contribute in any way to the protection or safeguarding of the interests, culture and development of the traditional way of life of the Indians living on the reserve.
> - The operations and activities of the credit union that paid the appel-lant the interest were not exclusively directed at the development of the Huron Nation.
> - Any financial or banking institution could have provided the same services to the Indians living on the reserve even if it was situated off the reserve.

- The services provided and offered by the credit union on the reserve were basically ordinary services related to the economic aspects of life; they had nothing to do with the Indians' culture and traditional way of life.
- The evidence established no connection between the *situs* of the credit union and the protection or safeguarding of the interests, culture and development of the traditional way of life of the Indians living on the reserve.
- The evidence basically showed that there was a closer, tighter bond between the credit union and its Indian members; the *situs* of the credit union no doubt contributed to that positive, harmonious and sustained relationship. However, the same could very well have been true of another institution situated off the reserve.
- The credit union had the same rights and duties as any other credit union, and its only distinctive characteristic was that it was favourably disposed towards its mainly Indian customers. This was appropriate behaviour for any organization the very essence of which was to do business with Indians.
- The interest paid to the appellant was neither spent nor invested on the reserve or for the benefit of the Indians living there. Like the capital that generated it, the interest resulted from economic activities that are common to all Canadians and was used for expenditures that are also usual, ordinary and common to all Canadians.

[64] Interests being property income, it is difficult if not impossible to determine where the income was generated, since the property is itself very volatile; in the instant case, the credit union's manager explained that most of the capital entrusted to it (contractual *situs* on the reserve) was sent to the traditional capital markets off the reserve. Where the only thing Indian about a credit union is the location of part of its operations, the fact that property income has gone through the credit union does not make it non-taxable. I do not think that the exemption provided for in the *Act* justifies or allows for an interpretation as broad and inclusive as that argued for by the appellant.

2. In *Sero*, there were two taxpayers. Both were Indians within the meaning of the *Indian Act*. One taxpayer (Mr. Frazer) resided on a reserve, but the other taxpayer (Ms. Sero) had never resided on a reserve. Both taxpayers excluded from their income interest earned on certain investments, including term investments and GICs. In addition, Mr. Frazer excluded from his income interest earned on a savings account. The term investments and savings accounts were all held at a branch of the Royal Bank situated on a Six Nations reserve. In reassessing Ms. Sero for 1995 and Mr. Frazer for 1996, the Minister included all of the excluded amounts in their income on the basis that the income was not exempt from tax pursuant to section 87 of the *Indian Act*. Both taxpayers appealed to the Tax Court of Canada and the Court dismissed both appeals.

The taxpayers argued that pursuant to section 461 of the *Bank Act*, S.C. 1991, c. 46, their bank deposits were deemed to be situated at the branch where the deposits had been made (that is, on the reserve) and accordingly should be deemed to be located on the reserve for the purposes of the *Indian Act* exemption. While the Court agreed that section 461 of the *Bank Act* deems the location of the bank deposit to be situated at the branch where the individual has placed his or her money, it found that section 461 of the *Bank Act* was merely one factor to be considered when applying the "connecting factors" test applied in *Williams* and *Recalma*.

Relying on the Federal Court of Appeal decision in *Recalma*, the Court considered the following connecting factors:

(a) the residence of the taxpayers;
(b) the origin or location of the capital used to buy the securities;
(c) the location of the bank branch where the securities were bought;
(d) the location where the investment income is used;
(e) the location of the investment instruments;
(f) the location where the investment income payment is made; and
(g) the nature of the securities (including the residence of the issuer, the location of the issuer's income-generating activity, and the location of the issuer's seizable property in the event of a default).

Weighing all of the factors in the cases of both Ms. Sero and Mr. Fraser, the Court found the income not to be situated on the reserve. In the case of Mr. Fraser, the Court found that although all connecting factors except the income stream were on-reserve, the greatest emphasis must be placed on the income stream and, accordingly, the exemption must be denied. The Court wrote (paragraphs 25-26):

> The facts in *Recalma* are somewhat similar to those in Mr. Frazer's appeal. In *Recalma*, all of the relevant factors, aside from the nature of the investment income, supported the finding that the income earned in that case was located on a reserve. However, in *Recalma*, this Court held that with respect to income derived from Bankers Acceptances and mutual funds, greater weight should be placed on the nature of the investment income, in particular the income stream. By placing greater emphasis on the income stream of the interests as well as the location of the bank and its assets, this Court reached the conclusion that income earned from investments in mutual funds and Banker's Acceptances was not situated on a reserve within the meaning of subsection 87(2) of the *Indian Act*. The Federal Court of Appeal affirmed this Court's findings in *Recalma*.
>
> A further reading of the Federal Court of Appeal's reasons in *Recalma* suggests that the Federal Court of Appeal went further to hold that the same analysis applied by the courts in *Recalma* is applicable to all cases involving investment income. Since the Federal Court of Appeal's decision in *Recalma*, this Court, in a line of case law, has applied the *Recalma* analysis to investment income other than income earned from investments in Banker's Acceptances and mutual funds. In the informal procedure case of *Hill* v. *R.* this Court held that interests earned on term deposits at the Royal Bank were not dissimilar from income derived from the Banker's Acceptances described in *Recalma*. Subsequently, this Court applied the Federal Court of Appeal's analysis in *Recalma* to the interests earned on term deposits and dismissed the appeal.

3. There has been much criticism of the courts' approach, making the tax exemption only applicable to traditional economic activities. For example, Professor Martha O'Brien has written about this line of cases in her article "Income Tax, Investment Income and the Indian Act: Getting Back on Track", (2002) 50 Canadian Tax Journal 1570 at 1588:

> The effect of the decisions in *Lewin* and *Frazer (Sero)*, drawn to their logical conclusion, would be to reduce the "protected reserve system" with

respect to Indian investment income to a separate, ring-fenced, exclusively traditional economy that has no direct or indirect connections or commercial analogues in the off-reserve world. This narrow application conflicts with current federal government policy with respect to First Nations, which aims to promote the development of modern economies with opportunities for employment and investment on reserves, to provide a framework for more extensive self-government, and to assist and encourage implementation of direct taxation on reserves for the benefit of the reserve community.

...The recommended approach would be based on the general legal and tax principles regarding the location of a source of income, and on real and substantial factual connections to a reserve, and would reject any considerations of the traditional Indian character of the income or its benefit to the reserve community. Such an approach would be more defensible in law, and more respectful of the economic and self-governance aspirations of First Nations, than are the recent decisions discussed above [*Recalma, Lewin* and *Sero*]. It would also be in keeping with the Supreme Court of Canada's decisions in *Mitchell, Williams* and *Union of NB Indians* [which you will read next].

Do you agree with Professor O'Brien's analysis?

Section 87 of the *Indian Act* has also produced litigation concerning the exemption of Indians from provincial sales tax.

E. SALES TAX

UNION OF NEW BRUNSWICK INDIANS v. NEW BRUNSWICK (MINISTER OF FINANCE)

[1998] 1 S.C.R. 1161

The judgment of **Lamer C.J.C.** and **Cory, McLachlin, Iacobucci** and **Major JJ.** was delivered by **McLachlin J.:** —

Introduction

This case requires the Court to rule whether Indians living in New Brunswick were required to pay provincial sales tax on goods purchased off the reserve for consumption on the reserve. ...

Analysis

This appeal requires us to decide whether s. 87 of the *Indian Act* applies to tax levied under the former New Brunswick *Social Services and Education Tax Act.* ...

The Application of Section 87 of the Indian Act

Section 87(1) of the *Indian Act* exempts certain property of Indians from taxation. This includes "the personal property of an Indian or a band situated on a reserve": see s. 87(1)(*b*). Section 87(2) describes the types, or modalities, of taxation on the exempted property that are prohibited: taxation "in respect of the ownership, occupation, possession or use of" the property mentioned in s. 87(1).

The purpose of the s. 87 exemption was to "preserve the entitlements of Indians to their reserve lands and to ensure that the use of their property on their reserve lands was not eroded by the ability of governments to tax, or creditors to seize". It "was not to confer a general economic benefit upon the Indians see *Williams, supra,* at p. 885.

In the past, s. 87(1)(*b*) has been confined to property physically situated on a reserve or property whose "paramount location" is on a reserve. ... [citations omitted]

These authorities suggest that s. 87 applies only to property physically located on a reserve at the time of taxation or property whose paramount location is on a reserve at the time of taxation. This comports with the purpose of s. 87 to protect the property of Indians on reserves and prevent that property from being eroded: see *Williams, supra.* In determining the applicability of s. 87, one must consider whether the property is located or has its paramount location on a reserve at the time and place that the tax would otherwise attach. In the context of retail sales taxes, this can be called the "point of sale" test.

The remaining question, therefore, is whether the sales tax here at issue is levied on property while it is situated, or has its paramount location on a reserve. The property described in the stated case consists of items for personal use and consumption like clothing and toiletries, purchased by Indians off the reserve for use on the reserve. The *Social Services and Education Tax Act* levies the tax on these items at the time of the off-reserve sale. At the point of sale, the property is not, and has never been located on a reserve. This, without more, suggests that the tax is not levied on goods situated on a reserve or whose paramount location is on a reserve. This would accord with the general view expressed by Richard H. Bartlett, *Indians and Taxation in Canada* (3rd ed. 1992), at p. 92:

The reasoning employed by the Supreme Court of Canada [in *Francis*] appears applicable to the imposition of sales tax at the point of sale off a reserve. In the vast majority of sales transactions involving Indian purchases in Canada the sales take place off the reserve, and according to *Francis* are not subject to the exemption conferred by section 87.

This, however, does not conclude the matter. The respondents raise a number of arguments in support of their position that s. 87 applies to the tax at issue in this case: (1) that the tax is not a sales tax but a consumption tax collected at the time of purchase but levied in respect of the on-reserve consumption of personal property by Indians; (2) that property purchased for use on-reserve has its paramount location on a reserve; and (3) that s. 87 must be applied to off-reserve purchases by Indians in New Brunswick in order to fulfill its purpose. I will address each of these arguments in turn. ... [The Court's discussion and rejection of the consumption tax argument omitted: they find the tax is a sales tax.]

The "Paramount Location" Argument

The respondents submit that tangible personal property which is intended to be consumed primarily on the reserve is "situated on a reserve" for the purposes of s. 87. In doing so, they seek to extend the "paramount location" doctrine to property which has never been on a reserve. ...

The concept of "paramount location" finds no application to sales taxes on tangible goods. Sales taxes attach at the moment of sale. At this point, the property has but one location -- the place of sale. It cannot have its paramount location elsewhere because no pattern of use and safekeeping elsewhere is established. The location of property after the sale and the imposition of tax is irrelevant. This means that goods purchased off-reserve attract tax, while goods purchased on-reserve are exempt, regardless of where the purchaser may intend to use them. To make taxation dependent on place of anticipated use of the article purchased would render the administration of the tax uncertain and unworkable. As Macfarlane J.A. put it in *Danes, supra,* at p. 259:

> An exemption must apply at the moment of purchase. To do so it must be certain. It must not depend upon the consideration of factors such as the extent to which the property may be used on or off the reserve.

In these circumstances, where the location of the property at the time of taxation is readily apparent, there is simply no need to apply the "paramount location" test and I conclude that it does not assist the respondents.

The "Purpose of Section 87" Argument

The respondents argue that s. 87 is intended to protect Indians from taxation in respect of their use of property on-reserve. Where Indians are obliged to purchase most of their goods off-reserve, as most are in New Brunswick, this protection is eroded. Therefore, they submit that s. 87 should be read as applying to sales tax levied off-reserve on goods purchased by Indians for use on the reserve. This was the view of the majority of the New Brunswick Court of Appeal.

The first difficulty with this argument is that it takes the purpose of s. 87 far beyond that articulated by this Court in *Williams* — to prevent Indian property on Indian reserves from being eroded by taxation or claimed by creditors. No support has been offered for the proposed extension, except that this would economically benefit Indians. But that, this Court has stated, is not the purpose of s. 87: see *Mitchell*; *Williams*. ...

The second difficulty with this argument is that it flies in the face of the wording of s. 87(1)(*b*), which confines the protection from taxation to property situated on a reserve. The respondents attempt to overcome this difficulty by relying on s. 87(2) which provides that "[n]o Indian or band is subject to taxation in respect of the ownership, occupation, possession or use of any property mentioned in paragraph (1)(*a*) or (*b*) or is otherwise subject to taxation in respect of any such property." But this section does not extend the ambit of s. 87(1)(*a*) and (*b*). Section 87(1) states what property is protected from taxation. Section 87(2) states that tax cannot be levied in respect of the ownership, occupation, possession or use of this property. It does not enlarge the class of property subject to the exemption, but merely states the types of tax that are prohibited on a particular type of property. It does not change the rule that for property to be exempt from taxation under s. 87, it must be situated on a reserve. Courts have consistently held that s. 87(1)(*b*) is confined to property physically situated on a reserve or whose paramount location is on a reserve: see *Francis, Mitchell, Williams, Lewis* and *Leighton, supra*.

A third difficulty with this argument is that the history of s. 87 belies the conclusion that Parliament intended it to provide general tax protection for off-reserve property. The tax exemption began in 1850 as a prohibition against taxes on Indians residing on Indian lands. It was amended in 1876 to prevent taxes on Indian property unless it was held outside the reserve. It now prohibits taxation in respect of Indian property that is situated on the reserve: see Bartlett, *supra*. Over the years Parliament has explicitly limited and narrowed the scope of what is now s. 87 to protect from taxation only property that is situated on the reserve.

A fourth difficulty with this argument is that it rests on the assumption that providing a tax exemption to Indians for property purchased off-reserve will benefit Indians uniformly. The argument is that Parliament must have intended the tax to apply to off-reserve purchases because this is required to protect and enhance the position of Indians. Yet it is far from clear that Indians across Canada would benefit from such an interpretation.

Confining s. 87 to property situated on a reserve and excluding off-reserve sales taxes will have varying effects. It is said that in New Brunswick the effects are negative. There are very few retail establishments on New Brunswick reserves where 65-75 percent of status Indians live. Delivery of goods to reserves may partially offset the problem; the trial judge, Savoie J., found that delivery of goods and services to Indians resident on reserves in New Brunswick was available from many of the retail establishments close to reserves. However, delivery may involve additional charges equivalent to a sales tax and, in any event, will not be available in many situations. The reality is that, at present, New Brunswick Indians are unable to live on their reserves without paying a certain amount of provincial sales tax.

At the same time, adopting the "paramount location" test would have adverse consequences for Indians who live off the reserve. They would presumably have to pay tax on purchases made on and off the reserve because the "paramount location" of the goods would be off-reserve. Indians who lived, and thus consumed their property, off the reserve would always be subject to taxation, while those living on the reserve would be effectively immune. In contrast, the "point of sale" test allows Indians living off-reserve to purchase goods tax-free on reserves regardless of where the goods are ultimately used.

In addition, the "point of sale" test is beneficial to on-reserve Indians in many parts of Canada. First, it provides an incentive for Indians to establish their own retail outlets on reserves and gives a competitive edge to reserve businesses, thereby increasing economic activity and employment. Although the exemption may not yet have been a catalyst in New Brunswick, where until recently off-reserve sales were exempt from tax, it has fostered aboriginal economic development elsewhere. For example, the intervener, the Attorney General of Manitoba, asserted that almost all Manitoba reserves contain some retail businesses. The fact that the exemption is closely tied to the reserve enhances reserve-linked benefits, promotes privatization of reservation economies and encourages an entrepreneurial spirit: see Robert A. Reiter, in *Tax Manual for Canadian Indians* (1990), at p. 1.1.

Second, the "point of sale" approach to the tax exemption permits reserves to impose their own taxes on reserve sales, thus creating a tax base for aboriginal governments: see Peter W. Hogg and Mary Ellen Turpel, "Implementing Aboriginal Self-Government: Constitutional and Jurisdictional Issues" (1995), 74 Can. Bar Rev. 187, at pp. 207 *et seq*. For example, in the *Budget Implementation Act, 1997*, S.C. 1997, c. 26, Parliament granted the Cowichan tribes the authority to impose a direct tax on the on-reserve purchase of tobacco by status Indians. This legislation enabled the Cowichan Tribes to fill the tax void created by s. 87 and raise revenue for the community. If s. 87 is interpreted to provide an exemption for all off-reserve purchases of tobacco destined for use on the reserve, the purpose of this amendment would be frustrated.

These considerations belie the conclusion that s. 87, by its object and purpose, must be read as intending to exempt Indians from all sales taxes, whether on or off a reserve, on property used on reserves. I conclude that the argument that s. 87 must, in keeping with its objects, be read expansively to apply to off-reserve sales cannot succeed.

Conclusion

I would allow the appeal and set aside the order of the New Brunswick Court of Appeal. I make no comment regarding the validity of the new Harmonized Sales Tax that replaced the tax here at issue.

The following constitutional question was stated:

Question: If as a matter of statutory interpretation, the *Social Services and Education Tax Act*, R.S.N.B. 1973, c. S-10, imposes a tax in respect of tangible personal property purchased at a location off reserve which is destined for use entirely or primarily by an Indian or an Indian band on a reserve, and further, if as a matter of statutory interpretation, s. 87 of the *Indian Act* prohibits such taxation, is the *Social Services and Education Tax Act* rendered inoperative to the extent of its inconsistency with s. 87 of the *Indian Act*?

Answer: Section 87 of the *Indian Act* does not prohibit taxation in respect of tangible personal property purchased at a location off reserve which is destined for use entirely or primarily by an Indian or an Indian band on a reserve. As such, the *Social Services and Education Tax Act* is not inconsistent with s. 87 of the *Indian Act* and is not rendered inoperative. ...

The reasons of **Gonthier** and **Binnie JJ.** were delivered by

Binnie J. (dissenting): — ...

Application of the Nowegijick Principle

As stated, the charging section (s. 4) of the Act says that it is a tax "in respect of the consumption" and I see nothing else in the Act to contradict that characterization. However, if I am wrong in that analysis, the very least that can be said is that the differences of opinion here and in the courts below about the interplay of the concepts of purchase and consumption in this statute show that reasonable people differ in their interpretation of the New Brunswick Act. In a word, some of the key provisions are ambiguous in their meaning and effect. In these circumstances, the applicable rule is that any ambiguities in the New Brunswick statute should be resolved in favour of the Indian taxpayers (*Nowegijick*). Unless the Court is now prepared to resile from the fundamental *Nowegijick* rule resolving statutory ambiguities in favour of the Indian taxpayer, then it seems to me s. 87 of the *Indian Act* applies and the appeal must be dismissed.

Giving Indian People a Meaningful Choice

In *Williams, supra*, Gonthier J. (for the Court at p. 887) outlined "the choice" confronting Indian people in respect of their personal property:
> Therefore, under the *Indian Act*, an Indian has a choice with regard to his personal property. The Indian may situate this property on the reserve, in which case it is within the protected area and free from seizure and taxation, or the Indian may situate this property off the reserve, in which case it is outside the protected area, and more fully available for ordinary commercial purposes in society. Whether the Indian wishes to remain within the protected reserve system or integrate more fully into the larger commercial world is a choice left to the Indian.

In the present case, we are dealing with personal property which, it is agreed, the Indians have chosen to locate and consume on the reserve. New Brunswick seeks to deny Indian people the tax benefit of that choice, not because the Indians have decided to "integrate more fully into the larger commercial world", but because the absence of appropriate retail stores on the reserve compels the Indians to shop off the reserve. The result of the majority decision to allow the appeal in this case is to defeat the assurance in *Williams, supra*, and in *Mitchell, supra*, that s. 87 is designed to give status Indian people a meaningful tax choice in the location of their personal property.

Subsequent Removal of Property from the Reserve

In the foregoing discussion, reference has been made to personal property "primarily located" on a reserve. The concept of "primary location" is intended to avoid the administrative inconvenience of shifting tax treatment every time the personal property in question crosses the boundary of the reserve. In *Mitchell, supra*, La Forest J. referred at pp. 132-33, with approval, to the concept of primary or paramount location:

> In another recent decision, *Leighton v. B.C. (Gov't)*, [1989] 3 C.N.L.R. 136, the British Columbia Court of Appeal again had occasion to consider the significance of the phrase "situated on a reserve" in s. 87(*b*) of the *Indian Act*. In what I take to be a sound approach, Lambert J.A. held that when considering whether tangible personal property owned by Indians can benefit from the exemption from taxation provided for in s. 87, it will be appropriate to examine the pattern of use and safekeeping of the property in order to determine if the paramount location of the property is indeed situated on the reserve. I have no doubt that it will normally be appropriate to take a fair and liberal approach to the problem whether the paramount location of tangible property or a chose-in-action is situated on the reserve: see *Metlakatla Ferry Service Ltd. v. B.C. (Gov't)* (1987), 12 B.C.L.R. (2d) 308 (C.A.).

It seems to me inconsistent with this "sound approach" for the Court in the present case to conclude that the one and only thread in the "pattern of use and safekeeping" which controls the tax treatment is the *situs* of the personal property at the moment of acquisition, irrespective of the fact that the "paramount location" of the use and consumption of the personal property is "situated on a reserve" in the literal and physical sense of the words in s. 87(1)(*b*) of the *Indian Act*. Even if some importance is to be attached to *situs* at the moment of acquisition, the issue here is not unidimensional, and acquisition should be placed in the larger context of the realities of life on a New Brunswick reserve. The "paramount location" approach endorsed by this Court in *Mitchell*, reflects a purposive approach to s. 87(1)(*b*). For this reason, as well, the provincial Attorney General's argument should be rejected.

Additional Policy Considerations

My colleague, McLachlin J., at the conclusion of her discussion of the purpose of s. 87 (paras. 41 to 45), reviews a number of policy arguments designed to show the mixed benefits and burdens for status Indian people across the country if the respondents' contentions are accepted. She points out, correctly, that taxes imposed by Indian bands themselves on retail sales on reserves may become an important source of income, and that there are real advantages for off-reserve Indians in being able to make on-reserve purchases free of tax if a "point of sale" exemption is allowed. On this theory, the goods would then be consumed tax free off the reserve. In my view, however, it is not the purpose of s. 87 to allow merchants on reserves to compete on a tax-free basis with off-reserve merchants for business in the broader community. Moreover, in terms of financing Indian self-government, the present wording of s. 87 is not immutable. The s. 87 exemption is the creature of an ordinary federal statute and can be expanded or redefined as Parliament sees fit. The successful financing of Indian government does not turn on the present wording of s. 87, or on the outcome of this appeal.

Disposition

I would dismiss the appeal with costs.

Justice La Forest in *Mitchell v. Peguis Indian Band*, [1990] 2 S.C.R. 85, 71 D.L.R. (4th) 193 suggested that "when Indians deal in the general marketplace, the protections conferred by these sections [sections 87-89 of the *Indian Act*] have the potential to become powerful impediments to their engaging successfully in commercial matters" [at p. 146]. This characterization, while accurate in one respect, does not capture the potential benefits these sections may hold for economic development more generally. The widely acclaimed *Report of the Royal Commission on Taxation*, 1966, suggested that "the existing tax system and recommendations for its improvement must be predicated on a widely accepted set of goals or objectives that the nation is seeking, and on a knowledge of the potential role that a tax system can play in the achievement of these goals". As a result, this Royal Commission posited four "fundamental objectives" on which it found wide agreement for the Canadian system of taxation:

1. To maximize the current and future output of goods and services desired by Canadians.
2. To ensure that this flow of goods and services is distributed equitably among individuals or groups.
3. To protect the liberties and rights of individuals through the preservation of representative, responsible government and the maintenance of the rule of law.
4. To maintain and strengthen the Canadian federation.

When Indian exemptions from taxation are judged by these standards (which are the standards for judging the entire tax system), there may be a greater role to consider for Indians aggressively employing their exemptions to secure benefits, even in the commercial mainstream. There is significant potential for these exemptions to: maximize output, ensure equitable flows of resources, protect the rule of law as embodied in Aboriginal rights, and strengthen the Canadian federation. Yet, despite the application of these standards more generally in the Canadian public, there is little sympathy for Indians "marketing their tax exemptions". While federal, provincial and municipal governments are able to manipulate their tax structures to secure economic development, in some sectors there is outrage when Indians attempt to follow the same logic. For example, while many (though not all) praise Alberta's or New Brunswick's use of tax incentives and exemptions to create development in these provinces, there are great cries of unfairness if Indians attempt to use their tax status to follow this same course. If one understands the history and contemporary economic realities of economic development among Aboriginal people, the application of this double standard can be troubling. It may be helpful at this point to inject some economic and empirical considerations relating to Indian taxation.

ANDRE LeDRESSAY, "A BRIEF TAX (ON A ME) OF FIRST NATIONS TAXATION AND ECONOMIC DEVELOPMENT" IN SHARING THE HARVEST: THE ROAD TO SELF RELIANCE, REPORT OF THE NATIONAL ROUND TABLE ON ABORIGINAL ECONOMIC DEVELOPMENT AND RESOURCES

(Ottawa: Ministry of Supply and Services, 1993) 215 at 218-223

87 and Economic Development — The Good, The Bad and The Uncertain

The section 87 taxation exemption employed to its potential can be an effective tool in successful First Nations economic development. It is unfortunately a double-edged sword, clearing a potential path to economic development with one edge, and creating confusion, tension, and red tape with the other. This section briefly reviews the role of the partial exemption in economic development.

The Good

The partial exemption offers several advantages to on-reserve First Nation businesses including the following:

• Exemption from GST, provincial retail sales taxes, and tobacco and fuel taxes means on-reserve First Nation businesses have a significant pricing advantage for their "status" customers. Assuming profit margins are high enough, and competition remains slim or nonexistent, this comparative pricing advantage could in theory be partially passed along to the larger non-status market in some First Nations.
• The income tax exemption for status employees could entail lower labour costs for on-reserve First Nation businesses and a subsequent comparative pricing advantage. This, though, is not a costless advantage, as discussed below.
• On-reserve corporations can distribute the business income to tax-exempt First Nation governments or individuals as a deductible fee, or possibly through dividends, thereby eliminating all its taxable income. This would provide such businesses with a comparative advantage since the opportunity cost (true cost) of doing business is lower.
• If First Nations governments can be considered municipalities and they control over 90 per cent of a corporation, then an exemption can be applied for under 149(l)(*d*) of the *Income Tax Act*. The situs of the income is irrelevant for this exemption (Merry, 1993, p. 17).
• First Nation partnership taxation exemptions will depend on the connecting factors of the business income. When the First Nation partner is tax exempt, this particular business structure may act as an investment incentive" since some of the taxable income can be allocated to the tax-exempt partner. This, however, does not apply to joint ventures.
• Band-operated businesses are tax-exempt if the source of income is situated on-reserve or if it uses the *Income Tax Act* municipality provisions alluded to above. It should be cautioned that as an unincorporated entity, the band may unintentionally expose its off-reserve assets to its creditors.

The Bad and The Uncertain

The section 87 exemption, however, is not always advantageous to successful First Nation business and economic development. In fact at least one First Nation business person has suggested that its handicaps almost outweigh its advantages, and may explain its apparent under-use on First Nation land. "Another band of not inconsiderable wealth indicated that on a scale of 1 to 10, the tax exemption didn't even register." (Brown and Strother, 1991, p. 120) Below are listed a few reasons why this may be the case:

- Many non-First Nation businesses believe that First Nation businesses are unfairly advantaged because of the partial taxation exemption. The media often perpetuate the myth that members of First Nations do not pay tax. This may discourage potential First Nation business persons who feel unwilling to wage a political battle just for developing a business.
- The situs provisions in the partial taxation exemption discourage off-reserve business development and expansion to larger markets.
- Use of the income tax exemption for First Nation employees often creates tension when these employees compare their before-tax income with non-First Nation workers doing similar work.
- The bureaucratic requirements of GST and provincial sales tax refunds from tax-exempt sales for on-reserve First Nation businesses (especially gas stations) can seriously affect these businesses' cash flow. Although the customer avoids sales tax at the time of purchase, the retailer may have to wait up to three months to be reimbursed for the tax exemption. For smaller businesses, obtaining these refunds often consumes a disproportionate amount of administrative time.
- There would appear to be a significant communication barrier between the methods for exploiting the section 87 taxation exemption and its effective economic application in First Nation communities. Interpretive difficulties such as the nature of an individual's property and the location of its acquisition complicate section 87. Beyond this the use of indecipherable legalese, economese, and bureaucratese seldom translates into First Nation community-based economic development action. The uncertainty surrounding the Williams case only exacerbates these problems.

Although it is undoubtedly true that the section 87 partial exemption provides a comparative advantage to First Nation business development, the case study statistical evidence presented in the next section clearly reveals its under-use. ...

Bungee Economics — A Case Study of a First Nations Economy

In order to understand the potential role between taxation and economic development for First Nations, it is crucial to comprehend the workings of a typical First Nations economy. To coin a phrase, most (if not all) First Nation economies are victims of "bungee economics." Money goes in and bounces right back out to the surrounding non-First Nation economy. Summary evidence extracted from "The Value of Co-operation — A Case

Study of Six Shuswap Nation Tribal Council Communities" describes ... the extent of this monetary rubber band.

The Shuswap Nation Tribal Council (SNTC) officially launched its statistics program in 1991. A component of this initiative was the collection of community based economic development survey information. ...

The communities of the SNTC, for the purpose of this document, are considered representative of most Canadian First Nations (rural, urban, and isolated). Statistics Canada 1991 Census and Aboriginal Peoples Survey data will be employed to validate these case study data nationally, as Statistics Canada releases the results throughout the current calendar year.

· · · · ·

Many First Nation leaders object to discussions on taxation because it may ultimately result in the removal of the section 87 tax exemption, and ultimately lead to the direct taxing of First Nation community members. It should be painfully obvious in the indicators above that even if First Nations did tax their own people, there is nothing to tax. Consider that mean household income in Canoe Creek is but 32 per cent of the average household income in Kamloops. Moreover, the percentage of UIC claimants is anywhere from 400 per cent to 600 per cent higher in the SNTC communities compared to Kamloops.

The Department of Finance conducted taxation case studies in six First Nation communities in Canada. The study concluded in support of the evidence above; only a small portion of First Nation households would pay tax if the current Canadian taxation system were applied to them. Most First Nation community members would receive tax rebates if they filed a tax return. ...

Highlights from more detailed analysis of this data contained in the "The Value of Co-operation — A Case Study of the Six SNTC Communities" include:

- 81 per cent of all expenditures from these six Shuswap communities (457 households) are spent off-reserve.
- The households of these communities contribute approximately $7.3 million annually into the non-First Nation economy. This amounts to an expenditure of over $16,700 per household; average household income is only about $20,600.
- This substantial off-reserve expenditure also destroys a myth concerning the payment of sales tax by First Nation peoples, since there are no tax exemption provisions for many of these off-reserve expenditures. The lack of business development on-reserve limits the usage of the tax exemption by consumers. "It was (generally) felt that in most situations involving purchases of a value less than $500, the additional effort and cost of delivery outweighed the GST (exemption) benefit" (Brown and Strother, 1991, p. 119).
- The estimated household multiplier for these communities is 1.25 (standard Keynesian techniques). This implies that every $10 that lands into the lap of an SNTC household produces an additional $2.50 for the

SNTC community-based economy. This points to a lack of economic co-operation among and between SNTC communities.

The Rubber Band Syndrome — First Nation Government Expenditures

The monetary rubber band persists. First Nation government and household expenditures bounce right off-reserve into the non-SNTC economy. Although it is false to assert that all First Nations governments are theoretically identical, it is safe to assume — given the administrative requirements of the Department of Indian Affairs and Northern Development system — that there are more than a few expenditure similarities.

The data of this subsection have also been extracted from "The Value of Co-operation — A Case Study of Six SNTC Communities" Table III summarizes the expenditures by location of selected SNTC governments organizations. Highlights from this study include:

- The selected SNTC governments are the major source of on-reserve employment.
- 52 per cent of all SNTC government organization expenditures are made off-reserve and the 48 per cent on-reserve expenditure is primarily wages and salaries.
- Approximately 80 per cent of all household expenditures is spent off-reserve, This implies that about 90 per cent of all SNTC government organization expenditures eventually occur off-reserve. The percentage translates to approximately $11.8 million into the non-SNTC economy. Add this amount to the household contribution and it translates to approximately $35,000 per household. Coincidentally, each household has an average income of just over $20,000 — hence the term bungee economics.
- Over 14 per cent of SNTC government organization expenditures is for communications.
- 11 per cent of SNTC government organization expenditures is paid to outside consultants.
- 39 per cent of SNTC governmental organization expenditures is paid direct to on-staff employees.

First Nation Economic Development and Taxation Jurisdiction

There are two conclusions relating to taxation from this case study analysis that might be generalized to other First Nations:

- The lack of a self-sustained reserve economy (reflected by the off-reserve expenditures by households and their governments) is undoubtedly a major cause of the well below average economic indicators for First Nations. These communities are clearly not exploiting the section 87 taxation exemption to its full potential.
- First Nations households and their governments significantly contribute not only to the non-First Nation economy but also to other governments through the payment of sales and income taxation.

F. CORPORATE/GOVERNMENTAL TAXATION

Some Indian communities have tried to remedy the economic issues identified in LeDressay's study by using economic development corporations and taxation planning. The *Gull Bay Development Corp. v. Canada* and *Otineka Development Corp. v. Canada* cases, on the following pages, explore these issues.

GULL BAY DEVELOPMENT CORP. v. CANADA

[1984] 2 F.C. 3 (T.D.)

Walsh J.: — Plaintiff in these proceedings is a corporation incorporated by Province of Ontario Letters Patent on February 28th, 1974, as a corporation without share capital having its Head Office on the Gull Bay Indian Reserve (No. 55), at Gull Bay, Ontario, a reserve of some 16 square miles on the west shore of Lake Nipigon some 120 miles north of Thunder Bay. The Letters Patent of the corporation provide that the objects of the corporation include:

> To promote the economic and social welfare of persons of native origin who are members of the Gull Bay Indian Reserve (No. 55) and to provide support for recognized benevolent and charitable enterprises, federations, agencies and societies engaged in assisting the development, both economic and social, of native people who are members of the Gull Bay Indian Reserve (No. 55).

They further provide that the corporation may hire employees, maintain offices, and incur reasonable expenses in connection with its objects, that the corporation shall be carried on without purpose of gain for members and that any profits or other accretions to the corporation will be used in promoting its objects. It is further provided that the directors shall serve without remuneration and no director shall directly or indirectly receive any profit from his position, provided only that he may be paid reasonable expenses incurred by him in the performance of his duties. In the event of dissolution of the corporation all remaining property is to be distributed or disposed of to incorporated Native Peoples Organizations in Ontario. ...

Plaintiff contends that it has from its inception been involved in working for the social and economic development of the Gull Bay Indian Reserve and its members and in the improvement of the social and economic conditions of the members of the Band living there, which activities include the establishment of a viable commercial logging operation to provide employment for members of the Reserve, the training of Indian students from the Reserve to work both as loggers and as managers in the office facilities, the carrying out of maintenance work on the recreational and administrative buildings and facilities on the Reserve, providing funds to Reserve programmes established to give food, clothing and other necessities to needy members of the Gull Bay Indian Reserve, providing of funds for travel expenses for school age children on the Reserve to enable them to take educational excursions that the school from time to time determines to be beneficial, providing of other assistance activities on the Reserve determined to be beneficial to social and economic welfare of the members off the Reserve, and that it was therefore a non-profit organizations within the meaning of that term as defined in Section 149(1)(*l*) of the *Income Tax Act*.

While a further argument was raised at trial based on Section 149(1)(*d*) of the *Income Tax Act* to the effect that the members and directors of Plaintiff are members of the Band Council which controls Plaintiff and that the Band Council carries out the functions of municipal government on the Reserve, so that Plaintiff is a municipal corporation, this was rejected by the Court at the trial. During the course of the argument Plaintiff also invoked Section 149(1)(*f*) of the Act which reads as follows:

> 149.(1) No tax is payable under this Part upon the taxable income of a person for a period when that person was
>
> (*f*)   a charitable organization, whether or not incorporated, all the resources of which were devoted to charitable activities carried on by the organization itself and no part of the income of which was payable to, or was otherwise available for the personal benefit of, any proprietor, member or shareholder thereof.

Section 149(1)(*l*) reads as follows:

> 149.(1) No tax is payable under this Part upon the taxable income of a person for a period when that person was
>
> (*l*)   a club, society or association organized and operated exclusively for social welfare, civic improvement, pleasure or recreation or for any other purpose except profit, no part of the income of which was payable to, or was otherwise available for the personal benefit of, any proprietor, member or shareholder thereof unless the proprietor, member or shareholder was a club, society or association the primary purpose and function of which was the promotion of amateur athletics in Canada. ...

On June 14, 1977 Plaintiff was assessed for corporate income tax for the year 1975 in the amount of $3272.40. A Notice of Objection was made but Defendant sent Notice of Confirmation. This action is an appeal from the assessment.

Defendant contends that in its 1975 taxation year Plaintiff carried out with a view to profit a logging business from which it earned a profit of at least $23,538.00, taking the position that Plaintiff was not exempt from tax as it was not a non-profit organization within the meaning of Section 149 (1)(*l*) of the Act nor a municipal corporation within the meaning of Section 149(1)(*d*) of the Act and that Plaintiff is not an organization described by subsection 149(1) of the Act.

While the issue is a clearly defined one, the extensive jurisprudence to which the Court was referred by both parties indicates that it is very controversial and to a considerable extent depends on the facts of each case so that it was necessary to introduce considerable factual evidence. ....

Chief Tim Esquega testified that he has lived on the Reserve all his life and has seven children. There are 323 people in all on the Reserve. Since 1962 he has worked as a caretaker employed by the Department of Indian Affairs and was elected Chief of the Band from 1972 to 1978 and again since 1980, as such being a member of the Band Council which administers the funds provided by the Department of Indian Affairs. The only work which could be done on the reserve prior to the formation of the Gull Bay

Development Corporation was some commercial fishing and trapping which is very poor and some seasonal work in firefighting. By 1972 membership on the Reserve was depleting and alcohol, vandalism and rape were prevalent. The Hudson Bay store in the community moved away as did the teachers. A few members of the Band worked outside the community in logging operations. The community had acquired a bad reputation so that the Government was taking the core funding back and administering it themselves. As Chief in 1972 he wanted to create some work in the community. He had helpful advice from John Blair, a Professor at Lakehead University, who was working on a contract basis with other Bands giving them advice on under-brushing and other forestry operations. The corporation was formed as a vehicle to provide employment. ....

The corporation had approximately 25 employees and initiated logging operations and gave work of a social nature, cleaning up the community, cutting wood for elderly residents, moving unsightly abandoned cars, moving a garbage dump which was objectionable on windy days, making hockey rinks, improving the fencing around the cemetery, and painting old buildings. Younger women were engaged to help older ones who could not do washing for themselves. Some members were taken on tours of the logging operation to show them how the work was done. A generating system was built as there were frequent power failures and fuel was sometimes bought for persons on the Reserve who could not afford it. An alcoholic control programme was initiated and a programme worker hired for this. The Government money was always slow in coming in even after the corporation was formed. The Government funds were provided for the Band, but the corporation was able to build up and improve the lifestyle of the community with the corporation and the Band Council working closely together. ...

Before setting up the corporation several community meetings were held. While it was enthusiastically received some concern was expressed by the trappers and guides who worked during the hunting and fishing season as to the damage which would be caused to the environment and wildlife by the logging operation. Moose hunting supplied a major source of food for the Band. He concluded that the logging must not be done in a conventional manner by large clear cuts but rather it was done by what might be described as a checker board pattern, areas of about 6 acres being cut with adjacent areas of similar size being left untouched. Cutting rights for the area in question belong to Northern Wood Preservers (Saskatchewan) Limited and an agreement was entered into with them to permit Plaintiff to do the logging and sell the wood to Northern Wood Preservers at a price fixed by the agreement. The area in question consisted largely of stands of jack pine and Northern Wood Preservers wanted it in tree lengths to use as telephone poles. Great Lakes Paper Company which had provided the corporation with a licence had an excess inventory of jack pine at the time and Domtar, the only other operator in the area would accept wood but wanted it in eight foot lengths and it was a long haul to their mill. He testified that marking the blocks to be cut is quite labour intensive, and also requires more roads. In a fully commercial operation an entire area would be cleared which would be more profitable, but would destroy the wildlife. He eventually increased the size of the areas marked to be cut from 6 acre blocks to 10 acre blocks so the equipment could be moved more readily, but about 50 per cent of the total timber was left uncut as a browse for the wildlife. Everybody including the timber licencees was happy with what they were doing. He testified that he was successful in working out a very favourable agreement with Northern Wood Preservers (Saskatchewan) Limited due to his friendship with a Mr. Headley their Vice-President. Initially the purchaser wanted wood delivered to the mill, but he was able to persuade them to build the roads as they had the equipment to do so, deducting the cost of the roads from the initial price. He was also able to arrange to have Northern Wood Preservers do the hauling of the wood themselves and they only charged a token amount for this. He was also able to persuade them to supply the necessary skidders and to assist in training the operators in the care and operation of these machines. Once a week a mobile repair truck was sent to the site to perform maintenance training for the loggers who were operating these machines. He was also able to persuade Northern Wood Preservers to do the scaling of the wood; if they had not done so somebody else would have had to be paid to do this work. Plaintiff therefore contends that the agreement with Northern Wood Preservers was almost of a quasi-charitable nature, as it would not have been able to make nearly as much profit, carrying on the operations as it did in a manner to preserve the environment if Northern Wood-Preservers had not been sympathetic with what they were doing for the community and given them a very generous contract. ...

With respect to the argument based on Section 149(1)(*l*) of the Act Plaintiff contends that the primary motive for setting up the corporation was to deal with problems on the Reserve and to create activity to raise funds to use for these purposes. The members (i.e. directors) were not themselves in a position to get any benefit from the corporation. ...

The real issue in the present case appears to be that the corporation was not set up, as its Letters Patent indicate, to carry on a commercial activity although it is no doubt true that the motive for forming the corporation may have been that it was desirable to provide employment and training to otherwise unemployed Indians on the Reserve by engaging in a commercial activity which would not only provide such employment but raise funds to be used for the very worthy social and charitable activities required on the Reserve. However, it was more efficient to carry on this activity through a corporation than to have the Band Council attempt to do it itself. Elections from time to time change the membership of the Band Council and different factions in the Band have different objectives, and while even the corporation was not immune from this, as appears from what happened during the brief period when Chief Esquega was replaced by another Chief and his associates, it was nevertheless more practical to operate as a corporation and negotiate as such with the company for whom the lumber was being cut. If this lumbering operation had been carried out by the Band Council itself it is unlikely that any attempt would have been made to tax the profits of the enterprise. It is certainly the policy of the Department of Indian Affairs to encourage Indian Bands to become self-reliant and to improve living and social conditions on the Reserves, and there is no doubt from the evidence in this case that a great deal has been accomplished in improving living conditions on the Reserve by the work done by employees of the Corporation with funds derived from the lumbering operations, and in providing gainful employment for members of the Band who would otherwise be on welfare.

I do not believe that because a corporation was formed for these purposes this should alter the liability for Income Tax.

The social and welfare activities of Plaintiff are not a cloak to avoid payment of taxation on a commercial enterprise but are the real objectives of the Corporation. ...

While the jurisprudence in this difficult area has led to varying results, depending on the facts applicable in each case, I have concluded that in the present case, whether by the application of Section 149(1)(*f*) or of Section 149(1)(*l*) Plaintiff's appeal should be maintained. The Corporation is operated "exclusively" for the purpose set out in Section 149 (1)(*l*) pursuant to its charter, even though it may raise funds for this purpose by its commercial lumbering enterprise.

OTINEKA DEVELOPMENT CORP. v. CANADA

[1994] 2 C.N.L.R. 83, [1994] 1 C.T.C. 2424 (T.C.C.)

Bowman T.C.J.: — These appeals were heard together and are, in the case of Otineka Development Corporation Ltd., from an assessment for 1986 and, in the case of 72902 Manitoba Ltd., from assessments for 1986 and 1987. In both cases the issue is whether the appellant corporations are subject to tax under the *Income Tax Act*. Their claim for exemption is based upon two alternative contentions:

(a) that they are organizations of the type described in paragraph 149(1)(*l*) of the *Income Tax Act*; or

(b) that they are corporations not less than 90% of the shares of which are owned by a Canadian municipality within the meaning of paragraph 149(1)(*d*).

A further contention was advanced that even if the appellants are not exempt under paragraphs 149(1)(*d*) or (*l*), the income upon which they have been assessed does not belong to them beneficially but rather is the income of The Pas Indian Band for whom they allege that they were agents or trustees.

FACTS

The Pas Indian Band is a "band" as defined in subsection 2(1) of the *Indian Act*. On September 14, 1992, by a resolution of the band council, it changed its name to Opaskwayak Cree Nation. The band consists of about 3,000 persons of whom approximately 2,000 live on the reserve which is situated adjacent to the town of The Pas, Manitoba, over 500 miles north of Winnipeg.

The band is a self-governing entity. It has passed by-laws for most of the purposes contemplated by sections 81 and 85.1 of the *Indian Act*. These purposes include the regulation of water supplies and sewers, the disposal of garbage, the destruction and control of weeds, the restriction of the use of slingshots and bows and arrows, the regulation and control of domestic animals, the regulation of beekeeping, the licensing of hawkers and peddlers, the control of public games and amusements, the observance of law and order, the provision of housing, the control of intoxicants, and the regulation of camping and traffic, to mention only some of the multitude of matters over which the band council has exercised jurisdiction.

On March 9, 1976 the Governor in Council declared, pursuant to subsection 83(1) of the *Indian Act*, that The Pas Indian Band had reached an advanced state of development. The result of this declaration was that the council of the band became entitled, subject to the approval of the Minister of Indian Affairs and Northern Development, to make by-laws for the purpose of raising money from band members by means of taxation. Such a by-law was passed by the council of the band in 1977 and was approved by the Minister but it was never implemented. It was said to be unwieldy and it was opposed by a number of band members, principally those living on the reserve on leased land.

The band provides services to the band members in a large number of areas, including education, health case, social services, including child and family services, employment and training services, alcohol and drug abuse counselling, and economic development.

The band has a complex and sophisticated structure relating to its governance. Its chief and council members are elected democratically and hold frequent meetings relating to all matters affecting the band and the reserve. There are extensive consultations by the council with the band members. The governmental structure resembles that of any municipal body and includes departments or committees with responsibility for such matters as public works, community services, education, economic development, community planning and finance. The band has its own police force, which operates with the RCMP. The band provides schooling for children from kindergarten to grade 12. It operates a modern home for senior band members. It has a sports and recreational department and has its own fire department.

I need not elaborate further. The Pas Indian Band, through its chief and council, is run on essentially the same lines as any other municipality and provides substantially the same services to its band members on the reserve as any municipality in Canada of comparable size. It has earned, deservedly, the reputation in Canada of being a model of self-government.

In 1973, the council of the band caused the appellant Otineka Development Corporation Ltd. to be incorporated under the laws of Manitoba. Since that time all of its issued shares have been owned beneficially by the band. In the years in question the appellant Otineka owned and operated on the reserve a shopping mall known as the Otineka Shopping Centre, which contained a number of retail outlets, including an IGA grocery store. The property on which the mall is situated is leased from the Government of Canada under a procedure whereby land on the reserve is "surrendered" to the Crown and is then leased to individuals or corporations. Rentals received from the leasing of the land are paid to the band. Otineka in turn subleases portions thereof to the various tenants who operate businesses in the mall. The band itself pays rent to Otineka for premises that it occupies there. Witnesses called for the appellant testified that Otineka was incorporated on the basis of advice from the Department of Indian Affairs and Northern Development, because lending institutions would not deal directly with the band since it was not an incorporated entity and it was believed that it did not have the capacity to contract or to give security.

Otineka had its own staff and payroll. Its officers and directors are band members. Financial statements were prepared and the year's profit or loss was shown as that of Otineka. Any excess cash not needed for operations or repairs was loaned to the band, and in most cases it appears that when the money was not repaid it was simply written off and the amount treated as a "contribution". Presumably the money was used by the band to assist in paying for the services that it provided to its members.

72902 Manitoba Ltd. was incorporated in 1986 to own and operate the Chimo Building Centre, a building supply business located on the reserve. It also leased from Her Majesty in right of Canada land surrendered to her by the band. 72902 had its own staff and payroll and kept separate financial statements. Its officers and directors were band members.

ANALYSIS

... One of the reasons for the incorporation of the appellants was that the council believed that the banks would not deal directly with the band because of its perceived lack of capacity to contract or to give security. Whether this view was correct or not, it was a reason for creating an entity that it was believed could contract and give security in its own right and not as agent for someone else. ... It is clear that the business, property and profits of the shopping mall and the building centre belonged both legally and beneficially to Otineka and 72902 respectively. They acted as principals throughout.

The second contention is that the appellants are exempt as organizations of the type described in paragraph 149(1)(*l*). That paragraph reads as follows:

> (*l*) a club, society or association that, in the opinion of the Minister, was not a charity within the meaning assigned by subsection 149.1(1) and that was organized and operated exclusively for social welfare, civic improvement, pleasure or recreation or for any other purpose except profit, no part of the income of which was payable to, or was otherwise available for the personal benefit of, any proprietor, member or shareholder thereof unless the proprietor, member or shareholder was a club, society or association the primary purpose and function of which was the promotion of amateur athletics in Canada;

There are at least two reasons why the paragraph does not apply.

In the first place the income was certainly available for the benefit of the shareholder, the band. Indeed it paid it to the band as a "contribution". In the second place, it cannot be said that the appellants were "organized and operated" exclusively for any of the purposes enumerated in paragraph 149(1)(*l*), or that it was organized and operated. ... "for any other purpose except profit". Their sole raison d'être was to own and run a business for profit. The fact that their profits, when distributed to the band, whether by way of dividend or as a "contribution", might ultimately be used for the social or civic welfare of the band does not mean that the corporate objectives and operations are something other than what they obviously are, the pursuit of profit, however worthy may be the ultimate use to which that profit is put.

Counsel for the appellants relied upon the decision of the Federal Court, Trial Division, in *The Gull Bay Development Corporation v. The Queen*, 84 D.T.C. 6040 in which Walsh J. held that the profits from a logging operation carried on by a corporation were exempt from tax both because the corporation was a charitable organization under paragraph 149(1)(*f*) or because it was a non-profit organization under paragraph 149(1)(*l*). The case does not assist the appellants. In *Gull Bay* the decision was based upon the activities that the corporation itself carried on using funds generated by its commercial operation. Here the corporations carried on commercial activities and distributed their funds to their shareholders. For this argument to have any chance of success there would have had to be a virtual identity between the corporations and the band. That conclusion is not open to me on the evidence. ...

The third contention is that the corporations are exempt under paragraph 149(1)(*d*).

Although paragraph 149(1)(*c*) was not relied upon and has no application, I set it out along with paragraph 149(1)(*d*):

> (*c*) a municipality in Canada, or a municipal or public body performing a function of government in Canada;
> (*d*) a corporation, commission or association not less than 90% of the shares or capital or which was owned by Her Majesty in right of Canada or a province or by a Canadian municipality,...

The appellants are 100 per cent owned by the band and no one else has the right to acquire the shares. The sole question is therefore whether The Pas Indian Band is a "municipality" within paragraph 149(1)(*d*).

The term "municipality" is not defined in the *Income Tax Act* and unless there is a reason to do otherwise it must be given its ordinary meaning of a community having and exercising the powers of self government and providing the type of services customarily provided by such a body. If its ordinary meaning is to apply, it is not necessary that it be incorporated.

The definition of municipality that was accepted by the Ontario Court of Appeal is one that was contained in the Shorter Oxford Dictionary and is set out in the following passage from the judgment of Robertson C.J.O. in *Re Gagnon et al. and Studer*, [1948] O.R. 634 at 640:

> *The Municipal Act*, in s. 1(m), defines a municipality as "a locality, the inhabitants of which are incorporated". It is beyond dispute that the Township of Norman is unorganized territory, and that its inhabitants are not incorporated. *The Interpretation Act*, R.S.O. 1937, c. 1, says, in s. 34: "The interpretation section of *The Municipal Act* shall extend to all Acts relating to municipal matters." It seems to me that the interpretation section of *The Municipal Act* should be an excellent place in which to look for the meaning of "municipality" as it is used in the several Acts relating to schools. However, appellants' counsel submits that the School Acts deal not with municipal matters, but with matters of education. I have not found any decision on the precise point whether s. 34 of *The Interpretation Act* has the effect of extending the interpretation section of The *Municipal Act* to *The Separate Schools Act*. I take, therefore, the meaning of the word "municipality" apart from any statutory definition. The word is derived from the Latin "municipalis". The Oxford English Dictionary gives as its meaning: "(1) A town, city or district pos-

sessed of privileges of local self-government, also applied to its inhabitants collectively; (2) The governing body of a town or district having municipal institutions." As part of an unorganized district, and itself unorganized, the Township of Norman is without the privilege of local self-government, or any governing body to administer it. It may have school boards to govern and administer the schools formed under the various School Acts, but it has no municipal organization. It has not even a municipal clerk to whom its residents, who are separate school supporters, can give a notice under s. 55 of The *Separate Schools Act.*

Similarly, the definition of "municipalité", the word appearing in the French version, in Robert, Dictionnaire de la Langue Française is as follows: "municipalité,... Le corps municipal; l'ensemble des personnes qui administrent une commune..."

It has been overwhelmingly demonstrated on the evidence that The Pas Indian Band, through its chief and council both in the powers that it exercises under the authority of the Indian Act and the services that it provides to its members, is a municipality within the definition quoted above. The very factors whose absence militated against the Township of Norman's being a municipality are here in abundance.

Counsel for the respondent, however, urges a more restrictive interpretation. Her argument, which was presented with skill and persuasiveness, is premised initially upon the distribution of legislative competence between the federal and provincial governments. She points out that, whereas the power to legislate with respect to Indians and lands reserved for the Indians lies within federal competence, the power to legislate in relation to "Municipal Institutions in the Province" is conferred upon the provinces under subsection 92(8) of the *Constitution Act, 1867.* From this she reasons that the federal government would not have the power to create a "municipality" within an Indian Reserve located in a province. She accepts that it is within the legislative competence of the federal government to confer upon the band the powers enumerated under sections 81, 83 and 85.1 of the *Indian Act*, and that the conferral of such powers gives to the band the attributes normally associated with conventional municipalities. This does not, however, in her submission, lead to the conclusion that the federal government has created a municipality but rather that it has created something analogous or similar to a municipality. Her position is that in Canada we have generally three levels of government — federal, provincial and municipal — and that in constituting an Indian band a self-governing body the federal government, within its constitutional powers, is creating a fourth category and that fourth category is not within the meaning of municipality in paragraph 149(1)(*d*). She contends therefore that we must look to a definition in the laws of the province having legislative competence over municipal institutions, in this case the Manitoba *Municipal Act*, R.S.M. 1988, c. M225.

Subsection 2(1) of that Act defines "municipality" as follows:

"municipality" means, subject to section 3,

    (*a*) a corporation comprising the inhabitants of an area in the province who are incorporated and continued under the authority of this Act or of another Act of the Legislature; or

(b)   the area the inhabitants of which are incorporated as stated in clause (a): but does not include a local government district.

She contends further that in the absence of a definition of municipality in the *Income Tax Act* we should look to a definition in a statute that is in *pari materia*, the *Excise Tax Act*. The definition of municipality in that act is as follows:

"municipality" means

(a)   an incorporated city, metropolitan authority, town, village, township, district or rural municipality or other incorporated municipal body however designated; or

(b)   such other local authority as the Governor in Council may determine to be a municipality for the purposes of this Act;

Notwithstanding Ms. Shield's able argument I am unable to accept it. In the first place it would clearly be within the legislative competence of Parliament to create a municipality on lands reserved for Indians in the exercise of its power under subsection 91(24) of *the Constitution Act, 1867*. Although it has not expressly purported to create a municipality, it has conferred powers upon the band under sections 81, 83 and 85.1 of the *Indian Act*. The result of that conferral of powers by the Government of Canada, and the exercise thereof by the band, has been to create a form of self-government that is an essential attribute of a municipality. It follows therefore that the entity exercising that form of self-government is a municipality within the ordinary understanding of that word. The question is not the nature of the authority that created the governmental body but rather the nature of the body that is created.

The *Excise Tax Act* is not in my view in *pari materia*. Indeed, I think it is more reasonable to infer from the absence of a definition in the *Income Tax Act* and the presence of one in the *Excise Tax Act* that Parliament did not intend the more restrictive definition to apply to the *Income Tax Act*. Nor can I find any legal justification for looking to the definition of municipality in the Manitoba *Municipal Act*.

> It must be recognized that paragraph 149(1)(d) has as its purpose the exemption from tax on corporations owned by Canadian municipalities. The rationale I presume is that the profits from businesses carried on by such corporations will be used for the public purposes of the municipalities, who will nonetheless have the protection of limited liability. There can be no justification for interpreting the paragraph to deny the exemption to corporations owned by a band of Indians that has all the attributes of a municipality on the ground that it derives those attributes from the *Indian Act* rather than from one of the provincial statutes that regulate municipal institutions.

In my opinion The Pas Indian Band was a Canadian municipality within the meaning of paragraph 149(1)(d) of the *Income Tax Act* and accordingly the two companies that it owned, Otineka Development Corporation Ltd. and 72902 Manitoba Ltd. were exempt from tax under paragraph 149(1)(d).

The appeals are therefore allowed with costs and the assessments vacated. There should be only one counsel fee for both appellants.

There is conflicting authority over whether a band may constitute a municipality as in the *Otineka* case. In *Tawich Development Corp. v. Deputy Minister of Revenue of Quebec*, [1997] 2 C.N.L.R. 187 (Que. C.A.), the Cree Nation of Wemindji incorporated an economic development corporation under the *Canadian Business Corporations Act*, R.S.C. 1985, c. C-44. Under the *Cree-Naskapi Act* (of Quebec), S.C. 1984, c. 18, the band is also a separately incorporated local government. Furthermore, the members of the Band are constituted as a municipality under the *Cree Villages Act*, R.S.Q., c. V-5.1. The issue in the case was whether the corporation could avoid capital tax by reason of being a "municipal corporation". The *Tawich* court distinguished the *Otineka* case and tacitly disapproved of its reasoning by saying that it relates only to that case's special circumstances. The Quebec Court of Appeal wrote (page 210): "A Canadian municipality cannot be created implicitly or by judicial interpretation. The status of a municipality cannot be acquired by analogy."

G. ABORIGINAL TAXATION POWERS

REPORT OF THE ROYAL COMMISSION ON ABORIGINAL PEOPLES, RESTRUCTURING THE RELATIONSHIP, VOL. 2

(Ottawa: Ministry of Supply and Services, 1996) at 290-293
(references omitted)

We want control of our destiny and a peaceful co-existence with Canadian society. In order for this to happen, First Nations must have an equitable share of lands, resources and jurisdiction, and fiscal capability to fulfill their responsibilities as self-determining peoples.

Chief Clarence T. Jules Kamloops First Nation Ottawa,
Ontario, 5 November 1993

...[A]ttaining a significant measure of fiscal autonomy is a fundamental prerequisite for effective self-government. A people that does not possess the means to finance its own government will be dependent on the priorities of others. This can be mitigated by negotiating long-term arrangements that commit other governments to fiscal transfers. But ultimately, a government that must look to others for most of its financial requirements remains dependent. Hence the importance of own-source revenues and authority for Aboriginal nations to tax their own resources and citizens.

Given the many responsibilities of Aboriginal governments, and assuming that Aboriginal people will want to receive a wide range of high quality services, Aboriginal governments will need to collect significant amounts of revenue. Other governments that support Aboriginal governments through transfers will expect them to do so. Indeed, transfers are likely to depend on the revenue collection effort of the recipient government, as is common in fiscal arrangements between governments in Canada.

———

There are different ways Aboriginal groups could raise funds and collect revenues through taxation.

1. Inherent Aboriginal Taxation Powers

Canada has not recognized the inherent right of Aboriginal governments to engage in taxation. However, it could be argued that wealth distribution was an activity integral to Aboriginal peoples prior to the arrival of Europeans, and therefore should receive protection under section 35(1) of the *Constitution Act, 1982*. There are many traditions where officially practiced wealth-redistribution was an important part of Aboriginal societies, such as potlatches, feasts, give-aways, gift-giving, etc.

The United States courts have been willing to recognize inherent or reserved powers of taxation vested in Indian tribes. For example, in *Washington v. Confederated Tribes of the Colville Reservation*, 447 U.S. 134 (U.S.S.C. 1980) the United States Supreme Court wrote: "The power to tax transactions occurring on trust lands and significantly involving a tribe or its members is a fundamental attribute of sovereignty, which the tribes retain unless divested of it by federal law or necessary implication of their dependent status". Similar conclusions are expressed in *Warren Trading Post v. Arizona Tax Commission*, 380 U.S. 685 (U.S.S.C. 1965); *McClanahan v. Arizona State Tax Commission*, 411 U.S. 164 (U.S.S.C. 1973); *White Mountain Apache Tribe v. Bracker*, 448 U.S. 136 (U.S.S.C. 1980); *Merrion v. Jicarilla Apache Tribe*, 455 U.S. 130 (U.S.S.C. 1982). While the plenary power of Congress to extinguish Indian rights to taxation is apparent in the Court's rulings (see especially *Atkinson Trading Company, Inc. v. Shirley*, 532 U.S. 645 (U.S.S.C. 2001), it is significant that the courts have recognized this power, and that the U.S. federal government has encouraged, not extinguished, the Indian taxation power. If Canadian courts and governments were to recognize inherent Indian taxation powers, this could have a positive impact on Aboriginal communities. The existence of inherent powers of taxation in the United States has helped many tribes become self-sufficient: see Stephen Cornell and Joseph P. Kalt, eds., *What Can Tribes Do? Strategies and Institutions in American Indian Economic Development* (Los Angeles: University of California, 1992), 1-61.

2. Indian Act Band Taxation

The primary way in which Aboriginal taxation powers have been utilized is under the *Indian Act*. In 1988 Parliament passed Bill C-115 (S.C. 1988, c. 23), known as the Kamloops Amendments, to allow band governments to assume powers of property taxation over non-Aboriginal interests in reserve lands. Since 1988, 90 of the more than 600 First Nations in Canada have assumed these taxation powers. First Nations tax revenues under this process have exceeded $42 million per year and have totalled $173 million since inception.

In particular, the Kamloops Amendments changed section 83 of the *Indian Act*, to read:

> 83 (1) ... the council of a band may, subject to the approval of the Minister, make by-laws for any and all of the following purposes, namely,
>
> (a) subject to subsection (2) and (3), taxation for local purposes of land, or interest in land, in the reserve, including rights to occupy, possess or use land in the reserve;
>
> (a.1) the licensing of businesses, callings, trades and occupations;
>
> . . . . .
>
> (f) the raising of money from band members to support band projects;

Thus, according to Parliament, the legislative basis of the Indian Band taxation power stems from section 83 of the *Indian Act*. There is no mention of any reserved or inherent rights of Aboriginal peoples to tax others through band by-laws.

In *Westbank First Nation v. B.C. Hydro and Power Authority*, [1999] 3 S.C.R. 134 the Supreme Court of Canada considered the constitutional basis for Indian Band taxation under section 83 of the *Indian Act*. Once again, no reference was made to any reserved or inherent rights that Aboriginal peoples might possess to tax others. As a result, the Court found that the constitutional basis for Indian band taxation powers was section 91(3) of the *Constitution Act, 1867* ("the raising of money by any mode or system of taxation"). In this case the Supreme Court of Canada found that the primary purpose of the taxation by-laws of the Westbank First Nation was in pith and substance taxation. The by-laws were not connected to a regulatory scheme, nor were they a user fee for services directly rendered. Because the by-laws were taxation by-laws, in their pith and substance, the Court found they were enacted pursuant to section 91(3) rather than section 91(24) of the *Constitution Act, 1867*. The Court found that Westbank's tax by-laws could not apply to B.C. Hydro, a provincial Crown agent, since section 125 of the *Constitution Act, 1867* prevents intergovernmental taxation.

The exercise of the taxation power under section 83 is assisted by an organization know as the Indian Taxation Advisory Board (ITAB). Soon after the amendment to section 83 of the *Indian Act*, ITAB was established to facilitate the approval of Indian taxation by-laws, since the power to tax under section 83 must be done through band by-law and ministerial approval. ITAB is made up of First Nations individuals and the organization assists the Minister in examining proposed by-laws and making recommendations before they are passed into law. Using ITAB's expertise, there are seven stages a band goes through to enact a taxation by-law:

1. Decision to tax: band expresses its intention to tax
2. Preparation: band collects legal information to produce draft by-law; discusses by-law with ITAB, Justice, and Indian Affairs
3. Communication: consult with potentially affected parties

4. Analysis: ITAB, Justice and INAC review
5. Recommendation to the Minister: ITAB forwards recommended decision to Minister based on analysis
6. Ministerial Decision: Yes or No
7. Implementation.

The principles ITAB applies when making recommendations are: conformity with the *Canadian Charter of Rights and Freedoms*, conformity with enabling legislation, comprehensiveness, compliance with principles of equity and justice, fairness, adequacy of notification and appeal procedures and absence of ministerial liability. The process to take a by-law from beginning to end can take up to eight months. ITAB is working to shorten this process, and actually hopes to replace ministerial oversight altogether. In its policy development guise, ITAB is working to create a First Nations Tax Commission as a statute-based institution to succeed it, and has initiatives to establish institutions such as The First Nations Financial Management Board, The First Nations Financing Authority and the First Nations Statistical Institute. Establishing an independent First Nations Tax Authority is important to ITAB because it believes this would increase expertise and build credibility in Indian tax matters throughout the country.

Despite the increasing use of Indian band taxation powers under the *Indian Act*, this approach has not been without controversy. Non-Aboriginal people and corporations hold most of the land subject to taxation under section 83 by-laws. The types of interests taxed include: commercial land use leases; oil, gas, timber and resources leases; utility leases (hydro, telephone and natural gas lines); rental leases; and agricultural permits and leases. Understandably, entities holding these interests seek to reduce their tax liabilities. As a result, most of the litigation before the Supreme Court of Canada has involved non-Aboriginal people and corporations appealing Indian band taxation decisions. A few examples include:

St. Mary's Indian Band v. Cranbrook (City), [1997] 2 S.C.R. 657

Prior to the Kamloops amendments in 1988, the definition of "reserve" made it doubtful that conditionally surrendered land remained part of the reserve for band taxation purposes. At that time it was therefore unlikely that a band taxation by-law could apply to the non-Indian developments on such land. However, when the *Indian Act* was amended, "Conditionally surrendered" lands were renamed "designated" lands. The definition of "reserve" was also changed so that designated lands, for most band by-law purposes, remained within the reserve.

In the *St. Mary's* case the Court was asked to consider the distinction between lands absolutely surrendered (which would not be subject to taxation) and conditionally surrendered or designated lands (which could be subject to taxation). In this case the band surrendered a portion of its reserve for full market value to the federal Crown for use as a municipal airport in 1966. The surrender was subject to the stipulation that it would revert to the band if it ceased to be used for public purposes. The band levied property taxes in 1992 on the ground that the reversionary stipulation to the surrender made the transfer "otherwise than absolut[e]" under the Kamloops amendments, with the result that the surrendered land fell within the "designated lands" category of the reserve. When the city r e-fused to pay, the band sued. The Supreme Court held that the band's re-serve lands were absolutely surrendered (and thus not subject to taxation) because at the time of surrender the band intended to part with the land on an absolute basis. The Court said that the mere fact the band included a rider in its surrender (i.e. reversion if land ceased to be used as an airport) does not necessarily mean that the surrender was "other than absolute". The Supreme Court held that "absolute" and "conditional" are not mutually ex-clusive terms — either conceptually or under the scheme of the *Indian Act*. Therefore, the definition of "designated lands" did not capture the airport lands, and these lands were not entitled to be subject to band taxation.

Canadian Pacific Ltd. v. Matsqui Indian Band, [1995] 1 S.C.R. 3

In *Canadian Pacific Ltd. v. Matsqui Indian Band* (1996), 134 D.L.R. (4th) 555 (F.C.T.D.), certain Indian bands tried to tax the railway lines of both the CNR and the CPR. They argued that the railways' interest in the rights of way was less than absolute, because they only held the land so long as it was needed for railway purposes. Thus, they said the railway lands should still be part of the reserves through which they passed, and thus subject to taxation under section 83. It was important to the band's argument that the lands be part of the reserve because band by-laws only have force and ef-fect within the geographical areas of the reserve and apply only to reserve lands. They do not apply to lands held outside the reserve by bands or to absolutely surrendered lands.

The first time the case went to the Supreme Court of Canada it consid-ered preliminary procedural questions: whether the assessment review board established by the band by-law was the proper forum to consider the jurisdictional question of whether land was in the reserve The railways argued successfully that the assessment review board was not the proper forum, and established the right to have the assessor's decision reviewed directly by the Federal Court on judicial review. Despite this holding, the Court did write:

> ... it is important that we not lose sight of Parliament's objective in creating the new Indian taxation powers. The regime which came into force in 1988 is intended to facilitate the development of Aboriginal self-government by al-lowing bands to exercise the inherently governmental power of taxation on their reserves. Though this Court is not faced with the issue of Aboriginal self-government directly, the underlying purpose and functions of the In-dian tax assessment scheme provide considerable guidance in applying the principles of administrative law to the statutory provisions at issue here. I will therefore employ a purposive and functional approach where appropri-ate in this ruling.

Following the Supreme Court of Canada's decision on the procedural questions, there was a series of actions that never did satisfactorily deter-mine the substance of the issue: see *Canadian Pacific Ltd. v. Matsqui Indian Band* (1996), 134 D.L.R. (4th) 555 (F.C.T.D.); affd. (1998), 162 D.L.R. (4th) 649 (F.C.A.); [1999] 2 C.N.L.R. iv (note) (S.C.C.); (1999), 176 D.L.R. (4th) 35 (F.C.A.). The second 1999 Federal Court of Appeal decision contains three sets of reasons. Two judges held that the by-laws' taxation of non-Indian property interests only was not discriminatory. Two judges found the Canadian Pacific rights of way were lands within the reserve, while one judge found that the Canadian Pacific rights of way were held in fee simple absolute and were not lands within the reserve. The Federal Court of Appeal decision was not appealed to the Supreme Court of Canada. Canadian Pacific and the five bands involved in the appeal (the Boothroyd, Cook's Ferry, Matsqui, Seabird Island, and Skuppah Indian Bands) concluded agreements that recognized the bands' property taxation jurisdiction and provided for the passage of a federal regulation under section 83(5) of the *Indian Act*.

Osoyoos Indian Band v. Oliver (Town), [2001] 3 S.C.R. 746

In the *Osoyoos* case the issue was whether expropriated Indian reserve land could still be considered reserve land and thus subject to band taxation. The technical framing of the question was whether lands taken pursuant to section 35 of the *Indian Act* were "land or interests in land" in a reserve of a band within the meaning of section 83(1)(a) of the *Indian Act* such that those lands are assessable and taxable pursuant to band assessment by-laws and taxable pursuant to band taxation by-laws?

The Supreme Court of Canada held that section 83(1)(a) of the *Indian Act* provides Indian bands with the jurisdiction to impose tax on a very broad range of interests in land, and should be given a broad reading. They held that since the Order in Council that expropriated the lands did not evince a clear and plain intent to extinguish the band's interest in the reserve land, resort must be had to the interpretive principles that impair the Indian interests as little as possible. The Court found that, in light of these interpretive principles, the Order in Council at issue should be read as granting only a statutory easement to the province, and that it be held that the canal land is still "in the reserve" for the purposes of section 83(1)(a), and thus subject to taxation.

Musqueam Indian Band v. Glass, [2000] 2 S.C.R. 633

Though not strictly a section 83 taxation case, the *Musqueam* decision may hold important implications for Indian band taxation. The Musqueam dispute arose in 1995 when rent renewal clauses contained in a large number of long-term ground leases of Indian reserve lands first took effect. The Musqueam lands are located adjacent to the City of Vancouver and they form a part of an Indian Reserve that was surrendered for development as a single-family residential development in the early 1960s. Each parcel of land was separately leased on 99-year terms and the rent was fixed in the lease for the first 30 years. The dispute arose because there was no agreement on a condition in the lease that provided that on renewal the annual rent was to be set at 6 per cent of "current land value". Unfortunately, the term "current land value" was not defined precisely enough in the lease. A lengthy and costly dispute followed. This conflict occurred because during the initial 30-year period land values had escalated dramatically. As a result, homeowners would be have been faced with significantly higher rents unless the phrase "current land value" was given some constrained meaning.

The phrase was given a restricted meaning by the Supreme Court. This was advantageous to the lease-holding homeowners and less favourable to the Musqueam. The Court resolved the dispute by holding that the annual rent payments should be based upon 6 per cent of the fair market value of fee simple land, less servicing costs, and discounted 50 per cent to adjust for the fact that the land was on an Indian Reserve. The decision has been criticized for reducing the fair market value of Indian reserve land. While the case is not, strictly speaking, a section 83 taxation case, it may become relevant for section 83 purposes (if the courts hold that Aboriginal taxation has to be at a lower rate on reserves because of the reserves' lower land values as compared to surrounding provincial lands).

3. Negotiated Aboriginal Taxation Powers

Aboriginal peoples can negotiate for recognition of taxation powers through treaties and agreements. A recent example of Indian taxation provisions relative to self-government is found in the Nisga'a Final Agreement. The Nisga'a are a people in northwestern British Columbia who were the subject of the *Calder v. British Columbia (Attorney General)*, [1973] S.C.R. 313, 34 D.L.R. (3d) 145 case in 1973 before the Supreme Court of Canada. This agreement, the product of 16 years of negotiation, sets out a scheme to assist the Nisga'a in operating their governments, and creating and distributing wealth for their people. It eliminates the taxation provisions of the *Indian Act* and replaces them with an entirely new scheme. The Nisga'a Agreement is a land and self-government agreement that is protected as a treaty under section 35(1) of the *Constitution Act, 1982* [being Schedule B of the *Canada Act 1982* (U.K.), 1982, c. 11].

Under section 1 of chapter 16 (Taxation) of the Nisga'a Final Agreement, the Nisga'a government has the power to make laws with respect to direct taxation of Nisga'a citizens on Nisga'a lands, including property taxation of Nisga'a citizens. That power does not include taxation of non-Nisga'a citizens. As Nisga'a lands are held in fee simple, and are not reserve lands, provincial property taxation laws would normally apply to all interests in those lands. However, under section 13 of chapter 16 (Taxation), certain Nisga'a lands held by the Nisga'a Nation and Nisga'a villages are exempt from real property taxation. These include unimproved lands, lands on which a Nisga'a citizen has a residence, and lands which are improved for public purposes. Provincial taxation laws have been amended to reflect these exemptions: see, for example, section 2.1 of the *Taxation (Rural Area) Act*, R.S.B.C. 1996, c. 448. The Nisga'a treaty provides for possible delegation to the Nisga'a government of provincial taxation powers over non-Nisga'a citizens on Nisga'a lands. For more information see Tom Falconer, "Fiscal Aspects of the Nisga'a Final Agreement" (2000) 48 Canadian Tax Journal 1829. Other agreements that contain negotiated taxation powers include: *Sechelt Indian Band Self Government Act*, S.C. 1986, c. 27; *Sechelt Indian Government District Enabling Act*, R.S.B.C. 1996, c. 416; *Yukon First Nations Self-Government Act*, S.C. 1994, c. 35.

Many people and groups have expressed concern about the fairness and constitutionality of Aboriginal taxation of non-Aboriginal people (see Jonathon Kesselman, "Aboriginal Taxation of Non-Aboriginal Residents: Representation, Discrimination and Accountability" (2000) 48 Canadian Tax Journal 1525; Dominic Belley, "Indian Taxation Powers: Sharing Canadian Prosperity" (2000) 60 La Revue du Barreau 185). Groups like the Canadian Taxpayers Federation, the Fraser Institute, the Saskatchewan Party, the Alliance Party and the B.C. Civil Liberties Association have all written in opposition to Aboriginal taxation of non-Aboriginal people without proper representation. For example, though more supportive than some groups, the B.C. Civil Liberties Association has expressed its position through the following series of principles (see www.bccla.org/positions/political/00nonaboriginal.html):

Principle 1

Aboriginal authority to impose property taxes on non-band/First Nations leaseholders under the *Indian Act* raises civil liberties concerns. The use of such authority is an example of a First Nation acting as a government authority, rather than as simply a party in private contract. Aboriginal taxation authority is part of a greater trend to provide First Nations with greater autonomy culminating in self-government treaties.

Principle 2

People who live in aboriginal jurisdictions, but are not band members, have no right to membership in the aboriginal political community.

Principle 3

Residents of aboriginal jurisdictions have a right to participate in decision-making regarding matters that directly affect them.

Principle 4

Canadian citizens who are not members of an Indian band have a right to participate in government decision-making that affects them in aboriginal jurisdictions because they retain some significant degree, though it may be necessarily attenuated in aboriginal jurisdictions, of their sovereign status throughout Canada. The right of citizens to participate meaningfully in decision-making is a fundamental characteristic of Canada's democracy.

Principle 5

To balance the competing principles of aboriginal self-government and non-aboriginal residents' right to participate in decision-making, when the non-Native population is close to, equals or outnumbers the aboriginal population in an aboriginal jurisdiction, then procedures must be weighted to respect aboriginal self-determination.

Principle 6

Non-Aboriginal residents' participation may reflect the process of decision-making used by the aboriginal community. For example, if an aboriginal community uses a consensus-based decision-making process, then non-aboriginal residents might sit at the table and participate as equals in the deliberations. If the aboriginal community uses democratic institutions like voting or appointing representatives, non-aboriginal residents might participate in the same way as First Nations people. A purely advisory body for non-aboriginal residents will only be "meaningful" if the residents agree to forego other types of participation. ...

H. CONCLUSION

The overriding aim of taxation is to provide governments with the funds they require to meet their obligations. As this chapter has demonstrated, however, other important objectives are also recognized and should be considered in the formulation of taxation policy. The 1966 *Royal Commission on Taxation* observed that:

> ... public facilities and services must be made available and public programmes instituted to transfer purchasing power from some individual and groups in the community to others, in order to create an environment which economic activity can expand rapidly and in which the generally accepted social and cultural needs of the people can be met. The government can satisfy these collective needs only if it commands the use of goods and the services of [people].
>
> In addition to obtaining command over goods and services for these purposes, the government must be able to influence the level of private command over goods and services so that it may be able to offset fluctuations in employment and prices, and to ensure that the total output of goods and services expands as rapidly as possible, given the choices of its citizens between present and future consumption, and between work and leisure. To meet this objective the government must be able to increase and reduce private demand over goods and services from time to time so that, together with the public command, all resources are fully utilized.

It is clear that the Canadian government has largely excluded Aboriginal people from its consideration of these wider objectives in taxation. Principles first articulated in outdated Victorian legislation (the *Indian Act*) have been left to develop on a case-by-case basis with little attention to the economic and cultural realities of contemporary Aboriginal communities. Aboriginal peoples have had to be creative in developing arguments that meet their current needs. Yet, since the time the *Indian Act* was first enacted, the Canadian approach to the formulation of taxation policy has undergone a remarkable change. Greater emphasis has been placed on participatory democracy and the development and more equitable distribution of wealth in Canada. While certain Aboriginal taxation initiatives represent the beginning of a greater attempt to weigh Aboriginal interests in tax policy, much work remains to be done. It is apparent from the legislative history and cases reproduced in this chapter that the purchasing power, social and cultural needs of Aboriginal people have not received the attention needed to enable them to capture a greater share of the wealth that circulates in and around their communities.

CHAPTER 11

CHILD WELFARE

A. INTRODUCTION

Children hold a special place in most communities around the world, and Aboriginal communities are no exception. There is a teaching in many Aboriginal communities that stresses today's decisions have to include the needs of the seventh generation of their children. This orientation demonstrates the importance attached to the intergenerational transmission of love, material resources, and cultural values. For many centuries, Aboriginal peoples lived by laws and customs that respected these teachings and promoted such values. Unfortunately, there has been a severe disruption of these laws that has had a devastating effect on child rearing practices. Aboriginal people have encountered numerous difficulties with Canada's treatment of their children. Residential schools, child welfare agencies, institutions of criminal justice, and the courts have all played a damaging role in this calamity. The reasons for this tragedy are numerous, and Canadian law has been among one of its causes. This chapter examines the law relative to Aboriginal child welfare and explores the relationship between government policies of assimilation and the faltering of Aboriginal child/family relationships. It also considers contemporary issues of reform, and raises some of the challenges Aboriginal people face in asserting greater responsibility for their children.

REPORT OF THE ROYAL COMMISSION ON ABORIGINAL PEOPLES, GATHERING STRENGTH, VOL. 3

(Ottawa: Ministry of Supply and Services, 1996) at 23 (references omitted)

Today we are in a time of healing for our children, our families, our communities and Mother Earth.

Judy Gingell Teslin, Yukon 27 May 1992

We believe our children are our future, the leadership of tomorrow. If you believe in that, then you have to believe also that you must equip your future with the best possible tools to lead your community and lead your nation into the twenty-first century.

Grand Chief Joe Miskokomon Union of Ontario Indians Toronto, Ontario, 26 June 1992

The Special Place of Children in Aboriginal Cultures

Children hold a special place in Aboriginal cultures. According to tradition, they are gifts from the spirit world and have to be treated very gently

lest they become disillusioned with this world and return to a more congenial place. They must be protected from harm because there are spirits that
would wish to entice them back to that other realm. They bring a purity of
vision to the world that can teach their elders. They carry within them the
gifts that manifest themselves as they become teachers, mothers, hunters,
counsellors, artisans and visionaries. They renew the strength of the family, clan and village and make the elders young again with their joyful
presence.

Failure to care for these gifts bestowed on the family, and to protect
children from the betrayal of others, is perhaps the greatest shame that can
befall an Aboriginal family. It is a shame that countless Aboriginal families
have experienced, some of them repeatedly over generations. Here we examine the genesis of that shame, the efforts to erase it, and the role of [law
and] public policy in restoring the trust of children, parents and grandparents in their future.

B. HISTORICAL TREATMENT

"CHILD WELFARE"

In A.C. Hamilton and C.M. Sinclair, *The Justice System and Aboriginal People:
Report of the Aboriginal Justice Inquiry in Manitoba*, Vol. 1
(Winnipeg: Queen's Printer, 1991) at 509-520 (references omitted)

... The intrusion by child welfare authorities in the past has been paternalistic and colonial in nature, condescending and demeaning in fact, and
often insensitive and brutal to Aboriginal people. Aboriginal children have
been taken from their families, communities and societies, first by the residential school system and later by the child welfare system. Both systems
have left Aboriginal people and their societies severely damaged. If Aboriginal people are correct, and we believe they are, part of the reason for
the high numbers of Aboriginal people in correctional facilities is the fact
that Aboriginal people still do not fully control their own lives and destinies, or the lives of their own children. Aboriginal people must have more
control over the ways in which their children are raised, taught and protected.

Failing this, we are convinced we will see more, not fewer, Aboriginal
people in our correctional facilities in the future. We will see more young
Aboriginal people falling into a pattern that is becoming all too familiar. It
takes them from institution to institution, from foster home to young offender facility and, finally, on to adult jails. As Oscar Lathlin, the then chief
of The Pas Band, asked our Inquiry, "Is the current system conditioning
our young for lives in institutions and not in society?"

The implications of these patterns are most obvious to people in Aboriginal communities. People there worry because they know their young
people make up a significant proportion of their populations today. The
numbers of young people in these communities are increasing at a rate far
higher than that of the general population. Aboriginal people worry about

the future survival of their languages, cultures and societies if yet another generation is swept into institutions and away from their communities.

It is for these and many other reasons that we have made a careful examination of the child welfare system. We felt it necessary because:

- We feel many of the problems Aboriginal people face with the criminal justice system today have roots in the history of government-Aboriginal relations. No analysis of the justice system can be complete without understanding the devastating effect these relations, guided by government policies, have had on Aboriginal Families. For many Aboriginal societies, existing child welfare practices have ranked as a major destructive force to their Families, communities and cultures.
- Some people have suggested that the child welfare and criminal justice systems are distinct and should function completely independently of each other. We do not agree. We believe many of the reasons why the numbers of Aboriginal people are so disproportionately high in the child welfare system are the same as the reasons why they are so over-represented in the criminal justice system. "Clients" of one system frequently become "clients" of the other system. It would be impossible to present a complete picture of the criminal justice system, and the youth justice system, without also analyzing the field of child and family services.
- The reforms we advocate, particularly in the youth justice area, involve the breaking down of artificial barriers between the criminal justice and child welfare systems. These systems, we believe, must work much more closely together. The needs and problems of Aboriginal families and communities are intertwined, and we feel we cannot separate them completely or relegate them to one system or the other.
- The available evidence indicates that the apprehension of Aboriginal children by the child welfare system tends to set a pattern of multiple foster home placements. The evidence also indicates this pattern often leads the children into young offender institutions and, ultimately, to "graduate" to the adult correctional system. Aboriginal families, communities and their leaders are rightly concerned about these patterns, and about their effects on the future of their children's lives and of their communities.
- There has been some remarkable progress in the child welfare system as Aboriginal people have assumed more control over the lives and well being of their children in their communities. The criminal justice system must move in a similar direction if it hopes to achieve similar success.
- The numbers of Aboriginal children will continue to increase at a rate exceeding that of the general population. Therefore, there is every indication that child and family services will play an increasingly important role in Aboriginal communities in the future.
- Finally, we believe it is essential to review the child welfare system in urban centres, particularly in Winnipeg, where there continue to be significant problems for Aboriginal persons requiring services. We will identify some of these problems and offer suggestions to make this system more effective.

Child Welfare and Education: An Historical Overview of Government-Aboriginal Relations

For some time, governments have undertaken to serve neglected children by taking them into their care or by helping the families of these children through what we now call child welfare services. Services may include family counselling, substance abuse counselling, assistance to an unmarried parent, or taking the child away from a disrupted home or family and placing the child in a foster home, a group home or with a new family, through adoption. In Canada, each province is responsible for developing and maintaining its own child welfare system. Each province gets financial help from the federal government under the Canada Assistance Plan, which pays approximately half the costs of these programs.

At first glance, this system appears to be one most people would support and encourage. It is certainly a far cry from the way Western or European societies have treated children in the past. Historically, the phrase "a man's home is his castle" meant just that. Society took a very dim view of interfering with the manner in which the head of a household treated his children. In ancient Rome, a father had "complete authority over his children, including the legal authority to sell them into slavery or even put them to death." Over time, a father's power over his children was tempered to a limited right of "reasonable chastisement," although this continued to mean a father could beat his children and even sell them into apprenticeship. Eventually, there were laws that forbade parents from killing or maiming their children or failing to provide them with the necessities of life. Nevertheless, children were still subject to abuse and forced labour in mines and factories.

Society's attitudes toward children began to change when social reformers became increasingly concerned at the plight of the working poor and, in particular, with the way children were treated. In the latter part of the 1800s, they pressured governments to pass laws to make the lives of children better. Private children's aid societies formed with the intent of caring for abused, abandoned or neglected children. Governments passed child labour laws and provided for public school systems. For the first time, governments adopted a policy allowing for the intervention by child care workers to protect the life of a child in extreme situations. These laws and policies make up the foundation of the modern child welfare system.

Most of these developments, however, passed by unnoticed in Aboriginal communities and reserves. The history of child welfare in these communities developed separately and much differently from the way it did in the rest of society.

Special Treatment for Aboriginal Children: The Residential School System

Since the time of earliest contact, Aboriginal people and European settlers have seen things from vastly divergent points of view, because their attitudes and philosophies differed. The interaction of the two groups has been characterized as one of "cooperation and conflict but, more importantly, by misconceptions and contradictions." One of the first, and perhaps the most enduring, of these misconceptions was that:

Europeans assumed the superiority of their culture over that of any Aboriginal peoples. Out of that misconception grew the European conviction that in order for the Indians to survive, they would have to be assimilated into the European social order. ...

This was an impossible task as long as Aboriginal people continued to live in vibrant, self-sufficient communities often far removed from the missionaries' influence. However, this did not prevent the missionaries from forming opinions about the ways Aboriginal people raised and taught their children, or from laying the foundation for future misconceptions of Aboriginal child-rearing methods.

> In view of the current ideal about child-rearing, it is interesting to reflect that no aspect of behavior shocked the French more than their refusal to use physical punishment to discipline their children. On general principles, the Huron considered it wrong to coerce or humiliate an individual publicly. To their own way of thinking, a child was an individual with his or her own needs and rights rather than something amorphous that must be molded into shape. The Huron feared a child who was unduly humiliated, like an adult, might he driven to commit suicide.

Aboriginal parents taught their children

> ... to assume adult roles in an atmosphere of warmth and affection. Learning emphasized such values as respect for all living things, sharing, self-reliance, individual responsibility and proper conduct. Children also had to learn how to utilize the environment most effectively for economic survival. Integral to all aspects of the education of the young was the spiritual, and events in the life cycle from birth to death were marked with ceremonies stressing the individual's link to the spiritual and sacred. Cultural continuity was thus ensured.

The early missionaries also condemned Aboriginal child-rearing methods as being negligent, irresponsible and "uncivilized." This stereotype was to endure even after Aboriginal people had lost much of their independence and "in the point of view of the European, the Indian became irrelevant." From then on, the relationship between Aboriginal people and Europeans became even more one-sided and paternalistic. Aboriginal people were reduced to being "wards of the state. All relevant decision-making power on financial, social or political matters, and even education, came to rest in the hands of the federal government. Eventually, the cause of "civilizing" Aboriginal people to European cultures and values evolved into the government policy of "assimilation," and education became "the primary vehicle in the civilization and advancement of the Indian race."

The federal government had little previous experience in "civilizing" Aboriginal people so it turned to the United States for an example. It sent Nicholas F. Davin to study the Americans' "aggressive civilization policy," based on sending Indian children to large, racially segregated, industrial schools. Davin was convinced the Americans were correct in their approach and the only way to "civilize" Aboriginal people was to remove them from the disruptive influences of the parents and the community. His final comment in the report to Ottawa was representative of attitudes of the time that "... if anything is to be done with the Indian, we must catch him very young." The federal government delegated the job of "civilizing" and "educating" Aboriginal people in Canada to religious organizations and churches. It encouraged the opening of large, industrial residential schools far from reserves and, later, of boarding schools for younger children nearer to their homes. There, every aspect of European life, from dress and behaviour to religion and language, was impressed upon the Aboriginal children. The belief was that Indians were a vanishing race and their only hope of surviving was to assimilate. Their uncivilized and pagan ways would be replaced by good Christian values.

The residential school system was a conscious, deliberate and often brutal attempt to force Aboriginal people to assimilate into mainstream society, mostly by forcing the children away from their languages, cultures and societies. In 1920, during debates in the House of Commons on planned changes to the *Indian Act*, Duncan Campbell Scott, the Deputy Superintendent of Indian Affairs, left no doubt about the federal government's aims:

> Our object is to continue until there is not a single Indian in Canada that has not been absorbed into the body politic and there is no Indian question, and no Indian department, that is the whole object of this Bill.

The experience of residential schools is one shared by many Aboriginal people all across Canada. That experience was marked by emotional, physical and sexual abuse, social and spiritual deprivation, and substandard education. "Even as assimilation was stated as the goal of education for Native people," one researcher wrote, "the assimilation was to take place under conditions which would cause no threat to the surrounding business and farming community." Few Aboriginal people achieved more than a grade five level of education.

The main goal of residential schools and the assimilation policy, however, was not further education, but, rather, to remove Aboriginal children from the influences of their parents and communities, and to rid them of their languages and cultures. The methods, as one former residential school student explained, often were brutally effective:

> The elimination of language has always been a primary stage in a process of cultural genocide. This was the primary function of the residential school. My father, who attended Alberni Indian Residential School for four year in the twenties, was physically tortured by his teachers for speaking Tseshaht: they pushed sewing needles through his tongue, a routine punishment for language offenders ... The needle torture, suffered by my father affected all my family (I have six brothers and six sisters). My Dad's attitude became "why teach my children Indian if they are going to be punished for speaking it"? So he would not allow my mother to speak Indian to us in his presence. I never learned how to speak my own language. I am now, therefore, truly a 'dumb Indian'.

After the Second World War, the federal government began to reconsider its assimilation policy. It wanted a more effective means of accomplishing the ultimate aims of the policy. This coincided with yet another revamping of the *Indian Act* and another set of hearings at the House of Commons. This also allowed another famous Canadian, noted anthropologist Diamond Jenness, to unveil his "Plan for Liquidating Canada's Indian Problems Within 25 Years." Jenness proposed abolishing Indian reserves, scrapping the treaties and integrating Indian students into the public school system. For the time being, the federal government shelved most of Jenness' proposals. It did, however, heed his suggestion to change the *Indian Act* to allow Indian children to be enrolled in public schools. This event signaled "the beginning of the end for many residential schools."

The effects upon Aboriginal societies of the federal government's residential school system, and its policy of assimilation, have been astounding. Residential schools denigrated Aboriginal cultures, customs and religions, and disrupted the traditional practices of Aboriginal child-rearing and education. They tore apart families and extended families, leaving the children straddling two worlds, the European one and that of their own Aboriginal societies, but belonging to neither. These policies have caused a wound to fester in Aboriginal communities that has left them diminished to this day. In testimony to our Inquiry, Janet Ross said:

> I'd like to begin at the boarding school. The boarding school is where the alienation began. Children were placed there, plucked out of their homes. The bonds between parents and children were fragmented severely — some lost forever. Some searched for the love between parent and child endlessly, searching for it in other ways, never to be restored. The boarding schools taught us violence. Violence was emphasized through physical, corporal punishment, strappings, beatings, bruising and control. We learned to understand that this was power and control.
>
> I remember being very confused when someone told me that my natural mother had died. Hence growing up for me not knowing whether my mother was really mine always created some more confusion. I searched for that love in [foster] parents, but that bond had been broken; you felt that it just wasn't there. The boarding schools were extremely influential towards our low self image and low self-esteem, because we were continuously put down by the use of text books portraying negative images of Indian people.

The loss of successive generations of children to residential schools, the destruction of Aboriginal economic bases, the decimation of their populations through diseases and the increasing dependence on government welfare have led to social chaos. This manifests itself in Aboriginal communities through staggering poverty rates, high unemployment rates, high suicide rates, lower education levels, high rates of alcoholism and high rates of crime. In individuals, the legacy of the residential schools has been lowered self-esteem, confusion of self-identity and cultural identity, and a distrust of, and antagonism toward, authority.

The residential school experience also resulted in a breakdown in traditional Aboriginal methods of teaching child-rearing and parenting. Entire families once took part in the raising of children. Young parents, like young parents everywhere, learned how to raise their children from their own parents, by example. Traditionally, they also drew upon the examples and advice of their extended families, their grand-parents uncles, aunts and siblings. The residential schools made this impossible. Without that example, many Aboriginal parents today feel that they have never learned how to raise their own children.

Aboriginal communities have not yet recovered from the damage caused by the residential schools. It is only in recent times that children are again being taught close to home. For the first time in over 100 years, many families are experiencing a generation of children who live with parents until their teens. The readjustment to this new situation has been difficult for both the parents and their children. The current generation of parents does not even have its own experiences as children growing up in a unified family upon which to draw.

The damage done by these schools is still evident today, as Aboriginal people struggle to recapture their cultural practices and beliefs. The return of self-identity and self-esteem is a slow process. Perhaps, if left alone, this social confusion might have corrected itself to some extent, once children returned to their communities. But, as we will see, there was another dramatic intrusion into their lives after the Second World War.

The Child Welfare System

The intrusion by state-run child welfare programs into the lives of Aboriginal children and families did not come about until quite recently, despite the devastating effects which colonization had wreaked on their communities and societies for more than a century. The modern child welfare system, for the most part, is a post-Second World War phenomenon.

. . . . .

However, the end of the Second World War brought about a number of new developments. There was a tremendous proliferation of government-operated and funded social services. These services, once concentrated in urban centres, were increasingly extended to more rural and northern communities, including Aboriginal communities.

This was mirrored by a corresponding proliferation in the new field of professional social work This profession was anxious to carve a niche for itself. More importantly, the profession provided a means by which the standards of the dominant society could be used to judge traditional Aboriginal family and child care practices. At the same time, Aboriginal peoples became much more visible because of increased mobility and, in particular because of their massive migration to urban centres in search of jobs, an education or a better life. This increased the contacts between Aboriginal people and the dominant society, and led to heightened awareness of the dire social and economic conditions in Aboriginal communities.

One of the first alarms about living conditions on reserves was sounded in 1947 by the Canadian Welfare Council and the Canadian Association of Social Workers. These groups presented a brief to a joint parliamentary committee examining possible changes to the federal *Indian Act*. The brief described living conditions as inadequate and the services delivered to Aboriginal communities as incompatible with similar services provided to non-Aboriginal communities.

In considering Indian adoptions and the role of the Indian agent, the brief stated that "the practice of adopting Indian children is loosely conceived and executed and is usually devoid of the careful legal and social protection afforded to white children." As "wards" of the federal government, "Indian children who are neglected lack the protection afforded under social legislation available to white children in the community." The council's submission also condemned the practice of sending Aboriginal children to residential schools.

In the minds of many experts of the day, the solution to these problems was obvious. They felt existing provincial child welfare programs should be extended to include federal Indian reserves, since the child welfare services provided by the Department of Indian Affairs were very limited or nonexistent. However, there were several problems with this apparently obvious solution.

The federal government had exclusive constitutional authority over "Indians and lands reserved for Indians" under s. 91(24) of the *British North America Act of 1867*. The *Indian Act* reinforced this exclusive federal jurisdiction. To complicate matters, at that time the federal government had no cost-sharing agreement with the provinces for social services, including child welfare programs, and it was reluctant to carry the costs of such programs itself.

Provincial governments, which were under pressure to extend their jurisdiction in certain areas such as education, policing and social services, including child welfare, were reluctant to extend their responsibilities without federal funding. In the end, neither level of government was prepared to provide child welfare to Indians living on- or off-reserve. This jurisdictional wrangling left Indians caught in a legal no-man's land, with devastating results for their children.

In 1951 the federal government amended s. 88 of the *Indian Act* to allow "all laws of general application ... in force in any province" to apply as well to Indians both on- and off-reserve. This included child welfare programs. Unfortunately, while the federal government changed the law, it did not provide any additional money to help pay for these new provincial responsibilities. The result was a patchwork of provincial child welfare services to reserves: some agencies in some provinces extended some services to some reserves, some extended none, and some acted to apprehend children only when they considered them to be in a "life or death" situation.

During the 1960s, public and political attention was once again focused on the living conditions endured by Aboriginal people on reserves and, specifically, on the welfare of Aboriginal children. In 1966 the federal Department of Indian Affairs and Northern Development completed an ambitious survey detailing all aspects of life for Canada's Aboriginal peoples living on reserves. It was called the Hawthorn Report, after its editor. In respect to child welfare services, the report found that "the situation varies from unsatisfactory to appalling."

In the same year, the federal government, attempting once again to expand existing child welfare services to Aboriginal communities, signed an agreement with the provinces to share the costs of extending social services under the Canada Assistance Plan. No Aboriginal people or organizations were consulted about these changes, and there was no commitment to preserve Aboriginal culture or to provide for local Aboriginal control over child welfare services. These services were to be delivered by non-Aboriginal agencies employing non-Aboriginal social workers.

Aboriginal Peoples and the Child Welfare System in Manitoba

The history of Aboriginal child welfare in Manitoba closely parallels the situation across the country. During the late 1970s and 1980s, however, the Manitoba government made a number of changes to its child welfare system in order to provide Aboriginal communities with better and more humane services through greater local control.

Like other provinces, Manitoba had passed various laws over the years, dealing with child welfare matters. In 1887, for example, Manitoba passed the *Apprentices and Minors Act* (S.M. 1877, c. 40), and established a superintendent of neglected and dependent children. The next year, the *Act Respecting Infants* (S.M. 1878, c. 39) was passed. In 1895 the *Humane Societies Act* was amended to provide for the establishment of societies which served children, as well as animals. In 1898 *An Act for the Better Protection of Neglected and Dependent Children* (S.M. 1898, c. 6) was passed, in which provision for the formal establishment of a Children's Aid Society was made. In the same year, the Children's Aid Society of Winnipeg was established. In 1922 Manitoba introduced the *Child Welfare Act.* (S.M. 1922, c. 2). Following the introduction of this legislation, the first foster homes were established and, in the 1950s, the first group homes.

The child welfare system had only a limited impact on Aboriginal people before the 1950s and the accompanying government-sponsored boom in social service programs. However, as we have seen, this changed as two things occurred coincidentally. First, there was a massive migration by Aboriginal people into southern and urban areas. Second, there was an expansion into the North of better communication and transportation, and industrial development. With this expansion came southern bureaucracy. Aboriginal and non-Aboriginal people were no longer separated by vast distances or artificial barriers, such as reserve boundaries. To its astonishment and dismay, the latter group quickly learned of the appalling inequities which affected all aspects of the lives of Aboriginal people. Unfortunately, its responses only worsened the situation.

The "Sixties Scoop"

Before the mid-1960s, there was no organized way to provide child welfare services to Aboriginal peoples in Manitoba living on reserves. Then, in 1966 the federal government and the government of Manitoba entered into an agreement that provided for the existing Children's Aid Societies of Central, Eastern and Western Manitoba to deliver child welfare services to 14 bands in southern Manitoba. Three-quarters of the bands in Manitoba were not covered by this arrangement. As in the past the northern bands continued to receive some services from the Department of Indian Affairs, but provincial child welfare authorities would intervene only in emergency or "life and death" situations.

This expansion of child welfare services to Aboriginal communities, which took place across Canada at this time, left a profound and negative impact on these communities. As the Canadian Council on Social Development documented:

> In 1955, there were 3,433 children in the care of B.C.'s child welfare branch. Of that number it was estimated that 29 children, or less than 1 percent of

the total, were of Indian ancestry. By 1964, however, 1,446 children in care in B.C. were of Indian extraction. That number represented 34.2 percent of all children in core. Within ten years, in other words, the representation of Native children in B.C.'s child welfare system had jumped from almost nil to a third. It was a pattern being repeated in other parts of Canada as well.

In most provinces, these child welfare services were never provided in any kind of meaningful or culturally appropriate way. Instead of the counselling of families, or consultation with the community about alternatives to apprehending the child, the apprehension of Aboriginal children became the standard operating procedure with child welfare authorities in most provinces.

In Manitoba, the child welfare system "protected" many Aboriginal children by taking them away from their families and placing them for adoption with non-Aboriginal families. This came to be known as the "Sixties Scoop," but it continued into the 1980s. Although the flaws in this approach would only become evident to most of society later, Aboriginal people immediately condemned the practice. ...

The child welfare system was doing essentially the same thing with Aboriginal children that the residential schools had done. It removed Aboriginal children from their families, communities and cultures, and placed them in mainstream society. Child welfare workers removed Aboriginal children from their families and communities because they felt the best homes for the children were not Aboriginal homes. The ideal home would instill the values and lifestyles with which the child welfare workers themselves were familiar: white, middle-class homes in white, middle-class neighbourhoods Aboriginal communities and Aboriginal parents and families were deemed to be "unfit". As a result, between 1971 and 1981 alone over 3,400 Aboriginal children were shipped away to adoptive parents in other societies, and sometimes in other countries.

Gradually, as education ceased to function as the institutional agent of colonization, the child welfare system took its place. It could continue to remove Native children from their parents, devalue Native custom and traditions in the process, but still act "in the best interests of the child." Those who hold to this view argue that the Sixties Scoop was not coincidental; it was a consequence of fewer Indian children being sent to residential school and of the child welfare system emerging or the new method of colonization.

As part of its comprehensive survey of Aboriginal child welfare policies and procedures, in 1983 the Canadian Council on Social Development compiled a statistical overview of Aboriginal children in the care of child welfare authorities across Canada. The director of the project, Patrick Johnston, found that Aboriginal children were highly over-represented in the child welfare system. They represented 40-50 per cent of children in care in the province of Alberta, 60-70 per cent, of children in care in Saskatchewan and some 50-60 per cent of children in care in Manitoba. Johnston estimated that, across Canada Aboriginal children were 4.5 times more likely than non-Aboriginal children to be in the care of child welfare authorities. Similar findings have been reported by other experts.

What began in the 1960s, with very few exceptions, carried on through the 1970s and 1980s. Patrick Johnston, in examining the history of Aboriginal children's involvement with the child welfare system, wrote:

In retrospect, the wholesale apprehension of Native children during the Sixties Scoop appears to have been a terrible mistake. While some individual children may have benefited, many did not. Nor did their families. And Native culture suffered one more of many severe blows. Unfortunately, the damage is still being done. While attitudes may have changed to some extent since the Sixties, Native children continue to be represented in the child welfare system at a much greater rate than non-native children.

C. BEST INTERESTS OF THE CHILD

Aboriginal children have been removed from their communities by different non-native ideologies and programs throughout the years. Federal "civilization" initiatives, residential schools, and provincial child welfare programs have all contributed to this tragedy. Despite the waning of these earlier intrusions, Aboriginal children continue to be over-represented in child welfare programs. The following extracts examine some of the reasons why Aboriginal children continue to be represented in the child welfare system at a much greater rate than non-native children, despite some of the changes that have taken place since the 1960s. Below, the role of the "best interests of the child" test is explored in this regard.

MARLEE KLINE, "CHILD WELFARE LAW, 'BEST INTERESTS OF THE CHILD' IDEOLOGY AND FIRST NATIONS"

(1992) 30 Osgoode Hall L. J. 375 at 389

... Child welfare law can [now] be understood as a new modality of colonialist regulation of First Nations, though one less explicit and apparently more "innocent" of colonialist intentions than the aggressive mechanisms of the past. Canadian child welfare law directs judges to make decisions that are "in the best interests of the child". Unlike earlier colonialist mechanisms that openly segregated Indians and treated them as inferiors, the apprehension of First Nations children from their communities and its negative effects are facilitated and legitimated by a legal system that is based upon ideals of universality and neutrality, and which purports to protect individual children and act in their best interests. In other words, there are ideological dimensions of child welfare law which make decisions arrived at within the system appear natural, necessary, and legitimate, rather than coercive and destructive.

RACINE v. WOODS

[1983] 2 S.C.R. 173, 1 D.L.R. (4th) 193

The judgment of the Court was delivered by

Wilson J.: — This appeal emphasizes once more, this time in an interracial context, that the law no longer treats children as the property of those who gave them birth but focuses on what is in their best interests.

Leticia Grace Woods ("Leticia") was born at Portage la Prairie, Manitoba, on September 4, 1976 to Linda Woods, an Indian, who was at the time the wife of Lloyd Woods. Lloyd Woods was not the father of the child and divorce proceedings were underway when Leticia was born. There are two children of the Woods marriage, Jason aged nine and Lydia aged eight. Mrs. Woods on her own admission had a serious alcohol problem and was unable to care for Leticia. First her brother and then her sister took the infant. The older children, Jason and Lydia, stayed with their father.

On October 20, 1976, when she was six weeks old, Leticia was apprehended by the Children's Aid Society of Central Manitoba pursuant to the protection sections of *The Child Welfare Act*, C.C.S.M., c. C80 ("the Act") and placed in a foster home. In February 1977 Judge Kimmelman, with her mother's consent, made her a ward of the Society for a one-year period which was subsequently extended for a further six months. On February 11, 1977 Leticia was placed in the foster home of Sandra Ransom (later Racine) and her husband Lorne Ransom. The Ransoms separated in the summer of 1977 and in September of that year Sandra started to cohabit with Allan Racine whom she subsequently married. Leticia remained in their home with the sanction of the Children's Aid Society until the wardship order expired in March 1978. Arrangements were then made by the Society to return her to her mother who was living in Brandon with her other two children. The Racines co-operated fully in this transfer which took place on May 4, 1978.

Mrs. Woods had made no effort to contact Leticia during the period of the wardship but had suggested to the Society early in 1978 that her sister might adopt her. The sister apparently had reservations about this and nothing came of it. The Racines by this time had, of course, developed an attachment to the child and were concerned as to whether she was being properly cared for. They therefore took up Mrs. Woods' invitation to pay her a visit. In fact they paid two visits to see Leticia and on the second visit in May 1978, with Mrs. Woods' consent, took Leticia home with them. The evidence as to Mrs. Woods' intention in relinquishing custody of Leticia to the Racines is conflicting. She says they were to have Leticia "just for a while" until she came for her in a couple of weeks' time. The Racines believed that she had surrendered the child to them on a permanent basis. She had confided to them that she was having difficulties with Lloyd Woods with whom she was periodically cohabiting and she appeared to be aware herself that she was in a state of emotional instability. Consistent with the Racines' understanding that they were now to have Leticia on a permanent basis they got in touch with the Children's Aid Society about the possibility of adopting her. Mrs. Woods by this time had returned to the Reserve with Lloyd Woods. The Society advised the Racines that it no longer had responsibility for the child and that if they wished to adopt her they should retain legal counsel. They followed this advice and on October 5, 1978 filed a Notice of Receiving a Child for Private Adoption under s. 102(1) of the Act.

The Racines heard nothing from Mrs. Woods until October 1978 when she arrived at their home announcing that she had left Lloyd Woods because he was abusing her, that she was on her way to Regina and wanted her sister to have Leticia. The Racines refused to give her up. They heard no further word from Mrs. Woods until January 1982 when she launched an application for *habeas corpus*. On February 24, 1982 the Racines applied for an order of *de facto* adoption.

It is apparent from the evidence that Mrs. Woods from January 1978 on was attempting with varying degrees of success to rehabilitate herself. She wanted to rid herself of her alcohol problem, to free herself of her association with Lloyd Woods, and to engage in a program of self-improvement. However, none of this was easy and periods of achievement when she underwent treatment for alcoholism and attended classes to upgrade her education would be followed by periods of backsliding. It took her five years and the support of friends, relatives and her extended family on the Reserve to accomplish her objective. By the time she did, Leticia was five or six years old and an established part of the Racine family. They had brought her up as if she were their own. The evidence discloses that they are a very fine couple, active and respected in their community, and excellent parents. They have two other children, Melissa aged four and two year old Jamie.

Leticia is apparently a well-adjusted child of average intelligence, attractive and healthy, does well in school, attends Sunday School and was baptized in the church the Racine family attends. She knows that Sandra Racine is not her natural mother, that Mrs. Woods is her natural mother, and that she is a native Indian. She knows that Allan Racine is not her natural father and that he is a Métis. This has all been explained to her by the Racines who have encouraged her to be proud of her Indian culture and heritage. None of this seems to have presented any problem for her thus far. She is now seven years old and the expert witnesses agree that the Racines are her "psychological parents".

An unfortunate incident occurred on February 3, 1982. When the court proceedings brought by Mrs. Woods in January 1982 were adjourned for the preparation of home study reports, she decided to take things into her own hands and with the assistance of friends attempted to abduct Leticia first from her school and then from the Racine home. Fortunately, the child was not in the home at the time. The R.C.M.P. had to be called. The Racines obtained an *ex parte* order granting them interim custody and enjoining Mrs. Woods from further attempts at abduction. Mrs. Woods moved to vary the order and was granted supervised access. On her first exercise of access she arranged for a reporter and a photographer from the Winnipeg Free Press to be present. The story was given considerable prominence in the newspaper with a photograph of Mrs. Woods and Leticia. The child was upset by the notoriety.

The Racines' application for adoption and Mrs. Woods' application for custody were heard by Judge Krindle in a trial lasting eight days. The application for custody was dismissed and the adoption order granted. Mrs. Woods appealed to the Manitoba Court of Appeal which overturned the adoption order, made Leticia a ward of the Court of Appeal, granted custody to the Racines and left it open to Mrs. Woods to apply subsequently for access or custody. The Court of Appeal subsequently on a motion for directions referred Mrs. Woods' application for access to Huband J.A., on being advised that an application was being made for leave to appeal to the Supreme Court of Canada, held the application for access in abeyance.

This Court gave the Racines leave to appeal on May 17, 1983 and ordered a stay of proceedings. Leticia continued to reside with the Racines and Mrs. Woods has had no access since Judge Krindle's order of adoption on May 12, 1982. Mrs. Woods cross-appealed in this Court on the ground that the Manitoba Court of Appeal erred in not restoring legal custody to her when they set aside the order of adoption in favour of the Racines.

The Racines' application for adoption was made under s. 103 of the Act, *i.e.* a *de facto* adoption based on the fact that Leticia had been cared for and maintained by them for a period of three consecutive years. Section 103(2) states that in the case of such an adoption the consent of the parents or guardian is not required. Judge Krindle found that the Racines had cared for and maintained Leticia for the required three-year period and indeed had rescued her as an infant from an intolerable situation, given her an excellent home, been devoted parents, were fully sensitive to the special problems of raising a native Indian child in a predominantly white environment and were coping with those problems in a mature and responsible fashion. She concluded that the Racines were well able to cope with any identity crisis Leticia might face as a teenager. Moreover, as a Métis Allan Racine was no stranger to the hurt racial prejudice could inflict on a sensitive soul and, in the view of the learned trial judge, was a model for Leticia of how to survive as a member of a much maligned minority. As to Mrs. Woods, Judge Krindle expressed respect and admiration for her courage and determination and the degree of success she had achieved in rehabilitating herself. At the same time, however, she expressed some concern as to whether she was going to be able to maintain her progress. She saw danger signals in "the venom of her anti-white feelings" and wondered what effect "her visible hatred for all things white" would have on her child. She also wondered whether Mrs. Woods' concern was for the child as a person or as a political issue. The media incident, in Judge Krindle's view, manifested an incredible indifference to the effect such an incident might have on her child. It made Leticia, a very private little girl, into a "cause celebre" in her school and community. Judge Krindle concluded that it was in the child's best interests that she remain with the Racines.

In addition to finding that it was in Leticia's best interests to remain with the Racines, Judge Krindle also made a finding that Mrs. Woods had abandoned Leticia between October 1978 and January 1982. She made this finding because of her concern as to whether s. 103(2) had the effect of dispensing with parental rights in the case of a *de facto* adoption. If it did have that effect, then the sole issue was the best interests of the child. However, if it did not, then under the common law a natural mother could lose custody of her child to a stranger in blood only by abandoning it or so misconducting herself that in the opinion of the court it would be improper to leave the child with her: *see Re Baby Duffell: Martin v. Duffell*, [1950] S.C.R. 737; *Hepton v. Maat*, [1957] S.C.R. 606; *Re Agar: McNeilly v. Agar*, [1958] S.C.R. 52.

Having made her findings as to abandonment and the child's best interests, Judge Krindle made the adoption order in favour of the Racines and dismissed Mrs. Woods' application for custody.

As already mentioned, the Court of Appeal overturned the adoption order. Each of the panel of three judges gave separate reasons. Mr. Justice

Hall would have affirmed the adoption order but, because his two col-
leagues were for overturning it, he yielded to the majority and then went
on to align himself with the alternate course advanced by O'Sullivan J.A.
rather than that advanced by Matas J.A.

O'Sullivan J.A. decided that the best course to follow was to make Leticia a ward of the Court with custody in the Racines, leaving it open to Mrs.
Woods at some future time to apply for access. Matas J.A., on the other
hand, did not think making the child a ward of the Court was a workable
alternative. He favoured a new trial as to custody (as opposed to adoption)
with interim custody in the Racines in the meantime and such access to
Mrs. Woods as might be agreed upon or as might be ordered by the Court.

On what grounds then did the Court of Appeal upset the judgment of the
learned trial judge? Hall J.A. identified the basis on which in his view it
should have been affirmed. He pointed out that the trial judge had the tremendous advantage of seeing and hearing the parties and their witnesses
and that she had accepted the evidence of some experts in preference to that
of others. She had the benefit also of home study reports and reflected in her
reasons the concern expressed in them about the consequences of moving
the child from the only permanent home she had ever known and separating
her from the *de facto* parents to whom she was now psychologically bonded.
He referred to the strong statement made by the trial judge after a review of
the whole of the evidence:

> I have absolutely no doubt whatsoever that the circumstances of this
> case demand the granting of an Order of Adoption of Letitia [sic] to the
> Racines. ...

He found that the findings and conclusions reached by the trial judge
were fully supported by the evidence. He pointed out that the trial judge
was well aware of the importance of Leticia's cultural background and
heritage and the potential difficulties involved in an interracial adoption.
She gave particular attention to the evidence of the expert who suggested
that Leticia could face a major identity crisis in her teenage years as a result of being reared in a predominantly white environment. She concluded
that the Racines would be well able to deal with such a crisis if it arose.

Matas and O'Sullivan JJ.A. had certain concerns in common about the
judgment of the learned trial judge. On the issue of abandonment they expressed the view that, when Mrs. Woods attempted to get her child back in
1978, the Racines refused to give her up. How can the Racines rely on
abandonment by Mrs. Woods when they at that time had no legal right to
keep the child? As Matas J.A. put it:

> The actions of the Racines, well motivated though they were, put roadblocks
> in the path of what Mrs. Woods might have been able to accomplish if she
> had been dealing with expected reactions of foster parents. In effect, Mr. and
> Mrs. Racine considered themselves as the equivalent of a court or a child
> caring agency, in deciding what they thought was best for the child at that
> time.
>
> In my view, Mr. and Mrs. Racine cannot now rely on a claim that Mrs.
> Woods abandoned her child when they deliberately refused to return the
> child to Mrs. Woods in 1978 and embarked on a three-year waiting period to
> simplify the legal procedures to be followed in adopting Leticia. And it is
> impossible for us to say now what may have been the result if an application

for adoption had been made properly in 1978. At least the court would not have been faced with the argument of the particularly long lapse of time. It is not enough for the Racines to say they have lived at the same address continuously and that Mrs. Woods should have known where to reach them. The custody claimed by the Racines cannot, in my opinion, be a foundation for an application under s. 103 of the Act.

O'Sullivan J.A. said:

... it is difficult to know what more Linda Woods could do to recover her child who was being held without legal right except to seek help from child caring agencies, legal aid lawyers and the police. The fact they were unable to help her does not show that she had abandoned her parental rights but that she was unable to assert them effectively.

The trial judge, of course, relied upon the period of four years from 1978 to 1982 for her finding of abandonment and the evidence seems to support her finding that Mrs. Woods:

... may have continued to feel for Letitia [sic] from time to time, but the fact is that for four years there was no contact between herself and Letitia [sic], not even an attempt on her part to see how the child was, to let the child know that her mother cared, to see if the child needed help. The only thing that could even be considered, I suppose, a "half-baked" stab at breaking the abandonment was the one time that Miss Woods got into a car with George Beaulieu, looked for the Racine residence, and then because George Beaulieu ran out of money and was low on gas, turned back and went back to Long Plains. That was one day in a period that extended from October of 1978 to January of 1982. During this period of time, from the point of view of the child, she may as well not even have had a natural mother.

It is apparent that Matas and O'Sullivan JJ.A. put an entirely different interpretation on the evidence from that put upon it by the learned trial judge and I agree with the appellants that it is not the function of an appellate court to reinterpret the evidence. In *Stein v. The Ship "Kathy K"*, [1976] 2 S.C.R. 802, this Court (*per* Ritchie J. at p. 807) put its stamp of approval on the following observation of Lord Sumner in *S.S. Hontestroom (Owners) v. S.S. Sagaporack (Owners)*, [1927] A.C. 37, at p. 47.

... not to have seen the witnesses puts appellate judges in a permanent position of disadvantage as against the trial judge, and unless it can be shown that he has failed to use or has palpably misused his advantage, the higher Court ought not to take the responsibility of reversing conclusions so arrived at, merely on the result of their own comparisons and criticisms of the witness and of their own view of the probabilities of the case. The course of the trial and the whole substance of the judgment must be looked at, and the matter does not depend on the question whether a witness has been cross-examined to credit or has been pronounced by the judge in terms to be unworthy of it. If his estimate of the man forms any substantial part of his reasons for his judgment the trial judge's conclusion of fact should, as I understand the decisions, be let alone.

Accordingly, even if a finding of abandonment was a prerequisite for an adoption order under s. 103, I am of the view that the evidence was there to support Judge Krindle's finding.

Nor do I accept the submission of counsel that the trial judge was precluded from finding abandonment by Mrs. Woods on the basis of some kind of estoppel operating against the Racines. The Racines' refusal to return the child to Mrs. Woods in October 1978 when she suddenly appeared at their home at a late hour in the evening and intimated that she had left Lloyd Woods, was moving to Regina and wanted to pass Leticia on to her sister was in my view a perfectly responsible act on the part of the Racines. I do not think they were, as Matas J.A. suggests, setting themselves up as a court to decide the ultimate fate of the child. They had had the care of Leticia since she was an infant except for a brief period in May 1978 following the expiry of the wardship order and had become very attached to her. I believe their conduct was prompted by concern for the child. No doubt they were of the view that if Mrs. Woods' intention in taking Leticia from them was to pass her on to her sister rather than to look after her herself, she might well be better off with them — at least until a proper authority had looked into the kind of home she would have with the sister. It must be recalled that the Racines thought that Mrs. Woods had given Leticia permanently into their care in May and were planning to adopt her. They had heard nothing from her from May until her sudden appearance in October and, indeed, heard nothing further from her until the writ of *habeas corpus* in January 1982. With all due respect to the majority of the Court of Appeal, I think it is quite inappropriate to characterize the conduct of the Racines as some kind of illegal assertion of title! We are dealing with a child who had been brought up in their home after being apprehended by the Children's Aid Society. It was for the Court to decide whether the Racines' conduct in refusing to give up Leticia in October 1978 was reasonable in the circumstances and whether it really prevented Mrs. Woods from pursuing her legal right to custody. The trial judge obviously concluded that it did not. She could have proceeded immediately with her *habeas corpus* application and not waited three years to do so. Matas J.A., in holding the Racines estopped from alleging abandonment by their refusal to give up the child in October 1978, states:

> In my view, Mr. and Mrs. Racine cannot now rely on a claim that Mrs. Woods abandoned her child when they deliberately refused to return the child to Mrs. Woods in 1978 and embarked on a three-year waiting period to simplify the legal procedures to be followed in adopting Leticia. And it is impossible for us to say now what may have been the result if an application for adoption had been made properly in 1978. At least the court would not have been faced with the argument of the particularly long lapse of time.

With respect, I see nothing "improper" about the Racines proceeding by way of *de facto* adoption. The statute contemplates it. Moreover, in my view the crucial question is not what a court would have done with an adoption application made in 1978 but what it would have done with a *habeas corpus* application. Mrs. Woods might have succeeded on such an application in 1978 had she proceeded with it. Her failure to do so permitted her child to develop a dependency on the Racines as her psychological parents. It seems to me that Mrs. Woods had a responsibility when her rights were challenged to pursue them in the court if necessary and not to wait until her child was bonded to the Racines with all the problems for the child that the disruption of that bond was likely to create.

I frankly cannot see this as a situation for the application of the doctrine of estoppel. I believe there was evidence before the learned trial judge on which she could make her finding of abandonment between October 1978 and January 1982 although I feel impelled to say that I myself would probably not have made that finding. I believe that the significance of a person's conduct must be assessed in the context of that person's circumstances. Acts performed by one may constitute abandonment when the same acts performed by another may not. I think I would have been disposed to take a more charitable view of Mrs. Woods' failure to contact her child given her circumstances than that taken by the learned trial judge.

Be that as it may, I do not think a finding of abandonment was necessary to the trial judge's decision. I think the statute is clear and that s. 103(2) dispenses with parental consent in the case of a *de facto* adoption. This does not mean, of course, that the child's tie with its natural parent is irrelevant in the making of an order under the section. It is obviously very relevant in a determination as to what is in the child's best interests. But it is the parental tie as a meaningful and positive force in the life of the child and not in the life of the parent that the court has to be concerned about. As has been emphasized many times in custody cases, a child is not a chattel in which its parents have a proprietary interest; it is a human being to whom they owe serious obligations. In giving the court power to dispense with the consent of the parent on a *de facto* adoption the legislature has recognized an aspect of the human condition that our own self interest sometimes clouds our perception of what is best for those for whom we are responsible. It takes a very high degree of selflessness and maturity — for most of us probably an unattainable degree — for a parent to acknowledge that it might be better for his or her child to be brought up by someone else. The legislature in its wisdom has protected the child against this human frailty in a case where others have stepped into the breach and provided a happy and secure home for the child for a minimum period of three consecutive years. In effect, these persons have assumed the obligations of the natural parents and taken their place. The natural parents' consent in these circumstances is no longer required.

Counsel for the respondent submits, however, that the word custody as used in s. 103 of the Act should be interpreted to mean legal custody and that Linda Woods never relinquished legal custody of the child and the Racines never obtained it. By legal custody I understood counsel to mean custody pursuant to a court order or some other lawful authority. Because they do not have this counsel submits that the Racines cannot meet the requirements of the section. I find no merit in this submission. Section 103 clearly provides for an application for adoption by a person having *de facto* custody of a child for the prescribed period of time. This is not to say that the means by which the *de facto* custody was obtained is irrelevant under the section. If it were obtained illegally, such as by kidnapping for example, this would certainly be a factor to be considered by the court in determining whether or not it was in the child's best interests to make the order. No such situation obtains here and I cannot read into the section something which is simply not there.

I turn now to the crucial issue on the appeal. Did the learned trial judge err in holding that Leticia's best interests lay with the Racines? The majority of the Court of Appeal thought she did. They appear to share a concern about the finality of an adoption order in terms of cutting Leticia off both from her natural mother and from her Indian heritage and culture. Matas J.A. said:

> As part of his submission, counsel for Mrs. Woods argued that a transracial adoption results in the loss of contact by the child with his heritage and culture and that this would not be in the best interests of the child. I would reject this argument if counsel meant that no transracial adoption order should ever be granted by the courts in this province. The legislation is not restrictive. In an appropriate case, the court may grant a transracial order of adoption. However, I agree that a child's culture and heritage should be considered by the court as one of the factors to be weighed as part of the circumstances envisaged by s. 89 of the Act. Depending on the circumstances, it is a factor which could have greater or lesser influence in the court's final decision. In the case at bar, the evidence supports the view that the factor is an important one.

Hall J.A. did not underestimate the importance of the fact that the child was an Indian. However, he adopted the conclusion the trial judge drew from the expert evidence before her as to the Racines' sensitivity to the interracial aspect and their appreciation of the need to encourage and develop in Leticia a sense of her own worth and dignity and the worth and dignity of her people. The trial judge found that they had amply displayed their ability to guide Leticia through any identity crisis she might face in her teenage years. Hall J.A. also accepted the trial judge's finding based on the psychiatric evidence that to risk the removal of Leticia from the Racines' home at this stage could cause her permanent psychological damage. This was the only home she had ever known and she was securely bonded to the Racines. Hall J.A. concluded that, important a factor as her Indian heritage and culture might be, the duration and strength of her attachment to the Racines was more important.

The majority of the Court of Appeal obviously saw in their alternate courses a means of keeping the door open for access to the natural mother. If the child were a ward of the Court the Court could grant her access while maintaining custody in the Racines if this seemed appropriate. Similarly, if a new trial were ordered as to custody, access rights could be claimed in those proceedings. The majority were loath to close the door on access by the finality of an adoption order. With respect, I think this overlooks something — something adverted to by Mr. Justice Hall when he said:

> In my opinion, it is quite unlikely that a solution to the problem will be found in either of the ways proposed by my colleagues. Rather, my forecast is lengthy, bitter and costly litigation which in itself would not serve the best interests of Leticia. A difficult choice has to be made. Either the order of adoption should stand or she should be returned to Mrs. Woods. The record is as complete as it is ever likely to be.

I agree with Mr. Justice Hall that this child should not be allowed to become a battleground — in the courts or in the media — and I believe that there is a very real risk of this if the Court refuses to "bite the bullet". In my view, when the test to be met is the best interests of the child, the significance of cultural background and heritage as opposed to bonding abates over time. The closer the bond that develops with the prospective adoptive parents the less important the racial element becomes. As the witness, Dr. McCrae, expressed it:

> I think this whole business of racial and Indian and whatever you want to call it all has to do with a parameter of time and if we had gone back to day one and Letitia [sic] Woods is now being relinquished by her mother in terms of priorities at that time, we would have said — supported a hundred times over "let's place the child with its cultural background." That would be a very — would have been very reasonable. But if that is not done and time goes by, that priority drops down. The priority is no longer there, the priority of ethnic and cultural background. That drops and now must go way down because now it's the mother-child relationship. It doesn't matter if Sandra Racine was Indian and the child was white and Linda Woods was white. This same argument would hold. It has nothing to do with race, absolutely nothing to do with culture, it has nothing to do with ethnic background. It's two women and a little girl, and one of them doesn't know her. It's as simple as that; all the rest of it is extra and of no consequence, except to the people involved, of course.

I think the learned trial judge recognized that reality, considered all the factors which were relevant to the determination of what was in the child's best interests including the fact that she was of Indian parentage, and weighed them in the balance. I cannot find that she erred in carrying out this rather difficult process.

Much was made in this case of the interracial aspect of the adoption. I believe that interracial adoption, like interracial marriage, is now an accepted phenomenon in our pluralist society. The implications of it may have been overly dramatized by the respondent in this case. The real issue is the cutting of the child's legal tie with her natural mother. This is always a serious step and clearly one which ought not to be taken lightly. However, adoption — given that the adoptive home is the right one and the trial judge has so found in this case — gives the child secure status as the child of two loving parents. While the Court can feel great compassion for the respondent, and respect for her determined efforts to overcome her adversities, it has an obligation to ensure that any order it makes will promote the best interests of her child. This and this alone is our task.

I would allow the appeal and reinstate the Order of Adoption made by the trial judge. I would dismiss the cross-appeal. I would make no order as to costs.

Appeal allowed and cross-appeal dismissed.

PATRICIA MONTURE, "A VICIOUS CIRCLE: CHILD WELFARE AND THE FIRST NATIONS"

(1989) 3 Canadian Journal of Women and the Law 1 at 11, 12, 14

First Nations distrust the child welfare system because it has effectively assisted in robbing us of our children and our future. This distrust is further complicated by the adversarial process itself, which is antithetical to the First Nations consensus method of conflict resolution. Judicial decisions on child welfare reinforce the status quo by applying standards and tests which are not culturally relevant. This is a form of racism.

These racist standards and tests of child welfare law were developed by judges. The most important tests is the "best interests of the child". Madame Justice Wilson wrote for the Supreme Court of Canada: "the law no longer treats children as property of those who gave them birth but focuses on what is in their best interests"....

There is evidence that the importance of heritage does not abate over time. The assertion that the importance of heritage abates over time really reflects a belief in the value and possibility of the assimilation of racial minorities — particularly in a racist environment. This belief is not grounded in First Nations tradition and culture, but is a reflection of government policies and "white" values. It is a belief that conceptualizes and prioritizes the rights of individuals over collective rights. And it is a test that effectively forces the assimilation and destruction of First Nations peoples. This is racism ....

Judges seem to "regret" removing First Nations Children from their communities. They express "compassion and sympathy for the mother". Judges feel compelled to indicate that in previous cases that "it was in the best interest of the native child to be raised with his or her own native people". But these comments do not reach the real harm that is being done by forced assimilation. Instead, they are patronizing and are sure flags of racism.

H. (D.) v. M. (H.)

[1999] 1 S.C.R. 761

Decision of the Court (**Lamer C.J.C.** and **L'Heureux-Dubé**, **Gonthier**, **Cory**, **McLachlin**, **Iacobucci**, **Major**, **Bastarache** and **Binnie JJ.**):

. . . . .

[2] The facts of this case are as follows. Ishmael was born March 8, 1995 and is four years old. The putative father is an African-American who lives in the United States, where the adoptive grandparents, the respondents, also live. The mother, Melissa, is an aboriginal Canadian. At birth, she was a member of the Swan Lake First Nation of Manitoba. She and her sister passed through a long list of foster homes in their infancy and were given up for adoption by the applicant and were adopted by the respondents when they were four and six years old respectively. After Melissa became pregnant with Ishmael, she resided with the respondents for some time both before and after his birth. Shortly following the birth, Melissa being unable or unwilling to look after Ishmael, the respondents took over his care. Ishmael was subsequently taken by his mother to British Columbia where, eventually, he came into the care of the British Columbia Ministry of Children and Families. In early 1995 Melissa made contact with her birth parents who were residing separately in Vancouver. In the spring of 1995, D.H. and N.H. paid for Melissa to visit Vancouver to meet her birth parents. Melissa went to Vancouver without Ishmael, made contact with her birth parents, and remained in Vancouver for about two and a half months. During this time, D.H. and N.H. cared for Ishmael. After returning

to Connecticut Melissa told the H.'s that she wanted to take Ishmael for a visit to see her sister Melanie in Hartford, Connecticut. On 6 November 1995 Melissa left with Ishmael on the pretense that she was going to visit her sister. Melissa did not go to Melanie's but instead she travelled with the infant by bus to Vancouver and moved into the home of the appellant, H.M. [The respondents found out in late November or early December of 1995 that Melissa and Ishmael were in Vancouver and they asked the Connecticut Department of Children and Families to liaise with the British Columbia Ministry of Children and Families. Ishmael was taken into care in British Columbia for a couple of months but ... interim custody was awarded to H.M. The H.'s have travelled to Vancouver on a number of occasions over the past two years to visit Ishmael. The evidence appears to indicate that Ishmael has interacted well with the H.'s during their visits.]

[3] The trial judge found that both the applicant and the respondents were sincere and loving grandparents and each were capable of offering a good home to Ishmael. In his reasons, he gave considerable emphasis to the aboriginal heritage of Ishmael's mother's side. He said that "aboriginal heritage and the ability of his biological grandfather to preserve and enhance it are important considerations" (para. 46), and that the claims of the applicant to custody were soundly based on "ties of blood, his obvious love and affection for Ishmael, his aboriginal heritage, [and] his demonstrated ability to provide a home and care for his family" (para. 49). At the same time, the trial judge extensively reviewed the other circumstances of the parties, including the stability of the respective homes, and concluded that "[t]he submission that Ishmael's aboriginal heritage is virtually a determining factor here, oversimplifies a very complex case" (para. 47). The trial judge did not agree that an order granting custody of Ishmael to the respondents would uproot him from his culture. Ishmael is African-American on his putative father's side, aboriginal Canadian on his mother's side, and has lived a significant part of his life with his adoptive grandparents, who are neither. As the trial judge said, "[t]his is not a case of taking an aboriginal child and placing him with a non-aboriginal family in complete disregard for his culture and heritage. The fact is that Melissa is the [adopted] daughter of [the respondents] and Ishmael is their grandson" (para. 46).

[4] The trial judgment was reversed by the Court of Appeal, which put emphasis on the apparent stability at the time of the appeal of the relationship between the applicant and J.S., and the fact Ishmael appeared "well integrated into the family unit of [the applicant], J.S., and their daughter, Sharleen. ... J.S. is proving to be a resource of stability to [the applicant] and the family and is able, together with [the applicant], to provide a good home milieu for Ishmael. ... As well, Ishmael has in his present home a young sibling, the child Sharleen, to whom he relates well" (pp. 551 and 554-55). We were advised at the hearing of the appeal that the applicant no longer lives with J.S. and Sharleen, but has returned to live in Manitoba.

[5] Both the trial judge and the Court of Appeal referred to the *Child, Family and Community Service Act*, R.S.B.C. 1996, c. 46, which provides a statutory direction to public authorities in British Columbia to have careful regard to the cultural identity of aboriginal children. In particular, s. 4(2) provides that: "If the child is an aboriginal child, the importance of pre-

serving the child's cultural identity must be considered in determining the child's best interests." The Court of Appeal noted that "[a]s a strict matter of law, the *Child, Family and Community Service Act* is not applicable to the proceedings" (p. 555). That court nevertheless concluded that the trial judge had "underemphasized ties of blood and culture" (p. 554). This Court, on appeal, disagreed. We concluded that in fact the trial judge had given careful attention to the aboriginal ancestry of Ishmael, together with all the other factors relevant to Ishmael's best interest, and that there was no error in his decision, which was reached after five days of evidence and two weeks of reflection, that justified its reversal by the Court of Appeal. The importance of the findings of the trial judge in custody cases cannot be forgotten. They should not be lightly set aside by appellate courts.

PINE TREE LEGAL ASSISTANCE, WABANAKI LEGAL NEWS,
Summer 1999

In February of 1999, the Supreme Court of Canada handed down a decision in a child custody case involving the young son of an aboriginal Canadian mother. The mother is a member of the Swan Lakes First Nation of Manitoba. For several years before the decision, the child had been living with his biological, aboriginal grandfather. The decision gave custody of the child to the mother's non-native, adoptive parents who live in Connecticut. The decision has deeply angered many in the Canadian aboriginal community.

According to Vice Chief Dennis White Bird, the Manitoba representative to the Assembly of First Nations in Canada, during the 1960's until the early 80's, the Canadian Government engaged in "exporting" First Nation children to the United States and Europe. Vice Chief White Bird called this policy "genocidal" and said that it resulted in "decimating our population." The Assembly of Manitoba Chiefs views this case as part of that policy. Vice Chief White Bird explained that the Assembly had been following the progress of this case for an extended period of time and has given its "moral support" to the biological grandfather as well as to the child. ...

ADOPTIVE FAMILY WINS CUSTODY OF NATIVE BOY SUPREME COURT WILL NOT DELIVER WRITTEN REASONS FOR RULING

Janice Tibetts, *National Post*, Thursday, February 18, 1999
(with permission of Southam News)

OTTAWA — The Supreme Court of Canada ordered yesterday that an aboriginal boy be taken from his poor blood family and returned to his white adoptive family in the United States.

The snap ruling from the bench overturned an earlier decision from the B.C. Court of Appeal that had found three-year-old [IH] was better off being raised by [HM], his biological grandfather, in native culture rather than grow up with adoptive grandparents on a sprawling farm in Connecticut.

The court's nine judges, immediately after hearing both sides in the dispute, instead sided with an earlier ruling from the B.C. Supreme Court, which had awarded custody to the adoptive grandparents, [N] and [DH], saying they offered a superior parenting and family environment compared with Mr. [M], a welfare recipient for the past decade who lives with his common-law wife, [JS], and their young daughter.

[DH] is a newspaper journalist who earns about $52,000 (US) and [NH] works part-time for a computer software company.

[I]'s mother, [MH], had given up custody of the child but intervened in the court case on Mr. [M]'s side.

Ms. [H], an Ojibway originally from Swan Lake, Man., was adopted by the [H]s when she was four years old and said in documents filed with the court that she didn't want her child to grow up like she did, with a feeling that she never belonged. ...

The decision means [I], who has lived with Mr. [M] for the past two years, will return to Connecticut, where he lived for the first eight months of his life.

Mr. [M] recently moved from Vancouver to his original Ojibway reserve north of Winnipeg with [I].

The [H]s had argued that a decision to side with the natural family would have been "excessive multiculturalism rooted in a regrettable form of political correctness." The Supreme Court, in choosing the [H]s, rejected the B.C. Court of Appeal's contention that the courts should abide by recent legislative trends to keep native children in native families. The B.C. Supreme Court also took into account other cultural considerations when it awarded custody to the [H]s. [I] is an American citizen and he has an absentee father who is black. The [H]s have promised to teach [I] about his aboriginal heritage along with his Afro-American heritage.

Both *H. (D.) v. D. (H.)*, [1999] 1 S.C.R. 761 and the following case *S. (K.J.) v. T. (M.)*, [2001] 4 C.N.L.R. 96 (N.S. Fam. Ct.) demonstrate the complexities of litigating child welfare cases in a multi-racialized context. Judges must weigh the importance of the child's racialized, cultural or community background against numerous other important factors. As Professor Annie Bunting has observed:

> Judicial decisions on the best interests of Aboriginal children or children of mixed cultural heritage are judgements about the value of culture, race and community in the lives of children and their families. ...Some commentators have asked whether the interests of Aboriginal communities ought to be given greater consideration in these decisions. The best interests of the individual Aboriginal child are often inseparable from the best interests of the wider community. To date such collectivist assumptions have not taken hold in child-placement decisions. For Aboriginal children in out-of-culture placements, other factors associated with best interests have tended to outweigh considerations of cultural background.

[Annie Bunting, National Judicial Institute, Aboriginal Law Seminar, Calgary Alberta, January 23-25, 2003].

As you think about *H. (D.) v. D. (H.)* and read the next case, ask yourself the following questions:

1. How do judges take race, culture and community into account, and do they undertake this task without reproducing discriminatory stereotypes?
2. Who should define the meaning and importance of a child's cultural identity?
3. Should children in different communities have different weight placed on their cultural heritage?
4. Is it possible for judges to be more explicit about their own assumptions in multi-racialized child placement cases?

S. (K.J.) v. T. (M.)

[2001] 4 C.N.L.R. 96 (N.S. Fam. Ct.)

Comeau C.J. Fam. Ct.: —

The Facts ...

[3] The child D.D.T. was born August 28, 1992, and prior to this in 1991 the parties resided together in Iqualuit. The Applicant is the father of the child and moved away from Nunavut before he knew the Respondent was pregnant with their child.

[4] In February of 1999, it was arranged with the assistance of a social worker in Cape Dorset that a letter of understanding between the parties confirmed the Respondent mother was not giving up her parental rights, but the child was to be sent to Nova Scotia to reside with his father. The agreement stated that this temporary arrangement was not to exceed a year unless agreed upon by the Respondent mother. The reason for this move appears to be a new relationship and the desire of the mother to have D.D.T. know his father better. At the time she was also having a baby and had problems with her older son (drug use).

[5] The father did not return the child but made an application to Family Court for custody. His reasons for doing this are that D.D.T. was experiencing academic and behavioural problems when he arrived in Nova Scotia. He has received help and the Applicant father believes that he could have a better life in Nova Scotia based on his experience in the north. In support of this, counsel on behalf of the Applicant called a number of witnesses.

[6] Lori LeBlanc a reading recovery teacher has been working with D.D.T. and noted that he has made very good progress. Her school principal described academic and behavioural problems when he first arrived, but there were items being addressed and much had been accomplished. This is also confirmed by his home room teacher, Pamela Smith. D.D.T. has and continues to participate in a Summer Day Camp program, T-Ball, minor hockey and other sporting activities (i.e. wrestling). Photos of D.D.T.'s residence and the family situation with the Applicant provide a picture of a very positive life there.

[7] A review of the evidence received from Cape Dorset, Nunavut, shows a mother who misses her son very much. She has not had what some may describe as an easy life. At the time the evidence was taken she did not have a permanent residence and was on the waiting list from housing. She resided with her mother and this amounted to a household of between ten and eleven people. This results in a number of people sleeping in one bedroom or in the livingroom. She resided with a boyfriend and slept on the sofa with her child. There was evidence she may be back in her mother's residence. The Respondent does not have a regular income but has started carving again and sells her art.

Inuit Culture

[8] The Respondent describes some of the Inuit culture and her concern over her son D.D.T. losing his language (Inuktitut):

Food

[9] Inuit food consists of caribou and fish and very few vegetables.

Language

[10] The Respondent finds that D.D.T. is speaking more English now when she speaks to him on the phone. An example of this is when she said to him "Qannuipit" and he guessed she was asking him to go play outside when in fact it meant "How old are you?"

Activities

[11] These include hunting, fishing and learning how to make hunting implements. There are also sporting events and camping in the summer.

Extended Family

[12] The extended family is very important in the Inuit culture and the Respondent describes many aunts, uncles and cousins of D.D.T. who he would and did have regular contact with.

[13] The evidence from Cape Dorset describe some negative things concerning the Respondent mother. Suicides have taken her nephew and niece and she knows of other families that have lost children to suicide. Counsel for the Applicant refers to an incident confirmed by the Applicant where she became very angry at D.D.T., took him outside, placed him on the ground and started kicking him in the head and stomach and then punching him until friends intervened.

[14] The Respondent admits to alcohol, drug and gambling abuse as problems she had in the past. Her mother testified that this past spring she found the Respondent not to be a very good mother, not with her youngest all the time and no permanent place to stay. There is no evidence that the Respondent is a child protection concern for the Department of Community Services.

[15] Counsel for the Respondent asks the Court in considering the best interest of the child to take into account, "That the Inuit culture is not that of the Nova Scotia, white community and that the standards used to judge the care, likewise should not be based on the standards of the Nova Scotia white community, but include the standard and accepted lifestyle of the Inuit brought out through the evidence on behalf of the Respondent." With this, the Court agrees.

Issue

[16] Which parent should have custody considering the best interests of the child. ...

Conclusion/Decision

[20] The application came before the Court in September of 1999, while the child D.D.T. has resided with his father the Applicant since February of 1999. This delay is outside the control of either of the parties. [There was a time delay because the court could not find an Inuktitut translator for the mother in this trial.] Counsel for the Respondent submits that because of the problem the Court should not take this status quo existing over two years into account. The paramount consideration of what is in the best interest of the child would require the Court to consider this as one of the factors to determine custody. The Court is aware of the action of the Applicant in establishing and promoting this status quo.

[21] ... the Respondent's physical environment does not compare to this of the Applicant, she does not have a permanent residence (a concern of her mother's) nor does she have steady income (means of support). These two items are necessities for parenting in the Inuit culture as well as the white Nova Scotia or any community (culture). On the other hand the Applicant has a permanent residence and a steady income. In answer to a question concerning her wishes for D.D.T. the Respondent mother indicated:

> I want to see happen is to get D.D.T. to be with me and to be with his father. To be with me sometime, to be with his father sometime. That's what me and his father should have did long time. I want to see D.D.T. to come — I want — I wish for D.D.T. to come home. I wish for D.D.T. to go to live with me and to share him with his father. That's my wish.

[22] There is no evidence concerning any problems at the Applicant's home. There appears to be a very positive atmosphere there with a good and happy family environment.

[23] D.D.T. is an Inuit and his long term parenting and life plan must include retaining his first language (Inuktitut) and the Inuit culture. This should be the duty of both parents. In the south as his mother describes Nova Scotia, he will be at times considered different and the consequences that flow from that. So far the community support, teachers and friends have helped him progress in the white Nova Scotian community, as counsel for the Respondent describes it. Particular help has come from his father and extended family and he has adapted well. His mother has a reason for

sending him to Nova Scotia, in additional to wanting him to know his father. She had her problems with her older child, with a new male relationship and with housing and means of support. September 2000 evidence does not disclose any change. It may be without any Court application she may have had to agree to extend the parties original agreement beyond the agreed year.

[24] The Court has great sympathy for the Respondent mother and the situation she found herself in. She was concerned about her son's welfare and sent him to Nova Scotia and her wish is that his parents share parenting of D.D.T. which is always the ideal.

[25] The dilemma the Court finds itself is to balance environment, parenting and cultural considerations. Given the situation the solution is not perfect, the Applicant father can provide the financial and environmental factors more satisfactorily while the Respondent mother has the cultural aspects which include an Inuit extended family and physical environment to enhance this and the Inuktitut language.

[26] Considering all the evidence before the Court, it is in the best interests of the child D.D.T., that custody be granted to the Applicant, his father. He has to spend considerable time with his mother to retain ties with her and his Inuit culture. Access will be every summer from the second week in July until and including the third week in August which is seven full weeks.

[27] For the purpose of this Order a week starts on Sunday and ends on Saturday and as further clarification access shall take place in the year 2001, starting July 8, 2001 (travel day) to August 25, 2001 (return travel day). Given the financial situation of the Respondent mother, it shall be the responsibility of the Applicant father to provide transportation costs both ways.

[28] Counsel for the Applicant shall prepare the Order and have counsel for the Respondent consent to it with form.

Custody awarded to father with seven weeks access to mother.

A leading anthropologist of Inuit culture has written: "The notion that meaning inheres in culture and that people receive it passively, as dough receives the cookie cutter, is being rapidly replaced by the idea that culture consists of ingredients, potentials, which people actively select, interpret, and use in various ways as opportunities, capabilities, and experience allow. But it is not *the* individual that creates meaning; but it is individuals who do so" (Jean Briggs, *Inuit Morality Play: The Emotional Education of a Three-Year-Old* (New Haven: Yale University Press, 1998) at 2). To what extent do the legal system and the judiciary play a role in the construction of Aboriginal culture through child placement decisions like those in *S. (K.J.) v. T. (M.)*, [2001] 4 C.N.L.R. 96 (N.S. Fam. Ct.) and *H. (D.) v. D. (H.)*, [1999] 1 S.C.R. 761?

D. SELF-GOVERNMENT INITIATIVES

Since Aboriginal peoples continue to run into significant challenges with provincially run child welfare agencies, many communities are seeking to make the delivery of these services more culturally appropriate. Others, having less faith in existing systems, seek to take control of Aboriginal child welfare away from the provinces to vest it in the community or Nation. Reform of the child welfare system relative to Aboriginal peoples continues to occupy a prominent place in discussions of self-government and community autonomy. The following case of *S. (E.G.) v. Spallumcheen Band Council*, [1999] 2 C.N.L.R. 318 (B.C.S.C.), and extracts from the Royal Commission on Aboriginal Peoples and the Manitoba Justice Inquiry illustrate how Aboriginal peoples are taking a larger role in Aboriginal child welfare.

S.(E.G.) v. SPALLUMCHEEN BAND COUNCIL

[1999] 2 C.N.L.R. 318 (B.C.S.C.)

[1] **Williamson J.**: — [FC] was born on October 27, 1996. Her mother, a member of the Spallumcheen Indian Band (the "Band"), found she was unable to care for the child. She asked the plaintiffs, Mr. and Mrs. [S], to act, in effect, as foster parents. The plaintiffs agreed to do so. However, concerned about this private arrangement, they asked the Provincial Ministry of Children and Families (the "Ministry") to become involved. As a result, the Ministry entered into a voluntary care agreement pursuant to which the [S]s would act as foster parents to [F]. The child's mother had visitation rights.

[2] In 1980 the Band passed a by-law, as it was then empowered to do by s. 81 of the *Indian Act*, R.S.C. 1970, c. I-6 (the "Act") in which it took responsibility for the welfare of children of the Band. This by-law was been approved by the Minister. It has the power of a regulation passed pursuant to the Act and is law.

[3] Thus, the welfare of children of the Spallumcheen Indian Band, unlike that of other children in British Columbia, is the responsibility of the Band rather than of the Ministry.

[4] The Ministry and the Band have a working relationship governed by protocols which have been amended from time to time since the by-law was first approved in 1980.

[5] Over the years the Band has developed a program which emphasizes cultural identity. The affidavits filed disclose the Band also has in place programs and personnel to deal with the physical and psychological health matters that may arise with individual children. The program currently employs three full-time staff, and has other professionals available for consultation. At the time of this application, 25 children were in the care of the Band. In [FC]'s case, several employees of the Provincial Ministry have been involved working with the Band staff.

[6] Although both of [F]'s biological parents are native persons, she was not registered as a member of the Band until February of 1998. When registration occurred, the responsibility for the welfare of [F] passed from the Ministry to the Band.

[7] Initially, the Band was content to leave the child with the plaintiffs and, therefore, entered into a foster parenting agreement with them. The Band decided, however, that it would be in the best interests of the child and consistent with the provisions of the governing by-law to work towards reuniting the child with her mother.

[8] On March 17, 1998, it was decided that the Band would maintain responsibility for [F], that she would continue to live with the plaintiffs, but that there would be increasing visits by the child's mother geared towards the eventual return of the child to her mother and the reunification of the family.

[9] At that stage, the mother's visits with the child were supervised.

[10] The affidavit material filed discloses that while the plaintiffs provided excellent care for [F] during the entire period that she was in their care, the plaintiffs' relationship with the Band began to break down over the spring.

[11] On June 16, 1998, the Band Council decided that while [F] would remain the responsibility of the Council for a further six months, she would be moved from her foster placement with the plaintiffs to the home of [F]'s maternal aunt and her family, [SW]. Ms. [W] is a member of the Band.

[12] Since [F] was moved to the [W]'s house on June 16, 1998, the plaintiffs have not had access to [F]. In this application, they seek an order for interim access and an order for a custody and access report, pursuant to s. 15 of the *Family Relations Act*, R.S.B.C. 1996, c. 128.

[13] They rely upon the inherent *parens patriae* jurisdiction of the court.

[14] I am not persuaded that this is a case in which that jurisdiction should be asserted.

[15] It is not disputed that pursuant to the by-law passed by the Band in 1980, it is the Band which has the responsibility for welfare of Spallumcheen children.

[16] The affidavit material discloses that the impetus for the passing of this by-law was the conclusion on the part of the Band that the best interests of its children were not being served by a child welfare regime geared to the general population. The Band had concluded that as a result of the loss of children to the residential school system and through apprehensions by Provincial authorities which resulted in Spallumcheen children being placed in non-native foster homes, the survival of the Spallumcheen First Nation was in jeopardy. The preamble to the by-law expressed that view in the following words:

> ... the removal of our children by non-band agencies and the treatment of the children while under the authority of non-band agencies has too often hurt our children emotionally and serves to fracture the strength of our community, thereby contributing to social breakdown and disorder within our reserve.

[17] The by-law went on to say that it was the Band that would have exclusive jurisdiction over any child custody proceeding involving a Spallumcheen child, notwithstanding the residence of that child.

[18] It also specified that where a child was to be placed with a family other than its own, a preference for such placement would be given in the following order:

1) a parent;
2) a member of the extended family living on the reserve;
3) a member of the extended family living on another reserve, although not a reserve to the Indian Band;
4) a member of the extended family living off the reserve;
5) an Indian living on a reserve;
6) an Indian living off a reserve; and
7) only as a last resort shall the child be placed in the home of a non-Indian living off the reserve.

[19] It is the contention of the Band that in placing [F] with her maternal aunt, they were carrying out the objectives of the by-law.

[20] They note that according to the terms of that by-law, it would be preferable to place [F] with a member of her extended family living off the reserve, such as her aunt, rather than with the plaintiffs who would be the preferred placement only as a last resort. Further, the Band says the decision was consistent with other enunciated goals in the by-law including the rebuilding, wherever possible, of the family of the child, and the paramountcy of the best interests of the child.

[21] While they concede the removal of [F] from the plaintiffs in June of this year was too abrupt, the Band says the fault for that cannot be laid at their feet. It is their submission that the relationship between the plaintiffs and the Band had deteriorated and that continued involvement of the plaintiffs would manifest an antagonism which would be apparent to [F] and could not be in her best interests. They observe that since the change in placement, the plaintiffs have been interviewed by the press and that the sensational and inaccurate reporting of this incident has been hurtful and damaging to the Band.

[22] Much of that press coverage was appended to affidavits. I agree that it discloses an apparent lack of verisimilitude and could be interpreted as reinforcing negative stereotypes of native peoples. Certainly there are blatant errors.

[23] For the purposes of this application, however, I am not prepared to accept that the inaccurate reporting in this case is the fault of the plaintiffs rather than the result of the apparent need of some journalists for material conducive to sensational headlines.

[24] The issue to be determined before me is, should this court exercise its inherent jurisdiction of *parens patriae* in the circumstances of this case? Courts once had wide powers pursuant to this inherent jurisdiction. However, in the last century, legislatures in the common law world have increasingly occupied the field. We are now at the stage where there are only limited circumstances where there should be resort to this jurisdiction. These include emergency situations where a child appears in need of some form of protection, in a judicial review of the exercise of a statutory power, or where there is found to be a gap in the legislation being considered. It is the latter which is relied upon by the plaintiffs in this case.

[25] The plaintiffs submit that the by-law, which gives the Band responsibility and power over the welfare of its children, is not as extensive a

code as the statutory framework which applies to non-Spallumcheen children in this Province. Thus, they argue, in a circumstance such as this where the best interests of the child arguably require that she continue to have a relationship with those foster parents who cared for her for most of her life to date, the court should intervene.

[26] While it may be that the by-law is not as extensive as the legislative scheme otherwise in effect, I am satisfied that it provides a clear statutory scheme whereby the Band, consistent with enunciated goals and priorities set out in the by-law, is to exercise its responsibility for the care of children within its care.

[27] I am cognizant of the observations of Associate Chief Judge Stansfield in his reasons given September 30, 1998 when he determined this application could be ruled upon only by a court of inherent jurisdiction. At paragraph 59, he wrote:

> But what of the best interests of a child who has been raised by, and presumably is bonded with, persons who are not within the classes enumerated by the By-Law? One can only presume that it is potentially contrary to the best interest of such a child, and thus could cause a grave injustice, to deny to such caregivers a fair process through which they can offer themselves in the continuing care of the subject child.

[28] The learned judge went on two paragraphs later to say there are "glaring deficiencies" in the by-law, and he suggested that these could and should be addressed through an amendment.

[29] It may be that the fact the legislative framework does not provide foster parents with status to apply for custody or access is a deficiency. But in this respect, the legislative scheme is no different from that applying to foster parents of non-Spallumcheen children in British Columbia.

[30] Foster parents who enter into an agreement with the Ministry to care for a child agree that they will relinquish that child at the request of the Superintendent. *The Family and Child Service Act*, S.B.C. 1980, c. 11, provided in s. 21, that:

> Nothing in this Act limits the inherent jurisdiction of the Crown, through the Supreme Court, over infants, as parens patriae, and the Supreme Court may rescind a permanent order where it is satisfied that to do so is conducive to a child's best interest and welfare.

[31] This legislation was reviewed by the Court of Appeal in *P. (E.) v. B.C. (Supt. of Fam. & Child Service)* (1988), 23 B.C.L.R. (2d) 329. In considering the *parens patriae* jurisdiction of the court, Anderson J.A. noted at p. 340 that as the responsibility for determining the best interests of children who are wards of the Ministry has been given to the Superintendent, the:

> onus is heavy on counsel for the foster parents to persuade us that the reference to the "parens patriae" jurisdiction of the Supreme Court was intended to enable the Supreme Court to "override or disregard the conclusions" of the Superintendent.

In that same case, the court concluded that foster parents have no status to make an application for access under s. 21 of the Act. Nothing in the current legislation renders that comment any less persuasive. See: the *Child, Family and Community Service Act*, R.S.B.C. 1996, c. 46, s. 99.

[32] In my view, foster parents who owe their status to an agreement with the Band Council pursuant to its by-law are in the same circumstance as other foster parents. They have no status to make an application for custody or access. If that be a gap, it is also a gap in the Provincial legislative scheme. And just as with that legislation, it is not a lacuna of such significance that the inherent *parens patriae* jurisdiction of the court should be invoked.

[33] Mrs. [S] deposes that she does not believe it is in the "best interests of the child that the Band be left as the sole decision maker regarding appropriate arrangements for [F]." She would have the court substitute its view of the child's best interests for that of the Band. To do so would be to usurp the very power which the legislation confers upon the Band.

[34] I agree with Judge Stansfield that if former foster parents' lack of a right to apply for access and other rights be a deficiency, the appropriate remedy is legislative action.

[35] The petitioners do not say the child is in need of protection. Rather, they seek access and assessment. I am satisfied, upon a review of the material, that in this case the Band is exercising powers which it has pursuant to the by-law and that there is nothing which would warrant the intrusion upon that jurisdiction sought by the petitioners in this application.

[36] The application is dismissed.

---

1.   The following exchange took place in the B.C. legislature concerning the *S. (E.G.)* case (Debates of the Legislative Assembly (Hansard), Wednesday, July 29, 1998 Afternoon, Volume 12, Number 11, Page 10678):

V. Anderson: To the Minister for Children and Families. Last week the official opposition pointed out to the Ministry for Children and Families that on June 22 the Spallumcheen band abruptly removed 20-month-old Baby F. from her foster home without any transition planning. Baby F. has fetal alcohol effect and cannot tolerate sudden and drastic changes. This child has already been separated from her biological mother, and she has now had another primary bond with a foster parent severed. As the Child and Family Review Board found last year in the Murphy case, destroying a developmentally challenged baby's bond with a caregiver is a violation of that child's rights. Why has the Ministry for Children and Families refused to even investigate whether or not this baby's rights have been violated?

Hon. L. Boone: The member probably knows — he should know — that the Spallumcheen band was given the right to deal with aboriginal children many years ago. ... In this case here, I certainly understand the concerns of the foster parent. I know that there's great attachment that comes with foster parents to the children. However, this case actually went before a judge. The judge accepted and approved the plan of care. So this is not something that is being done offhand; it is something that has been approved by the judge. We believe that it's in the best interests of the child.

The Speaker: First supplementary, member for Vancouver-Langara.

V. Anderson: That was the same thing that was said, in essence, in the Murphy case, which was proved to be false afterwards. All children in British Columbia deserve to have their rights protected under provincial law, and this is no exception. Now this government is debating whether or not they even have jurisdiction to protect this little girl. Will the minister acknowledge her responsibility to protect the rights of Baby F. under our provincial legislation and act immediately to ensure that the best interests of this child are put first, as we have committed ourselves to under the convention on the rights of the child?

Hon. L. Boone: It has gone before the courts. I believe that the courts have the final say as to whether the best interests of the child are at stake there. They approved the case plan for that child, so I believe that the best interests of the child are being taken care of.

2.   Members of the Spallumcheen Band had most of their children taken away from them before the by-law at issue in the *S. (E.G.)* case was passed in 1980. In fact, of the total Spallumcheen population of approximately 500 people, 80 children were in government care. One particularly poignant event was described as follows:

> A social worker chartered a bus and apprehended 38 children in the 1970's. Spallumcheen became a quiet, dispirited town of adults and Elders, with at times fewer than 14 children left on the reserve. Drinking and despair intensified rather than dissipated and it was generally known that once children were taken, they were never returned.

(Suzanne Fournier and Ernie Crey, *Stolen From Our Embrace* (Vancouver: Douglas and McIntyre, 1997). For a description of the by-law's development see: John A. MacDonald, "The Spallumcheen Indian Band By-Law and Its Potential Impact on Child Welfare Policy in British Columbia" (1983) 4 Canadian Journal of Family Law 76-95.

3.   The following extracts and notes outline the range of legislative and negotiated reforms that have recently developed to facilitate a fuller measure of aboriginal control in child welfare matters.

REPORT OF THE ROYAL COMMISSION ON ABORIGINAL PEOPLES, GATHERING STRENGTH, VOL. 3

(Ottawa: Ministry of Supply and Services, 1996) at 29-33
(references omitted)

Child Welfare Reform

Some things have changed as a result of efforts begun in the 1980s. Since 1981, when the first agreement was signed authorizing a First Nation agency to deliver child welfare services, responsibility for delivering child welfare services has been delegated progressively to agencies administered by First Nations and some Métis communities. Emphasis is being placed on supporting increased Aboriginal control of the development, design and delivery of child and family services. In 1990-91, DIAND funded 36 Aboriginal child and family agencies covering 212 bands. Also in 1990-91, a total of $1.5 million was allocated to First Nations, over a period of two years, for the development of Aboriginal child and family service standards.

Most Aboriginal child care agencies have adopted placement protocols specifying the following placement priorities: first, with the extended family; second, with Aboriginal members of the community with the same cultural and linguistic identification; and third, other alternative Aboriginal caregivers. As a last resort, placement is considered with non-Aboriginal caregivers. Some work has been done to develop culturally appropriate standards for selecting Aboriginal foster caregivers; however, as discussed later, it has been hampered by funding constraints and limited policy support for developmental work in new Aboriginal agencies.

The following summary illustrates the developments in child welfare in Aboriginal communities:

- Agencies established under the tripartite agreement with the Four Nations Confederacy of Manitoba, signed in 1982.
- Agencies authorized to administer child welfare, particularly in northern and northwestern Ontario under the 1984 *Child and Family Services Act*.
- Child welfare prevention services sponsored jointly by bands and the provincial government in southern Ontario.
- Agreements signed with single bands such as the Blackfoot at Gleichen, Alberta, and the Métis and Cree community of Sandy Bay, Saskatchewan, to provide services under provincial mandates.
- Regional Aboriginal services developed, including Mi'kmaq Family and Children's Service of Nova Scotia and Nuu-chah-nulth Community and Human Services in British Columbia.
- Child welfare and other human services, in regions where land claims agreements have been concluded, delivered through boards under Aboriginal control, such as Kativik Regional Social Services and Cree Regional Health and Social Services Board in Quebec.
- Social services in the Northwest Territories decentralized to increase community control.

Aboriginal child and family services have been established in metropolitan centres such as Toronto and Winnipeg. They report significant success in recruiting Aboriginal foster homes. For example, Native Child and Family Services of Toronto reported that 62 per cent of the agency's placements in 1993-4 were customary care arrangements, signifying voluntary involvement of parents and placement in Aboriginal homes.

Alberta has the distinction of sponsoring the only Métis-specific child welfare agency yet established. Métis Child and Family Services of Edmonton provides foster care placements and emphasizes traditional values as a component of the assessment process in home studies to screen potential caregivers. According to information provided to Brad McKenzie, who conducted a research study for the Commission,

> An orientation training program and ongoing support meetings for foster parents are provided. As a private agency [Métis Child and Family Services] did not qualify for a 1994 increase of 5 per cent paid to foster parents providing service within the provincial system. Barriers to the recruitment and retention of Aboriginal foster care identified by this agency respondent included limited funding, an inadequate training program for foster parents,

limitations in the number of potential families who are able to foster, and a failure on the part of the social service bureaucracy to involve foster parents as meaningful partners in meeting the needs of children in their care.

In the study McKenzie notes that such agencies, administered by Aboriginal people, have achieved considerable success in expanding the number of Aboriginal foster home providers, even though provincial agencies in diverse locations acknowledge difficulties in locating a sufficient number of homes.

Several provinces have moved to make their legislation more sensitive to Aboriginal identity in making plans for children. For example, Alberta specifies that an Aboriginal child must be informed of his or her status and that the chief and council of an Aboriginal child's community must be consulted before permanent wardship hearings. Newfoundland's legislation specifies that "the child's cultural and religious heritage" must be considered in determining a child's best interests." In the Northwest Territories, the objective of the 1994 *Aboriginal Custom Adoption Recognition Act* is "without changing aboriginal customary law, to set out a simple procedure by which a custom adoption may be respected and recognized". The adoptive parent or parents simply provide identification papers along with a written statement from the interested parties that an adoption took place in accordance with Aboriginal custom. Once the custom adoption commissioner is satisfied that the information provided is complete and in order, a certificate of adoption is issued and the adoption is registered in appropriate vital statistics files. Records of the adoption are not sealed. The Yukon provides that the child's "own cultural background" and "lifestyle in his home community" be considered in adoption cases. Quebec's *Youth Protection Act* stipulates that "Every person having responsibilities towards a child under this Act, and every person called upon to make decisions with respect to a child under this Act shall, in their interventions, take into account the necessity ... of opting for measures in respect of the child and the child's parents ... which take into consideration ... the characteristics of Native communities".

Ontario has the most extensive provisions in relation to Aboriginal child welfare in its *Child and Family Services Act* (1984). The Act seeks to include both status Indian people and others of Aboriginal ancestry by using the term "Native". Special provisions for all children's aid societies serving Aboriginal communities recognize "Indian" and "Native" status as a "best interests" category over and above the obligation to consider cultural background. The Act devotes an entire section to Aboriginal child and family service agencies. It also recognizes customary care and permits these agencies to seek exemptions from the application of any part of the law.

Alberta and Manitoba have created a child advocate office to provide impartial investigations into complaints concerning services rendered to children. About 20 years ago Quebec created a youth protection commission with a similar mandate. This commission was recently merged with Quebec's human rights commission to become the province's human rights and youth rights commission. Its mission is "to ensure ... that the interests of children are protected, and that their rights recognized by the Quebec youth protection act are respected."

In many jurisdictions, exceptions are permitted to culturally inappropriate requirements that might screen out Aboriginal people applying to foster or adopt Aboriginal children. Such exceptions may be explicit, as in Ontario's *Child and Family Services Act*; or implicit, as in the practice of agencies that encourage Aboriginal families to provide care for Aboriginal children.

Expenditures to improve the coverage and quality of Aboriginal-specific child welfare services have been increased substantially for services to registered Indians ordinarily resident on-reserve and Indian child-in-care costs charged back to the federal department of Indian affairs. In 1992-93 the department allocated $ 153.8 million to child and family services, representing 78 per cent of the welfare services budget, which also includes services to enable adults with functional limitations to maintain their independence. The welfare services budget increased from $38.7 million in 1981-82 to $204.8 million in 1992-93 — an annual increase of 16 per cent. Expenditures per child in care increased at an average annual rate of 17 per cent in the same period, rising from $6,754 in 1981-82 to $28,260 in 1991-92.

Despite these welcome reforms, and modest successes in placing children in Aboriginal foster homes, which have stemmed the flow of Aboriginal children out of their communities and nations, it is evident that services to care for neglected and abused children are insufficient to repair the ills plaguing Aboriginal families.

In 1992-93, about 4 per cent of First Nations children living on-reserve were in agency care outside their own homes, a reduction from the highs of between 6 and 6.5 per cent in the 1970s. During the same period, however, child welfare agencies serving the general population made an effort to keep children in their own homes, a move that reduced the general child-in-care rate to 0.63 per cent. The percentage of First Nations children in care is six times that of children from the general population in the care of public agencies. This disparity has increased since the 1970s, when First Nations children were placed in care at five-and-a-half times the rate of children in the general population. As with most statistics on social services, only data on First Nations services provided directly or funded by the federal government are available. The extent of service to Métis people cannot be discerned from existing sources.

A November 1994 publication of Alberta's Commissioner of Services for Children states that "While only nine per cent of all children in Alberta are Aboriginal, nearly 50 per cent of the children in care are Aboriginal". The terminology used would seem to imply that Métis and non-status Aboriginal children are included in the figures, despite the prevailing scarcity of data on the Métis population.

In a more localized study prepared for this Commission in 1994, an Aboriginal child and family service agency in southern Manitoba reported an on reserve child population (0-18 years) of 2,238 and an in-care figure of 257 at 31 March 1994, which translates to an in-care rate of 11.5 per cent. Child welfare agencies are set up to protect the interests of children at risk of neglect or abuse. The continued high rates of children in care outside their homes indicate a crisis in Aboriginal family life.

SONIA HARRIS-SHORT, "THE ROAD BACK FROM HELL? SELF-GOVERNMENT AND THE DECOLONISATION OF ABORIGINAL CHILD WELFARE IN CANADA"

(2003, unpublished)

There have been further developments towards Aboriginal control in child welfare matters since the Royal Commission reported in 1996. For example, British Columbia's *Child, Family and Community Service Act* [R.S.B.C. 1996] c. 46 states: "the cultural identity of aboriginal children should be preserved" and "kinship ties and a child's attachment to the extended family should be preserved if possible" (s. 2 (*e*) & (*f*)). It also stipulates that a child in care has the right "to receive guidance and encouragement to maintain their cultural heritage" (s. 70 (1)(*j*)). These general principles are reflected in several of the Act's more specific provisions. For example, the importance of an aboriginal child's cultural identity is given explicit recognition when determining the child's best interests (s. 4(2)) and the legislation provides that the director's interim plan for a child in care must include details of the steps to be taken to preserve the child's aboriginal identity (s. 35(1)(*b*)).

British Columbia's legislation also strongly recognizes the importance of keeping aboriginal children within their family and community. Therefore the Act contains provisions for voluntary care agreements between the Director and a person who has 'a cultural or traditional responsibility towards a child' (s. 8 (1)(*a*)). The Director can even provide some financial support for a placement arranged under this type of agreement (s. 8 (2)). The Act also contemplates a family conferencing model to enable the family to develop a plan of care that can take into account the role of the child's family, his/her culture and community. To this end, it includes a provision that the child can be placed with a relative or some other person with the director's consent (ss. 20-21).

The BC *Child, Family and Community Service Act* also provides for priority in aboriginal placements. The Act states:

71 (3) If the child is an aboriginal child, the director must give priority to placing the child as follows:
   (*a*)   with the child's extended family or within the child's aboriginal cultural community;
   (*b*)   with another aboriginal family, if the child cannot be safely placed under paragraph (*a*);
   (*c*)   in accordance with subsection (2), if the child cannot be safely placed under paragraph (*a*) or (*b*) of this subsection.

Greater community involvement in the design and delivery of aboriginal child protection services is also contemplated in the BC Act. For example, when an aboriginal child is removed from their family, or deemed to be in need of supervised care, a prescribed aboriginal organization or, in the case of a Nisga'a child the Nisga'a Lisms Government, must be given notice of the first presentation hearing (ss. 33.1(4), 34(3), 36(2.1)). Thereafter, the child's band (if the child is registered or entitled to be registered as a member of an Indian band), the Nisga'a Lisms Government (if the child is a Nisga'a child), or an aboriginal community identified by the child or the child's parents (if the child is aboriginal but not a Nisga'a child and not registered or entitled to be registered as a band member) is entitled to be served with notice of the proceedings and, if in attendance at the commencement of the proceedings, will be entitled to full party status (ss. 39(1), 49(3)). As regards service design and delivery, the guiding principles enshrined in the legislation state that:

- aboriginal people should be involved in the planning and delivery of services to aboriginal families and their children (3 (b));
- services should be planned and provided in ways that are sensitive to the needs and the cultural, racial and religious heritage of those receiving the services (3 (c));
- the community should be involved, wherever possible and appropriate, in the planning and delivery of services, including preventive and support services to families and children (3 (e)).

Pursuant to these principles of community participation, the legislative framework allows for a director to enter into an agreement with an Indian band, the Nisga'a Nation, a Nisga'a Village, or a legal entity representing an aboriginal community, to provide services under the Act (s. 93 (1)(g)(iii)). The director may also delegate any or all of his powers, duties and functions to a person or class of person (s. 92(1)). This has facilitated the development in British Columbia of aboriginal controlled child welfare agencies offering a range of child protection and family support services to aboriginal communities. To further this goal the BC government is also establishing five aboriginal regional authorities that will be responsible for the organization and delivery of all child welfare services to any aboriginal person living within the territorial region for which each new authority is responsible. The creation of these regional authorities is embodied in a Memorandum of Understanding entered into on September 9th, 2002 between the BC Government, the Union of British Columbia Indian Chiefs, the First Nations Summit, the Metis Provincial Council of British Columbia and the United Native Nations.

Other jurisdictions have also created an enlarged role for Aboriginal peoples in child welfare, see: See *Child and Family Services Act*, 1990 C-11 ss. 1(2)4, 1(2)5, 13(3), 34(2)(d), 34(10)(f), 35(1)(e), 36(4)(c), 37(3)3, 37(4), 39(1)4, 47(2)(c), 54(3)(f), 57(5), 58(2)(b), 58(4), 61(2)(d), 64(4)(d), 64(6)(e), 69(1)(e), 80(4)(f), Part X, 223 (Ontario); *Youth Protection Act*, 2002, P-34.1, ss. 2.4(5)(c), 37.5 (Quebec); *Child and Family Services Act*, C-7.2 1989-90, ss. 4(c), 23, 37(4)(c), 37(10), 37(11), 53, 61 (Saskatchewan); *Child Welfare Act*, 2000 C-12, ss. 2(f)(i), 2(h)(i), 2(h)(iii), 2(l), 107, 121, 122 and *Child and Family Services Authorities Act*, C-11 2000, Preamble (Alberta); *Children and Family Services Act* c. 5, 1990, Preamble, ss. 2(g), 7(2), 6(1), 9(i), 20(d), 36(3), 39(8)(c), 42(3), 44(3)(c), 47(5), 88(1)(e) (Nova Scotia); *Children's Act* c. 22, ss. 107, 109, 131(k) (Yukon); *Family Services Act* c. F-2.2 1980 ss 1(g), 3(1), 45(1)(a), 45(3)(a) (New Brunswick); *Child, Youth and Family Services Act*, c-12.1 1998, ss. 7(f), 7(g), 9(c), 75(2)(e) (Newfoundland); *Child and Family Services Act*, S.N.W.T.

1997, c. 13, Preamble, ss. 2(*f*), 2(*i*), 2(*l*), 3, 7(*l*), 7(*m*), 7(*n*), 15, 25 (*b*.1), 25 (*c*), 54 (*3*), 56, 57, 58, 58.1, 58.2, 59, 91(*i*) (North West Territories); *Consolidated Child and Family Services Act (Nunavut)* S.N.W.T. 1997, c. 13, Preamble, ss. 2(*f*), 2(*i*), 2(*l*), 3, 7(*l*), 7(*m*), 7(*n*), 15, 25 (*b*.1), 25 (*c*), 54 (3), 56, 57, 58, 58.1, 58.2, 59, 91(i) (Nunavut).

"CHILD WELFARE"

In A.C. Hamilton and C.M. Sinclair, *The Justice System and Aboriginal People: Report of the Aboriginal Justice Inquiry in Manitoba*, Vol. 1
(Winnipeg: Queen's Printer, 1991) at 520 (references omitted)

We believe that the Aboriginal child care agencies have been an outstanding success and that they warrant further support and encouragement. They are dealing with Aboriginal families with sensitivity, commitment and ability. At the same time, it must be recognized that their programs and activities sometimes will become the subject of controversy and criticism. Every time an Aboriginal agency stumbles, some critics inevitably will cry out for its dismantling and a return to the old way. But, as we and other inquiries have concluded, the old way was neither the only way, nor the best way. The need for ongoing support and a commitment to Aboriginal child welfare agencies must be recognized and reaffirmed.

Aboriginal people have enjoyed little influence or control over many of the issues which affect them, often adversely. Manitoba's experience in the field of child welfare, however, suggests that when a consensus develops that something must be done, then positive changes can take place. The reform of the child welfare system is an example of that. It is proof that Aboriginal people are ready, willing and able to exercise greater control over aspects of their lives which some erroneously believe can only be dealt with by non-Aboriginal professionals.

We must now do more to support and extend the reforms that have taken place. Positive steps have been taken, but not all Aboriginal people have benefited. Existing agencies must be strengthened and those Aboriginal people not served by Aboriginal agencies must now be afforded this opportunity. Aboriginal peoples must continue to gain more responsibility for the child and family programs and services that affect them. By expanding the range and number of mandated Aboriginal agencies as we have recommended, all Aboriginal Manitobans will have the opportunity to receive culturally appropriate child and family services. We believe that the rapid and positive development of reserve-based agencies augers well for the future success of Aboriginally administered programs.

In 1999, the Government of Manitoba announced a commitment to address the AJI's recommendations. Additionally, the government established the Aboriginal Justice Implementation Commission to advise the government on methods of implementing recommendations of the *Report of the Aboriginal Justice Inquiry* (1991).

The Commission prioritized issues of family and child welfare and recommended that:

> The Government of Manitoba seek to enter into agreement with the Assembly of Manitoba Chiefs and the Manitoba Metis Federation to develop a plan thdat would result in First Nations and Metis communities developing and delivering Aboriginal child welfare services.

Through negotiations with First Nations and Métis representatives, the Province of Manitoba signed three separate three-year agreements (Memoranda of Understanding) with the Manitoba Métis Federation (MMF) (February 22, 2000) representing the Métis; the Assembly of Manitoba Chiefs (AMC) (April 27, 2000) representing southern First Nations; and Manitoba Keewatinowi Okimakanak (MKO) (July 20, 2000) representing northern First Nations. All four parties subsequently signed the Child and Family Services Protocol. The overall purpose of these agreements was to establish a joint initiative under a common process to expand off-reserve jurisdiction for First Nations, establish a province-wide Métis mandate and restructure the existing child care system through legislative and other changes.

The parties have stated that the development of the regional authorities is the key feature of their approach to Aboriginal child welfare services. The authorities do not deliver services directly, but play an integral role in the coordination of services province-wide and are the governing bodies overseeing these services. The responsibilities of the authorities include:

- Delegating the mandate for service delivery to their respective service delivery agencies;
- Developing policies and procedures;
- Assessing needs, setting priorities, planning, funding and service management;
- Ensuring that children and families have access to quality services;
- Ensuring that policies and standards are followed;
- Monitoring and assessing service delivery;
- Working with other authorities, community partners, private bodies and government to coordinate service delivery;
- Promoting collaboration and cooperation among communities, service affiliates and authorities;

On June 10, 2002, legislation to create the new authorities and structure was introduced in The Manitoba Legislative Assembly. Royal Assent was received on August 9, 2002. The *Child and Family Services Authorities Act*, S.M. 2002, c. 35, will come into force upon proclamation, which is expected by Summer 2003. The legislation is viewed as an important first step toward a restructured child and family services system in Manitoba.

E. CHALLENGES OF ABORIGINAL CONTROL

There are significant developments and numerous experiments with Aboriginal control of child welfare throughout Canada. Many have begun to stem the tide of a century-long trend which devastated the lives of countless individuals and left communities without hope for their future. The well-documented successes of Aboriginally controlled child welfare agencies, however, does not mean they are without problems. As with other child welfare agencies in Canada, violence and abuse can just as easily find their way into Aboriginal institutions and cause great harm to children in care. For example, Manitoba Associate Chief Justice B.D. Giesbrecht reported many of the issues which some communities encounter when he investigated the death of Lester Desjarlais under the *Fatal Inquiries Act* in 1992.

In 1988 Lester Dejarlais took his life, by hanging, while under the supervision of the Dakota Ojibway Child and Family Services (DOCFS), an Aboriginally controlled child welfare agency. The Giesbrecht report made it clear that Aboriginally run child welfare services can at times present as many problems as provincially controlled agencies. He chronicled a sad tale of Lester's neglect at the hands of the DOCFS, which failed to intervene and take action on behalf of Lester when it had knowledge of the severely abusive circumstances he was in. Lester often became a pawn in the larger political struggles occuring within the agency, where people were working at contradictory and cross-purposes. The judge noted that it often seemed as if more attention was being paid to internal political struggles than was being given to the boy's needs. DOCFS failed to explain any special needs or concerns of children being placed in care when the foster placements were made. It did not take sufficient measures to protect Lester from known sex abusers. DOCFS mismanaged and suspiciously lost crucial files related to Lester's care. The agency was subject to political control and interference by the Dakota Ojibway Tribal Council and Band Councils, which led to extreme deference by many members of DOCFS to the disadvantage of children in their care. This enabled band councillors to "interfere" with agency matters and protect people from agency investigation on their reserves. Judge Giesbrecht wrote that "the chiefs and councillors insisted on injecting politics into the system at all levels, and meddling in the daily operation of the agency". He further noted that "The male Indian leaders are not only by and large uninterested in the horrific social problems that are paralyzing their communities, but they are, in too many cases, part of the problem themselves". The judge also observed that the Director of the agency was "virtually absent" and lines of responsibility and accountability for decisions were "completely mangled". These, and many other problems, illustrate the challenges Aboriginal child welfare agencies can encounter when assuming control of this function. While it bears repeating that there are numerous successes in Aboriginally controlled child welfare, the issues raised by the Giesbrecht report should not be ignored. It is absolutely crucial that the issues identified in Lester Desjarlais' death, and the *Jane Doe* case reproduced below, are also the subject of child welfare law reform. Consider the problems in this regard as you read the following case, and the recommendations of the Royal Commission on Aboriginal Peoples that immediately follow it.

JANE DOE (PUBLIC TRUSTEE OF) v. AWASIS AGENCY OF NORTHERN MANITOBA

[1990] 4 C.N.L.R. 10, 72 D.L.R. (4th) 738 (Man. C.A.)

Krindle J.: — This is an application by The Public Trustee to approve an infant settlement in an action in this court under the above style of cause.

. . . . .

This action arises out of the very tragic events which occurred to a youngster who has been permitted to be named in these proceedings under the pseudonym of "Jane Doe". The child was born on July 30, 1972, in Northern Manitoba. Her natural parents were members of an Indian Band and residents of an isolated reserve in Northern Manitoba. In the fall of 1973 the child was placed in the foster home of a couple living in a Northern mining community, in order that she receive medical treatment not available to her in her remote reserve. The child lived as a member of the foster parents' family for 13 years, moving with them from Northern Manitoba to Southern Manitoba, and ultimately to two locations in Alberta, where the foster parents have resided since 1983. The foster parents adopted the child in Alberta, but the adoption order was later set aside at the instance of the defendant Awasis because the natural parents had not been served. In July of 1986, some 13 years after she had been placed with the foster family, the child was removed (against her will) from the foster family by the defendant Awasis and returned to the care and custody of her natural parents on the isolated reserve in Northern Manitoba. She remained there for approximately six months, at which time she was admitted to hospital in the North, immediately transferred by the hospital to a Winnipeg hospital, and made a ward of this court in order to prevent the defendants, or any of them, from returning her to the Northern Reserve.

During the 13 years that the child lived with her foster family, her contact with her natural family was minimal. By the time she was returned to the reserve by the defendant, Awasis, she was unable to speak the local Dene language. Many of the reserve residents, including her natural parents, could not speak any English. In addition to the purely linguistic barriers between herself and her natural family, they were not well acquainted with one another and communication was extremely difficult. As well, the plaintiff mourned the loss of her foster family, who were the only people whom she knew as family. Life on the reserve was foreign to her. She was in no way accepted into the community and led the life of an outcast. On numerous occasions during the six months that the complainant was on the reserve, she was forcibly confined, sexually assaulted and raped by a number of the male residents of the reserve. She contracted venereal disease as a result of the sexual assaults and rapes. She wrote of her plight to her former foster parents, who contacted the defendants and attempted to seek assistance for her. The defendants did not come to the aid of the child. Ultimately, she was removed from the reserve by a fly-in doctor who had a regular circuit into the area, and to whom she made known her plight. Her former foster parents returned to Manitoba from Alberta to help her. The child was hospitalized in Winnipeg, and the court ordered that the child be returned to her foster parents to live in Alberta, as opposed to the custody of the defendant, Awasis, who wished to return the child to the reserve.

When the child was placed in hospital in Winnipeg she was depressed, suffering from an adjustment disorder, and suffering from a form of venereal disease. Subsequent to her return to Alberta she was referred to counseling in order to assist in resolving the various issues, and particularly to help in dealing with the repeated rapes. She has twice attempted suicide, and was hospitalized on two separate occasions in the year 1989 as a result of those gestures. She is residing in Alberta with her "family" and is undergoing counseling and therapy. The court records disclose that the rape allegations resulted in criminal charges having been laid against several individuals on the reserve. Convictions resulted. The child was required to go through numerous preliminary inquiries and trials in those cases. All of this, while necessary from the perspective of public protection, has exacted an additional toll on the plaintiff herself, who was required repeatedly to relive the incidents in court.

While the name of the child has never been publicized, this entire history of tragic events and the role of public agencies in it, was certainly a matter of media attention and broad public knowledge and concern.

The parties requesting this consent judgment asked that I order that the docket be sealed. I am not disposed to do so. In my opinion, the only thing that might justify removing the whole or any part of this proceeding from public scrutiny is the need to protect the identity of the victim. The child has been tragically and seriously victimized by this whole process. Anything that the courts can do to protect her from further humiliation should be done in her interest. I would not want, in any way, to see her publicly identified through these proceedings. That can be accomplished by referring to her as Jane Doe, and by removing from the docket and sealing or expunging only those documents or portions of documents which might tend to identify her. But having said that, where high profile cases are involved, particularly cases which involve public agencies whose duty it is to protect children, it is important that the public have access to those records, or so much of those records as can be made publicly available without disclosing the identity of the child. Accordingly, the sealing order which was sought is refused.

I order to be removed from the docket and sealed, or to be expunged, only those documents or portions thereof which might tend to identify the child. The rest of the pocket will remain open to the public and the pseudonym "Jane Doe" will continue to be used on these public documents.

Insofar as the proposed settlement is concerned, I approve it, albeit reluctantly. In my opinion the $75,000.00 figure for general damages is low. I recognize, however, the fact that damages in this case do not come within a predictable "range" because of the highly atypical nature of this case.

I recognize that the liability of certain of the defendants was arguable. Most important, however, I note what was said by the child herself and her worker, about the damage the child would likely sustain if she had to go through another trial. The criminal cases are now behind her. She seems to be making progress. She, her foster parents and everyone who is involved with her, stress the need to put the terrible experiences behind her so that she can get on with trying to rebuild her life. Part of putting it behind her involves ending the litigation which causes her to relive those horrors in the most brutal and insensitive of ways. Under those circumstances, I approve the proposed settlement.

I note that in addition to the general damage award, the Government of Canada is providing a fund pursuant to which specialized treatment will continue to be available to the child to help her recovery. I agree with the proposal to have the monies held for her benefit by the Public Trustee for the next few years. The costs charged by the Public Trustee, all of which are being borne by the defendants, are reasonable and are approved.

REPORT OF THE ROYAL COMMISSION ON ABORIGINAL PEOPLES, GATHERING STRENGTH, VOL. 3

(Ottawa: Ministry of Supply and Services, 1996) at 52-53
(references omitted)

Conclusion and Recommendations

Aboriginal institutions in the field of family and children's services are the way of the future. ...

> Our recommendations here focus on affirming and implementing the authority of Aboriginal nations and their communities to act in the field of family and child welfare, and on resolving the tensions between federal, provincial, territorial and Aboriginal authority that interfere with protecting the best interests of Aboriginal children.

While we consider that protecting children's interests can be achieved best in the context of revitalized Aboriginal families, communities and nations, we do not underestimate the difficulties of turning ideals into reality.

In the recent history of Aboriginal child welfare, the best interests of the child have at times been construed as being in conflict with community goals of self-determination. One highly publicized case was the death of Lester Desjarlais, a child who committed suicide while in the care of an Aboriginal agency in Manitoba.

Associate Chief Judge Dale Giesbrecht concluded from his inquiry into the death that political considerations in the local community had interfered with the agency's discharge of its responsibilities, that policies and lines of responsibility within the agency needed to be clarified and formalized, and that the provincial director of child welfare should take a more active role in monitoring the work of Aboriginal agencies. Concern about issues of political interference, organizational capacity and checks and balances in exercising of community responsibility are not confined to Manitoba.

The tension between individual and group priorities surfaces in another area of child welfare. ... Judgments about guardianship and adoption placements of minor children often entail balancing a child's need for stable parental relationships with the equally compelling need to have community support in developing a mature Aboriginal identity.

Aboriginal and non-Aboriginal agencies and personnel bring different perceptions and approaches to the work of child welfare. Tensions emerge precisely because the well-being of children is such a fundamentally important issue in both Aboriginal and non-Aboriginal societies.

As we reiterate often in this volume, non-Aboriginal institutions will have a continuing role in delivering services to Aboriginal people, even when Aboriginal self-government is fully operative across the country. The best interests of Aboriginal children will be served only by determined and sustained efforts on the part of Aboriginal and non-Aboriginal governments, institutions, and people to recognize and support each other's contributions to the common goal.

RECOMMENDATIONS

The Commission recommends that:

3.2.1 The government of Canada acknowledge a fiduciary responsibility to support Aboriginal nations and their communities in restoring Aboriginal families to a state of health and wholeness.

3.2.2 Aboriginal, provincial, territorial and federal governments promptly acknowledge that child welfare is a core area of self-government in which Aboriginal nations can undertake self-starting initiatives.

3.2.3 Aboriginal, provincial, territorial and federal governments promptly reach agreements on the authority of Aboriginal nations and their communities for child welfare, and its relation to provincial, territorial and federal laws respecting child welfare.

3.2.4 Block funding be provided to child welfare agencies mandated by Aboriginal governments or communities to facilitate a shift in focus from alternative child care to family support.

3.2.5 Until community of interest governments are established in urban and non-reserve areas, voluntary agencies endorsed by substantial numbers of Aboriginal people resident in the areas be authorized under provincial or territorial law to act in the field of child welfare (a) where numbers warrant; and (b) with levels of funding comparable to those of agencies providing comparable services to the general population and sufficient to meet the service needs of Aboriginal people.

F. CUSTOMARY CHILD AND FAMILY RELATIONS

Some Aboriginal communities are attempting to resolve the challenges of child care through their traditional customs and practices. The following commentary and case demonstrate how these customs are a living part of the fabric of contemporary Aboriginal nations. They illustrate the legal foundation on which these rights rest, and contain some important implications for the future exercise of Aboriginal jurisdiction in the area of child welfare.

REPORT OF THE ROYAL COMMISSION ON ABORIGINAL PEOPLES, GATHERING STRENGTH, VOL. 3

(Ottawa: Ministry of Supply and Services, 1996) at 87
(references omitted)

Constitutional scholars have concluded that the affirmation of Aboriginal rights in section 35(1) incorporates into Canadian law the common law principle of continuity. Under this principle the customary laws of Aboriginal peoples were deemed to have survived the Crown's acquisition of their territories, provided that this result was not incompatible with the sovereignty of the Crown.

... Two leading decisions of the United States Supreme Court, *Johnson v. M'Intosh* and *Worcester v. Georgia*, held that Indian tribes in the United States had the status of domestic dependent nations united by special ties to the Crown as ultimate sovereign. In Sioui, Justice Lamer of the Supreme Court of Canada used the words of the chief justice of the United States to describe British policy toward the Indians in the mid-eighteenth century:

> [S]he considered them as nations capable of maintaining the relations of peace and war; of governing themselves, under her protection, and she made treaties with them, the obligation of which she acknowledged.

It would appear, therefore, that at least to some extent Aboriginal customary laws survived the advent of the colonizers. Constitutional scholars seem to be in agreement that certain aspects of customary law pertaining to the family have survived. Customary laws on marriage and adoption have been upheld even in the face of legislation that might be taken to have abridged such laws. We referred earlier to the Quebec case, *Connolly v. Woolrich*, which upheld the validity of a marriage contracted under Cree customary law between a non-Aboriginal man and a First Nations woman in the Canadian northwest.

In *Re Katie's Adoption Petition*, Justice Sissons held that adoptions "made according to the laws of the Territories" within the meaning of section 103 of the *Child Welfare Act* included adoptions in accordance with Indian and Inuit custom."' In *J.T.K. v. Kenora-Patricia Child and Family Services*, the court issued a custody order in favour of relatives of the child's parents over the objections of the Crown. The court found that such an order was in accordance with the tribal tradition of customary adoption among the Ojibway people. ...

With the advent of self-government, Aboriginal nations will be in a position to make their own family law. Indeed, they can proceed with initiatives in this area now, since family law falls within the core of Aboriginal self-governing jurisdiction. While their customary laws in some areas have continuing validity under section 35(1) of the constitution, in other areas they have been preempted by federal or provincial laws. It seems likely, therefore, in view of the fundamental importance of family and family relationships, that Aboriginal people will wish to have their own laws in place as soon as possible. There would seem to be particular urgency in this regard concerning laws and policies affecting children — laws on apprehension, custody and adoption, for example — as well as other areas with an impact on children, including their quality of life and personal security, parental responsibilities with regard to support and maintenance, protection from violence, and property and inheritance. As Aboriginal people have told us, their children are their future.

The *Casimel* case, below, illustrates the court's recognition of the continuity of customary child welfare law within Aboriginal communities. As you read the case, think about the implications of the Royal Commission's finding that child welfare law is a core area of jurisdiction in Aboriginal self-government.

CASIMEL v. INSURANCE CORP. OF BRITISH COLUMBIA

[1994] 2 C.N.L.R. 22 (B.C.C.A.)

Lambert J.A. (for the Court, allowing the appeal): — The issue in this appeal is whether the plaintiffs, Louise Casimel and Francis Casimel, were dependent parents of Ernest Casimel when he was killed in an automobile accident on 9 November 1988. If they were, they would be entitled to receive "no fault" death benefits under Part VII of the Regulations under the *Insurance (Motor Vehicle) Act*.

The resolution of that issue requires a consideration of the interaction between aboriginal rights arising from aboriginal customary law, on the one hand, and the general statute law of British Columbia, on the other.

I

Louise Casimel is now 79 years old and has been blind for some years. Francis Casimel is 99 years old. They have been married to each other for many years. They are members of the Stellaquo Band of the Carrier People. Until recently they maintained their family home on the Stellaquo Reserve near Burns Lake. There they raised their family, including their two daughters, Mary Casimel and Charlotte Casimel.

In 1960, Mary Casimel bore a son, Ernest Casimel. Ernest's father was unknown. Mary took no interest in her son and from the beginning he was looked after by Mary's mother and father, Louise and Francis, the present plaintiffs, with the help of Mary's sister, Charlotte. Three or four years later Mary left home to marry. She moved to Vancouver with her husband and lived there for several years. She then returned to live on the Stellaquo Reserve but not with her parents. Charlotte also married and left home. The remaining family unit then consisted of Louise, Francis and Ernest. Ernest was raised by Louise and Francis and he was treated in all respects as their own son. He referred to them as "Mom" and "Dad", and they referred to him as their "son". Charlotte referred to Ernest as her brother and she treated him as her brother. Ernest did not maintain any significant relationship with his biological mother and rarely saw her, even after she returned to the reserve. When he did speak of her he called her "Mary".

As Ernest grew up and Louise and Francis became older, instead of Louise and Francis looking after Ernest, Ernest started looking after them. In due course he became eligible to have a house of his own on the Reserve but he never applied for one. He lived with Louise and Francis and he looked after them. In the words of the trial judge, Mr. Justice Wong: "Ernest washed the clothes, chopped wood for heat and took Louise and Francis shopping since neither of them was able to drive. Ernest did the cooking, washed the dishes and used his money to buy groceries for the whole household. As far as Charlotte can recall, Louise, Francis and Ernest did not have bank accounts and they would simply pool their money together for household expenses. Ernest would cash their cheques and look after the household money. Ernest worked from time to time and when he was not working he received social assistance or unemployment insurance benefits.

Shortly before his death, at age 28, Ernest was elected Chief of the Stellaquo Band. After his death he was succeeded as Chief by Robert Michell who, in an affidavit, said: "The late Ernest Joseph Casimel was raised and cared for by Louise and Francis Casimel and Louise and Francis Casimel were considered by the Stellaquo Band to be his parents."

II

The plaintiffs filed a Statement of Claim seeking "no fault" death benefits under Sections 92, 93 and 94 of Part VII of the Insurance (Motor Vehicle) Regulations as "dependent parents" of Ernest Casimel. The defendant denied that the plaintiffs were "dependent parents". The defendant then brought an application under Rule 18A for the dismissal of the action. The plaintiffs brought a cross-application under Rule 18A for judgment in accordance with their claim. Both 18A applications came on for hearing at the same time before Mr. Justice Wong in Supreme Court Chambers.

Mr. Justice Wong dismissed the action. He decided that the customary adoption under the customs of the Stellaquo Band of the Carrier People gave rise to moral rights and obligations but not to legal rights and obligations, and that for that reason the plaintiffs were not entitled to be treated as parents under the Insurance (Motor Vehicle) Regulations.

Mr. Justice Wong followed the decision of Judge Hutchinson in *Michell v. Dennis and Dennis*, [1984] 2 W.W.R. 449 (B.C.S.C.), where Judge Hutchinson decided that adoption by Indian custom did not give the adopting mother the capacity to sue as a parent under the *Family Compensation Act*.

Mr. Justice Wong's reasons in this case are reported at (1991), 58 B.C.L.R. (2d) 316. Since both the reasons of Mr. Justice Wong and the reasons of Judge Hutchinson *Michell v. Dennis and Dennis* are reported, I do not propose to refer to them at any length. Neither in set of reasons discusses the nature of an Indian customary adoption or the recognition of Indian customary rights by the common law.

I have reached a different conclusion than Mr. Justice Wong and I will set out my reasons for doing so. It is not necessary for me to express any opinion about the decision reached by Judge Hutchinson in *Michell v. Dennis and Dennis.*

III

In the course of his reasons Mr. Justice Wong stated the issue in this way, "At issue is whether the meaning of the words 'dependent parent' in the Regulation includes a dependant customary adoption parent. Mr. Justice Wong also described the plaintiffs as "biological grandparents and customary adoptive parents of [Ernest Casimel]".

I consider therefore that Mr. Justice Wong has found as a fact that a customary adoption in accordance with the customs of the Stellaquo Band of the Carrier People had taken place and that in accordance with those customs Ernest was treated by other band members as the son of Louise and Francis, and Louise and Francis, in turn, were treated by other band members as the parents of Ernest. Both parties to this appeal conceded that such a customary adoption had taken place. In view of Mr. Justice Wong's finding and in view of that concession, I propose to regard Ernest as having been adopted as their son by Louise and Francis in accordance with the customs of the Stellaquo Band of the Carrier People. I also propose to assume that under those customs not only were Francis and Louise regarded as the parents of Ernest, but that Mary was no longer regarded as a parent of Ernest and ceased to have any of the rights or obligations of a parent. That assumption is entirely consistent with the evidence though the precise nature of the customary adoption, which both parties agreed had occurred, was not explored in the evidence. Since the fact of the customary adoption had been agreed, there was no need to explore it.

I consider also that Mr. Justice Wong has found as a fact that Louise and Francis were dependent on Ernest within the meaning of "dependant parent," which is defined in Section 1(1) of the Insurance (Motor Vehicle) Regulations, in this way:

> "dependent parent" means a surviving parent of an insured who, at the date of an accident for which a claim is made, resides with the insured and receives most of his financial support from the insured.

Whatever may have been the case in Supreme Court Chambers, the defendant did not admit on this appeal that Louise and Francis were dependant on Ernest. But I consider that Mr. Justice Wong must have found such a dependency or he would not have stated the issue as he did. The defendant brought on an 18A application for dismissal of the claim and the plaintiff brought on an 18A application for judgment. Ernest was described in the evidence as the only member of the family unit who worked. When he was unemployed he received either unemployment insurance or social assistance. At the date of his death he was Chief of the Stellaquo Band. Louise and Francis received the old age pension but that was their only income. In short, there was evidence that Louise and Francis were dependant on Ernest within the terms of the definition and no evidence to rebut the inference of dependency. There is, in my opinion, no basis for interfering with the finding by Mr. Justice Wong that if Louise and Francis were parents of Ernest then they were dependent parents.

IV

The origin and the nature of aboriginal rights were argued very fully in this Court and considered at some length by this Court in *Delgamuukw v. The Queen*, [1993] 5 W.W.R. 97.

All five judges who heard that appeal concluded that aboriginal rights arose from such of the customs, traditions and practices of the aboriginal people in question as formed an integral part of their distinctive culture at the time of the assertion of sovereignty by the incoming power, (which in that case was taken to have occurred in 1846) and which were protected and nurtured by the organized society of that aboriginal people. Those aboriginal rights were then recognized and affirmed by the common law when the common law became applicable following the assertion of sovereignty with the result that those rights became protected as aboriginal rights under the common law. Existing aboriginal rights became constitutionally protected in 1982 as part of the constitutional amendments embodied in the *Constitution Act, 1982*, as Section 35.

When the rights in issue are rights in relation to the social organization of the aboriginal people in question, such as rights arising from marriage, rights of inheritance, and, I would add, rights arising from adoption, Mr. Justice Macfarlane, for himself and Mr. Justice Taggart, said this, at p. 151 (para. 163):

> No declaration by this court is required to permit internal self-regulation in accordance with aboriginal traditions, if the people affected are in agreement. But if any conflict between the exercise of such aboriginal traditions and any law of the Province or Canada should arise the question can be litigated. No such specific issue is presented on this appeal.

Mr. Justice Macfarlane, for himself and Mr. Justice Taggart, otherwise confined his consideration of aboriginal rights of social self-regulation to deciding that because of the distribution of legislative powers and judicial powers under the *Constitution Act, 1867* there were no remaining legislative or judicial functions exercisable by aboriginal peoples.

Mr. Justice Wallace confined his consideration of aboriginal rights of social self-regulation in the same way.

Mr. Justice Hutcheon, at p. 394 (para. 1164), said this:

> The traditions of the Gitksan and Wet'suwet'en societies existed long before 1846 and continued thereafter. They included the right to names and titles, the use of masks and symbols in rituals, the use of ceremonial robes and the right to occupy or control places of economic importance. The traditions, in these kinship societies, also included the institution of the clans and of the Houses in which membership descended through the mother and, of course, the Feast system. They regulated marriage and the relations with neighbouring societies.

I note that Mr. Justice Hutcheon referred specifically to marriage customs. I am sure that adoption customs would fall in the same category. Mr. Justice Hutcheon then asked this question: When was the right to practice those traditions lost? At p. 266 (para. 1168) Mr. Justice Hutcheon answered that question by saying that no one could argue that the traditions of the Feast and other traditions such as he was describing of the Gitksan and

Wet'suwet'en peoples had been extinguished. At p. 396 (paras. 1172 and 1173), Mr. Justice Hutcheon said this:

> The appellants accept that provincial laws of general application validly apply to aboriginal people subject, of course, to the test arising under s. 88 of the *Indian Act*. It is not necessary at this stage to decide, in a final way, the validity of any specific provincial statute.

What Mr. Justice Hutcheon said at p. 394 (para. 1164) was quoted by Mr. Justice Macfarlane at p. 150 (para. 158) and not disapproved, though Mr. Justice Macfarlane said, at para. 159, "However, what specific system of laws and customs have continued was not made clear."

At p. 363 (para. 1029), I said this:

> I propose to summarize. The Gitksan and Wet'suwet'en peoples had rights of self-government and self-regulation in 1846, at the time of sovereignty. Those rights rested on the customs, traditions and practices of those peoples to the extent that they formed an integral part of their distinctive cultures. The assertion of British Sovereignty only took away such rights as were inconsistent with the concept of British Sovereignty. The introduction of English Law into British Columbia was only an introduction of such laws as were not from local circumstances inapplicable. The existence of a body of Gitksan and Wet'suwet'en customary law would be expected to render much of the newly introduced English Law inapplicable to the Gitksan and Wet'suwet'en peoples, particularly since none of the institutions of English Law were available to them in their territory, so that their local circumstances would tend to have required the continuation of their own laws. The division of powers brought about when British Columbia entered Confederation in 1871 would not, in my opinion, have made any difference to Gitksan and Wet'suwet'en customary laws. Since 1871, Provincial laws of general application would apply to the Gitksan and Wet'suwet'en people, and Federal laws, particularly the *Indian Act*, would also have applied to them. But to the extent that Gitksan and Wet'suwet'en customary law lay at the core of their Indianness, that law would not be abrogated by Provincial laws of general application nor by Federal laws, unless those Federal laws demonstrated a clear and plain intention of the Sovereign power in Parliament to abrogate the Gitksan or Wet'suwet'en customary laws. Subject to those over-riding considerations, Gitksan and Wet'suwet'en customary laws of self-government and self-regulation have continued to the present day and are now constitutionally protected by s. 35 of the *Constitution Act, 1982*.

I think that the conclusion which should be drawn from the decision of the court in *Delgamuukw v. The Queen* is that none of the five judges decided that aboriginal rights of social self-regulation had been extinguished by any form of blanket extinguishment and that particular rights must be examined in each case to determine the scope and content of the specific right in the aboriginal society, and the relationship between that right with that scope and content and the workings of the general law of British Columbia.

Of course, if the aboriginal right had not been extinguished before 1982, it is now recognized, affirmed and guaranteed by s. 35 of the *Constitution Act, 1982*, not in its regulated form but in its full vigour, subject to the prima facie infringement and justification tests leading to a decision about ultimate justification, all as set out in *R. v. Sparrow*, [1990] 1 S.C.R. 1075.

V

That brings me to the decisive issue in this appeal, namely: the consequences under the general law of the province of a customary adoption brought about in the exercise of aboriginal rights.

I propose in this case to confine my consideration of that question to the narrow point about aboriginal rights which give rise to a particular status in the aboriginal community in question.

Before coming to the Canadian cases, I will refer to this passage from the majority reasons of Mr. Justice Brennan, with which Chief Justice Mason and Mr. Justice McHugh agreed, in the High Court of Australia in *Mabo v. Queensland* (1992), 107 A.L.R. 1:

> The incidents of a particular native title relating to inheritance, *the transmission or acquisition of rights and interests on death or marriage*, the transfer of rights and interests in land and the grouping of persons to possess rights and interests in land are matters to be determined by the laws and customs of the indigenous inhabitants, provided those laws and customs are not so repugnant to natural justice, equity and good conscience that judicial sanctions under the new regime must be withheld: *Idewu Inasa v. Oshodi*, [1934] A.C. 99 (J.C.P.C.).

(my emphasis)

That passage was framed in relation to the holding of native title (or aboriginal title as it is called in Canada), but in my opinion the fact that the acquisition of rights on death and marriage is specifically mentioned is an indication that rights arising from status may properly be determined by the laws and customs of the aboriginal people in question.

I propose now to turn to the Canadian cases. I have been much assisted in a search for the cases and in an understanding of them by an article written by Professor Norman Zlotkin: "Judicial Recognition of Aboriginal Customary Law in Canada: Selected Marriage and Adoption Cases", [1984] 4 C.N.L.R 1.

The leading case, and a most remarkable authority in this field, is the judgment of Mr. Justice Monk of the Superior Court of Quebec in *Connolly v. Woolrich* (1867), 11 L.C. Jur. 197; 17 R.J.R.Q. 75; 1 C.N.L.C. 70. The decision was rendered on 9 July 1867, just 9 days after Confederation. In 1802, William Connolly, at the age of 16, left Montreal as a clerk for the Northwest Company and went to live and work at Rivière-aux-rats in the Athabaska District. In 1803 he took to live with him, with her consent and her father's consent, and in accordance with Cree custom, Suzanne Pas-denom, a Cree. They lived together from 1802 to 1831 at a number of posts in the North-west country. They had six children or more, of whom the plaintiff was one. By 1831 William Connolly was a chief trader of the Hudson Bay Company and he and Suzanne and a number of their children moved to Montreal.

In 1832 William Connolly went through a form of marriage with Julia Woolrich in accordance with the Quebec civil law and their Catholic faith. William Connolly and Julia Woolrich lived together after that as man and wife and had two children. Suzanne was supported by William and, after his death, by Julia, at a convent at the Red River settlement. The contest in the lawsuit was between one of the children of William Connolly and

Suzanne Pas-de-nom, on the one hand, and the heirs of Julia Woolrich on the other.

Mr. Justice Monk decided that William Connolly and Suzanne Pas-de-nom had married in accordance with Cree custom and that for the purposes of Quebec law they were man and wife. Mr. Justice Monk decided further that the status of husband and wife conferred by Cree custom gave rise to community of property between William and Suzanne in accordance with the law of the domicile of origin of William, namely the law of Quebec. As a result the plaintiff was entitled to his proportionate share of half of the property of William Connolly. Mr. Justice Monk's decision was upheld by the Cour du Banc de la Reine, en appel. Chief Justice Duval, Mr. Justice Caron, Mr. Justice Badgley and Mr. Justice McKay agreed with Mr. Justice Monk's reasoning, conclusion, and result. Mr. Justice Loranger dissented. See (1869), 17 R.J.R.Q. 266; 1 R.L.O.S. 253; 1 C.N.L.C 151.

In *R. v. Nan-E-Quis-A-Ka* (1889), 1 Terr. L.R. 211; 2 C.N.L.C. 368 (N.W.T.S.C.), Mr. Justice Wetmore decided that Maggie, a woman married by Inuit custom, was not a compellable witness against her customary law husband. The status conferred by the Inuit customary law marriage was applied to the common law criminal law of evidence and she was not required to testify. A similar conclusion on similar facts was reached by Mr. Justice Gregory in *R. v. Williams* (1921), 30 B.C.R. 303 (B.C.S.C.), though he did not have time to research the point in the middle of an assize. In *Ex parte Côté* (1971), 5 C.C.C. (2d) 49 the Saskatchewan Court of Appeal reached the opposite conclusion on the same question. They considered that the presence of a clergyman was necessary for a simple consensual common law marriage.

In *R. v. Bear's Shin Bone* (1899), 4 Terr. L.R. 173 (N.W.T.S.C.), Mr. Justice Rouleau dealt with a marriage according to the customs of the Blood tribe and concluded that the marriage was valid and could give rise to a conviction for polygamy under the criminal law.

In *Re Noah Estate* (1961), 32 D.L.R. (2d) 185 (N.W.T.S.C.) Mr. Justice Sissons decided that a marriage between two Inuit, celebrated in accordance with Inuit custom in the Northwest Territories, involving simply a trial period and continuing consent of the parties, was a valid marriage and conferred marital status. When the husband had become part of the "white man's society" the Intestate Succession Ordinance of the Northwest Territories applied to confer benefits on his wife as "widow" and his children as "issue".

As Professor Zlotkin says at p. 5, the cases are consistent with the view that before a statute could remove the status confirmed by a marriage according to aboriginal custom the statute would have to be explicit on that point. Or, as the extinguishment cases say, the statute would have to demonstrate a clear and plain intention to extinguish the rights conferred by a marriage in accordance with aboriginal custom.

I propose to move now from the cases involving marriage by aboriginal custom to the cases on adoption by aboriginal custom.

In *Re Katie's Adoption Petition* (1961), 32 D.L.R. (2d) 686 (N.W.T.T.C.) Mr. Justice Sissons decided that an Inuit customary adoption conferred the status of parent and child on the respective parties to the adoption. Mr. Justice Sissons decided that the *Northwest Territories Act*, the Adoption Ordinance and the Child Welfare Ordinance did not end customary adoptions by Inuit custom.

In *Re Beaulieu's Petition* (1969), 3 D.L.R. (3d) 479 (N.W.T.T.C.) Mr. Justice Morrow followed *Re Katie* and decided that a Dogrib Indian customary adoption should be recognized.

In *Re Deborah* (1972), 27 D.L.R. (3d) 225 (N.W.T.S.C.) an Inuit customary adoption was challenged by the natural parents. Mr. Justice Morrow recognized the Inuit customary adoption and the status it conferred and he rejected the challenge of the natural parents. Mr. Justice Morrow's decision was appealed to the Northwest Territories Court of Appeal. Mr. Justice Johnson, for the court, upheld Mr. Justice Morrow's decision. See (1972), 28 D.L.R. (3d) 483 (N.W.T.C.A.). At p. 488, Mr. Justice Johnson set out the legal foundation for the recognition by the common law of adoption by aboriginal custom in this way:

> Custom has always been recognized by the common law and while at an earlier date proof of the existence of a custom from time immemorial was required, Tindal C.J. in *Bastard v. Smith* (1838), 2 Mood. & R. 129 at 136, 174 E.R. 238, points out that such evidence is no longer possible or necessary and that the evidence extending "as far back as living memory goes, of a continuous, peaceable, and uninterrupted user of the custom" is all that is now required. Such proof was offered and accepted in this case.

In *Re Wah-Shee* (1975), 57 D.L.R. (3d) 743 and in *Re Tagornak* (1983), 50 A.R. 237 the Supreme Court of the Northwest Territories declared adoption by aboriginal custom to be valid, notwithstanding that in each case one of the adopting parents was caucasian.

I conclude that there is a well-established body of authority in Canada for the proposition that the status conferred by aboriginal customary adoption will be recognized by the courts for the purposes of application of the principles of the common law and the provisions of statute law to the persons whose status is established by the customary adoption. That body of authority is entirely consistent with all of the reasons for judgment of the members of this court in *Delgamuukw v. The Queen* as those reasons discuss the jurisprudential foundation for aboriginal rights in British Columbia.

VI

I turn now to the provincial *Adoption Act* and to the federal *Indian Act* to see whether there is anything in either of those Acts which might be said to qualify, regulate, or in the case of the *Indian Act* extinguish, the status conferred by an aboriginal customary adoption.

Adoption was not known at common law. It is a creation of statute. The first *Adoption Act* in British Columbia was passed in 1920 as S.B.C. 1920 c. 2. There is nothing in that Act or in any amendment to that Act or in the present *Adoption Act*, R.S.B.C. 1979 c. 4, as amended, which could be thought to have qualified or regulated either before or after the constitutional amendment of 1982, the right of aboriginal people to continue their custom of adoption in accordance with the customs, traditions and practices which form an integral part of their distinctive culture.

Indeed, s-s. 11(5) and para. 13.6(1)(b) of the present *Adoption Act* indicate a sensitivity to the protection of aboriginal status in the adoption of Indian children by non-Indian or Indian adoptive parents. That sensitivity is entirely inconsistent with the abrogation of Indian customary adoptions.

Subsection 11(5) reads like this:

> 11. (5) The status, rights, privileges, disabilities and limitations of an adopted Indian person acquired as an Indian under the *Indian Act* (Canada) or under any other Act or law are not affected by this section.

In my opinion, if aboriginal customary adoptions were not to be recognized and only adoptions under the Adoption Act were to be recognized, then the subsection would have used the words "... an Indian person adopted under this Act ...", rather than the words "... an adopted Indian person ...".

I move on now to the federal *Indian Act*. In that Act "child" is defined in this way in ss. 2(1):

> "child" includes a child born in or out of wedlock, a legally adopted child and *a child adopted in accordance with Indian custom.*

(my emphasis)

That definition was placed in the *Indian Act* in 1985 to replace two former definitions which had been used for two different purposes. At the time of the change, the Honourable David Crombie, Minister of Indian Affairs and Northern Development, said this:

> If an Indian person is capable of transmitting status to his or her natural child, it seems logical to extend that capability to include a child whom the Indian person might adopt, either legally as defined by provincial or territorial law, *or by the custom of his or her people.* The equal treatment of children in an immediate family is important to the preservation and integrity of the family unit. *Band custom adoptions are not uncommon and very frequently involve a relative of the child in question.*

(my emphasis)

See Hansard [Canada, House of Commons, Commons Debates, Vol. IV at pp. 5564-5 (10 June, 1985)].

There is nothing in the *Indian Act* which might be thought to abrogate the status conferred by Indian customary adoptions and, indeed, the definition I have quoted of "child", and the passage I have quoted from Hansard, indicate quite the reverse.

I have discussed both the Provincial *Adoption Act* and the Federal *Indian Act*. Neither of them suggests the qualification, regulation or abrogation of aboriginal customary adoptions. It is therefore not necessary for me to deal with any question relating to the constitutional power to regulate or extinguish aboriginal rights, a subject discussed at some length in *Delgamuukw v. The Queen*.

VII

In my opinion, by the customs of the Stellaquo Band of the Carrier People, Ernest Casimel became the son of Louise Casimel and Francis Casimel, and Louise and Francis Casimel became the parents of Ernest Casimel. Such a customary adoption was an integral part of the distinctive culture of the Stellaquo Band of the Carrier People, (though, of course, other societies may well have shared the same custom or variations of that custom), and as such, gave rise to aboriginal status rights that became recognized, affirmed and protected by the common law and under s. 35 of the *Constitution Act, 1982*.

The status of parent, recognized by the common law and by the constitution of Canada, is sufficient to bring Louise Casimel and Francis Casimel within the definition of "dependent parent" in Part VII of the Insurance (Motor Vehicle) Regulations and so they are both entitled to the "no fault" death benefits provided under Sections 92, 93, and 94 of those Regulations.

I would allow the appeal and give judgment for the plaintiffs accordingly.

Lambert J.

Hutcheon J.A.: — I agree.

Hinds J.A.: — I agree.

G. CONCLUSION

As this chapter has illustrated, cultural chauvinism has often overshadowed the welfare of Aboriginal children in Canada. While this has largely been evident by the way Aboriginal children have been treated by Canadian governments, unfortunately, it can also exist in Aboriginal communities. Residential schools, the "sixties scoop", and some interpretations of the "best interest of the child" test illustrate the devastating impact that cultural chauvinism can have. However, cases like that of Lester Desjarlais and *Jane Doe (Public Trustee of) v. Awasis Agency of Northern Manitoba* illustrate that cultural chauvinism can also cut the other way. Despite these challenges, there are some hopeful signs that Aboriginal children will be better cared for in the future. The re-emergence of traditions and customs which respect and strenghten the extended family, and implement teachings of sharing, kindness and respect, present some cause for optimism about the future. In any event, no matter what path reform takes to help Aboriginal children, knowledge of the issues identified in this chapter will form the basis upon which the regeneration of Aboriginal peoples is built.

CHAPTER 12

ABORIGINAL PEOPLES AND CRIMINAL JUSTICE

The justice system has failed ... Aboriginal people on a massive scale. It has been insensitive and inaccessible, and has arrested and imprisoned Aboriginal people in grossly disproportionate numbers. Aboriginal people who are arrested are more likely than non-Aboriginal people to be denied bail, spend more time in pre-trial detention and spend less time with their lawyers, and if convicted, are more likely to be incarcerated. It is not merely that the justice system has failed Aboriginal people: justice also has been denied to them.

A.C. Hamilton and C.M. Sinclair,
Report of the Aboriginal Justice Inquiry of Manitoba,
Vol. 1, The Justice System and Aboriginal People
(Winnipeg: Queen's Printer, 1991), at 1.

A. INTRODUCTION

The justice system has failed Aboriginal people. These words preface the Aboriginal Justice Inquiry of Manitoba, one of Canada's most comprehensive inquiries into Aboriginal people and the criminal justice system. Unfortunately, their findings are not unique. Numerous reports have identified and repeated this same sad fact — "that notwithstanding the hundreds of recommendations from commissions and task forces, the reality for Aboriginal people ... is that the justice system is still failing them". The Royal Commission on Aboriginal People suggested that this failure has most strongly represented itself through over-representation and systemic discrimination within the system. And in some disturbing and astonishing news, they report that "these problems are getting worse, not better".

This dismal view of the tragic impact of Canada's criminal law on Aboriginal people has generated a search for positive solutions. Various initiatives have been undertaken in an attempt to heal the horrific scars this law has left on many communities. Change has manifested itself in many ways, from the greater involvement of Aboriginal people in the administration and reform of Canada's current criminal laws, to the creation of more autonomous, Aboriginally controlled systems. Some of these ventures have met with great success, while others have struggled or failed under the weight of a variety of circumstances.

The materials in this chapter illustrate the problems Aboriginal people encounter in the criminal justice system, and the opportunities its reform potentially offers them. The search for criminal justice promises to remain a very fluid area of law. Great innovations and upheavals will, no doubt, continue as the disturbing legacy of the failure of Canada's criminal law continues to be felt by Aboriginal peoples.

B. THE FAILURE OF CRIMINAL LAW FOR ABORIGINAL PEOPLES

1. *Historical Realities*

THE ROYAL COMMISSION ON ABORIGINAL PEOPLES, BRIDGING THE CULTURAL DIVIDE: A REPORT ON ABORIGINAL PEOPLE AND CRIMINAL JUSTICE IN CANADA

(Ottawa: Ministry of Supply and Services, 1996) at xi, 7
(references omitted)

It is rare today to read a newspaper, listen to the radio or watch television without being confronted with issues of crime and punishment, whether in news reports, documentaries or dramatizations. However, the criminal justice system and its effects on the Aboriginal people of Canada reveal themselves in places far removed from the glare of television cameras and reports' microphones. For Aboriginal people the criminal justice system is not the stuff of drama, real or imagined, but a system in which they, more than any other Canadians, are more likely to become involved, but as victims of crime and as offenders. The over-representation of Aboriginal people in federal, provincial and territorial court systems and prisons casts a long shadow over Canada's claim to be a just society.

Over the last seven years, commissions of inquiry from coast to coast have reviewed the experiences of Aboriginal people with the criminal justice system and have concluded that the system is failing them. Far from addressing the problems they face in their nations, their communities, and their personal lives, it is aggravating them. In large measure these problems are themselves the product of historical processes of dispossession and cultural oppression. ...

We believe that it is essential to frame our discussion of Aboriginal justice issues in the broadest possible context and we have sought to do that. From what we have heard and from what we have read in the reports of the many other justice inquiries, understanding the contemporary realities facing Aboriginal people in the justice system must occur in a historical context of the relationship between Aboriginal and non-Aboriginal people. The sense of oppressiveness, the sense of illegitimacy that has come to characterize Aboriginal peoples' perception and experience of the justice system has deep historical roots.

The trial and execution of Louis Riel for his actions in seeking recognition and respect from Canadian authorities for a Métis homeland have left indelible scars on the collective memory of the Métis people. The perceived injustice of the trial has been compounded by the history of dispossession of Métis people. The trial and execution of eight Cree chiefs who allied themselves with Riel and the Métis, and who were hanged on a single scaffold in the North West Mounted Police courtroom at Battleford, Saskatchewan, on 27 November 1885, continue to cast a long shadow over the descendants of those who were executed for the "crime" of defending their land.

However, the trials of Louis Riel, of Poundmaker and Big Bear, and of the other Métis and Indian "criminals" were not unique. Many other episodes that have rarely penetrated the history books of Canada remain alive in the oral histories of Aboriginal peoples and provide not simply a back-drop but the bedrock of Aboriginal peoples' experience of "justice" according to Canadian law.

REPORT OF THE CARIBOO-CHILCOTIN JUSTICE INQUIRY (BRITISH COLUMBIA)

Judge Anthony Sarich, Commissioner (1993) at 1

Over the years, the native people of the Cariboo-Chilcotin complained about how they were being treated by the various components of the justice system. Recently, those complaints became louder and more insistent. As a result I was asked by the Honourable Colin Gabelmann, the Attorney General of British Columbia, to check into those complaints. ...

In the Chilcotin ... in every village, the people maintained that the chiefs who were hanged in Quesnel Mouth in 1864 as murderers were, in fact, leaders of a war party defending their land and people. Much has been written but little is known with any certainty of the facts that led to the trials of those chiefs before Judge Matthew B. Begbie. The people of the Chilcotin have long memories. They hold the memory of those chiefs in high esteem and cite the effect of smallpox on their ancestors, the incursions onto their land, and the treatment of their people by the road builders hired by Alfred Penderill Waddington as justification for the war. Many natives consider the trial and subsequent hanging as a political event in a deliberate process of colonization. ...

It became apparent early in the course of the inquiry that the native people of the Cariboo-Chilcotin area were complaining not only about the police and the justice system, but also about all non-native authority structures bearing on their lives. These complaints are long-standing and insistent. They are a product of a conflict of cultural values and beliefs and are driven by the past and present conduct of non-native authority figures. And these complaints go back to the first contact with Europeans.

In every community west of the Fraser River, there was still barely concealed anger and resentment about the trickery that led to the hanging of the Chilcotin Chiefs in 1864 at Quesnel. The village Chiefs spoke with passion about the desecration of their graves, the spread of smallpox that killed so many of their people, and the brutish conduct of Waddington's road builders.

In accusatory tones the Chiefs also spoke about how their land was taken by government agencies, particularly those lands now used by the Canadian army as a weapons proving ground. They railed as well against the many fenced ranches carved from what they considered their traditional lands, and the forced move of a whole village to accommodate a ranching enterprise. ...

It appears that even Judge Begbie was concerned about the fairness of the trial of the Chilcotin Chiefs of Quesnel Mouth in 1864. There was genuine concern that the Chiefs were induced to surrender and give inculpatory statements on a promise of immunity by Magistrate Cox. Many natives still feel that the trial and hangings were more a show piece to impress the natives than an honest search for truth. Whatever the correct version, that episode of history has left a wound in the body of Chilcotin society. It is time for that wound to heal.

---

2. Contemporary Realities

(a) Donald Marshall Jr.

On the night of May 28, 1971, Donald Marshall, a 17-year-old native youth in Nova Scotia, was involved in a confrontation that resulted in 11 years in prison for a crime he did not commit. During his trial in November of 1971 Marshall was convicted of murder on the strength of false testimonies obtained through coerced police action. During the trial one of these key witnesses admitted to the Crown that he had lied on the witness stand. This was not pursued. Ten days after the trial the police received important evidence strongly implicating another as the perpetrator of the crime for which Marshall had been found guilty. The police did not question Marshall again, and accepted the denials of the other suspect.

After 11 years of numerous investigations and references, the Nova Scotia Court of Appeal finally heard the truth of Marshall's innocence in the spring of 1982 from the witnesses who had testified at his earlier trial. The Crown also admitted that Marshall should be acquitted. However, in a disturbing turn of events, the Crown asked the court to exonerate the police to preserve the criminal justice system's credibility, and the court appeared to oblige. The court accepted arguments that Marshall's supposedly "evasive" statements to the police, and his presumed attempt to "rob" the man with whom he had the confrontation were the cause of his misfortune. They seemed to imply that Marshall, and not the criminal justice system, was to blame for the tragedy which had befallen him. Five judges of the Court of Appeal declared "any miscarriage of justice is ... more apparent that real".

Many were shocked by the court's comments. Public outcry led to a Royal Commission.

EXCERPTS FROM SUMMARY OF FINDINGS OF THE ROYAL COMMISSION ON THE DONALD MARSHALL, JR. PROSECUTION, NOVA SCOTIA JUDGMENTS

[1990] N.S.J. No. 18

The criminal justice system failed Donald Marshall, Jr. at virtually every turn, from his arrest and conviction in 1971, up to — and even beyond — his acquittal by the Supreme Court of Nova Scotia (Appeal Division) in 1983. The tragedy of this failure is compounded by evidence that this miscarriage of justice could have and should have been prevented, or at least corrected quickly, if those involved in the criminal justice system had carried out their duties in a professional and/or competent manner.

These are the inescapable, and inescapably distressing conclusions this Royal Commission has reached after sifting through 16,390 pages of transcript evidence given by 113 witnesses during 93 days of public hearings in Halifax and Sydney in 1987 and 1988; after examining 176 exhibits submitted in evidence during those hearings; after listening to two-and-one-half days of presentations by experts on the criminal justice system's treatment of Blacks and Natives and on the role of the office of the Attorney General in that system; and after examining five volumes of research material prepared for the Royal Commission by leading academics and researchers.

The Royal Commission was not established, however, just to determine whether one individual was the victim of a miscarriage of justice, or even to get to the bottom of how and why that miscarriage occurred. The Nova Scotia Government, which appointed this Royal Commission on October 28, 1986, also asked us to "make recommendations" to help such tragedies from happening in the future. ...

We find...

- that Marshall was not the author of his own misfortune.
- that the miscarriage of justice was real and not simply apparent.
- that the fact that Marshall was a Native was a factor in his wrongful conviction and imprisonment.
- that the fact that Marshall was a Native was one of the reasons [the investigating police officer] identified him as the prime suspect.
- that the Crown prosecutor and the defense counsel in Donald Marshall, Jr.'s 1971 trial failed to discharge their obligations, resulting in Marshall's wrongful conviction.
- that the cumulative effect of incorrect rulings by the trial judge denied Marshall a fair trial.
- in the Appeal Process that counsel for Donald Marshall, Jr. failed to put arguments before the Court of Appeal concerning fundamental errors of law during the trial, and that this failure represented a serious breach of the standard of professional conduct expected and required of defence counsel.
- in the Reference Decision that the Court of Appeal made a serious and fundamental error when it concluded that Donald Marshall, Jr. was to blame for his wrongful conviction.
- that the Court selectively used the evidence before it — as well as information that had not been admitted in evidence — in order to reach its conclusions.
- that the Court took it upon itself to "convict" Marshall of a robbery with which he was never charged.
- that the Court was in error when it stated that Marshall "admittedly" committed perjury.
- that the Court's suggestion that Marshall's "untruthfulness ... contributed in large measure to his conviction" was not supported by any available evidence and was contrary to evidence before the Court.
- that the Court's decision amounted to a defence of the criminal justice system at Marshall's expense, notwithstanding overwhelming evidence to the contrary.
- that the Court's gratuitous comments in the last pages of its decision created serious difficulties for Donald Marshall, Jr., both in terms of his

ability to negotiate compensation for his wrongful conviction and also in terms of public acceptance of his acquittal.

REPORT TO THE CANADIAN JUDICIAL COUNCIL OF THE INQUIRY COMMITTEE ESTABLISHED PURSUANT TO SUBSECTION 63(1) OF THE JUDGES ACT AT THE REQUEST OF THE ATTORNEY GENERAL OF NOVA SCOTIA

(1991) 40 U.N.B.L.J. 211

Report of Inquiry Commitee Members, Richard C.J., Laycraft C.J., Abella, and Bellemare

August 27, 1990

The mandate of this Inquiry Committee, appointed under subsection 63(3) of the *Judges Act* of Canada, arises out of a request of the Honourable the Attorney General of Nova Scotia dated February 9, 1990 to the Canadian Judicial Council:

> ... to commence an inquiry as to whether, based upon the conduct which has been examined by the *Royal Commission on the Donald Marshall, Jr., Prosecution*, and commented upon in its report, the Honourable Ian M. MacKeigan (former Chief Justice and now a supernumerary judge), the Honourable Gordon L.S. Hart (supernumerary judge, the Honourable Malachi C. Jones, the Honourable Angus L. Macdonald, and the Honourable Leonard L. Pace, or any of them, should be removed from office for any of the reasons set out in paragraphs 65(2)(a) to (d) of the *Judges Act.*

On April 11, 1990, after the establishment of our Committee, the Honourable Ian MacKeigan, then a supernumerary judge and former Chief Justice of Nova Scotia, reached the mandatory retirement age and left the Bench. On April 5, 1990, the Honourable Leonard Pace left the Bench due to ill health. These retirements were verified by Orders in Council filed with us as Exhibits 8 and 9 respectively. Accordingly, this Inquiry Committee has no jurisdiction over them.

Under the *Judges Act*, the Canadian Judicial Council must carry out an inquiry when requested to do so by the Attorney General of a Province. Accordingly, this Committee was appointed to inquire, and to recommend to Council, whether the judges named by the Attorney General should be removed from office. The Canadian Judicial Council designated three of its members as members of the Inquiry Committee; the Honourable Minister of Justice for Canada appointed the two members of the Bar. ...

The applicable sections of the *Judges Act* state:

> 65(2) Where in the opinions of the Council, the judge in respect of whom an inquiry or investigation has been made has become incapacitated or disabled from the due execution of the office of judge by reason of
>
> (*a*) age or infirmity,
> (*b*) having been guilty of misconduct,
> (*c*) having failed in the due execution of that office, or
> (*d*) having been placed by his conduct or otherwise, in a position incompatible with the due execution of that office the Council, in its

> report to the Minister under subsection (1), may recommend that
> the judge be removed from office. ...

We were directed by the Canadian Judicial Council:

> that the Inquiry be held in public except when in the Inquiry Committee's
> view the public interest and the integrity of the judicial process require that
> it be held in private.

The Issues of This Inquiry

In view of the way the issues were argued before us, we find it unnecessary to discuss the Commission's specific criticisms of the judgment of the
Reference Court. We say this because, in our view, the serious criticisms of
the Reference Court by the Commission may be merged into a single,
comprehensive question which may be stated as follows:

> Was it misconduct justifying removal from office for the Court to character-
> ize the conduct of Mr. Marshall as it did having regard to all the circum-
> stances it knew from the record which it had before it? ...

It seems to us that during the course of argument in this ease, the emphasis shifted from error demonstrating bias to allegations of a lack of
fairness in the way the Court characterized the conduct of Mr. Marshall.

We wish at the outset to state our strong disapproval of some of the
language used by the Reference Court in its comments about Mr. Marshall.
In reviewing the record before the Reference Court, we cannot help but be
struck by the incongruity between the Court's legal conclusion that Mr.
Marshall's conviction in 1971 was "unreasonable" and "not now supported by the evidence" and its *obiter* observations that nonetheless "any
miscarriage of justice" was "more apparent than real." Surely it cannot be
seriously argued that the conviction of an innocent person, let alone one
who was at the time an adolescent, who was then unfairly incarcerated for
more than ten years, was anything but a blatant miscarriage of justice.

The wrongful conviction and imprisonment of any person constitutes a
real miscarriage of justice; it cannot be termed "more apparent than real."
This is especially so when the conviction is based upon perjured evidence
obtained with the complicity of the agencies of the crown. The miscarriage
is greater still when crown agencies, subsequent to conviction but while an
appeal is pending, receive conclusive or practically conclusive evidence of
innocence but do not move promptly, or at all, to have the conviction reviewed. The miscarriage of justice, of course, becomes worse each day the
innocent person remains imprisoned. There is no formula that it is possible
to suggest that can be applied to redress completely more than ten years of
wrongful imprisonment or which will accurately reflect the horror of what
happened to Mr. Marshall. We have no difficulty in assuming that any
reasonable person, knowing the circumstances adduced in evidence before
the Reference Court, would regard some of its language to be at least inappropriate.

Nevertheless, in making findings of credibility, the Court was within its
jurisdiction. It was entitled to believe or disbelieve any of the witnesses
before it, including Mr. Marshall. Accepting part of Mr. MacNeil's evidence, the Court concluded that an attempted robbery had been in prog-

ress. There was evidence before the Court from which this finding could honestly be made. We do not say that this is what happened, or that another court would have so concluded.

In disbelieving part of Mr. Marshall's testimony, the Court concluded, from the evidence, that his "evasions" had unleashed the tragic consequences he experienced and that he had thwarted his own defence. The Court also apparently concluded that Mr. Marshall would probably not have been convicted if he had told his lawyers, as he did not, where the real murderer could be found. And the Court concluded that Mr. Marshall was at least an unsatisfactory witness who did not tell the truth. It is not for us to substitute our own opinion about the findings of credibility made by the Reference Court. We are left to conclude that those findings lead the Court to the impression which found expression in the *obiter* paragraphs.

The real question, however, is whether inappropriate language, even grossly inappropriate language, constitutes judicial misconduct in the circumstances of this case, keeping in mind that the Reference Court was entitled in the performance of its judicial duty to analyze the evidence and to comment upon it.

What we must observe is that in the six *obiter* paragraphs the Court focused upon Mr. Marshall to the exclusion of the other destructive factors which had a role in the wrongful conviction. A court is entitled to comment on the evidence before it and upon the conduct of the parties or witnesses. Nevertheless, by referring exclusively to Mr. Marshall, the six paragraphs give the impression that the Court was ignoring the grossly incorrect conduct of other persons and concentrating on the victim of the tragedy. ...

Whatever its intention in choosing to refer only to the person it acquitted, there can be no doubt that the impact of the Court's derogatory *obiter* statements created the strong impression that it was not responsive to the injustice of an innocent person spending more than ten years in jail. ...

We would go so far as to suggest that the Court, in seeming to attribute to Marshall exclusive responsibility for the wrongful conviction, and thereby inferentially exculpating the other persons and factors demonstrated in the record to have played a key role in that conviction, so seriously mis-characterized the evidence before it as to commit legal error (*Desgagne v. Fabrique de St. Philippe D'Arvida*, [1984] 1 S.C.R. 19 at 31, *per* Beetz, J.).

We take it as a presumption, however, that judges ought not to be removed from office for legal error. Having found that the five judges in the collegial decision-making capacity were inappropriately harsh in their condemnation of the victim of an injustice they were mandated to correct, we nonetheless accept the submissions of all counsel that their removal from office is not warranted. While their remarks in *obiter* were, in our view, in error, and inappropriate in failing to give recognition to manifest injustice, we do not feel that they are reflective of conduct so destructive that it renders the judges incapable of executing their office impartially and independently with continued public confidence. The three remaining judges collectively had 58 years of judicial experience prior to deciding the Reference and have each served since for seven more years. Moreover, the Court did in fact acquit Mr. Marshall and find his conviction unsustainable.

We do not make our criticisms lightly. We are deeply conscious that criticism can itself undermine public confidence in the judiciary, but on balance conclude in this case that confidence would more severely be impaired by our failure to criticize inappropriate conduct than it would by our failure to acknowledge it.

Conclusion

While we cannot condone or excuse the severity of the Reference Court's condemnation of Donald Marshall, Jr., and in particular its extraordinary observation that any miscarriage of justice was "more apparent than real", we do not find that the comments can lead to the conclusion that the judges cannot execute their office with the impartiality, integrity and independence the public rightly expects from the judiciary. We therefore, do not recommend their removal from office.

---

3. Aboriginal Over-representation

THE ROYAL COMMISSION ON ABORIGINAL PEOPLE, BRIDGING THE CULTURAL DIVIDE: A REPORT ON ABORIGINAL PEOPLE AND CRIMINAL JUSTICE IN CANADA

(Ottawa: Ministry of Supply and Services, 1996) pp. 28-33
(references omitted)

Injustice Personified — Aboriginal Over-Representation

The justice inquiries that preceded our work documented extensively how this failure has affected the lives of Aboriginal men, women and young people. The clearest evidence appears in the form of the over-representation of Aboriginal people in the criminal justice system. This was first documented in 1967 by the Canadian Corrections Association report, *Indians and the Law*, and in 1974 by the Law Reform Commission of Canada in *The Native Offender and the Law*. *Reports and inquiries since then have not only confirmed the fact of over representation but, most alarmingly, have demonstrated that the problem is getting worse, not better.*

The over-representation of Aboriginal people in Canadian prisons has been the subject of special attention and appropriately so, because the sentence of imprisonment carries with it the deprivation of liberty and represents Canadian society's severest condemnation. The Canadian Bar Association focused its attention on Aboriginal imprisonment in 1988, arguing that lawyers have a particular responsibility to bring these issues to the forefront of the public and governmental agenda.

As Members of the Bar we see the people that lie behind the statistics. We see them in the courts and prisons of this country and are witnesses to the continuing injustice towards them which we as a society practice in the name, paradoxically, of a criminal justice system.

The Association provided this bleak overview of the measure of this injustice:

> Statistics about crime are often not well understood by the public and are subject to variable interpretation by the experts. In the case of the statistics regarding the impact of the criminal justice system on Native people the figures are so stark and appalling that the magnitude of the problem can be neither misunderstood nor interpreted away. Government figures which reflect different definitions of 'Native' and which probably underestimate the number of prisoners who consider themselves Native show that almost 10 per cent of the federal penitentiary population is Native (including about 13 per cent of the federal women's prisoner population) compared to about 2 per cent of the population nationally. In the west and northern parts of Canada where there are relatively high concentrations of Native communities, the over-representation is more dramatic. In the Prairie region, Natives make up about 5 per cent of the total population but 32 per cent of the penitentiary population and in the Pacific region Native prisoners constitute about 12 per cent of the penitentiary population while less than 5 per cent of the region's general population is of Native ancestry. Even more disturbing, the disproportionality is growing. Thus, in 1965 some 22 per cent of the prisoners in Stony Mountain Penitentiary were Native; in 1984 this proportion was 33 per cent. It is realistic to expect that absent radical change, the problem will intensify due to the higher birth rate of Native communities.
>
> Bad as this situation is within the federal system, in a number of the western provincial correctional systems, it is even worse. In B.C. and Alberta, Native people, representing 3-5 per cent of the province's population constitute 16 per cent and 17 per cent of the admissions to prison. In Manitoba and Saskatchewan, Native people, representing 6-7 per cent of the population constitute 46 per cent and 60 per cent of prison admissions.
>
> [A] Saskatchewan study brings home the implications of its findings by indicating that a treaty Indian boy turning 16 in 1976 had a 70 per cent chance of at least one stay in prison by the age of 25 (that age range being the one with the highest risk of imprisonment). The corresponding figure for non-status or Métis was 34 per cent. For a non-Native Saskatchewan boy the figure was 8 per cent. Put another way, this means that in Saskatchewan, prison has become for young Native men, the promise of a just society which high school and college represents for the rest of us. *Placed in a historical context, the prison has become for many young Native people the contemporary equivalent of what the Indian residential school represented for their parents.*

The Association cautioned that "absent radical change, the problem will intensify." The surest evidence that there has been no radical change, and the most damning indictment, is found in the commissions of inquiry appointed since the publication of *Locking Up Natives in Canada*. The Aboriginal Justice Inquiry of Manitoba reported that whereas Aboriginal people accounted for 33 per cent of the population at Stony Mountain Federal Penitentiary in 1984, by 1989 the figure had risen to 46 per cent. In 1983 Aboriginal people accounted for 37 per cent of the population of the provincial Headingly Correctional Institution; by 1989 they accounted for 41 per cent. By 1989 Aboriginal women accounted for 67 per cent of the prison population at the Portage Correctional Institution for Women, and in institutions for young people, the proportion of Aboriginal people was

61 per cent. All together, Aboriginal people made up 56 per cent of the population of correctional institutions (both federal and provincial) in Manitoba in 1989. Aboriginal people account for just under 12 per cent of Manitoba's total population and "thus, Aboriginal people, depending on their age and sex, are present in the jails up to five times more than their presence in the general population."

The figures received by the Task Force on the Criminal Justice System and its Impact on the Indian and Métis People of Alberta also confirmed that Aboriginal over-representation is getting worse in the province of Alberta. Indeed, because Alberta has the second highest rate of imprisonment per person charged in the whole country, over-representation has even harsher effects than elsewhere. Aboriginal men now make up 30 per cent of the male population in provincial jails and Aboriginal women 45 per cent of the female jail population. The most alarming conclusion of the task force is that for Aboriginal young offenders, "over-representation in the criminal justice system is even more dramatic" than it is for adults, and future population projections indicate that the situation will get much worse.

> Projections indicate that by the year 2011, Aboriginal offenders will account for 38.5 per cent of all admissions to federal and provincial correctional centres in Alberta, compared to 29.5 per cent of all such offenders in 1989... In some age categories, for example, the 12-18 years of age group, Aboriginal offenders are projected to account for 40 per cent of the admission of population to correctional facilities by the year 2011.

The fact that in some provinces the coercive intrusion of criminal laws into the lives of Aboriginal people and Aboriginal communities is increasing, not receding, is reflected in the most recent figures from Saskatchewan. John Hylton, a human justice and public policy adviser who has kept a close watch on the situation in Saskatchewan, has broken down total and Aboriginal admissions to provincial correctional centres for the years 1976-77 and compared them to the figures for 1992-93. The breakdown reveals several startling findings:

1. Between 1976-77 and 1992-93, the number of admissions to Saskatchewan correctional centres increased from 4,712 to 6,889, a 46 per cent increase, during a time when the provincial population remained virtually unchanged. The rate of increase was 40.7 per cent for male admissions and 111 per cent for female admissions.
2. During the same period, the number of Aboriginals admitted to Saskatchewan correctional centres increased from 3,082 to 4,757, an increase of 54 per cent. Male Aboriginal admissions increased by 48 per cent, while female Aboriginal admissions increased by 107 per cent.
3. In terms of overall rates of admission, Aboriginals were 65.4 per cent in 1976-77 and 69.1 per cent in 1992-93.
4. Increases in Aboriginal admissions accounted for 77 per cent of the increase in total admissions between 1976-77 and 1992-93.

These data indicate clearly that the problem of disproportionate representation of the Aboriginal people in Saskatchewan's justice system is growing worse, not better. ... Predictions that were prepared in the early 1980's and that were rejected by some as too extreme, have in some instances proven to be conservative, particularly in the case of female Aboriginal admissions.

Aboriginal over-representation in the country's prisons, while presenting the face of injustice in its most repressive form, is only part of the picture. The Aboriginal Justice Inquiry of Manitoba commissioned a great deal of research on the other parts of a system that from beginning to end treats Aboriginal people differently. The Inquiry reported that

> Aboriginal over-representation is the end point of a series of decisions made by those with decision-making power in the justice system. An examination of each of these decisions suggests that the way that decisions are made within the justice system discriminates against Aboriginal people at virtually every point ...
>
> • More than half of the inmates of Manitoba's jails are Aboriginal
> • Aboriginal accused are more likely to be denied bail
> • Aboriginal people spend more time in pre-trial detention than do non-Aboriginal people
> • Aboriginal accused are more likely to be charged with multiple offences than are non-Aboriginal accused
> • Lawyers spend less time with their Aboriginal clients than with non-Aboriginal clients
> • Aboriginal offenders are more than twice as likely as non--Aboriginal people to be incarcerated

The over-representation of Aboriginal people occurs at virtually every step of the judicial process, from the charging of individuals to their sentencing.

In a society that places a high value on equality before the law, documenting the appalling figures of over-representation might seem to be enough, without any further analysis, to place resolution of this problem at the very top of the national human rights agenda. However, as compelling as the figures are, we believe that it is equally important to understand what lies behind these extraordinary figures, which are a primary index of the individual and social devastation that the criminal justice system has come to represent for Aboriginal people. Understanding the root causes is critical to understanding what it will take by way of a national commitment to bring about real change.

---

4. Systemic Racism

Aboriginal people observe that their overrepresentation in the criminal justice system can be explained by reference to systemic racism. The *Report of the Commission on Systemic Racism in the Ontario Criminal Justice System* (Toronto: Queen's Printer, December 1995) defined systemic racism as "the social production of racial inequality in decisions about people in the treatment they receive". The Commission noted that systemic racism is produced through the combination of:

• social constructions of races as real, different and unequal (racialization);

- the norms, processes and service delivery of a social system (structure); and
- the actions and decisions of people who work for social systems (personnel).

As the cases and materials in this book have illustrated, Aboriginal people have often been racialized as different and unequal. Albert Memmi, the influential Tunisian Jewish writer of the post World War II African decolonization movement, observed that racism had the following elements:

1. Stressing the real or imaginary differences between the racist and his victim;
2. Assigning values to these differences, to the advantage of the racist and the detriment of the victim;
3. Trying to make them absolutes by generalizing from them and claiming that they are final;
4. Justifying any present or possible aggression or privilege (*The Colonizer and the Colonized*, 1965).

Through these processes of selection, sorting, attribution and action, the criminal justice system has sustained and promoted systems which negatively impact Aboriginal people. This has led to legislative and institutional processes that support, transmit and tolerate their unequal and adverse treatment. These patterns are also apparent in the treatment they receive at the hands of the criminal justice system. The operating norms, decision-making processes, service delivery, and actions of the courts' participants have contributed to the high degree of Aboriginal over-representation in the criminal justice system. Consider these ideas in the Court's treatment of racism in the *Williams* case which follows.

R. v. WILLIAMS

[1998] 1 S.C.R. 1128

The judgment of the Court was delivered by

McLachlin J.: —

Introduction

Victor Daniel Williams, an aboriginal, was charged with the robbery of a Victoria pizza parlour in October, 1993. Mr. Williams pleaded not guilty and elected a trial by judge and jury. His defence was that the robbery had been committed by someone else, not him. The issue on this appeal is whether Mr. Williams has the right to question (challenge for cause) potential jurors to determine whether they possess prejudice against aboriginals which might impair their impartiality.

The *Criminal Code*, R.S.C., 1985, c. C-46, s. 638, provides that "... an accused is entitled to any number of challenges on the ground that ... a juror is not indifferent between the Queen and the accused". The section confers discretion on the trial judge to permit challenges for cause. The judge should do so where there is a realistic potential of juror partiality. The evidence in this case established widespread racial prejudice against aboriginals. I conclude that in the circumstances of this case, that prejudice established a realistic potential of partiality and that the trial judge should have exercised his discretion to allow the challenge for cause. ...

At his first trial, Williams applied to question potential jurors for racial bias under s. 638 of the *Code*. In support of his application, he filed materials alleging widespread racism against aboriginal people in Canadian society and an affidavit which stated, in part, "[I] hope that the 12 people that try me are not Indian haters". ...

Analysis

What is the Rule?

The Prevailing Canadian Approach to Jury Challenges for Lack of Indifference Between the Crown and the Accused

The prosecution and the defence are entitled to challenge potential jurors for cause on the ground that "a juror is not indifferent between the Queen and the accused". Lack of "indifference" may be translated as "partiality", the term used by the Courts below. "Lack of indifference" or "partiality", in turn, refer to the possibility that a juror's knowledge or beliefs may affect the way he or she discharges the jury function in a way that is improper or unfair to the accused. A juror who is partial or "not indifferent" is a juror who is inclined to a certain party or a certain conclusion. The synonyms for "partial" in *Burton's Legal Thesaurus* (2nd ed. 1992), at p. 370, illustrate the attitudes that may serve to disqualify a juror:

> bigoted, ... discriminatory, favorably disposed, inclined, influenced, ... interested, jaundiced, narrow-minded, one-sided, partisan, predisposed, prejudiced, prepossessed, prone, restricted, ...subjective, swayed, unbalanced, unequal, uneven, unfair, unjust, unjustified, unreasonable.

The predisposed state of mind caught by the term "partial" may arise from a variety of sources. Four classes of potential juror prejudice have been identified — interest, specific, generic and conformity: see Neil Vidmar, "Pretrial prejudice in Canada: a comparative perspective on the criminal jury" (1996), 79 *Jud.* 249, at p. 252. Interest prejudice arises when jurors may have a direct stake in the trial due to their relationship to the defendant, the victim, witnesses or outcome. Specific prejudice involves attitudes and beliefs about the particular case that may render the juror incapable of deciding guilt or innocence with an impartial mind. These attitudes and beliefs may arise from personal knowledge of the case, publicity through mass media, or public discussion and rumour in the community. Generic prejudice, the class of prejudice at issue on this appeal, arises from stereotypical attitudes about the defendant, victims, witnesses or the nature of the crime itself. Bias against a racial or ethnic group or against persons charged with sex abuse are examples of generic prejudice. Finally, conformity prejudice arises when the case is of significant interest to the community causing a juror to perceive that there is strong community feeling about a case coupled with an expectation as to the outcome.

Knowledge or bias may affect the trial in different ways. It may incline a juror to believe that the accused is likely to have committed the crime alleged. It may incline a juror to reject or put less weight on the evidence of the accused. Or it may, in a general way, predispose the juror to the Crown, perceived as representative of the "white" majority against the minority-member accused, inclining the juror, for example, to resolve doubts about aspects of the Crown's case more readily: see Sheri Lynn Johnson, "Black Innocence and the White Jury" (1985), 83 *Mich. L. Rev.* 1611. When these things occur, a juror, however well intentioned, is not indifferent between the Crown and the accused. The juror's own deliberations and the deliberations of other jurors who may be influenced by the juror, risk a verdict that reflects, not the evidence and the law, but juror preconceptions and prejudices. The aim of s. 638 of the *Code* is to prevent effects like these from contaminating the jury's deliberations and hence the trial: see *R. v. Hubbert* (1975), 29 C.C.C. (2d) 279 (Ont. C.A.). The aim, to put it succinctly, is to ensure a fair trial.

The practical problem is how to ascertain when a potential juror may be partial or "not indifferent" between the Crown and the accused. There are two approaches to this problem. The first approach is that prevailing in the United States. On this approach, every jury panel is suspect. Every candidate for jury duty may be challenged and questioned as to preconceptions and prejudices on any sort of trial. As a result, lengthy trials of jurors before the trial of the accused are routine.

Canada has taken a different approach. In this country, candidates for jury duty are presumed to be indifferent or impartial. Before the Crown or the accused can challenge and question them, they must raise concerns which displace that presumption. Usually this is done by the party seeking the challenge calling evidence substantiating the basis of the concern. Alternatively, where the basis of the concern is "notorious" in the sense of being widely known and accepted, the law of evidence may permit a judge to take judicial notice of it. …

Judicial discretion, however, must be distinguished from judicial whim. … To guide judges in the exercise of their discretion, this Court formulated a rule in *Sherratt, supra*: the judge should permit challenges for cause where there is a "realistic potential" of the existence of partiality. *Sherratt* was concerned with the possibility of partiality arising from pre-trial publicity. However, as the courts in this case accepted, it applies to all requests for challenges based on bias, regardless of the origin of the apprehension of partiality.

Applying *Sherratt* to the case at bar, the enquiry becomes whether in this case, the evidence of widespread bias against aboriginal people in the community raises a realistic potential of partiality.

Identifying the Evidentiary Threshold

. . . . .

(1) The Assumption that Prejudice Will be Judicially Cleansed

Underlying the Crown's submissions (as well as the judgments of Esson C.J. and the Court of Appeal) is the assumption that generally jurors will be able to identify and set aside racial prejudice. Only in exceptional cases is there a danger that racial prejudice will affect a juror's impartiality. In contrast, the defence says that jurors may not be able to set aside racial prejudices that fall short of extreme prejudice. Is it correct to assume that jurors who harbour racial prejudices falling short of extreme prejudice will set them aside when asked to serve on a jury? A consideration of the nature of racial prejudice and how it may affect the decision-making process suggests that it is not.

To suggest that all persons who possess racial prejudices will erase those prejudices from the mind when serving as jurors is to underestimate the insidious nature of racial prejudice and the stereotyping that underlies it. As Vidmar, *supra*, points out, racial prejudice interfering with jurors' impartiality is a form of discrimination. It involves making distinctions on the basis of class or category without regard to individual merit. It rests on preconceptions and unchallenged assumptions that unconsciously shape the daily behaviour of individuals. Buried deep in the human psyche, these preconceptions cannot be easily and effectively identified and set aside, even if one wishes to do so. For this reason, it cannot be assumed that judicial directions to act impartially will always effectively counter racial prejudice ...

Racial prejudice and its effects are as invasive and elusive as they are corrosive. We should not assume that instructions from the judge or other safeguards will eliminate biases that may be deeply ingrained in the subconscious psyches of jurors. Rather, we should acknowledge the destructive potential of subconscious racial prejudice by recognizing that the post-jury selection safeguards may not suffice. Where doubts are raised, the better policy is to err on the side of caution and permit prejudices to be examined. Only then can we know with any certainty whether they exist and whether they can be set aside or not. It is better to risk allowing what are in fact unnecessary challenges, than to risk prohibiting challenges which are necessary...

(2) Insistence on the Necessity of a Link Between the Racist Attitude and the Potential for Juror Partiality

The Court of Appeal, *per* Macfarlane J.A., stated that the existence of a significant degree of racial bias in the community from which the panel is drawn is, by itself, not sufficient to allow a challenge for cause because bias cannot be equated with partiality. The court held that in order for the appellant to be successful, there must be some evidence of bias against aboriginal persons which is of a particular nature and extent; evidence which only displays a "general bias" against a racial group is insufficient to warrant a challenge for cause. The Crown goes even further, arguing that racial prejudice in the community must be linked to specific aspects of the trial in order to support a challenge for cause. More particularly, it asserts that where, as here, the defence was that another aboriginal committed the crime, race could have no relevance because the jury was obliged to decide between two aboriginals.

I cannot, with respect, accept this contention. In my view, it is unduly restrictive. Evidence of widespread racial prejudice may, depending on the nature of the evidence and the circumstances of the case, lead to the conclusion that there is a realistic potential for partiality. The potential for partiality is irrefutable where the prejudice can be linked to specific aspects of the trial, like a widepread belief that people of the accused's race are more likely to commit the crime charged. But it may be made out in the absence of such links.

Racial prejudice against the accused may be detrimental to an accused in a variety of ways. The link between prejudice and verdict is clearest where there is an "interracial element" to the crime or a perceived link between those of the accused's race and the particular crime. But racial prejudice may play a role in other, less obvious ways. Racist stereotypes may affect how jurors assess the credibility of the accused. Bias can shape the information received during the course of the trial to conform with the bias: see *Parks*, *supra*, at p. 372. Jurors harbouring racial prejudices may consider those of the accused's race less worthy or perceive a link between those of the accused's race and crime in general. In this manner, subconscious racism may make it easier to conclude that a black or aboriginal accused engaged in the crime regardless of the race of the complainant: see Kent Roach, "Challenges for Cause and Racial Discrimination" (1995), 37 *Crim. L.Q.* 410, at p. 421.

Again, a prejudiced juror might see the Crown as non-aboriginal or non-black and hence to be favoured over an aboriginal or black accused. The contest at the trial is between the accused and the Crown. Only in a subsidiary sense is it between the accused and another aboriginal. A prejudiced juror might be inclined to favour non-aboriginal Crown witnesses against the aboriginal accused. Or a racially prejudiced juror might simply tend to side with the Crown because, consciously or unconsciously, the juror sees the Crown as a defender of majoritarian interests against the minority he or she fears or disfavours. Such feelings might incline the juror to resolve any doubts against the accused.

Ultimately, it is within the discretion of the trial judge to determine whether widespread racial prejudice in the community, absent specific "links" to the trial, is sufficient to give an "air of reality" to the challenge in the particular circumstances of each case. ...

(3) Confusion Between the Two Phases of the Challenge for Cause Process

Section 638(2) requires two inquiries and entails two different decisions with two different tests. ...

The Crown conflates the two stages of the process. Instead of asking whether there is a potential or possibility of partiality at the stage of determining the right to challenge for cause, it demands proof that widespread racism will result in a partial jury. The assumption is that absent such evidence, no challenge for cause should be permitted. This is not the appropriate question at the preliminary stage of determining the right to challenge for cause. The question at this stage is not whether anyone in the jury pool will in fact be unable to set aside his or her racial prejudices but whether there is a realistic *possibility* that this *could* happen.

(4) Impossibility of Proving That Racism in Society Will Lead to Juror Partiality

To require the accused to present evidence that jurors will in fact be unable to set aside their prejudices as a condition of challenge for cause is to set the accused an impossible task. It is extremely difficult to isolate the jury decision and attribute a particular portion of it to a given racial prejudice observed at the community level. Jury research based on the study of actual trials cannot control all the variables correlated to race. ...

"Concrete" evidence as to whether potential jurors can or cannot set aside their racial prejudices can be obtained only by questioning a juror. If the Canadian system permitted jurors to be questioned after trials as to how and why they made the decisions they did, there might be a prospect of obtaining empirical information on whether racially prejudiced jurors can set aside their prejudices. But s. 649 of the *Code* forbids this. So, imperfect as it is, the only way we have to test whether racially prejudiced jurors will be able to set aside their prejudices and judge impartially between the Crown and the accused, is by questioning prospective jurors on challenges for cause. In many cases, we can infer from the nature of widespread racial prejudice, that some jurors at least may be influenced by those prejudices in their deliberations. Whether or not this risk will materialize must be left to the triers of impartiality on the challenge for cause. To make it a condition of the right to challenge to cause is to require the defence to prove the impossible and to accept that some jurors may be partial.

(5) Failure to Read s. 638(1)(b) Purposively

The object of s. 638(1)(*b*) must be to prevent persons who may not be able to act impartially from sitting as jurors. This object cannot be achieved if the evidentiary threshold for challenges for cause is set too high.

As discussed above, to ask an accused person to present evidence that some jurors will be unable to set their prejudices aside is to ask the impossible. We may infer in many cases, however, from the nature of racial prejudice, that some prospective jurors, in a community where prejudice against people of the accused's race is widespread, may be both prejudiced and unable to identify completely or free themselves from the effects of those prejudices. It follows that the requirement of concrete evidence that widespread racism will cause partiality would not fulfill the purpose of s. 638(1)(*b*).

Similarly, an evidentiary threshold of extreme prejudice would fail to fulfill the object of s. 638(1)(*b*). Extreme prejudice is not the only sort of prejudice that may render a juror partial. Ordinary "garden-variety" prejudice has the capacity to sway a juror and may be just as difficult to detect and eradicate as hatred. A threshold met only in exceptional cases would catch only the grossest forms of racial prejudice. Less extreme situations may raise a real risk of partiality. Yet there would be no screening of jurors in those situations. The aim of the section — to permit partial jurors to be identified and eliminated — would be only partially achieved.

. . . . .

This raises the question of what evidentiary standard is appropriate on applications to challenge for cause based on racial prejudice ...

. . . . .

[I]t is not correct to assume that membership in an aboriginal or minority group always implies a realistic potential for partiality. The relevant community for purposes of the rule is the community from which the jury pool is drawn. That community may or may not harbour prejudices against aboriginals. It likely would not, for example, in a community where aboriginals are in a majority position. That said, absent evidence to the contrary, where widespread prejudice against people of the accused's race is demonstrated at a national or provincial level, it will often be reasonable to infer that such prejudice is replicated at the community level. ...

(6) Failure to Interpret s. 638(1)(b) in Accordance with the Charter

Parliament's laws should be interpreted in a way that conforms to the constitutional requirements of the *Charter*: see *Slaight Communications Inc. v. Davidson*, [1989] 1 S.C.R. 1038. ...

The s. 11(*d*) of the *Charter* guarantees to all persons charged in Canada the right to be presumed innocent "until proven guilty according to law in a fair and public hearing *by an independent and impartial tribunal*". [Emphasis in original.] A *Charter* right is meaningless, unless the accused is able to enforce it. This means that the accused must be permitted to challenge potential jurors where there is a realistic potential or possibility that some among the jury pool may harbour prejudices that deprive them of their impartiality. ...

The challenge for cause is an essential safeguard of the accused's s. 11(*d*) *Charter* right to a fair trial and an impartial jury. A representative jury pool and instructions from counsel and the trial judge are other safeguards. But the right to challenge for cause, in cases where it is shown that a realistic potential exists for partiality, remains an essential filament in the web of protections the law has woven to protect the constitutional right to have one's guilt or innocence determined by an impartial jury. If the *Charter* right is undercut by an interpretation of s. 638(1)(*b*) that sets too high a threshold for challenges for cause, it will be jeopardized.

The accused's right to be tried by an impartial jury under s. 11(*d*) of the *Charter* is a fair trial right. But it may also be seen as an anti-discrimination right. The application, intentional or unintentional, of racial stereotypes to the detriment of an accused person ranks among the most destructive forms of discrimination. The result of the discrimination may not be the loss of a benefit or a job or housing in the area of choice, but the loss of the accused's very liberty. The right must fall at the core of the guarantee in s. 15 of the *Charter* that "[e]very individual is equal before and under the law and has the right to the equal protection and equal benefit of the law without discrimination". ...

Although allowing challenges for cause in the face of widespread racial prejudice in the community will not eliminate the possibility of jury verdicts being affected by racial prejudice, it will have important benefits. Jurors who are honest or transparent about their racist views will be removed. All remaining jurors will be sensitized from the outset of the proceedings regarding the need to confront racial prejudice and will help ensure that it does not impact on the jury verdict. Finally, allowing such challenges will enhance the appearance of trial fairness in the eyes of the accused and other members of minority groups facing discrimination: see *Parks, supra.*

(7) The Slippery Slope Argument

The Crown concedes that practical concerns cannot negate the right to a fair trial. The Court of Appeal also emphasized this. Yet behind the conservative approach some courts have taken, one detects a fear that to permit challenges for cause on the ground of widespread prejudice in the community would be to render our trial process more complex and more costly, and would represent an invasion of the privacy interests of prospective jurors without a commensurate increase in fairness. Some have openly expressed the fear that if challenges for cause are permitted on grounds of racial prejudice, the Canadian approach will quickly evolve into the approach in the United States of routine and sometimes lengthy challenges for cause of every juror in every case with attendant cost, delay and invasion of juror privacy.

In my view, the rule enunciated by this Court in *Sherratt, supra,* suffices to maintain the right to a fair and impartial trial, without adopting the United States model or a variant on it. *Sherratt* starts from the presumption that members of the jury pool are capable of serving as impartial jurors. This means that there can be no automatic right to challenge for cause. In order to establish such a right, the accused must show that there is a realistic potential that some members of the jury pool may be biased in a way that may impact negatively on the accused. A realistic potential of racial prejudice can often be demonstrated by establishing widespread prejudice in the community against people of the accused's race. As long as this requirement is in place, the Canadian rule will be much more restrictive than the rule in the United States. ...

In the case at bar, the accused called witnesses and tendered studies to establish widespread prejudice in the community against aboriginal people. It may not be necessary to duplicate this investment in time and resources at the stage of establishing racial prejudice in the community in all subsequent cases. The law of evidence recognizes two ways in which facts can be established in the trial process. The first is by evidence. The second is by judicial notice. ...

Conclusion

Although they acknowledged the existence of widespread bias against aboriginals, both Esson C.J. and the British Columbia Court of Appeal held that the evidence did not demonstrate a reasonable possibility that prospective jurors would be partial. In my view, there was ample evidence that this widespread prejudice included elements that could have affected the impartiality of jurors. Racism against aboriginals includes stereotypes that relate to credibility, worthiness and criminal propensity. As the Canadian Bar Association stated in *Locking up Natives in Canada: A Report of the Committee of the Canadian Bar Association on Imprisonment and Release* (1988), at p. 5:

> Put at its baldest, there is an equation of being drunk, Indian and in prison. Like many stereotypes, this one has a dark underside. It reflects a view of native people as uncivilized and without a coherent social or moral order. The stereotype prevents us from seeing native people as equals.

There is evidence that this widespread racism has translated into systemic discrimination in the criminal justice system: see Royal Commission on Aboriginal Peoples, *Bridging the Cultural Divide: A Report on Aboriginal People and Criminal Justice in Canada*, at p. 33; Royal Commission on the Donald Marshall Jr., Prosecution, Volume 1: *Findings and Recommendations* (1989), at p. 162; *Report on the Cariboo-Chilcotin Justice Inquiry* (1993), at p. 11. Finally, as Esson C.J. noted, tensions between aboriginals and non-aboriginals have increased in recent years as a result of developments in such areas as land claims and fishing rights. These tensions increase the potential of racist jurors siding with the Crown as the perceived representative of the majority's interests.

In these circumstances, the trial judge should have allowed the accused to challenge prospective jurors for cause. Notwithstanding the accused's defence that another aboriginal person committed the robbery, juror prejudice could have affected the trial in many other ways. Consequently, there was a realistic potential that some of the jurors might not have been indifferent between the Crown and the accused. The potential for prejudice was increased by the failure of the trial judge to instruct the jury to set aside any racial prejudices that they might have against aboriginals. It cannot be said that the accused had the fair trial by an impartial jury to which he was entitled.

I would allow the appeal and direct a new trial.

Appeal allowed.

Is there evidence of widespread bias against Aboriginal peoples in your community? What sources would you look to in answering this question? If you found there was no widespread bias where you live, what would be your response to Justice McLachlin's opinion in *Williams*? If on the other hand you found evidence of widespread bias in your community, would you agree with the Court that such bias could raise the potential for partiality amongst jurors? Should an individual's partiality be questioned because of the community in which he or she lives?

On the other hand, if you agree that widespread bias could lead to partiality, do you agree with the further proposition that such bias can be "judicially cleansed"? Furthermore, if you agree with the Court's opinion, that widespread bias against Aboriginal peoples can lead to partiality in jurors and must therefore be judicially cleansed, should there be any issue about the impartiality of judges drawn from communities where there is widespread bias? As you have studied the cases and materials in this book, have you seen any evidence of widespread bias and partiality amongst members of the judiciary? If you do not see bias in the cases, what explains the impartiality of judges? If you do see widespread bias against Aboriginal peoples by judges in the courts, what can be done? Does the *Williams* case hold any answers if this is the case?

As part of this issue, many criticize the judiciary for failing to recognize and give effect to Aboriginal law and traditions in their decisions. These critics say Aboriginal peoples would not experience the same degree of problems in the criminal justice system if Aboriginal justice traditions had been followed. As you read the materials in the next section, ask yourself whether it is discriminatory to fail to recognize the pre-existing laws and traditions concerning justice in Aboriginal communities.

C. ABORIGINAL TRADITIONS AND JUSTICE

All Aboriginal societies relied upon a complex and sophisticated array of mechanisms to maintain order in their societies prior to the arrival of Europeans. For example, after analyzing Ojibwa, Cree and Iroquois methods of justice, Michael Coyle (in "Traditional Indian Justice in Ontario: A Role for the Present?" (1986) 24 Osgoode Hall L.J. 605) reported that "a number of methods were universally used by Ontario's Indian peoples to prevent anti-social behaviour". These included:

1. Regular teaching of community values by elders and other respected persons in the community;
2. Warning and counselling of particular offenders by leaders or by councils representing the community as a whole;
3. Use of ridicule or ostracism by the community at large to shame offenders and denounce particular wrongs;
4. Public banishment of individuals who persisted in threatening peace in the community;
5. Mediation and negotiations by elders, community members, or clan leaders, aimed at resolving particularly dangerous private disputes and reconciling offenders with the victims of misconduct;
6. Payment of compensation by offenders (or their clans) to their victims or victims' kin even in cases as serious as murder; and
7. In the case of wrongs that posed a grave threat to the community (such as sorcery, murder, and perhaps theft or adultery), physical coercion or execution of the offender, either directly by the community (after investigation and deliberation by a council) or by the victim of the wrong, who was recognized by the community as having the right to take such action.

The values underlying these mechanisms of social order were of vital significance to the proper functioning of Aboriginal communities. These laws and legal principles varied from nation to nation, and one must be careful not to universalize the rules of one group as being consistently applicable to others. However, the study of most First Nations reveals that they each had their own laws, adapted to their unique circumstances. Many of these same laws and systems can still be found in contemporary Aboriginal communities, and they are regarded by some as just as significant for the proper functioning of Aboriginal communities today. The existence of these traditions among the Anishinabe (Ojibway) of central Canada can be traced through the following three accounts taken from the 1840s, the 1890s and the 1990s — the report of Mayakaming, the case of *Machekequonabe*, and the *Jacko* case. Consider the possible role of traditional Anishinabek law in contemporary communities in light of the principles these cases reveal.

JARVIS PAPERS COLLECTION # 5 S-125, VOLUME B. 57

Jarvis Papers, Metro Toronto Reference Library,
Collection # S-125, Volume B57
(William Jarvis was the superintendent of Indian Affairs in the 1840s)

Account given by Mayamaking of the murder of an Idiot [*sic*] last winter by a band of Indians near French river during the winter of 1838:

He came among us at the very beginning of last winter having in most severe weather walked six days without either kindling a fire or eating any food.

During the most part of this winter he was quiet enough, but as the sugar season approached got noisy and restless. He went off to a lodge and there remained ten days, frequently eating a whole deer at two meals. After that he went to another lodge when a great change was visible in his person. His form seemed to have dilated and his face was the colour of black. At this lodge he first exhibited the most decided professions of madness and we all considered that he had become a Windigo (giant). He did not sleep but kept on walking round the lodge saying "I shall have a fine feast". Soon this caused plenty of fears in this lodge, both old and young. He then tore open the veins at his wrist with his teeth and drank his blood. The next night was the same, he went out from the lodge and without an axe broke off many saplings about 9 inches in circumference. [He] never slept but worked all that night, and in the morning brought in the poles he had broken off, and at two trips filled a large sugar camp. He continued to drink his blood. The Indians then all became alarmed and we all started off to join our friends. The snow was deep and soft and we sank deeply into it with our snow shoes, but he without shoes or stockings barely left the indent of his toes on the surface. He was stark naked tearing all his clothes given to him off as fast as they were put on. He still continued drinking blood and refused all food eating nothing but ice and snow. We then formed a council to determine how to act as we feared he would eat our children.

It was unanimously agreed that he must die. His most intimate friend undertook to shoot him not wishing any other hand to do it.

After his death we burned the body and all was consumed but the chest which we examined and found to contain an immense lump of ice which completely filled the cavity.

The lad who carried into effect the determination of the council has given himself to the father of him who is no more, to hunt for him, plant and fill all the duties of a son. We also have all made the old man presents and he is now perfectly satisfied.

This deed was not done under the influence of whiskey. There was none there, it was the deliberate act of this tribe in council.

Mayamaking's case illustrates the operation of Anishinabek law outside of the Canadian legal structure. It is an excellent example of protective and restorative justice in traditional Anishinabek communities. Yet it can be difficult to understand these laws without an appreciation of the cultural context from which they grow. Can you identify the legal process followed by the community in coming to its decision? Can you identify the legal principles followed by the Anishinabek in this case? Do you need more information to properly answer these questions? Often, the operation of Aboriginal law has been judged without a fuller appreciation of this background information. Imagine a common law judge from Ontario being called upon to civil trial in Quebec. What difficulties do you think they would encounter?

Eventually, Canadian courts were called upon to evaluate the operation of Aboriginal law in cases similar to Mayamaking's.

R. v. MACHEKEQUONABE

(1897), 28 O.R. 309 (Div. Ct.)

Ontario Divisional Court, **Armour C.J.**, **Falconbridge** and **Street JJ.**, 8 February 1897

A pagan Indian who, believing in an evil spirit in human shape called a Wendigo, shot and killed another Indian under the impression that he was the Wendigo was held properly convicted of manslaughter.

This was a case reserved under the *Criminal Code* 1892 Statement and amending Act 58 & 59 Vict. ch. 40 (D.) as to whether the prisoner was properly convicted of manslaughter.

The trial took place at Rat Portage on the 3rd of December, 1896, before **Rose**, J., and a jury.

Langford, for the Crown.

Wink, for the prisoner.

It appeared from the evidence that the prisoner was a member of a tribe of pagan Indians who believed in the existence of an evil spirit clothed in human flesh, or in human form called a Wendigo which would eat a human being.

That it was reported that a Wendigo had been seen and it was supposed was in the neighborhood of their camp desiring to do them harm.

That among other precautions to protect themselves, guards and sentries, tho prisoner being one, were placed out in pairs armed with firearms (the prisoner having a rifle); that the prisoner saw what appeared to be a tall human being running in the distance, which he supposed was the Wendigo; that he and another Indian gave chase, and after challenging three times and receiving no answer fired and shot the object, when it was discovered to be his own foster father, who died soon afterward.

The jury found affirmative answers to the following questions:

> Are you satisfied the prisoner did kill the Indian?
>
> Did the prisoner believe the object he shot at to be a Wendigo or spirit?
>
> Did he believe the spirit to be embodied in human flesh ?
>
> Was it the prisoner's belief that the Wendigo could be, killed by a bullet shot from a rifle?
>
> Was the prisoner sane apart from the delusion or belief in the existence of a Wendigo?

The learned trial Judge then proceeded with his charged as follows: — "Assuming these facts to be found by you, I think I must direct you as a matter of law that there is no justification here for the killing; and culpable homicide without justification is manslaughter, so that unless you can suggest to yourselves something stated in the evidence to warrant a different conclusion, I think it will be your duty to return a verdict of manslaughter. You may confer among yourselves if you please, and if you take that view, I will reserve a case for consideration by the Court of Appeal as to whether he was properly convicted upon this evidence."

The jury found the prisoner guilty of manslaughter recommending him to mercy, and the learned Judge reserved a case for consideration whether upon the findings of the jury in answer to the questions he had submitted and upon his direction to them and upon the evidence the prisoner was properly found guilty of manslaughter.

The case was argued on February 8th, 1897, before a Divisional Court composed of **Armour, C.J.**, and **Falconbridge**, and **Street, JJ.**

J.K. Kerr, Q.C., for the prisoner. The evidence shews the Indian tribe were pagans, and believed in an evil spirit clothed in human form which they called a Wendigo, and which attacked, killed and ate human beings. The man that was shot was thought to be a Wendigo, a spirit as distinguished from a human being. It is true there was a mistake, but there was no intention even to harm a human being much less to kill. The evidence shews the mistake was not unreasonable. At common law the following of a religious belief would be an excuse. The trial Judge wrongly directed the jury to find the prisoner guilty. There should be a new trial at least. I refer to *Levet's Case*, 1 Hale 474; 1 Bishop on Criminal Law, 7th ed., sec. 305 and note; *Territory v. Fish*, cited in note p.185, is almost a parallel case; *Plummer v. The State*, 4 Texas App. 310; *Regina v. Rose*, 15 Cox C.C. 540; *Regina v. Wagstaffe*, 10 Cox C.C. 530; *State v. Nash*, 88 N. Car. 618; *Regina v. Mawgridge*, Kelyng's C.C. 167 [119].

John Cartwright, Q.C., Deputy Attorney-General was not called on.

The judgement of the Court was delivered by

Armour C.J.: — Upon the case reserved if there was evidence upon which the jury could find the prisoner guilty of manslaughter it is not open to us to reverse that finding, and the question we have to decide is whether there was such evidence.

We think there was, and therefore do not see how we can say that the prisoner was not properly convicted of manslaughter.

Whose standards should have the court applied in determining the reasonableness of *Machekequonabe's* actions? Should *Machekequonabe's* belief in Wendigos have been a justifiable defence to manslaughter? Consider what you might do if, in 1897, you were living as an Anishinabe person in a small, isolated community, and you believed a serial murderer, as Wendigo, was attacking you? Do you think your reactions would be influenced by the fact that you had a pre-existing system of custom and conduct that for centuries had enabled you to deal with such issues?

A Canadian court recently examined a defence against a charge of manslaughter in relation to another Anishinabek belief, concerning a Bearwalker. In reading the following decision, ask yourself whether the judge's decision was appropriate in light of all the circumstances?

R. v. JACKO

[1998] 1 C.N.L.R. 164 (Ont. Gen. Div.)

Trainor J.: — ... Two years have elapsed since this death. ... This 19 year old Accused, Leon Gavin Jacko, is charged that on the 30 June, 1995, at the First Nation of Sheguiandah, he unlawfully killed Ronald Wilfred Thompson and did thereby commit manslaughter.

The Accused had been charged with murder but the Crown elected to proceed on a manslaughter indictment...

THE EVIDENCE

The Accused and Ronald Thompson (Tab), the victim, were friends. They both resided at the First Nation of Sheguiandah, on Manitoulin Island. The Victim was 45 years old at the time. They were drinking heavily on the 30 June, 1995. The Victim had a lifelong history as a heavy binge drinker. The Accused had not been a drinker until a short time before this tragic day. The two had been consuming alcohol for a number of days prior. On the 30th they received their welfare checks and headed for the closest liquor store. Tab had the shakes so he asked his friend and long time drinking companion, Chris Aguonie, to buy two large bottles of wine for him. Leon purchased a bottle of Bacardi rum and a bottle of Bailey's Irish Cream. Caroline Aguonie had driven the three men to get their welfare checks and then to Little Current to the liquor store. ...

[E]vidence showing extreme levels of alcohol ingested by both men and its impact on them is vividly portrayed in a brief description by Caroline Aguonie. She said that at 4:20 p.m. she drove the two men to Leon's residence. He resided in his father, Julien Aguonie's home. A relative, Orville Aguonie, and his wife also lived in the same residence. They were away at the time. Caroline said that when they arrived at the east door of the residence and she stopped the vehicle to let them out they did not even know they had reached their destination. She yelled at the Victim and offered to help him out of the car. He got mad, got out of the car and immediately fell to the ground. Earlier when they got into the car they both fell, with Tab landing on top of the Accused. Leon got out of the car at his home, staggered around and then sat beside Tab on the ground. Both men found support from a wooden pallet located near the entrance. Their liquor and wine bottles were placed beside them on the pallet. As Caroline drove away she heard Leon say "oh f..., I don't have any keys". The Forensic Centre analysis revealed that at 7:30 p.m. that day the accused had a reading of about 200 milligrams of alcohol in 100 millilitres of his blood. The Victim's reading was in excess of 400 milligrams. The evidence is that as drunk as they were the two were not arguing or fighting and seemed to be getting along fine. Tab was not seen alive after Caroline left at 4:30 p.m., except by Leon. It is clear that their friendly relationship deteriorated dramatically in the next few hours.

At 7:30 p.m. Ronald Roy was at his mother's residence for dinner and cards. She resides at the foot of Indian Mountain Rd. The Julien Aguonie residence is at the top of the hill. Roy was outside the home when he heard a loud bellowing noise, like bears fighting, coming from the top of the mountain. He said he had never heard a sound like that coming from a human being. He had in the past heard the sound from bears fighting. He then heard voices cursing and yelling. He thought one of the voices was Tab's.

He said that about 20 minutes later Leon was in the driveway. He was badly cut to the left outer wrist. He was hysterical, screaming words to the effect "I am a warrior — I got the Bearwalker." He repeated this over and over with his arms raised in a V. as in victory salute. He was breathing heavily.

Roy said that Tab was known by some people in the community of Sheguiandah 1st Nation as the Bearwalker, a person who practices witchcraft or black magic.

Winifred Trudeau, Roy's mother, testified that Leon came to the door about 8 p.m. wanting a light for a cigarette. He said he cut his wrist by "killing a f... Bearwalker." He was emotional at times, screaming about "killing the Bearwalker," at other times he cried. He said he "won the victory, the Bearwalker won't bother us anymore." Winifred Trudeau drove Leon to the Chris Aguonie home. On the way he talked about "the militia coming but he had a 25 magnum." When he said this he tapped his right chest. She described Leon as small in stature and frail.

Caroline Aguonie and her sister Brenda Whiteduck decided to investigate the whereabouts of Tab. They went to Leon's where they proceeded to the trailer or more properly the camper located behind and to the north of the residence, where she had dropped Leon and Tab off that afternoon.

Near the camper they discovered the Victim's body laying on the ground, face down. He was dead ...

Several witnesses described Tab. Caroline said she was fond of him even though he had two personalities. She said that when he was drinking he said he used bad medicine. She saw him strangle a cat and cut off its ears to use for bad medicine. She testified that he killed her father's dog and told her he could hurt others. She said he had a reputation as a Bear-walker. She said she was not afraid of him but did not trust him. She was careful to keep her hair out of his reach as she knew if he got a lock of her hair he could bring bad medicine to her. She said that when he was drinking he would go from happy to angry out of the blue and for no reason. She said he had a very dark side. She had seen him become violent on a number of occasions. He had not been violent when she saw the two men together on June 30.

Chris Aguonie was Tab's uncle. Leon is his nephew. He was a life long drinking buddy of the Victim. ... He said Tab and he drank together for 20 years. Tab had taken Leon under his wing and for a week prior to his death they drank together. The witness described Tab as a powerful man when drunk and mad. When drinking it was usual for him to become quite violent. He said that 2 months prior to his death Tab told the witness "I don't know what is wrong but I just feel like killing somebody — something big is coming down."

The witness said Tab told him he had learned bad medicine from an old lady up north. He said he could hurt people and make them suffer. The witness said Tab told him about hurting others. Chris said at times Tab was obsessed with bad medicine. The witness came to fear Tab. He said that when sober Tab was a different person. ...

Allison Manitawabi ... described the Accused as shy and quiet. She said he was a native traditionalist who enjoyed the outdoors, crafts and bead-work.

Orville Aguonie ... said Leon was physically very weak. He was a person interested in native spirituality and had been so interested since his early teens. This witness has known Tab for years. Tab was often drunk and when drunk bragged about his spiritual powers as a Bearwalker. He would say he knew a lot of medicine and could hurt people. When sober he was pleasant. When drunk he fought. He had no fear when he was drinking. He talked about his fights when he was intoxicated. The witness had not seen Tab fight for years. ...

THE DEFENCE EVIDENCE

The defence called Julien Aguonie, the father of the accused. The Accused, the Victim and a majority of the witnesses called in this trial were aboriginal people of the Ojibwe culture and were members of the Sheguiandah 1st Nation. The Accused and his father live in the traditional way of native people and have done so for a number of years prior to June 30th. Julien said Leon came to live with him when he was 12 years old. The witness had stopped drinking when his wife died in 1981. He returned to the traditions of native spiritualism, learning from the elders and studies. During the years he was reunited with Leon he taught him to live in the traditional way. The traditional way is to live in harmony with nature by gathering herbs and creating medicines: gathering food from the land: hunting and fishing and joining in ceremonial traditions such as elders gatherings, pipe ceremonies, sweat lodges and vision quests.

The witness explained that in a pipe ceremony a connection is made with the Creator and with nature. From the directions of the compass, knowledge and wisdom come from the east: a new life from the south: a cleansing from the west and healing and purifying from the north. In a sweat lodge cleansing, healing and guidance take place. The spirits enter through the fire and rocks. In a vision quest the spirit world is contacted and you refocus a troubled life. Food and water is excluded for 4 days. You travel to a secluded place in the forest, after participating in a sweat lodge. Your spirit travels and meets other spirits in the spirit world. You are given directions for your life.

Mr. Aguonie described a positive and negative aspect to the traditional way. The creator makes only good medicine but people, instead of healing others with medicine, cross over and misuse powers by making bad medicine. That is, they use spiritual power to cause harm, get revenge, satisfy greed and use power to harm others. He said Leon was a good student because he is very humble and eager to learn. Leon became a hunter, gathered herbs and made medicine.

The witness explained that a Bearwalker is a belief, known to him since he was a child, when his mother smudged the house to protect it. A Bearwalker is a person who causes harm to others by the use of bad medicine. The Bearwalker can transform himself to animal forms such as a bear. This is known as "shape shifting." The Bearwalker travels as a ball of fire. The Bearwalker strikes fear into people that may result in sickness or death if not treated by good medicine. This witness testified that he has treated 10 people in the past 4 years. A secret herb is placed in hot coals. The victim of the Bearwalker is covered with a white sheet. The hair of the Bearwalker, symbolizing power, comes through the sheet and is picked up on a Kleenex, wiped across the sheet. The hair tells the healer and victim that the Bearwalker has lost its power and evil influence. The fear and terror is removed. The Bearwalker, according to tradition and belief, has more than normal physical strength when he is transformed into a bear.

Julien told his son Leon about the Bearwalker. He gave him medicine to protect him, telling him to carry it with him. ...

This witness has known the Victim all of his life. He testified that Tab's reputation, in the small community of Sheguiandah, is that he is passive when sober but aggressive when drunk. Tab, he said, was drunk a lot of the time. He would brag about his fights and his power as a Bearwalker. He told the witness he could hurt him or his family. He said, "if I can't get the parents because they are too strong I cause them to suffer by getting their children." The witness said he believed Tab had this power. He was not afraid because he had good medicine but he was wary and warned Leon. He told him about Tab's drinking and his evil power.

THE ISSUES

The issues in this trial are narrowly focused. It is not contended nor argued that the Victim's death was caused by someone other than this Accused. The sole issue is, whether the death of Ronald Thompson was caused by the unlawful act of Leon Jacko, beyond a reasonable doubt. If the Accused acted in self-defence then he did not commit an unlawful act in killing the Victim. The narrow issue is whether the Accused acted in self defence as that term is defined in s. 34(2) of the *Criminal Code*.

Everyone who is unlawfully assaulted and who causes death or grievous bodily harm in repelling the assault is justified if:

(a) he causes it under reasonable apprehension of death or grievous bodily harm from the violence with which the assault was originally made or with which the assailant pursues his purposes; and

(b) he believes, on reasonable grounds that he cannot otherwise preserve himself from death or grievous bodily harm

The Crown must prove, beyond a reasonable doubt, that one of the essential elements of the section is missing and therefore the Accused is not entitled to rely on the section.

The essential elements are:

1. Has the Crown established that the Accused was not unlawfully assaulted? If the answer is no then,

2. Has the Crown established that the Accused was not under a reasonable apprehension of death or grievous bodily harm from the violence with which the assault was originally made or with which the assailant pursued his purposes? If the answer is no, then,

3. Has the Crown established that the Accused did not believe, on reasonable grounds, that he could not otherwise preserve himself from death or grievous bodily harm? If the answer to any of the questions is yes, beyond a reasonable doubt, then the Accused is not entitled to rely on Section 34(2).

THE LAW

... The uncontradicted evidence, in my view, is that the Accused was aware of the Victim's propensity for violence and his powers and reputation as a Bearwalker; *R. v. Scopelliti* (1981), 63 C.C.C. (2d). 481, *R. v. Pintar* (1996), 110 C.C.C. (3d) 402, *R. v. Cameron* (1995), 96 C.C.C. (3d) 346. The reasonableness of the Accused's belief or apprehension must be that of a sober man: *Reilley v. Q.* (1984) 15 C.C.C. (3d) 1...

R. v. Lavallee, [1990] 1 S.C.R. 852 was a self-defence case founded on battered wife syndrome. Wilson J. said the question is "whether, given the history, circumstances and perceptions of the appellant, her belief that she could not preserve herself from being killed by [her common-law spouse] that night except by killing him first was reasonable."

CONCLUSION

The only living eyewitness to this case is the Accused. The circumstantial evidence is capable of any number of interpretations and inferences. The difficulty is to draw logical inferences of fact and not conclusions based on speculation.

It has been established beyond a reasonable doubt that this Accused struck at least two blows to the Victim's head with a walrus bone that caused extensive damage to the left side of the skull behind the left ear. Identity is not an issue.

The only direct evidence as to how the altercation unfolded comes from the utterances made by the Accused. His utterances and any reconstruction of the events must be viewed in light of his culture, beliefs and native spirituality.

There is no evidence that would lead me to conclude that the Crown has come close to establishing that his Accused was the instigator of the fight that took place in or beside the camper. It is clear that the Accused was unlawfully assaulted by the Victim. I rely on the utterances and statements to that effect, made by the Accused to a number of witnesses, including the police. In addition, the evidence of the victim's propensity to fight when drunk, coupled with the evidence that the Accused is normally shy and mild mannered, small in stature, not a strong person compared to the Victim and the fact that their is no evidence that the Accused has a violent disposition, even when he is drinking is persuasive.

The fact that the Victim was the aggressor and that he is a powerful man compared to the Accused is significant. It sets the stage in examining the remaining questions in issue.

The difficult issues in this case relate to the reasonableness of the Accused's apprehension of death or grievous bodily harm and the reasonableness of his belief that he could not otherwise preserve himself from death or grievous bodily harm, except by striking out with the walrus bone.

The first of the utterances made by the Accused at the Trudeau home were preceded 20 minutes earlier by a bellowing noise like bears fighting, a sound Ronald Roy had never heard from a human. They were followed by human voices cursing and yelling. One of the voices sounded like Tab's, according to Roy. The utterances made to Roy and other native witnesses, included statements that "I am a warrior." "I got the Bearwalker." "I won the victory." "I cut my wrist by killing a Bearwalker — the bearwalker won't bother us anymore." The native witnesses described the Accused as crying, dazed, looking like a cornered animal, emotional, and screaming as he uttered the words.

Witnesses said his clothes were dirty, his face bloody, he was frail looking, he was talkative, nervous, laughing at times.

His utterances to the aboriginal witnesses must be understood in the context that he was talking to his own people.

Utterances to Constables Goodwin and Rosser were summarized by Constable Goodwin in these words, "his constant theme was Tab went crazy — I had to defend myself — it was an accident." The Accused was now talking to police officers.

His description of himself as a warrior, who killed the Bearwalker, must be understood, not as an act of aggression but as an act of self defence, an act to protect others from an evil spirit.

The Accused referred to Tab's death as an accident. It is clear to me the word accident, repeated many times, is not used in a narrow legal sense but in the sense that he did not mean to kill.

The Accused described the Victim as getting crazy when he drinks wine. The statement reflects his knowledge of the propensity of the Victim for violence, knowledge gained in part from his father. In other utterances he said words to the effect that Tab went crazy. There is no description in the evidence as to how Tab went crazy and what specific action he took. There is, however, evidence of Tab's strength compared to the accused and his reputation for violence. In addition, the Accused knew of his reputation and power as a Bearwalker, including his ability to transform himself into a bear, adding to his power and strength. That reputation and spiritual belief is not to be looked at or judged by the standards of non-native society. I accept the evidence about native spirituality as being sincerely held beliefs by which I must judge the reasonableness of the Accused's apprehension and belief as to the danger that he was facing when the Victim attacked the Accused.

There is evidence, from which it is not unreasonable to infer, that the Victim attacked the Accused with the jagged end of a wine bottle, after breaking a full bottle to create a dangerous weapon.

... It is not unreasonable to infer from the physical evidence and the utterances that Tab attacked Leon with the bottle. I do not mean to suggest that the evidence leads solely to this conclusion. However, it is as persuasive as any other reconstruction of the facts. The fact that I cannot say with conviction, based on the evidence, exactly how Tab "went crazy," tends to show that the Crown has not made its case. The obligation on the Crown is to prove, beyond a reasonable doubt, that the Accused did not have a reasonable apprehension of death or grievous bodily harm or that he did not believe on reasonable grounds that he could not otherwise escape. ...

I do not say that the evidence points solely to the Accused being the unsuspecting victim of a Bearwalker but I do say the evidence in this case is not so clear and convincing that the Crown has satisfied me beyond a reasonable doubt that the Accused did not strike the fatal blow or blows in self defence under s. 34(2) of the *Code*.

I find the Accused not guilty.

Did the judge apply the appropriate standards in judging Tab's actions? Who might be harmed and who might benefit as a result of these standards? Are there dangers that could arise in employing the court's standards?

The continued existence of Aboriginal traditions of justice, and the unremitting individual and systemic discrimination that Aboriginal people face, has led to many proposals for the reform of the criminal justice system. Proposals for such reform are often contrasted with calls for Aboriginal people to abandon the system altogether and seek justice within their own separate systems. Although there is great attraction to both arguments, in practice there can be a relationship between the two strategies. People often attempt to reform the existing system *and* set up separate processes to deal with conflict in more culturally appropriate ways. In such efforts there may be the thought that experience gained in one system can assist in the development of another one. Others, working on both models, may start from the assumption that simultaneous cultural participation and intercultural relationships create the need to recognize constructions of *both* Aboriginal similarity and difference. The post-colonial writer Edward Said, in his book *Culture and Imperialism* (New York: Vintage Books, 1993) at 336, observed:

> [n]o one today is purely *one* thing. Labels like Indian, or woman, or Muslim or American are not more than starting points, which if followed into actual experience for only a moment are quickly left behind. Imperialism consolidated the mixture of cultures and identities on a global scale. But [its] worst and most paradoxical gift was to allow people to believe they were only, mainly exclusively, White, or Black, Western or Oriental. Just as human beings make their own history, they also make their cultures and ethnic identities. No one can deny the persisting continuities of long traditions, sustained habitations, national languages and cultural geographies, but, there seems to be no reason except fear and prejudice to keep insisting on their separation and distinctiveness, as if that was all human life was about.

Intercultural forces of education, urbanization, politics, economic participation and inter-marriage each have a significant influence in drawing Aboriginal peoples into closer relationship with Canadian society. Many people consider such developments as necessitating work on reforming the existing system, as well as working on separate processes of conflict accountability and resolution. Mary Ellen Turpel wrote "that we have spent several years in a distracting debate over whether justice reform involves separate justice systems or reforming the mainstream system. This is a false dichotomy and a fruitless distinction because it is not an either/or choice. The impetus for change can better be described as getting away from the colonialism and domination of the Criminal Justice system" (*Continuing Poundmaker's and Riel's Quest*, R. Gosse, J.Y. Henderson & R. Carter eds. (Saskatoon: Purich Publishing, 1994) at 208). The commentary and cases in this section illustrate the issues and struggles involved in the process of reforming the Canadian criminal justice system. By focusing on one type of innovation in this effort, elders' panels and sentencing circles, a greater appreciation of the strengths and weaknesses of this approach can be formulated. The *Naqitarvik, Moses* and *Gladue* cases are reproduced in the following pages to assist in this evaluation.

D. REFORMING THE CRIMINAL JUSTICE SYSTEM

THE ROYAL COMMISSION ON ABORIGINAL PEOPLE, BRIDGING THE CULTURAL DIVIDE: A REPORT ON ABORIGINAL PEOPLE AND CRIMINAL JUSTICE IN CANADA

(Ottawa: Ministry of Supply and Services, 1996) at 109, 110, 116
(references omitted)

... Much progress has been made in opening up the sentencing of Aboriginal people to greater Aboriginal input. This advance has come about through the initiative of Aboriginal communities and the support of judges concerned about the problems the justice system causes for Aboriginal people. The development of these initiatives sprang originally from the Yukon and Northwest Territories. ...

Generally speaking these initiatives have come in two forms — elders panels and sentencing circles. In the case of elders panels, elders or clan leaders sit with the judges and provide advice about the appropriate sentence in a case. This advice is given in open court or in private. In a sentencing circle, individuals are invited to sit in a circle with the accused and discuss together what sentence should be imposed. In both cases, the ultimate decision about the sentence rests with the judge.

Regardless of the precise mechanism established, the purpose behind the process is the same — to give the court meaningful input from the people who are most directly affected by his or her conduct. The experience with these programs is that the offender responds more deeply to concerns and suggestions expressed by members of the community that by a judge who is removed in all ways from the offenders world.

The notion of obtaining community input to the sentencing process has spread from the far North to other areas as well. Similar initiatives are in place in Ontario, British Columbia, Quebec, Manitoba and Saskatchewan. ...

Sentencing circles and elders panels should not be seen as an end in themselves. Rather ... they are perhaps best seen as stages in an evolutionary process. The idea of community circles in the Yukon has recently been expanded, so that now they act as an alternative to courts. These initiatives must be allowed to grow and develop on their on. They are helpful not only continuing reform of the existing system, but as useful models in the development of distinct Aboriginal justice systems.

R. v. NAQITARVIK

(1986), 26 C.C.C. (3d) 193 (N.W.T.C.A.);
leave to appeal to S.C.C. refused May 20, 1986

Laycraft C.J.N.W.T.: — In this case the Crown appeals a sentence of 90 days imprisonment to be served intermittently, followed by two years probation for a major sexual assault on a 14 year old girl at Arctic Bay, N.W.T. His Honour Judge Bourassa of the Territorial Court stated the ground for this disposition as being the existence at Arctic Bay of a system of traditional Inumarit Committee counselling which is a suitable alternative to the longer sentence of imprisonment which would ordinarily be imposed.

I have had the opportunity to consider the Reasons for Judgment of my brother Belzil. I agree with his summary of the facts of this offence but I regret that I am unable to concur in the conclusion which he has reached. I would allow the Crown's appeal and substantially increase the sentence.

Neither Belzil, J.A. nor Judge Bourassa has treated this as a case, such as *R. v. Fireman* (1971) 4 C.C.C. (2d) 82, where a very unsophisticated person must be sentenced for an offence against the laws of a more complex society which has intruded upon his culture. In this view, they are, in my respectful opinion, correct. I shall review the personal attributes of the respondent later in these reasons, but he has had considerable contact with, and experience of, the way of life of Canadians outside his own remote community.

There is no doubt that for the last quarter century, much of northern Canada, particularly its more remote region, has been a land in transition. The traditional institutions and the old cultures of its people are being replaced or modified, in collision with influences from the south. But while the community of Arctic Bay is remote in distance from other parts of Canada, being situated on the northern coast of Baffin Island, it has many of the facilities of other towns and cities in other parts of Canada. Its people have been exposed for some time to the same laws and customs as other Canadians.

The witnesses in this case do not describe a culture markedly different than that in the rest of Canada. Rather the incident itself arose as the victim and her sister played music on a modern player for which there was an electric cord. The complaint of sexual assault was conveyed to the police by telephone and the victim was taken to a modern nursing station for examination and treatment. Both victim and accused have at least grade school education. A large and modern mine is in the vicinity and several of the witnesses, including the accused, had worked there at some time.

My brother Belzil has described in his reasons the traditional Inumarit Committee. It is a traditional governing body of the Inuit, consisting of the experienced elders of the community. Among its functions is the counselling of offenders. If required, that counselling was traditionally relentless and continuous until effective. The offender reformed or he was excluded from community life. In a harsh and hostile environment where the offender could no longer be part of community cooperation in hunting and other food gathering, that exclusion could have fatal consequences.

The present Inumarit Committee in Arctic Bay is not a direct successor to the traditional governing body described by the witnesses. The witness Koonoo Ipkirk, the chairperson of the Committee, has lived in Arctic Bay since childhood. She did not say when the traditional Committee last existed but the present body was started in 1975. In that year 6 members were elected by the community. Since that time "anybody who wants to become a member becomes one". The ages of the members range "from 50 and up", and "a member should have more experience than other people".

Witnesses who spoke of relentless counselling by a committee of Inumarit standing in a circle around the offender were describing a tradition rather than the present situation in Arctic Bay. Ms. Ipkirk said that the present membership of the Committee is 6 and that an individual member was assigned to counsel the respondent. That counselling is done much as it would be done in any other Canadian community. Indeed, one member of the Committee, who gave evidence, brings to his assignments a sophisticated background in counselling; he was trained as a counsellor while serving with the Canadian Armed Forces in the United Kingdom and gained experience counselling under-privileged children in Liverpool, England.

The modern reincarnation in Arctic Bay of the traditional Inumarit Committee resembles the usual community counselling service rather than the traditional governing and counselling body of earlier times. I am unable to see, given its recent origin, the community which it serves, its methods of operation, and the absence of the traditional ultimate sanction on the offender, that it is a remanent of ancient culture. Its counselling service, admirable as it undoubtedly is, cannot, in my opinion, replace the sentence of imprisonment which is required in virtually all cases of major sexual assault.

In *R. v. Curley, Nagmalik & Issagaetok*, [1984] N.W.T.R. 281, McGillivray, C.J. said:

> We wish at this point to say something of cultural circumstances. There are people who suggest that members of an isolated community should be judged in and by that community and by the standards of that community. The judge did not accede to any such suggestion. There is one criminal law of Canada. What he said was that the accused were ignorant of that law and that ignorance is relevant to sentencing as a mitigating factor, just as deliberate flouting of the law is relevant as an aggravating factor. He recognized, and we recognize, that knowledge of the law is an evolving factor. This case will assist the community to better understand the law. A second factor in cultural consideration is that to take these accused out of their own community and imprison them in a totally foreign environment adds a harshness to a jail sentence that must be recognized.

In this case the accused committed a most serious offence. He attacked a 14 year old girl, tied her hands behind her back and forced her to have sexual intercourse with him despite her shouted objections, her struggles, and her attempts to bite him as she attempted to defend herself. The respondent was her cousin and the trial judge found as fact that they had had consensual sexual intercourse previously.

The respondent had a criminal record, though it is unrelated to this offence. In March 1982 he was sentenced to 6 months imprisonment and 2 years probation for 6 offences of breaking and entering. He actually served some five months of this sentence, presumably in the Territorial correctional facility away from Arctic Bay. In June 1984 he received a suspended sentence and probation for one year for possession of a narcotic. The present offence occurred on July 20, 1984 while he was on probation for the narcotics conviction.

There are a number of points to be made in mitigation of sentence. The respondent ceased the sexual assault when the victim's sister came into the room. He untied the girl's hands at her request. He tried to apologize to her within a few minutes and some time later made a full apology to her in public. There is considerable evidence that he is genuinely remorseful and the learned trial judge so found. Moreover, in the six month interval before the imposition of the sentence now appealed, he had reacted to counselling in a very positive manner.

The respondent has a common law wife and a child born in August 1984. He "dropped out" of school in 1979 after completing Grade 7. He has also attended a Housing Maintenance Course given at Frobisher Bay. He has worked at a nearby mine and has also been employed as a roofer by housing contractors in the area. He is described as a reliable employee.

There is little in the material before us to show the effect on the victim. She gave evidence briefly on the sentencing hearing when the respondent denied she had shouted during the attack and her evidence was accepted by Judge Bourassa. However, both counsel chose not to examine on the traumatic effect of the incident and no medical evidence was called. In *R. v. Sandercock* (1985) 62 A.R. 382 at 386, Kerans, J.A. said on this aspect of sexual assault:

> The other aspect which creates a major sexual assault is the effect on the victim. Notwithstanding statements in some authorities to the contrary, the tradition is to assume, in the case of a rape for example, that the victim has suffered notable psychological or emotional harm aside entirely from any physical injury. Of course, once this assumption is brought into question, the Crown must prove it. Nevertheless, harm generally is inferred from the very nature of the assault. This harm includes not just the haunting fear of another attack, the painful struggle with a feeling that somehow the victim is to blame, and the sense of violation or outrage, but also a lingering sense of powerlessness. What we mean by this last is that, while we all are aware in an intellectual way about the fragility of normal existence, to experience a sudden and real threat to one's well-being, a threat so intense that one must beg to be spared, tends to destroy that sense of personal security which modern society strives to offer and humanity so obviously wants. It matters little in this respect whether that threat comes from a robber, a rapist, or any swaggering bully.

I follow *Sandercock* in using a sentence of imprisonment for 3 years as a starting point in cases of major sexual assault. No doubt some of the aggravating and mitigating factors mentioned in that case may be somewhat modified when applied to northern Canada. In particular one must have careful regard to the degree of sophistication of both the offender and the victim. Nevertheless, *Sandercock* offers a general guideline of the starting point and of the various factors involved in upward or downward revision of that starting point in the light of aggravating or mitigating factors.

It is unfortunate that there has now been a considerable lapse of time since the offence was committed. The respondent has served the intermittent sentence of imprisonment imposed on him. Nevertheless on a consideration of all of the factors in this case, I consider the sentence to be wholly inadequate, though the mitigating factors justify a considerable reduction from the starting point. I would substitute for the sentence imposed in Territorial Court, a sentence of imprisonment for eighteen months.

Haddad J.A.: — I concur.

Belzil J.A.: — This appeal raises important considerations in the imposition of sentence in a remote and isolated Inuit community for a serious offence committed there by a member of that community. ...

I turn to an examination of the evidence before the learned sentencing judge, with the caution that this evidence comes to the transcript through untrained interpreters.

The trial judge first heard the testimony of Rebecca Williams. A native of Arctic Bay, social worker and probation officer of the community, she prepared a pre-sentence report recommending against incarceration outside of the community. She testified that before preparing the report she had consulted with the Social Services Committee of Arctic Bay and also with the Inumarit and she explained to the court the status of these groups in the community...

Miss Williams then described the Inumarit:

Q. Who are the members of the Inumarit?

A. The Inumarit people are the age from fifty and up, and they form themselves in order to rectify some of the problems in the community that they can see or to be and assistance to anybody who is in need.

Q. Do you know how members of the Inumarit are chosen?

A. I am not really sure on that, but I can — I think it would be fair to say that you have to be a mature person. You have to have some experience in life in dealing with problems or anything, maybe hunting, sewing, anything that is traditional."

She was asked in cross-examination whether rape was always considered an offence with her people and how it was traditionally punished, and she said:

Q. ... Since my friend asked you questions about the historical facts of your people, can you tell me whether or not the sexual assault of a young lady while tying her up and then having forced sex with her was an accepted part of the ways of your people?

A. No, it is not accepted behavior.

Q. It never has been?

A. Not as far as I know.

Q. People who did that were punished by your people historically always?

A. The punishment would be getting the people for confrontation and counselling after that. ...

I then turn to the reasons expressed by Judge Bourassa imposing the light sentence which he did:

Now, I have to say a few words about the community of Arctic Bay. I have been coming to Baffin Island for three years now, and I think I can say quite fairly that there is something here in Arctic Bay that isn't found in very many other communities. I don't know exactly what it is, I don't know how it works. I only had a small description this afternoon from the testimony of the Inumarit members. But what is important to the court is that whatever control mechanism there is in this community, it has kept it crime free. There are few other communities like Arctic Bay, but not many. Igloolik and Lake Harbour for example are two. In each of those communities, and Arctic Bay, it seems as though there are enough people that care, and are involved in such a way that people don't commit crimes. If all of the communities in the Northwest Territories were like Arctic Bay and Igloolik, we wouldn't need any jails.

It is obvious to me that what has been said in evidence today that the community is willing to act, the Inumarit is willing to act and social services are willing to act in this case is not an empty promise. It is true. It is a fact. It is proven in the past by the very absence of crime or disturbance. This special part of Arctic Bay is something that I would be very sad to see in any way taken away or diminished. The very things that the Inumarit are trying to do is what the court is trying to do: rehabilitating an offender, reconciling the offender, the victim and the community so that there is unity in the community and a program of education. Can any of us really say that jails do that? For the person that responds, the Inumarit, the Social Services Committee and the whole community together can obviously heal; They can unite; They can reconcile, and they can reform. ...

I am impressed with the Inumarit. They promise and appear in the past to have delivered more than what jails can do. I accept what they say without reservation because as I say for the last three years that I have been here we hardly ever come to Arctic Bay, because there is simply no trouble in this community. ...

There is precedent for the imposition of a comparatively lesser sentence for serious offences in isolated communities of the North under the recognition of a very broad discretion by the trial judge in fixing sentence when particular local conditions warrant it. ...

The trial judge properly took into account the special circumstances disclosed in evidence of a small isolated group striving to preserve its cultural heritage by maintaining its cultural unity, not for the purpose of blocking the imposition of criminal law but by gradually introducing it by bridging the gap between traditional law and the new law. The crime free record of the community obviously satisfied the trial judge that this community was much more successful in this than had generally been the unfortunate case in too many communities of the far North.

I am unable to detect any error in principle in the reasons of the sentencing judge. The preservation of cultural heritage is given new recognition by the Charter and it was proper to take it into account. The trial judge weighed this and all other factors and imposed a sentence which in my view was fit in the circumstances disclosed by the evidence before him.

I would refuse the Crown leave to appeal.

What are the dangers in using *R. v. Fireman* as a guide for deciding whether community justice initiatives are appropriate? Remember that *Fireman* stands for the proposition that a judge can exercise broad discretion in crafting a sentence "where a very unsophisticated person must be sentenced for an offence against the laws of a more complex society which has intruded upon his culture". What are the problems for the community, the accused, and the victim in applying this standard? How are each group's problems similar and/or different from one another using the *Fireman* principle? What are the potential solutions to these problems? Would it help if the courts approached their jobs differently, and applied different legal standards to these problems, as in the following case? Or do you see other problems that may arise from such action? Read *R. v. Moses* with these questions in mind.

R. v. MOSES

(1992), 71 C.C.C. (3d) 347 (Y.T. Terr. Ct.)

Stuart Terr. Ct. J.: — The reasons for this sentence will take us on an unusual journey. Unusual, because the process was as influential in moulding the final decision as any substantive factors. Consequently, this judgment examines the process as well as the traditional stuffings of sentences, mitigating and aggravating circumstances.

Many might debate the extent any decision-making process shapes the result, but indisputably process can be as determinative as content. In sentencing, process profoundly influences the result. The process influences, not just what, and how matters are addressed, but who participates and what impact each person has in shaping the final decision. ...

1. Process

(A) Overview

Rising crime rates, especially for violent offences, alarming recidivist rates and escalating costs in monetary and human terms have forced societies the world over to search for alternatives to their malfunctioning justice systems. In the western world much of the energy expended in this search has focused on sentencing. While the underlying problems of crime and the gross inadequacies of the justice system stem from much broader, deeper ills within society, significant immediate improvement within the court process can be achieved by changing the sentencing process.

Currently the search for improving sentencing champions a greater role for victims of crime, reconciliation, restraint in the use of incarceration, and a broadening of sentencing alternatives that calls upon less government expenditure and more community participation. As many studies expose the imprudence of excessive reliance upon punishment as the central objective in sentencing, rehabilitation and reconciliation are properly accorded greater emphasis. All these changes call upon communities to become more actively involved and to assume more responsibility for resolving conflict. To engage meaningful community participation, the sentence decision-making process must be altered to share power with the community, and where appropriate, communities must be empowered to resolve many conflicts now processed through criminal courts.

An important step, towards constructive community involvement must involve significant changes to the sentencing process, before, during and after sentencing.

(B) Before Sentencing

The court circuit flew to Mayo for a special one day circuit to deal with several charges against Philip Moses.

He was found guilty of carrying a weapon, a baseball bat, for the purpose of committing an assault on Constable Alderston. ... Philip picked up a baseball bat to confront Constable Alderston who was standing by his vehicle behind an open car door. Despite several warnings from the Constable to stop, Philip continued to approach in a menacing and angry manner. Philip did not know that behind the vehicle door, the Constable had drawn his revolver. The situation was extremely dangerous. At the last moment, the Constable leapt into his vehicle and sped off. By seeking a less dangerous manner of arresting Philip, the Constable avoided potentially disastrous consequences. Within the hour, the constable arrested Philip without incident. The prudence, and courage of Constable Alderston averted a violent showdown.

Philip was also found guilty of theft. Philip had stolen clothes from a home within Mayo. Philip pled guilty to a breach of probation.

By evening all trials were completed. A brief adjournment was called to enable counsel and the court to review pre-sentence reports, psychiatric and alcohol assessments that had been before the court in 1989. These documents described an incredulous life history.

Philip, a 26-year-old member of the Na-cho Ny'ak Dun First Nation of Mayo, Yukon, is the third youngest in Tommy Moses and Catherine Germaine's family of four sons and five daughters. Tommy Moses, a respected member of the First Nation, works full-time as a heavy equipment operator and spends all of his spare time pursuing a traditional lifestyle through trapping, hunting and fishing. He suffers from the adverse health ramifications of a survivor from long standing problems of alcohol abuse. Catherine works as a native culture instructor in the Mayo school. A source of strength and stability in the family, she has been sober for eight years. All of Philip's brothers have suffered from substance abuse, and all but one have long criminal records. Philip's sisters survived an early childhood amid extreme alcohol abuse and now raise their own families. Philip has a six year old son, whom he rarely sees and plays no part in parenting.

The litany of desperate, destructive circumstances engulfing Philip's early childhood are sadly typical of families caught in the turmoil of alcohol abuse and poverty. Abuse, and neglect within his home launched Philip from age ten until he was 16 into a series of foster homes, group homes, and ultimately into juvenile centres. Along this painful, destructive road of State imposed care, Philip was physically and sexually abused.

Any hope for a formal education was lost through placements in a series of juvenile facilities. Unable to advance past elementary school, Philip functions at approximately a grade six level. Handicapped by extremely poor reading and writing skills, he encounters severe difficulty with basic literacy and other educational courses.

His limited education frustrates attempts to find gainful employment. With virtually no marketable work skills or work experience, without money or a sober home, without a positive personal support system, and with ready access to others addicted to drugs or alcohol, Philip, once out of jail, quickly drifts into the maelstrom of poverty, substance abuse and crime. He commits crimes while impaired by alcohol or drugs, or to support his addictions.

These circumstances explain the short turnaround time from the street back to jail. With such grim prospects on the street, jail continues to be his primary home. His criminal record of 43 convictions, has imposed jail sentences totalling almost eight years. Jail, as did long stints in juvenile facilities, destroys his self-image, what little there may be, and induces severe depression and suicidal tendencies.

Since 1980, each in depth assessment has described Philip as extremely sensitive, lacking the ability to trust, and suffering from numerous personal problems with significant dysfunctional coping skills. In each assessment, the same theme is repeated: Philip needs "extensive personal counselling, needs to bond with an important helping person who can offer one to one counselling". This has never been provided. Most treatment recommendations have not been carried out. Philip's distrust, anger, lack of discipline, ability to disappear into the street, and poor self-image partially explain why prescribed treatment has not been employed to release Philip from his severe personal problems. ...

... He has extremely poor insight into his behaviour and demonstrates neither the judgment nor perspective to adopt a sensible or realistic course of action.

Against this abjectly dark picture, given his extensive criminal record, and a sentence of months imposed at his last appearance in 1989, common practice marked out a simple task for counsel and judge. How much jail time would be appropriate? Had Mr. Moses now proven by his criminal conduct that a sentence of two years was warranted; a sentence which would send this relatively young aboriginal person out of the Territory to a Federal penitentiary!

The court was being asked once more to remove this violent offender from the community, to again demonstrate the power of society to punish those who break "our" laws.

It was late in the evening, everyone was tired. The police plane waited to return Mr. Moses to jail. The charter plane waited to return the court circuit to Whitehorse. Everyone — including myself — expected the sentencing hearing would be short, directed only to the question of how much time in excess of the last sentence of 15 months would be imposed. Numerous factors which never appear in sentencing decisions but often affect sentencing, pressed the court to "get on with it".

We did not.

Somehow the pernicious cycle plaguing the life of Mr. Moses, has to be broken before he tragically destroys himself or someone else.

Insidiously and predictably, Mr. Moses had for ten years travelled from alcohol abuse, to crime, and then to jail. Each time emerging from jail, angrier, more dysfunctional, and more deeply entrenched in a marginal existence that featured alcohol abuse and crime, which inescapably closed the circuit back to jail. His long history with the criminal justice system had proven two unmistakeable conclusions.

First, the criminal justice system had miserably failed the community of Mayo. Born and raised in Mayo, his family in Mayo, Philip instinctively returned to Mayo after each of the previous seven jail sentences. He would again return after any further jail sentences; each time returning, less capable of controlling either his anger or alcohol abuse; more dangerous to the community and to himself. The criminal justice system had not protected, but had endangered the community.

Secondly, the criminal justice system had failed Mr. Moses. After ten years, after expending in excess of a quarter of a million dollars on Mr. Moses, the justice system continues to spew back into the community a person whose prospects, hopes and abilities were dramatically worse than when the system first encountered Philip as a wild, undisciplined youth with significant emotional and general life skill handicaps. His childhood had destined him for crime, and the criminal justice system had competently nurtured and assured that destiny.

If the criminal justice system had failed, what could the community do? It was hardly the model case to experiment with community alternatives. What could be lost in trying!

Court was adjourned for three weeks. The probation officer was asked to enquire if the First Nation and Philip's family wished to become involved. The local RCMP Corporal was asked to enlist other community involvement. Crown and defence counsel were asked to consider what else might be done in addition to incarceration to break the vicious cycle that had inextricably captured Philip.

Another special circuit to Mayo was set for on January 9 to sentence Philip and to thereafter hold an open community meeting to discuss how the community, especially the First Nation might constructively participate in the justice system.

Parts of the plan to involve the community were not pursued. However, the crucial parts were implemented. The probation officer met with the Chief and other members of the First Nation. They would assist in searching for a solution. Equally important, the probation officer met with Philip and his family to encourage their participation. A visit to Mayo two days before the sentencing hearing by Crown counsel and the senior Crown, enhanced their knowledge about the community and its concerns. Their time with the local RCMP, the First Nation, the probation officer and others within the community contributed to the collective search for a solution to a difficult case.

The successful use of sentencing remedies primarily depends upon the work invested by counsel, probation officers and the community in exploring and developing proposals for sentencing before a sentencing hearing.

(C) Sentencing Hearing

In any decision-making process, power, control, the overall atmosphere and dynamics are significantly influenced by the physical setting, and especially by the places accorded to participants. Those who wish to create a particular atmosphere, or especially to manipulate a decision-making process to their advantage, have from time immemorial astutely controlled the physical setting of the decision-making forum. Among the great predator groups in the animal kingdom, often the place secured by each member in the site they rest or hunt, significantly influences their ability to control group decisions. In the criminal justice process (arguably one of contemporary society's great predators) the physical arrangement in a courtroom profoundly affects who participates and how they participate. The organization of the courtroom influences the content, scope and importance of information provided to the court. The rules governing the court hearing reinforce the allocation of power and influence fostered by the physical setting.

The combined effect of the rules and the courtroom arrangements entrench the adversarial nature of the process. The judge, defence and Crown counsel, fortified by their prominent places in the courtroom and by the rules, own and control the process and no one in a courtroom can have any doubt about that.

For centuries, the basic organization of the court has not changed. Nothing has been done to encourage meaningful participation by the accused, the victim, or by the community; remarkable, considering how the location of a meeting, the design of the room, furniture arrangements, and the seating of participants are so meticulously considered in most decision making processes to ensure the setting reinforces the objective of the process. If the objective of the sentencing process is now to enhance sentencing options, to afford greater concern to the impact on victims, to shift focus from punishment to rehabilitation, and to meaningfully engage communities in sharing responsibility for sentencing decisions, it may be advantageous for the justice system to examine how court procedures and the physical arrangements within courtrooms militate against these new objectives. It was in this case.

(D) Advantages of Circle

In this case, a change in the physical arrangement of the courtroom produced a major change in the process.

(1) Physical setting

For court, a circle to seat thirty people was arranged as tightly as numbers allowed. When all seats were occupied, additional seating was provided in an outer circle for persons arriving after the "hearing" had commenced.

Defence sat beside the accused and his family. The Crown sat immediately across the circle from defence counsel to the right of the judge. Officials and members from the First Nation, the RCMP officers, the probation officer and others were left to find their own "comfortable" place within the circle.

(2) Dynamics of the circle

By arranging the court in a circle without desks or tables, with all participants facing each other, with equal access and equal exposure to each other, the dynamics of the decision-making process were profoundly changed.

Everyone in turn around the circle introduced themselves. Everyone remained seated when speaking. After opening remarks from the judge, and counsel, the formal process dissolved into an informal, but intense discussion of what might best protect the community and extract Philip from the grip of alcohol and crime.

The tone was tempered by the close proximity of all participants. For the most part, participants referred to each other by name, not by title. While disagreements and arguments were provoked by most topics, posturing, pontification, and the well worn platitudes, commonly characteristic of courtroom speeches by counsel and judges were gratefully absent.

The circle setting dramatically changed the roles of all participants, as well as the focus, tone, content and scope of discussions. The following observations denote the more obvious benefits generated by the circle setting.

(i) Challenges monopoly of professionals

The foreboding courtroom setting discourages meaningful participation beyond lawyers and judges.

The judge presiding on high, robed to emphasize his authoritative dominance, armed with the power to control the process, is rarely challenged. Lawyers, by their deference, and by standing when addressing the judge, reinforce to the community the judge's pivotal importance. All of this combines to encourage the community to believe judges uniquely and exclusively possess the wisdom and resources to develop a just and viable result. They are so grievously wrong.

Counsel, due to the rules, and their prominent place in the court, control the input of information. Their ease with the rules, their facility with the peculiar legal language, exudes a confidence and skill that lay people commonly perceive as a prerequisite to participate.

The community relegated to the back of the room, is separated from counsel and the judge either by an actual bar or by placing their seats at a distinct distance behind counsel tables. The interplay between lawyers and the judge creates the perception of a ritualistic play. The set, as well as the performance, discourages anyone else from participating.

The circle significantly breaks down the dominance that traditional courtrooms accord lawyers and judges. In a circle, the ability to contribute, the importance and credibility of any input is not defined by seating arrangements. The audience is changed. All persons within the circle must be addressed. Equally, anyone in the circle may ask a direct question to anyone. Questions about the community and the accused force discussions into a level of detail usually avoided in the courtroom by sweeping assumptions and broiler plate platitudes. In the courtroom, reliance upon technical legal language imbues the process with the air of resolutely addressing difficult issues. In fact, behind the facade of legalise, many crucial considerations are either ignored or superficially considered. The circle denies the comfort of evading difficult issues through the use of obtuse, complex technical language.

(ii) Encourages lay participation

The circle setting drew everyone into the discussion. Unlike the courtroom, where the setting facilitates participation only by counsel and the judge, the circle prompted a natural rhythm of discussion.

The physical proximity of all participants, the ability to see the face of the person speaking, the conversational tone, the absence of incomprehensible rituals, and the intermingling of professionals and lay members of the community during breaks, all a consequence of the circle, broke down many barriers to participation.

The highly defined roles imposed upon professionals by the formal justice process creates barriers to communication. The circle drew out the person buried behind their role, and encouraged a more personal and less professional contribution. The circle, in revealing the person behind the professional facade fostered a greater sense of equality between lay and professional participants in the circle. This sense of equality and the discovery of significant common concerns and objectives is essential to sustain an effective partnership between the community and the justice system.

(iii) Enhances information

The justice system rarely acquires adequate information to competently target the sentencing process on the underlying causes of criminal behaviour. ...

The rituals and specialized language of the sentencing process produce an aura of competence. Rising crime rates (especially rising recidivism) despite staggering increases in expenditures, debunk this illusory aura. Sentencing could be vastly improved by enhancing the quantity and quality of information. ...

Community involvement through the circle generates not only new information, but information not normally available to the court. Through the circle, participants can respond to concerns, fill in gaps, and ensure each new sentencing option is measured against a broader, more detailed base of information. In the circle, the flow of information is alive, flexible and more readily capable of assessing and responding to new ideas. ...

Courtroom procedures and rules often preclude or discourage many sources from contributing crucial information. The circle removes or reduces many of the impediments blocking the flow of essential information into court.

(iv) Creative search for new options

Public censure often focuses on the differences in sentences meted out for the same crime. There should be more, not fewer differences in sentences.

. . . . .

In this case the circle promoted among all participants a desire to find an appropriate sentence that best served all of the above objectives. Their creative search produced a sentence markedly different from customary sentences for such crimes, and radically departed from the pattern of sentences previously imposed upon Philip for similar offences. The circle forged a collective desire for something different, something unlike the sentences imposed in the past ten years, something everyone could support, something they believed would work. Fuelled by the expanded and responsive flow of information, the circle participants worked towards a consensus, towards a unique response to a problem that had plagued the community for ten years and had stolen ten years of productive life from Philip.

I was surprised by the result, but the new information and the option provided by the community rendered the final sentence obvious and compelling. The combination of new information and an array of new sentencing options can dramatically change sentencing dispositions from those based on information normally available and dependant upon the limited range of conventional sentencing remedies.

(v) Promotes a sharing of responsibility

In traditional courtroom settings, all inputs, all representations are directed to the judge. Not surprisingly, all participants, including the community, expect the judge after hearing all submissions to be responsible for rendering a sage and definitive edict. The circle redirected the flow of discussion from a single channel leading to the judge to a flow that followed the natural rhythms of interest around the circle. This in turn redirected expectations over responsibility for developing a workable solution. The circle by engaging everyone in the discussion, engaged everyone in the responsibility for finding an answer. The final sentence, evolved from the input of everyone in the circle. The consensus-based approach fostered not just shared responsibility, but instilled a shared concern to ensure the sentence was successfully implemented. Time will tell how much each participant, especially the offender, will continue to act upon their obligation to the circle and to the decision collectively developed.

This was a first run at a new process. Failures must not daunt further attempts. It may take time for the feelings of shared responsibility inspired by the circle to be translated into concerted and sustained action. There are many well-entrenched bad habits to break. The indolence, apathy and easy but imprudent reliance upon professionals, characteristic of most communities, will not be easily overcome in developing proactive community involvement. Current community leaders now strained beyond normal breaking points cannot be stretched to provide the input necessary to assume meaningful responsibility for community justice. Other community members must be inspired and encouraged to become involved.

However difficult inspiring citizens to become involved may be, the most difficult task will be breaking down the monopoly over conflict resolution tenaciously held by professionals within the justice system. Forging new and meaningful partnerships between professionals and communities will not be easy, we are the professionals after all, we know what to do, we have the power, we know what is best. To many, the existing criminal justice system is sacrosanct. Tampering with its rituals is tantamount to heresy.

The circle provided an important opportunity for both citizens and professionals to put into practice an emerging desire to work together in responding to crime.

(vi) Encouraging the offender's participation

Philip Moses, as is typical of most offenders, had not significantly participated in any of the previous seven sentencing hearings which had instrumentally shaped his life. Most offenders, during formal court proceedings, sit with head bowed, sometimes in fear, more often in anger as incomprehensible discussions ramble on about their life, crimes, and about how communities must be protected from such hardened criminals. ...

In the circle, the police, mother, brother, Chief of the First Nation, the probation officer, and other community members expressed constructive concern about Philip. They repeatedly spoke of the need to "reintegrate" Philip with his family and his First Nation.

This was the first time Philip heard anyone from his community, or from his First Nation offer support. He could no longer believe that the police and the community were solely interested in removing him from their midst.

These comments within the circle drew Philip into the discussion. His eloquence, passion, and pain riveted everyone's attention. His contribution moved the search for an effective sentence past several concerns shared around the circle. No, he did not convince everyone, nor did he ultimately secure what he sought, but his passion and candour significantly contributed to constructing the sentence.

(vii) Involving victims in sentencing

Many offenders perceive only the State as the aggrieved party. They fail to appreciate the very human pain and suffering they cause. Absent an appreciation of the victim's suffering, offenders fail to understand their sentence except as the intrusion of an insensitive, oppressive State bent on punishment. An offender's remorse is more likely be prompted by a desire to seek mercy from the State or by a recognition that they have been "bad". Only when an offender's pain caused by the oppression of the criminal justice system is confronted by the pain that victims experience from crime, can most offenders gain a proper perspective of their behaviour. Without this perspective, the motivation to successfully pursue rehabilitation lacks an important and often essential ingredient.

Much work remains to find an appropriate means of including the victim, or in the very least, including the impact on the victim in the sentencing process. The circle affords an important opportunity to explore the potential of productively incorporating the impact upon victims in sentencing.

(viii) Creates constructive environment

The courtroom, ideally suited to meting out punishment with its potentates on raised podiums, appropriately robed in black, retains its historic function as a degradation ceremony. This atmosphere is counter-productive to developing a constructive rehabilitative plan or to genuinely inspiring offenders (except out of fear) to pursue rehabilitation.

Punishment, if required, can be imposed in a circle as readily as in a courtroom. It is not the trappings surrounding the announcement of punishment, but who imposes, and what is imposed that engages the benefits (if any) of punishment. There is a significantly different sting to a punishment imposed by a community, than to a similar sentence imposed by a circuit court judge.

The circuit court judge is a stranger, in town only for the court circuit. The shame and embarrassment of the few moments of sentencing by the judge quickly dissipates.

Punished by a community, the offender must face his sentencers daily. Punished by a court, the offender confronts the disapproval of a stranger, enforcing strange laws whose punishment carries the authority of the State. Punished by the community, the offender faces the disapproval of his neighbours, friends, and of those within his most immediate environment, whose punishment carries the authority of a consensus within the community.

For purely punitive sanctions, particularly where jail sentences in excess of two years are expected, the circle may be inappropriate. In all other cases where the primary objective is rehabilitation, or reconciliation, the circle in contrast to the courtroom creates a more constructive atmosphere. Whatever sentence is imposed, whether it is purely designed for rehabilitation or punishment or a combination of both, the degrading courtroom ceremony proclaiming the moral inferiority of the offender serves little constructive purpose in achieving contemporary sentencing objectives.

(ix) Greater understanding of justice system limitations

Despite the appalling track record in either stemming the rising tide of crime or in rehabilitating offenders, communities persist in placing excessive reliance upon the justice system. Many conflicts currently channelled into the justice system could be far better processed within the community. For far less money, communities could achieve far better results. Support for families in stress, timely interventions in the budding criminal lives of young offenders, help desperately needed to maintain positive momentum for people faced with crippling pressures that often lead to crime, community involvement in all of these matters could often be more effective than the existing justice system.

For far too long, the expensive, formal, slow, and blunt instruments of the justice system have been employed for too many conflicts within communities. In effect, conflicts are stolen from the community by the justice system. Properly processed, conflict is an essential element in building the foundation of community spirit and pride, and most importantly in building the ability to co-operatively develop community based solutions to social problems.

(x) Extending the focus of the criminal justice system

Our criminal justice process has an obdurately narrow focus. Too much attention, too much blame and too much responsibility is placed upon the offender. The court's process, often too engrossed in the administration of the law, is not sufficiently alive to the reality of what happens in the community before and after a sentence is imposed. Within the community, lies many answers to what causes crime, what will prevent crime and what can be done to rehabilitate offenders. The circle, by injecting an awareness of the larger community environment engulfing the offence can immeasurably improve the utility of the sentencing process.

The circle discussions force community members to see beyond the offender, and to explore the causes of crime. This search inevitably leads to assess what characteristics in the community precipitate crime, what should be done to prevent crime, and what could be done to rehabilitate offenders.

(xi) Mobilizing community resources

After several offenders have been processed through the circle, circumstances within the community that directly or indirectly influence criminal behaviour will become patently obvious. For example inadequate recreational activities for teenagers may be a significant part of the reasons they resort to drinking, drug abuse and ultimately to crime to find excitement or the funds to sponsor their expensive substance abuse. Dropping out of school, indolence, unemployment, and strained relationships within the family are only the first ripple of adverse ramifications emanating from early teenage substance abuse. Circle participants, in gaining an appreciation of factors contributing to crime, may exert pressure to realign community expenditures from new roads to new recreational initiatives, and may stimulate local businesses to recognize their best interests are served by developing community based alternatives to prevent crime.

Similarly the circle may discover why, despite heroic efforts to control or cure their substance abuse, anger or other personal problems, some offenders relapse into crime. Circle discussions with repeat offenders may reveal what community based support systems are necessary to reinforce and sustain courageous struggles against substance abuse or other personal difficulties.

Most importantly, the circle stimulates the community to be proactive. Circle discussions generate a collective will to constructively intervene to help individuals or families obviously in trouble. Community support can be more purposefully employed before rather than after crime. ...

(xii) Merging Values; First Nation and western governments

Because aboriginal people use the same language, engage in similar play and work, western society assumes similar underlying values govern and motivate their conduct. Particularly within the justice system, this widely spread erroneous assumption has had a disastrous impact on aboriginal people and their communities.

Much of the systemic discrimination against aboriginal people within the justice system stems from a failure to recognize the fundamental differences between aboriginal and western cultures. Aboriginal culture does not place as high a premium on individual responsibility or approach conflict in the direct confrontational manner championed by our adversarial process. Aboriginal people see value in avoiding confrontation and in refraining from speaking publicly against each other. In dealing with conflict, emphasis is placed on reconciliation, the restoration of harmony and the removal of underlying pressures generating conflict.

After extensive exposure to the justice system, it has been assumed too readily that aboriginal people have adjusted to our adversarial process with its obsession on individual rights and individual responsibility, another tragically wrong assumption. Similarly, we have erroneously assumed by inviting their involvement in our system they will be willing and eager participants. If we generally seek their partnership in resolving crime, a process that fairly accommodates both value systems must emerge.

The circle has the potential to accord greater recognition to aboriginal values, and to create a less confrontational, less adversarial means of processing conflict. Yet the circle retains the primary principles and protections inherent to the justice system. The circle contributes the basis for developing a genuine partnership between aboriginal communities and the justice system by according the flexibility for the respective values to influence the decision making process in sentencing.

(3) Safeguards: protecting individual rights in merging the community and justice in the circle

Courage, patience, and tolerance must accompany all participants in the search for a productive partnership between communities and the justice system. The search need not be foolhardy. Many safeguards can be adapted to protect individual rights while opening the process to community involvement. In this experiment with the circle, the following safeguards were used to cushion any adverse impact on individual rights. Within the justice system, a critical assessment must be made about what is truly inviolable and what has by convention been presumed to be. Many conventions have survived long past the justification for their original creation.

(i) Open court

The courtroom remained the same, only the furniture was rearranged. The door was open, the public retained free access to the room.

The long standing reasons for open court may not be as persuasive in some sentencing hearings where privacy may be essential to precipitate frank exchanges which reveal extremely sensitive family or personal information. Normally such information, vital to competently employing any sentencing option, is rarely available as participants are understandably reluctant to share intimate circumstances of their life in an open public courtroom, especially in small communities where anonymity is impossible.

In most cases there will be no need to limit access. However, where clear advantages flow from a closed session, the long standing reasons for open court must be dusted off and reexamined in light of the advantages derived from acquiring extremely sensitive and personal information from offenders, victims or their families and friends.

(ii) Transcripts

The court reporter remained a part of the circle.

In some cases, there are good reasons to question why a transcript embracing all circle discussions is necessary. Some aspects of the discussion may be best excluded from the transcript, or where the circle is closed to the public, the transcript retained in a confidential manner, available only if required by a court of appeal.

To establish appropriate guidelines in assessing the competing values of an open versus a closed process on a case by case basis, some of the ancient icons of criminal procedures need an airing and reassessment.

The tradition of a circle — "what comes out in a circle, stays in a circle" — runs counter to the justice tradition requiring both an open court and transcripts. A more flexible set of rules for exceptions must be fashioned to establish a balance in merging First Nation, community, and justice system values in the circle.

(iii) Upper limits to sentence

The circle is designed to explore and develop viable sentencing options drawing upon, whenever possible, community based resources. The circle is not designed to extract reasons to increase the severity of punishment. Accordingly at the outset of the circle process, Crown and defence counsel were called upon to make their customary sentencing submissions. Based on these submissions, I indicated the upper limit sentence for the offence.

By stating at the outset an upper limit to the sentence based on conventional sentencing principles and remedies, the offender enters the circle without fearing a harsher jail sentence provoked by candour or anger within the circle. This constitutes an important basis to encourage offenders to participate.

The upper limit also provides a basis for the circle to appreciate what will happen in the absence of community alternatives. The utility of the upper limit sentence can be measured against any new information shared in the circle. Any community based alternative developed by the circle may be substituted for part or all of this sentence.

(iv) Opportunity for offender to speak

The *Criminal Code*, s. 668, ensures the offender has an opportunity to speak in his own words before a sentence is imposed. This opportunity is generally offered after all submissions have been made, and the court has all but formally concluded what the sentence will be. It is generally a perfunctory step in the process, rarely used and generally of little effect.

Defence counsel bears the primary and often exclusive responsibility to represent the offender's interest. How far we have come from the time when lawyers were banned and offenders left to make their own submissions. Somewhere on this journey from exclusive reliance upon the offender to essentially exclusive reliance upon defence counsel, we passed a more fitting balance in the participatory roles of counsel and offender. It may be too cute to suggest courts currently sentence defence counsel not offenders, but the thought does highlight how much sentencing depends upon the work, competence, knowledge, and eloquence of defence counsel. ...

(v) Crown and defence counsel

The traditional and essential functions of Crown and defence counsel are not excluded by the circle.

The Crown at the outset placed before the circle the interests of the State in sentencing the offender. The Crown's participation through questions, and by engaging in the discussions retains the circle's awareness of the larger interests of the State. Aware of community-provided alternatives, having acquired first hand knowledge of a broad spectrum of community concerns and armed with detailed information about the offender, the Crown at the end of the circle discussions can more competently assess how the interests of the State, and the interests of the community are best addressed in sentencing. ...

(vi) Disputed facts

Any disputed fact must be proven in the customary manner. Proof of a disputed fact can be carried out in the circle by the examination of witnesses under oath. Alternatively, during a break in the circle discussions, court can be resumed and all the traditional trappings of the courtroom engaged to resolve a disputed fact.

The circle moves along a different road to consensus than the adversarial character of the formal courtroom hearings. The process in a circle can either resolve disputes in a less adversarial manner, or render the disputed fact irrelevant or unimportant by evolving a sentencing disposition principally relevant upon community based alternatives. However, the formal court process provides a "safe guard" to be called upon by either counsel at any time a matter in the circle necessitates formal proof.

(4) Summary: the circle

These changes to the sentencing process are not the makings of a panacea. They are relatively small steps in a very long journey to move the criminal justice system from its destructive impact on people and communities to doing what it should working closely with communities to prevent crime, protect society, rehabilitate offenders and process conflict in a manner that builds not undermines a sense of community. ...

The circle may not be appropriate for all crimes or all offenders. Experience will explore and test the utility of each new initiative. We must however, continue to search for a less expensive, more purposeful, more humane manner to respond to crime. The current thrust to involve communities in processing and resolving conflict and crime within the community is essential and unavoidable. Costs in monetary and human terms allow no alternative.

Even if funds were unlimited, crime cannot be resolved solely by hiring legions of professionals. This lesson has been repeatedly and expensively learned by many communities who tried to buy their way out of crime. ...

A struggle for a safe community must be led by the community. They, not the justice system must be in the front line of defence against crime. All members of the community must appreciate and accept responsibility to carry their share of the burden in establishing and maintaining a safe community. The safety and overall health of each community is directly related to the extent each citizen participates. This is a fact of family well-being as much as it is of community well-being. The twentieth century is replete with examples of the demise of communities and families that failed to accord the time and take the responsibility to process conflict in a constructive manner. Conflict will always be a part of community life. Creating constructive processes for dealing with conflict is the primary challenge facing society and the criminal justice system.

The current justice system is a very expensive failure, and in many respects undermines the very objectives it champions. There is an increasing recognition within and without the legal community that something more than mere tinkering must be done to create a criminal justice system that is just and offers genuine protection to the community. The existing system notoriously does neither. ...

2. *Primary Sentencing Considerations*

(A) *Criminal Record*

Philip began his criminal record as an adult in 1982 with two minor offences. A decade later Philip had amassed a criminal record comprising 43 offences, over eight years of jail sentences, and numerous probation orders. In the past three years his criminal behaviour has significantly intensified (27 offences). The State, despite spending at least a quarter of a million dollars on Philip in the past ten years, has worsened his chances for rehabilitation and lessened public security. ...

(B) *Appropriateness of Jail*

Jail is an undeniably important part of the numerous options required to competently address the infinite variety of offenders and offences. In Philip's case, as with many others, jail sentences are unfortunately not simply the last resort, but the most expedient means of sweeping out of the community, off the court docket, a difficult problem. Crime will mysteriously disappear, society naively presumes, if criminals are sent away to jail. Sweeping offenders into the hands of prison officials simply moves the problem from one incompetent process to another. The dust bins of society, the jails, are so overwhelmed that prison officials struggle with maintaining security and desperately attempt against impossible overcrowding to provide more than an expensive method of warehousing offenders. An undue reliance upon jail sentences, creates an intolerable task for prison officials. Despite resourceful, imaginative, and dedicated efforts by many prison officials, overall their efforts do little to rectify the problems dumped upon them by the courts.

Judges and prison officials elude responsibility for the abysmal failures of incarceration by shifting blame to the "system". This is partly true. The absence of reasonable alternatives creates a difficult choice. Faced with the prospect of leaving an offender in the community without any programs offering a reasonable prospect of rehabilitation, or sending the offender to jail, where at least any question of control is resolved, begrudgingly, often in frustration, jail is chosen. The tenaciously held belief against over-whelming evidence to the contrary that jail can be rehabilitative provides an illusory solace for the court, and enables communities and courts to avoid confronting reality. The destructive impact on offenders and ulti-mately future victims, and the squandering of scarce public resources is reason enough to exercise restraint in relying upon punishment and espe-cially upon jail to protect the public.

Public protection is diminished when we throw away the key and re-turn offenders to the street unreformed and unsupervised. Lengthy sen-tences employed to punish offenders increase the chance the offender will offend again.

Courts call upon ancient incantations to bless the process of sending of-fenders to jail: "The public must be protected"; "A clear denunciatory sentence must be imposed to send a clear message to others and to reaf-firm society's values"; "Only jail can rehabilitate the offender, all else has failed".

For many years experiences in countries the world over have debunked these reverently expressed ancient myths. The legal community, and par-ticularly the courtroom can no longer comfortably hide behind principles and practices universally questioned by other disciplines. The intended purpose of jail sentences must be subject to the scrutiny of what actually takes place in jail and of what objectives jail can realistically achieve. ...

The criminal record, the information shared by Philip in the circle about his experiences in jail, and the singularly constant theme in all professional assessments, provide compelling reasons to conclude that further punish-ment, particularly incarceration, would continue to lock Philip into a life of crime and self-destruction. For any prospect of rehabilitation, something other than punishment, something other than jail must be used. ...

(C) Jail: Unique Circumstances of Each Offender

. . . . .

In this case, the evidence revealed the particularly harsh and destructive impact of jail on Philip. The prison system expressed as much trouble with Philip as he did with it. Degradation, depression, and suicidal tendencies provoked by jail, bitterly flowed through Philip's story of his life as a "dog" in jail. Previous psychiatric assessments and pre-sentence reports indicated why jail was particularly difficult and potentially destructive for Philip. ...

Anyone reading Philip's personal history would simply not believe someone could be subjected to such abuse and survive. Conversely, most justice professionals who read such personal histories, having been condi-tioned by reading so many similar stories, tend to discount its significance in affecting the offender's ability to function within society.

The standard measure of what offenders can or ought to do is based upon western middle class values, opportunities and lifestyles, which bear little relevance to evaluating either Philip's past or what he can do in the future. There is simply no appropriate basis within the justice system to properly consider the devastating impact a life like Philip's can have on the ability to function, least of all, avoid criminal behaviour. Failing to take properly into account the cultural or personal life circumstances of offenders may help explain why we repeatedly err, repeatedly increase the prospect that the very thing we so religiously strive to prevent will happen again. Each time we punish Philip with jail, and the more severe the sentence, the sooner once on the street, Philip returns to crime. Perhaps if we knew more about Philip's personal circumstances, then if protecting society and rehabilitating Philip were our primary goals, punishment would not be our primary remedy.

(D) Rehabilitation: A New Direction

The probation officer vividly described why, despite a commonly shared perception that Philip had been given many chances for rehabilitation in the past, that Philip persisted in believing that he had never been given a chance. Most of Philip's chances were incorporated in a probation order that came into play upon the termination of a lengthy jail sentence. Philip's *bona fide* intentions to change his life at the time of sentencing were obliterated by jail. His self image, courage, and will to change were drained by his experience in jail. Upon his release the "good times" of "bad company" and substance abuse easily recaptured a despondent, defeated, and angry Philip whose self image had once again been severely damaged by jail. ...

(E) First Nation Involvement

In First Nation communities, the first challenge in exercising control over their future must be in healing and rehabilitating their members. The impact of incarcerating so many of their members adversely affects the community's ability to. First Nation's have the best knowledge and ability to prevent and resolve the long list of tragedies plaguing their communities.

Philip's First Nation and his family responded to the challenge. Their involvement was the singularly most important reason for focusing the sentence on rehabilitation. Without their involvement, the destructive cycle would be sustained, as the justice system could only turn once again to jail. ...

3. Sentencing Plan

(A) Overview

By the end of the circle discussion, the search for an appropriate sentence had shifted from punishment to rehabilitation. The resources contributed by Philip's family, his First Nation, and his community created a practical, realistic alternative to incarceration. Without this investment, despite the obvious need for rehabilitation, jail once again would have been the only option. ...

The leaders of the community where Philip will live out his life are willing to risk their safety in a rehabilitative program, his family and First Nation are willing to invest in Philip. After many years of counselling

Philip, the local probation officer, a long time resident of Mayo, believes Philip deserves an opportunity to try and believes he can succeed. Philip recognizes all of this support and spoke eloquently of his motivation to try to change his life. In the face of all of these compelling grounds for a rehabilitation sentence, neither the offences before the court, nor his criminal record deny taking a risk. What risk could there be. We knew the risks of jail (further offenses)! Neither a trial judge nor an appellate court should hesitate to take a calculated risk when satisfied by so doing there is a reasonable possibility that the offender may change his life.

The doubts properly raised and fairly expressed by Crown counsel were simply not enough to offset the support of the community for Philip and for the plan that had evolved. The Crown and judge who do not live in the community and are not familiar with the community must be cautious in opposing, on the basis of a need to "protect the public", a rehabilitative plan developed by the community.

(B) The Plan

A suspended sentence, coupled with a two-year probation order provides the legal packaging for the sentencing plan that contains three distinct parts.

The first part commences Philip's rehabilitation by immediately calling upon his family to reintegrate him into their family and lifestyle. Foster homes, juvenile facilities and eight years of jail sentences, removed Philip from any positive interaction with his family and directed his life into an urban context. Consequently, he lost contact with the culture and practices of his family. Philip is required to reside with his family on the trapline located 60 miles outside Mayo. His family will ensure a member of the family will stay with Philip.

The plan's second part sends Philip from the trapline to a two month residential program for native alcoholics in southern British Columbia. Other members of his First Nation have benefited from this program. His brother may attend with him and in the very least, his family, First Nation and the probation officer will maintain regular contact. Unfortunately as yet, no such program exists in the Yukon. (A local program, reliant upon local resources, constructively engaging local community and family support systems, would significantly increase the likelihood of success at significantly less cost per patient.)

The plan's third part brings Philip back to Mayo where his family will provide an alcohol free home. The First Nation will develop a support program for Philip to upgrade life and employment skills, and provide continuing counselling for substance abuse. The probation officer will add additional support and counselling services. All efforts will be made within the community to help Philip acquire gainful employment.

At each stage, a court review will be held in the circle to fine-tune the plan and offer whatever further support may be required. The plan depends upon a concerted investment from Philip, his family, his First Nation, his community and from government. Combining all of these resources created for the first time a viable alternative to jail, and incorporates the values and concerns of the First Nation, the justice system, and most importantly, Philip.

4. *Conclusion*

. . . . .

Tragically, Philip's is not a unique story. There are many other victims of the current justice system and will be many more if we irresponsibly believe simply keeping the current machinery of justice in gear defines the parameters of our "professional" responsibility. Unless the system is changed, the community will be victimized by the very system charged with the responsibility of protecting it. We must find a way to change. We must find communities, First Nations, professionals and lay people willing to work together to explore "truly new ways". We will; we have no choice. In making the circle work, the Na-cho Ny'ak Dun First Nation took an important first step. Can we follow?

Judgment accordingly.

In 1996 the Parliament of Canada set out the purposes and principles of sentencing in an amendment to the *Criminal Code*. As a result of these amendments, section 718.2(e) of the *Code* now reads:

> 718.2 A court that imposes a sentence shall also take into consideration the following principles: . . .
> (e) all available sanctions other than imprisonment that are reasonable in the circumstances should be considered for all offenders, with particular attention to the circumstances of aboriginal offenders.

Three years later the Supreme Court of Canada considered this provision in the case of *R. v. Gladue.*

R. v. GLADUE

[1999] 1 S.C.R. 688

The judgment of the Court was delivered by **Cory** and **Iacobucci JJ.**: —

I. *Factual Background*

. . . . .

[2] ... The appellant and the victim Reuben Beaver started to live together in 1993, when the appellant was 17 years old. Thereafter they had a daughter, Tanita. In August 1995, they moved to Nanaimo. ... By September 1995, the appellant and Beaver were engaged to be married, and the appellant was five months pregnant with their second child, a boy, whom the appellant subsequently named Reuben Ambrose Beaver in honour of his father.

[3] In the early evening of September 16, 1995, the appellant was celebrating her 19th birthday. She and Reuben Beaver, who was then 20, were

drinking beer with some friends and family members in the townhouse complex. The appellant suspected that Beaver was having an affair with her older sister, Tara. During the course of the evening she voiced those suspicions to her friends. The appellant was obviously angry with Beaver. She said, "the next time he fools around on me, I'll kill him". ...

[4] The appellant's sister Tara left the party, followed by Beaver. After he had left, the appellant told her friend, "He's going to get it. He's really going to get it this time." The appellant, on several occasions, tried to find Beaver and her sister. She eventually located them coming down the stairs together in her sister's suite. The appellant suspected that they had been engaged in sexual activity and confronted her sister, saying, "You're going to get it. How could you do this to me?"

[5] The appellant and Beaver returned separately to their townhouse and they started to quarrel. During the argument, the appellant confronted him with his infidelity and he told her that she was fat and ugly and not as good as the others. A neighbour, Mr. Gretchin, who lived next door was awakened by some banging and shouting and a female voice saying "I'm sick and tired of you fooling around with other women." The disturbance was becoming very loud and he decided to ask his neighbours to calm down. He heard the front door of the appellant's residence slam. As he opened his own front door, he saw the appellant come running out of her suite. He also saw Reuben Beaver banging with both hands at Tara Chalifoux's door down the hall saying, "Let me in. Let me in."

[6] Mr. Gretchin saw the appellant run toward Beaver with a large knife in her hand and, as she approached him, she told him that he had better run. Mr. Gretchin heard Beaver shriek in pain and saw him collapse in a pool of blood. The appellant had stabbed Beaver once in the left chest, and the knife had penetrated his heart. As the appellant went by on her return to her apartment, Mr. Gretchin heard her say, "I got you, you fucking bastard." The appellant was described as jumping up and down as if she had tagged someone. Mr. Gretchin said she did not appear to realize what she had done. At the time of the stabbing, the appellant had a blood-alcohol content of between 155 and 165 milligrams of alcohol in 100 millilitres of blood.

[7] On June 3, 1996, the appellant was charged with second degree murder.

[9] There was ... evidence that Beaver had subjected the appellant to some physical abuse in June 1994, while the appellant was pregnant with their daughter Tanita. Beaver was convicted of assault, and was given a 15-day intermittent sentence with one year's probation. ... However, the trial judge found that the facts as presented before him did not warrant a finding that the appellant was a "battered or fearful wife".

· · · · ·

[13] The appellant was sentenced to three years' imprisonment and to a ten-year weapons prohibition. Her appeal of the sentence to the British Columbia Court of Appeal was dismissed.

· · · · ·

IV. *Issue*

[24] The issue in this appeal is the proper interpretation and application to be given to s. 718.2(*e*) of the *Criminal Code*. The provision reads as follows:

> 718.2 A court that imposes a sentence shall also take into consideration the following principles: ...
>
> (*e*) all available sanctions other than imprisonment that are reasonable in the circumstances should be considered for all offenders, with particular attention to the circumstances of aboriginal offenders.

. . . . .

V. *Analysis*

[27] This is the first occasion on which this Court has had the opportunity to construe and apply the provision.

. . . . .

[33] In our view, s. 718.2(*e*) is *more* than simply a re-affirmation of existing sentencing principles. The remedial component of the provision consists not only in the fact that it codifies a principle of sentencing, but, far more importantly, in its direction to sentencing judges to undertake the process of sentencing aboriginal offenders differently, in order to endeavour to achieve a truly fit and proper sentence in the particular case. It should be said that the words of s. 718.2(*e*) do not alter the fundamental duty of the sentencing judge to impose a sentence that is fit for the offence and the offender. For example...it will generally be the case as a practical matter that particularly violent and serious offences will result in imprisonment for aboriginal offenders as often as for non-aboriginal offenders. What s. 718.2(*e*) does alter is the method of analysis which each sentencing judge must use in determining the nature of a fit sentence for an aboriginal offender. ...

[34] ... In our view, s. 718.2(*e*) creates a judicial duty to give its remedial purpose real force.

. . . . .

[36] Section 718.2(*e*) directs a court, in imposing a sentence, to consider all available sanctions other than imprisonment that are reasonable in the circumstances for all offenders, "with particular attention to the circumstances of aboriginal offenders". The broad role of the provision is clear. As a general principle, s. 718.2(*e*) applies to all offenders, and states that imprisonment should be the penal sanction of last resort. Prison is to be used only where no other sanction or combination of sanctions is appropriate to the offence and the offender.

[37] The next question is the meaning to be attributed to the words "with particular attention to the circumstances of aboriginal offenders". ... [T]he logical meaning to be derived from the special reference to the

circumstances of aboriginal offenders, juxtaposed as it is against a general direction to consider "the circumstances" for all offenders, is that sentencing judges should pay particular attention to the circumstances of aboriginal offenders *because those circumstances are unique*, and different from those of non-aboriginal offenders.

. . . . .

[43] Section 718 now sets out the purpose of sentencing in the following terms:

> 718. The fundamental purpose of sentencing is to contribute, along with crime prevention initiatives, to respect for the law and the maintenance of a just, peaceful and safe society by imposing just sanctions that have one or more of the following objectives:
> (*a*) to denounce unlawful conduct;
> (*b*) to deter the offender and other persons from committing offences;
> (*c*) to separate offenders from society, where necessary;
> (*d*) to assist in rehabilitating offenders;
> (*e*) *to provide reparations for harm done to victims or to the community*; and
> (*f*) *to promote a sense of responsibility in offenders, and acknowledgment of the harm done to victims and to the community.* [Emphasis added by Court.]

Clearly, s. 718 is, in part, a restatement of the basic sentencing aims, which are listed in paras. (*a*) through (*d*). What are new, though, are paras. (*e*) and (*f*), which along with para. (*d*) focus upon the restorative goals of repairing the harms suffered by individual victims and by the community as a whole, promoting a sense of responsibility and an acknowledgment of the harm caused on the part of the offender, and attempting to rehabilitate or heal the offender. The concept of restorative justice, which underpins paras. (*d*), (*e*), and (*f*)..., involves some form of restitution and reintegration into the community. ...

[44] Just as the context of Part XXIII supports the view that s. 718.2(*e*) has a remedial purpose for all offenders, the scheme of Part XXIII also supports the view that s. 718.2(*e*) has a particular remedial role for aboriginal peoples.

. . . . .

D. *The Context of the Enactment of Section 718.2(e)*

. . . . .

[50] The parties and interveners agree that the purpose of s. 718.2(*e*) is to respond to the problem of overincarceration in Canada, and to respond, in particular, to the more acute problem of the disproportionate incarceration of aboriginal peoples. ...

[51] The fact that the parties and interveners are in general agreement among themselves regarding the purpose of s. 718.2(*e*) is not determinative of the issue as a matter of statutory construction. However, as we have suggested, on the above points of agreement the parties and interveners are correct. A review of the problem of overincarceration in Canada, and

of its peculiarly devastating impact upon Canada's aboriginal peoples, provides additional insight into the purpose and proper application of this new provision.

(1) [Discussion on the problem of over-incarceration in Canada is omitted]

(2) The Overrepresentation of Aboriginal Canadians in Penal Institutions

[58] If overreliance upon incarceration is a problem with the general population, it is of much greater concern in the sentencing of aboriginal Canadians. In the mid-1980s, aboriginal people were about 2 percent of the population of Canada, yet they made up 10 percent of the penitentiary population. In Manitoba and Saskatchewan, aboriginal people constituted something between 6 and 7 percent of the population, yet in Manitoba they represented 46 percent of the provincial admissions and in Saskatchewan 60 percent: see M. Jackson, "Locking Up Natives in Canada" (1988-89), 23 *U.B.C. L. Rev.* 215 (article originally prepared as a report of the Canadian Bar Association Committee on Imprisonment and Release in June 1988), at pp. 215-16. The situation has not improved in recent years. By 1997, aboriginal peoples constituted closer to 3 percent of the population of Canada and amounted to 12 percent of all federal inmates: Solicitor General of Canada, Consolidated Report, *Towards a Just, Peaceful and Safe Society: The Corrections and Conditional Release Act — Five Years Later* (1998), at pp. 142-55. The situation continues to be particularly worrisome in Manitoba, where in 1995-96 they made up 55 percent of admissions to provincial correctional facilities, and in Saskatchewan, where they made up 72 percent of admissions. A similar, albeit less drastic situation prevails in Alberta and British Columbia: Canadian Centre for Justice Statistics, *Adult Correctional Services in Canada, 1995-96* (1997), at p. 30.

. . . . .

[61] Not surprisingly, the excessive imprisonment of aboriginal people is only the tip of the iceberg insofar as the estrangement of the aboriginal peoples from the Canadian criminal justice system is concerned. Aboriginal people are overrepresented in virtually all aspects of the system. As this Court recently noted in *R. v. Williams*, [1998] 1 S.C.R. 1128 at para. 58, there is widespread bias against aboriginal people within Canada, and "[t]here is evidence that this widespread racism has translated into systemic discrimination in the criminal justice system".

. . . . .

[64] These findings cry out for recognition of the magnitude and gravity of the problem, and for responses to alleviate it. The figures are stark and reflect what may fairly be termed a crisis in the Canadian criminal justice system. The drastic overrepresentation of aboriginal peoples within both the Canadian prison population and the criminal justice system reveals a sad and pressing social problem. It is reasonable to assume that Parliament, in singling out aboriginal offenders for distinct sentencing treatment in s. 718.2(*e*), intended to attempt to redress this social problem to some

degree. The provision may properly be seen as Parliament's direction to members of the judiciary to inquire into the causes of the problem and to endeavour to remedy it, to the extent that a remedy is possible through the sentencing process.

[65] It is clear that sentencing innovation by itself cannot remove the causes of aboriginal offending and the greater problem of aboriginal alienation from the criminal justice system. The unbalanced ratio of imprisonment for aboriginal offenders flows from a number of sources, including poverty, substance abuse, lack of education, and the lack of employment opportunities for aboriginal people. It arises also from bias against aboriginal people and from an unfortunate institutional approach that is more inclined to refuse bail and to impose more and longer prison terms for aboriginal offenders. There are many aspects of this sad situation which cannot be addressed in these reasons. What can and must be addressed, though, is the limited role that sentencing judges will play in remedying injustice against aboriginal peoples in Canada. Sentencing judges are among those decision-makers who have the power to influence the treatment of aboriginal offenders in the justice system. They determine most directly whether an aboriginal offender will go to jail, or whether other sentencing options may be employed which will play perhaps a stronger role in restoring a sense of balance to the offender, victim, and community, and in preventing future crime.

E. *A Framework of Analysis for the Sentencing Judge*

(1) What Are the "Circumstances of Aboriginal Offenders"?

[66] How are sentencing judges to play their remedial role? The words of s. 718.2(*e*) instruct the sentencing judge to pay particular attention to the circumstances of aboriginal offenders, with the implication that those circumstances are significantly different from those of non-aboriginal offenders. The background considerations regarding the distinct situation of aboriginal peoples in Canada encompass a wide range of unique circumstances, including, most particularly:

(A)   The unique systemic or background factors which may have played a part in bringing the particular aboriginal offender before the courts; and

(B)   The types of sentencing procedures and sanctions which may be appropriate in the circumstances for the offender because of his or her particular aboriginal heritage or connection.

(a) Systemic and Background Factors

[67] The background factors which figure prominently in the causation of crime by aboriginal offenders are by now well known. Years of dislocation and economic development have translated, for many aboriginal peoples, into low incomes, high unemployment, lack of opportunities and options, lack or irrelevance of education, substance abuse, loneliness, and community fragmentation. ...

[68] ... However, it must be recognized that the circumstances of aboriginal offenders differ from those of the majority because many aboriginal

people are victims of systemic and direct discrimination, many suffer the legacy of dislocation, and many are substantially affected by poor social and economic conditions. Moreover, as has been emphasized repeatedly in studies and commission reports, aboriginal offenders are, as a result of these unique systemic and background factors, more adversely affected by incarceration and less likely to be "rehabilitated" thereby, because the internment milieu is often culturally inappropriate and regrettably discrimination towards them is so often rampant in penal institutions.

[69] In this case, of course, we are dealing with factors that must be considered by a judge sentencing an aboriginal offender. While background and systemic factors will also be of importance for a judge in sentencing a non-aboriginal offender, the judge who is called upon to sentence an aboriginal offender must give attention to the unique background and systemic factors which may have played a part in bringing the particular offender before the courts. In cases where such factors have played a significant role, it is incumbent upon the sentencing judge to consider these factors in evaluating whether imprisonment would actually serve to deter, or to denounce crime in a sense that would be meaningful to the community of which the offender is a member. In many instances, more restorative sentencing principles will gain primary relevance precisely because the prevention of crime as well as individual and social healing cannot occur through other means.

(b) Appropriate Sentencing Procedures and Sanctions

[70] Closely related to the background and systemic factors which have contributed to an excessive aboriginal incarceration rate are the different conceptions of appropriate sentencing procedures and sanctions held by aboriginal people. A significant problem experienced by aboriginal people who come into contact with the criminal justice system is that the traditional sentencing ideals of deterrence, separation, and denunciation are often far removed from the understanding of sentencing held by these offenders and their community. The aims of restorative justice as now expressed in paras. (d), (e), and (f) of s. 718 of the *Criminal Code* apply to all offenders, and not only aboriginal offenders. However, most traditional aboriginal conceptions of sentencing place a primary emphasis upon the ideals of restorative justice. This tradition is extremely important to the analysis under s. 718.2(e).

[71] The concept and principles of a restorative approach will necessarily have to be developed over time in the jurisprudence, as different issues and different conceptions of sentencing are addressed in their appropriate context. In general terms, restorative justice may be described as an approach to remedying crime in which it is understood that all things are interrelated and that crime disrupts the harmony which existed prior to its occurrence, or at least which it is felt should exist. The appropriateness of a particular sanction is largely determined by the needs of the victims, and the community, as well as the offender. The focus is on the human beings closely affected by the crime. ...

[72] The existing overemphasis on incarceration in Canada may be partly due to the perception that a restorative approach is a more lenient

approach to crime and that imprisonment constitutes the ultimate punishment. Yet in our view a sentence focussed on restorative justice is not necessarily a "lighter" punishment. Some proponents of restorative justice argue that when it is combined with probationary conditions it may in some circumstances impose a greater burden on the offender than a custodial sentence. ...

[73] In describing in general terms some of the basic tenets of traditional aboriginal sentencing approaches, we do not wish to imply that all aboriginal offenders, victims, and communities share an identical understanding of appropriate sentences for particular offences and offenders. Aboriginal communities stretch from coast to coast and from the border with the United States to the far north. Their customs and traditions and their concept of sentencing vary widely. What is important to recognize is that, for many if not most aboriginal offenders, the current concepts of sentencing are inappropriate because they have frequently not responded to the needs, experiences, and perspectives of aboriginal people or aboriginal communities.

[74] ... What is important to note is that the different conceptions of sentencing held by many aboriginal people share a common underlying principle: that is, the importance of community-based sanctions. Sentencing judges should not conclude that the absence of alternatives specific to an aboriginal community eliminates their ability to impose a sanction that takes into account principles of restorative justice and the needs of the parties involved. Rather, the point is that one of the unique circumstances of aboriginal offenders is that community-based sanctions coincide with the aboriginal concept of sentencing and the needs of aboriginal people and communities. It is often the case that neither aboriginal offenders nor their communities are well served by incarcerating offenders, particularly for less serious or non-violent offences. Where these sanctions are reasonable in the circumstances, they should be implemented. In all instances, it is appropriate to attempt to craft the sentencing process and the sanctions imposed in accordance with the aboriginal perspective.

(2) The Search for a Fit Sentence

[75] The role of the judge who sentences an aboriginal offender is, as for every offender, to determine a fit sentence taking into account all the circumstances of the offence, the offender, the victims, and the community. Nothing in Part XXIII of the *Criminal Code* alters this fundamental duty as a general matter. However, the effect of s. 718.2(*e*), viewed in the context of Part XXIII as a whole, is to alter the method of analysis which sentencing judges must use in determining a fit sentence for aboriginal offenders. Section 718.2(*e*) requires that sentencing determinations take into account the unique circumstances of aboriginal peoples.

[76] ... [T]he appropriateness of a sentence will depend on the particular circumstances of the offence, the offender, and the community in which the offence took place. Disparity of sentences for similar crimes is a natural consequence of this individualized focus.

. . . . .

[78] In describing the effect of s. 718.2(e) in this way, we do not mean to suggest that, as a general practice, aboriginal offenders must always be sentenced in a manner which gives greatest weight to the principles of restorative justice, and less weight to goals such as deterrence, denunciation, and separation. It is unreasonable to assume that aboriginal peoples themselves do not believe in the importance of these latter goals, and even if they do not, that such goals must not predominate in appropriate cases. Clearly there are some serious offences and some offenders for which and for whom separation, denunciation, and deterrence are fundamentally relevant.

[79] Yet, even where an offence is considered serious, the length of the term of imprisonment must be considered. In some circumstances the length of the sentence of an aboriginal offender may be less and in others the same as that of any other offender. Generally, the more violent and serious the offence the more likely it is as a practical reality that the terms of imprisonment for aboriginals and non-aboriginals will be close to each other or the same, even taking into account their different concepts of sentencing.

[80] As with all sentencing decisions, the sentencing of aboriginal offenders must proceed on an individual (or a case-by-case) basis: For this offence, committed by this offender, harming this victim, in this community, what is the appropriate sanction under the *Criminal Code*? What understanding of criminal sanctions is held by the community? What is the nature of the relationship between the offender and his or her community? What combination of systemic or background factors contributed to this particular offender coming before the courts for this particular offence? How has the offender who is being sentenced been affected by, for example, substance abuse in the community, or poverty, or overt racism, or family or community breakdown? Would imprisonment effectively serve to deter or denounce crime in a sense that would be significant to the offender and community, or are crime prevention and other goals better achieved through healing? What sentencing options present themselves in these circumstances?

[81] The analysis for sentencing aboriginal offenders, as for all offenders, must be holistic and designed to achieve a fit sentence in the circumstances. There is no single test that a judge can apply in order to determine the sentence. The sentencing judge is required to take into account all of the surrounding circumstances regarding the offence, the offender, the victims, and the community, including the unique circumstances of the offender as an aboriginal person. Sentencing must proceed with sensitivity to and understanding of the difficulties aboriginal people have faced with both the criminal justice system and society at large. When evaluating these circumstances in light of the aims and principles of sentencing as set out in Part XXIII of the *Criminal Code* and in the jurisprudence, the judge must strive to arrive at a sentence which is just and appropriate in the circumstances. By means of s. 718.2(e), sentencing judges have been provided with a degree of flexibility and discretion to consider in appropriate circumstances alternative sentences to incarceration which are appropriate for the aboriginal offender and community and yet comply with the mandated principles and purpose of sentencing. In this way, effect may be

given to the aboriginal emphasis upon healing and restoration of both the victim and the offender.

(3) The Duty of the Sentencing Judge

[82] ... The provision expressly provides that a court that imposes a sentence should consider all available sanctions other than imprisonment that are reasonable in the circumstances, and should pay particular attention to the circumstances of aboriginal offenders. There is no discretion as to whether to consider the unique situation of the aboriginal offender; the only discretion concerns the determination of a just and appropriate sentence.

[83] How then is the consideration of s. 718.2(e) to proceed in the daily functioning of the courts? ... In all instances it will be necessary for the judge to take judicial notice of the systemic or background factors and the approach to sentencing which is relevant to aboriginal offenders. However, for each particular offence and offender it may be that some evidence will be required in order to assist the sentencing judge in arriving at a fit sentence. Where a particular offender does not wish such evidence to be adduced, the right to have particular attention paid to his or her circumstances as an aboriginal offender may be waived. Where there is no such waiver, it will be extremely helpful to the sentencing judge for counsel on both sides to adduce relevant evidence. Indeed, it is to be expected that counsel will fulfil their role and assist the sentencing judge in this way.

[84] However, even where counsel do not adduce this evidence, where for example the offender is unrepresented, it is incumbent upon the sentencing judge to attempt to acquire information regarding the circumstances of the offender as an aboriginal person. Whether the offender resides in a rural area, on a reserve or in an urban centre the sentencing judge must be made aware of alternatives to incarceration that exist whether inside or outside the aboriginal community of the particular offender. The alternatives existing in metropolitan areas must, as a matter of course, also be explored. Clearly the presence of an aboriginal offender will require special attention in pre-sentence reports. Beyond the use of the pre-sentence report, the sentencing judge may and should in appropriate circumstances and where practicable request that witnesses be called who may testify as to reasonable alternatives.

[85] Similarly, where a sentencing judge at the trial level has not engaged in the duty imposed by s. 718.2(e) as fully as required, it is incumbent upon a court of appeal in considering an appeal against sentence on this basis to consider any fresh evidence which is relevant and admissible on sentencing. In the same vein, it should be noted that, although s. 718.2(e) does not impose a statutory duty upon the sentencing judge to provide reasons, it will be much easier for a reviewing court to determine whether and how attention was paid to the circumstances of the offender as an aboriginal person if at least brief reasons are given.

. . . . .

VII. *Was There an Error Made in This Case?*

[94] From the foregoing analysis it can be seen that the sentencing judge, who did not have the benefit of these reasons, fell into error. ...

[95] The majority of the Court of Appeal, in dismissing the appellant's appeal, also does not appear to have considered many of the factors referred to above. ...

[96] In most cases, errors such as those in the courts below would be sufficient to justify sending the matter back for a new sentencing hearing. It is difficult for this Court to determine a fit sentence for the appellant according to the suggested guidelines set out herein on the basis of the very limited evidence before us regarding the appellant's aboriginal background. However, as both the trial judge and all members of the Court of Appeal acknowledged, the offence in question is a most serious one, properly described by Esson J.A. as a "near murder". Moreover, the offence involved domestic violence and a breach of the trust inherent in a spousal relationship. That aggravating factor must be taken into account in the sentencing of the aboriginal appellant as it would be for any offender. For that offence by this offender a sentence of three years' imprisonment was not unreasonable.

[97] More importantly, the appellant was granted day parole on August 13, 1997, after she had served six months in the Burnaby Correctional Centre for Women. She was directed to reside with her father, to take alcohol and substance abuse counselling and to comply with the requirements of the Electronic Monitoring Program. On February 25, 1998, the appellant was granted full parole with the same conditions as the ones applicable to her original release on day parole.

[98] In this case, the results of the sentence with incarceration for six months and the subsequent controlled release were in the interests of both the appellant and society. In these circumstances, we do not consider that it would be in the interests of justice to order a new sentencing hearing in order to canvass the appellant's circumstances as an aboriginal offender.

Appeal dismissed.

Should Aboriginal peoples be singled out as requiring particular attention in sentencing decisions? One opposition Member of Parliament discussing the passage of section 718.2(e) stated in Commons debate:

> Finally, again with respect to the purpose and principles of sentencing, it is deplorable that the bill tries to sneak through the back door the concept of a parallel system of justice for Aboriginals. It is so well hidden that it is almost necessary to read Clause 718.2(e) twice to discover this enormity hidden under nine sneaky words. (*House of Commons Debates*, 20 September, 1994 at 5876 by Ms. Venne)

Do you agree with the Member's characterization of the *Gladue* decision?

E. ABORIGINAL JUSTICE SYSTEMS

"THE ARGUMENT FOR ABORIGINAL JUSTICE SYSTEMS"

in A.C. Hamilton and C.M. Sinclair, *The Justice System and Aboriginal People:
Report of the Aboriginal Justice Inquiry of Manitoba*, Vol. 1
(Winnipeg: Queen's Printer, 1991) at 256-264 (references omitted)

The call for separate, Aboriginally controlled justice systems was made repeatedly in our public hearings throughout Manitoba as one solution to all or most of the problems with the present system. ...

Aboriginal self-government is a reality. It exists. It benefits the Aboriginal person and his or her community, and takes nothing away from Canadian society. In fact, we believe that Aboriginal self-government adds to the overall positive growth and development of Canada.

It is time to apply similar advances to the administration of all aspects of the justice system. Aboriginal governments need to establish systems to deal appropriately with those people causing problems in their own communities and provide a means for other community members to provide them with culturally appropriate ways to achieve the ultimate result of restoring and ensuring peace among individuals, and stability in the community.

To enable this to be done, Aboriginal communities must have the right, as part of self-government to establish their own rules of conduct, to develop means of dealing with disputes (such as courts and peacemakers), appropriate sanctions (such as holding facilities or jails), and the full range of probation, parole, counselling and restorative mechanisms once applied by First Nations. ...

The reality is that approaches taken by a non-Aboriginal justice system in Aboriginal communities will not address the social needs, development, culture or right to self-determination of those communities. A court system is not seen as an institution that belongs to them, and that is able to adapt to their indigenous concepts and mechanisms of justice, will not work in Aboriginal communities. ...

This means that in establishing a system of justice for Aboriginal people, the laws enacted by Aboriginal peoples themselves, or deliberately accepted by them for their purposes, must form the foundation of the system's existence.

BRYAN SCHWARTZ, "A SEPARATE ABORIGINAL JUSTICE SYSTEM?"

(1990) 28 Manitoba Law Journal at 77-91

The Aboriginal Justice Inquiry may well be considering proposals that would set up special, and to a greater extent, separate system of justice for Aboriginal people. A variety of worthy initiatives are possible that would enhance local self-government in aboriginal communities that would facilitate their contribution to the direction of programmes elsewhere. This submission will, however, caution against going to far in the direction of separatism and special status for Aboriginal people. ...

It must be emphasized that this submission is not proposing the assimilation of Aboriginal people, nor is it disregarding the real inequalities that exist. On the contrary, we should encourage the development of aboriginal communities on reserves that have a strong measure of local self-government; we should ensure that the system of justice does respect the cultural values of Aboriginal people, but it is my view that we can achieve these goals without weakening the bonds that hold us together as a national political community and without granting extensive privileges to some groups or individuals that are denied to others.

The model of quasi-independent Aboriginal communites and courts may have some attractions to the Inquiry, but it has drawbacks that the Inquiry should carefully consider.

I. Drawbacks to a Separate Aboriginal Justice System

A. Problems with Separatism

1. SEPARATISM LEADS TO INDIFFERENCE FROM THE LARGER COMMUNITY INSTEAD OF SUPPORTIVE INTERVENTION

The interweaving of aboriginal communities with the larger community of a province and the nations can be poorly done. It can involve ignorant and paternalistic meddling; however, it can, and should be, an involvement that benefits both sides. Aboriginal communities can benefit from the fiscal and administrative support of a larger entity. Even smaller Canadian provinces rely heavily on federal fiscal transfers; grants to support their governmental structures; economies of scale achieved by having a national bureaucracy assist with administration...; sharing information, expertise, and experience with national politicians and bureaucrats; and, having a national government to advocate and support their position with larger powers such as the United States of the European Economic Community. Federal-provincial interaction also is an integral part of the justice system. The provinces rely on the federal government to do the research, consultation, and hard politicking necessary to define society's attitudes towards the most serious offences. Canadians everywhere benefit from being tied to a system that draws from the widest range of experience and perspectives, and that moderates the responses to local passions. All parts of Canada learn from the precedents established elsewhere and, ultimately, by the Supreme Court of Canada. Most provinces and municipalities further rely on a larger partner to establish and carry out policing.

Aboriginal communities no less that provinces can benefit fiscally, intellectually, and politically from participation in a larger community. If aboriginal justice systems are detached from the larger network, the consequences will not be benign, "no-strings-attached" support. It will likely be increasing indifference and neglect. Why should voters and politicians care about communities that are not strongly connected to their own?

2.   SEPARATISM CAN LIMIT THE REAL AND PERCEIVED RIGHT TO
      PARTICIPATION FULLY IN THE POLITICS OF THE LARGER
      COMMUNITY

Former Prime Minister Pierre Trudeau always made this point about special status for Quebec: Canadians in other provinces are not going to accept Quebeckers as equal partners in national government if Quebeckers
have special exemptions from national laws. If you have no say over how
another person is governed, why should that person have any voice over
how you live?

Most Canadians, however, want Aboriginal people to be full and accepted participants in the national and political system. We want aboriginals to be able to serve as members of Parliament, to be judges in the provincial and federal courts, and to occupy other high positions in the general political system.

Another fact that should not be overlooked is that an extremely high
proportion of persons born on reserves end up living in the cities. Part of
the preparation for that life should be contact with the legal and political
systems that are exclusively in place in the rest of Canada. It is possible to
have some unique or adapted institutions for aboriginal communities;
even if modified somewhat though, the general criminal justice system
should be present and operating in aboriginal communities, just as in the
rest of Canada.

3.   SEPARATISM DOES NOT ALLOW FOR THE "CHECKS AND BALANCES"
      EFFECT OF HAVING DIFFERENT ORDERS OF GOVERNMENT

In a small community, it is fairly easy for one faction to take over, to
dominate all aspects of life, to favour its own and discriminate against others. If a small community participates in a larger system, as well as having
some local self-government, there can be effective checks and balances.
Provinces check abuses at the local level; national governments can stem
overbearing provincial governments. Conversely, local autonomy helps
prevent central governments from being arrogant and insensitive.

If aboriginal communities participate in the life of a larger federation or
aboriginal communities, then some of the necessary, mutually correcting
interaction of local and larger government can occur. Still, even a federation of aboriginal communities in Manitoba would be a "small world".

4.   THE PROPER ADMINISTRATION OF JUSTICE REQUIRES A LEVEL OF
      IMPARTIALITY THAT CAN BE DIFFICULT TO ACHIEVE IN SMALL
      COMMUNITIES

If Justice is solely administered by the inhabitants of small communities,
all of whom know each other, the possibility for personal favouritism and
discrimination is high.

5.   A SEPARATE SYSTEM OF ABORIGINAL JUSTICE WOULD TOO GREATLY
      DEPART FROM THE PRINCIPLE OF EQUALITY FOR ALL CANADIANS

Canadians rightly expect that a reasonable measure of political and legal
equality is maintained among citizens. When the stakes are high, as when

for example a serious criminal offence is alleged, the ideal should be that an accused will not be treated any more harshly or leniently on account of his ethic origin. Nor should the group affiliation of the victim or the place where the offence occurred diminish the demands of equal justice. Even the American model has limited the extent to which tribal courts are autonomous. The American Supreme Court has held that a tribal court has no inherent criminal jurisdiction over a non-member. The American congress has insisted, largely at the urging of Indians themselves, that tribal courts must observe the criminal process guarantees of the American constitutions. Furthermore, jurisdiction over the most serious offences is denied to tribal courts, regardless of who the accused and victims are.

6. SEPARATE OR PRIVILEGED TREATMENT FOR ABORIGINAL OFFENDERS WOULD MAKE LESS VISIBLE A SYMPTOM OF UNDERLYING SOCIAL AND POLITICAL DISORDER RATHER THAN DEALING WITH ITS CAUSES

The number of aboriginal persons accused of crimes and incarcerated in the system is an expense and an embarrassment to the larger system. Giving off aboriginal people in a special system might reduce the "public relations" embarrassment to the general community and ease consciences, but it would do little to address the underlying social and political causes. By making the problem less visible and expensive or by creating an impress that "something has been done", it might even discourage responsible conduct by politicians.

Do you agree with Professor Schwartz's criticisms concerning separate Aboriginal justice systems?

In the United States, separate tribal justice systems have been an important part of Aboriginal community development. The Harvard Project on Economic Development found that the existence of a separate justice system was crucial to the creation of social, political and legal stability within a tribe. While the organization of tribal courts was initially suspect because of their heavy reliance on the Bureau of Indian Affairs, in the last 25 years many have grown to become independent bodies capable of addressing the most challenging issues courts can face.

One particularly strong example of this power comes from the decision *In Re Certified Question II: Navajo Nation v. MacDonald*. In *MacDonald*, where the Navajo court was asked to consider, among other things, whether their tribal chairman had breached any fiduciary duties by receiving "bribes and kickbacks from contractors doing business with the Navajo Nation" [*In Re Certified Question II: Navajo Nation v. MacDonald* (1989), 16 Indian Law Reporter 6086 (Navajo Supreme Court)]. This case was significant for the Navajo courts because it asked them to solve their nation's most pressing problem without resorting to external legal institutions.

In *MacDonald*, the Navajo Court drew upon "Western" principles of law to articulate the fiduciary duty a tribal executive officer owes to tribal members. In finding this duty the Court did that which any other court would have done. It examined general principles of law and applied them to the facts of the case to arrive at an appropriate solution. However, in finding that the chairman owed and violated fiduciary duties to the nation, the court referred to other legal norms that only it would be qualified to draw upon in facing down this problem. In particular, the Navajo justices drew on Navajo common law to give meaning to the fiduciary duty in the context of principles of normative order within their communities. The Court wrote of a story concerning two "Hero Twins" who slew monsters and overcame other troubles faced by the Navajo at the time of their creation. The court held that this story embodied the "Navajo traditional concept of fiduciary trust of a leader (*naat'aanii*)". In applying the principles embedded in this story the court wrote:

> After the epic battles were fought by the Hero Twins, the Navajo people set on the path of becoming a strong nation. It became necessary to elect *naat'aaniis* by consensus of the people. A *naat'aanii* was not a powerful politician nor was he a mighty chief. A *naat'aanii* was chosen based on his ability to help the people survive and whatever authority he had was based upon that ability and the trust placed in him by the people. If *naat'aanii* lost the trust of his people, the people simply ceased to follow him or even listen to his words. ... The Navajo Tribal Council can place a Chairman or Vice Chairman on administrative leave if they have reasonable grounds to believe that the official seriously breached his fiduciary trust to the Navajo people. ...

The court's explanation of how an ancient story about Hero Twins gave rise to fiduciary duties for a tribal chairman gives a different view from Professor Schwartz's about the utility of tribal justice systems. It suggests that these systems enable Native American tribes to solve pressing legal problems more appropriately by fitting general legal principles to the specific realities of their community.

While Canadian Aboriginal peoples do not have separate justice systems to the extent found in the United States, some communities are beginning to experiment with innovative systems of dispute resolution. The following example from the Royal Commission's report on the Hollow Water Healing Project illustrates this development.

THE ROYAL COMMISSION ON ABORIGINAL PEOPLE, BRIDGING THE CULTURAL DIVIDE: A REPORT ON ABORIGINAL PEOPLE AND CRIMINAL JUSTICE IN CANADA

(Ottawa: Ministry of Supply and Services, 1996) at 159-167
(references omitted)

Hollow Water First Nation's Community Holistic Circle Healing Project

History and development

Community holistic circle healing (CHCH) deals with cases of sexual abuse in the northern Manitoba First Nation community of Hollow Water and in the surrounding Métis communities of Manigotagan, Aghaming, and Seymourville. CHCH has fashioned a unique response to the particular needs of people affected by this offence.

The idea behind CHCH took root first in the Ojibwa community of Hollow Water in 1984, when a group of residents and other people involved in providing social services to the community sought to grapple with the legacy of decades of alcoholism and family abuse, suicide and cultural loss. By 1987 a resource group had been formed, and based on their work — and the first trickle of what was to become a stream of disclosures — they became convinced that many of the community's problems could be traced to sexual abuse. The degree to which sexual abuse was a problem undermining the very fabric of the community was illustrated by the fact that the resource group believes that 75 per cent of the community have been victims of sexual abuse and 35 per cent are victimizers.

In 1988 members of the resource group traveled to Alkali Lake to learn about the successful efforts of that community to address the problems of alcohol abuse and sexual abuse. The resource group found the trip to Alkali Lake a moving and profound experience. Upon their return to Hollow Water, the group launched a number of initiatives, among them CHCH.

A sub-committee of the resource group, the assessment team, was responsible for the development of CHCH. Before any initiatives were undertaken specifically to respond to cases of sexual abuse, those interested in participating in the process went through a two-year training program. The program included cultural awareness; alcohol and drug awareness; team building; networking; suicide intervention; family counselling; communications skills; nutrition; and human sexuality.

CHCH focuses on cases of sexual assault, as it is felt that the root problems of the community can be dealt with only when the issue of sexual abuse is addressed. At the same time, resource group members feel it is important that people realize that CHCH is not about addressing a particular problem; rather it is integral to the healing and development of the community.

> CHCH is not a program or project. It is a process with individuals coming back into balance. A process of a community healing itself. It is a process which one day will allow our children and grandchildren to once again walk with their heads high as they travel around the Medicine Wheel of Life.

At its core, CHCH addresses sexual abuse by providing support, counselling and guidance to everyone affected by the crime, including the victim, the victim's family, the victimizer, and the victimizer's family.

The CHCH method of treating sexual abuse contains thirteen steps:

Step 1.	Disclosure
Step 2.	Protecting the Victim/Child
Step 3.	Confronting the Victimizer
Step 4.	Assisting the Spouse
Step 5.	Assisting the family(ies)/the Community
Step 6.	Meeting of the Assessment Team/RCMP/Crown
Step 7.	Victimizer Must Admit and Accept Responsibility
Step 8.	Preparation of the Vicitmizer
Step 9.	Preparation of the Victim
Step 10.	Preparation of All the Families
Step 11.	The Special Gathering

Step 12.   The Healing Contract Implemented
Step 13.   The Cleansing Ceremony

Progress through the entire 13 steps is estimated to take five years.

Project operation

While CHCH is often referred to as a Hollow Water initiative, it actually serves four communities: Manigotagan, Aghaming, Seymourville, and Hollow Water. Using the first initial of each community produces the acronym MASH. The community has taken to this acronym for several reasons:

1.   We live in a war zone. It's not the guns and bombs kind of war. Ours is a more insidious conflict that has consumed the best energies of our best people for several generations. The enemies in this war are alcohol and drug abuse, sexual abuse, interpersonal and family violence, welfare dependency, dysfunctional family and community relations, and extremely low self-esteem. We've been at war with these enemies for quite a while now.

2.   MASH is also a good name for us because we are in the business of healing our communities, and the team of us who work together (sometimes referred to as the Resource Group) from our four communities are continually struggling to cope with casualties of the war while at the same time planning and executing strategies for winning it.

While Hollow Water is a First Nations community, the other three communities are largely Métis. The total population of the four communities is about 1,500 people. All members of the community can take part in CHCH; it is a status-blind program. The only time status plays a role in the program is in relation to funding for psychological services. The Medical Services Branch provides this service for status Indians but not for others.

The overall operation of CHCH is handled by the assessment team, while specific tasks are undertaken by a management team. The assessment team provides all the resources necessary to restore balance to those affected by sexual abuse. In particular, the team is responsible for prevention and intervention activities; developing support systems; providing assessments of those involved in the process; and maintaining liaison with lawyers, Crown attorneys and child welfare agencies.

CHCH is currently staffed by an executive director, seven community and family violence workers, an administrative assistant, and the volunteers and/or professionals who make up the assessment team. In addition to CHCH staff, the assessment team calls on volunteers and professionals from virtually all local social services providers in the community.

The actual process of treating sexual abuse is quite extensive and cannot receive its full due here. The key to all interventions is the protection, support and healing of the victim. Once a disclosure of sexual abuse has been made, the assessment team conducts a detailed interview with the victim.

Steps are then taken immediately to protect the victim and to ensure her or his long-term safety. Only after these steps have been taken is the victimizer confronted. In most cases the victimizer is confronted before the RCMP is notified and charges are laid. The CHCH process is explained to the victimizer at this time. It is emphasized that if the victimizer wishes to enter CHCH he must accept responsibility for the offence and plead guilty in court. The agreement to plead guilty is important because it spares the victim the trauma of testifying in court. The victimizer has five days to decide whether to participate in CHCH. In some cases, victims do not wish to bring formal charges against the victimizer. While the absence of charges limits some of the things CHCH can do, workers nevertheless continue to assist the victim.

Following confrontation of the victimizer, the team meets with the victimizer's spouse to provide support. In her review of CHCH for the federal solicitor general, Theresa Lajeunesse describes the role of team members in dealing with victims, victimizers and their families:

> In some cases, the family of the victim and victimizer will be the same, in other cases they are different. In most cases, they will be from the same community. In all cases, the pain brought about by a disclosure will have a rippling effect throughout the community and members of both immediate and extended families will be affected. As with the victim and the victimizer, individual workers will work with members of all affected families. Often workers must deal with not only the sexual abuse, but past trauma which occurred in the lives of all the participants.

The non-Aboriginal criminal justice system puts the bulk of its energies into securing the conviction of the offender. In cases of sexual assault, it is now recognized that victims too have a legitimate claim on the services of the justice system. There is no comparison, however, between the way the non-Aboriginal justice system understands the impact of sexual assault and the way it is understood in Hollow Water. Rupert Ross describes the energies that go into creating a support network for all those involved:

> At all times, from the moment of disclosure through to the cleansing ceremony, team members have responsibility to work with, protect, support, teach and encourage a wide range of people. It is their view that since a great many people are affected by each disclosure, all of them deserve assistance, and just as important, all of them must be involved in any process aimed at creating healthy dynamics and breaking the inter-generational chain of abuse. I watched them plan for a possible confrontation with a suspected victimizer, and the detailed dispersal of team members through the community to support those whom the disclosure would touch reminded me of a military operation in its logistical complexity.

CHCH has entered into a protocol with the Manitoba Crown attorney's office to govern the way their intervention is respected. Enough time is taken before sentencing to allow the assessment team to work with the victimizer. Generally, victimizers who plead gully receive three years' probation. During those three years they are required to continue their work with CHCH. Failure to follow through with the program would result in a charge of breach of probation. No such charges have yet been brought against a victimizer. The three-year probation term is the maximum permitted by the

Criminal Code. As noted earlier, in the opinion of CHCH staff, five years are required to see a person through the entire program.

An understanding of the process of healing is crucial to an understanding of this initiative in particular and of Aboriginal justice programs in general. With reference to CHCH, Rupert Ross describes the healing process in the following manner:

> This healing process is painful, for it involves stripping away all the excuses, justifications, angers and other defences of each abuser until, finally, confronted with a victim who has been made strong enough to expose his or her pain in their presence, the abuser actually feels the pain he or she created. Only then can the re-building begin, both for the abuser and the abused. The word "healing" seems such a soft word, but the process of healing within the Hollow Water program is anything but.

In a newspaper article about CHCH, Peter Moon discussed the experience of those who participate in the process.

> These circles are wrenching experiences in which all hurt by disclosure talk about their feelings. They dredge up painful suppressed memories. There are tears, anger, sharing and forgiveness. Sometimes offenders and victims participate in the same circles.

> "My body feels strong outside, but not inside," one offender told a recent survey. He wept as he talked in a barely audible voice about the abuse he had suffered as a boy and the sexual assaults he had committed as a man.

> The circles are not an easy path to healing, said Burma Bushie, an Ojibwa child and family worker who coordinates the Hollow Water Healing Programme. But they are crucial...

> All circles open and close with a prayer to the Creator, and although people taking part in the program are not compelled to do so, they are given every opportunity to take part in traditional ceremonies.

> "The spiritual program is the key," Mr. Hardesy [a member of the Hollow Water band council] said. "It helps people to understand why they have hurt and been hurt and makes them feel better.

> "It makes all the difference in the world. The ceremonies, the sweat lodge, even the prayers in the circle. And the burning of the sweet grass, the sage, cedar and the tobacco. It's all part of the spiritual healing process."

Understanding the healing process at work in Hollow Water helps also to understand the position CHCH now takes on the incarceration of offenders. Initially, CHCH dealt with the sentencing process by providing a pre-sentence report for the court. By 1993, however, dissatisfaction with this role led CHCH to re-evaluate the need for incarceration in the cases they were handling. The issue was important enough that CHCH wrote a paper setting out its position:

> CHCH'S position on the use of incarceration, and its relationship to an individual's healing process, has changed over time. In our initial efforts to break the vicious cycle of abuse that was occurring in our community, we took the position that we needed to promote the use of incarceration in cases which were defined as "too serious." After some time, however, we came to the conclusion that this position was adding significantly to the difficulty of what was already complex casework.

As we worked through the casework difficulties that arose out of this position, we came to realize two things:

- that as we both shared our own stories of victimization and learned from our experiences in assisting others in dealing with the pain of their victimization, it became very difficult to define "too serious." The quantity or quality of pain felt by the victim, the families and the community did not seem to be directly connected to any specific acts of victimization. Attempts ... to define a particular victimization as "too serious" and another as "not too serious"...were gross oversimplifications, and certainly not valid from an experiential point of view, and

- that promoting incarceration was based on, and motivated by, a mixture of feelings of anger, revenge, guilt and shame on our part, and around our personal victimization issues, rather than the healthy resolution of the victimization we were trying to address.

Thus our position on the use of incarceration has shifted. At the same time, we understand how the legal system continues to use and view incarceration — as punishment and deterrence for the victimizers ... and protection and safety for the victim(s) and community. What the legal system seems not to understand is the complexity of the issues involved in breaking the cycle of abuse that exists in our community.

The use of judgment and punishment actually works against the healing process. An already unbalanced person is moved further out of balance.

What the threat of incarceration does do is keep people from coming forward and taking responsibility for the hurt they are causing. It reinforces the silence, and therefore promotes, rather than breaks, the cycle of violence that exists. In reality, rather than making the community a safer place, the threat of jail places the community more at risk.

In order to break the cycle, we believe that victimizer accountability must be to, and support must come from, those most affected by the victimization — the victim, the family/ies, and the community. Removal of the victimizer from those who must and are best able to, hold him/her accountable, and to offer him/her support, adds complexity to already existing dynamics of guilt and shame. The healing process of all parties is therefore at best delayed, and most often actually deterred.

The legal system, based on principles of punishment and deterrence, as we see it, simply is not working. We cannot understand how the legal system doesn't see this ...

We do not see our present position on incarceration as either "an easy way out" for the victimizer, or as the victimizer "getting away." We see it rather as establishing a very clear line of accountability between the victimizer and his or her community. What follows from that line is a process that we believe is not only much more difficult for the victimizer, but also much more likely to heal the victimization, than doing time in jail could ever be.

Our children and the community can no longer afford the price the legal system is extracting in its attempts to provide justice in our community.

As a result of this shift in perspective, CHCH moved away from providing pre-sentence reports and looked at more community-based ways of providing justice in sexual abuse cases. In December 1993, CHCH took a step toward greater control over the justice process when a sentencing circle was held for two victimizers. The circle, the first in Manitoba, involved 250 residents of the community. The assessment team felt that the sentencing circle approach better met the needs of all those affected by the offence. In outlining their support for this initiative the assessment team wrote:

> Up until now the sentencing hearing has been the point at which all of the parties of the legal system ... and the community have come together. Major differences of opinion as to how to proceed have often existed. As we see it, the legal system usually arrives with an agenda of punishment and deterrence of the "gully" victimizer, and safety and protection of the victim and community; the community on the other hand, arrives with an agenda of accountability of the victimizer to the community, and restoration of balance to all parties of the victimization.
>
> As we see it, the differences in the agendas are seriously deterring the healing process of the community. We believe that the restoration of balance is more likely to occur if sentencing itself is more consistent in process and in content with the healing work of the community. Sentencing needs to become more of a step in the healing process, rather than a diversion from it ...
>
> As we see it, the sentencing circle plays two primary purposes (1) it promotes the community healing process by providing a forum for the community to address the parties of the victimization at the time of sentencing, and (2) it allows the court to hear directly from the people most affected by the pain of victimization. In the past the crown and defence, as well as ourselves, have attempted to portray this information. We believe that it is now time for the court to hear from the victim, the family of the victim, the victimizer, the family of the victimizer, and the community-at-large.

By June 1995, CHCH had dealt with 409 clients, including 94 victims (32 of whom have completed the healing program), 180 family members of victims (27 of whom have completed the healing program), 52 victimizers (4 of whom have successfully completed the program), and the family members of victimizers. Two victimizers have re-offended since entering the program.

Next steps

As with other justice initiatives, the continued funding of CHCH is still unsettled. Funding from the federal Aboriginal Justice Initiative, which has supported the program, is time-limited, and it is not clear where the funds will come from once this funding ceases. Given the intense, holistic approach taken by the project, the per case cost can appear high for a community of approximately 1,500. But comparisons with the cost of other programs, completely miss the point. CHCH is a program without precedent in Canada — one that truly addresses the needs of all those affected by sexual abuse and attempts to find solutions that deal with the root causes of behavior and prevent the cycle of abuse from continuing.

Interest in the project from other communities is quite high, and CHCH staff receive a great number of requests to speak about the program and conduct workshops. It is precisely the holistic approach of the program that is generating such interest from other Aboriginal and non-Aboriginal communities.

As the program develops it will undoubtedly come up with new and innovative approaches to the issues arising from sexual abuse in a manner that is grounded firmly in cultural traditions. One area where innovation can be expected is sentencing. Circle sentencing has begun in Hollow Water, but this is not seen as the end point of the process. Ultimately, the resource group sees a move away from the non-Aboriginal justice system altogether, although this can happen only over time. As they say in their report on circle sentencing:

> We realized that, at least until the community mandate was stronger, the community healing process needed the support of the legal system in holding accountable those people who were victimizing others.

Where CHCH moves next in this area will be of interest to everyone with a specific concern for aboriginal justice issues, as well as for those with a general interest in innovative approaches to solving complex human problems in the criminal law context.

Despite the longevity and success of many Aboriginal initiatives in the criminal justice system some, like Emma LaRoque below, wonder about their authenticity and impact. How would you answer Professor LaRoque's concerns and critiques?

EMMA LAROQUE, "RE-EXAMINING CULTURALLY APPROPRIATE MODELS IN CRIMINAL JUSTICE APPLICATIONS"

in Michael Asch, *Aboriginal and Treaty Rights in Canada*
(Vancouver: U.B.C. Press, 1997) at 75 (references omitted)

In the winter of 1993, the *Winnipeg Free Press* reported on the first Aboriginal community to exercise justice presumably based on "tradition" by forming a "healing circle" to "pass sentence on the crimes of their neighbours." The crime was committed by a couple from Hollow Water, Manitoba, a reserve 160 kilometres northeast of Winnipeg. This couple had raped their two daughters numerous times. For these unspeakable acts the Hollow Water community of 450 "sentenced" the couple to three years of supervised probation "during which time the couple must continue healing under the guidance of the circle members."

I received so many telephone calls from Native women across Canada, women expressing horror and outrage at the Hollow Water "sentence," that I decided to follow up on some cautionary questions and issues I had raised about the Hollow Water Project in a previous article on "Violence in Aboriginal Communities" (1993). There are a number of unsettling ramifications that come with the Hollow Water model with respect to victims of violence in Native communities. Involved are numerous complex issues, many necessarily beyond the scope of this paper. The Hollow Water incident is very important in the consideration of not only culturally appropriate models but also of gender issues, especially in view of Aboriginal self-goverment aspirations.

This paper will examine assumptions of "tradition" upon which Aboriginally controlled justice systems seem to be based. By "traditions" I am referring largely to ideas, theories, and assumptions relevant to this discussion, not to spirituality or associated rituals. Also, I am not in any way suggesting that traditions are no longer extant in Aboriginal lives, nor that Aboriginal peoples cannot "borrow" other traditions. The concern is the misuse of "traditions." Because these "traditional" perspectives on "culturally appropriate" justice models as practiced on victims of violence may be having drastic effects on the victims and therefore on the Native community, they must be questioned and re-evaluated.

Terms such as "traditional" or "culturally appropriate" appear as a matter of course in discussions on Aboriginal·governance, or for that matter, on any community-oriented programs related to justice, violence, women, and "healing." As a recent federal discussion report on family violence prevention puts it: "The issue of cultural appropriateness is now accepted as central to creating effective services for Aboriginal individuals, families and communities." Native peoples have fought long and hard for cultural recognition. Within this often politically charged atmosphere, a considerable number of "traditions" and "values" have been recalled. The result has been a growing complex of reinvented "traditions" which have become extremely popular even while lacking historical or anthropological contextualization. This is particularly true with respect to notions of justice and the role of women in Aboriginal societies, past and present. In effect, much of what is unquestionably thought to be tradition is actually syncretized fragments of Native and Western traditions which have become highly politicized because they have been created from the context of colonization. ...

The Hollow Water sentencing must be re-evaluated in light of real traditional justice. The decision to merely "supervise" two adults who had committed horrific crimes poses, or at least should pose, many disturbing questions with respect to certain uses of "traditions" such as "healing circles" within Aboriginally controlled justice systems. Frankly, it is difficult to comprehend the Hollow Water decision given the mind-boggling nature of the crime. ...

Upon whose "tradition" is the Hollow Water decision based? Clearly, no one considered those Aboriginal traditions that punished sexual offenders with severity. If programs are claiming to apply traditional measures, then they should.

But traditional justice is unrecognizable here, as in most other mediation and healing circle programs.

Origins of Current Notions and Practices

If Hollow Water and other mediation programs are not exactly practicing traditional methods of justice, the question must be asked: Have they, in fact, fallen prey to contemporary, white, leftist/liberal, Christian, and even New Age notions of "healing," "forgiveness," and offender "rehabilitation"?

Most of the culturally appropriate programs being promoted as alternatives to the existing justice system rely on assertions of "healing" and "forgiveness." For example, in a tone reminiscent of a pacifist church pamphlet, Sawatsky claims Aboriginal justice entails "encouragement for apology, forgiveness and healing with a view to making peace" (item 14 on his chart). Sawatsky goes on to claim: "From an aboriginal perspective, victims need to meet the offender face to face, receive personal restitution and be directly involved in a fair settlement." This is a highly questionable assertion from any perspective. As established above, there is no anthropological basis for asserting it is Native tradition for victims to either "forgive" or meet "offenders." It is, however, traditional to pursue 'healing' in the form of justice. A "fair settlement" would mean the victims or their families would seek some form of justice in kind, not rehabilitation as such. There is every indication in human history that the ancients had learned there is no healing without justice. ...

Political Factors in the Defence of Offenders

I believe there are a number of significant political factors that help explain the persistence of "culturally appropriate" rhetoric, factors that can only be briefly introduced here. As colonized peoples, Natives have been forced to use whatever arsenal is at their disposal in response to relentless political pressure — pressure that amounts to sociological and cultural warfare — from Canadian governments, especially on issues of land rights and identity. Native peoples have been forced to make their case for Aboriginal (land) fights on the basis of cultural differences, when it should simply be on the basis of inherent rights that flow from aboriginality. Justices have made appalling decisions on the basis of what they perceive as Native culture, whether it concerns sexual assault or land fights. Native leaders, faced with convoluted, self-serving, and shrewd legal arguments, have had to scramble for proof of cultural differences.

The issue of "individual" versus "collective" rights is a perfect example of Natives resorting to a cultural framework when boxed in by Western liberal democratic traditions that are associated with individualism. Perhaps unavoidably, Native leaders have had to overemphasize collective rights to make the point that such fights are even culturally feasible. However, the fact that Native cultures were egalitarian in organization does not mean Native peoples acted on some instinct akin to a buffalo herd with no regard for the well-being of individuals! Native people have had to emphasize collective fights on the issue of land, but it must be remembered that the framework around which Aboriginal fights are pursued originates in European theory and law. Further, Native "collectivity" was in many ways invented through the creation of reserves and a legalized collective identity via the *Indian Act*. Obviously, there is much more to consider on the matter of land rights and the Aboriginal collective. ... In response to the Euro-Canadian theft of Aboriginal history and of the ground upon which Aboriginal cultures are based, contemporary Native peoples have been trying to prove they do have cultures — and often morally better ones at that — hence the romanticization evident in most culturally appropriate models, as well as the reluctance to critique them.

There is such hunger within the Native community for an identity separate from the Canadian mainstream that a number of issues have become hopelessly entangled. Take, for instance, the notion of forgiving and healing the offender. It seems that spirituality has become a precondition of being accepted as Native, and spirituality, or "following traditional teachings," entails having to "forgive." What arises from this belief is the confused expectation that Native victims must forgive the offender in order to qualify as being truly Native. ...

One of the most persistent and frustrating stereotypes about Native cultures is their relegation to the past, which has led to the false dichotomization of many contemporary issues. Making individual rights antithetical to collective rights, confusing spirituality with healing, and identity are among the problems delving from the ossification of tradition. Further, freezing Native culture in the past makes it virtually impossible for Native people to engage in contemporary rights debates such as freedom of religion, speech, personal choice, citizenship, or women's rights.

When Native women turn to contemporary analysis to explicate their double oppression, they are often accused of using "white" instead of Native traditions — clearly an instance of the double standard, since white traditions are heavily borrowed for culturally appropriate programs. When Aboriginal women demand justice in a contemporary context, they are accused of betraying "solidarity," putting them, in effect, in an absolutely no-win situation between justice and community. Clearly, "tradition," "culture," and "history" are political handles with many twists that result in the continued oppression and silencing of women.

The strident insistence by the Native leadership on our cultural differences has pushed Aboriginal people to the extreme margins. We have given the message that we are so fathomlessly different as to be hardly human. We are supposedly so different as to be exempt from the Canadian Charter of Rights and Freedoms, as if our history of oppression has made us some how immune to ordinary human evils, as if we do not require basic human rights that other Canadian citizens expect. As evidenced by statistics and court decisions regarding Native sexual violence, "otherness" can be carried to rather chilling extents by both communities. It is ironic that today as we struggle to decolonize, we ourselves are turning to the stereotypes that have segregated and defined us as inferior in the first place. ...

The point remains that we live in a contemporary world, whether in a rural or urban setting. This means we have many worlds from which to draw with respect to ideals of human rights or healing. ... I am not arguing that Native peoples cannot or should not control their programs, but it is possible to construct new models that accommodate real, multidimensional human lives. Traditions can be and must be used in a contemporary context in such a way as to bring meaning to our young people, justice and equality to women, and safety and human rights protection to everyone.

Nevertheless, tradition cannot necessarily or always be of value or relevance in our times. "Healing," for instance, cannot be the sole means of dealing with the sexually violent in our midst. There comes a time when, for ethical and moral considerations, a people must confront or change their own traditions. There is no need to wait for external forces to make us change. And we must never assume that our historical oppression has somehow made us extraordinarily moral. If there is one thing we can learn from history, it is that human beings do not become better people, that is, more morally sensitive, just because they have been oppressed. Morality is an ongoing dialogue, it is not innate. Our traditions and cultures cannot be immutable. For this reason, we must be vigilant in our suppositions and behaviors as to what constitutes the good, the bad, and the moral. Even seemingly "good" notions such as "family" or "forgiveness" need to be reexamined; there are things human beings, human families, do that are so dehumanizing and destructive that the only word and concept we can use to describe them is "evil." ...

Freedom of Expression

I am aware of the depth of emotion the Hollow Water sentencing generated. I have received many calls from concerned people expressing the view that Hollow Water is a travesty of justice and a cruel disregard for human dignity. In particular, Native women expressed shock, disgust, and outrage. Many said that if Hollow Water is any example of things to come with respect to "culturally appropriate" applications of justice to women, they would fear to live under Aboriginal self-governments. One Native woman who was in law school considered challenging the decision under the Canadian Charter of Rights and Freedoms. Even white journalists urged me to make a statement and told me they were not politically free to question the Hollow Water decision. All those Native women who called asked to remain anonymous because they too did not feel free to publicly challenge Hollow Water. I have not felt free either.

What have we come to in our community? It is this fear of free expression that has provided the impetus for me to write this paper. It appears that culturally appropriate applications are increasingly becoming rigid and doctrinaire, leading to the alienation of valuable community members. Such a path is more Western in tradition than it is Native, for as has been amply indicated already, the best of Native traditions place high regard on freedom, democracy, justice, and gender inclusiveness.

If Aboriginal self-government or any other community-based organizing model is to be created under the healthiest of circumstances, everyone must be free to examine issues in a context of freedom, honesty, creativity, caring, and gender equality.

F. CONCLUSION

Aboriginal peoples continue to encounter a criminal justice system in which they do not receive justice. It has failed them on a massive scale. Individualized and systemic racism have adversely impacted these populations and left them with severe disproportional representation in charges laid, court appearances, and rates of incarceration. For most Aboriginal people the system remains vast and inaccessible. It does not promise to heal lives, but continues to grind up the bodies and souls of those who are pulled into its clutches. Anishinabe elder Art Solomon observed this truth when he wrote:

> They say that
>
> The wheels of "Justice",
>
> They grind slowly.
>
> Yes we know.
>
> But they grind
>
> And they grind
>
> And they grind
>
> And they grind.
>
> It seems like they grind
>
> Forever ...
>
> (*Songs for the People: Teachings on the Natural Way*
>
> (Toronto: W.C. Press, 1990) at 126.)

This chapter has examined this sentiment and some of the causes for the criminal justice system's spectacular failure for Aboriginal peoples.

This chapter has also attempted to present some of the initiatives being taken to transform and revolutionize criminal justice for Aboriginal peoples in Canada. While Aboriginal legal traditions have been submerged in Canada for many years, their reappearance is providing creativity for both the reform of Canada's criminal law and the development of separate practices. While this process has not been without its setbacks or problems, it holds some promise for individuals and communities. Despite these reforms however, at present, the problem Aboriginal people encounter in the criminal justice system is getting worse, not better.

In the *Report on the Cariboo-Chilcotin Inquiry*, at page 28, Judge Sarich wrote:

> One constant drum beat that followed the commission from reserve to reserve was the message that native people want to control their own lives and manage their own affairs. That means a process of justice that is comprehensible and culturally acceptable to them. To achieve these ends some of the communities will institute their own justice process and others will experiment with an adaptation with of the non-native process.

Aboriginal peoples will continue to search for ways in which they can receive justice. These will not be easy discussions, proposals or actions. The deep dysfunction the system has participated in creating will not immediately disappear. There will be many successes, set-backs and reformulations.

INDEX

[A page number in boldface type
indicates materials excerpted in the text.]

A

Aboriginal Justice Inquiry of
Manitoba, **2, 5-11, 419, 490-92,
597-605, 830-39, 869-71, 955**
Aboriginal rights, *see also*
Aboriginal title
as pre-contact rights, 68, 371-73,
381, 384-85, 406, 754
as *sui generis*, 61, 65, 67, 344-45,
355, 496
commercial fishing rights and,
350-51, 376, 383-94, 401
Crown-Native fiduciary
relationship and, 329-31, 334,
379
European influence and, 375
extinguishment, 349, 387-88, 754
as opposed to regulation, 349
clear and plain intent, 349-50,
388-89, 413-14
frozen rights and, 333-34,
347-50, 360, 366-67, 372-73,
378-81, 385, 390
incidental rights and, 323,
373-74, 385-88
independent existence of, 345,
367-69
inherent versus contingent,
360-64, 420-21
origins of, 337, 378, 880
relationship to aboriginal title, 1,
76, 375-76, 379, 402, 404, 405,
408, 413-14, 501
relationship to treaty rights,
379

test for identification, 368-73,
389, 410, 412, 706
versus treaty rights, 418-19
Aboriginal title, *see also* Aboriginal
rights
aboriginal understandings of,
1-2, 3-4, 36, 42-43, 44, 46
as *sui generis*, 59, 61, 71, 74,
410-411
comprehensive claims and,
94-101
connection of group to land,
doctrine of, 4-20,
origins of, 4-5
extinguishment, 51, 52-54, 65,
95-97. *See also* Royal
Proclamation of 1763;
Sovereignty
clear and plain intent, 51, 94,
comprehensive claims and,
95, 96
frozen rights and, 72-75
independent existence of, 1, 50,
57, 58
land interests (non-Aboriginal
title), 85-93
Law of Nations (*jus gentium*)
and, 5-11. *See also* Sovereignty
nature and incidents of, 29-34,
36-37, 45-46, 49-50, 58-60,
70-77, 271, 378
onus of proof, 81-85
origins of, 4, 74
relationship to aboriginal rights,
1, 76, 375-76, 379, 402, 404, 405,
408, 413-14
reserves and, 121

973